The Soviet Revolution

The Soviet Revolution

1917-1939

By

RAPHAEL R. ABRAMOVITCH

Introduction

By

SIDNEY HOOK

INTERNATIONAL UNIVERSITIES PRESS, INC., NEW YORK

Library of Congress Catalog Card Number: 62-13964

Manufactured in the United States of America

To the memory of my son:

MARK REIN

Introduction

by SIDNEY HOOK

This history by the lone remaining public figure in the leadership of the Russian Social Democratic Party is an important contribution to the understanding of the Soviet October Revolution of 1917. It provides not only a fresh perspective upon one of the major historical experiences of our era, but a flood of little-known details which helps make the events more intelligible. It is, in a sense, a part of history commenting on itself.

The truth about any great historical event is inexhaustible. No one can describe or interpret it except from some perspective of selective interest. The desire to tell the truth is necessary but not sufficient, for unless the truths of history are related to the primary causal factors which determine social change, they may be trivial, irrelevant or peripheral. No perspective, therefore, can tell the whole story; but without some perspective nothing at all can be told of moment. Three features of this history contribute to the creation of a unique perspective.

First, it is written from the standpoint of a participant, of someone who knew intimately the leading figures of the Bolshevik Party, and who debated with them until they sought to silence his arguments by threat of imprisonment and the executioner's bullet. Second, this book may be characterized as a socialist history of the Soviet Revolution. It is an account by someone who never approved of any move to restore the prerevolutionary regime and who opposed every attempt at foreign intervention in the Soviet Union as violating the right of the Russian people to determine their own destiny. On the contrary, the author was sympathetic to the ideals of an early peace, which the Bolsheviks under Lenin and Trotsky exploited for their own purposes when they seized power, and to the ultimate socialist ideals to which the Bolsheviks gave lip allegiance. To those in the West, especially in the United States, who have been confused by the semantic deceptions of the Communist regime, the author's allegiance to socialism, and his description of the price his fellow socialists, and above all the Russian people had to pay for it, should be very revealing. Third, and most far-reaching, this history is written by a socialist who is a democrat—and because a democrat, one who believes that the means of achieving a goal are integral to the goal itself, that the future of society depends not upon the abstractions men proclaim, but upon the means they use.

Raphael Rein Abramovitch was born in 1880 in Dvinsk, then as now under Russian rule. He matriculated at the Riga Polytechnical Institute as a student of mechanical engineering but was expelled in 1901 for revolutionary activities. From that time until the present, he has been a man totally dedicated to the struggle for his secular humanist and socialist ideals. From 1900 to 1917 he worked in Russia and Europe. He was elected a member of the Central Committee of the Jewish Labor Bund and represented it in the Russian Social Democratic Labor Party with which it was affiliated. The Bund opposed the Bolshevik faction of Lenin, and Abramovitch became one of the leaders of the Menshevik group. He was never "a professional revolutionary" in that he refused to be supported by his party. He made his living by teaching physics and mathematics at a high school in Vilna and, from 1908 to 1917, by examining technical patents in a patent office in Vienna.

At the outbreak of the Russian Revolution in February 1917, he returned to his native country and was elected to the Petrograd Soviet. He opposed the Bolshevik seizure of power both before and after the coup which destroyed the democratic regime set up in February 1917, the regime that Lenin himself had declared to be the freest in the world. Although Abramovitch engaged in no illegal activities against the Bolsheviks, he was arrested in 1918 on trumped up charges because of his growing influence among the workers of Petrograd and Moscow. Slated to be shot, he was saved at the very last moment, after being permitted a farewell visit from his wife, by the intervention of some liberal elements of the Central Committee of the Bolshevik party and by the plea of his friend Friedrich Adler, himself a political prisoner in Austria, whom Lenin held in great esteem.

In 1920 the Soviet government gave the Mensheviks permission to send a delegation abroad. This delegation consisted of Julius Martov and Raphael Abramovitch. They became cofounders of the Vienna International and the leaders in the attempt to create a united front embracing all the labor and socialist parties of Europe. When this and subsequent efforts were shattered on the rock of Bolshevik intransigence and duplicity, the Labor and Socialist International was formed in May 1923 without the Communists. Raphael Abramovitch —after the death of Martov—became instrumental in the forming of the new organization and shaping its social and political philosophy.

Abramovitch's major interest has always been Russian affairs. In 1921 he became the founder and co-editor of the Russian language magazine, *Socialist Courier*—the most knowledgeable journal on Soviet affairs published anywhere, which called the turn on every change in Soviet policy. He was elected to the leadership of the Russian socialist movement in exile. In 1931 Abramovitch became one of the central figures in the first Moscow frame-up Trials. He was charged with visiting the Soviet Union secretly to plot against the regime—during the very period when he was in Brussels attending a meeting of the Labor and Socialist International. After Hitler came to power in 1933 Abramovitch fled Berlin. In 1940 he narrowly escaped Hitler's legions in France and reached the United States. During the Spanish Civil War his only son, Mark Rein, was kidnapped, tortured and slain by the Barcelona agents of the Soviet G.P.U. in Spain. From the time of his arrival in the United States Raphael Abramovitch has been active in the cause of labor, refugee relief, peace, and freedom. He has been a columnist in the *Jewish Daily Forward,* to which he began contributing in 1922, the editor of the magazine, *Modern Review,* and co-editor of the *Jewish Encyclopaedia.* In the middle of the eighth decade of his life, he undertook to write this history which is at the same time his intellectual testament.

Raphael Abramovitch symbolizes in his person and career the history of a remarkable group of noble men and women, who refused to compromise their basic moral ideas, and who foresaw with a terrible prescience the fate of those who sought either power or survival at any price. Although they stood, so to speak, in the antechamber of history, aware of the program of peace and social change which was necessary to save Russia from chaos in 1917, they were defeated by the insensitivity of the West to the acute Russian needs of the time, and by the ruthlessness of the Bolsheviks who reinforced their demagogy with brute force. Defeated but not embittered, they put their knowledge and insight at the disposal of all working-class parties and groups that wished to achieve the promise of a welfare economy without sacrificing their dignity and freedom as human beings. Although the author of this history was an active participant in the events he describes, he recalls them with objectivity and an unusual tranquility of spirit. He does not regard himself as an instrument of History. As a Marxist he allows full scope for the operation of economic forces, but he also makes the reader aware of the importance of organization, of personality, and of chance in determining the pattern of events. Nor does he inflate his own role in the story he tells or suppress the evidence of his own ineffectuality. This absence of the histrionic element, this almost too sober account of an experience which must have been full of anguish, gives the narrative a sense of authenticity. It brings home to the reader, as no mannered literary account can, the mixture of grandeur and horror, of the drab and the tragic, which marks sudden historical change.

The second noteworthy feature of this history is that in a strange and paradoxical way it vindicates some of the key insights of the Marxist philosophy of history and social change. From one point of view, the Bolsheviks who claim to be the only true heirs of Marx have actually refuted the theory of historical materialism by creating an economic system—call it state socialism, state capitalism, bureaucratic collectivism—by *political* means in the absence of the preparatory, material foundations. Nothing is so clear as the fact that, far from the mode of production determining the political and cultural superstructure of the Soviet Union, it was the mode of political decision, the unlimited use of terror, based on no law except the will of the Politbureau of the Communist Party, which determined the change in the mode of production both in industry and agriculture. The consequences of this attempt to substitute political fiat for the process of gradual economic growth were predicted by the author and his circle. They warned that the result of seizing power by a small minority, in an overwhelmingly agrarian society, would mean the merciless coercion of the majority. They warned again of the consequences for the lives and liberties of the Russian workers and peasants of abandoning the New Economic Policy, and of instituting the forced collectivization of agriculture, and the absurdly ambitious five-year plans. They never dreamed that the Bolsheviks would be prepared to pay such a ghastly price in human suffering and death for the accumulation of capital and the industrialization of the country required by their grandiose plans. The Bolshevik economist, Preobrazhensky, was not jesting when he referred to the peasantry as an "internal colony" to be exploited by the Communist government for the sake of industrialization. The Bolsheviks succeeded at a cost far greater than that paid by other countries in the course of their industrial development. What they achieved could have been done more humanely and more efficiently by gradual processes through a coalition of workers, peasants, and intellectuals. The great merit of this history is to pose the problem of social determinism or historical maturity within the context of socialist humanism and political freedom.

The third and most important feature of Raphael Abramovitch's history is the light it throws on the assessment of the Soviet Union today, its future course, and the relationship between the communist and the free worlds. These problems cannot be pursued in all their complexity, but the emphasis which the author puts on the interrelatedness of means and ends, of the indispensability of political democracy for any genuine system of social democracy, and of the consequences of disregarding these principles, provides a reliable guideline.

This history reaches its climax with the complete triumph of Stalin, and the creation of a system which is the closest approximation in recorded time to the ideal type of a totalitarian society. It is published at a moment when Stalin is being posthumously downgraded, his remains removed from its marbled mausoleum, and his political reputation shrunk to fit the lines of the postscript of Lenin's testament. There are some who see the dawn of a new day in the Kremlin's discovery that what Abramovitch and his circle have been saying about Stalin for the last thirty years is true.

As I read this history I find no ground for sanguine expectations. What it establishes is that although the emergence of Stalin and his full-fledged totalitarian system would have surprised Lenin—as it did Trotsky!—and although Stalin was capable of doing what Lenin and Trotsky were too intelligent to do, nonetheless the system which Lenin and Trotsky created made Stalin possible. The Soviet Union today, in which the authority of the leader (Khrushchev) has replaced "the cult of personality" (Stalin), still suffers from greater oppression and terror than existed even under the dictatorial rule of Lenin. So long as a minority political party enjoys the monopoly of all political power and no legal political opposition is possible, so long as the press is not free, and the creative spirit chained by the power of police, there will always be a well-founded probability that Khrushchev may act in the future as he did in the past in the Ukraine, when he sought to endear himself to Stalin by the thoroughness of his purges. And if not Khrushchev, then his successor.

This seems to me to be the abiding moral of Raphael Abramovitch's history. The day in which it will be circulated and read within the confines of the Soviet borders will be a day of rejoicing for free men everywhere.

Author's Preface

A noted British author once remarked that the Russian Mensheviks, a group never lacking in literary talent, should have turned out at least one authoritative work expressing its concept of the Bolshevik revolution.

This mild reproof calls for explanation. In the 1920's when—as political expatriates—we made our home in Germany and later in France, we still were a political movement, closely connected with numerous comrades in Russia, who represented the only organized opposition to the Soviet regime. None of us thought of writing a history of the Russian revolution, much less of its Bolshevik period.

Our bi-weekly organ *Sotsialistichesky Vestnik* (*The Socialist Courier,* published in Russian) provided analytical comments on all significant developments in Russia. At the same time, we published bulletins in other languages, summarizing items that had appeared in the *Courier* for the information of the international labor movement. Several of us regularly attended the sessions of the Socialist International, delivering reports on current developments in the Soviet Union, which were followed by critical discussions of its policies. Our lecturers on Soviet affairs toured Europe and occasionally the United States. Some of us were regular contributors to the German, Austrian and French Socialist press, or to some English and Yiddish-language publications in America.

Absorbed as we were in a ceaseless political activity, we felt no particular need to write a large-scale historic treatise on the Russian Revolution. Men of action rather than scholars, we published works on vital current economic issues, or on the working class and labor unions in Russia. This author published a report on a Soviet anti-

Socialist drive in Russia and Georgia, which appeared simultaneously in several languages.

Our opposition to Bolshevik rule in the first decades was based on the belief that Bolshevism was an anomaly—a utopian terrorist aberration, incidental to the world Socialist movement. We believed that it was historically doomed to failure, since the victory of a proletarian socialism seemed inconceivable in a backward country such as Russia, with her predominantly peasant population.

This premise was no longer tenable after Stalin had carried out forced collectivization of agriculture and rapid industrialization. During this period, strong differences of opinion arose within our group. Former concepts of the nature of Bolshevism had to be drastically revised. Some in our group resembled the paleontologists in an old story who thought they had identified prehistoric eggs on a Pacific island as those of a harmless giant diplodocus, but after a few years learned that the prehistoric animal was a ferocious carnivorous beast. The majority of our group accepted the analysis of Rudolf Hilferding, who ranged the Bolsheviks in the category of totalitarian regimes.

The 1930's—the years of an intellectual crisis in the Menshevik party—were also the years of Hitlerism, approaching war, and, finally, our exodus to the United States.

The first two decades in a new land were taken up by a day-to-day struggle to keep the *Socialist Courier* alive—apart from problems of personal adjustment (no easy matter, for any of us). Not until we had settled down in this country did we become conscious of a serious historical challenge. No one, before us, had come forward with a satisfactory and comprehensive account of the Bolshevik Revolution, its peculiar features and its specific problems. To write such a history, we now felt, was our responsibility, not alone for the sake of historic truth but also to further our struggle against the Bolsheviks. Critical onslaughts alone could not recreate a true picture of the Bolshevik Revolution. What we needed was a detailed step-by-step report on the essential phases of its development.

To a far greater extent than any other group, Russian or non-Russian, our group had accumulated an enormous amount of relevant material. A mere glance at the shelves holding forty volumes of the

Socialist Courier brought to mind the wealth of facts, figures, and first-hand accounts by direct participants or eyewitnesses of the Russian experience. To be sure this was a mere fraction of what was needed. We had to dig through tons of stenographic reports to keep track of Soviet and Communist party conferences and meetings. Our recollection of past events had to be refreshed by looking through countless newspapers, journals and other periodicals, going back to 1917.

Several persons had to be engaged for several years to carry out such laborious work. This raised the question of how the project could be financed. Various American foundations, known to have extended generous grants sponsoring scientific and historic research, were approached without success. The author then turned to those organizations which had helped him and his group through the years of their European exile, long before they came to the United States. We were confident that our old friends would not turn us down—and we were not wrong. The author is deeply indebted to the Amalgamated Clothing Workers of America, Inc., the Atran Foundation, the International Ladies Garment Workers Union, the Jewish Labor Committee, the *Jewish Daily Forward,* the Tamiment Institute, and the Workmen's Circle which all helped generously.

We have been able to accomplish the larger portion, though by no means all, of our program. The publication, as originally planned, was to include two volumes, one covering the period up to 1939, the other dealing with the second world war, its aftermath and the years following Stalin's death. A work of such scope has proved beyond our means. Relations between the various national groups in the USSR were a major factor in the Soviet revolution, but this area too had to be omitted from our discussion. The reader is referred to the works by Richard Pipes: *The Formation of the Soviet Union* (Syracuse University Press, 1954); Solomon M. Schwarz: *The Jews and the Soviet Union* (Syracuse University Press, 1951); and Walter Kolarz: *Russia and her Colonies* (London, 1952).

The present book took almost four years to complete. The work was written in Russian and simultaneously translated into English. The entire text was dictated by the author, who alone is responsible for its contents. The author could not possibly have accomplished this work if not for the kind help rendered by his many loyal friends. My deeply felt thanks must go, in the first place, to all those who helped me overcome many difficulties and handicaps. I am greatly indebted to Mrs. Xenia G. Chikalenko and Mrs. Genia M. Wasser for their kind assistance, as well as to my friends and associates who have helped in the compilation of material and the presentation of various chapters. My special thanks are extended to N. V. Volsky (Valentinov), Y. P. Denike, B. L. Dvinov, M. V. Vishniak, as well as to Mrs. L. O. Dan, Vera Aleksandrova and Mrs. Julia A. Kammermacher.

The bulk of this work was translated into English by Mrs. Vera Broido-Cohn, daughter of my late lamented friend Eva Broido, and edited by Anatole Shub. Jacob Shapiro translated several chapters. The late S. M. Levitas, Boris Souvarine, Daniel Bell and Alexander Ehrlich furnished valuable suggestions and criticism. B. I. Nikolaevsky, Mrs. A. M. Bourgina and Dr. Leo Magerovsky have provided not only their friendly advice, but much-needed books and materials. Special thanks are extended to Harvard University for permission to use the materials from the Trotsky archive.

Note: All mention of my "Memoirs" refer to a book published in Yiddish, in two volumes, under the title, *In Tsvei Revoluties* (New York, Workmen's Circle, 1944). All quotations from Lenin's writings and speeches are taken from the official Moscow publication (4th Edition) and translated by me from the Russian original.

Contents

Prologue

Russia Before the War (1907-1914)

If there was a single cause for the Russian Revolution of 1917, it was undoubtedly the First World War. The war's defeats and inevitable demoralization were the primary source of all the disruptive changes in Russian society, in the Russian economy, and in Russian politics which contributed to the upheavals of February and October 1917. To ascribe such a decisive significance to the war is not to ignore the century-old Russian revolutionary tradition: the Decembrist rebels of 1825, the utopian terrorists of the *Narodnya Volya* who assassinated Tsar Alexander II in 1881, or any number of lesser known revolutionary groups of the 19th century. Nor is there any desire to slight the agrarian movements of the half-century before 1917, nor the glorious Revolution of 1905, which nearly toppled the throne of the Romanovs. Indeed, it is with full consciousness of these tendencies and events—and particularly of the 1905 Revolution—that one must assign primary importance to World War I in determining the shape and character of the 1917 Revolution. For, as a result of the events of 1905 and the social processes then set in motion, Russia on the eve of the war was well advanced on the path of evolution toward a modern democratic state. Had the war not intervened, she could have advanced much further, peacefully, through the pressures of the growing labor movement, the liberal middle classes, and the socially-conscious intelligentsia.

This is not to say that Russia in 1914 was already a modern nation. That was hardly the case. The 1905 Revolution neither overthrew the Tsarist regime nor compelled the nobility and the large landowners to agree to any extensive redistribution of the lands. And a radical agrarian reform, traditionally one of the most cherished dreams of poor and landless peasants, represented one of the basic prerequisites for the modernization of Russian society. Indeed, while some peasants did participate in the upheaval of 1905, the peasants' sons in the army largely obeyed the Tsar and their officers: Guards' regiments were instrumental in putting down the Moscow uprising of December 1905.

What happened afterward was the establishment of a mixed regime in Russia. It was no longer the old autocratic regime which had existed before 1905; nor was it a truly constitutional regime comparable to those of the Western democracies. The Tsar and his ministers were compelled to reckon with the existence of the State Duma, a representative Chamber elected by the broad masses of the people. Because of the Duma the autocracy could not revoke the liberal concessions which Tsar Nicholas II had been forced to make in his manifesto of October 17, 1905, during the general strike which had paralyzed the nation. On the other hand, the Duma's predominantly democratic majority lacked the power to compel the government to accept its leadership, which the laws of the land continued to proclaim after two "illegal" operations performed on its constitution by the Tsar during 1906 and on June 3, 1907.

The co-existence of the two antagonistic systems—the autocratic Ministry and the democratic Parliament—was not harmonious, nor could it be since the Executive was still not responsible to the Duma or to the people the Duma broadly represented. Nevertheless, on balance, the civil and political rights of the population were greatly expanded as a result of the 1905 Revolution, although many autocratic tendencies survived intact. A limited freedom of the press, of assembly and of association continued to exist even after the reaction of 1906-07. Moderate political parties, labor unions, co-operatives and similar social institutions were established in Russia, though their activities and achievements were not so secure as in the democratic countries. Even in the worst days of the reaction, daily newspapers were sponsored by socialist parties, from the moderate right to the Bolsheviks, who gave them neutral titles to disguise their origins.

In the Duma itself, all political viewpoints were represented in some way. Every shade of opinion had its Duma group. The right was represented by the extreme monarchists and reactionaries, the center by the Octobrists (moderate conservatives) and the more liberal Constitutional Democrats (Kadets). Somewhat to the left sat the so-called Trudoviki or Populists, many of whom were very close to the illegal Socialist Revolutionary (S-R) Party. Then came the Social Democrats, a Marxist party, already divided into Bolsheviks and Mensheviks, both of which remained relatively intact until the very outbreak of the War, though many of their most prominent leaders had been arrested in the reaction of 1907 and others had preferred to seek asylum abroad. Each group in the Duma after 1907 was free to proclaim its name and program openly and its members enjoyed parliamentary immunity from arrest and other harassments. At the same time, mass socialist parties were not tolerated: they conducted their work underground or through ingenious semi-legal devices.

That Russia in this period was neither an autocracy nor a democracy did not hamper the country's social and economic development, which began moving forward at an amazing pace. From 1908 to 1914, the output of Russian industry rose by 50%, as did its foreign trade, both imports and exports. The relative freedom which the bourgeoisie acquired in Russia as a result of the political changes after 1905 acted as a great stimulus. Limitation of the autocratic privileges of the Tsarist bureaucracy and of the *dvorianstvo* (the landed gentry) further released the free initiative of the resourceful, energetic middle-class. New industries, new enterprises, new markets sprang to life. The economic standstill characteristic of the Russia of 1905 gave way to a period of steadily growing prosperity.

Although some historians of contemporary Russia have uncritically accepted the Communist thesis that Russia before 1917 was a country practically without industry, without modern engineering and with antideluvian techniques,[1] this is absolutely untrue. Lenin did not have to start from scratch. Russia had made considerable advances in the development of heavy industry, iron, coal, oil, machinery and lumbering even before the Revolution of 1905. And after that Revolution and especially from 1908 on, Russian industry and technology advanced by leaps and bounds.

As for the workers, they had achieved under the leadership of socialist intellectuals, both political and—even more—economic organization, the latter in the form of legal trade-unions. And so, while the number of political strikes diminished after the failure of the 1905 uprising, the number of economic strikes—for higher wages, shorter hours, better working conditions—rose from year to year. After the great strike of 1907, as a result of which the national average wage rose from 213 to 242 roubles a year, the labor movement came to a standstill for several years. In 1911, as the economic condition of the country became quite prosperous, the workers began to strike again. These strikes involved 97,000 workers in 1911, 176,000 workers in 1912 and 385,000 in 1913. As a result, wages again rose considerably. After 1912, the workers began to organize health insurance funds, which were recognized by law and which spread throughout the country. On the eve of the war there were 2,826 local health funds with more than 2 million members in the machine industry and 252 locals with over 587,000 members in the mines.

The relative improvement of the economic and social position of the workers resulted in a considerable weakening of revolutionary fervor. In each of the old revolutionary groups, the S-R's, the Mensheviks and the Jewish Socialist Bund, a rising number of intellectuals and party workers withdrew from revolutionary activity. The same phenomenon took place among the industrial workers. Hope for the revival of the revolutionary wave, and for the overthrow of the government by a new uprising, fell to the vanishing point even for those who remained in the party and supported the Social Democratic groups in the Duma. A better future seemed to depend on winning new political concessions from the government through mass pressure by legal societies and clubs, lectures, congresses of trade unions, meetings of professional groups, etc. Those who urged this strategy of piecemeal reform no longer were mockingly called "liquidators." They were, in fact, people who did not believe in the possibility of restoring the old clandestine revolutionary parties and instead tried to concentrate on the open, legal activities and methods permitted by the new constitutional practice.

Moreover, the party of the Bolsheviks, which officially condemned any idea of "liquidation" or compromise with the existing semi-constitutional regime and which called for the organization of armed shock-troop units of 5-10 members with the objective of initiating a new uprising, was deteriorating as fast as the Mensheviks and the S-R's. The Bolshevik Party at that time was actually split into a number of different groups. In Switzerland, Lenin and others tried to maintain Bolshevik orthodoxy. But important former leaders of the party had separated from Lenin. A. Bogdanov, Goldenberg, Prof. Rozhkov, V. Bazarov, A. Lunacharsky and others organized various separate political groups under such names as the "Boycottists," the "Otsovists," the "Religion Seekers," the "Vpered" group, etc. The great monolithic Marxist Party with iron discipline had more and more become a myth. In its place was a multitude of separate groups, incessantly quarreling with one another and with everybody else. Lenin and his Central Committee in Switzerland had no funds and could hardly support a small magazine. A similar plight faced the S-R group headed by Victor Chernov and the Mensheviks around Axelrod, Martov and Martynov.

The Duma functioned as the center of political life. The left factions of the Duma, which enjoyed legal status and could address the nation from its rostrum, were for all practical purposes the only well-known recognized leaders of the socialist and labor movements.

Even efforts to solve the problem of the peasantry and of agrarian reform made considerable progress during the semi-constitutional period. The most resourceful of the Tsarist ministers, Peter Stolypin, adopted a definite agrarian policy which enabled individual peasants to acquire land with government loans and establish themselves as individual farmers outside the village communes. Each peasant now had the right to leave the commune, to acquire a plot of the communal land, and to set himself up as an independent farmer. With aid from the Peasants' Bank, he could buy land from the community or emigrate to Siberia, where the land reserves at this time were limitless. During the years 1907-1915, over 16 million desiatinas (one desiatina—1.09 hectares) of community lands were sold to 2,470,000 individual applicants. Hundreds of thousands set up farms on the virgin lands of Siberia. But this reform had barely begun to operate when war intervened. And then the young peasants were called to arms.

It seems clear to me, in sum, that, had peace been maintained in Europe for another decade or two, a peaceful evolution in Russia toward modernization, democratization and rapid economic growth would have taken place.[2] Under the pressure of the Duma, of the growing middle-classes, and last but not least, of the workers,[3] Russia might have taken her place among the other democratic nations without a new revolution. But the war of 1914 prevented any such development. A major war is always a revolution for any country which participates in it, and a lost war usually weakens the prestige and confidence of the regime which conducts it. But for Russian society, which was still in a state of flux unstabilized, the First World War was a veritable earthquake.

[1] A British author wrote in his book on Stalin that prior to 1917 Russia was not even capable of manufacturing matches; but in precisely that period Russia was the biggest manufacturer of "safety matches" in all Europe.

[2] Lenin had the right intuition when in January 1913 he wrote to Maxim Gorki: "What we need right now is a war but I am afraid Franz Joseph and little Nicholas wouldn't do us such a favor." *Leninski Sbornik,* I, p. 137.

[3] That the Russian workers were not at that time in a state of apathy and political indifference can be seen from the fact that the brutal action of the Tsarist gendarmerie against the striking workers in the Lena gold fields in Siberia in 1912 provoked a strike of 215,000 workers throughout all Russia.

CHAPTER 1

The War and The February Revolution

Russia's Early Defeats

Russia was drawn into the First World War completely unprepared —psychologically, politically and even militarily. In spite of its population of over 180,000,000 the trained military forces of the gigantic Russian Empire on August 1, 1914 did not exceed the combined strength of Germany and Austria-Hungary.[1] To be sure, the German forces were divided: about 1,500,000 men were thrown into the battle on the western front. Nevertheless, Russia's numerical advantage on the eastern front was to a large extent outweighed by Germany's geographical position in the heart of Europe, her superior railroad transportation, her shorter lines of supply and excellent technical equipment. Russian industry was unable to meet the requirements of prolonged warfare under modern conditions. At the outset of military operations, Germany and Austria-Hungary had 11,232 pieces of light and 2,244 pieces of heavy artillery, while the Russian army had 6,848 light and only 240 heavy guns. German industry remained the most powerful on the continent of Europe, while Russian industry could not satisfy even the minimum demands of the army. The supply of arms and ammunition to Russia from France and England was limited by the naval blockade which Germany successfully maintained. From the start, then, the relative material and industrial strength of Russia and the Central Powers made a Russian victory improbable.

Within three weeks, the Russian army had suffered a grave defeat. An attempt to invade East Prussia, after meeting with initial success, turned into a disaster which cost the Russians 250,000 in dead, wounded, captured. The Russians, however, had compelled the Germans to transfer two corps[2] from the western front at the height of the decisive fighting on the Marne at the end of August. This enabled the French to win the battle of the Marne, and thus saved Paris —Russia's greatest single military contribution to the Allied cause.

On the Austrian front, as in East Prussia, the Russian armies were at first successful, occupying Lvov on September 3; but a counterattack launched by German troops forced a retreat. A second Russian attack threw the Austro-Hungarian forces back in the direction of Warsaw-Ivangorod. Then, for a time, military operations took the form of siege warfare, as in the west. But while the disposition of forces on the western front was stable for a long time, the eastern front became mobile again in the spring of 1915.

Conditions in the Russian army grew difficult after only a few months of war. In December 1914, Alexander I. Guchkov, the chief representative of the Russian Red Cross, reported after a tour of the front:

> The problems of food supply have not been solved in the army. The troops go hungry. Many have no boots. Their feet are wrapped in strips of cloth . . . Particularly alarming is the shortage of ammunition for the artillery. I read an order of the corps commander to the effect that each gun was to fire only from three to five rounds per day. Our infantry, which is under constant shelling by the enemy, has no artillery protection.[3]

In the spring of 1915 the General Staff calculated that the Russian armies needed monthly replacements of 500,000 men, 350,000 rifles and 1,500,000 shells.[4] But it was exceedingly difficult for the country to meet these requirements. The Germans' technical superiority, particularly in heavy artillery, which they deployed in incredibly large numbers before every decisive engagement, became overwhelming. Add to this the incompetence of some Russian commanders and the corruption of others, the inadequate technical training of the soldiers, general backwardness in the special arts of modern war (the Russian radio code was easily broken by the Germans), primitive logistics and inadequate railroads; and one can understand why the

General Staff on February 23, 1915,[5] should declare that it was impossible, given the condition of the Russian armies, to wrest the initiative from the enemy. All the Russian commanders could hope to do was to weaken the impending German spring offensive by various diversionary movements. As it turned out, even this was no longer feasible.

On May 2, 1915, General von Mackensen began an attack in western Galicia, between Gorlice and Tarnov, which had been prepared by an extraordinary concentration of cannon and mortars. The victories gained by German-Austrian forces led to a general Russian retreat. By September the Germans had occupied almost all the Baltic states and Poland, and partly re-occupied Austrian Galicia. The new front line followed the West Dvina as far as Dvinsk and, thereafter, the tributaries of the Nemen and the Pripet, along a line defined by Riga-Dvinsk-Pinsk-Chernovitsi.

The Bankruptcy of the Old Regime

In the face of these defeats, the prestige of the Russian government was seriously undermined, at home as well as abroad. The opposition currents which had characterized Russian public opinion before the war were now intensified by a sense of national humiliation. Since the middle of the nineteenth century, defeat in the field had been accompanied, in Russia, by opposition at home, which, in turn, led to reforms. Thus, after the Crimean war of 1854-56, Tsar Alexander II instituted a number of basic administrative and social reforms, such as the abolition of serfdom in 1861. The ill-fated Russo-Japanese war of 1904-1905 was the prelude to the Revolution of 1905, and the semi-constitutional regime.

In the autumn of 1915, opposition began to manifest itself among the Russian people in various ways. The so-called Progressive Bloc, uniting the moderate and liberal parties, was formed in the State Duma; it strove to turn the Duma into a real parliament and to form a government responsible to it, a government capable of introducing necessary reforms and reorganizing the nation's defenses. Meanwhile patriotic industrialists formed a network of War-Industry Committees, which attempted to utilize the creative initiative of both industrialists and workers in the national defense. Over government resistance, the War-Industry Committees organized affiliated "Workers' Groups," which sought to unite the patriotic workers; these groups later became the arena for labor's political activities, since all its other economic and political organizations had been dispersed, suppressed or driven underground at the outbreak of war.

Yet, neither the intensified opposition of the liberal bourgeoisie, nor the growing pressure from the working class, nor even the dissatisfaction in the army, which had reached the highest ranks, succeeded in affecting the Tsarist court. The weak and spineless Tsar, and the energetic and strong-minded Tsarina, both continued to live in an unreal world. Among the Tsarina's entourage, a pernicious cabal existed in which an increasingly important part was played by the "holy man" Gregory Rasputin, a semi-literate Siberian peasant with hypnotic powers. Rasputin was not distinguished by the holiness of his conduct—he often sought and enjoyed the favors of the ladies-in-waiting—but he remained first among the Tsarina's advisers, and came to have real influence on the decisions of the Tsar himself. Moreover, the Tsarina was a former German princess, Alice of Hesse, and rumors of her pro-German leanings and friends circulated freely in the court, and later throughout the country.

This state of affairs aroused indignation even among the courtiers and within the royal family—a fact confirmed recently in the memoirs of the former protopresbyter of the Orthodox Church, Shavelsky,[6] who regularly dined with the imperial family. Devoted men in the Tsar's entourage—such as the Commander-in-Chief, General M. V. Alexseev, V. Gurko of the State Council, and the increasingly popular war-leader, General N. Ivanov—warned the monarch of the impending catastrophe, but to no avail. "Once," writes Shavelsky, "P. M. Kaufman, member of the State Council, came to see him. He was the chief Red Cross representative at GHQ and had always been considered a special favorite of the Emperor, with whom he lunched and dined daily, and to whom he was very devoted. This time (it was November 9, 1916, at 10 a.m.) Kaufman had resolved to speak quite frankly to the Emperor and to tell him the whole truth. When he had finished speaking, he asked Nicholas: 'Do you believe me? Do you believe that I am your devoted subject and that I love you deeply?' 'I believe you,' answered Nicholas. 'Then allow me to kill Rasputin.' Nicholas burst into tears and embraced and kissed Kaufman."[7] A month later, on December 9, Kaufman was removed from his post and deprived of his position at the court.

Shavelsky himself determined to have a frank talk with the Tsarina, but was refused an audience. The refusal was communicated by the lady-in-waiting, Madame Vyrubova, considered closest to the Tsarina. Vyrubova indignantly accused the courtiers, including the grand dukes, of intrigue and maintained that the rumors of the Tsarina's unpopularity were untrue; on the contrary, the people everywhere acclaimed her enthusiastically, she received letters from officers' groups begging her to resist the pressure of the mob, etc.[8]

Shavelsky writes: "The impending storm could only have been averted by generous reforms which would have met the needs and rights of the people and by self-sacrifice on the part of the upper classes; not by bullets and not by the betrayal of the honor of a great people."[9] But the Romanovs were incapable of recognizing the gravity of their own plight. Disaffection continued to spread, and even members of the imperial family began to think of a palace revolution. On the night of December 17-18, 1916, Rasputin was assassinated; the plot had been organized by Grand Duke Dmitri Pavlovitch, Prince Yusupov and the monarchist Purishkevich, who was the leader of the extreme right in the State Duma. But even this failed to jolt the court into decisive action.

Meanwhile, the economic crisis was gradually deepening. A report transmitted to the Tsar by M. Rodzianko, in the name of a group of leading citizens, summarized data gathered in an investigation in Moscow, Petrograd and various other centers. The report showed that food was in dangerously short supply, that Moscow's daily ration was adequate for "just over half the population," and that a similar situation prevailed in Petrograd. Things were no better in the provinces. The Perm district, one of the centers of war production, expected its reserves of bread would be exhausted by March. The fuel picture was equally alarming: in the Moscow industrial area, several factories were idle because of a shortage of fuel; in Petrograd, first 39 and later 11 additional industrial plants were compelled to suspend production. The output of pig iron and steel fell sharply in

February, production of steel in southern Russia had decreased by more than half, and in the Urals the situation was even worse.[10]

This, then, was Russia at the beginning of the fateful year 1917.

The February Rising

On February 22 (March 7), 1917, the Tsar left Petrograd for General Headquarters. His departure was uneventful. "Nothing seemed to foretoken a storm," wrote a well-informed observer. "Although there was unrest in the factories, and often an angry mood among the queues at the shops, there was nothing unusual in that. The surface of political life was smooth and untroubled. In the State Duma, debates over the food supplies dragged on . . . The newspapers, under the thumb of war-censorship, were lifeless and emtpy . . . The frost was severe . . . Silence and quiet reigned over the immense, snow-covered Russian plain. There was a lull along the whole front and the everyday routine of army life went on sluggishly in trenches half-buried in snow . . . That lull deceived everybody."[11]

The very next day, February 23, strikes began in several factories; here and there, workers went out into the streets, demanding food. There was no bread, and working women, tired of endless queues, lost their patience and protested loudly. The unrest spread with amazing rapidity. There were 90,000 people on strike on the 23rd, about 200,000 on the 24th, and over 240,000 on the 25th.

These demonstrations were entirely spontaneous. They had not been organized either by any of the old political parties or by any newly-formed political body. Neither the Bolsheviks nor the Mensheviks nor the Socialist Revolutionaries, whose underground groups were almost extinct in those days, ever claimed to have played any part in the outbreak of unrest.[12] The strikes not only surprised everyone in Petrograd; they were an even greater surprise to the political exiles in Geneva, Berne, Stockholm and Zurich.[13]

Although neither the strikes nor the demonstrations in the working-class suburbs (such as the Vyborg district) had a political character, the desultory efforts of the police to stop the movement quickly gave it political significance. On the second day, red flags began to appear, and the slogans "Down with the war!" and "Give us bread!"

were heard. The same day, 14,000 workers of the Obukhov plant unfurled a red banner inscribed: "Down with the autocracy! Long live the democratic republic!"

The police could not cope with the spreading unrest, so the commander of the Petrograd military district, General Khabalov, turned to the military authorities. Army patrols were posted in all parts of the city, and the Cossacks were called out. But the Cossacks appeared without their whips, while the Grenadier Guards assured the workers that they would not load their rifles.[14] Thus, until February 25, both the crowds and the authorities generally behaved with restraint and good humor.

Then, in answer to the stream of telegrams arriving at General Headquarters from Petrograd, the Tsar sent the following order to General Khabalov: "I command that the disorders in the capital cease by tomorrow, *as being inadmissible* in this time of war with Germany and Austria." On the 25th, Khabalov prepared the various regiments for their tasks; the decisive offensive was to begin on Sunday the 26th. That day the workers were at home, and both the industrial suburbs and the center of the city were comparatively deserted.

In the afternoon, however, a crowd began to gather in Znamensky Square. It was composed not so much of workers, who largely lived on the outskirts, as of somewhat more prosperous folk. When a mass meeting spontaneously developed, similar to those held in the outlying districts the two preceding days, the training unit[15] of the Volynsky Regiment was ordered to disperse it. Suddenly, without warning, shots were fired. Some of the soldiers fired above the heads of the crowd, but others fired into it, and the panic-stricken people were horrified to see the dead and wounded on the pavement.

The crowd dispersed, but the government's victory was a Pyrrhic one. The bloodshed outraged not only the civilian population; the soldiers of the Volynsky Regiment itself were shaken by the behavior of their training group. Early next morning (February 27), small groups of soldiers stood about the regimental barracks discussing the incident. When the commanding officer of the training group appeared, accompanied by a subaltern, the soldiers shot them both, to shouts of "Hurrah!" The Volynsky Regiment then went over to the the people. It left the barracks in full battle order and marched to the

Liteyny Bridge to "relieve" the Moscow Regiment on duty there. On the way the Volynsky were joined by detachments of other regiments —the Preobrazhensky and the Litovsky. Later, workers began to fall in step and, after a short dispute with its officers, the Moscow Regiment, too, marched with them.

The news of these events spread through the town like wildfire, and all the intersections along Nevsky Prospect were soon blocked by wildly cheering crowds. Then, soldiers and civilians surrounded the district court building, freed all the prisoners, including the recently arrested "Workers' Group" of the War-Industry Committee, and set the building on fire. Fires were also started in a great many police precincts, which the police had abandoned. The dense smoke signaled the victory of the revolution. Petrograd was now in the hands of the soldiers and workers. Only the Winter Palace, the Admiralty, and the Schluesselburg Fortress were guarded by army units still loyal to the regime.

The issue had been decided by the soldiers' support of the revolution. The State Duma, which Nicholas had first "dissolved" by telegram, now ceased to waver, overcame the resistence of the conservatives and moderate liberals who remained loyal to their Emperor, and seized the authority which had slipped from the hands of the old government. A "Provisional Committee of the State Duma," composed mainly of moderates, was created; it became in effect the new government.

In the Tauride Palace, which now became the official residence of the "Provisional Committee," the popular Duma deputy, Alexander Kerensky, stationed the sentries, welcomed deputations, gave orders; his prestige was high, and his every appearance was greeted with an ovation.

At General Headquarters, meanwhile, Tsar Nicholas remained happily ignorant of the developments in his capital. He had been informed, by a telegram from Khabalov on the 26th, that the unrest had been suppressed and that the State Duma, with its "mutineers," had been dissolved. So he went home to his palace in Tsarskoye Selo undisturbed. He did not know that one guards' regiment after another, led by its officers, was marching armed to the Tauride Palace and swearing allegiance to the new regime. One of these regiments was led by Grand Duke Cyril Vladimirovich, wearing a red cockade of the revolution on his breast. All came to Petrograd to declare their loyalty to the new regime—the garrisons of Schluesselburg, Kronstadt and Tsarskoye Selo, and the commander of the Baltic Fleet. In Mocow, at the same time, a Popular Committee assumed authority, and the garrison placed itself at its disposal. Even at General Headquarters, where the news arrived somewhat belatedly, the *fait accompli* was accepted by the Commander-in-Chief and the entire corps of generals. Without any recorded protest, they endorsed Rodzianko's proposal that Nicholas should be asked to abdicate and that a new government be formed that would have the confidence of the country. Neither in the army, nor in the cities, nor among the upper classes could any sympathy for the Romanov dynasty be discerned. Even the most convinced monarchists now knew that nothing could save the autocracy. On March 2 (15), Nicholas signed his abdication.

Power had been snatched from the weak grasp of Tsarism by the Provisional Committee of the State Duma, by General Headquarters, and by the various public bodies in Russian society. But soon a very significant addition appeared. The formation of Soviets (councils) of workers in the factories, after the pattern of those created in October 1905, was proposed by "individual socialists" as early as February 25 (March 10). Two days later, the leaders of the "Workers' Groups" of the War-Industry Committee (K. Gvozdyev, B. Bogdanov and others) were freed from prison and went immediately to the Tauride Palace. Then and there, they assembled a number of leading socialists from the Duma and founded the Provisional Executive Committee of the Soviet of Workers' Deputies. This was on February 27 (March 12). The Committee included representatives of the Mensheviks, the Bolsheviks, the Socialist Revolutionaries, the Popular Socialists, the Trudoviks (Kerensky among them), the Jewish Workers' "Bund," and the Polish and Latvian socialists; and it instantly set to work forming a network of Soviets in the city.

"The Tauride Palace," wrote the observers quoted above, "then became divided in two. In one half, there was the Provisional Committee of the State Duma, composed mainly of right-wing and moderate elements, which, precisely for that reason, had made the revolution acceptable to the conservative element in Russian society;

in the other half there ruled the newly founded Soviet, which had grown into a mass organization with the speed of an avalanche." The worker deputies to the Soviet were joined by "soldier deputies," and it became abundantly clear that the Petrograd Soviet, and the whole system of Soviets, had emerged as the representative of the broad, popular masses.

Although the new generation of soldiers and workers, who had entered Petrograd during the war years, were ignorant of the events of 1905, they immediately embraced the Soviets as their own organization. The same factors which had attracted the workers to the Soviets in October 1905—in spite of the opposition of the Bolsheviks—were also operating in March-April 1917. The workers were in a generally revolutionary mood, but they steered clear of the existing parties and party leaders. Gravitating more naturally to their own, non-party organizations, they followed the non-party men who, in the course of events, rose from their midst. In January 1905, the Petrograd workers had followed the priest Gapon and his group, rather than the Socialist Revolutionaries or the Social Democrats. In October 1905, they had chosen as their idol neither Lenin, Plekhanov nor Martov, but the unknown young lawyer Khrustalev-Nossar—only to forget him soon afterwards. Trotsky owed his popularity at that time precisely to his activities within the Soviet and to his brilliant speeches at the trial of its arrested members. Even more alien to political parties and devoid of political training were the workers' closest partners in February-March 1917, the soldiers. The masses' cherished leader was Kerensky, who was considered a non-party revolutionary, and who was the natural link between the two parts of the dual system of power.

The Soviets and the Political Parties

Yet, as time went on, the political parties gained an increasing hold on the masses, even in the non-partisan Soviets. With the possible exception of Prince Lvov's first cabinet, negotiations among the parties determined the composition of the successive cabinets of the Provisional Government.

The Kadets (Constitutional Democrats), who had carried considerable weight in all four Dumas, became, after the abolition of the monarchy, the unchallenged representatives of bourgeois liberalism. (The monarchists of various shades had found no mass support and ceased to figure in the political arena.) The parties of the left determined the policies of individual Soviets, and of the central organs of the whole network of Soviets.

The least radical of these was the Trudovik Party (Popular Socialists), which had originally been the right wing of the Narodniki and later became an independent party. The revolutionary socialists, at the outbreak of the February revolution, fell into two main groupings: the Socialist Revolutionaries, founded in 1900 and representing the so-called populist or agrarian (Narodnik) outlook, and the two Marxist parties, known as the Mensheviks and Bolsheviks. These two were originally parts of one and the same party, the Russian Social Democratic Labor Party, founded in 1898, which had split into a majority and a minority group at its Second Congress, held in London in 1903. The breach originated over an apparently minor issue, but widened so much with the passage of time that, by 1912, they were two completely separate and rival parties, quite hostile to each other. The Bolsheviks, under Lenin, favored extreme tactics; the Mensheviks, led by Paul Axelrod, Julius Martov and others, were moderate in their methods, although not in their program.

Trotsky, who was to play such an outstanding part in October, was at one time a Menshevik. He did not switch over to the Bolsheviks until 1917. Ideologically, however, he differed from both. The two Marxist parties had maintained—right up to the outbreak of the war and even afterward—that the revolution in Russia would, inevitably, be anti-feudal and bourgeois-democratic in character. In view of the general social backwardness of Russia, and of the smallness of its industrial working class, the Russian Marxists did not envisage that the revolution would immediately enter a socialist-proletarian stage. Trotsky, on the other hand (supported abroad by the Russo-German Social Democrat, Parvus, and the prominent German Marxist writer, Rosa Luxemburg), refused to subscribe to this "class asceticism," as he ironically termed it. Instead, he advanced the thesis that, when the revolution took place in Russia, it would be the prologue to a world socialist revolution.[16] Consequently, it would unavoidably itself become a proletarian socialist revolution, in spite of all obstacles.

Such, then, were the parties' beliefs before the war.[17] They underwent considerable ideological change as a result of the war, and under the impact of the February revolution.[18] When the war broke out, the socialist parties' central organizations in Russia were smashed by the Tsarist police, and contact between the various local organizations as far as they managed to survive could not be maintained. Ideological discussion could only thrive thenceforth in the emigré party centers abroad, or among groups formed by political deportees in some parts of Siberia. Only under such conditions could theory and ideology be sustained—and the war had engendered ample dissension in socialist movements throughout the world. Nevertheless, after the February revolution, the socialist parties came to life with unexpected vigor—and became powerful organizations commanding the allegiance of millions of people. By November 1917, when the elections for the All-Russian Constituent Assembly were held, 20.9 million people, over half of all the voters, voted for the Socialist Revolutionary parties, the Russian and those of other nationalities; and the various socialist parties together won 88 per cent of the seats in the Assembly.

To comprehend this fantastic growth on the part of the socialist parties after February 1917—a time when the Russian people seemed in a non-party mood—one must examine the sociological and psychological changes that had taken place during the war.

The Birth of a New "Class"

During the years 1907-1914, Russia had advanced considerably, as stated in the Prologue, toward becoming a fully-developed industrial, capitalist country, but it had by no means completed the transformation. Although, in the fight against Tsarism, the bourgeois groups in the State Duma (the "Progressive Bloc") had commanded support among workers and peasants, the Russian bourgeoisie had had little impact on Russian spiritual and social life until the beginning of the 19th century, and the concepts underlying capitalism and private property still meant little to the Russian people as a whole.

Despite Stolypin's[19] agrarian reforms, the Russian peasantry had not yet produced any considerable number of conservative, property-minded, independent farmers of the type of the Central European *Bauer* or the 19th century French peasant; nor were the urban middle classes in Russia as self-assertive as those of Western Europe. For its part, the intelligentsia had in the decades preceding the war been drawn more and more from the lower classes in town and country; it was traditionally radical, and strongly attracted to various kinds of socialism. And, paradoxically, though it had come to dominate Russia's economic life, capitalism had little real influence in administration or government.

For these reasons, when the Romanov regime was swept away in February, the capitalist class was neither mature nor experienced enough to seize and hold the reins of government, as the middle class had done in France, for example, in the 19th century. Only Lenin in far-off Switzerland could possibly imagine, in the first days of the February revolution, that the people who had replaced the Tsarist regime—A. Guchkov, M. Rodzianko and the others—represented a "counter-revolutionary bourgeoisie," capable of either establishing a constitutional monarchy or creating a stable conservative regime in its stead.[20] In fact, neither the first provisional government headed by Prince Lvov, nor the coalitions that followed it, were "bourgeois" either in their programs or their social aims. The rapid emergence of dual power—with the popular Soviets soon becoming far stronger than the legitimate government and its broken-down state administration—proved that the bourgeoisie had been incapable at the very start of mastering the situation on its own. From the first, the bourgeoisie was only the junior partner of the revolutionary and socialist intelligentsia, with its following of workers, soldiers, and peasants.

The character of the working class had been considerably transformed during the war. Quite a number of the older workers, who had been part of the Revolution of 1905 or who had been acquainted with the Social Democratic parties or the trade-union movement under the semi-constitutional regime, had been absorbed into the army and lost to industry. Meanwhile, the defense industries, greatly expanded, had received an enormous influx of new workers. Some of these came from among the urban poor, but many more came from the peasantry—a politically unschooled mass which knew little of the traditions of an industrial working class. Nor could such traditions be rapidly acquired, since the working-class movement was stifled in war time.

Still more decisive was the mobilization of soldiers itself, on a scale that was unprecedented in Russian history. Between 12 and 15 million peasant lads, from villages in remote Siberia and other far-flung districts of the vast empire, had been put in military uniforms and crowded into urban areas, most of them along the northwestern and southern frontiers. Since the disastrous summer campaign of 1915, the Russian army had been inactive and, though new recruits continued to be drafted, there were no major military operations. Here then, was an enormous new social formation—a soldiery that had ceased to be peasants in the social and economic sense, that was falling under the influence of urban political ideas, and yet had no material roots in the working class. Toward the end of 1916, vague ideas of revolution and socialism had come to permeate these young men. But their basic concern was peace; they wished to be free of the haunting menace of death or mutilation and to return to normal life, either in the towns or in their distant villages, where their families and land awaited them.

The urban workers were also strongly attracted by the idea of peace, and the desire for an end to the war gave new appeal, among soldiers and workers alike, to revolution and agrarian reform. Sometimes the soldiers did not quite understand the various covert or overt socialist agitators who came among them. But the workers were better organized, more articulate and purposeful, so they followed the workers and their socialist parties. In their peasant minds, of course, socialism and communism were seen from the viewpoint of the consumer; to them it meant a sharing-out, a redistribution of goods, rather than a fundamental reorganization of the means of production. A considerable number of the "new" workers, who had also only recently left the countryside, pictured socialism in much the same manner. "The army will always and everywhere be an enormous 'consumers' commune' "—wrote the well-known socialist sociologist, A. Bogdanov, in early 1918[21]—"because the army takes no part in production or in economic life in general."

Where the organs and the authority of the government remain intact the army will remain its obedient instrument, even when some parts of it are disintegrating morally under the impact of prolonged war and defeat (as was the case in France, Italy and sporadically in Germany and even in England). In Russia, where the apparatus of government was practically destroyed in a few days, the army soon became the main force of the revolution. The pressure from millions of soldiers, the only armed force in the country, proved overwhelming.

The coalition of workers and soldiers was to a considerable extent supported by the peasantry in the villages. But at that stage of the revolution, the influence of the peasantry in 1917 was insignificant. In the cities and towns, ideas, slogans and leadership were supplied by the socialist intelligentsia and the workers. But the decisive influence, on balance, was the sentiments, aspirations and demands of the soldiery. Without or against them, nothing could be done even by those socialist parties which were closest to them—the Mensheviks and the S-R's before the autumn of 1917, and the Bolsheviks thereafter.

The Urge of the Masses for Peace

Russia's heavy defeats in the war were deeply humiliating to her intellectuals, her middle classes, and, above all to the vast numbers of the army officers. Their frustrated patriotism caused them to seek a scapegoat, and none so obviously suited the part as the autocratic Tsarist regime, which had plunged the unprepared country into a disastrous war. The intelligentsia's opposition to autocracy, which had deep roots in the nineteenth century, was intensified by its desire for more vigorous national defense against Germany. In the spring and summer of 1917, broad sections of the intelligentsia believed that freedom would revitalize the nation and renew the army's fighting spirit. But the peasants, workers, and enlisted men in the army expected something else. The first banners to appear in the streets on

February 22 and 23 (March 7 and 8) had proclaimed "Stop the War!" and "Give us Bread!" As the revolution developed, and Germany continued to hold the upper hand on the battle fronts, the masses became increasingly determined that the revolution should bring an end to the war.

Not that Russia was clearly divided in this manner at the very beginning of the revolution. On the contrary, at first all were in favor of a more vigorous defense effort. The defense-minded socialists commanded a large majority in all the Soviets and, until Lenin arrived, even the Bolsheviks—Kamenev, Stalin, and Molotov, for instance—endorsed the majority opinion. The general feeling was indicated in the resolution proposed by Irakly Tseretelli on March 30 (April 12) at the First All-Russian Conference of Workers' and Soldiers' Soviets, which was attended by about 500 delegates. The resolution, after reaffirming the general desire for an early peace, went on to say:

> Collapse of the army—a weakening of its strength, resilience, and *preparedness for active operations*—while the war is still on would be felt by all Russian democrats as a grave blow to the freedom and vital interests of the country.

The italicized words, proposed as an amendment by Romm, the delegate of the 12th Army, were inserted in the draft resolution with Tseretelli's approval. Their meaning is clear: the Conference included the ability to counter-attack in its definition of defense. The resolution, with this amendment, was carried by 325 votes, with 20 abstaining and 57 voting for a different resolution proposed by Kamenev on behalf of the Central Committee of the Bolshevik Party and the internationalist wing of the Socialist Revolutionaries. Kamenev's resolution ended on the following note: if any of the belligerent countries should reject proposals of peace, then

> the revolutionary people of Russia would take war into their own hands and turn it, in agreement with the proletariat of Western Europe, into a war for the freedom of nations. Until such a time, we oppose the disintegration of the army, and consider it essential to maintain the army as a strong bulwark

> against counter-revolution. We appeal to all soldiers and workers to remain at their posts and to preserve complete discipline.

The resolutions passed by army units, Soviets, and factory meetings in these days were, similarly, all outrightly defensist in character. When the Bolsheviks organized a triumphal reception for Lenin on the 3rd (16th) of April, they sent to Kronstadt for a special guard of honor, to be composed of sailors of the Second Baltic Fleet. Later these sailors issued a resolution stating that they had agreed to honor Lenin for his many services to the revolution; but had come to regret their participation in the reception; had they known "by what route he had come to Russia, then, instead of the jubilant 'Hurrahs,' the indignant cry would have been heard: 'Go back to the country you came through!' "

The revolutionary masses could not consciously accept the idea of capitulation to the German emperor, or of a separate peace and a betrayal of Russia's allies; yet, without realizing it, they began to yield to defeatism as time went on—to the alluring vision of an immediate peace at any price that would put an end to their sufferings and permit revolutionary change to proceed. The peasants, in particular, felt the connection between agrarian reform and peace. For, while the war was still on, millions of peasants were away from home and unable to participate in radical redistribution of land. It might have been easy, after the collapse of the old order, to stretch out a hand and seize a long-coveted field from one of the landowners; but the government had forbidden any such actions until the Constituent Assembly had been elected and convened.

The early weeks of the revolution provided a striking illustration of the attitude of the peasants. Even before the revolution, desertions from the army had increased enormously. When the revolution broke out and local organs of government temporarily lost control, many soldiers seized the opportunity to take off and visit their families. Soldiers' Soviets, both at the front and in the rear, urban Soviets and other organizations all recognized the danger in this mass desertion, and bombarded the villages with resolutions and demands. But it was to no avail. until a rumor began to circulate that deserters would be deprived of their share in the future redistribution of the land. Then the army depots were thronged with crowds of deserters, all clamoring to be returned to the front. They went back accompanied by military bands, red flags, and the singing of revolutionary hymns. But, as a chronicle of the times records, the stream of repentant deserters returning to the front was met by another, even larger, stream of new deserters moving in the opposite direction. The incessant two-way "migration" of deserters seriously disrupted the already strained railroad system and imperiled the flow of supplies to the front.

Not only the agrarian, but all other social reforms hinged on the ending of the war. With the administration and the economy in chaos, with food, raw materials, and fuel in short supply, and with a rising inflation under way, the government was in no position to start raising the living standard of the workers or enact any other far-reaching social changes. Until the end of the war, privations had to be patiently endured. But in the revolutionary Russia of 1917, endurance and patience were wearing thin.

In the heated atmosphere generated by any revolution, social processes tend to develop much more rapidly than in a normal time of peace. It was in this psychological atmosphere that the Soviets and the socialist parties began to develop into mass organizations, embracing millions of workers, soldiers, and peasants under the leadership of the Russian revolutionary intelligentsia. These masses were animated by manifold social, economic and political interests, sometimes coinciding but often divergent and conflicting. All moral considerations, however, gave way to the one most urgent need—to put an end to the war which blocked the implementation of their various social, economic, and political desires. With the passage of time, the desire for immediate peace became the obsession of millions and millions of Russian men and women, in the cities and in the country at large.

The Socialist Parties and Their Leaders at the Beginning of the Revolution

Immediately after the formation of the Provisional Government, a general amnesty had opened the road to freedom to imprisoned and deported revolutionaries, and within a few days the old leaders of the socialist parties, the trade unions, and various social organizations began arriving in Petrograd.

For the emigrés abroad, return was not so easy. With Russia cut off from western Europe by the war, the only routes open were by sea (via England, Scandinavia, and Finland), or through the German front. The sea route was closed to many emigrés because the Allied intelligence services had blacklisted the names of all those who had adhered to the program of the anti-war Zimmerwald Conference of 1915; these included not only such extremists as Lenin and Trotsky, but also a number of moderates. Such emigrés could not get transit visas, and were refused passage on Allied ships; furthermore, no women and children had been allowed on ships at all since early 1917, as all shipping was in danger of attack from German submarines and sailed under naval convoy.

The situation of the fairly large Russian colony that had gathered in Switzerland during the war was particularly difficult. At a joint meeting of emigrés of all parties in Zurich, a special committee was appointed to handle the problem of returning home. The secretary of the committee was Dr. Bagotsky, the chairman S. Semkovsky. A general agreement among all the groups, including the Bolsheviks, barred separate action by any individual group; the committee was to handle all the efforts made, including negotiations with the new Russian government and Soviets and the governments of the Allies. The ensuing negotiations, however, were practically hopeless, for even if the Allied governments had been sympathetic, which they were not, the transportation of some eight hundred emigrés and their families to Russia would have taken more than a year. The leaders of the emigré groups refused to remain cut off from home at such an historic moment.[22]

Without the knowledge of other groups of emigrés, Lenin and his group had been conducting talks with the German government through the Swiss socialist, Fritz Platten, pupil and friend of Lenin. Within a short time they had received permission to board a train which was to cross Germany non-stop. The train would take a group of emigrés of various parties (the German government agreed not to check the composition of the group) to Sweden, whence the travelers were to make their own way through Finland to Russia.[23] This was the famous "sealed train"; it left on April 10 (European calendar) and Lenin arrived in Petrograd six days later.

Lenin had made this move without consulting the joint emigré committee or any other group.[24] When he had successfully made his way to Petrograd, without any noticeable protest from the revolutionaries, the numerous emigrés remaining in Switzerland decided to make use of the precedent. The emigrés were aware that the German government had accorded Lenin's group a preferential treatment because it was known to oppose Russia's prosecution of the war—which fit in with German policy. Precisely because of this, the stranded emigrés decided to put pressure on the German officials. They demanded, through the Swiss Red Cross, that Germany allow the Russian citizens and their families remaining in Switzerland to return to Russia via Germany, as Lenin and his group had, without conditions or interference with the composition of the traveling party. In return, the emigrés would promise (as had Lenin and his group) to urge the Russian government to repatriate an equal number of German citizens who had been stranded in Russia during the war. The emigrés reasoned that a refusal on the part of the German government would reveal its real purposes in permitting Lenin's journey—and might thus impede those purposes.

The reasoning proved correct.[25] After some hesitation, the German government granted permission for the passage of 280 emigrés and their families. The train carrying the emigrés left Zurich on May 13 (new style); among the passengers were the Mensheviks Martov, Martynov, Paul Axelrod, Semkovsky, Astrov, Abramovitch and others; the former Bolshevik Lunacharsky, the future Bolshevik Ryazanov, and the active Bolshevik Karl Radek; the old Bolsheviks Manuilsky and Lebedev-Polyansky; the Polish socialists Paul Lapinsky, Felix Kohn and Bronsky; the Social Revolutionaries, Mark Natanson, Gavronsky, and Ustinov. They were accompanied by the chairman of the Zimmerwald Union, the Swiss socialist Robert Grimm, and its secretary, Angelica Balabanova.

Later a third group of Russian emigrés was allowed to pass through Germany from Switzerland, and another group from Bulgaria; among the latter were the Menshevik "Kuzma" (Sborovsky) and the Bolshevik Dr. Semashko. A number of emigrés from France and French Switzerland (Avksentyev, Fundaminsky, Victor Chernov, G. Chicherin, A. Troyanovsky, and others) returned by sea via England. At almost the same time, Trotsky, Bukharin, and Volodarsky returned from the United States. British Intelligence detained Trotsky in Halifax for some time, and he was allowed to proceed only after intervention from Petrograd.

The emigrés soon discovered that the February revolution had caused profound ideological reappraisals among the revolutionary parties. The relative strengths of the "defensist" and "Zimmerwaldist" wings of the Menshevik and S-R parties had shifted greatly. It was one thing to urge an unqualified defense effort under the Tsarist regime, quite another to be a defensist, and even take part in military resistance to enemy armies, when Russia had become a democratic republic practically governed by socialists and democrats. The dividing line between the defensists and the internationalists shifted accordingly.

An overwhelming majority of Mensheviks and S-R's (including those who, prior to February, had considered themselves Zimmerwaldists) now became defensists or, as they styled themselves, "revolutionary defensists." Not one prominent Menshevik, S-R, or Bolshevik leader (and the Bolsheviks included Kamenev, Stalin, Molotov), who was in Russia in the days immediately following the February revolution would have denied the necessity of resisting the German aggressor who had invaded the Russian Democratic Republic. The resolution passed by the Petrograd Soviet left no doubt about the matter. The division between "defensists" and "internationalists" took on a new meaning among the Mensheviks and S-R's. Both the revolutionary defensists (men like Tseretelli, Dan, Gotz, Liber, and Erlich) and the internationalists (such as Martov and Chernov) shared the same desire for immediate peace on the terms formulated at Zimmerwald and reaffirmed by the Petrograd Soviet—that is, peace without annexations or indemnities and without victors or vanquished. Later, a new point, formulated by President Wilson—national self-determination—was also supported by both defensists and internationalists. The only serious difference between the revolutionary defensists, who commanded an overwhelming majority in the Soviets, and the internationalists, who were a small minority, concerned the tactics most likely to achieve their common aim. (This divergence of opinion will be described in greater detail below.)

However, the very opposite tendency was developing among the Bolsheviks and their followers, such as the left S-R's and various small groups (for instance, Trotsky's *Mezhrayontsy* and the Internationalists, or United Internationalists, a small group assembled around the daily newspaper *Novaya Zhizn*, published by Maxim Gorki and Sukhanov). While the Mensheviks and the S-R's were, broadly speaking, moving to the right, and their policy was no longer dictated by a simple repudiation of the Tsarist regime, taking the interests of the state and the nation more into account, the Bolsheviks, under the influence of Lenin, were rapidly becoming more radical in their approach to the problem of war and peace.

The Bolshevik Party After Lenin's Return

In the first week after the revolution, when Lenin was still in Zurich, his letters and speeches still reflected the ideology that he had originally formulated for the Zimmerwald left wing. His main slogan was the conversion of the imperialist war into civil war inside each country, that is, the fomenting of proletarian revolutions in the most advanced of the belligerent countries. He argued that the capitalists had unleashed a world war which they would be unable to bring to a close, since that would produce intolerable conflicts within the capitalist system. Peace could be achieved only after a series of socialist revolutions which would transfer political power to the working class in the major European countries. The possibility of peace was thus inextricably linked, in Lenin's mind, with the success of a world socialist revolution.

In Russia, Lenin maintained, the revolution had already broken out, but it was still in its first phase: it had not yet become a socialist revolution. The country was still governed by the bourgeoisie, through the Provisional Government. True, a network of Soviets had already been created which had the lower classes of the population behind it. But the Soviets, however popular and proletarian in composition, did not consciously aim at the immediate achievement of a socialist regime. This, Lenin argued, was because the Soviets were still influenced by those socialist parties which sought a compromise with the bourgeois classes in order to continue the war. To achieve the socialist program, Lenin reasoned, "and to make the Russian revolution an effective prologue to a world revolution," it was necessary, first, to remove all political power from the hands of the bourgeoisie and transfer it to the Soviets; and then to remove the Soviets from the control of the moderate socialist parties and place them under the control of the Bolshevik Party. Consequently, the struggle for world peace required that the Bolshevik Party become the sole ruler of Russia.

Subsequent history showed how fantastic and unreal Lenin's postulates were. The bourgeois classes in the belligerent countries proved quite capable of bringing the war to a close, as the Treaty of Versailles showed. Lenin's seizure of power in Russia by no means ignited a world revolution or even revolutions in the most important capitalist countries. Lenin achieved the opposite of what he had hoped for. His Brest-Litovsk Treaty did not end the war, even for Russia, and it was not world revolution, but the might of the youngest capitalist country, the United States, that brought the bloodshed to an end.

Nevertheless, from his completely utopian analysis, Lenin managed to draw strategic and tactical conclusions for his party which led to a degree of success. That was to surprise even Lenin himself. This strategy as formulated in Lenin's "April Theses," was, from the point of view of pure theory, couched in the spirit of the old, conservative Russian Marxism of the 1890s. In the "Letters from Afar," which Lenin had written in Zurich before his return to Russia, it was stated: "We Marxists still regard the Russian revolution as bourgeois-democratic in essence."[26] In accordance with this analysis, he urged not the immediate nationalization of the Russian economy but simply "the introduction of supervision of general production and the distribution of produce, by the Soviet of Workers' Deputies" (Thesis 8).[27]

Lenin's tactical recommendations were likewise moderate and cautious. Neither in the "Letters from Afar" nor in the "April Theses" is there any mention of an overthrow of the Provisional

Government, or of the establishment of a dictatorship of the proletariat, or even of a dictatorship of the proletariat and peasantry. On the contrary, he merely called on his party to achieve a majority in the Soviets. Moreover, he later publicly condemned the Petrograd Committee of his party for demanding the overthrow of the Provisional Government during the so-called "April Days." In a polemic with Plekhanov's paper *Edinstvo,* which had accused him of provoking civil war, Lenin pointed out that even the very words "civil war" were never mentioned in his theses and speeches. This was, of course, a subtle evasion. Lenin did, in reality, aim precisely at provoking a civil war and establishing a dictatorship of the proletariat or, more particularly, of his own party. But in the early months of the revolution, with the masses generally unreceptive to such notions, Lenin, for tactical reasons, hid behind vague formulations, which he later could interpret as he wished, according to circumstances.

However, if the sections of his theoretical analysis which concerned a social-economic program for Russia held to the traditions of orthodox Marxism, an uncommonly radical and revolutionary note emerged in other parts of the document. For Lenin envisaged the Russian revolution as the prelude of a world revolution in the more advanced capitalist countries on both sides of the battle lines; and this world revolution would help Russia overcome her general backwardness and enable the only genuinely revolutionary party, the Bolsheviks, to turn her into a socialist country. This concept shocked the Russian Marxists in April 1917; they considered it a betrayal of scientific socialism, a reversion to the old, utopian, Bakuninist, maximalist-anarchist ideas, which Russian Marxism had been combatting for three decades before the revolution. Many of Lenin's friends and pupils were embarrassed by these views. Even his wife, N. Krupskaya, was worried. She is reported to have told an old personal friend: "I am afraid it looks as if Lenin has gone crazy."[28]

Shortly after his return to Russia, Lenin gave two addresses on "The Tasks of the Proletariat in Our Revolution," in which he publicly discussed his "Theses" for the first time. His first address was given at the meeting of the Bolshevik fraction of the All-Russian Conference of Soviets, which was then in session; it was later repeated in the White Hall of the Tauride Palace, at a joint meeting of the Bolshevik, Menshevik, and Internationalist fractions.

At the first meeting, it was obvious that Lenin's views had isolated him even within his own party circle. At the second meeting, he distinctly broadened the gulf which separated him from the non-Bolshevik Marxists. N. Sukhanov, who attended the second meeting, wrote that "the Bolshevik sect was lost, perplexed and confused." Goldenberg, a formerly prominent Bolshevik, said at the meeting: "Today, Lenin has put forward his claim to a throne in Europe that has been vacant for thirty years: it is Bakunin's throne . . . Lenin has raised the flag of civil war within our democracy." The Menshevik Boris Bogdanov, one of the founders of the Petrograd Soviet, declared the address to be "the delirium of a madman."[29]

The overwhelming majority of those at the second meeting, including many Bolsheviks, shared the view expressed by Tseretelli, who quoted the well-known passage from Engels' *The Peasant War in Germany,* asserting that "a revolutionary party is irretrievably lost if it attempts to seize power in a society which is not yet mature for the domination of the class which it represents."[30] In *Pravda,* which at that time was edited by Kamenev and Stalin, Kamenev pronounced Lenin's "Theses"—which had been printed in the April 7 (20) issue —unacceptable to the party, "as they were based on the assumption that the bourgeois-democratic phase of the revolution was complete and that it could immediately enter upon its socialist phase."

But although the overwhelming majority of Russian Marxists, including many Bolsheviks, strongly disagreed with Lenin's "Theses," his authority within the Bolshevik Party and his prestige with its old guard had long been such that it was impossible to "defeat" him within his party. Moreover, Lenin was helped by radical undercurrents of mass feeling, which were growing noticeably stronger. After two Bolshevik Party conferences—the conference of the Petrograd city organization, of April 14 (27), and the All-Russian Conference of the Bolshevik Party, of April 24-29 (May 7-12)—Lenin emerged as uncontested leader of the party. Only a few of his opponents, among them Kamenev, Rykov, and Milyutin (Zinoviev joined them in October), remained unconvinced and continued, without much success, to oppose Lenin's views until, and even after, the Bolshevik seizure of power on November 7.

Lenin's victory within his party did not produce an immediate change in the cautious policy he had adopted on his return to Petrograd. He still maintained that the Bolsheviks' first task should be to secure a majority in the Soviets, and, for that reason, he in the first weeks carefully avoided advocating publicly the overthrow of the Provisional Government or the immediate forcible seizure of power. He even sternly reprimanded the extremists in the Petrograd Committee of the Bolshevik organization when, during the Milyukov crisis, it appealed to the workers to seize power at once:

> Our slogans were intended to give a peaceful character to the demonstrations, but some comrades from the Petrograd Committee gave out a different slogan; we annulled it, but too late, and the masses followed the slogan of the Petrograd Committee . . . We intended to reconnoitre, to test the strength of the enemy forces, not to give battle, but the Petrograd Committee went just a little further to the left, and this, at that moment, was, of course, a serious crime.[31]

This condemnation of the leftists was rather a tactical manouver on Lenin's part, since at that time he was trying to reconcile himself with his party, to win over Kamenev and others and to minimize the difference between himself and his opponents. In the sequel to the passage quoted above, he said: ". . . the differences of opinion between Kamenev and myself are not very great." This assertion was to be repeatedly belied in the next few months, for Lenin's cautious approach was not to last too long. A few weeks later, during the "June Days," he risked a much bolder policy—a policy much like that which he had rejected in April.

[1] The Russian army kept under arms, in peace-time, 1,284,000 men, as against 1,246,000 in Germany and Austria. Of trained reservists, there were 5,650,000 in Russia, as against 7,900,000 in Germany and Austria-Hungary.

[2] Capt. S. T. H. Wilton, in vol. 23 of the *Encyclopaedia Britannica* (14th edition). The *Great Soviet Encyclopedia*, vol. 44, p. 566, speaks of two corps and one cavalry division. Characteristically, the *GSE* (in vol. 44, issued in 1939, after the purges and on

the eve of the Second World War), in describing Samsonov's East Prussian operation, does not mention any losses at all and gives no figures. The new line of Soviet patriotism, as then prescribed by Stalin, avoided evoking memories painful to Russian national self-esteem.

[3] *Great Soviet Encyclopedia,* Vol. 44, p. 575.

[4] *Ibid.,* p. 580.

[5] *Ibid.*

[6] G. Shavelsky, *Memoirs,* Chekhov Publishing House, New York, 1956.

[7] Shavelsky, *Memoirs,* Vol. II, pp. 224-225.

[8] *Ibid.,* p. 238.

[9] Shavelsky, *Memoirs,* p. 229.

[10] The report handed to the Tsar in the name of a group of public men is quoted from *The Red Archive,* Vol. 10, 1925, pp. 69-86.

[11] D. S. Zaslavsky and V. A. Kantorovich in *The Chronicle of the February Revolution,* Petrograd, 1924, pp. 17 ff.

[12] We shall return to this problem below.

[13] Lenin put the intrigues of British Ambassador Buchanan first among the immediate causes of the revolution. (See his first "Letter from Afar," written from Zurich on March 7 [20] 1917). To Buchanan he ascribed a plan to replace the Tsar by a more bellicose monarch with the help of "English money" and the support of Guchkov and Milyukov. But he made no mention of his own party groups in Petrograd (Lenin, *Collected Works,* 4th Edition, Vol. 23, p. 296). Before it happened, Lenin had had little faith in the immediacy of a revolution; on January 22, 1917, in a lecture to Swiss students he had declared that his generation was probably not destined to live to see the revolution *(ibid.,* p. 246).

[14] From the testimony of General Khabalov before the Extraordinary Committee of Inquiry, quoted by S. P. Melgunov, "How Legends are Created," *Vozrozhdenye,* issue 11, p. 128.

[15] Preparatory courses for training of non-commissioned officers.

[16] This theory of Trotsky's, known as the theory of permanent revolution, found no partisans among Russian Social Democrats before 1917. But in October 1917 it was precisely this estimate of the Russian Revolution that became predominant, though Lenin never formally accepted the whole theory.

[17] In a number of towns, notably in Petrograd, Moscow, Odessa and Kronstadt, Anarchist groups also came into being. But though popular with certain sectors of the working class, they did not play an independent part anywhere and often joined forces with the Bolsheviks—until the Bolshevik dictatorship started to exterminate them.

[18] The history of socialist ideologies in Russia is worthy of further study.

[19] Peter A. Stolypin, premier of Russia from 1907 until his death in 1912, was assassinated by a revolutionary terrorist.

[20] Lenin, V., "Letters from Afar." Letter I, *Collected Works,* 4th edit., Vol. 23, pp. 296, 297, 299.

[21] Bogdanov, A., in *Novaya Zhizn,* January 26 and 27 (February 8 and 9), 1918.

[22] See the correspondence between the Paris committee of the emigrés, the secretary of which was G. Chicherin, and the above-mentioned committee in Zurich (*Neue Züricher Zeitung,* May 14, 1917) .

[23] Werner Halweg, *Lenin's Reise durch Deutschland.* Vierteljahrshefte fur Zeitgeschichte, Heft 4, October 1957.

[24] See letter by A. Lunacharsky, written in Zurich on April 3, 1917 (copy in the archives of the author).

[25] Hahlweg, *Lenin's Reise durch Deutschland, op. cit.*

[26] Lenin, *Works,* vol. XXIII, p. 299.

[27] Lenin, *Works,* vol. XXIV, p. 5. It should be noted that the phrase used by Lenin

(*control za*) is correctly translated into English not as "control over" but as "supervision of."

[28] See *Memoirs of G. Denicke,* Harvard University (unpublished).

[29] N. Sukhanov, *Journal of the Revolution,* Berlin, 1922, vol. III, pp. 40, 41, 49.

[30] F. Engels, *The Peasant War in Germany.* N. Y., pp. 105-106.

[31] Lenin, *Works,* vol. XXIV, p. 214.

CHAPTER 2

The Debate Over Peace Aims, March-April 1917

The Second Coalition and the Campaign for Peace

On March 6 (19), four days after the Tsar's abdication, Prince Lvov affirmed the Provisional Government's intention to respect all the treaties which the Tsarist government had concluded with the Allies during the war. (Kerensky alone within the Provisional Government dissented from these views.) On the strength of this declaration, the Provisional Government was recognized on March 11 (24) by all the Allied governments.

But the Soviets could not permit the government to pledge itself, without reservation, to carry the war on to total victory. On March 14 (27), the Petrograd Soviet issued its historic first proclamation "to the peoples of the world," urging them, in the name of the Russian revolution, "to oppose with the utmost determination any expansionist tendencies of the governments of all the belligerent countries" and "to take the problem of war and peace into their own hands."

Perhaps moved by protests from Allied governments against these Soviet attitudes, Paul N. Milyukov, the Minister for Foreign Affairs, responded with an interview on March 23 (April 5) which discussed Allied peace aims. He declared that Austria-Hungary should be compelled to grant independence to those of its peoples who craved it, such as the Czechs, Slovaks and Croats, and also to return such territories as had originally belonged to Italy and Rumania. At the same time, Milyukov averred that the cession of Constantinople and the

Straits to Russia "would not constitute a violation of Turkey's national rights." Milyukov's interview evoked furious opposition from the Soviets and from the members of the Cabinet (Kerensky, Nekrasov, Prince Lvov) who favored modification of these extreme war aims. The debate within the government ended in a compromise, considerably closer to the position of the Soviets. A declaration of war aims was issued by the government on March 27 (April 9), and published the following day. It was addressed, not to foreign governments, but to the citizens of Russia. It said:

"The defense, at all costs, of our national heritage and the liberation of our native soil from the invading enemy—such are the primary and most vital duties of our soldiers, who are standing guard over the freedom of our people . . . Relying on the will of our free people, in close unity with our Allies, to solve the problem of the war and its termination, the Provisional Government wishes to declare officially that the ultimate aim of free Russia is neither to dominate other nations, nor to seize other nations' possessions, nor to annex foreign territory, but to establish a lasting peace based on the self-determination of nations."

The declaration ended, however, with a renewed pledge to keep all the obligations "which have been entered into with our Allies." This last phrase was probably inserted by Milyukov to alleviate Allied doubts about the Provisional Government's intentions concerning the old treaties, among them the 1914 agreement forbidding conclusion of a separate peace between any Allied government and the German coalition. But this pledge did not represent the view of the Soviets. The All-Russian Conference of Soviets decided on March 30 (April 12), after prolonged deliberation, to make the following announcement:

"The Executive Committee of the Soviet Workers' and Soldiers' Deputies has entered into negotiations with the Provisional Government, in which it is stressing the urgent necessity for the Provisional Government to publicly repudiate all and any of the annexationist aims of Russia's old regime . . . The Executive Committee reaffirms the *necessity for negotiations between the Provisional Government and the Allies for a new agreement on these lines* . . . An official disavowal of expansionist policies *by all governments* would constitute a powerful means toward ending the war" (italics added).

Some two weeks later, on April 18 (May 1), the Provisional Government, to satisfy the Soviets, decided to inform the Allies of the March 27 (April 9) proclamation to the citizens of Russia. But Milyukov appended to this document an "accompanying note," which gave it a sense opposite to that which the Soviets had intended; furthermore, he dispatched the document to the Allies and the press without showing his note to the other ministers or to the representatives of the Soviets.

In an emergency night session, on the night of April 18 (May 1), the leaders of the Soviets unanimously condemned Milyukov's behavior and decided to take precautionary measures against any repetition. But the very next morning, the newspapers announced in bold headlines, the Provisional Government's intention of carrying on the war until complete victory—and the effect in Petrograd was explosive. The next afternoon, at 3 o'clock, Fedor Linde, a teacher of mathematics and philosophy, serving in the Finland Regiment as a private, led his regiment in perfect military order to the Maryinsky Palace, where the Provisional Government was sitting. The soldiers carried banners inscribed: "Down with Milyukov!", "Milyukov—resign!", "Peace without annexations or indemnities!" They were later joined by the Moscow, Pavlovsky and Keksholm regiments, detachments of the fleet and other units. Members of the Soviet and finally the Commander-in-Chief, General Lavr Kornilov, spoke to calm them. They listened attentively to all the speeches and returned peacefully to their barracks, but the next day the disorder had spread to the factories.

In the meantime the Kadet Party had organized processions and demonstrations in support of Milyukov. Petrograd was now divided: the center was in the hands of the Kadets, the well-to-do folk, the patriots; in the working-class suburbs, meetings were conducted by the parties of the left, notably the Anarchists and the Bolsheviks.

By April 21 (May 4), the slogans carried by the demonstrators in the working class districts had become more pointed. The Petrograd committee of the Bolshevik Party now urged the immediate overthrow of the Provisional Government and seizure of power by the workers. The Mensheviks and the Socialist Revolutionaries appealed vainly for calm, but the workers continued to come out in great numbers, profoundly disturbed by the prospect of an endless war. Finally, the Executive Committee of the Soviets warned the soldiers not to leave their barracks without a special order signed by two members (specifically mentioned by name) of the praesidium of the Executive Committee.

Though life in the city slowly returned to normal and there were no further demonstrations, the Central Soviet was inundated by resolutions from local Soviets and other working-class organizations demanding a radical change in the foreign policy of the government. It became obvious that the Provisional Government of Prince Lvov and Milyukov could not survive and that it would have to make way for a government enjoying greater confidence.

The Kadet Party stubbornly continued to support Milyukov. But, annoyed because, in a cabinet reshuffle, his own party was now offering him the Ministry of Education instead of that of Foreign Affairs, he handed in his resignation on May 2 (15). General Kornilov had already resigned as Commander-in-Chief, and the Minister for War, Alexander I. Guchkov, had stepped down on April 30 (May 13). The first Provisional Government was falling apart.

The coalition had thus far been dominated by moderate bourgeois liberals; it was definitely a cabinet of the center because the socialist parties were firmly convinced of the bourgeois-democratic nature of the revolution and had refused to participate in it. The events of April showed, however, that real power was largely held by the socialist parties, through their command of the Soviets. The practical solution seemed to be for these parties to assume an important, perhaps decisive role in a new government. Yet this was a difficult step for the Russian Social Democrats and Socialist Revolutionaries to take in May 1917.

Today, even the most dedicated socialist would find it hard to understand their hesitation. We have since 1917 experienced forty years of co-operation in war and in peace, between socialist and non-socialist parties all over the world—in Germany, Great Britain, Austria, France, Belgium, the Scandinavian countries. Whether or not socialists should enter a coalition with bourgeois parties is no longer a problem of basic importance. But in 1917, European socialism still regarded such coalitions as dangerous opportunism and the socialist parties had been cautioned by the International Socialist Congress of Amsterdam in 1905 against such experiments. It was difficult, even for broad-minded Russian socialists like Liber, Tseretelli and Dan, to overcome the traditional aversion to participation in a bourgeois government.

At a meeting of the Organizational Committee of the Menshevik Party with the editorial board of the *Rabochaya Gazeta* (Workers' Gazette) and the Bureau of the Petrograd Party Organization, on April 24 and 25 (May 7 and 8), it was decided, by an overwhelming majority, that the party would not participate in a coalition government.[1] Neither the Socialist Revolutionaries nor the Executive Committee of the Soviet as such were prepared to join in a coalition without the Mensheviks. Therefore, at a meeting on April 28 (May 11) the Executive Committee decided—by 23 votes to 22, with several abstentions—against the participation of representatives of the Soviet in a coalition government.

But that position could not be maintained indefinitely. The right had lost the confidence of a majority of the people and the army. A special delegation from front-line troops to the Executive Committee of the Soviet declared emphatically that only the formation of a strong coalition government under the leadership of the Soviet could save the army from complete disintegration. The speeches of the army delegates made a deep impression. At a subsequent meeting of the Executive Committee, which lasted through the night of May 1-2 (14-15), the balance began to tip in favor of participation. During a recess, the parties held separate meetings. A majority of the Mensheviks voted to reverse the line laid down by the Organizational Committee, even though this was contrary to the statutes of their party. The Socialist Revolutionaries, too, decided to participate. In the Executive Committee of the Soviet, a motion in favor of participation in a new government was then carried by 41 votes to 18, with 3 abstentions. The Soviet was to be represented in the new government by Kerensky; the Mensheviks, N. Skobelev and Tseretelli; the Socialist Revolutionary, Victor M. Chernov; and the Popular Socialist, Peshekhonov. The new government, formed officially on May 6 (19), was again headed by Prince Lvov; Michael I. Tereshchenko was appointed Minister of Foreign Affairs; Kerensky, Minister of the Army and Navy; Chernov, Minister of Agriculture; and Skobelev, Minister of Labor. Tseretelli was nominally Minister of Posts and Telegraphs, but from the start he played a leading role in the cabinet.

The tasks of the new coalition were evident: to introduce the most urgent social reforms, and particularly to prepare the agrarian reform; to strengthen the local administration; to provision the front and raise the morale of the army; to restore order to the chaotic economy; and to convene a Constituent Assembly. But its most essential and immediate task, the core of all its policies, was to induce the Allies to modify their peace aims so that the war might be brought to a speedy close. In this effort the chief mover was Tseretelli.

The formation of the new government temporarily allayed the public's anxieties, although the people were not inclined to give the government much time. Shortly after the new cabinet had taken office, one of the army delegates, speaking at a meeting of the Executive Committee of the Soviet, said: "Comrade Tseretelli has been Minister for ten whole days. What has been done for peace?" Actually, Tseretelli had been quite active.

The formation of the new government had coincided with an event —kept strictly secret by all concerned—which might have proved a decisive turning point in international relations: Austria-Hungary was trying to leave the war. As Tseretelli tells us in his memoirs,[2] this highly confidential news was communicated to him by Foreign Minister Tereshchenko at the end of May. According to unofficial information passed on by Lloyd George, the Emperor Charles of Austria had sent a highly-placed personage to France with a direct offer for a separate peace with the Allies. Austria was ready to withdraw from the war and abandon her conquests in the Balkans and in Russia, in return for an assurance that Austrian territory would remain inviolate. Had this Austrian offer been accepted, the war might have been shortened by a year, perhaps more. The United States had already entered the war, and the pressures on the German government would have become quite formidable. And, certainly, the entire course of the Russian revolution would have been profoundly affected.

For this reason the episode deserves more careful attention than it has yet received.

From January 1917 on, Austrian agents had been seeking suitable channels through which to start open separate peace negotiations. Baron von Mensdorff even went to Oslo in the hope of gaining the assistance of the King of Norway. The rumors of these activities seemed substantial enough for the British government to send Sir Francis Hopwood (later Lord Southborough) to Oslo to make unofficial inquiries. But they led to nothing, until the appearance on the stage of a Belgian artillery officer, Prince Sixtus of Bourbon Parma, a brother of the Austrian Empress Zita.[3] Prince Sixtus was summoned from his regiment to Switzerland on January 29, 1917, to meet his mother, who had just returned from Vienna. She conveyed to her son the Emperor Charles' request that he serve as an intermediary between Austria and the Allies. Prince Sixtus agreed to negotiate, on the condition that the peace terms should be acceptable to France. The Emperor Charles consented. On February 13, Prince Sixtus began a series of secret journeys to Vienna, Paris, and London.

The conditions which the Emperor Charles was prepared to accept were, briefly, these: the return of Alsace-Lorraine and the left bank of the Rhine to France, in fulfillment of French demands; the creation of a new southern Slav state, and the restoration of Belgian independence. On the other hand, Charles stipulated that he should not be asked to conduct military operations against Germany. Nothing was said of Italy or of Italian demands on Austria.

Lloyd George was well-disposed toward this offer and even hopeful of obtaining, in due course, some concessions for Italy about that part of the Tyrol which was populated by Italians. The French, however, were much less eager. They insisted that Italy must be informed before any decisions could be taken. The Ministers of France, Great Britain and Italy met on April 19, in the French Alpine village of St. Jean de Maurienne. Great Britain was represented by Lloyd George, France by Ribot, and Italy by Sonnino and Boselli. In deference to the Emperor Charles, who had insisted that his name be kept secret,[4] Lloyd George and Ribot represented the Austrian offer as based on well-founded rumors coming from Scandinavia, rather than on terms coming directly from the Austrian government. The immediate reaction of the Italian delegates toward a separate peace with Austria was extremely adverse, and the French supported them. In the end it was agreed that the negotiations should be broken off, since they threatened to disrupt Allied unity. This was, in fact, the end of the story, although Prince Sixtus continued to transmit to Great Britain Austrian proposals which offered still further concessions.

At the same time that the Emperor Charles was making overtures to France and Great Britain, King Victor Emmanuel of Italy was offering a separate peace directly to the Emperor Charles. He acted with the full agreement of his general staff and of many Italian politicians, including Giolitti and Tittoni, all of whom feared the disaffection of an army which was growing wearier and wearier of the unsuccessful war. Moreover, Victor Emmanuel was prepared to forego all annexations and territorial expansion—which had been so stubbornly demanded by Sonnino and Boselli at the conference at St. Jean de Maurienne. The King asked only for the return of that part of the Tyrol which was populated by Italians. The Emperor Charles informed Lloyd George and Ribot of this offer through Prince Sixtus on May 9.[5]

The King of Italy's proposal offered good prospects of a separate peace, on terms acceptable to France and Great Britain as well as Italy. But France, according to Lloyd George, feared that such a peace would immediately release Italy from the war, while France would have to keep fighting until Germany was totally defeated if her own demands were to be realized. These demands included not only the return of Alsace-Lorraine and the left bank of the Rhine, but also far-reaching territorial readjustments in Europe, the Middle East and elsewhere. So France simply sabotaged all further talks with Austria and on June 5, wearied by his fruitless mission, Sixtus rejoined his regiment in Belgium. Lloyd George, disillusioned, entered in his diary some reflections on the excessive nationalism of the French and remarked sadly that, when blinded by prejudice, "the shrewdest man is often no better than the fool."[6]

The difference in the two countries' attitude to the affair is obvious when one compares the memoirs of Lloyd George with those of Raymond Poincaré, the French president. Lloyd George devotes a long chapter to the Austrian episode,[7] but Poincaré mentions it only four times and gives it only a few lines altogether.[8] Moreover, from Poincaré's entry of April 3, before the meeting with the Italians, it is quite clear that Ribot never intended to pursue the negotiations seriously. Throughout, the affair remained secret. Only from Ribot's speech in the French Chamber of Deputies on October 19, did Russia and the whole world learn that Austria had offered a separate peace, which had been rejected out of consideration for Italy's interests.

The members of the Provisional Government in Petrograd and leaders of the Soviet who had learned of the Austrian overtures from Tereshchenko, through Tseretelli, remained unaware for months that their hopes in this direction had already been doomed. They never relaxed their efforts to persuade the Allies to negotiate a compromise peace rather than insist on unconditional surrender. But whatever illusions they may have harbored were shattered by the Allied reply to Milyukov's note of April 27 (May 9). The bad impression this reply left with even the most defense-minded Russian socialists can be seen from an editorial in the Menshevik *Rabochaya Gazeta,* entitled "The notes from the British and French governments": "The British and French bourgeoisie is ready to change the flag it flies on its ship, but under the new flag it still intends to carry the same cargo. On such a basis there can be no agreement between them and us. . . . Should we, therefore, send an ultimatum to the Allies, and, in case of a negative reply, break with them altogether? No, certainly not. We must try to revise our treaties with them at the special conference of representatives of the Allied governments."

It did not seem probable, however, that the Allies could easily be induced to bring their war aims more into line with the program of the Soviets. The pessimistic view that was gaining ground among socialists was reinforced by the talks which leaders of the majority in the Soviet held with the British Ambassador in Petrograd, Sir George Buchanan. At Buchanan's request, Tereshchenko arranged the meeting at his home, on May 26 (June 6). The three socialist Ministers, Tseretelli, Chernov and Skobelev were present. Buchanan wanted to gain, through direct, personal contact, a true impression of the opinions of the real rulers of the new Russia. In the course of the conversation, Buchanan disclosed the contents of the Allied reply to Milyukov's note, which had not yet been officially handed to the Provisional Government. This reply formed the basis of a lengthy exchange of views between Tseretelli and Chernov, on one side, and Buchanan on the other.

Tseretelli said that, at that moment, Russian socialists were most interested in the Allied reaction to their proposal that the war aims be revised. He did not, he said, share the view of the left-wing opposition (the internationalists) that "the abolition of the treaties in their original form was an essential precondition for the continuance of the Alliance." Did the Ambassador think that "we are wrong in hoping to find, among some sectors of the British public, sympathy and understanding for the aspirations of revolutionary Russia?" Buchanan replied that the British government, acting in complete accord with public opinion, including the majority opinion in the Labour Party, would be sure to find a common ground with revolutionary Russia when the time came to formulate the broad principles of democracy on which the future world would be built. Thereupon, Tseretelli asked outright whether Russia's renunciation of all expansionist plans would not constitute sufficient grounds "for Britain and France to renounce, in their turn, all conquests made in the course of this war? . . . Can we be sure that, at the forthcoming conference (of the Allies), the British government will support our proposal for a new Allied program, in which the peace terms would be based on the liberation of occupied territories by both sides and a renunciation of all further territorial claims?"

At this, Buchanan's manner changed abruptly. He looked displeased, and said guardedly that he was not prepared to reply to such a question without consulting his government. As for the conference of the Allies, he was not at all certain whether war aims—and, in principle, the British government still stood by the original war aims—would be discussed, or whether the subject would be considered instead through diplomatic channels, by the ambassadors. The meeting closed with mutual assurances of friendship; but the question which was most vital to the leaders of the revolutionary Soviets had, by implication, been answered in the negative.

It now seemed useless to try further to obtain a revision of war aims through governmental channels. Tseretelli and his friends reasoned that other means of pressure would have to be employed and that such pressure could only come from the people, who in all countries were showing unmistakable signs of fatigue and dissatisfaction (mutinies in the French army, etc.). The time had come to appeal to the working masses and to the socialists of all belligerent countries to apply pressure for the conclusion of a negotiated peace without victors or vanquished. So the organization of an international socialist conference became central to the strategy of Tseretelli and his friends, and, eventually, to that of the whole coalition government.

The Conflict over the Stockholm Conference

An international socialist conference had already been suggested by members of a number of individual socialist parties—in both neutral and belligerent countries. Resolutions to this effect were adopted by the socialists of Italy, Denmark, Norway, Switzerland, South Africa, Canada, Australia, Rumania, Portugal, Russia and Great Britain. The February revolution gave new impetus to the peace effort. On April 13, 1917, leaders of the Dutch party met with Camille Huysmans, secretary of the Second International, and they decided to put forward the idea of a conference of socialists of all the belligerent countries. At a meeting of Swedish, Danish, Norwegian, Dutch and Belgian socialists, on May 3, it was agreed that a Dutch-Scandinavian Committee should be formed in Stockholm, with the participation and co-operation of Huysmans. This committee originally consisted of Troelstra, Albarda, Van Col, Vliegen and Wibaut of Holland; Hjalmar Branting, Gustav Moller and Sodoesberg of Sweden, Stauning and Nina Bang of Denmark, and Vidnes of Norway.[9] The Dutch and Scandinavian socialists had doubtless been encouraged in their mediation efforts by the report brought back from Russia by the leader of the Swedish Socialist Party, Hjalmar Branting. Branting had spent several days in Petrograd at the end of March and had established very cordial relations with the socialist leaders of the Soviets. In addresses to the Soviet and to the socialist parties in Petrograd, Branting had pointed out that the German working-class was undergoing a change of heart as a consequence of the exhaustion of Germany's resources, the weariness of her people and, above all, America's entry into the war. The nationalists in the German Social

Democratic party—Philip Scheidemann and his supporters—now seemed ready for peace talks, though their writing still employed the characteristic tones of German imperialism.[10] Branting warmly approved the peace policy of the Russian socialist parties, and encouraged them to persevere in it. A plan was then put forward to send a delegation from the leading Russian socialist parties abroad, so that the prestige of the Russian revolution could help to strengthen the endeavors of the Dutch-Scandinavian Committee. That committee planned to convene in Stockholm a conference of socialists from all the belligerent countries, with the object of evolving a peace program acceptable to all. The questions connected with such a conference were discussed at a meeting of the Dutch-Scandinavian Committee on May 18, with Branting in the chair. A prominent member of the Belgian socialist party, Louis de Brouckere, was in Stockholm on his way to Russia; and he declared categorically that the Belgian socialists would not participate together with socialists of the Austro-German bloc, unless the latter repudiated their policy of *Burgfrieden* ("national unity") and co-operation with the Kaiser's government. It was, therefore, agreed that delegations from the various countries should be asked to come to Stockholm one at a time—though the idea of a general conference was not abandoned. The declaration issued at this meeting of the Dutch-Scandinavian Committee acknowledges the inspiration of the "Russian revolution and the immense hopes aroused by it."

* * *

But in Petrograd events were moving faster and faster. The conference would have to meet soon if the uneasiness of the Russian people was to be allayed. For these reasons, the Executive Committee of the Petrograd Soviet, by-passing the Dutch-Scandinavian Committee, issued, on May 20 (June 2nd), a direct appeal to the socialist parties and the trade unions of the world. The appeal recalled that the principles of peace without annexations or indemnities, and based on national self-determination, had been accepted by the workers and the Soviets of Russia, and by the coalition government. It now urged working-class organizations and parties, which agreed with these principles, to send their representatives to an international conference to be held in Stockholm on July 8. This conference would bring together all parties and groups, from both neutral and belligerent countries, that were ready to abandon the policy of "national unity" and co-operate in devising ways of bringing peace. The Soviet expressed "its conviction that all the parties and organizations that accept the invitations will also undertake to put into effect all decisions reached at the conference." The appeal was immediately communicated to all countries by the Petrograd Telegraph Agency.

But the leaders of the Soviet had overestimated both the influence of the Russian revolution on the governments of the West and their own influence on the friendly socialist parties of Europe. The day after the publication of the appeal, they received a collective protest from a group of prominent western socialists then in Russia: the Belgians Emil Vandervelde and Louis de Brouckere, the Frenchman Albert Thomas, and Arthur Henderson, a member of the British Cabinet. These men had been engaged in talks with the leaders of the Soviets; they expressed their surprise that the Soviet should have even drafted such a declaration without waiting for the conclusion of the talks, and before a delegation from the British Labour Party, which the Soviets had invited to Petrograd, had even arrived there.

"We could not have supposed," they wrote, "that you would convene the conference on terms which it was impossible to expect on the basis of our previous talks . . . We readily agreed to accept the formulation of conditions for peace advanced by the Soviet, but on condition that the formulation be made very precise and be expounded in such a way as to make misinterpretation impossible. Particularly, for instance, the term annexation should not be stretched to include liberation of territories when it is desired by the local population, or the term indemnity be made to cover compensation for losses inflicted in occupied regions by the very fact of aggression." The parties they represented would not be able, the four western socialists emphasized, to take part in the proposed conference until they and the Soviets had agreed on terms in which a peace policy could be formulated that were so precise as to leave no room for further misunderstanding. Their written protest was followed by a number of personal talks and exchange of letters, all very friendly on the surface but sharp in substance.

Relations between the Soviets and the British Labour Party, in particular, were soon to deteriorate further. The executive of the British Labour Party invited the Soviets to a conference of the socialist parties of Allied countries that was to be held in London in mid-July. The Soviets politely declined the invitation. The British, the French and the Belgians insisted that Russians participate, since a refusal to do so might be taken to indicate a desire to stand above the two belligerent sides, to be a kind of "third force." The Soviets said they had no such wish, but that they did not want to be bound by the decisions of a conference which was limited to the Allied countries, at the very moment when they were organizing a conference of all the belligerent and neutral countries. The Soviets preferred to put forward their own program at the broader conference. Tseretelli told the foreign socialists that the International could succeed only if it heeded the voice of revolutionary Russia, which stood outside the two hostile camps into which European socialism was divided.[11]

On June 3 (16), the First Congress of Soviets opened, so that international discussions were interrupted. But a delegation from the Soviets went abroad soon afterward. On June 19 (July 2), the Social Democrats, V. N. Rozanov, A. N. Smirnov and Goldenberg (Meshkovsky), arrived in Stockholm; they were joined a few days later by the Menshevik H.M.Erlich and the S-R, N. Russanov. Their political adviser in Stockholm was old Paul Axelrod, one of the founders of the Russian Social Democratic movement. The delegation had a number of talks with the Dutch-Scandinavian Committee; with the Bolshevik delegation abroad, which consisted of Radek and Ganetsky; with Angelica Balabanova, representing the Berne Committee of the Zimmerwaldists; with the representatives of the German Social Democratic majority led by Hermann Mueller; and, finally, with a delegation from the German Independent Socialist Party led by Hugo Haase and Georg Ledebour. The Bolsheviks and the Berne Committee refused to take part in the conference planned by the Soviets, but the two German delegations gave the impression that they might be open to persuasion, despite the fact that there was a very wide divergence between the viewpoint of the Soviets and the attitude of the Germans, especially of the SPD-group headed by Hermann Mueller. The Soviet delegation also prepared plans for its forthcoming meeting in Paris with other socialists from Allied countries, a meeting arranged by the Stockholm Committee.

After the discussions in Stockholm the Russian delegation—with the exception of Rozanov, who remained as a permanent representative with the Stockholm Committee—moved on to London. There they were warmly received and soon found common ground with the British Labour Party, mainly through the good offices of Arthur Henderson. They were greeted even more cordially by members of the Independent Labour Party, such as Ramsey Macdonald and Philip Snowden, who were basically opposed to the war. The executive council of the Labour Party decided to take part in the Paris meeting and deputized Henderson, and the Independent Socialists Wallhead and Macdonald, to accompany the Russian delegation there. In Paris, the Russians and the British met with representatives of both factions of French socialism, Pierre Renaudel for the majority and Jean Longuet for the minority, and of the Dutch-Scandinavian Committee. The Paris talks were conducted in a generally friendly atmosphere although there were disagreements. One stumbling-block was the demand of the Labour Party and the French majority group that the agenda of the international conference being planned should include the question of responsibility for the war—an issue that had divided the Socialist International from the very outbreak of the war. Another much-discussed question was whether the decisions of the conference should be binding for all participants; disagreement on this point almost brought the Paris talks to an abrupt end. Henderson rose from his seat and began gathering up his papers, ready to leave. He said that the Labour Party delegates could not undertake to obey the decisions of the conference if they were at variance with those of their own party. The situation was saved by a proposal that Paul Axelrod had advanced earlier, during the preliminary consultations in Stockholm: that each party should be asked to declare, immediately after a decision had been adopted at the conference, whether and how it was prepared to carry out that decision. This compromise satisfied Henderson, and the talks were concluded in complete harmony. It was agreed (1) to invite to the conference all member organizations of the Socialist International, including the splinter groups which had broken away from their parties during the war, and all trade unions belonging to the International Federation of Trade Unions; (2) to put the question of responsibility for the war on the agenda of the conference; (3) to have the participants announce after each decision whether and how they intended to carry it out; and (4) to convene the conference in Stockholm between September 9 and 16. These unanimous decisions of the conference were transmitted to the Stockholm Committee on August 1.

From Paris, the Russian delegation went on to Italy where it was enthusiastically cheered by workers at many mass meetings. The delegations met the Italian socialist leaders (Giuseppe Modigliani, Treves, Morgari) and reached the same agreement as they had with the French and the British.

The international socialist conference now seemed assured, but those opposed to it were not idle. At the French War Council (*Conseil de guerre*) on May 31, 1917, President Poincaré asked Marshal Pétain: "If the international conference were to take place in Stockholm and the French were to meet the Germans there to discuss peace terms, would you be able to maintain order in the army and would it continue to fight?"

Pétain answered firmly with one word: "No." This monosyllabic reply made an overwhelming impression. The War Minister, Painlevé, then asked whether a prohibition of the Stockholm conference would not adversely influence the performance of the Russian army and thus permit Germany to transfer some of her divisions from the eastern to the western front. Petain replied that new German divisions on the western front would worry him less than the demoralization of the whole French army.[12] This settled the question. The war council decided to refuse exit visas to the French delegates and to request the other Allies to do likewise.

As in the case of the Emperor Charles's peace offer, the British attitude was somewhat more sympathetic than the French. Nevertheless, in England, too, many insisted that the war be fought to a total victory. A campaign was started in the press. The Russian delegation was described as a tool of German imperialism and the Labour Party was sharply criticized. The French government's intransigence had strongly affected the British government. Alarmed by these developments, Henderson wired the Russian delegation, which was still in

Italy, to come and address a conference of the Labour Party which was to begin on August 10.

As the Italian socialists would not let all the Russian comrades leave before their next mass meeting, the Russian delegation split up and Russanov and Erlich left for London. In spite of all their efforts, they were delayed on the journey and reached London on the evening of August 10, to find that the Labour Party Conference had already voted by an overwhelming majority (1,876,000 votes to 555,000) in favor of participation in the Stockholm conference. However, in the war cabinet, Lloyd George attacked Henderson for disloyalty and Henderson was forced to resign from the government. Bonar Law then declared, on behalf of all the Allied governments, that exit visas would be refused to socialists who wished to go to Stockholm. (The previous decision of the French War Council remained unknown to the socialist parties.) The British declaration effectively killed the conference and put an end to the attempts by the Russian socialists to exert pressure for peace through the labor movements of the belligerent countries. And the failure in the spring and early summer of 1917, to bring closer a negotiated peace had an immense effect on the future course of the February revolution.

[1] Nikolaevsky, B. I., *The Mensheviks in the First Years of the Revolution (1917-18)*, pp. 55, ff. (unpublished manuscript).

[2] Tseretelli, I. G., *Unpublished Memoirs of the February Revolution*, chapter XI, pp. 4-6. Russian Institute at Columbia University.

[3] His identity did not become known until much later. At the time his name was kept a close secret even from the British and French cabinets, and was known only to Lloyd George, King George V, French President Raymond Poincaré and the French Foreign Minister, Ribot.

[4] That the Emperor Charles was sincere in his intentions emerges clearly from a book by Gooch, published in 1925. It appears that on April 3, 1917, the Emperor Charles and his foreign minister, Count Czernin, visited Emperor William of Germany in Bad Homburg and told him: "Our military resources are coming to an end. We must begin negotiations before our enemies are fully aware of our exhaustion. Another winter campaign is absolutely out of the question. The burden on our people is intolerable now. The bow is so taut that it may snap at any moment." The German foreign minister, von Kuehlmann, received Charles' suggestions with approval, on the whole, and considered that the only obstacle to peace was the question of Alsace-Lorraine. G. P. Gooch, *Germany*, New York, 1925, p. 148.

[5] The same communication from the Emperor Charles to Lloyd George also mentions four offers of a separate peace received by Austria from Russia. The details and the dates of these offers are not given, but clearly they were all made before the February revolution: David Lloyd George, *War Memoirs*, Vol. IV, p. 2011.

[6] David Lloyd George, *War Memoirs*, Vol. IV, p. 2027.

[7] *Ibid.*, Vol. IV, chapter LXI, "The Austrian Peace Move," pp. 1983-2035.

[8] Raymond Poincaré, *Au Service de la France*, Vol. IX, *L'année troublée*, 1917, pp. 65-66, 100, 116, 394-395.

[9] *Stockholm*, Commité Organisateur de la Conference Socialiste Internationale de Stockholm, Ed. Tiden Forlag, Stockholm, 1918, pp. V-IX.

[10] Tseretelli, I. G. *Unpublished Memoirs of the February Revolution*, chapter XL, Russian Institute at the Columbia University.

[11] Tseretelli, I. G. *Unpublished Memoirs of the February Revolution*, chapter XI, pp. 73-77.

[12] Raymond Poincaré, *L'année troublée*, 1917, p. 149.

CHAPTER 3

The Disintegration of the February Revolution

The June Days

The inability of the moderate leaders of the February revolution to solve the problem of peace, and the growth of Bolshevism, were two facets of the same process. The process began in April when Lenin, arriving from Switzerland, succeeded in getting his "April theses" accepted by the still small Bolshevik Party in place of the party line that had been worked out by the Bolsheviks in Russia itself. His aggressive new policy was strengthened by the demonstrations of workers during the Milyukov crisis, and advanced further during the so-called "June Days."

The First All-Russian Congress of Soviets opened on June 3 (16) in Petrograd. To the Cadet Corps Building on Vassilyevsky Island had come from all parts of Russia, workers' and soldiers' delegates, representatives of political parties, well-known personalities of the left, and a great number of guests. Of the 1,090 delegates, 822 had the right to vote; the rest were present in a consultative capacity. Since only 103 were Bolsheviks, the Congress was dominated by the Socialist Revolutionaries and Mensheviks. The leaders of these two parties were greeted with enthusiastic applause whenever they appeared; among them, Tseretelli was by now most prominent. Replying to the remark by Tseretelli that the government had to be composed of many parties, including the bourgeois parties, because there was no single political party which would be prepared and able to rule alone, Lenin interjected boldly: "Tseretelli is wrong, it is not so. There is such a party—my party, the party of the Bolsheviks which is ready to take over the government all alone, at any time, in fact, at once."

Lenin was then by no means widely known, except possibly among the workers of the Vyborg district in Petrograd, and his announcement was received with astonished laughter. Even some of the Bolsheviks present (Kamenev, Zinoviev, Nogin and their friends) seemed embarrassed. But soon it was no longer possible to jeer at Lenin. Taking advantage of the preoccupation of the Provisional Government and leaders of the coalition parties with preparations for a military offensive and with other urgent matters, Lenin decided to organize a party demonstration, ostensibly in honor of the Congress. Not only workers but also the soldiers of the garrison were invited to take part, and the soldiers were to arrive fully armed and carrying banners inscribed: "Down with the ten capitalist ministers!", "All power to the Soviets!", "War must end!", "No separate peace with the Kaiser, no secret treaties with the Allies!", "Bread, peace, freedom!" etc.

Material later published by Sukhanov[1] and Tseretelli[2] shows that Lenin's plan for an armed demonstration aroused heated discussion among the Bolshevik leaders. The left wing, which according to the mentioned sources included H. Stassova, Stalin, Semashko,[3] a young commander of the First Machine Gun Regiment, and members of the Bolshevik organization in the army, such as Nevsky, Latsis, Smilga, and Rakhia, advocated an actual armed uprising in the guise of a demonstration. Their plan[4] was for the units friendly to the Bolsheviks, in particular the First Machine Gun Regiment, to surround the Maryinsky Palace, arrest the ministers, and proclaim a new government. The right wing, composed of Zinoviev, Kamenev, Tomsky, Kalinin, Nogin and others, argued that, even in Petrograd, the workers were not behind the Bolsheviks and were certainly not inclined to fight on the barricades against the majority socialist parties.

Lenin and his supporters put through a compromise between these two positions. They proposed that the armed demonstration should take place on June 10 (23). If circumstances were propitious, the seizure of power should be attempted. But if the masses were not favorable, the undertaking was to be limited to a mere skirmish. Such a clash might result in bloodshed, of course, but that would bring further discredit on the coalition government. An appropriate resolution to this effect was adopted (by 131 votes to 6, with 22 abstentions)[5] at a meeting with representatives of local Bolshevik groups, on June 8 (21).

Through the vigilance of the Petrograd printers, the leaders of the socialist parties learned of the sortie planned by the Bolsheviks; and of the copy of *Pravda,* already set up and made up into pages, containing the Bolshevik Central Committee's call to join in the armed demonstrations in the streets. The leaders of the majority in the praesidium of the Congress violently protested. In the course of a series of meetings, most speakers condemned the Bolsheviks, calling upon them to cancel the armed demonstration. The praesidium of the Congress then issued an order forbidding all demonstrations for three days. Numerous "go-betweens"—Lunacharsky, Nogin, Kamenev and others—urged Lenin to give up his plan. But Lenin stubbornly refused, insisting that preparations were complete, that no danger was involved and that nobody could deprive the Bolsheviks of their right to hold their own rallies and demonstrations. In the end, the pressure from all sides was so great that Lenin had to give in. The demonstration was cancelled, but the praesidium of the Soviet promised, as a kind of compensation, to arrange a joint demonstration of all the Soviet parties on June 18, which would give to each party, including the Bolsheviks, a chance to display its forces. In this demonstration, as all eye-witnesses agree, the Bolsheviks' banners and placards occupied a conspicuous place.

That very day, on which the huge crowds of demonstrators in the streets of Petrograd revealed the rapid growth of Bolshevik influence among the workers and soldiers, a military engagement opened in distant Galicia. It was the combined offensive by the Seventh, Eighth and Eleventh Armies on a front stretching from Galich to Kalush. The Provisional Government had long cherished the hope of launching an offensive, and its plans had been carefully laid out. The attack was to be delivered at a point where the Russian armies were facing the demoralized and exhausted Austrians, and it was hoped that a victory would raise the prestige of the Provisional Government with the Allies, with the other nations, and with the Russian people. It would confirm the defensist thesis that Russian military capacity had been strengthened, not weakened, by the revolution, and it would strike a blow at Bolshevism. A defeat, of course, would lead to exactly the opposite consequences, but neither the Provisional Government nor the High Command thought of the possibility of a defeat.

In the first two days the offensive achieved a resounding success. The Russian forces broke through the Austrian defenses; Kornilov's Eighth Army occupied the towns of Kalush and Galich; the Austrians were surrendering almost without resistance, and the Russians took hordes of prisoners. The telegrams announcing these victories made a tremendous impression in Petrograd. Government circles were jubilant. The leaders of the majority parties went about with their heads high, condescendingly accepting congratulations from such confirmed Bolsheviks as Lunacharsky. Even Lenin was perturbed. As recently as June 19 (July 2),[6] he had written that only a minority of the people followed the lead of the Socialist Revolutionaries and the Mensheviks. Now, in *Pravda* for June 21 (July 4), he admitted grudgingly that the Provisional Government and those parties scored a victory: "This general and basic fact," Lenin concluded, "the fact that a majority (of the people) should have trusted the petit bourgeois policies of the Mensheviks and the Socialist Revolutionaries . . . . dependent as these are on the capitalists, will determine the position and behavior of our party."[7] This could only mean that the Bolsheviks would in future take a more careful approach to the problem of national defense.[8]

The Provisional Government's triumph was short-lived. The Central Powers threw fresh reinforcements of German troops into the battle and the Russians could not withstand the counter-attack. They retreated with such haste that complete catastrophe followed: the operation ended in a redrawing of the front line much farther to the east. Great numbers of Russian prisoners were left in German hands. There were no further attempts to reactivate the battle front. Nobody thereafter dared to mention active defense or counter-attack. The Russian army was in fact no longer in the war.

The July Days

The most disastrous consequences of the ill-fated offensive were political: the disintegration of the February bloc now proceeded much more quickly, while Bolshevism received another powerful impetus. The masses were tired of the appeals for patience and self-control which were being made by the leaders of the socialist parties; they were looking elsewhere for guidance, and the influence of extremist groups was everywhere on the increase.

The decline of the socialist parties became particularly evident during the events that have come to be known in history as the "July days." The immediate causes of these events were several. To begin with, the economic position of the workers was deteriorating due to inflation and insufficient food supplies. There was dissatisfaction in the barracks after the failure of the offensive of June 18 (July 1). The general ferment was aggravated by Bolshevik and Anarchist propaganda. But above all there was impatience with the inability of the government and the Soviets to lead the way out of an intolerable situation. The soldiers particularly were impervious to the argument that there was no immediate solution for their troubles, that they would have to mark time and wait patiently.

Keenly aware of the growing discontent, the Bolsheviks now decided (as Lenin himself later admitted) to conduct a "reconnaissance in depth": to test the masses' readiness for the final battle of which Lenin never ceased to dream. The Bolshevik leadership was almost as divided over this new venture as it had been in June, as Trotsky, for one, testifies; but, once again, Lenin's view prevailed.

Even the Bolsheviks, however, could not control turbulent Petrograd. They had planned to start with a peaceful street demonstration, so as not to arouse the suspicions of their opponents. But from the start the patrols of their own military organizations began to stop and confiscate private cars, to arrest people, and to search houses. The soldiers acted entirely on their own. For two whole days, starting July 3 (16), trucks packed with soldiers, sailors and some workers, all armed with loaded rifles, roamed up and down the Nevsky Prospect. Shots were fired in all directions, sometimes at houses where snipers were supposed to be hiding. Quite a number of people were wounded or killed. Bolshevik organizers had the utmost difficulty in directing the movement, which had spread to some units of the garrison—notably the First Machine Gun Regiment—and to many factories. In some factories all the workers, often with their wives and children, joined in the disorders. In the Obukhov works, for instance, the excitement had been high even before the disorders began.

On July 4 (17), 20,000 sailors arrived from Kronstadt to join the demonstration. This numerous band was led by Lunacharsky, the poet and playwright, the future People's Commissar for Public Education, who seemed somewhat ill at ease in his new role. A little later, a regiment carrying red flags, as well as the yellow and blue flag of the Ukrainian nationalists, appeared at the Tauride Palace. For two days the Central Executive Committee of the Soviet (VTsIK) was besieged by passing columns of soldiers and workers, with slogans "All power to the Soviets" and "Bread, Peace and Freedom." Some of the columns paused at the Palace, and their leaders entered the VTsIK hall to proclaim their demands from its platform—not always in friendly terms. When the Kronstadt sailors arrived at the Tauride Palace, some members of the VTsIK went out to address them. Victor Chernov, the leader of the S-R Party, was suddenly seized by a group of people and thrust into a car amidst an uproar from the crowd. But Trotsky, who at that time was already very popular among the workers and the soldiers, appeared at the gate. His resounding voice not only demanded Chernov's release, but he stepped boldly forward, with a few of his comrades, and led Chernov away.[9]

From July 3 to July 5 (16 to 18), the VTsIK, in session day and night at the Tauride Palace, was virtually without protection except for a few armed sentries at the gates. On the second day two armored cars arrived at the gates of the Palace. It later became known that they were manned by supporters of the Bolsheviks. Since the VTsIK had no protection other than its sentries, the Bolsheviks might have seized power then. But Lenin lacked the resolution to do it. On the third of these eventful days, his hesitation might have vanished. But at dawn on July 5 (18), just as Tseretelli was summing up at a meeting of the VTsIK, the sound of marching troops broke the morning stillness and a military band struck up the "Marseillaise."[10] A detachment, hastily gathered from all parts of the Petrograd garrison, had been brought to the aid of the VTsIK by two socialist officers, the Mazurenko brothers. The presence of this force, small but loyal to the government, at once altered the situation. Demonstrations and open-air meetings came to an end and life returned to normal.

The government had won a moral victory without having fired a single shot in self-defense. The casualties, according to the Bolshevik Shlyapnikov, were 400 wounded and dead; according to the findings of a special investigating commission, 114 had been wounded and 20 killed by demonstrators firing from their trucks.[11] Since neither the "militia" (city police) nor government military detachments had been summoned, not a single one of these casualties was caused by defenders of the government. (This well-established fact is falsified by Bolshevik historians. An official Soviet textbook on the history of the USSR tells its young readers: "Despite the fact that the demonstrations were completely peaceful, the Provisional Government and the Central Executive Committee of the Soviets, then composed of Mensheviks and S-R's, decided to take bloody revenge on the demonstrators. The streets of Petrograd were profusely stained with blood. There were 400 dead and wounded"—*Istoria USSR*, "Epokha Socialisma, 1917-1957," Moscow, Gosizdat., p. 46.)

At the time, the Bolsheviks persistently denied all responsibility for the July disorders, but the minutes of the meetings of the Central Committee of the Bolshevik Party, published many years later, showed beyond a shadow of doubt that Lenin and many other Bolshevik leaders had played a very active part. They blamed the unpreparedness of the masses for the defeat of the July movement.[12]

The Provisional Government at once took repressive measures against the Bolsheviks. Some Bolshevik leaders, among them Kamenev, were arrested; others went into hiding. Trotsky, too, was arrested and charged with organizing an armed demonstration. Simultaneously, the Provisional Government accused Lenin, Ganetsky, Koslovsky and other Bolsheviks of having accepted money from the Germans. The government had had the accused under observation for some time, but it was delaying the arrests until it had complete proof of their guilt. The "July days" persuaded the Minister of Justice, Pereverzev, to strike at once. But his public denunciation, it turned out, was premature, for it spoiled his chance of securing some of the most important evidence. Lenin and Zinoviev escaped before they could be arrested, and made their way to Finland.

The failure of the July demonstrations, and the charge of having taken German money, so discredited the Bolsheviks in the eyes of the masses that the life of the party came almost to a standstill. The government and the Menshevik-Socialist Revolutionary majority in the Soviet could now breathe more freely. In closed meetings of the praesidium of the VTsIK, some of the internationalist wing of the Mensheviks (this author and others), pressed for an end to the indecision on the problem of peace which had almost led to catastrophe in the "July days." But the defensist majority could not be moved. They were determined to avoid friction with the western Allies, and reluctant to jeopardize their coalition with the center parties at home. The center parties, for their part, stigmatized any attempt to deal with the problem of peace independently of the Allies as high treason. Thus, despite the failure of the military offensive and the near disaster of the "July days," the deadlock continued.

Meanwhile, the coalition was severely shaken by the resignation of four ministers over the Ukrainian question. In a visit to Kiev in June, three leading members of the cabinet, Tereshchenko, Nekrassov and Tseretelli, had succeeded in reaching a compromise with the Ukrainian Rada on Russo-Ukrainian relations, which entailed concessions to Ukrainian autonomy. The Kadets considered that these concessions were too far-reaching and endangered the territorial integrity of Russia. Prince Lvov, Konovalov, Shingarev and Godnev resigned from the government on July 8 (21). Kerensky was now elected President of the Council of Ministers in Lvov's stead, while the places of the other three were left vacant until the broader composition of the future government could be settled. Discussions were held throughout August and September in an attempt to find a new basis for coalition between the socialists and the parties to their right, in other words, to find a common approach to the problem of peace.

The Kornilov Rebellion

In the summer of 1917, Russia's political life became more and more polarized. While the right-wing parties broke away from the government after the resignation of the Kadet Ministers, the masses on the other hand, moved steadily to the left, despite the Bolshevik defeat in July.

The polarization of Russian politics became evident at the State

Conference held in Moscow from August 12 to 15 (25-28). The 2,414 delegates included representatives of all public bodies, professional associations, Soviets and political parties, ranging from extreme right to the Bolsheviks, and including national minorities. The government was anxious to maintain a proper balance among the various sections of the population and between the right and the left, and so, because of the growing tendency of the rightist groups to boycott the Provisional Government, Kerensky deemed it prudent to give them a slight numerical edge. Nevertheless, the rightist politicians were no longer in a mood for reconciliation. They cherished the idea of a "strong government," which at that time could mean only government by a military man. And they were sure they had found their man in General Lavr Kornilov, once again the Commander-in-Chief of the Russian armies.

Preparations for a military *coup d'etat* had begun well before the start of the State Conference. The plot involved influential army commanders (Generals Kaledin, Kornilov, Denikin and Krymov, Colonel Golitsyn), prominent conservative politicians (Milyukov and Prince Lvov), the Union of Army and Navy Officers, industrialists and financiers (such as Putilov), and a great number of adventurers and irresponsible military figures.[13] Their plan called for officers from various units to come to the capital and spread false rumors of a Bolshevik "St. Bartholomew's night" allegedly fixed for August 27. These *agents provocateurs* were to be directed by a group that met at the Villa Rode—a swanky restaurant frequented by the *jeunesse dorée*.[14] As soon as their efforts had provoked disturbances, the officers were to gain control of the armored division and other military formations, to seize the Soviets, and to arrest the leaders of the left and the ministers of the Provisional Government if they refused to co-operate with the conspiracy. Finally, on the pretext of re-establishing order in the unruly capital, Kornilov would order the so-called Savage Division of cavalry, commanded by General Krymov, to enter Petrograd on August 28 (September 10). This was the plot. In order to implement it, Kornilov, on August 7th, ordered General Denikin to move the Savage Division in "the agreed direction." Denikin summoned Krymov to General Headquarters and entrusted command of the operation to him.

When Kornilov arrived in Moscow for the State Conference, a street demonstration was organized in his honor. He drove to the conference in a white car and was received by the right with rapturous applause that left no doubt that it looked to him for the salvation of Russia.

Kerensky had received incomplete information about the Kornilov plot by August 12 (25). He wished to warn the public of the impending danger but, still uncertain of the accuracy of his information, he did not dare call things by their right names. As a result he made a very confused speech at the State Conference, one of the strangest of his career, which threw out many dark hints and hysterical-sounding warnings but puzzled even the better-informed persons in his audience.

The next day, August 13 (26), Kornilov informed Milyukov at the State Conference that preparations had been made for the *coup* to take place on August 27 (September 9). A few hours later, at a secret meeting with several former members of the State Duma, officers from GHQ declared that "everything was ready for the overthrow of Kerensky."[15]

Every eventuality seemed to have been foreseen and every precaution taken, but in reality the whole plot was built on sand and most poorly organized. No account was taken of the mood of the masses, and particularly of the soldiers. On the night of August 27 (September 9), the conspirators were celebrating their future victory at the Villa Rode, when Colonel Clergé, one of the plotters, arrived with the news that the conspiracy had been discovered. The "general staff" of the plotters immediately fled and the attempt to provoke disturbances in Petrograd failed. The Savage Division, instead of marching into Petrograd to restore order on the morrow of a successful *coup,* was now advancing on a peaceful city without any provocation—and, what is more, was expected to carry out the *coup* itself.

On August 28 (September 10), the country learned that the former Prime Minister, Prince Lvov, had, on August 26 (September 8), handed Kerensky an ultimatum from General Kornilov, which demanded an immediate and complete surrender of "all civil and military powers" to himself. When Kerensky telephoned Kornilov at General Headquarters, the latter confirmed that these were indeed his demands. On August 27 (September 9), Kerensky in a telegram rejected Kornilov's ultimatum as an attempt to deprive the Russian people of the rights and liberties they had won in the revolution. He ordered Kornilov to hand over his command immediately to General Klembovsky, the commander in the North, and he appealed to all ranks of the army and navy to remain at their posts. At the same time, Kerensky announced that the government had authorized him to take all necessary measures to protect freedom and peace, and that this had been done. He asked all citizens to remain calm.

Kornilov answered Kerensky's telegram with a counter-accusation, declaring that the Provisional Government "under pressure from the Bolshevik majority, was acting in complete agreement with the plans of the German General Staff." Determined to save Russia from an evil fate, he, General Kornilov, the son of a Cossack peasant, was taking upon himself the task of restoring order and was resolved to give his life for his country. Simultaneously it was announced that the Savage Division, under the command of General Krymov, was marching on Petrograd.

The news of Kornilov's revolt electrified the nation, and especially the left. The Soviets and their affiliated organizations, the railroad workers and some sections of the army, declared themselves ready to resist Kornilov by force if necessary. Military detachments were sent out to meet him, while the advance of the Savage Division and other hostile forces on Petrograd was impeded in every way by the railroad men, who kept in constant touch with Petrograd by telephone.

From a purely military point of view, there was small chance of successfully defending Petrograd. At a meeting of the praesidium of the VTsIK, a military commission, which had just surveyed the front, asserted unequivocally that the armed ring on which the defense of Petrograd rested showed a gap of nearly 50 kilometers, which could not be closed. Many expressed very pessimistic views, but Vladimir S. Woytinsky, the commissar of the Fifth Army, insisted that purely military considerations were of no importance, since there would be no fighting: Kornilov's cavalry was no more prepared to engage in fratricide than the forces of the Petrograd garrison, and his troops would scatter before it came to a military engagement.

And that is how it was. The hundreds of agitators—workers, soldiers, members of the Soviets—who infiltrated Kornilov's camp before Luga encountered little resistance. Only the officers remained intransigent; most of the soldiers soon began to echo the argument that their numbers were insufficient, that there was no infantry to support them, and that to fight the entire Petrograd garrison would be sheer folly. Others simply responded to the appeal to avert fratricidal strife.

Kornilov's attempted *coup* simply collapsed. Krymov, who had come to Petrograd in advance of his troops, committed suicide in his hotel room. Bagratuny, the commander of the attacking troops, surrendered and led a delegation from his corps to the Soviet, where members of the Savage Division fraternized with the VTsIK. "Long live Tseretelli!" shouted the representatives of the division after a speech by the latter. "Long live the Savage Division!" responded the members of VTsIK.[16] Kornilov was dismissed from his post, arrested and brought to trial, after interrogation by a special commission of the VTsIK headed by M. Liber.

Though the Kornilov plot was militarily a shameful failure, its political consequences were disastrous. For the threat of a counter-revolutionary revolt roused and united the entire left, including the Bolsheviks, who still exerted considerable influence in the Soviets. It seemed impossible to reject their offers of co-operation at such a dangerous moment. The Bolsheviks exploited the situation to raise their prestige, strengthen their organization, and arm their own Red Guard. Delegations from the Bolsheviks were constantly demanding arms, allegedly for use against Kornilov, and obtaining them from the VTsIK under this or that pretext. At the same time the Bolsheviks demanded the freeing of Trotsky, who in their view, was indispensable to the organization of resistance against the counter-revolution.[17] After the "July days," the Kornilov plot was a godsend to Lenin, second only to the ill-fated military offensive of July 1-3 as an impetus to power.

As for the right, it was now irrevocably split between the supporters and opponents of Kornilov. An inquiry by the Central Committee of the Soviets revealed the General's complete political naiveté and utter unfitness for the role of Russia's savior. Nevertheless, in the eyes of most officers, "the honest soldier Kornilov" had been martyred by the revolution; while Kerensky, whom Kornilov had accused of duplicity, was regarded by many as a traitor with whom they would not shake hands. From that time on, Kerensky and the Provisional Government became more hateful to the right than socialists like Tseretelli and Gotz, or than even the Bolsheviks, whom in fact they did not yet take seriously.

The Democratic Convention and the Pre-Parliament

The Provisional Government had survived a third time, but this was due more to the weakness and indecision of its foes than to its own efforts. For the third and last time, the government failed to take advantage of its victory. It could not do the one thing that might have preserved the esteem of the masses—namely, launch an energetic and unequivocal drive for peace. The leaders of the Menshevik defensists and of the Socialist Revolutionaries still wished to maintain the coalition with the liberal bourgeois groups and maintain harmony in the Allied camp. The internationalist Mensheviks, for their part, insisted on a break with the liberals, not for any "class" reason, but because they felt that coalition with the patriotic groups prevented the government from taking independent initiatives toward a general peace. That such initiatives had to be independent was becoming quite obvious. Even Tseretelli, who was committed to the support of Allied unity, now admitted that France and Britain could not be shaken in their resolve to continue the war "to a victorious conclusion." Nevertheless, despite disaffection among the peasants and even among the rank-and-file Mensheviks and Socialist Revolutionaries, the leaders of the two parties adamantly refused to dissolve the coalition with the liberals.

However, some action was clearly indicated after the Kornilov affair and so, yielding to the feeling prevailing on the left, the government decided to convoke an All-Russian Democratic Convention. It was not to be on the model of the Moscow State Conference, but to be drawn from a narrower sector of "Russian public life," to be confined to the left and the liberal center, and to exclude participation by the organizations and parties of the right. This convention was to make a definite decision to settle the question of a new government.

The 1,200 delegates, who assembled in Petrograd on September

14 (27), represented workers', peasants' and soldiers' Soviets; trade unions; *zemstvos,* municipal authorities, political organizations on the front lines; consumer co-operatives; and political parties. The delegates of the co-operatives occupied the right-wing position, while the Bolsheviks were on the left. At an unending succession of meetings—plenary, sectional, fractional—and in various subcommittees, the urgent problems of the Russian revolution and the world were discussed yet once more from every possible angle. In the absence of Lenin, who was still in hiding in Finland, the chief spokesman for the Bolsheviks was Trotsky, who had now officially joined the party. The brilliant oratorical duels between him and Tseretelli, the chief speaker for the socialists, contributed some striking polemics to political literature, but had no other noteworthy effects.

The debates at the Democratic Convention centered around the composition of the new government and the question of coalition with the liberals. The Bolsheviks, as well as some left-wing Mensheviks and left-wing Socialist Revolutionaries, urged the transfer of all power to the Soviets, as the only way out. The defensists, on the other hand, maintained their belief in a continued coalition with the "best elements" of the democratic bourgeoisie. In the course of protracted sessions, it became obvious that the Convention was split so nearly in half that it would be impossible to reach a clear-cut decision. And, indeed, in the voting of September 19 (October 2), 766 were for continuing the coalition, and 688 against. Strangely enough, an amendment to exclude the Kadets from the coalition passed by 595 votes to 493; yet a resolution proposing a coalition cabinet without the Kadets was defeated by 813 votes to 183.

These highly contradictory and confusing results seemed to permit the inclusion of at least some individual Kadets in the cabinet, and Kerensky's government quickly acted on this interpretation. A cabinet was formed to include the liberal industrialists, Konovalov and Tretyakov, and the physician, Kishkin, a left-wing Kadet to whom the left was sympathetic. Thus, the new coalition cabinet was in effect not different from the old. Its only innovation was the decision to establish, for the period before the convocation of the Constituent Assembly scheduled for November 28 (December 11), a consultative body which would be a kind of pre-Parliament and to which the Provisional Government would be responsible morally if not legally. This pre-Parliament, which was officially named the Provisional Council of the Republic, was composed of 550 members, including 156 from non-Soviet (that is, bourgeois) groups. The other 394 represented the various shades and sections of the Soviet groups and parties, including the Bolsheviks. The Bolsheviks, however, after a furious struggle within their party, eventually refused to participate in the Provisional Council. Their delegates came to the opening of the pre-Parliament on October 7 (20), but later Trotsky read a declaration on behalf of their group which included the following statements:

". . . the bourgeois classes which are directing the policies of the Provisional Government are determined to sabotage the Constituent Assembly . . . The privileged classes are openly relying upon 'the bony hand of hunger,' hoping that it will strangle the revolution and put an end to the Constituent Assembly.

". . . the Provisional Government, under the thumb of Kadet counter-revolutionaries and of the imperialist Allies, is allowing the suicidal war to drag on, senselessly, with no energy and no plan; aimlessly sacrificing more and more hundreds of thousands of soldiers and sailors and paving the way for the surrender of Petrograd and the strangling of the revolution . . . We, the delegates of the Social Democrats (Bolsheviks), refuse to have anything to do with this government of national treason and with this Council of counter-revolutionary connivance . . . In leaving the Provisional Council, we appeal to the vigilance and valor of the workers, soldiers and peasants of all Russia."

The declaration ended with the slogans: "All power to the Soviets! All land to the people! We demand an immediate, honorable and democratic peace! Long live the Constituent Assembly!"

Of course, even Trotsky, when mouthing his absurd accusations against "this government of national treason" and "counter-revolutionary connivance," must have known that there was not an atom of truth in them. He must have known that the overwhelming majority of the pre-Parliament had no thought of surrendering Petrograd to the enemy or of strangling the revolution by means of a planned famine. And he certainly knew that there was not one among the various powerful groups behind the government that would have wished to sabotage the Constituent Assembly. The hypocrisy of the Bolshevik oath of loyalty to the Constituent Assembly must have been as apparent to him as it was to Lenin, who had long since decided that the Bolshevik Party would not tolerate a Constituent Assembly that did not have a Bolshevik majority.

Among Trotsky's many demagogic lies, one accusation, unfortunately, was true, and that was, fundamentally, the most serious accusation of all. It was his indictment of the majority for having no clear view of the future, for "allowing the war to drag on" with neither the energy nor the will to stop it. Earlier (p. 43) we quoted from the Menshevik paper *Rabochaya Gazeta* to illustrate the resentment of the Mensheviks and Socialist Revolutionaries toward the Allies' refusal to make any significant change in their peace aims. Still, *Rabochaya Gazeta* categorically declined to urge applying pressure on the Allies. On the other hand, the internationalists, Martov and others, insisted on a more exacting attitude towards the Allies' imperialist aims. This was an important difference, but it was a difference in tactics, not in policy. Martov argued that "if the Revolution does not kill the War, the War will kill the Revolution," and demanded that the Provisional Government take a much firmer attitude toward the reluctant Allies—and even resort to complete freedom of action if absolutely necessary. Tseretelli and others, on the other hand, believed that this would be dangerous and ill-advised both for the Russian government and for the socialist parties. Friendship and harmony with the western Allies, in their opinion, was as vital to the success of the revolution as close co-operation with the Russian liberals and progressives. Preserving the government coalition between the Soviets and the "best elements of the bourgeoisie" internally was closely linked with maintaining friendship and co-operation among the Allies externally.

To understand this attitude, one must recall that the ruling group in the Soviets as well as in the government was the Russian intelligentsia, which had for some generations been inspired by the French

Revolution and British constitutionalism. They knew the backwardness of Russia, had a high opinion of western civilization and political institutions, and were deeply convinced that, as Russian patriots and democrats, it would be unpardonable for them to loosen Russia's ties with the Allies and assume a measure of independence in their foreign policy, which might weaken the cause of the western democracies and help imperial Germany.

This state of mind produced a certain timidity in the relations of the democratic leaders with the Allied governments. For their part, the Allies gave the revolutionary leaders little sympathy. After the Milyukov incident, when the Provisional Government and the Soviets requested a conference on war aims between the Allies and the representatives of the new Russia, their polite request was tacitly rejected. Even the half-promise of British Ambassador Buchanan to Tseretelli, Chernov and Skobelev that this problem would be discussed through diplomatic channels was never honored. The Allies acted as though the Russian government did not exist—except to be criticized for not doing enough for the war effort. The Austrian Emperor's peace proposal was brought to the attention of the Russian Foreign Ministry three weeks after it had been sabotaged by France. The political leaders in Petrograd still continued to hope that a separate peace with Austria might bring relief to the Russian revolution and further the cause of general peace, but until October 19 nobody bothered to tell the Russians that France and Italy had terminated the negotiations with Austria, without permitting their Russian allies even the chance to be heard. In the case of the Stockholm Conference, the Russian delegation left Russia in June and the main negotiations took place in July and August; even Tseretelli and his friends did not suspect that the conference had been doomed May 31 by Marshal Petain at the French War Council in Paris. Surely the Russian socialists would have been deeply shocked to learn that the Allied military leaders had discounted the Russian army as a real force as early as the spring of 1917. Months later, when the Bolsheviks had seized power and were starting the Brest-Litovsk negotiations, the British Ambassador to Petrograd, Sir George Buchanan, made his famous proposal that Russia be permitted to leave the war.

But at the Allied War Council on November 30, Clemenceau violently rejected the idea of "thanking the pickpocket for having stolen our purse."[18]

In his memoirs, Sir Robert Bruce Lockhart, who was a British diplomatic agent in Russia in 1917, writes:

> After the February Revolution of 1917, the diplomatic endeavors of both France and Great Britain were directed to keeping Russia in the war at almost any cost. Although both France and Britain owed much to the Russian military effort in the early days of the war, the French were bitter almost from the start of the February Revolution. British diplomacy, exercised by the gentle and sympathetic Sir George Buchanan, was more suave in manner, but its purpose was the same: to cajole or bully Russia into continuing the war.[19]

Such were the Allied governments and statesmen. And yet, in their political inexperience, some Russian socialist leaders were deeply convinced that to remain the partners of the western Allies and perhaps to sacrifice the revolution for the sake of Allied unity was the sacred duty of Russian revolutionary democracy.

Another British historian, the well-known military analyst, B. H. Liddell Hart, summed up the attitude of the Russian revolutionaries toward the Allies in the following sentence:

> Let us not forget how many times Russia had sacrificed herself to save her Allies; preparing the way for their ultimate victory as surely as for her downfall.[20]

The vicious circle which the socialist parties were unable to break all those months was not of their own creation. It was a product of the early defeat of Tsarist Russia in the war and the insurmountable contradiction between the necessity of radically rebuilding the country under war conditions, and the impossibility of ending the war without betraying democracy and socialism. In fairness to the Russian leaders, who were tyros in war and statecraft, one must note that not one of the leaders of the West understood the tragedy of the Russian revolution. Not one could suggest a means of reconciling the conflict between natural Russian patriotism and the need to save

Russian democracy by making the concessions that had to be made, in the face of rising extremist utopianism and an irresistible urge for peace at any price. Neither President Wilson, nor his Secretary of State, nor his ambassador in Petrograd, knew anything about the tremendous difficulties of Russia at that period. As is made clear by George Kennan's *Russia Leaves the War,*[21] Lloyd George, Clemenceau, and the other European statesmen took it for granted that the Russians would manage somehow. It was naive to expect these men—completely absorbed in the life-and-death struggle of their own countries—to show any initiative in helping the Russians with their very difficult problems. And so the deadlock over war and peace, evident since the spring, continued to paralyze the revolutionary leaders.

One need only reread the numerous speeches delivered at the pre-Parliament during the two weeks of its existence to see that such was, in fact, the state of affairs. The democratic intelligentsia of revolutionary Russia included many outstanding personalities, brilliant orators, highly educated people; yet during this critical fortnight they failed to come to any practical decision whatever. Some spoke more or less brilliantly, but all the speeches were well reasoned and most of them were sincere. Only the Minister for Foreign Affairs, Tereshchenko; the War Minister, General Verkhovsky; and the Navy Minister, Admiral Verderevsky, carefully weighed every word in their public pronouncements, aware of the presence of foreign correspondents and diplomats.[22] But the former Commander-in-Chief, General Alexeev, was less diplomatic. He declared that the army was disorganized and discipline non-existent, and that the offensive of June 18 (July 1) had shown it was impossible to arouse a fighting spirit in the ranks. He saw only one hope: to make the country and the army realize that Germany, too, was in bad shape and that one supreme national effort might yet save Russia in its tragic crisis.

It would have been difficult to find weightier arguments in favor of immediate peace negotiations than those advanced by the former Commander-in-Chief. It was obviously a national necessity for the country to get out of the war as quickly as possible, even at a high price. And one, at least, of the internationalist Mensheviks[23] clearly formulated this necessity.[24]

The Russian intelligentsia understood that, in the interests of the country's future, Russia's military defeat had to be frankly admitted and that certain unavoidable conclusions had to be unflinchingly drawn, however galling they might be to national self-esteem. And yet for the most part, the democratic leaders were psychologically and morally incapable of facing that necessity. In the course of prolonged debates, the minority consistently argued that military defeat was a fact which could not be altered. If no reasonable way out of the war were found now, what would happen if the Bolsheviks seized power? The Bolsheviks would accept any peace terms which Germany chose to offer them, despite Trotsky's boast that they would consider only "a democratic and honorable peace"; for Lenin had bluntly announced that they would be prepared to accept even an "obscene" peace. The Bolsheviks would surely get worse terms than those which the legitimate and united government of Russia might hope to obtain.

But the most eloquent arguments were lost on the defensist leaders. Only at the very end of the last meeting did the internationalists (now supported by the former defensist Dan, by General Verkhovsky, and by those left-wing Socialist Revolutionaries who had not walked out with the Bolsheviks) succeed in putting through a resolution demanding the immediate opening of peace negotiations and the immediate transfer of land to the land committee. The final vote took place at dawn of October 25 (November 7), only a few hours before the Bolshevik commissars and their detachments occupied the Maryinsky Palace.

[1] Sukhanov, *Journal of the Revolution*, Vol. IV, pp. 316, ff.

[2] Tseretelli, "The June Days," *op. cit.*

[3] Not to be confused with the future commissar for health, Dr. N. A. Semasko.

[4] This plan of Lenin's is described in Sukhanov's *Zapiskie o Revolutsii*, Vol. IV, pp. 316-324. Sukhanov states that he learned about it several years later from a very well-informed and reliable person whom he trusted absolutely but whose name he could not divulge at that time (1922). Trotsky, who wrote his *History* in the early '30's, brushed aside this account on the ground that Sukhanov had accepted unconfirmed rumors. But Sukhanov was referring to the testimony of an important witness, not to rumors.

As for Trotsky, who had not yet joined the Bolshevik Party at the time and was still leader of a small Petrograd group of intellectuals called the *Mezhrayontsi*, he did not personally agree with the course adopted by Lenin in June; but afterward he felt it his duty, even as late as 1932, to support and justify all Lenin's actions, though he interpreted them in his own fashion. (Trotsky, *The October Revolution*, Vol. I, pp. 484-485.)

[5] Trotsky, *The October Revolution*, Vol. I, p. 484.

[6] Lenin, *Works*, Vol. XXV, p. 92.

[7] *Ibid.*, p. 95.

[8] The sudden change in Bolshevik tactics is confirmed by the memoirs of V. Belsky, who at that time was in the battle near Minsk. He writes that at the beginning of the offensive the leaders of the Bolsheviks in the front army suddenly assumed a patriotic position, in direct contradiction to their previous attitude. Even after the collapse of the offensive, they put the blame for the disaster not on the "petit bourgeois parties" but on the rightist defeatists and counter-revolutionaries: V. Belsky, *The Year 1917 in the Western Provinces and on the Western Front*, unpublished memoirs in the Russian Archives of Columbia University. Part 2, pp. 95-96.

[9] Later Trotsky declared that the men who had seized Chernov had been recognized as criminals and agents of the Tsarist police.

[10] The "Marseillaise" was a traditional revolutionary song at that time.

[11] Chamberlin, W. H., *The Russian Revolution (1917-1921)*, Vol. 1, pp. 173-174.

[12] *Minutes of the Central Committee*, Lenin's speeches in preparation for the October rising. "We did many silly things in July," Lenin used to say later in private conversation. He also mentioned, as far as I remember, at the meeting with the German delegation where the events of March 1921 in Germany were discussed, "What kind of silly things? Such things, for instance, as probing the situation too deeply and doing our reconnoitering too vigorously. Unless one risks such sorties from time to time, it is easy to lose touch with the masses. It is well known, however, that a sortie may lead willy-nilly to a major battle. That is exactly what almost happened in July. But the retreat was sounded just in time." (Trotsky, *On Lenin*, pp. 67-68.)

[13] Kerensky, "The Kornilov Affair," *Novoye Russkoye Slovo*. October 21, 1956.

[14] Vinberg, *The Captives of the Monkeys*, pp. 104-107.

[15] See *Posledniye Novosti* of November 4, 1920. According to the paper, on August 23 (September 5), that is, four days before the intended *coup*, Kornilov gave orders to the Cossack General Kaledin to move to Moscow.

[16] Raphael Abramovitch, *Memoirs*, Vol. II, p. 118.

[17] *Ibid.*, p. 153.

[18] Poincaré, *op. cit.*, Vol. 9, p. 395.

[19] *Foreign Affairs*, January 1957, Vol. 35, No. 2, p. 333.

[20] *Encyclopaedia Britannica*, Fourteenth Edition, Vol. 23, p. 776-B.

[21] American indifference to Russia was matched by an amazing lack of interest, among the Russian political leaders, in the United States as an international factor. Only two among the score of speakers at the pre-Parliament even mentioned America. Milyukov, the former Foreign Minister, praised Wilson for having changed his attitude toward Germany and for accepting, as a war aim, the complete destruction of German militarism. And the Polish internationalist, P. Lapinski, predicted that the American entry into the war would probably only prolong it by about two years.

[22] Admiral Verderevsky, and especially General Verkhovsky, spoke quite differently at the private meetings of the committees in the pre-Parliament. There they advocated substantially the same policy as the internationalists—influenced not so much by political principles as by the hopeless position at the front.

[23] This author.

[24] General Alexeev himself summed up the situation equally clearly when he was asked in the lobby about his attitude to immediate peace negotiations. He answered (*Russkive Vedemosti*, No. 230, October 8 [21], 1917): "We could complete a peace at any time, but who would dare propose it?" This described the historical impasse with complete accuracy.

CHAPTER 4

The October Revolution

The Rising Tide of Extremism

From the time of the Kornilov episode on, great masses were drawn irresistibly toward Bolshevism. In the army and among the workers, the Bolsheviks captured one important position after another in September and, particularly, in October. We may note the following more striking events in October, as compiled by Ryabinsky, the official historian:[1]

> On October 1 (14), the garrison in Rostov-on-Don organizes a peaceful demonstration of soldiers and workers under Bolshevik slogans.
>
> On October 3 (16), the soldiers stationed in Kyshtym unanimously decides to demand the transfer of power to the Soviets. The same demand is also voiced by the soldiers of the First Siberian Army Corps.
>
> The second congress of sailors of the Baltic Fleet urges the immediate resignation of Kerensky.
>
> A joint meeting of the soldiers of the 61st, 62nd, 63rd, 64th, 526th, 527th and 528th Regiments, of the First Petrograd Brigade of the 8th Heavy Artillery Division, and of the 23rd Railroad Battalion of the First Siberian Army Corps, at the front, demands an immediate truce and peace without annexations or indemnities.
>
> At a meeting of the workers' section of the Petrograd Soviet, delegates from the Rumanian front describe the unbearable sufferings of the soldiers, caused by the bread shortage: "If peace

is not concluded soon, the soldiers will simply go home. Already they refuse to fire. In another two or three weeks they will proclaim a truce and lay down arms."

The delegates from the 33rd Corps, who have come to Petrograd with demands for peace, land, etc., warn that if their demands are not met they will seize power and proclaim a truce.

The executive committee of the Soviet of the Latvian sharpshooters promises armed support to the Bolsheviks.

On October 12 (25) a soldiers' meeting in Kazan demands the immediate conclusion of peace.

Officers and other ranks of the Volynsky Regiment of Guards ask for arms for the workers and for the transfer of power to the Soviets. Similar resolutions are passed at the general meetings of the Chasseur Regiment of Guards and the 125th Infantry Reserve Regiment.

On October 13 (26) the 85th Infantry Reserve Regiment urge that "power be seized by the proletariat and the poor peasants."

On October 14 (27) at a meeting of the Executive Committee of the Soviets, numerous delegates from the front demand the transfer of power to the Soviets and an immediate peace. They declare that the mass of soldiers are completely obsessed by the desire for peace and that before long nobody will be able to keep them at their posts.

From mid-October onwards the overthrow of the government is the talk of the barracks in Petrograd. On October 18 (31) and 19 (November 1) the following army and navy formations vote for an overthrow of the Provisional Government: the Chasseur Regiment of Guards, the Moscow, the Volynsky, the Pavlovsky, the Keksholm, the Semenovsky, the Izmaylovsky, the Grenadier, the Finland, the First Chasseurs and the 3rd Reserve Regiments, the Second Baltic Fleet, the Electro-Technical Battalion, the Artillery Division of Guards, the Pioneer Battalion of Guards and the Regiment of Sailors.

Meanwhile, the balance of forces within the all-important Soviets had shifted radically. One Soviet after another was slipping out of the control of the Socialist Revolutionaries and Mensheviks and into the hands of the Bolsheviks and their allies, the Left Social-Revolutionaries. Thus, at the Executive Committee of the Moscow Soviet on September 19 (October 2), the Bolsheviks secured a majority; and

Victor Nogin, a member of the Central Committee of the Bolshevik Party, was elected chairman. At the Congress of Soviets of the Moscow Region, the Bolsheviks won a majority, too, and the new Executive Committee ranged itself solidly behind them. A similar trend manifested itself in many other places.

> On October 3 (16), the Vladivostok Soviet adopted a resolution proposed by the Bolsheviks.
>
> On October 8 (21), the congress of Soviets of the Lysvensk mining region fell into the hands of the Bolsheviks.
>
> At an election in the soldiers' section of the Feodosia Soviet (in the Crimea), the Ukrainian Bolsheviks were victorious.
>
> At an election of the executive of the Minsk Soviet, the praesidium was entirely Bolshevik, the Mensheviks and Socialist Revolutionaries having refused to take part in the elections.
>
> On October 14 (27), the Minsk regional congress of Soviets adopted a Bolshevik resolution.
>
> At the conference of the Soviets of the western region at Minsk, the Bolsheviks were predominant.

And so on. The most important single fact was the Bolshevik victory in the Petrograd Soviet. On September 25 (October 8), Trotsky, who had only recently been released from prison, was elected chairman of the Soviet and immediately became the head of its newly-formed Military Revolutionary Committee. This committee's official aim was to combat counter-revolution; its real task was to seize power for the Bolsheviks. From that point on, the organization of the *coup* was officially conducted under the banner of the Soviets. This was immensely useful to Lenin, since many soldiers and workers would respond only to a call from the Soviets and not to an appeal from the Bolshevik Party.

Among the workers in Petrograd, the atmosphere was becoming increasingly tense as the second congress of Soviets approached. Bolshevik slogans were winning support in most of the large factories —in such industrial giants as the Putilov and Obukhov plants, with their tens of thousands of workers, and in other large plants like the Old and the New Parviyanen, Trubochny, Siemens and Schuckert, Gvozdilny, Leisner, and the Sestroretsky small-arms plant. The same was true in many plants in Moscow and other industrial centers.

The country, as a whole, however, was not nearly so uniform. Thus, on October 1 (14), the old Central Executive Committee of the Soviets received from various towns 169 resolutions on the question of the character of the government. Of these 58 were for a democratic government of all the socialist parties (at that juncture this was a non-Bolshevik slogan); 31 for transfer of all power to the Soviets (which was the official slogan of the Bolsheviks); 5 for the dictatorship of the proletariat and the poor peasants; and 1 for the dictatorship of the proletariat alone.

Nevertheless, the trend in October was unmistakable. On October 7 (20), the Bolshevik paper *Rabochiy Put* published 34 resolutions, from various organizations, calling for the transfer of power to the Soviets. On October 11 (24), *Izvestia*[2] published 14 resolutions demanding that the All-Russian Congress of Soviets be summoned immediately for the purpose of assuming power. Meanwhile, there was a growing peasant movement, influenced by the sentiments of the soldiers. Agrarian disorders, violent in some places, were reported from the Ryazan and Penza *gubernias,* the Caucasus, the Zadonsky district near Voronezh, and the *gubernias* of Podolsk, Volyn, Chernigov, Nizhny-Novgorod and Tambov.

The Socialist Revolutionaries and Mensheviks were aware that the rising tide of political and social discontent was carrying the Bolshevik Party toward victory. But, unable to end the war and refusing to undertake radical social reforms before the Constituent Assembly had been elected and convened, the two democratic socialist parties could merely attempt to mark time as long as possible. They tried to postpone the date of the second All-Russian Congress of Soviets, but the pressure from the Bolsheviks was too strong. And so the Congress was convened by the old Executive Committee, though the democratic parties were fully aware that disaster lay ahead.

Struggles within the Bolshevik Party

After the "July days," when an order for his arrest was issued, Lenin had gone into hiding, first at Razliv, a railroad station near Petrograd, and later in Finland. From Finland he kept in constant touch with his party, receiving frequent visits from members of the Bolshevik

Central Committee, and, in turn, incessantly bombarding them with letters, articles and oral messages conveyed by trusted friends. It is difficult to imagine Lenin's feverish intensity at this time. Having been insufficiently prepared to seize power in June and again in July, he now sensed, almost physically, that the moment he had so long awaited was at hand: the Kornilov plot had helped the Bolsheviks emerge from political isolation.

Although Lenin's superhuman "foresight" is a Bolshevik myth, and bears little relation to reality, it cannot be denied that none among the Bolshevik leaders pressed for a speedy armed uprising so passionately, fanatically or incessantly as Lenin. To be sure, Trotsky, whose talents and revolutionary fervor were valued highly, shared Lenin's view, but as a former Menshevik he was not yet a full-fledged member of the Bolshevik "inner circle." And that inner circle, in October, was rent by profound disagreements, not only over technical details and estimates of armed strength, but also over the fundamental strategy and principles of an armed uprising. The documentary material now available fully establishes the lack of unanimity in Boshevik counsels throughout September and the first half of October.

An example of these divided counsels was the Central Committee meeting of September 15 (28), attended by Trotsky, Kamenev, Rykov, Nogin, Stalin, Sverdlov, Bubnov, Bukharin, Lomov (Opokov), Kollontay, Dzherzhinsky, Uritsky, A. Ioffe, Shaumyan, Sokolnikov and Milyutin. At this meeting two letters from Lenin in Finland were read. ("The Bolsheviks must seize power" and "Marxism and the uprising.")[3] Both called for immediate revolt. Stalin proposed that the letters be circulated among the chief party organizations; but this proposal was turned down as too dangerous. Kamenev proposed to inform all party organizations that the party line would continue unaltered, and he declared at the same time that he, personally, was opposed to all plans for an uprising. This position found no support either.[4] It was finally decided, by 6 votes to 4, with 6 abstentions, to keep only one copy of each letter and destroy all others.[5] In other words, less than six weeks before the armed uprising took place, the Bolshevik Central Committee was split in half over this all-important question. At a meeting on September 21 (October 4), the Central

Committee was again split nearly equally over the question of the party's participation in the pre-Parliament: 8 voted for participation while 9 were in favor of staging a walk-out to suggest Bolshevik readiness for armed revolt. Because of these divisions a special meeting to discuss the question was arranged by the Bolshevik delegation to the Democratic Convention. A majority of 77 to 50 voted to stay in the pre-Parliament. The Central Committee could only endorse the motion.[6]

But the tide of extremism was rising, and the pressure of Lenin and his associates grew more intense. On October 5 (18), the Central Committee reaffirmed its former decision to walk out of the pre-Parliament; this time the only one to vote against it was Kamenev, who also asked to be relieved of the duty of representing the party in important Soviet institutions.[7] From that point on, the left wing of the party dominated the Central Committee. Even so, members of the Central Committee continued to differ over the question of the armed rising. On October 10 (23), Lenin was present for the first time at a meeting of the Central Committee, having arrived in Petrograd three days earlier, and hidden with friends. His speech at the meeting reiterated the themes of his letters, adding that he was convinced that much time had been wasted and urging that preparations for the rising should be speeded up immediately. Lenin was enthusiastically supported by Trotsky, who had by then acquired a firm grip on the Military Revolutionary Committee, and also by the Bolsheviks' Moscow regional bureau, represented in the Central Committee by Lomov (Opokov). Yet two members of the Central Committee, Zinoviev and Kamenev, still voted against an armed uprising.[8]

A more revealing picture of the hesitations among the Bolshevik leaders is provided by the Central Committee meeting on October 16 (29), only nine days before the actual rising, when representatives of various party organizations reported on local conditions in and near Petrograd. The chairman of the meeting, Jacob Sverdlov, made a fairly optimistic speech on the state of the party: he said it was growing at an extraordinary rate, already numbered 400,000 members, was winning elections in various working-class organizations, etc. But the report by Bokiy, himself an ardent advocate of an armed rising, was in significant contrast. Surveying the situation in different parts of Petrograd, Bokiy said that there was no fighting spirit in the Vassilyevsky Ostrov in spite of energetic preparations for the rising; a similar report came from the Vyborg district; it was difficult to assess the mood in the first metropolitan district; things looked a little bit better in the second metropolitan; in the Moskovsky district the mood was "reckless" but the people would "rise only if called by the Soviets, not by the party"; in the Narva district there was no desire to rise; in the big Putilov plant, Anarchist influence was growing; in the Nevsky district the mood had radically changed in favor of the party and "everybody will follow the call of the Soviet"; in the Okhta district things looked bad; in the district of Peterburgskaya Storona the mood was to "wait and see"; in the Rozhdenstvensky district there was no doubt that the rising was necessary and the Anarchists were growing strong; in the Prokhovsky district the situation had changed in the party's favor; finally, in the Schluesselburg, the mood was favorable.

The situation was painted even more soberly by Volodarsky, the New York tailor who had returned to Russia with Bukharin, and who enjoyed great popularity in the factories. He declared that "if the rising is planned for tomorrow, then we must frankly admit that we are quite unprepared," and added that in factories in which he had occasion to address the workers, "the masses received our call with bewilderment." Shlyapnikov, on behalf of the steel workers' union, said that although Bolsheviks wielded considerable influence in the union, yet "the rising planned by the Bolsheviks is not popular; rumors about an imminent rising even started a panic." Schmidt, on behalf of the central trade-union body, spoke in a similar vein. The organization was growing and comprised about half a million men, but "the mood was such that it was futile to expect any active revolt, particularly because of the fear of lay-offs for participation in the revolt."

This unoptimistic appraisal of the trade unionists, who were of course in closest touch with the workers, was echoed by those active among the soldiers. Thus, Shotman, an old Bolshevik, a worker who had been converted to Bolshevism by Lenin himself in 1903, reported that the mood at the city conference of the Petrograd party committee and of the military organizations was even more pessimistic, and concluded: "We are not ready to strike."

Stepanov, on behalf of the district organization of the party, spoke about the depressed mood among the Narva workers because of the fear of lay-offs, and added: "As for the garrison, the mood there is very gloomy, although Bolshevik influence is very strong. In New Peterhof our work in the regiment is very weak and the regiment is disorganized." In Krassnoye Selo, he continued, the 176th Regiment was solidly behind the Bolsheviks, and the 172nd almost as much so. (But Bokiy remarked that according to his information "the situation in Krassnoye Selo is not that rosy," and in Kronstadt "morale is low and the local garrison is in no fighting mood at all.") Continuing, Stepanov reported that in Luga, where the garrison was 30,000 strong, the Soviet was defensist but the workers were pro-Bolshevik. The Regiment in Gdov was solidly behind the Bolsheviks. In contradiction to these reports, the Finnish worker Rakhia maintained that "the masses are with us" and were eager for a fight. Krylenko supported Rakhia, stating that the "water is boiling."

Another group of speakers—Milyutin, Nogin (at that time chairman of the Moscow Soviet) and Rykov—insisted that the Bolsheviks should not take the initiative but should try to provoke the enemy to start an armed conflict; otherwise the risk would be too great. To this argument Stalin countered: it is said that we should wait for an attack, "but let us understand what constitutes an attack; a rise in the price of bread, the dispatch of Cossacks to the Don region, and so on —all this is attack."[9]

Lenin intervened in the discussion several times, repeatedly arguing for an immediate uprising. He pointed out that it would not be a fight of workers against the army, but between two parts of the army. The international situation and the internal difficulties were arguments for the uprising, not against it. In Petrograd, there was bread for only one day, and that is when people revolt. Politically, the revolution was ripe. All that remained to be done was to organize the uprising skillfully.

Thus far, the speakers at the meeting had differed only in their appraisal of the mood of the workers and soldiers, agreeing in support of the idea of the rising. But at least two men, Zinoviev and Kamenev, rejected the idea, and advocated a policy of gaining power by political methods—through propaganda and victory in the elections to the Constituent Assembly. An armed conspiracy, they argued, was not the only way for the party to achieve its aims—and it might fail. On the other hand, while the Constituent Assembly was obviously not a panacea, it would be a significant achievement in itself. The peasants, in time, would become more sympathetic to Bolshevism, and there was no reason to believe that they would waver on the land question. It was quite possible that the Bolshevik Party, together with the Left Social-Revolutionaries and the internationalists, would secure a majority in the Constituent Assembly. In that case, the work of the Assembly could be run on truly revolutionary lines and the party would keep growing all the time.

But this policy of faith in "the immanent power of the Russian revolution" (Kamenev's expression) found no support in the Central Committee. It turned down, by an overwhelming majority, Kamenev's proposal that the party's central organ announce that no armed uprising would take place before the opening of the Congress of Soviets. Instead, Lenin's resolution for an uprising before the Congress was carried by 19 votes to 2, with 4 abstentions. The die was cast.[10]

Unable to reconcile themselves to the Central Committee's decision, Kamenev gave an interview, and Zinoviev wrote a letter, to the newspaper *Novaya Zhizn* to inform the public that they opposed such a rising. Although their protest was couched in veiled terms (*Novaya Zhizn,* October 18 [31], 1917), Lenin flew into a terrible rage. He wrote an article, printed in *Rabochiy Put* on October 21, 1917, which under the guise of an attack on V. Bazarov's comments on the interview and letter in *Novaya Zhizn* was actually a brutal criticism of Kamenev and Zinoviev.[11]

This journalistic cross-fire between prominent Bolshevik leaders gave rise to rumors that there was a great split in the party over the question of the rising and that it was therefore unlikely to take place. The paradoxical result, therefore, was that the protest of the dissenters helped, rather than hindered, the success of the rising, for it served to lull the vigilance of its opponents.

The Coup

The feverish preparations for the armed rising which were being made by Trotsky and the Military Revolutionary Committee were now speeded up, with the stress on the military and technical sides of the operation. By comparison, the Day of the Petrograd Soviet, a mass operation organized on October 22 (November 4), in favor of the rising, was quite unimpressive. Official Bolshevik reports of that day mention only a large meeting in the People's House and "a number of meetings" in unspecified factories, and describe some quite minor gatherings—a clear indication that the Bolshevik appeal to the workers was not very successful. There were no signs of great activity even in the large plants, where only recently, between October 8 and 12 (21 and 25), huge meetings (held before the Congress of Soviets of the Northern Region was to convene on October 11 [24]) had demanded the overthrow of the Provisional Government and the transfer of power to the Soviets. The general impression of these days, noted by some contemporary observers,[12] was that, with the approach of the decisive moment, the Petrograd workers grew restive: they became dubious of the wisdom of the great leap into the unknown that the Bolsheviks were urging upon them. Volodarsky was right after all when he warned that the workers accepted the call to arms with "bewilderment."

But if most of the workers were hesitant, the soldiers, with their profound hatred of the war, represented an active and determined revolutionary force. And it was on the soldiers, together with the sailors, whom Trotsky called "the pride and glory of the revolution," that Lenin based his entire strategy.

The Bolsheviks had spared no effort to draw workers into the plot. Red Guard groups had been formed in the factories and drilled by Bolshevik instructors from the army and navy. They received weapons practice, at first secretly and later quite openly, on the training grounds of the local regiments. Yet, at the decisive moment, on the night of October 24-25 (November 6-7), it was almost exclusively army formations that appeared on the scene—according to the official survey published by the Bolsheviks themselves, who were always eager to stress the proletarian character of their movement.

The exclusively military character of the rising, which was to enter history under the name of "the great proletarian-socialist October Revolution," emerges clearly from the chronology compiled by the official Bolshevik chronicler, Ryabinsky.[13] The first important step was the assignment by the Petrograd Soviet (or, more precisely, its Military Revolutionary Committee) of commissars to all parts of the Petrograd garrison. This was done for the alleged purpose of "defending the revolution and its achievements from any attack by the counter-revolution." No order from the Provisional Government was to be carried out without the endorsement of these commissars, who were also to take control of the military telephone system. The government was thus virtually cut off from the armed forces of Petrograd. The Military Revolutionary Committee was even bold enough to send representatives to the General Staff, demanding that its authority be recognized. The reception they received was "hostile in the extreme" and was reinforced by a threat of arrest for unlawful activities, but this did not deter the committee.

On the night of October 23 (November 5), the Military Revolutionary Committee circulated the following telephone message:

> The Petrograd Soviet of Workers' and Soldiers' deputies is in danger. The counter-revolutionary conspirators have tried to assemble officer-cadets and shock brigades from the outskirts of Petrograd, by night. The newspapers *Soldat* and *Rabochiy Put* have been closed. We order you to put your regiment into battle order and to await further directives. Any delay or disobedience of this order will be considered treason to the revolution.
>
> Signed for the Chairman—Podvoysky
>
> Secretary—Antonov-Ovseyenko

When it received news that the cruiser *Aurora* and other naval vessels had been ordered out to sea, the Military Revolutionary Committee countermanded the order, and also summoned a large number of warships from Kronstadt and Helsinki to Petrograd.

These acts were openly defiant of the Provisional Government. Further defiance followed. But the Military Revolutionary Committee also used trickery. The Petrograd Soviet had long been in conflict with the Ministry of War over that Ministry's decision to send certain units of the Petrograd garrison (Bolshevik-controlled) to the front. For obvious reasons, the Petrograd Soviet (that is, the Military Revolutionary Committee) was firmly opposed to the removal of any of the Bolshevik-controlled regiments from the capital. It therefore denounced the Ministry's decision as a counter-revolutionary move, in preparation for the surrender of Petrograd to the Germans. And, although a conference of Soldiers' Soviets at the headquarters of General Cheremissov, the commander of the northern front, unanimously endorsed the troop transfer, the Petrograd Soviet vetoed it. This was obvious sedition, and the government would have been fully justified in adopting very severe measures. To prevent such measures, the Petrograd Soviet hypocritically declared (at 3 a.m. of October 23 [November 5]) that it "accepted in principle" all the points of the ultimatum that the General Staff had presented.

Another piece of deception, intended to persuade the public that the Bolsheviks had no aggressive intentions, was the following declaration on the evening of October 24 (November 6): "In face of all kinds of rumors and loose talk, the Military Revolutionary Committee wishes to make it clear that it was set up not for the purpose of seizing power but solely for the defense of the interests of the Petrograd garrison and of democracy, against the counter-revolution." A few days earlier, on October 18 (31), Trotsky had proclaimed in the Petrograd Soviet that "neither the Bolsheviks nor the Petrograd Soviet were preparing any *coups* or risings for the immediate future and no armed revolts were planned."[14] To this Kamenev added that he "subscribed to every word of Trotsky's pronouncement"; and, since Kamenev was widely known to be opposed to an armed rising, his words served even better to allay suspicion.

In reality, the rising had been carefully prepared and the various formations were already at their posts. On October 24 (November 6), the regional military commander, loyal to the government, ordered the bridges across the Neva to be raised in an effort to cut communication between the various parts of Petrograd and the center. This order was carried out by cadets, and met with only slight resistance from the Red Guards on duty at the bridges. Thereupon, the Military Revolutionary Committee ordered the cruiser *Aurora,* which in defiance of the government order, had not put out to sea, to ensure the resumption of traffic across the Nikolaevsky Bridge; and an armed detachment of sailors and mechanics from the cruiser did so. At 4 p.m. of the same day, the Bicycle Battalion adopted a resolution in support of the Soviets and deserted its post outside the Winter Palace.

The main phases of the rising took place during the night of October 24-25 (November 6-7). At 2. a.m., the Nikolaevsky and Baltiysky railroad stations and several bridges were occupied by the soldiers of the Sixth Reserve Engineer Battalion. Formations of the Pavlovsky Regiment posted themselves in Millionnaya Street, cutting all communications from the Winter Palace.

> At 3:30 a.m. the *Aurora* cast anchor at the Nikolaevsky Bridge, opposite the Winter Palace.
>
> At 5 a.m. the first convoy of sailors left Helsingfors for Petrograd.
>
> At 6 a.m. a detachment of sailors occupied the State Bank.
>
> At dawn, torpedo boats arrived from Helsingfors and entered the Neva.
>
> At 7 a.m. detachments of the Keksholm Regiment occupied the telephone exchange; the telephone lines of the General Staff were disconnected; the Palace Bridge was occupied.
>
> At 8 a.m. the Warsaw railroad station was occupied.
>
> At 9 a.m. detachments of the Semenovsky and the Chasseur Regiments occupied the printing plant of the *Russkaya Volya,* an important bourgeois newspaper, and the issue of the Bolshevik *Rabochiy Put* containing Lenin's article on the uprising was printed there.
>
> The cadets defending the Winter Palace were given an ultimatum from the Military Revolutionary Committee, ordering them to leave the Palace.
>
> At 10 a.m. the Military Revolutionary Committee announced that power was now in the hands of the Petrograd Soviet.
>
> During the night and into the morning the Committee gave the garrison orders for the arrest of officers who refused to obey the new authority. Anti-aircraft guns, armored cars and one cannon arrived at the Smolny Institute (headquarters of the Committee).
>
> Shortly after mid-day, detachments of the Izmaylovsky Regiment and sailors of the Guard began to surround the Maryinsky

Palace, where the pre-Parliament was in session. The members dispersed under protest.

At 1 p.m. the Nevsky Prospect, the main street of Petrograd, and the adjacent streets were occupied by the Pavlovsky Regiment.

At approximately 2 p.m. the warships *Amur, Yastreb* and others, with 5,000 sailors, arrived from Kronstadt and stationed themselves near the *Aurora,* opposite the Winter Palace. The sailors of the cruiser *Dawn of Freedom* were ordered by Antonov-Ovseyenko to prepare to fire on the Winter Palace.

The Baltic railway line was occupied by a detachment from the *Dawn of Freedom.* The same detachment disarmed the cadets in Oranienburg and in Peterhof. The *Dawn of Freedom* was placed at the entrance of the Morskoy Canal, to keep the Baltic railway covered.

At 3:15 p.m. a unit of the Pavlovsky Regiment occupied the Polizeysky Bridge and stopped all traffic along the Nevsky Prospect. Two armored cars, with machine guns and 3-inch guns, were stationed on the bridge.

At 3:45 p.m. Kazan Square was occupied by the troops of the Military Revolutionary Committee.

During the day, guns in the Peter-Paul Fortress were placed in readiness to bombard the Winter Palace. But when the order to fire was given, the gun crews declared that the guns were out of order; the crews were replaced by naval gunners.

At an order from Antonov-Ovseyenko, the torpedo boats made for the Nikolaevsky Bridge and spread out to face the Winter Palace. Of the six armored cars on guard before the Palace, five went over to the Bolsheviks.

At 6 p.m. the Winter Palace was surrounded by the troops of the Military Revolutionary Committee. Armored cars of the Committee appeared in the Palace Square; one of them drove up to the main entrance of the Palace, disarmed the cadets on guard, and departed unobstructed.

At the same time, at an order by the head of the Mikhailovsky Artillery School of War, under pressure from the Military Revolutionary Committee, most of the cadets of the school left the Winter Palace and made for the school; they were arrested by soldiers of the Pavlovsky Regiment near the Nevsky Prospect. Two machine guns were placed on the bridge across the Moyka, pointing at the Winter Palace.

During the evening, five warships from the operational Baltic Fleet arrived in Petrograd to help the Military Revolutionary Committee—the cruiser *Oleg,* two destroyers of the *Novik* type and two torpedo boats.

> At 9 p.m., after a refusal to surrender had been received from the Provisional Government and one blank signal shot had been fired from the Peter-Paul Fortress, a blank round from the six-inch gun of the *Aurora* was fired. This was followed by a general rifle and machine-gun attack on the Winter Palace (supported by the armored gun-carriers), which lasted until 10 p.m. At 11 p.m. the attack was resumed. Between 30 and 35 rounds were fired from the Peter-Paul Fortress, only two hitting the target. At 2:10 a.m. the Winter Palace was occupied.

A multitude of similar details could be added, showing that the main forces in the "proletarian" revolt were soldiers and sailors, armored cars and guns. The famed workers' Red Guard acted only as a police force—the official report declares that "the militia (police) in all parts of the city acted in full co-operation with the Red Guard."[15]

If the workers were unable to get to the Winter Palace or the Smolny Institute because of military obstacles, there was nothing to prevent them from holding meetings at the factories to give moral support to the insurgents and so share at least indirectly in the "victory of the proletariat." Yet the documents and official Bolshevik reports for the days of the actual fighting, or even the days following it, say almost nothing about workers' meetings or resolutions, or about their attitude. There is but one mention of a meeting: at 8 a.m. on October 25 (November 7) a thousand cigarette-workers, mostly women, passed a resolution expressing "full support for the Soviets and complete readiness to rally to the flag of the revolution at the first call."[16]

A few days later we do find some resolutions passed by various Bolshevik-influenced organizations, such as the Soviet of the trade unions, the central council of factory committees, the central and regional strike committees of the wood workers' union, and the head office of the union of clerical workers in trade and industry. As for the workers themselves, the official chronicler could find only three resolutions: in Petrograd, where the workers of the Neva shoe factory decided to contribute 1,000 roubles for the Petrograd Soviet and another 1,000 for the Second Congress of Soviets and promised support against counter-revolution; by the workers of the Sestroretsk arms plant; and by the workers of the Schluesselburg cotton mill, which employed mostly women.[17]

In brief, the "proletarian revolution" was accomplished while the working masses of the capital stood by passively. The struggle for the "world socialist revolution" was won by war-weary peasant lads in soldiers' or sailors' uniforms.

Thus far we have been examining the strength of the Bolsheviks—and of their temporary associates, the Left Social Revolutionaries and Anarchists, who then had some influence in Petrograd.[18] What of the Provisional Government and the parties supporting it? And what of the army at the front, and the right, which had great influence on the army high command?

With the complete freedom of the press which the February Revolution preserved, information concerning the Bolsheviks' plans, although not always correct, was fairly widespread. Thus, the socialist parties and the government knew that there was an internal struggle among the Bolsheviks and that the group headed by Lenin and Trotsky was for an immediate rising. But the memory of the Bolshevik fiascos in June and July was still fresh; many people were skeptical about the chances of a third Bolshevik *coup*. Even the Bolsheviks themselves were worried about "the enormous organizational apparatus" of the existing regime (Zinoviev). When Lenin argued that the fighting would not be between workers and the army, but "between one part of the army and another," he was assuming that a considerable part of the army would side with Kerensky. It is no wonder then, that the people around the Provisional Government were convinced that not only the overwhelming majority of the public but also the greater part of the army would inflict a resounding defeat on the Bolshevik usurpers. When the Bolshevik plans were discussed at an all-night session of the political committee of the pre-Parliament, Kerensky declared that he would almost welcome a third attempt by

Lenin to seize power, since that would most certainly be the end of the Bolsheviks.

The government appointed a committee of three to organize resistance to the approaching uprising: the commander of the Petrograd military region, Colonel Polkovnikov; the right-wing Social Revolutionary Rogovsky, who was acting chief of police of Petrograd; and Colonel Bagratuni. They were to take all necessary precautions, both inside Petrograd and by summoning more troops from outside. The tone of the pronouncements by Kerensky and a number of prominent right-wing Socialist Revolutionaries, such as A. Gotz, was so reassuring as to leave little room for anxiety. One delegate to the pre-Parliament, an internationalist Menshevik, has recorded in his memoirs[19] that he was so convinced that all possible precautions had been taken that, in his naiveté, he warned Gotz to beware of possible excesses in the suppression of the expected rising.

The reality was not at all so reassuring. First, it developed that the chairman of the triumvirate, Colonel Polkovnikov, hated the Provisional Government and particularly Kerensky more than he did the Bolsheviks. He not only failed to take any precautions, but also systematically gave Kerensky false information, assuring him that all was well and the defense prepared. In acting thus, Colonel Polkovnikov reflected a general attitude among the rightist officers, which was shared by some civilians. These people saw Kerensky and the Provisional Government, and not the Bolsheviks, as their chief foes; the latter, they thought, would only last a couple of weeks. As we will see, the same opinions prevailed in anti-Bolshevik units of the Petrograd garrison, notably among the Cossacks. All these troops were convinced of the ultimate victory of the right. As the popular cabaret song had it:

First came the Mensheviks,
then came the Bolsheviks,
then came the Anarchists,
and then will come the Monarchists!

But even among the left-oriented, revolutionary-minded public, the prestige of the Provisional Government was extremely weak. Within the Socialist Revolutionary Party, the left wing, which was prepared to ally itself with the Bolsheviks, was growing steadily. In the Menshevik Party left-internationalism was growing stronger as the political paralysis of the government coalition became ever more apparent.

When the crucial moment came, in the days between October 21 and 25 (November 3-7), the Provisional Government was caught completely unprepared; stranger still, it was ignorant of what was happening in the working-class districts of Petrograd and in the units of its garrison. Not until the night of October 23 (November 5) did Kerensky discover, to his utter horror, how hopeless his position was. We know from his memoirs[20] that he had been working on plans to transfer some troops from the front to the capital; the first convoys were to come from the northern front, which was commanded by General Cheremissov. Kerensky has written: "Colonel Polkovnikov reported personally to me every morning; and he invariably repeated that the armed forces at his disposal were sufficient . . . to cope with the threatened rising." On learning the truth about Polkovnikov, he replaced him with Bagratuni and rushed to the Maryinsky Palace, where the pre-Parliament was in session. There he demanded an immediate vote of confidence, emergency powers to deal with the insurrection, and a resolution expressing a determination to quell the insurrection and calling on the troops to resist the insurgents.

But the pre-Parliament, split from the very beginning, could not arrive at a firm decision even then. The far right predictably refused to give the government a vote of confidence. The moderate right and the center—that is, the Kadets and the representatives of the co-operatives—agreed on a short resolution expressing confidence in the government and demanding immediate measures against the uprising. But the left, the socialist groups of various shades and nationalities, divided into defensists and internationalists of varying shades of conviction, spent a long time debating. The internationalists (Mensheviks and some left-wing Socialist Revolutionaries) argued that a military campaign against the insurgents had no chance of success unless it was accompanied by a proclamation of such radical measures as an immediate start of peace negotiations and the transfer of land to the peasant committees. There was no majority for such a program. As already mentioned in the account of the last night session, the internationalists did win a majority—122 votes to 102, with 26 abstentions

—but it was too late. Kerensky was, of course, right when he declared in his memoirs that this resolution was both belated and useless, but this was largely due to the sterile policy of the coalition at the head of which Kerensky stood.

What was the balance of forces on the fateful night? Numerically, the Cossacks stationed in the capital would probably have sufficed by themselves to rout the forces of the Military Revolutionary Committee. But the Cossacks were not eager to fight. Thus, a meeting of regimental committees of the 1st, 4th, and 14th Cossack Regiments, held on October 25 (November 7), decided to ignore the orders of the Provisional Government and to refuse to fight against the "Petrograd Soviet and the Central Executive Committee."[21] To be sure, almost at the same time there was a meeting of the Soviet of the Union of Cossack Regimental Committees (under the leadership of Boris Savinkov), at which the Soviet of the Union appealed to the Petrograd Cossacks to "carry out in the strictest possible manner all orders from the government."[22] But the decision not to resist the Bolsheviks was clearly more in keeping with the feelings of the Cossack lower ranks; for, when they were actually asked to defend the Provisional Government, the Cossacks refused to do so without the support of some infantry units.[23] Even the cadets, who had been always looked upon as the most reliable supporters of the Provisional Government, were not altogether unanimous. At their meetings and discussions, many spoke against defense of the government, some for reasons which were borrowed from the right, and others reflecting the position of the left. Later, however, the cadets proved the only force to try, bravely but hopelessly, to defend the Winter Palace.

Kerensky's Last Effort

Kerensky decided to go to the northern front, in the hope that his own prestige would enable him to gather the necessary forces and direct them toward Petrograd before it was too late. This story deserves to be told in detail, as it serves to show the deeper causes of the crisis and at the same time reveals the element of pure chance that so often plays a major part even in the greatest events.[24]

On the morning of October 25 (November 7), after several fruitless trips from the Winter Palace to General Staff Headquarters, Kerensky resolved to go to Gatchina to find the troop detachments he had requested of General Cheremissov, which he expected now at any moment. He managed to slip out of the Winter Palace only a few minutes before the besiegers' ring closed around it, and drove unmolested out of the city. He found no fresh troops in Gatchina, and proceeded to Cheremissov's headquarters in Pskov. Lacking confidence in Cheremissov, he first called at the private quarters of General Baranovsky, whom he trusted implicitly. There Kerensky learned that Cheremissov was co-operating openly with the local military revolutionary committee, which had already seized power in the town.[25] Vladimir S. Woytinsky, who was then chief commissar of the Fifth Army and was working directly with Cheremissov, gives the following characterization of the general in his memoirs:[26] "Cheremissov, a comparatively young general, who had made a name for himself as a divisional commander during the June offensive, was very skillful at political intrigues. He was ambitious, lacking in moral scruples, and set upon making a great career; he was eager for popularity among the soldiers, professing political opinions somewhat to the left of those of the soldier-elected army committee. But his impudence was checked by his cowardice . . ."

This was the man who held the fate of the Bolshevik rising and the Provisional Government in his hands. He had been ordered by Kerensky, his Commander-in-Chief, to send troops to Petrograd, yet he had procrastinated. And when Kerensky arrived in Pskov, Cheremissov persuaded him to cancel the order, on the ground that a transfer of troops would be useless if not actually dangerous. According to Woytinsky, who arrived in Pskov some time later, Kerensky was in a state of nervous exhaustion and had even, in a fit of despair, told Cheremissov that he would resign as Commander-in-Chief and would like to appoint the general in his stead.

Kerensky himself does not mention this episode, but Woytinsky's testimony is confirmed by the recorded text of messages over the direct wires from the chief of staff to the commanders on various fronts. Thus, on the evening of October 25 (November 7), Cheremissov told the Chief of Staff, General Dukhonin, of Kerensky's intention to lay down the duties of Commander-in-Chief and to appoint him. (Dukhonin asked his permission to pass the information on to the Provisional Government, with which GHQ was still connected.) Later Cheremissov told the same story to the deputy chief of staff, General Vyrubov.[27]

Meanwhile, according to Woytinsky, some army units agreed to move to Petrograd against the Bolsheviks, but only on condition that the order came from the Central Executive Committee of the Soviet[28] and not from the Provisional Government. While Woytinsky was trying to communicate with the people who could meet this condition, Cheremissov countermanded the previous order to move on Petrograd. Woytinsky, alarmed, rushed to Pskov, where he was told by Cheremissov that the original order had been cancelled by Kerensky himself. Woytinsky immediately went to see Kerensky, who now countermanded his second order, cancelling his cancellation. But this came too late.

Late the same night, General Krasnov, commander of the Third Cavalry Corps, arrived at General Baranovsky's quarters, also with the intention of learning the reason for the puzzling cancellation of orders. After much discussion, it was decided that Kerensky would go to Krasnov's headquarters in Ostrov, and that Krasnov's troops would move from there towards Petrograd. But the infantry, without which the Cossacks had refused to move, was not yet available, and because of the confusion and delay caused by Kerensky's orders and counter-orders, none could be found in time to take part in the intended campaign.[29]

After Kerensky had had several consultations with Krasnov, with his officers and with the commissars, and had addressed a general meeting of the Cossacks, many of whom were hesitant and at loggerheads with each other, the moment came to board the train which was to take Krasnov's troops from Ostrov to Gatchina. But the railway workers were sabotaging the departure of the train. Woytinsky then had a long political talk with the engine drivers, who first said that the locomotive was out of order and that repairs would take the better part of two days. This was later reduced to two hours. The locomotive was actually ready in twenty minutes.

In his account of these events, Kerensky has admitted that he erred in authorizing an inadequate military force to move on Petrograd. Instead of staking everything on this one weak force, he should have gone to General Headquarters to mobilize all the units he needed. But on the spur of the moment and under the influence of too many advisers, Kerensky gave the order to march to his troops—by his own estimate not more than 600 to 700 men.[30]

The Battle of Gatchina

The campaign started well enough; Gatchina was occupied almost without resistance. The pro-Bolshevik troops defending it, to whose assistance the Military Revolutionary Committee had dispatched 100 sailors and 1,500 soldiers of the Semenovsky and the Izmailovsky Regiments,[31] showed little stamina and ran off in all directions, abandoning their rifles and machine guns and even an armored car.

The next morning, the Cossacks were supposed to move on towards Tsarskoye Selo, but now things began to take an ugly turn. It seemed likely that Tsarskoye Selo could be occupied easily, and the road would then be open for an advance to Petrograd. But something had gone wrong. Krasnov's attitude seemed to have changed, and so had that of the Cossacks. There was an inexplicable delay, and Kerensky soon discovered that this was due to political hesitation. On the one hand, the Cossacks were under pressure from Bolshevik agitators, who pointed to the great number of officers in Kerensky's force—officers who had flocked to join it from all sides and who made no effort to disguise their anti-revolutionary sentiments. On the other hand, Krasnov himself had come under the influence of the delegates of the Soviet of the Union of Cossacks, who had soon convinced him that for the future good of Russia the rightists had been correct in refusing to defend Kerensky's Provisional Government. Having come under this cross-fire from Bolshevik and reactionary propagandists, the Cossack force of 600 to 700 men was being rapidly demoralized under Kerensky's very eyes. Only late in the evening did Kerensky—with the help of the commissar for the northern front, Stankevich—succeed in getting Krasnov to order an attack on Tsarskoye Selo. The town surrendered without a shot being fired.

The decisive battle was to be fought the next morning. But the Bolsheviks had made good use of the day wasted by the Cossacks, and had managed to bring up reinforcements, which were estimated by the government command to be 10,000 to 12,000 strong. They also fortified the hills at Pulkovo and manned them with sailors, who proved to be excellent fighters. For his part, Kerensky disposed of the 600 to 700 Cossacks, plus a regiment which just arrived via Luga, and a well-equipped armored train.[32] According to Kerensky, none of the reinforcements which had been promised him over the telephone from various places, and which were reported on the way, had arrived.

The decisive battle was joined. And although the Bolsheviks had been feverishly increasing their numbers and the Kronstadt sailors on their right flanks fought well, the outcome was on the whole favorable to the government.[33] But the government forces were too weak to consolidate their successes or even to pursue the Bolshevik infantry, which had run away from a few cannon-shots. At this point, General Krasnov began a "strategic withdrawal" to Gatchina. This might have been the correct move prescribed by classic military strategy, wrote Kerensky, but in a civil war it was in fact the beginning of the end. For the withdrawal completed the demoralization of the Cossacks. Thus the Bolsheviks owed their final victory in this theatre of war not to strength of their arms but to the skill of their propaganda and to the moral disintegration of the enemy, especially the Cossacks.

That this was so can be now proved from documents of the Bolsheviks themselves.

On October 27 and 28 (November 9 and 10)—at the very time when Kerensky and the Cossacks were conducting their chaotic military operations at Gatchina—disorder also seems to have prevailed among the Bolsheviks. They too were ignorant of the strength and intentions of their adversaries. According to the Bolshevik Podvoysky, then head of the Military Revolutionary Committee, who wrote his memoirs in 1948 (printed in *Kommunist,* no. 1, 1957), the position was far from satisfactory:

"We received only scanty news from the front. It was known that Comrade Chudnovsky's group had failed to halt the enemy advance and was in difficulties. Chudnovsky himself was wounded and his unit cut off and in danger of annihilation. There was no overall command. Each unit—the garrisons of Krasnoye and Tsarkoye Selo and the Red Guard—operated independently . . . . Comrade Antonov-Ovseyenko went personally to the front, but returned very depressed by the disorder and muddle there."

Antonov-Ovseyenko soon collapsed from nervous exhaustion. After hurried consultation with Lenin, Podvoysky replaced Antonov-Ovseyenko, but the position was still critical. "The regiments which had brought about the socialist revolution considered that their work was completed and that they were heroes. The defense of Petrograd from the internal enemy they did indeed accept as a sacred duty. But as for fighting against Kerensky's troops somewhere near Gatchina, that, they felt, should be left to the local garrison . . ."

The Volynsky Regiment, like most of the other regiments, refused to go anywhere; the soldiers contended that they were needed in Petrograd. The workers, Podvoysky continues, tried feverishly to arm themselves under the personal guidance of Lenin, who had appointed himself as second in command but who, one can guess from Podvoysky's tone, only interfered with the latter's work. (In rather humorous fashion, he described Lenin putting a table behind Podvoysky's and making endless telephone calls. His conversation was so loud that Podvoysky was compelled to ask Lenin to speak more softly.) But it was impossible to make soldiers of workers in 24 or even 48 hours. Having surveyed the situation, Antonov-Ovseyenko and Podvoysky came to the conclusion that "given our general lack of co-ordination and in the absence of a unified command, the enemy . . . could easily, with very small forces, completely crush us" and, in the ensuing panic of the retreat, engineer a counter-revolutionary *coup*.

Podvoysky's account substantially confirms that given by Trotsky in his little-known book, *Notes on the October Revolution,* published in New York in 1918, in Russian.[34] He too describes the confusion in the Military Revolutionary Committee at that time. But whereas Podvoysky, to judge from the published part of his memoirs, attributes Bolshevik survival exclusively to Lenin's genius, and does not mention Trotsky at all,[35] Trotsky's account is very different.

In his opinion the situation was saved by the munitions workers, who supplied missing parts for cannons, and by his own energetic efforts. On his initiative the garrison, at an emergency meeting, elected a commission of five with Trotsky as chairman; and this commission entrusted the post of Commander-in-Chief to Lt.-Col. Muraviev, an old Socialist Revolutionary, who had joined the left wing of his party shortly before the October days. At dawn Trotsky and Muraviev went in a car to Pulkovo on the Gatchina front. There Muraviev appointed Colonel Walden commander of the Pulkovo sector and it was there that, with the help of the sailors, Krasnov's Cossacks were halted. It was Trotsky himself who published a signed victory communiqué in *Pravda* which ended with the words: "This night will enter history."

The subsequent course of events is well known. When Krasnov's Cossacks retreated to Gatchina, having missed the psychological moment for pressing home their advantage, their morale collapsed and the Bolsheviks skillfully exploited this opportunity. The Bolshevik command sent a delegation led by the sailor Dybenko to promise the Cossacks that they would be demobilized and sent home immediately, with their horses and arms, if they agreed to hand over Kerensky. The Cossacks agreed, but Kerensky, warned by friends, managed to escape in time. And the road to Petrograd was now closed against all attempts to overthrow the Bolsheviks.

Chance and contingency, on both sides of the line, had been largely responsible for the Bolshevik victory. The Pulkovo battle could have ended in disaster for the Bolsheviks if Cheremissov had not deliberately delayed sending troops to Kerensky, or if, on the other hand, there had not been that band of sailors, whose bravery tipped the balance to the Bolsheviks at the critical moment. The outcome, of course, might have been quite different if a single regiment in good fighting order had rallied to Kerensky. But no such regiment was available. And this was in large measure due to the policies of the Provisional Government itself.

[1] Ryabinsky, K., *The Revolution of 1917 (Chronicle of Events).* State Publishing House, Moscow-Leningrad, 1926.

[2] Until October 25 (November 7), 1917, the Central Executive Committee had a non-Communist majority and its organ, *Izvestia,* had a non-Communist editor.

[3] Lenin, *Works,* Vol. XIV, part 2, pp. 133-140.

[4] *The Minutes of the Central Committee,* pp. 13-15, 65. Moscow, 1927.

[5] Bukharin later humorously told the story of how the Central Committee, frightened by the dangerous frankness of Lenin's letters, had decided to burn them—see Trotsky, *The History of the Russian Revolution,* Vol. II, part 2, p. 147.

[6] *Ibid.,* pp. 70-71.

[7] *The Minutes of the Central Committee,* pp. 90-91.

[8] *Ibid.,* pp. 101-102.

[9] This remark is particularly interesting in the light of Stalin's definition of the methods of the proletarian revolution, given on November 19, 1924, at a meeting of the Bolshevik

faction of the All-Russian Federation of Trade Unions: "Note one striking peculiarity of the revolutionary tactics for that period. It is that every, or almost every, step forward was taken under the pretense of self-defense . . . It is as if the revolution was making its advance under the cloak of self-defense so as to be better able to draw into its orbit all those who were hesitant or unstable. This probably explains the seemingly defensive tone of most speeches, articles and slogans of that period, while underlying it all there was a firm determination to attack": Stalin, *Works,* Vol. VI, p. 324.

[10] *The Minutes of the Central Committee,* pp. 10-126.

[11] Lenin, *Works,* Vol. 26, pp. 185-188, 192, 196.

[12] Abramovitch, R., *Memoirs,* Volume II, pp. 146-157.

[15] Ryabinsky, K., *The Revolution of 1917 (Chronicle of Events),* Vol. V, p. 183. State State Publishing House, Moscow, 1926.

[14] *The Minutes of the Central Committee,* p. 137.

[15] Ryabinsky, K., *The Revolution of 1917 (Chronicle of Events)*, Vol. V, p. 183. State Publishing House, Moscow, 1926.

[16] *Ibid.*, p. 176.

[17] *Pravda* of October 28, 1917; *Izvestia* of October 27 and 28.

[18] The rapid growth of anarcho-syndicalist tendencies among the Petrograd workers was generally acknowledged at that time. It is mentioned also in the minutes of the Bolshevik Central Committee dealing with local reports (October 16 [29]) and in various newspaper articles (the article by Bazarov in *Novaya Zhizn,* others in *Rabochaya Gazeta,* etc.).

[19] Abramovitch, R., *Memoirs,* p. 155.

[20] *Sovremennye Zapiski,* Vol. X, p. 148, Paris, 1922.

[21] Ryabinsky, K., *op. cit.*, p. 184.

[22] *Ibid.,* p. 184.

[23] *Ibid.,* p. 176.

[24] Kerensky, A., "Gatchina," *Sovremennye Zapiski,* Vol. X, 1922, p. 171.

[25] An official report of the Military Revolutionary Committee for that period says: "General Cheremissov behaves in a friendly manner towards the Military Revolutionary Committee." (See Ryabinsky, *op. cit.,* p. 190, citing the Moscow Soviet's *Izvestia,* No. 2.)

[26] Woytinsky, V., *Memoirs,* p. 654.

[27] *The Archives of the Russian Revolution,* Vol. VII, pp. 298-299, 303.

[28] They meant, of course, the old Central Executive Committee, which was still functioning when Woytinsky was negotiating wtih the soldiers and officers at the front.

[29] Woytinsky, V., *Memoirs,* p. 704.

[30] Kerensky, A., *Sovremennye Zapiski,* Paris, 1922. Vol. X, pp. 171, ff.

[31] Melgunov, "How the Bolsheviks seized power," p. 161. (Cited from the *Minutes of the Military Revolutionary Committee.*)

[32] The origin of this regiment and the armored train could not be traced by this author.

[33] In Petrograd there were rumors of 2,000 dead and wounded. These figures proved to be wildly exaggerated. The only available report, published in *Novaya Zhizn,* October 31 (November 13), 1917, speaks of 60 bodies brought to the Obukhov Hospital.

[34] Trotsky, L. *Notes on the October Revolution* (Russian), pp. 77-78. New York, 1918.

[35] Podvoysky may actually have mentioned Trotsky's role at the time. It is not unlikely that the numerous omissions in the text published in *Kommunist,* indicated by dots, referred to Trotsky. But nothing can be proved in the absence of the original manuscript.

CHAPTER 5

Point of No Return

The Second Congress of Soviets

While historic battles were being fought on the hills of Pulkovo, political battles were taking place at the sessions of the Second Congress of Soviets at the Smolny Institute. Here, to the accompaniment of passionate speeches and under the deceptive slogan of "All power to the Soviets," began the death agony of the Soviets as the system of free, non-partisan organizations of the lower classes that had developed almost spontaneously in the first hours of the February Revolution. This system was now dying from the blow dealt to it by the party and the men who were to introduce the word "Soviet" into the dictionaries of the whole world.

When Lenin had demanded that the rising must take place at all costs before the opening of the Second Congress, when he refused to postpone it even for one day (as Trotsky suggested at the last moment),[1] it was not because he feared that the Provisional Government might start to deploy its "gigantic organizational apparatus." Rather, he feared the temper of the Congress, even though the local elections had already practically ensured a majority of Bolsheviks and Left Socialist Revolutionaries and internationalists. The Bolsheviks had organized their rising under the ostensible authority of the Petrograd Soviet, but in reality they had carried it out in their own interest. The Soviets had served them as a cover, and they intended to go on using it—but only if the Soviets could be made into a reliable tool of the Bolshevik Party. That is exactly what happened. The Congress of Soviets, which opened at 10:45 on the evening of October 25 (November 7), found itself confronted with the *fait accompli* of a Bolshevik seizure of power, accomplished by the Military Revolutionary Committee through its soldiers and sailors, though without the participation of the working masses of Petrograd. Not only were the Bolshevik troops surrounding the Winter Palace; the Second Congress also met under the vigilant eyes of the Military Revolutionary Committee's sentries, armed units and armored cars and the close personal attention of Lenin and Trotsky who spent the night in the same room lying on blankets on the floor![2]

When Theodore Dan, on behalf of the outgoing Central Executive Committee, officially opened the Congress, everything was already decided. The Mensheviks and the Socialist Revolutionaries knew the game was lost, that the Bolshevik rising had caught the government unawares and that it was too late to try to organize serious resistance in the capital. The feeling of doom was particularly strong at a meeting of the Menshevik and Socialist Revolutionary delegations in Chkheidze's study. Chkheidze, tormented by a severe attack of migraine, sat with his head swathed in wet towels, and the meeting gave the impression of being held at the bedside of a very sick man. The sick man was the democratic revolution, wounded by the Bolshevik *coup d'etat*.

After the usual formalities, the Bolshevik faction of the Congress nominated Kamenev for the chair. Dan, amid thunderous applause, ceded to the new chairman. Kamenev behaved from the start like the representative of a new regime, in possession of full power and no longer in need of official recognition by the Soviets, although it was obvious that the majority in the Congress would in fact give retrospective sanction to the Bolshevik revolt.

On the platform in the great hall, with its slender white columns, one speaker followed another with short declarations protesting the Bolshevik *coup*. Their speeches were punctuated by the roar of the cannons of the Peter-Paul Fortress bombarding the besieged Winter Palace. Martov, speaking for the internationalist Mensheviks, passionately declared that the *coup* which transferred power to the Revolutionary Military Committee had been accomplished by a single party, by conspiracy and violence, on the very eve of the Second Congress of the Soviets. He urged that the immediate task of the Congress was to create a new government acceptable to all the revolutionary parties. Otherwise civil war was sure to follow and that could lead only to a victory for counter-revolution. In conclusion, Martov asked the Congress to appoint a representative committee to deal with this problem.

Martov's proposal was supported by the left Socialist Revolutionaries and by R. Abramovitch on behalf of the internationalist section of the Bund. The latter regarded the recent events in Petrograd as a disaster for the revolution and saw the only way out in an agreement among all the socialist parties. Lunacharsky, on behalf of the Bolsheviks, stated that his party did not object to Martov's proposal since it wanted all the groups to clarify their views and formulate concrete proposals. So Martov's resolution was carried unanimously.

The defensists at the Congress, however, had an entirely different position. Gendelman, of the Socialist Revolutionaries, declared that his group considered the *coup* illegal and was leaving the Congress under protest. L. Khinchuk, of the Mensheviks, spoke similarly: "We see the only way out in the formation of a new government that will unite all parts of the people. We regard the Bolshevik seizure of power as illegal, and we are leaving the Congress under protest."

Henryk Erlich, speaking for the defensist wing of the Bund, supported Khinchuk. He urged the Social Democratic delegates to leave the session and to repair to the town hall, where a meeting of democratic anti-Bolshevik groups was in progress and a Committee to Defend the Motherland and the Revolution was being formed. From there they would march to the Winter Palace to cast their lot with the Provisional Government.[3] The representatives of the 12th Army, A. Kharash and G. Kutchin, strongly supported the Menshevik protest. The Bolshevik Lukianov and the delegate of the Latvian sharpshooters, Peterson, retorted that Kutchin and Kharash did not represent the soldiers. Trotsky challenged Martov's assertion that the Bolshevik seizure of power was a military conspiracy: "It wasn't a conspiracy, it was a revolutionary uprising. We steeled the revolutionary energy of the Petrograd workers and soldiers, we openly hardened the will of the masses and then the uprising came. It was an open revolt, not a secret plot." Trotsky then enumerated a long series of misdeeds allegedly committed by the Mensheviks and the Socialist

Revolutionaries against the workers, peasants and soldiers, and concluded that the exodus of the Mensheviks and the Socialist Revolutionaries would not weaken the revolution but strengthen it.

Lenin, who spoke the next day, October 26 (November 8), was much less arrogant. He even made a remarkable promise: "As a democratic government we cannot ignore the will of the people even if we disagree with it. In the acid test of reality . . . . the peasants will soon find out by themselves where the truth was. And even if the peasants continue to follow the Socialist Revolutionaries, even if they give that party the majority in the Constituent Assembly, we will say: so be it." Needless to say, Lenin never honored this solemn pledge.[4]

The defensist, Mensheviks and Socialist Revolutionaries had left the Congress and begun their attempt to organize a struggle against the Bolsheviks. But the small group of internationalists took a somewhat different position. Long aware that the Bolsheviks had been advancing rapidly, the internationalists had insisted, both in the Central Executive Committee of the Soviet and in the pre-Parliament, on adoption of policies which would deprive the Bolsheviks of most of their appeal. They doubted that sufficient military force could be rallied to defeat the Bolsheviks, who had the support of revolutionary soldiers fighting for immediate peace. Sufficient military forces could be recruited only from the supporters of General Kornilov, and that would mean civil war.

The internationalist Mensheviks had been told by the Left Social Revolutionaries that there was strong opposition to Lenin andTrotsky within the Bolshevik Party; they also repeatedly assured Martov and Abramovitch that they had great influence in the Military Revolutionary Committee and would go to any length to prevent a dictatorship of the Bolshevik Party. Consequently, the Martov group did not call its followers to go to the town hall or to join in the solemn unarmed procession to the Winter Palace. Instead, it instructed two of its members, R. Abramovitch and Professor A. Pinkevitch, to sound out those Bolsheviks who were known to favor an agreement with the socialists in forming a government. They decided first to approach Felix Dzherzhinsky, whom Abramovitch knew personally, who had opposed Lenin's April theses, and who now occupied a prominent position in the Military Revolutionary Committee.[5] Dzherzhinsky received them at 2 a.m. on October 25 (November 7), in the presence of A. Bubnov, a member of the Bolshevik Central Committee. Abramovitch asked two questions: first, what the general policy of the Bolsheviks would be; and second, what Dzherzhinsky thought of the idea of an all-socialist government composed of all the socialist parties from the Popular Socialists to the Bolsheviks. To the first question, the Pole Dzherzhinsky answered the Bundist Abramovitch in terms familiar to both. The program of the revolution, he said, would resemble that of the Left PPS (Polish Socialist Party); that is, the Bolsheviks would combine with the democratic revolution certain elements of socialism, thus creating a system embodying transition from capitalism to socialism. As for a government of all the socialist parties, Dzherzhinsky replied that he would have to consult his party comrades.

Thus began the episode which entered the history of the October Revolution under the name of the "Vikzhel" negotiations.[6]

"Vikzhel"

The next morning October 26 (November 8), an emergency conference convened of all the internationalist groups which were active in advocating a coalition government embracing all the socialist parties. These groups included the Martov wing of the Mensheviks, the left wing of the Jewish Bund, and the so-called "United Internationalists," a small but influential group of writers. The conference soon realized that not only were the socialist parties divided in their attitudes toward a coalition with the Bolsheviks, but that among the leading Bolsheviks themselves there was a similar division of opinion. The conference therefore decided to put the problem of the coalition squarely before the Central Committee of not only the Menshevik and S-R parties but before the Bolshevik Central Committee as well. At the same time it became known that the All-Russian Executive Committee of the Railwaymen's Union ("Vikzhel" in the Russian abbreviation) had in a published statement, questioned the legality of the new government and condemned the seizure of power by a single party. "Vikzhel" was composed of liberals and socialists of various political leanings, including even a few Bolsheviks. It was believed that the Bolshevik Party would accept "Vikzhel" as mediator in the planned negotiations, because the outcome of the battle with the Kerensky forces depended largely on the good will of the railwaymen. Contact was immediately established with two influential members of "Vikzhel": the president of the union, the lawyer Planson, and the railway engineer Malitsky They were eager to undertake the task of mediating the negotiations if requested to do so. The same afternoon, the Central Committee of the Menshevik Party agreed to take part in the "Vikzhel" negotiations without prejudice to their final position. A similar resolution was adopted by the S-R.

Next some of the left S-R's and left internationalists tried to establish contact with the Bolshevik Party. It was well known that Lenin and Trotsky resolutely opposed any compromise with the Mensheviks and the S-R's—in their opinion this would despoil the victors of their victory. But the majority of the Bolshevik Central Committee felt otherwise. For various reasons they considered it inopportune to take an intransigent position and thus expose themselves to the charge of standing in the way of establishing unity in the ranks of revolution. But it was not an easy matter for the majority to ignore the opposition of two most important leaders. The result was hesitation and an attempt to delay the agonizing decision.

"Vikzhel," apprehensive about the delaying tactics of the Bolsheviks, then issued a proclamation "To all, to all, to all," in which it insisted on ".... the immediate formation of an all-socialist government of all parties from the Trudoviks to the Bolsheviks, as being the only way of avoiding an economic disaster and complete chaos in the country." All local committees of the railwaymen's union were instructed to prepare for a general railway strike in case the Bolsheviks refused to take part in the negotiations. The strike was to begin at midnight October 29 (November 11).[7]

This ultimatum produced an immediate effect. On October 29 (November 11), the Bolshevik Central Committee met (with Lenin, Trotsky and Zinoviev absent) and unanimously decided that it would be desirable to enlarge the Bolshevik government by the inclusion of those parties in the Soviet that remained outside the then-ruling Soviet majority. It was also decided that the government should be nominated by VTsIK and be responsible to it. The meeting elected a delegation to the forthcoming negotiations to be held under the auspices of "Vikzhel."

Almost simultaneously with this meeting of the Bolshevik Central Committee, however, a meeting of the Petrograd City Committee of the party, at which Zinoviev and Molotov made addresses, took a much less favorable attitude toward a coalition with other socialist parties. The resolution adopted by the Petrograd City Committee demanded as a precondition to co-operation with the socialist parties the continuation of the merciless fight against all "counter-revolutionaries," among whom it specifically included not only Kerensky, but a number of prominent Mensheviks and S-R's such as Tseretelli and Gotz.

The "Vikzhel" proclamation calling for the immediate formation of an all-socialist government was brought officially to VTsIK by the engineer Krushinsky, who invited VTsIK to send delegates to the "Vikzhel" talks. The invitation was accepted, and Kamenev, Ryazanov, and the Georgian Menshevik internationalist, Sagarashvilli, were elected as delegates. VTsIK's promise of participation, sanctioned by the Bolshevik Central Committee, settled the matter.

The first "Vikzhel" meeting took place on October 29 (November 11) in the White Hall of the Ministry of Transport, with Planson in the chair. Among those present were Kamenev and Sokolnikov of the Central Committee of the Bolshevik Party; T. Dan and H. Erlich of the Central Committee of the United Menshevik Party; Martov, Martynov, Abramovitch, and Semkovsky of the internationalist wing of the Mensheviks; Yacobi and Gendelman of the Central Committee of the S-R; Malkin of the Left S-R; Gutman of the Jewish Social Democrats; Lapinsky of the Polish Socialist Party; Baru of the Zionist Socialists (Poale-Zion); Kastrel and Bloom of the United Internationalists; Rykov of the Soviet of People's Commissars; Sagarashvilli and Ryazanov of VTsIK; Znamensky (Trudovik) and Weinstein (Menshevik) of the newly-formed Committee for the Defense of the Motherland and the Revolution; Pokrovsky (S-R) of the Executive Committee of the All-Russian Soviet of Peasant Deputies; and representatives of the Petrograd City Council, the Clerical Workers' Union, and the

Postal Workers' Union—26 persons in all, not counting the members of "Vikzhel."

Kamenev was the first to address the meeting. He was prepared, on behalf of VTsIK, to agree to the formation of an all-socialist government incorporating all member parties of the Soviets from Trudoviks to Bolsheviks, provided this government adhered to the policy laid down by the Second Congress of Soviets and held itself responsible to VTsIK. Aware that many present would have liked to exclude Lenin and Trotsky from the future government, if not the whole Bolshevik Party, Kamenev concluded with the following remark: "VTsIK is concerned above all with the policy of the government, not with the composition of its personnel."

Speaking next, from the viewpoint of the right-wing socialists, Weinstein, Gendelman, and especially Dan made impassioned pleas for a coalition, but stressed the necessity of first removing the basic obstacles in its way—the insistence of one party on keeping the power it had seized by force.

In contrast to Dan, Martov suggested that "the only way out of the present situation is to bury the past and to forget former quarrels; the various parties must stop mutual recrimination and their attempts at face-saving." It was essential, he said, to concentrate on the main task —to avert the threat of an imminent collapse of the revolution; and this could not be achieved by the victory of one side, for neither side was by itself strong enough to rescue the country from catastrophe.

Sokolnikov, on behalf of the Central Committee of the Bolshevik Party, seconded Kamenev's view, adding that the Bolshevik Party had never wanted to seize power alone: "At the Democratic Convention we offered to form, together with all the socialist groups, a socialist government, but at that moment you refused."

Abramovitch agreed with Martov in urging both sides to drop the squabbles about legitimacy. At the present moment, he said, the old government was gone and there was as yet no new government; clearly, this offered a chance of creating a third government from the united strength of all revolutionary democratic parties. What was needed in this internal quarrel was an agreement without victors or vanquished; it would be a crime to fall out over the question of the composition of the future government.[8] In conclusion, Abramovitch suggested that the practical points of agreement should be worked out without delay, and that a special subcommittee should now be appointed which could get down to business. The suggestion was accepted and the following were named to the subcommittee: Dan, Abramovitch, Kamenev, Ryazanov, Sokolnikov, and the representatives of "Vikzhel," the Petrograd City Council, and the Central Committee of the S-R. The moment the subcommittee began its work, "Vikzhel" cancelled its order for the strike at midnight of the same day. The strike committees, however, were instructed to keep themselves in readiness.

At the first meeting of the subcommittee, the Bolsheviks' position was cautious and flexible. Their military situation at the moment was quite uncertain. There were rumors that anti-Bolshevik divisions were being moved from the front to Petrograd; the battle for Moscow was having intermittent success. Meanwhile, the right-wing socialists were profoundly hostile to any agreement with the Bolsheviks. The internationalist groups tried to find a compromise acceptable to both sides. After a long session, it appeared that agreement between the internationalists and the Bolsheviks was possible. The right wing, however, continued to insist stubbornly on certain conditions, among them the exclusion of Lenin and Trotsky from the future government—Lenin on the grounds that he had declined to stand trial when he was accused of having received money from the German government, and Trotsky because he had organized the October rising.

At this point the meeting ended. The internationalists left with the firm resolve of carrying the problem to the working masses and military forces in Petrograd. Therefore, the internationalist factions in the Second Congress of Soviets (with the exception of the Bolsheviks) issued a joint proclamation "To the workers, soldiers and peasants" under the title "The revolution is in peril." The proclamation urgently called upon all workers and soldiers and all political parties

> ... to try to reach an agreement for the creation of a unified democratic government capable of repulsing the counter-revolutionary coalition of the propertied classes. We appeal to both camps within the democracy to restore the united revolutionary

> front, so that the revolution may not be drowned in the blood of the workers, soldiers and peasants.

The proclamation was published in a number of socialist morning papers on October 30 (November 12) and found an immediate and enthusiastic response in the factories. The Petrograd workers, who in the first few days after the Bolshevik uprising had been in a state of indecision, were electrified by the news that a way might be found to reunite the revolutionary forces and avert civil war. After a long interval of passivity, meetings and discussions began to be held in the factories. The consensus favored union, a united socialist government, and support for "Vikzhel." Scores of delegations from the factories converged on the Ministry of Transport, where "Vikzhel" was meeting, and telegrams and resolutions arrived from all parts of the country.

The enthusiastic response of the revolutionary masses to the possibility of an understanding between the Bolsheviks and other socialist parties had its effect on both camps. The right wings of the Trudoviks, the S-R's and the Mensheviks, which had been suspicious of the negotiations, had to change their tactics under pressure from delegations of workers. The Bolsheviks, too, were affected by the rising clamor for conciliation in the working-class districts of Petrograd, which was becoming ever stronger and more insistent.

Meanwhile, however, the Military Revolutionary Committee continued its policy of arbitrary persecution of non-Bolshevik publications, arrests of individuals and groups, searches without warrants, and the issuance of orders for the arrest on sight of well-known right-wing socialists whom they accused of counter-revolutionary activities. On October 30 (November 12), at the second plenary meeting of the "Vikzhel" Committee, Martov immediately rose on a point of order and lodged a strongly-worded protest against these practices. Lozovsky also condemned the terrorist activity of the self-appointed prosecutors and tribunals. Martov and Lozovsky were then appointed to draft a resolution declaring political terror inadmissible and demanding the abolition of extraordinary tribunals. The draft was approved, and the resolution, addressed to "All, All, All," was then circulated by telegraph to the whole country by "Vikzhel." The meeting also received a resolution from a conference of representatives of all army organizations at the front and in the rear, district military committees, and the Military Revolutionary Committee of the Fifth Army demanding the formation of an all-socialist government.

When the S-R's raised the question of the actual composition of the future government, Kamenev declined to discuss it, declaring that the Bolsheviks envisaged the future union as "an honest coalition of the socialist parties participating in the Soviets."

Next it was suggested that the incomplete VTsIK, elected after the majority socialists had walked out of the Second Congress of the Soviets, should be replaced by a new and much larger body, to be called the "People's Soviet" and that a special subcommittee be entrusted with the task of working out its composition. Dan declared, on behalf of the Menshevik Central Committee, that even if the composition of the new government were not in accordance with the principles advocated by his party, his party was still prepared to support it, though it would not participate in it. The meeting passed a majority resolution (with the Bolsheviks abstaining) demanding immediate cease-fire between all warring parties and organizations. This resolution, too, was circulated as a telegram (No. 5223) to "All, All, All," on October 31 (November 13). A copy was sent to Kerensky at Gatchina,[9] but it had no effect there. At the conclusion of the meeting, a subcommittee was elected to start work the next day on the composition of the "People's Soviet" and of the future government.

On October 31 (November 13), a highly significant conversation, over a direct wire, took place between a representative of the Committee of Army Organizations at the Ministry for War in Petrograd and Perekrestov, the representative of the army committees at the front. Perekrestov declared that the occasion called for an all-socialist government, without the Bolsheviks, but above all for an immediate agreement. Should agreement be possible only at the price of letting the Bolsheviks into the government, then this compromise should be accepted, but only if the Bolsheviks were in a minority.[10]

The workers of Petrograd were most active in urging agreement. They sent not only resolutions but delegations to "Vikzhel." Workers of the huge Obukhov factory, who came to the "Vikzhel" meeting of October 31 (November 13), were particularly vociferous in their demands that the agreement be immediately implemented.[11] This was true not only of the non-Bolshevik part of the Petrograd workers but of the Bolsheviks as well. Statistical data published later by the prominent Communist, V. Nevsky, in the historical magazine *Krassnaia Lietopis,* No. 2-3, pp. 312, ff., proved that after October 25, the Bolshevik district party organizations in Petrograd ("Rayons") were, in the great majority, for an agreement with the other socialist parties. Only three out of the ten Rayons (the Esthonian, the Latvian and the local Vassilievsky Ostrov) were against the "Vikzhel" plan, while the remaining seven (Nevsky, Peterburgsky, Narvsky and Moskovsky etc., some of them with qualifications) were for a pact with the other socialist parties and for preventing strife in the ranks of labor.[12] This same Obukhov delegation conducted itself even more resolutely at the City Council. Thumping the table with their fists, the delegates called for action, not words, and repeated the epithets current in the working-class districts: to hell with all the leaders—Lenin, Kerensky, Trotsky—it's their fault we are in trouble. The workers' delegation from another huge plant, the Putilov works, acted in a similar spirit and insisted on a speedy agreement between the parties and an end to the fratricidal civil war, threatening that otherwise the workers would take matters into their own hands.[13] At about the same time a delegation of workers of the Baltic plant went to the Military Revolutionary Committee to demand an end to the fighting at any cost.[14]

The vigorous support given "Vikzhel" by the Petrograd workers improved the atmosphere at the next meeting of the subcommittee which was to consider the candidates for the future-government and the constitution of the new "People's Soviet."[15] At this meeting, held on October 31 (November 13), the subcommittee almost reached agreement on the list of members of the future cabinet, which was to include Bolsheviks, but not Lenin and Trotsky. Kamenev and Ryazanov, the Bolshevik representatives on the subcommittee, assented to this provision. The proposed list was made up of experts rather than political figures. Only for the post of Foreign Secretary were prominent political leaders suggested: Avksyentev of the right S-R's, Skobelev of the Mensheviks, Trotsky or Pokrovsky from the Bolsheviks. Trotsky and Skobelev were eliminated after debate.

The accord reached at the night session of October 31-November 1 (November 12-13) was considered so definite that Kamenev, at the end of the meeting, said that posters would be placed all over the city that morning announcing that a provisional agreement had been signed. This was intended to put an immediate end to the inter-party warfare. But Kamenev proved unable to carry out his promise. On November 1 (14) an internal *coup d'etat* occurred in the Bolshevik Party which led to a serious crisis in the Bolshevik Central Committee and made any agreement with other parties impossible. Up to that moment, Lenin and Trotsky, taking account of the unsettled military situation, had permitted Kamenev and his friends to play along with the socialists. But now Kerensky was beaten and had to flee, and Moscow was firmly in the grip of the Red Guard. "Diplomacy" was no longer necessary, and Lenin took to the stick.

The Bolshevik Central Committee met on November 1 (14). Invited to this meeting were members of VTsIK, the Bolshevik organization in the army, the Soviet of People's Commissars, and the trade unions. Lenin was the first to speak: "Kamenev's policy must be abandoned at once. This is not the time for talks with 'Vikzhel.' We must send troops to Moscow." Next, Trotsky denounced "the parties which had no part in the October rising and which now propose to snatch the power from those who have overthrown them." He insisted that

> . . . . we cannot agree to less than 75% of the seats in the VTsIK and we cannot agree to the exclusion of Lenin . . . We must break with them not over details but over the very program . . . But we must show the masses what we stand for and to do this we must have the governmental apparatus.[16]

Dzherzhinsky accused the delegation to the "Vikzhel" talks of having failed to carry out the instructions of the Central Committee, that is, to insist on responsibility to VTsIK and on the inclusion of Lenin and Trotsky in the list of ministerial candidates. He proposed a vote of no confidence and the replacement of the present delegation by another. He was seconded by Uritsky.

Lenin repeated that an end must be made to Kamenev's policy; the talks were intended only as a diplomatic move to divert attention from the military operations. To this, Rykov replied that he had taken the talks seriously: "If we suspend the negotiations, we will alienate those groups which are supporting us now, and we shall not be able to retain power." Sokolnikov, on the other hand, asserted that the talks had never represented anything more than a diplomatic maneuver and must now be stopped. Next, Milyutin declared that "we will be unable to sustain a prolonged civil war," and insisted that an agreement with other parties was absolutely necessary. Ryazanov and Kamenev admitted that the conditions put forward by the right-wing socialists were not acceptable in their present form, but nevertheless insisted that a compromise be reached. Sverdlov took the position that some members of "Vikzhel" should be arrested, which would explode the whole business. When a vote was taken, four were in favor of an immediate suspension of the "Vikzhel" talks, and ten—for various and often contradictory reasons—were in favor of continuing them.

Trotsky made a new proposal, which was supported by Lenin: that all the previous Bolshevik tenets which had been serving as a basis for the talks should now be presented in the form of an ultimatum to all other parties. This resolution was adopted by the Bolshevik Central Committee and, on the same night (after some hesitation by the Left S-R's) by VTsIK. Only the internationalist Bazarov and his group understood that the resolution amounted to a breaking off of the talks; in protest, the group left VTsIK.

The intra-Bolshevik struggle that began on the night of November 1 (14) was not yet at an end, however. Having lost the battle in the Central Committee, the leaders of the opposition (Kamenev, Zinoviev, Rykov, and Milyutin) sought, and apparently found, support among leading Bolsheviks outside the Central Committee. On November 2 (15), Lenin tried to resolve the struggle by getting yet another resolution passed by the Central Committee. In this, all further talks were openly rejected:

> ... the Central Committee affirms that any capitulation to the threats and ultimata of the Soviet minority would mean a complete repudiation of the power of the Soviets and of the laws of democracy, as it would express reluctance on the part of the majority to asserting its supremacy and would therefore amount to a surrender to anarchy, thereby leaving the door open to new threats from any new minority.[17]

The resolution ended by accusing the Left S-R's of having caused the failure of the talks by declining the Bolshevik offer to join the Soviet of People's Commissars.

Having suffered a second defeat in the Central Committee, the opposition now decided to transfer the struggle to VTsIK. The opportunity presented itself when this resolution was read at a meeting of VTsIK. It provoked strong indignation among the Left S-R's and the few remaining internationalists. The former composed a counter-resolution which bitterly protested that

> . . . the tactics assumed lately by the ruling Bolshevik Party must lead to a schism in the working class. A virtual dictatorship by one political group has been established and this will lead, with *inexorable* logic, towards acts of brutal repression not only against the propertied but also the needy classes. . . .

The resolution concluded that Bolshevik tactics were preventing the formation of an all-socialist government and were thus pushing the country towards civil war.

Kamenev decided to take advantage of the situation in VTsIK to oppose Lenin. He demanded that the resolution of the Central Committee be discussed by the Bolshevik fraction in VTsIK. This was an unheard-of breach of party tradition: the highest law for any Bolshevik, in no matter what public body he might be serving, was to obey unquestioningly the decision of the Party Central Committee. On the surface, Kamenev, Zinoviev and the other dissenters appeared to have succeeded: the Bolshevik fraction passed a resolution agreeing, in the main, with the opposition, though it differed on one crucial point: it insisted on the inclusion of Lenin and Trotsky, whereas Kamenev, Ryazanov, and Zinoviev had not so insisted at the "Vikzhel" meetings of October 29 and 31 (November 11 and 13).

Kamenev's victory was pyrrhic. His attempts were doomed to fail in the face, on the one hand, of Lenin's resistance, and on the other, of the hostility of the right-wing socialists, to whom a government that would include Lenin and Trotsky was anathema. The situation was aggravated by the growing arrogance of the Bolsheviks, who had won military victory more easily than Lenin and Trotsky in their most optimistic expectations had dared to hope. "Capitalism" had surrendered almost without a struggle; the "proletariat" had won almost without bloodshed.

Although in the south the Cossack General Kaledin, General Denikin, and other generals still threatened, at this time the Bolsheviks were marching from one victory to another, seizing Petrograd, Moscow, Kazan, and a number of other cities. Each day brought them the allegiance of more divisions at the front, and they advanced with ever greater determination toward their goal. This, was, of course the establishment of a dictatorship of the Bolshevik Party; *Pravda* now talked openly about it, *Izvestia* only a little less frankly.

More confident, the Military Revolutionary Committee now began to threaten "Vikzhel" with arrests. On November 2 (15), the Committee met twice. At 11 p.m. on November 2 (15), it received a telegram from "Vikzhel" demanding that it remove its commissars from the railway telegraph offices within two hours, otherwise the railway telegraph operators would go on strike. The Military Revolutionary Committee decided to ignore "Vikzhel's" ultimatum; at the same time, the Headquarters of the Petrograd Military District was notified that it was under the jurisdiction of the Military Revolutionary Committee. The Military Revolutionary Committees in Petrograd and Moscow also stopped the publication of the entire bourgeois press and a large number of socialist papers as well. In this respect, Colonel Muravyev particularly distinguished himself after he was appointed to command the defense of Petrograd. The general tactics of the Military Revolutionary Committee, which branded as a "counterrevolutionary" anyone who did not agree with the Bolsheviks; the constant clashes with the railway workers, who tried to observe strict neutrality and stopped trains transporting the forces of the Military Revolutionary Committee—all this produced an atmosphere of terror and imminent civil war.

Many of those who were working for an agreement among socialists realized, particularly after the Bolshevik resolutions of November 1 and 2 (14 and 15), that even though some Bolsheviks and most of the Left S-R's were sincerely trying to avert civil war by an honest agreement among all the socialist parties, the intentions of the real leaders of the Bolshevik Party were quite different. These leaders were not concerned with shortening or preventing the civil war; on the contrary, they saw in the civil war the best opportunity to consolidate their power and of winning in the end, in spite of all the obstacles which they could not fail to see. The knowledge that such was their real attitude paralyzed even those who, like the Martov wing and the

United Internationalists, were prepared to make the greatest concessions to reach an agreement. It became increasingly obvious that the only real test of the sincerity of the Bolshevik intentions would be a public renunciation of terror, at least against the socialists. There was a distinct danger that the Bolsheviks, while they had no intention of reaching a real agreement, would create a fiction of unity under cover of which they would contrive a capitulation of all other parties to their own dictatorship. In view of this danger, and supported by the atmosphere prevailing in the working-class districts of Petrograd, the internationalist Mensheviks resolved to unmask the group of intransigent Bolshevik leaders who then held all the key positions. The Central Committee of the Menshevik Party, on the recommendation of Martov and Abramovitch, decided to make the question of terror a public test. Accordingly, at the next plenary meeting of "Vikzhel," on November 3 (16), at which Stalin had joined the Bolshevik delegation, Martov and Abramovitch protested against the terror that was being intentionally fomented by the Bolshevik Party, pointing out that agreement could not be reached in such an atmosphere. How could one persuade the Trudoviks to join the united front if their paper had just been closed down? How could one persuade the right-wing S-R's to abandon their intransigent attitude when Kerensky had just been declared an enemy of the people and leader of the counter-revolution? It was impossible to have it both ways. The Bolsheviks must make their position in the matter clear. If they really desired unity, then the atmosphere of hatred and civil strife must be changed into one of conciliation, and if this were not done, further negotiations would be useless.

The Left S-R, Karelin, tried to smooth matters over by proposing that an agreement be concluded first; then afterward the Bolsheviks would make concessions in the matter of terror. An ultimatum of this kind, he added, only delayed the agreement. Karelin may have been sincere, but it was difficult to believe in the good faith of Sokolnikov, who attacked the Menshevik criticism as an attempt to sabotage the negotiations; for Sokolnikov was known to belong to that group among the Bolsheviks which did not want any agreement but was taking part in the negotiations for diplomatic reasons alone.[18]

After the ultimatum issued by Martov and Abramovitch, the "Vikzhel" meeting adjourned. The representatives of VTsIK declared that the subject of political terror would be discussed in the near future in VTsIK (as the highest organ of power), and a final decision would then be taken. Before the close of the meeting, Abramovitch was commissioned to persuade those groups that were not present at the meeting (right-wing S-R's, Trudoviks, representatives of the City Council) to attend the next one.

When the adjourned meeting was resumed at 3 p.m. on November 4 (17), the right-wing socialist groups were present, although the S-R's declared that they were attending as observers only. But the Bolsheviks were absent—they were at a meeting of their Central Committee.

Rumors of a crisis in the negotiations spread throughout the city and soon the White Hall of the Ministry of Transport was packed with delegations from various organizations and factories. Everyone waited impatiently for the meeting to open. Then news reached the Hall from various sources that there was a serious crisis, possibly even a split, in the Bolshevik Party, that several members had left the Central Committee, that several people's commissars had resigned. Agitation and indignation mounted. At last, losing all patience, the delegates from the Putilov works proceeded to the Smolny Institute to find out what was happening. They returned towards 3 a.m. in a very gloomy mood and reported that there was almost no chance of an agreement between the parties. But, they added, they would not allow the Bolsheviks to ignore the wishes of the working class. Since the Bolsheviks clearly were not coming, the meeting dispersed.

Not until the following morning did it become known what had actually taken place at the long meeting of the Bolshevik Central Committee on that memorable night. We know of the events leading up to it: how the majority of the Bolshevik Central Committee had made a show of continuing the talks with other parties, but without intending to come to any agreement; how Kamenev had tried to foil that maneuver by appealing to VTsIK (which was a bloc of moderate Bolsheviks with Left S-R's and other groups) against his own party. Lenin was not the man to be thwarted in this manner. If we can trust the evidence of Bubnov, a member of the Bolshevik Central Committee, events took the following course: Bubnov drew Lenin's attention to Kamenev's stratagem and insisted that this "fiddle-faddle" be stopped. Lenin, furious at Kamenev's "desertion," instantly drew up a resolution and had all the members of the Central Committee called to him, one by one, and asked them to sign it. When the majority of the Central Committee (Lenin, Trotsky, Stalin, Sverdlov, Uritsky, Dzherzhinsky, Yoffe, Bubnov, Sokolnikov, Muranov) had signed it, Lenin presented it to the minority as an ultimatum.[19]

> The resolution read as follows:
>
> At a time when the outcome of our work may decide the fate of the party, the fate of the revolution, [the party cannot allow the opposition] to blackmail the party bodies, to sabotage the work of the party. [Therefore the Central Committee demanded of the minority] a definite answer, in writing, whether it undertakes to observe party discipline . . . In case of a negative or evasive answer . . . the Petrograd and Moscow party committees and the Bolshevik faction of VTsIK, and the Petrograd City Organization will be immediately informed and a party congress convened. If it approves your line, then the congress will entrust you with the authority to dictate policy in conformity with your views. [If, on the other hand,]—and we have no doubt about this—the party approves our line—then you will have to remove yourselves and your activities from our party. This will mean a split, but an honest split is better than internal sabotage.[20]

The minority answered this ultimatum with several declarations signed separately by several groups, all dissenting from Lenin on the question of agreement with other parties. Kamenev, Zinoviev, Milyutin, Rykov and Nogin of the Central Committee handed in their resignations, accompanied by full statements of their grounds for resigning; the following People's Commissars and members of VTsIK also resigned: Ryazanov, Larin, Derbyshev, Teodorovich, Arbusov, Yurenev, Federov, and Shlyapnikov. The grounds given for the resignations were all the same. First, that the Bolshevik Party alone—without the other parties as allies—would not be strong enough to face the civil war, restore peace, and overcome Russia's economic and other social difficulties. Second—and this argument was particularly stressed by the People's Commissars—that even if the Bolsheviks succeeded in retaining power, their insistence on ruling alone would inevitably drive them to the use of terror and thus "the working-class organizations would be eliminated from leadership in politics, an irresponsible regime would be established, and a downfall of the revolution and of the country would follow."[21] A more succinct statement of the differences between the supporters and opponents of an all-socialist agreement could hardly have been formulated.

Lenin, replying to the declaration of the 11 commissars at the meeting of VTsIk on November 4 (17), turned to Nogin and Rykov, saying that some comrades "have adopted a point of view that has nothing whatsoever to do with Bolshevism." But both on this occasion and in the later document in which he gave his version of the conflict in the Bolshevik Party,[22] Lenin carefully bypassed the question of dictatorship by a minority, which was basic to Bolshevism as conceived by Lenin and his supporters. His argument rested on purely formal considerations—that the party commanding a majority at the Second Congress of Soviets (a claim for the Bolshevik Party that is disproved by the facts) had not only the right but the duty to rule and lead the people towards a socialist revolution; that as the representatives of the Soviet majority, that is, of millions of workers, peasants, and soldiers in the trenches, the Bolshevik Party must lead the people to victory. In passing, Lenin accused the minority (Kamenev, Zinoviev, and others) of deserting the party, and recalled that these same comrades had disagreed at the outbreak of the rising and had even campaigned in the press against it. He concluded that these people were not "sufficiently resolute" revolutionaries if they were ready to yield to the ultimatum of "Messrs. Abramovitch and Martov," behind whom he saw ranged the Purishkevichs, the Kaledins, and the rest of the counter-revolution.[23]

The Organization of the Bolshevik Government

At the time of the "Vikzhel" negotiations, it was beyond doubt that the establishment of an all-socialist coalition, including all parties from Trudoviks to Bolsheviks, would be highly satisfactory to the great majority of the so-called "revolutionary democracy," that is, the left sector of the Russian public, including a considerable part of its Bolshevik fringe. A government based on such a coalition and committed to convening a Constituent Assembly (without any underhand intention of dissolving it later) would probably have been the most authoritative government possible at that time. Such a government could probably have prevented the tragic civil war which was to last for more than two years. But with the establishment of a one-party dictatorship which completely disregarded the political sentiments of the majority of the population, civil war became unavoidable.

From the very first, Lenin and his supporters had aimed at nothing less than the establishment of a *purely* Bolshevik dictatorship. Yet, after the failure of the "Vikzhel" plan, Lenin had to maneuver for a time before he could form a stable government which would follow him without hesitation. The first step was to entice the Left S-R's into participating in the government; this was primarily intended to disguise the reality of one-party government, but it was also necessary to ensure an official majority in VTsIK, in which the Bolsheviks alone were in the minority. Then, the All-Russian Peasant Union, which had been dominated by the Socialist Revolutionaries, had to be captured; and the resistance of the trade unions which were not yet in Bolshevik hands, such as the Union of Railwaymen, had to be overcome.

It was not difficult to come to terms with the Left S-R's, a group which was, on the whole, ideologically unstable and politically inexperienced. The Left S-R's had sincerely supported the idea of a coalition in the "Vikzhel" talks and they had protested against Lenin's terrorist "press decree."[24] Nevertheless, their most influential leaders—Mark Nathanson, Maria Spiridonova, Kamkov and Alexandrovich—did in fact, pursue a policy close to Lenin's line. Immediately after the October rising, when Lenin offered the Left S-R's three seats in the Soviet of People's Commissars, they had declined them; but after the collapse of the "Vikzhel" negotiations, they reversed themselves by maintaining the fiction that an agreement had in fact been reached. Spiridonova insisted, perhaps more from naiveté than from cunning, that the enlarged VTsIK was, in fact the same "People's Soviet" that the decisive meeting of "Vikzhel," on the evening of October 31 (November 13), had decided to create; consequently, she declared, the left S-R's, by joining the government, were effecting that union of all revolutionary forces which had been the object of "Vikzhel." The Soviet of People's Commissars was now enlarged to include six Left S-R's.[25] As we shall see, the heterogeneity and instability of the Left S-R group led later (in July 1918) to a revolt against Lenin's government and finally to the total disintegration of this short-lived group.

The Bolsheviks found it somewhat more difficult to deal with the Peasant Union. Nevertheless, they applied certain organizational methods which have since become familiar in the history of Communism. The Second Congress of the All-Russian Peasant Union was convened by the new VTsIK, bypassing the old Executive Committee of the Peasant Union. VTsIK appointed a special organizational committee, composed of Left S-R's and Bolsheviks, with the obvious intention of packing the Convention. The manner in which this preparatory work was carried out provoked constant protests from the democratic wing of the Peasant Union. Nevertheless, despite all the efforts of Bolsheviks and Left S-R's, the mood of the peasants was such that at the opening of the Convention on November 26 (December 9), the pro-Bolshevik and non-Bolshevik wings were found to be almost equal in strength. The Left S-R, Maria Spiridonova, was elected chairman of the Convention by a small majority, and on the first set of resolutions, 360 votes went to the resolution proposed by the pro-Bolsheviks and 320 to the opposing resolution.[26] The Convention became so tense that by the second day a split occurred. The pro-Bolshevik delegates, having adjourned to another hall to hear Trotsky speak on the negotiations at Brest-Litovsk, promptly claimed for themselves the exclusive right to conduct the Convention—thus simply excluding the other half of the delegates.

"Vikzhel" and other independent associations of workers were swept out of the way by similar techniques. The first attempt to get rid of "Vikzhel" took the form of organizing a parallel conference of railway workers a week in advance of the official, regular Second All-Russian Railwaymen's Convention, which had been fixed for December 19 (January 1). The preliminary unofficial conference was organized with the view toward infiltrating the regular Convention, but the plan failed. The official Convention showed from the start a determined anti-Bolshevik attitude. The proposal to elect Lenin honorary chairman was rejected, and all attempts to incorporate the Bolshevik-organized unofficial conference into the main Convention were vigorously resisted.

After lengthy debates during which the Convention heard speeches by Zinoviev, Skobelev, Kamkov, Cherepanov and Abramovitch, a resolution in support of the coming Constituent Assembly, proposed by the internationalists, was carried, on January 4 (17), by 273 votes to 261, with three abstentions.[27] Thereupon the Bolshevik minority, by the arbitrary decision of the People's Commissar for Transport, Elizarov, declared the Convention dissolved and confirmed instead, as the only legitimate representatives, the minority consisting of the Bolsheviks, the Left S-R's and some internationalists.The name of the central organ of the Railwaymen's Trade Union was changed from "Vikzhel" to "Vikgedor," and the socialists in it were expelled.

This technique of closing down refractory trade-unions and replacing them by minorities dominated by Bolsheviks became a standard tactic. A few unions managed to survive until 1920; generally speaking, the trade-union movement, as a free and voluntary workers' movement, was completely obliterated within a few months after Lenin proclaimed the dictatorship of the "proletariat."

The Constituent Assembly

The demand for a constituent assembly was firmly rooted in the traditions of the Russian revolutionary movement. It was incorporated in the programs of all the socialist parties that had come into being at the turn of the century. The Bolshevik and Menshevik wings of the Social Democrats, the S-R's and the moderate Narodniki, and the democratic Liberals all agreed that the victories won by the revolution would be properly confirmed and consolidated by an all-Russian constituent assembly elected by universal, direct and secret suffrage. In their own writings Lenin and other Bolsheviks had incessantly reiterated the demand for a constituent assembly.

But Lenin's views underwent a radical change ofter the outbreak of the February revolution, when a huge network of Soviets spread all over Russia. If in October 1905, the first appearance of Soviets in several large towns evoked no great Bolshevik enthusiasm, their reappearance in the early days of the February revolution was at once interpreted by Lenin as the emergence of a new and higher form of democracy. To be sure, he at first did not openly oppose the constituent assembly.[28] But, characteristically, the demand for a constituent assembly was not mentioned in Lenin's "April Theses." Somewhat later, Lenin realized that mass support for a constituent assembly was too strong, and so he began accusing the Provisional Government of deliberately delaying the convening of the assembly.

When the Bolshevik fraction was about to walk out of the pre-Parliament on October 7, Trotsky read out the Bolshevik declaration in which the bourgeois classes directing the policies of the Provisional Government were accused of attempting to sabotage elections to the constituent assembly. The Bolsheviks declared that only the transfer of power to the Soviets would ensure the convening of this assembly. There was little logic in this argument but it was readily enough believed by the masses at that time.[29] The day after the October rising, *Pravda* announced on its front page: "Comrades! By shedding your blood you have made sure that the master of the Russian lands—the All-Russian Constituent Assembly—will be able to start work at the appointed hour!"

In reality, neither Lenin nor Trotsky was at all sure that the convening of the constituent assembly would strengthen their power. Some Bolsheviks hoped that their party would, together with the Left S-R and other left groups, win a majority in the assembly, but nobody could be certain of the outcome of the elections. The results in fact gave the lie to the Bolsheviks' claim that they represented a majority of the people. According to Lenin himself, who based his calculations on the data given by Svyatitsky in *The Year 1918 in the Russian Revolution* (Moscow, 1918), the Bolshevik Party received 9.02 million votes or 25 per cent; the Socialist Revolutionaries (Russian and other national groups taken together) received 20.9 million votes or 58 per cent; and all the right-wing groups, including the Kadets, received 4.62 million votes, or 13 per cent.[30] The elections had been held after Lenin took power: on November 12 (25) in most districts, and on November 19 and 26 (December 2 and 9) in a few others. Some 60 to 80 per cent of the rural and roughly 50 per cent of the urban electorate voted. These elections had been held under conditions of complete freedom—except in a few districts, where pressure had been exerted by the new Bolshevik government. The results showed, in other words, that three to four weeks after the seizure of power by the Bolsheviks, not less than 75 per cent of the population had voted against them, leaving Lenin's party and its Left S-R allies in direct opposition to the people.

Having solemnly promised on behalf of his "democratic government" to honor the wishes of the majority of the people, Lenin, aided and abetted by the Left S-R's, now decided to ignore those wishes altogether. A brief debate within the Bolshevik Party ended in unanimous acceptance of Lenin's 19 theses, in which he laid down his justifications for the dissolution of the Constituent Assembly in spite of its overwhelming socialist majority. As for the Left S-R's, Lenin at first feared that they would raise objections, but against all expectations the most influential leader of that party, old Mark Nathanson, declared himself in favor of dissolution.[31] Thus the All-Russian Constituent Assembly was dissolved by the sailor Dybenko, only 20 hours after it had been opened by Victor Chernov, its elected president.

Later, Lenin felt it necessary to justify his behavior, under moral pressure both from public opinion in Russia itself and sharp criticism from abroad—especially western socialist parties. To these latter, especially, it became necessary to explain why the Bolsheviks dissolved an assembly in which all socialists together had a majority of more than 80 per cent, and which, consequently, was ready to enact the most radical socialist and democratic reforms. A socialist united front would also have prevented the civil war, at least in that terrible form that resulted precisely from the dissolution of the Constituent Assembly. The Assembly enjoyed at that moment the general confidence of the whole country and nobody, save perhaps some small groups of diehard reactionaries, would have dared question its authority. A government based on the majority vote of the Assembly would have been the strongest since the February Revolution. Its position in negotiations for a compromise peace with Germany would have been much more favorable than the position of the weak Bolshevik Council of People's Commissars, with nothing behind it but part of the demoralized soldiery.

It could be argued that if the further development of Russia had been directed by the Constituent Assembly—as Kamenev and Zinoviev, in the memorable meetings of the Bolshevik Central Committee of October 10 and 16 (23 and 29), had insisted—the civil war could have been avoided, and Russia would have been spared what she endured in the years that followed: the creation of a dictatorship over the great majority of the people by unrestricted terror, the loss of political freedom for the people, and terrible bloodshed and famine. In other words, if Lenin had put his faith in the inherent strength of the Russian revolution (as the right wing of his party demanded in the "Vikzhel" Conference) and had formed in the Constituent Assembly a coalition government with other socialist parties, there need not have been a Brest-Litovsk capitulation. The Allied governments might have accepted the proposal put forward (too late)—by the British Ambassador to Russia, Sir George Buchanan—and released Russia from her obligation not to conclude a separate peace.

But Lenin and his followers in the Bolshevik Party were concerned above all in retaining full and unqualified power in the hands of their party alone. Their goal was establishment of a dictatorship of the Bolshevik Party for the purpose of achieving integral socialism in Russia and thereby kindling socialist revolution all over the world. In the pursuit of this goal, Lenin had no use for coalitions or peaceful democratic evolution in conformity with the will of the people. He manipulated the election figures so as to make it appear that in "reality"—though not formally—"the majority of the revolutionary masses" had voted for the Bolsheviks. At the same time he tried to prove that the Left S-R's should by rights have won more than their 40 seats in the Assembly, that they had been "shamefully tricked" by the right S-R's, with whom they shared a common list.

Yet Lenin could not answer the argument advanced by Bazarov in an article in *Novaya Zhizn* on December 5, 1917. Bazarov asked a simple question: if indeed the right S-R's had put themselves at the top of their list, and if indeed the peasants were against them, why did the peasants vote for the list at all? The supporters of the Left S-R's could instead have given their votes to the Bolsheviks, who "adopted the S-R revolutionary land program and were in all other respects even more determined and outspoken than the Left S-R's." Had leftist peasants indeed voted for the Bolsheviks, the total Bolshevik vote would have been much higher than 25 per cent. But Lenin was not concerned with numerical majorities. For him the crux of the matter lay elsewhere:

> However much the petty-bourgeois democrats who call themselves Socialists and Social-Democrats (the Chernovs, Martovs, Kautskys, Longuets, Macdonalds and Co.), may worship the goddesses of 'equality,' 'universal franchise,' 'democracy' and 'total democracy'—none of it will remove the blatant economic and political fact of the *inequality* that exists between town and village . . . . *Village cannot be equal to town* . . . The crucial question is which *class* among the urban classes will be able to make the village follow it. . . .[32]

Contrary to this sweeping sociological generalization, in November 1917 the Russian village did not follow the lead of the town but pursued its own path. It certainly did not follow the Bolshevik Party. Had Lenin been honest, he would have admitted frankly that he and his party did not care whether the peasants were with them or not. What was decisive in their view was that in Petrograd they disposed of sufficiently strong police and army units to shoot down demonstrating workers and intellectuals and to dissolve the Constituent Assembly by force.

As early as September 1917, Lenin had made a highly significant observation in his well known article, "Can the Bolsheviks Retain State Power?" He wrote:

> If after the 1905 revolution Russia was ruled by 130,000 landowners, why then should Russia not now be ruled by 240,000 members of the Bolshevik Party—ruled in the interest of the poor and against the rich?[33]

Was it not strange that Lenin should refer to the number of Bolshevik Party members when discussing the retention of power? Would it not have been much more fittingfor him asa nominal Social Democrat to argue that the Bolsheviks would retain power because, ruling in the interest of the people, they would have the support and the votes of the grateful workers, citizens of a free Soviet democracy? But Lenin's thoughts were already running on quite different lines. In old Russia the 130,000 land-owners had been the privileged ruling class, with the entire police apparatus of Tsarism at its beck and call; in the new Russia the members of the Bolshevik Party were to become a new ruling class, which would maintain and tighten its hold on the country with the help of its own new apparatus of violence and repression.

The dispersal of the Constituent Assembly was carried out after careful military preparations by the Soviet of People's Commissars. Police precautions were taken to prevent the deputies' reassembling. The checking of the credentials and the preparatory work for the opening of the Assembly were entrusted to a special commission under the chairmanship of Uritsky, second-in-command of the terroristic "Extraordinary Commission" (Cheka). All non-socialist papers were closed down; all suspect meetings were raided and the participants arrested. (For example, one such meeting held on the premises of the Free Economic Society on December 18—five days before the official opening of the Constituent Assembly—was interrupted by the Bolshevik police—accompanied by the Minister of Justice, the Left S-R Steinberg, and the S-R Karelin—who came to arrest those in attendance at the "illegal" meeting.) Orders were issued for the arrest of all Kadet deputies to the Constituent Assembly and even of some S-R's and Mensheviks, including Chernov, Avksentyev and Tseretelli. Reliable troops were brought to Petrograd, while in the barracks of the Petrograd garrison all weapons were placed under special guard so that the ordinary soldiers could not get at them. Machine guns were placed on the roofs adjoining the Tauride Palace where the Assembly was to meet. The Constituent Assembly found itself defenseless; yet even so it was possible to organize an impressive demonstration in its support in which (at the most conservative estimate) 20,000 people took part. On December 3 (16) a meeting of some 50,000 took place in Moscow. There were no incidents.

On the day of the opening of the Assembly, the streets leading to the Tauride Palace in Petrograd resembled a military camp. Soldiers and sailors armed with revolvers and machine guns stopped all comers, letting no one pass except those who held deputies' cards. Nevertheless a large crowd—workers with banners, office workers, and intellectuals—assembled and moved towards the palace, where it was met by fire from the military guards. It was officially admitted that there were 21 dead[34]; the number of wounded was never known. The shattering impression which the shooting of these demonstrators and the dissolution of the Constituent Assembly made on the minds of Russian intellectuals, workers and peasants, was given vivid expression by Maxim Gorki, who wrote:

> The best among the Russian people have for almost a hundred years lived for the idea of a constituent assembly—a political forum where the entire Russian democracy could freely express its will. For this idea thousands of intellectuals, tens of thousands of workers and peasants have perished in prisons, in exile and at hard labor, died on the gallows or under the bullets of the firing squads. Rivers of blood have flowed as a sacrifice to this sacred idea—yet now the 'people's commissars' gave the order to shoot down the crowd demonstrating in honor of this idea . . . .
>
> On January 5 they fired on the unarmed workers of Petrograd. They fired without previous warning, fired from ambush, through gaps in the railings, like cowards, like true assassins. . . .[35]

Not only the democratic sectors of the Russian public, but also the international working-class movement was critical of Lenin because of the dispersal of the Constituent Assembly. Perhaps the strongest blow to Lenin and Trotsky was the fierce fundamental criticism from Rosa Luxemburg, who had been Trotsky's associate in promoting the theory of "permanent revolution." Trotsky had defended the dissolution of the Constituent Assembly on the grounds that in revolutionary epochs representative bodies can never keep in step with popular moods and always reflect yesterday, not tomorrow. Rosa Luxemburg, then in a German prison for anti-war propaganda, attacked these superficial and historically baseless arguments. She cited the examples of the English Revolution of the 17th century, the French Revolution of the 18th century, and even of the 4th State Duma in Russia itself. To Trotsky's assertion that the composition of the Constituent Assembly contradicted the real sentiments of the masses, Rosa Luxemburg replied with a striking question: why, then, were not new elections held immediately afterward to ascertain the real feelings of the people? Rosa Luxemburg made the prophetic observation that, though democratic representative bodies were not free of weaknesses and faults, the remedy concocted by Lenin and Trotsky—the destruction of democracy itself—was many times more dangerous than the disease it pretended to cure. She wrote:

> The suppression of political life in the whole of the country must bring in its wake a progressive paralysis of life in the Soviets themselves. In the absence of universal franchise, of unrestricted freedom of press and assembly and of free discussion, life in any public body is bound to wither, to become a mere semblance of life, in which only bureaucracy can remain an active element. This is a law from which nobody is exempt. Public life gradually becomes dormant while a few dozen party leaders of inexhaustible energy and boundless idealism do the ruling and directing; from among these a dozen outstanding intellects do the real leading while an elite from the working class is summoned from time to time to meetings, there to applaud the speeches of the leaders and to give unanimous approval to the resolutions laid before them—in fact, power in the hands of cliques, a dictatorship certainly, but a dictatorship not of the proletariat but of a handful of politicians . . . .[36]

It would be difficult to find a better description of the dynamics of dictatorship by a terrorist minority—the "totalitarian spiral" so characteristic of the further development of the Soviet state and the Bolshevik Party itself—than that given by Rosa Luxemburg on the basis of genuinely Marxist reasoning. But Lenin and Trotsky were quite incapable of Marxist reasoning when success had turned their heads.[37] Intoxicated with their unexpectedly quick victory, they were confident—against all the teachings of Marxism and of history—that their iron will and the dawning world revolution would make the impossible come true. They did not ask themselves what it would cost Russia's workers and peasants in blood and suffering when they took this leap into the unknown and ordered Dybenko to disperse the Constituent Assembly by force of arms.

[1] "The Bolsheviks during the preparatory period," Moscow, 1947.
[2] Trotsky, L., *My Life*, pp. 48-49.
[3] *Pro domo sua:* In the Petrograd newspapers of the next day Erlich's speech was

mistakenly attributed to R. Abramovitch. From the press this mistake was carried into John Reed's *Ten Days that Shook the World* and even into the official minutes of the Second Congress, published in Moscow in 1928. See R. Abramovitch, Vol. II, p. 167.

[4] Lenin, *Works*, Vol. 26, p. 228.

[5] See Abramovitch, *Memoirs*, Vol. II, p. 162.

[6] *Ibid.*, Vol. II, p. 176.

[7] Lyubimov, I. N., *Revolution 1917*. Moscow, 1930. Vol. VI (October-December), pp. 436-37.

[8] Vompe, "The Days of the October Revolution and the Railwaymen" (*Istprofstran*), published by the Central Committee of Railwaymen, Moscow, 1924, pp. 29-32.

[9] *Ibid., pp.* 36-37. The author notes that the minutes of this meeting do not show how the Bolsheviks voted on this question.

[10] *Novaya Zhizn*, November 1 (new style), 1917.

[11] *Novaya Zhizn*, November 1, 3, 4, 7, 12, 15 and December 5 (old style), 1917; also Lyubimov, p. 60. These were the same workers from the Obukhov factory who, at a general meeting on October 10 (23), had unanimously demanded the transfer of power to the Soviets.

[12] See B. Nikolaevski, *Lietopis Revolucii*, Berlin 1923, p. 287.

[13] *Novaya Zhizn*, November 4 (17), 1917.

[14] Lyubimov, p. 67.

[15] There were several proposals concerning the composition of the "People's Soviet." It was to have altogether 420 members: by mutual agreement 100 from the old and 100 from the new VTsIK; 75 from the peasants; 80 from the army and navy; 100 from the local governments of Petrograd and Moscow; 40 from the trade unions, including "Vikzhel," and 25 from those parties that were not yet represented in the new VTsIK.

[16] *Minutes of the Central Committee.*

[17] Lenin here intentionally ignores the fact that the Bolshevik Party as such did not command a majority in either the Congress or VTsIK.

[18] At a meeting of the Petrograd Soviet of October 31 (November 13), Sokolnikov reported on the course of the negotiations with the socialist parties at "Vikzhel." The meeting issued an appeal to the railway workers to "force 'Vikzhel' to surrender its credentials."

[19] *Izvestia*, November 7, 1927.

[20] Lenin, *Works*, Vol. XXVI, pp. 247-49.

[21] *Minutes of the Central Committee*, pp. 167-68.

[22] Lenin, *Works*, Vol. XXVI, pp. 269-73.

[23] *Ibid.*

[24] See "The Dispute Over the Freedom of the Press," chapter 13.

[25] The following Left S-R's were included in the Soviet of People's Commissars on the evening of December 9 (22): Proshyan, Commissar of Posts and Telegraph; Algassov, Commissar of Home Affairs; Trutovsky, Commissar of Local Government; Mikhailov, Commissar of the Navy; Steinberg, Commissar of Justice; Izmailov, Commissar of Administration of Former Tsarist Palaces. Not one of these was a prominent leader of the Left S-R's with the possible exception of Proshyan; nor did the appointees include any politically influential members of the group which had taken part in the "Vikzhel" talks and had worked for the all-socialist coalition, such as Karelin, Kalegaev, Malkin, Sablin, Spiro, or Cherepanov.

[26] *Novaya Zhizn*, No. 191, December 2 (15), 1917.

[27] *Novaya Zhizn*, January 5 (18), 1918.

[28] An eyewitness, who was present at the farewell meeting on March 14 (27) held by the Zurich emigrés, describes how one of the speakers asked why Lenin's speech had avoided all reference to the constituent assembly and whether this meant that, having accepted the idea of a Soviet republic, Lenin now considered the constituent assembly as unnecessary, or even harmful to the progress of the revolution. Lenin gave no answer

to this question and only smiled in reply to a renewed and more pressing request to make his position clear (see Abramovitch, R. A., *Memoirs,* Vol. II).

[29] See chapter 3 of this book for a discussion of "The Democratic Convention and the Pre-Parliament."

[30] Lenin, V. I., vol. XXX, pp. 230-251.

[31] *Pravda,* April 20, 1924; also Trotsky, L., *Memories of Lenin,* p. 92. Moscow, 1924.

[32] Lenin, V. I., vol. XXX, p. 234.

[33] Lenin, V. I., vol. XXVI, p. 87.

[34] This admission was made in a speech by the chairman of the VTsIK, Sverdlov, at the meeting of the Congress of Soviets on January 11 (24), 1918. *Novaya Zhizn,* January 13 (26), 1918.

[35] *Novaya Zhizn,* January 9 (22), 1918.

[36] Rosa Luxemburg, *Die Russische Revoluzion,* Berlin, 1922, pp. 103, 113-114. This prophecy reached the workers only in 1922, when Paul Levy published R. Luxemburg's pamphlet on the Russian revolution. It is still not included in the complete edition of Rosa Luxemburg's writings published in East Germany.

[37] Trotsky writes in his book *O Lenine* that on the morning of November 8 when the victory of the rising was evident, Lenin told him in German: "es schwindelt" (it makes you dizzy). Trotsky, *O Lenine.* Moscow 1924, p. 77.

CHAPTER 6

From Brest-Litovsk to Civil War

The Brest-Litovsk Negotiations

Lenin had been swept to power on the tide of war-weariness. An end to the war, therefore, was his first imperative. The "decree on peace" passed by the Second Congress of Soviets at its second session on October 26 (November 8) urged the peoples and governments of all belligerent countries to open peace negotiations at once. As the news of this proposal spread throughout the world, the Allies soon made clear their alarm at Russia's evident intention to negotiate a separate peace. The Germans, however remained silent for two full weeks—which troubled the Soviet of People's Commissars and raised faint hopes among some of their opponents.

On November 9 (22) the world was startled by a report that the German government had refused to parley with the Bolsheviks and was insisting that it would deal only with a government backed by the Constituent Assembly.[1]

The Bolsheviks tried, through their men in Stockholm, to contact representatives of the German government and some right-wing members of the German Social Democratic Party, but to no avail. When anxiety had become intolerable, the Bolsheviks repeated their peace offer. On November 8 (21) Trotsky sent telegrams to the ambassadors of all Allied countries in Petrograd suggesting that they consider the peace decree of the Second Congress of Soviets "as a formal proposal to conclude immediately a cease-fire agreement on all fronts and to start negotiations for a general peace." The previous night—November 7 (20)—Lenin, Stalin and Krylenko had spoken over a direct wire to the Commander-in-Chief, General Dukhonin, suggesting that he immediately approach the "military authorities of the enemy armies" with an offer to begin armistice talks. General Dukhonin refused to comply: he would accept such an order only from a government "supported by the army and the country." Thereupon, he was relieved of his command and replaced by the trusted Bolshevik, Ensign N. Krylenko. An order signed by Lenin and Krylenko was then radioed to every regiment at the advanced front positions "to elect immediately delegates for formal armistice negotiations" with the opposite German units. In compliance with this order, a group of negotiators crossed the front from Dvinsk on the night of November 12 (25). It was passed through the German lines and spoke to the German Command, which agreed to enter into negotiations. Thus were initiated the Brest-Litovsk talks, which lasted more than two months and which concluded with the ratification of the peace treaty by the Fourth Congress of Soviets on March 3 (16), 1918.

Throughout these complicated and lengthy negotiations, the Germans played with the insecure Soviet government like a cat with a mouse. The Russian army had, in fact, disintegrated after the dismissal of General Dukhonin (and his brutal murder by soldiers who had accompanied Krylenko at his installation as the new Commander-in-Chief). Though the Central Powers, for various political reasons, played at negotiating, the outcome was determined in advance by the obvious "relation of powers." Lenin understood the situation well, and had no illusions, but not all his comrades in the Bolshevik Central Committee were able to assess the situation so realistically. Consequently the agonizing negotiations were accompanied by fierce struggle, ideological and political, within the Central Committee. As on the eve of the October rising and during the "Vikzhel" conferences, the Bolshevik Party, theoretically "monolithic," was once again deeply divided. This emerged with extraordinary clarity with the publication, much later, of minutes of the meetings of the Central Committee, of the various Bolshevik Party conferences, and of the congresses of Soviets. It was, indeed, thanks to Lenin alone that the Soviets agreed to ratify the Brest-Litovsk peace treaty—a pitiful capitulation to the demands of German Generals von Hoffmann, Ludendorff, and

Hindenburg—and thus it was Lenin who saved the Soviet government at that critical moment.

While Trotsky, Zinoviev, and in particular such left-wing Bolsheviks as Bukharin and Radek speculated that the threat of a German revolution or of a prolonged Russian guerilla war might effectively influence the German government, Lenin apparently never shared these illusions although he sometimes talked in public in these terms. His opponents within the party, less cynical, proved helpless before the mailed fist of General von Hoffmann. Only six days before the arrival in Brest-Litovsk of the first Soviet delegation, under A. Yoffe, on December 3 (16), Trotsky told the Second Peasant Congress that a general democratic peace would be concluded, and threatened the Germans with a revolutionary war should they fail to comply with the just demands of the Russian revolution. But, as press correspondents noted, the same audience that had greeted each brilliant sally by Trotsky with thunderous applause was conspicuously silent when he came to call for a revolutionary war. Zinoviev was somewhat more cautious when he addressed the Bolshevik-organized Conference of Railway Workers a month later, on December 13 (26). In saying that those who were against the Brest-Litovsk talks had been proved wrong, that the Bolshevik delegates had won, and that "the conclusion of a general democratic peace is now assured," Zinoviev was indulging in wishful thinking; but at least he no longer talked of waging a revolutionary war.

After preliminary technical details had been arranged, the armistice negotiations began at Brest-Litovsk on November 20 (December 3). On December 2 (15) an agreement was signed for a cease-fire to take effect on December 4 (17). The talks thus far had been strictly confined to the conditions of the armistice. The Germans rejected all attempts of Yoffe and Kamenev to broaden them into a discussion of peace terms. They also declined a Soviet proposal to transfer the negotiations to a neutral city such as Stockholm.

On December 9 (22), the full delegations of the Central Powers and Russia met in Brest-Litovsk to negotiate peace terms. The Central Powers were represented by professional diplomats and important military figures. The German delegation was led by von Kühlman, and the Austrian delegation by Count Czernin. Russia was represented by A. Yoffe (leader of the delegation), Kamenev, Mrs. Anastasia Bitsenko (Left S-R), L. Karakhan (secretary to the delegation), and several civilian and military consultants. It was agreed that the talks should be held in public and that all speeches be reported by press, telegraph, and radio.

The Bolshevik delegation advanced the principles of a general democratic peace in accordance with the tenets of the Russian revolution —a peace without annexations or indemnities, based on the self-determination of nations. The Germans, on the surface, seemed to accept all these principles, but "interpreted" them in their own fashion. Soviet propaganda, particularly as expressed by Trotsky, aimed at convincing the world that the Germans and Austrians had accepted the revolutionary Bolshevik formulas. "We have forced the German generals," Trotsky declared triumphantly at workers' meetings, "to accept the terms laid down by the Russian revolution"; we "cornered them" so they could not escape. The real situation belied these verbal formulas. For example, the Central Powers guaranteed not to transfer any divisions from the Russian front to the West—but the guarantee included the proviso: "except for those divisions which are already on the way there." Obviously, all military units that were needed on the western front had been included in the list of those "on the way" even before the talks began; there had never been any intention of transferring the others. The Central Powers also accepted the principle of self-determination—but saw no conflict with this principle if some Latvian, Lithuanian, or Esthonian territories or towns were "voluntarily" (under German occupation!) to join Germany. The matter of indemnities was subjected to similar "interpretations."

After an exchange of declarations, Yoffe suggested an adjournment of ten days to give the countries which had not thus far been participating in the talks to decide the question of their future participation. The suggestion was accepted, and the Soviet delegation left for Petrograd on December 12 (25).

A large conference of the Bolshevik Party, convened on 15 (28) December, soon after the return of the delegation, became the scene of a passionate struggle. The Moscow city and district party organizations, as well as the majority of the Petrograd Bolsheviks, favored a determined fight, even, if need be, a revolutionary war. Lenin's position was diametrically opposed: "If we do not succeed in obtaining peace now, we shall be overthrown, and then conditions will be even more difficult." Trotsky's famous formula of "neither war nor peace" amounted to declaring the war finished while refusing to sign a peace treaty with Germany. In the end, 32 votes were cast in support of a revolutionary war, 15 in support of Lenin's proposal, and 16 in support of Trotsky's proposal.[2]

Talks resumed in Brest-Litovsk on December 27 (January 9). This time Trotsky was present. On arrival, the Soviet delegates found representatives of the Ukrainian Rada negotiating a separate peace on behalf of the Ukraine, which had just been declared independent by the second "universal" (decree) of the Central Rada, the Ukrainian National Council. Count Czernin has described in his memoirs how pitiful it was to see Trotsky blanch when he saw the Ukrainians. However, when formally asked by von Kühlman whether he objected to the presence of the Ukrainian delegates, Trotsky replied that out of respect for the principle of self-determination he could not object. It was nevertheless clear to all that the position of the Soviet delegation was much weakened.

After eight days of discussion, it became evident that the Germans were not accepting any of the Bolshevik principles but were merely trying to trap the Soviet delegation by ambiguous formulations. On December 30 (January 12) General von Hoffmann had asked Trotsky to drop his arrogant manner of speech and remember that it was victorious German armies that were on Russian territory and not the other way around. A few days later—January 5 (18)—during a luncheon at which all the delegates were present, General von Hoffmann spread a map of Russia on the table before him and, tracing a thick blue line with his finger, said that this represented the future frontier of Russia. According to this line, Russia, out of respect for the principle of self-determination, would lose Poland, part of Byelorussia, and the Baltic states; at the same time, as reparations for war damages, Russia was to pay six billion gold marks. The play was over, the pretense of negotiations was dropped. Instead there was an ultimatum, backed by the still unbroken might of the German army.

The Soviet delegation asked for an adjournment of a few days for consultation with its government. Trotsky was still hoping in his heart of hearts that a miracle might happen and the German revolution break out at that very moment. But no such miracle happened.

The delegates returned to Petrograd. The decisive meeting of the Bolshevik Central Committee took place on January 11 (24). The conflicts of the December meeting were repeated once again. The results of the voting were as follows: first, Lenin's proposal to prolong the peace negotiations as long as possible was passed by 12 votes to 1; next, Trotsky's proposal not to sign any treaties, but to declare the war ended, was accepted by nine votes to seven. Although Lenin voted against this proposal, Trotsky was entitled to claim that his line was supported by the majority of the Central Committee.

Lenin's position in the Central Committee had obviously been weakened. His prestige had suffered from the fact that in his attacks on the Provisional Government he had never tired of boasting that only a Bolshevik government, when it came to power, would be able to conclude a general democratic peace instead of a separate capitulation to the Germans. And now the Bolshevik Soviet government was facing an implacable enemy, helpless, with no power to fight back, praying for a miracle.

The bewilderment among the Bolshevik leaders became manifest at the second enlarged plenary meeting of the Central Committee, which included party activists. The only thing on which all could agree was the need to drag out the peace negotiations. This, however, the Germans would not allow. Trotsky had tried to get them to drop at least a few of the demands listed by von Hoffmann, and to this end he had sought the mediation of Count Czernin of Austria, who was more inclined to compromise than were Ludendorff and von Hoffmann. But this scheme came to nothing. On January 27 (February 9) the Germans concluded a peace treaty with the Ukrainian Rada; on the strength of this agreement, the German High Command decided, at a special meeting in Bad Homburg attended by the Kaiser, to yield no further and to confront the Bolsheviks with an ultimatum.

At the Brest-Litovsk meeting of January 28 (February 10), Trotsky delivered one of his most brilliant speeches, which moved even some of the representatives of the Central Powers. He concluded that the Soviet government could not be a signatory to such a peace treaty, but that, to prevent further bloodshed, Soviet Russia would consider the war as ended. The Central Powers simply refused to accept Trotsky's declaration; they took it instead to mean the end of the armistice. They announced that they considered themselves free to resume military operations within seven days if the Soviet government had not by that time agreed to the peace terms.

The return of the Soviet delegation to Petrograd plunged the Bolsheviks into despair and panic. They tried to save face by proclaiming the "fatherland in peril"; they appealed to soldiers and citizens to continue the fight and resist further penetration by the Germans, to dig trenches; Krylenko was ordered to destroy military stores and to blow up ammunition factories at the approach of the enemy. But when the Germans began their advance on February 5 (18), they met with no resistance whatever. The next day, the Soviet of People's Commissars hastily dispatched a telegram to Berlin expressing its readiness to sign on the dotted line.

The Germans, however, were in no hurry, and continued to capture still more territories and towns. The German High Command's answer, which finally arrived on February 9 (22), contained new and harsher terms of surrender. The Germans further demanded that the new terms be accepted within 48 hours and that the Soviet delegation leave immediately for Brest-Litovsk, where the treaty would have to be signed within three days and ratified within two weeks thereafter.

The period between February 5 (18) and February 12 (25) was a most critical one for the Soviet government. In the uninterrupted sessions of the Central Committee and at various party conferences there was still no stable or sufficiently strong majority. Lenin had made his position quite clear: the attempt to ignore the real balance of power only made the situation worse; there was no choice but to capitulate; the only thing that mattered was that the Bolsheviks should retain power. But at the Central Committee meeting of February 4 (17) there were at first only five votes in support of Lenin, while six members of the Central Committee, headed by Bukharin, voted against him. After several counts, with varying results, the final vote was six (including Trotsky) in support of Lenin, one against, and four (Bukharin, Lomov, Uritsky, and Krestinsky) abstaining.

An open revolt against the Central Committee and Lenin followed. The Petrograd and Moscow city and district party organizations were now joined by the Ural and Ukrainian district organizations in protesting that the Central Committee had no right to take decisions on the basis of such a small majority and should lay the questions before a party congress. Trotsky characterized the situation by noting that by parliamentary standards there were already two parties instead of one.[3] After a heated discussion accompanied by mutual recrimination, a vote was taken. This time the result was: seven in support of Lenin's proposal to sign a treaty, four against, and four, including Trotsky, abstaining. Lenin rejected Stalin's suggestion that a new attempt should be made to draw out the negotiations. A second telegram was sent to Berlin which stated that Germany's ultimatum was accepted. Although the Central Committee was now inundated with protests and resignations, Lenin took no account of them. He put his proposal before VTsIK, where he received a more impressive majority of 116 to 84.[4]

When confirmation was received from Germany, a new delegation left for Brest-Litovsk, headed this time by Sokolnikov and Chicherin; Trotsky and Yoffe had refused to go. At Brest-Litovsk the Soviet delegation signed the treaty without discussing it or even reading the text. The terms proved even more severe than those announced in the German telegram of February 9 (22). Thus, on demand of the Turkish delegation, Russia was obliged to return to Turkey the towns of Kars, Ardagan and Batum[5] in the Caucasus, which had been captured 70 years earlier. The treaty was signed on February 18 (March 3) and ratified two weeks later by the Fourth Congress of Soviets.

The S-R's and the Mensheviks protested the signing of the treaty; some Left S-R's, too, spoke against it. To one of the latter, Lenin rudely commented that he would not answer any queries, since one fool could ask more questions than ten wise men could answer. On the other hand, another Left S-R, I. Steinberg, People's Commissar for Justice, consoled himself with the reflection that frontier demarcations no longer had any meaning, since the coming world-revolution would soon sweep them all away.

The signing of the treaty was a great disappointment to some of the Allies, who had hoped that at the last moment the Bolsheviks would change their minds. On the strength of this hope, France and Britain had offered their support to the Bolshevik government on condition that it continue to resist the Germans; representatives of the United States in Petrograd and Moscow were vainly trying to get President Wilson[6] to make a similar promise. In the Bolshevik Central Committee, Trotsky advocated the acceptance of Allied aid but Lenin brushed all such suggestions aside. Again as during the days before October, Lenin's personal prestige broke the resistance of the majority in his party and swung Bolshevik policy in the direction that he considered correct.

The Change in 1918

Russia's withdrawal from the war as a result of the Bolshevik rising brought deep changes in the life of the country, which were of the utmost consequence for the future of Russia. The opening of the peace negotiations and, even more, the ratification of the Brest-Litovsk Treaty were signals of the demobilization of the army—at first unauthorized, later official. Millions of soldiers went back to their villages, thus dissolving the peculiar "class" of soldiers which had given the Bolshevik Party its most powerful support.

The war veterans who came back to the villages, heavily laden with "war souvenirs" in the form of rifles, small arms, hand grenades, and sometimes even machine guns, soon became peasants again. The urgent task for them now was to see to the redistribution of the land. They had some good words for the Bolsheviks who had put an end to the war and assisted their agrarian reforms, but they interpreted the land decree issued by the Second Congress of the Soviets, not according to the programs of the various socialist parties, but in their own way: the land was their private property, the horse and the cow were their private property, and so was the product of their labor. Once this dream of their lives had been achieved, they had no further use for the Communists, as Lenin's party now called itself. At that time one frequently heard peasants say that they were Bolsheviks all right, but not Communists.

The Communists, however, needed a great deal from the peasants, primarily bread for the cities, for the newly-organized Red Army, for the workers in industry. Since private trade had been abolished by Communist decree and since the government had practically no industrial products to exchange for farm produce, the government was compelled to requisition grain, potatoes, dairy products, etc., and this soon met with growing peasant resistance. Moreover, despite all the Bolshevik efforts, the cities and towns remained hungry owing to the paralysis of industry and the destruction of the country's entire trade apparatus. Thus, the special "class" of soldiers had disappeared into thin air; the Bolsheviks had lost to a considerable degree the support of the peasants; and now it also began to lose the sympathy of the urban workers.

In this social context, the Bolshevik dictatorship found itself, in the spring of 1918, suspended in a vacuum. A small party which loses its influence over major classes of society can either relinquish power or hold it by means of terror. The Bolsheviks chose the second alternative. The organizers of the terror were the Central Committee and the local organizations of the Bolshevik Party, as well as the newly-created Extraordinary Commission for the Struggle Against Speculation and Counter-Revolution (Cheka). The Red Guard, which was recruited partly from among demobilized soldiers who did not want to return to civilian life and partly from among the more fanatical Bolshevik workers, became the main armed instrument of terror. The Red Guard was numerically not large but, after the dissolution of local militias and the demobilization of the army, it remained the only organized armed force in the Soviet-dominated part of Russia.

THE BOLSHEVIKS AND THE PEASANTS

We turn now to several incidents which illustrate the tense relations which existed (from January 1918 to the start of the Civil War in the autumn of the same year) between the Soviet administration and the principal classes of the population, primarily the workers but also the peasants.

We have felt obliged to discuss some of these incidents because histories and studies of the early Soviet period are most deficient in this matter. The data are particularly difficult to obtain because they can be found only in the daily press of that time; and such publications are rarely available even in the best Western libraries. However, without a knowledge of this period, it is difficult to understand the Civil War of 1918-19—especially because the Civil War can not be separated from the social and political conditions within Soviet Russia during the first year of Communist power.

Russia's food-supply system had been strained by the war and was already quite inadequate in the summer and fall of 1917; it broke down altogether when the local municipal organs and the *zemstvos* were abolished and the inexperienced Soviets took over. Although transportation was disorganized and grain reserves in Soviet territory were low, a government concerned with establishing friendly relations with the bulk of the Russian peasants might have overcome some of these difficulties while averting many unnecessary hardships. Lenin and his party chose a very different course, which has gone down in history under the name of War Communism.

Alliance with the main body of the peasants had long been a mainstay of Lenin's doctrine, and even at the beginning of 1918 he still proclaimed that the Bolshevik Party should never use coercion against either the poor or the middle-income peasants.

The Bolsheviks hoped that, with sufficient effort, they could get the poor peasants (*bedniaks*) to join forces with the city workers almost immediately, and thus lure the middle-income peasants (*seredniaks*) away from the influence of the village bourgeoisie (*kulaks*). Propaganda and the force of example were to be the chosen means of this effort. The party created 70,000 committees of poor peasants (*kombeds*) to intensify the class struggle in the countryside. From the cities, teams of armed workers would roam the countryside, asking the peasants for voluntary delivery of grain in order to maintain the industrial enterprises which were now the property of the whole people.[7]

But the propaganda of the *kombeds* antagonized the *seredniaks*, and the grain-collecting squads received a chilly welcome.[8] The government was compelled to shift from propaganda and persuasion to physical coercion. On May 9 and 27, a decree of the VTsIK introduced a "food dictatorship." The food supply was reorganized and centralized, and the People's Commissariat of Food Supply was granted unlimited power to collect grain by any means. According to the decree, only the surplus which remained after meeting the needs of the peasants themselves was to be collected; but the requisitioning detachments were given an armed escort which had the right to confiscate grain by force of arms, if necessary. The "socialist plan" was thus transformed in a perpetual battle for grain. Not only the rich peasants, but the *seredniaks* as well, fiercely resisted the requisition detachments. Later, all private grain trade was made illegal and a network of special "barrage" detachments was posted—around the cities, at railroad intersections, etc.—to block any "illegal" flow of grain from the villages. Despite this effort, Lenin's plan failed dismally. During the 1918 grain campaign, the requisitioning detachments collected only 74,300,000 poods throughout the Soviet territory of that time; in 1916-1917 the same territory had sent 776,000,000 poods of grain to the free market —more than ten times as much.

The results of these coercive methods, however, was a small civil war. Not only those non-Communist newspapers which remained in existence until July 1918, but also government papers, printed daily accounts of violent clashes and even peasant uprisings in the war for bread. We shall cite a few of the many thousands of such clashes:

In *Novaya Zhizn* for February 11 (24) 1918,[9] a dispatch from Rovno reported that for the fifth time the Zhelich district food administration had been looted in retaliation for the requisitioning of grain; another dispatch from Lyudvipol in the same district, reported that the local food-administration building had been set on fire. The same issue reported pitched battles between peasants and Red Army units in the Dankov district, Ryazan *gubernia.* The peasants descended on the town, disarmed the militia, and used their weapons to rout the soldiers of the food-requisitioning detachments. There were scores of casualties. In Kologriv district, Kostroma *gubernia,* the peasants disarmed a fighting detachment of the Red Army and arrested some members of the local executive committee (*Ibid.,* March 10 [23], 1918).

In the village of Tishanka, Bobrov district, there was a bloody clash between the peasants and the sailors of a naval grain-requisitioning detachment. The peasant Soviet also organized resistance to a punitive expedition, ambushed the expeditionary force and wiped out its vanguard of 19 mounted soldiers (*Ibid.,* March 26 [April 8]). The same issue reported the killing of a member of the provincial executive committee, four Red Guards, and a grain accountant in Shlykov district, Perm *gubernia.*

Peasant resistance was particularly stubborn in Tver *gubernia,* which was frequently visited by the requisition units. Thus, *Novaya Zhizn* of July 4 and 5 reported that the peasants of the Staritsky district had killed the commissar of a punitive unit and disarmed the soldiers; that the peasants of the Zalischensky district had tried to disperse the unit which was requisitioning grain; that in the village of Spasskoye the crowd had killed three Red Guards; that in clashes between peasants and requisitioning units in the Maslovsk district five peasants were wounded and disarmed by soldiers

The peasants of the Chmerovsk district offered stubborn resistance to a requisitioning unit. Men from the entire countryside formed themselves into squads armed with rifles and hand grenades. The Red Guards were forced to retreat. The next day they returned with reinforcements, but the peasants had entrenched themselves near the village of Savino, and again put the Red Guards to flight.[10]

Sometimes the peasants tried to rid themselves of their local dictators by purely legal means: Thus, on April 22, in Chembar, in Penza *gubernia,* 200 peasant delegates assembled at a conference. The report of the credentials committee showed at once that the government could not count on a majority, and this was confirmed when the praesidium was elected. Thereupon Red Guards were sent to the conference hall, but the delegates voted against their attendance and they were forced to leave. They were soon back again, however, led by Commissar Shuvaev, who shouted at the peasants, threatening to take away all their bread and punish them as "counter-revolutionaries," "saboteurs," and "bourgeois." The peasants, intimidated, gave in (*Novaya Zhizn,* May 18).

Peasants in certain northern *gubernias* and those living near certain big towns were in a particularly disadvantageous position. Local organs of food distribution repeatedly warned that the central government's food policy would plunge the north into famine, and these warnings were fully borne out. Famine set in and large numbers of peasants left the villages and wandered through the forests, seeking the roads to the richer areas.

Not all the ruined peasants took to the forests. Some of those living near the big towns tried to rob railway cars loaded with grain that passed through. Thus, on May 30, about 300 unarmed hungry local peasants assembled at the Jeshemlya station of the Northern Railway as food train No. 119, bound for Petrograd, was due to arrive. They stopped the train and timidly begged for bread. The Red Guards opened fire and killed and wounded many. Workers and employees of the railway who witnessed the scene protested against the brutality of the Red Guards, some of whom bayoneted the wounded, while others fired at the houses of the railway employees (*Novaya Zhizn*, June 6).

At the Chikhachevo station of the Moscow-Vindava-Rybinsk Railway, a crowd of 400 peasants unlocked two freight cars from a stalled food train and began to unload them. A detachment of Red Guards arrived on the scene and fired a blank round over the heads of the crowd. The crowd dispersed, but the next day it returned, 700 strong, many of the peasants carrying rifles. The papers contained no information on the outcome of this incident (*Novaya Zhizn*, June 20).

By the end of June 1918, peasant resistance became more determined and merged with the civil war, which was then in full swing in the south and east. The peasants bitterly resented the requisitioning of their grain and the ban on free trade in grain; in addition, the introduction of the so-called "barrage" detachments, which effectively prevented any trade or barter between town and country, still further enraged the peasants and made them receptive to the propaganda of the Whites. It is true that the mood of the peasantry often changed abruptly after the arrival of White armies, who attempted to restore the large land-owners to their estates. The several changes of temper on the part of the peasants had a decisive influence on the course of the civil war.

The Government and the Workers

The food shortage in the cities aggravated the discontent of the workers, who already had grounds for disillusion with the Bolshevik regime: the dissolution of the Constituent Assembly, the abolition of the liberties which the cities had enjoyed in the first months of the revolution, disappointment over the Brest-Litovsk capitulation. As the cities came to the very brink of famine, incessant clashes broke out in the factories between the workers and the Communist managers and between the urban populace and the local Soviet administrations. This was the case in Petrograd, Moscow and other industrial centers (such as Tula, Sormovo and Briansk) as well as in many other provincial towns. A partial list of the towns in which disturbances and risings occurred (as given in *Pravda* during June-July, 1918), included: Yaroslavl, Gorodishche (near Kostroma), Murom, Vologda, Tsaritsin, Petrovsk, Arzamas, Tula, Luga, Tashkent, Vyatka, Vitebsk, Archangel, Tyumen (Tomsk province), Orenburg, Rybinsk. To these could be added Kolomna, Vyazniki, Voronezh, Sormovo, Rzhev, Vyshniy Volochok (factories of Ryabushinsky, Prokhorov, Bolotin), Suma (Kharkov province), Soligalich, Roslavl, Irkutsk, Byisk, Saratov, Samara, and hundreds of other towns.

Needless to say, *Pravda* described all these incidents as fomented by the "White Guards," and so on. But in almost every case the conflicts arose either between workers and the dictatorial commissars, or between railwaymen and the narrow-minded Kobozev, the People's Commissar for Transport (Lenin eventually had to remove him). In other instances clashes occurred when townspeople tried to exercise their lawful right (as laid down in the Soviet constitution) to elect a new Soviet in place of an old and unpopular one; such people were dispersed and fired on by military units.

The most frequent conflicts of this type occurred when townspeople or workers attempted to replace Soviets which had formed in the period before Brest-Litovsk, when an overwhelming proportion of the electors were soldiers of the local garrison. After the demobilization the composition of many Soviets was in sharp contrast to the composition of the local populations: workers, peasants, townspeople were now much more numerous than soldiers, yet their representatives still remained a small minority in the local Soviets. Their demands for new elections, however, met with stubborn resistance from the Bolshevik authorities. Where the Bolsheviks were forced to concede new elections, they invariably insisted that only Communists and Left S-R's could be elected to the Soviet—no independents, Mensheviks, or right-wing S-R's.

Where risings occurred in the towns, they were usually the result of a clash between local workers and the Soviet administration. From the enormous mass of reports on such risings, a few will be cited as most typical:[11]

On January 2 (15), 1918 in Minsk, a demonstration of workers and townspeople carrying banners with the inscription "Give us bread!" was fired on and dispersed by soldiers. (*Novaya Zhizn,* February 9 [22]).

On January 14 (27) a general meeting of railway craftsmen, workers and employees of the Tula station, which had assembled to discuss the murder of two railway workers, Soshnikov and Illaryonov, by the Bolshevik Khazarinov, was fired on and dispersed by the Red Guard (*Novaya Zhizn,* January 19 [February 1]).

In mid-February, the discontented citizens of the city of Soligalich (in Kostroma *gubernia*) drove out the unpopular Soviet, beat and arrested some of the most hated and corrupt commissars, elected a provisional new Soviet, and organized a temporary civil guard. On February 21 (March 6) a punitive expedition arrived, with a list of people marked for the firing squad. Fifty-two persons were arrested and taken to prison, where 20 of them were shot the next day. The condemned prisoners were ordered to undress and stand shoulder to shoulder; then they were mowed down by a machine gun. Those who still moved were finished off with bayonets. Relatives were not allowed to remove the bodies for burial; instead, the bodies were loaded on carts and taken to the cemetery. The trail of blood on the snow led the bereaved to the scene of burial. The bodies, dressed only in torn remnants of underwear, were thrown into a single mass grave by laughing and jeering men in army uniform (*Novaya Zhizn,* March 13 [26]).

On April 5 (18) the local Soviet from the town of Byisk, in the Altai mountains of Siberia, which had long been unpopular, enraged the citizens by placing a tax on geese and chickens in the sum of three million roubles. The citizens demanded new elections and sent a delegation to Commissar Bedarev. When he answered mockingly, one of the delegates lost his temper and struck him. Suddenly shots were fired by Commissar Evgenyev and other members of the Soviet. One delegate was killed and four wounded. Evgenyev ran from the house, climbed the bell-tower, and began to ring the alarm to summon the

Red Guard; instead, a crowd of townspeople dragged Evgenyev from the tower and beat both him and another commissar, Fomichenko. According to the reporter, the Red Army soldiers remained neutral in this clash (*Novaya Zhizn*, May 2).

At about the same time, at the other end of Russia, similar events were taking place in Roslavl, near Smolensk. Again the discontent centered around the local Soviet, which had been elected before the demobilization and consisted mainly of soldiers. After the demobilization, the remaining members of the Soviet ordered new elections. But the railway workers, who had hitherto been supporting the Bolsheviks, now cast their votes for the Mensheviks. Thereupon the old Soviet declared the elections illegal on the grounds that the socialists, as opponents of the Soviet government, could not be tolerated. The angry railway workers arrested the old Soviet; and the Red Guards offered no resistance but surrendered, though they had several machine guns and 700 rifles. Soon afterward, troops arrived from the neighboring town, and their commander negotiated a peaceful agreement—no one was to be arrested or punished, the newly elected Soviet was cofirmed in office, consideration would be given to the demand that the Red Guards cease to receive special rations. The satisfied workers peacefully dispersed to their homes, but during the night they were treacherously seized, disarmed and allegedly taken to Moscow. Yet the bodies of some of them were later found buried in the sand; others were recovered by fishermen from the river. In the local hospital, to which the recovered bodies were taken, it was established that the victims had first been tortured and then shot; some had had their eyes gouged out. "The town population is depressed and has lost all interest in the elections. The demobilized soldiers continue to rule in the local Soviet" (*Novaya Zhizn*, May 2).

Between May 3 and May 6 there was a mutiny of new Red Army recruits in the town of Saratov, on the Volga. It started over economic demands, but when the authorities refused these, the discontented Red Army men staged a mutiny in which they made political demands as well ("the restoration of democratic organizations, new elections to the Soviet, surrender of all power to a Provisional Executive Committee composed of representatives from all socialist parties," etc.). A two-day battle followed, with machine guns and artillery. The supporters of the Soviet, finding themselves outnumbered, pretended to accept the demands while they waited for reinforcements. These entered the town by stealth, seized the artillery, and dealt brutally with the "victors." The town was once again in the hands of the Bolsheviks (*Novaya Zhizn*, May 16).

At the beginning of June the authorities dissolved the local Soviet in Tambov after it had demanded the restoration of the Constituent Assembly. This action was carried out with the help of new recruits who had been drafted under a recent decree of mobilization.

Toward the end of June, hostility to the Soviets in the industrial center of Oziory, near Moscow, had reached such a pitch that 8,000 workers surrounded the building of the local Soviet and demanded its resignation. Inside the building at the time were three members of the Executive Committee, eight Red Army soldiers, and six militiamen. The members of the Executive Committee vainly appealed to the workers to disperse peacefully, but the workers refused to go. Thereupon the militiamen and soldiers fired into the crowd, wounding several. Former soldiers among the workers then fetched rifles and hand grenades and launched an attack on the besieged Soviet, killing two and wounding four. When the men still refused to surrender, the crowd set fire to the building. Meanwhile, a train carrying reinforcements had been summoned by telephone and was now approaching the station. The workers failed to destroy the railway tracks in time, and the troops were able to rescue the Soviet. The press did not report the number of arrested, killed, or wounded (*Nashe Slovo,* July 2).[12]

As the summer progressed, an increasing number of reports in the Soviet newspapers (all the others had been closed down on July 6-8) described risings in all parts of Russia, variously attributed to the "White Guards," *kulaks*, "counter-revolutionaries," and "conspirators." It is not always easy to determine from these reports how the disturbances had started. Nevertheless, precise information is available with respect to some towns, and this invariably shows the large part played by discontented industrial workers, railwaymen, poor townspeople, and other segments of the population that had nothing whatever to do with counter-revolution or foreign intervention. Sometimes, indeed, the accumulated popular resentment was actively exploited by anti-Bolshevik groups, notably the Union for the Defense of the

Fatherland and the Revolution, and the Union for the Rebirth of Russia. But these organizations, in the first place, were democratic and not counter-revolutionary—above all, they were too insignificant themselves to initiate risings; the risings sprang from the unrelenting struggle between the government on the one hand and the workers and peasants on the other.

The rising of June 6 in Yaroslavl is a typical example. It followed a fierce and prolonged struggle between the local workers and the Bolsheviks. In October 1917, the Yaroslavl Soviet, thanks to the vote of the soldiers, was dominated by Bolsheviks and Left S-R's, although the Mensheviks were strong among the workers. After the demobilization in February, the Mensheviks pressed for new elections on the grounds that the Soviet should reflect the real situation among the local workers. The Bolshevik authorities arrested many Mensheviks and tried them on a charge of "counter-revolutionary agitation against the Soviet government." During the trial, the court was packed with numerous delegations from the factories, furiously protesting the accusation. The court finally had to acquit the accused after the proceedings had developed into a public denunciation of Bolshevik policy. Nor could the Bolsheviks any longer prevent new elections, which resulted in giving 47 seats to the Mensheviks, 13 to the S-R's, and 38 to the Bolsheviks and Left S-R's. The new Soviet was installed on April 9. The Bolsheviks immediately demanded that the 23 members of the old Executive Committee for the province (all Bolsheviks and Left S-R's) be co-opted. When the Mensheviks rejected this demand, the Soviet was dissolved by force, and the town was left without a legitimate local government. In practice, the old Executive Committee and Revolutionary Committee continued to rule even though the majority of the workers had clearly expressed their lack of confidence. Discontent became more pronounced as the food situation worsened. There was a strike at the oil refinery where the bread ration fell to a quarter-pound a day. Such were the local conditions in which the right S-R, Boris Savinkov, of the Committee for the Defense of the Fatherland and the Revolution, and his emissary Colonel Perkhurov, succeeded in organizing the uprising of June 6, in which some workers joined. The revolt was suppressed after two weeks of shelling by government troops.[13]

With some variations this pattern was characteristic of most of the risings of that period—such as those in Kolomna, Rybinsk, Vetluga, in the villages of Matrenka, Dryazgi, in Tallinsk-Chemlyk, in the Gruzin district of the Novgorod *gubernia,* in the village of Stolbishche (Sergachov district), in Ligov, Volsk (Saratov *gubernia*), Zhizdra, Murom, in the *gubernia* of Cherkask, Vladimir, and Novgorod in the Volga district, and in hundreds of other towns, districts and villages (*Pravda,* July 16-25, 1918).

The Petrograd Workers

The change in the attitude of the workers in the large factories after December 1917 was most striking in Petrograd, where the food shortage had an especially severe effect. The very workers who before October had been intoxicated by Bolshevik slogans now began to manifest an often aggressive disillusionment. Thus, the workers of the cannon plant, who had been regularly paying a voluntary 2 per cent of their wages to the Petrograd Soviet, voted to discontinue the contribution (*Nash Vek,* December 9 [21], 1917). The workers of the 4th workshop of the Trubochny plant showed such rebellious spirit that the Soviet authorities decided to arrest their food distribution committee and the Soviet of Foremen elected by the workers. At about the same time the workers' representatives in the Obukhov plant, Kuvaghin and Kuzmin, were also arrested.[14]

In January 1918, workers at a general meeting in the Siemens and Schuckert works demanded the immediate recall of their comrades from the Red Guard. The Red Guards instead arrested some of the leaders of the workers, among them the S-R, Pavlov, which led to another general meeting. Thereupon, twenty-five armed Red Guards arrived and, after warning the Bolsheviks and the left S-R's to leave, dispersed the remaining workers by force. The chairman was arrested at the point of a revolver. This was followed by systematic arrests of S-R's—some of whom, however, were able to escape (*Novaya Zhizn,* January 17 [30], 1918).

The behavior of the Red Guards, who, together with the Communist cells, were becoming the real rulers of the factories, aroused many protests from the workers. They resented the Red Guards' high-handed disregard of their own representatives as well as the high rations and other special privileges enjoyed by the Guards (a Guard's bread ration was often fixed at one and a half pounds, as against a quarter of a pound for others). But the workers also understood the broader implications of government policy and they protested against the anti-peasant "crusade" carried out by the government with forces recruited from the working class. A typical resolution was passed by the workers of the Trubochny plant, who opposed the dispatch of the Red Guards to the countryside and expressed their disgust in these words: "Go away and stay away—we have no use for people like you."[15] A meeting of 5,000 workers of the Neva shipbuilding works condemned the Bolshevik policy of trying to turn workers into policemen and loosing them upon the "comrade peasants."[16] Contempt for the Red Guard became so strong that some Guards asked to be dismissed from their units and returned to their work; this happened at the Retchkin plant and other plants in the Neva, Narva and Vyborg districts of Petrograd.[17] On all sides there was a clamor for new elections to the local Soviets; instead the government issued a decree giving it the option of not ordering new elections in the event of the Soviets' dissolution. With this decree, Soviet democracy became wholly fictional.[18]

In February 1918, the interruption of the Brest-Litovsk talks, the threat of a new German advance, and the necessity of evacuating the factories brought about a temporary standstill in the internal struggle. But after the ratification of the Brest-Litovsk treaty, the struggle flared up once again, and the dictatorship increasingly resorted to terror. The most vivid manifestation of this terror was the brutal murder in a Petrograd hospital of the former progressive Kadet deputies, Shingarev and Kokoshkin, on January 7 (20), 1918. The group of sailors who perpetrated this outrage were never indentified, let alone punished, despite the efforts of the Commissar for Justice, the Left S-R, Steinberg, and despite all sorts of appeals to Lenin. The murder came only two days after the firing on the demonstration for the Constituent Assembly, and from then on the capital was in the grip of a terror which was only thinly veiled. People were shot in the streets, armed bands entered and searched private houses and printing shops. In reply to protests in the few surviving newspapers or to complaints of notables like Maxim Gorki,[19] Lenin simply shrugged his shoulders. At the beginning of March, a band of Red Guards stopped a few young men in the street; among them were the four Ganlez brothers, French citizens who had voluntarily joined the Russian army. Their behavior was perfectly peaceful and they carried no arms, but they were shot on the spot. This pointless murder, too, caused great indignation. A public meeting of the Military Medical Academy on March 6 (19), addressed by many prominent personalities, protested strongly; but the murderers were never found.

Amid this atmosphere of violence the food situation continued to deteriorate, and chronic malnutrition led to epidemics in Petrograd. In early February the newspapers reported that 370 patients suffering from typhus and over 200 suffering from recurrent typhoid fever were in the Botkin Hospital; 120 typhus cases were in the Semenov Hospital, and a great number of others in the Obukhov Hospital. The normal incidence of typhus in Petrograd was not above 70 cases a year (*Novaya Zhizn,* January 26 [February 8]).

The economic position of the printing workers was particularly desperate because almost all newspapers had been closed. A meeting of the printers in the Chiniselli Circus witnessed a fierce clash between the Menshevik, Mark Kefali, and the Bolsheviks (*Novaya Zhizn,* March 13 [26]).

Such was then the atmosphere at the beginning of April, when the workers of the giant Putilov works began discussing their possible participation in the May Day celebration (in Russia, using the old-style calendar, this took place on April 18). The predominant opinion was, that since power was now allegedly held by the workers, the best way to celebrate would be to stay home; but if there was to be a demonstration, then "the banners should carry the inscription: 'Give us bread and work; and down with the Brest-Litovsk' " (*Novaya Zhizn,* April 6 [19]). Zinoviev admitted to the Petrograd Soviet on April 17 (30) that the Putilov workers had refused to celebrate May Day, but added that elections were being held at the works at that very moment and that the Bolsheviks were winning. He disputed the Menshevik statement that 5,000 Putilov workers had decided to boycott the official demonstration (*Novaya Zhizn,* April 18 [May 1]).

How little Zinoviev's words reflected the true situation became obvious from further developments. On May 8 (21), a general meeting of Putilov workers passed a decidedly anti-Bolshevik resolution, which was published in almost all the remaining non-Bolshevik newspapers. Thereupon the administration called another meeting for May 9 (22), at which a great number of Red Guards turned up. The result was a pro-Bolshevik resolution. The following day, May 10 (23), 10,000 workers (out of a total of just under 14,000 still employed at the Putilov works[20]) held a protest meeting and decided (1) to determine the real opinion of the workers by a secret ballot on both resolutions under supervision of a special commission, and (2) to elect two delegates from each of the workshops to investigate the stocks of food available in town. In addition the following resolution was accepted, with only two men voting against and 10 abstaining:

> 1. We, the workers of the Putilov Works and Docks, wish to protest against the resolution proposed by Volodarsky and passed on May 9 (22), and declare that it was passed not by the workers but by the Red Guards—with their one-and-a-half pounds of bread a day—who came to our meeting.
>
> 2. Let it be known once again that the Bolsheviks express not the opinion of the starving working class but that of the Red Guards by whose bayonets they are supported.
>
> 3. We reaffirm that the resolution passed by us on May 8 and reported in all the newspapers is the only true expression of our opinion.

Meanwhile, in Kolpino on May 9, women waiting in a bread queu became restless and demanded to see the chairman of the local food office. The town square was soon crowded with excited people, and armed Red Guards were sent to disperse them. The Guards were using rifle butts on the crowd when a boy in the crowd blew a whistle. The assistant commander of the Guards, Toropilov, fired a revolver shot and the Guards followed with a volley from their rifles. The boy was wounded; the crowd fled, leaving dead and wounded behind. When the workers tried to get to the square, they were stopped by the Red Guards. Then they held a mass meeting at which they passed a resolution protesting against the shooting and demanding immediate new elections to the local Soviet. They also sent a delegation to inform the

Petrograd workers of the outrages in Kolpino. When the workers returned home after this meeting they were fired on; one was killed and several wounded. During the night there were house searches and arrests—the authorities had even summoned some cavalry units from Petrograd to help them. The news of the brutal repression at Kolpino roused further anger in Petrograd. Protest meetings were held at all of the industrial plants without exception; delegations were sent to Kolpino to investigate and there were demands for the punishment of those responsible.[21]

Almost at the same time, in Sestroretsk, where there was a large munitions plant, workers attacked the Soviet, beat up some of its members and entered the houses of others, apparently in search of food. The authorities retaliated with numerous arrests and many workers were tried on the charge of "inciting to assault on members of the Soviet." For a long time the town remained in a state of high excitement, and the Petrograd workers were greatly concerned over the events at Sestroretsk.

The food situation in Petrograd continued to deteriorate rapidly. On April 27 (May 10), Lenin and the Commissar for Food Supplies, Tsuriupa, appealed to the whole country. In a most exalted tone, the appeal described the desperate plight of Red Petrograd—on the brink of famine and starvation, the workers having only potatoes and bran to eat—and asked for immediate help: "The situation can be saved only if all Soviet organizations take immediate steps . . . to ensure the dispatch of food trains." However, the appeals were of little use. The bread ration was reduced from 4 to 2 ounces at the end of May, which stirred the Petrograd workers to further resentment. A new decree announcing another reduction in the bread ration for the general public, together with an increase of 2 ounces in the ration for workers still employed in the factories, was received badly by its beneficiaries. In the Pahl plant, the factories of the Neva district, the Obukhov works, the Maxwell plant, the workshops of the Nikolaevsky railway, the Siemens and Schuckert works, the Retchkin plant, the tramway depot of Vassily Island, the City Electric Station—everywhere the workers passed resolutions against "supplementary rations at the cost of those doomed to die of starvation." The workers of the Skorochod plant, where the Bolsheviks were supposed to be strong, were even prepared to stage a one-day protest strike (*Novaya Zhizn,* of May 17-18 [30-31]).

Opposition to the government was extremely strong at the Thornton textile plant, where the dictatorial manners of the commissars had led to very strained relations with the workers. Thus, at a general meeting on May 15(28), Commissar Medovikov, a left S-R, brandished a revolver while he was trying to dissuade the workers from going on strike (on another occasion, he had threatened the workers with a hand grenade). A few days later, Zhukov, a worker who had taken the revolver away from Medovikov, was arrested together with the captain of the company's steamer, Dybov, who had formerly served on a torpedo boat. Dybov's wife immediately carried this information to the sailors of the torpedo boat on which he had served. The sailors got up steam, readied their guns and moved along the Neva to the Red headquarters. A group of sailors armed with rifles disembarked and demanded the immediate release of the prisoners. The demand was complied with (*Novaya Zhizn,* May 17-18 [30-31]).

The Assembly of Factory Representatives

The opposition of the Petrograd workers to the Soviet government grew from such spontaneous beginnings as these into an authentic movement with an official organization at its head, called the Assembly of Factory Representatives. This body openly proclaimed its existence and its activities were fully reported in the socialist press—notably in the papers published by unemployed members of the Printer's Union on Saturdays and Sundays and called *Petrograd's Evening* and *Petrograd's Morning* (later a parallel edition began to appear in Moscow under the name *Moscow's Evening* and *Moscow's Morning*).

Judging from the newspaper reports, regular meetings of the Assembly of Factory Representatives began to be held about the middle of March, 1918. The nucleus of the Assembly, which already existed in January, consisted of such outstanding Petrograd labor leaders as the old Mensheviks, Alexander Smirnov and K. Gvozdev, of the metal workers; M. Kefali, leader of the printing workers; the S-R, E. Berg, leader of the Putilov workers; F. Yudin, originally a baker and later a prominent labor writer; I. Shapakovsky and V. Borisenko;

and the Menshevik intellectuals, B. Batursky, B. Bogdanov, G. Denike and A. Dubois.[22]

The movement grew until soon it embraced practically every factory of any size in the Petrograd area and the Petrograd Soviet was forced to reckon seriously with it.

The chairman of the "Northern Commune,"[23] Zinoviev, tried to capture the movement for the Soviets. He planned a series of district conferences of workers convened by the district Soviets, that is, the Bolsheviks; but the invitations to these conferences were to come from workers of various factories in the districts concerned.[24] One such experiment was carried out in the Rozhdestvensky district, where the streets were plastered with appeals from the Petrograd Soviet to come to a conference at the local Soviet—a conference at which the workers could "unite and without delay discuss their situation and try to find means of protecting themselves against future calamities so as to be better able to survive the coming tribulations."[25] This conference was held and actually lasted five days.

On the first day, the internationalist Menshevik, Gorin, was elected chairman; two Left S-R's, one internationalist Menshevik, one S-R, one Anarchist and one Maximalist were elected to the praesidium. At its first session the conference decided to admit on equal terms to all discussions both a representative of the Petrograd Soviet and a representative of the "Assembly of Factory Representatives." The first item on the agenda was the activities of the Petrograd Soviet, which were criticized with brutal frankness. Two resolutions were offered. One, by the Bolsheviks and the Left S-R's, admitted defects in the work of the Soviet and proposed that, where the workers considered it necessary, they should replace their delegates to the Soviet by new men—with reservation that only supporters of the Soviet government should be elected. The second resolution, proposed by the Mensheviks, accused the Soviet of having lost touch with the masses and insisted on new elections—without any reservations with regard to the candidates.

The balance of opinion at this point was unfavorable to the Bolsheviks, but at the last moment before voting, the credentials' committee suddenly reported that a big thread manufacturing factory[26]—a Bolshevik stronghold—had sent 32 delegates instead of the 11 allotted to them. The Bolsheviks with support from the Left S-R's and a few non-party delegates, insisted that all 32 be confirmed. And this enabled the Bolshevik resolution to be passed by 70 votes to 53.[27] Pleased with this victory, the Bolsheviks repeated the trick with two other factories in which they commanded support: the cotton mill and the tramway depot were now accorded extra delegates. Then they voted down the chairman, Gorin, and elected a Bolshevik in his place.

Yet this episode, although it gave the Bolsheviks an inflated majority at the conference, persuaded many anti-Bolshevik workers that the Soviet government would stoop to any deceit in order to retain power. The conference itself confirmed the depressing state of affairs among the working class. It appeared that, with the exception of the thread plant (which still had 14 million roubles worth of raw material and equipment left behind by the former British owners), most factories were slowing down, and great masses were being thrown out of work. Factory delegates declared: "We were promised the dictatorship of the proletariat—it was a lie; we were penniless and so we still are; nobody cares about the unemployed; we are fed on paper decrees." The printers' delegates spoke of terrible unemployment since the closing of the press and declared that they had been instructed to demand freedom of the press. The delegate from the state printshops complained that the government did not pay the printers regularly. The delegate from the Molodstov factory, a Left S-R, announced that some 500 workers dismissed from his factory demanded secure employment and cheap food. The delegate from the tramway depot of the Rozhdestvensky district reported that the workers were depressed. They had been promised a punctual opening of the Constituent Assembly, but instead the Assembly had been dissolved. They had been promised peace but were now confronted with war; they had been promised bread but got famine instead; the workers were disillusioned; there was no freedom; one party ruled over them all—"our only hope," concluded the speaker, "lies in the Constituent Assembly."

The delegate from a cork factory said that of the usual 500 workers in his factory only 40 were still working; the families of the unemployed cried for help, but the response they got from the "government of the workers" was no different from what they used to get from Kerensky's government. The authorities took no steps to provide fuel, and the factory would soon stop to work altogether. The delegate of the "Helios" electric-power station told the conference that when the electricity workers demanded a wage increase from the new "workers' " city council they were told: "Give us, the new (Bolshevik) city council, your recognition and you will get the increase." So the workers had recognized the council for the sake of the wage increase. However, during the German advance, when they were told that their station was to be blown up, they replied: "Though we have given your city council our recognition and though you are proud of your pretty government of workers and peasants, this time we are going to disobey you." And the workers had organized their own armed guard to prevent it.[28]

The Moscow worker, Chirkin, reported on the feelings among the workers in greater Moscow. He said that, though conditions were not yet ripe for the organization of anything like the Petrograd Assembly of Factory Representatives, the mood of the workers was changing rapidly. In the Prokhorov works, the women workers complained during an address by Trotsky that their brothers and sons, who had been sent to the fertile regions to collect bread, had been charged with speculation and shot. Trotsky replied that the people's commissars, too, had to go short on food. The women, enraged, shouted: "You lie, it's not true, you lie," and would not let him finish.

In Kolomna, Sormovo and Nizhny Novgorod, Chirkin said that the opposition to the Bolsheviks was felt in the large factories, particularly during the days of the German advance. Mammoth meetings were then held at the Sormovo works which passed anti-Bolshevik resolutions protesting against Soviet terror and demanding reconvening of the Constituent Assembly. After these meetings several workers (Mensheviks and S-R's) were arrested, but the others demanded their release; and when the Bolsheviks hesitated, the session of the Soviet was swamped by a huge mass of workers many thousand strong. The prisoners were set free. Chirkin also reported that the idea of new free elections to the Soviets had won ground in Ekaterinoslav, Kharkov and several other provincial towns, but that the Bolshevik government would doubtless go to any lengths now to prevent new elections. Chirkin told how he himself had been arrested and dragged through the Bolshevik prisons when he tried to speak at the workers' meeting at the Kolomna works.[29]

After the Rozhdestvensky district conferences, the Bolsheviks ceased to experiment with free conferences of workers. The conference arranged for the Vasilyevsky Ostrov district, for which the delegates had already been elected and assembled, was postponed by an order from Zinoviev and Commissar Lashevich "until a more propitious moment . . . in view of the grave danger to Petrograd." The order was issued on April 24th, when there was no danger to Petrograd at all—except that the preliminary counts showed that there was no Bolshevik majority. The assembled delegates were highly indignant.[30]

It appeared that a sharp conflict had developed with the Red Guards, who demanded that their pay should be raised to 300 roubles, and the Soviet authorities, who refused. It also appeared (mainly from the speeches of Mensheviks and S-R's) that during the elections to the conference several fraudulent returns had been made—notably at the Siemens-Halske works, where the workers had even passed a resolution of protest. But the conference was cancelled, and the Bolsheviks made no further attempts along these lines. Meanwhile, the Assembly of Factory Representatives was becoming more and more openly political in character. Whereas at first it had limited its scope to protests against individual acts of Soviet terrorism, against unlawful arrests and the closing down of newspapers, by May and even more by June 1918 it had acquired a political character which was very definitely anti-Bolshevik.

The Petrograd workers were convinced that no protests, resolutions or appeals would make the Bolshevik government modify its dictatorial policy; gradually they began to feel more and more strongly that the Soviet of People's Commissars had to resign and that the Constituent Assembly would have to be reconvened for the purpose of establishing a representative government. In some factories the old "Vikzhel" idea of an all-socialist government was revived. Countless meetings now demanded the reconvening of the Constituent Assembly, the reorganization of the government, the abolition of the dictatorship, and an end to the strangling of the press and the coercion of the workers.

Now that branches of the Assembly of Factory Representatives were established in Petrograd and Moscow, various political leaders began to think of extending the organization to the whole country. Many

Mensheviks (notably Abramovitch and Alexander Smirnov) brought this new thought into relation with Paul Axelrod's old idea of a workers' congress. Their argument ran as follows: the Russian working class was at a crossroads; one part of it had followed the Bolsheviks and was helping them to establish a minority dictatorship over the rest of the huge Russian people, while the other part was firmly opposed. The Bolsheviks were trying to settle this difference of opinion by acts of terror and civil war. It was imperative to force the Bolsheviks to heed the voice of the working class; and to this end a freely elected congress should be called, representative of all working class groups and parties, which would face up to all the enormous problems confronting the country. All groups taking part in the congress would have to agree that the freely expressed decisions of the working class would be binding on majority and minority. Even the preparations for such a congress would offer the opportunity to clarify the ideas of the working class in an atmosphere of free discussion. Accordingly, the Assembly decided to send emissaries to the provinces to organize local assemblies which would later fuse into district conferences and ultimately—it was hoped—into a large All-Russian Congress.

At the same time, the leaders of the Petrograd Assembly increasingly favored the idea of a one-day political strike as a gesture of working class protest. This plan so captivated the leaders of the Assembly that, once having fixed the strike for July 2nd, they used their influence to stop the small, local strikes which at the beginning of June had involved the greater part of Petrograd workers. (There had been strikes in the Maxwell, Pahl and Thornton factories, at the locomotive and at the railway buildings works of the Nikolaevsky railway, at the Vargunin factory, the Neva shipbuilding yard, the electricity section of the Putilov works and at the Obukhov works.)[31] Within the Assembly of Factory Representatives one group, headed by Alexander Smirnov, felt that the existing spontaneous strike-movement should be supported and enlarged to the size of a general strike. But others, particularly F. Izmaylov, opposed this plan because they felt that, under the conditions of Bolshevik terror and propaganda, a strike needed to be thoroughly organized if it were to succeed. At the preliminary voting on this subject, a huge majority of the factory representatives cast their votes in favor of a well-organized strike. Many of them said that the factories they represented were ready to down their tools at the first call of the Assembly.[32]

In response to these plans, the Bolsheviks began to concentrate Red Guard units in the Neva district, where the ferment among workers was especially strong. At the strike date they mobilized all their available armed forces (including railway guards), alerted all workers who were still faithful to them and deployed their propaganda to the full. Thus, the district Soviet ordered the factory committee of the Pahl works to put up posters no later than 6 a.m., July 2, with the inscription: "The White Guards are on strike" and "Long live the Soviet government." Machine guns were placed at the gates of the Skorokhod shoe factory, and similar measures were taken at other factories.[33]

Despite these preventive measures, many factories did indeed come out on strike: the Obukhov works, the Neva shipbuilding yard (where of a total of several thousand workers only 200 Bolsheviks stayed at work), the Izhora factory in Kolpino, the Pahl factory (despite the posters), a great number of printing plants, and the tobacco factories of Kolobov, Bobrov, Shaposhnikov, Shapovalov.[34] Nevertheless, the strike as a whole was not a great success. At the last moment many workers hesitated, some because they feared that a "third party" ("the Whites") would make capital out of a quarrel between the Bolsheviks and the industrial workers, and others because they were not yet ready to fight the Bolsheviks actively. A number of economic and practical reasons also deterred various workers from striking. Finally, it is possible that individual acts of terrorism against Bolshevik leaders, such as the murder on June 20th of the popular Bolshevik, Volodarsky, had had a certain psychological effect.

After the partial defeat of July 2nd, the Petrograd Assembly of Factory Representatives concentrated on helping Moscow, Sormovo, Tula and other industrial towns of central Russia to organize assemblies on the Petrograd pattern. The first delegation of Petrograd workers left for Moscow at the beginning of June. It included the representatives from the Setroretsk factory, Krakovsky and the workers Kuznetsov and Venderovich, who were warmly received by their fellow workers in Moscow and succeeded in organizing several successful meetings in the factories. From the provinces, too, there was a lively response—workers in Briansk, Maltsevo, Kolomna, Sormovo, Tula and Mytishche (a suburb of Moscow) eagerly accepted the Petrograd challenge, elected delegates to maintain contact, and promised every support.

A dramatic episode crowned the visit of the Petrograd delegates to the towns of Oziory and Kolomna: When the delegates went to have informal talks with the Oziory trade-union council, militiamen followed them into the trade-union building, asked for their papers, and interrogated them. They were then accused of distributing seditious literature, engaging in anti-Soviet agitation, and taken away to prison. But as soon as the news spread, the local workers downed their tools and flocked to the Soviet where the prisoners were being held. Three times the militia vainly attempted to disperse the crowd by firing shots into the air. Finally, hand grenades were thrown into the crowd, but still to no avail—a group of workers, armed with heavy picks, climbed to the second floor of the Soviet, broke the bars in the window of the delegates' cell and set them free. The delegates made good their escape by walking to the railway station at Kashira, where they boarded a train for Moscow. From the window of their compartment they could see a great cloud of smoke rising above Oziory; later they learned that the enraged crowd had set fire to the Soviet building. The army units that had been summoned to the scene arrived too late to help, for the railway workers in Kolomna had deliberately delayed their train.[35]

When the Petrograd delegates, Krakovsky and Kuznetsov, were finally arrested in Moscow, there were protests from workers of the Alexander railway, the Sytin printing works, the Muir-Meriles department store, the Moscow-Kazan railway, the Siemens works and other plants.[36] A delegation of Moscow workers went to the VTsIK, which was in session at the time, and demanded an opportunity to protest against the arrests. But the VTsIK refused to see the delegation. Martov rose to object against the "workers' " own parliament refusing to receive a delegation from the workers. To this, Sverdlov replied that the people in question had been arrested not as workers but as members of a political party.[37]

Obviously the Bolshevik government was no longer prepared to tolerate the Assembly of Factory Representatives. Nevertheless, the organizers continued with their preparations for the first of the series of workers' conferences, which was to be held on July 20. Neither the arrest of the 56 members of the Moscow Assembly of Factory Representatives[38] nor the failure of the Petrograd strike on July 2nd deterred the organizers who realized that if this last appeal to the workers themselves were abandoned, there would be no alternative but to take sides in a civil war. But socialists of all shades were unanimous in abhorring civil war as a disaster to the revolution, whoever might be victorious.

All socialist parties, including the Bolsheviks, were officially invited to send delegates to the conference. The Moscow newspapers that were still appearing published an unofficial announcement, giving the time and place of the conference—the building of the Moscow co-operative societies on Arbat Street.

The conference opened on the appointed day, July 20, with 150 participants, including delegates from the Petrograd Assembly, numerous Moscow factories, Tula, Viazma, Sormovo, Briansk, Kolomna and Jaroslavl, among others. Raphael Abramovitch was elected chairman. But the Bolsheviks had sent no delegates, a sign that the experience would be short-lived.

The first day of the conference was given over to local reports, which taken together, showed revulsion from the Bolsheviks and lack of confidence in their promises and plans. A party that had been so consistently wrong, both internationally and domestically, was clearly unfit to lead the working class; in particular, its basic conception of an imminent and total socialist revolution had been proved, by events abroad and by the attitude of the peasantry at home, to be a fantasy. The delegates' reports on the situation in their factories and localities strengthened the conviction that to prolong the existing situation would lead to more uprisings by peasants and workers against the Soviet regime (as had happened in Yaroslavl, Rybinsk and other places) and finally to social collapse.

The political debates were to begin at the afternoon session of the following day, July 21, but at noon that day the staircase and the corridors of the building on Arbat Street suddenly echoed with the clatter of arms and shouts of "Hands up! Surrender arms!" The doors of the conference hall flew open and an armed unit of the Cheka burst in. The delegates, frozen in their seats, watched silently as the Cheka men, revolvers drawn, searched the hall and the individual delegates for arms, and confiscated all papers. This done, all present were herded into trucks and driven through the busy Moscow streets to the prison in the Lubyanka. In the prison they were interrogated singly and in groups by a young Cheka officer with a huge revolver on the desk in front of him. All were accused of plotting against the Soviet government and threatened with the death penalty.[39]

After some hesitation the Bolsheviks decided to bring the prisoners to trial before the Supreme Revolutionary Tribunal on a charge of participation in an armed plot to overthrow the Soviet government. Krylenko was appointed public prosecutor in the case. But no preliminary investigation was carried out and no proper charge was brought against the accused, who continued to be kept in prison. After the attempted assassination of Lenin by Fanny Kaplan in August 1918 and the wave of Red terror which followed, it appeared that the members of the workers' conference might be shot without trial. At least one of the accused, Abramovitch, received late one night at the end of September an unexpected visit from the Bolshevik Ryazanov, who happened to be a friend of his family. Ryazanov had brought Abramovitch's wife with him so that she should say goodbye to her husband before his execution. This, Ryazanov said, had been definitely decided on—even though one part of the Bolshevik Central Committee was much opposed to this kind of shooting and a special meeting to discuss the fate of the workers' conference had been called for that very evening. A few anxious days followed, until at last Ryazanov sent news that the execution had been canceled.[40]

Gradually the delegates were set free; the most prominent among them—Alexander Troyanovsky, Raphael Abramovitch, Victor Alter, George Denike, Alexander Smirnov, M. Kefali (Kammermacher) and E. Berg—were released after the November 1918 revolution in Germany, which was followed in Russia by a relaxation of terror. For the Bolsheviks were hopeful that the German revolution would spread until it transformed the entire world situation.

[1] *Novaya Zhizn*, No. 178, November 1917.

[2] *Minutes of the Central Committee*, p. 200.

[3] *Minutes of the Central Committee*, No. 44.

[4] E. H. Carr, *History of Soviet Russia*, Vol. III, p. 40.

[5] Kars and Ardagan were immediately occupied by the Turks, but Batum escaped

Turkish occupation owing to a separate agreement between the government of then independent Georgia and the German Commander, General von Lossow. By this agreement, Batum was occupied by German military units formed from German prisoners of war living in the town. This arrangement prevented Turkish troops from entering.

[6] George F. Kennan, *Russia Leaves the War*, pp. 372-376.

[7] According to the *Minutes of the Second Trade Union Congress* (State Publishing House, Moscow, 1921, p. 169), 7,200 workers from Petrograd and about 7,000 from Moscow took part in this operation.

[8] Kostelovskaya, *op. cit*. Following the August 1918 decree authorizing all collective food-supplying agencies or factory committees to send grain-collecting groups to the villages, 30,000 persons rushed to the countryside. Half came back empty-handed, for instance, in Moscow and Voznesensk. *Ibid*., p. 174.

[9] In January 1918, the Soviet government abolished the old-style Russian Calendar and introduced the European style.

[10] *Nashe Slovo,* July 4; *Svobodnaya Zhizn,* July 5. Quoted from James Bunyan, *Intervention, Civil War, and Communism in Russia,* Baltimore, Johns Hopkins Press, 1936, pp. 158-69.

[11] It is worth reflecting that in some of the incidents in which authentic right-wingers did take part, workers were driven by desperation to side with former officers against their own government as the only way of defending their most elementary rights.

[12] Quoted from Bunyan, *op. cit*., pp. 164-65.

[13] For full details of the Yaroslavl rising, see the unpublished work by B. I. Nikolaevsky, *The Menshevik Party in the Period December 1917 to July 1918*, pp. 33-37; also the newspapers *Novaya Zhizn, Pravda, Izvestia,* etc., for June-July, 1918.

[14] "The Logic of Terror," *Novaya Zhizn*, December 16 (29), 1917.

[15] *Nash Vek*, No. 15, December 1917.

[16] *Novaya Zhizn,* May 18 (31), 1918.

[17] *Ibid.*

[18] N. Sukhanov, "The Soviet Government on the Position of the Working Class," *Novaya Zhizn,* May 29 (June 11), 1918.

[19] In *Novaya Zhizn* for March 4 (17) Gorki wrote: ". . . innocent and honest men, Shingarev and Kokoshkin, are killed, but our government has neither the strength nor the integrity to bring the murderers to trial . . . all integrity is dead . . ."

[20] *Novaya Zhizn,* March 9 (22), May 11, 1918.

[21] *Novaya Zhizn,* May 12, 13, 14, 15, 16, 21, 26, 28, 30, June 1, 2 (new style).

[22] Some relevant data can be found in P. Garvi, *The Trade Unions in Russia.* (New York, 1958) and in the unpublished work by G. Aronson, *The Turning Point: A Contribution to the Analysis of the Tendencies in the Working Class in the First Half of 1918.*

[23] This was the somewhat pompous name at that time for greater Petrograd.

[24] According to official instructions "each district Soviet, upon receiving the information about the free district conference, should publish a detailed address to all the workers of the district on the aims of the conference 5 days before the election of the delegates . . . and should elect an organizational committee, composed of representatives of *all* political groups represented in the Soviet, for the organization of elections and the convening of the conference" (*Novaya Zhizn* of April 19th, 1918).

[25] *Novaya Zhizn* of March 8th (21st), 1918.

[26] *Nitochnaya Manoufactourah* in Petrograd.

[27] *Novaya Zhizn* of March 13th (26th), 1918.

[28] *Novaya Zhizn* of March 26, 1918.

[29] *Novaya Zhizn* of March 29th, 1918.

[30] *Novaya Zhizn* of April 26th, 1918.

[31] *Novaya Zhizn* of May 18th, June 2nd, 5th and 23rd.

[32] *Novaya Zhizn* of May 31st, June 2nd and 23rd.

[33] *Novaya Zhizn* of July 5th.

[34] *Ibid.*, July 3rd and 5th.
[35] *Novaya Zhizn,* June 12, 1918.
[36] *Ibid.*, June 11, 1918.
[37] *Ibid.*, June 16, 1918.
[38] *Novaya Zhizn* of June 26, 1918.
[39] A few days after these arrests, *Pravda* and *Izvestia* published mocking notices about the "conference of the workers" led by such "workers" as Abramovitch. One article described how one of the women delegates was found to be wearing many jewels (!). But nowhere in the Soviet press was there any information about the real aims of the conference or the participation of the workers. Even the opening date was given wrongly —July 23 instead of July 20. Nor were the subsequent closing of the case and the release of the prisoners ever reported.
[40] R. A. Abramovitch, *Memoirs,* Vol. II, pp. 234-255.

CHAPTER 7

The Civil War

When Lenin took power in November 1917, neither the western Allies, nor the Germans, nor the Bolsheviks foresaw that the world war would end a year later in an Allied victory. The collapse of the eastern front led the German High Command to believe it could defeat the western Allies before United States forces could be brought into effective action. As General Fuller has described the situation, "the British were bled white, the French were morally exhausted, the Italians nearly out of the war, and the Americans were not yet sufficiently involved to make good a fraction of the enormous losses sustained." After the dismissal of Chancellor Bethmann-Hollweg, who favored negotiations for a compromise peace, Ludendorff became *de facto* dictator of a Germany bent on continuing the war even over the opposition of Austria.

Although, after the abortive Russian offensive in June 1917, the Allies could no longer rely on active help from Russia, as long as she remained in the war, she pinned down considerable German forces. The Brest-Litovsk Treaty deprived them of this advantage, and threatened other complications as well. For one thing, Rumania was isolated when contact with the Russian forces was disrupted. Britain's position on the Turkish front would be jeopardized if the Caucasian front ceased to exist. There were also large quantities of arms and ammunition that the Allies had supplied to Russia which were stockpiled in Murmansk, Archangel and Vladivostok; it was feared they might fall into German hands.

These were the conditions which determined the Allied reaction to the Bolshevik *coup* and the Brest-Litovsk negotiations. On October 10, 1917, speaking on the military outlook if Russia were to accept a separate peace, United States Secretary of State Lansing estimated that it would prolong the war against Germany by two or three years. While in America this might not have been an unbearable prospect, to the European Allies it was. And this desire to keep Russia in the war at all costs led ultimately to the Allied intervention in the Russian Civil War. The original aims of the intervention were to maintain centers of resistance to the Germans. Once it became clear that the Soviet government would not continue to resist, the Allies sought out anti-Bolshevik movements. Their object was to keep Russia in the war and their efforts were not especially directed against the Soviets out of political considerations, particularly since there was a widespread feeling that the Bolshevik regime would be short-lived.

Until the end of 1918, Allied intervention was confined to the Don region and the Kuban, to Murmansk and Archangel in the north, and to the Volga region and Siberia, including Vladivostok, in the east. Much of the rest of pre-revolutionary Russia—Poland, the Baltic countries and the Ukraine—was occupied by the Germans.

The Allies soon discovered, in the winter of 1917-18, that the Russian movements then in resistance to Bolshevism were of no help in the war against Germany. All such hopes proved futile, although for a time they were entertained by many, even in the United States. Thus, Kennan writes:

> Throughout the latter part of November and the first weeks of December, the pages of the American press, as well as the official reports received by the State Department, were full of items dealing with General Kaledin and his Don Cossacks, portraying them as a powerful center of resistance to Bolshevik power, in fact as the likely source of its overthrow, as well as a possible nucleus for a revived "eastern front" against Germany.[1]

England and France displayed even greater interest in this possibility of a new "eastern front," and it was in connection with Kaledin and his Cossacks that the idea of intervention took shape. Although Kaledin's army was not the "powerful center of resistance" the Allies wished, it still held some attraction for those Russians who wanted to continue armed resistance to the Germans and their Bolshevik "agents."[2] Prominent generals gathered on the Don, and thousands of officers who had escaped from the disintegrating combat units. Thus sprang up the so-called Volunteer Army, which was to fight under successive commanders (Alexeev, Kornilov, Denikin and Wrangel) for nearly two years, until November 1920.

Early in December 1917, the British government, while still avoiding direct intervention, authorized its agents in southern Russia to give financial aid to all those prepared to resist the Central Powers. After an Anglo-French meeting in Paris on December 22 and 23, 1917, a memorandum was issued which rejected direct support of the anti-Bolshevik movements, but declared it desirable that contact be maintained with the Ukraine, the Cossacks, Finland and Siberia, and that financial aid be given to the Ukrainians and the Cossacks. It appears that this aid was quite limited, for the leaders of the Volunteer Army constantly faced financial difficulties. The United States had not participated in the Paris conference, although the matter of secret financial help to Kaledin through England and France was discussed in Washington.[3] Some contact was established on the initiative of the American consul general in Moscow, Maddin Summers, who on December 16 sent De Witt C. Poole, one of his subordinates, to the south. On December 22, Poole reached Novocherkassk, which served as the capital for Kaledin's Cossack government. His report exploded the myth of Kaledin's power. Poole estimated the army at 1,500 to 2,000 men, with no infantry to speak of, and no ammunition for the artillery. His pessimistic impressions were confirmed when Kaledin killed himself in despair some weeks later. Soon after this suicide, the Volunteer Army renounced all hope of holding the Don region and decided to move to the northern Caucasus, to the Kuban. This move, accomplished under extremely difficult conditions, became known as the "Frozen March." The Volunteer Army had several battles with the Bolsheviks and in one of them its Commander, Kornilov, was killed. He was succeeded by Denikin, who was to lead the army in its most important engagements.

At the beginning of April, when the Cossacks of the Don region rose against the Bolsheviks, the Volunteer Army turned in its tracks. On April 16 it started back to the Don from the Kuban—another epic march with almost uninterrupted fighting. Meanwhile, the Cossack uprising spread and after a few days of fluctuating fortunes, the Cossacks took Novocherkassk. However, the same day, April 25, German forces marched into Rostov-on-the-Don. Since the Volunteer Army considered itself still at war with Germany, it was obliged to return once again to the Kuban.

Meanwhile representatives of Cossack camps, mostly those around the Cossack capital, Novocherkassk, held a congress ("Circle for the Salvation of the Don") in that city. This congress adopted a sort of provisional constitution of the "Sovereign Army of the Don" and on May 3 elected General P. N. Krasnov as its Ataman. Unlike the Volunteer Army's commanders, Krasnov assumed an outspokenly pro-German orientation. In the fall of 1918, Krasnov mustered an army of 45,000 bayonets and sabers and 93 cannon and tried to break through to Tsaritsyn. When his repeated attempts failed, he was forced to retreat. Then the German collapse led to evacution of all the German forces, and radically altered the disposition of forces in this area, as elsewhere.

Meanwhile, on the eastern front of the Civil War, in the Volga region and Siberia, operations soon exceeded those of the Volunteer Army in scope. Two forces, hostile to the Bolsheviks but independent of each other, had appeared almost simultaneously. The larger was the Czech Legion that had been formed from among the Austro-Hungarian war prisoners and incorporated into the Russian army as an autonomous body. During the Brest-Litovsk talks, this unit was stationed in the Ukraine. With the signing of the Brest-Litovsk Treaty the Czechs wished to leave Russia by way of Siberia and the Far East, so that they could return to pursue the war on the western front. France supported the Czech demand, and on March 26, 1918 the Soviet government signed the Penza Agreement with the Czechs and the French government, authorizing passage of the legionnaires through Siberia and Vladivostok. The Czechs were to travel as private citizens, but were authorized to keep some light arms and machine guns and a limited amount of ammunition, to be used in the event they were attacked during their journey. The rest of their arms were to be handed over to the Soviet command in Penza.

At first, the evacuation of the Czech units proceeded smoothly. The

Czechs and the Red Army even jointly repelled some small-scale German attempts to break through on the Russian front. As the Czechs were leaving the Ukraine, the Soviet commander there, Antonov-Ovseyenko, presented them with a document expressing fraternal gratitude to their legions. It ended with these words:

> The Revolutionary Armies of South Russia will never forget the brotherly help of the Czech corps in the struggle of the working people against the vile imperialist hordes.[4]

Thus, 10,500 Czechs made their way across Siberia and reached Vladivostok unmolested. The remainder were delayed by the scarcity of transportation as well as by all sorts of difficulties that arose between them and local Soviet authorities. Then something occurred which the available materials do not explain. The only hard facts at our disposal are that the Czech delegates in Moscow were arrested and that Trotsky's assistant, Aralov, sent out two wires (May 21 and 24) directing that the Czech detachments be detained, disarmed and disbanded, by every possible means. This was followed by Trotsky's famous telegram, which was relayed all along the route followed by the Czechs, ordering that all Czechs be disarmed and interned and that those who resisted be shot on the spot. The Czechs refused to submit, and turned against the Soviet authorities in self-defense.

The Czechs were, relatively, a solid military force, and by the end of May, General Cecek, leading the almost unarmed Czech troops, had taken Penza, where he found large stores of arms and ammunition. Then his units occupied Syzran and Samara. Other Czech forces took Chelyabinsk (May 27) and Ekaterinenburg. Soon Czechs were also in possession of all the Siberian towns west of Irkutsk. After these initial successes, the Czechs slowed down. In some districts, especially in the Transbaikal region, they met with stiffening resistance. In far-off Vladivostok, however, they took over control of the city, for all practical purposes, after overthrowing the local Soviet. Local governments under the protection of the Czechs began to spring up in various parts of Siberia and in the Volga region.

The Czechs were then approached by the Constituent Assembly Committee, formed after the successful uprising in Samara and consisting of seventy members of the Constituent Assembly, mostly Socialist Revolutionaries. There had been no preliminary agreement between the Samara movement and the Czechs, but when the committee learned of their uprisings in Chelyabinsk, Penza and Syzran, it established close co-operation with the Czechs, many of whom were democrats and socialists.

The formation of the Constituent Assembly Committee, and the creation of its "People's Army" as a democratic, anti-Bolshevik force, had been planned at the clandestine 8th Congress of the S-R Party, held in Moscow in May 1918. This congress pledged the S-R Party to fight

> for the restoration of Russia's independence and for the restoration of her national and political unity, on the basis of the principles proclaimed by the February Revolution.

There were strong anti-Bolshevik currents among the peasants of the Volga region and so a meeting of Constituent Assembly members, mostly S-R's, chose Samara (now Kuibyshev) as the seat for the Constituent Assembly Committee which would serve as nucleus of a new, all-Russian democratic government. The practical implementation of this plan was entrusted to I. Brushvit, P. Klimushin, I. Nesterov, B. Fortunov and V. Volsky. Even before this, the committee of the Volga region had concluded an agreement with the Cossack Ataman, Dutov, who had overthrown the Soviet authorities in Saratov, based on mutual recognition of the Constituent Assembly. Then followed the establishment of close ties with the Czechs, and formation of the "People's Army."

Reinforced by these volunteer Russian units, the Czechs moved up the Volga, entering Stavropol on May 14 and Simbirsk on May 22. After repelling the first Soviet counter-offensive, on August 7 they took Kazan, where they seized the gold reserve that had been transferred there during the war by the Russian Treasury. This was the high-water mark of the anti-Soviet campaign. According to Trotsky, even Lenin wavered for the first time and was beset with doubts.[5] The All-Russian Central Executive Committee decreed a general mobilization on May 29. In the military districts of the Volga, the Urals and western Siberia, which were directly threatened, the mobilization went into effect immediately. Moscow and Petrograd factory workers were drafted into the army on June 17. The Bolsheviks succeeded in opening an eastern front by mid-June. Its first commander was Colonel Muraviev, later replaced by Colonel Vatsetis, former commander of the Latvian sharpshooters. By July 15 the Soviet government's eastern army was about 45,000 strong. But Lenin considered the situation so perilous that he forced the adoption of a resolution declaring the "Socialist Fatherland in Danger." In August, party members were drafted and sent to the eastern front. According to the Central Committee's report to the 8th Party Congress, a fifth of the total party membership was called up. Many party officials left for the front to serve as political commissars and propagandists.

An important part was played by Trotsky, who was chairman of the highest military organ, the Revolutionary Military Council. An extraordinarily able organizer with indefatigable energy, he would race in his special train along the front lines, delivering speeches to the men, encouraging and instructing the commissars and conferring with the commanders. His popularity with the troops and the officers was great. And it was on Trotsky's initiative that the party decided to employ former Tsarist officers in the Red Army on a large scale. One of these, Colonel S. S. Kamenev, was later appointed commander of the eastern front.

On August 29, 1918, at Svyazhsk, the Red Army won its first victory. On September 10 it re-took Kazan, and on September 12 Simbirsk; Syzran fell on October 3, and Samara on October 7. By October the Soviet regime was restored in the Volga region and in the lower Kama Valley. Until the following spring, the eastern front remained relatively calm.

Meanwhile, in an effort to co-ordinate anti-Bolshevik efforts, a conference of all the anti-Bolshevik organizations was held in Ufa in the first half of September 1918. Twenty-three organizations took part in the debate that lasted two weeks. Finally, on September 23, an all-Russian provisional government was formed, which has gone down in history as the Ufa Directorate. The Socialist Revolutionary, N. Avksentiev, was elected president; and General V. Boldyrev, N. Chaikovsky, N. Astrov, P. Vologodsky and others were members. In the absence of the three last named, V. Zenzinov (S-R), V. A. Vinogradov (Kadet) and Professor V. V. Sapozhnikov (Liberal), were seated in their stead.

In November, the Soviet offensive in the Urals began and the Ufa Directorate moved to Omsk. And there the coalition government was unseated on November 18, 1918 by right-wing elements with the support of the Allies. The *coup* was carried out by a military clique including Colonels Annenkov, Volkov and Lebedev, General Andogsky and others. Behind them were several ministers of the Directorate, headed by the Minister for the Army and Navy, Vice-Admiral Kolchak, who had the backing of British General Alfred Knox. The S-R members of the Directorate, Avksentiev, Zenzinov, Argunov and Rogovsky, were arrested and escaped death only because of Allied intervention. Here was another illustration of a frequent occurrence in British diplomacy: subordinates on the spot had carried out their own policy, without the knowledge or approval of London. In his *Ordeals of a Diplomat*, V. Nabokov, the Russian chargé d'affaires in London, writes:

> Although the local (British) officials in Siberia reported that the Directorate was not stable and that there was bickering between the S-R's and the "War Party," it was decided that the Directorate should be recognized and, on November 17, a telegram to this effect, to be sent to Omsk, was drafted. The *coup* of November 18, the dispersal of the Directorate and the proclamation of Kolchak as supreme ruler delayed the sending of that telegram. On November 19, I went to see Lord Robert Cecil and he told me: "We were ready to recognize the Directorate. It was swept away by force. Who can guarantee that the same thing won't happen to Kolchak three weeks from now? In such circumstances, it's very difficult for us to make a decision. Let's wait and see!"

It may well be that the *coup* was planned for November 18 precisely because the conspirators had learned that British recognition was being prepared in London on the 17th.

When Kolchak came to power as "Supreme Ruler," he refused to release the arrested members of the Directorate unless they renounced all future political activity. Avksentiev indignantly refused. Thus, the suppression of the Constituent Assembly, begun by Lenin, was completed by rightists.[6]

Other Theaters of Intervention

In the summer and fall of 1918, the eastern front was by far the most important sector in the Civil War. In the fall the Bolshevik Central Committee issued a circular letter to the party membership explaining that the "inspired effort of September" which had brought about the successes on the eastern front, had been due to the "correct, common conviction that, if the Czechs were not defeated, the end of the Soviet Republic would follow within a more or less brief period." Neither the operations of the Allies in the Murmansk and Archangel districts nor Krasnov's two attempts to capture Tsaritsyn presented comparable threats. As to the Allied intervention in Vladivostok, it did not actually present a threat to Russia or the Soviet regime; on the contrary, it effectively blocked Japan's aggressive designs on the Russian Far East and Siberia. Before returning to the story of the two main battlefronts, manned by the armies of Denikin and Kolchak, it would be well to summarize these lesser theaters of civil conflict and foreign intervention.

Archangel: The first Allied landings in Archangel and Vladivostok took place simultaneously. The anti-Soviet uprising in Archangel of August 2 occurred because Allied support was expected. The small Soviet force fled the city and on the following day the Allied Expeditionary Force made its first landings. Allied occupation of Archangel (and, to a lesser degree, of Murmansk) was a purely military move.

Following the Archangel *coup,* a democratic, moderately socialist government came into being. This government immediately became the object of the irreconcilable hostility of the monarchists, especially those officers who had the support of General Poole, the senior British officer. During the night of September 4-5, a Russian naval officer named Chaplin, who was attached to Poole's staff, arrested all but two members of the government and deported them to the Solovki Islands. The two ministers who remained free appealed to the population; the workers went on strike, and the unrest soon spread to the surrounding countryside. The Allied diplomats stationed in Archangel thereupon opposed Poole and supported Chaikovsky. Within three days, the ministers were brought back to Archangel. Poole, too, was soon replaced by Ironside. Chaikovsky's government was reorganized along less "leftist" lines and consequently lost all influence.

Murmansk: The first Allied landing on Russian territory took place at Murmansk. It was on a very limited scale: 150 British Royal Marines in April and 370 in May. Gradually, the British contingent came to exceed 18,000 men, besides small units of the French, Italians and Serbs. The Murmansk operation pursued the purely military objective of preventing German and Finnish forces from moving into Murmansk. Finland was at war with Soviet Russia, which had at first recognized its independence and then, at the end of January, moved an army into Finland. The situation in Murmansk became quite paradoxical. The British concluded an agreement with the Murmansk Soviet (approved by Moscow), and the British and the Bolsheviks joined in military operations against the Finns. Then Moscow changed its position and began demanding the evacuation of the Allied forces. Thus, for some time the Allies and the Bolsheviks were fighting jointly against Finnish-German forces in one place, while elsewhere they were fighting each other.

Siberia and the Far East: As early as December 1917, an attempt was made to form an autonomous Siberian Socialist Republic in Tomsk, with a government including parties ranging from the Popular Socialists to the Bolsheviks. A Siberian regional Duma was created. Then the Bolsheviks seized power, and when the Duma convened at the end of January 1918, they dispersed it. A small group of its members, who had managed to avoid arrest, elected a "provisional government" headed by the S-R, Derber. But this "government" had to move as far east as Harbin, where it found little support. In Harbin, a sort of government under General Horvat, the director of the Chinese Eastern Railway, had been in office since the Chinese troops had cleared the Bolsheviks out of the railway zone. Many other anti-Bolshevik movements sprang up in that zone, to which many officers had escaped. The most important of these was headed by the self-proclaimed Ataman, Semyonov, who attempted to seize the Transbaikal region. With the exception of the United States, the Allies had once placed some hope in the Semyonov movement, its main supporter being Japan. Semyonov and Kalmykov, another "Cossack leader," looted and robbed the population, including Chinese shopkeepers, and killed without discrimination. Their "movements" did not affect the course of the Civil War in Siberia.

Vladivostok: The Allied occupation of Vladivostok had the most serious consequences of all their actions in Siberia and the Far East. The Allies feared, after Brest-Litovsk, that Germany would be able to open a new eastern front by using the numerous German and Austrian prisoners of war in the Siberian camps. From the end of February through March, the mood among the Allies was panicky. Washington was bombarded by telegrams and warnings. In addition to the Japanese and French governments, Lord Balfour and others advocated immediate intervention.

General Foch expressed this view in an interview he gave to a correspondent of the *New York Times* on February 26, 1918:[7]

> If America will look ahead, I am sure she will see another field in which she can render immense service, without relaxing her efforts on the western front. She should give her attention to the Orient. Germany is walking through Russia. America and Japan, who are in a position to do so, should go to meet her in Siberia. Both for the war and after, America and Japan must furnish military and economic resistance to German penetration. There should be immediate steps in this important matter. Don't wait after it is too late.

President Wilson was reluctant to invite Japan into Siberia because of the traditional American policy of barring Japanese expansion on the Asian continent at the expense of either China or Russia. About three months later, however, when fighting broke out between the Soviet government and the Czech legion, the advocates of intervention could now argue effectively that the Czech force had to be rescued, as a valuable asset to the Allies. Wilson could no longer withstand the Franco-British pressure, but wished to entrust the intervention not to Japan alone but to the Entente as a whole.

On July 6, 1918, Wilson agreed to intervention in terms that limited its scope, excluded any interference in Russia's internal affairs, and made it impossible for Japan to seize Russian territory. The Japanese voiced their formal agreement with Wilson on August 3: "The Japanese government affirm their avowed policy of respecting the territorial integrity of Russia, and of abstaining from all interference in her national politics." A British batallion landed in Vladivostok on August 3, a Japanese division landed on August 12; and on the 16th, 1,500 Americans arrived. The French sent 500 men who had been stationed in Peking. Canada sent a contingent of 800. However, even after the troops had been reinforced, the Allied contingent in the Far East remained inadequate for important military operations (the United States force was gradually brought up to 7,700 men). In historical perspective we can see that American participation in the Vladivostok operation actually forestalled Japan's attempt to seize Siberian territory which the Soviet government by itself could not possibly have done. An American historian actually concludes that the intervention "introduced America's greatest offensive against Japanese expansion on the Asiatic continent prior to World War II."[8]

The War at its Height

After the armistice with Germany, the Allied attitude toward intervention rapidly changed. There was no longer any question of keeping Russia in the war, and popular feeling in the Western democracies was increasingly hostile toward any foreign adventures. Before the armistice, the French generals stationed in eastern Europe had been preparing, on orders from Clemenceau, a plan for operations in southern Russia in which twelve Allied divisions (French and Greek) were to be used. On November 23, an Anglo-French naval squadron, consisting of two cruisers and two destroyers, arrived in Novorossiysk. On December 3, a British military mission arrived, headed by General Poole, who had commanded the Allied forces in Archangel. On December 18, the first French division landed in Odessa. A period of indecision followed. England did supply considerable arms to the Volunteer Army but the small British detachments were not used to support this army, but were dispatched instead to Transcaucasia (Baku, Batum, Tiflis) and Russian possessions beyond the Caspian Sea. In December 1918, we have learned since, Britain and France had agreed on their respective "spheres of influence." The French sphere was to include Poland, the Ukraine, the Crimea, and the territory west of the Don, while the British zone was to encompass northern Russia, Finland, the former Baltic provinces, the eastern part of the Don province, Kuban and the Caucasus. Moreover, the Allies sympathized with the creation of independent states: Finland, Poland, and the Baltic and Caucasian countries. All this caused considerable friction with the leaders of the Volunteer Army, whose program was a "Russia united and indivisible."

Even if some of the Allies were pursuing traditional power-politics in their dealings with anti-Bolshevik movements, the United States, and Britain to a lesser extent, made attempts to play the honest broker between the Soviet government and its various opponents. At the end of January 1919, a resolution was adopted at the Versailles Peace Conference which Denikin has called "the first serious blow struck at the Russian national movement by the Allies." On January 22, the Allies appealed by radio to "all organized political groups, in power or aspiring to it, in European Russia and Siberia," to send their representatives to Prinkipo Island by February 15 for negotiations. This would require "an armistice agreement among all the invited groups and the cessation of all offensive operations." The Soviet government and Estonia accepted the invitation, all the others rejected it. The Prinkipo conference never took place, but still another attempt was made to mediate between the belligerents. In March, William C. Bullitt arrived in Moscow as a representative of Wilson and Lloyd George, and renewed the offer of a peace agreement. Again the Soviet government expressed its willingness. A year later, Lenin was to say this about these negotiations: "When we offered Bullitt . . . an agreement so very unfavorable to us, by which a huge expanse of territory was to remain under Denikin and Kolchak, we were certain that if the peace were signed no White Guard government could ever maintain itself in power." Lenin understood, in any case, that the White armies would refuse to negotiate on the basis of a truce which left the Bolsheviks in control of Petrograd, Moscow, and the heartland of European Russia. Considering the difficult position of the Soviet regime and the menace of a possible Allied intervention in force, Lenin sought by ths demonstration of peaceful intentions to gain sympathy in the western countries and make intervention more difficult. In any event, intervention by Allied military forces soon ceased, although the substantial material aid enabled the Whites to equip and arm hundreds of thousands of men.

On March 11, 1919, Franco-Greek forces attacked Soviet troops approaching Odessa. Their attack near Kherson was beaten back and they were forced to evacuate by sea to Odessa. This was the only Allied participation in the military operations of the Civil War. The French soldiers refused to fight on, and there was a mutiny on a French warship in Odessa harbor. In April, the French evacuated Odessa and then Sebastopol, after which they were sent home. At about this time, the Russian Ambassador in Paris, Maklakov, wrote: "It is beyond the power of any (Allied) government, now, after the Armistice, to make their forces fight for Russia."[9] After the terrible hardships of four years of war, the longing for peace was irresistible, especially in France. Furthermore, there were so many reactionaries among the Whites that support of that movement by the western countries was politically impossible. As Denikin wrote: "They advised us often from Paris that Allied aid was inadequate because the armies of the south (Denikin) and that of the east (Kolchak) were not popular among the European democracies; that in order to gain their sympathy we had to pronounce two words: republic and federation. We did not pronounce them." But Denikin also maintained that even such a pronouncement would not have seriously altered the situation.

Meanwhile, the Bolsheviks were consolidating their forces. Defense was the central topic at the 8th Communist Party Congress from March 18 to 23, 1919. The Congress decided to modify Soviet agrarian policy and, by a series of concessions (disbanding the Committees of Poor Peasants), to gain the sympathy of the *seredniaki* (the middle-income peasants). The Congress also witnessed long debates on the organization of the Red Army and on methods of waging the Civil War. The so-called Military Opposition insisted on continued adherence to guerilla warfare and vehemently rejected the use of former officers of the Tsarist army, which Trotsky and Lenin advocated. Once Lenin's viewpoint was adopted, the Civil War took on the character of an authentic war between two regular armies.[10]

Trotsky relates how Lenin, during a visit to Moscow in the spring of 1919, suggested that perhaps the Soviets should rid themselves of all the former Tsarist officers. Trotsky asked: "How many of them do you think we have in our army?" Lenin: "Don't know." Trotsky: "How many would you say?" Lenin: "Don't know." Trotsky: "We've got 30,000 of them." "What?" Lenin exclaims. Trotsky repeats: "30,000. For every traitor, 100 fight loyally; for every one who deserts to the enemy, two or three get killed. With whom do you expect to replace them all?" Lenin then recognized that Trotsky's policy was correct and passionately defended it at the Party Congress. In his speech on building Communism, he said: "When Comrade Trotsky told me that there were tens of thousands of (former) Tsarist army officers in our army, I saw concretely the secret of how the enemy could be used for the building of Communism. We are picking up the bricks which the capitalists collected to use against us."[11]

The Party Congress was still in session when Kolchak's offensive began. According to Soviet sources, the total size of the armed forces opposing the Red Armies in the Urals, Siberia and the Far East was 400,000. According to the same sources, Kolchak concentrated about 130,000 infantry and cavalry, with 210 cannon and 1,300 machine guns. These forces were originally opposed, on the Soviet side, by 101,000 infantry and cavalry, with 365 cannon and 1,817 machine guns. The Soviet forces were divided into six armies. The commander was Sergei Kamenev, a former Tsarist colonel. One of the six armies was under a former Tsarist general, Shorin; another army, after April, was under Mikhail Tukhachevsky.

Even if these figures are assumed to be correct, they give a misleading idea of the forces at Kolchak's disposal. The 400,000 men said to be under Kolchak, to start with, included the Czechs, most of whom were no longer taking part in military operations. They had only one thing in mind: to return to their homeland, which had become an independent republic. Furthermore, they were indignant over Kolchak's *coup* in Omsk. Almost all of them were democrats, many were socialists, and they could not sympathize with the Kolchak regime. Of the Allied contingents, only the Japanese was of any size. Japan recognized the Kolchak government, although it did not treat it in a friendly fashion. The Japanese, trying to strengthen their position in the Far East, mostly supported Semyonov, who was more of a liability than a help to Kolchak.

For the Soviets, maintaining the minimum food supply necessary to keep the population at work was a most difficult problem. The great hopes in 1918 of supplies from the rich, corn-producing Ukraine proved unfounded. After the departure of the German and Austrian armies, the Bolsheviks had suppressed all organized opposition in the Ukraine and had established a Soviet regime there, but they were unable to cope with the anarchy that had spread through the land. The only field in which some results were registered was the production of armaments. Thanks to the fact that the old centers of this industry were now in Soviet hands, the regime was able by July 1919 to produce 43,000 rifles, 34,000,000 rounds of ammunition, and 720 machine guns a month, instead of the 13,000 rifles and 17,000,000 rounds of ammunition turned out in April.

Kolchak's initial military superiority enabled him to gain a greater victory than he could have hoped for. Among his commanding officers, this created an exaggerated notion of weakness and unreliability in the Soviet forces. The Kolchak armies advanced rapidly toward the Volga, and, although the poor state of the roads slowed them down, by April 1919 they had seized a vast territory inhabited by 5,000,000 people and including many fertile provinces.

On April 28, the southern group of the Soviet armies began its counter-offensive. From the first battles it became evident that the fighting quality of Kolchak's forces had been seriously impaired but their resistance was broken only after fierce fighting. Then other Soviet units passed to the offensive. Kolchak's armies were rolled back about as rapidly as they had advanced. Around June 20, they were back to the starting line of their offensive. Kolchak's forces never recovered.

On the southern front, in the meantime, the Soviets faced a most difficult situation. A letter from the party's Central Committee to the party organizations, headed, "Everybody to Fight Against Denikin," opened with these words: "One of the most critical moments, perhaps the most critical moment, of the Socialist Revolution has arrived." Events fully vindicated this evaluation. Numerically the Soviet forces were inferior to those of the White Army, especially on the southern front. According to the Soviet High Command, on June 15—i.e., at the start of Denikin's offensive—they had 77,000 men on the southern front. On the eastern, where the campaign against Kolchak continued, they had 125,000; and on the western front, where many operations originating in the Baltic provinces were being carried out, they had 139,000.

The Whites began their offensive with a numerical advantage of about 100,000 men. On June 13, Denikin's western army entered Kharkov. The first major thrust, under General Wrangel, began in the direction of Tsaritsyn three days later and resulted in a total rout of the Soviet forces. Soviet losses, according to Lenin, were "huge."

By June 29, White units had occupied the Crimean peninsula. The advance of Denikin's armies seemed irresistible, its main direction being Moscow. At the same time, General Yudenich's anti-Soviet army threatened Petrograd from the west.

In this critical situation the Bolsheviks ordered emergency mobilizations—training, outfitting and arming new recruits. In the course of Denikin's advance on the southern front, the Red Army had had to abandon a considerable part of its equipment and the soldiers suffered from an acute shortage of ammunition. Thanks to "superfrenetic" efforts, as Lenin put it, the Red Army's numerical strength on the southern front was more than doubled. At the same time, Vatsetis, the new Soviet commander, insisted on transferring troops from the Siberian front to the southern. He reasoned that instead of sending poorly-trained recruits to the southern front, it would be more effective to transfer battle-tested troops from the Siberian front, where they were no longer needed for operations against Kolchak. Although this proposition was supported by Trotsky, it was twice voted down by the party's Central Committee. If Vatsetis' advice had been heeded, Denikin would have probably been defeated sooner, with fewer Soviet losses.

The numerical superiority achieved by the Soviet armies by mid-July did not make them stronger on the southern front than Denikin's force. The first Soviet counter-offensive in August failed. Even before it began, Denikin sent Mamontov's cavalry corps into the Soviet rear. Mamontov reached Tambov and not only disrupted the Red Army's lines of communication and supply, but even provoked a series of peasant uprisings or, as the Soviet historians refer to them, "mutinies."[12] The Soviet counter-offensive began with some initial successes, but a shortage of reserves, especially cavalry, prevented them from being pressed further. Denikin's cavalry units (under Mamontov and Shkuro) then broke through into the rear of the Soviet armies. Soon Denikin had occupied Kursk and was advancing toward Orel, which he captured on October 13. This was the most critical moment of the Civil War, for at the same time Yudenich was advancing on Petrograd. Leo Kamenev wrote that Lenin said: "Only a miracle can save us."

However, all the troops that could be spared from the White Sea front were transferred to defend Petrograd, while on the southern front, most of the Soviet forces were ordered to confine themselves to holding operations at the approaches to Moscow, thus releasing several units for the Orlov-Voronezh sector. The Soviet lines held, and Denikin's attempts to interfere with the Red troop movements failed. Yudenich was defeated in December 1919; and Denikin retreated to Rostov-on-Don, where he was again defeated on March 27, 1920. He then embarked on a French warship in Novorossiysk and was taken to the Crimea, where he was followed by the remnants of the Volunteer Army and by a part of the Don Cossack forces. In Sebastopol, Denikin resigned, naming Wrangel as his successor, and left for Constantinople.

The rout of Denikin's armies marked the virtual end of the Civil War; only mopping-up operations remained. In the east, the pursuit of Kolchak went on for several months; his retreating army was meanwhile harassed by uprisings and guerilla warfare. When he reached Irkutsk, he found a government of the "Political Center" composed of non-Communist socialists, who arrested him and brought him to trial. But a few days later, Irkutsk was in Bolshevik hands and, on February 7, 1920, Kolchak was shot. The Soviet armies continued their advance until they reached the Pacific. At the same time, the Soviet government was compelled to assent to the formation of several independent states within what had previously been the Russian Empire: Finland, the Baltic republics (Estonia, Lithuania and Latvia), the Transcaucasian republics (Georgia, Armenia and Azerbaijan) and the Far Eastern government, composed of various groups of socialists. The Transcaucasian republics and the Far Eastern government were short-lived.

The decisive element in the victory of the Red Armies was not any purely military advantage over the Whites, but rather the political factor. All in all, the two armies were fairly evenly matched numerically. In the quality of their troops, the Whites possibly had an edge at the beginning, since they had more of the officers of the old Tsarist army; however, toward the end, the Soviet side also had experienced and battle-tested units, and they always had their share of former Tsarist officers. As to equipment and supplies, the Soviets had Russia's largest military plants, where by propaganda and coercion, they were able to get the workers to increase their output immensely. Moreover, they found supplies that had not been used during the World War. All this enabled them to match, and ultimately surpass, the equipment and armies supplied to the Whites by the Allies.

Politically, however, the Soviet side proved much the stronger. Denikin himself was no advocate of restoring the old regime. In a speech which he quotes in his memoirs[13] he wonders what should follow the revolution, counter-revolution or evolution; and he expresses his preference for the latter. As commander, he was *ex officio* the dictator of the territory occupied by his army. However, the government under him, called the Advisory Committee, consisted of representatives of various political groupings, of which the Kadets formed the left wing; the remainder were extreme right-wing and reactionary elements. This coalition was enthusiastically counter-revolutionary. In view of other profound disagreements, Denikin could not maintain any consistent policy, right-wing or left-wing. The greatest stumbling-block to the White movement was the agrarian question, and Denikin failed to enunciate a policy to satisfy the peasants—which proved fatal to the White movement.

When it first had entered the Ukraine, the White Army was received with enthusiasm by the peasants, who had enough of the Bolsheviks with their War Communism. In his book Denikin quotes from a pamphlet by the Menshevik, Kutchin-Oransky: "The Volunteer Army's advance was supported by peasant unrest, which prepared the ground for them." The anti-Bolshevik mood was also strong among the workers. Kutchin gives Bolshevik behavior in occupied territory as the reason for this: "Thousands of crimes and senseless acts were perpetrated. Blood ran in streams as never before." Everything favored the Whites, while the Reds suffered mass desertions. In June 1919, Lenin mentioned "tens of thousands" of deserters. Then suddenly the picture was reversed: the deserters began to rejoin the Red Army, while mass desertions started to plague Denikin's forces.

What was actually happening was that, while the members of Denikin's Advisory Committee debated how the agrarian question should be settled, Denikin's armies, as he writes himself,[14] "were followed by landowners forcibly re-establishing their rights, sometimes with the help of the military, settling personal accounts. . . . In some areas, where a certain measure of calm had been restored, the returning landowners brought back unrest by outrageously increasing the rent for holdings." Denikin tried to prevent this: "I threatened to try the perpetrators of violence," he writes. But he was powerless.[15]

Denikin gives a metaphorical description[16] of the churchbells used to welcome his armies at first and then being used later to sound the alarm when "the wave of Cossack and Volunteer forces left behind it a muddy residue of violence, looting and anti-Jewish pogroms." There was much "mud" left in the wake of the Red Army, too, but the Soviet government had at its disposal Communist Party members who could be dispatched wherever discipline needed to be restored.

For many members of Denikin's forces, war was merely an opportunity for looting. Writing about Mamontov's brilliant raid that opened the path to his attack, Denikin says: "Roads were opened and columns of carts, miles long and heavily laden with loot, moved south, toward the Cossack villages in the Don region. They were accompanied and guarded by long lines of combat personnel."[17] During the withdrawal, many of the officers were in an "Eat, drink and be merry, for tomorrow we die" mood. They wasted precious time in wild orgies and looted indiscriminately. As Wrangel described in his report to Denikin, dated December 9:

> The war was becoming a means of growing rich, requisitioning has degenerated into pillage and speculation. Each unit tries to secure as much as possible for itself. What cannot be used on the

> spot is sent to the interior and sold at a profit . . . Many officers absent from the front areas, ostensibly on lengthy missions, are engaged in selling and trading loot. The Army is completely demoralized and is rapidly turning into a bunch of tradesmen and profiteers . . . Corps commanders and division chiefs report that most units have altogether lost their fighting capacity. This is the bitter truth. The Army has ceased to exist as a fighting force.[18]

Such was the state of the army that had begun the fight as a crusade, which counted in its ranks many enthusiasts, people capable of heroism but having no conception of a program that could gain them solid support among wide sections of the population. Without that support, the army became isolated and lost the restraints which would have guarded it against demoralization. The fact that the Civil War against dictatorship became a war against the peasantry as well, was fatal. In a conversation with Denikin, Wrangel sadly summed up the situation: "The Volunteer Army has discredited itself by looting and violence. Here everything is lost. We cannot again follow the same path, carrying the same flag. We need another flag." Of one thing Wrangel was certain: it must "not be the monarchist flag."[19]

When the war with Poland drew the main strength of the Red Army to the Polish front, Wrangel forgot his brooding and tried to take advantage of the situation. Hoping to receive support from the Allies, who he was sure would want to help Poland, he began his offensive on May 25 with four army corps having a total strength of 25,000 men. He overcame a weak Soviet screening force and moved ahead rapidly. But this spark of activity rapidly burned out. On November 14 and 15, his army was beaten back and hurriendly evacuated to Constantinople.

The Civil War, in the course of which the Soviet government had repeatedly been on the very brink of defeat, was thus won by the Bolsheviks. But, as Lenin himself later admitted, the balance had tipped in their favor only because the peasantry had grown seriously afraid of a White victory that would deprive them of their newly acquired land. The peasants did not actually always support the Red Army; and when they did, it was not out of a genuine devotion to the Soviet regime. On the contrary, in the period immediately preceding the outbreak of the Civil War on the Volga and in southern Russia, the Soviet requisitioning of food and the suppression of free marketing met with general peasant opposition. But when the alternative threat began to loom in the course of the Civil War, the peasants finally went over to the side of the Red Army.

The workers were in a similar position, for, with few exceptions, they were altogether incapable, psychologically and politically, of making common cause with the Whites, however disappointed and disgusted they had been with Bolshevik tactics in early 1918. Moreover, the outbreak of the German revolution in November 1918 seemed to bear out the Bolshevik prophecies of imminent world revolution and so strengthened the determination of workers and revolutionary intellectuals to resist the Whites. Behind this determination was a vague hope that once the Civil War was won, the internal family quarrel with the Bolsheviks could somehow be settled.

Thus, the Bolshevik Party defeated the White armies, suppressed nationalist uprisings and peasant revolts, and coped with the foreign intervention of 1918-19. In the course of the Civil War, Russia suffered not only colossal material and economic losses (in industry production figures fell to 13% and in agriculture to 50% of the pre-war levels) but also a loss of human life on a scale hitherto unimaginable. The Bolshevik economist and writer, Stepanov-Skvortsov, reported to the Tenth Congress of the Bolshevik Party, on March 9, 1921, that, on his journey from Siberia to Moscow, he had seen the dreadful devastation of towns and villages: "Instead of towns—ruins and ashes. Instead of homes—gutted walls without roofs, with the blind eyes of empty windows. Not a place, not a trace—and this in the most brutal and literal sense."[20] Stepanov-Skvortsov noted that in the Urals and the Don district, the whole population had been diminished by one third, while, among men, the loss in some places was as high as 90%.[21]

Stepanov-Skvortsov's observations were by no means isolated. L. Kritsman, in his book, *The Heroic Period of the Russian Revolution*,[22] gives the following data, based on the findings of the well-known Soviet statistician, S. Strumilin.[23]

> The living standards of the Russian worker in 1919-1920 were at least three times lower than before the war . . . Famine and cold, disease and infant mortality are hidden behind these figures. There were over 5 million typhus cases during these two years, raising the incidence of the disease to 37 times that for 1914. The number of prematurely dead is calculated as above 7 million for the period January 1, 1918 to July 1, 1920, in those territories in which registration of the dead was carried out.

Applying the same calculation to the entire population under Soviet rule, 130 million at that time, one obtains a total figure of over 9 million dead—and this does not include the military casualties of the Civil War. Soviet statistics supply no details explaining these figures. But it should be noted that Russia's 2.5 million dead in the World War amounted to only a quarter of the losses suffered by the country in 1918-20.[24]

Naturally, Kritsman and Strumilin, both devout Bolsheviks, blame these dreadful losses on the "capitalist encirclement" which forced the Bolsheviks to resort to extreme measures and the working class to fight with "extraordinary heroism." However, as we have already pointed out, these extreme measures, particularly the economic measures which constituted War Communism, had been adopted by the Bolsheviks for ideological reasons before the beginning of the Civil War. (Later, when he had already decided to introduce the New Economic Policy, Lenin was to ridicule in biting words the "leftists" who had been so eager to nationalize and confiscate more than was necessary.[25]) These extreme measures of 1918-1920 in no way helped the Bolsheviks to win the Civil War, but only added countless new victims to those already claimed by the fighting. From countless descriptions, we also know only too well the means by which the Soviet government induced the workers and peasants to fight "heroically," while their wives and children were dying in mass famines and epidemics.[26]

[1] Kennan, *op. cit.*, p. 161.
[2] Kennan, pp. 167-169.
[3] Kennan, p. 171.
[4] Chamberlin, Vol. 2, p. 3.
[5] Trotsky, *Diary in Exile*, 1935, p. 46. Harvard University Press, 1958.

[6] As late as 1927, some Bolshevik leaders were still concerned with the idea of a constituent assembly. In a conversation with Radek, reported in *Izvestia* for November 1, 1927, Kamenev asked whether he kept a diary and then said: "If you do, write down what I am going to tell you: We are moving toward a re-birth of capitalism and the Constituent Assembly! It was bound to happen! I was right all along!"

[7] This interview has been reprinted in the English edition of the *History of the Communist Party of the Soviet Union: Short Course.* (Foreign Languages Publishing House, Moscow, 1945, p. 215).

[8] Betty Miller Unterberger: *America's Siberian Expedition, 1918-1920.* Duke University Press, 1956, p. 3.

[9] Denikin, *Ocherki Russkoi Smuty,* Vol. IV, p. 242.

[10] See L. M. Spirin, "The Communist Party—The Organizer of Kolchak's Rout," *Voprosy Istorii,* No. 8, 1956.

[11] L. Trotsky, *My Life,* 1930, pp. 180-181.

[12] Spirin, pp. 26-27.

[13] Denikin, Vol. V, p. 135.

[14] Denikin, Vol. IV, p. 223.

[15] Denikin, Vol. V, p. 136.

[16] Denikin, Vol. V, p. 122.

[17] *Ibid.*

[18] Denikin, Vol. V. p. 263.

[19] *Ibid.*

[20] *The Tenth Congress of the Bolshevik Party,* p. 70.

[21] *Ibid.*

[22] Kritsman, L. *The Heroic Period of the Russian Revolution,* 2nd ed., State Publ. House, Moscow, 1926, p. 187.

[23] Strumilin, S., "Labor Losses in Russia During the War," in *Narodnoye Khoziaistvo,* December 1920, p. 104.

[24] Loss of life was particularly heavy in the capitals and in certain districts fought over during the Civil War. Thus, in the Saratov district, the mortality rose to 20% of the population.

[25] Lenin, *Works,* Vol. XXVII, p. 301.

[26] A curious light is thrown on the situation at the front by a secret telegram, now in the unpublished part of Trotsky's archives kept at Harvard University. This telegram from Trotsky was sent over the direct wire to Lenin, with copies to People's Commissars Sklyansky and Muralov, and said, among other things: "The lack of revolvers creates an impossible situation at the front. *It is impossible to maintain discipline without revolvers.* I suggest that Comrades Muralov and Pozern take revolvers away from all those who are not on active duty . . . *Without revolvers, it is impossible to conduct a war.*" No. 20, Sviazhsk (File No. 23 for 1918, part I, pp. 13-14. Secret. Chairman of the Revolutionary Military Soviet of the Republic).

CHAPTER 8

The Revolt Against War Communism

Victory in the Civil War strengthened the Bolshevik leaders' belief in the soundness of their basic premises and policies. They had consolidated their government in the Civil War and created not only a large well-equipped army but a powerful police apparatus. In various debates with democratic socialists at trade-union and other congresses held during 1919 and 1920, Trotsky often argued that a social system capable of creating so great a force as the Red Army could not be regarded as inferior. Lenin did not resort to such arguments, but neither did he yield an inch in pursuing the general policy of War Communism after the defeat of Kolchak and Denikin.

The monopoly in the grain trade, enforced by "requisitioning detachments" and "barrage detachments," was not only maintained but was made more exacting. Under a new plan each industrial worker was to be mobilized and his place of work and job designated by the high command of the "labor army." A new measure was applied to combat the passive resistance of the peasants who were reducing their sowing area so as not to produce a surplus (for which they would receive no compensation). Sowing committees were created in every region and county to supervise the peasants, who were compelled, under penalty of severe punishment, to plant as much as possible, in accordance with state instructions. Thus state intervention in agriculture took place not only in the sphere of distribution but also in the process of agricultural production.

In 1920, the peasants again resorted, as they had in 1918, to mass resistance. The death grip of War Communism so vividly described by Boris Pilnyak in his famous novel, *The Hungry Year,* led to real famine and made life unbearable for the townspeople and the urban working class. Once again, as in early 1918, the Bolshevik Party began to find itself isolated from workers and peasants alike.

The dissatisfaction of the peasants was undoubtedly the most dangerous, as Lenin and other Bolshevik leaders frankly admitted. Poor harvests and drought led to famine which, as the spring of 1921 approached, had already cost hundreds of thousands of lives in southern Russia and on the Volga. Attempts to seize the last remnants of hidden grain from the peasants met with bitter resistance.

The minutes of the 10th Party Congress, held March 8-15, 1921 describe a series of armed peasant uprisings in various regions. In July 1920, the commander of a Red Army cavalry division, a Communist named Sapozhkov, began a mutiny, called his division "The Army of Truth," and occupied a number of villages in the Samara *gubernia.* The uprising was crushed by the end of July.[1] A couple of months later, another guerilla army sprang up in Khoper, Ust-Med-veditsa and Tsaritsin regions of the lower Volga.[2] Still another peasant army, called the "Peasants' Union" was created beyond the Urals in the regions of Altai, Omsk and Semipalatinsk.

The most important outbreak of peasant resistance took place in the Tambov *gubernia* in central Russia, where a former S-R and army officer, A. S. Antonov, organized a well-equipped peasant guerilla force. According to the *Great Soviet Encyclopedia,*[3] the revolt spread over the following districts of the Tambov *gubernia*: Borisoglebsk, Kirsanov, Kozlovsk, Morshansk and Tambov (particularly in the villages of Inzhavino, Sampur and Kamenka). The regular Cheka detachments failed to check the revolt, and a special army had to be formed to fight the Antonov guerillas. The insurrectionary mood even affected groups of the local Communist Party, which urged the central party office and Lenin himself to change their policy toward the peasants. According to the *Great Soviet Encyclopedia,*[4] Lenin received a delegation from the Tambov peasants on February 14, 1921, and ordered the discontinuation of food requisitioning in the Tambov *gubernia.* By conceding to the peasants' main demand, Lenin—according to this official Soviet source—did much to undermine the insurrection.

The Tambov revolt was followed by unrest in Petrograd and other working class centers, and among the revolutionary sailors of Kronstadt. The workers in the industrial towns faced widespread unemployment (at a time when there was no state compensation to the jobless) and food shortages—actual famine in some areas, such as the Donets Basin. A galloping inflation further depressed the real value of wages. The workers expressed their dissatisfaction openly and violently; even the Bolshevik press wrote about it. The workers' ferment aggravated the chaos in industry caused by the shortage of fuel and raw materials and the extreme disorganization of transportation.

The most violent clashes between the government and the workers again occurred in Petrograd. The Menshevik leader, Theodore Dan, who arrived in the city in early February 1921, has given the following description of the situation there.[5]

> In November-December, the government started production at several industrial plants, but it soon became obvious that mistakes had been made in the allocation of fuel and raw materials. The factories had to stop or slow down; workers were deprived of their ration cards and they and their families were left without bread or other food. An attempt was made to replace industrial fuel with wood from the surrounding forests: workers were sent to the forests to cut trees without enough warm clothing or boots, without enough tools. Sufficient fuel could hardly be supplied in this manner.
>
> Bread (half a pound to a pound) and from time to time a little sugar—that was all that was issued on food coupons. And even then, bread was not issued every day, and the quality of the bread!

Dan writes that even the soldiers of the Red Army went short of bread:

> I had to walk past the barracks on my way to the office and every day I was stopped in the streets near the barracks by Red Army soldiers literally begging for "a crust of bread" . . . Factories and workshops were seething with unrest. Workers assembled to discuss the situation and most of their demands were concentrated on abolition of the barrage detachments and the lifting of all restrictions on the free marketing of food. The workers would not listen to Bolshevik speakers in the factories; in the

> streets, Bolshevik officials were thrown out of their cars and some of them were threatened with beating. By February 20th, the movement had grown into a general strike.[6]

The Petrograd Soviet headed by Zinoviev had no influence with the workers. An attempt was made to revive the methods of 1918 by calling a conference of "non-party workers" with the assurance that the government would attempt to draw them into the government machinery. But the first such conference ended in a fiasco, in an incident characteristic of the political atmosphere of the time. The harassed Menshevik Party organization in Petrograd still managed, with the help of sympathizers among the printers, to issue leaflets and distribute a number of them in the factories. The leaflets demanded the release of all arrested socialists, the termination of the state of emergency, free elections to the factory Soviets and other Soviet bodies, and the reintroduction of the free trade in food. And so Mensheviks continued to be arrested, the latest victims being Kamensky and Kazukov, two active party members, and Theodore Dan himself. At a session of the "non-party" conference, Zinoviev made several sarcastic remarks about the Marxism of the Mensheviks. Thereupon a Menshevik worker replied: "Why argue with us half-educated workers who have never studied Marxism; why not get into your car, Comrade Zinoviev, and drive to the prison where you will find the Menshevik leader, Dan —bring him here with you, then the workers will be better able to understand the difference between the Bolshevik and the Menshevik interpretations of Marxism." Zinoviev, embarrassed, announced a recess, and that was the end of the conference.

Although the Mensheviks, whom Zinoviev attacked, called for neither a general strike nor an uprising, the strike movement swelled and grew, beyond the control not only of the government but also of the opposition leaders. At the eleventh hour—on February 26—the Petrograd Soviet yielded to the demands of the workers and withdrew the "barrage detachments" around Petrograd, but it was too late. The movement had now spread to Kronstadt.

The Kronstadt Rebellion

The sailors of the Baltic Fleet, and in particular those of Kronstadt, had formed the extreme left vanguard of the February Revolution, and their part in the October rising is well known. In Kronstadt they had established a revolutionary commune of a special kind. The Kronstadt sailors were the first in the Russian armed forces to introduce the election of officers and to forbid the wearing of epaulettes. At one time they had even proclaimed themselves an independent socialist commune. There were no Mensheviks among the sailors of Kronstadt and very few S-R's; on the other hand, Maximalists, Anarchists, left S-R's and Bolsheviks were very strongly represented among them from the start. During the "July days," Lunacharsky had led a huge crowd of sailors of the Baltic Fleet to the Tauride Palace. Trotsky called the sailors "the pride and glory of the Russian Revolution."

But, with the end of the Civil War, even this ultra-leftist revolutionary group came to oppose the economic policy of War Communism, as well as the government's extreme terror, which could no longer be excused on the grounds of the threat of counter-revolution. The sailors, as sons of peasants, were against an economic policy which led to famine, against the universally hated barrage-detachments, and against the dictatorship which weighed so heavily on the entire country.

During the election of delegates to the Tenth Congress in December 1920, the Bolshevik Party branch in Kronstadt, consisting of several thousand sailors and workers, had condemned Trotsky's attempts to convert the trade unions into tools of the government. The rank-and-file sailors also condemned the dissolution of political cells in the fleet. They especially resented the "Political Administration" of the Baltic Fleet, a kind of Bolshevik political police. As a result of these conflicts, 5,000 sailors had resigned from the Bolshevik Party even before the rising.[7] A few thousand sailors from the naval base had been transferred, as a precautionary measure, to the Black Sea and the Caspian Fleets and to the ports of the Far East.[8] Relations between the sailors and the remnants of the split Bolshevik Party at the base became extremely strained. On March 1, 1921, the tension in Kronstadt reached its peak.

The previous day there had been a conference of sailors on board the battleship *Petropavlovsk.* Its decisions were endorsed first by the sailors of the battleship *Sebastopol* and then by those of other ships, and by some Red Army units in the Kronstadt garrison.[9]

On March 1, a mass meeting of sailors of the active fleet, of Kronstadt workers, and of soldiers of the local garrison assembled in the open air, in Yakornaya Square. Among the speakers were M. Kalinin, the chairman of the VTsIK, and Kuzmin, the chief commissar of the Baltic Fleet. They were received with military honors, but their arguments and threats had no effect. The meeting passed the following historic resolution with only two abstentions:

1. In view of the fact that the present Soviets do not express the will of workers and peasants, new elections should be immediately held by a secret ballot, and the elections should be preceded by free electoral propaganda among workers and peasants.
2. Freedom of speech and press to be granted to workers and peasants, to Anarchists and to left-wing socialist parties.
3. Also freedom of assembly and of trade-union and peasants' associations.
4. A non-party conference of workers, Red Army soldiers, sailors of Petrograd city and district, and of Kronstadt, to be convened not later than March 10, 1921.
5. All political prisoners belonging to socialist parties[10] and also all workers and peasants, Red Army soldiers and sailors arrested in connection with workers' and peasants' disturbances, to be set free.
6. A commission to be elected to review the cases of all those held in prisons and concentration camps.
7. All political cells to be dissolved, as no one party can be allowed to possess privileges in propagating its ideas and to receive government money for that purpose.[11] Instead, locally elected cultural-educational commissions to be introduced, financed by the government.
8. Immediate removal of all barrage detachments.
9. Rations to be the same for all toilers, with special allowances for those in harmful occupations.
10. Bolshevik shock-troops to be abolished in all army units, as well as all Bolshevik watchers in the factories. If needed, those should be appointed by the respective army units and by the factory workers themselves.
11. Full freedom to be granted to peasants to cultivate their land as they think best, and to keep cattle by their own efforts, that

is, without hired labor.

12. All army units and the comrades in military schools are requested to support our resolution.
13. We demand that all resolutions be widely reprinted in the press.
14. A mobile control bureau to be appointed.
15. It is demanded that free production by individual craftsmen using only their own labor should be allowed.

This resolution is passed by the Brigade, meeting unanimously, with two abstentions.
Chairman of the Brigade-Meeting—Petrichenko.
Secretary—Perepelkin.[12]

The next day, March 2, a conference of Kronstadt workers, soldiers, sailors and trade-union delegates was convened to organize free elections to the Kronstadt Soviet. During the discussions, the Bolsheviks Kuzmin and Vassilyev (chairmen of the Kronstadt Soviet) threatened those present with dire retribution. Their pronouncements were so aggressive and provocative that they were arrested and placed in a special cabin on board the *Petropavlovsk*. Bolsheviks who conducted themselves in an orderly manner, however, were given complete freedom of speech. The conference elected a provisional revolutionary committee of 15 members: sailor Petrichenko, who was in charge of food supplies on the battleship *Petropavlovsk*; telephone operator Yakovenko; engineer of the *Sebastopol*, Perepelkin; chief electrician of the *Petropavlovsk*, Petrushev; sanitary orderly Kupulov; sailor Vershinin; electrical engineer Tukin; docker Romanenko; headmaster Oreshin; timber cutter Valk; miner Pavlov; master of fortification works Voykov; and pilot Kilgast.[13] This committee, with Petrichenko as chairman and Tukin as secretary, established its headquarters on the *Petropavlovsk* and immediately had strategic points in the city and fortress occupied by reliable troops. At the same time, the Provisional Revolutionary Committee issued a proclamation to the people of Kronstadt, stating its determination to avoid bloodshed and appealing to workers to remain at their work benches and to sailors and soldiers to remain at their posts. "Let us go forward, comrades, with order, tranquility and self-control towards a new and honest socialist construction for the good of all toilers."[14]

The Bolshevik authorities in Petrograd, with no intention of solving the conflict by peaceful means, prepared to suppress the Kronstadt rebels. They appointed a Committee of Three (Troika), consisting of Lashevich, a member of the Revolutionary Military Council; Antselovich, of the Central Executive Committee of the Petrograd Soviet; and Avrov. In addition, local Troikas were formed in each section of Petrograd consisting of the local party secretary, the commander of local troops, and one officer of the cadet school. At the same time, all able-bodied party members and officer cadets were hurriedly assembled in Petrograd in an emergency mobilization. The military advance on Kronstadt was entrusted to a commission consisting of Trotsky, Commander-in-Chief S. Kamenev, and Tukhachevsky.

In order to make the ensuing carnage more acceptable politically, the Bolsheviks declared that the Kronstadt movement was really a military plot organized by the Tsarist General Kozlovsky as part of a conspiracy with spies and agents of the Entente and "counter-revolutionary officers." In Petrograd, everyone suspected of membership in the Menshevik or S-R Parties was thrown into prison. Theodore Dan, Professor Rozhkov and the others arrested before the Kronstadt events were now accused of complicity in the movement and transferred to the Peter-Paul Fortress for execution. Their lives were saved only by the personal intervention of some members of the Bolshevik Central Committee.[15]

The Bolsheviks realized that the disorders in Petrograd itself had to be quelled first. A state of emergency was declared and the strike was ruthlessly put down. Trotsky boasted that the Petrograd disorders were quelled with "an iron hand" in just two days. At the same time, the Petrograd Soviet temporarily removed the barrage detachments around the city, and the workers and their families were allowed to go to the countryside for food; extra allocations of meat, shoes and clothes were issued in the factories. The tension in the working class relaxed, and the onslaught against Kronstadt could now begin.

In the Kronstadt Provisional Revolutionary Committee, there was not a single military man capable of the complex task of defending the fortress. Nor did the Committee wish to engage any old Tsarist officers as military instructors or commanders. True to their initial determination to avoid bloodshed, the men of Kronstadt did not think in terms of counter-attack. In view of the shortage of guns and ammunition, it is doubtful whether a counter-attack would have been possible, especially in the absence of an experienced military commander.

Restricting their activities to issuing leaflets, electing Soviets and building Soviet democracy, the sailors and their leaders showed much human decency. Thus, having arrested local Bolsheviks to prevent them from assisting the advancing government army, they did not, as the Bolsheviks did, arrest their families as hostages or threaten them with execution. They only took away 280 pairs of boots, urgently wanted at advance posts in winter time—giving the owners bast sandals instead.[16]

The Kronstadt outposts bravely repulsed the Bolsheviks' first attack. On March 8, the official records declare, the government troops began an offensive that "ended unsuccessfully."[17] Many of Trotsky's and Tukhachevsky's soldiers went over to the insurgents, groups of as many as 20 to 30 men, and even some complete companies.[18]

Once in Kronstadt, 700 such men passed a resolution greeting the insurgents and offering them help in the fight against the commissars from the Kremlin.[19]

But more and more troops from other parts of Russia were concentrated on Kronstadt, and all possible pressure was brought to bear to make the soldiers fight. In some regiments, military tribunals worked incessantly, shooting or severely punishing anyone who seemed unreliable or who was caught spreading news about the situation in Kronstadt. Party members were mobilized *en masse* and sent to the Kronstadt front as observers, commissars and propagandists. Moreover, special detachments were formed from Cheka forces and party members to shoot from behind all soldiers who seemed to hesitate, refused to advance, or tried to desert. Eyewitnesses affirmed that some government lines had lost up to half their strength even before coming under fire from Kronstadt—they had been mowed down by government machine-guns.[20]

In spite of all difficulties and the constant desertion of army units to Kronstadt, the Soviet government succeeded in assembling enough fanatical Bolsheviks to form, together with the cadets, the needed units for battle. At the last moment, even the Tenth Party Congress was temporarily suspended, and 300 of the delegates were sent to the Kronstadt front.[21]

Taking advantage of a snowfall which had shrouded everything in white, the Bolsheviks, dressed in white sacks, forced an entry into the town and fortress, although the defenders fought bravely and retreated only when the last round of ammunition was fired. During the last two days on March 17 and 18, there was hand-to-hand fighting in the streets. The losses were enormous on both sides. Some indication of the government losses is given in an official report of the health authorities of the Petrograd area. In the Kronstadt hospitals from March 3 to 21 there were 4,127 wounded, 158 shock cases and 527 dead. These figures do not include the many wounded who had died on the ice from exposure or loss of blood.[22]

If the Kronstadt sailors behaved like the Paris *communards* of 1871, their victors behaved little better than the Versailles government that suppressed the Paris Commune. There were mass executions and mass arrests. Exile and the most brutal punishment were the lot of all suspected by the Bolshevik Cheka of having helped the Kronstadt rebels. The Petrograd professors who were in prison at the time told of the merciless beating of the arrested Kronstadt men. In their words, the sailors, when brought back to the cells after interrogation, were masses of bleeding flesh. The exact number of those shot, arrested and sent to the camps is unknown, but rumor put the number of sailors shot at 2,000. A special commission examined the reliability of sailors, and 15,000 were dismissed from the fleet. However, some 8,000 Kronstadt sailors who had taken part in the rising managed to escape to Finland during the night of March 17.[23]

The official charge that the White General Kozlovsky had organized the rising was pure invention. There was a general named Kozlovsky in Kronstadt, but he took no part in the rising. He was one of a number of old officers who had been sent to Kronstadt, on the orders of Trotsky himself, as an artillery expert. For purposes of propaganda, Trotsky now turned him into a White general and represented him as the organizer of the rising. Neither were there any foreign agents or, for that matter, Mensheviks or right S-R's. The official representation of the Kronstadt rising as a White revolt is morally on a par with the trials that Stalin was later to stage against his enemies. The same alleged White contacts, the same spies—except that in the case of Kronstadt the accused were humble sailors with anarchist or socialist leanings, and the false-tongued prosecutor was not Vyshinsky but Trotsky himself.[24]

The Bolsheviks understood quite well that the Kronstadt "rising" was a protest by Russian workers and peasants, or their sons, against the deception practiced upon them by the Bolshevik Party. The fifteen points of the Kronstadt rebels showed no trace of a desire to return to the capitalist order, or even to "bourgeois democracy"; in fact, their whole social philosophy faithfully echoed the teachings of Lenin, Trotsky and the Left S-R's. In a long article printed in No. 10 of the "Announcements of the Provisional Revolutionary Committee" of March 12, the tenets of the Kronstadt men appear to be exactly the same as in July or October 1917. This is what it says:

> The three-centuries-old autocracy had fallen . . . The capitalists and the landowners rejoiced that at last they no longer needed to share their profits with the Tsar and his minions but could pad their pockets the better, still continuing to prosper on the toil of the worker and the peasant. They were hoping to get the toilers firmly into their clutches after tricking them out of their rights at the Constituent Assembly, to which Kerensky slowly but surely was leading . . . The inexperienced peasants and workers were also hoping for the Constituent Assembly, little knowing what was in store for them . . . But the patience of the toilers snapped and the joint effort of sailors, soldiers, workers and peasants swept away the bourgeoisie in October 1917. It seemed that the toiling masses had at last come into their own. But now the self-seeking Bolshevik Party seized power. This party decided to rule the country through its commissars after the model of the landowners in old Russia. The time has come to sweep away the autocracy of the commissars. The vigilant sentry of the social revolution—Kronstadt . . . is the first to raise the flag of revolt in the name of the Third Revolution of the toilers.

When the Bolsheviks were ruthlessly massacring the Kronstadt sailors, they were fully aware of the meaning of the Kronstadt protest. None other than Bukharin found it necessary to declare at the Third

Comintern Congress in 1922: "Who says that the Kronstadt rising was White? No. For the sake of the idea, for the sake of our task, we were forced to suppress the revolt of our erring brothers. We cannot look upon Kronstadt sailors as our enemies. We love them as our true brothers, our own flesh and blood . . ."[25]

The Famine

As early as April 3, 1919, Fritjof Nansen of Norway, moved by reports of starvation among the Russian population and the high mortality of its children, wrote to Wilson, Clemenceau, Orlando and Lloyd George, proposing the formation of a humanitarian commission to dispatch food and medical supplies to Russia. On April 9, Nansen was notified that the heads of the four governments were willing to accept his plan: the commission was to be of a non-political character. The Soviet reply to this proposal did not arrive until May 13. It accepted the offer in principle, but declined to suspend military operations on those sectors of the front through which the transports of food and medical supplies were to pass. Subsequently, in 1919 and 1920, the American Relief Administration (ARA), the YMCA and other charitable organizations made repeated attempts to work out a plan for sending supplies to the starving children of Russia, but all these attempts failed because the Bolsheviks were suspicious of a dark plot on the part of the "western imperialists."

Meanwhile, the famine had assumed catastrophic proportions. Millions of hungry peasants, with their wives and children, began to march in endless columns to the cities in the hope of finding relief. Cannibalism was common. Under these circumstances, the Soviet government finally decided to accept foreign help. The first step was to break the official silence. On June 26, 1921, *Pravda* published an article which revealed that "about 25,000,000 people" were suffering from the famine.[26] Then the Patriarch of the Russian Orthodox Church, with the permission of the Soviet government, publicly appealed to the Christians of the entire world to help the hungry women and children of Russia. Next, the writer and novelist, Maxim Gorki, on July 23, 1921, appealed to all "the honest men and women in Europe and America to render help to the Russian people . . . Give us bread and medical supplies." Gorki's appeal was cast in the form of a telegram to Herbert Hoover, then director of ARA. The same day (July 23), Gorki received Mr. Hoover's reply, indicating the readiness of ARA to start sending relief supplies to Russia. But the first meeting between the ARA representative, Brown, and Deputy People's Commissar for Foreign Affairs, Maxim Litvinov, did not take place until August 10. The discussions were held in Riga and lasted 10 days; on August 21, Brown and Litvinov, in the presence of the official representatives of Latvia and a group of journalists, signed an agreement regulating the work of ARA in Russia. The agreement granted ARA workers the right of free movement throughout Russia, but limited ARA activities to relief for children and the sick.

The first free kitchen for children was opened in Petrograd on September 7, and another was opened in Moscow on September 11. In November, *Pravda* began to carry, on page 4, a column under various headlines which often reported, in highly realistic detail, how people on the Volga and elsewhere disinterred corpses, or chopped up and ate their own children who had died.[27] This column was soon discontinued, however, at the request of People's Commissar for Health, Semashko, who wanted to protect the mental health of the citizens of Moscow.

In June 1922, ARA succeeded in obtaining permission to extend its activities to all famine victims. During that month it distributed food to 7,322,000; in July to 8,967,000; and in August to 10,492,000 (4,174,000 children and 6,318,000 adults). In September 1922, the number of famine victims had dropped by two million, and in October by seven million. In addition, at the suggestion of the Chairman of the War Committee of the U.S. House of Representatives, Julius Kahn, the United States Army turned over to ARA, for distribution in Russia, $4,000,000 worth of drugs and medical equipment from its own stores, all of which was duly sent to Russia.

The generous help provided by the United States during those critical years saved millions of lives in Soviet Russia, but the work of ARA was not allowed to run smoothly. Thus, at one point grain transports were arriving very late because the railways were not functioning properly and because the railway workers (who had received no wages for a whole year) were demanding payment in kind—

that is, in American grain or flour. The representatives of the Soviet government on ARA, the Cheka man Eydook and his assistant Penas, requisitioned ARA deliveries and rerouted them according to their own fancy. The ARA representative in Russia, Colonel Haskell, had to intervene in the most energetic manner: he telegraphed Hoover on April 10, 1922 to stop all further consignments to Russia in view of the breach of the Riga agreement by the Soviet authorities. This brought to the scene Leo Kamenev, whom the ARA representatives had till then been unable to locate, and who now promised that no further incidents would occur. The same Eydook tried, in October 1921, to stop ARA from entering the Ukraine on the spurious grounds that there was no famine there. After a ten-day struggle, Eydook had to give way. On November 26, the ARA representatives were allowed to enter the Ukraine, and on November 30 they called on the Deputy Chairman of the Soviet of People's Commissars of the Ukraine, Mikola Skrypnik. Here a new and completely unexpected obstacle arose, this time of a political character. The Ukrainian government would not consider the Riga agreement binding on the Ukraine, and was not prepared to accept American aid until ARA signed a separate agreement with the Ukraine as an independent republic. So ARA signed a separate agreement with the Ukraine. When the ARA representatives went to Minsk, the Byelorussian government also tried to hold out for a separate agreement, but this time ARA was adamant and the Byelorussians had to yield.

This buffoonery was taking place while millions were dying of starvation and epidemics—when, for instance, in the town of Orenburg, 150 people were dying of hunger each day, and a refugee train there was found to contain 450 dead and 250 dying. On the roads, crowds of people were in flight from the famine in the towns, among them large numbers of homeless children (*bezprizornye*) whom the Soviet government could not save from hunger and disease. In 1922 the *bezprizornye* numbered almost 7,000,000.

The work of ARA was hampered throughout by the police, who constantly arrested ARA employees as counter-revolutionaries, Socialist Revolutionaries, or whatever. To complaints from ARA representatives, the Soviet authorities replied that the police were not arresting ARA employees as such, but only as counter-revolutionaries, etc. This did not prevent Trotsky from writing that ARA was helping the famine victims with one hand and Wrangel with the other.[28] Since Wrangel's army had been defeated about three years earlier, these words could refer only to the fact that one or two former officers of that army were among the ARA employees.

But while Trotsky was busy heaping demagogic slander on ARA, Lenin went further. At the very moment that the Soviet government was admitting that the famine had not yet been conquered, Lenin decided to export Russian grain. At the Third Comintern Congress, on November 13, 1922, he announced that, to finance the industrial plan, another 80,000,000 roubles had to be found. For this purpose the State Bank and the Central Grain Office had already begun buying up bread for export abroad in exchange for foreign currency.[29] Thus, at the very time that the Americans were bringing bread into the country to save sick and starving children, the Russian government was exporting its own grain.

The summer and fall of 1922 were the periods when, at least on the Volga, epidemics and cannibalism reached their peak. In Bashkiria, authorities had reported over 2,000 cases of cannibalism up to July 1, 1922. This is mentioned in a book published in Petrograd in 1922.[30] Another book, published in Samara (Kuibyshev), gives more detailed descriptions of the widespread cannibalism of that period:

> Reports on cases of cannibalism and the eating of human corpses have begun to come in almost daily. Thus we hear from Pestravka, Pugachovsky district, that women cut the hands and feet off a human corpse and ate them. Children who die are not taken to the cemetery but kept for food . . . Houses where people turned cannibal had long been without a crumb of food . . .[31]

Cannibalism became such an everyday occurrence in the famine-stricken area that "a group of citizens of Idrissovsk division of the Zlatoustovsk district officially petitioned the divisional Executive Committee for permission to slaughter their children for food."[32]

In December 1922, the head of ARA in Russia reported to Herbert Hoover that there were still about 3,000,000 children and sick persons in Russia who would require feeding. ARA decided to continue the relief operation, and it was not until June 4, 1923, that Colonel Haskell informed Kamenev that ARA was terminating its work in

Russia. The last ARA food consignment arrived from Riga on June 13, 1923.

According to official Soviet data published later,[33] the number of deaths during 1921-1922 "from famine and its after-effects" was approximately 5,000,000. To this figure must be added the number of those who died during the first few months of 1923, when there were still about 3,000,000 children suffering from illness or undernourishment. It may be confidently estimated that the intervention of ARA saved the lives of two or three million, if not more.

Toward the end of 1922, Maxim Gorki was writing to Herbert Hoover: " . . . in the whole history of practical humanitarianism I know of no achievement that could compare, in greatness and compassion, with the help that you extended . . ." The thanks of the Soviet government were considerably more reserved. The Soviet of People's Commissars wrote: "The people of the Soviet Union will never forget the generous help of the American people." But on the very day that the ARA representatives left, Soviet authorities in all parts of the country began to arrest Russian employees of ARA. Although some were released, many disappeared forever.

What little confidence the Soviet government had in the Russian people and the Russian intelligentsia was demonstrated very clearly in the case of the Civic Relief Committee which had been formed under Kamenev's chairmanship in the summer of 1921. The democratically-minded intellectuals of Russia considered it their duty to lend all their energies to the campaign for famine relief. The Civic Relief Committee organized by Kamenev, who was considered one of the more liberal Bolsheviks, was joined by many members of the Moscow intelligentsia. Foremost among these were the well-known Sergei Prokopovich, his wife, the writer Ekaterina Kuskova, and the famous doctor, Nikolai Kishkin.[34] But not all those who wanted to join the committee were allowed to do so. For instance, Mensheviks were not admitted; they addressed an independent appeal to the socialist and other workers' parties of Europe to come to the help of the starving Russian masses.[35]

While the Soviet government was gratefully accepting help from religious and charitable societies conducted by "western capitalists," and even from Christian sects in the United States (the Mennonites), it would not permit the Russian intelligentsia to take a part in saving its own people. On the day that the first representative of ARA arrived in Moscow and was due to meet the Civic Relief Committee, specially convened for the purpose, a Cheka man turned up—to declare the committee dissolved and to arrest all those present, with the single exception of Vera Figner, the famous revolutionary and former prisoner in the Schluesselburg Fortress. Those arrested were later exiled from Russia, as were the Mensheviks still resident there. It was at first intended to send the Mensheviks to western Siberia or Turkestan, but the Mensheviks went on a hunger strike and in the end succeeded, through Martov and Abramovitch, in making their plight known to the German Independent Socialists and other socialist parties which had just united in the Vienna International. The resulting wave of protests from abroad persuaded the Soviet government to substitute banishment for confinement in Siberia, and the Mensheviks went abroad early in 1922.

[1] *Minutes*, 10th Party Congress, pp. 864-865.

[2] *Minutes*, 10th Party Congress.

[3] *Great Soviet Encyclopedia*. Vol. II, 1950, p. 528, 2nd ed. Moscow, 1950.

[4] *Ibid.*

[5] Dan, T., *Dva Goda Skitaniy* (Two Years of Roaming) (1919-1921), Berlin, 1922, pp. 101, ff.

[6] The strike began on February 24th. The picture painted by Dan is borne out by a speech delivered by Lashevich, a member of the Revolutionary Military Soviet, at the session of the Petrograd Soviet on February 26th, and reported in the *Krasnaya Gazeta* of February 27, 1921.

[7] Scheuer, Georg. *Von Lenin bis. . .* Vienna, 1954, pp. 209, ff; and *Socialist Courier*, No. 4, March 18th, 1921, p. 1.

[8] Mett, Ida, "La commune de Kronstadt," p. 57.

[9] Scheuer, Georg. *op. cit.*, p. 213.

[10] Point 2 had mentioned only *left-wing* socialists.

[11] This shows that the Kronstadt sailors did not at all intend to exclude the Bolsheviks from the parties admitted into the Soviets or, as is often said, want "Soviets without Communists." They only insisted that the Communist Party should enjoy no privileges not granted to the other left-wing socialist parties.

[12] "Announcements of the Provisional Revolutionary Committee of sailors, Red Army soldiers and workers of Kronstadt," No. 1, March 3, 1921.

[13] This list was published in No. 10 of the "Announcements of the Kronstadt Soviet," March 12, 1921, under the title "Our Generals."

[14] "Announcements of the Provisional Revolutionary Committee," No. 1.

[15] Dan, Th., *op. cit.*, p. 130.

[16] "Announcements of the Provisional Revolutionary Committee," No. 9, March 11, 1921.

[17] *Minutes of the Tenth Congress*, Moscow, 1933, p. 841.

[18] The troops in question were those of the 561st Regiment, several companies of which, "coming into contact with the enemy, surrendered." (See Zhakovstchikov, *The Smashing of the Kronstadt Revolt, 1921*. Leningrad, 1941, p. 61.)

[19] "Announcements of the Provisional Revolutionary Committee," Issue of March 9, 1921.

[20] Ida Mett, *op. cit.*, p. 53.

[21] *Minutes of the Tenth Congress*, p. 841.

[22] Ida Mett, *op. cit.*, p. 56.

[23] *Ibid.*, p. 57.

[24] Trotsky would, no doubt, have regarded as mad anyone who had told him then that in 1939 the Political Administration of the Red Army would issue a leaflet for soldiers, telling them that "Judas Trotsky" had prepared the rising by sending as early as 1920 many of "his own men" to Kronstadt, including bandits, deserters and notorious White Guards, while early in 1921 he had deliberately deflected the attention of the party to a discussion on trade unions (see Leonidov, L., *The liquidation of the counter-revolutionary Kronstadt revolt,* Military publication, p. 139). Still more intriguing is the booklet by K. Zhakovstchikov, *The smashing of the Kronstadt counter-revolutionary revolt,* published in 1941, which lays the blame for organizing the Kronstadt rising not only on Trotsky but also on "his protegé, the commander of the Seventh Army, Tukhachevsky," and on "the old Trotskyist Raskolnikov, the commander of the Baltic Fleet," and other Trotskyists, and affirms that the rising was put down, almost single-handedly by "the true Leninist, the closest comrade-in-arms of the great Stalin, the outstanding proletarian army leader, Klementy Voroshilov" (p. 62).

[25] *Minutes of the 3rd Congress of the Comintern,* 1922.

[26] The figures given in the *Pravda* article were a gross underestimate. According to the *Great Soviet Encyclopedia,* 35 *gubernias* with a total population of 90,000,000 were stricken by famine, and no less than 35,000,000 were actually starving at that time (*Great Soviet Encyclopedia,* 1st ed., vol. 17, p. 463).

[27] *Socialist Courier,* No. 5, March 5, 1922, p. 12.

[28] *Izvestia,* March 14, 1922.

[29] During 1923, when the famine was still far from over, Soviet Russia exported twice as much grain to Germany as in 1913, a bumper-crop year in Russia. (See article by M. Orlov, "On the History of Soviet-German Relations," in *International Life,* No. 8, 1955.)

[30] *Book on the Famine,* by Drs. L. A. and L. M. Vassilevsky, 3rd ed., Kniga Publishing House, Petrograd, 1922, pp. 175-76.

[31] *Book on the Famine,* published by the Samara Commission for Famine Relief, State Publishing House, Samara Division, 1922, p. 125.

[32] *Book on the Famine,* by Drs. L. A. and L. M. Vassilevsky, *op. cit.*, p. 178.

[33] *Great Soviet Encyclopedia,* 1st ed. vol. V, 1927, p. 463.

[34] The initial letters of these three names made up the popular nickname of the Committee, "Prokukish," a word which has a far from flattering symbolic meaning in Russian and is untranslatable into any other language

[35] This appeal was issued on July 6, 1921 by the Central Committee of the Menshevik Party, which still existed in Russia. In addition, the representatives of the Menshevik Party abroad, Martov and Abramovitch, appealed to all socialist parties to support the campaign for famine relief in Russia and suggested that the Amsterdam Trade Union International organize the relief. This appeal was acted upon and such modest help as was possible at the time was given. In February 1923 one trainload of food was taken to Russia by one of the secretaries of the Trade Union International, Karl Volmerhaus.

The Amsterdam International was given permission to feed 50,000 children through local Soviet organizations. The district allocated to it was distant Chuvashia, where there was absolutely no industry and consequently no workers among whom the representatives of the International could develop their "yellow" propaganda. The only thanks that the Amsterdam International ever got from the Soviet government for feeding these children was an order from Lozovsky, the then Secretary of the red Trade Union International, to the Soviet press to stop calling the Amsterdam International "yellow." (See *Socialist Courier,* No. 4, February 23, 1922, p. 14; No. 6, March 21, 1922, p. 5.)

CHAPTER 9

Lenin and Marxism

The Two Souls of Lenin

Lenin had always combined an analytical Marxist outlook with a strong streak of romantic utopianism. After the February Revolution the utopianism gradually became dominant. Lenin, at this point, turned to the early Marx, who, in the draft agreement for an alliance between Communists and revolutionary Blanquists (April 1850), wrote:

> The aim of the Association is the abolition of the privileged classes, their subjection to the dictatorship of the proletariat through the maintenance of a permanent revolution, until Communism, the ultimate form of organization for mankind, is achieved.[1]

This kind of social utopianism, which Marx repudiated in the 1860s and 1870s, brought Lenin close to Trotsky in 1917; until then, his attitude to Trotsky's idea of "permanent revolution" had been rather critical.

In the Marxist tradition there had long been warnings against utopianism. Back in 1850, Friedrich Engels had warned the leaders of the revolutionary party of the inescapable peril threatening those who took power in a society which was not yet ripe to be ruled by the class which the party represented.[2] Engels' advice applied precisely to a country such as Russia in 1917, where the workers were an insignificant minority of the population. Back in 1905, and even as late as 1915-1916, Lenin was still a staunch supporter of Engels' views. In a debate with the Menshevik leaders Martov and Martynov, Lenin emphatically denied that his plan for a revolutionary coalition of the Social Democrats with the peasants and the urban petty-bourgeoisie was intended to bring about a "pseudo-socialist" society, as Engels called it. Quite the contrary—its goal, Lenin asserted, was a democratic "middle-class" revolution which would leave the foundations of bourgeois property intact.[3]

In another discussion, this time between himself and Parvus, Lenin welcomed Parvus as an ally in the fight against the Mensheviks, but at the same time drew Parvus' attention to the fact that a provisional government, in a country such as Russia, with a small number of workers and a large number of peasants and middle-class property holders, would never have a socialist majority. "Our party," said Lenin, "should, of course, be a revolutionary one in the broadest sense of the word, but we could not claim to be more revolutionary than any other party. To make such a claim would be an error." Lenin went on to explain again and again that in Russia the revolution was bound to be one of a bourgeois-democratic, not of a socialist, nature. The very real interests of the peasantry made it unthinkable that this class would go so far as to become socialist, even in a major revolution. For the same reason, he said, it was "unthinkable that the revolution and the government in which we shall participate will be a socialist government with a socialist majority. This cannot happen in Russia, if we exclude ephemeral historic accidents, which leave no trace in history."[4]

Lenin concluded by reminding Parvus that "leaders of the revolutionary peasants cannot at this time become socialists, because their class instincts do not permit it, not only for the reason of their backwardness but because the objective logic of the historic development has put before them the problem of a democratic revolution, not of a socialist one."[5]

Indeed, it would be difficult to formulate a more convincing and more Marxist defense of Plekhanov's theses postulating the bourgeois character of the forthcoming Russian revolution and the historic necessity of political self-limitation of the Russian proletariat.

Thus taught Lenin—before, during and after the 1905 revolution. In his book, *The Two Tactics of the Social Democrats in a Democratic Revolution,* he wrote:

> Marxism has irrevocably broken with the silly twaddle of the Populists and the Anarchists, who claim, for example, that the development of capitalism in Russia could . . . be bypassed . . . The idea of seeking salvation . . . in anything but the further development of capitalism . . . is reactionary.[6]

Lenin pointed out that the ultimate victory of the revolution would require a temporary dictatorship; but, he added,

> It will be of course not a socialist but a democratic dictatorship. The latter will not get at . . . the roots of capitalism, but will at best introduce a radical redistribution of landed estates for the benefit of the peasantry; establish a complete and consistent democracy, including a republican regime; eradicate all Asiatic slavery, and lay the foundation for a real improvement in the workers' condition and raise their standard of living . . . Such a victory will by no means have turned our bourgeois revolution into a socialist one; the democratic upheaval will not directly expand beyond the limits of bourgeois socio-economic conditions.[7]

In conclusion, Lenin wrote:

> . . . the democratic revolution will be bourgeois in nature. The slogan, 'radical redistribution of land' . . . is likewise bourgeois. Yet we, the Marxists, must understand that there is not, and cannot be, any path toward true freedom for the proletariat and the peasantry other than the path of bourgeois freedom and bourgeois progress.[8]

A great many statements such as those quoted can be found throughout Lenin's writings. The point is that Lenin remained true to the fundamental thesis of Russian Marxism, even as late as the initial phase of the 1917 revolution. Thus, in an article entitled "Left Populism and Marxism," published in the first issue of *Rabochaya Pravda*, he wrote:

> The economic development in Russia, as in the rest of the world, proceeds from serfdom to capitalism and by way of large-scale mechanized capitalism to socialism.[9]
>
> Dreaming of a 'different' road to socialism other than by way

> of the *further* development of capitalism and large-scale mechanized *capitalist* industry is typical in Russia either of liberal-minded sons of the rich or of backward petty-bourgeoisie. These dreams, with which the left Populists still litter their brains, reflect the backwardness and ineptitude of the petty bourgeoisie.[10]

Despite the categorical nature and apparent firmness of statements such as these, repeated scores and even hundreds of times, Lenin was irresistibly driven to the old Populist dreams. In Lenin's mind there revolved two ideas, each not always in perfect harmony with the other. Surely the passion and sharpness with which Lenin denounced as absurd the idea that Russia could bypass capitalism was, from the psychological point of view, but a reflection of the inner struggle in Lenin's mind. It was not the Populists, the Maximalists, or the ignorant whom he was trying to convince; it was himself.

How did this dualism develop in Lenin's mind? An explanation may be found in a remarkable book by N. Valentinov, which traces an entirely new ideological biography of the young Lenin.[11]

According to Valentinov, young Vladimir spent a year after the execution of his brother in the country house of the Ulianovs near Kazan. During this time his favorite reading was the work of Chernyshevsky, the most famous revolutionary Populist writer of that time. So powerful was the influence of Chernyshevsky that Lenin himself wrote in his diary, which Valentinov had the chance to read: "... he turned all my ideas inside out ..."

Three years later, while living in Samara, the young Lenin used to meet Yaseneva, a close collaborator of another old-time revolutionist, Zaichnevsky, the leader of "Young Russia." This organization, which was active in 1861-62, had been created by a group of Russian Jacobins whose philosophy was based on ruthless terrorism and dictatorship. Yaseneva introduced Lenin to the history of this movement and to its leader's teachings.[12]

Lenin's third and last teacher was Marx. After reading the first volume of *Das Kapital,* Lenin became a loyal disciple of Marx. However, as Valentinov points out, he would at times retrogress to his old Populist utopianism. This tendency manifested itself not when he defined the *substance* of the approaching revolution, in sociological formulas that adhered strictly to Marxist standards, but when he went on to define the revolutionary *strategy* of the Social Democrats. It was this concept of his relations with the other Russian political groups that led him to highly utopian conclusions.

In the *Proletarii* (No. 3, dated September 14, 1905), Lenin wrote that from the overthrow of absolutism, from the democratic bourgeois revolution, " . . . we shall at once begin the transition to the socialist revolution . . . . We are for a *permanent revolution*. We shall not halt midway."[13]

While Lenin continued to reject "utopian nonsense," he often defined the political tasks of our "bourgeois revolution" in such a manner that it automatically became an anti-bourgeois revolution, i.e., a proletarian, socialist revolution. Thus, Lenin argued that the "leading" revolutionary class, which determined the course of events, could be only the proletariat. He consigned to the camp of the counter-revolution every section of the urban bourgeois population, including the liberal and democratic parties of every shade. The Social Revolutionaries and the Mensheviks were considered the allies of the counter-revolution.

In criticizing Lenin's idea, the Mensheviks pointed out to him that he wanted to make a bourgeois revolution without the bourgeoisie, against the bourgeoisie, by means of a dictatorship of the proletariat over the bourgeoisie. To this Lenin retorted:

"A victorious bourgeois revolution in our country is impossible as a victory of the bourgeoisie."[14]

The only possible ally of the proletariat, the "leading" class of the revolution, Lenin said, was the peasantry, insofar as the peasants sought the expropriation of the landed gentry. An alliance of these two forces, in his opinion, was "nothing other than a revolutionary dictatorship of the proletariat and the peasantry."[15]

The relationship between these two classes in the development of the Russian revolution had from the outset been one of the major strategic and tactical problems confronted by the Social Democrats in Russia. In 1902, when the draft of a new party program was discussed by the Editorial Board of *Iskra,* this problem was the subject of disagreement among the members of the Board. Vera Zasulich, looking over a preliminary draft of Lenin's comments on the program drafted by Plekhanov, called Lenin's attention to the inner contradictions in his argument. She pointed out that the party program, insofar as it concerned the peasants, should be so formulated that the peasants would feel drawn to the proletariat. Yet, Lenin threatened the peasants with the dictatorship of the proletariat. To this Lenin's rejoinder was: "The 'kinder' we are to the small producer (such as the peasant) in the practical portion of our program, the 'sterner' our attitude must be, in our basic tenets, toward these vacillating, double-faced social elements. We must not retreat one iota from our essential position. The point should be made very clear: to those who accept our ideas we shall be 'good' in every way. Those who do not—will have to suffer the consequences. Once the dictatorship is ours, we shall not waste words, but use force."[16]

Commenting on this remark, V. Zasulich exclaimed: "Use force on millions? Just try! You had better convince them! Woo them!"[17]

This exchange clarifies the issue. Lenin's intention was to draw the peasants into a common struggle against Tsarism, not only in the interests of the workers, but for the benefit of the peasantry as well. In his opinion, collaboration between these two social groups was possible, even though their class interests were not fully compatible and, in fact, conflicted in certain areas. Such collaboration was possible, he reasoned, if the leading class (the workers) would deliberately limit its objective in the coming revolution to the replacement of the semifeudal autocratic regime by a modern democratic state, without attempting to advance beyond the confines of capitalist bourgeois society —a task which should be left for the future (the maximum program). At the same time, the collaboration of the working class (Social Democrats) with the peasantry was conceived quite obviously by Lenin not as a partnership of equals but rather in terms of a group which was leading and a group which was being led. Should the latter, at some stage of the game, refuse to follow the leaders, the working class would use its dictatorial powers to subdue forcibly its recalcitrant and none-too-reliable partner.

Thus, Lenin's intellectual dualism cannot be doubted. On the one hand, Lenin maintained that there was no other path to progress and the liberation of the working class except that of large-scale capitalist industry; on the other, Lenin taught that there was no other path to a regime of bourgeois freedom except through the dictatorship of the proletariat. There was no rational link between the Marxist and the utopian halves of his mind. For if one attentively examines all of Lenin's strategic and tactical plans, one can readily see that he concentrated his entire attention on the problem of power. The one and only question with which he was preoccupied all those years and in all his political studies was the question of the forces and levers to be used in seizing power.

But the basic difference between utopian Populism and the Russian Marxism of Plekhanov lay not in the methods for seizing power, but in the different evaluation of the degree to which Russian society, in the second half of the nineteenth century, was mature enough for the building of a socialist order.

The notion of a society being mature for socialism was basic for both Marx and Engels. They had asserted more than once that a new system of economy and social order must first ripen in the womb of the old society if the overthrow was to be practicable and successful. The basic argument against utopian socialism during that era was the consideration that the socio-economic, political, material and general cultural conditions in the country were not sufficiently ripe. For such ripening, not only the "revisionist" Bernstein and his followers, but also orthodox Marxists of the school of Kautsky, Bebel, and Wilhelm Liebknecht, considered that decades of capitalist social and political development were needed.

With the possible exception of Trotsky, whom Lenin had nicknamed "the windbag," the leading Russian Marxists thought that the numerically weak working-class, submerged as it was in the enormous mass of a hundred million peasants and the lower middle-class urban population, would, if it came to power, find itself completely incapable of assuming the burden of power within the framework of a bourgeois-democratic order emerging in the place of the autocracy.

All of these considerations were fresh in Lenin's mind when it came to opposing the Populists, but he promptly forgot them whenever he visualized the prospect of the establishment of a revolutionary dictatorship of the proletariat and the peasantry, with the aid of the very peasants who were to be deceived—that is, in the final analysis, of rule by the Bolshevik Party. At these times, his Marxism was temporarily discarded and the "second" Lenin—the utopian—appeared on the scene.

The World War played a decisive role in making the utopian elements dominant in Lenin's *Weltanschauung*. Only a few weeks before the outbreak of the war, Lenin still held to the standpoint of the inevitability of a capitalist development in Russia. But during 1915-1916 he became increasingly convinced that a long and cruel war, which had shaken the entire capitalist world deeply, could end only in a world revolution which, in its turn, could be only a socialist revolution. Here, at last, was a solution for his dualism. For if the war was bound to end in a world revolution, the Russian revolution would no longer have to reckon with the degree of ripeness of Russia herself, but would become part of, or perhaps the prelude to, the world revolution. The latter, by liquidating the capitalist system the world over, would enable the numerically-limited Russian proletariat to undertake a socialist revolution.

However, the following quotation from a letter by Lenin to Alexandra Kollontai, written on February 17, 1917, only two weeks before the outbreak of the revolution in Petrograd, shows how deeply Lenin's mind was split and also how profoundly he had been influenced by Plekhanov. Thus, Lenin had just been shocked by the news from the United States that the Socialist Labor Party was preparing to jettison its entire "minimum program"; and he wrote: ". . . what a temptation and danger this would present to our Bukharin, who has been stumbling over this question ever since 1915" (*Leninski Sbornik,* No. 2, second edition, Moscow-Leningrad, p. 282).

Lenin and War Communism

The unexpectedly easy victory in October 1917 turned Lenin's head. In his book, *On Lenin,* published in Moscow in 1924, Trotsky relates:

> In Lenin's theses on peace, which he wrote at the beginning of 1918, he says that a socialist success in Russia requires time, at least several months . . . Today, these words do not seem to make sense: isn't there a misprint? Could he have meant several years, several decades? But no, it is not a misprint. It must be possible

> to find more declarations like this one, made by Lenin. I remember very well now, during the Smolny days, Lenin constantly repeated, at every meeting of the Soviet of People's Commissars, that in six months we were going to have socialism and become the most powerful state.[18]

Analyzing his 1918 plans, at the Second Congress of Committees for Political Education, in October 1921, Lenin declared in a speech: "We made the mistake of deciding to change over directly to Communist production and distribution. We sought to obtain a sufficient quantity of grain from the peasants by the way of the *razverstka* (compulsory grain delivery quotas), then to apportion it to the industries, and that thus we would obtain Communist production and distribution. I would not affirm that this was exactly how we visualized it, but we did act in this spirit."[19]

Following this plan, the Bolsheviks banned free trade as early as the spring of 1918 and began to send food-collecting detachments to the villages. These requisitioned the peasants' "surpluses," and, as Lenin himself later recognized, "not only the surpluses." They began, systematically, to fan a class war in the countryside through the Committees of Poor Peasants.[20]

By June 1918, the nationalization of all industrial enterprises, including small workshops, was completed. Shortly after that, on November 21, all private trade was banned—not only grain, but all other commodities, retail as well as wholesale. In attempting to realize integral socialism within a few months, Lenin refused to face the real state of affairs, and imagined that victory was near. Here is how he depicted the triumphant march of socialism in the Soviet Union:

> . . . . The Soviet republic now sends detachments of armed workers, in the first place those who are the most politically advanced, from the two capitals to the countryside. These workers carry socialism to the countryside, bring the poor peasants over to their side, organize them, enlighten them, help them to *suppress the resistance of the bourgeoisie* . . .
>
> . . . The actual number of those on the side of Bolshevism is *growing limitlessly*: tens and tens of millions of poor peasants are waking up to political life as they are freed from the tutelage and influence of the *kulaks* and the village bourgeoisie.

Having thus completed the bourgeois-democratic revolution together with the peasantry as a whole, Russia's proletariat started the socialist revolution, after it succeeded in splitting the village, rallying the village proletarians and semi-proletarians against the *kulaks* and the village bourgeoisie.[21]

The extent of Lenin's self-deception is surprising. Lenin must have already realized that the policy of fomenting a class war in the countryside was antagonizing the rank-and-file peasants and would cause great damage to the Red Army in the Civil War. Indeed, the Committees of Poor Peasants were dissolved and Lenin began advocating an alliance with the bulk of the peasantry. However, a most important aspect of the policy of War Communism had not been revoked: The January 11, 1919 decree introducing the *razverstka* gave new legal sanction to this old practice. When, in February 1920, Trotsky proposed that the *razverstka* be replaced by a tax in kind, only four Central Committee members voted for this proposal; eleven, headed by Lenin, voted against it.[22]

In the spring of 1920, the Menshevik Party, which was still legally recognized and still invited to the congresses of the Soviets, presented its program, "What is to be Done?", proposing a new policy toward the peasants and the abandonment of the utopian system of integral Communism. Lenin, together with Trotsky, who had himself put forward an essentially Menshevik policy in February, accused the Mensheviks of being agents of the bourgeoisie. Theodore Dan, the Menshevik spokesman, speaking at a December 1920 session of the 8th Congress of the Soviets, was able to complete his speech only because many delegates demanded that he be allowed to do so. All this happened only three months before the 10th Congress of the Communist Party, at which Lenin decided to renounce his utopia. But then, he was forced to do so by the "stubborn facts," which, as a rule, he treated with respect.

Writing about the Kronstadt revolt, Bukharin's pupil, Professor A. Slepkov, declared that the delay in introducing the New Economic Policy was a mistake. Had the NEP been proclaimed a month earlier, there would have been no Kronstadt uprising. But, Slepkov wrote, "the great architect wanted to take his bearings, to calculate, to check, he wanted to make sure."[23] This idealized account is not quite accurate, for Lenin was not guided by calculations. Rather, it was the machine guns of Antonov's rebels, and the guns of the Kronstadt sailors, that compelled him to give in.

In his speech at the 10th Party Congress, March 8, 1921, in the midst of the Kronstadt uprising, Lenin continued to insist that it was dangerous to yield to the chief demand of the Kronstadt sailors and of the Petersburg workers: the abolition of the *razverstka* and free trade in grain. Lenin said: "Freedom of trade, even if originally it was not as closely connected with the White Guards as was Kronstadt, would still unfailingly lead to the rule of the White Guard, to the triumph of capitalism, to complete restoration of the old regime. And I repeat: we must clearly recognize this political danger."[24]

Apparently, to the very last moment, Lenin had not overcome the utopian half of his soul. In his speech at the Second Congress of Committees for Political Education (October 1921),[25] in which he conceded that "we made the mistake of deciding to change over directly to Communist production and distribution," Lenin still refused to acknowledge that the roots of the error were planted in the Bolsheviks' utopian approach to the very nature of the Russian revolution. How, otherwise, could he have written the following, in his book on Kautsky, which contained his plan for the socialization of the peasantry within a few months:

> If the Bolshevik proletariat, in October and November 1917, had failed to wait out the differentiation of the classes in the villages, had failed to prepare it and to see it through—if it had tried to 'decree' civil war and the 'introduction of socialism' in the countryside, if it had tried to do so without the temporary alliance with the bulk of the peasantry, without making concessions to the *serедniaks,* etc.—this would have been a *Blanquist* distortion of Marxism, this would have been an attempt on the part of a *minority* to impose its will upon the majority, this would have been a theoretical absurdity, a failure to understand that the all-peasant revolution is still a bourgeois revolution and that, without a *series of transitions* and of *transitional stages,* this revolution could not have been made a socialist revolution in a backward country.[26]

This is expressed in Marxist language, but all that differentiates it from Blanquism is the delay of a few months—from October-November 1917 to March 1918—in introducing socialism.

Lenin's Conception of the NEP

The New Economic Policy, or NEP, was unofficially introduced by Lenin's famous speech on taxation in kind, at the Tenth Party Congress, on March 15, 1921. On the basis of a resolution at that Congress, the All-Union Executive Committee (VTsIK), on March 21, promulgated the decree replacing the requisition of "surpluses" with taxation in kind, while reducing by half the amount of grain to be taken from the peasants. The dry wording of this historic decree fails to convey the tremendous significance of the NEP. The abolition of grain requisitioning and its replacement by taxation in kind, the fact that the assessment of the total tax came to half of what the peasants had to contribute under the old system, amounted, in fact, to a revolution. To a considerable extent, the peasant became an independent agricultural producer again, and once he had delivered his tax in kind, he was entitled to sell his produce or barter it in the free market for the goods he needed. Thereby, the bread monopoly was abolished and the freedom of private trade was re-established, not only for the peasants, but for the entire population. In other words, after having spent three years in the strait-jacket of War Communism, the Russian peasantry returned to their normal state.

By this time Lenin seems to have understood that the re-education of the peasants, their breaking up into different classes, and their alliance with the proletariat was a long-term process. He said then: "The re-education of the small land-holders, the reshaping of their entire psychology and habits, will take generations. . . . When I say it will take generations, I do not mean that it will take centuries . . . but you understand very well that this must be reckoned . . . at least in decades."[27]

Lenin repeated that it would take decades to improve technology and living standards, to develop industry and introduce electrification, and to create the other prerequisites of socialism, especially to acquire social experience, and carefully re-educate and psychologically reshape the people. In 1922, little more than a year before his death, Lenin told the 11th Congress that it was necessary to form a bloc with the peasant mass, with the rank-and-file laboring peasant, and to begin the forward movement, incomparably, infinitely more slowly than we had hoped."[28]

In 1923, already bed-ridden, Lenin dictated to his secretary: "Remember about the bloc with the peasantry, remember that we are riding an exhausted peasant nag. Attempts to jump onto the back of the industrial steed, an inability to wait for the peasant horse, would indicate that the proletariat is a bad master, inexperienced and miscalculating."[29]

In his "testament," Lenin returned for the last time to his basic idea —the possibilityof the peaceful co-existenceof the proletariat with the bulk of the peasantry. There he points out that the regime is based on the co-operation of the two classes, and that a disruption of this co-operation could have catastrophic results for the Soviet state. It would seem that, during the last two years of his life, Lenin was genuinely convinced that the NEP had been introduced in earnest and for a long time.

Illness and then death prevented Lenin from thinking through all the prospects, possibilities and contradictions of the NEP. All he could do was formulate a few improvisations, but he left no worked-out conception of the new course to his successors. These improvisations were interesting, but in the long run inadequate.

One of Lenin's most fascinating ideas was that foreign capital should be encouraged to take over the task of creating modern industrial enterprises in Russsia. Going back to the Marxist concept that the road to economic progress and socialism was through large-scale capitalist industry, Lenin, having annihilated the last remnants of domestic capitalism, was prepared to "entrust" this role to foreign capital. In his pamphlet, "Taxation in Kind," Lenin expressed the hope that "if successful, the policy of concessions will give us a number of big enterprises, far superior to our own, meeting the standards of modern capitalist technology: after a few decades these enterprises will have passed into our hands." He declares further that "the transition from concesssion to socialism is a transition from one form of large-scale production to another form of large-scale production."

At the Tenth Party Congress, Lenin was already saying that the aid of foreign capital would be the only possible salvation for the Soviet regime.[30] Lenin added that this foreign capital-aid was worth a good price: ". . . and here we won't grudge millions, nay, billions of our unlimited wealth, of our rich raw-material resources, in order to get the aid of big modern capital . . ."

Lenin was aware that foreign capital would have to be paid for helping Russia, and that the price would be high. He realized that the results he sought would take several decades to be achieved. But not once did he try to work out a realistic formula for the harmonious, fruitful co-existence of the Soviet regime and foreign capital. He seemed to have forgotten that Russia had become a land dominated by the terroristic methods of a proletarian dictatorship; that the social, political, judicial and moral climate of such a country could not be propitious for the thriving of capitalist enterprises; that foreign capitalists and companies would not feel safe in a country that had neither proper protection for capitalist property nor an independent judiciary, a country where the entire official propaganda of the regime was concentrated on propagating the annihilation of capitalism in all countries of the world. No wonder the theoretically sound idea of large capitalist concessions in Russia proved a failure.

Lenin's second improvisation was electrification. Despite his countless discussions with his old friend, the engineer Krzhizhanovsky, Lenin had only a vague notion of the scope of the technical problems, of the difficulties involved in the electrification of a country the size of Russia, or of how much time it would take. In a letter to Krzhizhanovsky, Lenin wrote that within ten to twenty years, the whole of Russian industry and agriculture would be electrified and that this would put Russia on a high technological level. He said: "Socialism is Soviet power plus electrification."

Once again, Lenin proved to be a utopian. The electrification of industry required tremendous capital investment and industrial prerequisites, which could not possibly be achieved in ten to twenty years in such a huge, backward country. Furthermore, Lenin did not realize that even in highly developed countries, electric power is less important in agriculture than the supply of automotive power needed for the tilling of the soil, harvesting, transportation, etc.[31]

Even his most sober improvisation—the fostering of the co-operative method in agriculture—proved, in the long run, to be unrealistic. Lenin reckoned that, at the same time as concessions were being made in big industry, the co-operative system could spread widely among Russia's peasants, small manufacturers and artisans (as a matter of fact, it had in pre-revolutionary Russia), and that the consumers' and producers' co-operatives would become schools of socialism and collective economy. He wrote that "under our conditions, the co-operative movement, again and again, coincides with socialism," and further that "now, we have the right to say that the simple growth of co-operatives is, for us, tantamount to the growth of socialism." Lenin pointed out that the Russian working people had left behind them the times when the question of socialism was centered mainly around the struggle for power. "Today, the center of gravity has been transferred to peaceful organization, to the 'cultural' effort." But, having made this statement, Lenin immediately called attention to the fact that this development of co-operatives, which would result in "the Soviet regime having both feet on socialist ground," required a preliminary "general, cultural revolution."[32] Lenin spoke of co-operatives in very general terms, without specifying how his plan would apply in different areas and to various forms of co-operatives.

To understand the problem of co-operatives at that time, we must note that the Bolsheviks, from the moment that they acceded to power, began to take over the old pre-revolutionary co-operatives, to which great numbers of peasants and small producers belonged. They did this primarily for political considerations, in much the same way as they seized control of the trade unions. In place of the dissolved voluntary co-operatives, which had operated in the fields of supply, credit, retailing and, to a considerable extent, production (the artels), the Bolsheviks set up groups which were kept under the vigilant surveillance of the Communist Party and administration, and which became, in fact, agencies of the state administration. These Soviet "co-operatives" became weaker and weaker and gradually lost all importance in the country's economy.

Apparently, Lenin was not thinking of these "political co-operatives" when he spoke of basing his far-reaching plans for socialization on co-operatives. Nor, apparently, did he have in mind what later became known as *kolkhozy*. Again and again, Lenin reiterated his belief that peasants should not be forced into *kolkhozy* (collective farms), *sovkhozy* (state farms) or into communes, which were not at all the same as free co-operatives formed voluntarily by peasants or groups of peasants in various regions.[33]

Under Lenin's influence, the Communist Party began to make solemn pledges to sponsor co-operatives. But in the political atmosphere created by the Communist dictatorship, genuine co-operatives were not viable. In the period preceding the introduction of the NEP, the authorities dealt with the co-operatives as though they were governmental agencies, sending them directives to amalgamate here or to come under such-and-such a jurisdiction there. In the following years, up to 1924, the co-operatives were mostly viewed by the authorities as a political instrument. Thus, at the 13th Party Congress, at which a report on the state of the co-operatives was presented and the pertinent problems discussed, it became evident that, in the countryside, the co-operatives were nothing but alliances of poorer peasants formed to fight the *kulaks*.

Thus, the third of Lenin's improvisations also proved illusory. The co-operatives played no part in the building of Soviet socialism. Nor could they, so long as the political system established by Bolshevism was maintained.

The political aspect of the NEP, as conceived by Lenin, consisted of the undiluted theory and practice of proletarian dictatorship through the Communist Party. Although the Civil War police regime was relaxed somewhat, there were no political concessions: no freedom of political activity for democratic socialists, or freedom of the press for non-Communist publications. On the contrary, while during the Civil War, the Bolsheviks had tolerated the Mensheviks as well as the internationalists and a small group of S-R's as a "legitimate opposition," with the introduction of the NEP, Lenin decided that Mensheviks and S-R's could no longer be tolerated. In the very pamphlet in which he proclaimed the introduction of the NEP, Lenin wrote that the regime of the NEP, with its concessions to small capitalism, would automatically generate the "chemical precipitation" of the Mensheviks and the S-R's and that therefore they would have to be "handled with care—but kept in jail."[34]

In loosening the restraints on economic growth, Lenin simultaneously tightened the clamps on political heterodoxy. He reasoned that, at a time when the "proletarian dictatorship" was forced to exist surrounded by prosperous petty-bourgeois classes, the party, more than ever, needed complete insulation against the infiltration of democratic, liberal and social-democratic elements and ideas. The more economic concessions were to be made to the Russian petty bourgeoisie and to the foreign big bourgeoisie, the sterner the regime had to be in order to keep the Communist Party in power.

Trotsky agreed with Lenin. In his economic report at the 12th Party Congress, in April 1923, Trotsky pointed to the danger that private trade and private industry would grow excessively under the NEP. But he reassured his audience by reminding them that the Soviet government still held the knife of power by means of which, like a gardener, it could prune those capitalist shoots which grew too fast. The NEP presented no danger as long as that knife was kept well sharpened. Thus, technical and economic progress would go hand in hand with the maintenance of undiluted dictatorship, in the country as well as within the ruling party itself.

The economic progress under the NEP was real enough. Once the Russian peasant became the true owner of his own land and could trade his produce freely, he quickly began to display his economic capabilities. The areas under cultivation grew larger and larger, the land was worked with greater and greater care and efficiency, and its yields continued to increase. Farm animals reappeared in peasant households, first the smaller animals, then cattle. Soon, in the private markets of many cities and towns of Russia, sufficient quantities of bread, dairy products and meat began to appear. Cordwood, an important fuel in richly forested Russia, made its appearance and was followed by oil, kerosene and coal; the railroads came to life, smoke began to pour from the factory stacks, and working women no longer had to stand in line to get bread for their hungry children. Russia began to live an almost normal life.

The area under grain, which was 94,400,000 hectares in 1913 and had dropped to 66,200,000 hectares in 1922, increased again to 87,300,000 hectares by 1925. Thus, by 1925 the total production of grain crops had reached almost the prewar level (94%). The same recovery was made by the technical crops (beets, flax, hemp). The smaller farm animals (pigs, goats, and sheep), which had been completely exterminated in 35 provinces during the famine years, began to multiply again. There were 22,200,000 pigs in 1924 as compared to 23,000,000 in 1916. The number of goats and sheep in 1925 was 122,900,000, as against 114,600,000 in 1916. There were 62,100,000 head of cattle in 1925, as against 58,400,000 in 1916.[35]

In 1925 the number of fallow farm-holdings was reduced; the number of middle-sized peasant holdings with an average acreage markedly increased. In the same way, the number of above-average areas sown by well-to-do peasants, the so-called *kulaks,* went up. There were about a million such well-to-do peasants and the land they farmed totaled 10,000,000 desyatinas (one desyatina equals 2.7 acres). The land reorganization, which reshaped farmsteads to avoid lot-crossing and reduced the distance between the peasant's farmhouse and his holding, made it possible to increase the area of rationally utilized land to over 32,000,000 desyatinas, and 1,300,000 homesteaders practiced crop rotation on more than 10,000,000 desyatinas of land.

The deep wounds inflicted upon Russia's agricultural economy by World War I, the Civil War and War Communism, were healed. By 1928 total agricultural production had exceeded the prewar level, though this was not true of per capita production, because of the increase in population.

The wholesome effects of the NEP were felt not only in agriculture, but in trade and industry as well. The freedom of small trade and of small-scale, private-capital industry stimulated new activity. The Communists, who had hoped for immediate realization of socialism, now had to accept the existence of a class of small traders, small and medium contractors, intermediaries, speculators, *nouveaux riche* or *"Nepmen."* But, along with the appearance of these undesirable elements, the freedom of private initiative brought a considerable invigoration of the national economy, filling many gaps that large-scale, nationalized industry could not fill. Generally speaking, the "restoration process" came to an end by 1926, and at that time the party leaders had to face all the problems and contradictions associated with the NEP in the "country of triumphant socialism."

For non-Communists—social democrats and liberals—the NEP was a return to realistic thinking. They saw in it nothing incompatible with their objectives. But to the Communists the NEP represented an ideological and psychological retreat from their dogma.

The retreat had saved the regime by averting an otherwise inevitable economic catastrophe and general collapse. The more realistic Soviet leaders felt that the NEP had been worth the gamble; that at the price of a temporary retreat they had been able to buy time to continue their experiment; and that this withdrawal had considerably strengthened the regime. They had accepted the NEP because the salvation and consolidation of the regime had always been the fundamental tenet of their world view. Nevertheless, it was a retreat, tantamount to a return to capitalism, which they had officially buried during the October Revolution and which they had proclaimed to be dead not only in Russia, but, potentially, in the world at large.

Thus the collective thinking of the Communist Party was caught on the horns of this contradiction. This was felt by Communists of all shades, and caused a state of ideological turmoil that became evident again and again, in the breaking off of new splinter groups, in debates during which individual Communists often re-examined the very foundations of Leninist dogma. During the last months of his life, Lenin maintained that the NEP was there to stay for a long time, for generations, and he apparently believed this sincerely. For Lenin, the central figure of Russian history was now the individual peasant, the private owner, who wanted no part of socialism. It was impossible to attract him to the collective farms. All attempts to do so had failed. Even at the high-water mark of the class struggle, in 1918, only 4% of the peasants, at most, joined the state or collective farms; moreover, these were very poorly organized. In his speech at the 10th Congress, Lenin conceded that these collective farms were the targets "of the sneers and ill wishes of the peasants all around them."[36]

Lenin believed that an alliance had to be contracted with the individual peasant based on the "peaceful co-existence" of petty-bourgeois agriculture and nationalized large industry.

How far certain Bolsheviks went, in this respect, may be gauged from a curious document preserved in the unpublished part of Trotsky's archives.

> The following proposal was made to the Central Committee of the party by V. Obolensky (Osinsky), a Central Committee member. Copy. Top secret. Note by Comrade Lenin to Comrade Molotov: "I suggest this should be handed to the CC members and request it should be returned to the secretariat with their written comments. Its return should be checked because the whole thing is secret." Lenin, 23/V/1921. "My comment will follow." (signed:) Lenin.
>
> Central Committee of the Russian Communist Party. With reference to the Creation of a Peasant Union.
>
> A "peasant union," founded on principles similar to those of the Young Communist League, must be created. Formally, the Komsomol is a non-party organization, although it comes under the ideological and organizational hegemony of the Russian Communist Party. The Soviet Peasant Union must be organized along similar lines.
>
> V. Obolensky (Osinsky).

According to rumors circulating in Moscow at that time, prominent Bolsheviks were encouraging socialistically-oriented specialists outside the party to work on the organization of a peasant union. But Lenin decided to postpone this risky experiment. In Osinsky's letter, there is written in Lenin's own hand:

> I believe it is still too early. We should think up some safer measures in preparation for this . . . to put on the order of the day in the Party Bureau. All members of the Central Committee are requested to comment briefly. May 23, 1921, Lenin.[37]

Lenin, of course, saw as clearly as anybody the dangers of the NEP from the viewpoint of pure Communism. With the presence of individual farming in the countryside, the seeds of capitalism and the capitalist spirit were planted in the entire country. In industry, the necessity of allowing small and medium-scale private enterprises to compete with the nationalized plants, threatened to evoke comparisons unflattering to the latter. Menshevik-oriented economists, the higher executives and even many Bolsheviks saw nothing disastrous for the cause of socialism in Russia in the further development of the NEP. What they criticized was not the idea of a compromise with the peasantry but the theory and practice of dictatorship, which barred the working class from all free political activity, from forming political and class organizations and from any possibility of exerting pressure on governmental policies. But the reaction of the orthodox Communists to the deepening influence of NEP was quite different.

The appearance and growth of the large class of *Nepmen* filled them with horror and disgust: what had these *Nepmen* to do with Communism? The speculators, the most repulsive scum of the bourgeoisie, who had unlimited opportunities for profiteering with full immunity in the streets of socialist towns, were, for them, an unbearable sight. To Trotsky, even more dangerous was the inundation of the lower levels of the national administration and of the party by people from petty-bourgeois or peasant environments. To him they were the symbols of deterioration and decay of Russia's Communist system. How long could the "dictatorship of the proletariat" last, submerged as it was in the petty-bourgeois flood? There were about 100 million peasants as against four or five million workers and proletarians of all categories; what is more, a considerable proportion of the latter were not class-conscious proletarian socialists.

[1] See Russian editions of the *Works* of Karl Marx and Friedrich Engels, vol. VIII, Moscow-Leningrad 1930. Preface by D. Riazanov, p. XXVIII.

[2] Friedrich Engels, *The Peasant War in Germany*. International Publishers, p. 135.

[3] Lenin, Vol. 8, p. 253.

[4] *Ibid.*, p. 262.

[5] *Ibid.*, p. 263.

[6] *Ibid.*, Vol. 9, p. 33.

[7] *Ibid.*, p. 40.

[8] *Ibid.*, pp. 92-93.

[9] *Ibid.*

[10] *Ibid.*, Vol. 20, p. 346.

[11] *Encounters with Lenin*. Chekhov Publ. House, N. Y., 1953.

[12] The historian Prof. M. Pokrovsky had good reason to write in his memoirs (M. N. Pokrovsky: *The October Revolution*, Moscow, Communist Academy, 1929, pp. 35-37) that Lenin's Bolshevism had been anticipated in the 1861 program of "Young Russia." Pokrovsky correctly grasped the Jacobin essence of Leninism. He was in error when he wrote that Lenin had never heard of Zaichnevsky and was not familiar with his teaching.

[13] Lenin, *op. cit.*, Vol. 9, p. 213.

[14] Lenin, Vol. 15, p. 41.

[15] *Ibid.*

[16] *Leninski Sbornik*, Moscow, II., p. 83. Comments by V. I. Lenin and V. I. Zasulich on the program drafted by Plekhanov.

[17] *Ibid.*
[18] Trotsky, *On Lenin,* p. 112.
[19] Lenin, Vol. 33, p. 40.
[20] Lenin, Vol. 28, pp. 273-280.
[21] Lenin: *The Proletarian Revolution and the Renegade Kautsky* (Sept.-Oct., 1918).
[22] Trotsky, *Autobiography,* Part two, p. 199.
[23] A. Slepkov, *The Kronstadt Revolt.* Moscow Worker Publishing House, Moscow, p. 15.
[24] This passage stood out so sharply from the rest of his speech that, although it appears in the Minutes of the Congress published in Moscow in 1933 (p. 36), it is left out of Lenin's *Collected Works.* (See Vol. 32, p. 161.)
[25] Lenin, Vol. 33, p. 40.
[26] Lenin, Vol. 28, p. 281.
[27] *Ibid.*
[28] *Minutes of the 10th Congress,* pp. 408-409.
[29] Quoted from the notes of B. I. Nikolaevsky.
[30] A declaration of this kind was tantamount to the abandonment of all hope of a world revolution in the near future. In Lenin this change was crystallized in March 1921, after the failure of the March Communist uprising in Germany. Unlike Lenin, such Bolsheviks as Trotsky, Zinoviev and others, continued to cling to the idea of a world revolution which alone, in their opinion, could save Russia's socialist system.
[31] This author was certain, as far back as 1921, that Lenin's enthusiasm for electrification, especially in agriculture, stemmed from a widely discussed article by the Populist writer, Gleb Uspensky, "There Will be a Holiday for Us, Too," in which Uspensky colorfully depicts the use of wind-generated electricity to drive engines in Russian villages. This pseudo-scientific fantasy so fired Lenin's imagination that he extended it to electrification in general.
[32] Lenin: "Second Article on Co-operatives," Jan. 6, 1923, Vol. 33, pp. 434-35.
[33] When a French Communist delegation came to Moscow in 1922, it brought along a draft for a new Communist program in which, in the event of a Communist victory, the private ownership of the land by peasants would be preserved. Lenin greatly approved this idea and added that he wholeheartedly approved, among other points of the draft, the sixth, which read that those small proprietors who till their own soil should be granted "permanent and hereditary ownership of their land." (Lenin, Vol. 33, pp. 106-107.)
[34] Lenin, Vol. 32, pp. 340-343.
[35] See Liashchenko, *Istoria Narodnogo Khozyaistva USSR* (*History of the National Economy of the USSR*), Moscow, 1956, Vol. 3, pp. 113-35.
[36] *Minutes of the Tenth Congress,* Moscow, 1933, p. 408. This sentence has been left out in Lenin's *Collected Works* (see Vol. 32, p. 194).
[37] Trotsky Archives, No. 657, Harvard University, Cambridge, Mass.

CHAPTER 10

Lenin and the Weimar Republic

The German Revolution and the Bolsheviks

In making the October Revolution, in concluding the Brest-Litovsk Treaty, in risking and fighting a civil war, Lenin was guided by a supreme faith that was to prove unjustified. This was his belief, expressed many times between 1917 and 1921, that the war had strained capitalism in the advanced countries of central and western Europe beyond its capacities; that the October Revolution would resound beyond Russia's borders, and particularly into Germany, the most advanced industrial nation in Europe, with its strongest labor movement; and that a mass, proletarian uprising in Germany would usher in a world revolution.

In fact, however, when Germany's war effort faltered, the revolution envisioned by Lenin did not take place in the form he had imagined; the heirs of Imperial Germany were moderate Social Democrats to whom Lenin's visions of global revolutionary adventure were unappealing as well as unfeasible; and the revolutions which took place in Austria and Hungary proved to be of purely local importance. And so, even before the smoke had cleared in postwar Europe, Lenin and his aides made the same sort of "realistic" adjustment toward Germany that they had made toward the Russian peasants through the NEP. Hopes of a German Communist revolution were never completely set aside; but, parallel with the "proletarian" activities of the German Communist Party and the new Communist International, the Soviet government in Lenin's lifetime embarked on a wide-ranging diplomatic and military collaboration with German nationalist forces—and particularly with the German army—directed against the western Allies. In both its aspects, Soviet Communist policy toward Germany was to influence world history profoundly—by helping to undermine the fledgling German democracy and by creating the cadres of the Wehrmacht which was, in 1941, to ravage Russia and threaten the Soviet regime itself. From the German policies developed by the Soviet regime under Lenin, to the pact which Stalin concluded with Hitler, ran the continuous thread of consuming animosity toward liberal democracy.

By 1918, the exhaustion of Germany's economic resources and food shortages among the people as well as in some units of the army had produced widespread demoralization. Russia's withdrawal from the war, following the Brest-Litovsk Treaty, revived flagging hopes, but it did not markedly improve Germany's economic or military situation. The military vacuum left by the Russians was filled by the entry of the United States into the war. And when the "Hindenburg offensive" of 1918 failed, the German people lost all hope of victory. Although the American forces had not yet gone into combat in great numbers, they were standing by, ready to do so, and the prospect of fighting fresh, well-equipped divisions was dismaying to Germans both in the field and at home.

It is untrue to say—as the nationalist "stab-in-the-back" legend later had it—that at that moment a popular revolt broke out in the rear, hamstringing the still undefeated German army. In fact, by September, a willingness to end the war, by capitulation if necessary, was quite evident at German GHQ. This willingness hardened into a firm resolve when Bulgaria capitulated on September 26, 1918. When Austria's surrender followed, Hindenburg and Ludendorff categorically demanded that their government open peace negotiations with the Allies without a day's delay—on the ground that only thus could catastrophe be averted.

The Reichstag began feverish preparations. The "imperial" government became a "parliamentary" government responsible to the Reichstag. The constitution was hurriedly amended to read that decisions to declare war or to make peace were no longer the prerogative of the Emperor but of the Reichstag. A new cabinet was formed, headed by the liberal Prince Max of Baden with the representation of the two largest parties in the Reichstag—the Catholic Center and the Social Democrats. Prince Max took office on October 3, and almost immediately sent a telegram to President Wilson, requesting negotiations for a truce based on his Fourteen Points. There was, then, an exchange of telegrams which continued for almost three weeks. Wilson demanded that the German command immediately discontinue submarine warfare and put a stop to all demolitions in Allied territory from which the Germans were withdrawing. The Germans agreed to these conditions. Wilson's second note hinted that the peace terms would be more lenient if the political character of the German regime were changed, and influential members of the Reichstag began to press for the immediate abdication of the Kaiser. But the Kaiser hesitated, and it was only at the last moment, when confronted by demonstrations of soldiers, sailors, and workers in a number of German towns, that he agreed to leave the GHQ in Spa for Doorn in Holland.

The masses of the people, realizing at last that the war was practically over, now began to assert themselves. On November 3rd, a revolt broke out in a part of the fleet based at Kiel. It was followed by disturbances among sailors and workers in other ports, by uprisings of workers in Munich and Stuttgart, and then, on November 9th, by workers' strikes combined with revolts among sailors in Berlin. The hour of the revolution had struck.

Prince Max of Baden hastily surrendered the post of Chancellor to Friedrich Ebert, a former saddler who was the leader of the Social Democrats; and another Social Democratic leader, Philip Scheidemann, proclaimed Germany a republic from the balcony of the Reichstag. Workers' councils began to spring up in the towns. In Berlin a Council of People's Representatives—composed of three Social Democrats (Ebert, Scheidemann, and Landsberg) and three Independent Socialists (Haase, Dittmann, and Barth)—was established, which roughly corresponded to the Soviet of People's Commissars in Petrograd.

Although it was not immediately obvious, the German revolution took a quite different course from that taken by the Russian revolutions of February and October 1917. The German government never fell—it simply passed into other hands, quite legally. The revolutionary tide in Germany did not create chaos, as it had in Russia in February; nor did it end in a military dictatorship of one party as in Russia in October. All of Germany's political and social institutions remained intact, and attempts by sailors and others to stage a complete overthrow of the existing order soon miscarried, owing mainly to the resistance of the workers. The administrative apparatus of the state never lost its authority among the people. The broad mass of workers followed the lead of the organized workers' parties and trade unions, headed by the Social Democrats, who were supported on all important issues by the Independent Socialists. The Social Democratic leaders, even those of the left wing, realized that increased social disorders could bring final ruin to Germany, which was already at the mercy of the victorious Allies. Germany in 1918 did not contend with a disintegrated, demoralized soldiery such as that which, in October 1917, had acted as the most powerful revolutionary stimulus in Russia. Nor did it face a peasantry longing for agrarian revolution, for the German agrarian revolution had taken place in 1848 and the peasantry had since become a conservative class. Political parties were not replaced by non-party Soviets; the two wings of the Social Democratic Party retained the allegiance of the majority of workers, and the existing Communist Party—the Spartacists—was insignificant numerically and was not at all eager to imitate the policies of Lenin and Trotsky.

Perhaps most important, the army expressed immediate loyalty to the new regime. On November 9, the very day Ebert became Chancellor, he received a telephone call from General Groener of the German General Staff. The general offered Ebert full support of the army and its officer corps on condition that Ebert promise to respect and defend the army's autonomy as a body. Ebert accepted without hesitation. He telephoned Hindenburg himself at GHQ, to check whether the proposal had come from Groener alone or had been made in agreement with other army leaders. Hindenburg endorsed the proposal. And from that moment on, a gentlemen's agreement existed between the two main forces effective in Germany—the organized workers and the army.

The first Congress of Workers' and Soldiers' Deputies met December 16-19 and passed several resolutions for the establishment of a democratic republic and various social reforms. It delegated the question of nationalization to a special study commission under Karl Kautsky. It decided, almost unanimously, against trying to take over the government of Germany and resolved instead that elections to a Constituent Assembly should be held on January 19, 1919. It agreed that this Assembly should settle the question of the peace treaty and adopt a constitution for a new, genuinely democratic German republic. The German Constituent Assembly met in Weimar on February 6th. After stormy and prolonged debate, it ratified the Versailles Treaty and accepted the new republican constitution, which was considered the completion of the revolution.[1]

The Bolsheviks had placed the highest hopes in a German revolution. Their hopes had soared toward the end of September, when news of political ferment in Germany reached Moscow. On October 3, Lenin laid before the VTsIK a special decree proclaiming the formation of a grain fund to feed starving Germany during the first days of the revolution. He also proposed increasing the Red Army to 3,000,000 men to give military support to Germany if the "Anglo-French bloc" tried to crush the revolution.[2] At the same time, revolutionary propaganda inside Germany—mainly in co-operation with the anti-war Independent Socialists—was vastly intensified. Great zeal was shown by the Soviet Ambassador, Adolf Yoffe, who transmitted large sums of money to the German revolutionaries. Crates of propaganda pamphlets in German, printed in Russia, were also sent to Berlin via the diplomatic pouch. The suspicious German police persuaded the porters to drop one of these crates on the steps of the Embassy, and bundles of the revolutionary pamphlets fell out.[3]

In the early days of November, the Bolshevik leaders lived in a fever of expectation. For at almost the moment that Scheidemann proclaimed the German Republic from the balcony of the Reichstag, Karl Liebknecht, newly released from prison, was promulgating a German Socialist Republic from the balcony of the Imperial Palace. But how could these stirring events be reconciled with the expulsion at that very moment of Yoffe? Lenin had his own theory. Radek relates in his memoirs that Lenin suggested then that "Germany was bowing to the Entente and offering its services to fight the Russian revolution."[4] However, Radek's memoirs themselves supply sufficient material to belie Lenin's "intuition."

The Bolsheviks at that moment were in fact torn betwen doubt, hope and apprehension. Unable to endure the painful uncertainty about what was happening in Germany, Radek and Chicherin tried desperately to get in touch with Kiel or Berlin. Attempts to establish radio communication were jammed by the powerful German station at Nauen. There remained the direct telegraph line between the German Embassy in Moscow and Berlin, but for a long time no response could be obtained from Berlin, because the cable passed through Kovno, still held by anti-revolutionary German troops.

At last the Ministry for Foreign Affairs in Berlin replied—in the person of the teletype operator. Radek rushed to the machine:

"I want to speak to the people's representative, Herr Haase."

"He is not in the building."

"Then call his deputy, Solf."

"He is not here either."

"Who is deputizing for them then?"

"There is nobody here, they have all left."

"Then send somebody to find Haase or Liebknecht."

"There is nobody here to send."

Whereupon the quick-witted Radek dictated this command to the operator: "I order to fetch them in the name of the All-Russian Central Executive Committee of the Soviets, and I make you responsible to the Soviet of Workers' and Soldiers' Deputies in Berlin."

Silence. The machine continued to print: Berlin, Berlin, Berlin. While waiting for the reply, Radek went to a workers' meeting at the Prokhorovsk textile plant, then spoke from the balcony of the Palace of the Soviets. Lenin was also there, sunk in gloom. At last the German Embassy sent a message to say that Berlin was calling Moscow. On his way to the Embassy, Radek picked up Chicherin. When they arrived, they found that Reichstag deputy Oskar Kohn, an Independent Socialist, was on the line. He informed Radek and Chicherin briefly of the events in Berlin, and then Hugo Haase took over.

Haase began by expressing his gratitude for the Soviet offer (transmitted by radio) to send trainloads of grain to the starving population of Berlin. Haase then paused for a minute, and Radek writes: "Comrade Chicherin and I stood still, our eyes glued to the teletype tape. I felt my heart pounding." "However," said Haase after the pause, "we hear that there are many starving in Russia itself and we think that the Soviet government would do better to give its stores of grain to its own starving people." As for Germany, President Wilson of the United States had undertaken to supply Germany with grain and oils during the coming winter.

Radek and Chicherin reeled under the blow, but worse was to come. When they asked Haase about Yoffe and his chances of returning to Germany, he answered evasively that the question had not been settled yet. Next, Radek raised the matter of General von der Holtz's troops, which were still occupying the Baltic countries even though the Treaty of Brest-Litovsk had been annulled and Moscow now regarded these countries as Russian. On this subject, too, Haase was evasive. Here, Radek lost his temper and, although he had no authority and no government decision to back him, he announced furiously: ". . . if we do not receive a definite answer to all our questions within three days, the Red Army will feel free to act, and all responsibility for any complications during the evacuation of your troops will be yours and yours alone."

The conversation was broken off. After opening with mutual congratulations and offers of brotherly help, the first encounter between the young German revolution and the Russian revolution had ended in the threat of an attack by the Red Army. In actuality, the relations between Bolshevik Russia and the German revolutionary movement proved even more disappointing from the Soviet point of view than Radek and Lenin feared at this time. The German workers had received a thorough political training in the ranks of the Social Democratic Party under the leadership of Wilhelm Liebknecht, August Bebel, Karl Kautsky, Eduard Bernstein, and their pupils, and they were not at all favorably disposed toward Bolshevism or Communism. The German Social Democrats, both those of the right wing and those of the internationalist left-wing, proved to be staunch supporters of democracy and of democratic socialism. Worse still from the point of view of the Kremlin, the Spartacus group, nurtured during the war by Rosa Luxemburg, Karl Liebknecht and Leo Yogiches (Tyshko), turned out, when put to the test, to be insignificant in numbers and influence.

Luxemburg, Liebknecht and Tyshko were present at the founding congress of the German Communist Party which met in Berlin at the end of December 1918, but attendance was very poor and the "masses" supporting it could be counted in the hundreds. Radek, the Russian representative, tried vainly to fashion the new-born German Communist Party in the image of Russian Bolshevism. He was opposed by Rosa Luxemburg, who expressed the view that the Spartacus group was much too small to be anything but an ideological *avant garde* and was quite unfit for the task of organizing a revolutionary movement.

Despite this disappointment, a semi-spontaneous, unprepared and disorganized revolt with some proletarian support broke out in Berlin only a few days after the conclusion of the congress. A few buildings were seized but the movement had no definite objectives or aims, and it was quickly suppressed by cavalry detachments stationed near Berlin. A group of officers took this opportunity to murder Rosa Luxemburg and Karl Liebknecht. A short time afterward, Tyshko was also assassinated. Thus, at its very inception, German Communism lost its outstanding leaders. Those who replaced them were mediocrities and thenceforth the party was ruled entirely by the Kremlin—through Zinoviev, president of the Comintern.

Inevitably, neither the German working class movement nor even the Communist Party itself could be effectively directed from Moscow. As one of its early leaders, Thalheimer, rightly remarked,[5] Moscow knew nothing about Germany or about the character and peculiarities of the German working class. The men in the Kremlin, wrote Thalheimer, fixed a plan of action for the German Communist Party four to eight weeks in advance and, instead of studying German conditions, based their calculations on the assumption that, in the period from "August" to "October," events would take precisely the same course in Germany as they had in the corresponding period in Russia in 1917. This type of planning was patently absurd; but the rather unintelligent Zinoviev and his aides, and even greater men like Lenin and Trotsky, failed to see this absurdity. (True, among the Soviet leaders there was one, Radek, who had some understanding of Germany. But he was not influential enough.) As a result, one fiasco followed after another. In vain did Zinoviev, in the spring of 1920, call upon the German proletariat to "arm themselves," "form their own Soviets," and "create their own Red Army." The fact that Zinoviev addressed himself to the German workers directly, over the heads of the German Communist party, showed how ineffective that party was and how slight were the chances of a Communist revolution in Germany. An attempted uprising by leftist workers in the Ruhr, who formed a German Red Army, was crushed by the Reichswehr.

One event revived Zinoviev's hopes: the German Independent Socialist Party split in two at its congress in Halle in October 1920. This party had grown considerably at the expense of the majority Social Democrats whose policy many workers regarded as too moderate and not sufficiently socialist. On January 19, 1919, the Independents had polled 2,300,000 votes and the Social-Democrats 11,500,000; but in the Reichstag elections of 1920 the Independents polled over 5,000,000 votes and possessed a membership of 800,000, the largest in its history. The party was not homogeneous. Its right wing differed little from the Social Democrats, while its strong left wing idealized the Bolshevik revolution.

Moscow decided to exploit this situation and encouraged the left wing to precipitate a schism. In the summer of 1920, a delegation of the Independent Socialist Party went to Moscow during the Second Congress of the Comintern. As soon as it arrived, the delegation virtually split in two: its right-wing members (Crispin and Dittmann) immediately got in touch with the Mensheviks—Martov and his friends—while the left wingers (Stöcker and Däumig) established close ties with the Bolsheviks. The results of this Moscow visit were visible at the party congress in Halle in October, at which the question of affiliation with the Comintern came up for discussion.

Zinoviev came to Halle especially for the congress. His speech was a sensational success, mainly because Zinoviev was capable of speaking for four hours with a demagogy and fervor in sharp contrast to the usual run of speeches to which socialist audiences in Germany were accustomed. For at least part of the audience, however, Zinoviev's speech was considerably blunted by the address of another Russian, the Menshevik leader, Julius Martov. Martov was already suffering from a disease of the throat, and could not deliver his speech in person. It was read, in a German translation, by Alexander Stein, an old former Menshevik who had long lived in Germany and had become one of the leading Independents. Martov's profound criticism of the terrorist dictatorship of Lenin and Trotsky received a sympathetic hearing from the more thoughtful, better educated members of the party. Nevertheless, the majority favored Zinoviev's position, which received 237 votes against Martov's 156. In December of that year, at a conference in Berlin, the small Communist Party fused with the majority faction of the Independents. The new Communist Party numbered 350,000 members, 300,000 of them former Independents. Thus, although the Comintern had failed to capture the entire Independent Socialist Party, for the first time a mass Communist Party entered the German political scene in 1921.

In the spring of 1921, a mine strike in the Mansfeld region and increased political ferment centering in the towns of Halle and Moerseburg seemed to increase the chances of a revolution. The Comintern ordered the German Communist leaders to issue a call for a general strike. The Comintern's strategists calculated that the party could count on the support of some 2,000,000 to 3,000,000 workers in this region. Zinoviev attributed the greatest importance to this revolt and sent the leader of the Hungarian Revolution of 1918, Bela Kun, and two other Comintern agents to Germany to ensure its proper organization. On March 16th, the police attempted to break the miners' strike and met with armed resistance. To Zinoviev the long awaited moment seemed at hand. But when Brandler, the Communist leader, called on all Germans to take up arms and beat back the attack by the forces of reaction, the response was lukewarm: only 300,000 workers heeded the call. Even more unfortunate was the physical resistance by workers to local Communist attempts to picket factories, so that the Communists had to fight both workers and police. The so-called "March putsch" led to an internal crisis in the Communist Party and eventually to a split. Party membership fell to 180,000. After this dismal failure, the German Communist Party refrained from provoking any new mass disorders for almost two years.

By the summer of 1921, the Weimar Republic seemed, for the time being, relatively secure. It had weathered not only uprisings by Spartacists and other extreme leftists, but had also withstood an assault from the right—the so-called Kapp putsch of March 1920.

Aided by troops who had been evacuated from the Baltic countries, a group of right-wing politicians and reactionary nationalists, led by

Kapp, proclaimed themselves the government. Ebert and Scheidemann fled from Berlin to Stuttgart. For three days the situation remained critical. The Reichswehr generals, notably von Seeckt, refused to use their troops against the insurrectionary forces, which included a brigade led by the naval officer, Ehrhard; the generals argued that German soldiers who had only recently fought side by side in battle could not now be instructed to fire on each other. But von Seeckt, at least, honored the gentlemen's agreement between Ebert, Hindenburg and Groener: if he did not take action against Kapp and Ehrhard, neither did he move against the legitimate government. Meanwhile, the Social Democrats and the trade unions carried out a successful general strike throughout Germany. After three days Kapp fled, his putsch a failure.

Thus, by 1921, the leaders of both Soviet Russia and of Weimar Germany were to re-examine their relations. They discovered that they had much in common—principally their mutual hostility to the system which the Allies had imposed on Europe at the Treaty of Versailles. Lenin was quick to adapt to the new situation created by the Versailles system and the frustration of so many of his prophecies of the pre-October period.

The world revolution had failed to materialize, and the war had been brought to an end by that very bourgeoisie which Lenin had been absolutely convinced could not terminate it. Contrary to the expectations of the Zimmerwald peace program, the war had been followed not by a peace without victors or vanquished, but a victory for the Entente and the severe punishment of a defeated Germany. At the Versailles Conference, victorious Britain, France and Italy succeeded —despite President Wilson's opposition—in putting through their maximum demands, which included the reorganization of Europe, the Near East and the African colonies. New, independent states—Poland, Czechoslovakia and Yugoslavia—were created and moved into the French sphere of influence. Austria and Hungary were split, and the Hapsburgs banished; the Turkish empire was dismembered, and a host of new Arab states (under French and British influence) was created; Germany's overseas colonies were divided among the victors (France, Britain, Japan and Italy); Denmark was given a piece of Schleswig-Holstein; a corner of East Silesia was sliced off and Poland obtained the port of Gdynia (near Danzig) and a corridor which gave it free access to the Baltic, thereby cutting East Prussia in two.

The reparations imposed on Germany reached astronomic proportions: 226 billion gold marks to be paid over 45 years. Moreover, the Versailles Treaty bound Germany to abolish general military conscription and forbade it to rebuild its former army, to maintain a General Staff or a military air force, and to manufacture tanks or heavy artillery, poison gas or anything else that might help restore its former military might. At the same time, demilitarized zones were created on both the left and right banks of the Rhine. Two inter-Allied control commissions were set up in Germany—one to ensure that German demilitarization would be carried out, the other to supervise the payment of reparations and indemnities.

The European victors felt that they were the masters of the world, especially after the United States withdrew from Europe, declined to join the League of Nations, and entered on a long period of isolation. They were confident that Germany could never again become a danger to peace.

Yet in the long run, the victorious Allies proved to be no more far-sighted or sagacious than the narrow-minded German generals had been at Brest-Litovsk. Had the German military and court circles been endowed with greater political foresight and historical intelligence, they would have seized the moment of Russia's exit from the war and the temporary weakness of the Allies that followed it to offer a genuine compromise peace without victors or vanquished, and without indemnities or reparations. If they had done so, the war might have been brought to an end early in 1918, and Germany would have been spared the humiliation of the Versailles Treaty. But the German generals, who considered themselves great "realists," calculated that they would win the war and adopted an uncompromising attitude at Brest-Litovsk. The Allies, in their turn, adopted exactly the same attitude at Versailles and thereby threw away their chance of building a new world. They, too, thought they were being "realistic" by taking great pains to work out a military and diplomatic system to reduce Germany to a permanent state of impotence. But the disarmament of Germany proved to be a myth. Equally naive was the belief of the Allies that "*le Boche payera,*" that the Germans would pay for all the war damages. The Germans paid practically nothing, and the idea of indemnities and reparations was never more than a mirage. Within less than a decade, the weakness of the Versailles system was plain for all to see.

* *
*

In 1920, Germany and Russia, the two largest countries in Europe, found themselves outside the Versailles system. They had been excluded on different grounds—Germany because of its war crimes, Russia mainly because of Brest-Litovsk and revolutionary and political transgressions (confiscation of foreign enterprises, refusal to repay foreign loans, etc.). The community of interests created by the similarity of their positions *vis-à-vis* the Versailles system was reinforced by the fact that the two nations complemented each other in the economic field. Russia had become even more of an agrarian country than before the war. Its pre-war industry lay in ruins and could only be restored with German assistance. It needed industrial credits and technical assistance and could get them only in Germany, since the Entente nations continued to boycott Russia in all matters diplomatic, financial or commercial, even after the end of the Civil War. To Germany, on the other hand, Russia had always been a market for industrial exports.

There were other, less obvious reasons for a German-Russian rapprochement. In the first place, the German military did not accept defeat and considered the humiliating peace treaty an undeserved stain on the honor of the German army and the German people, a stain to be removed at all costs. Consequently, the German regular army officers, who formed a class apart even during the Kaiser's time, did not for a moment seriously accept any of those paragraphs of the Versailles Treaty which forbade the restoration of German military power. They determined on rearmament to rectify, in whatever manner necessary, "the injustices of the peace settlement."

A Germany bent on revenge could regain its armed might only with the help of the Soviet Union, which stood outside the Versailles system. For their part, the Communist rulers of Soviet Russia had never given up their *idée fixe* of a world revolution. They believed that it was necessary for them as quickly as possible to revive industry and build up the Red Army, in order to be ready to support revolution in other countries. In backward Russia, military as well as industrial power could most easily be created with the help of German industry, capital and technical assistance. Thus, in both Germany and Russia—the two pariahs of the Versailles system—the need for a close partnership was clearly recognized from the start. In industry and trade, co-operation was open and sometimes was even given a great deal of deliberate advertisement in the press; co-operation in military matters, on the other hand, was kept totally secret, but was no less real and effective.

For such a policy to be carried out over many years, it was, of course, essential that both Germany and Russia be ruled by regimes which combined steadfast dedication to their chosen aims together with Machiavellian skills at conspiracy. By a whim of history, Russia was then ruled by Bolsheviks who possessed these attributes to a high degree: Lenin, Trotsky, Chicherin, Krassin, Radek and later Stalin might have been especially created for such designs. As for Germany, the Weimar Republic was indeed based on entirely different principles; but the secret rearmament in preparation for a war of revenge was conducted not by President Ebert, the Reichstag or the main political parties but by the officers' caste, which found such ideal leaders as General von Seeckt, and by eager helpers such as the diplomat Ago von Maltzan, an aristocrat raised on Bismarck's thesis that German-Russian rapprochement was imperative. Von Seeckt, a man of strong character and supple intelligence with an iron will, was of course the leading architect of this policy. Members of the government and political leaders danced to his tune, and he knew how to maneuver skilfully in the most difficult and dangerous situations. His group was later joined by the man whom the entire world in the mid-Twenties believed represented the democratic, Western and pacifist wing in the German government—Gustav Stresemann. Later documents established that Stresemann had been a firm supporter of von Seeckt, and thus played a large part in starting Germany on the road to Hitlerism.

Another prominent figure was Brockdorff-Rantzau, an aristocrat and diplomat who had been German ambassador in Copenhagen during the war and had taken a deep interest in the Russian revolutionary movement, due mainly to the influence of the imaginative

Russian-German revolutionary, Dr. Alexander Helfand (Parvus). Parvus, who had been Trotsky's close friend and associate in the Russian revolution of 1905, became convinced after the outbreak of the war that the interests of the proletarian revolution required a German victory, and he approached Brockdorff-Rantzau in Copenhagen toward that end. Thus, the two formed a working alliance aimed at fomenting revolution in Russia with the help of German money. During the Versailles negotiations, Brockdorff-Rantzau served as chairman of the German delegation and became convinced of the necessity of a German surrender. But later he was appointed German ambassador to Moscow and found a congenial colleague in Lenin's foreign minister, the Russsian aristocrat Chicherin. As German ambassador, Brockdorff-Rantzau did everything in his power to cover up the highly secret transactions between Moscow and General von Seeckt.

From the Soviet side, one of the most intriguing figures was Karl Radek, and the story can properly be said to begin with Radek's secret mission to attend the first inaugural congress of the German Communist Party—after which he was arrested and held in Moabit Prison, Berlin, where he received an unusual array of visitors.

Radek's personality was outstanding: he was exceptionally gifted, widely read, and capable of talking entertainingly in several languages (though he never completely mastered some, including Russian). A Galician Jew, born Sobelsohn, he joined the Polish Social Democratic Party and at an early age, possibly only 18, was appointed editor of the party journal. He was a pupil of Rosa Luxemburg, as well as of Varsky (a veteran leader of the Polish Social Democrats), but created a position in his own right and was constantly at loggerheads with everybody. A typical Bohemian, always out of funds, he successfully compensated for his material indigence by an abundant wealth of intellect.[6]

Among the men close to Lenin, Radek was undoubtedly one of the most talented, witty and cultured. Like Lenin, he belonged to a breed of revolutionaries who, convinced of the rightness of their cause, cared little about the methods they used to advance it. In politics they had no use for moral principles; their sole criterion was success.

Before the war, Radek had lived in Germany where he was prominent among Social Democratic journalists. During the war, he went to Switzerland and there became one of Lenin's most trusted, talented and informed aides. After the February Revolution he settled in Stockholm for a time and, together with Ganetsky, edited a Bolshevik bulletin in foreign languages—its Russian name was *Pravda*. For years after the October Revolution, most anti-Soviet jokes were attributed to Radek's malicious tongue.

Radek's cell in the Moabit Prison became a political *salon*, in which the most unexpected visitors were announced. The most important, for our story, was the former Turkish minister of war, Enver Pasha, who was the go-between linking Radek and General von Seeckt. Much impressed by the Russian Revolution and the Red Army, Enver Pasha believed that the best hope for the losers at Versailles was to ally themselves with the growing power of the Soviet Union. He enjoyed close relations with several German generals, and particularly von Seeckt. In any case, Enver Pasha passed on to von Seeckt the gist of several talks with Radek. Von Seeckt himself did not meet Radek until later, but the idea shared by Enver Pasha and Radek—that all the victims of the Versailles Treaty should rally around Soviet Russia—made an impression upon him.

Though some of the dates have not been definitely established, it is now known that the military-technical negotiations between Soviet Russia and Germany go back to the end of the Russo-Polish war of 1920. During that war, von Seeckt had declared:

> I refuse to support Poland even at the risk of its being swallowed up by Russia. On the contrary, I am counting on that. Even if we cannot now help Russia to restore its former frontiers, we should certainly not obstruct it.

The logical consequence of such an attitude was co-operation with Soviet Russia. Krestinsky's admission at his trial in 1938 that Russo-German negotiations were conducted as early as the autumn of 1920 through Victor Kopp, then Soviet representative in Berlin, was probably the truth.[7]

The German-Soviet Collaboration (1921-1926)

Somewhat later, in the winter of 1920-21, these negotiations took on concrete shape. A special section "R" (Russland-Russia) was formed at the German War Office and soon brought tangible results. According to documents preserved in the Trotsky archives (at Harvard and Amsterdam), the Politburo held a special meeting in Moscow on April 7, 1921, to discuss a report from Kopp on the situation. The report was addressed to Trotsky as chairman of the Military Revolutionary Soviet and copies were sent to Lenin and Chicherin. It mentions "what was discussed in Moscow" (obviously referring to Kopp's visit in January) and describes the progress of negotiations with respect to three large firms in Russia: the Albatross works, to build airplanes; Bloem and Voss, for submarines; and Krupp, to manufacture shells and other munitions.[8] Lenin approved the proposals contained in Kopp's reports.[9]

Next, a German military preparatory commission arrived in Russia. After this commission had departed on September 10th, 1921, the Politburo met again. According to the same document in Trotsky's archives, Lenin approved the idea of combining industrial and military negotiations and of camouflaging munitions factories as German concessions in Russia. Lenin also recommended "playing the Polish card" for all it was worth, that is, luring the Germans with the prospect of a joint war against Poland.

Formal talks began soon after the preparatory commission had returned to Berlin. They were held at the house of Major Kurt von Schleicher, who later, as a general, played an important part in Hitler's seizure of power. The Germans were represented by von Schleicher and General Hasse, von Seeckt's successor as commander of the new and growing German army. The Russian group was headed by Krassin—who was, at the very same time, buying arms for Russia from the United States.[10] Krassin deliberately publicized his dealings with leading German industrialists and never failed to mention his frequent lunches and dinners with them to British Ambassador d'Abernon, whom he also visited frequently, Thus Britain knew that Krassin was actively promoting trade with Germany, but the other side of his activities went unsuspected.

Shortly after an October meeting at von Schleicher's house, Hasse visited Russia. But then the negotiations were interrupted, as attention shifted to the preparations for an all-European conference at which both Russian and German economic problems were to be considered. The initiative for a conference to deal with Russia's economic relations with her former Allies came from the Soviet government. On October 28, 1921, Foreign Commissar Chicherin proposed to the Allied governments an international conference to review Russia's pre-war debts and the claims of the Allied countries and their nationals against the Soviet government.[11] Chicherin made it clear that the Soviet government would be prepared under certain conditions to recognize debts incurred by the Tsarist government before the war.

At a session of the Supreme Allied Council in Cannes on January 6, 1922, Lloyd George insisted on the necessity of restoring normal commercial relations throughout all Europe. He argued in favor of making considerable concessions to both Russia and Germany, so that, after the long interruption of economic ties, normal economic life might at last be restored in Europe. Lloyd George's point of view prevailed and it was decided at Cannes to convene an international conference in Genoa in March 1922 with both Russia and Germany invited.[12]

The Bolshevik leaders could not agree among themselves on the tactics to be followed at the Genoa conference. By and large, however, they were optimistic about the outcome. Lenin was already enthusiastically planning to widen the scope of the NEP by granting greater concessions to private enterprise and, in any case, expected Allied economic relations with Soviet Russia to be resumed sooner or later. He declared that "we will go to the Genoa conference as business men."[13]

A large Soviet delegation, led by Chicherin, Litvinov, Rakovsky, Radek and Krassin attended the Genoa Conference, which opened on April 10th. In reply to the claims against Russia, estimated by a special commission at almost 40,000,000,000 pre-war roubles, the Soviet delegation presented counter-claims which included compensation for the losses caused by foreign intervention in Russia, estimated at 50,000,000,000 French francs in gold.

Both before and during the Genoa Conference, various complex international negotiations were carried on, some of them secret, some open. For Russia and Germany, all these talks had the same result: they underscored the necessity of their mutual co-operation. And yet, the first bids to capture the Russian market came not from Germany, which was still too weak to undertake such an initiative, but from the Allies. One of the earliest moves had been the Anglo-Soviet trade agreement of March 16, 1921. Krassin's success in obtaining this agreement was Soviet Russia's great diplomatic breakthrough. It did not, it is true, imply *de jure* recognition of the Soviet government, but the very fact that such an agreement had been reached cut right through the postwar *cordon sanitaire* around Soviet Russia and, in addition, gave Russia a trump card in its negotiations with Germany.

Another Allied move in the commercial and industrial sphere was the proposal to create an international consortium to regulate trade relations between Russia and the Allied countries. This proposal was advanced by French and British industrialists with the support of their governments. It was based on the belief that, in negotiating with a government which had nationalized industry and turned foreign trade into a state monopoly, an international organization would be able to obtain better terms and safer guarantees than private industrialists of any single country. It was also thought that the centralization of all trade with Russia in one international body would ensure a more even distribution of agreements and prevent any one country from dominating the market. This move was clearly dictated, at least in part, by fear of a possible German hegemony in trade relations with Soviet Russia, a fear that was strong among the French and the British.

But the idea of an international consortium was opposed by German heavy industry which, unlike German light industry, had had few dealings with Russia before the war. The Soviet government, of course, did not favor a consortium; it preferred to deal with individual industrialists or industrial firms rather than with a powerful international organization. Even before the Genoa Conference, moreover, signs of a gradual alignment of German heavy industry (and the army) with the Soviet government had not been lacking.

Throughout the Conference, the Germans watched the behavior of the Soviet delegation with suspicion. They were particularly aroused by mysterious talks between the Soviet and British delegates in the latter's headquarters at the Villa d'Alberti. These German suspicions sprang from anxiety over Clause 116 of the Versailles Treaty which provided that Russia could demand reparations from Germany if it ever signed the treaty. Such a move by Russia was most improbable, but the possibility worried the German representatives at Genoa, where the complex question of German reparations was being reviewed as a whole. Knowing that the German representatives and particularly their leader, Foreign Minister Walter Rathenau, were filled with anxiety on this score, the wily Bolshevik delegates made a point of advertising their frequent visits to the Villa d'Alberti and displaying a smug satisfaction which seemed to indicate that their relations with Britain were rapidly improving. Moreover, the British really hoped to make a deal with the Bolsheviks and pointedly abstained from holding private talks with the Germans. Several requests made by Rathenau, a liberal and a well-known Anglophile, for a meeting with Lloyd George were refused. The German suspicions deepened, and the Bolsheviks chose this moment to put their long-prepared and carefully thought-out plan into effect.

Long before the Genoa Conference, Soviet Russia, through its official diplomatic and commercial representatives and particularly through its military and semi-military representatives, had been systematically preparing for a rapprochement with Germany against the Allies. To be precise, it planned to conclude a pact of mutual friendship with Weimar Germany in the middle of the Genoa Conference. In mid-April the Bolsheviks judged the time to be ripe. The Soviet delegation was housed outside Genoa in the nearby town of Rapallo. At two o'clock one morning, Chicherin, who was in the habit of working at night, telephoned the hotel in Genoa which housed the German delegation and asked for von Maltzan, the German deputy minister. Von Maltzan came to the telephone in his pajamas and Chicherin (or, according to another account, Rakovsky) asked him whether the Germans would be prepared to come to Rapallo the first thing in the morning to sign a Russo-German agreement that had been prepared by both parties in advance. Greatly surprised, the pro-Russian von Maltzan readily agreed and immediately roused his superior, Rathenau. Chicherin's offer, said von Maltzan, must be accepted; at last the time for action had come. In the early hours of April 16th, the German and Russian delegates met in Rapallo and signed the agreement. Rathenau himself still harbored some misgivings and hesitated, but von Maltzan and the Soviet delegates persuaded him that refusal to sign would be dangerous. To the Allies the news of the signing of the so-called Rapallo Treaty came as a thunderbolt.[14] So violent was their reaction that the German delegation frantically telephoned the Russians later that same day, imploring them to expunge their signatures and say that the treaty had not yet been signed. But the Soviet representatives would not agree. The Rapallo Treaty remained in force, and the whole Genoa Conference came to nothing—together with the German hopes of a reduction in reparations.

In substance the Rapallo Treaty was neither threatening nor particularly sensational. The two parties to the treaty agreed to resume full diplomatic and economic relations, and to forego all claims to compensation for losses suffered during the war, the civil war, etc. Germany agreed not to claim compensation for such property of German nationals or of the German state as had been nationalized in Russia, with the proviso that this point might be reconsidered should other countries receive compensation. Finally, both parties agreed to hold discussions prior to any international conference on economic or commercial matters. But it was not the substance of the treaty that aroused the special interest, indeed the fury, of the Allies but the very fact of its conclusion, since it was so obviously directed against them. Moreover, the Allies could not help suspecting that, in addition to the published provisions of the treaty, there were other, secret clauses concerning military and technical collaboration between the two countries. Both the Germans and the Russians flatly denied these charges, but they were not believed. In reality, as we now know, these Russo-German denials were true up to a point: the Rapallo Treaty did not contain any secret clauses, but that did not mean that no understanding existed concerning technical and military collaboration. Exactly two weeks after the Rapallo Treaty was signed, a military-technical agreement was concluded at a highly secret meeting between representatives of the German Reichswehr and the Russian General Staff.

Shortly after the signing of the Rapallo Treaty, a representative of the Soviet General Staff, under the assumed name of Rosenblatt, met with General von Seeckt, and the agreement was concluded on July 29th. On August 11th, von Seeckt sent an envoy (according to one version, Colonel Nicolai, and another, Colonel von Niedermayer), to Moscow to sign the treaty. It formalized years of co-operation between Bolshevik Russia and the nationalist German military.

It is interesting to note that von Seeckt met Radek for the first time in February 1922, on the eve of the Genoa Conference,[15] and again in November of that year. Radek used all his eloquence to persuade von Seeckt that Germany had nothing to fear from Russia and that, in any case, Russia's immediate aims were compatible with German national aims.

The secret Russo-German Treaty of July 29th, 1922, has since been published.[16] Under this agreement, the German military undertook to create a large underground organization in Germany, its existence a secret from the Entente, the German government and, of course, the German people. In Russia, over which the Entente had no control, a sister organization was set up jointly by the German military and the Soviet government.

An army could not, of course, be formed outside Germany. But the illegal German General Staff, which the Versailles Treaty had dissolved, but which had never gone out of existence, was most ingenious at making the most of Germany's right to maintain a small army of 100,000 men. Inasmuch as conscription had been forbidden, this army was made up of volunteers who were required to sign up for a long period: twelve years for enlisted men and twenty-five for officers.

The unambiguous stipulations of the treaty seemed to make it impossible to create a large army or to train any appreciable number of young men in the art of war. In particular, it seemed impossible to build up a sufficiently large reserve of well-trained, disciplined officers, pilots, and other personnel. But the General Staff, with the connivance of the right-wing political parties and of many civil servants, succeeded in circumventing all the obstacles and prohibitions imposed at Versailles. Thus, non-commissioned officers often left the army on fictitious grounds—illness, travel abroad, etc.—and were replaced in a way that did not contravene the Versailles clauses. In this way, the Reichswehr's first 100,000 men were replaced almost entirely within the first three to four years. Thus, there were many more than 100,000 well-trained soldiers and non-commissioned officers in Germany, although all of them could not be found on the army lists. To train officers many scientific groups, clubs and private military-technical institutes sprang up to give young men of suitable temperament and interests a reasonably solid basic knowledge of military theory and practice. The whole country was dotted with clubs for rifle practice and gymnastics. In these traditional German institutions (*Vereine*) hundreds of thousands of German youths of military age received what amounted to basic military training.

All these subterfuges would have been useless, however, if the German war lords had not been able to test their new tanks and airplanes and their new chemical inventions, all forbidden by Versailles, in Russia. The Germans even staged regular military maneuvers on Russian soil to train their officers. Factories which produced supplies for the German army but were camouflaged as industrial concessions were built on Lenin's suggestion in Fili near Moscow (Junkers), in Kazan (a tank factory—the tank troops were also trained there), in Zlatoust, Tula, Leningrad (a munitions factory), and in Trotsk on the Volga (poison-gas grenades).

The air base at Lipetsk played a particularly important role in the preparation of German military aviation. It contained all the latest equipment, comfortable living quarters and canteens for the German personnel who lived and trained there, halls for meetings and conferences, up-to-date laboratories, etc. The importance of the Lipetsk air base was emphasized by General Speidel, who was the organizer of the "special group R" at that time. He wrote[17] that as its main contribution to German aviation the base gave the pilots a chance to master flying techniques under conditions comparable to real war and foster the spirit of the future Luftwaffe. The all-metal Dutch Fokkers was tested at this base, as well as all the new types of military aircraft which, from 1926 onward, were designed and constructed in Germany itself. At Lipetsk, future German pilots and some Soviet pilots, too, were taught to fly these aircraft.

At the Kazan training field, tests were conducted of the German *Panzer* which later, in the Second World War, helped Guderian and other originators of the new armored warfare to overrun the continent of Europe, including European Russia.

In addition, German generals attended Soviet maneuvers, and Soviet generals came to German maneuvers. The Soviet public were led to believe that these German generals, who usually wore mufti, were delegates of the German workers or of the Comintern. Some Soviet generals, among them Tukhachevsky and Zhukov, attended

German schools of military theory at which the highest Reichswehr commanders received their tactical instruction.

The preparatory work done between 1920 and 1922 and even the treaty of July 29th, 1922 were at first kept secret from President Ebert, the Chancellor and most of the members of the Reichstag. In military circles, too, those in the know could be counted on the fingers of one hand. Needless to say, the Soviets observed absolute secrecy. From time to time, rumors arose but they could never be confirmed and were hotly denied by the Soviet and German military.

Once the preparatory stage was concluded, large sums of money were required for execution of the plans. Since the Soviets did not have such funds, it had to come from German sources, and it was necessary, therefore, to include all those involved in the allocation of Reichstag funds in the conspiracy. At this point von Seeckt confided in Chancellor Wirth, the Minister of Finance, the President and a few members of the Reichstag Finance Committee. Freund writes that there are grounds for suspecting that the Social Democratic member of that Committee, one Schönlein, must have known what was afoot, but that he probably followed Ebert's directive and kept his knowledge to himself. It is difficult to say what other members of the Reichstag had a part in this game. But when the Social Democratic leader, Scheidemann, heard of it, he at least had the courage to expose and publicly condemn the alliance between the Reichswehr and the Kremlin.

The "R" group and all other camouflaged organizations (notably the notorious GFU—*Gesellschaft für Förderung gewerbschaftlicher Unternehmungen*—continued their activities undisturbed. These organizations had ostensibly been created to carry on private commercial and financial transactions; in reality, they transmitted hundreds of millions of marks to Soviet Russia for the secret rearmament of Germany. Even after Germany had entered the League of Nations, and was apparently committed to a pro-western policy, secret rearmament continued with the Soviet Union's help and on its territory.

Then on December 2nd, 1926, the great British liberal newspaper, the *Manchester Guardian*, published a sensational dispatch from its obviously well-informed Berlin correspondent. He reported in general terms but with great accuracy that Soviet factories were manufacturing grenades, poison gas and airplanes for the German Reichswehr. This dispatch was immediately reprinted in *Vorwärts,* the organ of the German Social Democrats, and the Social Democrat Scheidemann told the Reichstag of the sums secretly transmitted by various firms to German factories on Soviet soil, the goods produced in these factories, how these operations were camouflaged, etc. The speech caused a great uproar in the Reichstag, and Scheidemann was accused of slandering the Fatherland.

The German government made known unofficially that anyone responsible for such "false accusations" would be tried for high treason. Since the German judiciary at that time was very reactionary, German courts would undoubtedly have dealt most harshly with such "slanderers." This threat more or less silenced those newspapers which were opposed in principle to rearmament with Russia's help. The leading German papers refrained from comment when another Social Democrat, Franz Künstler (a former Independent who later became chairman of the Berlin organization of the Social Democratic Party), wrote a pamphlet describing a visit he had made to Stettin, where Soviet ships unloaded. He named the ships and indicated what their cargo was. He had spoken to Social Democratic dockers working in the harbor and they had told him that once they had seen a crate break open and poison-gas grenades with Soviet markings fall out. Yet all this material, though it was very detailed and obviously factual, caused little controversy in the press.

On January 19, 1927, the *Manchester Guardian* published another article, giving the names of the German officers who had gone to Moscow to sign the agreement on military and technical collaboration with the Soviet Union. Inside Germany, one fearless paper, the *Weltbühne,* edited by Karl von Ossietzky, a pacifist, had the courage to reprint this article. And Karl Martens, another German pacifist, who fled to escape trial for high treason, published in Switzerland all the details of the treaty of July 29, 1922, between the General Staffs of Germany and the Soviet Union.

On February 25, 1927, at a secret session of the Reichstag, the Social Democrat Breitscheid, a former Independent Socialist, asked the government to name the source of the enormous sums which were being sent to Soviet Russia for secret rearmament. War Minister Gessler gave an evasive answer, observing only that it was necessary to import ammunition and other military supplies into Germany for defense against a possible attack by Poland. At the same time he promised that these imports would be discontinued. This was a deliberate lie. In reality, the military and technical co-operation was continued until 1934 on a very large scale and with only occasional interruptions. Carr, a historian who has been repeatedly cited in this book, writes that it is impossible to understand why France, Britain and the other Allies did not take action against such an obvious and undeniable breach of the Versailles clause forbidding German rearmament. This is very fully and plausibly explained by another British historian, John W. Wheeler-Bennett, in his book *Nemesis of Power.*[18]

> The German application for admission to the League in March 1926 had been accompanied by the demand that all controls should be abolished, on the grounds that all the requirements of the Treaty of Versailles had been complied with. The Control Commission was therefore instructed by the British, French and Belgian Governments to make a final inspection of Germany's armaments with a view to satisfying this demand. Contrary to the expectation of London, Paris and Brussels, the Commission's report, a document of some five hundred pages, stated in essence that "Germany had never disarmed, had never had the intention of disarming, and for seven years had done everything in her power to deceive and 'counter-control' the Commission appointed to control her disarmament." So anxious, however, were the Governments concerned to place the final coping-stone upon the edifice of Locarno, so confident were they in the validity of Stresemann's pledges of Germany's peaceful intentions, that they deliberately suppressed and ignored this final report and issued a communiqué on December 13, 1926 that of more than a hundred questions of disarmament outstanding in June 1925 there remained now but two, that the Powers had agreed to continue negotiations on these two items and that the Commission of Control would be withdrawn on January 31, 1937.

Of all political parties in Germany only the small group of pacifists and the Social Democratic Party consistently and courageously opposed the policy of preparing for a second World War. The German

Communist Party kept a cowardly silence on the subject of rearmament or else savagely attacked the Social Democrats for their "slanderous persecution" of the Soviet Union. The German Communists, by this time, had been prepared for tacit or open collaboration with reactionary nationalists in the Ruhr crisis of 1923.

The Ruhr Crisis and Moscow

The crisis was set off by the announcement of the Cuno Cabinet in Berlin that it had decided to postpone reparations payments for five years. In response, France and Belgium sent troops into the Ruhr on January 12, 1923. The Germans replied with a total resistance. Industrialists suspended operations, the workers went on strike and all economic life in the huge Ruhr basin came to a standstill. Somehow, however, it was necessary to feed the people and this required enormous sums of money. The German government, which shared responsibility for the whole stoppage with the trade unions, the workers' organizations and all the parties in the Reichstag, could raise the necessary funds in only one way—it printed paper money. A galloping inflation, such as had never been known in the history of a modern state, resulted. In the course of a few months the value of the mark fell so sharply that 1,000,000,000 paper marks to the dollar were offered, in contrast to the previous rate of slightly more than four gold marks to the dollar. All private savings, both in bank deposits and in government bonds, became completely valueless; a package of cigarettes cost 1,000,000 marks and more; money was worthless and each evening found prices higher than they had been in the morning. Commercial deals became meaningless. The workers suffered dreadful privation. The whole middle class, the main bearer of the German liberal and democratic tradition, was plunged into ruin. The rising tension sought outlets during 1923 in revolts, strikes, the attempt of an armed uprising by the Communists and the abortive Hitler putsch of November 9th. Finally, the fall of the Cuno government, brought about by the Social Democrats, saved the German Republic. A new coalition government of the Center Party and the Social Democrats came to power, headed by Chancellor Gustav Stresemann, who favored fulfillment of the Versailles Treaty, and stopped the struggle for the Ruhr.

In 1924, the United States intervened in the matter of reparations. A commission headed by Charles Dawes went to Germany and helped stabilize the currency and economy. After the Locarno Conference of September 15, 1925, at which Weimar Germany under Stresemann's leadership decided to join the League of Nations, the stabilization of the Weimar Republic became an established fact.

However, the dramatic events of 1923—the Ruhr occupation, the inflation, the deep changes in the economic situation and ideology of the middle classes—left a deep impression on the social and political life of the Weimar Republic. The consequences came to the surface only after the Great Depression of 1929.

During the crisis of 1923, the Social Democratic Party had, albeit unwillingly, supported the strike of the Ruhr workers but it had made no ideological concessions to the nationalist tide that was rising in the country. In sharp contrast, the German Communists started a blatant flirtation with the extreme nationalists and chauvinists. Radek, Zinoviev and other Comintern leaders attempted to concoct an ideological justification of the wildest and most senseless German nationalism. During his term in the Moabit Prison in 1920, Radek had attacked the "National Communist" schemes of the Hamburg Communists, Lauffenberg and Wolffheim, as contrary to true Communism. In 1923, he completely reversed himself. He wrote:

> In 1920, National Bolshevism meant an alliance to save the generals, who would have wiped out the Communist Party immediately after the victory. Today, National Bolshevism means that everyone is penetrated with the feeling that salvation can be found only with the Communists. Today we are the only way out. Great emphasis on the nation in Germany is a revolutionary act, like emphasis on the nation in the colonies.[19]

In addition, Radek argued that, with Russia's support, the German Communist Party was strong enough not to fear an alliance with the nationalists: "German nationalism is a broad movement of the people, which has great revolutionary importance."[20] Despite the protests from the right-wing German Communists who disliked this new view of fascism, Radek's opinions, of which Zinoviev, Trotsky and Lenin (as far as he was still capable of active work) approved, undoubtedly influenced the policy of the Third International and the Soviet government.

Radek expressed his viewpoint particularly clearly in a brilliant speech in memory of Leo Schlageter, a Nazi who was caught and executed by the French authorities for attempting to blow up railroads in the Ruhr. Schlageter had already become a hero among German nationalists, a martyr of the German struggle against French oppression. At his funeral in Munich one of the speeches was delivered by Field Marshal von Ludendorff. At the enlarged plenary meeting of the Executive Committee of the Comintern, Radek said: "Schlageter was a brave soldier of the counter-revolution" who fought for the liberation of his people. Radek argued that Schlageter's fate would force a decision upon the German masses: to side with the capitalists and reactionaries of the Entente against the Russian people, or to side with the Russian people against the capitalists of the Entente and thus bring nearer the liberation of Germany and of the whole world.[21] Even Klara Zetkin, who at the beginning of the meeting had said that the fight against fascism must take priority over everything else, declared that she had been deeply moved by Radek's speech.

When Radek's speech became known in Germany, it greatly impressed the nationalists, who affirmed that his point of view represented a form of National Bolshevism with which they were prepared to collaborate. A mass meeting organized by the Nazis in Stuttgart on August 2nd was addressed by Remmele, a member of the Central Committee of the German Communist Party. On August 10th, a Communist mass meeting was addressed, in its turn, by a Nazi representative who called for a national brand of socialism as opposed to international socialism. The Nazis, he said, would be willing to collaborate with the Communists, especially if they could get rid of their Jewish leaders. The Nazi paper *Gewissen* praised Radek's speech on Schlageter and went so far as to say that the Nazis would willingly yield the leadership of the proletariat to the German Communists. Radek was also complimented by Count Reventlow, later closely linked to Hitler. A pamphlet published in Germany in July contained articles by Radek and Fröhlich, both Communists, beside those of Möller van den Bruck, an extreme nationalist, and Count Reventlow.

Later in 1923, the German Communists sacrificed whatever standing they retained by another inept attempt at an uprising. A cache of arms for the revolutionaries was seized in Berlin, and on September 25, 1923, the Berlin daily *Vorwärts* disclosed that the warehouse where the arms were stored had been rented in the name of a certain Petrov, an employee of the Soviet Embassy. In a note of October 6th, Chicherin protested—with more heat than plausibility—this "slander" against the Soviet government.[22]

After the local elections in Thuringia and Saxony in early October 1923, the Socialists and the Communists formed coalition united-front governments in both states. Having achieved this much, the Communists immediately demanded a revolutionary policy including, if need be, preparations for an actual uprising. Before the Executive Committee of the Comintern, Zinoviev had cautiously estimated in June that the German revolution was surely coming, but that this did not mean "it would come in a month or even a year. It might need much longer."[23]

As autumn approached, Zinoviev became more inclined to share Trotsky's view that the German revolution was just around the corner.

However, President Ebert dissolved the coalition governments of Thuringia and Saxony, whereupon the Communists cancelled a rising that had been planned for October 22-23. The Hamburg Communists did not receive news of the cancellation in time, and rose on the appointed day. They suffered an overwhelming defeat. Later, it was learned that the "rising in Hamburg had had at its command 50 men, three revolvers and two rifles."[24]

For the next few years, the Communist Party no longer played a significant part in German politics. But its flirtation with German nationalists, like the more deeply grounded collaboration between the Kremlin and the Reichswehr, helped lay the groundwork for Communist policy when the great crisis of the Weimar Republic began in 1930.

[1] At the elections of January 19th, the Social Democratic majority polled 11,509,000 votes and the Independent Socialists 2,137,000. In effect the socialist wing of the Constituent Assembly had obtained almost 14 million votes, nearly half the total of 30,401,000.

On points of democratic political reform, the Social Democrats were able to gain support in the Assembly from some bourgeois-democratic deputies, but on purely socialist issues they were invariably in the minority. It is interesting to compare this with the Russian Constituent Assembly in which a socialist coalition of all workers' parties, had it been formed, would have commanded more than 75% of the votes. This alone clearly demonstrates the difference in the political make-up of post-war Germany and post-October Russia.

[2] Lenin, vol. 28, p. 84.

[3] The British historian, E. H. Carr, had such confidence in the Bolsheviks that in 1951 he put forward the suggestion that the pamphlets might have been planted by the German police (see *German-Soviet Relations*, p. 3). In this respect he outdoes Yoffe himself, who admitted supplying the German revolutionaries with money but said nothing about a police plant in the matter of the pamphlets (see Yoffe's letter of December 16, 1918 in Jane Degras, *Soviet Documents on Foreign Policy*, New York, Oxford University Press, 1957, vol. 1, p. 127).

[4] See K. Radek's article, "November," in *Krassnaya*, Nov. 1926, p. 41.

[5] A. Thalheimer, *1923: Eine verpasste Revoluzion*, Berlin, 1931, p. 21.

[6] On one occasion Radek, being low in funds, stole a watch from a comrade who was staying the night with him and pawned it. When accused of the theft, he was not at all abashed and cynically turned the incident to good use: from then on he signed his witty, malicious articles with the *nom de plume*, K. Radek, the word *kradek* meaning thief in Polish.

[7] Carr, *Germany and the USSR*, pp. 56-60.

This date for the beginning of negotiations between Moscow and Berlin is also that given by former German war minister, Gessler (see Wheeler-Bennett).

[8] Carr, *German-Soviet Relations*, p. 57.

[9] Trotsky's archives, quoted by Carr in *German-Russian Relations*, p. 57 seq.

[10] *Ibid.*, p. 58.

[11] Degras, *op. cit.*, pp. 270-272.

[12] In the middle of February an international conference met in Paris "for protection of foreign private investments in Russia"; and the decisions reached there were communicated to the Allied governments. On the basis of all these deliberations the Allies were able to prepare a draft resolution on financial claims against the Soviet government for the Genoa conference.

[13] Lenin, vol. 33, p. 187.

[14] It is extremely interesting to note that the conclusion of the Rapallo Treaty was almost as great a surprise to President Ebert. As a long-time, convinced Social Democrat he was highly suspicious of the Bolsheviks. Knowing this, his foreign minister kept the news of the secret negotiations at Rapallo from him until the last moment. Only on the night of the signing of the treaty did Rathenau telephone him from Genoa to inform him. Ebert was furious but he was unable to do anything: the army was completely in favor of the treaty. (See Freund, p. 120—reference to F. Stampfer, *Die vierzehn Jahre der ersten deutschen Republik*, Karlsbad, 1936, p. 270.)

[15] Freund, p. 110.

[16] H. Speidel, "Reichswehr und Rote Armee" in *Vierteljahrhefte für Zeitgeschichte*, 1 Jhrg, Heft 1, p. 18 (Stuttgart, January, 1953).

[17] *Ibid.*, p. 28.

[18] Wheeler-Bennett, J. W., *Nemesis of Power*, London, 1954, pp. 185-186.

[19] *Internationale Presse-Korrespondenz*, No. 103, June 21, 1923, p. 869.

[20] Radek's speech at the enlarged plenary meeting of the Executive Committee of the Comintern, 12th-23rd June, 1923 (cited from Carr, vol. IV, p. 179).

[21] Carr, vol. IV, p. 178.

[22] Degras, *op. cit.*, vol. I, pp. 410-412.

[23] Enlarged plenary meeting of the Executive Committee of the Comintern, June 12-23, 1923, p. 103. (Cited from Carr, vol. IV, p. 178.)

[24] Ruth Fisher, *Stalin and German Communism*, Cambridge, Mass., 1948, pp. 338-340.

CHAPTER 11

The Comintern

The Bolsheviks swore by the world revolution, feverishly shifting their interest from West to East.[1] They hoped it would come, not only for the cause of the world proletariat but, perhaps unconsciously, so as to fortify their own power in Russia. With characteristic energy, they did their utmost to hasten the coming of the millenium.

Early in 1919, Lenin decided to lay the foundations for a new, third, Communist International which would assume the leadership of the world's workers under the banner of the Soviets. He was obviously inspired by Marx's feat of creating the first International in 1864 and making it into a real power in the relatively small international working-class movement of his day. As Lenin saw it, the Second International had fallen from grace in 1914, and a complete break between reformism and revolution was needed. The new International was to be rooted in Marx's original teachings on the dictatorship of the proletariat and the expectation of an immediate social revolution. It seemed quite natural, both theoretically and practically, to establish the headquarters of the world revolution in the Kremlin, in the "land of triumphant socialism."

The foundations of this new organization in 1919 were as yet unstable. The Civil War was not yet over; Russia itself was threatened with famine and even possible counter-revolution. Nevertheless, the first conference of what was to be the Third International opened in Moscow on March 2, 1919.

The Communist International—or Comintern—had to be formed without its component parts—Communist parties. There were none except the Russian party and the beaten remnants of one in Hungary. But that did not deter Lenin. He argued that individual parties would quickly be organized as soon as there was a Third International to provide them with agents, emissaries and financial backing.

The conference opened with 35 delegates. With very few exceptions these "delegates" were members of the Russian party who had simply been appointed by the Central Committee to play the part of foreign delegates. The only genuine delegate, Eberlein, came from Germany; towards the end of the conference, Steinhardt arrived with a mandate from a group of Communists in Austria. There were several other individuals from abroad; these did not represent organized Communist parties but rather small groups of left-wing socialists in Switzerland, France, Sweden and Norway. Poland was represented by Unschlicht (a member of the Russian Military Revolutionary Council), the Ukraine by Skrypnik, Finland by Sirola, the Volga Germans by Klinger, and the "peoples of Eastern Russia" by Yalymov. In the debate on whether the International could be formally organized in the absence of all the leading workers' parties of the world, Lenin carried the conference with him: it was decided to transform the meeting into the constituent congress of the Third International. Only Eberlein, the delegate of the German Spartacists, opposed this decision. He had come to Moscow with instructions from Rosa Luxemburg to oppose the formation of an International at that moment with the utmost determination, and under no circumstances to agree to such a step in the name of the Spartacists. For a while, Eberlein was adamant and neither Lenin's insistence nor the eloquence of other "delegates" could sway him. Only the persuasion of the Austrian Steinhardt finally prevailed upon Eberlein to abstain from voting against the motion.[2] Thus the creation of the International was decided upon by 35 votes with one abstention. Angelica Balabanova was appointed its first secretary—she was informed over the telephone by the Central Committee of the Bolshevik Party. The Central Committee also appointed Zinoviev chairman of the Executive Committee of the new organization.[3]

At this stage the Executive Committee of the Comintern could only be an international adjunct of the Central Committee of the Bolshevik Party. But Lenin and his colleagues were firmly convinced that it would not remain so for long. They counted on many revolutionary elements scattered throughout the world to rally to the new center. And events proved them right. Fifteen months later, on July 19, 1920, the Second Congress of the Comintern was attended by genuine representatives of foreign organizations, some of them fairly large and influential. At this Second Congress, 169 full delegates and 48 others in a consultative capacity were present. One of the parties represented was the German Independent Socialist Party, which at that time had over half a million members.

Even though large groups of revolutionary socialists from all over the world flocked to the Comintern, it still remained, in effect, an international section of the Bolshevik Party. On the face of it, the majority on the Executive Committee was made up of non-Russians, but this was in no way decisive. All real authority was vested in the Russian Bolsheviks, partly because they occupied the main posts and also because the foreign Communists who came to Moscow looked up to the Soviet leaders with such respect and admiration that it took little effort by Lenin and Trotsky, or even by Zinoviev and Radek, to make the Comintern follow their lead. The enormous extent of Lenin's and Trotsky's prestige can be judged from remarks of the Italian delegate, Serrati. He told a group of Mensheviks that, when he spoke to Lenin at a reception and put various questions to him, his Italian comrades watched him almost fearfully, horrified at his daring to argue with Lenin.

At this congress, Lenin formulated the basic theory and outlined the political and organizational strategy for his Third International. He viewed the International as the organizer of Communist revolutions all over the world. He did not conceive of his universal revolution as a historical process that would mature in the distant future, as had been assumed by the parties of the Second International before the First World War, but rather saw it as the most urgent immediate task. To accomplish it, the old methods of parliamentary struggle, democratic preparation for socialism, long years of propaganda to attract millions of enlightened workers into the party, were no use. What was needed was the direct militant action of an *élite* which, as in Russia, would sweep the revolutionary-minded masses into pseudo-spontaneous risings. In accordance with this policy, the Communist parties were urged to foreswear the reformism of the Second International and to turn themselves for all practical purposes into conspirational organizations, which would not merely prepare Communist revolutions by normal political methods but would also exploit all conflicts inside the workers' movements of their respective countries. In many countries (particularly in the West) in which large, well-established socialist parties existed, the first task was to split and break them up because they were reformist, drive a wedge between the masses and their leaders ("traitors incapable of revolutionary action"), and build parties of a new type, either from the remnants of the old or from scratch.[4]

Lenin and Zinoviev worked out these fundamental principles at the Comintern's Second Congress in their 21 conditions for the affiliation of socialist and other workers' parties with the Third International. All parties had been free to join previous Internationals, provided only that they agreed with the program and tactics. That was not true of the new Communist organization. To join the Third International, a party was required to pass a most rigorous test and, above all, to fulfill the 21 conditions. In brief, they stipulated that the party should cast out all treacherous, reformist, non-revolutionary leaders; create a secret organization parallel to an official legal one to carry out the actual preparation of the revolution; and, most important, accept the ideological leadership of the Russian Communist Party and of the Soviet Union.

In the early 1920s, as Bolshevik prestige, both political and military, rose steadily, the Comintern in Moscow became a veritable Mecca for revolutionary elements from all over the world. Delegations, pilgrims and sympathizers from the furthermost ends of the earth streamed to it. It was visited by representatives of all major socialist parties in Europe: the German Independent Socialists, the socialist parties of France, Italy, Spain and Czechoslovakia, the left-wing Polish Socialist Party, the Polish Bund, the Labor parties of Sweden, Norway, Denmark and even Britain (the Independent Labour Party and the trade unions). Simultaneously an equally long file of secret Comintern agents moved out from Moscow to all these countries. They carried with them large quantities of diamonds and other valuables, together with wide powers to exploit the local situation to foment workers' uprisings. Various former members of the Communist parties of those days have since told much about these agents' activities. More direct evidence has been supplied by Comintern agents who have become disillusioned with Communism. One agent who remained a Communist even published his memoirs in Moscow and related his adventures fairly candidly.[5]

This man, Vladimir Degot, was resident agent of the Third International in Italy in 1921. He later described how

> After the congress [of the Socialist Party] Nitti, a very cunning politician, wanting to deceive the revolutionary masses, suggested to those Socialists from the Socialist Party who were members of the Comintern that they should stage an internal parliamentary coup, that is, remove the King, proclaim a republic and thus save Italy . . .

When the socialist leader Bombacci asked Degot how the Comintern would react to this proposal, which was supported by many socialists:

> I took up a determined position against it, and argued that they were only deflecting the revolutionary impetus, throwing dust in the eyes of the working class. The Socialist Party must have no part in this comedy.
>
> And it would be indeed a comedy because all that this parliamentary revolt could achieve would be the departure of the King; and in any case Nitti's proposal was of no importance as the revolutionary movement was so strong that the immediate issue was the seizure of power by the working class.[6]

At a meeting of the Central Committee of the Socialist Party, Bombacci secured acceptance of the Comintern line. Nitti's proposal was rejected and the Socialist Party embarked on a path that led to splits within the party, an endless series of strikes and the whole unhappy history of Italy which preceded Mussolini's march on Rome. It is quite possible that, in rejecting Nitti's proposal, the Italian Socialist Party threw away its last chance of barring the fascists from power. At least, such was the opinion of Modigliani[7] and Nenni[8] in those days.

As we have seen, the Comintern played a fateful part in Germany in the split of the Independent Socialist Party, in the creation of a mass Communist Party and in the fanning of its revolutionary ambitions. Bela Kun, his assistant Guralski, General Skoblevski, "Walter" (Krivitsky), Joseph Pógany (John Pepper) and other Comintern agents directed the German Communist Party, and were later responsible for its final defeat.

There were similar events in other countries, where the Bolsheviks succeeded in gaining influence in the old parties, and split them. Between 1920 and the Second World War, schisms rent the socialist parties of France, Belgium, Holland, Denmark, Sweden, Norway, Switzerland, Italy, Rumania, Poland, Czechoslovakia, Yugoslavia, Austria, Spain, the United States, Argentina, Brazil, and many other countries.

The Comintern and its constituent parties were weapons in the hands of their Soviet masters. In the final instance it was the Kremlin, through Zinoviev, Bukharin, Manuilsky, Dimitrov, Stalin and the rest, which decided who was to head this or that party; and it did so without bothering about local conditions. In some cases, leaders with only a small following were given control of the party, and the majority of the membership was expelled. Party tactics were decided by the Kremlin without regard for differences of opinion or the balance of forces inside the parties. The parties were often impecunious and dependent on the Kremlin for financial and technical assistance; and to them every directive of the Kremlin was an order. The entire Comintern was built on the basis of an absolute obedience to the interests, plans and wishes of the Bolshevik leaders.

The history of the Comintern, from the hour of its formation to its inglorious end at Stalin's hands in 1943, is an endless chain of defeats, fiascos, errors, none of which advanced the world proletariat in the least along the road to its mythical Communist revolution. In reality, the very existence of the Comintern, its intrigues and its opposition to the socialist parties, weakened the world proletariat and acted as an impediment to its progress throughout the whole period between 1920 and the Second World War.

The emergence of the Comintern forced the socialist parties to close ranks and to reaffirm their adherence to the Marxism of Engels in the 1890s, especially as this was interpreted by his pupils Kautsky and Bernstein, and, to a certain extent, Rosa Luxemburg.

After the arrival of Martov and this author in Europe, efforts were made to form an all embracing International composed of all leftist, revolutionary socialist parties, including the Communists. Insisting on such "unity," leftist socialist leaders stubbornly refused even to discuss the policy of the Soviet government.

After a preliminary meeting in Berne, in December 1920, a conference was held of the new International Association of Socialist Parties in Vienna, the citadel of Austrian Marxism, led by Otto Bauer and Friedrich Adler. This conference lasted from February 22 to 27, 1921 and was attended by 79 delegates representing 19 socialist parties in various countries of Europe. A declaration of the principles of democratic socialism, which took into account the main changes that had occurred in the world during the war, was adopted. A number of specific issues were discussed, notably a report on the situation in Russia and a telegram from the socialist government of the democratic Georgian (Caucasus) Republic which violently protested against an unprovoked attack by Soviet troops. The discussions revealed great differences of opinion among the representatives of the various parties. There was such unwillingness to criticize Soviet Russia that the conference could not agree on a condemnation of the occupation of Georgia by Soviet troops, thoug the facts laid before it were unambiguous and the participants in the conference had complete personal confidence in Martov and his friends, who were present, and in the Georgian socialist leaders, Tseretelli and Jordania, whom many of them knew. Nevertheless, the conference agreed on the formation of the Vienna Association of Socialist Parties, usually referred to as the Vienna International (Radek maliciously nicknamed it the "Two-and-a-half International"), which was committed to work for the unification of all socialist parties.

While Martov remained in Russia, little had been heard of him abroad. But when socialists met him on his appearance in Halle in October 1920, and in December 1920 at the first meeting of the initiators of the new International in Berne and in Vienna, personal contact with him strengthened the will of the left-wing socialist leaders to take a critical look at the Comintern and the excesses of the Bolshevik dictatorship.

The left-wing socialists of western and central Europe were confirmed and strengthened in their opposition to the Bolshevik terror by the example of Martov and his comrades. It seemed obvious that there must be something very wrong about the Bolshevik dictatorship if such a convinced internationalist as Martov, a patently sincere and honest man, found it impossible to collaborate with Lenin and his party. If Martov's comrades in Soviet Russia were arrested, imprisoned and even sometimes shot, then the dictatorship was unacceptable to democratic socialists, however revolutionary their feelings.

* * *

After the fiasco of the March 1921 Communist putsch in Germany, the Comintern decided to adopt the tactics of the "united front." The reason for this stratagem was very simple: to enable the German Communist Party to extricate itself from complete political and moral isolation. Lenin wrote of this with his usual frankness. He said that its purpose was to smuggle Communists into "the locked, well-guarded building, so that, once inside, they would have the possibility, however slight, of addressing the workers who had hitherto been the exclusive property of the reformists."[9]

The leaders of the Vienna Association saw through these Bolshevik plans, but they were unwilling to ignore any opportunity, however small, of uniting all sections of the European proletariat. And so they not only agreed themselves to take part in a joint conference of all three Internationals, but even persuaded the leaders of the Second International to do so too. Some of the member parties of the Second International, which had belonged to the extreme right wing and had collaborated with their governments during the war, were extremely hostile to the Bolsheviks. But they considered it important enough to maintain their link with the Vienna Association to let themselves be persuaded.

The conference of the three Internationals took place April 4 in the Reichstag building in Berlin. It was the first and last of its kind. The Third International was represented, among others, by Klara Zetkin, Radek, Frossard and Bukharin; the Second International by Ramsey Macdonald, Emile Vandervelde, Otto Wells, Hjalmar Branting and Irakly Tseretelli; and the Vienna Association by Otto Bauer,

Friedrich Adler, Dittmann, Crispin, Wallhead and Martov. In addition to these official delegates, the other members of the respective executive committees were invited to attend as guests.

It became obvious from the very beginning that it would not be possible to reconcile the different points of view. Nevertheless, agreement was reached on a point raised by the Russian Menshevik delegation (Martov, Dan and Abramovitch) concerning the fate of the twelve Russian S-R's who were then awaiting trial by the Supreme Tribunal in Moscow. They were to be tried for "terrorist" acts and plans dating back to the Civil War which, as we know, had started by acts of terror perpetrated by Bolsheviks—the violent dissolution of the Constituent Assembly and mass executions without trial. The possible fate of these comrades, who were in danger of execution, worried not only the Russian Mensheviks and their S-R friends but many European socialists as well. An amnesty had been declared at the end of the Civil War and the death penalty had been abolished three times in Soviet Russia by official decrees of the Soviet government. But there was reason to fear, nevertheless. The case was hotly debated in a secret session of a subcommittee and, the pressure from most of those present, including the present writer, proving too great for them, Klara Zetkin, Radek and Bukharin promised on behalf of the Soviet Communist Party that the S-R's would not be sentenced to death and that representatives of the Vienna and the Second Internationals would be admitted to the trial as defense counsel. This concession turned out to be the only positive achievement of this conference which had excited so many hopes and provoked so much comment.[10]

The main result of the Berlin conference of the three Internationals—and that an indirect one—was the drawing together of the Vienna and the Second Internationals. The participants in the Vienna meeting shed most of their former illusions when they saw for themselves that the Communists had no real intention of yielding on any important point, that their attendance at the conference was not motivated by a genuine desire for proletarian unity but was just a fraudulent maneuver. They concluded that, in view of the existence of the Comintern and the "proletarian dictatorship" in Moscow, unity was possible only among those sections of the working classes which held socialism to be inseparable from democracy and the self-determination of the workers, and that the Social Democratic movement was incompatible with dictatorial organizations or parties dominated by a handful of conspirators believing in rule by force and terror. After their experience in Berlin, the rapprochement between the Vienna and the Second Internationals proceeded at a much quicker pace.[11]

A joint committee, consisting of five representatives of the Vienna International and five of the Second, was set up. After careful preparation, the first congress of the new, united international association, known as the Hamburg International, opened in May 1923 in Hamburg. This "Labor and Socialist International" (LSI) was composed of the socialist parties of 28 countries. At the congress, the Russian question was given great prominence. R. Abramovitch (Martov had died shortly before of tuberculosis of the throat) delivered a report on the situation in Russia. The admission of Russian democratic socialists to the new International also came under discussion. This problem was considered by the political subcommittee of the congress, presided over by Beatrice Webb, who already at that time was extremely pro-Communist. She argued that people fighting against a socialist government in their own country should not be permitted to join the International. The representatives of the Russian socialist parties opposed this contention. After a long and bitter fight, Beatrice Webb was defeated; the political subcommittee considered the participation of Russian Mensheviks and S-R's in the International not only desirable but essential. No fewer than seven Russian socialists (Mensheviks and S-R's) were given seats both on the Executive Committee and on the Bureau of the International. The congress also passed a resolution condemning the use of terror against socialists in Russia and offering its sympathy and a promise of moral and material help to Russian socialists fighting against the dictatorship.

The Communist International did not succeed in capturing a decisive section of the working class in Europe or elsewhere. Communists remained in the minority almost everywhere between the two world wars. During this period no attempts were made to start revolutions in any country, least of all during 1925-1930, the years of capitalist stabilization.[12] On the other hand the Hamburg International and the International Federation of Trade Unions, which the Bolsheviks called the "Amsterdam International," won more and more influence for the working class in the economic, social and political fields. The Marseilles Congress of 1925 and the Brussels Congress of 1928 showed that democratic socialism in Europe was growing continuously and increasing in strength.

[1] Trotsky's memorandum (archives)—India, Asia.

[2] Eberlein, in *The Communist International*, Nos. 9-10, 1929.

[3] Angelica Balabanova, *Erinnerungen*, Berlin, 1927, pp. 229-30.

[4] One of the methods which the Comintern, on the direct advice of Lenin, used in the process of splitting and rebuilding groups, was corruption. The Soviet government had at its disposal very large funds which it could use at will. Angelica Balabanova, who at the beginning was appointed secretary of the Comintern and resided in Stockholm, tells in her new book, *Lenin* (German translation, 1961, Verlag für Literatur und Zeitgeschehen, G.m.b.H., Hanover), the story of how Lenin urged her not to skimp with money but to spend "the money freely by millions and tens of millions" for the above purpose.

[5] Degot, V. A., *Under the Banners of Bolshevism: Notes of a Revolutionary*. Second revised edition. Publ. by the All-Russian Society of Political Prisoners and Settlers, Moscow, 1931, pp. 224-225.

[6] *Ibid.*

[7] See *La vie socialiste* of March 5, 1952.

[8] See the journal *Gesellschaft* and the newspaper *Avanti* of March 1 and 12, 1932.

[9] Lenin, vol. 33, pp. 296, 297.

[10] As might be expected, the Bolsheviks kept only one of their promises—the representatives of the Second International, Emil Vandervelde, Theodore Liebknecht (Karl's older brother), the German socialist Kurt Rosenfeld and others were admitted to the trial. But they did not, strictly speaking, fulfill their second promise. The accused were sentenced to death but the date of execution was not fixed; the sentences were to be carried out immediately if and when the Social Revolutionary Party resumed its terrorist activities. It is interesting to note that Lenin severely condemned the "inadmissable concessions" made by the Communist delegates to the conference. In his article "Too High A Price," to which Trotsky fully subscribed, Lenin said that to call off the execution of the S-R "terrorists" was too high a price to pay for the chance of enlarging Communist influence in a specific sector of the working class. In future, said Lenin, they were not to pay "such altogether disproportionate prices." People who talk about Lenin's humanity would do well to read this article.

[11] A further milestone in this development was the so-called Congress of Peace in mid-December 1922 at the Hague and attended by 600 delegates and countless guests from various workers' organizations, trade unions, peace societies, etc. At this congress a verbal clash occurred between Radek and this writer, who represented Martov's group. Radek, defending the Bolshevik aggression in Georgia, said with undisguised cynicism that Georgia had to return to Russia because Russia needed oil. His speech was not well received, whereas the speech of his opponent, which was an exposition of the Menshevik attitude in the matter, received a prolonged and enthusiastic ovation from the entire congress. The left-wing, non-Communist part of the world proletariat obviously inclined toward the point of view of the Mensheviks, who were morally, though not numerically, a challenge to world Communism and Bolshevism.

[12] In Bulgaria and Estonia there were revolutions started by Soviet agents—both in 1925—but they found no mass support and were quickly suppressed.

CHAPTER 12

Lenin, Trotsky and Stalin

The Rise of Stalin

Throughout the revolutionary period, the Bolshevik Party leaders looked upon their colleague Joseph Stalin as a very average sort of man—uneducated, ignorant of foreign languages, bad speaker, poor writer, colorless, intellectually indolent,[1] and lacking in all breadth or originality of thought. They thought of him as a fairly good organizer and administrator, but intellectually a mediocrity at best. Trotsky contemptuously described him early in his career as "the most outstanding mediocrity of our party."[2] Such was also the opinion of Zinoviev, Kamenev, Bukharin, Piatakov, Preobrazhensky, and virtually every other Bolshevik leader.

Lenin's estimate of him may have been somewhat higher, but even Lenin valued Stalin above all as a reliable and willing subordinate, an efficient organizer of various party enterprises (including some very "special" ones) and an adroit intriguer in internal party politics. He also recognized in him a man who knew the party apparatus well and was eminently suited to become a party secretary. But Lenin certainly did not admire him for his intellectual talents or his knowledge, even in the early days, 1912-1913, when he called him "the marvellous Georgian," or when Stalin submitted the draft of a piece on the nationalities problem, which Lenin had asked him to write.

Stalin knew exactly what the other party leaders thought of him, particularly those who were educated and talented. He repaid them with equal amounts of contempt and hatred. To him they were empty chatterers—some, like Kamenev, simply spineless, others, like Zinoviev, downright cowardly, but all lacking strength of character, self-control and the will to fight. Yet Stalin was profoundly convinced that it was these qualities, together with unhesitating ruthlessness, that were needed in men who aspired to bring about a violent revolution and rule over a great people.

As a result of these convictions and much thought about his prospects in the party, Stalin adopted a farsighted policy. At the beginning of the October Revolution his colorless personality was overshadowed not only by Lenin—a titanic figure in the eyes of the Bolsheviks—but also by the brilliant and immensely energetic Trotsky. Stalin gave no outward sign of his mounting irritation with Lenin, or even his jealousy of Trotsky and all the others whom he regarded as unworthy of the prominent positions they occupied. He used his enormous willpower and self-discipline to control his ambition. He knew that his strength did not lie in surface brilliance, the art of oratory, a ready pen or theoretical knowledge, but in organization.

In the organizational sphere, it is true, the foremost position was at first held by another man, Jacob Sverdlov, a young man gifted with exceptional energy and a wonderful memory, who was well liked by Lenin. In the second half of 1917 and in 1918, Sverdlov served as secretary of the Central Committee and chairman of the VTsIK. Stalin, who already occupied an important position, did not try to compete with Sverdlov but waited patiently. Like an experienced chess player, Stalin foresaw not only the next but also the second and third moves of his opponents in the party game. Slowly he worked to clear the way to become second to Lenin in the party machine and the Central Committee. He reached his goal with unexpected rapidity: Sverdlov died of typhus at the end of 1918 and Stalin had little trouble succeeding him. At the Eleventh Congress, in March 1922, he was elected General Secretary of the Central Committee. And soon fate came once again to his assistance—on May 26, 1922, Lenin suffered his first stroke and exhibited the symptoms of a fatal disease, sclerosis of the brain. This development opened up prospects for Stalin far beyond anything previously conceivable. He began to move towards becoming not only the boss of the party machine but also the successor of Lenin himself.

The dedicated, systematic and skillful manner with which Stalin pursued his double aim and developed the full potentialities of his character can be traced in the organizational changes within the Bolshevik Party from the Civil War to the death of Lenin.

In the period between October and the beginning of the Civil War, the party was ruled by a triumvirate consisting of Lenin, Stalin and Sverdlov. The latter, in fact, was the party secretary; but there was no secretariat, and his sudden death left the organization of the rapidly growing party in chaos.

When the Eighth Congress, in March 1919, considered the reorganization of the Central Committee, it adopted a plan prepared by Stalin and Lenin to distribute the work of the Central Committee among three newly created bodies: the Political Bureau (Politburo), Organizational Bureau (Orgburo), and Secretariat. The Politburo was alloted responsibility for the political leadership of the party, the Orgburo for filling appointments in the party machine and the various party organizations, and the Secretariat for all the technical duties which had previously rested on Sverdlov alone. The first Politburo[3] was composed of Lenin, Stalin, Trotsky, Kamenev and Krestinsky, with Bukharin, Zinoviev and Kalinin as alternates. Stalin was, in addition, elected to the Orgburo, and, with a foot in both leading organs, was certain of a key position in the Central Committee.

At the Ninth Party Congress, in March-April 1920, the Secretariat was reorganized and three intellectuals were appointed to it: Krestinsky, Preobrazhensky and Serebryakov. As Stalin must have hoped, these men proved quite unsuited for the task. It was therefore easy for him at the earliest opportunity to fill not only the Orgburo but also the Secretariat with his friends and favorites. At the Tenth Party Congress, in March 1921, Molotov, Yaroslavsky and Mikhailov became members of the Secretariat. Thus, at the Eleventh Congress (March-April 1922), when the creation of the post of General Secretary was approved, Stalin was the logical man for the job.[4]

At the same time, Stalin carefully chose new members and alternates for the Central Committee. During this period the party hierarchy was filled with many new figures, all supporters and cronies of Stalin, who formed his personal clique for the next decade or more. Thus, Yaroslavsky became an alternate member of the Central Committee at the Eighth Congress and a full member at the Tenth Congress;

Andreyev and Rykov were elected to the Central Committee at the Ninth Congress; Molotov and Petrovsky became alternates at the Ninth and full members at the Tenth Congress; Ordzhonikidze and Mikhailov were elected members and Kirov, Ouglanov, Kuibyshev and Chubar alternate members at the Tenth Congress. All these men were not intellectuals but party "apparatchiki" who had made their career through organizational activity in the party apparatus.

In the early Twenties, various dissident elements also developed rapidly in the Bolshevik Party. The victorious conclusion of the Civil War and the economic retreat represented by the NEP lured many who had so far shunned the Bolshevik Party to join it. On the other hand, it also led to ideological misgivings among old Bolsheviks, notably those who had fought in the Civil War under War Communism and had believed in the imminence of socialist construction.

This situation was doubly perilous. New elements, who had joined not to fight and die for the revolution but merely to reap its harvest, threatened to swamp the party. Dissatisfied old-timers were not prepared to capitulate to "capitalism" or even to accept the "respite" offered by Lenin in the shape of the NEP. The vital double task of weeding out opportunist elements and cracking down on ideological dissenters severely challenged the firmness and ingenuity of the leadership.

The Ninth Party Conference, held in September 1920, added to the three executive organs (Politburo, Orgburo and the Secretariat) a fourth, the Central Control Commisssion (CCC), to coordinate the work of all local party control bodies. In time, the CCC became a most powerful lever in the hands of the reorganized Secretariat.

Soon the organizational structure of the Central Committee was made even more complex. At the Twelfth Congress, in April 1923, when Lenin was already on his sickbed, the CCC was fused with the Commissariat of Control into a new organ for the supervision of party members. It included representatives of the Cheka, the military political police, and the Commissariat of Justice. It was in fact a kind of special Cheka for Communists, who were thus removed from the jurisdiction of the ordinary state institutions and transformed into a class apart, endowed with duties and rights of their own not shared by the rest of the population. Beside the punitive organs, a special tribunal for Communists only, the so-called party collegium, was created and endowed with far-reaching powers.

In this manner the party was shackled by a regular web of organizations which left it entirely at the mercy of the Central Committee. Thus was realized Lenin's old plan, whereby the Central Committee was able to keep a grip on every individual party member. Stalin became the unquestioned boss of these new control organs, as he already dominated the Secretariat and the Orgburo. His friend Kuibyshev was chairman of the united CCC; and his old friend and supporter Aaron Solts, chairman of the party collegium.

In this manner, from congress to congress, from conference to conference, the highest organs of the party came to be more and more uniformly composed of Stalin's nominees, friends and agents. The power thus concentrated in the hands of one man was, as Lenin remarked shortly before his death, almost boundless.

Lenin's first stroke, on May 26, 1922, was followed by a second on December 16 of the same year and a third on March 9, 1923; he died on January 21, 1924. In the intervals between strokes he rallied temporarily, renewed his activity, wrote copiously, dictated, but was not in full possession of his energies.

In 1922 Lenin tried to take an active part in the day-to-day life of the party, gave interviews, sent a great number of personal messages and even took the chair at several meetings of the Central Committee and of the Soviet of People's Commissars. But from the end of the year his activities slowed down and his interests centered on working out problems connected with the NEP and on trying to combat the growing influence of Stalin in the central organs of the party.

Lenin's Illness

In the years 1922-23, the period of Lenin's illness, the formerly close relations between Lenin and Stalin became increasingly strained. Lenin was more and more distrustful of Stalin and felt impelled to look for people to counterbalance Stalin's hegemony in the Central Committee. Lenin knew Kamenev and Zinoviev and the other members of the Central Committee well enough to realize that only one among them was sufficiently independent and popular to oppose Stalin on any issue. That man was Trotsky.

Lenin had no illusions about Trotsky's shortcomings: he knew him to be an ambitious, egotistical man who could not bear to be second to Lenin and struggled to be his equal. But Lenin had a high regard for Trotsky's talents, especially his organizing abilities, and therefore always treated him with a certain respect. In October 1917, when Trotsky, after much inner struggle, had led the Bolshevik delegation out of the pre-Parliament,[5] Lenin had called him "the best Bolshevik" of all. And he was full of admiration for Trotsky's energy during the Civil War.

Nevertheless, however closely one examines the relations between the two men, one finds no signs of personal friendship—at least not on Lenin's side—or even of human warmth. Indeed there is no indication in Trotsky's diary that he and Lenin ever met privately, for other than official reasons. In their correspondence they addressed each other formally—"Comrade Trotsky," "Comrade Lenin." It is true that Lenin normally adopted the official form of address in correspondence, but sometimes he used the more intimate Russian form. (For instance, he invariably addressed Fedoseev as Nicolai Evgrafovich, and even referred to him by that name in letters to others.) Similarly, as his life in Zurich showed, Lenin could be on sufficiently good terms with other Bolsheviks to drop in unannounced with his wife for a cup of tea, or be visited by them without ceremony.

With these reservations, the two men became, in the course of Lenin's illness, as intimate as the official nature of their relationship permitted. Trotsky tells us how on one occasion the ailing Lenin, obviously worried about what would happen to the party after his death, summoned Trotsky to his sickbed and outlined to him changes of the greatest importance which he proposed to make in the leadership of the government and the party. According to Trotsky, Lenin wanted the Central Committee to appoint a special commission including both of them to struggle against bureaucracy in the party. Lenin also proposed that Trotsky should become his deputy as chairman of the Soviet of People's Commissars; he clearly regarded all his former deputies, such as Kamenev, Tsuriupa and Rykov, not fit for the job. But Trotsky declined this offer. Later, when Trotsky complained about the increase of bureaucracy in the government and the party, Lenin asked him point blank: "You mean the Orgburo?" Trotsky replied in the affirmative and added that in his view the Orgburo was the center from which bureaucracy spread throughout the party and country. Thereupon, Lenin suggested to Trotsky the formation of an alliance to fight the evil, even within the Orgburo itself, where Stalin of course predominated. To this, Trotsky replied: "It is a pleasure to form a good alliance with a good man."[6]

In November 1922, in the absence of both Lenin and Trotsky, the Central Committee unanimously accepted Sokolnikov's proposal, supported by Bukharin and Stalin, to relax restrictions on foreign trade. This decision was dictated by practical considerations, but both Lenin and Trotsky considered it opportunistic and opposed it most energetically. Their joint attack at once produced the desired effect and the Central Committee unanimously revoked its own decision. Lenin wrote triumphantly to Trotsky on December 21, 1922: "Comrade Trotsky, it seems we succeeded in taking the fort without a single shot, by a simple maneuver. I suggest we do not stop there but press our attack."[7]

The conflict over foreign trade was only indirectly related to Lenin's fight against Stalin; two other conflicts were directly involved. One was the so-called Georgian problem. When Soviet troops conquered independent Menshevik Georgia in February-March 1921, the Bolshevik Central Committee was divided on future policy towards the newly reoccupied country. The existence in Georgia of strong nationalist feelings presented a special difficulty. Ordzhonikidze and Stalin, both Georgians, and another member of the Central Committee, Dzherzhinsky, a Pole, were sent to Georgia and behaved in a manner which Lenin regarded as "Great-Russian chauvinism." Lenin firmly condemned this policy, especially in view of the fact that the Mensheviks still enjoyed widespread influence in Georgia, and he favored granting a certain measure of autonomy to the republic. He attacked Ordzhonikidze, Dzherzhinsky and particularly Stalin, whom he considered the chief culprit, for approaching the problem of the nationalities in a completely false fashion; he added significantly that "assimilated non-Russians always tended to excessive Russian nationalism."[8]

Lenin, determined to inform himself more fully on the state of affairs and on the difference of opinion in the Georgian Bolshevik Party, instructed his secretary, Fotyeva, to get the file on Georgia from Dzherzhinsky. But Dzherzhinsky expressed his regrets—the file was with Stalin, and Stalin was out of town. A few days later Mrs. Fotyeva repeated Lenin's request to Stalin himself, and he replied that he could not give the file to Lenin without formal permission of the Politburo.[9] For the next several days Lenin incessantly asked his secretary whether the Politburo had met and decided on the matter, and Fotyeva hardly knew what to say. At last the documents arrived, but they were far fewer than Lenin had expected. No doubt some had been withheld by Stalin. In one of his conversations with Fotyeva about these Georgian documents, Lenin made a most curious slip of the tongue. He began to say: "If only I were free . . . ," then stopped, laughed and resumed: "If only I were free, I could easily do all this myself."[10] Lenin obviously felt himself not only a patient but also a prisoner, whom Stalin was depriving of freedom of action. Trotsky, who relates this episode, also repeats the account of Lenin's secretary, Fotyeva, to whom Lenin is supposed to have mentioned "the bomb" which he was preparing for Stalin "at the Congress."[11]

Because his illness took a turn for the worse, Lenin was unable to carry through the attack on Stalin over the nationalities question. On December 30 and 31, 1922, however, he wrote two letters to the Central Committee in which he demanded a change of policy. He sent these letters, which he wanted to be read at the Twelfth Party Congress, to Trotsky with the request to take over the defense of his point of view in the Central Committee against Stalin and the others.[12]

Trotsky received these letters on March 5, 1923, and immediately forwarded copies to all members of the Central Committee. He added a note of his own to the effect that Lenin desired the letters to be read to the Congress, but that permission was required since three members of the Central Committee were mentioned by name. Kamenev at once went to see Trotsky with an offer of peace and promised that the resolution on the Georgian problem would be couched in terms acceptable to Lenin. But on March 9, Lenin suffered his third stroke and his appearance at the Congress was out of the question. The resolution passed by the Congress completely disregarded Lenin's position and reflected Stalin's ideas.

The second conflict between Lenin and Stalin involved the reform of the Commissariat of Workers' and Peasants' Inspection, or *Rabkrin,* headed by Stalin. Lenin was extremely dissatisfied with the work of this department. He attached such importance to the problem of control that he dictated two articles from his sickbed on the subject: "How To Reorganize *Rabkrin*" and "Better Less, But Better." The first was, as usual, immediately printed in *Pravda,* but the second was kept out by the editor, Bukharin, because Lenin attacked Stalin's activities in extremely sharp terms. Though Lenin never mentioned Stalin by name, it was obvious whom he had in mind. The failure of this article to appear in *Pravda* greatly disturbed Lenin. He could not miss its implications and insisted repeatedly on its immediate publication. But it was published only much later.[13]

And so, in his attempts to arrest Stalin's rise to ever greater power, Lenin was frustrated by illness. Stalin made good use of the illness and, under the pretense of protecting Lenin's precious health, isolated him from the Central Committee and the party. Whenever possible, he kept Lenin in ignorance of what was happening in the Politburo and the Central Committee.

Lenin's suspicions of Stalin must have been strengthened by two incidents which occurred in 1923. From the moment that Lenin fell ill, Stalin abruptly changed his attitude toward Krupskaya. Indeed, his manner to Lenin's wife became so rude that soon she could not bear it any longer. Not wanting to upset Lenin himself, she complained to Kamenev and Zinoviev, but eventually the story came to Lenin's ears. He became terribly agitated and, on March 5, 1923, dictated a note to Stalin, with copies for Kamenev and Zinoviev. In it he declared that he considered the insults to his wife as being offered to him personally and he demanded that Stalin should either make an immediate apology to Krupskaya or consider all personal relations with him at an end.[14] Stalin sent a written apology.

The last drop of bitterness was provided by an even more annoying incident.

An agricultural exhibition was held in Moscow, with the Comintern's participation, and had aroused much talk and admiration. Lenin wanted very much to visit it, and though his doctors and Krupskaya were much opposed to the idea, he insisted and was driven by car from Gorki, where he resided, to Moscow. Instead of going straight to the exhibition, however, he decided to stop at his apartment in the Kremlin to collect some papers. On opening his desk, he discovered that some of his papers had disappeared. He was so shocked and upset that he no longer thought of going to the exhibition, but returned directly to Gorki.[15]

The Struggle for Lenin's Succession

In January 1923, a year before his death, Lenin made another attempt to stop Stalin's rise. Almost in despair, he decided to make a last, as it were, a posthumous effort—he left a document behind in which he intended to deal a heavy blow against Stalin. This document, known as "Lenin's Testament," consists, strictly speaking, of two parts. The first is a letter to his comrades, which in its final form was committed to paper on December 25, 1922 (a few days after his second stroke). The second part is an addendum, written ten days later on January 4, 1923.

In the letter, Lenin starts out from the premise that the worst fate that could befall the party—which, it must be admitted, was most fervently desired by Russian counter-revolutionaries—was a schism. Lenin admonishes those whom he considers outstanding among the leaders to make every effort to avoid a split. Of Stalin, who as General Secretary has concentrated "limitless power" in his hands, Lenin expresses doubt whether he will always use this power judiciously. Next, of Trotsky, Lenin says that for all his shortcomings he has also demonstrated tremendous virtues and is undoubtedly the most gifted member of the Central Committee. Peaceful relations between Stalin and Trotsky would be the best guarantee against a schism in the party. The Central Committee must ensure peace between them, or the split may come quite suddenly. Then Lenin refers to Zinoviev and Kamenev—their wrong policies during the October days were, of course, no accident, but their mistakes, nevertheless, ought not to be held against them, just as the fact that Trotsky had not always been a Bolshevik ought not to be held against him.

Lenin discusses no other member of the Central Committee, but mentions only Bukharin and Piatakov as the "most gifted" among the younger set. Bukharin is an outstanding theoretician and a general favorite in the party, and Piatakov a man of great talent and strong will. Lenin points to their shortcomings, too, but hopes that they will learn by experience.

The addendum to the letter constitutes an unexpected and deadly thrust at Stalin. It says:

> Stalin is too rude, and this shortcoming, though bearable in internal relations among us Communists, becomes quite unbearable in a General Secretary. I therefore suggest to you, comrades, that you remove Stalin from his post and replace him with someone else who is superior to Stalin in this respect, namely, is more tolerant, more loyal, more polite and more attentive to the needs of the comrades, is less capricious, etc. This may seem a trifling detail. But as regards the avoidance of schism and as regards the relations between Stalin and Trotsky, which I have discussed earlier, this is not a mere detail, but a detail that might one day acquire decisive importance.[16]

Lenin's desire to see Stalin removed from the post of General Secretary is here expressed clearly enough; but in discussing Stalin's successor, Lenin took refuge in ambiguity. Why did he not simply name the man whom he wanted to replace Stalin? The answer is obvious. When he tried to think the problem out fully, he could not find a suitable man. In effect, Lenin left undecided not only the further development of the NEP but also the most important problem of the party—his choice for General Secretary.

The helpless perplexity revealed by the very phrasing of the testament expresses what at that time Lenin already understood but was not yet ready to admit—that Stalin no longer could be replaced or removed from the post of General Secretary. The actual course of events after Lenin's death showed how justified his apprehensions had been.

The testament was handed by Krupskaya to the Politburo—that is, to Stalin—immediately after Lenin's death. But the Politburo decided unanimously against making it known or even divulging its contents at the forthcoming Thirteenth Party Congress. Of course, news of the document spread through the upper stratum of the Bolshevik Party, and a brief summary even reached the *Socialist Courier* in Berlin.[17] But the Soviet people could learn about it only from the *Communist* in 1956, thirty-two years later, after Khrushchev's speech to the Twentieth Congress.

The suppression of this historic document, which bore witness to Lenin's desire to remove Stalin as General Secretary, greatly assisted Stalin in his rise to supreme power. Lenin's posthumous blow at Stalin was, so to speak, arrested in mid-air. And after Lenin died on January 21, 1924, Trotsky, Krupskaya and others were forced not only to suffer the concealment of Lenin's will but even to support Stalin by declaring publicly that no such will existed.[18]

In the last year of Lenin's life, the actual leadership of the party had already passed into the hands of the so-called "Troika": Stalin, Zinoviev, and Kamenev. They were united to a large extent by fear of Trotsky, who was still War Commissar and, next to Lenin, the most "charismatic" of the Bolshevik leaders.

In 1923, Trotsky and his friends, largely excluded from leadership in the party machine, embraced the issue of democracy within the party. Trotsky had had no such concern when the Workers' Opposition and other dissident groups had been throttled at the Tenth Party Congress in 1921. However, in a letter to the Central Committee on October 8, 1923, Trotsky—while agreeing that a democratic regime for the working class was incompatible with party dictatorship—at the same time charged that the party was undergoing a rapid bureaucratization or a "secretarization." The General Secretary appointed provincial secretaries, who in turn appointed district secretaries, and so on, down to the smallest cell. As a result, the party rank and file participated less and less in party life and had very little say regarding its organization or general policy. The secretaries tended to think of themselves as omnipotent and omniscient, even when they knew nothing of the questions they were called upon to settle."[19]

Trotsky's appeal for a return to democracy within the party met with a strongly favorable response among workers, whose economic and political situation was lamentable, and university students who still believed in the freedom that Bolshevism was supposed to defend. Of twenty-five university Communist cells, only one had a non-Trotskyist secretary. (The one non-Trotskyist, according to some accounts, was Georgi Malenkov, whose subsequent career was fostered by Stalin.) In working class districts a similar situation prevailed. In the fall of 1923, only oppositionists were elected to the district committee at the District Conference held at Khamovniki, a Moscow suburb.[20] By October 1923, however, Trotsky was already isolated within the Politburo, whose members feared him as the most dangerous rival in the struggle for Lenin's succession. Trotsky suspected, as witnesses later confirmed, that the majority of the Politburo held "illegal" meetings without him, for the purpose of working out strategy against him.[21] At one such clandestine meeting, it was decided to introduce the slogan, "Trotskyism versus Leninism." Kamenev himself admitted this later, in a conversation with Trotsky.

During this period, forty-six outstanding Bolsheviks published a statement sharply criticizing the prevailing party regime, the working methods of the Central Committee and the inconsistency of its policies. In order to remedy the situation, they suggested that the Central Committee should

> . . . as a first and urgent step, convene a conference of the members of the Central Committee and other active party workers, provided that the attendance will also include comrades whose view of the situation differs from that of the majority of the Central Committee.

This statement was signed, among others, by E. Preobrazhensky, L. Serebriakov, A. Beloborodov, Danishevsky, Antonov-Ovseyenko, Iu. Piatakov, N. Muralov, V. Osinsky (Obolensky), T. Sapronov, A. Bubnov, A. Voronsky and V. Kossior.[22]

This memorandum produced an immediate response. On October 25, a meeting of the Central Committee and the Central Control Commission was convened. In addition to members of those two bodies, delegates from the ten largest party organizations and twelve members of the opposition were invited.

The conference, however, yielded no positive results. After meeting for three days, it adopted, with only two opposing votes and ten abstentions (those attending by special invitation were not allowed to vote), a resolution condemning the position of the forty-six and approving the action taken by the Politburo in the matter of activating intra-party work and strengthening "workers' democracy." At the same time, the conference decided to publish neither its own records, nor the memorandum of the forty-six, nor Trotsky's letters. In other words, except for the adoption of a hypocritical resolution, nothing was changed. This resolution enabled Zinoviev to say in his article in *Pravda* of November 7, 1923, that

> . . . instead of paying lip-service to the sanctity of the principles of workers' democracy, we must put into effect workers' democracy within the party by affording greater freedom of discussion of political, economic and other questions . . .

A formal resolution adopted on December 5th at a joint meeting of the Politburo and the Praesidium of the Central Committee affirmed that "all members of the party must be free to discuss the most important questions of party life, while all officers and organs, from the lowest to the highest, should be elected." But it added that, under the New Economic Policy, some restrictions would have to be maintained, such as the right in some cases to confirm secretaries, provided that "the right to confirm elected secretaries must not be allowed to become the right to appoint them."[23]

This resolution was adopted unanimously. It was accepted by Trotsky, who had been prevented by illness from attending the meeting; but three days later he withdrew his signature. Apparently he found the last paragraph of the resolution unsatisfactory, because it might leave the door open to the equivalent of wholesale appointments. In any event, his first "Letter on Party Consultations of December 8" upset the compromise arrangement, and debate broke out anew.[24] In order to offset the deep impression made by Trotsky's letter, Stalin on December 14 sent a telegram to all party organizations stating that:

> The Central Committee recognizes the timeliness of deepening and widening workers' democracy in the field of intra-party organizational work . . . The Central Committee invites you to keep it posted on your discussions, submitting proposals and resolutions. The Central Committee expects your first reports not later than the 20th of this month.

"Democracy by telegraph" became the current joke in party circles. But this was only the beginning of the fight. Other letters by Trotsky followed and were later published in a pamphlet entitled "The New Course," which had strong repercussions in party circles. But the ruling group was ready to fight back. The first to react against Trotsky's attack was Kamenev, the boss of the Moscow Soviet, who made a speech opposing Trotsky, stating the issue in broader terms. He declared that to maintain democracy under a dictatorship was a very difficult and complex matter. For if

> they say today, let us have democracy in the party, tomorrow they will say, let us have democracy in the trade unions; the day after tomorrow, workers who do not belong to the party may well say: give us democracy too . . . and surely then the myriads of peasants could not be prevented from asking for democracy.[25]

On December 15, *Pravda* carried an article by Stalin, sharply attacking the opposition and Trotsky in particular. On the same day, Zinoviev spoke against Trotsky in Leningrad.

The debate spread until it reached outlying party sectors which could hardly have been expected to take a stand on matters of this sort. Not only factory workers, various party organizations and student party cells, but even army organs and, strangest of all, cells of the special units of the Cheka, began to adopt resolutions in favor of democracy within the party and to report them to the Central Committee. Thus, on December 24, 1923, Antonov-Ovseyenko, who was then chief of the Political Administration of the Red Army, sent out a circular letter on matters of intra-party democracy in the spirit of Trotsky's "The New Course." Another important Red Army figure, I. N. Smirnov, a Trotskyist sympathizer, acted in the same manner.

A conference of the party workers of the Red Army (the Moscow Military District and the staff of the special Cheka units) adopted a resolution expressing mistrust of the forthcoming 13th Party Conference for having been convened by the "party machine" and demanded that the principles of workers' democracy be applied in the army. Communist cells of the special units, numbering 2,000 members, voted for this resolution.

Understandably, the ruling group was alarmed that the discussion should have spread to the Red Army and even to the special units of the Cheka. At the same time the situation suggested a possible counter-attack: alleged dissension among the soldiers might furnish sufficient justification for removing Trotsky and his assistants from their major posts in the Red Army.

Stalin was to relate this incident with great bitterness at the 13th Party Conference. He ended with the telling remark: "Comrades such as these cannot be trusted with the education of the Red Army."[26]

After Lenin's death, Stalin, Kamenev and Zinoviev continued in every possible way to undermine Trotsky's position in the party. With disconcerting frequency, however, Trotsky himself involuntarily assisted his enemies by his peculiar behavior.

Shortly before Lenin's death, Trotsky became ill and his doctors advised him to go to the Caucasus for a cure. As Trotsky's train stopped at Tiflis, the decoded telegram from the Kremlin bearing the news of Lenin's death was handed to Trotsky. Despite his illness, Trotsky immediately telephoned the Central Committee and asked about the date of the funeral. He was told that it would be held on Saturday and he was advised not to interrupt his treatment in as much as he could not arrive in time for the funeral anyway.

The date given to Trotsky was not the true one; the funeral, or more precisely, the removal of the body from Gorki to Moscow, took place a day later, on Sunday, January 23, and Trotsky probably could have managed to return in time if he had not been deliberately and cunningly misled by Stalin. Still, it is difficult to understand Trotsky's behavior at the time. It is possible, as he later affirmed, that he was physically exhausted and therefore lacking in decision. At any rate, he did not make the obvious suggestion to Stalin—a suggestion that should have occurred to him—that the funeral should be delayed a day. Moreover, as chairman of the Revolutionary Military Council, he could have commandeered a military airplane and arrived in time even for the date given him by Stalin. Or he could have communicated with his friends in the army or in the Central Committee and obtained correct information about the arrangements. Altogether, he could have shown greater initiative in an event whose crucial importance he could not have failed to perceive.[27]

Whatever the reason, Trotsky absented himself from the funeral, and the plotters had it all their own way. The Central Committee now officially gave all power into the hands of a committee (collegium) of three—Stalin, Kamenev and Zinoviev—who henceforth were free to act as they pleased. At first, Stalin modestly remained in the background. Kamenev was made chairman of the triumvirate, while all political speech-making, notably the official Central Committee report to the Thirteenth Party Congress, was left to Zinoviev. This distinction greatly flattered Zinoviev, who became persuaded that even Stalin, supreme though he might be in the party machine, was compelled to acknowledge that in the political leadership of the party or of the revolution the place of honor rightfully belonged to him. Was he not indeed the closest ideological collaborator of Lenin, chairman of the Comintern, and spiritual leader of world Communism?

As for Trotsky, even after his return to Moscow, he did nothing to alter the situation. After writing his book, *On Lenin,* full of unprecedented adulation, Trotsky remained inactive, leaving the triumvirate to its machinations. This defeatist attitude made things easy for Stalin. All he needed now was to weaken the position of his two other colleagues in the triumvirate. By playing on the vanity and ambition of Zinoviev and the mild character of Kamenev, Stalin systematically prepared the ground for an open attack on them both. Again, the future victims of Stalin's duplicity helped him in that task. As early as the summer of 1922, Zinoviev and Kamenev had noted to their great annoyance that Stalin was steadily usurping more and more power and was elbowing them out of the way. Zinoviev, the more agile and aggressive of the two, thereupon hit on the idea of building an alliance against Stalin's bid for autocratic power.

This idea led to the curious episode known as "the council in the cave"—one of the famous caves near Kislovodsk, the spa in the Caucasus where the notables used to take their rest in those years. In September 1923, Zinoviev, Bukharin, Lashevich and Evdokimov went there for their vacations. In the course of private conversations among them (the last two were Zinoviev's devoted adherents), the discussion touched on the need for a more harmonious balance in the structure of the Central Committee. To one such conference, held in a cave, Zinoviev had sent a telegram summoning Ordzhonikidze and Voroshilov, who happened to be in Rostov. Zinoviev proceeded, in the absence of Lenin, to express his views on the situation in the Central Committee and in the Secretariat.

> ... the Secretariat is one thing with Vladimir Ilyich about and quite another without him. When Vladimir Ilyich is there, whoever is the secretary, whoever else is in the Secretariat—all play subordinate limited parts. It is just an organizational instrument, made to carry out a definite policy. With Vladimir Ilyich away, it is obvious to all that the Secretariat of the Central Committee is bound to acquire an absolutely decisive importance. We are all wondering what to do to make sure of a certain balance of forces.[28]

Later, at the Fourteenth Party Congress in 1925, Voroshilov told the story of that meeting in the cave and explained that he personally was extremely skeptical about the desirability of any changes:

> . . . At this meeting, I . . . gave it as my opinion to the comrades that all such machinations could lead to nothing but harm and fiasco.[29]

Bukharin, aware of the estrangement between Lenin and Stalin and of the joint campaign by Lenin and Trotsky against Stalin, decided, for reasons of his own, that an attack on Stalin should be averted for the sake of the unity of the Central Committee. In the end the "council in the cave" agreed to charge Ordzhonikidze with delivering a letter to Stalin setting forth the various proposals. It is curious that the conspirators were naive enough not to see that they were in fact asking Stalin for help in limiting his own power.

In reply, Stalin sent a "familiarly blunt" telegram, roughly as follows: "Why are you fooling about, boys? I will be with you soon and we will talk then."[30] Stalin did join them for several chats. What Zinoviev, Evdokimov and Lashevich did not realize was that Voroshilov had kept Stalin posted about everything his rivals were doing. Well-briefed, Stalin arrived with a plan and offered it to the others as his solution. Zinoviev, in his speech to the Fourteenth Congress, described this plan as "not very practical." But from Stalin's point of view it was supremely practical. It proposed leaving the Secretariat unchanged and instead to introduce three members of the Politburo into the

Orgburo. This was supposed to ensure close contact between the administrators and the political leaders. The plan was adopted and the three men elected were Trotsky, Bukharin and Zinoviev.

The outcome of this reform was just what the wily Stalin had foreseen. The three politician-intellectuals had never taken any part in practical party work, were fundamentally not interested in organizational detail, hardly knew the rank and file, and stood no chance at all of penetrating Stalin's net of intrigues and skillful placement of personnel. They could have done so only by entering actively into organizational work and gaining access to the materials and archives of the Orgburo. But none of the three could or would undertake this task. Zinoviev attended the meetings of the Orgburo twice, Trotsky and Bukharin not once.

The "reform" thus proved illusory, but it suited Stalin. It deflected the intended blow at the Secretariat, which remained intact and continued to play an "absolutely decisive" role. The attempt to reorganize the apparatus of the Central Committee and to redress the "balance of forces" failed dismally.

As for Trotsky, on October 15, 1924, he further isolated himself from the other Politburo members by the publication of his strange pamphlet, "The Lessons of October." This work contained transparent hints that the October *coup d'état* had been the logical outcome not of Lenin's conception of revolution but of Trotsky's. It suggested that Lenin and his group had required some time to re-orient themselves and to accept Trotsky's formerly rejected theory of permanent revolution. These allegations would alone have sufficed to bring Lenin's old guard down on Trotsky's head. But Trotsky incurred the special enmity of Zinoviev and Kamenev in this pamphlet by reviving memories of their opposition to the October *coup* and their vehement attacks on their "great teacher," Lenin. Zinoviev, an ambitious and emotionally unstable man, was so enraged that he demanded Trotsky's trial and expulsion from the party. Kamenev and others disputed Trotsky's statement in a calmer but no less forceful manner.

At a joint meeting of the Central Committee and the Central Control Commission on January 17, 1925, Stalin declared that the members would have to choose among three proposals for punishing Trotsky: (a) expel him from the party; (b) expel him from the Politburo;

and (c) remove him from his post as Chairman of the Revolutionary Military Council. Stalin strongly opposed Trotsky's expulsion not only from the party, but even from the Politburo, and so the third proposal was adopted. Stalin had, in the debates of 1923 and 1924, maintained that reprisals should not be taken against the opposition. Indeed, during the 1923 debates the Politburo published a special resolution in which it

> brands, as a malicious fabrication, the idea that there is a single comrade in the Central Committee of the party who can conceive of the work of the Politburo, the Central Committee and the organs of state power being carried on without the most active participation of Comrade Trotsky.[31]

In the 1924-25 discussions, Stalin took a similar position: Trotskyism must be destroyed, but repressive measures should not be taken against Trotsky himself.[32]

Perhaps Stalin's generous attitude had something to do with the fact that Trotsky had attacked Zinoviev and Kamenev in his pamphlet. Why had Trotsky done so? He must certainly have been aware—for he had talked and written to Lenin about it—that the center of bureaucracy in the party was Stalin and not the weak-kneed Zinoviev and Kamenev. His attack on them was so little called for by the needs of the intra-party struggle that Aleksandrov,[33] a careful observer, noted that it was difficult to avoid the suspicion that Stalin himself had incited Trotsky to quarrel with Zinoviev and Kamenev, since any blow to their prestige suited his long-range purposes.

In any event, Trotsky's removal from his historic post as Chairman of the Revolutionary Military Council temporarily calmed the troubled waters of the party, and for a time peace reigned in the Central Committee and the Politburo. In May 1925, Trotsky was appointed to a number of governmental posts: Chairman of the Concessions Committee, head of the Electrotechnical Administration, and Chairman of the Scientific and Technical Industrial Administration.[34] He threw himself enthusiastically into this new work and for a time abandoned the factional struggle within the party. The central group, headed by Stalin, held power firmly in its hands, and the party machine, represented by the Central Committee, ran smoothly.

[1] Trotsky, L., *My Life*, vol. II, p. 184: " 'The most striking quality in Stalin is his indolence,' Bukharin impressed upon me."

[2] *Ibid.*, p. 225. If one wanted to complete the list of Stalin's negative qualities one ought to add—in the light of later developments—his lust for power and limitless ambition, as illustrated by some striking examples given by Khrushchev to the Twentieth Party Congress.

[3] Schueller, in his book, *The Politburo* (Stanford Univ. Press, 1951), dates the history of the Politburo from the plenary meeting of the Central Committee which was held on October 10, 1917, to discuss the preparation for the rising. This is straining historical facts too much. The political commission elected on that occasion was meant merely to exercise political control over the preparations for a rising, nothing more. It was not a permanent institution or section of the Central Committee but an *ad hoc* commission appointed for a definite task and a limited time only. Moreover, this political commission, which was obviously appointed for the purpose of pacifying the rebellious Kamenev, never met and thus proved still-born.

[4] According to Trotsky, the nomination of Stalin to this immensely important position was opposed at the time by Lenin, but he was overruled. (See Trotsky, *Stalin*, pp. 457-458).

[5] See pp. 93-94, ff.

[6] Trotsky, L., *My Life*, vol. II, pp. 216-217.

[7] *Ibid.*, p. 219.

[8] The *Socialist Courier*, Nos. 23-24, p. 14, December 17, 1923.

[9] Fotyeva, L. A., *Memories of Lenin*. Problems of the Russian Communist Party, No. 4, 1957, pp. 160-161.

[10] *Ibid.*, p. 162.

[11] Trotsky, L., *My Life*, vol. II, p. 220.

[12] These two letters or memoranda, written in the period between December 30, 1922 and March 6, 1923, were not read at the Twelfth Congress despite Lenin's request, and remained unpublished in the Soviet press and unknown to the Soviet readers. A copy of the documents, however, found its way into the Berlin Menshevik *Socialist Courier*, Nos. 23 and 24 of December 1923. After 33 years of silence, Lenin's views on the national question emerged in Russia only after the speech by Khrushchev at the 20th Congress in 1956. They were published but only in part in the Soviet *Communist*, No. 9, July 1956. But Lenin's letters to Trotsky and others which accompanied his memoranda still remain unpublished in the Soviet press. So does Lenin's note to the Georgian opponents of Stalin, the Bolsheviks Mdivani and Makharadze. In this note, written on March 5, 1923, Lenin wrote: "Dear Comrades, I am following the developments of your affairs with my whole heart. I am disgusted with the rudeness of Ordzhonikidze and the maneuvers of Stalin and Dzherzhinsky. Am preparing a memo and some speeches for you. Your Lenin." These letters can only be found in the above-mentioned issues of the *Socialist Courier*.

In the complete edition of Lenin's writings (4th edition, vol. 33), Lenin's position on this point is misrepresented in an extraordinarily crude manner. On p. 496, in a list of Lenin's writings composed during his illness, the following entry appears under the date October 21, 1922: "A telegram sent to the Central Committee of the Georgian party demanding that immediate measures should be taken to suppress the anti-party activities of the nationalist-deviationists of the Mdivani group." The text of the telegram is not given. But as we already know from Lenin's notes, this transcript of the telegram completely falsifies Lenin's true position. In reality Lenin demanded action not against Mdivani's group, which had his full support, but against Stalin, Ordzhonikidze and Dzherzhinsky, whose policy he considered anti-party, chauvinistic and harmful.

[13] The Politburo found itself in a difficult position. The Stalinist majority did not want to undermine Stalin's prestige by publishing Lenin's article, yet it could not altogether disregard Lenin's insistence. At one of the meetings of the Politburo, Kuibyshev suggested publishing the article in a special edition of *Pravda*, printing only one copy and sending it to Lenin: this episode is mentioned in a memo sent by Trotsky to the Politburo on October

24, 1923, and published on May 28, 1924, in the *Socialist Courier,* No. 11 (pp. 11-12).

Kuibyshev's suggestion was rejected and the article was published in *Pravda,* though belatedly. In the complete edition of Lenin's works the article is given under a fictitious date, March 2, obviously with the intention of covering up all traces of this incident. As Carr points out (*Interregnum,* vol. IV, p. 265), the first edition of Lenin's works, edited by Kamenev, omits the date of the article altogether, but in subsequent editions the fictitious date appears.

[14] This episode is mentioned briefly in Trotsky's memoirs (vol. II, p. 223), but the full text of the letter was made known only in 1956 by Khrushchev in his speech to the Twentieth Congress. Fotyeva describes in her memoirs (Fotyeva, L. A., *Memories of Lenin,* p. 167) how on March 6 Lenin, who was again running a temperature, called her, asked her to read out once more the letter which he had dictated the day before, sealed it and told her to deliver it to Stalin personally and wait for an answer.

[15] This version of Lenin's journey to the exhibition is given by Volsky (N. Valentinov, *Memoirs,* Columbia University Russian Archives), who lived in Moscow at that time, worked in the Ministry of Economic Affairs and there mixed with many prominent Bolsheviks, some of whom were his old friends. The official version reads differently. In Lenin's *Works,* Vol. 33, on p. 500, the incident is described as follows: "Lenin came to Moscow for a few hours, visited his study; on the return journey to Gorki he visited the Agricultural Exhibition."

[16] *Communist,* No. 9, Moscow, 1956, p. 181.

[17] No. 15, July 24, 1924.

[18] Trotsky's and Krupskaya's declarations in the magazine *Bolshevik,* No. 16, 1925.

[19] *Socialist Courier,* No. 11, May 28, 1924, p. 10.

[20] Iakovlev, "Khamovniki," *Sputnik Komm,* X, 1927, p. 82.

[21] Trotsky, *My Life,* Berlin, 1932, Vol. 2, pp. 240-241.

[22] Carr, *Interregnum,* pp. 367-373.

[23] *Discussion, 1923* (Materials and Documents), edited by K. A. Popov, Moscow-Leningrad, 1927, pp. 269-274.

[24] *Pravda,* December 11, 28, 29, 30, 1923 and January 1, 4, 1924.

[25] *Socialist Courier,* No. 2, 1924, p. 5, footnote.

[26] Trotsky, *My Life,* Vol. 2, p. 256.

[27] It is interesting to note that Trotsky's elder son Lev, at that time a youth of 17, wrote his father a reproachful letter pointing out that his absence at Lenin's funeral was an irreparable mistake. (I. Deutscher, *The Prophet Unarmed,* London, 1959.)

[28] *Minutes of the Fourteenth Party Congress,* p. 455; A-v, p. 99.

[29] *Ibid.,* p. 398; A-v, p. 99.

[30] *Minutes of the Fourteenth Party Congress,* p. 456; A-v, p. 100.

[31] *1923 Debates,* pp. 25-26.

[32] Stalin, speech made before a section of the All-Union Central Council Trade Unions on November 19, 1924.

[33] Aleksandrov, *op. cit.,* p. 127.

[34] Trotsky, *My Life,* Vol. 2, p. 261.

CHAPTER 13

Soviet "Normalcy": Russia in the Mid-Twenties

The mid-Twenties form, in the history of the Soviet regime, a period of relative quiet and stability, of consolidation after the cataclysmic events of the War, Revolution and Civil War. Russia was not to enjoy similar tranquility for another generation. Thus, for many of the Soviet citizens of the 1940s and 1950s, the 1920s became "the good old days," remembered fondly in later Soviet literature. In fact, this period proved an illusory calm before the storm which was to burst with the launching of agricultural collectivization under Stalin toward the end of the decade. Moreover, the horrors which were to shock the world in the 1930s had been institutionally prepared in the previous decade. Tools had been forged and tempered in the 1920s which were put to use with deadly effect later on.

One reason for the political stability in the Soviet Union in the 1920s was the simultaneous stabilization of the entire international situation, particularly in Europe, as a result of which military hostilities or revolutionary outbreaks were for a time most unlikely. For all its ingenuity and persistence, the Comintern was unable to whip up any serious revolutionary unrest in Europe. In these circumstances, Soviet Russia tended to become a "normal" state, and country after country established diplomatic and trade relations with it.

Inside Russia, the principal and indeed decisive stabilizing factor was the introduction and development of the New Economic Policy (NEP), thanks to which the Soviet regime succeeded in neutralizing the peasantry. Instead of promises, the NEP gave the Russian peasants real and tangible benefits which seemed to justify, in retrospect, the dreadful sacrifices they had been called upon to make during and after the Civil War. The Russian peasants, 100,000,000 strong, now felt themselves to be the real owners of their 20,000,000 homesteads. Now they had horses, a few head of livestock and some farm implements. Their yields increased, and the so-called "middle" peasants were able to live fairly well from the sale of their produce, without interference from above. The village Soviets bore a strong resemblance to the peasant village-administration which existed before the Revolution, with the significant difference that the land formerly held by landowners now belonged to the peasants. The more progressive, industrious and successful peasants were anxious to learn modern farming methods and to acquire new machinery, and Soviet newspapers were full of reports that the peasants dreamed of obtaining small "Fordson" tractors from the United States.

The urban population was also better off. The revival of industry reduced the army of unemployed; real wages, which at the peak of the inflation had dropped to one and a half gold roubles a month, began to rise; the workers abandoned the manufacture of cigarette lighters and other small gadgets to return to normal jobs. Opposition to the party and the government, which had been rampant during the period 1920-1923, tended to decline. Though the workers were not entirely reconciled to Communist dictatorship, their objections to it now took a far less violent form. The socialist parties had been crushed, their newspapers had been closed, and their leaders had been banished abroad or exiled to Siberia. Underground resistance groups were penetrated by secret agents and arrested by the Cheka. No longer was strong opposition forthcoming from the freedom-loving Russian intelligentsia; the outstanding professors, writers and journalists had been arrested and exiled during the famine of 1922-1923.

Scientists and technicians found themselves in a different position, for the revival of industry and the construction of new plants and factories opened up a new sphere for their activities. At that time, the Bolsheviks did not yet require every plant manager or member of a planning commission to belong to the Communist Party or to be at least "politically reliable." The State Planning Commission and all its sub-commissions were full of Mensheviks (such as Groman, Ginzburg, Valentinov, Kafenhaus and Grintser) and Populists (such as Chaianov, Kondratev and Makarov). Dzherzhinsky himself, the "Grand Inquisitor" of the Cheka, who had taken over the direction of all planning, had been known to say that the Menshevik specialists were useful and diligent and that he held them in high esteem.

Economists, engineers and statisticians found the work of industrial reconstruction particularly attractive because it enabled them to influence the planning and shaping of a state-operated industry, to take an active part in an experiment for which there was no precedent in the history of mankind. Without sacrificing their convictions, which was not then demanded of them, they were able to feel themselves useful and essential participants in a great enterprise. They were aware, of course, that the methods used were not those of a Social Democratic regime, but they consoled themselves with the thought that in time all this would be taken care of and that the government would gradually evolve towards some form of democracy.

Another important factor in the stabilization of Soviet power was the emergence of a new professional army which, even in its primitive state, had proven capable of putting down the White movement and of protecting Russia's national interests in the war against Poland in 1920-1921. Reorganized and mechanized by Tukhachevsky and others. the army, now largely staffed by officers of Soviet rather than Tsarist origin, furnished the military framework which the Soviet regime required for stability.

Yet peaceful economic development, the use of nonpolitical technicians and the emergence of a professional army do not adequately characterize Russia in this period. These are characteristics of all sorts of "normal" societies, more or less autocratic as the case might be. Russia's embryonic totalitarian society can best be characterized by an examination of other tendencies and institutions.

In *The Peasant War in Germany,* written in 1850, Friedrich Engels, analyzing the underlying causes of the failure of the peasant revolutions in sixteenth-century Germany, makes the following generalizations:

> The worst thing that can befall a leader of an extreme party is to be compelled to take over a government in an epoch when the

> movement is not yet ripe for the domination of the class which he represents . . . What he *can* do depends not upon his will but upon . . . the degree of the material means of existence, the relations of production and means of communication . . . What he *ought* to do . . . again depends not on him . . . Thus he necessarily finds himself in a dilemma. What he can do is in contrast to all . . . his principles and to all the present interests of his party (class); what he ought to do cannot be achieved. In a word, he is compelled to represent not his party or his class but the class for whom the conditions are ripe for domination. In the interest of the movement itself he is compelled to defend the interests of an alien class and to feed his own class with phrases and promises, with the assertion that the interests of that alien class are their own interests. Whoever puts himself in this awkward position is irrevocably lost . . .[1]

In other words, the leaders of a utopian revolution may in certain circumstances survive and retain power, but only at the cost of systematic deception and concealment of the true state of affairs.

In the Twenties, the Soviet government, after surviving the Civil War and setting up a vast machinery of domination that could not be overthrown by internal rebellion or foreign intervention, expounded its official ideology in the very manner foretold by Engels. According to official theory the Soviet regime was a dictatorship of the proletariat. But, as everyone realized, that was merely a fiction, one of the many fictions which have served as the ideological foundation of the Communist system from its very inception.

Actually, neither the numerically weak working-class nor the large peasantry was at that time the ruling class in Soviet Russia. Such a ruling class was the Communist Party, i.e., a heterogeneous grouping, sociologically speaking, of members of the intelligentsia, petty bourgeoisie and peasantry with a very small admixture of the more educated workers. The Communists were united not by any common social characteristics but solely by their ideology. It was an ideocratic dictatorship of men who shared not a class origin but a certain specific philosophy. Thus, they represented a new social formation, not unlike the priesthood of ancient Egypt or of the even more ancient Mesopotamian states of Assyria and Babylon. It was a caste of

Communist priests recruited from different classes of society, welded together into a pyramid-shaped authoritarian organization in which each lower stratum mutely accepted the authority of the next higher stratum—a caste composed of the most active and dynamic elements of many groups and governed by an ideology which, according to another fiction, had been originated by Marx and Engels but which in point of fact stemmed rather from purely Russian utopian terrorism and Jacobinism.

In the Soviet state, the Communist Party, which in theory is the bearer of the proletarian idea but which is itself not composed of proletarians, has become a true dominating class or caste that has arrogated unto itself the right to dispose—as it sees fit—of the land, economic resources, industry and means of transport; the right of life and death over every citizen and over entire social groups; and the right to direct the spiritual life of the people with none to say it nay. It is, in fact, the "alien class," the new social formation, about which Engels wrote. It is the "new class" whose existence the Yugoslav Communist, Milovan Djilas, stumbled upon in Tito's Yugoslavia, a discovery which shattered his Communist convictions and led him to embrace the ideas of the Social Democrats.[2]

The principle that the Soviet government was a government of the workers, or even a government of the workers and peasants, was a fiction. The dogma that there existed in Russia a dictatorship of the proletariat, as Marx understood the term, was a fiction. The oft-repeated statement that the factories belonged to the workers and the land to the peasants was another fiction. The Constitution may have deeded the factories to the working class but every Russian worker knew from daily experience that the actual right of ownership and the practical management of these factories, as of all other means of production and distribution, were not exercised by the working class. It was never asked for its views and was not allowed an active part in the direction or planning of industry and agriculture. All such powers were exercised wholly by the Communist Party, to which the people had never transferred any such rights nor asked to assume any such responsibility.

In the early NEP years, the fiction that the land belonged to the peasants was a reality for a while. For this reason, the peasant masses changed the attitude they had taken towards the Soviet government during the period of War Communism. Subsequent developments, however, made it brutally clear that the peasants' title of ownership to the land was fictitious. The land belonged to the state—in other words, to the Communist Party. It remained the property of the party from the collectivization of 1929 onward, and the party disposed of it without accounting to anyone.

Still another fiction was Lenin's claim that the Soviet system represented a higher form of democracy than the bourgeois system, because it allegedly afforded the people a far greater measure of active participation in government than any capitalist state had ever done. In fact, the introduction of the Soviet system very soon resulted in the elimination of the Soviets as an independent institution and their transformation into a mere camouflage for the arbitrary rule of the Communist Party. In order to emphasize the dominant position of the workers and to penalize the widespread opposition to Communism among the peasants, the government promulgated electoral regulations which gave each worker ten times the electoral rights of each peasant: a factory employing one hundred workers elected one deputy, whereas it took a thousand peasants to elect a single delegate. As a general rule, however, neither the workers nor the peasants were permitted to elect a Soviet composed of representatives of their own choice. The party and police saw to it that they elected only those who could be counted upon to strengthen the domination of the Communist Party. No Soviet could be elected that did not contain an overwhelming majority of Communists—or, if elected, it was not allowed to function, though workers in some cities and factories almost unanimously voted for non-Communists. Such a Soviet was instantly dissolved and new elections were held at which non-Communist candidates were ruled out. A Soviet had to be Communist-dominated or there would be no Soviet at all—and the city or area in question would be governed by a committee appointed by the Communist Party. In important institutions in cities and villages, to say nothing of national institutions, none but Communists could hold positions of power. This principle became so firmly entrenched that important leaders of the Communist Party proclaimed it quite openly and cynically for all the world to hear.

In 1928, an American correspondent who was touring Russia discussed the subject with Bukharin and Tomsky. When the American asked whether political parties other than the Communist Party could exist in the USSR, they both replied almost in the same words, but Bukharin's answer was the more colorful. "It's nonsense to say that different political parties may not exist in Russia," said Bukharin. "On the contrary they may—provided only that one party—the Communist—is lodged in the Kremlin, and all the rest in jail."

The policy applied not only to the Soviets, the highest organs of government, but also to purely working-class organizations and trade-unions. From 1918 on, trade unions which did not have a safe Bolshevik majority were dissolved as a matter of policy. No trade union could exist unless it scrupulously followed the party line and carried out the party's plans and instructions. The last free trade-unions in Russia were closed down in 1920-1921.

In her well-known book on the Russian Revolution, Rosa Luxemburg sharply criticized the tactics of Lenin and Trotsky in dispersing the Constituent Assembly of 1918. She wrote this work in jail, before the German Revolution, and did not use the term "totalitarianism," but the process itself was described with great accuracy and thorough understanding. If free elections, political freedom and individual rights are abolished, she predicted, the Soviets themselves would die out and all political life in Russia would be smothered. She foresaw that the political stage would be occupied only by a small elite containing great leaders endowed with inexhaustible energy, but the people itself would be forced to remain silent. "This will be a dictatorship, certainly, but a dictatorship not of the proletariat, but of a handful of politicians."[3]

When Rosa Luxemburg painted this horrifying prospect of the degeneration of Soviet democracy into the dictatorship by a clique, she apparently intended to frighten the Bolsheviks and persuade them to abandon this fatal course. After 1924, however, the Communist Party deliberately set out to fulfill her worst fears. It did its utmost to create an atmosphere of trance-like political apathy, precisely in order to establish the dictatorship of a clique which it called the dictatorship of a party that was allegedly representing the proletariat.

Myth-making propaganda can be fully successful only when objective information is completely lacking. How was it possible to keep alive for decades the myth that workers abroad were the starving, impotent slaves of capitalist tyrants? Or to contrast their servitude with the "great freedom" and "increasing prosperity" which the Russian workers allegedly enjoyed? This feat could be achieved only by sealing off all the cracks through which the truth could penetrate to the people, by stifling freedom of the press and assembly, by refusing to admit foreign literature, by making it impossible for the great masses of people to read foreign newspapers or listen to foreign broadcasts.

As far as freedom of the press is concerned, there exists a document which proves beyond doubt that in the days of the October Revolution Lenin did not envisage—at least not publicly—the establishment of a complete monopoly for the Communist press and total abolition of non-Communist newspapers, journals, etc.

The mentioned document is known in the literature as Lenin's "Decree on the Press," which was adopted at the meeting of the VTsIK (All-Russian Central Executive Committee) on November 4 (17) by 25 votes against 23. In this document Lenin found it necessary to explain and to justify the repressive measures taken against a number of Petrograd newspapers by the Revolutionary Military Committee.

This is how this remarkable document runs (*Novaya Zhizn,* October 29 [November 11], 1917):

> DECREE ON THE PRESS
>
> At the crucial hour of the revolutionary upheaval and in the harrowing days that followed, the Provisional Revolutionary Committee was forced to take various measures against counter-revolutionary publications of every description.
>
> Immediately, a hue and cry was raised in all quarters. The Soviet government, it was claimed, had violated the principle of freedom of the press, which had been a vital part of its own program.
>
> The workers' and peasants' government wishes to call the people's attention to the fact that, in our society, what hides behind this screen of liberalism is actually freedom for the propertied classes to monopolize the lion's share of the press and thus to be able to confuse the masses and poison the people's minds.

Everyone knows that the bourgeois press is one of the most powerful weapons possessed by the middle class. At this critical time, while the new government of the workers and peasants is still in the process of consolidation, this weapon, more dangerous than machine guns and bombs, cannot be left entirely in the hands of the enemy. It was for this reason that drastic temporary measures have been taken to stop the barrage of filth and slander put forth by the yellow and reactionary press, eager to see a collapse of the victorious young people's state.

As soon as the new order has been consolidated, all administrative controls of the press will be lifted. The press will be granted full freedom, within the limits of legal responsibilities, as interpreted by the most liberal, progressive legislation.

At the same time, considering that even in a period of stress, restrictions on the press can be tolerated only within the bounds of absolute necessity, the Council of People's Commissars has decreed as follows:

GENERAL PROVISIONS CONCERNING FREEDOM OF THE PRESS

1. No publication can be suppressed unless it 1) urges open resistance, or insubordination, to the workers' and peasants' government; 2) spreads discord, by means of deliberate and slanderous distortion of the facts; 3) incites people to criminal acts, i.e., acts of a felonious nature, punishable by law.
2. No publication can be suspended, or discontinued, except by an executive order of the Council of People's Commissars.
3. *The present ruling is a temporary one, and will be rescinded by a special decree when social conditions have returned to normal.*

Chairman of the Council of People's Commissars,
Vladimir Ulyanov (Lenin).

That Lenin did not, at the time, contemplate the suppression of all publications except the Communists' is evidenced not only by the facts cited above but also by the discussion which developed at the same session of the VTsIK. Lenin's proposal was sharply criticized by Larin, a Communist Party member, whose arguments were vigorously supported by the Left Socialist Revolutionaries, Karelin and Kalegaiev. Trotsky alone, and after him Avanesov, later a prominent figure in the Cheka, sided with Lenin, in urging a total ban on bourgeois publications in a socialist country. The rest of the speakers took the traditional stand of democratic socialists, who preferred to combat the bourgeois mentality by means other than resorting to the party abolition of the freedom of the press. It should be pointed out that neither Lenin himself nor any of the other speakers proposed closing the Social Democratic papers—not even those organs that might not fully approve of the ideological position of the practical measures undertaken by the Soviet government. In fact, no mention of such a step was made by any speaker.

The editorial board of *Novaya Zhizn* (The New Life), commenting on this session of the VTsIK, justly emphasized the fact that Lenin's decree had passed by a majority of only two votes. Moreover, two of the Bolshevik members, Riazanov and Kirichenko, who were distinctly at odds with Lenin in this matter, abstained from voting for the sake of party discipline. Had it not been for them, Avanesov's motion of confidence in the government would not have been adopted and Lenin's decree would have been formally rejected by the VTsIK.

It should be added that among the various drafts of this decree which Lenin left, there was one version which established the principle that any citizens' group numbering 10,000 had "the right to issue a regular publication." The government, furthermore, was "obligated to grant these citizens an equal claim to the necessary quota of newsprint and printing services" (see Lenin's *Collected Works*, vol. 26, p. 250).

A very different situation prevailed in the Bolshevik Party in 1924, at the time when, after Lenin's death and Stalin's accession to power, the question of a free press, as well of other political rights for Soviet citizens, was once more brought up for decision.

By that time not only the capitalists but also all the socialist parties had been destroyed in the Soviet Union. The Socialist Revolutionaries, right-wing and left-wing alike, had been outlawed and made political hostages, following the 1922 trial; they were no longer free men. The Mensheviks, who outlasted the others, had been forced to go underground. As late as 1919 and 1920, a few Menshevik papers and journals still appeared in Soviet Russia. However, after Lenin had publicly declared that with the advent of the New Economic Policy, the Mensheviks and Socialist Revolutionaries should be "handled with care—and kept in jail," there could be no question of permitting the Mensheviks to publish books or periodicals.

In 1924, after introduction of the NEP, the social life of the Soviet Union came back to normal. But the promised decree, which was to remove the "temporary" restrictions against the free press, was never issued. Freedom of the press was not restored, either while Lenin was alive, nor after his death.[4] It was then that the unique system was developed under which publishing houses, magazines, newspapers and pamphlets were subjected to a censorship far exceeding in severity and scope the censorship exercised in the old Russia of Nicholas I. Not a single book, magazine, pamphlet, or leaflet could be printed without first passing through censorship and being given an official publication number by the Central Administration for Literature and Publishing (*Glavlit*). Besides, all printed matter and information reaching or leaving the country, all incoming and outgoing mail, all long-distance telephone calls and telegrams were censored and registered.

After the revolution, the large public and academic libraries, as well as the whole network of innumerable small libraries in the cities and some villages, still contained books in which it was possible to find information the Communist Party regarded as harmful to Soviet readers. The libraries of pre-Communist Russia contained Marxist, socialist, democratic and bourgeois literature which treated their subjects in a way quite different from the Bolsheviks. It was now removed in order to make it impossible for the people to obtain information in any branch of science or knowledge that did not conform to the government's propaganda.

Many years ago this writer had the good fortune to obtain a printed copy, probably the only one existent outside the USSR,[5] of a secret circular published by the Division of Libraries, then headed by Krupskaya, and part of the Ministry of Public Education, headed by A. Lunacharsky. This circular, bearing the number 12,706 of the Central Administration for Literature and Publishing (*Glavlit*) and issued in 5000 copies, began as follows:

> In 1920 the Board of Political Education of the People's Commissariat of Education sent out instructions to review the book lists and to remove obsolete literature from the public libraries.

Whereas libraries all over the world endeavor to amass the greatest possible number of books, old and new, on every subject, the circular emphasizes that Soviet libraries would be able to perform their educational function only:

> 1. If they clear their shelves of counter-revolutionary and harmful literature.

The circular complains that local authorities have not always shown the proper zeal in carrying out this task:

> In certain areas the GPU was compelled to intervene before the work of removal began.

The circular sets different standards for small local libraries on the one hand, and for scientific, academic and "central" libraries on the other. In the small popular libraries serving ordinary readers, all books listed as "undesirable, counter-revolutionary or harmful" were simply to be removed and destroyed. In the larger or specialized libraries, two copies of each of the more basic and valuable works listed in the index were to be retained and kept in "specially locked bookcases." Such books were to be made available only for "literary and scientific work" and "on the strict responsibility of the person in charge, who shall undertake not to permit general circulation thereof."

The purging of the libraries was to be carried out with all haste and:

> The Boards of Political Education and the commissions on the review and removal of books are ordered to prepare a time-table for this work so that the entire operation may be completed by January 1, 1924.

The index of prohibited works is too long to be cited here in its entirety, but a few examples may be given in order to convey some idea of the principles which guided the authors of the circular.

Under the heading of religion, every work was to be removed with the exception of the anti-religious literature published by the Soviet government. The recommendation for the large libraries was that

> Especially valuable and basic books on the history of religion and the church and works containing religious dogma—the Gospel, the Koran, the Talmud, etc.—and also books describing localities, monasteries and other monuments of art should be kept in special bookcases.

As for philosophy, religion and ethics, the following were to be removed from the smaller libraries (again with the proviso that two copies were to be kept in special bookcases): *"the biographies and works* of Descartes, Kant, Mach, Plato, Spencer, Schopenhauer, Höffding, William James, Taine, Thomas Carlyle, Kropotkin, Maeterlinck, Nietzsche, Nordau, Ruskin, Leo Tolstoi, Faure, Vl. Soloviev, Lange, Grot, Lossky, Chelpanov."

It may be of interest to note that the removal of the following political works was ordered:

> Propaganda pamphlets directed against the Communist movement, the Bolsheviks and the pacifists, published during the 1914-1917 War, and propaganda literature of 1917 supporting a democratic constitution, a democratic republic, civil freedoms, the Constituent Assembly, universal suffrage, etc.

The reference to these publications was not accompanied by the usual recommendation that two copies were to be retained in the larger libraries. These works were, therefore, no longer to be available even for scientific research. Even more interesting from the point of view of the internal development of the Communist Party itself is the following directive:

> Obsolete propaganda and reference literature published by Soviet organs (1918, 1919, 1920) on questions which are now being given a different solution by the Soviet government (agrarian question, system of taxation, free trade, food supply, policy, etc.) must be removed from the smaller libraries serving the ordinary reader.

The writer was unable to obtain later circulars with additional indexes of prohibited books and is therefore in no position to say precisely what ravages the Boards of Political Education wrought in the libraries in the fields of sociology, economics, the history of socialism and the labor movement, the natural sciences, biology, etc. However, there can be no doubt—for this is a matter of common knowledge—that in the 30's and 40's the ordinary libraries in Soviet Russia did not contain any of the classical works on socialism and "capitalist" economics, or the works of socialist leaders who opposed Bolshevism, including Rosa Luxemburg. These writings were available only to university students for their studies; in recent years, it is said, many students have exercised this privilege.

When we compare the Soviet "coordination" of the libraries, accompanied by the censorship of new books, with the "coordination" (*Gleichschaltung*) in the realm of ideas by the Italian fascists under Mussolini and the German Nazis under Hitler, it must be admitted that the Russian Bolsheviks were more efficient and absolute in the control of information and human thought. Neither Mussolini nor Hitler could boast of such an absolute achievement.

Even during the most liberal phase of the Soviet regime, the government quietly but most successfully proceeded to seal off Russia's channels of communication with the outside world. A young man with an inquiring mind who had heard of Dostoyevsky was nowhere able to lay his hands on *The Possessed*. A student who wanted to study a book on the history of the French Revolution was unable to obtain the works of Kautsky or Jaures, or of other non-Bolsheviks on this subject. A student of philosophy could not read any of the authors whom Lenin criticized—among others, Mach, Avenarius and Bogdanov; they had been removed from the libraries. In Soviet Russia, history did not even begin with the October Revolution, since a few years later Trotsky's works were also included in the index of prohibited literature.

At the same time, the Soviet government exercised strict control over the production of new literature—fiction, stories, novels and even children's books as well as works in the social sciences. Aided by Communist writers and their unions, the government—by placing orders with appropriate persons, selecting writers, and regulating their royalties and earnings, censoring and criticizing works—was able to ensure that writers portrayed in a narrowly tendentious manner the processes taking place in Russia, and that they did so with the deliberate aim of arousing emotions in the reader which would promote his education in the spirit of the directives, plans and purposes of the Communist Party. Subsequently, this literary trend was named "socialist realism," although it had nothing to do with either socialism or realism. Genuine realism was anathema, because the daily life and evolution of Soviet society, as they really were, were still too unattractive to win the Soviet reader to Communism. Reality had to be touched up and glossed over. Only persons who defended the Communist Party and its dictatorship could be the heroes in such works; all others had to be made to seem unattractive, repulsive, ludicrous and unworthy of acceptance. Thus, if "realism" stood for deliberate falsification, the word "socialist" came to mean the current political tack of the Soviet leadership. A reader of the Soviet press and literature, during virtually this entire period, was not given an overall picture of the true course of development of Soviet society, its members and its genuine heroes. Instead, he was presented with a purely fictitious and artificial portrayal of what that development should have been had it followed the party's plans and directives.

To the relatively non-violent controls exercised through the Communist Party organization, with its monopoly of expression and power, through a vast propaganda apparatus and through the control of literature past and present, were added the powers granted to and exercised by the political police—by the organization known successively to the world as the Cheka, OGPU, NKVD, MGB and KGB.

The Cheka—All-Russian Extraordinary Commission for the Suppression of Counter-Revolution, Sabotage and Speculation—was organized in mid-December 1917, that is, before the outbreak of the Civil War or the popular uprisings against the Soviets. The new institution was endowed with unlimited judicial, as well as police, powers, "to fight the enemies of the Soviet government and of the new order."[6]

In describing the work of the new institution, Felix Dzherzhinsky, its chief architect, told a correspondent of the newspaper *Novaya Zhizn*[7] that it was a mistake to regard the Cheka as a police or judicial organization intended for normal times. "We represent organized terror—this must be said openly—a terror which is absolutely essential in the revolutionary period we are passing through."

"Nevertheless," he went on, "you must not think that we are an inhuman organization. The Commission is composed of 18 old party workers, members of the Central Committees of Bolsheviks and Left Socialist Revolutionaries and of the Central Executive Committee [of the Soviet]. Death sentences require complete unanimity. If a single member of the Commission disagrees, the accused is pronounced not guilty." Rumors that interrogations were accompanied by violence were proclaimed by Zaks, Dzherzhinsky's assistant, a left-wing S-R, to be "absolutely false."

This description of the Cheka's methods of operation is quite idyllic when we consider what this situation developed into. As far as the use of torture is concerned, the rumors were far from false, Zaks's assertion to the contrary notwithstanding. The question was openly discussed by the personnel of the Cheka, as may be seen from *The Cheka Red Book* published in Moscow in 1922. It would appear that some sections and individual investigators went in merely for intimidation, while others resorted to beatings and torture. In any event, the Commission executed a tremendous number of people, especially during the period of the Civil War and the uprisings of peasants and workers. Bokiy, the Commissar of the Petrograd Cheka and an old Bolshevik, wrote in a report on the Cheka's activities that in Petrograd "during the period from March to October 1918, the Cheka considered 5,423 cases and effected 6,229 arrests; during the period of the Red terror, 800 persons were shot. Of these, 500 were shot in a single day."[8]

In the course of its development, this institution, despite Dzherzhinsky's pious intentions and undoubted sincerity, became an object of dread to every Soviet citizen; and the 18 "Saints of the Revolution," who at the outset discussed each individual case on its merits and whose unanimous consent was required for every verdict of "guilty," evolved into a soulless machine which destroyed hundreds of thousands of innocent men and women and which extorted "sincere confessions" by means of the most cruel and most refined tortures.[9]

In a few years, the small group of Central Committee and Central Control Commission members, with a few Red Army detachments, grew into a vast police machine employing hundreds of thousands, holding the entire country in a grip of iron, stationing its agents in every village, every city block, every apartment house, and relying in addition on the "voluntary services" of millions of informers. The

GPU not only had its own building in every city but its own prisons, and in many cases its own cemeteries and torture laboratories (for example, the notorious Lefortove Prison in Moscow in the Thirties). It had its own military divisions, its own aircraft, its own tank troops, its own telegraph system and radio stations equipped with the latest devices. Its card-index files were housed in a vast building staffed with hundreds of clerks and containing a separate file on everyone who had ever been investigated or suspected.

In the early Twenties, the GPU concentrated its attention on speculators, saboteurs and so-called *Nepmen,* on the one hand, and Mensheviks, S-R's and dissident Communists, on the other. By the mid-Thirties, however, when Yagoda, Yezhov, and later, Beria, were put in charge, the machinery of terror had become a state within the state.

[1] Friedrich Engels, *The Peasant War in Germany,* p. 135, International Publishers, New York.

[2] Milovan Djilas, *The New Class,* New York, 1957.

[3] Rosa Luxemburg, *Die Russiche Revoluzion.* Berlin, 1921.

[4] Moreover, it is worthwhile to point out that the post-Lenin Bolsheviks took great pains to let the Soviet people forget about Lenin's "Decree on the Press" and his solemn pledge to rescind the decree of November 4 (17) and to restore to the people of Russia the complete and far-reaching freedom of the press.

And even in the *Collected Works* of Lenin (4th edition, vol. 26, pp. 250-252), a curious reader cannot find the text of this decree, but instead there is given an entirely falsified account of the whole procedure in order to cover up the omission of this historic document. (Lenin, vol. 26, p. 495, footnote 68.)

[5] In the archives of B. I. Nikolaevsky.

[6] Interview with Dzherzhinsky, *Svoboda Russii,* No. 43, June 9, 1918, p. 3.

[7] *Novaya Zhizn,* June 9, 1918.

[8] Records of the Conference of the Chekas of the Northern Region, held in Petrograd on October 15, 1918, cited by Bunyan, *op. cit.,* pp. 351-352.

[9] In memoirs written in 1937, I cited a story told to me by an old friend in January 1920. He himself was very friendly with Kamenev, who told him in strict confidence that at a New Year's Eve party in the Kremlin attended by the top leaders of the Communist Party, Dzherzhinsky got drunk and went from one person to another begging to be executed. "A man who shed so much human blood has no right to live!" he wept. A comparison between Dzherzhinsky, consumed by remorse at having shed human blood, and Yezhov or Beria gives a clear indication of the transformation undergone by the Cheka between 1917 and the mass purges of the Thirties and Forties.

CHAPTER 14

The Birth of the General Line

Stalin Changes His Course

In August 1917, in the Kornilov days, at the Central Executive Committee canteen in the Smolny Institute, Felix Dzherzhinsky turned to the author, who was standing in line behind him and whom he had known for years, and asked:

"Abramovitch, do you remember Lassalle's speech on the essence of a constitution?"

"Yes, of course."

"He said that a constitution is determined by the correlation of real forces in a country. How does such a correlation of political and social forces change?"

"Oh, well, through the process of economic and political development, the evolution of new forms of economy, the rise of different social classes, etc., as you know perfectly well yourself."

"But couldn't this correlation be altered? Say, through the subjection or extermination of some classes of society?"[1]

The remark shocked me, but I attached no great importance to it, since at that time Dzherzhinsky appeared emotionally unbalanced. He apparently realized that it was quite impossible in a brief period to increase the number of industrial workers in Russia to anything more than a negligible minority in a vast petty-bourgeois peasant society, and he was seeking a way out of this historical impasse. He apparently had reached the conclusion that in revolutionary Russia the only way to change the existing balance of class forces in a hurry was through the method of "subjection or extermination."

The dreadful holocaust of 1920-21 caused many leaders, including Lenin, to doubt that even brute force could overcome the laws of social development. Yet, after seven years of the NEP had restored Russia to something resembling pre-war "normalcy," it was in the manner sketched by Dzherzhinsky that Stalin sought to overcome the contradictions imposed on a dictatorship of a small minority in a society composed of a majority of classes socially alien to the ruling party.

The NEP was a realistic attempt by the Communist Party to establish co-operation between the working class and the peasants, including (on certain conditions) the richer peasants and the middlemen and traders or *Nepmen.* This policy of the NEP, conceived by Lenin, was followed after his death because the outstanding members of the ruling group in this period belonged to the camp of "moderate" or "rightist" Communists, who opposed the "leftist" or "extremist" partisans of War Communism and "anti-peasant deviationists." This "rightist" ruling group included Stalin, Molotov, Rykov, Kalinin, Dzherzhinsky, Tomsky, Tsuriupa and A. P. Smirnov (the People's Commissar of Agriculture, not to be confused with the other two Smirnovs). The theoretician of the group was Bukharin.

The resolutions and key speeches of the 14th Conference and the 14th Congress of the Party were imbued with the spirit of realistic rightist Communism. Its clearest expression was found in the reports and statements of Bukharin. Thus, at the Moscow Province Conference of April 17, 1925, Bukharin said:

> Now that our industry has been growing in strength, we must change our policy with a view to diminishing the squeeze . . . We must fight private capital not in order to close a man's store, but in order to produce goods of better quality and sell them more cheaply that he can . . . Petty-bourgeois stimuli must be allowed to develop in such a form that they should help us and we help them, thus strengthening our economy. The petty bourgeoisie can now be made to participate with us in the construction of socialism . . . Because of the administrative pressure brought to bear on the *kulaks,* the middle peasants are afraid to improve their farms, lest they be listed among the *kulaks* and be subject to the same pressure . . . Our policy towards the village should be to decrease and, on occasion, to remove the restrictions which hamper the

growth of well-to-do and *kulak* farms. The peasants, all the peasants, must be told to grow rich, to develop their farms, and not to worry that they will be clamped down on.

Rykov, whose approach to the economic policy of the Soviet Union was practical and pragmatic, and who acquired great experience as Lenin's successor in the Council of People's Commissars, spoke in the same vein. He said: "The development of a bourgeois system in the village is no danger to us; we will be able to make use of the funds accumulated by the growing bourgeois stratum . . ." (*Stenographic Record, 14th Party Conference.*) He added: "We must stop the administrative squeeze of this (bourgeois) stratum. If we want to insure the further economic growth of the village, we must make it possible for the peasants to hire farm labor legally and facilitate the leasing of land."

Where the cities were concerned, Rykov took the view that: "We must not fight private capital now by administrative measures. The relationship between the state and private capital should be based on economic competition." (*14th Conference of the Russian Communist Party, Stenographic Record,* Moscow, 1925, p. 85.)

Stalin agreed with Bukharin and Rykov at this time—although he made a sharp about-face two or three years later. In his report to the Moscow party organization on the decisions of the 14th Conference, Stalin said:

The important thing is not to incite class struggle in the village. The important thing now is to unite with the great peasant masses, to raise their standard of living and their cultural level, and, together with these masses, to start out on the way to socialism.

He said further:

There are people in the party who maintain that, inasmuch as we have the NEP and capitalism is being temporarily stabilized, our task is to tighten the screws both in the party and in the state apparatus, so that the sinews should creak. I must say that such a policy is erroneous and fatal. What we need now is not a maximum squeeze but maximum flexibility, both in political and in organizational leadership. Otherwise, in the present complex situation, we will be unable to remain at the helm.[2]

Stalin's loyal lieutenant, Molotov, went even further:

> Close attention should be paid to the fact that we must in no circumstances place the hardworking, intelligent peasants, whose prosperity the party desires to promote, in the same category with the *kulaks*. But in the present state of development of trade relations ... we must tolerate the development of a strong agriculture, at least during the immediate future, and the strengthening of capitalist elements, i.e., the *kulaks*.

Dzherzhinsky, who had left the Cheka and had become president of the Council of the National Economy, approached the peasant question from the same angle. At the plenary meeting of the Central Committee held in July 1926, he said:

> It is unfortunate that there are statesmen among us who are afraid of prosperity in the village. We cannot hope to industrialize the country if the idea of prosperity in the village fills us with terror.[3]

What the rightist Communists advocated was a long-range policy. If the peasants and the petty bourgeoisie in town and country were permitted to prosper, the state would be unable to increase substantially its capital investment in industry. To derive considerable profits from trade, the state would be obliged to charge high prices for the industrial goods it produced. On the other hand, any increase in the taxes and duties levied on the peasants, particularly the richer peasants, would inevitably defeat the policy of harmonious co-existence with the petty bourgeoisie. Thus, the rightist Communist policy implied that the development of heavy industry and the formation of a large class of urban industrial workers would be quite slow and gradual.

In the beginning, many Communists, including Lenin himself, had hoped that foreign capital would play an important part in Russian industrialization. In practice, foreign capital was not readily available, especially after the failure of the Genoa conference. As a result, all in all, 1,937 offers for concessions were submitted, but the Soviet government concluded only 135 (relatively small-scale) agreements. In 1926 the number of offers was greatly reduced, and in 1927 steps were taken to annul the existing concessions. In the absence of foreign capital, the only source from which to draw investment capital was the peasantry, but under the rightist policy its contribution was inadequate. This situation lay at the heart of the various "leftist" opposition movements which gathered during the 1920s, under the leadership of Trotsky, Zinoviev, Kamenev and others.

Many Communists had been in a state of chronic dissatisfaction since the introduction of the NEP, which they considered a retreat in the face of the class enemy. The policy of War Communism, which held out the prospect of transforming Russia into a socialist country in a few years (if not in months, as Lenin had promised in the spring of 1918) remained dear to their hearts. They reacted as if they had lived through the golden age of Communism—that pure, unadulterated, unforgettable, majestic Communism, in Lenin's phrase—which made daily life under the New Economic Policy, with its grave limitations, its lack of militancy, its modest goals and its "Menshevik tendencies," seem like an insult to its memory.

The brilliant fireworks were over; instead, little kerosene lamps flickered all over Russia. Many Communists who had exhibited great valor and self-abnegation during the years of the Civil War and War Communism now found themselves misplaced; heroic Red Army commanders worked as bookkeepers in various government agencies; important leaders of the early years now occupied secondary posts, or no posts at all. To the romantically minded, the atmosphere of mediocre tranquillity and contentment which had succceeded the years of storm and stress was intolerable, and Trotsky was not alone in deeply deploring the crowding into the party of men from the lower middle classes. The lower levels of the Soviet administration were flooded by the peasantry. On the other hand, quite a few stalwart Communists suffered a "sea change" into entrenched bureaucrats, to whom words like Communism, the International, and the World Revolution were so many clichés devoid of real content.

Had the Communist Party not intended the NEP to be a temporary breathing spell to enable it to "*reculer pour mieux sauter*"; had the Communist Party accepted the NEP *in principle* and decided to promote the gradual evolution of peasant Russia toward industrialization and the progressive introduction of necessary social reforms, it would eventually have had to give up the very idea of dictatorship over the peasants and the working class. Communism would have become a Social Democratic doctrine adapted to the peculiar social and cultural conditions prevailing in Russia; it would have led to a more or less democratic state governed by a coalition of the peasantry, the proletariat and the intelligentsia. But such an ideology and program would have meant the liquidation of the Communist Party as it had been created by Lenin, Trotsky, Stalin and the rest, and its transformation into a party along Menshevik and S-R lines. (As we have seen, precisely such a program had been worked out by representatives of the Menshevik Party back in 1919-20.)[4]

Such a reappraisal of the basis of Communism was utterly unacceptable to the Bolshevik leaders for numerous reasons. They devoutly believed that the Communist Party must remain in being; that its rule must not be changed but only strengthened; and that socialism in backward Russia could not be built through piecemeal reforms and democratic processes, but through the iron dictatorship of the party. In addition, they were convinced that the party must not only introduce socialism into Russia but must work for a world revolution, without which the Bolshevik regime could not feel secure in Soviet Russia.

Therefore, the left protested against the rightist policies on the ground that they deviated in the direction of Menshevism and Social Democracy, towards what it called Thermidorianism. Their fears and accusations were far from groundless. Although the opposition was divided into several factions, each with its own leaders, platform and strategy, in essence all agreed on the same policy. They all opposed the aims of rightist Communism and the very idea of forming a bloc with the peasant class—and particularly with village bourgeoisie and the town *Nepmen*. They advocated a campaign against the capitalist elements in town and country, the concentration of all available resources and energies to push rapid industrialization and—in order to change party policy—the restoration of democracy in the Communist Party.

The undisputed leader of the so-called United Opposition, which developed after 1926, was Trotsky. Its main economic theorist, however, was Preobrazhensky, a very able and erudite Communist.

Preobrazhensky's theory had a certain merciless logic. The party could not, he assumed, wait several decades for state industry to develop to the point at which it would itself create the needed capital for rapid industrial development. Since long-term foreign loans were not available on acceptable terms, for the Soviets the only possible solution was greatly to reduce the people's level of consumption: the lower the consumption, the higher the rate of accumulation. In practice, this meant taking away from the peasantry, as the main sector of the population, an exorbitant share of its income and turning it into an economic milk cow, or—as Preobrazhensky himself once put it—into an internal colony, to be exploited by the government for the sake of industrialization.

There was no point in concentrating on despoiling the *kulaks* only, for they formed as little as two percent of the peasantry, and their confiscated property would not have sufficed to finance a large-scale program of industrial construction. The entire peasantry, including the 25,000,000 poor and middle peasant-households, had to be heavily taxed if the party was to bestride the "race horse of industrialization," to use Lenin's phrase.

But such a policy would clearly result in new peasant uprisings, in a civil war in reverse—fought not in order to give the land to the peasants, as the Civil War of 1918-20 had been fought, but in order to take it away. While the process of reconstruction lasted, and agricultural and industrial output increased, it was possible for the ruling group to ignore these problems and to continue as before in the hope that all would come out right in the end. After all, what the opposition called "laws" were merely theoretical suppositions which had not been tested by experience. Preobrazhensky spoke in general terms, as though there were many precedents for the industrialization of backward peasant countries by dictatorships of the proletariat. Stalin and his supporters were in no hurry to review their position; they were content to leave the peasantry well enough alone. But as time went on and as the differences of opinion regarding the methods and tempos of industrialization provoked sharp conflict within the party,[5] the nature of the problems which the party faced became increasingly clear—and the need to solve them increasingly more urgent.

At bottom, there could be no question of the Communist Party adopting a Social Democratic position on economic development.

True, there were many democratic socialists among the specialists and technicians, particularly among the economists, gifted and able men who honestly approached the problems of industrialization and might have enabled the party to espouse a "middle way" to achieve considerable industrialization while maintaining or expanding the NEP. But such a way required a relaxation of the party dictatorship and a certain democratization, which meant, for the Bolsheviks, an emulation of the vulgar "pettiness of Menshevism."

For orthodox Communists, then, the only remaining course left was abolition of the New Economic Policy. This meant a departure from the position clearly taken by Lenin during his last years, and a return to War Communism—on a much larger scale and in peacetime at that. The change was a fundamental one—and its achievement required strong and flexible leadership. The risk involved was tremendous.

Stalin was the only one of the party's leaders bold enough to steer the course which the contradictions of the New Economic Policy made necessary. Stalin's virtues and—even more important—vices supremely fitted him to head the party's new line. He was a man of great animal cunning, sharp wits, iron will, and firm character, combined with inhuman cruelty, vindictiveness, and utter contempt for the opinions of others. We do not know at what point Stalin decided that the only way for the Soviet regime to achieve its goal was the crusade to liquidate by force the peasantry as a social class. It would appear that he reached the decision gradually, in the course of his discussions and arguments with the Trotskyists and other leftist Communists, who in the end—paradoxically enough—managed to convince him of their approach even as he was already smashing them brutally.

The Grand Maneuver

Stalin used great caution in shifting his position from the rightist views, held in 1925 by Bukharin, Rykov and himself, to the ideas and policies of the ultra left. He continued for a long time to pay lip service to the old doctrine of the right. He could not possibly confess openly that Trotsky, Preobrazhensky, Piatakov, Larin, Kamenev and Zinoviev had won him over to their views; such an admission would have obliged him to support them in the internal party debates against his own former friends of the right. Even more important, the ruling party group, which had grown up under his leadership and had surrounded itself with an army of bureaucrats, would have been thrown into a panic at the idea of a sudden change, a fierce internal struggle. Stalin had no intention of alarming prematurely his own bureaucracy, which was still convinced that the rightist policy was the best way to insure economic growth and to raise the standard of living. Many of these people were not greatly concerned with long-range problems and future trends, but some who really believed in the right-wing views held key posts, and thus it was necessary for Stalin to find ways to deceive or circumvent them. Stalin executed this far from simple task with amazing patience and skill. No less a person than Kamenev admitted at the 17th Party Congress that Stalin's grand maneuver was a "stroke of genius."

First, Stalin dealt with the leftist opposition-bloc headed by Trotsky, Zinoviev and Kamenev. Here, he was backed not only by his own party clique, but by the right-wing leaders—some of whom, however, objected to the use of "organizational sanctions," such as dismissal from government posts and expulsion from the party, against the oppositionists.

The strategy of the campaign against the opposition was scheduled to be settled finally at a joint meeting of the Central Committee and the Central Control Commission held on October 23-26, 1926. Forewarned, the leaders of the opposition decided to engage in a diversionary maneuver prior to the joint meeting. In recognition of their impending defeat, the opposition leaders issued a simulated capitulation. On October 16, they published a statement, which *Pravda* called "a historic document," in which they virtually threw themselves at the mercy of the victors. The declaration was signed by Zinoviev, Trotsky, Kamenev, Sokolnikov, Piatakov and Evdokimov.[6] They said that while they did not "repudiate their views" and continued to regard them as correct, they nevertheless rejected "the theory and practice of the freedom to form factions and groups, recognizing that such tactics are contrary to the bases of Leninism and the decision of the party." They recognized that "in fighting for their views" they and their followers had on many occasions after the 14th Congress permitted steps to be taken which constituted a violation of party discipline and "exceeded the limits, established by the party, of ideological struggle within the party itself" and had embraced "the course of factionalism." They further stated that, "considering these steps utterly mistaken," they definitely renounced "factionalist methods" of defending their views and called for "the immediate dissolution of all factional groups which had formed around the opposition." In their declaration they stated, *inter alia,* that they entirely agreed with Lenin's earlier criticism of the "workers' opposition" headed by Shliapnikov-Medvedov. The declaration ended with the statement that the opposition "regards as absolutely binding" the decisions of the 14th Congress, the Central Committee and the Central Control Commission and would "obey them unreservedly and put them into effect."

The Berlin *Socialist Courier,* which at the time published comprehensive and well-informed reports on the struggle between the opposition and the Stalinist majority, described this declaration as a deliberate deception by both sides. The leaders of the opposition knew full well that they had not given up the fight, while Stalin and his adherents realized that they had not yet seen the last of the opposition. Temporarily, however, both sides were willing to settle for a semblance of reconciliation, and this conciliatory attitude was to some extent reflected in the theses regarding the opposition bloc prepared by Stalin for the 15th Party Conference.

These theses, approved by the Central Committee and published in *Pravda* before the opening of the Conference (October 25, 1926), stressed that:

> The opposition bloc is the exponent of defeatist attitudes in one portion of the party . . . These attitudes are based on disbelief that socialism can be built in a single country. Such views have nothing in common with Leninism and essentially represent a Menshevik deviation in the party.
>
> [In international politics] the party assumes that the advanced capitalist countries are going through a period of temporary stabilization . . . The opposition bloc . . . denies that there is such stabilization and embraces the course of revolutionary adventure.

> [In domestic politics] the party assumes that the highest principle of dictatorship is to maintain the alliance between the proletariat and the peasantry, as stated by Lenin. At the same time, the oppositionary bloc "proposes economic and financial measures which are likely only to break the tie between city and village, disrupt the alliance between the working class and the peasantry, and thereby to make effective industrialization utterly impossible."

In intra-party matters, the opposition bloc "seeks to set the party rank and file on the party officials," allegedly in order to democratize the party. The party, on the other hand, believes that those "who in any way weaken the iron discipline of the party of the proletariat—in effect side with the bourgeoisie against the proletariat."

For these reasons, and in view of the fact that Trotsky's former opponents (Zinoviev, Kamenev, et al.) had now espoused his point of view, "now speaking for Trotskyism with the same ardor with which they formerly spoke against it," and that the opposition bloc meant the creation of factions within the party, the conference resolved: "To conduct an ideological struggle against the Social Democratic deviation in our party, by explaining to the masses the erroneousness of the views of the opposition bloc . . ."

Thus the conference resolved "to strive to bring the opposition bloc to recognize the erroneousness of its own views," and systematically nip in the bud "any and all attempts to reintroduce factionalism and infractions of discipline."[7]

The entire conference had undoubtedly been planned for the sole purpose of putting an end to the left opposition. In order to make capitulation easier, Stalin carefully avoided uncompromising or insulting terms and any definite indications of concrete measures to prevent further opposition activities.

Furthermore, the very agenda of the conference was unusual. As a rule, the first item was a report of the Central Committee, delivered by whoever was currently considered Lenin's successor. But this time the opening speech was made by Bukharin, reporting on the international situation. He was followed by Rykov, with a report on the economic situation and on the tasks facing the party. Next came Tomsky, with a report on the work of the trade unions. Only then was it Stalin's turn to make a report on the last item of the agenda which both politically and psychologically should have come first, but which had been deliberately postponed until the very end.

Stalin was greeted by a standing ovation and proceeded to attack the opposition in forty-two pages of the stenographic record. The only thing not proposed in Stalin's theses was a statement on "organizational sanctions." Trotsky had charged that the adoption of these theses would result in the expulsion of the opposition leaders from the party. Stalin protested: "I must state that this remark of Comrade Trotsky is void of all foundation and is utterly false." He went on to say that the party did not intend to take any punitive measures against the opposition. The "liberal statesmen" could rest content; the opposition would not be crushed by force.

The opposition leaders completely ignored the first three reports and concentrated their fire on Stalin; Trotsky alone spoke for about an hour. The longer they talked, however, the less sympathy they received from the carefully chosen pro-Stalin delegates to the conference. Stalin's theses were adopted unanimously, and the opposition had no choice by Communist custom but to capitulate completely.

The opposition's defeat in the Soviet Union was followed up by another defeat at the plenary meeting of the Executive Committee of the Communist International on December 7-13, 1926. The chairman of the meeting, the German Communist Ernst Thaelmann, refused to permit discussion of the internal struggle in the Russian Communist Party, and when the opposition leaders tried to speak they were met by hooting, whereas Stalin was given another tumultuous ovation. How Trotsky, Zinoviev and Kamenev attempted to defend their position can only be learned from the German rightist-opposition newspaper[8] which published a record of this meeting. The record shows that here, too, they were forced to acknowledge their factional errors, and accepted the discipline of the Communist Party and the Communist International. Their declaration ended with the words: "We will defend the unity of the Russian Communist Party and the Communist International. We will fight against factionalism."

Although the resolution of the 15th Conference made no mention of organizational sanctions, organizational measures were soon taken against the opposition, including dismissal from government posts, transfer to outlying areas, and, later still, expulsion from the party. Immediately after the conference and the meeting of the Comintern Executive Committee, Zinoviev, chairman of the Communist International, and Lashevich, member of the Revolutionay Military Council, were removed from their posts. History must record, however, that to some extent the opposition had brought this fate upon itself. It had no intention of fulfilling its pledges to refrain from factionalism. While avoiding *public attacks* on the policies of the Central Committee outside the party, it engaged in violent propaganda *within* the party. It presented its own draft resolutions, dissenting opinions and critical comments to the different party organizations, making an effort to keep within the strict boundaries of "expressing opinions" which the party had always permitted. At the same time, it published its documents illegally, and thus created a clandestine literature which frequently found its way outside the party. (A number of these documents were printed in the *Socialist Courier.)* Members of the opposition held clandestine meetings at factories or elsewhere. In the summer of 1926, for example, they gathered at a certain milepost in a forest near Leningrad. One such meeting was surprised by GPU agents, who were astonished to find among those present one of their own men, Belenkiy, as well as the above-mentioned Lashevich.[9] Young people were especially active; they frequently resorted to the old prerevolutionary method of scattering leaflets in motion picture theatres when the lights were out. The opposition's activities became so widespread that a special section of the GPU, headed by Agranov,[10] was organized to combat them.

The 15th Party Congress

The opposition's efforts continued in 1927. During the November festivities in Moscow, open clashes occurred between its members and the pro-Stalin Communists. The people of Moscow were treated to a rare spectacle: one group of Communists would snatch banners and portraits of their leaders from another group of Communists and tear them to tatters. Fights, arguments and insults went on continuously.

This sad spectacle was recorded not only by Trotsky in his memoirs, but also by an independent non-Communist witness, who watched the parade and described it for the *Socialist Courier*.[11]

The worst fighting took place on the Tverskaia near the Hotel Paris. A group of opposition leaders, including Preobrazhensky, Sapronov and Smilga, stood on a second story balcony and harangued the passing crowd on the dangers of the course on which the party had embarked. Some of the paraders shouted approval, others booed. Young Stalinists tried to climb up on the balcony to silence the speakers but were pushed down. Finally, a group of men wearing identical caps and coats approached the hotel; they completely drowned out the speakers on the balcony by blowing whistles.[12] Then they broke down the locked doors of the hotel, made their way to the second floor, and after a skirmish dragged the speakers inside. Riutin, secretary of the Krasnopresny district committee, walked out onto the balcony and declared that nothing would now "darken the harmony of our festivities." In fact, according to the same eye-witness, the festivities were also "darkened" elsewhere, especially on the Nikitskaia, in an area frequented by university students, where hand-to-hand fighting went on for hours and the pavements were littered with pieces of torn red banners, and on the Mokhavaia, where soldiers surrounded a large crowd and kept it confined for several hours.

A similar demonstration took place in Leningrad, organized by Zinoviev. The oppositionists crowded around the speakers' platform, were pushed back by the authorities, and many of them, including Zinoviev, were hurt. Parades in other cities, too, were accompanied by clashes. Shortly before the November 7 celebrations, the opposition in Leningrad felt very optimistic, and Zinoviev wrote: " . . .there has been a great shift in our favor. We have no intention of leaving here." The next day, however, he went to Moscow and insisted on capitulation.[13]

It must be admitted that there was nothing else for the opposition to do. Its attempt to arouse a mass movement among the working-class Communists had failed. Outside the party, its policies were unpopular with the peasants, the technicians and the intelligentsia, and within the party, minor officials rejected them for fear of reprisals and dismissal at a time when there was considerable unemployment in the country. For this reason, its most active partisans were to be found among university students, who held no jobs, whose interests were not linked with the party, and who cared least for the possible consequences.

In the meantime, the Stalin group had begun to extend its organizational sanctions. At the October 1927 meeting of the Central Control Commission, Trotsky and Zinoviev were excluded from the Central Committee. After the November parade, Smilga was transferred to a post in distant Khabarovsk, an occasion which the opposition seized upon for one of its last mass demonstrations. Trotsky and Zinoviev spoke to some 2,000 persons gathered at the railroad station to see Smilga off. A little later, Trotsky's disciple and admirer, A. Ioffe, an oversensitive intellectual, who had headed the Soviet delegation at Brest-Litovsk, and was the ambassador to Germany up to the revolution, became so depressed that he committed suicide. His parting note to Trotsky, a dramatic document, was never delivered. Ioffe's funeral was attended by a great many people (1,500 according to some sources and 5,000 according to others). While the statements of government spokesmen were received coolly, Trotsky was given a tumultuous ovation. Nevertheless, the left opposition was breathing its last. Within a year, Trotsky was to be banished to Alma Ata, in central Asia; later he was exiled to Constantinople and the Prinkipo Islands.

Stalin now decided that the time had come to deal a final blow to the left opposition. Even as he launched his attack against it, however, he began with great caution the shift over to its policies.

The Fifteenth Congress of the party took place in an atmosphere of high tension. The workers were worried and restless, as unemployment had reached some two million. Factories often interrupted operations for lack of imports and raw materials; the economic planning agencies were notoriously divided over the prospects of the First Five-Year Plan.

Unlike the 15th Conference, the 15th Congress opened with a political report by Stalin on behalf of the Central Committee. During the discussion of the report, in which some thirty persons spoke and paid considerable attention to the struggle against the opposition, a symbolic clash occurred between Kamenev and Rykov. In a very conciliatory manner, Kamenev assured the Congress that inasmuch as the opposition found itself in the minority, it had only two possible courses of action: to form a second party or to submit to the discipline of the Communist Party. Since the first course was contrary to all of Lenin's teachings about the dictatorship of the proletariat, there remained only the second alternative, which the members of the opposition accepted honestly and wholeheartedly. They would abandon all factional activities within the party and disarm completely, without mental reservations or qualifications.

But, he went on, no one could ask them to give up their convictions. No party in the world could require anything of the sort from sincere and honest members, since it would mean imposing hypocrisy on them. The Communist Party did not want hypocritical obedience. It was harder for the opposition to abandon its views because some of its predictions had been borne out by events, as the party itself had been forced to admit. Kamenev cited the growth of the *kulaks* and the fact that the *kulaks* were able to regulate and control the export program and industrialization plans.

"We still have differences of opinion," Kamenev said, "and we accept party discipline, for we are united in spirit and our unity stems from Lenin's teachings. But don't put us into an intolerable position by forcing us to remain silent when a revolutionary like Mrachkovsky is in jail. We cannot and we will not repudiate comrades who have behaved like honest revolutionaries."

Rykov, who spoke next, quickly accepted Kamenev's challenge: "I must begin by saying that I do not dissociate myself from those revolutionaries who put in jail some members of the opposition for their activities against the party and against the Soviets."[14] Rykov's remark was greeted by "lengthy and tumultuous applause, shouts of 'hurrah!' " The delegates rose to their feet. Shouts of "Long live Lenin's Central Committee!" were heard.

Thus the Fifteenth Congress witnessed the consolidation of a bloc between the future rightist opposition and the Stalinist center. The Congress, controlled by this bloc, decided to expel from the party seventy-five Trotskyists, and twenty-three members of Sapronov's Democratic Centralism group. Among the expelled Trotskyists were Kamenev, Radek, Piatakov, Rakovsky, Smilga, Lashevich and Evdokimov. Trotsky and Zinoviev were expelled even before the Congress, a decision which the Congress approved.

Yet, at this very Congress, at which the rightists approved "organizational sanctions" against the left oppositionists, Stalin perfidiously deceived his rightist allies and laid the groundwork for the new "general line" of forcible collectivization of agriculture and accelerated industrialization. This was done in a very cunning and skillful way in order not to provoke the suspicions of the rightist partners.

With regard to Rykov, their principal leader in the field of practical politics, we have the testimony of N. Volsky: "Shortly before the 15th Congress, I had an opportunity to talk to Rykov, and I said to him, phrasing it rather vaguely, that I had heard rumors about a forthcoming abolition of the NEP. Were they true? Rykov fell into a rage and, pounding on the table, shouted: 'That's all nonsense, idiotic gossip by people who don't realize that to abolish the NEP now they would have to have our heads, my own among them, and I am not a man to allow that to happen.' "[15]

Rykov's closing speech at the Fifteenth Congress indicates that he was utterly unaware of what had really happened at this Congress. It is the speech of a man consciously making "leftist" concessions without realizing their implications and consequences:

> The very fact that the question of the Five-Year Plan was placed on the agenda of the Congress indicates that we are beginning to put into effect a broad program of socialist construction. At this Congress we have approached, for the first time, a major practical task, the question of building socialism in the village through the collectivization and socialization of the peasant economy . . . The very nature of the question decided at this Congress is a reflection of the interrupted forward march of socialism.[16]

Rykov apparently failed to understand that what he was extolling as the march towards socialism would necessarily lead to the abolition of the NEP. Stalin may well have persuaded him that such verbal concessions to leftist Communism were intended only for show and as part of a plan to destroy the leftist opposition.

Nevertheless, careful analysis of the main decisions taken by this Congress reveals a number of equivocal and hypocritical phrases, the use of which enabled Stalin to deceive not only the left opposition but right-wing Communists as well. For example, here is the most important part of the resolution adopted on Molotov's report on work in the village:

> The 15th Congress of the All-Russian Communist Party (B) deems it necessary . . . to stress that the level of agriculture still remains extremely low, and the Congress, therefore, instructs the Central Committee to take practical measures to raise agricultural production. One of the basic measures is, in the view of the Congress, the speedy passage of a new agrarian law. The first task to be carried out must be the gradual transfer of scattered peasant households to the system of large-scale production in the form of peasant co-operatives (collective working of the land through the intensification and mechanization of farming), every measure being taken to support and encourage socialized agricultural work. This raising of the level of agriculture is essential in the interest of increasing the prosperity of the main body of the peasants, in the interest of increasing the market (sales of raw materials) for big industry, and in the interest of altering the structure of, and introducing socialist co-operation in the village, thereby displacing the capitalist element in the village.[17]

As the phrases used by Molotov were customarily interpreted by the party's right wing, they contained nothing that might have indicated an abandonment of the NEP. The idea of co-operative agriculture had been stressed by Lenin in introducing the NEP, while the need for "improving the conditions of the main body of the peasantry" had never been denied. The *gradual* introduction of collective agriculture could not antagonize Rykov and his friends. Even the reference to "socialized agricultural work" was no cause for alarm, inasmuch as the Soviet government had always deemed it necessary to encourage co-operative farming.

To further allay rightist suspicions, Molotov stated in the report: *"The party can no longer have any doubt what path to follow towards socialism. That path is the NEP and an alliance with the peasantry."* And he stressed the principle of a gradual transition: "There can be no question of a quick jump from individual to large-scale farming. We can proceed only through the gradual development of large collective farms. That is the only correct course. We cannot allow any flights of fancy, *any coercion of the peasants,* during the transition to large-scale farming."[18]

In reality, Stalin was to lay the stress not on gradual socialization, not on raising the standard of living of the peasants, and certainly not on the inadmissibility of coercion, but on accelerating the pace of collectivization and overcoming "the capitalist elements in the village." What Rykov and his friends took to be mere technicalities and verbal concessions to the beaten leftists were in fact the real achievements of the Congress. What they thought to be its essentials were merely Stalin's verbal concessions to them in the twilight of rightist Communism.

The Congress ratified action in two spheres which were to lay the foundation of the new general line. One sphere was that of industrialization and the Five-Year Plan. The other was the law of land tenure.

As to industrialization, Stalin took advantage of the existence of a number of quite different plans, worked out by various agencies and commissions, to prevent the Fifteenth Congress from adopting a clear resolution. In this maneuver, he was greatly assisted by Rykov, the avowed enemy of all far-reaching "Utopias." At the Congress, the unsuspicious and credulous Rykov said half jokingly:

> At the present time we already have several versions of the Five-Year Plan. I know of no less than five versions of the Five-Year Plan for the development of the national economy. Certain better informed comrades maintain that by now there are even more versions of the Five-Year Plan, namely seven. The last of these versions, that of the State Planning Commission, was prepared just before the Congress and has not been reviewed.[19]

In view of this abundance of plans, Stalin was able to put across a proposal "to instruct the Central Committee to insure the elaboration of the Five-Year Plan with a view to its being placed before the next Congress *of the Soviets* for consideration."[20] In other words, by submitting the plan not to this Congress of the Communist Party, in which there might have been considerable difference of opinion, the vital matters of industrialization and capital investment were handed over for decision to Stalin's machine.

The same was true of the collectivization of agriculture. In order to abolish the NEP in the countryside, it was essential, first, to withdraw all the rights, freedoms and privileges that the middle and well-to-do peasants had been granted in 1922-1925. It was indispensable to amend the laws which protected the peasants from the confiscation of their land, property and income and to annul the law of 1922 which had revoked the 1917 decree socializing the land. The government also had to put itself in a position to crush any peasant resistance to new policies.

Molotov's long report at the Fifteenth Congress—full of deliberate omissions, platitudes, qualifications and ambiguities—made the point, almost in passing, that it was necessary for a number of technical reasons, particularly in order to review land tenure conditions and to carry out a land reform for the poorer peasants, to amend the old land law. The very last point of the resolution adopted on Molotov's report stated that the Congress: "Recognizes the urgent need to establish the basic principles of land tenure and land use on an all-Union scale."[21] As in the case of industrialization, the final decision of the land laws was left wholly and unconditionally to Stalin.

A draft of the new agrarian law was submitted directly to the Executive Committee of the Soviets, bypassing all party organs, as early as April 28, 1928, adopted late that year, and put into effect in 1929. The crucial character of the change may be gauged by comparing the older Soviet agrarian law of 1922 and the new Stalinist act of 1928.[22]

Land Code of 1922	New Act, 1928
Art. 9. All citizens of the RSFSR (without distinction as to religion or nationality) who wish to work the land by their own labor *have the right to the use of land* for agricultural purposes.	Para. 7. All citizens of the USSR without distinction as to sex, religion or nationality, and also working aliens who reside in the territory of the USSR and enjoy political rights, who wish to work the land by their own labor, have the right, in the manner established by law, to receive land for farming *by joining one of the existing associations of land users or by forming new associations of this type.*

Art. 10. The right to land may be exercised by *the land user:* (a) as a member of a land users' association . . . or (b) *individually, without joining a land users' association.*	Para. 8. *Agricultural collectives* and also the poorest peasants who have little or no land shall have a preferential right to receive land for farming purposes.
(This limitation does not exist.)	Para. 9. Persons who have been deprived of the right to vote in elections to the Soviets shall have the lowest priority in receiving land for farming purposes.
Art. 11. A person who has been given land for farming shall enjoy his right to the land *indefinitely;* this right may be revoked only on grounds *stipulated by law.*	Para. 10. Land is given for farming purposes *without specifying in advance the period for which it is given.*

This act—adopted as a result of the Fifteenth Congress—proved a veritable time-bomb inserted under the very foundations of the NEP. For in operation, forced collectivization was to assume the following pattern: for objecting to collectivization, the peasant was deprived of his electoral rights; for losing his electoral rights, he was deprived of his land; for losing his land, he was deprived of his house; he was also forced to leave all his property behind with the exception of a pair of shoes and a change of underwear. In theory, the law entitled him to a new grant of land, but since his was the lowest priority of all, his turn never came.

With the Fifteenth Congress, the way was clear to pursue the late Dzherzhinsky's chimera—altering the correlation of forces in Russia through the "subjection or extermination" of the peasants.

[1] R. Abramovitch, *Memoirs,* Vol. 2, p. 148, New York, 1944. D. Y. Dallin quite independently reported this conversation, which he had happened to overhear, in much the same words (*The New Leader,* N. Y.).

[2] Stalin, *Problems of Leninism,* 9th Edition, pp. 127-130.

[3] It was at this plenary meeting of July 20, 1926 that Dzherzhinsky died of heart failure after engaging in bitter polemics with the leftists Piatakov (his assistant in the Council of the National Economy) and Kamenev.

[4] The so-called platform, "What should be done," which T. I. Dan put forward at the 8th Congress of the Soviets when representing the Menshevik Party.

[5] See Alexander Ehrlich, *The Soviet Industrialization Debate, 1924-28.* Harvard University Press, 1960.

[6] *Communist Revolution,* No. 16-17, August-September, 1927, pp. 99-100.

[7] *15th Congress of the All-Union Communist Party (B), Stenographic Record,* pp. 811-822.

[8] *Mitteilungsblatt* (Linke Opposition), Berlin, Nos. 1-3, January-February, 1927.

[9] *Socialist Courier,* No. 15-16, 1926, pp. 17-18.

[10] *Socialist Courier,* No. 22, 1926, p. 11.

[11] *Socialist Courier,* No. 1, 1928. "Demonstracija opposicii," p. 12.

[12] According to a memorandum submitted to the Central Committee by several oppositionists, this group included Riutin, secretary of the Krasnopresny district committee, Moroz, secretary of the Moscow Control Commission, and other members of the Moscow Committee and Moscow Control Commission. They were joined by the head of the circuit political administration, and several of his officers. (See Trotsky Archives, Harvard University, Document No. 983 [1103].)

[13] Trotsky, *My Life,* Vol. 2, pp. 280-81.

[14] *15th Congress of the All-Union Communist Party (B), Stenographic Minutes,* State Publishing House, Moscow, 1928, pp. 251-256.

[15] N. Volsky, *Memoirs,* Part 3, p. 2. Columbia University, Russian Archives.

[16] *Stenographic Records of the Congress,* pp. 1271-1272.

[17] *15th Congress,* pp. 1281-1282.

[18] *Stenographic Records of the 15th Congress,* pp. 1063, 1077 and 1081.

[19] *15th Congress,* p. 769.

[20] *15th Congress,* p. 1304.

[21] *15th Congress,* p. 1315.

[22] *Izvestia,* April 25, 1928.

CHAPTER 15

The Great Leap

THE MIGHTY COLLECTIVIZATION MOVEMENT

Even the most determined enemies of Bolshevism failed, until the beginning of 1930, to foresee the scope of Stalin's policies of total collectivization and forced industrialization. The forced abolition of the NEP and a new civil war against one hundred million Russian peasants seemed too insane, too risky a course, to be put into practice. Few believed that the Stalinist party machine and police would be able to cope with peasant resistance. According to the general opinion of that time, such a course would inevitably result in Stalin's downfall.

Contemporaries simply could not imagine the monstrous power of the police machine that had already been organized in Russia by the end of the 1920s. Nor could they conceive the incredible strength that could be mustered by a fanatical party, organized on a military basis, which had at its disposal all the resources of a modern state and which was not restricted in its actions by moral inhibitions.[1]

The words totalitarian and totalitarianism had been introduced into popular usage at that time by Benito Mussolini. But their meaning was still largely theoretical. For what Fascism was then doing in Italy was mere child's play compared with what Stalin was to do in the Soviet Union, and Hitler in Germany.

In the summer of 1929, the *Berliner Tageblatt* ran a series of articles by its Moscow correspondent, Paul Schaeffer, reporting interviews with important Communists and well-informed Germans in Moscow. On the basis of these interviews, Schaeffer declared that the Soviet government aimed at nothing less than the eradication of the Russian peasantry as a class by turning the peasants into hired hands on huge state-owned or nominally co-operative farms. Schaeffer's reports were met with general scepticism. In Berlin, London and Paris, even experts on Soviet affairs declared that these reports were mere sensationalism based on scraps of conversations picked up in the corridors of the Kremlin. As a result, the events which started in the fall of 1929 came as a shock.

The reaction to forced industrialization was the same. Everybody had known for a long time about the various plans for a forced-march industrialization. But when it turned out that Stalin had approved the version of the plan calling for a 176% increase in industrial output and a 70.5% increase in real wages, public opinion in Russia and abroad was stunned by the scope of the program and the inner contradictions it contained. What capital could the Bolsheviks use to build their new industry? Where would they obtain the huge sums necessary for such investment if not by the most callous lowering of the people's living standards?

To be sure, the detailed objectives were not quite fulfilled. Nevertheless, despite the failure of many parts of the First Five-Year Plan, the overall objective was achieved: Soviet industry began its rapid growth. This "growth" was not accompanied by raising the living standards by 70.5%; on the contrary, it was marked by a lowering of the standard of living by more than 50%. That is, it was founded on the hunger and privations inflicted on the Soviet people.

Stalin laid the political groundwork for the campaign against the peasants in 1928. On May 16, *Pravda* published a Central Committee circular urging local organizations to intensify socialist construction in the villages, and on June 3, it published a similar appeal to all party members and workers.

On September 30, 1928, Bukharin published an article in *Pravda*, criticizing Stalin's new policy. Stalin counter-attacked at once. He aimed his first blow at Uglanov, a leading rightist who was secretary of the Moscow Party Committee. On October 18 and 19, Stalin delivered speeches to the Moscow Committee and the Moscow Control Commission in which he declared the rightist view to be an anti-party deviation and contrary to the decisions of the Fifteenth Congress. In November, the Moscow Committee of the party was reorganized,

Uglanov and his aide Kotov were removed from their posts, and a new Committee composed of faithful Stalinists installed. At its November plenary meeting, the Central Committee declared that the rightist deviation was the main danger faced by the party. The Central Executive Committee of the Soviets enacted the new agrarian law at its session, December 3-15, 1928. On January 1, 1929, *Pravda* published an address by the party's Central Committee to all local committees regarding new elections to the Soviets in the spirit of "an intensified attack on capitalist elements in city and village." On June 29, *Pravda* printed the "Act concerning the widening of the powers of local Soviets in assisting in the fulfillment of all-Union directives and plans." A decision of the Central Committee of July 1 and July 18 empowered the party rural-district organizations to assume direct control over Soviet, co-operative and trade-union organizations.

With these political preparations complete, the campaign began to "liquidate the *kulaks* as a class." The first blow was delivered in connection with state grain purchases. Groups of party members, sometimes with the support of the poorer peasants, volunteers and GPU men, began to challenge one *kulak* after another and demand immediate delivery of the quantity of grain assigned to him; refusal or resistance called forth severe reprisals. Anyone who failed to comply with the demand, even if it was physically impossible for him to deliver the grain, was arrested on the spot; his house and property were confiscated; and he was told to report somewhere with his "personal effects" (a change of underwear). Such people seldom reported of their own free will, but were usually brought under guard by the GPU, the militia, or armed party members. Their families were evicted and their entire property, agricultural machinery and fodder were confiscated for the benefit of poor peasants who wished to join collective farms.

This campaign, which started in the Crimean Autonomous Republic on February 11, 1929, was only the beginning.

After the grain offensive, the government proceeded with collectivization itself, mixing persuasion with outright intimidation. General meetings were called in the villages at which government representatives would make statements on the advantages and benefits of collectivization. Then a vote would be held. Of the fifty or sixty peasants who might attend, ten or fifteen would be poor peasants. During the vote, the great majority would abstain, while the poor peasants for the most part voted for the immediate collectivization of all rural property. A few bold spirits might possibly vote in the negative, but that would not change matters. A resolution would also be adopted, transferring land and livestock to the collective farm. In most cases, small livestock and poultry, as well as horses and cattle, were taken away from the peasants.

With the fate of the *kulaks* still fresh in their minds, the middle peasants did not even dream of resisting. In most cases, they obeyed orders silently, though a few, fearing reprisals, went into hiding. Collectivization proceeded apace, with relatively few cases of stubborn resistance recorded. Reports of the "victory of socialism in the village" piled up in the People's Commissariat of Agriculture and in the sections of the Central Committee which conducted the collectivization drive. Ordzhonikidze was able to state at the Moscow Regional Party Conference on September 18, 1929 that "the collective movement has assumed gigantic proportions," and at a meeting of Marxist agrarians on December 27, Stalin referred with unusual eloquence to the mighty collectivization movement "growing like an avalanche." On January 6, 1930, the Central Committee published a directive calling for total collectivization in the areas of the Lower and Middle Volga and Northern Caucasus by the fall of 1930 or, in any event, not later than the spring of 1931.

To reach this goal, it was necessary to use even harsher methods of coercion. A directive published in the *Socialist Courier* during 1930 gives some idea of what these methods were. This directive—the authorship of which the correspondent of the *Socialist Courier* attributed to Kaganovich, Bauman and the chief of the GPU, Yagoda—instructed the heads of Communist squads and members of the GPU, in charge of carrying out wholesale collectivizations, as follows: The local authorities were directed to divide all the *kulaks* in their territory into three categories. The first category was comprised of *"kulaks"* who actively opposed the Soviet government or were suspected of being secret counter-revolutionaries. All these *"kulaks"* were to be arrested and shot summarily on the order of the local authorities, without asking for approval by any central authority. The speedy extermination of the possible ring-leaders was necessary in order to prevent any *"kulak"* uprising.

The second group embraced the *"kulaks"* who regularly employed hired labor. Their entire property was ordered confiscated and, in accordance with a special directive, transferred to the collective farms. The *"kulaks"* themselves and members of their families were to be deported to the northern provinces to do forced labor, such as cutting roads through the taiga, drainage work, lumbering, and work in the mines.

The third group was composed of all *"kulaks"* not included in the first two categories. It could be stretched to include almost any peasant, for the directive refers simply to *"kulaks,"* without taking the trouble to define the term. Peasants in this last group were to have all their property confiscated and to be driven out of the area with only a pair of shoes and a change of underwear in their possession.

It may be that the archives of the GPU contain full and exact data on the number of persons arrested, deported and shot during the collectivization years 1929-32. Without access to such material, we can only speculate. Nevertheless, some information available to us provides an indirect indication of the tremendous numbers of victims involved. Thus, serious friction arose between the People's Commissariat of Railways and the GPU regarding the trains used to transport the *"kulaks"* to the North and the Far East. The demand for engines and railway cars for this purpose was so great that it seriously interfered with the Commissariat's transport plans and schedules. The two agencies argued and bickered for some time before they agreed on the maximum number of trains to be made available to the GPU for the transportation of its "white coal"—the official term used in the negotiations.

The *"kulaks"* were transported in appalling conditions. So many of them were crammed into freight and cattle cars that often there was no room to sit down; they were sent off without adequate rations, sometimes without water, usually without warm clothing and frequently without shoes. As a result, in winter (particularly in the winters of 1929-30 and 1931-32) these nightmare trains became veritable "echelons of death"; and, at nearly every stop, corpses of people who had starved or frozen to death were thrown out. Epidemics were rife, and the arduous working conditions at the places of deportation claimed still more victims. Their families were not much better off; they were driven from their homes to beg for bread in other villages, whose inhabitants were well aware that it was dangerous to help the relatives of a "*kulak*."

But the government was heedless of the mounting number of victims. Yagoda insisted that the only way to fight the *kulaks* was with bullets. Even the moderate Kalinin supported him, saying that during a great social revolution there was no time for humanitarian considerations. Another "prominent Communist," whose name the *Socialist Courier* withheld, declared: "We must destroy five million people," in order to put through socialism in the villages.[2]

However, barely a year after the campaign had begun, Stalin decided to apply the brakes. His main consideration was not the staggering number of lives sacrificed to wholesale collectivization, but the economic difficulties which it had brought in its wake. By exceeding all expectations in its scope, collectivization had upset all the government's carefully prepared plans and schedules. The peasants meekly obeyed orders, joined the collective farms, and surrendered their property, even if with great inner reluctance. The cases of overt opposition were relatively rare. According to reliable sources, from 1929 to 1931 the GPU recorded some 1,000 instances of resistance, open rebellion, rioting, etc.[3] For a country the size of Russia, this was not much. But the absence of overt resistance did not mean that the peasants were reconciled to the new order. They worked on the collective farms without any real desire for achievement. Sowing and harvesting were carried out lazily, carelessly and late in the season; agricultural machinery was kept in poor repair; the losses suffered in animal husbandry, for lack of skilled and devoted personnel, were particularly large. Many cattle died because of poor fodder, polluted water and lack of care; calves perished and the milk yield sank to a very low level. Even greater were the losses in horses, which no longer received the loving care of their former owners. The losses in livestock were so extensive that it took Russia more than a generation to recover. As Khrushchev stated in his report to the plenary meeting of the Party Central Committee in September 1953, butter production in 1953 was still 40% lower than it had been in 1928, milk production 35%

lower and that of eggs 60% lower. The number of pigs had increased —by only 3%.

The grain harvests, too, were disastrously poor. The drops in grain production cannot be estimated authoritatively. They have not yet been shown in official Soviet statistics, which deliberately exaggerated the harvest figures for 1931-33 in order to prove to the world that collectivization had greatly increased the productivity of Soviet agriculture. In point of fact (according to the reliable calculations of N. Jasny), agricultural production was reduced as much as 20% in 1931-32. Some of the decrease may have been due to the weather, less favorable than in 1930, but the rest must be attributed to the inefficiency of forced collective farming. In 1933, the government resorted to a radical method of concealing these decreases—a method which continued to be practiced until after Stalin's death. Instead of citing the amount of grain actually harvested, Soviet statistics began to publish figures for what it called "biological harvest"—in other words, an estimate of the grain in the field before harvesting. This figure was more than 20% higher than the real harvest. Thus, the 1933 harvest seemed on paper to be larger than the 1930 harvest, although in fact the opposite was the case.

Even before these economic consequences became fully clear, Stalin began to sense the dangers of unlimited, unconstrained collectivization. Political restlessness throughout the country, and depressed morale on the new collective farms in particular, had become so threatening that Stalin was forced to call overzealous collectivizers to order and to give the peasants some measure of relief and reassurance. This he did in his "historic" article, "Dizzy With Success," published on March 2, 1930. With unparalleled cynicism, Stalin laid the entire blame for the collective "avalanche" on the local officials who, as he admitted, had not always abided by the law and had on occasion resorted to illegal coercion of the peasants. With seeming innocence, he insisted that such methods must be abandoned.

This article was followed on March 15 by a Central Committee order making a number of concrete concessions. It countermanded the socialization of dwellings, small livestock, poultry, and dairy cattle whose products were not intended for sale; it ordered a review of the lists of former *kulaks* and the immediate correction of any mistakes that had occurred. It threatened the dismissal of officials who were unable or unwilling to fight against deviations from the new party line.

Stalin himself made no provision for allowing peasants to leave the collective farms which they had been forced to join, but the peasants themselves remedied this omission. They began to abandon the collective farms in ever increasing numbers, using Stalin's letter as their excuse (many peasants carried a newspaper clipping of the letter in their pockets as a sort of safe conduct). According to official statistics, there were 14,264,500 peasant households in collective farms on March 1, 1930, and only 5,778,000 were left.[4]

But these concessions afforded no more than a temporary respite. The ceaseless harrying of individual peasants was soon resumed. They were squeezed out of existence by high taxation, confiscation, nondeliveries of agricultural tools, and various other methods short of outright coercion. After the Sixteenth Party Congress (June 26 to July 13, 1930), which issued stern new directives to intensify wholesale collectivization, the numbers of collective farmers began to swell again. By 1933, the number of households which had joined collective farms had risen to 15,200,000.[5]

At the Sixteenth Congress, not a word of criticism was heard from either the left or right Communist oppositionists. The Trotskyists and leftists were silent; they could hardly have objected to what they had themselves so long advocated. Many of them, no doubt, felt that they themselves would have carried out that vast operation with greater efficiency and perhaps greater concern for human lives, but they failed to say so. Even Trotsky, already in exile and free to write as he chose, never raised his voice (in the *Bulletin* of the opposition which he published after 1929 in Paris) against the cruelty of forced collectivization. In one article (No. 14 of the *Bulletin*), he criticized rather mildly "certain methods, bad planning and exaggerated tempi of the collectivization and industrialization." But that was all. The right-wing Communists, who had boasted of their willingness to fight to the bitter end against the abolition of the NEP, surrendered meekly. Rykov confessed at the Congress that he had failed to realize that the resources of the Soviet state were already powerful enough to overcome any resistance of the Russian peasants. He added that, if anybody tried to restore individual farming and dissolve the collectives, the peasants themselves would not permit it and would fight for the *kolkhozes.*

An incontestable official document of the Soviet government proves beyond any possible doubt how false this was, how naked and bloody was the coercion against the peasants. It is a circular of May 8, 1933, signed by Stalin and Molotov, a copy of which appeared in the so-called "Smolensk Archive" and was published *in extenso* in the *Socialist Courier* in 1955 by S. Wolin.[6] This secret circular stated explicitly that peasants were still being arrested by any official who so desired, and that the country's jails were crammed with peasant prisoners. The circular estimated the number of peasants in jails alone, without counting camps and labor colonies, at 800,000. It called for a reduction in the number of arrested and, for practical guidance, included a table listing the maximum number of arrests of peasants permissible in any given area in the course of the year. The table follows:

"Eviction is permitted only from the following areas and only in the following numbers":

	Households		*Households*
Ukraine	2,000	Western Siberia	1,000
Northern Caucasus	1,000	Eastern Siberia	1,000
Lower Volga	1,000	Byelorussia	500
Middle Volga	1,000	Western Region	500
Central Black Earth Region	1,000	Bashkiria	500
Ural	1,000	Transcaucasia	500
Gorki Territory	500	Central Asia	500
		Total	12,000

The total number of families to be deported was quite modest compared to the number of evictions and arrests recommended by the local "*kulak*-fighters" (in 1933). According to the circular, these amounted to 100,000 families. The circular called for a reduction of the peasant jail-population in the whole USSR to 400,000 before the end of 1934.[7] (In addition, the peasants sent to corrective camps and to so-called labor settlements and colonies probably numbered from 1.5 to 2 million.)

To explain why a more liberal attitude was needed, Stalin and Molotov wrote: "The work of *kulak*-fighting must be streamlined, or else it will harm the interests of the Soviet state, for these old methods of work are now obsolete." At no point did the authors of the circular admit that these methods had been wrong. On the contrary, they asserted that "the last three years of our work in the village were years of struggle for the liquidation of the *kulaks* and the victory of the collective farm." It had been necessary to conduct this struggle by means of mass deportations, arrests and shootings because the *kulaks* had offered "desperate" resistance as early as 1929. Under the present conditions, they explained, drastic reprisals were no longer necessary, but this did not mean that the struggle against the "class enemy" by any means whatsoever was entirely excluded. On the contrary, it might well become more violent in the near future. Nevertheless, the new policy substituted reprisals against "dangerous" individuals for mass reprisals. The circular introduced a number of restrictions which deprived "the chairmen of district executive committees, district and territorial officials, chairmen of village Soviets, chairmen of collective farms and collective farm associations, secretaries of party cells, etc.," of the power to decide arrests, sentences and deportations. These powers were now confined to "the offices of the public prosecutor, the OGPU, and chiefs of militia."

This circular, which was discovered and published by the merest chance, deals a death blow to the official myth of collectivization as an irresistible surge on the part of the great masses of the peasantry towards socialism. This hyprocritical official doctrine of the Stalin epoch was merely a repetition of the pious lie of which Lenin himself was guilty when he asserted, in his book attacking Kautsky in November 1918, that tens of millions of peasants were flocking to the Bolsheviks and were enthusiastically setting up socialist farms and a socialist exchange between city and village. Lenin made similar statements, partly out of ignorance, partly out of wishful thinking. In Stalin's case, the lie was coldly deliberate and calculated.

To the losses, probably in the millions, suffered in the "civil war" between the government and the peasantry, must be added the millions of victims of the dreadful famine which broke out in Russia, in the Ukraine, in the Volga regions and in Kazakhstan in 1932-33.

This catastrophe was kept secret for a long time. Whereas a large amount of historical material exists on the famine of 1921-22, including fairly accurate data in official Soviet publications,[8] no official reports were published concerning the famine of 1932-33, and the very fact of its existence was stubbornly denied in the Russian press. Only the reports of a handful of foreign correspondents, who happened to travel in the Soviet Union during the famine, provide some direct impression of its scope and consequences. The most striking description of the famine and of its shocking human cost may be found in William Henry Chamberlin's book, *Russia's Iron Age,* published in 1934 (pp. 66-92). The American journalist, Harry Lang, after a trip through the Ukraine, also gave a graphic description of the famine in the *Jewish Daily Forward* and, in a condensed form, in a special supplement to the *New York Evening Journal* of April 16, 1935.

Chamberlin traveled through many Cossack settlements in the Kuban and visited a number of western and southern towns such as Belaya Tserkov and Poltava. After interviewing the local authorities wherever he went, he reached the conclusion that about ten per cent of the area's population had perished in 1932-33. Since the famine raged over a territory populated by about 60 million persons, this percentage represents a total number of six million—or, making allowances for normal mortality, of perhaps four million persons killed by the famine.

Harry Lang was told by an important Soviet government official that about six million persons had starved to death. Lang's description of the hideous scenes of famine in the Ukrainian villages and of the city crowds of hungry women and children who no longer seemed human, cannot be read, even today, without horror. Many cases of cannibalism had occurred, and a poster against cannibalism hung in the official's office. Pointing to the poster, the official said, shaking his head sadly, "Our people are still very primitive." He was trying to convince the American correspondent that cannibalism was the result of the cultural backwardness of the Russian people, rather than the famine.

In fact, within twelve years (1921-1933), the Russian people were stricken twice by appalling famines, and each time this disaster was brought on them not by a natural cataclysm but by deliberate government policy. The direct and immediate cause of the first famine was the policy of Civil War and War Communism; the cause of the second was the policy of forcible collectivization. In each case, millions of human lives were deliberately and remorselessly sacrificed.

Whatever doubt there may be that the famine was in the deepest sense deliberate is dispelled by the movement of Russian grain exports abroad in these years of agricultural crisis. In order to promote "socialist industrialization" and to obtain foreign currency, the Soviet government dumped Russian grain on the world market (seriously depressing grain prices in consequence). On January 10, 1930, as large quantities of Russian rye suddenly appeared on the market, rye sold in Hamburg at 9 to 9.15 Dutch guldens per double hundredweight, while on May 23, Khlebotorg, the Soviet grain sales agency, sold 10,000 tons of the same kind of rye in Hamburg at only 5 guldens.[9] Even in 1931, according to Chamberlin, 4,600,000 tons of grain were exported from the USSR, and in 1932, when the famine was as its height, 1,819,914 tons.

If, instead of sending abroad these six million tons of grain which it had wrested from half-starved peasants, the government had sent them to the stricken territories, the famine might have been prevented. Surely the Soviet government, which boasted of organizing the country's entire economy in accordance with a prepared central plan incorporating the minutest details of production and distribution, export and import, should have foreseen this dreadful catastrophe and taken measures to prevent it.

Moreover, once the catastrophe had occurred, the Soviet government made absolutely no attempt to organize famine relief, to feed the starving or give medical treatment to the millions ill from hunger, epidemics and all the other consequences of malnutrition. On the contrary, it was forbidden to aid the *kulaks,* and those who did so laid themselves open to severe penalties. There were no soup-kitchens or feeding-stations for children; and the Soviets permitted no foreign Hoover to come to rescue the starving. Maxim Gorki, who had ten years before dramatically appealed to the United States for help, now remained silent; the famine evoked no reaction on the part of Trotsky, who found time and space to write of the "dreadful persecution" of his own partisans in Russia and to denounce Stalin for the latter's falsification of Trotsky's biography. The "proletarian humanist" Bukharin and the tempestuous Rykov likewise remained silent. None of these famous Bolsheviks of the left and right dared to mention the hundreds of thousands of children's corpses with horribly swollen bellies strewn on the highways of the Ukraine, the Volga region, Kazakhstan and the northern Caucasus.

Although it remains impossible to estimate how many Russians died of the famine itself, how many peasants were killed in the course of collectivization, how many died in deportation or exile, the total cost of Russia's agricultural upheaval is no secret.

According to the calculations of Lorimer, a well-known demographer who was not concerned with exposing Soviet policy, the annual population increase in the USSR dropped from 2.9 million in 1928 to 100,000 in 1933—in effect, it became almost non-existent. Population increases resumed only in 1936. Consequently, from 1928 to 1935, the population failed to increase at all, when it should normally have increased by some twelve million. In part, this may be explained by a lowering of the birth rate for a number of political, economic and social reasons, including mass executions and deportations of men, women in factories, etc. But a large part of the "population gap" must be attributed to the frightful increase in mortality as a result of the famine of 1932-33 and its attendant epidemics. Lorimer himself estimates the loss in human lives resulting from collectivization at 5.5 million persons.[10]

An indirect confirmation of these enormous losses is furnished by the population figures for the national republics. Thus, the Ukraine, which had a population of 31,194,000 in 1926, had—according to Lorimer—only 28,070,000 in 1939. Kazakhstan, with 3,968,000 in 1926, had only 3,098,000 in 1939. These heavy losses in peasant regions outweighed the increase in the Great-Russian population, from 77,791,000 in 1926 to 99,019,000 in 1939.[11] The Ukraine, Kazakhstan, the Middle Volga Region and Kuban were most severely stricken by the famine, the human losses running over three million persons for the Ukraine alone.

Stalin's own version of collectivization, in Churchill's *Memoirs,* confirms the ferocity of this period. According to Stalin, forcible collectivization had been indispensable, for the conservative Russian peasants categorically rejected modern agricultural techniques; force had had to be used. Stalin said: "The collective farm policy was a terrible struggle . . . . It was fearful. Four years it lasted."[12]

Reorganization of the Communist Party

Collectivization of the peasantry was one side of Stalin's general line; the other was laying the foundations of modern heavy industry. The same Fifteenth Party Congress which launched collectivization (in the guise of a gradual, voluntary transition of twenty million peasant households to a socialist system) also adopted the general outline of the First Five-Year Plan for the development of large industry. While collectivization was supposed to have taken place slowly, however, industrialization was to proceed with breakneck speed. The target figures of the first version of the plan called for an 80 per cent increase in the industrial output in five years. At the same time, the plan provided both for a 56 per cent increase in agricultural production and a 70 per cent improvement in the real wages of the workers. In fact, Stalin proceeded to carry out another, much more grandiose version of the plan, calling for an increase not of 80 per cent, but of 179 per cent in industrial production. If these fantastic targets had remained on paper, no great harm would have been done. In practice, however, the government, eager to attain unattainable results, exerted cruel and unremitting pressure on the working people.

A very superficial examination will suffice to show that even the first, relatively modest and "realistic" version of the plan was deliberately intended to deceive. The first version of the plan called, for example, for a capital investment of 64.5 billion roubles. Now, the investment in 1928 had been 3.7 billion a year. Considering the growth of industry, the plan might realistically have called for some 20-25 billion roubles in investment over five years. However, the Soviet government undertook to furnish some 40-45 billion roubles more than could rationally have been expected. How could it obtain such a huge sum? Obviously not through foreign loans or through confiscating the property of the wealthier town dwellers or the *kulaks*. It could get the money only by taking it away from the great masses of the peasantry, the workers and the city poor. That meant, literally, that "socialism" would have to be built by systematically reducing the general consumption and even the food-rations of the entire population almost to the physiological minimum.

Furthermore, the First Five-Year Plan, like all the subsequent ones, concentrated on increasing the means of production, especially heavy industry, while the production of essential consumer goods was pushed into the background. Thus, under the First Five-Year Plan, in which more than half the funds (51.7 per cent) were allocated to industry, 45.2 per cent was allocated to heavy industry ("production of the means of production") and only 6.5 per cent for the manufacture of consumer goods. The government proceeded to build machines, factories and heavy armament for the Red Army while ever smaller percentages of its funds were devoted to clothing, shoes, textiles, processed foods, house and kitchen wares, furniture, bicycles, etc. Machines were everything, man nothing.

Apologists of Bolshevism claim that Soviet industry was built through the heroic effort of workers and peasants who gladly went hungry in order to build socialism. Ph. I. Liashchenko, an official historian of Soviet economic development, writes: "Labor, which had been a compulsory penal servitude under capitalism, became a matter of honor, a matter of glory, a matter of valor and heroism."[13] To be sure, some Communist youth were inspired by the idea of industrial construction on a gigantic scale, and saw glory and honor in it.[14] But the overwhelming majority of Russian workers were compelled to bear a grievous burden not of their own choice without getting the barest essentials. The standard of living of the industrial workers, whose number increased greatly as a result of the rapid industrialization, declined by 50 per cent or more during the First Five-Year Plan, and the 1928 level was not again within reach for some three decades. In practice, what saved the workers from starving to death was the fact that wives and older children of working-class families went into the factories. According to reliable statistics, 1.45 persons per family were employed in industry in 1931.[15] This ratio enabled families to survive —at subsistence levels. Socially speaking, however, the Soviet government now had three workers for roughly the price of two. The process was at least as brutal as the nineteenth-century "primitive capital accumulation" described by Marx.

The life of the workers recruited for construction, who cleared the ground, uprooted the tree stumps, dug the foundations and performed the other jobs necessary for erecting the new plants and factories, was almost intolerable. Labor for these operations was recruited from among the former *kulaks,* shopkeepers, unskilled unemployed, and inmates of concentration camps. Their living conditions were unimaginably squalid. They were kept on short rations and housed in mud huts or in poorly heated, jerry-built barracks, often full of dirt and crawling with vermin.

By this time, the right-wing Communists had been removed from leadership in the trade unions, and the trade unions themselves had become occupied wholly with propagandizing the workers to work harder despite their low pay and miserable working conditions. Although the workers no longer had anyone to defend them, often—driven by hunger and desperation—they showed their discontent in no uncertain terms, although in those days to protest openly was a very dangerous matter.

The radical changes in economic policy and the general line were inevitably accompanied by equally drastic changes in the Communist Party, in the organization of its governing bodies, particularly the Central Committee, and in its method of governing the country. In order to react quickly to every change in the situation and take measures called for by each new turn or zigzag of the party line in its headlong rush to "socialism," the Central Committee cut itself loose from the government, eliminated the delays occasioned by the passage of laws and regulations, and bypassed the cumbersome administrative machinery of the Soviet state. The façade of state power gave way to naked dictatorship by the party Central Committee. It had once pretended to guide the state; now it ruled it openly. Decisions were made by the Central Committee and transmitted directly through party channels.

To enable the party leaders to act with lightning speed and apply unlimited pressure, far-reaching changes were made in the organization of the Central Committee. The Politburo was virtually removed from the chain of command. Stalin's Secretariat became the center of action and decision. Stalin was assisted by the most influential and important party men, grouped in the Organization Bureau, which during this period in Russia had far more power not only than the Council of People's Commissars or the Central Executive Committee of the Soviets, but more power even than the Central Committee of the party and the Politburo. After Stalin's death, the Politburo (re-named the Praesidium) and the Central Committee again assumed roles. In the Stalin era, however, Stalin's Secretariat framed the major decisions and the Organization Bureau supervised their implementation.

Here is a brief excerpt from the Organization Bureau's work-program for 1931:

> The questions to be settled were divided into the following categories: 1. Industry, 2. Agriculture, 3. Transport and Communication, 4. Finance, 5. Food Supplies and State Grain Purchases, 6. Trade Unions and Soviets, 7. Skilled and Unskilled Labor, 8. Culture and the Press.

Industry in turn was divided into various branches: A. Metallurgy, B. Fuel and Power, C. Chemistry, D. Tractor Building, E. Agricultural Machinery, etc.

Here, for purposes of illustration, is a short excerpt from the subsection on Metallurgy:

> A. Metallurgy and Machine Building: Control of the implementation of the decisions of the Central Committee of the All-Russian Communist Party (B) regarding the improvement of party and professional work and the training of specialists at 'Kuznetskstroy' with a view to putting plants into operation on target date and fulfillment of the indices of the industrial and financial plan (lowering the costs, increase in labor productivitiy, etc.).
>
> Reports by the Western Siberian Regional Committee of the All Russian Communist Party (B), the Secretary of the District Committee and head of construction of 'Kuznetskstroy,' 'Vostokostal,' the Supreme Council of the National Economy, the central committees of the appropriate trade unions and sections of the Central Committee of the All-Russian Communist Party (B).[16]

This is not the work program of the Council of the National Economy or any of the government's economic agencies; it is the work program of the Organization Bureau of the party Central Committee.

Government economic or administrative state organs were mere appendages of local party committees and party organizations. Thus, Russia became a "partyocracy."

With such vast power concentrated in such few hands, and utilized to such devastating effect throughout Russia, it was, perhaps, inevitable that even the victorious Stalin faction of the party, which had crushed the left and right oppositions, would soon be rent by passionate disagreements, suspicions and rivalries. Such disagreements had begun to appear within the first year of full-scale collectivization (as indicated by Stalin's "Dizzy with Success" speech, and then the renewed militancy of the Sixteenth Party Congress). They grew more serious—threatening to limit Stalin's power—as forced collectivization and breakneck industrialization proceeded.

The anatomy of the struggle within the Stalin faction was described in detail in the famous "Letter of an Old Bolshevik," published anonymously in the *Socialist Courier* of December 1936 and January 1937. For twenty-three years, the name of its author remained a closely-guarded secret. On November 23, 1959, the editorial board of the *Socialist Courier* decided formally to reveal that the author of this remarkable account was Bukharin, whom Lenin had called the ablest theoretician of the party. By that time, many of the details of Bukharin's account had been directly confirmed by Stalin's successor, Nikita Khrushchev.

Bukharin's letter describes how Stalin began to lose the trust and confidence of even the party's inner core, which had backed him unconditionally in promulgating the general line. The enormous amount of human suffering, the disorder in the countryside, the breakdowns in industry provided food for thought and cooled the enthusiasm of many of Stalin's followers. The dissatisfaction increased still further in 1932 with the onset of the disastrous famine—which party leaders were aware had been, to a large extent, deliberately caused by Stalin in an effort to break the peasants' passive resistance to collectivization. The leaders of the Stalin faction, in contrast to rank and file party members, were not concerned so much by moral, political or humanitarian considerations as by the fact that the famine almost completely paralyzed the progress of the Five-Year Plan. Because the workers as well as peasants were hungry, their productivity was dangerously low. A critical situation prevailed in the Donets Basin and other industrial centers.

Since, throughout this period, party leadership had been concentrated in the enlarged Orgburo run by Stalin, the primary responsibility for this disastrous state of affairs clearly rested with Stalin. Thus, many party leaders who had unquestioningly followed the lead of the Central Committee now clamored for a revision of party policy. The plenary meeting of the party's Central Committee in September 1932 was one of the most turbulent in the party's history. It was the scene of a violent struggle which placed Stalin in the minority. At the meeting of the Politburo on the same occasion, only Kaganovich sided with Stalin, while Ordzhonikidze, Kuibyshev, Kossior, Kalinin and Rudzutak spoke against him. All these men had been enthusiastic Stalinists in the intra-party struggles of the 1920s.

This "inner opposition" found a leader in one of the younger members of the Politburo, Sergei Kirov. A former worker who had risen to influence in the party, Kirov had become, after the defeat of Zinoviev's "Leningrad opposition," one of the most popular leaders in Leningrad. A staunch defender of working-class interests, he had exerted himself to insure that workers received their food rations. The workers affectionately called him by his patronymic "our Mironych." Kirov had supported the plans for total collectivization without reservation, but he thought Stalin's methods for carrying them out were too drastic and thus dangerous. Kirov also opposed the argument of Stalin, Kaganovich and Molotov that the resistance of the "class enemy" would increase as collectivization and industrialization progressed. On the contrary, he argued that a truce between the government and, at least, the democratic strata of the population would become possible once the peasants had accustomed themselves to the *kolkhozes* and their standard of living had begun to rise. He warned against the danger of antagonizing broad masses of the people by indiscriminate use of terror, arrests and deportations. Like many others, he was particularly indignant at the deliberate creation of a widespread famine.

These disagreements became even more pronounced at the next plenary meeting of the Central Committee on January 7-12, 1933. Boris Nikolaevsky[17] tells how this meeting resolved "to send special commissions into the more important agricultural districts with special assignments to study the local situations and with special rights to free the arrested . . . one such commission, working in the Middle Volga region, was headed by Krylenko, the Chief Prosecutor of the Soviet Union and a member of the Central Committee; and his report made a deep impression in Moscow at that time, particularly the part dealing with the visit to the prison in Samara, where, to accommodate the arrested peasants, a many-storied cellar had been constructed underground; here lay thousands of peasants, the living alongside the dead."

One result of this plenary meeting was the decision to relax the terror in the villages by cancelling the sentences of deportation and by freeing many of the imprisoned peasants. (This is the decision documented in the "Instruction" of May 8th, 1933, previously mentioned in this chapter.)

The opposition to Stalin represented by Kirov continued to gain ground in 1933. Kirov himself was triumphantly elected delegate from Leningrad to the 17th Congress, and spontaneous street demonstrations took place in his honor. His reputation in the Politburo stood so high that the Congress decided to transfer him to Moscow and appoint him a secretary of the Central Committee with the special task of coordinating all ideological and propaganda work. This promotion meant, in effect, a new division of leadership between Stalin and Kirov.

This fact alone would have been enough to put the suspicious and wary Stalin on his guard. His mistrust was all the greater because the man who had become his colleague and to a certain degree his rival had, from 1932 onwards, successfully opposed his vengeful policies within the party. This was revealed in the episode of the so-called "Riutin plot."

In our account of the struggle between the Trotskyist "left" opposition and the Stalinist Central Committee, the name of Riutin—secretary of the Krasnopresny district of the Moscow Communist Party—figured as an active participant and ardent Stalinist, in the famous demonstration of November 7, 1927. Nevertheless, as collectivization became a fierce reality, Riutin, the son of a peasant from Siberia and a village teacher by profession, became an arch opponent of Stalin's general line and of Stalin personally. Bukharin's "Letter of an Old

Bolshevik" describes how Riutin collected around him a group of anti-Stalinists and wrote a lengthy statement of their views which soon began to circulate within the party in mimeographed form. In this statement, 50 pages, out of a total of 200, dealt with Stalin personally, representing him as the evil genius of the Bolshevik revolution, the man who would ruin both the revolution and the Communist movement. The statement called on the party to rid itself of Stalin if it did not wish itself to perish and the revolution to miscarry.

A copy of this statement soon fell into Stalin's hands, and drove him to such a rage that he demanded that Riutin be tried and executed for incitement to murder of a party leader. However, the other heads of the party were still mindful of Lenin's warning not to repeat the Jacobins' mistake of "devouring their own children." It was agreed that all kinds of punitive measures might be taken against oppositionists and other offenders against party discipline; it was conceded that an occasional execution might even be permitted if the victim happened to be someone on the fringes of the party or had been wrongly admitted to it. But to enforce the death penalty against a member of the inner circle, an old and tested Bolshevik—that seemed a betrayal of Lenin's legacy. In any case the GPU declined to act on Stalin's demands. Stalin, infuriated, put the case before the Politburo and the Central Committee at the stormy sessions of September 1932. He was defeated by the bloc led by Kirov, and including Ordzhonikidze, Kuibyshev, Kossior and Rudzutak. Riutin was not executed, but exiled to a remote area of Russia.

Two months later came what was undoubtedly the most politically significant event of Stalin's domestic life. On November 9, 1932, his young wife, Nadezhda Alliluyeva, was shot in the Kremlin. Various accounts indicate that she had been critical to some degree of the excesses of collectivization. Most authorities believe that Stalin killed her in a fit of rage.[18] The incident doubtless affected him personally, intensifying the pathological tendencies in his character. It became ever more difficult for him to retain his self-control.

In the next two years, Stalin clashed with the group led by Kirov on at least three other occasions. On still other occasions, doubtless, Stalin modified his policies in order to prevent the Kirov group from launching an all-out attack on his power. Disagreement was kept within the bounds of the ruling Central Committee, for the left and right oppositionists had only been defeated fairly recently, and the ruling faction remained united by belief in the correctness of the general line. That belief had been strengthened by the fact that, by the end of 1933, the party had indeed proved strong enough to carry out a vast social transformation which its critics had thought impossible. Perhaps Kirov and his associates believed that the concessions and compromises which they had urged on Stalin had insured the success of the general line of which he had indubitably been the chief architect.

Accordingly, at the 17th Party Congress (January 26 to February 10, 1934), the reception given Stalin was reminiscent of a Roman triumph. Every appearance of Stalin, every one of his words, every mention of his name, was greeted with tumultuous applause. Not only did his Politburo colleagues praise him highly, but all his former foes and critics were invited to the Congress as guest-delegates and each had to deliver a speech in which Stalin was glorified. Rightists like Bukharin, Rykov and Tomsky, leftists like Radek, Zinoviev, Preobrazhensky and Kamenev headed a parade of flagellants who repented their crimes and errors and hailed the great Stalin as the greatest theoretician of Marxism after Lenin and the great organizer and father of the peoples all over the world.

This was the so-called Congress of Victors, the congress of a totalitarian party that had in fact won a victory over a hundred million peasants as well as over a working class which, in theory, it represented. But did that victory represent, as the orators claimed, the triumph of socialism in Russia?

Opinions may differ on how successfully the Soviet government carried out its industrialization plans. It must be said that the industrialization of a country like Russia was without precedent and that mistakes were inevitable; now, in historical perspective, it seems quite immaterial which target figures were met and which were not, or by what percentage any given branch of industry fell below or exceeded its goal. What is beyond doubt is that the First Five-Year Plan and the succeeding Five-Year Plans resulted in a tremendous growth of industry despite all the mistakes, failures, shortcomings and miscalculations. It is also beyond doubt that, in creating large-scale industry, Stalin ruined Soviet agriculture, to the point where its low production menaced the health and thus also the productivity of the industrial workers. It is an indisputable consequence of Stalin's general line that the Soviet government has proved unable, even as late as 1961, to make agriculture keep pace with industry. The peasants' passive resistance, long after collectivization, has defeated every one of the state plans for agricultural development.[19] After three decades of collectivization, Soviet agriculture has been unable to match that of more advanced countries, particularly in the production and delivery of meat, dairy products, and other high-calorie foods. In the 1960s, the Soviet government was still struggling to regain the dietary levels of 1913 and 1928. In terms of strict economic efficiency, this was a high price to pay for heavy industry.

However, from the viewpoint of genuine socialist development—from the viewpoint, that is, not of the power of the Soviet state but of the welfare of the Soviet citizen—all the industrial, technical and economic achievements of the Soviet Union cannot alter their cost—the fact that the then half-starved Soviet people have had to pay for them in blood, privation and tears as no other civilized people has been called upon to do in modern times.

In the social calculus which Communism shares with fascism and some other modern movements, the yardsticks of success are technological progress, the power of the state and the nation's military strength—all opening up the prospect of dominating other peoples. In this philosophy, the state, governed and guided by a single party, becomes a goal in itself. It is a Hobbes' Leviathan of a much higher potency. Man, his freedom, his welfare, his happiness and his dignity are viewed as entirely secondary. No sacrifice is great enough to drive faster the Juggernaut which crushes under its wheels the men who fling themselves or are thrown in its path; they must perish in the belief that their sacrifice is "necessary."

The basic concept of this philosophy, which rests on the denial of the rights of man and the citizen, is that the masses must be ruled by force because they are unwilling to sacrifice themselves; they fail thereby to understand where their true happiness lies and must therefore be guided by the elite—the party—which knows best how to achieve the ultimate happiness of mankind. This philosophy flagrantly contradicts the philosophy of humanitarian socialism which inspired the entire socialist movement from Thomas More through Karl Marx.

Marx's doctrine is based on German classical philosophy, and in particular on principles formulated by the great humanitarian philosopher, Ludwig Feuerbach; Plekhanov, who translated Feuerbach into Russian, added a foreword in which he fully associated himself with Feuerbach's philosophy of social progress achieved by liberating and uplifting the individual. Since the 1860s, the entire labor movement throughout the world has been guided by that same philosophy, which is still professed by democratic socialists everywhere. Lenin's views in 1903 and the Bolshevik doctrine taught by Lenin and Trotsky in 1917 already contained many elements of totalitarian philosophy. Trotsky's theory of permanent revolution necessarily involved dictatorship from above, i.e., dictatorship by a revolutionary party rather than by the working class, acting as the majority of the nation. Mistrust of the working masses, who allegedly would never attain socialism on their own and who needed forceful mentors in the form of an organization of professional revolutionaries, emerges clearly from the organizational plans worked out by Lenin in 1903.

These Communist ideas, which had only begun to germinate in 1917 and in the years of transition from the NEP, became a bloody and gruesome reality under Stalin. In declaring unremitting war against Russia's peasant majority, in deliberately and drastically depressing the meager living standard of the workers in whose name he pretended to rule, Stalin crossed the Rubicon which henceforth was to separate irrevocably Bolshevik "Communism" from humanitarian and democratic socialism.

During the tragic years 1935-1938, when the totalitarian spiral was unfolding all over the land and Soviet Russia was enveloped in a bloody fog of mass arrests, executions and medieval tortures, when intellectual and political life came to a standstill—no one in the country itself or abroad was able to grasp the true historical meaning of the great tragedy developing before the eyes of the world.

The few European socialists who were observing closely, as far as it was possible, the developments behind the iron curtain—were misled by Stalin's "general line," allegedly introducing socialism in agriculture in the form of forcibly created collective farms and accelerated industrialization which was to transform the working class into serfs. Despite the official misinformation, they knew what kind of "socialism" it was. Yet they could not deny the success of collectivization in the countryside and the rapid growth of industrialization in the cities. A good many of them felt, in fact, that, historically speaking, Stalin, in spite of the appalling inhumanity of his methods, was creating in Russia the essential elements of a socialist economy. To be sure it was not democratic or humanitarian socialism: it was a terroristic, dictatorial socialism, but socialism nevertheless.

The foremost theoretician of the Austrian Socialist Party, Otto Bauer, wrote that in Europe two parallel processes of socialization were taking place—the experiment in democratic socialism, carried on by the Social Democratic parties of Europe and led by the Socialist and Labor International, and the Russian experiment in socialist tyranny.[20]

Neither of the trends, Bauer believed, could be eliminated or supplanted by the other, since both were firmly rooted in the historical past. He felt, therefore, that democratic socialists both in Europe and in Russia should recognize this reality and work together with the Russians in harmony when the right time came. Within a few years, Bauer predicted, Russia's general standard of living would be substantially raised and the economy would be shifted from heavy industry to the production of consumer goods. The Russian dictatorship would then be able gradually to relinquish its rule of terror and would finally evolve toward democracy. All that was necessary to achieve this goal was patience and mutual tolerance for a certain period of time. Thus the old controversy between Communism and Social Democracy would be eliminated and peaceful co-existence would be established in the world's labor movement.

Quite a few left-wing socialists in Europe accepted Bauer's thesis. The Russian socialists however—not only the right-wing fraction of Russian Mensheviks but also such notorious left-wingers as Dan,[20a] Yugov and others—disagreed completely with Bauer. They maintained that Bauer's concept was mere wishful thinking, a sheer utopia with no relation to reality.

The controversy between the proponents of Bauer's ideas and the Russian Social Democrats was given a new dimension by Rudolf

Hilferding, an eminent Marxist writer and author of *Das Finanzkapital* who advanced the theory that the Bolshevik regime was a new form of society which was neither socialism nor capitalism but belonged in the group of totalitarian states along with Hitler's Germany and Musssolini's Italy.[21]

Hilferding refuted the view of R. L. Worrall, a British Trotskyist. Worrall maintained that the Soviet economy had become actually a system of state capitalism, with the Soviet bureaucracy as its ruling class.[22] Hilferding demolished Worrall's concept in a few masterly strokes as he wrote:

> The concept of 'state capitalism' can scarcely pass the test of serious economic analysis. Once the state becomes the exclusive owner of all means of production, the functioning of a capitalist economy is rendered impossible by destruction of the mechanism which keeps the life-blood of such a system circulating. A capitalist economy is a market economy.

But a state economy or a managed economy must be a consumer's economy.

> ... it is no longer price but rather a state planning commission that now determines what is produced and how. Formally, prices and wages still exist, but their function is no longer the same. They no longer determine the process of production, which is now controlled by a central power that fixes prices and wages.[23]

Hilferding went on to show that the Soviet bureaucracy was never a ruling class but remained an obedient servant of the actual ruling group which, since October 1917, had been the Communist Party, or more exactly, the upper strata of the Communist Party apparatus. The Soviet bureaucracy, according to Hilferding, receives orders but does not give orders. The real power is concentrated in the hands of the leading group of Communists, and it is this group that shapes and plans the economy to suit its own ends. It is not the economy that dominates the state and the political order. It is, on the contrary, the state and the political machine of the ruling party that dominate the economy and the whole life of the nation. This situation existed since the first days of Soviet rule, when Lenin, Trotsky and a few other Bolsheviks "created the first totalitarian state in modern history ... even before the name was invented." "The totalitarian power lives by the economy but not for the economy ... it does not even live for the economic welfare of the classes it claims to represent." Hilferding adds: ". . . an analogy may be found in the era of the late Roman Empire, in the regime of the Praetorians and their emperors."

A different historical analogy was offered by K. A. Wittfogel in his book, *Oriental Despotism* (A Comparative Study of Total Powers. 1957, Yale University Press).

"The emergence of the state as an independent power," Hilferding goes on to say,

> greatly complicates the economic characterization of a society in which politics (i.e., state) play a determining role . . . From this point of view the controversy whether Soviet society is socialist or capitalist becomes immaterial.

It is neither, says Hilferding. It *"represents a totalitarian state economy . . ."*

The Bolshevik state, Hilferding maintains, "can hardly be called 'socialist,' for, to us, socialism is indissolubly linked to democracy. According to our concept, socialization of the means of production implies the freeing of the economy from the rule of one class and investing it in a society as a whole—a society which is democratically self-governed. We never imagined that the political form of that 'managed economy' which was to replace capitalist production for a free market, could be unrestricted absolutism . . ."[24]

When Engels wrote in his *Anti-Dühring* that under socialism the governing of people would be replaced by the administering of things, he could not foresee, as Hilferding pointed out, that the administration of things could be itself transformed into an unlimited "administering of people"—the source of monstrous power created by the modern totalitarian states.

Hilferding did not discuss the international aspect of Communist totalitarianism; but the full extent of the moral rift, which since then has divided Soviet Communism from democratic socialism, will be revealed with particular clarity if we examine the international situation at the time when Stalin's "general line" was carried out in Russia.

[1] Even on the top echelons of Stalin's machine some people were worried by the scope of this enterprise. Out of these considerations came the project of mobilizing a special division of 25,000 Communist city workers who would participate in the collectivization drive as organizers, propagandists and, if necessary, as auxiliary military units. These 25,000 volunteers played quite an important role physically and morally in the collec-

tivization drive. See Zombe, "Dvadtsatipiatitysiachniki," *Voprosyi Istorii*, No. 5, Moscow 1947. The writer of the article, an old Communist worker, explains to the reader of the Communist magazine that the collectivization drive was a social revolution necessary from the viewpoint of the proletariat but added that this was, of course, a "revolution from above" and not a voluntary movement of the peasants themselves.

[2] *Socialist Courier*, No. 6-7, 1930.

[3] Uprisings are known to have occurred in Pskov, Armavir (Transcaucasia), Shushe (Azerbaijan) and other Caucasian localities. Detailed reports of one uprising were published in the *Socialist Courier* (see the *Socialist Courier*, No. 12, p. 14, 1929 and No. 9, pp. 11, 15, and 16, 1930).

[4] *Economic Bulletin*, Prof. S. Prokopovich, 1931, No. 85, p. 11.

[5] Ph. I. Liashchenko, *History of the National Economy of the USSR*, Vol. 3, p. 368.

[6] See also M. Fainsod, *Smolensk Under Soviet Rule*. Harvard Univ. Press, 1958, p. 263.

[7] Some sinister indications about the methods by which the population of the prisons was reduced can be found in the story of Vinnitsa: in August 1943 the Germans who at that time occupied the Ukrainian city of Vinnitsa made a gruesome discovery. At the "Park for Culture and Recreation" of the former Soviet city, a huge mass grave was unearthed. The Germans invited neutral experts—including physicians from Scandinavia, Italy, Switzerland and other countries—to determine that it was not German propaganda, but a fact: 10,000 corpses were counted, all shot in the neck, the typical trade-mark of GPU executions. All the dead were Ukrainians or Russians; some of them had identification papers, photographs and letters in their clothes. To cover the crime, the GPU buried them in the square near the GPU building and erected the park over the mass grave. (The author has the testimony of a Russian military doctor, Dr. Georgi Aleksandrov, who at that time was a German prisoner of war, now in this country.)

[8] *Great Soviet Encyclopedia*, Vol. 5, first edition, 1927, p. 463.

[9] *Socialist Courier*, No. 14, July 26, 1930, pp. 6-8.

[10] Frank Lorimer, *The Population of the Soviet Union (History and Prospects)*. League of Nations, Geneva, 1946, p. 133.

[11] *Ibid.*, p. 138.

[12] Churchill, *Memoirs*, Vol. IV, *Hinge of Fate*, p. 498.

[13] Liashchenko, p. 327.

[14] See Gladkov's novel, *Cement*.

[15] S. Schwartz, *Labor in the USSR*, p. 144.

[16] *Pravda*, No. 63 of March 5, 1931. Quoted from Aleksandrov's book, p. 318.

[17] "The Murder of Kirov," *Socialist Courier*, No. 5, May 1956, p. 93.

[18] A truly reliable witness, personally known to the author, recalls that "toward the morning of November 9, 1932, the head of the Kremlin Hospital, Dr. K., was awakened by a telephone call from the Kremlin and asked to come immediately. On arrival, she saw the lifeless body of Alliluyeva on the floor. Nearby, leaning against the writing desk, stood Stalin, pale and stunned and almost insensible. On the desk lay the revolver. Alliluyeva never had a revolver." (*Novoye Russkoye Slovo*, December 21, 1949, article by M. Vishnyak, "Guile and Love.")

[19] N. Jasny, "Is the Seven-Year Plan Realistic?," *Socialist Courier*, 1959, No. 6, p. 113.

[20] O. Bauer, *Kapitalismus und Sozialismus nach dem Kriege*, Vol. 1. Vienna, 1931.

[20a] In the interest of historic truth I would like to add that a few years later Dan and his friends left the "Delegation Abroad" of the Menshevik group and completely revised their attitude toward Bolshevism. See: T. Dan, *Proischozhdenie Bolshevisma*. New York, 1946, pp. 455-490.

[21] R. Hilferding, "State Capitalism or Totalitarian State Economy," *Socialist Courier*, April 25, 1940. Hilferding's brilliant article was later published in the *Modern Review* (March 1947) and in *Verdict of Three Decades* (New York, 1949), an important book edited by Julian Steinberg.

[22] In the London magazine, *Left* (December 1939).

[23] Hilferding, *op. cit.*

[24] *Ibid.*

CHAPTER 16

The Changing International Situation

STALIN AND EUROPE

The relationship between Stalin's policies at home and abroad in the period between 1928 and 1934 is expressed in the somewhat cryptic phrase, "socialism in one country." The phrase reflected the belief of Stalin and his colleagues that the round of mass revolutions which had begun in 1917 was over; that the promise of a proletarian revolution in advanced Germany, which was to rescue Russia from backwardness, was illusory; and that, therefore, until the contradictions of capitalism revealed themselves anew, the best—indeed, the only—path to world revolution lay in the strengthening of Soviet power. The apparent "stabilization of capitalism" in the mid-Twenties lent urgency to the drive for industrialization and collectivization.

Following the Locarno Conference and Germany's entry into the League of Nations, relative calm was established over the continent of Europe—the post-Versailles order appeared stabilized. This period was marked by a simultaneous speeding up of economic development and the growth of the labor movement in various European countries. Economic progress varied from country to country and, in some countries, was accompanied by quite sharp social conflict.

A severe coal crisis hit England after the war. But the country soon recovered and the labor movement forged ahead to become one of the dominant political economic forces in the country. For the first time in British history, a Labour government was formed, headed by Prime Minister Ramsay Macdonald, Arthur Henderson, Philip Snowden and others. It was a minority government, and only lasted from

January to November 1924. But in 1926, Labour came into office a second time and, with the sharp decline of the Liberals, assumed the role of Britain's second party.

In Germany, economic progress was accompanied by an intensification of political conflicts, in which the German Communist Party played an active part, although it had temporarily given up the methods of putsch and uprising. However, the election of Field Marshal von Hindenburg to the presidency, following the death of Ebert, helped consolidate the Weimar regime for a while; all the right-wing and bourgeois parties, which had opposed the Social Democrat Ebert, were willing to support a regime headed by Hindenburg.

France and its Little Entente played the leading roles in Continental policy. England played a secondary role, beset by internal political troubles as well as increasing difficulties with her colonies—especially India, where the nationalists headed by Mahatma Gandhi engaged in a huge passive-resistance campaign aimed at achieving national independence.

Austria had become a large head with a small body, beset by chronic economic insolvency. The large and militant Social Democratic Party dominated the city of Vienna, but not the country at large. It was constantly forced to fight off the Christian Social Party, which owed its strength to the peasant provinces.

The problems of the newly-formed Czechoslovak state were met by a bloc formed by the National Socialists of Masaryk and Benes and the Social Democrats headed by Nemetz, Soukup and others.

In Italy, Mussolini and the Fascists remained in power. Italian socialists and Communists were only able to survive as small refugee groups abroad, most of them in France, England and Germany. At this time, too, Mussolini began to toy with plans to restore the former greatness of the Roman Empire.

The socialist movement in Europe made considerable strides. Despite the split of the old socialist parties caused by Zinoviev's 21 points, the Communist parties were very weak, except in France, Czechoslovakia and, in the nineteen-thirties, in Germany. The Socialist International, set up in Hamburg in May 1923, together with its associated Amsterdam International of the Trade Unions, occupied the dominant position in European labor.

For Europe's Social Democrats, the Soviet problem was primarily one of the interrelationship between Communism and Social Democracy. In this respect, the excesses of the Bolshevik terror and European Communism kept pushing the Social Democrats toward the right. In Russia itself, especially after Stalin's rule had began, the unceasing terror directed against the socialists and all other oppositionists constantly disturbed the consciences of the European socialist parties. At the top levels of the International, the representatives of the Russian, Georgian and other socialist parties were a constant reminder of the bleeding wound inflicted by anti-socialist terrorism which never ceased in Russia, even in the relatively quiet years—1924-27.[1]

At the same time, in such European countries as France, Germany, Austria, Czechoslovakia, and Belgium, a constant adaptation to democracy took place in the growing labor movements. This process made it necessary to re-examine the outmoded tactical and theoretical postulates on which European Social Democracy had been based before the First World War.

After the First World War, the workers, their unions and the Social Democratic parties began to play a most important role in national affairs. It was very difficult for any democratic government, even a conservative one, to run a country against or even without them. The socialist parties, especially if one includes the trade-union membership which followed the parties or co-operated with them, were numbered in the millions. Socialist representation in central and local legislative bodies had vastly increased and socialists held the majority in various localities and municipalities. In Poland and Czechoslovakia, to name but two examples, the socialist parties had played a significant, even a crucial role, in the very formation of these countries as national states (the PPS in Poland, and Masaryk's and Benes' National Socialists in Czechoslovakia).

The old concept of the social and political role of the working class in relation to the state, expressed in such dramatic formulas as "the proletariat has no Fatherland" and "the workers have nothing to lose but their chains," had become an anachronism in many countries even

*Affiliated Parties:**

Country	Party Membership	SOCIALISTS Popular Vote	Trade-Union Membership
1. Austria	698,181	1,517,251	737,277
2. Belgium	600,964	803,369	530,575
3. Czechoslovakia:			
Czech, S. D.	155,483	963,462	573,727
German, S. D.	67,459	506,750	573,979
4. Denmark	171,407	593,191	339,265
5. Finland	33,930	385,820	76,000
6. France	125,500	1,700,000	840,000
7. Germany	1,037,384	8,575,240	5,353,885
8. Great Britain	2,541,000	8,364,883	4,870,326
9. Holland	74,461	804,714	292,500
10. Sweden	276,474	873,931	599,208
11. Switzerland	46,500	226,000	180,000

* Taken from: *The 4th Labor and Socialist International,* Zurich, 1931.

before the War—increasingly, in this era of democratic progress all over the continent of Europe. These obsolete concepts (dating from the "Communist Manifesto" of 1848) stood in obvious contradiction to real life.

Pre-war socialists had believed that socialist and labor parties could not co-operate with bourgeois parties, political blocs, and government coalitions. This view, formulated in the resolution of the International Socialist Congress held in Paris in 1900, was now completely reversed. In several countries—Scandinavia, Germany, Belgium, Holland, Czechoslovakia—the Social Democratic parties joined in government coalitions with peasant, liberal and petty-bourgeois parties. The labor parties came to consider themselves an organic part of the state and nation. They modified their attitude towards the possibilities of social and political progress within the framework of a democratic-bourgeois state.

This new pragmatic approach of European socialism gave rise to a continuous re-examination of the old theories and programs inherited from the era before World War I. Such a pillar of orthodox Marxism as Karl Kautsky—who before the war had led a furious campaign against "revisionists" like Bernstein, David, Vandervelde and Jean Jaures—now took to revising obsolete concepts and formulas him-

COMMUNISTS

Represent. in the Centr. Parl.	*Party Membership*	*Popular Vote*	*Trade-Union Membership*
72 of 165		21,004	0
70 " 187	500	—	1
39 " 300	35,500	753,444	30
21 " 300			
61 " 149	400	3,656	0
66 " 200	Communist Party illegal		
109 " 612	30,000	1,000,000	12
143 " 577	134,000	4,590,160	77
279 " 615	2,000	—	—
24 " 100	Unknown	67,482	2
90 " 230	12,000	149,096	8
50 " 198	4,000	14,816	2

self. Kautsky did this, in 1922, in a book devoted to the new program of German Social Democracy, and in 1927, in two big volumes on historical materialism. This new revisionism was marked not only by a re-evaluation of the old values in the light of the latest social developments but also by the need for a theoretical rearming of European Social Democracy in the struggle against the political and ideological aggression of world Communism.

In this context of democratic stabilization, peaceful economic development, and socialist "revisionism" in Europe, where could the Kremlin look for the "new round of wars and revolutions" which Lenin had once mentioned and of which Stalin spoke constantly? For a time, the Bolsheviks saw China as the great hope. But Chiang Kai-shek's break with the Communist Party and the slaughter of its Shanghai militants put an end to this hope in 1927. There was little hope for Communism in Japan and still less in India, where the Tolstoyan philosophy of Gandhi and the Fabian outlook of Nehru dominated the independence movement.

Communism's opportunity, therefore, had to be created in Europe—if not by the will of its workers, then out of the "contradictions of capitalism" as intensified by Soviet foreign policy and Comintern strategy.

There seems little doubt that by 1928, when the NEP was abandoned, Stalin had definitely ceased to believe that the proletariat of the western countries was capable of making a revolution. Later, in his report to the 18th Party Congress, in March 1939, Stalin admitted that capitalism in the more advanced countries in the world continued to exist not because of the inherent force of the system but mainly because the workers of these countries did not have enough faith in their own strength: "The capitalists and their agents succeeded in poisoning the mind of the workers with the venom of doubt and disbelief" (*Minutes of the 18th Congress,* p. 38). He no longer reckoned that a revolutionary situation could be created by the working masses alone—even with moral, organizational and material support from Moscow. He became quite scornful of the Comintern and its potentialities. (W. W. Krivitsky has reported that among intimates, Stalin always spoke of the Comintern as a racket. "How is your racket?" he would ask.)

But if socialism could not be achieved through the revolutionary efforts of the working masses in the west, how else could it triumph? So far as we can reconstruct Stalin's ideas of that period, it appears that his alternative was to carry the revolution into the west (and the east) on the bayonets of the Red Army. Just as the French Revolution had developed from a Jacobin phase to one in which the revolution had been brought to other countries by the armies led by the former Jacobin, Napoleon Bonaparte, so the Soviet Union would install world Communism through its own power as a state. This required a more dynamic revolutionary regime as well as a more aggressive foreign policy. It was necessary first to transform the Soviet Union into an adequate, technological, industrial and military base. The NEP was not suitable for such a mission.

At the same time, the Kremlin had to act to check the progress of democratic socialism in the western countries, and to foster the international contradictions and rivalries which appeared to have abated. For a Europe at peace, with the prospect of democratic-socialist governments in several countries, was intolerable to the Bolshevik dictatorship and its international ambitions. In examining the prophecy that "the stabilization of capitalism had ended," made by the Sixth Comintern Congress in 1928, it is impossible now to tell whether it was made out of genuine conviction or was, rather, what philosophers call a "self-fulfilling prophecy"—that is, a prophecy made in the deliberate hope that it would itself influence the conditions with which it dealt in the direction indicated. There can be little doubt, however, that the policy of combatting Social Democracy as the main enemy—under the slogan "down with social fascism"—had the effect of destroying German democracy and bringing Nazism to power. And this event ended the post-Locarno "stabilization" which the Kremlin feared and raised new hopes for a "new round of wars and revolutions." From 1930 to 1945, the fates of Hitler and Stalin were intricately, but indissolubly, linked.

The German Crisis and the Growth of Nazism

Hitler's rise to power has been ably described by Konrad Heiden, John Wheeler-Bennett and other historians. In this volume, we must concentrate on the responsibility borne by the German Communists and the Kremlin for Nazism's triumph.

The first event to note is the German Presidential election of 1925. In the initial campaign, the rightist parties formed an alliance called the Reichsbloc and backed the candidacy of Dr. Karl Jarres, the conservative mayor of the city of Duisburg. The Social Democrats nominated Otto Braun, the Prussian Prime Minister. The Catholic "Center" Party nominated one of its leaders, Wilhelm Marx; the Nazis put forward Field Marshal von Ludendorff; and the Communists nominated Ernst Thaelmann. The results were: Jarres—10,400,000 votes, Braun—7,800,000, Marx—3,900,000, and Thaelmann—1,900,000.

Since no candidate had won a majority, a second ballot was needed. At this juncture, von Hindenburg was substituted for Jarres and gathered 14,600,000 votes. The Social Democrats supported the Centrist Marx, who received 13,600,000. The Communists, however, failed to withdraw Thaelmann, who received 1,900,000. Had the German Communists joined forces with the democratic left and center parties, Marx and not Hindenburg would have been elected president of Germany in 1925. History might well have followed a very different course.

This became increasingly clear after the economic and financial crisis radiated from the great recession in the United States to Europe after 1929. Germany's economic situation deteriorated rapidly, and the orthodox fiscal policies of Chancellor Bruening failed to help. The number of unemployed reached a total of more than six million in 1932, an incredible number for a country with a population of approximately 66,000,000. The streets were full of desperate people, many from the lower middle classes, with no way of earning a living. Young people rushed headlong into the ranks of the extremists movements, Communist as well as Nazi.

German National Socialism was basically a nationalistic protest against Germany's defeat in the First World War. Its chief demand was that Germany must struggle against enslavement by the Allies, who allegedly were ruining the economy through reparations and were turning a powerful empire into a second-rate country.

The Nazis' main appeal was to the "declassed" elements from the middle classes which had been ruined during the 1923 inflation; to youths of the lower-middle income group who had been deprived of the possibility of a career in the army, the colonies or foreign trade by the Versailles settlement; to unemployed intellectuals and intellectual failures who could not find an outlet for their talents under the Weimar regime, where they had to compete with the children of trade-union workers and peasants; to the former officers of World War I; and, finally, to the unemployed, whose numbers kept increasing catastrophically month after month through 1930, 1931 and 1932.

German National Socialism was not a reaction of the capitalist class against an approaching proletarian revolution, as has been averred by the Communists and by some left-wing socialists. Nazism, to the extent that it was ever made intelligible in programs and theories, never aimed at the preservation of a capitalist society and the maintenance of the sacred principles of private capitalism. Hitler's Twenty-Five Points show clearly that he was no champion of social conservatism but, if anything, a revolutionary of sorts, the incarnation of an elemental protest against the reign of capital which he declared to be a typically Jewish system. Hitler opposed monopoly in trade which, to the small shopkeepers who supported him, was symbolized by the expanding department-store chains, many of them belonging to Jewish firms.

Nazism was, thus, primarily a movement of revenge against the west which, among other things, used social radicalism in its demagogic propaganda, a social radicalism which took the form of a nationalistic rather than a Marxist socialism. Its program promised immediate repudiation of the Versailles Treaty, immediate restoration of military conscription and the re-creation of a powerful German army (built around the Reichswehr created by von Seeckt and von Schleicher with Moscow's assistance), and immediate cessation of reparations payments.

One must not slight the fact that this program found little mass support until the Great Depression. In 1928, Hitler seemed nothing more than the leader of a splinter sect. The Nazis scored their first significant victory in the September 1930 elections to the Reichstag. (The Communists also registered a gain but only of 23 seats as compared with the Nazis' 95.) Nazi clubs for young people then began to spring up in all sorts of places, including boys' and even girls' secondary schools. At the same time, the official Reichswehr forces supported all kinds of Nazi organizations which sported a variety of caps, badges and flags but all of which displayed the swastika. The older groups were formed into illegal paramilitary formations and trained in the use of weapons by Reichswehr officers. They wore civilian clothes and disguised themselves as teachers of gymnastics or sport coaches. The tang of civil war filled the air.

The Social Democrats and trade unions had, as early as 1924, organized a force for the support of the republic called the Reichsbanner, made up of republican war veterans, as opposed to the right-wing veterans of the Stahlhelm. As the Nazis grew in strength, the Reichsbanner was re-organized into the Iron Front, a paramilitary, uniformed force with a red-black-and-gold (the republican colors) arm band and its own emblem: three arrows. This organization contained at least five to six million members. It did not have too many weapons, but everyone knew where the weapons would come from if they were required.

The republican and democratic forces were in the strongest position in Prussia, the largest German state with two-thirds of the population of Weimar Germany. For several years, Prussia was governed by a bloc composed of the Catholic Center, the Democrats, and the Social Democrats. Throughout this period, the Prussian Prime Minister was Otto Braun, a Social Democrat and a man of strong character. The Minister of the Interior, who headed the Prussian police force of 50,000, was another Social Democrat, Karl Severing, also a determined and able man. Severing purged the police force of reactionary elements in most Prussian towns, and the police chiefs in almost all the large cities were Social Democrats or members of the Center. Many police officers belonged to the Social Democratic Party and even more were members of the Social Democratic trade unions. In an emergency, the Iron Front could have obtained arms from the depots of the Prussian police, and its members could have been made auxiliary police officers.

The Communists also created their own revolutionary militia, the Red Front. They, too, had their own badges, a special greeting—a raised clenched fist—and hidden weapons which they obtained by various means. One of their slogans was "strike the fascist in the face," which contributed mightily to the disorders on which Hitler counted and which undermined the government's authority among the middle class elements interested mainly in internal peace.

At the same time, the Communists joined with the Nazis in opposition to all existing authorities. The opposition ultimately forced the dissolution of the Reichstag and facilitated rule by Presidential decree—setting an unfortunate precedent. Nazis and Communists also collaborated in opposition to the Braun-Severing government in Prussia, and to the Social Democratic municipal government of Berlin. Communist spokesmen continually repelled proposals for "working class unity" of Social Democrats, Catholics and Communists against the Nazi menace.

Stalin justified the Communists' *de facto* alliance with the Nazis on the basis of the notion: "After Hitler, us." The theory[2] was that, after the fall of the main enemy—the Social Democrats or the "social fascists"—the Communists would be able to cope with Hitler quite easily even if he did come to power temporarily. Within a short time, this theory went on, Hitler's mad policy would turn the German masses against him. The Social Democrats having demonstrated their inability to cope with the Nazis, the masses would join the Communists. Then the Communist Party would head a broad popular movement, overthrow Hitler and establish a Soviet regime in Germany.

In fact, Stalin was not quite so naive. He knew that, after the defeat of the Social Democrats, no Communist revolt could possibly prevail against the powerful Nazi organization supported by the new German army. Stalin's real policy was based not on a revolt against the Nazis but on the hope that, once in power, Hitler would immediately proceed to realize the aims of the German military and the nationalists dedicated to the destruction of the Versailles system. Stalin reckoned that, ideological differences notwithstanding, there was a solid basis for co-operation between a Nazi Germany and Soviet Russia: fundamental antagonism toward the western democracies.

Thus came 1932—unemployment rising steadily, Nazi and Communist propaganda against the "system" increasing in intensity, three private armies (Socialist, Communist, Nazi) in the streets, the orthodox conservative policies of Chancellor Bruening growing steadily more irrelevant, the Reichswehr—in the person of General Kurt von Schleicher, an apt pupil of von Seeckt—edging closer to power in the Presidential Palace.

President von Hindenburg was by then a very old man incapable of rapid decisions. For a long time he had looked down with aristocratic scorn upon the uncouth Nazis, and refused to take them seriously. He would not consider even the possibility of handing over limited power to a man like Hitler, with his hysterical outpourings, his lack of moderation and complete absence of a sense of statesmanship in the Bismarckian tradition.

Hindenburg epitomized the attitude of the aristocratic old nationalists of Prussia who dominated the Reichswehr as well as respectable German conservatism generally. These forces received a bitter shock in the elections of the spring of 1932. The Nazi candidate for President this time was Hitler himself. The left and center parties (except the Communists) united behind Hindenburg in what was called the Great Coalition, comprised of the Social Democrats, the Democrats, the Center and smaller moderate groups. In the first ballot, no candidate obtained an absolute majority: Hindenburg obtained 18,600,000 votes, Hitler 11,300,000 votes, and the Communist Thaelmann 5,000,000 votes. At the second ballot, Hindenburg was elected with 19,300,000 votes against Hitler's 13,400,000 and Thaelmann's 3,500,000 votes. As many as 1,500,000 voters who had voted Communist on the first ballot probably became frightened and switched to Hindenburg. But 3,500,000 Communists still remained faithful to the Comintern principle: "the worse the better."

That a former Austrian corporal could muster over 13,000,000 votes against Field Marshal von Hindenburg marked a virtual landslide for the nationalist extremism represented by the Nazis. The entire face of the Reichstag had been changed since 1930: a considerable section was filled with young people in Nazi shirts, the swastika on their arm bands, arrogant and rude.

Good German *burghers* were shocked by the Nazis' wild speeches in which they demanded a St. Bartholomew's night to destroy their opponents. It was obvious, however, that the Nazis had strength behind them and this brought them a certain consideration even from those who were repelled by their ways. The big capitalists and industrialists had begun looking at the Nazis with interest in 1936, as a definite factor in politics which they could possibly utilize to their advantage. They were attracted, if not by Nazi theory, at least by that part of Nazi practice aimed at the "fat bureaucrats" of the trade unions. These big industrialists were not worried by the Nazis' social demagogy, which was mostly directed against Jews and referred more to commerce than to big industry. The Nazis never spoke of nationalizing plants and of handing them over to the management of the workers, as the Social Democrats and trade unions did. The industrialists connected with the Reichswehr and illegal armament were fully aware of Hitler's plans to recreate Germany's military might. These plans held out the promise of a fantastic increase in arms manufacture and government contracts as well as a huge leap forward in Germany's international prestige.

The Nazis were clever in changing masks, in making use of varied groups, in promising different and often contradictory things to different people, in gaining the confidence of the banks, even those whose main depositors were Jewish. They drew close to big industrialists, especially to steel magnates who put at their disposal the sums necessary for large-scale propaganda and for maintaining Hitler's vast private army.

The only hope, therefore, of checking Hitler lay with the parties of the left and center. Yet they, too, ultimately proved unequal to the task. There is a striking analogy between the attitude of the socialist and bourgeois parties toward the Russian Bolsheviks in 1917-20 and the attitude of the German Social Democratic and bourgeois parties before the Nazis took over. In both cases, neither those who sympathized nor those who opposed these regimes fully realized what a totalitarian dictatorship was; what forces, potentialities and resources it possessed; and how radically it could transform a country. In the Russia of 1917, not a single political group, from the right extremists to the left extremists, ever grasped, even at the last moment, what a victory of Lenin and Trotsky would bring in its wake. In the Germany of the 1930s, neither the rightists nor the moderates nor the Social Democrats ever succeeded in imagining what a victory by Hitler would mean to Germany.

When the Nazis began to rise in Germany, the only people in socialist circles who fully understood the nature and future course of the Nazis were—strange to say—the Russian Mensheviks who were refugees in Germany. There are documents, memoirs and factual evidence to demonstrate that these Russian emigrés, who had experienced the rise and victory of Bolshevism, rightly warned the German Social Democrats as well as others in both Germany and France, that a totalitarian dictatorship was imminent, that it would destroy every trace of freedom and democracy in Germany, rule by terror, and energetically prepare for a new war. "The Nazis," we used to tell our German comrades," are not the classical reaction against the workers' victories. At this time, they are only an embryo—although a rapidly growing one—of a totalitarian dictatorship whose only political purpose and historical task is to unleash a war of revenge against the west and set out to conquer the world."

This writer went to Zurich, from Berlin, to attend the meeting of the Executive Committee of the Socialist International in March 1933, a few days after the Reichstag fire. After giving a detailed report on the situation in Germany, he ended his speech with the words of the Good Soldier Schweik, the hero of the famous Czech novel: "And so, my friends, we shall meet again at 6 p.m., after the *Second* World War." The German comrades, however, stubbornly refused to understand the meaning of what was happening before their eyes. They considered the Nazis to be a temporary boil, a kind of mass psychosis which had taken possession of the Germans as a result of inflation and economic crisis, and they thought that a wise and careful policy would enable them to overcome the Nazi infection. So they were not disposed to act with determination, to take revolutionary steps, to adopt the radical measures which the Russian Mensheviks advised them to take.

Much of what the German democrats said was quite correct. In the first place, the Social Democrats and the trade unions had at their disposal the 6,000,000-man Iron Front, with the expectation of arms from the Prussian police force. When the time came, Severing would give the signal to march. "Our Berlin *Polizeipresident*, Grzezinsky, and his lads will show the Nazis what's what," declared the Prussian deputy, Heilmann, at a conference between the representatives of the International and the leader of the Reichsbanner.

But after the Nazi and Communist gains in the elections to the Landtag in the spring of 1932, the Braun-Severing government of Prussia lost its majority. On the motion of Wilhelm Pieck, the Communists and the Nazis won a vote of non-confidence in the government (they mustered 253 votes out of 400), and the whole scheme upon which the Social Democratic strategy had been built went up in smoke. The Nazi-Communist majority in the new Landtag, it is true, could not possibly form a new government, and the Braun-Severing ministry could remain in power until a new election. But Franz von Papen, a diplomat and well-known industrialist, was already Chancellor. Close to Hindenburg, he played along with Hitler, whom he thought he could easily manage and "civilize." The ruling group, headed by von Schleicher and von Papen, decided to send Dr. F. Bracht, Mayor of Essen, to dismiss the old Prussian government and assume power as provisional administrator of Prussia. This was the last moment for the Social Democrats and the Iron Front. Braun and Severing could have rebuffed Bracht, declared his appointment unconstitutional, mobilized the Iron Front, and armed it with the weapons still in the hands of Severing, Grzezinsky and the other socialist police chiefs. They could have called a general strike and forced the government of the Reich to choose between backing down or unleashing a civil war.

That memorable July night, representatives of the Social Democratic Party and Iron Front came to Berlin from all over the country. A long and painful conference took place in the *Vorwaerts* building. The main opponents of any move that might possibly be interpreted as illegal were the trade-union chiefs, headed by Leipart and others. They insisted that, above all, it was necessary to preserve the foundations of German democracy. If they were the first to violate them (a refusal to obey the government of the Reich could, under certain conditions, be interpreted as illegal), their entire position would lose its moral strength and they would become the violators instead of defenders of the Constitution.

Others pointed out that, in view of the fact that the working class was split, the Iron Front would not only be opposed by the Nazis but also by the Red Front, which seemed to have formed at least a *de facto* bloc with the Nazis. The whole strategy of the Iron Front was based on the idea of fighting a Nazi *coup,* i.e., fulfilling the role of the defender of the Constitution and democracy. Behind this idea was the belief that Hindenburg, von Papen and von Schleicher would not, of their own free will, call upon Hitler to take office and that the impatient demagogue would try to seize power through mass revolts.

But now, things were taking a very different turn. The Nazis had not attempted to stage a revolt; all they had done was to bring down the government constitutionally—through the ballot. The government of the Reich had acted with full legality in appointing a Reichskommissar to act as caretaker for a fallen Prussian government. "What legal reason is there for us to come out into the streets?" the opponents of such a step kept asking.

Of course, with sufficient will, a very just reason could have been found. The appointment of a commissioner was not mandatory. The Prussian government, which had been in power for a long time, could have carried on in a "caretaker" status for a few more months, as was usual in parliamentary regimes all over the world. Besides, the Iron Front could at the very least have staged a huge and perfectly legal demonstration against von Papen's arbitrary decision.

But, among the Social Democrats, the advocates of inaction prevailed. The leaders of the party insisted that Hitler would not be called to office and that his popularity and strength had already begun to decline. In the second half of 1932, unemployment had just begun to decrease and the Nazis actually lost votes between the July and the November 1932 elections to the Reichstag. They now had fewer deputies in the Reichstag. Some of Hitler's more cautious financiers had begun to withhold their contributions; and within the Nazi party, sharp clashes had occurred between the group led by the Strasser brothers and Hitler, and also between Hitler and Captain Ernst Roehm. It became known that Hitler had run into financial difficulties, and that the Nazis were not paying the bills of the printing presses which issued their literature in enormous quantities.

However, just as these Nazi reverses began in the country at large, Hitler's stock among the immediate entourage of the President shot unexpectedly upward. By this time, the clique around Hindenburg had completely isolated him from the outside world. This clique included Oskar Hindenburg, the President's son; Meisner, secretary of the Chancellory, an unscrupulous civil servant; von Papen and von Schleicher. It would serve no useful purpose to analyze here all the unsavory ingredients of the "witches' brew" which was cooking in the last months of 1932 and at the beginning of 1933 in Hindenburg's palace: intrigues, treachery, treason, blackmail and big lies which were the specialty of the supreme chef, the master of intrigue, von Schleicher.

However, the main factor which kept the leaders of the Social Democratic Party from acting was not von Schleicher's misinformation but their own underestimation of Nazi dynamism. Germany, they said, was no Russia, and it was wrong to expect events to follow a similar pattern there. They also said that the devil (Hitler) was not as black as he was painted. Even if Hitler were to be appointed to a government position, it would only be a secondary one and, caught in the mesh of German parliamentarianism, he would gradually lose his grip on the masses. Even German Jews, who were directly threatened by Hitler, remained relatively unperturbed by his threats, repeating that Germany was a land of law, order and culture and that there was no need to expect horrors to occur there. The Communists, until the last moment, confidently expected to reap the whirlwind.

At last, the intrigues carried on around Hindenburg brought Hitler to power. On January 31, 1933, Hindenburg entrusted Hitler with the post of Reichschancellor. Until the very last moment, the leaders of the Nazi Party themselves were by no means sure of final success. Konrad Heiden describes how, in the Nazi headquarters in the flashy Hotel Kaiserhof, the Nazi leaders, armed with powerful binoculars, watched the entrance door of the Chancellor's Mansion to gauge from Hitler's facial expression whether he had won or not. And while they were all still gathered by the window with their glasses, the door opened and, with tears pouring from his eyes, Hitler entered the room.[3]

That same night, 30,000 Nazi storm troopers staged a torchlight victory parade to mark the victory of their Fuehrer.

What followed is all too well known. In the first few weeks many people were arrested and killed, and the Reichstag was set on fire. The Communists were accused of the crime and, in the interests of "security," the Constitution was abolished, the dictatorship was established, and everything fell into the pattern of a terroristic dictatorship by a single, totalitarian party.

[1] R. Abramovitch and I. Tseretelli, *Der Terror gegen die Sozialisten in Soviet-Russland und Georgien,* Berlin, 1925.

[2] The author has at his disposal documents which establish that such really were the theoretical justifications offered by the Soviet Ambassador in Berlin, Mr. Khinchuk, and by the German Communist leaders for their queer flirtation with Hitler. There is the testimony of Friedrich Stampfer, the former Editor-in-Chief of the Social Democratic newspaper, *Vorwaerts,* as well as a letter received by the author from the Mayor of Hamburg, Max Brauer, a former worker and an old-time Social Democrat, who in 1932 was trying to explain to Khinchuk the real situation in Germany.

[3] Heiden, *Der Fuehrer,* p. 535.

CHAPTER 17

The Totalitarian Spiral

Purge of the Technical Intelligentsia

If Stalin had kept a diary, he would have marked January 31, 1933 as a red-letter day. For this was not only a day of triumph for Hitler, but also a turning point for Stalin, who had foreseen the course of events in Germany and had doomed the Weimar Republic by ordering the Communists in the Prussian Diet to vote down the Braun-Severing government, thus opening the door for Hitler to become Chancellor. Hitler in 1933, of course, was not yet ready for the major European war which Stalin expected, but Stalin knew that he had no time to lose in preparing his country, his army and his party for the greatest test of his career.

Stalin's first task was to silence the Russian intelligentsia, which, in the Twenties was still trying to remain independent of the Kremlin. Not only ideologists and politicians but even the technical intelligentsia tried to raise its voice.

With the launching of collectivization and all its chaos, the party began to seek scapegoats for the failures of its grandiose plans. In the early trials, from 1928 to 1934, the scapegoats were "class enemies" in Russia and abroad—capitalists, manufacturers, former owners of nationalized enterprises and their "agents" who, according to Soviet propaganda, were organizing conspiracies for wrecking and sabotage in the Soviet Union. The defendants in the early trials were engineers, economists and plant managers who allegedly had been bribed by former factory owners living abroad to engage in various forms of wrecking and sabotage and who were made to shoulder the blame for all Soviet mismanagement in the field of industrial construction.

To judge by the Soviet press, the first example of this kind of show-trial was the case of setting fire to the Dubrov industrial complex. This case was tried by a court martial, whose chairman, Ulrich, stated that the court had "established" that the arsonist had acted on the orders of the former owners of the plant living abroad. The framework of the next trial, the Don mines case, was the same: the former mine owners and managers had allegedly distributed large sums through agents for purposes of sabotage and wrecking.[1] Dozens of people were jailed and many were threatened with court martial and capital punishment.

Basically, all of the trials in this series were staged along the same lines. Foreign money and foreign espionage were darkly hinted at, but in no trial was any genuine evidence brought forward. With monotonous regularity, the accused were tried and convicted solely on the basis of their own "confessions." The proceedings were so many judicial tragi-comedies—staged by the prosecution, the GPU, and the accused themselves, who were forced to go along for fear of reprisals against themselves and their families.

In some cases, this procedure would backfire. Thus, one of the accused in an early trial was a "German agent," Koster, who was alleged to have supplied enormous sums to certain engineers. It later developed that Koster was in the first place not a German but a Soviet citizen, and that he had not given away any money; the German engineers who had worked with Koster were able to return to Germany due to the intervention of the German government. During the Don mines trial, frequent references were made to Riabushinsky, a big industrialist well known in Tsarist Russia, who was alleged to have transferred vast sums to Russia for wrecking and sabotage. Professor Ramzin, an important figure in engineering circles, offered a "sincere confession" in which he told in detail about the amounts he had received from Riabushinsky, on what dates and for what purposes. In the course of the trial, however, it was shown that Riabushinsky had died years before, so that Ramzin's entire testimony was seen to be a sheer fabrication, suggested to him by the GPU investigator. The prosecution then hastily dug up a son or nephew of Riabushinsky, who had no money or connections and had never been an industrialist; the dead man's part was reassigned to this newcomer, and the trial calmly continued as if nothing had happened.

These public trials were accompanied by widespread terror which was not publicized. A well-informed correspondent of the *Socialist Courier* (No. 6-7, April 3, 1931) reported:

> Of the 35,000 engineers in the country, a figure which includes the latest graduates, over 7,000 have been arrested by the GPU. All of them have been accused of wrecking under the notorious Article 58. Confessions of crimes they never committed are being extorted from them by various means. Very few manage to hold out. Most of those who resist for any length of time commit suicide or are driven to insanity. Those with stronger nerves are summarily shot or are sentenced to long terms of imprisonment in concentration camps by a GPU board.[2]

A special case in this series of trials was the so-called "Menshevik trial" of 1931.

The Menshevik Trial

The crusade against the technical intelligentsia was undertaken largely with an eye on political gains to be achieved on the home front. Later, Stalin conceived a political trial that would, above all, produce strong repercussions abroad. After lengthy preparations, the necessary groundwork had been laid for the "Menshevik trial," officially referred to in the Soviet press as the "Trial of a counter-revolutionary Menshevik organization." It was held in Moscow, March 1 through 9, 1931.

The trial, as planned, was to achieve a threefold objective. It was to demoralize politically the Menshevik Party, which no longer had any broad following (but still enjoyed a measure of influence among the intellectuals and in some workers' circles). The second goal was to discredit the Mensheviks in the eyes of European workers and in the Labor and Socialist International (LSI). The trial, it was thought further, would deal a crippling blow to the LSI itself, since it would bring to light the political misdeeds and counter-revolutionary activities of the Mensheviks sponsored by LSI. By 1931, Stalin had new reasons for his bitter dislike of the Mensheviks and the LSI. From the very start of forced collectivization the Mensheviks had launched a vigorous campaign abroad, denouncing the strong-arm methods of coercion used against the peasants.

In the spring of 1930, this writer, then touring the USA as lecturer on Soviet Russia, spoke of the collectivization of agriculture at every public appearance throughout the country.

In May 1930 the Menshevik Delegation Abroad submitted to the LSI a memorandum which described Soviet policy with regard to the peasants as utterly objectionable and without justification.

The memorandum ended in an appeal to the world's proletariat and the International to voice a vigorous protest against the detrimental and dangerous policy of the Bolshevik dictatorship.

At a meeting of the Executive Committee of the LSI in Zurich (May 11-30, 1930), after an opening address delivered by this writer and speeches by Otto Bauer and T. Dan, the Executive Committee approved by unamimous vote the text of an appeal to the Soviet government and to the workers and peasants of Russia. The appeal, which was published in the socialist press throughout the world, pointed to the grave danger implicit in Stalin's peasant policy, which imperiled both the Russian revolution and the people of Russia: "This policy signified an open break with the peasantry and, if continued, was bound to drive the vast peasant population, including its poorest elements, toward a counter-revolution."

The LSI appeal ended in the following words:

"In this effort to save the revolution, the hearts of the socialist proletarians the world over will beat in unison with the hearts of the Soviet workers. In the name of this proletariat the LSI is always ready to extend a helping hand to the fellow workers of the Soviet Union. Moreover, should reactionary world capitalism attempt a counter-revolution, taking advantage of your present difficulties, we shall oppose such an attempt with all our strength."

To achieve its overall purpose, Stalin's Moscow trial had to establish the fact that the Mensheviks no longer represented a socialist political party but had degenerated into a counter-revolutionary organization, subsidized by foreign agencies. Menshevik intellectuals on the staff of Soviet economic organizations had earned a good reputation as hard-working, conscientious men. Dzherzhinsky, at one time head of all economic agencies, spoke very highly of the Mensheviks.[3] Now these loyal men were to be "exposed" as deliberate saboteurs, wreckers and foreign spies, whose job was to disrupt the economic life of the country.

Dozens of Mensheviks, some of them key men in Soviet economic agencies—intellectuals, workers, writers—were subjected for months to relentless interrogation in order to obtain the desired testimony, prepared in advance by the GPU investigators under the supervision of the chief prosecutor, N. Krylenko.

The trial opened in Moscow with much pomp, on March 1, 1931. Among the fourteen men in the dock were old Mensheviks: V. G. Groman, a well-known economist, highly respected in government circles; V. V. Sher, for many years not active in the party, now holding a key post in the State Bank; A. M. Ginsburg, member since 1928 of the All-Russian Council of National Economy, also member of the commission for revising the scheduled figures of the State Economic Plan—a man dedicated to his work in the Soviet economic organizations and long out of touch with the party (he had become, specifically, a prominent figure in the field of metallurgy); N. N. Sukhanov, a well-known writer, co-editor of Maxim Gorki's publication, *Novaya Zhizn* (The New Life), who for a short time, in 1918, thought of himself as a Menshevik, but later came out with a blistering attack on the party; Fin-Yenotayevsky, the renowned economist and financial expert, who was never a Menshevik and had taken no part in any political activity; M. P. Yakubovich, a Menshevik until 1921, who later drifted away from political work and the party, and now held an important position in the Ministry of Domestic Commerce; A. L. Sokolovsky, who had been a member of the Central Committee of the United Jewish Socialist Party until 1920.

The rest of the defendants had the same tenuous relationship with the Menshevik Party, except I. I. Rubin, professor at Moscow University, who had actually been a member of the Social Democratic Bund and a Menshevik until about 1923, and in the following years kept in touch with the party. The only defendant at the trial who had in effect been active in the underground Menshevik organization was Ickov, a veteran party member since 1901. Deported by the Bolsheviks, Ickov remained in exile for many years and did not return to Moscow until 1928. Ickov had actually corresponded with the Menshevik

Delegation Abroad, sent reports and received letters from the members, of a personal as well as political nature. This lone activist was made to appear as the head of a far-flung underground organization. To render the exaggeration more plausible, the GPU decided to build up Ickov's tieup with the Menshevik Delegation Abroad to a more significant level, not only through his correspondence but by associating his name with an alleged trip to Russia made by R. Abramovitch.

According to the charges, which were corroborated by the defendants' testimony, the Socialist International, partly because it was "aware of its own weakness" and partly under the influence of the Menshevik Delegation—Dan, Abramovitch, Garvi, Nikolaevsky and others—had adopted a new policy line which called for aiding a foreign intervention in Russia, preparing the ground for a popular uprising, carrying on acts of sabotage and espionage in collaboration with foreign intelligence agencies, etc. To further these plans, R. Abramovitch, provided with a German passport, allegedly went to Moscow, after numerous conferences and consultations with his colleagues in the international socialist movement—with Kautsky, Emil Vandervelde, then chairman of the LSI, Leon Blum, Hilferding, Breitscheid, and others (cited from the testimony of Groman and Berlatsky, pp. 17 and 64, respectively, of the court records). Starting out on this secret trip, Abramovitch, curiously enough, had not even bothered to change his appearance and was seen wearing the same beard he had always worn in the past.

The defendants, when questioned, replied readily and succinctly, acknowledging every charge without hesitation. Not so Sukhanov, who missed no chance to deliver himself of a political diatribe against the Mensheviks and, specifically, against the LSI. He made continuous references to vague, unofficial decisions, to speeches and authoritative statements. Yet all attempts on the part of Krylenko to verify names, dates or the authentic texts remained unsuccessful. Sukhanov's memory invariably failed him, or else the necessary sources were not available at the moment, and the like. True enough, Sukhanov did mention one document, supposedly in the court files, but it was never produced during the trial. As a matter of fact, the court first learned of its existence from the testimony given by Rubin (p. 140 of the court records). The defendant stated that while all documents passed on to him by Scher were subsequently destroyed, there was one letter—a voluminous communication from the LSI on the matter of intervention—which he remembered well enough to relate its contents in detail. This statement was followed by an oral account occupying 2½ printed pages.

The major domestic purpose of the trial was thus achieved, at least for the time being. A very different situation developed abroad, where the plan to vilify the Russian socialists misfired. An iron-clad alibi had been brought forth as incontrovertible proof that Abramovitch could not possibly have gone to Russia and stayed there for "at least two weeks in June or July, 1928." From July 3rd to mid-August, Abramovitch was attending the congress of the LSI and was seen by hundreds of socialist delegates from various countries. Later on, when he filed a libel suit against two Communist papers published in Berlin, which had been reporting on the Moscow trial, the attorney for the defendant, a Communist member of the Reichstag, Löwenstein, had to concede that Abramovitch could not possibly have visited Russia at the time specified in the indictment and in the court testimony as given by the accused. Löwenstein made a half-hearted attempt to convince the court that even though Abramovitch could not have been to Russia in July 1928, he may have gone there at some other time. The Communist editor, adjudged guilty of libel, was ordered by the court to publish a notice of the verdict, which was to be prominently displayed in his paper, and to pay the court expenses.

What was interesting about Stalin's Menshevik trial was the evidence that it could not and did not bring to light any Menshevik activity in Russia. For example, in November 1927, Eva Broido, for two decades an active member of the party, for a time an inmate of the Tsarist *katorga,* and a member of the Menshevik Delegation Abroad, made an illegal journey through Russia for an on-the-spot look at what was left of the party and its underground struggle. Arrested and incarcerated within a short time after her arrival in Russia, Eva Broido did not appear at the trial. It would seem that the legal comedy could have been made far more plausible by producing a flesh-and-blood diversionist who had actually come to Russia from Germany to engage in subversive work. It was obvious, however, that she had flatly refused to participate in the legal farce. Thus, the name of Eva Broido was never mentioned, either in the defendants' testimony, or by Krylenko himself.[4]

In 1928 another major contributor to the *Socialist Courier* and a member of the Menshevik Party, M. A. Braunstein (whose articles appeared under the pen-name, "Valeryanov"), went to Moscow from Berlin, carrying another man's passport on his person. He managed to reach Moscow without any mishap, but was soon arrested and jailed. There had been occasional rumors filtering through concerning Braunstein, who was being transferred from one Soviet prison to another, yet he, too, was conspicuously absent at the Menshevik trial. This despite the fact that Braunstein's name, in association with his illegal visit to Russia, was mentioned in court testimony by some of the defendants. It was at the Menshevik trial that the ugly methods of slander and deception, to which the Bolsheviks resorted in combatting their socialist opponents, were brought into the open. Friedrich Adler published a pamphlet on the "Witches' Trial"; meanwhile, at the World Socialist Congress in Vienna (June 1931), R. Abramovitch was unanimously elected chairman, at the suggestion of the Swiss delegates.

The Labor Camps

It was between 1930 and 1934, that the system of forced-labor camps was introduced in Russia on a large scale. Several million Soviet peasants, industrial workers and intellectuals were interned. Many of them had never been sentenced by a court, had never committed any criminal or even political offense. They had only, in some way, manifested their discontent over the unprecedented sacrifices imposed on them by the regime in pursuit of collectivization and industrialization.

Following the "death echelons" of *Kulaks* which we have already mentioned, new waves of deportees (peasants, technicians, economists, doctors and others) were forced to build settlements in the tundra, in virgin forests of Siberia, in wild and isolated places far removed from any human habitat. These people had to dig up frozen soil, erect the first barracks for the guards and for themselves, cut down the virgin forests, dig wells—and all without proper equipment, clothing, boots or mittens, without sufficient food. The first contingents often perished during such work. Of the hundreds of people who worked on the opening of a camp, only a few individuals managed to survive. Their replacements showed an amazingly high percentage of mortality from cold, hunger, and epidemics. Yet waves upon waves of new immates kept pouring in.

It would be futile, in this necessarily brief mention of the camps, to try to describe the daily existence of the inmates or the economic implications of the camps. A vast literature in many languages has accumulated on the camps, and the reader should consult these works—particularly that of David Dallin and Boris Nikolaevsky,[5] as well as the thorough and comprehensive book by P. Barton.[6]

As a rule, the persons interned in the labor camps for "re-education" were stubborn opponents of the Soviet regime, violators of labor discipline, people who had resisted collectivization, saboteurs either imaginary or real from among the technicians and industrial workers. Officially, these people were supposed to be tried by a special tribunal attached to the GPU. In actual fact, however, the lists of the future inmates of the camps were already made up when they were sent to the GPU administration for approval. There they were summarily handled by a committee of three ("Troika") which never even saw the accused. Thus the latter could not say anything in his own defense.

As to re-education, there was none in the camps. There was no training in the inmates' trades or professions. Dr. Yu. Margolin, in his remarkable book, *The Journey to the Land of Z. K.* (Chekhov Publishing House, New York, 1952), notes very accurately that one of the basic camp rules was never to give an inmate a job in his specialty. On the contrary, the jailers seemed to want to make him forget his profession in hard unskilled labor under conditions that soon destroyed the average man—insufficient clothing, impossible output quotas, shortage of food and medical help. Since the individual food ration depended on the output of each worker, those who were incapable of producing the minimum norm of work received less food, which in turn decreased their output even further. Then the inmate became what was called a *dokhodiaga,* a slang expresssion for those who were on their last lap toward death. He could no longer go out to work and therefore received no rations and was doomed to feed on the bits that were thrown to him by the more merciful of the inmates. Such a person knew he was sentenced to die.

Surrounded by electrified barbed wire which was interspersed with watch towers manned day and night by soldiers, guarded by dogs, these camps were places from which there was no escape other than death.

Around 1930, the Soviet government decided to put more order and system into the concentration camps. A special office was established in Moscow at the OGPU under the name of GULAG (Central Administration of the Labor Camps) for administration, direction and supervision of the labor camps. Due to the great number of peasants and other citizens who were arrested and deported during collectivization, the GULAG turned into a gigantic organization, an industrial empire with hundreds of camps all over Russia. Some territories of Russia were transformed into a land of camps harboring many hundreds of thousands of inmates (Vorkuta, Bamlag, Dalstroi and others).

After Stalin's death, these camps began to acquire a different character. But in the period before World War II, millions of Russians who were not guilty of any crime perished in the camps.

It is true that among the inmates there were also some criminal elements, especially young criminals who were known as the *oorki* (criminal offenders), while the others were called *contry*. The *oorki* were in a privileged position since, according to the Soviet concept, they were not "enemies of the people" but socially backward elements. The *oorki*, in fact, helped the camp administration to illtreat the counter-revolutionary saboteurs and other persons guilty of crimes against the Soviet state. Thus the common-law criminals were in many cases the aristocracy of the labor camps.

It is impossible to give any accurate statistical data on the population of the Soviet concentration camps. According to certain secret documents that found their way abroad, and according to the estimates of former members of the GULAG staff, about 14 million persons passed through the Soviet camp system between 1930 and 1937. How these 14 million were distributed over the years, it is impossible to estimate.

The concentration camps confirmed the prophecy of Karl Kautsky in his book published as far back as 1921—*From Democracy to State Slavery*.[7] Kautsky had predicted at that time that, under a proletarian dictatorship in the Soviet Union, slave labor would become the fate of tens of millions of workers, peasants and intellectuals.

The Murder of Kirov

At the 17th Congress of the Soviet Communist Party, as we have noted, a rapturous reception was accorded to the chief victor, Stalin. The vanquished leaders of the right and left oppositions were specially rounded up from all corners of the Soviet Union and brought to the Congress to make self-accusing speeches from the platform, confessing their own terrible errors, and extolling with shameful self-abasement the wisdom, the farsightedness, the strategic genius and the iron will of the great Stalin. Two or three years later, all these speakers were executed by Stalin. In fact, according to Khrushchev's speech at the 20th Congress in February 1956, the same fate was meted out to 80% of all those elected to the Central Committee at the 17th Congress of 1934, and to 1,000 of the 1,901 delegates who had cheered Stalin so enthusiastically.

Stalin made the necessary preparations for a large-scale purge at the 17th Congress itself. There he secured the establishment of special punitive police machinery independent of Yagoda's GPU and directly responsible to the Secretariat—as it proved, to Stalin himself. This agency, which for a time was known as Stalin's personal secretariat, was later given the name of "Special Sector." It was headed in Stalin's last years by Alexander Poskrebyshev; but Malenkov, Molotov, Kaganovich, Khrushchev and others also took an active part in its manifold operations at one time or another.

Bukharin's "Letter of an Old Bolshevik" first described the origins of the Great Purges in the mounting tension between Stalin and the group led by Kirov and including Kuibyshev, Kossior, Ordzhonikidze and Rudzutak. This letter first hinted that the assassination of Kirov on December 1, 1934—less than a year after the 17th Congress had assigned him to the central party apparatus in Moscow—was planned by Stalin himself. Since then, the suspicion has been confirmed by a host of facts, some of them revealed by Nikita Khrushchev in his speeches to the 20th and 22nd Party Congresses. Khrushchev also confirmed the extent to which the purges which followed were directed at the leaders of the former Stalin faction, as represented at the 17th Congress.

A detailed reconstruction of the Kirov murder may be found in the book by Alexander Orlov, a former high official of the GPU, published in 1953. Orlov revealed that in 1934, Stalin appointed one of his trusted agents, "Vania" Zaporozhets, to work in the Leningrad GPU with instructions to arrange the murder of Kirov.[8] In Leningrad, Zaporozhets soon noticed a certain Leonid Nikolaev, a young Communist who was nursing a grievance because he had failed to find suitable employment in the government or the party apparatus. He had taken part in the Civil War, yet was condemned to a miserable existence working in a small office of a minor department. He was disgruntled because no better use was made of a man with his past, and he inscribed his thoughts, sorrows and longings in a diary which fell into the hands of the GPU. In the diary Nikolaev indulged in dreams of revenge against those members of the Personnel Control Commission who, in his view, stood between him and a great career.

When Zaporozhets read this diary, he decided that the author might well serve his purpose. He sent a young GPU agent to strike up a friendship with Nikolaev. This "friend" soon persuaded Nikolaev that the murder of some unknown and insignificant member of the Leningrad Personnel Control Commission would do the revolution no good, whereas the murder of, for instance, a member of the Politburo would alarm the whole country and focus the attention of the whole party on the disorders and injustices which they were suffering. Nikolaev was won over by this line of reasoning and eager to put it into effect. The same persuasive friend supplied him with a revolver, and they began to discuss the details of the murder. It was decided that Nikolaev would obtain a pass to the Smolny, enter Kirov's office and kill him. Everything was ready, and Zaporozhets even once arranged to meet Nikolaev in order to get a personal impression of the man on whom Stalin's plans depended.

The decisive moment came in the second half of November. Nikolaev went into the country for some shooting practice, and on his return made straight for the Smolny, carrying the revolver and diary in his briefcase. All went smoothly at first, but as he was walking down a corridor he was stopped by a sentry and his case was taken from him. The loaded revolver was discovered and Nikolaev was detained. To his astonishment, the incriminating briefcase was returned to him after a few hours and he was set free with a warning not to come back to the Smolny. Nikolaev returned home in a state of complete dejection—all was lost and the whole plan ruined. But his friend urged him not to give up so easily.

After ten days, Nikolaev recovered his nerve and was once again ready to make the attempt. This time Zaporozhets took the necessary precautions to remove all obstacles from Nikolaev's path. Nikolaev encountered no difficulty in obtaining another pass; he was not stopped on the way; there were no sentries around; and he reached Kirov's secretariat unmolested. Kirov, however, was not in his room; only his elderly servant or bodyguard by the name of Borisov was there. Kirov himself was at that moment presiding at a meeting of the Leningrad Party Committee in an adjacent room. Borisov first carried a tray with tea and snacks for Kirov into the committee room; later he entered a second time to inform Kirov that he was wanted for a telephone call from Moscow. Kirov left the meeting and closed the door behind him. A few minutes later a shot was heard from his room. The members of the Committee hurried into the corridor and pushed open the door which was blocked on the inside by the body of Kirov lying in a pool of blood. Next to him lay another inert body—that of Nikolaev, who had fainted. There was no sign of sentries in the corridor. Several minutes passed before GPU agents arrived on the scene and arrested Nikolaev. Thus Zaporozhets had carried out his mission.[9]

On the very night of the murder, Stalin personally went to Leningrad to take over the investigation and to unmask the criminal plot by the enemies of the people against "one of the best sons of the Soviet Union and the Communist Party." Stalin's quick move had a two-fold aim: to ensure that the investigation was led in the "right" direction by suppressing all undesirable evidence, and to use the murder of Kirov as a pretext for launching a furious campaign against all "enemies of the people." That very night, mass arrests were carried out in Leningrad and all other big cities, and all those whose names were on the lists of the GPU—compiled long in advance—were cast into prison.

A decree was issued the same day over the signatures of Abel Yenukidze[10] and N. Kalinin, the Secretary of the Central Executive Committee of the Soviets. In this decree—quoted by Khrushchev at the 20th Congress—the following instructions were issued:

> (1) Investigating agencies are directed to speed up the cases of those accused of the preparation or execution of acts of terror.
>
> (2) Judicial organs are directed not to hold up the execution of death sentences pertaining to crimes of this category in order to consider the possibility of pardon, because the Praesidium of the Central Executive Committee of the USSR does not consider as possible the receiving of petitions of this sort.
>
> (3) The organs of the Commissariat of Internal Affairs are directed to execute the death sentences against criminals of the above-mentioned category immediately after the passing of sentences.[10]

Two years later, while the terror was still raging, Stalin (together with Andrei Zhdanov, another member of the Politburo and the Secretariat) sent a coded telegram from the Crimea to the Politburo in Moscow, suggesting the appointment of Nicolai Yezhov as Commissar for Home Affairs and head of the GPU. This telegram was sent on September 25, 1936. In it Stalin reproached Yagoda, who had "proved incapable of mastering the task of uncovering and eradicating the Trotsky-Zinoviev bloc. In this respect the GPU was four years too late."[12] This reference to four lost years becomes intelligible if we recall that the GPU under Yagoda—and the Politburo majority led by Kirov—had refused to apply the death penalty in the Riutin case of 1932. The years between 1932 and 1936 were the "four wasted years" lamented by Stalin.

Yezhovshchina

The appointment of N. Yezhov in 1936 inaugurated the most terrible and bloody period of Stalin's reign. A few months after the death penalty was made legal and its application extended to include even the highest Communists, the Central Committee agreed to legalize the physical torture of prisoners suspected of terrorist intentions or of espionage. (Although this was not publicized until 1939, it had been decided in 1937.) The fact that torture was legally permitted and widely used was confirmed by Khrushchev in his speech to the 20th Congress.[13]

The so-called "Yezhovshchina" was the longest St. Bartholomew's night in history; it lasted for at least three years. Hundreds of thousands of party members, as well as their relatives who did not belong to the party, were arrested. Many were shot without trial. Others died of their tortures. The great majority was deported to concentration camps—either the general forced-labor camps or specially-organized camps in which the inmates were kept "incommunicado." There they remained until the war—if their talents were specially needed—or till Stalin's death, if they lived that long.

Some of the casualties of this period—an illustrious few—were publicly mourned by Stalin; yet they, too, appear to have been victims of his "Special Sector." Maxim Gorki, the famous writer, died of poisoning. Sergei Ordzhonikidze was found dead under strange circumstances, which Khrushchev has since laid to Stalin's doorstep. Sergei Kuibyshev, Kirov's loyal supporter, died at an appropriate moment for Stalin. Mikhail Tomsky, the rightist trade-union leader, was a suicide, as was the theatrical director, Vsevolod Meyerhold.

While this silent guillotine was felling the leaders of the 17th Party Congress and, indeed, the leaders at all levels of the old Stalin "centrist" faction, the attention of the world was claimed by the so-called show trials of the old left and right oppositionists.

At the show trials which began in 1935, however, the defendants were not non-political technicians or socialists, but world-famous leaders of the Communist Party, friends and close collaborators of Lenin, former members of the Central Committee and the Politburo, People's Commissars and heads of the GPU. In all these trials, as in secret trials of Soviet Army leaders, the accused were charged with heinous and implausible crimes. No factual or documentary evidence was ever presented in court, and the indictment rested essentially on the "sincere confessions" of the defendants themselves. The verdicts in all cases were most severe. With few exceptions, the accused in the show trials of 1936, 1937 and early 1938 incurred the death penalty; a handful escaped with lengthy imprisonment.

The first of these trials, which took place almost immediately after Kirov's assassination, was the so-called Leningrad trial of Zinoviev, Kamenev and others. It was not entirely representative of the later trials because the accused were not forced to confess to crimes they had not committed, and no death sentences were then imposed.

The defendants at the Leningrad trial of January 15-16, 1935, were 19 in number: Zinoviev, Kamenev, Gertik, Kuklin, Sakhov, Sharov, Evdokimov, Bakaev, and others. They were accused of having plotted the murder of Kirov and sentenced to from five to ten years in prison. In connection with this case, Zalutsky, Vardin and others (49 persons in all) were sentenced to imprisonment in concentration camps for a term of four to five years, and other persons were sentenced to deportation for two to five years. All in all, 97 ex-leaders of the former Zinoviev opposition were sentenced.[14]

The Court found it necessary to explain the mildness of the sentences by stating that "the investigation failed to establish facts which would provide a basis for a direct accusation of the members of the 'Moscow Center' of giving their consent or issuing any instructions in organizing the terrorist act against Comrade Kirov." This mildness proved illusory.

In the summer of 1935, only a few months later, a second trial involving Zinoviev and Kamenev was apparently held—this time in Moscow on charges of organizing Kirov's assassination. Zinoviev and Kamenev were brought to Moscow from the Upper Ural Solitary Confinement Prison and this time charged with directly taking part in preparing and carrying out Kirov's assassination. Worse, they were compelled to confess that they had acted in collaboration with the German Gestapo. Radek and Piatakov also appeared as defendants in this case.

This trial was never reported in the Soviet press. The only mention of it may be found in an article by Anton Tsiliga, "Something is Rotten in the State of Denmark."[15] Tsiliga did not know the names of all the defendants or the verdict in this second preparatory trial. In any event, according to his report, Zinoviev immediately agreed to confess to whatever was asked of him, and was rewarded, upon his return to the Upper Ural Solitary Confinement Prison, with a better cell. Kamenev, on the other hand, put up strong resistance and was given an additional five years.

Tsiliga's report gains in credence from the fact that Radek, Piatakov and others were put on trial publicly shortly after the article appeared. In this second preparatory trial, it seems, the defendants were subdivided into two groups: one headed by Zinoviev and Kamenev, who were again (for the third time!) brought to trial on August 19, 1936; and a second group, headed by Radek and Piatakov, who were tried in January 1937.

The Big Show-Trials

The Trial of the Trotskyist-Zinovievist Center

The first big show-trial was that of the Trotskyist-Zinovievist Terrorist Center, held in Moscow, January 19-24, 1936. The sixteen defendants included Zinoviev, Kamenev, Mrachkovsky, Ter-Vaganian, I. N. Smirnov, Dreitser, Goltsman and a number of hitherto unknown young men, several of whom later proved to be agents of the GPU. The charges were broad and serious. The chief prosecutor—the renegade Menshevik Andrei Vyshinsky—stated that, during the months which had passed since the earlier trial, a number of facts had been brought to light which had established beyond all doubt that the defendants had organized Kirov's assassination and had planned many other terroristic acts. In truth, the prosecution was unable to produce a single bit of factual evidence; its only weapons were the "sincere confessions" of the defendants and their mutual denunciations.

This trial, like the great trials which followed, was a spectacular public performance in which the two parties—the prosecution and the accused—jointly prepared both the charges and the defense by the methods of collusion and "persuasion" which in most cases included threats against the members of the defendants' families (moral torture) and outright physical torture. By the time the court was opened to the public and the press, everything had already been discussed, agreed and rehearsed. In a few exceptional cases, a defendant forgot or deliberately departed from the agreed text, whereupon the prosecutor immediately attacked him. If the prosecutor's shouting was not enough, the presiding judge took a hand in the proceedings. In the end, the prosecution obtained the testimony it needed to sentence the defendants to death.

Each of these trials had a definite political purpose for Stalin and was needed to support a well-defined propagandistic thesis. The trials of Zinoviev, Kamenev and others aimed to prove that it was the "Trotskyists" who had started terroristic tactics within the party against Stalin and his group. The term "Trotskyist" was indiscriminately applied to anyone on Stalin's liquidation list. It did not matter whether the victims were really followers of Trotsky or, as in many cases, his staunch opponents. At every public trial, the name of Trotsky was prominently exhibited in the form of an "Amalgam," and each time the defendants were accused of being members of a terrorist group headed or connected with Trotsky (the Trial of the Trotskyist-Zinovievist Terrorist Center; the Trial of the Anti-Soviet Trotskyist Center; and the Anti-Soviet Rightist-Trotskyist Bloc). Stalin wanted to eradicate completely from the mind of the Soviet Communists the traditional image of Trotsky as Lenin's closest partner in organizing the October Revolution and as the leader of the Red Army in the Civil War.

At the same time, starting with 1936, Stalin's goal was to liquidate not only physically but morally all the Communist opposition groups real or suspected—left, right, center. The trials demonstrated that any opposition to the ruling group fatally and unavoidably brought the oppositionists to political and moral decay, to corruption and rottenness, to collaboration with the foreign capitalists and fascists, to betrayal of the fatherland and the revolution, to vulgar espionage and other crimes against the revolution and the country.

In many cases, Stalin had a more limited object in organizing a trial in a certain way. This applies especially to the trials of Zinoviev and Kamenev, who were accused of having plotted or executed the murder of Kirov. The reason Stalin ordered them tried three times may be found in the rumors—widespread in the Communist Party and even abroad—that Stalin himself had been the real organizer of Kirov's murder. In order to counteract these rumors, Stalin found it necessary to stage the public trial of August 1936, at which, before representatives of the world press and a large local audience, such old Communists and close friends of Lenin's as Zinoviev and Kamenev, such great heroes of the Civil War as Mrachkovsky, and such old St. Petersburg workers as Bakayev publicly confessed that in the fall of 1934 they had organized Kirov's assassination on Trotsky's instructions.

Thus began the orgy of mutual denunciations, fabrications, and utterly fantastic confessions reminiscent of the darkest days of the middle ages when, as Friedrich Adler so well put it, the witches sincerely confessed at trials at which they were sentenced to be burned at the stake, that they had caused tempests, rains, and storms by waving their skirts.[16]

The following excerpt from the official report on the trial exposed blatantly the real purpose of its organizers:

"Vyshinsky: Was it your center that organized the assassination of Comrade Kirov? Was the assassination of Sergei Mironovich Kirov organized by your center or by some other organization?

"Zinoviev: Yes, by our center.

"Vyshinsky: In that center were you, Kamenev, Smirnov, Mrachkovsky and Ter-Vaganian?

"Zinoviev: Yes.

"Vyshinsky: So you all assassinated Comrade Kirov?

"Zinoviev: Yes.

"Vyshinsky: Sit down."[17]

The Soviet press was full of ferocious attacks against the defendants. An editorial in *Pravda* of August 23 demanded that "the mad dogs be shot." Beria, who was not yet head of the GPU, said in *Pravda* of August 19, that "the enemies of socialism must be crushed into dust." In *Pravda* of August 20, D. Zaslavsky, another renegade from the ranks of the Mensheviks, listed the various monstrous accusations in detail and added his own description of the defendants. On another date, *Pravda* carried a collective letter from Soviet writers entitled: "To be wiped off the face of the earth."

Similar articles appeared under signatures which seem like tragic omens. The first was signed by Alexei Rykov, who demanded in *Pravda* of August 21 that no mercy be shown to the organizers of the assassination. The second was signed by Yuri Piatakov, who called for "the merciless annihilation of the despicable murderers and traitors." Both men would stand in the same dock shortly. Their articles evidently were not independent acts: they had apparently been given to understand that it would be better for them to show their solidarity with Stalin.[18]

The Trial of the Anti-Soviet Trotskyist Center

Whereas the purpose of the Zinoviev-Kamenev trial had been to shield Stalin from any suspicion in connection with Kirov's murder, the Piatakov-Radek trial was intended to prove another major thesis of Stalin's propaganda—that Trotsky maintained close liaison with fascism and Nazism and worked with them against Soviet Russia and the Soviet government.

We have cited above Tsiliga's report to the effect that at the second (closed) Zinoviev trial, in the summer of 1935, the original intention had been to accuse the Zinoviev-Kamenev group of collaboration with the Gestapo as well, but that, at the last moment, because of "higher considerations," it was decided to launch this accusation instead against the Piatakov-Radek group and, in order to make it more convincing, to organize a special preliminary trial for this purpose. That trial was held in Novosibirsk and concerned a mythical German Nazi group which allegedly existed at the Kemerovo coal mines in western Siberia. The mines employed a fairly large number of German as well as Russian workers and engineers. These Germans were for the most part anti-Nazis, both Communists and non-Communists, who had succeeded in escaping from Hitler's Germany. So many people in that country wanted to be employed in the USSR that the Soviet government organized a special GPU section in the Soviet Embassy in Germany to consider applications and investigate the applicants for admission to Russia.

In November 1936, arrests of German workers and engineers began in Kemerovo.[19] The German Embassy protested to the Minister of Foreign Affairs, Litvinov, who replied that forming a fascist group in the territory of the USSR was punishable under the law and that the accused had already confessed that it had been their intention to overthrow the Soviet government, to organize wrecking and to carry out terroristic acts.

The threatening tone of the German press, however, compelled

Moscow to abandon its plan of staging a trial of the fictitious Nazi group. Of all the Germans arrested, only one was added to the group which was brought to trial in Novosibirsk on November 19-21, 1936. His name was Emil Stickling. He and nine Soviet co-defendants, four of whom the prosecution termed Trotskyists and the rest counter-revolutionaries and White Guards, were sentenced to death for collaboration with the Germans, espionage, wrecking, etc.

After this verdict was published in *Pravda,* von Ribbentrop, German Ambassador in London, requested the British Prime Minister, Stanley Baldwin, to inform the Soviet government that if the death sentence imposed on Stickling were carried out, the German government would break off diplomatic relations with Moscow.[20] Moscow thereupon beat a retreat and in the case of Stickling and two Russian "White Guards" (*not* Trotskyists), the VTsIK commuted the death penalty to ten years imprisonment.

After the Novosibirsk trial had "proved" the existence in the USSR of a German Nazi group acting as a link between Trotsky abroad and his followers in the USSR, the stage was set for a trial to "prove" that Trotsky himself was closely linked with Hitler. Seventeen such men —Radek, Piatakov, Sokolnikov, Muralov, Drobnis, Serebriakov, Boguslavsky and others—appeared as defendants at the trial, supplemented by a number of less famous Communists and also several persons who had been convicted but not shot at the Novosibirsk trial. Among the latter, two, Stroilov and Grashe, both of them experienced GPU agents who masqueraded as members of a Trotskyist group, played outstanding parts as witnesses. The trial was held from January 23 to January 30, 1937, and was known as the "Trial of the Anti-Soviet Trotskyist Center." The defendants were accused of "treason to their country, espionage, diversionism, wrecking, and planning terroristic acts."

The trial of the seventeen followed exactly the same pattern as that of the Zinoviev-Kamenev group. All the defendants admitted everything, even the wildest charges against them; no factual or documentary proof was ever submitted; and the entire performance proceeded in accordance with the "gentlemen's agreement" between the executioners and their victims. The only point which is still unclear is whether all the defendants were actually awarded the exact penalties promised them for their co-operation in the trial. There is some reason to believe that Stalin deceived a number of them, and that after promising them mercy, at the last moment ordered them shot. There are indications that just this happened to Yuri Piatakov.

Orlov relates[21] that Sergei Ordzhonikidze, one of Stalin's closest friends and collaborators, did everything in his power to save Piatakov, whom he greatly valued as an administrator and whom he needed in his commissariat. According to this version, Piatakov resisted for a long time and stubbornly refused to give false testimony. He was a strong and resolute man, and everyone was aware that he had broken with the Trotskyists long ago, whereupon he had zealously carried out Stalin's directives. Consequently, Piatakov failed to see any reason why he should be implicated in the case of terrorist-wreckers and punished for imaginary offenses.[22]

For a fairly long time, Piatakov would not surrender. One day, Ordzhonikidze appeared at the prison and wanted to speak to Piatakov. Despite his high position, he was not allowed to see Piatakov immediately; inquiries had to be made first, apparently. In a little while Piatakov was brought into the prison office. Ordzhonikidze rushed up to him and tried to embrace him but Piatakov waved him aside. Ordzhonikidze began by assuring him that no one intended to harm him, that he was in no danger, etc. At this point Piatakov was left alone with Ordzhonikidze and they held a long conversation in private.

A few days later Ordzhonikidze again came to the GPU prison and held a second long talk with Piatakov. Before leaving, he summoned Agranov, one of the GPU's senior officers, and in Piatakov's presence transmitted to him Stalin's personal order that Piatakov's wife and his private secretary, Kolia Moskalev, were to be excluded from the list of defendants and were not to be summoned to court even as witnesses. Whether Ordzhonikidze at the same time also transmitted a promise from Stalin that Piatakov himself would be spared, is not known, but Ordzhonikidze's entire behavior would seem to indicate as much. After this, Piatakov gave way. He was shot nonetheless. No one knows whether or not Piatakov's execution was the reason for the serious quarrel which ensued between Stalin and Ordzhonikidze, and it would be difficult to prove that Ordzhonikidze's sudden death was a consequence of this quarrel, but there is some reason to think that this may have been the case, for Ordzhonikidze was found dead only three weeks after Piatakov's execution.

The last statements of Piatakov and Radek are worth citing as strikingly representative of the temper of the times.

Piatakov declared:

"I am foregoing a speech for the defense, because the charges brought by the state were correct both in establishing the facts and in defining my crime. But I cannot agree, I cannot reconcile myself to one assertion of the state prosecutor: that I am a Trotskyist now."

Piatakov finds this accusation intolerable. He does not ask for mercy; he has not deserved it. But he says:

"Don't deprive me of the right to feel—only of the right to feel—that although too late, I did nevertheless reject all this filth and nastiness."

Radek's closing statement was even more revealing of the political impact of the second trial. After a very devious and confusing "theoretical" introduction, Radek clearly formulated the political purposes of this propaganda trial. According to Radek, the trial was necessary in order to disorganize, disarm and dissuade

> not only Trotskyists—for they are very few—and the GPU can easily get the better of them—but all those half-Trotskyists one-fourth Trotskyists, one-eighth Trotskyists, who followed Trotsky out of liberalism or rebellion against the party, without any suspicion that they were promoting treason against their country, the restoration of capitalism and an alliance with fascism . . .
> . . . Finally, we want the whole world to know that the Trotskyists are war mongers and that this has been proved by our frank and truthful testimony, which we have found so difficult to give and for the truth of which we shall pay with our heads.

As he spoke these words, did Radek really think he would pay with his head? We doubt it. For at the very end of his closing statement, he suddenly remarked that he had told the truth, the whole truth, at the trial, except for one single point. This was the existence of a parallel terroristic group headed by Bukharin. He had long concealed this fact out of personal friendship, he said, but in the end had been able to overcome this scruple and now wished to state that this parallel group actually existed.

This was a denunciation of Bukharin, which Radek must have known to be false. He had clearly sacrificed Bukharin, his comrade, because the GPU had promised him his life in return. The GPU kept its word. Radek was sentenced to ten years in a concentration camp, whereas all the other defendants were shot.[23]

The Trial of the Military Chiefs

More than a year elapsed, however, between the Radek and the Bukharin trials. In order to amass sufficient "proof" against the former leaders of the rightist opposition, it was first necessary to stage a number of public and secret minor trials against various groups and individuals in the different national republics.

Meanwhile, there occurred what was in some ways the most intriguing trial of all—that of the leading marshals and generals of the Red Army. It was intriguing because it was secret, and to this day one can only guess at the political realities behind it.

For nearly two decades, the only information ever published in the Soviet press on this trial, which was held on June 11, 1937, and resulted in the execution of all the defendants, was a brief report in *Izvestia* of June 12, 1937:

> Yesterday, June 11 . . . the trial chamber of the Supreme Court of the USSR, composed of Comrade Ulrich, presiding judge and chairman of the War College and of member judges A. M. Alksniss, Deputy People's Commissar of the Commissariat of Defense, S. M. Budenny, V. I. Blukher, Shaposhnikov, P. E. Dybenko, N. D. Kashirin, E. M. Goryachev, I. P. Belov, examined in closed proceedings in accordance with the law of December 1, 1934, the case of M. I. Tukhachevsky, N. Z. Yakir, M. P. Uborevich, A. I. Kork, A. M. Eideman, B. M. Feldman, M. V. Primakov and V. Putna.
>
> The above named persons were accused of breach of military duty and oath of allegiance, treason to their country, treason against the peoples of the USSR and treason against the workers' and peasants' Red Army.
>
> All the defendants were condemned to the supreme penalty, which was duly carried out.

Marshal Tukhachevsky had been one of the most capable and most famous Red Army chiefs in the Civil War, after which he had apparently played a decisive part in reorganizing and modernizing the Soviet army. He had been a member of the Communist Party since 1918, and a candidate-member of the Central Committee since 1934. General Uborevich was Commander-in-Chief of the Byelorussian military district, party member since 1917 and candidate-member of the Central Committee since 1930. General Yakir had been a member of the Communist Party since 1917, candidate-member of the Central Committee since 1930, and member of the Central Committee since 1934. Eideman, who had been a Red Army leader during the Civil War, was a well-known Latvian writer, member of the Communist Party since 1917, and chairman of the Central Soviet of "Osoviakhim."[24] One seat on the defendants' bench had been reserved for General Ian Gamarnik, a member of the Communist Party since 1916 and an outstanding party and military figure, but he had committed suicide before the trial.

The execution of such outstanding chiefs of the Red Army, with decades of service behind them, was bound to make the strongest impression throughout the world. The absence of any specific charges of treason against them arroused widespread perplexity. Little was clarified when Voroshilov two days later issued Army Order No. 96, which, after citing the composition of the court, the verdict and the names of the defendants, added this note:

> Some time ago the Supreme Court meted out a merciless sentence to the members of the band of Zinoviev, Kamenev, Trotsky, Piatakov, Smirnov, *et al* . . . (*Izvestia*, June 14, 1937.)

The imputation was that the military "criminals" had been linked in some manner with the leftist opposition, but this has never been confirmed.

The published official material on the various military trials is so inadequate that it is altogether impossible to establish the complete list of defendants, the charges, the evidence, and even the exact composition of the court itself. The indications are that several hundred high-ranking Soviet officers were liquidated, and that many more perished secretly than were ever announced in the Soviet press. At the same time, hundreds of junior officers and thousands of soldiers and non-commissioned officers were sent to the concentration camps, where a considerable number of them were executed. We know, moreover, that two of the judges at the Tukhachevsky trial were themselves shot later. They were Marshal Blukher, Soviet commander in the Far East, member of the Communist Party since 1916, and candidate-member of the Central Committee since 1934, and Dybenko, a Bolshevik since 1912, a sailor famous in 1917 and subsequently a member of the Central Executive Committee of the USSR.

Unlike all the other big trials of 1936-1938, the trial of the military chiefs was reviewed by the Soviet government after Stalin's death and Khrushchev's famous speech. The main defendants were in fact "rehabilitated," although why they had been killed was never fully explained. Marshal Tukhachevsky was described as a brave and loyal military chief at the Twentieth Congress, and brief biographies of Gamarnik, Tukhachevsky, Uborevich, Yakir and Eideman were inserted in Vol. 51 of the second edition of the *Great Soviet Encyclopedia.* (Why this volume does not also contain the biographies of Feldman, Primakov, Putna and Kork remains a mystery.) In any case, there has now been official recognition of the fact that the principal defendants had been innocent of the crimes imputed to them. There has been no such review of any of the other famous public trials of 1936-1938.

It is easy to understand the reason—the pressure arising from the "esprit de corps" of the victorious Red Army leaders of World War II. It was intolerable for the Marshals Zhukov, Konev, Malinovsky, etc., to leave unchallenged the humiliating and dishonoring indictment of their predecessors and teachers as traitors to the fatherland, agents of the Germans, and spies for a foreign government. Thus, the pressure of the army leadership after Stalin's death compelled the Communist Party to agree to drop the malicious slander by which Stalin unintentionally smeared the honor of the Russian armed forces as a whole.

No such pressure was issued by any part of the Communist Party in the direction of restoring the honor of the Communist Party, of Lenin and his closest collaborators, pupils and friends, blackened, slandered and executed on absolutely false and dishonoring accusations or confessions extorted by inhuman tortures. Thus, the defendants in all the publicized and non-publicized political trials of 1936-38 remain (up to this moment) inscribed in the annals of Soviet history, in the textbooks and encyclopedias, as traitors, bandits, spies, vulgar murderers and paid agents of capitalism and fascism.

But if the rehabilitated military leaders were absolutely innocent, the question arises: why did Stalin find it necessary to condemn and execute a number of valuable military commanders?

In the opinion of the writer, the most plausible explanation is that Stalin—having decided that Russia should become a partner in Hitler's war for the redistribution of the world—found it imperative to purge not only those Communists who might oppose this policy in the party, but even more the military figures who might fight or sabotage it when the test came. On the other hand, the suddenness of the Tukhachevsky trial indicates that in this case Stalin may have been the prey of his own diseased suspicions.

We have been given indirect information on the background of the Tukhachevsky trial, in a public statement made after the Second World War by Leon Blum. The former French socialist Premier relates that when his son Robert had visited Prague late in 1936, President Benes had summoned him and declared cautiously that Czech military intelligence had learned of some mysterious dealings between Soviet military chiefs and Hitler. Benes sought to warn the French government to be on its guard when high-ranking Soviet officers arrived in France in connection with the conclusion of the Franco-Soviet mutual assistance pact. The senior Blum wrote that he was stunned by this information, but that, when the press reported Tukhachevsky's trial in June 1937, he understood whom Benes had had in mind. Blum added that it was this knowledge of strange things going on between high-ranking Soviet officers and the Germans which paralyzed him in his efforts to transform the Franco-Russian alliance into an effective and broad military co-operation.[25] It was only natural that Benes should have warned not only the French government but London as well. Benes actually did so and his warning was formulated in almost the same words as his message to Blum. No names were given, just the following lines were transmitted according to Churchill:

> He [Benes] became aware that communications were passing through the Soviet Embassy in Prague between important personages in Russia and the German Government. This was a part of the so-called military and Old-Guard Communist conspiracy to overthrow Stalin and introduce a new regime based on a pro-German policy. President Benes lost no time in communicating all he could find out to Stalin.[26]

But the better informed and more sceptical Churchill hastened to add the following footnote on the same page.

> There is, however, some evidence that Benes' information had previously been imparted to the Czech police by the OGPU, who wished it to reach Stalin from a friendly foreign source.

Much has been written on this episode, and a number of different hypotheses have been advanced. One theory is that some GPU or "Fourth Sector" (Military Intelligence) agents, acting on Stalin's orders, forged some documents for transmission to the Gestapo through double agents, and that this information was in turn leaked from the Gestapo through Czechoslovak double agents to Benes, who passed it on to Stalin at the same time as he took steps to inform his French and British allies. It is also possible that the Gestapo planted the false report, in the hope of disorienting the Red Army, and that the suspicious Stalin fell for the dodge. In any case, as soon as he received this information, Stalin used it to convince a number of important people in the Red Army and in the Politburo, whose support he required, that his suspicions against a good many marshals and generals had been well-founded and to demand their execution—without a public trial and probably without any trial at all.

In connection with Stalin's purge of the Red Army, it should be noted that his hostility toward it goes back at least to the Russo-Polish War of 1920. At that time, Stalin (with the assistance of Budenny, his friend) sabotaged the war effort. By perverting the orders of the General Staff and by ignoring the opinions of Tukhachevsky (opinions in which Lenin and Trotsky concurred), Stalin and Budenny weakened the position of the Russian forces and contributed greatly to the military defeat at Warsaw. From then on, a bitter but disguised rivalry existed between Stalin and Tukhachevsky. Stalin had to wait seventeen years; but he was finally able to revenge himself on Tukhachevsky and on Tukhachevsky's friends and supporters in the Red Army.

As Khrushchev has in effect admitted, this liquidation of the ablest and most experienced Red Army chiefs greatly weakened Russia's military effectiveness in World War II.

The Trial of the Anti-Soviet Rightist-Trotskyist Bloc

The climax of the whole series of trials was that of the rightist Communists, officially known as "The Trial of the Anti-Soviet Rightist-Trotskyist Bloc," held on March 2-13, 1938. Vyshinsky again served as the state prosecutor, Ulrich as the presiding judge. A motley group occupied the defendants' bench: Bukharin and Rykov, right-wing ideologists of the Communist Party; Yagoda, ex-chairman of the GPU; N. Krestinsky, ex-secretary of the Central Committee of the Communist Party and former ambassador to Germany; Ch. Rakovsky, ex-chairman of the Soviet of People's Commissars of the Ukraine and Soviet ambassador to many countries; A. Rozengolts, former head of foreign trade; Grinko, former People's Commissar of Finance; Ikhnamov and Khodzhaev, leaders of "National Republics"; the well-known medical professor, Pletnev, before the Revolution a rightist liberal; and Dr. L. G. Levin. To them were added a number of lesser Communists, including several GPU *agents-provocateurs,* whose function was established during the trial without objection from Vyshinsky. The accusation stated in part:

> As has been established, the defendants in the present case organized a conspiratorial group known as the "Rightist-Trotskyist Bloc," whose purpose was to overthrow the socialist, social and political regime existing in the USSR, to restore capitalism and the power of the bourgeoisie in the USSR, to dismember the USSR and to split off from it, for the benefit of the capitalist countries, the Ukraine, Byelorussia, the Central Asian Republics, Georgia, Armenia, Azerbaijan and Primorye.

This trial followed the same monotonous pattern as its predecessors. Each defendant readily admitted all the charges against him, glibly recited the lessons he had learned by heart, and finally repented of monstrous crimes, fitting the noose around his own neck. As in each of the trials, one person tried at the last to deny at least a single charge. At this trial, that person was Bukharin. When Vyshinsky proceeded to question him in a highly insulting manner on his alleged connection with various foreign secret services, Bukharin lost his temper. Vyshinsky baited him and the presiding judge intervened. Here is this highly typical little scene (Testimony of Bukharin, Official Record, March 2-13, 1938, pp. 186-187):

"Vyshinsky: Did you live in Austria?

"Bukharin: I did.

"Vyshinsky: For a long time?

"Bukharin: 1912-1913.

"Vyshinsky: Did you have connections with the Austrian police?

"Bukharin: No.

"Vyshinsky: Did you live in America?

"Bukharin: I did.

"Vyshinsky: For a long time?

"Bukharin: About seven months.

"Vyshinsky: Did you have relations with the police in America?

"Bukharin: Absolutely not.

"Vyshinsky: When you left America you travelled to Russia through . . .

"Bukharin: Through Japan.

"Vyshinsky: Did you stay there long?

"Bukharin: One week.

"Vyshinsky: Were you recruited during this week?

"Bukharin: If you choose to put such questions . . .

"Vyshinsky: I have a right to put such questions under the Code of Criminal Procedure.

"Presiding judge: The prosecutor is all the more entitled to ask such a question because you, Bukharin, are accused of attempting to assassinate party leaders back in 1918; you are accused of plotting, even back in 1918, against the life of V. I. Lenin.

"Vyshinsky: Then why did you so readily join a bloc which engaged in espionage?

"Bukharin: I know absolutely nothing about espionage.

"Vyshinsky: And what was the bloc doing?

"Bukharin: We have heard two statements here about espionage—by Sharangovich and by Ivanov—which is to say, by two *agents-provocateurs.*

"Vyshinsky: Do you regard Rykov as an *agent-provocateur?*

"Bukharin: No, I do not.

"Vyshinsky: (addressing Rykov) Defendant Rykov, are you aware that the Rightist-Trotskyist Bloc engaged in espionage?

"Rykov: I know that there were some organizations which did espionage work.

"Vyshinsky: Tell me, did the Byelorussian Nazi-Fascist organization, which was a part of your Rightist-Trotskyist Bloc, and was headed by defendant Sharangovich, engage in espionage?

"Rykov: It did.

"Vyshinsky: It maintained liaison with Polish military intelligence?

"Rykov: It did.

"Vyshinsky: You knew of this?

"Rykov: I did.

"Vyshinsky: And Bukharin did not know of it?

"Rykov: In my opinion, Bukharin did, too.

"Vyshinsky: So you see, Defendant Bukharin, this is being said not by Sharangovich, but by your dear friend Rykov.

"Bukharin: Nevertheless, I knew nothing of it."

And so this last flare-up of human dignity on the part of Bukharin, who still had a little fight left in him, was extinguished by the concerted efforts of the public prosecutor,[27] the presiding judge, GPU agents and former friends. Even a strong and proud man like Bukharin was unable to escape the traps set for him. The trial took its usual course, except that one session had to be hastily adjourned when Krestinsky refused to follow the script. At the next session, he was compliant. All the defendants were condemned to death and shot.

When the Soviet government began its show-trials of engineers, technicians, plant directors, etc., the world was mystified by the eagerness of the majority of the accused to confess to crimes of which the court was unable to produce the necessary evidence. What made the defendants act in this incongruous way, which seemed to be absolutely against their basic vital interests?

The Enigma of "Sincere" Confessions

The enigma of "spontaneous sincere confessions" had become still darker after the big political trials of 1936-1938.

It became clearly evident that there was a previous collusion between the prosecution and the defendants. But what made a group of irreproachable men of unimpeachable honesty play such a despicable role? Nobody knew.

In the summer of 1936, public opinion was struck by the unimaginable spectacle of old and famous Bolsheviks, confessing to murder plots against other Bolshevik leaders, to espionage, to a plot against the Soviet Union and the revolution in connivance with Hitler and the Gestapo. By what means could Stalin compel these great men of Bolshevism to such shameful behavior?

If we accept the competent and certainly very well informed opinion of Khrushchev given in his speech at the 20th Congress, this result was achieved simply by inhuman tortures. Khrushchev said:

> I may be asked how it happened that loyal Communists confessed to crimes which they never committed; this is achieved in one way only—by applying physical pressure and by using tortures which reduced the accused to a state of semiconsciousness, inability to reason and loss of human dignity (p. 34).

By way of illustration. Khrushchev cited a letter written by one of the executed, Robert Eikhe, to the Central Committee, a letter which the most hardened cannot read without a shudder. Eikhe, a former member of the Central Committee, the Politburo, the Revolutionary Military Council, People's Commissar of Agriculture and First Secretary of the District Committee of Western Siberia, was arrested on April 29, 1938, and accused of a number of fantastic crimes. On October 27, 1939, he wrote to Stalin as follows (pp. 28-29):

> . . . On October 25 of this year I was informed that the investigation in my case has been concluded and I was given access to the materials of this investigation. Had I been guilty of only one

> hundredth of the crimes with which I am charged, I would not have dared to send you this pre-execution declaration; however, I have not been guilty of one of the things with which I am charged and my heart is clean of even a shadow of baseness. I have never in my life told you a word of falsehood, and now, finding my two feet in the grave, I am also not lying. My whole case is a typical example of provocation, slander and violation of the elementary basis of revolutionary legality . . .
>
> . . . I am now alluding to the most disgraceful part of my life and to my really grave guilt against the party and against you. This is my confession of counter-revolutionary activity . . . The case is as follows: not being able to suffer the tortures to which I was submitted by Ushakov and Nikolaiev—and especially by the first one —who utilized the knowledge that my broken ribs have not properly mended and have caused me great pain, I have been forced to accuse myself and others . . .
>
> . . . I am asking and begging you that you again examine my case, and this not for the purpose of sparing me but in order to unmask the vile provocation, which, like a snake, wound itself around many persons in a great degree due to my meanness and criminal slander. I have never betrayed you or the party. I know that I perish because of vile and mean work of the enemies of the party and of the people, who fabricated the provocation against me.

But there was no response to this plea of Eikhe: according to Khrushchev, Stalin in 1941 ordered the execution of Eikhe after he had been acquitted by the Court.

Stalin's guiding principle in extracting confessions—according to Khrushchev—was "beat, beat and beat again." Other witnesses have recounted other forms of torture; forty-eight hours of standing still, until blood vessels of the defendants' legs would burst; "assembly-line" interrogation; the "manicure," red-hot needles stuck under the nails of the accused; and the maiming of the internal organs—the kidney and the liver—by blows below the belt. Still another torture was designed to make the old Bolshevik lose all human dignity: the guards forced him to lie on the floor, and the investigator urinated on his face.[28]

Sometimes—as in the case of Eikhe—even the most brutal tortures would not break a defendant's spirit. We do not know how many of the victims of the purges went to their deaths without implicating their comrades. In other cases, the tortures applied to others were sufficient to make a suspect confess all.

According to rumors which were widely circulating in Moscow in the years 1937-39, still more atrocious tortures were applied to political prisoners at the Lefortovo Prison in Moscow.

Only very important prisoners would be brought by the GPU to Lefortovo as the last resort of the investigators for the extortion of the confessions. One of such prisoners was Victor Alter, the well-known Jewish Polish socialist leader, who was arrested in Poland in 1939 and brought to Moscow. He was released after Hitler's attack against Russia, together with his friend, Henryk Ehrlich; but both were subsequently executed by Stalin in Kuibyshev (December 1940). The Soviet aviation designer, Tupolev, for some reason suspect to Stalin, was placed in the Lefortovo Prison in the same cell with Muklevich—a high official in the Soviet navy who was questioned many times before he confessed. Whatever Muklevich told him, it was enough for poor Tupolev. He immediately "confessed" what the GPU asked and was released: he was too important to Russian aviation to be hurt.[29]

However, the widespread use of tortures was not the whole story. There were some "sincere confessions." In order to understand this phenomenon, we will cite cases described in the available literature. Walter Krivitsky (*Socialist Courier,* No. 8, April 1938, pp. 6-7) described the case of Mark Mrachkovsky, one of the Bolshevik guerilla heroes in the Civil War, as recounted to him by Slutski, the GPU investigator:

> When Mrachkovsky was first led into my office, I saw that he limped heavily from the effects of a leg wound he had received in the civil war. I offered him a chair. He sat down. I opened the examination with the words: "You see, Comrade Mrachkovsky, I have received orders to question you."
>
> Mrachkovsky replied: "I have nothing to say! In general, I don't want to enter into any conversations with you. Your kind are much worse than any gendarmes of the Tsar. Suppose you tell me what right you have to question me. Where were you in the revolution? Somehow I don't recall ever hearing of you in the days of the civil war."

Mrachkovsky caught sight of two Orders of the Red Banner which Slutski was wearing and continued: "I never saw your type at the front. As for those decorations, you must have stolen them!"

Slutski kept silent. He gave his prisoner an opportunity to pour out his bitterness. Mrachkovsky went on: "You have addressed me as Comrade. Only yesterday I was examined by another of your kind. He used different methods. He called me a reptile and a counter-revolutionist. He tried rough stuff on me. Yet I was born in a Tsarist prison. My father died in exile in Siberia. My mother there too. I joined the revolutionary movement and the Bolshevik Party when I was almost a child."

At this point, Mrachkovsky rose and with one swift motion removed his shirt and exposed the scars of the wounds he had received in battles for the Soviet regime. "Here are *my* decorations!" he exclaimed.

Slutski continued his silence. He had tea brought in, and offered the prisoner a glass and some cigarettes. Mrachkovsky seized the glass and the ashtray which was put before him, threw them on the floor and shouted: "So you want to bribe me? You can tell Stalin that I loathe him. He is a traitor. They took me to Molotov, who also wanted to bribe me. I spat in his face."

Slutski finally spoke up: "No, Comrade Mrachkovsky, I did not steal the Orders of the Red Banner. I received them in the Red Army, on the Tashkent front, where I fought under your command. I never considered you a reptile and do not regard you as one even now. But you have opposed and fought against the party? Of course you have. Well, the party has now commanded me to question you. And as for those wounds, look at this."

And Slutski bared part of his body, exhibiting his own war scars. "These, too, came from the civil war," he added.

Mrachkovsky listened, pondered and then said: "I don't believe you. Prove it to me."

Slutski ordered that his official biographical sketch he brought from the files of the OGPU. He gave it to Mrachkovsky to read. Then he said: "I was connected with the revolutionary tribunal after the civil war. Later the party switched me to the OGPU administration. I am now only doing my assignment, carrying out orders. If the party orders me to die, I shall go to my death."

"No, you have degenerated into a police hound, into a regular Okhrana agent," broke in Mrachkovsky. Then he stopped, hesi-

> tated and continued: "And yet, apparently, all the soul has not yet gone out of you."
>
> For the first time Slutski felt that some spark of understanding had been generated between him and Mrachkovsky . . .
>
> The interrogation lasted 90 hours without interruption. Mrachkovsky had not a minute of rest. Slutski took 4 hours off and was replaced by his secretary. Every two hours came a call from Stalin: "Did you crack him?"
>
> The end was that Slutski succeeded in convincing Mrachkovsky that the sincere confessions were necessary to save the revolution in this dangerous national and international situation. And Mrachkovsky confessed everything as a supreme sacrifice of a devoted Communist.

To which we may add that, eighteen months later, it was announced that Slutski had committed suicide.

The second case is that of Yuri Piatakov. N. Volsky[30] tells the story of a long conversation with Piatakov in the summer of 1928, in Paris, where the latter was then Soviet Trade Representative. Volsky, an old acquaintance, made a critical remark about Piatakov's rather sudden change of attitude toward Stalin's policies. Piatakov answered by a monologue of more than an hour in which he explained his conception of the Bolshevik Party as a unique phenomenon in the world.

"According to Lenin," Piatakov said, "the Communist Party is based on the principle of coercion which doesn't recognize any limitations or inhibitions. And the central idea of this principle of boundless coercion is not coercion by itself but the absence of any limitation whatsoever—moral, political and even physical, as far as that goes. Such a party is capable of achieving miracles and doing things which no other collective of men could achieve."

"A real Communist," Piatakov went on to say, "that is, a man who was raised in the party and had absorbed its spirit deeply enough becomes himself in a way a miracle man." An ordinary man, Piatakov noted, cannot honestly change his views quickly, but a Communist, by an effort of his own free will, can honestly and earnestly call white today what was black for him yesterday, and vice versa. This mystical conception smacks more of Dostoyevsky than of Lenin, but whether it relieved Piatakov's mental sufferings in his last hours is dubious.

Finally, there is the unrealistic behavior of Bukharin in the last years of his life. He, too, visited Paris—in the spring and summer of 1935—and, unannounced, dropped in on the Mensheviks, Theodore and Lydia Dan. In the ensuing conversation, they discussed Russia and Stalin at length. Bukharin said that Stalin's trouble was that he was insanely ambitious. "It even makes him miserable that he cannot convince everyone, including himself, that he is a taller man than anybody else. That is his misfortune; it may be his most human trait and perhaps his only human trait; but his reaction to his 'misfortune' is not human—it is almost devilish; he cannot help taking revenge for it on others, any others, but especially those who are in some way better or more gifted than he is . . .

"Any man who speaks better than he does is doomed; Stalin will not permit him to live, for this man will serve as an eternal reminder that he is not the first, not the best speaker; if any man writes better than he does, he is in trouble, for Stalin, and only Stalin, must be the greatest Russian writer . . . Yes, yes, he is a small, malignant man—or rather not a man but a devil . . ."

When Dan, shaken by this characterization, asked why Bukharin and other Communists had so blindly entrusted their fate to this devil, Bukharin shifted ground and said with considerable emotion: "You don't understand, it's not like that at all. It is not *him* we trust but the man in whom the party has reposed its confidence. It just so happened that he has become a sort of a symbol of the party. The lower classes, the workers, the people trust him; this may be our fault, but that's what has happened. That's why we all put our heads in his mouth . . . knowing for sure that one day he will gobble us up. He knows it, too, and merely waits for a propitious moment . . ."

When Lydia Dan broke in to ask Bukharin why he was returning to Moscow, Bukharin replied: "What, stay here? Become a refugee? Oh no, I could not live as you do, in exile from my country . . . No, come what may . . . Besides, perhaps, nothing will come."[31]

Bukharin's last remark, with its somewhat optimistic ring, was related to the rumors then current in Russia and abroad that Stalin had decided to change his course. It was said that he had drawn closer to Bukharin, whom he asked to take part in drafting the new Soviet Constitution, which, on the face of it, appeared to make important concessions to democratic ideas. News came from Russia that, under Bukharin's influence, Stalin had decided to embrace a policy of "proletarian humanism." Yet all this was wishful thinking, for Kirov, the hope of the opposition at the 17th Congress, had already been murdered, and Bukharin already suspected Stalin of the crime. His return to Russia in these circumstances betrayed a naiveté uncommon in a Bolshevik.

The Silent Guillotine

In addition to the high party leaders who were executed with or without a trial, there were the tens of thousands of lesser officials and rank-and-file Communists who were deported to forced-labor camps in the North, in Siberia and the Far East. News of what went on in these camps did not reach the West for a decade. After the end of the Second World War, a new wave of Soviet refugees included a number of persons who could bear witness to the "silent guillotine" which operated in the camps. Two episodes of many stand out, the bloodbath of the Trotskyists at Vorkuta, and the "camp of death" in the Far East.

Mass deportations of Trotskyists began immediately after Kirov's assassination. In the fall of 1936, the Trotskyists were moved from political isolation prisons and various city jails to far-away camps. Many of them were sent to the copper mines of Vorkuta, in the Arctic region of European Russia. Living conditions there were far harsher than in the jails and isolation prisons which they had left behind. The climate was extremely rigorous; the work they were required to do was beyond their physical strength; the entire regimen was hopeless. Some of the Trotskyists at Vorkuta hit on the idea of a hunger strike. From the total camp population of 3,500 political prisoners and criminal offenders, 340 deportees, belonging to various opposition groups, went on a hunger strike late in October 1936. The main core of the group was made up of Trotskyists, who issued a lengthy declaration in which they denounced the recent trial of Zinoviev and Kamenev, and asked that they themselves be either released or returned to the urban prisons.

In the first few days, the authorities took no steps against the hunger strikers. They were left alone, and no attempt at coercion was made even when they refused to go out to work. Sympathetic criminal prisoners tried to smuggle food to them, but were offended when their offerings were refused. After a few days the hunger strikers began to get weak, and the authorities decided to isolate them from the rest of the camp population. They were transferred to tents and mud huts, some distance from the main barracks. Despite the iron stoves, the canvas of the tents and the roofs of the huts let in the bitter cold. The hunger strikers were placed on wooden bunks, without mattresses or blankets. They had to use most of their energy to fight the cold. According to participants in the strike, the hunger pangs soon disappeared, but the cold became almost unbearable.

After a while, the strikers were so weak that they could not even talk to one another. At this point, the authorities resorted to forced feeding. The tents were visited by a doctor, accompanied by orderlies and armed guards. The doctor would take a striker's pulse and, depending on his condition, force about 200 grams of sweetened milk down his throat. The orderlies held the prisoner's legs, arms and head; the physician forced open his mouth, and inserted a rubber tube to pour down the milk. At first many of the strikers resisted, so that the milk spilled over their clothes, making them feel all the colder. A little later, the doctor stopped choosing the weakest and fed all of them by force. This lasted through November 1936. The most stubborn of the strikers held out until March 1937, but by then they were being forcibly fed twice a day. Several attempted suicide.

In the fall of 1937, the GPU began to pay a great deal of attention to the Trotskyists. The questioning showed that the GPU was interested not only in imaginary new "crimes" but in small incidents, conversations and remarks which had taken place five or six years previously. Those who had been questioned were transferred to other sections of the camp and kept in isolation from the other deportees. Sergei Sedov, Trotsky's younger son, a prisoner in this camp, was spirited away by airplane to Moscow, where, according to rumors, he was executed. Criminal prisoners were also questioned frequently about the conversations of the political prisoners.

A special GPU investigation commission was flown to Vorkuta in December 1937 to open a new phase of the campaign against the Trotskyists. This commission occupied an abandoned brick plant, closed some years previously, fifteen kilometers from the camp, and a school building which had been used for instruction. Small groups of political prisoners were taken to the brick factory. These men were usually not brought back to the camp, but were locked up in some of the barracks near the factory. Soon after, a brigade of ski troops from Obdorsk passed through the camp and went straight to the factory. Arrivals of prisoners from Obdorsk became more and more numerous. It was learned later that political prisoners were being brought to the brick factory from many different camps and numbered about 1,300 in all. The lights in the school and the sounds from it indicated that questioning was being carried on without interruption. Sometimes screams and explosions were heard. A little later, the brick factory requested horses and sleighs from the camp. The sleighs were returned after twenty-four hours, covered with frozen blood which had to be scraped off with knives and hacked off with axes. The next day, an announcement was made by loud-speaker from the factory that the GPU had shot forty-seven men and several women for "counter-revolutionary sabotage, attempts to escape from the camp, refusal to work and breaches of camp discipline."

The interrogations and explosions continued all winter, until March 1938. In April, a joyful rumor that the commission had left for Moscow spread through the camp. At the same time, seventy prisoners returned to the camp from the now deserted brick factory. From these survivors and from one of the members of the camp management, the few political prisoners remaining in the camp learned the gruesome truth about the factory.

After "confessing" or refusing to confess, the prisoners were condemned to be shot. However, they were not executed at the factory itself, but were taken to another camp in the hills, and there, in a ravine, stripped naked and shot, their clothes dumped into a pile, sprinkled with gasoline and set on fire. The bodies were buried in shallow graves. It appears that the explosions heard in the camp were connected with the executions. An examination of the brick factory showed that, before leaving, the commission caused to be shot all the criminal prisoners who had acted as servants at the brick factory and who knew too much. Some of the commission's own members were also shot. The head of the commission, GPU Lieutenant Kashketin, and his aide left safely for Moscow, but, according to rumor, both were liquidated by Lavrenti Beria—Yezhov's successor—upon their arrival. The seventy Trotskyists whom even Kashketin had spared were later condemned by a special session of a camp court, and they were duly executed.[32]

The "correctional labor camp" in the Far East[33] was established in 1930 at the time the second track of the Baykal-Amur Railway was laid. At first it had been populated by peasants who had been deported to the Far East in great numbers during the collectivization years. By 1937 it had grown into a tremendous enterprise, stretching over 1,500 kilometers from Chita to Khabarovsk. It embraced 22 divisions, each containing 50 camp units, with a total population of nearly a million persons. The abbreviated name of this camp was Bamlag (Baykal-Amur Railway Camp). Its Division No. 3 had a special prison for political offenders, known as the Central Isolation Prison of Bamlag Division No. 3 in the Far East.

A worker from the Donbas, "P. Georgiev," who was deported there for three years as a "socially dangerous person," was assigned to work in this prison. He was first ordered to break up the frozen soil in the prison's vegetable garden, but he was soon assigned to a building about which there were many mysterious rumors.

The isolation prison at the camp consisted of three buildings, known by their numbers. Buildings No. 2 and No. 3 were indeed prisons, but Building No. 1 served different purposes: interrogation, torture and execution "Georgiev" was assigned to Building No. 1. A deep veil of mystery covered all that occurred there. A Ukrainian named Vasilenko sat in the furnace room, with orders to admit no one. However, "Georgiev" caught a glimpse through the half-open door of piles of the most varied objects: clothing, costly fur coats, suitcases and mounds of papers, documents, notebooks, etc. "Georgiev" worked there for two years, 1937-1938. From his own observations and the remarks of others, he ascertained that the building was used for executions.

The victims were told that they were being transferred, and their effects were carefully packed in valises with name tags. From a waiting-room they were called out singly for "a final check on their documents." The floor of the dark corridor had been carpeted to deaden sound. When the prisoner opened the door at the end of the hall, he was suddenly blinded by a powerful search-light. Two executioners grabbed him by the arms from behind, while a third forced a gag into his mouth. His arms and legs were bound with twisted wire and, packed neatly, unable to move or make a sound, he was laid on a bench like a log. When enough such "logs" were assembled, they were loaded through the front door into a truck, covered with tarpaulin or blankets, and carted off. Usually several such trucks were followed by a car with a GPU physician and GPU agents who were required to be present at the execution. The prisoners were taken to a predetermined spot, shot in the back of the head, stripped and thrown into shallow graves. The bodies were then covered with layers of quicklime and earth. According to "Georgiev's" calculations, some 50,000 persons were executed while he worked in this building.

How many victims, in all, did the great purges claim? It is difficult to make an estimate of the toll among the middle-level Communist officials and rank-and-file party members. We have already noted that more than half the members of the Central Committee elected at the 17th Congress perished. We have this on the testimony of Khrushchev, many years later. No figures have yet been given on the incidence of executions in the power ranks.

However, we do have some indirect evidence, provided by Stalin in his report to the 18th Party Congress in March, 1939. Between the 17th and 18th Congresses, he said, "the party assigned over 500,000 young workers, more than twenty per cent of them women, to responsible posts." Half a million new party officials meant in fact that nearly that number of older officials had been removed. In other words, several hundred thousand old Bolsheviks in the party machine and the government apparatus had been either killed, jailed or removed from public life.

This fact offers a partial explanation for the lack of resistance in the middle and lower layers of the party to the systematic extermination of the top ranks. Surely, very few party members fully believed that virtually all of Lenin's closest comrades, collaborators and disciples had from the very beginning of the October Revolution actually been the agents of imperialistic powers, spies, traitors and renegades. To the average Communist functionary, however, the removal of these party leaders opened up intoxicating prospects of personal advancement. The removal of his superiors might become his great opportunity. Soviet publications described how men in the lower ranks of the administration, factory management and engineering staffs helped the secret police to uncover "crimes" and "plots" allegedly committed by their superiors—and were then promoted to the vacant posts. Apart from its broader effects, Stalin's reign of terror resulted in an epidemic of the rankest sort of careerism, for it enabled the young, ambitious Communists to rise rapidly—often by vile means—to positions which they would have taken years to attain otherwise.

Stalin was fully aware of this state of affairs. In the 1920s he had found it more convenient to tolerate graft and corruption than to have constant trouble with honest but rebellious oppositionists. A similar phenomenon now took place on a much vaster scale: Stalin exterminated the party's ideologists and allowed go-getters and time-servers to come to the top, fully aware that such officials rarely opposed their superiors. In these circumstances, Stalin and his immediate henchmen became the only possible source of wisdom, knowledge and experience, without any rivals for the leadership of the party or the administration of the state. The result was a concentration of power in the hands of one man which was unprecedented in world history. Stalin made no attempt to conceal it. At the 18th Congress, he declared proudly that the purge had greatly strengthened the Soviet government and made it the most stable and powerful in the world.

To appreciate Stalin's cynicism, we must read that part of his speech at the 18th Congress in which he attempted to explain how it happened:

"We learned of the espionage and conspiratorial activity of the leaders of the Trotskyists and Bukharinists only very recently, in 1937-1938, although, as the documents show, these gentlemen had been spies of foreign powers and had engaged in conspiratorial activity from the very first days of the October Revolution. How is it that we failed to learn of such a serious matter? How is this failure to be explained? The explanation is that we underestimated the strength and importance of surrounding states and their intelligence services which sought to use these people's weaknesses, ambition and lack of character to trammel them in espionage nets and to infiltrate the organs of the Soviet government. The explanation is that we underestimated the role and importance of our own socialist machinery of state . . ." (Verbatim record, p. 32.)

Had there been one bold man at the Congress, he might have pointed out that Lenin was responsible for the "failure." How could Lenin have accepted as his assistants and collaborators before the revolution such traitors as Zinoviev, Piatakov, Bukharin and Radek? How could he have appointed Rykov, a spy and traitor, as his own successor in the Soviet of Peoples' Commissars? How could he, in October 1917, have entrusted leading roles in the October Revolution to those two spies, Trotsky and Antonov-Ovseyenko? How could he have assigned the creation and leadership of the Red Army during the Civil War to Trotsky, Tukhachevsky and all those other generals who were later shot? And how could all these vile traitors have won the Civil War against such heavy odds that Lenin himself had called their victory a miracle? Was the entire doctrine of Marxism-Leninism, according to which history was the product of objective forces, to be replaced by the secret-police philosophy of Stalin, who held that the course of history was really shaped by the intelligence and counter-intelligence of capitalist countries?

At the 18th Congress no one dared any longer to put such questions to Stalin. The few top Bolsheviks who had survived the holocaust, such as Molotov, Zhdanov, Mikoyan, Kaganovich and Khrushchev, vied with one another in barbaric public worship of "the greatest," "the genius," "the god-like" Stalin. (Khrushchev was the most sycophantic of the lot.) The party had been silenced. The military leaders, too, had either been exterminated or intimidated. Stalin was now free to act.

[1]*Socialist Courier*, No 7, 1928.

[2] The resourceful GPU also found another approach to subduing Russia's technical intelligentsia. As an experiment, "technical bureaus" were organized by the GPU in prisons in Kharkov and Moscow; they were composed of jailed engineers, plant directors, professors and so on. In prison, they were given some technical assignment on which they could work. The members of these groups and their employees were accorded a special prison regime. They were given access to scientific literature, both domestic and foreign, and even permitted to receive short visits in jail from their families. Each bureau was headed by a GPU official, with one of the imprisoned specialists acting as his deputy. The first experiments were regarded as satisfactory and were imitated in other cities and prisons. The Leningrad, Caucasian and Ural branches of the GPU followed the example

of Kharkov and Moscow. Thus, it may be noted, the police extended its role in the economy.

[3] See Memoirs of N. Volsky, Russian Archives, Columbia University, New York.

[4] During the 30 years which have elapsed since the Menshevik trial neither the family of Eva Broido nor her friends have been able to obtain any reliable information as to her fate. According to unofficial reports she was punished by 20 years' imprisonment and there were rumors that she had been sent to the Orel Prison. Whether Eva Broido was still in Orel during the German occupation of 1942-1943 could not be verified.

[5] D. Dallin and B. Nikolaevsky, *Forced Labor in Soviet Russia,* Yale University Press, 1947.

[6] Paul Barton, *L'Institution concentracionnaire en Russie,* Paris, 1959.

[7] Berlin, 1922.

[8] Orlov, Alexander, *The Secret History of Stalin's Crimes.* New York, 1953, pp. 10-19.

[9] This account of Kirov's murder is borne out by an official document emanating from the Soviet government. On page 253 of the official report on the trial of the "Rightist-Trotskyist Center," involving Bukharin, Rykov and others, we read how the defendant Yagoda, former deputy chairman of the GPU, now declared a traitor and plotter, testified that the murder was indeed organized by Zaporozhets. He stated that "Zaporozhets informed him that Nikolaev had been detained by the NKVD agents and that a revolver and a map of Kirov's movements was found on him. Nikolaev was set free. Soon afterwards, Kirov was killed by this same Nikolaev."

As this statement was contradicted by neither the prosecutor nor the chairman of the court it would seem that this part of it, at least, was authentic. To be sure, Yagoda went on to state that Zaporozhets was under orders from the rightist plotters, but this was an obvious fabrication; all crimes committed at that time in the Soviet Union were laid at their door.

[10] Some two years later Yenukidze himself was executed after one of the trials, swept away by the same wave of terror which was officially unleashed by his decree.

[11] *The Crimes of the Stalin Era,* by Nikita Khrushchev, annotated by Boris I. Nikolaevsky, New York. 1956, p. 22.

[12] *Ibid.,* p. 23.

[13] Khrushchev's speech, p. 35. In his annotations, Boris Nikolaevsky quotes the relevant circular issued by the People's Commissar for Home Affairs, Boris D. Berman, in the winter of 1936/37.

[14] *Bulletin Oppositsii,* No. 52-53, p. 11.

[15] *Socialist Courier,* No. 16, August 30, 1936, p. 13.

[16] Friedrich Adler, "The Wild Trials in Moscow, 1938."

[17] *Reports of Court Proceedings,* August 19-24, 1936, pp. 44-45.

[18] Despite this ferocious and blood-thirsty campaign, some observers noted certain facts which seemed to indicate the possibility that some of the main defendants might be pardoned. Thus, five days before the trial, the newspapers carried a decree by the Praesidium of the VTsIK repealing a clause in the decree of December 1, 1934, prohibiting applications for pardon. Some observers, therefore, concluded that the particularly damaging and passionate self-accusations of the defendants had been exchanged for indirect promise of a pardon. Nevertheless, no pardons were granted at this particular trial. All sixteen defendants were shot.

[19] See unpublished work by D. Y. Dallin.

[20] *The New York Times,* November 25, 1936, p. 9.

[21] Orlov, *op. cit.,* pp. 181, ff.

[22] This author's personal view is that Piatakov had to be publicly discredited and removed from the scene for the reason that his was one of the six names mentioned in Lenin's testament as possible party leaders. At a time when Trotsky had been discredited and exiled (although not yet assassinated) and when Zinoviev and Kamenev had been

both discredited and executed, apart from Stalin only Bukharin and Piatakov still remained—those whom Lenin had termed as highly promising young party theoreticians. It is clear that they had to be smeared and liquidated so that Stalin should remain on the scene as the only party leader and theoretician who had Lenin's blessing.

[23] Krivitsky has written: "When Radek refused to answer the young investigator Kedrov, they took him to Stalin." . . . When he returned from the Kremlin, Radek was in an altogether different mood . . . He said to Kedrov: "You can go to sleep, Kedrov. I will do the rest." (Walter Krivitsky, *Stalin's Secret Service*. New York, 1940.)

[24] Society for Promotion of Aviation and Defense against Chemical Warfare.

[25] Leon Blum, "Déposition," *Populaire de Paris*, January 4, 1952.

[26] Churchill, Vol. I, p. 288.

[27] Twelve years later the learned jurist and professor of criminology, A. Y. Vyshinsky, called in his book (*Theory of Trial Evidence in Soviet Law*. Moscow, 1950, pp.261-267) "medieval" and "radically wrong" the "practice when admission of one's guilt was deemed to be a solid and incontrovertible truth, even though this admission was extorted by torture."

But it would be wrong to think that Mr. Vyshinsky was alluding in this quotation to his own investigation methods in the big show-trials of 1936-1938. On the contrary: speaking of the political trials of this period, he explains that in that time "the administration of justice made it necessary for the judge to decide a question not from the viewpoint of absolute truth but from that of maximum probability of given factors which the court is called upon to appraise." (*Sovietskoie Gosudarstvennoie Pravo,* No. 2, 1946, pp. 8-9).

The above words and the words of the defendants show clearly what Vyshinsky had in mind when speaking of the "absolute truth" and "maximum probability" . . .

[28] See Ivanov-Razumnik, *Tiurmy i Ssylki*. Chekhov Publishing House, New York, 1953, p. 271.

[29] *Ibid.*, p. 280.

[30] Unpublished Memoirs of N. Volsky, Columbia University Russian Archives, pp. 20-21.

[31] Written down from memory by Lydia Dan in 1949.

[32] This information is based on a report by Eduard Dunne, a Latvian worker who had taken part in the October Revolution in Moscow and had fought in the Civil War. A party member of long standing, he had once joined an opposition group known as "Democratic Centralism" and was one of the fifteen signers of the manifesto which the group had submitted to the Communist Party Congress on June 27, 1927. Dunne died in Paris in 1953. His information has been confirmed and supplemented by another survivor of Vorkuta now in the United States. The latter has reported that among those shot at Vorkuta were some foreign Communists, including the secretary of Ernst Thaelmann, the German Communist leader who had taken refuge from Hitler in Moscow in 1933. Another Vorkuta victim was the American Communist, George Andreychin, who had been once sentenced to 15 years imprisonment in Boston, but had preferred Soviet "freedom" to a "capitalist" jail. Both witnesses agree that mass extermination on the Vorkuta scale took place in a number of other camps, in Chibiu and Usa, which was a Pechora camp center, also in the Far North. There are also reports of mass shootings in Cherdyn, where according to available information only a few dozen prisoners survived out of 500.

[33] P. Georgiev, "A Soviet Buchenwald," *Socialist Courier*, 1951, No. 1, p. 19, and No. 3, p. 74.

CHAPTER 18

The Road to the Second World War

Peace at any Price

Although Hitler's rise to power in Germany marked a turning point in world history, this crucial moment was not immediately recognized by European public opinion. As in Germany itself, where Nazism was first considered an incidental phenomenon which could not last long, so in Europe the political leaders tended to view Nazism as a temporary aberration, doomed to disappear soon without serious consequences. True, the frontier posts in France and Switzerland were flooded with streams of refugees from Germany, including many Jews and left-wing politicians fearing persecution and arrest. But, for Europe, this was nothing new and failed to cause any great concern.

England and France in particular felt reassured by the diplomatic cordon set up by the Entente to encircle Germany and by the limitations imposed by Versailles. A few powerless groups of emigrés, who now included, besides the Russian refugees, those from Germany (Rudolf Hilferding, Otto Wells, and many other leaders of the Social Democratic Party), demanded vainly that the European democracies do something while there was still time. But the prevailing spirit was that of "business as usual." Though everyone knew that Germany's military preparations were in flagrant violation of the Versailles Treaty, no one did or said anything that implied "interference" in Germany's internal affairs. Only Pilsudski suggested that Western Silesia should be occupied by Polish troops (according to another version, he wanted to occupy the strategic territory of Spiegelplatte in Pomerania) and the right bank of the Rhine by French troops. But his proposals were indignantly rejected by France, England and the other powers.

It may be interesting to quote the testimony of Leon Blum in this connection. In the period between the two wars, Blum was the recognized leader of the French Socialist Party. We have his testimony of June 18, 1947, before the Commission of the French Chamber of Deputies appointed to study the causes of the Second World War. Leon Blum began his statement of the problem by directly posing the question whether it had been possible or not to prevent the war in 1933. "After many years and much meditation," he had arrived at the opinion that it would have been possible to prevent the war through the same policy with which the successor states of the Austro-Hungarian Empire—Czechoslovakia, Rumania, Yugoslavia and Poland—had successfully prevented the restoration of the Hapsburg monarchy in 1932, namely, by adopting the position that "every attempt to restore the monarchy in Hungary would be regarded as a *casus belli*" and that every practical measure leading to a restoration would be met by collective military action.

In a similar way, England, France and Poland could have jointly declared that the establishment of a Nazi government in Germany would be regarded as a war provocation and treated accordingly by the military forces of the three powers. But Blum frankly admitted that, if this was not done, the guilt did not rest exclusively with the governments. The responsibility was also shared by the socialist movement.

> I am saying now, with all my heart and conscience, that England, France and Poland, joined together, could and should have undertaken a preventive action against Hitler in 1933. I am telling you this with a sentiment which approaches remorse, because if the other socialist parties and we, who were regarded at that time as bleating pacifists and sometimes even as defenders of Germany, had demanded that our governments prohibit under the threat of force the establishment of a Nazi government in Germany, I am convinced that we would have had public opinion and a majority in the parliament with us. We didn't do so.

Blum added that the motives for inaction were completely honorable, but misguided just the same.[1]

In the same vein, Blum depicted the fatal result of the events of March 7, 1936—the day Hitler sent detachments of the Wehrmacht to reoccupy the German territory on the left bank of the Rhine, which had been barred to the German armed forces by the Versailles Treaty. It was entirely in the power of the French government to prevent the re-militarization of the Rhineland by simply sending a small detachment of the French army to meet the German troops and telling them to move back. We now know that Hitler expected the French to do just that, and the German officers had orders, signed by Hitler himself, to turn back the moment they made contact with French troops. But the French government acted very strangely. The first reaction of the Premier, Albert Sarraut, was to declare that if German troops tried to penetrate the forbidden zone, France would take the necessary measures to prevent them. But this declaration provoked a storm of protest on the left. Delegations of socialists, Communists and various pacific organizations led mostly by Communists besieged Sarraut with the demand to revoke this order. Hundreds of telegrams of various peace societies protested against the "war provocation." The Communists and the pacifists jointly organized a feverish compaign against the "war-mongering policy" of the Sarraut cabinet. Sarraut gave in and withdrew his order.[2] Thus, without any incident or even moral resistance, German troops reoccupied the vital zone which had been forbidden to them since 1918. It is hard to find words to characterize the colossal repercussions of this capitulation of France as a great power. Leon Blum said: " . . . The day of March 7th, 1936, created an invisible Siegfried Line which separated France from the rest of Europe . . ."[3]

When Blum himself became Premier in June 1936, the former Prime Minister of Yugoslavia, Stojadinovich, came to congratulate him. He told Blum that he was deeply sorry that Yugoslavia could not maintain its old traditional friendship with France, because "you yourself permitted the German danger to install itself and to develop . . . now things have changed and the Yugoslavs are compelled to adjust themselves to the changed situation. We have to reckon now with the German danger and to find a way of dealing and establishing friendly relations with them."

In almost identical terms, a minister from Rumania confessed to

Blum that the relations between Rumania and France were deteriorating under the pressure of Germany's growing military force. In 1937, when Blum was Vice Premier under Camille Chautemps, he visited Prague to represent France at the funeral of the late Thomas Masaryk, the beloved first President of Czechoslovakia. Before a joint session of French, Polish, Rumanian, Czechoslovakian, and Yugoslav diplomats, Blum tried to put forward the idea of creating a solid bloc of their countries, but he came to realize that it had already become impractical. The reason was always the same: Now that the Germans had remilitarized the Rhineland, how would France come to their rescue if they were attacked by Germany? Each of France's former allies asked for arms, money and other things, but something had snapped in the relations between them and France—"a principle was broken and confidence betrayed." (See *Populaire*, January 3, 1952.)

It must be realized that in 1933, less than 15 years after the Armistice, the countries of Europe had not yet fully recovered from the material, demographic and psychological upheavals of World War I. A revulsion against war and a deep certitude that another world conflagration could not be tolerated had deeply permeated the masses, the intelligentsia and even the politicians of the Allied countries, including the United States, which, though not a member of the League of Nations, was still an important international factor. The League of Nations met regularly, and occupied itself more and more with disarmament problems. The clownish figure of Hitler, who was considered merely a noisemaker, rather spoiled the picture of a general striving for peace. Europe had already to deal with one dictatorship of the same type—the Italian. But the rise to power of Mussolini and his Blackshirts caused no special alarm in European governmental circles. In Italy itself, the people grew accustomed to the regime, the trains began to run on time, new buildings rose and new archaeological work was carried on to make the Eternal City even more beautiful. Why should anyone believe that Hitler would be more dangerous than Mussolini? Hitler, of course, was associated with the persecution of Jews, and from time to time pogroms occurred in Germany. But, after all, there were pogroms against the Jews in Pilsudski's Poland, Rumania and other countries.

The socialists also engaged in some rather distorted thinking. The socialists were even more militantly pacifist than other European political groups, as shown by the conference of the Socialist International in Paris in August 1933. It was the first meeting of the International since Hitler's rise to power. The German trade unions had already been dissolved or seized by the Nazis. The Social Democratic Party had been ejected from the Reichstag and outlawed. It was represented at the conference by a refugee delegation from Czechoslovakia. By then, Leipart, the leader of the German trade unions, knew that von Schleicher had proven to be no Machiavelli but an idle wordmonger and that no agreement between the trade unions and Hitler was possible. Otto Wells, chairman of the German Social Democratic Party, had quoted Leipart against the Mensheviks to prove that, above all, democratic principles could not be sacrificed in the fight against the Nazis; later, at a closed meeting of the International's executive committee, Wells humbly admitted that the Mensheviks had been right and his own hopes for a peaceful liquidation of Hitler had been illusory.

Some speakers at the conference demanded energetic measures. Rudolf Hilferding's group declared that only intervention by England, France, Poland and other countries could prevent Europe from slipping fatally into a new war. Hilferding pointed out that the dangers of intervention would be minimal, since Hitler had just embarked on his armament program and could not yet put up a serious resistance. Indeed, Hilferding insisted, Hitler would not even try to fight but would simply retreat and thus demonstrate the utter helplessness of the new German militarism and the emptiness of his promises in the face of the Western powers' determination. Moreover, he contended, the Reichswehr would not allow itself to be dragged into a conflict without far greater support behind it.

However, when the question of preventive action was put forward at the joint session of the executive committee of the Social International and the Amsterdam Trade Union Federation, the solution proposed by the International remained very much what it had been before: immediate, controlled, international disarmament. How disarmament was possible in a country ruled by Hitler and his SS, the International did not explain.

While refusing to see this basic flaw in the old pacifist position, the International continued to insist that "the *private* production of weapons must be completely forbidden" and that arms control, "functioning unceasingly in all countries," must be set up. The countries which rejected these demands should be viewed as "aggressors" and "organized labor should use the general strike in these countries." It was the duty of the workers in other countries to "support this movement and to organize boycotts against the aggressor country."[4]

But how could the German proletariat call a general strike in a country which, by that time, was totally controlled by the Nazi Party with its secret police and an army that had passed over to its side completely? It was tantamount to asking the German workers to start a bloody revolution under the most unfavorable conditions. The practical impossibility of this "revolutionary" resolution was self-evident. But even among those who thought of themselves as revolutionaries, obsolete concepts were deeply entrenched. The Socialist International and the International Federation of Trade Unions failed to guide the German workers and the rest of the world's working classes in this tragic situation. The one right solution was an increase in the armament of Britain and France to counterbalance the Nazis' secret arming. But this measure, too, was rejected by public opinion in both countries.

So it proved impossible for the European community as a whole to agree on intervention.

At that time, moreover, the British government did not believe that Nazism presented a serious threat to Britain and to the rest of Europe.

No greater insight was displayed by the British Labour Party. It was frozen in its pacifist tracks and refused to depart from its policy of avoiding war at almost any price and maintaining peace through the League of Nations and the policy of disarmament. After Hitler came to power, the British Labour Party formed the hard core of the disarmament advocates within the Socialist International. Its leader, Arthur Henderson, acted as chairman of the League's Disarmament Committee. Among the leaders of the Labour Party, however, some showed signs of grasping the gravity of the situation and giving it a lot of thought. Walter Citrine, President of the International Federation of Trade Unions, and some of his colleagues took part in a discussion club devoted to international affairs organized by Winston Churchill for MPs of various parties and groups.

The French situation was still more complicated. Despite the shock caused by Hitler's rise to power in Germany, popular attention was distracted by a moral crisis in French political life. Instead of concentrating on international problems, France's politicians immersed themselves in an internal political crisis caused by the sensational exposure of widespread corruption in the parliamentary and governmental machinery of the Third Republic.

When Edouard Daladier tried to implicate the former Paris Prefect of Police, Jean Chiappe, a right-wing politician compromised in the corruption scandals, a political storm broke loose. Its high point was a demonstration staged by the "Croix de Feu," a fascist war veterans' organization, with the support of royalist and Communist students (February 7). The demonstrators failed only by a hairbreadth to capture the Chamber of Deputies. The Third Republic was saved by the loyalty of a section of the Gardes Republicains which dispersed the demonstration by force.

This incident profoundly influenced the workers, who had until then been little interested in parliamentary struggles and scandals. The socialist and labor leaders—especially Leon Jouhaux, the General Secretary of the French trade union movement (*Confederation Generale du Travail,* C.G.T.)—decided to call mass anti-fascist demonstrations all over the country. The demonstrations took place on February 12, and at the last moment, the Communists joined the demonstration. This move indicated that Moscow had adopted a different policy for France than it had for Germany—it came out for a united front between the socialists and the Communists in France. The crisis was temporarily resolved by the formation of a right-of-center cabinet headed by former President Gaston Doumergue. But the workers' demonstrations and the new Communist line soon cleared the way for the Popular Front, i.e., a bloc of the Radical Socialist, the Socialist and the Communist parties. This new alignment—in which the Socialist Party leaders took care to forestall Communist intrigues—brought France its most progressive government, under Leon Blum in 1936.

The Austrian situation was different. Although the Social Democrats had long been the dominant party in the Austrian cities, the peasants mainly supported conservative, reactionary and clerical groups, and two varieties of fascism had begun to raise their heads. The so-called Christian Social Party had come more and more under the influence of a Mussolini-type of fascism, while a splinter group from the Christian Social Party had turned to the Nazis especially after Hitler's accession to power in Germany. The Social Democrats had formed a defense organization composed of workers—the Schutzbund—with weapons hidden in various places; the peasant parties maintained their own paramilitary force, the Heimwehr, armed by the police where the local administrations were fascist.

By February 1934, relations between the two camps—the Social Democrats and the two forms of fascism—had reached the point of open conflict. Linz was a major industrial center, with a large working-class population, but it was surrounded on all sides by peasant strongholds. In the first days of February 1934, the Heimwehr concentrated all its military units around Linz and presented the Social Democratic Party with an ultimatum. It demanded the dissolution of the administrative Council of the province of Upper Austria, which had a socialist majority; its replacement by a governing committee to be composed of the leaders of the fascist paramilitary formations; and the resignation of all Social Democrats who occupied municipal posts in the city of Linz and in the province of Upper Austria. The Linz socialists realized that the Linz maneuver would be repeated in all other Austrian towns unless they acted immediately, and decided to fight.

At dawn on February 12, the police tried to occupy the headquarters of the Linz workers' organizations. The workers resisted, and shooting began in all parts of the city. A few hours later the news of the uprising in Linz reached Vienna, and the Viennese Social Democratic Party and the Schutzbund immediately joined the movement. For four days Vienna was the scene of armed battles between the workers (who barricaded themselves in the municipal houses), the police and army-units equipped with modern weapons. The uprising spread to other cities of Austria. For a few days Austria was in a state of civil war but the old rifles of the workers could not win against a regular army.

Hundreds of workers, women and children were wounded, many were killed, thousands were arrested and imprisoned, while other thousands went into hiding. Vienna was now in the hands of the fascist government and the Heimwehr. After destroying democracy, the fascist Heimwehr could resist neither Mussolini nor Hitler. Its "Anschluss" with Nazi Germany did not occur till 1938, but its fate was sealed in February 1934.

In 1933 and in the following 6 years, Stalin still had to accomplish many vital tasks in the field of domestic policy and in that of international policy as well, before he could be ready for his ultimate goal, of which he never stopped dreaming. He had to reorganize radically the economy of the Soviet state, create the heavy industry which was absolutely indispensable for a big war, and crush the resistance to his grandiose plans which existed within Soviet society. This included, of course, a giant purge in the apparatus of the state, in the army and last but not least, in the Communist Party itself. All that had to be achieved in time for the Great Hour.

At the same time, it was necessary for Stalin to watch carefully the man of whom he was never completely sure as to whether he was his most dangerous foe or his future comrade-in-arms. The trouble was that Hitler himself was not sure of the way he was going to act. He was looking for "Lebensraum" and generally was convinced that this "Lebensraum" lay in the East, within and beyond the borders of the Soviet state.

And then, was it not his historic mission to destroy the barbaric Bolsheviks and the Soviet state? On the other hand, Hitler knew that Germany could never become really great as long as the British world empire had not been dismembered and France had not been severely punished for the humiliation of the "Vaterland" at Versailles. Stalin was following closely Hitler's ideological zigzags and was trying to adjust his own strategy to the changes of Hitler's mind.

This led to a dual policy toward Hitler, which was to ensure that in the "next round of wars and revolutions" Soviet Russia would be in a position to avert the full force of Hitler's thrust; and at the same time, to witness the collapse of the Versailles system. Because of the Western policy of appeasement, the strongest Central European barrier to Nazism—Czechoslovakia—was sacrificed, and Hitler could avenge

1918 in France with little fear for his rear, once he had come to terms with Stalin.

But Stalin could never, in the six-and-a-half years between Hitler's advent and the beginning of the Second World War, be completely sure of the West either. His early overtures toward Nazism having failed, he launched, in 1934, the new Communist line of the united front against fascism. (This line, it should be noted, was always limited in the sense that Stalin never wished the socialist-led coalitions to prove too successful, for fear of the corrosive effects on the Communist movement; thus, Stalin helped the Spanish Republic avert defeat in 1936, but he never gave it enough for victory.) Concomitantly with this public anti-Nazi policy, Stalin continued secretly to woo Hitler. He made no firm commitments till the last, although there was a great show of anti-fascist diplomacy which many Communists, including perhaps several who carried it out, took quite seriously.

This anti-fascist diplomacy is associated with the name of Maxim Litvinov, who in 1930 became Soviet Foreign Minister in place of the ailing Chicherin. Litvinov was an old Bolshevik and a Jew besides, and there seemed little doubt that he was sincerely committed to an anti-Nazi course. Nevertheless, during his tenure, other agencies of the Soviet regime maintained periodic contacts with the Nazis. And when the time came for Stalin to make his devil's pact with Hitler, Litvinov was dismissed.

Litvinov's diplomacy was at first centered on the conclusion of bilateral non-aggression pacts with Russia's immediate neighbors. In 1926, Chicherin had offered Poland a non-aggression pact but Poland had made her acceptance conditional on similar Soviet pacts with all the other neighboring states. Chicherin had refused to accept this condition; but in 1931, Litvinov accepted it. He followed up by approaching Finland, Latvia, and Estonia. A non-aggression treaty with Finland was concluded on January 21, 1932, with Poland on January 25, with Latvia on February 5, and with Esthonia on May 4. On February 12, 1932, Litvinov put forward his famous proposal for total disarmament, proposing at the same time an alternative plan for arms cuts.

When Hitler came to power, Litvinov was ordered to attempt diplomatically to isolate Hitler. In July 1933, the League of Nations agreed upon the definition of an aggressor,[5] and the definition was accepted by Soviet Russia, although it was still outside the League. In 1934, Russia joined the League and her delegate, Litvinov, became one of the most eloquent and popular champions of the idea of collective security against aggression.

The Comintern line was also modified to correspond to Litvinov's new policy. The French Communists, who had marched on February 6, 1934 alongside the fascist Croix de Feu and the royalist Camelots du Roi, were ordered on February 12th to join the anti-fascist demonstrations of trade-unionists and socialists, as already mentioned. Obviously, the thought of a fascist France, in league with Germany and Italy, was a terrifying one for Stalin. In time, Moscow formally proposed a united front with the socialists. It also gave all possible support to the leading pacifist organizations, which at that time, under the skilled leadership of Willi Munzenberg and other Moscow agents, were Communist-front organizations. Their line shifted from pacifism to anti-fascism with little disturbance.

But did all this really mean that Stalin was allying himself with the West against Hitler? In the *Socialist Courier* of April 15, 1938, Walter Krivitsky, until 1937 a high Soviet military intelligence officer, revealed that behind the façade of anti-fascism, Stalin was still committed to the establishment of friendly relations with Germany. In Stalin's opinion, this was the country the Soviets had to fear most and, therefore, its friendship was most vital. This basic concept of Stalin's foreign policy, Krivitsky insisted, had not in the least been altered by Hitler's efforts to organize an international anti-Communist bloc. On the contrary, Krivitsky maintained, Hitler's hostility only made Stalin try still harder to establish friendly ties. Stalin considered it a great achievement to renew the Soviet-German trade pact in 1934. He instructed his representatives in economic negotiations with Germany to make all possible concessions. The main thing, he would tell them, was to achieve agreement.

At one time, Stalin hoped to reach an agreement with Poland. According to Krivitsky, this matter was discussed at a special meeting of the Politburo to which the representatives of the interested Soviet agencies were invited:

> The question of what Poland would do was thoroughly analyzed. Litvinov, Radek, and the representative of the People's Commissariat of Defense thought that at a given moment Poland could join the Soviet Union. Only Artuzov, the representative of the NKVD, opposed this view. He considered the prospects of a Polish-Soviet agreement as pure wishful thinking.

Poland balked at an agreement with the Soviets, and Stalin became even more convinced that the Kremlin was compelled to reach an understanding with Hitler.[6]

Krivitsky writes:

> By all possible means, official and unofficial, Stalin tried to persuade Hitler's entourage that his attempts to reach an agreement with Germany were sincere. And, although he failed to receive any hopeful reaction to his advances, Stalin continued stubbornly to press his objective . . . Then came June 30, 1935 when Hitler, with one blow, annihilated the Roehm-Schleicher group. At the Politburo meeting with the representatives of all the interested agencies, Stalin again returned to his pet idea—the necessity of of reaching an agreement with Hitler.[7]

Stalin believed that Hitler's dictatorship, far from having weakened, had gained in stability from the destruction of its internal opposition. He was further impressed by the skein of fascist successes which testified to Hitler's power and the weakness and disunity of the Western forces. In February 1934, there was the triumph of the Austrian fascists.

On August 2, 1934, the German Reichswehr had to take a personal loyalty oath to Hitler as Commander-in-Chief. On February 28, 1935, Hitler re-established the German General Staff which had been abolished by the Versailles Treaty. On March 5, he announced the re-creation of Germany's military Air Force. On March 16, he reinstituted universal military service, prohibited at Versailles. That spring, too, Hitler started to build a navy, also prohibited at Versailles. Instead of protesting, England concluded a naval pact with Hitler on June 18, 1935. On June 30 came the "blood purge" which wiped out the "Nazi left" (Roehm, etc.) and the "Army right" (von Schleicher). On March 7, 1936, Hitler remilitarized the left bank of the Rhine—with no opposition whatever. This, surely, was a major turning point from which Stalin was bound to draw conclusions about the policy of the leading statesmen of England and France. As John Wheeler-Bennett has correctly pointed out:

"Totally unprepared for war, reaping the bitter fruit of five years' neglect of national defenses and armaments and of blindly and willfully ignoring the storm signals so blatantly displayed across the Rhine, the French and British governments were bent upon the preservation of peace at any price, even at the sacrifice of their own vital interests and, in the case of France, of her bounded duty and plighted word."

By November 1937, the overall design of Hitler's diplomatic and military strategy had been completed. His plans and considerations were communicated, in a solemn report, to a small group of German diplomats and military men summoned to a secret meeting. The plan was based on demanding the "liberation of all Germans living under foreign domination," and their reunification with the Greater Germany. This meant "Anschluss" with Austria, wresting the Sudetenland away from Czechoslovakia, and the annexation of German-populated territories in Poland. In reality, it was an attempt to expand toward the East, first into Central Europe, and then in the direction of the Ukraine. Eastward aggression was first on the schedule, both from considerations of nationalist demagogery and in order to secure the neutrality of the Western powers. What Hitler counted on was that the Western powers, because of their desire for peace, would accept his crusade against the Slav nations placidly.

The conservative generals and diplomats warned that England and France would resist Germany in the East. But Hitler coolly predicted that England and France, far from interfering with his plans, would in fact assist him in the annexation of German-populated territories.

Hitler proved right. The "Anschluss" with Austria (March 1938) aroused no Western opposition. And, having started a skillfully organized propaganda for the protection of Sudeten Germans, Hitler succeeded in securing recognition by the West of the principle of national self-determination for the Sudeten. On this basis, France and England undertook the task of convincing Czechoslovakia that this region should be voluntarily ceded to Germany. True, such a concession meant a complete collapse of Czechoslovakia's defenses, as it did away with the strong fortifications in the Sudeten mountains. But had not the Fuehrer himself made a statement, in a talk with Chamberlain, that the Sudetenland was his last aspiration, and that no other demands would be made upon any of the great powers? Negotiations were conducted in September 1938, first at Godesberg and then at Munich, which ended in the cession of the Sudetenland to Germany, by a solemn international agreement which within a year of its signing had become notorious.

It would, however, be wrong to blame Munich solely on the shortsightedness and incompetence of a handful of diplomats and political leaders in England and France. Their policy, in fact, correctly expressed the current temper of their peoples; this is evident from the outbursts of jubilant joy with which the announcement of the Munich pact was greeted in both France and England. In France, Daladier, back from Munich after signing the agreement, received a hero's welcome at a joint session of both Houses in which every member, on the left and the right alike, took part. There was a similar demonstration in England's House of Commons. In the memoirs of Lord Waltham we find a description of this historic session.

Even in the USA, President Roosevelt on August 28, 1938 (a month before the Munich agreement) sent word to Mr. Chamberlain saying that he was a "good man" if he could avert war by making a few concessions to Germany. True, George S. Messersmith, Assistant Secretary of State, remained extremely skeptical and pessimistic. On the other hand, Truman Smith, the Military Attaché in Berlin, thought that visions of Hitler as a future world conqueror were grossly exaggerated. All that Hitler needed was one or two decades of undisturbed peace for carrying out his program.[9]

The Munich agreement, of course, paved the way for the Second World War. A chronological listing of the events of 1938 will prove the point. In March of that year, after Dollfuss had been assassinated by the Nazi followers, little Austria was subjected to tremendous pressure from Germany, which insisted that the lesser country must voluntarily join its Big Brother, the German Reich. Formal guarantees of Austria's independence, however, had been given not only by France and England but by Italy as well, and for a while Mussolini's policy was to prevent the unification of Germany and Austria. The situation changed in 1938. When the ministries for foreign affairs of the larger states were sounded out, as a preliminary move, it became clear that none of the great powers was willing to get itself involved in a war with Germany over Austria. Next came Marshal Goering's telephone order to the Austrian government—which had a few Nazi members—to surrender without resistance to the German troops, already marching on Austria. When German tanks rolled into Austria, they were greeted by women bearing flowers.

On March 14, 1939, Dr. Hacha, who had replaced Benes as president of Czechoslovakia, was summoned to Berlin by Hitler. There he was told that already on March 15th German troops had been ordered by Hitler to occupy Prague. Any resistance would be crushed by aerial bombardment. The Czech state must immediately accede to the German demands ("independence" for Slovakia, a German protectorate over the Czech lands) if Prague and other cities were to be saved from destruction. Dr. Hacha, on the verge of collapse, saw no alternative but to submit to Hitler's ultimatum. Czechoslovakia was wiped off the map.

France and England, which had guaranteed the inviolability of Czech borders following the cession of the Sudetenland, at last realized that they had been tricked.

This did not mean that the Conservative cabinet of Chamberlain, or the French government headed by Daladier and Bonnet, at once decided to abandon the policy of appeasement. True, England and France addressed a formal protest to Hitler over his breach of the Munich agreement, and even recalled their ambassadors from Berlin. This did not, however, stop the London government from transferring Czech funds in the amount of 6 million pounds, kept in the Bank of England, to the Treasury of the Third Reich through the International Clearing House.[10]

Still, the seizure of Prague and the dismemberment of Czechoslovakia dealt a heavy blow to the "Munich" policy. England became the scene of a "diplomatic revolution." This was clear in the House of Commons on March 16th when the Minister for Foreign Affairs, Sir John Simon, rose to answer questions by members of the House regarding the developments in Prague. Sir John tried to ridicule the idea of going to the aid of Czechoslovakia, the victim of aggression. Why, argued Sir Simon, had not Hitler himself declared that Czechoslovakia no longer exists? How, then, can we render assistance to a non-existent country? But Sir John Simon's speech was received with distinct disapproval.

The next day, March 17th, on the eve of his seventieth birthday, Chamberlain was scheduled to deliver an important political speech at Birmingham, in the evening. After the debate in the House, Chamberlain made a few revisions in the prepared speech, to which he added a pointed, unambiguous warning to Hitler. He omitted any regrets over the past, but stated clearly and unequivocally that Hitler had not fulfilled the obligations stipulated at Munich and that Great Britain would brook no further deception. Chamberlain's speech made a strong impression and greatly enhanced the will to resist further aggression from Hitler, not only in England but in the rest of the world as well. The new line adopted by the British government won full approval of both Parliament and the people.

In France, where "appeasement" trends proved more deeply rooted, the reaction was far less intense. Georges Bonnet, immediately before the Munich parley, had privately told Ribbentrop that once the pact was signed, France would never again place the question of Czechoslovakia on the agenda of diplomatic negotiations.[11] This, in fact, was the policy to which France adhered even after the seizure of Prague. The climate of Western Europe began to change, nevertheless, as Hitler's plans for further eastward advance were becoming increasingly clear. German troops occupied Memel; and Danzig, still a Free City, was subjected to a *de facto* blockade. All signs pointed to Poland as the next objective on Hitler's agenda. These reports were confirmed and reinforced by warnings which the London government received from some of the German generals, diplomats and public leaders who opposed Hitler. According to Wheeler-Bennett[12] and Wenzel Jaksh,[13] shortly after the occupation of Prague, Schacht, Goerdeler and a group of military men working with them sent a warning to London that Hitler was going to attack Poland not later than the fall of the same year.

Stalin and Hitler

It was natural, under the circumstances, that England, the leading power of the Allied camp, should now turn her attention to the position taken by the Soviet Union. An attempt was made to sound out the Kremlin on its true intentions, which remained completely inscrutable. Litvinov's speeches in the League of Nations and elsewhere seemed perfectly clear and direct. The Soviet Union, Litvinov said, was ready to join the common front against Hitler and to stop Nazi expansion into Central and Eastern Europe. In 1935 certain steps had been taken by Litvinov toward creating a rapprochement between the Soviet Union, Czechoslovakia, France and Rumania. On May 2nd and 14th of the same year, after long negotiations, a pact for mutual assistance in the event of German attack had been signed by France and Russia, at Paris and Moscow. In addition, a similar pact had been signed with Czechoslovakia on May 16th. But this pact bound Russia to defend Czechoslovakia only if France did—and was never tested because of Munich.

On March 18, 1939, after the fall of Prague, Litvinov informed Berlin that the USSR did not recognize the annexation of Czechoslovakia. Yet Russia, unlike England and France, did not recall her ambassador from Berlin. Meanwhile former prominent GPU officials who had opposed a rapprochement with Hitler—such as Krivitsky (see our pp. 436-437) or Ignats Reiss, whom agents of the GPU killed in Switzerland in 1937 (the latter left a diary)[14]—warned that Stalin, inspired both by fear and by anticipation of an impending revolution, was attempting to exploit both sides, with Hitler his first concern.

After the occupation of Prague, the British Foreign Office made a new attempt to sound out Moscow's attitudes. London knew of the conversation which had taken place in Geneva somewhat earlier between Leon Blum and Litvinov. In a confidential, man-to-man talk, Blum had asked Litvinov: Would the Soviet Union honor the obligations it had assumed in its pacts with Czechoslovakia and France? After a moment's hesitation, Litvinov replied: "If by that time I am still the Minister for Foreign Affairs, it certainly will."[15]

Thus, on March 23, 1939, the British Minister for Foreign Trade, Hudson, arrived in Moscow for preliminary negotiations on a trade agreement. He had long talks with Litvinov, Mikoyan and Molotov, but did not see Stalin. Some time later, on April 15 and 16, 1939, the British Ambassador in Moscow, Seeds, was received by Litvinov and raised an official question as to the possibility of a triple alliance between England, France and the USSR. There was no mention of this occasion in the Soviet press, although Seeds was received by Litvinov twice. Two days later, on April 18, the Soviet Ambassador in Berlin, Merkalov, called on the German Assistant Minister for Foreign Affairs, Weizsacker, but no details of this meeting were reported either in the German or in the Soviet press. Nevertheless, the general feeling in London was one of optimism, and Soviet Ambassador Maisky became a frequent visitor at 10 Downing Street.

Just then, however, Litvinov was removed from office. On May 3rd he had received Seeds in the morning. That very evening, Litvinov's retirement was announced. Molotov was appointed Minister for Foreign Affairs. Apparently Stalin, after some deliberation, had finally made up his mind to cast his lot with Hitler rather than with the Allies. This was confirmed indirectly in the programmatic speech delivered by Molotov on May 31st at a session of the Supreme Soviet of the USSR. One of the key points of the speech was Molotov's statement that the Soviet Union was ready to maintain trade relations with Germany and Italy.

London and Paris sounded the alarm. In June and July military missions were sent to Moscow for secret talks on the price Moscow might exact for not going over, in one way or another, to the side of the Nazi-Fascist Axis. The full story of these negotiations remains obscure to this day. A few suggestive details can, however, be found—particularly in the collection of diplomatic papers, German as well as Soviet, published by the United States government in its White Book entitled *Nazi-Soviet Relations, 1939-1941,* as well as in Churchill's memoirs. Chamberlain's policy, Churchill bitterly comments, was not equal to the occasion. The civilian and military envoys sent to Russia were men of relatively minor rank, with little influence and limited authority. As Stalin saw it, this was a sign of neglect; it showed lack of respect for the Soviet government as well as for himself. Moreover, it smacked of insincerity and deliberate evil intent. When Stalin requested, through Molotov, a tripartite pact between

France, England and the USSR, the British envoys became evasive. The boundaries of Poland and Rumania had already been guaranteed by England against the German aggressor, by treaties concluded directly with these countries. All that was needed, in Chamberlain's opinion, was a similar guarantee given by Russia. Moscow was strongly suspicious. The mission entrusted to a high functionary of the Foreign Office, Lord Strang, in June, proved unsuccessful. Strang made no headway at all, mainly because earlier negotiations with other British envoys had left the Soviet government with the impression that London could not be counted on for substantial assistance in the way of shipping across large contingents of military forces. On the other side, a serious obstacle to the pact had been created by the flat refusal on the part of Poland and Rumania to allow the Soviet troops to cross their territories in the event of war. There were perfectly good reasons for this refusal. Quoting from Paul Reynaud, Churchill wrote that the attitude of the Poles could be stated in these words: "Under the Germans we would have to give up our freedom; under the Russians, our very soul."[16] The Baltic countries—Latvia, Estonia and Lithuania as well as Finland, took the same stand as Poland and Rumania. These states flatly refused to admit Russian troops.

Thus, the gist of Stalin's negotiations with the Allies was simply this: the Soviet government demanded the right to occupy the Baltic states, Finland, Poland and Rumania in the event of war as the price for concluding a triple alliance with England and France. These were countries with which France and Great Britain were bound by pacts of one sort or another. Although Moscow in no case demanded annexation of these countries to the Soviet Union—the point under discussion was solely their temporary occupation to protect Russia's borders against a German flank attack—Moscow's true aims were too well understood for London and Paris to trust in words.

By the end of June or the beginning of July, it had become clear that the die was cast. The June issue of the *Socialist Courier,* commenting on the military negotiations, wrote that the whole thing was completely baffling. "Is it simplicity—or duplicity?" queried the *Socialist Courier,* describing the Soviet position. This writer, who was responsible for the editorial, had, it goes without saying, no idea of the actual content of these negotiations, which were conducted in absolute secrecy. Yet, knowing well Stalin's mind, he sensed that something very dangerous was under way.

What actually was taking place were simultaneous negotiations, in two separate halls of the Kremlin, with representatives of both the Entente and Germany, who knew nothing of each other's presence, and a good deal of shrewd haggling by the Soviets. Far more interesting than the talks with the Allies, were the parleys between Germany and the Soviet Union, conducted after Litvinov had been replaced by Molotov as Minister for Foreign Affairs.

The first sign of trouble emerged in Molotov's speech on May 31st. There were no reasons whatsoever, said Molotov, why Russia should not establish normal economic relations with Germany and Italy. Molotov was echoing Stalin's speech at the 18th Party Congress in March. Ideological differences, the Soviet dictator had said, should not be regarded as an obstacle to peaceful co-existence of nations. "Take Italy," said Stalin. "We now have most amicable relations with that country." Molotov's reiteration of this theme was noted in every world chancellery. There were, indeed, weighty considerations behind Molotov's words. While England sought a rapprochement with Russia in a vacillating, half-hearted manner, the same intention was manifested far more determinedly and persistently by German diplomats. The democratic powers drew back from proposals which involved betrayal of their lesser allies and division of the latter into spheres of influence. Germany, on the other hand, objected neither to the partition of Poland nor to dividing up spheres of influence in the East. The Germans, as a matter of fact, had precisely that objective in mind. This did not mean, however, that negotiations between the Soviet rulers and Hitler's government proceeded painlessly along a straight course. The barometer fell and rose continually in the hall where Soviet negotiators sat at the table with Hitler's envoys, just as it did where negotiations were in progress with the Allies.

The men whom Hitler used as his intermediaries in the preliminary negotiations were as undistinguished as the Allied envoys. Schnurre Tippelskirch, and the like were by no means leading figures among German diplomats, although in Count von der Schulenburg, Germany had a first-rate ambassador in Moscow. Nevertheless, the choice of envoys was not decisive; rather, it was Britain's unwillingness—and

Hitler's willingness—to give Russia a free hand in Eastern Europe that swung the balance. This was the time-table of Nazi-Soviet negotiations:

On May 4, the German Chargé d'Affaires at Moscow, Tippelskirch, reported to the Foreign Ministry in Berlin on the significance of the fact that Litvinov, a Jew, had been replaced by Molotov. The following day, May 5, the Soviet Chargé d'Affaires, Astakhov, met with the Counselor of the German Foreign Ministry, Schnurre, and ". . . suggested to Schnurre the revival of economic negotiations and stressed the significance of Molotov's appointment."

May 9: Astakhov expresses pleasure at the changed tone of the German press.

May 17: Astakhov is skeptical concerning the prospects of an Anglo-Soviet agreement, and is optimistic on the improvement of Soviet-German relations.

May 20: Molotov says the construction of "political bases" must precede new economic negotiations; he refuses to elaborate.

May 27: Germany hesitates to make advances until the outcome of the Soviet negotiations with Britain and France is known.

May 29: Foreign Office Memorandum: Arguments for and against negotiations with the USSR. On the same day: A proposal that Weizsacker explore the possibility of agreement.

May 30: Both Weizsacker and Astakhov, in conversation on economic questions, hint that a German-Soviet political agreement is desirable and possible. In a telegram from Foreign Office to Ambassador Schulenburg: Government had decided to undertake negotiations.

May 31: The above-quoted major speech by Molotov at the Supreme Soviet, favoring the establishment of normal economic relations with Germany and Italy.

June 5: Telegram by Schulenburg to Berlin that Molotov at the interview of May 20 almost invited political discussions.

June 18: The German Chargé in the Soviet Union, Tippelskirch, says the Soviet government is skeptical of German sincerity. Mikoyan termed the German reply on economic negotiations "not entirely favorable."

June 27: Schulenburg stresses the Soviet fear that Germany is pushing economic negotiations only to block an Anglo-Soviet agreement and that Germany will allow the negotiations to lapse when this objective is achieved.

June 29: Hitler orders negotiations with the USSR ended.

June 29: Molotov shows desire to maintain contact with Germany.

July 22: The Soviet press announces the opening of economic negotiations.

July 27: Schnurre, in a friendly conversation at a dinner party with Astakhov and Babarin, explore problems of German-Soviet relations. He stresses common ideological ground.[17]

July 29: The German Foreign Office suggests that Schulenburg let Molotov know that the Germans are prepared to respect Russian interests in Poland and the Baltic states.

August 3: Germany must know whether or not the USSR is prepared to settle all problems, so that German policy can be adjusted to meet the Soviet position.

August 10: Schnurre warns Astakhov that Soviet interests in Poland can be protected only by a German-Soviet agreement concluded before the outbreak of war.[18]

The pact was concluded. On August 23, Ribbentrop came to Moscow to sign it. Stalin watched. Now no one doubted that war was merely a matter of days. On September 1st, Hitler's troops moved into Poland, and a new era in the history of mankind began.

[1] Leon Blum and the French Socialist Party did not support in the beginning of 1933 the already mentioned plan put forward by Rudolf Hilferding and his friends that the socialist parties should undertake a preventive action to dislodge, if necessary by force, the Nazi government. See *Populaire,* January 3, 1952.

[2] At this time, both the broad strata of the French people and the intelligentsia were paralyzed by fear of a new war. This spirit moved socialists, anti-fascists and anti-Bolsheviks to accept appeasement of Hitler, rather than call for resistance, which might lead to an armed conflict. In March 1936, at the Toulouse Congress of the C.G.T. (Confederation of Labor), M. Mathé, delegate from the Postmen's Union, delivered a speech in which he declared that he ". . . preferred servitude to war . . ." Two years later, Mathé repeated the speech at the 1938 Congress of the Confederation of Labor in Nantes.

[3] *Populaire,* January 3, 1952.

[4] *Stenographic Protocols of the Socialist International,* Paris, August 1933.

[5] The definition used in the League.

[6] Both Poland and Rumania were refusing an arrangement which, in case of hostilities, would enable the Soviet Union to move its armed forces onto Polish and Rumanian territory. This refusal was motivated by the conviction that the Soviet troops would never evacuate their territory. As we shall see, this particular point also prevented agreement in the last talks that Moscow conducted in 1939 with the representatives of the Anglo-French bloc.

[7] *Socialist Courier* of April 15th, 1938, No. 7, p. 7.

[8] John W. Wheeler-Bennett, *The Nemesis of Power,* Macmillan & Co., Ltd. London, 1954, p. 414.

[9] Collection of Diplomatic Papers on Foreign Relations of the US in the year 1938. State Department, Washington, D. C., 1958. (*New York Times,* May 15, 1958).

[10] Wheeler-Bennett, *Munich,* p. 358, footnote.

[11] *Ibid.*, p. 361.

[12] *Ibid.*

[13] *Europas Weg nach Potsdam,* Deutsche Verlagsanstalt, Stuttgart, 1959.

[14] See "The Bulletin of the Opposition," No. 60-61.

[15] At that time Leon Blum told some of his personal friends in Paris, the present author included, about this talk with Litvinov. It can hardly be doubted that he had informed the London and Paris governments of this extremely important conversation.

[16] Churchill's *Memoirs,* vol. 1, p. 408.

[17] At that dinner Schnurre remarked that "despite all the differences in *Weltanschauung,* there was *one* thing in common in the ideology of Germany, Italy and the Soviet Union: opposition to the capitalist democracies. Neither we nor Italy had anything in common with the capitalism of the West. Therefore it would appear to us quite paradoxical of the Soviet Union, as a Socialist state, were to side with the Western democracies." See *Nazi-Soviet Relations,* p. 33.

[18] *Ibid.*, pp. 3-44.

Epilogue: The War and After

Although the Molotov-Ribbentrop pact made it clear that another world war could not be averted, the governments of the major Western powers continued to hope that the worst would not happen.

On the night of September 1, 1939, when the war had actually begun, I accidentally heard on a shortwave radio a speech by Hitler, declaring war on Poland and ordering his troops to march. Since nothing of the sort had yet been reported on the French broadcasts, I called Dan to tell him the news. He remained sceptical. Half an hour earlier, he had talked to the well-informed Leon Blum, who had told him that the worst crisis was over.

Despite the late hour, Dan was finally persuaded to get in touch with Blum once more and let him know of the broadcast I had heard. Blum, aroused from sleep, inquired at the Ministry of Foreign Affairs and was advised that, according to official reports, war had been averted at the last moment. The morning papers carried huge headlines announcing the beginning of the Second World War.

This minor episode remains to me a symbol of what is usually called wishful thinking. After August twenty-third, the day on which the Stalin-Hitler pact was signed, no man of sober judgment could fail to see that a way had been cleared for German aggression in Eastern Europe, beginning in Poland.

The official Soviet version is that the pact was necessary to keep the Nazis from attacking the Soviet Union. Yet, the German General Staff, to a man, opposed a war on two fronts and a march on Poland. Defiance of a Soviet pact with the Allies was bound to lead to just such a war. There was some reason to believe, in fact, that if a move were made to involve Germany in a war on two fronts, the German generals might move to arrest Hitler and overthrow his regime. Such a mutiny seemed a distinct possibility, although this has been denied by some writers reminiscing about the Hitler years.[1] Nowhere, however, is the mendacity of Stalin's official version exposed with such ultimate clarity as in the documents that accompanied the German-Soviet nonaggression pact and trade agreement—that is, the "secret protocol" stipulating the terms for a division of Poland and of all of Eastern Europe.

The official text of the protocol[2] reads as follows:

Secret Additional Protocol

On the occasion of the signature of the Nonaggression Pact between the German Reich and the Union of Socialist Soviet Republics the undersigned plenipotentiaries of each of the two parties discussed in strictly confidential conversations the question of the boundary of their respective spheres of influence in Eastern Europe. These conversations led to the following conclusions:

1. In the event of a territorial and political rearrangement in the areas belonging to the Baltic States (Finland, Estonia, Latvia, Lithuania), the northern boundary of Lithuania shall represent the boundary of the spheres of influence of Germany and the USSR. In this connection the interest of Lithuania in the Vilna area is recognized by each party.

2. In the event of a territorial and political rearrangement of the areas belonging to the Polish State, the spheres of influence of Germany and the USSR shall be bounded approximately by the line of the rivers Narew, Vistula and San.

The question of whether the interests of both parties make desirable the maintenance of an independent Polish State and how such a State should be bounded can only be definitely determined in the course of further political developments.

In any event, both Governments will resolve this question by means of a friendly agreement.

3. With regard to Southeastern Europe attention is called by the Soviet side to its interest in Bessarabia. The

German side declares its complete political disinterestedness in these areas.

4. This protocol shall be treated by both parties as strictly secret.

Moscow, August 23, 1939.

For the Government of the German Reich:	Plenipotentiary of the Government of the USSR:
von Ribbentrop	V. Molotov

The division of Poland proceeded according to plan and was completed in September, 1939. Even as Hitler's armies were storming Warsaw and pressing on toward the demarcation line separating the German from the Soviet sphere of influence, which ran along the Narew, Vistula and San rivers, Stalin's troops were deployed in combat readiness East of the same boundary, while other Soviet units overran Eastern Galicia and the other Polish regions ceded to the Soviets by the secret agreement of August 23. In October the Soviet Union went to war with Finland, and this was followed by the capture of the Baltic States, under the guise of popular referendum.[3]

In the West, General Guderjan's armored divisions and Goering's dive bombers scored one victory after another. France, Belgium, Holland, Denmark and Norway fell. The Battle of Britain was on. By October, 1940 Hitler became convinced that the surrender of England was only a matter of time and that the war had virtually been won. At this point he attempted to persuade the Kremlin to join the threepartite alliance ("Axis") of Germany, Italy and Japan.[4]

The attempt began with von Ribbentrop's letter to Stalin dated October 13, 1940. The letter was held over for five days at Molotov's office, pending a verified translation, and was not delivered to Stalin until October 17.

In his reply on October 20, Stalin thanked von Ribbentrop for his "instructive analysis of recent events" and expressed his willingness to do what he could toward further improvement of Russia's relations with Germany "on the permanent basis of long-range delineation of their mutual interests." With a view to more detailed discussions, he promised to arrange for Molotov's visit to Berlin on or about November twelfth. The talks between Hitler and Molotov began on that date in the presence of von Ribbentrop and Dekanozov. The next day Hitler again received Molotov and stressed "an agreement on the division of the British Empire." Molotov insisted that this must be preceded by recognition of Soviet interests in Finland, in the Balkans and in Turkey (the Straits). Two days later there was another Molotov visit which took place "in an atmosphere of mutual confidence" and resulted "in agreement on all important questions between the Three-Partite Alliance and Russia."

On November twenty-sixth, however, Molotov put forward additional demands, requesting the withdrawal of German forces from Finland, a mutual assistance pact with Bulgaria, and the renunciation by Japan of her oil and coal concessions in Northern Sakhalin. These demands were accepted and the draft was amended. Its text[5] reads as follows:

Secret Protocol No. 1

1. Germany declares that apart from the territorial revisions in Europe to be carried out at the conclusion of peace, her territorial aspirations center in the territories of Central Africa.
2. Italy declares that apart from the territorial revisions in Europe to be carried out at the conclusion of peace, her territorial aspirations center in the territories of Northern and Northeastern Africa.
3. Japan declares that her territorial aspirations center in the area of Eastern Asia to the South of the Island Empire of Japan.
4. The Soviet Union declares that apart from the territorial revisions in Europe to be carried out at the conclusion of peace, its territorial aspirations center South of the national territory of the Soviet Union in the direction of the Indian Ocean.

In addition, Germany, Italy and Russia made an agreement concerning Turkey, the Straits and the Black Sea, favoring Russia.

None of this helped Russia very much. For weeks afterward Hitler issued his secret order for "Operation Barbarossa"—the invasion of the Soviet Union. Delayed by the unexpected resistance to Nazi demands offered by Yugoslavia, the invasion began on June 22, 1941, in circumstances which even now appear to be a matter of some controversy among Stalin's heirs. In any case, whatever the degree of Russia's political and military preparedness, the losses were frightful —nearly 30 million dead, many other millions wounded and uprooted, material losses almost beyond calculation. Stalin's "realism" in concluding a pact with Hitler turned out to be utter folly which brought the Soviet regime itself to the brink of destruction. It was redeemed through the patriotic valor of the Soviet people, with the aid of the Western allies whom Stalin rebuffed before the war and was to attack afterward. For the governments of Stalin's democratic allies in the Second World War proved as naïve and shortsighted with regard to the Soviet dictatorship as with respect to Hitler in the days of Munich. When Roosevelt's personal envoy, Harry Hopkins, arrived in Moscow for the first time to discuss joint action against the Axis, Stalin asked on what condition such collaboration was proposed. "No conditions whatever," Hopkins explained magnanimously. None of the Western leaders imagined that Stalin, striving desperately to drive the German invaders out of the Soviet homeland, would at the same time be working to take over all non-Russian territories freed from the Nazis. The war-ravaged Soviet economy was in sore need of financial help. Huge sums were required to rebuild Russia's industries, transportation, urban centers, etc. The Russians, it seemed, would be grateful if the Allies provided them with the necessary means for the great task of reconstruction. Stalin, however, had other things on his mind—uppermost among them, the Communization of Central and Eastern Europe. This was eventually accomplished despite the Moscow declaration of October 1943, in which the powers pledged themselves "to make no attempt to exploit the fact of their armed forces holding the territories freed from Hitler's troops for the purpose of changing the political or social order existing in related countries." The upshot was that, after a brilliant victory over fascism and reaction, the world found itself split again into two hostile camps, facing each other as implacable rivals and foes.

Much as the peoples and governments of Britain, France and the United States sincerely strive for peaceful coexistence with world communism, the communist movement continues on its aggressive path—Russia itself contending in bellicosity with more recent adherents to communism (China, Albania, East Germany, North Korea, North Vietnam).

What has become of socialism—the kind of socialism taught by Marx and Engels? Its last vestiges have long since disappeared in the immense territory now under Communist rule. The world socialist labor movement, beginning with the First International founded by Karl Marx in 1864, has been guided by the ideals that inspired the French Revolution nearly two centuries ago: the ideals of freedom, equality and universal brotherhood.

The socialist ideal envisioned by Marx was predicated on the transition of the old social order, with its capitalist ownership of the means of production, to a completely emancipated, self-governing society free of any ruling classes. In the so-called communist, i.e., totalitarian, states there is no capitalist ownership, but neither is there any freedom, or self-rule. Socialism cannot be equated with anticapitalism as such, since history has shown that fascist states as well as other societies based on despotic rule (the ancient Oriental empires, the Inca autocracy, etc.) may be equally anticapitalist in their organization. Communist-controlled community is split into many classes and groups, some more privileged than others. The principle of equality has been replaced by the ideal of leadership, in a social system approaching a military hierarchy. The small minority entrenched in the position of power—less than five per cent of the total population even in the Soviet Union—has every advantage associated with a ruling class, such as the French aristocracy before the revolution of 1789, or Russia's landed gentry under the czars.

The Soviet Union today is inordinately proud of its superrockets, long-range missiles and hydrogen bombs. But it was the freedom and happiness of men, rather than their destruction by superweapons, that the founders of socialism had in mind when they elaborated their basic tenets and their programs. Nikita Khrushchev sees these technological successes as an extraordinary manifestation of "cultural" progress. But similar "success" was last witnessed in 1942-1945 when Nazi Germany outstripped all the major powers in the production of tanks, Stuka bombers and V-2 rockets. Is it conceivable that "victorious socialism" can develop no better formula for human progress than the designing of ever more powerful weapons for destruction?

France's great socialist tribune, Jean Jaures, author of a socialist history of the French Revolution, once remarked that all revolutions have been a fairly savage means of achieving a measure of progress. The English Revolution in the seventeenth century and the French Revolution in the eighteenth century were no exception. But can it be said that the Russian, or for that matter the Chinese revolution, are steps along the road to progress? We do not think so. No one who has lived in a totalitarian state and is familiar with its internal functioning can believe that this savagery will ever contribute to the cultural development or well-being of mankind. For totalitarian rule is not so much anticapitalist as it is antihuman.

[1] Hans Bernd Gisevius: *To the Bitter End.* Boston, 1947, pp. 374-375.
[2] *Nazi-Soviet Relations,* p. 78.
[3] S. M. Schwarz: How the Baltic Countries Were Taken Over by the Soviets. *The Socialist Courier,* Nos. 11 and 12, Nov. 15 and Dec. 5, 1940.
[4] *Nazi-Soviet Relations,* pp. 217-225.
[5] *Nazi-Soviet Relations,* pp. 216-258.

Index

DESIGNING AND MANAGING THE SUPPLY CHAIN

Concepts, Strategies, and Case Studies

THIRD EDITION

DESIGNING AND MANAGING THE SUPPLY CHAIN

Concepts, Strategies, and Case Studies

THIRD EDITION

David Simchi-Levi

Massachusetts Institute of Technology (MIT), Cambridge, Massachusetts

Philip Kaminsky

University of California, Berkeley

Edith Simchi-Levi

LogicTools, Inc., Lexington, Massachusetts

Ravi Shankar

Indian Institute of Technology Delhi, India
&
School of Management, Asian Institute of Technology, Thailand

Tata McGraw-Hill Publishing Company Limited
NEW DELHI

McGraw-Hill Offices

New Delhi New York St Louis San Francisco Auckland Bogotá
Caracas Kuala Lumpur Lisbon London Madrid Mexico City Milan Montreal
San Juan Santiago Singapore Sydney Tokyo Toronto

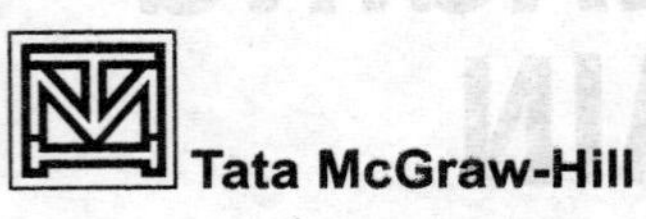

Tata McGraw-Hill

Designing and Managing the Supply Chain: Concepts, Strategies, and Case Studies, 3/e

Indian Adaptation done by arrangement with the McGraw-Hill Companies, Inc., New York

Sales Territories: India, Pakistan, Nepal, Bangladesh, Sri Lanka and Bhutan

Tata McGraw-Hill Edition 2008

ISBN-13: 978-0-07-066698-6
ISBN-10: 0-07-066698-9

Published by the Tata McGraw-Hill Publishing Company Limited, 7 West Patel Nagar, New Delhi 110 008, typeset at Script Makers, 19, A1B Block, DDA Market, Paschim Vihar, New Delhi and printed at Avon Printers, 271, FIE Patparganj, Delhi 110 092

Cover Designer: K.Anoop

Cover Printer: SDR Printers

RAXYCDDYRYRQB

The ***McGraw·Hill*** *Companies*

To our children, Sara and Yuval, who have the patience and humor to survive our work together

D.S.L., E.S.L.

To my family, for their support and encouragement

P.K.

To my doting children Pratyush and Snigdha, who find my smile when I lose it. And to my wife Poonam, for her pragmatic prudence and unassailable love.

R.S.

ABOUT THE AUTHORS

DAVID SIMCHI-LEVI is Professor of Engineering Systems at the Massachusetts Institute of Technology (MIT). Prior to joining the faculty at MIT, he taught at Northwestern University and Columbia University. Professor Simchi-Levi received his Ph.D. in Operations Research from Tel-Aviv University and has won awards for his work in supply chain management, logistics, and transportation. At MIT he teaches logistics and supply chain management at the Leaders for Manufacturing program as well as Executive Programs at the MIT Sloan School of Management. In 2000, he was named the "Master of Design" by *Supply Chain Management Review*. He is co-author, together with Xin Chen and Julien Bramel, of *The Logic of Logistic,* published by Springer, and a co-founder and former CEO of LogicTools, a Division of ILOG. LogicTools is a leader in strategic and tactical supply chain planning software.

PHIL KAMINSKY is Associate Professor of Industrial Engineering at the University of California at Berkeley. He received his Ph.D. in Industrial Engineering from Northwestern University. Prior to his graduate studies, he worked for the production division of Merck & Co., Inc. He has consulted in the areas of supply chain and production management.

EDITH SIMCHI-LEVI is a co-founder and Vice President of Operations of LogicTools Inc., a Division of ILOG. She has extensive experience in software development and has engaged in numerous consulting projects in logistics and supply chain management. She received her B.S. in Mathematics and Computer Science from Tel-Aviv University.

RAVI SHANKAR is Associate Professor of Operations and Supply Chain Management at Dept.of Management Studies, Indian Institute of Technology (IIT) Delhi, India. Currently, he is also associated with School of Management, Asian Institute of Technology Thailand as Associate Professor in the same area. He received his Ph. D. from IIT Delhi. He has over twenty five years of experience in teaching, research, consultancy and conducting management development programs. He has co-authored over one hundred journal research papers in Operations and Supply Chain Management area.

FOREWORD

In the last few years we have seen an explosion of publications on supply chain management; numerous books have been published and many articles have appeared in academic, trade, and popular magazines. These publications either are too technical—and therefore inaccessible to practitioners and students—or lack the breadth and depth that the topic deserves. Certainly, it is difficult to find a book appropriate for teaching supply chain management to business or engineering students. *Designing and Managing the Supply Chain* solves this problem!

The book is an important contribution and major milestone for the supply chain community. It is the first book that covers a comprehensive breadth of supply chain topics in depth, and addresses the major challenges in this area. It was written by experts from academia and industry who have been researching, consulting, and developing software for supply chain management for many years.

This book includes many classic and new case studies, numerous examples as well as in-depth analyses of some of the technical issues involved in inventory management, network design, and strategic partnering, to name a few. It is therefore an ideal textbook for classes on supply chain management at the undergraduate, Master's, and M.B.A. levels. Since each chapter is self-contained, instructors can pick the chapters they want to use depending on the length of the class and its requirements. The book comes with three computerized games. The Computerized Beer Game provides an excellent instructional tool that engages students in managing a supply chain and provides a starting point for discussing the value of information in the supply chain, strategic partnering, centralized decision making, and so forth. The Risk Pool Game allows students to gain insight on an important concept in supply chain management, called risk pooling. The Bidding Game illustrates important procurement strategies. The authors have been most creative in using games to motivate and expose students to challenging subjects.

Finally, since many companies view supply chain management as the core of their business strategy, this book also will be of interest to managers involved in any of the processes that make up the supply chain.

I want to compliment the authors for having written such an outstanding textbook for the supply chain community.

Hau L. Lee

Kleiner Perkins, Mayfield, Sequoia Capital Professor
Director, Stanford Global Supply Chain Forum
Stanford University

PREFACE

Three years ago, when the second edition of this text was published, we mentioned our goal of building on the positive elements of the first edition and including what we had learned subsequently. We are pleased to note that that revision was successful; as with the first edition, we received a tremendous response from adopters, students, executives, and consultants. Nevertheless, new concepts have subsequently been developed, technological changes continue at an ever-increasing rate, and we have discovered a variety of important new teaching approaches and concepts, so the time is right for a newly revised edition.

The original edition of this book grew out of a number of supply chain management courses and executive education programs we taught at Northwestern University, as well as numerous consulting projects and supply chain decision-support systems we developed at LogicTools. Since then, we have continued teaching executive and regular courses, both at Massachusetts Institute of Technology and at the University of California, Berkeley, and have continued to develop a variety of supply chain decision-support tools. These courses have spawned many innovative and effective supply chain education concepts. The focus in these programs has always been on presenting, in an easily accessible manner, recently developed state-of-the-art models and solution methods important in the design, control, and operation of supply chains. Similarly, the consulting projects and decision-support systems developed by LogicTools have focused on applying these advanced techniques to solve specific problems faced by our clients. In the last three years, we have continued to add new models and techniques to these courses as they have been developed, and we continued the process of integrating these approaches, models, and solution methods into frameworks so that students can better put these ideas into perspective. We have also integrated the contents with examples of Indian supply chains.

Interest in supply chain management, both in industry and in academia, has grown rapidly over the past two decades, and continues to grow. A number of forces have contributed to this trend. In the 90s, many companies recognized that they have reduced manufacturing costs as much as practically possible. Many of these companies discovered the magnitude of savings that can be achieved by planning and managing their supply chains more effectively. Indeed, a striking example in the 90s was Wal-Mart's success, which is partly attributed to implementing a new logistics strategy called cross-docking. At the same time, information and communication systems were widely implemented, and provide access to comprehensive data from all components of the supply chain.

In particular, the influence of the Internet and e-commerce on the economy in general and business practice in particular has been tremendous. Changes are happening extremely fast, and the scope of these changes is breathtaking! For instance, the direct business model employed by industry giants such as Dell Computers and Amazon.com enables customers to order products over the Internet and thus allows companies to sell their products without relying on third-party distributors or conventional stores. Similarly, the Internet has made a significant impact on business-to-business transactions and collaborations. At the same time, deregulation of the transportation industry has led to the development of a variety of transportation modes and reduced transportation costs, while significantly increasing the complexity of logistics systems.

Finally, new forces contributed to the increased interest in supply chain management in the last five years. As offshoring and globalization of manufacturing operations continue to grow, supply chain complexity and risks have significantly increased. This, together with rising energy costs and the acceleration of merger and acquisition activities, has motivated many companies to reevaluate their supply chain strategies in order to better utilize existing resources and infrastructure.

It is therefore not surprising that many companies are involved in the analysis of their supply chains. In most cases, however, this analysis is performed based on experience and intuition; very few analytical models or planning tools have been used in this process. In contrast, in the last two decades, the academic community has developed various models and tools for supply chain management. Unfortunately, the first generation of this technology was not robust or flexible enough to allow industry to use it effectively. This, however, has changed over the last few years, during which improved analysis and insight, and effective models and decision-support systems, have been developed; however, these are not necessarily familiar to industry. Indeed, to our knowledge there is no published work that discusses these problems, models, concepts, and tools in an accessible manner and at an appropriate level.

In this book, we intend to fill this gap by providing state-of-the-art models, concepts, and solution methods that are important for the design, control, operation, and management of supply chain systems. In particular, we have attempted both to convey the intuition behind many key supply chain concepts and to provide simple techniques that can be used to analyze various aspects of the supply chain.

The emphasis is on a format that will be accessible to executives and practitioners, as well as students interested in careers in related industries. In addition, it will introduce readers to information systems and decision-support tools that can aid in the design, analysis, and control of supply chains.

The book is written to serve as

- A textbook for M.B.A.-level logistics and supply chain management courses.
- A textbook for B.S. and M.S. industrial engineering courses on logistics and supply chain management.
- A reference for teachers, consultants, and practitioners involved in any one of the processes that make up the supply chain.

Of course, supply chain management is a very broad area, and it would be impossible for a single book to cover all of the relevant areas in depth. Indeed, there is considerable disagreement in academia and industry about exactly what these relevant areas are. Nevertheless, we have attempted to provide a broad introduction to many critical facets of supply chain management. Although many essential supply chain management issues are interrelated, we have strived wherever possible to make each chapter as self-contained as possible, so that the reader can refer directly to chapters covering topics of interest.

The discussion ranges from basic topics of inventory management, logistics network planning, distribution systems, and customer value to more advanced topics of strategic alliances, the value of information in the supply chain, supply contracts, procurement and outsourcing, product design and the interface between product design and supply chain strategies, business processes and information technology including decision-support systems, technology standards and risk management, and international issues in supply chain management. Each chapter utilizes numerous case studies and examples, and mathematical and technical sections can be skipped without loss of continuity.

NEW IN THE THIRD EDITION

The third edition of the book represents a substantial revision. Indeed, while we kept the same structure and philosophy as in the previous editions, we have placed an increasing importance on finding or developing effective frameworks that illustrate many important supply chain issues. At the same time, motivated by new development in industry, we have added material on a variety of topics while increasing the coverage of others. This edition lays special emphasis on supply chain issues in the Indian context. Many new examples and cases from Indian supply chains are the important inclusions in this edition.

In brief, the major changes include

- New case studies such as Amazon.com's European Distribution Strategy; Dell Inc.: Improving the Flexibility of the Desktop PC Supply Chain; Maruti Udyog Limited: A case study of Vender Management; H. C. Strack, Inc.; Steel Works Inc.; Selectron: From Contract Manufacturer to Global Supply Chain Integrator; Zara; and Mumbai Dabbawalahs.
- New topics such as network planning, strategic inventory, risk management strategies, global sourcing strategies, and technology standards.
- New chapters on network planning, distribution strategies, supply contracts, pricing, technology standards and local issues in supply chain management.
- New concepts such as the development supply chain, strategic sourcing, and service-oriented architecture.

Specifically,

- We have introduced the concept of the "development supply chain" (Chapter 1) and applied it to product design and supply chain strategies (Chapter 11).
- We have expanded our discussion of network planning and increased our emphasis on strategic safety stock and inventory planning in supply networks (Chapter 3).
- We have added a chapter on supply contracts for strategic and commodity components (Chapter 4).
- We have enhanced our discussion of the impact of lead time on supply chain strategy (Chapter 6).
- We have added a chapter on distribution strategies where we focus on the impact of inventory pooling and customer search (Chapter 7).

- We have substantially revised the chapter on procurement and outsourcing strategies, focusing on framework for outsourcing, strategic purchasing, and supplier footprint (Chapter 9).
- We have developed a new framework for risk management in global supply chains (Chapter 10).
- We have added a chapter on smart pricing and revenue management in supply chains (Chapter 13).
- We have added a chapter on technology standards such as service-oriented architecture and RFID (Chapter 15).
- We have added and updated numerous examples, including many Indian ones, to illustrate various concepts, frameworks, and strategies.

The book also includes three software package—the **Computerized Beer Game,** the **Risk Pool Game,** and the **Bidding Game**—that help to illustrate many of the concepts we discuss in the book. Indeed, in teaching executives and M.B.A. students, we have found that these games help students better understand issues and concepts such as the bullwhip effect, the value of information in the supply chain, and the impact of lead times, centralized decision making, risk pooling, and supplier competition on supply chain operations. As in the second edition, we have included a Microsoft Excel spreadsheet to help students understand many of the supply contracts concepts introduced in Chapter 4.

Parts of this book are based on work we have done either together or with others.

- Chapters 1 and 3 borrow extensively from *The Logic of Logistics*, written by J. Bramel and D. Simchi-Levi and published by Springer in 1997; second edition (with X. Chen and J. Bramel) appeared in October 2004.
- The development supply chain concept was first introduced by C. H. Fine from MIT and then applied by C. H. Fine and D. Simchi-Levi to develop effective supply chain strategies. Some of their ideas are discussed in Chapters 1 and 11.
- Some of the material on the bullwhip effect appears in an article by F. Y. Chen, Z. Drezner, J. K. Ryan, and D. Simchi-Levi in *Quantitative Models for Supply Chain Management*, edited by S. Tayur, R. Ganeshan, and M. Magazine, and published by Kluwer Academic Publishers in 1998.
- The material in Chapter 6 is taken from two papers, one written by D. Simchi-Levi and E. Simchi-Levi and the second written by these two authors and M. Watson. This latter paper appeared in *The Practice of Supply Chain Management*, edited by T. Harrison, H. Lee, and J. Neale, published by Kluwer Academic Publishers in 2003.
- The material on inventory pooling and customer search discussed in Chapter 7 is based on the paper "Centralization of Stocks: Retailers vs. Manufacturer," by R. Anupindi and Y. Bassok, published in *Management Science* in 1999. This paper motivated D. Simchi-Levi to develop (together with X. Chen and Y. Sheng) a simulation model used in Examples 7-2 and 7-3.
- Some of the material in Chapter 9 is based on teaching material received by the authors from C. P. Teo from the National University of Singapore and V.M. de Albeniz from IESE, Spain.
- Chapter 14 borrows extensively from an article by C. Heinrich and D. Simchi-Levi published in *Supply Chain Management Review*, May 2005.
- The discussion on RFID in Chapter 15 is based on a chapter written by D. Simchi-Levi in the book *RFID and Beyond: Growing Your Business Through Real World Awareness*, edited by C. Heinrich and published by Wiley in 2005.

- The Computerized Beer Game is discussed in an article by P. Kaminsky and D. Simchi-Levi that appeared in *Supply Chain and Technology Management*, edited by H. Lee and S. M. Ng and published by The Production and Operations Management Society.
- The Bidding Game is based on an article by V. Martinez de Albeniz and D. Simchi-Levi "Competition in the Supply Option Market," Working Paper, MIT, 2005.
- Some of the material on risk management is taken from an article by D. Simchi-Levi, L. Snyder, and M. Watson published in *Supply Chain Management Review* in 2002.

ACKNOWLEDGMENTS

It is our pleasure to acknowledge all those who helped us with the three editions of this manuscript. First, we would like to thank Dr. Myron Feinstein, former director of supply chain strategy development at Unilever, New York City, who read through and commented on various chapters of the first edition. Similarly, we are indebted to the instructors who reviewed the manuscript of the first edition, Professors Michael Ball (University of Maryland), Wendell Gilland (University of North Carolina, Chapel Hill), Eric Johnson (Dartmouth College), Douglas Morrice (The University of Texas, Austin), Michael Pangburn (Pennsylvania State University), Powell Robinson (Texas A&M University), William Tallon (Northern Illinois University), and Rachel Yang (University of Illinois, Urbana-Champaign).

We are also grateful to Dr. Deniz Caglar of Booz Allen Hamilton for his comments on earlier drafts of the book.

The second edition benefited from comments and suggestions we received from many people. These include Professors Arjang Assad, Michael Ball, and their colleagues from the University of Maryland–College Park; Chia-Shin Chung (Cleveland State University); Brian Gibson (Auburn University); Boaz Golany (Technion, Israel); Isaac Gottleib (Rutgers University); Shelly Jha (Wilfrid Laurier University, Ontario, Canada); Dana Johnson (Michigan Technical University); Mary Meixell (George Mason University); Dan Rinks (Louisiana State University); Tony Arreola-Risa (Texas A&M University); and Joel Wisner (University of Nevada– Las Vegas). These comments were invaluable in improving the organization and presentation of the book.

Professor Ravi Anupindi (University of Michigan, Ann Arbor), Professor Yehuda Bassok (University of Southern California), Dr. Jeff Tew (General Motors), and Professor Jayashankar Swaminathan (University of North Carolina, Chapel Hill) provided valuable insights that we incorporated into the second edition of the text.

We also are indebted to those who reviewed the second edition in preparation for the third edition: Kyle Cattani (University of South Carolina, Chapel Hill), Zhi-Long Chen (University of Maryland), Deborah F. Cook (Virginia Technical University), Sriam Dasu (University of California, Los Angeles), Mark Ferguson (Georgia Technical University), Manoj K. Malhotra (University of South Carolina, Columbia), Charles Petersen (Northern Illinois University), and Young K. Son (Baruch College). The third edition has greatly benefited from their comments.

The third edition also benefited from comments by Professor Chung-Lun Li (The Hong Kong Polytechnic University) and Professor Victor Martinez de Albeniz (IESE, Spain). Professor Kanshik Sengupta of Hofstra University prepared the PowerPoints and Instructor's Manual, and we are grateful for his contribution.

We are grateful to our colleagues at Massachusetts Institute of Technology; the University of California, Berkeley; Indian Institute of Technology, Delhi and LogicTools who have provided us with opportunities to interact with some of the brightest minds in our field and to learn from their research and development. A few people stand out in this regard: Professors Charles H. Fine and Stephen C. Graves (MIT), with whom Professor Simchi-Levi has closely collaborated in the last five years, as well as Peter J. Cacioppi, Derek Nelson, and Dr. Michael S. Watson from LogicTools.

Dr. Shankar is grateful to his colleagues and mentors: Prof. S. G. Deshmukh, Prof. Surendra S. Yadav, Prof, D. K. Banwet, Prof. Sushil, Prof. P. K. Jain, Prof. Vinayshil Gautam, Prof. Rajat K. Baisya, Prof. Arun Kanda, all from IIT Delhi; Prof. Prem Vrat (UP Technical University); Prof. I. M. Pandey (AIT Thailand); Prof. S. K. Garg (DCE); Prof. K. N. Singh (IIM Lucknow); Prof. Kripa Shanker and Prof. V. K. Jain (IIT Kanpur); Prof. A. Subash Babu (IIT Bombay); Prof. Pradeep Kumar (IIT Roorkee), Prof. B. S. Sahay (IMT Ghaziabad); and Dr. M. K. Tiwari (IIT Kharagpur) for their support. Dr. Shankar also acknowledges his doctoral students, who were the part of his journey in understanding and resolving some of the supply chain complexities. They are: Sanjay Jharkharia (IIM Kozhikod), Ashish Agarwal (IGNOU, New Delhi), V. Ravi (ITM Mussoorie), N. Faisal (AMU Aligarh), V. K. Khanna (IMT, Ghaziabad), M.D. Singh (NIT Allahabad), Tilak Raj (YMCA Faridabad), Manoj Kumar, Shiri D. Vivek, Vanita Ahuja (QUT, Brisbane Australia), M. llyas, Akhilesh Barve, Parikshit Charan, Rohit Joshi, A. Ramesh, and Nirmal Kumar. As a industry consultant, Dr. Shankar acknowledges all, his industry sponsors, specially Mr. Joe Dyer (Executive Director) and Devesh Shankar (General Manager: Supply Chain) of Xerox India for understanding and appreciating the improvement plans in the supply chain.

We thank Dr. Kathleen A. Stair and Ms. Ann Stuart for carefully editing and proofreading many chapters. Ms. Ann Stuart also provided invaluable assistance in preparing the second edition.

Finally, we wish to thank Ms. Colleen Tuscher, who assisted us in the initial stage of the project; our editor, Mr. Scott Isenberg; and our developmental editor, Ms. Cynthia Douglas, who encouraged us throughout and helped us complete the book. Also, thanks to James Labeots and the production staff at McGraw-Hill for their help.

Dr. Shankar acknowledges the excellent effort of the editorial team of Tata McGraw-Hill, specially Mr. Tapas Maji and Ms Anubha Srivastava. Without their professional touch, this work would have never reached this stage. Dr. Ravi Shankar is also thankful to Mr. Biju Kumar, Mr. B.L. Dogra and Mr. Manohar Lal without whom this book would never have been published.

David Simchi-Levi
Cambridge, Massachusetts

Philip Kaminsky
Berkeley, California

Edith Simchi-Levi
Lexington, Massachusetts

Ravi Shankar
IIT Delhi, India

LIST OF CASES

BRIEF CONTENTS

CONTENTS

CHAPTER 1

Introduction to Supply Chain Management

1.1 WHAT IS SUPPLY CHAIN MANAGEMENT?

Fierce competition in today's global markets, the introduction of products with shorter life cycles, and the heightened expectations of customers have forced business enterprises to invest in, and focus attention on, their supply chains. This, together with continuing advances in communications and transportation technologies (e.g., mobile communication, Internet, and overnight delivery), has motivated the continuous evolution of the supply chain and of the techniques to manage it effectively.

In a typical supply chain, raw materials are procured and items are produced at one or more factories, shipped to warehouses for intermediate storage, and then shipped to retailers or customers. Consequently, to reduce cost and improve service levels, effective supply chain strategies must take into account the interactions at the various levels in the supply chain. The supply chain, which is also referred to as the *logistics network,* consists of suppliers, manufacturing centers, warehouses, distribution centers, and retail outlets, as well as raw materials, work-in-process inventory, and finished products that flow between the facilities (see Figure 1-1).

In this book, we present and explain concepts, insights, practical tools, and decision support systems important for the effective management of the supply chain. But what exactly is *supply chain management*? We define it as follows:

> Supply chain management is a set of approaches utilized to efficiently integrate suppliers, manufacturers, warehouses, and stores, so that merchandise is produced and distributed at the right quantities, to the right locations, and at the right time, in order to minimize systemwide costs while satisfying service level requirements.

This definition leads to several observations. First, supply chain management takes into consideration every facility that has an impact on cost and plays a role in making the product conform to customer requirements: from supplier and manufacturing facilities through warehouses and distribution centers to retailers and stores. Indeed, in some supply chain analysis, it is necessary to account for the suppliers' suppliers and the customers' customers because they have an impact on supply chain performance.

Second, the objective of supply chain management is to be efficient and cost-effective across the entire system; total systemwide costs, from transportation and distribution to inventories of raw materials, work in process, and finished goods, are to be minimized. Thus, the emphasis is not on simply min-

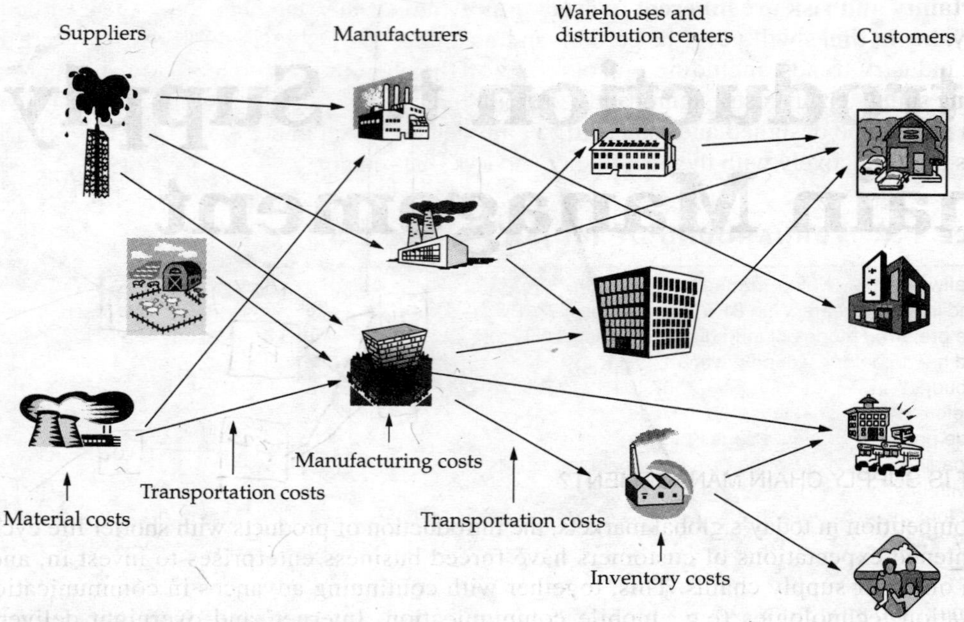

FIGURE 1-1 The logistics network.

imizing transportation cost or reducing inventories but, rather, on taking a *systems approach* to supply chain management.

Finally, because supply chain management revolves around efficient integration of suppliers, manufacturers, warehouses, and stores, it encompasses the firm's activities at many levels, from the strategic level through the tactical to the operational level.

What about logistics management, or value chain management, or demand chain management? Various companies, consultants, and academics have developed a variety of terms and concepts to stress what they believe are the salient issues in supply chain management. Although many of these concepts are useful and insightful, for the purposes of this text, we will use supply chain management as the generic name for the set of concepts, approaches, strategies, and ideas that we are discussing.

What makes supply chain management difficult? Although we will discuss a variety of reasons throughout this text, they can all be related to some or all of the following observations:

1. **Supply chain strategies cannot be determined in isolation. They are directly affected by another chain that most organizations have, the *development chain*** that includes the set of activities associated with new product introduction. At the same time, supply chain strategies also should be aligned with the specific goals of the organization, such as maximizing market share or increasing profit.
2. **It is challenging to design and operate a supply chain so that total systemwide costs are minimized, and systemwide service levels are maintained.** Indeed, it is frequently difficult to operate *a single facility* so that costs are minimized and service level is maintained. The difficulty increases exponentially when an entire system is being considered. The process of finding the best *systemwide* strategy is known as *global optimization*.

3. **Uncertainty and risk are inherent in every supply chain;** customer demand can never be forecast exactly, travel times will never be certain, and machines and vehicles will break down. Similarly, recent industry trends, including outsourcing, offshoring, and lean manufacturing that focus on reducing supply chain costs, significantly increase the level of risk in the supply chain. Thus, supply chains need to be designed and managed to eliminate as much uncertainty and risk as possible as well as deal effectively with the uncertainty and risk that remain.

EXAMPLE 1-1 TURNAROUND OF INDIAN RAILWAYS

Indian Railways (IR), which manages one of the largest railways networks of the world, has shown remarkable turnaround in recent years. With 81,511 km of track, 7429 locomotives, 253186 wagons and 40775 coach vehicles, it is one of the preferred modes of long distance transport in India. In 2001, when it had a fund balance of a paltry Rs. 3.59 billion and had to defer dividend payment, experts started saying that it has gone into a serious debt trap. In the annual railways budget presentation in Feb. 2007, Mr. Lalu Prasad, the Union Minister of Railways announced that the cash surplus before dividend has gone up to Rs 200,000 million as against Rs 147,000 million in the previous year. This has been made possible through a series of measures like technology upgradation, improved freight loading by increasing the axel-loading capacity of wagons, market-oriented approach, use of IT and telecommunication, etc. According to Mr. Prasad, with an increase of just 1 ton in the loading capacity of a wagon, the annual loading capacity goes up by about 10 million tons. Just this measure has improved the IR annual loading capacity by a whopping 170 MT in the last three years [227, 228].

In the next three sections, we discuss these issues in more detail.

1.2 THE DEVELOPMENT CHAIN

The *development chain* is the set of activities and processes associated with new product introduction. It includes the product design phase, the associated capabilities and knowledge that need to be developed internally, sourcing decisions, and production plans. Specifically, the development chain includes decisions such as product architecture; what to make internally and what to buy from outside suppliers, that is, make/buy decisions; supplier selection; early supplier involvement; and strategic partnerships.

The development and supply chains intersect at the production point, as illustrated in Figure 1-2. It is clear that the characteristics of and decisions made in the development chain will have an impact on the supply chain. Similarly, it is intuitively clear that the characteristics of the supply chain must have an impact on product design strategy and hence on the development chain.

EXAMPLE 1-2

Hewlett Packard (HP) was one of the first firms to recognize the intersection of the development and supply chains. A case in point is the inkjet printer introduction, where decisions about product architecture were made by taking into account not only labor and material cost, but also total supply chain cost throughout the product life cycle. More recently, HP has focused on making decisions such as what design activities to outsource and the corresponding organizational structures needed to manage the outsource design process by considering the characteristics of both the development and the supply chains.

Unfortunately, in most organizations, different managers are responsible for the different activities that are part of these chains. Typically, the VP of engineering is responsible for the development chain, the VP of manufacturing for the production portion of the chains, and the VP of supply chain or logistics for the fulfillment of customer demand. Unless carefully addressed, the typical impact of this organizational structure is a misalignment of product design and supply chain strategies.

To make matters worse, in many organizations, additional chains intersect with both the development and the supply chains. These may include the reverse logistics chain, that is, the chain associated with returns of products or components, as well as the spare-parts chain. In this book, we explore the various characteristics of each of these supply chains in order to better understand the impact of these on product and supply chain strategies. We illustrate how the consideration of these characteristics leads to the development of frameworks to assist in matching products with strategies.

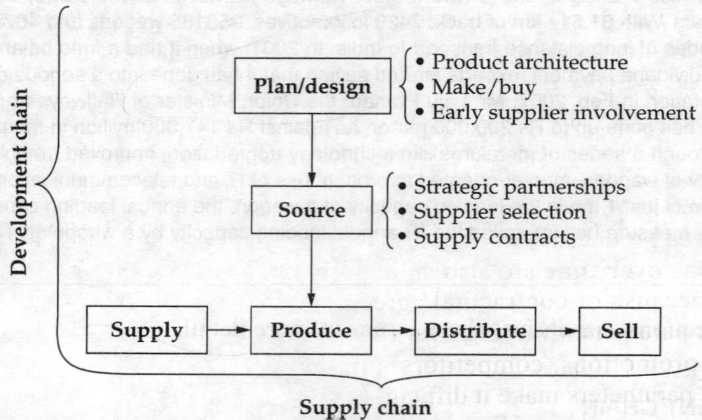

FIGURE 1-2 The enterprise development and supply chains.

1.3 GLOBAL OPTIMIZATION

What makes finding the best systemwide, or globally optimal, integrated solution so difficult? A variety of factors make this a challenging problem:

1. **The supply chain is a complex network** of facilities dispersed over a large geography, and, in many cases, all over the globe. The following example illustrates a network that is fairly typical of today's global companies.

EXAMPLE 1-3

National Semiconductor, whose list of competitors includes Motorola Inc. and the Intel Corporation, is one of the world's largest manufacturers of analog devices and subsystems that are used in fax machines, cellular phones, computers, and cars. Currently, the company has four wafer fabrication facilities, three in the United States and one in Great Britain, and has test and assembly sites in Malaysia, China, and Singapore. After assembly, finished products are shipped to hundreds of manufacturing facilities all over the world, including those of Apple, Canon, Delphi, Ford, IBM, Hewlett-Packard, and Siemens. Since the semiconductor industry is highly competitive, short lead time specification and the ability to deliver within the committed due date are critical capabilities. In 1994, 95 percent of National Semiconductor's customers received their orders within 45 days from the time the order was placed, while the remaining 5 percent received their orders within 90 days. These tight lead times required the company to involve 12 different airline carriers using about 20,000 different routes. The difficulty, of course, was that no customer knew in advance if they were going to be part of the 5 percent of customers who received their order in 90 days or the 95 percent who received their order within 45 days [109, 268].

2. **Different facilities in the supply chain frequently have *different, conflicting objectives*.** For instance, suppliers typically want manufacturers to commit themselves to purchasing large quantities in stable volumes with flexible delivery dates. Unfortunately, although most manufacturers would like to implement long production runs, they need to be flexible to their customers' needs and changing demands. Thus, the suppliers' goals are in direct conflict with the manufacturers' desire for flexibility. Indeed, since production decisions are typically made without precise information about customer demand, the ability of manufacturers to match supply and demand depends largely on their ability to change supply volume as information about demand arrives. Similarly, the manufacturers' objective of making large production batches typically conflicts with the objectives of both warehouses and distribution centers to reduce inventory. To make matters worse, this latter objective of reducing inventory levels typically implies an increase in transportation costs.
3. **The supply chain is a dynamic system** that evolves over time. Indeed, not only do customer demand and supplier capabilities change over time, but supply chain relationships also evolve over time. For example, as customers' power increases, there is increased pressure placed on manufacturers and suppliers to produce an enormous variety of high-quality products and, ultimately, to produce customized products.
4. **System variations over time** are also an important consideration. Even when demand is known precisely (e.g., because of contractual agreements), the planning process needs to account for demand and cost parameters varying over time due to the impact of seasonal fluctuations, trends, advertising and promotions, competitors' pricing strategies, and so forth. These time-varying demand and cost parameters make it difficult to determine the most effective supply chain strategy, the one that minimizes systemwide costs and conforms to customer requirements.

EXAMPLE 1.4 SUPPLY OF ONION

India has seen quite a few dramatic situations in the vegetable market place when price of onion, which is a common man's daily use agriculture produce, sky-rocked to an unprecedented level. For example, its price jumped from Rs. 6 per kg in May 1998 to Rs. 60 per kg in October 1998. According to analysts, on a majority of such occurrences the cause is not only a shortfall in production or inflation in demand. Generally, it is due to poor supply management practices. The possible reasons are excessive export, hoarding, poor warehousing and distribution, late decision-making in controlling the problem, etc. On quite a few occasions, the unprecedented price rise of onion had significantly contributed towards the defeat of ruling Governments in Centre or State during the election following the price rise, [292, 300, 301].

Of course, global optimization only implies that it is not only important to optimize across supply chain facilities, but also across processes associated with the development and supply chains. That is, it is important to identify processes and strategies that optimize or, alternatively, synchronize both chains simultaneously.

1.4 MANAGING UNCERTAINTY AND RISK

Global optimization is made even more difficult because supply chains need to be designed for, and operated in, uncertain environments, thus creating sometimes enormous risks to the organization. A variety of factors contribute to this:

1. **Matching supply and demand** is a major challenge:
   a. Boeing Aircraft announced a write-down of $2.6 billion in October 1997 due to "raw material shortages, internal and supplier parts shortages and productivity inefficiencies" [251].
   b. "Second quarter sales at U.S. Surgical Corporation declined 25 percent, resulting in a loss of $22 million. The sales and earnings shortfall is attributed to larger than anticipated inventories on the shelves of hospitals" [252].
   c. "EMC Corp. said it missed its revenue guidance of $2.66 billion for the second quarter of 2006 by around $100 million, and said the discrepancy was due to higher than expected orders for the new DMX-3 systems over the DMX-2, which resulted in an inventory snafu" [218].
   d. "There are so many different ways inventory can enter our system it's a constant challenge to keep it under control" [Johnnie Dobbs, Wal-Mart Supply Chain and Logistics Executive].
   e. "Intel, the world's largest chip maker, reported a 38 percent decline in quarterly profit Wednesday in the face of stiff competition from Advanced Micro Devices and a general slowdown in the personal computer market that caused inventories to swell" [86].

   Obviously, this difficulty stems from the fact that months before demand is realized, manufacturers have to commit themselves to specific production levels. These advance commitments imply huge financial and supply risks.

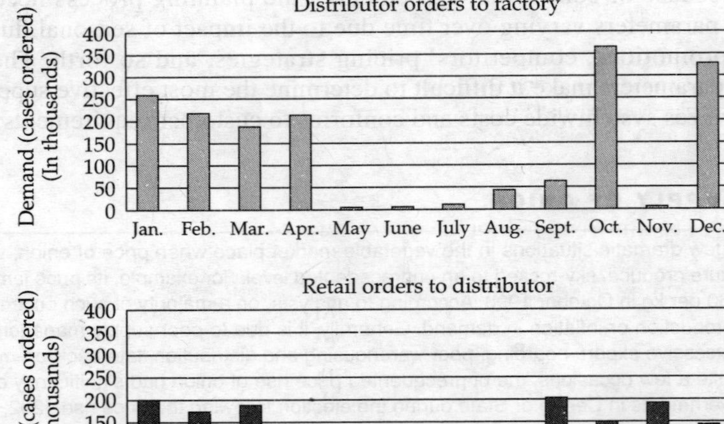

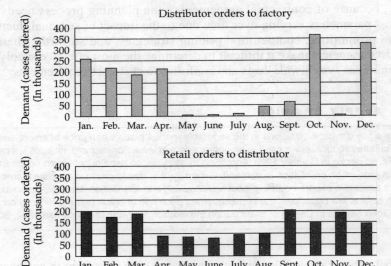

FIGURE 1-3 Order variations in the supply chain.

2. **Inventory and back-order levels fluctuate considerably across the supply chain,** even when customer demand for specific products does not vary greatly. To illustrate this issue, consider Figure 1-3, which suggests that in a typical supply chain, distributor orders to the factory fluctuate far more than the underlying retailer demand.
3. **Forecasting doesn't solve the problem.** Indeed, we will argue that the first principle of forecasting is that "forecasts are always wrong." Thus, it is impossible to predict the precise demand for a specific item, even with the most advanced forecasting techniques.

4. **Demand is not the only source of uncertainty.** Delivery lead times, manufacturing yields, transportation times, and component availability also can have significant supply chain impact.
5. **Recent trends such as lean manufacturing, outsourcing, and offshoring that focus on cost reduction increase risks significantly.** For example, consider an automotive manufacturer whose parts suppliers are in Canada and Mexico. With little uncertainty in transportation and a stable supply schedule, parts can be delivered to assembly plants "just-in-time" based on fixed production schedules. However, in the event of an unforeseen disaster, such as the September 11 terrorist attacks, port strikes, January 26, 2001 earthquake in the Indian state of Gujarat, or weather-related calamities, adherence to this type of strategy could result in a shutdown of the production lines due to lack of parts.

   Similarly, outsourcing and offshoring imply that the supply chains are more geographically diverse and, as a result, natural and man-made disasters can have a tremendous impact.

EXAMPLE 1-5

- On August 29, 2005, Hurricane Katrina devastated New Orleans and the Gulf coast. Procter & Gamble coffee manufacturing, with brands such as Folgers that get over half of their supply from sites in New Orleans, was severely impacted by the hurricane. Six months later, there were, as a P&G executive told the *New York Times,* "still holes on the shelves" where P&G's brands should be [204].
- A 2002 West Coast port strike shut down ports from Seattle to San Diego. Economists estimate that this strike cost the economy up to $1 billion a day, as stores could not be stocked, fruits and vegetables rotted, and factories were shut down due to lack of parts [94].
- In September 1999, a massive earthquake devastated Taiwan. Initially, 80 percent of the island's power was lost. Companies such as Hewlett-Packard and Dell, who source a variety of components from Taiwanese manufacturers, were impacted by supply interruptions [11].
- Fabric shipments from India were delayed in the wake of the January 26, 2001, earthquake in the Indian state of Gujarat, impacting many U.S. apparel manufacturers [77].

Although uncertainty and risk cannot be eliminated, we will explore a variety of examples that illustrate how product design, network modeling, information technology, procurement, and inventory strategies are used to minimize uncertainty, and to build flexibility and redundancy in the supply chain in order to reduce risks.

1.5 THE EVOLUTION OF SUPPLY CHAIN MANAGEMENT

In the 1980s, companies discovered new manufacturing technologies and strategies that allowed them to reduce costs and better compete in different markets. Strategies such as just-in-time manufacturing, *kanban,* lean manufacturing, total quality management, and others became very popular, and vast amounts of resources were invested in implementing these strategies. In the last few years, however, it has become clear that many companies have reduced manufacturing costs as much as is practically possible. Many of these companies are discovering that effective supply chain management is the next step they need to take in order to increase profit and market share.

Indeed, logistics and supply chain costs play an important role in the U.S. economy: the annual "State of Logistics Report," which is sponsored by the Council of Supply Chain Management Professionals, first published in 1989, provides an accounting of the nation's total logistics bill and tracks trends in transportation costs, inventory-carrying costs, and total logistics costs. As you can see from Figure 1-4, U.S. logistics costs were over 12 percent of GDP in the early 80s, steadily decreasing until 2003. The absolute numbers are quite staggering: for 1998 the amount was $898 billion, while in

2005 it was $1.18 trillion. This $1.18 trillion represents an increase of $156 billion over 2004, which is even more striking if one considers that while the U.S. economy slowed down in 2005, logistics costs increased by about 15 percent. This increase was driven, according to the "State of Logistics Report," by "high fuel costs, truck driver and rail capacity shortages, offshoring and outsourcing and the costs of security."

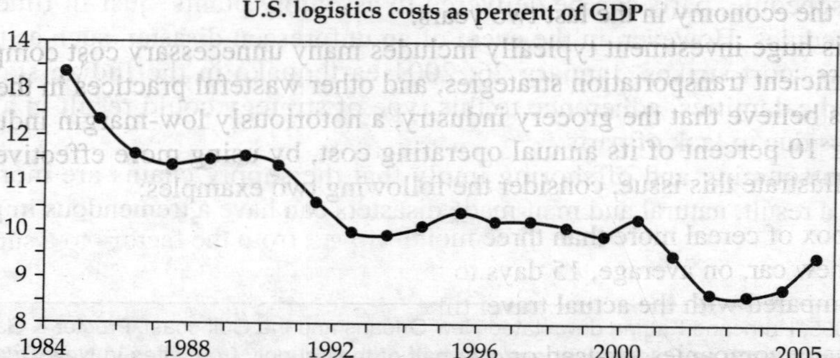

FIGURE 1-4 Logistics costs' share of the U.S. economy.
Source: Based on www.dcvelocity.com/articles/20060801/news.cfm.

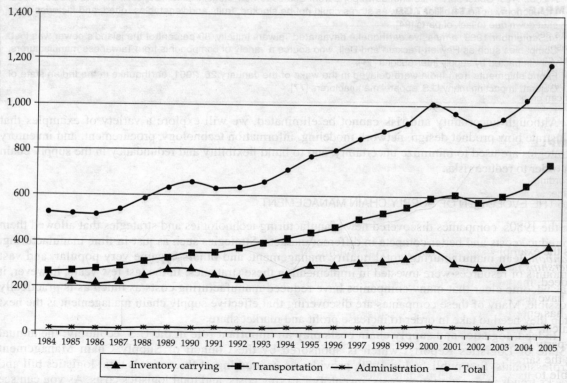

FIGURE 1-5 Total U.S. logistics costs between 1984 and 2005.
Source: Based on www.dcvelocity.com/articles/20060801/news.cfm.

It is also interesting to understand the magnitude of the various cost components that constitute the U.S. logistics costs. These data are presented in Figure 1-5 (taken again from the "State of Logistics Report"), where transportation cost is by far the largest cost component; inventory cost is slightly higher than half of the transportation costs. Both costs have steadily increased in the last few years, except that, until 2003, total logistics costs increased slower than the economy growth, while they have increased faster than the economy in the last two years.

Unfortunately, this huge investment typically includes many unnecessary cost components due to redundant stock, inefficient transportation strategies, and other wasteful practices in the supply chain. For instance, experts believe that the grocery industry, a notoriously low-margin industry, can save about $30 billion, or 10 percent of its annual operating cost, by using more effective supply chain strategies [109]. To illustrate this issue, consider the following two examples:

1. It takes a typical box of cereal more than three months to get from the factory to a supermarket.
2. It takes a typical new car, on average, 15 days to travel from the factory to the dealership. This lead time should be compared with the actual travel time, which is no more than four to five days.

Thus, in the 1990s many companies focused on strategies to reduce their costs as well as those of their supply chain partners.

EXAMPLE 1-6 TATA MOTOR

India's second-largest and longest-established conglomerat's Chairman, Mr. Ratan Tata, has an ambitious plan to tap the aspiration of the Indian middle class, which owns and drives two wheelers, to switch over to their own family car. The Tata's car has passed the major design and testing stages and according to Mr. Tata it would initially cost less than Rs. 1 lakh or about $ 2200. The car is going to be gearless with lighter rear engine and will have a seating capacity of five people. The vehicles would be produced primarily in the form of a kit for assembly at several places around India. This can create local employment and save production and logistics cost [299].

EXAMPLE 1-7

Procter & Gamble estimates that it saved retail customers $65 million in a recent 18-month supply chain initiative. "According to Procter & Gamble, the essence of its approach lies in manufacturers and suppliers working closely together . . . jointly creating business plans to eliminate the source of wasteful practices across the entire supply chain" [248].

As the example suggests, an important building block in effective supply chain strategies is *strategic partnerships* between suppliers and buyers, partnerships that can help both parties reduce their costs.

Indeed, manufacturers such as Procter & Gamble and Kimberly-Clark and giant retailers like Wal-Mart have used strategic partnering as an important element in their business strategies. In India, Wal-Mart has entered into a strategic partnership with Bharti. Firms such as 3M, Eastman Kodak, Dow Chemical, Time Warner, and General Motors turned over large portions of their logistics operations to third-party logistics providers.

At the same time, many supply chain partners engage in *information sharing* so that manufacturers are able to use retailers' up-to-date sales data to better predict demand and reduce lead times. This information sharing also allows manufacturers to control the variability in supply chains (known as the bullwhip effect; see Chapter 5), and by doing that, reduce inventory and smooth out production.

EXAMPLE 1-8

Among the first companies to utilize real-time information was Milliken and Company, a textile and chemicals company. Milliken worked with several clothing suppliers and major department stores, all of which agreed to use point-of-sale (POS) data from the department stores to "synchronize" their ordering and manufacturing plans. The lead time from order receipt at Milliken's textile plants to final clothing receipt at the department stores was reduced from 18 weeks to 3 weeks [215].

The huge pressure during the 90s to reduce costs and increase profits pushed many industrial manufacturers towards *outsourcing;* firms considered outsourcing everything from the procurement function to production and manufacturing. Indeed, in the mid 90s there was a significant increase in purchasing volume as a percentage of the typical firm's total sales. More recently, between 1998 and 2000, outsourcing in the electronic industry has increased from 15 percent of all components to 40 percent [216].

Finally, in the late 90s, the *Internet* and the related *e-business models* led to expectations that many supply chain problems would be solved merely by using these new technologies and business models. E-business strategies were supposed to reduce cost, increase service level, and increase flexibility and, of course, increase profits, albeit sometime in the future. In reality, these expectations frequently were not met, as many e-businesses failed. In many cases, the downfall of some of the highest-profile Internet businesses can be attributed to their logistics strategies.

EXAMPLE 1-9

Furniture.com, launched in January 1999, offered thousands of products from many furniture makers, although only a few brand names. The company had $22 million in sales in the first nine months of 2000 and one million visitors a month to its Web site. Its downfall in November of 2000 was due to logistics details, and, in particular, inefficient delivery processes. Initially, Furniture.com used carriers to ship its products from a central warehouse to the customers. Since transportation costs were too high, the firm formed an alliance with six regional distributors. Unfortunately, these relationships were hard to maintain and left many problems unsolved, including handling of repairs and returns.

Of course, in many cases, the Internet introduced new channels and helped to enable the direct-to-consumer business model. These new channels required many companies to learn new skills, and added complexity to existing supply chains.

EXAMPLE 1-10

According to the Stern Stewart EVA 1000 database, Dell Computers outperformed the competition by over 3,000 percent in terms of shareholder growth over the eight-year period from 1988 to 1996. Dell's success over this period can be attributed to its virtual integration, a strategy that blurs the traditional boundaries between suppliers, manufacturers, and end users. Dell's decision to sell computers built from components produced by other manufacturers relieved the firm of the burdens of owning assets, doing research and development, and managing a large workforce. At the same time, the Dell model of direct sales to consumers and production to order virtually eliminated finished goods inventory. These business decisions allowed Dell to grow much faster than its competition and maintain only eight days of inventory.

The landscape has changed in recent years. Industry recognized that trends, including outsourcing, offshoring, lean manufacturing, and just-in-time, that focus on reducing manufacturing and supply chain costs significantly increase the level of risk in the supply chain. As a result, over the past several years, progressive firms have started to focus on strategies that find the right balance between cost reduction and risk management.

A number of approaches have been applied by industry to manage risk in their supply chains:

- Building redundancy into the supply chain so that if one portion fails, for example, a fire at a warehouse or a closed port, the supply chain can still satisfy demand.
- Using information to better sense and respond to disruptive events.
- Incorporating flexibility into supply contracts to better match supply and demand.
- Improving supply chain processes by including risk assessment measures.

Of course, many of these approaches rely heavily on technology. Indeed, the implementation of ERP systems, motivated in many companies by year 2000 concerns, as well as new technology such as tools for supplier performance assessments, have created opportunities to improve supply chain resiliency and responsiveness. Similarly, advanced inventory planning systems are now used to better position inventory in the supply chain, and to help firms better understand the impact of product design alternatives on supply chain costs and risks, thus facilitating the integration of the development chain and the supply chain.

EXAMPLE 1-11

United Technologies Corp. (UTC) continuously measures and evaluates suppliers' performance using third-party vendor software. The software relies not only on historical delivery data but also on external financial data on each supplier to create supplier risk alerts. UTC complements the supplier performance and risk alert system with teams that help tier 1 suppliers improve their supply chain and reduce risks with their own suppliers. According to UTC, these initiatives significantly increased inventory turns and reduced cost of nonquality (unplanned overtime, scrap, etc.) [1].

As we saw in Figure 1-4, the urgency of supply chain challenges has not diminished over the years with the recent increase in supply chain costs. With complexity driven by globalization, high transportation costs, poor infrastructure, weather-related disasters, and terrorist threats, managing the supply chain has become even more challenging. Throughout this text, we demonstrate how new technology and supply chain strategies can help companies deal with these challenges.

1.6 THE COMPLEXITY

The preceding section describes a number of supply chain management success stories: Procter & Gamble, Wal-Mart, UTC, and others. They suggest that, in some industries, supply chain management is perhaps the single most important factor determining the success of the firm. Indeed, in the computer and printer industries, where most manufacturers use the same suppliers and identical technologies, companies compete on cost and service levels, the two key elements in our definition of supply chain management.

The examples also raise an important question. If these firms have improved supply chain performance by focusing on strategic partnering, using information sharing and technology, or by applying risk mitigation strategies, what inhibits other firms from adopting the same techniques to improve their supply chain performance?

The earlier discussion suggests that the answer involves three critical abilities that successful firms must possess:

- The ability to match supply chain strategies with product characteristics. Indeed, it is clear that the supply chain strategy for products and industries where the technology changes frequently, the so-called fast clock speed products, must be fundamentally different than that of slow clock speed products. Similarly, product design strategy depends not only on characteristics of the development chain but also on supply chain characteristics. Thus, the intersection of the development chain and the supply chain has an impact on both product design and supply chain strategy.

- The ability to replace traditional supply chain strategies, in which each facility or party in the chain makes decisions with little regard to their impact on other supply chain partners, by those that yield a *globally optimized* supply chain.
- The ability to effectively manage uncertainty and risk. As observed earlier, initiatives such as outsourcing and offshoring and manufacturing strategies such as lean and just-in-time have significantly increased the level of risk for the enterprise. This is complemented by the significant increase in the level of demand uncertainty. Indeed, in high-tech industries, product life cycles are becoming shorter and shorter. In particular, many computer and printer models have life cycles of only a few months, so the manufacturer may have only one order or production opportunity. Unfortunately, since these are new products, no historical data are available that allow the manufacturer to accurately predict customer demand. At the same time, the proliferation of products in these industries makes it increasingly difficult to predict demand for a specific model. Finally, significant price declines in these industries are common, reducing the product value during its life cycle [167].

EXAMPLE 1-12

A Korean manufacturer of electrical products such as industrial relays is facing a service level of about 70 percent; that is, only about 70 percent of all orders are delivered on time. On the other hand, inventory keeps piling up, mostly of products that are not in demand. The manufacturer's inventory turnover ratio, defined as the ratio of the annual flow to average inventory at the manufacturer's main warehouse, is about four. However, in the electronics industry, leading companies turn inventory over about nine times a year. If the Korean manufacturer can increase its inventory turns to this level, it will be able to significantly reduce inventory levels. The manufacturer is thus searching for new strategies that will increase service levels over the next three years to about 99 percent and, at the same time, significantly decrease inventory levels and cost.

Just a few years ago, most analysts would have said that these two objectives, improved service and inventory levels, could not be achieved at the same time. Indeed, traditional inventory theory tells us that to increase service level, the firm must increase inventory and therefore cost. Surprisingly, recent developments in information and communications technologies, together with a better understanding of supply chain strategies, have led to innovative approaches that allow the firm to improve both objectives simultaneously. Throughout the rest of this book, we endeavor to present these approaches and strategies in detail. We will focus on demonstrating why certain strategies are adopted, what the trade-offs are between different strategies, and how specific strategies are implemented in practice.

1.7 KEY ISSUES IN SUPPLY CHAIN MANAGEMENT

In this section, we introduce some of the supply chain management issues that we discuss in much more detail throughout the remaining chapters. These issues span a large spectrum of a firm's activities, from the strategic through the tactical to the operational level:

- The *strategic level* deals with decisions that have a long-lasting effect on the firm. This includes decisions regarding product design, what to make internally and what to outsource, supplier selection, and strategic partnering as well as decisions on the number, location, and capacity of warehouses and manufacturing plants and the flow of material through the logistics network.
- The *tactical level* includes decisions that are typically updated anywhere between once every quarter and once every year. These include purchasing and production decisions, inventory policies, and transportation strategies, including the frequency with which customers are visited.
- The *operational level* refers to day-to-day decisions such as scheduling, lead time quotations, routing, and truck loading.

Below we introduce and discuss some of the key issues, questions, and trade-offs associated with different decisions.

Distribution Network Configuration Consider several plants producing products to serve a set of geographically dispersed retailers. The current set of warehouses is deemed inappropriate, and management wants to reorganize or redesign the distribution network. This may be due, for example, to changing demand patterns or the termination of a leasing contract for a number of existing warehouses. In addition, changing demand patterns may require a change in plant production levels, a selection of new suppliers, and a new flow pattern of goods throughout the distribution network. How should management select a set of warehouse locations and capacities, determine production levels for each product at each plant, and set transportation flows between facilities, either from plant to warehouse or warehouse to retailer, in such a way as to minimize total production, inventory, and transportation costs and satisfy service level requirements? This is a complex optimization problem, and advanced technology and approaches are required to find a solution.

Inventory Control Consider a retailer that maintains an inventory of a particular product. Since customer demand changes over time, the retailer can use only historical data to predict demand. The retailer's objective is to decide at what point to reorder a new batch of the product, and how much to order so as to minimize inventory ordering and holding costs. More fundamentally, why should the retailer hold inventory in the first place? Is it due to uncertainty in customer demand, uncertainty in the supply process, or some other reasons? If it is due to uncertainty in customer demand, is there anything that can be done to reduce it? What is the impact of the forecasting tool used to predict customer demand? Should the retailer order more than, less than, or exactly the demand forecast? And, finally, what inventory turnover ratio should be used? Does it change from industry to industry?

Production Sourcing In many industries, there is a need to carefully balance transportation and manufacturing costs. In particular, reducing production costs typically implies that each manufacturing facility is responsible for a small set of products so that large batches are produced, hence reducing production costs. Unfortunately, this may lead to higher transportation costs.

Similarly, reducing transportation costs typically implies that each facility is flexible and has the ability to produce most or all products, but this leads to small batches and hence increases production costs. Finding the right balance between the two cost components is difficult but needs to be done monthly or quarterly.

Supply Contracts In traditional supply chain strategies, each party in the chain focuses on its own profit and hence makes decisions with little regard to their impact on other supply chain partners.

Relationships between suppliers and buyers are established by means of supply contracts that specify pricing and volume discounts, delivery lead times, quality, returns, and so forth. The question, of course, is whether supply contracts also can be used to replace the traditional supply chain strategy with one that optimizes the entire supply chain performance. In particular, what is the impact of volume discount and revenue-sharing contracts on supply chain performance? Are there pricing strategies that can be applied by suppliers to provide incentives for buyers to order more products while at the same time increasing the supplier profit?

Distribution Strategies An important challenge faced by many organizations is how much should they centralize (or decentralize) their distribution system. What is the impact of each strategy on inventory levels and transportation costs? What about the impact on service levels? And, finally, when should products be transported by air from centralized locations to the various demand points? These questions are important not only for a single firm determining its distribution strategy, but also for competing retailers that need to decide how much they can collaborate with each other. For example, should competing dealers selling the same brand share inventory? If so, what is their competitive advantage?

Supply Chain Integration and Strategic Partnering As observed earlier, designing and implementing a globally optimal supply chain is quite difficult because of its dynamics and the conflicting objectives employed by different facilities and partners. Nevertheless, Dell, Wal-Mart, and Procter & Gamble success stories demonstrate not only that an integrated, globally optimal supply chain is possible, but that it can have a huge impact on the company's performance and market share. Of course, one can argue that these three examples are associated with companies that are among the biggest companies in their respective industries; these companies can implement technologies and strategies that very few others can afford. However, in today's competitive markets, most companies have no choice; they are forced to integrate their supply chain and engage in strategic partnering. This pressure stems from both their customers and their supply chain partners. How can integration be achieved successfully? Clearly, information sharing and operational planning are the keys to a successfully integrated supply chain. But what information should be shared? How should it be used? How does information affect the design and operation of the supply chain? What level of integration is needed within the organization and with external partners? Finally, what types of partnerships can be implemented, and which type should be implemented for a given situation?

Outsourcing and Offshoring Strategies Rethinking your supply chain strategy involves not only coordinating the different activities in the supply chain, but also deciding what to make internally and what to buy from outside sources. How can a firm identify what manufacturing activities lie in its set of core competencies, and thus should be completed internally, and what product and components should be purchased from outside suppliers, because these manufacturing activities are not core competencies? Is there any relationship between the answer to that question and product architecture? What are the risks associated with outsourcing and how can these risks be minimized? When you do outsource, how can you ensure a timely supply of products? And when should the firm keep dual sources for the same component? Finally, even if the firm decides not to outsource activities, when does it make sense to move facilities to the Far East? What is the impact of offshoring on inventory levels and the cost of capital? What are the risks?

Product Design Effective design plays several critical roles in the supply chain. Most obviously, certain product designs may increase inventory holding or transportation costs relative to other designs, while other designs may facilitate a shorter manufacturing lead time. Unfortunately, product redesign is often expensive. When is it worthwhile to redesign products so as to reduce logistics costs or supply chain lead times? Is it possible to leverage product design to compensate for uncertainty in customer demand? Can one quantify the amount of savings resulting from such a strategy? What changes should be made in the supply chain to take advantage of the new product design? Finally, new concepts such as mass customization are increasingly popular. What role does supply chain management play in the successful implementation of these concepts?

Information Technology and Decision-Support Systems Information technology is a critical enabler of effective supply chain management. Indeed, much of the current interest in supply chain management is motivated by the opportunities that appeared due to the abundance of data and the savings that can be achieved by sophisticated analysis of these data. The primary issue in supply chain management is not whether data can be received, but what data should be transferred; that is, which data are significant for supply chain management and which data can safely be ignored? How frequently should data be transferred and analyzed? What is the impact of the Internet? What is the role of electronic commerce? What infrastructure is required both internally and between supply chain partners? Finally, since information technology and decision-support systems are both available, can these technologies be viewed as the main tools used to achieve competitive advantage in the market? If they can, then what is preventing others from using the same technology?

Customer Value Customer value is the measure of a company's contribution to its customer, based on the entire range of products, services, and intangibles that constitute the company's offerings. In recent years, this measure has superseded measures such as quality and customer satisfaction. Obviously, effective supply chain management is critical if a firm wishes to fulfill customer needs and provide value. But what determines customer value in different industries? How is customer value measured? How is information technology used to enhance customer value in the supply chain? How does supply chain management contribute to customer value? How do emerging trends in customer value, such as development of relationships and experiences, affect supply chain management? What is the relationship between product price and brand name in the conventional world and in the online world?

Smart Pricing Revenue management strategies have been applied successfully in industries such as airlines, hotels, and rental cars. In recent years, a number of manufactures, retailers, and carriers have applied a variation of these techniques to improve supply chain performance. In this case, the firm integrates pricing and inventory (or available capacity) to influence market demand and improve the bottom line. How is this done? Can "smart" pricing strategies be used to improve supply chain performance? What is the impact of rebate strategies on the supply chain?

Each of these issues and strategies is discussed in great detail in the remaining chapters. As you will see, the focus in each case is on either the development chain or the supply chain and the focus is on achieving a *globally optimized* supply chain or managing risk and uncertainty in the supply chain, or both. A summary is provided in Table 1-1.

Local Issues Supply chain is important not only to a big corporate house but also to common people, for whom many local issues are important. These could be supply and distribution of common use

TABLE 1-1

KEY SUPPLY CHAIN MANAGEMENT ISSUES

	Chain	Global optimization	Managing risk and uncertainty
Distribution network configuration	Supply	Y	
Inventory control	Supply		Y
Production sourcing	Supply	Y	
Supply contracts	Both	Y	Y
Distribution strategies	Supply	Y	Y
Strategic partnering	Development	Y	
Outsourcing and offshoring	Development	Y	
Product design	Development		Y
Information technology	Supply	Y	Y
Customer value	Both	Y	Y
Smart pricing	Supply	Y	

items like food and water. During natural calamities like earthquake, *tsunami,* etc and also during unexpected events like 9/11, the role of proper deployment of supply chain strategy is very important. How can supply chains be effective during these temporary phases? An effective but quickly designed supply chain is important as these are vital to save many lives. How can one approach towards this? In some of the developing nations like India, organized retail is coming in a big way. The skill sets needed to manage their supply chains will require an understanding of local dynamics, customer preferences, government policies, infrastructural constraints, and strength and weaknesses of supply chain partners. How can one approach these issues? Issues like reverse logistics and environment concerns necessitate a new look on supply chain design and planning. How can we manage the reverse logistics?

1.8 BOOK OBJECTIVES AND OVERVIEW

For many reasons, interest in logistics and supply chain management has grown explosively in the last few years. This interest has led many companies to analyze their supply chains. In most cases, however, this has been done based on experience and intuition; very few analytical models or design tools have been used in this process. Meanwhile, in the last two decades, the academic community has developed various models and tools to assist with the management of the supply chain. Unfortunately, the first generation of this technology was not robust or flexible enough to be effectively utilized by industry.

This, however, has changed in the last few years. Analysis and insight have improved, and effective models and decision-support systems have been developed—but these may not be familiar to industry.

This book fills this gap by presenting state-of-the-art models and solution methods important in the design, control, operation, and management of supply chain systems. We intend this book to be useful both as a textbook for MBA-level logistics and supply chain courses and as a reference for teachers, consultants, and managers involved in any one of the processes that make up the supply chain. Each chapter includes case studies, numerous examples, and discussion questions. In addition, each chapter is mostly self-contained, and mathematical and technical sections can be skipped without loss of continuity. Therefore, we believe the book is accessible to anyone with an interest in some of the many aspects of supply chain management. For example, transportation managers deciding which modes of transportation to use, inventory control managers wanting to ensure smooth production with as little inventory as possible, purchasing/supply managers designing contracts with their company's suppliers and clients, and logistics managers in charge of their company's supply chains all can benefit from the contents of this book.

The book includes chapters covering the following topics:

- Inventory management.
- Logistics network planning.
- Supply contracts for strategic as well as commodity components.
- The value of information and the effective use of information in the supply chain.
- Supply chain integration.
- Centralized and decentralized distribution strategies.
- Strategic alliances.
- Outsourcing, offshoring, and procurement strategies.
- International logistics and risk management strategies.
- Supply chain management and product design.
- Customer value.
- Revenue management and pricing strategies.
- Information technology and business processes.
- Technical standards and their impact on the supply chain.
- Local issues in supply chains.

In addition, three software packages, the **Computerized Beer Game,** the **Risk Pool Game,** and the **Procurement Game,** as well as a set of spreadsheets, are included with the book. The Computerized Beer Game is an advanced version of a traditional supply chain management role-playing simulation, first developed at MIT. In addition to replicating the traditional board-based game, the Computerized Beer Game has many options and features that enable the reader to explore a variety of simple and advanced supply chain management concepts that cannot be easily taught using the traditional game. This includes the value of information sharing, the impact of long and short lead times, and the difference between centralized and decentralized decision making on supply chain performance. This game complements much of what we discuss in the text; in particular, it helps to clarify many of the points raised in Chapter 5.

Similarly, the Risk Pool Game was developed to illustrate important issues in inventory management and, in particular, an important concept in supply chain management referred to as *risk pooling,* a concept that we discuss in Chapter 2. In the game, the player simultaneously manages both a supply chain with a single warehouse and a supply chain without any warehouse. In the latter case, the player delivers finished goods directly from the suppliers to the retail outlets. Throughout the game, the software records the profits of both supply chains, so that the player can compare the performance of the centralized and decentralized systems.

The Procurement Game was developed to illustrate the impact of flexible (option) contracts and supplier competition on the behavior of both the suppliers and the buyer. The game presents a realistic situation in the high-tech industry where demand uncertainty is high and buyers need to reserve capacity in advance of the selling season with one or more suppliers. The game complements the material on procurement strategies in Chapter 9. The three software packages are described in detail in the appendix.

Finally, a series of spreadsheets is included with the book. These spreadsheets illustrate the various inventory concepts and *supply contracts* described in Chapters 2 and 4.

DISCUSSION QUESTIONS

1. Consider the supply chain for a domestic automobile.
   a. What are the components of the supply chain for the automobile?
   b. What are the different firms involved in the supply chain?
   c. What are the objectives of these firms?
   d. Provide examples of conflicting objectives in this supply chain.
   e. What are the risks that rare or unexpected events pose to this supply chain?

2. Consider a consumer mortgage offered by a bank.
   a. What are the components of the supply chain for the mortgage?
   b. Is there more than one firm involved in the supply chain? What are the objectives of the firm or firms?
   c. What are the similarities between product and service supply chains? What are the differences?

3. What is an example of a supply chain that has evolved over time?

4. A vertically integrated company is a company that owns, manages, and operates all its business functions. A horizontally integrated company is a corporation consisting of a number of companies, each of which is acting independently. The corporation provides branding, direction, and general strategy. Compare and contrast the supply chain strategies of the two types of companies.

5. If a firm is completely vertically integrated, is effective supply chain management still important?

6. Consider the supply chain for canned peaches sold by a major food processing company. What are the sources of uncertainty in this supply chain?

7. Consider a firm redesigning its logistics network. What are the advantages to having a small number of centrally located warehouses? What are the advantages to having a larger number of warehouses closer to the end customers?

8. Consider a firm selecting a supplier of transportation services. What are the advantages of using a truckload carrier or a package delivery firm such as UPS, Safe Express, etc.

9. What are the advantages to a firm of high inventory levels? What are the disadvantages? What are the advantages of low inventory levels? The disadvantages?

10. What are some ways that redundancy can be built into a supply chain? What are the advantages and disadvantages of building redundancy into the supply chain?

11. Consider Figure 1-5. What are the reasons for the increase in transportation costs? Inventory costs? Does one affect the other? How?

12. Through secondary research, identify the salient features of supply chain of following companies: Maruti Udyog Limited (MUL), Asian Paints, Public Distribution System in India, a major retail chain of your country, and a groceries store.

CASE: Meditech Surgical

Three years after Meditech was spun off from its parent company, Meditech captured a majority of the endoscopic surgical instrument market. Its primary competitor, National Medical Corporation, had practically invented the $800 million market just over a decade ago. But Meditech competed aggressively, developing new, innovative instruments and selling them through a first-class sales force. The combination paid off, and Meditech had become a phenomenal success in a short period of time. Despite the success, Dan Franklin, manager of Customer Service and Distribution, was concerned about growing customer dissatisfaction. Meditech had recently introduced several new products that were central to the entire Meditech product line. New product introductions, which were critical to Meditech's strategy of rapid product development, needed to be introduced flawlessly to protect Meditech's reputation and sales of other products. But Meditech consistently failed to keep up with demand during the flood of initial orders. Production capacity became strained as customers waited over six weeks to have their orders delivered. Poor delivery service, which is fatal in the health care industry, was jeopardizing Meditech's reputation.

COMPANY BACKGROUND

Endoscopic surgical techniques fall under a class of surgical procedures described as minimally invasive. Minimally invasive surgery, as opposed to traditional open surgery, requires only small incisions to perform an operation. As a result, procedures using endoscopic techniques often provide substantial benefits for the patient both physically and financially. The procedures often shorten patient recovery, which can translate into reduced surgical expenses overall. Despite the benefits and the multidecade history of endoscopic technology, the procedures have only become popular in the last 10 years. Only three years ago, the market for endoscopic surgical instruments was expected to double its size in five years. Growth beyond five years also looked promising. Largo Healthcare Company, Meditech's parent company, decided to spin Meditech off as an independent company focused solely on producing and selling endoscopic surgical instruments. Largo management hoped that the new company would prosper without the distractions of other Largo businesses and capture market share of endoscopic instruments as quickly as possible.

Since its inception just over six years ago, Meditech has produced innovative, low-cost products. New products were brought to the market quickly and pushed by an aggressive sales force. Old products were updated with innovative features and presented to the market as new products. Consequently, the competition between Meditech and National Medical centered on the continuous development and introduction of new products by both companies. A dozen or more new products would typically be introduced by Meditech in any given year.

While the development strategies were similar, the sales strategies differed dramatically. National Medical concentrated on selling to surgeons. Meditech's sales force concentrated on selling to hospitals, material managers as well as to surgeons. Material managers tended to be more concerned with cost and delivery performance. The surgeons, on the other hand, focused on product features. As the pressures increased on health care costs, the importance of the material manager's purchasing position also increased. Meditech was well positioned to take advantage of this important shift.

The success of Meditech's strategy quickly became evident. Within six years, Meditech had captured the leading share in the endoscopic surgical instrument market. This was no small feat by any market's standards, but with surgical instruments this was especially impressive. Market share changes in the professional health care industry tended to take place gradually. Surgeons and doctors often held onto preferred manufacturers. Hospitals frequently used group purchasing organizations (GPOs) that took advantage of extended contracts with suppliers. The process of "converting" a hospital to a new supplier often took months of negotiation and convincing.

Most endoscopic surgical instruments are small enough to fit into the palm of a surgeon's

---

 This case was prepared by LFM Fellow Bryan Gilpin under the direction of Professor Stephen C. Graves as the basis for class discussion.

hand. They are mechanical in nature, typically having several intricate mechanisms to provide the required functionality. Materials used to produce the instruments include plastic injection–molded parts, metal blades, springs, and so forth. In all cases of use, surgeons use the instrument for one operation and then immediately dispose of it. Instruments are never resterilized and reused for another patient. All in all, the Meditech product line consists of over 200 separate end-products.

DISTRIBUTION

Meditech distributes all its goods from a central warehouse, using two primary channels—domestic dealers and international affiliates—to distribute its products from the central warehouse to end-customers (i.e., hospitals). The first channel, for domestic sales only, uses domestic distributors, or dealers, to ship to hospitals. The dealers order and receive products from multiple manufacturers, including Meditech, typically stocking hundreds of different products. Stocked products range from commodity items, such as surgical gloves and aspirin, to endoscopic surgical instruments. By using dealers to supply products, hospitals do not need to order directly from manufacturers for their diverse needs. Additionally, since dealers maintain regional warehouses all over the United States, the distance between dealer warehouses and most hospitals tends to be quite small. The short distance permits frequent replenishments of hospital inventories; in some cases, trucks from dealers drop off supplies once or twice per day. Hospitals enjoy the frequent replenishments, which reduce hospital inventory and, consequently, reduce material costs.

The regional dealer warehouses act as independent entities, autonomously determining when to order new supplies and how much to order. Therefore, while Meditech uses only four or five major distribution companies, it still receives orders from, and ships to, hundreds of regional, individually run warehouses. Each warehouse in turn ships to about a dozen or more hospitals, resulting in thousands of hospitals that receive Meditech products.

The distribution channel for international sales uses Largo Healthcare's international affiliates. International affiliates are wholly owned subsidiaries of Largo Healthcare residing outside of the United States. As with domestic dealers, affiliates distribute to hospitals in their regional area. However, in contrast with domestic dealers, which may locate within just a few miles of customer hospitals, an affiliate ships product throughout an entire country. From Meditech's point of view, affiliates' orders essentially look no different than dealers'—international affiliates submit orders to Meditech and Meditech fills them with available product.

INTERNAL OPERATIONS

The production processes to manufacture endoscopic instruments are composed of three major steps: assembling of component parts into individual or "bulk" instruments, packaging one or more bulk instruments into a packaged good, and sterilizing the packaged goods. Each of these steps is described below.

Assembly

The assembly process is manually intensive. Component parts arrive into the assembly area from suppliers following a brief inspection by Quality Assurance (QA). The parts are placed into inventory until ready for use by one of several assembly lines. Each assembly line is run by a team of cross-trained production workers who can produce any of several instruments within a product family. Line changeovers within a family are quick and inexpensive, merely requiring a warning from the production team leader and a supply of the appropriate component parts. The typical cycle time for assembly of a batch of instruments—the time required to schedule assembly of a batch of instruments and then actually assemble them, assuming that component parts are available in component parts inventory—is on the order of two weeks. Lead time for component parts is on the order of 2–16 weeks. Assembled instruments are moved from the assembly area into bulk instrument inventory, where they wait to be packaged.

Packaging

The packaging process makes use of several large packaging machines. The machines direct bulk instruments into plastic containers and then adhere a flexible sheet of material over the top of the container. The entire plastic container is then placed into a finished 16-cardboard container and shipped immediately to the sterilizer. Capacity at the packaging area has not restricted output.

Sterilization

The sterilization process uses a large Cobalt radiation sterilizer. After batches of packaged instruments (cardboard container, plastic container, and instruments) are placed into the sterilizer, the sterilizer is turned on for about an hour. The radiation penetrates cardboard and plastic to destroy any potentially harmful contaminants. The sterilizer can sterilize as much product as will fit inside its four walls. Capacity limitations have not been a problem thus far. Sterilized instruments are immediately moved into finished goods inventory.

The Operations Organization

The entire operations organization reports up through the vice president of Operations, Kenneth Strangler (see Figure 1-6 for an organization chart for Operations). Functions immediately reporting to Strangler include several plant managers (one for each of Meditech's four manufacturing facilities), a director of supplier management, and a director of planning, distribution, and customer service. Other vice presidents (not shown) exist for marketing and sales, product development, and finance. All vice presidents report to the highest officer in the company, the president of Meditech. The plant managers in the organization have responsibility for production personnel, engineering technicians, quality

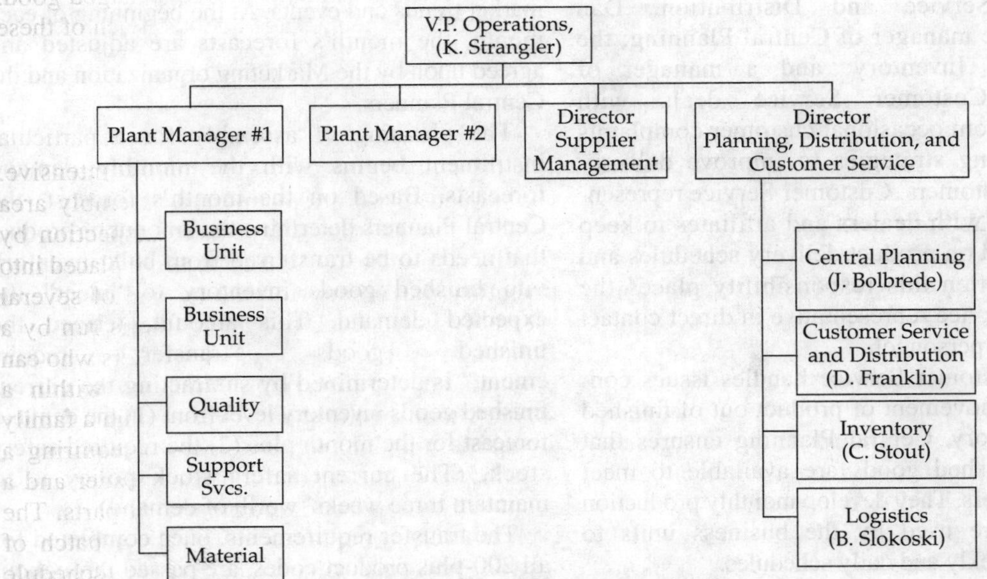

FIGURE 1-6 The Meditech organization chart for operations.

assurance, support services, and material supply for their respective facilities. Reporting directly to the plant managers are several business units. Each business unit has full responsibility either for the assembly of a particular product family or, in the case of packaging and sterilization, for an entire production process. The most important job of each assembly business unit is to meet the production schedule every week. Meeting the schedule ensures a constant supply of bulk instruments to the packaging/sterilization process. The process of determining assembly and packaging/sterilization schedules will be discussed below.

Also reporting to the vice president of Operations are Supplier Management and Planning, Distribution, and Customer Service. Supplier Management works on relationships with suppliers, including establishing purchasing contracts and finding new suppliers if necessary. The Planning, Distribution, and Customer Service department does everything it can to ensure that customers receive product when needed. The positions within the Customer Service department include the manager of Customer Service and Distribution, Dan Franklin; the manager of Central Planning; the manager of Inventory; and a manager of Logistics. Customer Service deals with everything from occasional customer complaints to establishing strategies to improve delivery service to customers. Customer Service representatives work with dealers and affiliates to keep them updated on product delivery schedules and problems. Often this responsibility places the Customer Service representative in direct contact with hospital personnel.

While Customer Service handles issues concerning the movement of product out of finished goods inventory, Central Planning ensures that adequate finished goods are available to meet incoming orders. They develop monthly production plans that are used by the business units to determine weekly and daily schedules.

Charles Stout, the Inventory manager, determines the finished goods inventory policy and establishes parts and bulk inventory guidelines for the business units. When a mandate to reduce inventory is passed down from higher levels of management, the Inventory manager must determine where inventory can be reduced and then begin enforcing those reductions. Through recent efforts, Stout had successfully eliminated several million dollars of obsolete and slow-moving inventory.

PRODUCTION PLANNING AND SCHEDULING

The production planning and scheduling process is broken down into two parts: planning, based on monthly forecasts, of assembly and component parts orders and daily scheduling of packaging and sterilization based on finished goods inventory levels. During the fourth quarter of each fiscal year, the marketing and finance organizations determine an annual forecast. The annual forecast is then broken down proportionately, based on the number of weeks in the month, into monthly forecasts. As the year progresses, the Central Planners work with the Marketing organization to make forecast adjustments according to market trends and events. At the beginning of each month, the month's forecasts are adjusted and agreed upon by the Marketing organization and the Central Planners.

The planning of assembly for a particular instrument begins with the monthly demand forecasts. Based on the month's forecast, the Central Planners determine the amount of product that needs to be transferred from bulk inventory into finished goods inventory to "meet" the expected demand. This amount, termed the finished goods "transfer requirement," is determined by subtracting the current finished goods inventory level from (1) the demand forecast for the month plus (2) the required safety stock. (The current safety stock policy is to maintain three weeks' worth of demand).

The transfer requirements, once completed for all 200-plus product codes, are passed throughout the organization for approval. This process typically takes place one to two weeks into the current month. While not actually used to schedule assembly or to alter the packaging and sterilization processes, the transfer requirements provide an estimate of the required overall production for the month. Any problems in being able to deliver to the plan can then be identified and resolved.

Assembly schedules and replenishment orders for parts are based on the monthly demand forecasts and current inventory levels. By mid-month, the completed monthly plans, which contain the monthly forecasts, are sent to the assembly business units. A planner in the business unit plugs the forecasts into a Materials Requirement Planning (MRP) system, which determines weekly production schedules and component parts orders for each finished product. The MRP system determines assembly schedules and parts orders based on (1) the monthly forecasts; (2) the lead times for assembly, packaging, and sterilization; and (3) current parts, bulk, and finished goods inventory levels. Although the MRP calculation may be run several times each week, the planner is careful not to change weekly production schedules with less than a week's notice. (A schedule change often requires rescheduling workers and procuring more component parts. One week's notice for responding to scheduling changes, therefore, has been deemed adequate by the business unit managers.)

In contrast to the forecast-based scheduling of the assembly operation, the packaging and sterilization operations are scheduled based on as-needed replenishment of finished goods inventory. For purposes of scheduling, the packaging and sterilization operations are considered one operation because bulk instruments flow through packaging, into the sterilizer, and into finished goods without being inventoried. (See Figure 1-7 for a diagram of the entire production process.) The entire packaging/sterilization process can be completed for a batch of instruments in about one week. The scheduling of packaging/sterilization is done on an order point/order quantity (OP/OQ) basis (i.e., when finished goods inventory drops below the predetermined order point, OP, a replenishment order for more packaged/sterilized product is initiated; the size of the order in terms of number of instruments is always equal to the predetermined order quantity, OQ).

Another way to view the scheduling process is to think of material as being "pushed" through assembly into bulk instrument inventory and as being "pulled" through packaging/sterilization into finished goods inventory. The push through assembly is based on the monthly forecast determined before the month's demand actually arrives. The pull through packaging/sterilization simply replenishes what was sold from finished goods the day before.

NEW PRODUCT INTRODUCTIONS, HIGH LEVELS OF INVENTORY, AND POOR SERVICE LEVEL

Over the past several years, Meditech has introduced dozens of new products into the market, mostly by updating existing products. Meditech plans to continue this strategy of continuously obsoleting its own products by constantly introducing innovations. While the innovative products have been well accepted by the marketplace, each new product introduction has resulted in a nightmare of supply problems. Dan Franklin felt that customers were beginning

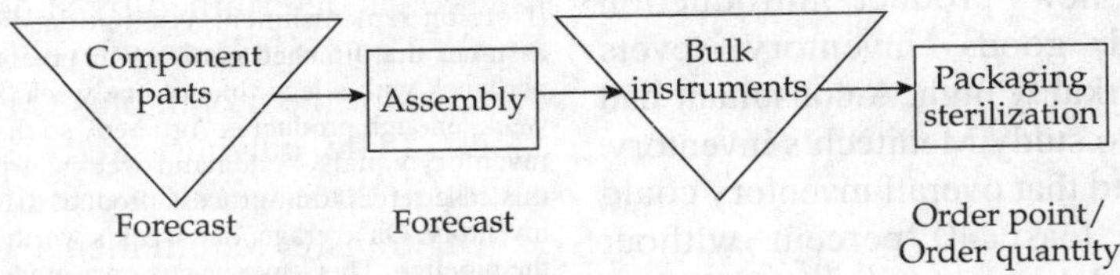

FIGURE 1-7 The Meditech production process.

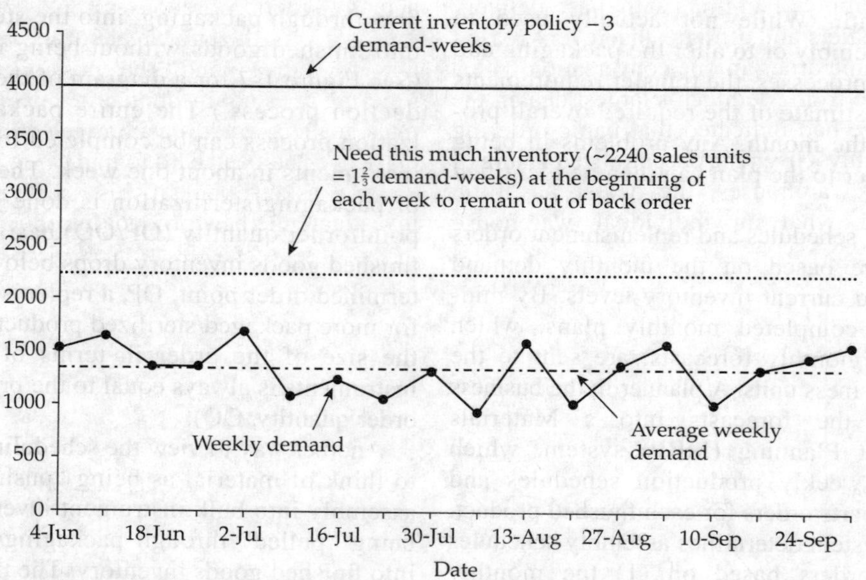

FIGURE 1-8 Weekly demand pattern for a representative stable product demonstrating current levels of inventory versus consultant's recommended inventory policy.

to tire of the poor service resulting from each introduction. Through many meetings with hospital material managers, Dan began to realize the full scope of his customers' frustrations.

Franklin could not figure out why Meditech consistently had shortages with each introduction. Forecasting had definitely been a problem, but determining its extent was difficult. Data to measure forecast accuracy had not previously been tracked, nor had forecasts and demand information been kept. Data gathering requires a lengthy process of going back through hard copies of prior monthly plans and entering the information by hand into a computer. Even if a better methodology could be determined, forecasts can only be improved by so much.

In addition to new product introduction problems, finished goods inventory levels appeared to be remarkably high. A consultant had recently been hired to study Meditech's inventory. Her findings indicated that overall inventory could be reduced by at least 40 percent without an impact on the delivery service level (see Figure 1-8).[1] Despite the high levels of inventory, the actual service level over the past year was disappointing and below corporate objectives. Management feared that reducing inventory would further damage the already subpar level performance.

Another possible cause of the problem is "panic ordering" from dealers and affiliates. Panic ordering occurs when a dealer or affiliate is unsure of whether or not product will be received in time and therefore increases the size of its orders hoping that Meditech will deliver at least part of the order. The increased orders would cause demand to temporarily rise, helping to explain Meditech's problems with demand consistently

[1]Note on replenishment assumption: For simplicity, this chart assumes that finished goods (FG) inventory is replenished once per week with a lead time of one week. At the beginning of each week, enough product is "ordered" so that the "pipeline" plus FG inventory equals $2/3$ demand-weeks of product. The pipeline in this case refers to in-process product that has not yet reached FG inventory. On average, one week's worth of demand will reside in the pipeline. This leaves, again on average, $2\frac{2}{3} - 1 = 1\frac{2}{3}$ demand-weeks in FG inventory at the beginning of each week.

exceeding supply. Familiar with past delivery problems, dealers and affiliates had every reason to want to panic order. In one conversation with a representative from Meditech's largest dealer, the representative had indicated that panic ordering was a possibility. Given the decentralized nature of the regional warehouses, the dealer has little control over what an individual warehouse actually orders. Warehouses could therefore panic order without the knowledge of the central dealer. On the other hand, the possibility of panic ordering does not mean that it actually occurs. To make matters worse, data proving or disproving its existence had been hard to find.

Dan asked one of his staff members to investigate the new product introduction problem

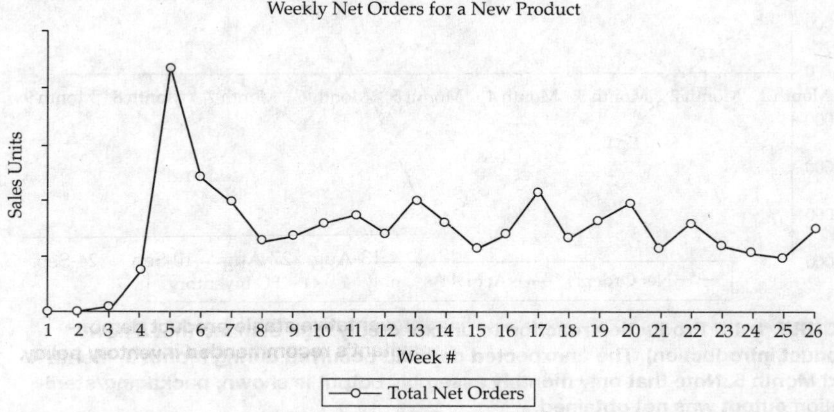

FIGURE 1-9 Typical demand pattern for a new product introduction. The product was officially introduced near the end of week #4.

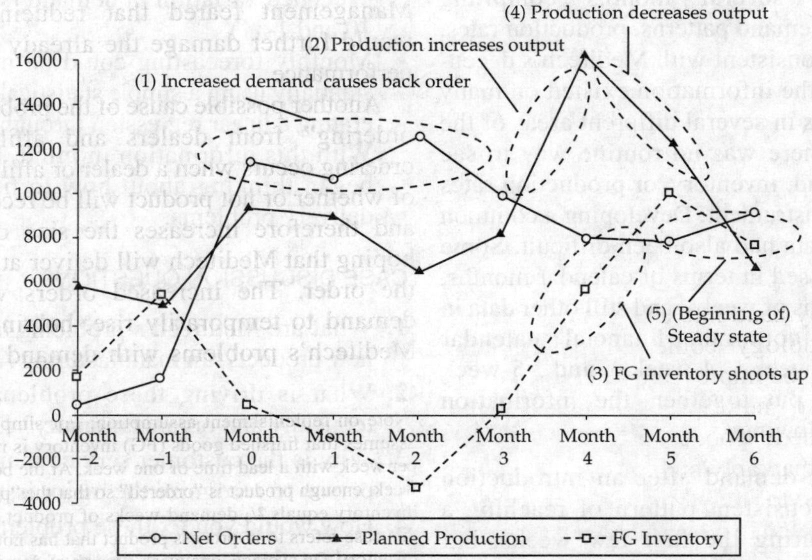

FIGURE 1-10 Production reaction to a new product introduction. The product was introduced in the last 2 weeks of Month 0.

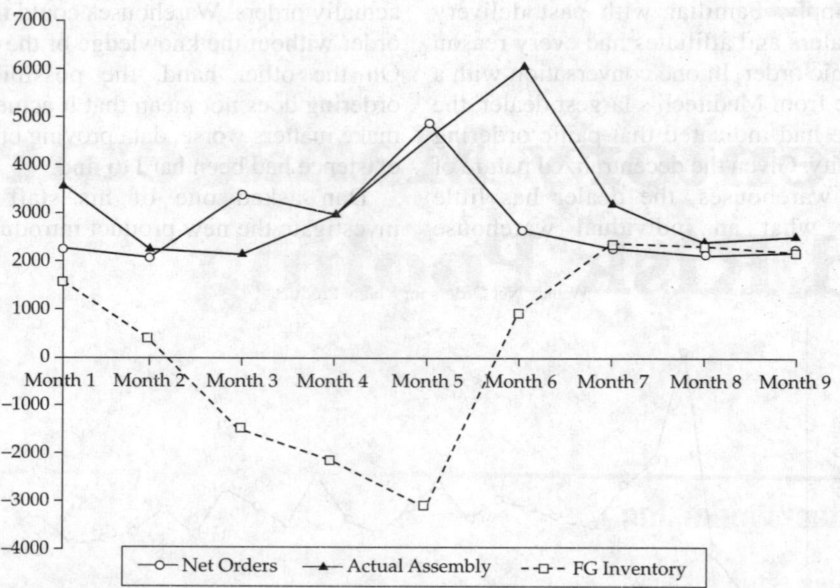

FIGURE 1-11 Production reaction to unexpectedly high demand (not a new product introduction). The unexpected demand occurred during Month 3, Month 4, and Month 5. Note that only monthly assembly output is shown; packaging/sterilization output was not obtained.

and inventory/service level paradox. The staff member spent several months compiling information on demand patterns, production rates, and forecasts. Consistent with Meditech's decentralized nature, the information existed on many different systems in several different areas of the organization. There was no routine way to see incoming demand, inventory, or production rates for a particular instrument. Developing a common format for the data had also been difficult. Some data were expressed in terms of calendar months, other data in terms of weeks, and still other data in terms of the corporate financial calendar (alternating 4-week, 4-week, and 5-week months). Once put together, the information conveyed the following:

- New product demand after an introduction followed a consistent pattern of reaching a high peak during the first few weeks, but becoming relatively stable immediately afterward (see Figure 1-9).
- Variation in production schedules often exceeded variation in demand (see Figures 1-10 and 1-11).
- Monthly forecasting could be improved substantially using a simple statistical method: generating a linear regression through past data.

With this information in mind, Dan Franklin began thinking about how to fix Meditech's delivery problems.

CASE DISCUSSION QUESTIONS

1. What are Meditech's problems in introducing new products? In manufacturing ALL products?
2. What is driving these problems, both systemically and organizationally?
3. Why is the customer service manager the first person to recognize the major issues?
4. How would you fix these problems?
5. Relate the learning of this case to a similar supply chain with which you are familiar.

CHAPTER 2

Inventory Management and Risk Pooling

CASE: Steel Works, Inc.

Gary Lemming sat in his new corner office and tapped his pencil on the desk. Lemming had just been named head of Steel Works, Inc.'s new centralized logistics group. After a decade of experience implementing MRP (Materials Requirements Planning) systems throughout the company's manufacturing facilities, Lemming was confident he could handle the job. Until this morning.

"Our inventory levels are ridiculous!" barked Jean Du Blanc, the company's Chief Financial Officer. "Our customer service is the worst in the industry, and getting worse," grumbled Kirk Callow, the CEO. Lemming started to explain, "You see, I've already set up a team to look at all of that. . . ." But before he could finish, Callow stood up. "Sales are down 30 percent and expenses are up 25 percent. Our best customers are calling me and telling me they're going to our competitors, and at the rate we're losing market share we won't be in business in a year. I don't want to hear about teams; I want you back in here in a week telling me how you're going to fix this thing."

Lemming looked over the list of people he'd asked to meet with him this week. He shook his head—how do I lower expenses and improve performance? How will I ever find the right answer?

BACKGROUND

Steel Works, Inc., is a manufacturer of custom and specialty use steels with annual sales of $400 million in 1993. Founded in 1980 by three brilliant material scientists from MIT, the company now employs more than 2500 people at 5 different locations. With its first product, DuraBend™, the company earned a reputation as a high technology provider and quickly established a niche position in what is typically regarded as a commodity market. Its two divisions, Specialty Products and Custom Products, are very separate and distinct businesses.

CUSTOM PRODUCTS

Lemming's first interview of the morning was with Stephanie Williams, President of the Custom division. "Our motto is 'The Customer Comes First, Second, and Third, But Never Last,'" explained Ms. Williams. "The Custom division

Source: This case was prepared by research assistant David Kletter under the direction of Professor Stephen C. Graves as the basis for class discussion rather than to illustrate either effective or ineffective handling of an administrative situation. The company, people, data, and events depicted herein are entirely fictitious. Any resemblance to actual people, businesses, or situations is purely coincidental.

develops most of its products under contract for a single customer, for sale exclusively to that customer, and works very closely with them from before a product is invented until our product is a part of their product. We have the best scientists and engineers in the world, and that is why the biggest companies in the U.S. come to *us*. We've designed the metals that make our customers' products work great. That's why we typically aren't allowed to sell our products to anyone but the original customer—our customers' competitors would love to buy from us."

Williams went on to explain that eventually when a product is no longer leading-edge, the Custom division will negotiate with the customer to allow Steel Works to sell the product to anyone. "Such discussions are an art form," explains Stephanie, "but it can make a huge difference in sales revenues for us."

"Take DuraFlex™ R23, for example. We developed that under contract for one of the big three auto companies. It took us over a year to develop, and there is still no product like it in the marketplace. Yet we were able to convince our customer to allow us to sell it openly on the market at a 30 percent premium over what we charge them. We still sell in large volumes to our customer, and Specialty Products makes a small fortune manufacturing the exact same steel and selling it at a higher price to four other auto manufacturers and a copier company."

Williams displayed a schematic of Custom Products' manufacturing system. The three manufacturing sites were each located within a few miles of one of Custom Products' three R&D centers, which served the West, Midwest, and Eastern regions of the U.S. Customers and their products were each assigned to a specific plant and R&D center. Steel Works operated several warehouses located near the plants.

The only question on Lemming's mind was why the inventory levels were so high. The reply was direct and blunt: "We've got to keep our customers happy. Customers aren't satisfied when you tell them that they have to wait three weeks for delivery! We listened to that corporate inventory reduction mandate in 1991 and cut our inventories back 20 percent and we were running out of product every week!"

SPECIALTY PRODUCTS

"Let me tell you something," Barry White said as he stormed into the room, "we are *nothing* like Custom." Mr. White was President of the Specialty division, whose sales have been the most hard hit in recent months.

"That Custom division has nothing to do all day but play in laboratories. We're the ones out in the marketplace selling every day and bringing in 67 percent of this company's revenue. I've got the best sales force around, and they are what makes this business work."

"Custom thinks they're so special because they've got some big customers; well guess what, so do we. Our largest customer in Specialty brings in 10 percent of the revenue for this company, and it is with blood, sweat and tears that we keep them and everyone else as our customer. You want to solve some problems? Manufacturing is where the problems are; you should talk to them. I've got my plant managers screaming at me every day that the CSR's [customer service representatives] are screaming at them because the customers are screaming at the CSR's for not having any steel in the warehouse to ship. And that's not the CSR's fault, it's manufacturing's fault."

"Last week the IS department comes knocking on my door telling me how great it would be if all of Steel Works was on a common computer system, and wants me to pay $12mm for my division. They think they understand our business but they don't. We don't need centralized computer systems, we need to fix manufacturing!"

White explained that like the Custom Products division, Specialty attempted to manufacture its products in a single plant. The division operated three plants that manufactured 6 different product lines. The division's general strategy was to exploit economies of scale in production and to

Big customers (> $25mm)	5
Small customers (< $1mm)	107
All others	18
Total	130

FIGURE 2-1 Profile of Specialty Products customers.

rely on the logistics network to distribute the product nationwide. To achieve further efficiency, product families were almost always manufactured in the same plant to save manufacturing costs: the change-over costs between products in the same family were often considerably lower than across different families. Products were produced in a rotating sequence. For example, DuraFlex™ R23 is always produced during the first week of the month.

And before Lemming knew it, White had stormed out of the room.

ANALYSIS

It was now Tuesday and 20 percent of the week was gone. Debby Klein, a senior logistics analyst, sat across from Lemming.

"Well it's just like you said it would be. Custom has a lot of products, and something like 90 percent of them are sold to only one customer. On the other hand, Specialty has something like 130 customers for some 120 products. They've got so many products I can't even keep track!"

Debby then related the grim news about customer service levels. "Based on data collected by our order entry systems, approximately 70 percent of the orders entered into the system are scheduled to be shipped from stock within 48 hours. The rest of the orders (30 percent) are either canceled by the customer at the time of entry or placed in a backorder file. I couldn't find out how many of the backorders are canceled, and I wasn't sure if we needed to know that."

Lemming then asked about the big customer. "Yep, they're big all right. They're like 15 percent of the Specialty sales for 1993 but they buy a lot of

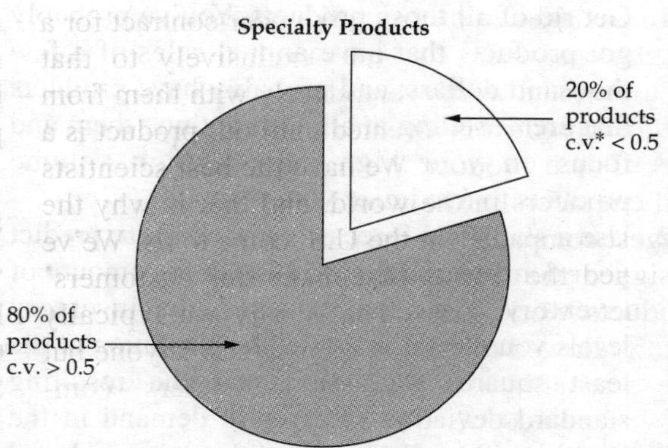

Note: c.v. means coefficient of variation of one month's demand, equal to the standard deviation of demand over one month, divided by the mean monthly demand.

FIGURE 2-2 Demand variation in Specialty Products.

different products. There are other big customers, though. And small ones, and medium-sized ones too" (see Figure 2-1) "Thanks Debby," said Lemming, feeling more confused than ever.

After lunch, Lemming had the production plan for Specialty's Ohio plant faxed to him. The Ohio plant manufactured the DuraBend™ and DuraFlex™ product families. Production at the plant followed a regular rotating schedule, producing each family about once per month. The plan seemed consistent with Barry White's account of the division's manufacturing strategy.

At the end of the day, a young forecasting expert named Maria stopped by, looking quite upset. "I looked at all the products like you asked. It's a mess just like you said, 80 percent of the products fall in this 'highly volatile' category (see Figure 2-2). With standard deviations that large, I don't think a demand forecasting tool is going to help you very much."

CONSULTING

Bright and early on Wednesday morning, Fred Chow, a logistics consultant, walks into Lemming's office. "From what you described on the phone, the answers are all very simple. There are three things you need to do:

1. Get rid of all those products. You've probably got products that have annual sales of a few thousand dollars, and probably have products that aren't selling at all. Discontinue them and focus on your high margin, high volume products to maximize your revenue.
2. Use a statistical forecasting package to predict your demand and this will lower the amount of inventory you need. You see, the inventory levels you need to hold will be a function of the least squares regression and the resulting standard deviation of error in demand in the leadtime. So reduce that and you've reduced your inventory. Violá!
3. You've probably got too many warehouses. Everybody knows that fewer warehouses mean less inventory."

Lemming was now excited. Although he didn't understand about the least squares-thing, and although Maria said yesterday that forecasting wouldn't work, now he was getting somewhere. Accidentally calling the consultant "Jonah" at one point, Lemming was forever grateful.

REALITY SETS IN

The businesses completely rejected the idea of discontinuing the slow-moving products. "We can't do that! Our most important customers buy those products!" So much for that idea.

If that weren't bad enough, Debby happens to stop back in. "Reduce our warehouses? What are you talking about? If we have to ship from fewer warehouses, it will take longer, cost more and that will *really* make the divisions mad. Plus, just because you combine two warehouses doesn't mean you're going to save that much money. Some fixed costs certainly, but that won't make up for those added transportation costs you're going to have to swallow."

Lemming didn't believe this, so he mounted an effort to get to the bottom of the warehouse consolidation issue. Several hours and several hundred sheets of paper later, Lemming realized that he had underestimated the data collection and number-crunching involved with this type of analysis. Although the idea had the potential to reduce costs, his team did not have enough time to look at it this week.

THE CLOCK CHIMES ELEVEN

It's Thursday, close to midnight, and Lemming is now sweating. Debby, Maria, and John Thompson, a recent Sloan graduate, are all gathered in the corner office. They've listed a dozen ideas on the blackboard: ABC analysis, customer segmentations, EOQs, and many more . . . and crossed them all off. Lemming can see Callow's angry face now—his career is slipping away.

Now what do you do, John Thompson?

OVERVIEW OF STEEL WORKS, INC., DATA

Since it would be nearly impossible to analyze all of Steel Works' data, a representative sample of products from 1994 has been provided to you. Specific data has been provided for portions of two of the product lines: DuraBend™ and DuraFlex™.

Five spreadsheets are available in the book's CD-ROM to assist you in your analysis:

S0121958.XLS Sales of DuraBend™ R12 for each month and for each customer.

MONTHVOL.XLS Total sales of DuraBend™ and DuraFlex™ for each month.

PRODBAT.XLS Production batch sizes for DuraBend™ and DuraFlex™.

FINCLDAT.XLS Unit costs and 1994 selling prices for DuraBend™ and DuraFlex™.

EOMINV.XLS DuraBend™ and DuraFlex™ inventories at the end of each month.

Note: In the spreadsheets provided, all data (including dollar figures) are in thousands.

When drawing inferences from the data, you can safely assume that the DuraBend™ and DuraFlex™ product lines are representative of the entire Specialty division.

By the end of this chapter, you will understand the following issues:

- How firms cope with huge variability in customer demand.
- What the relationship is between service and inventory levels.
- What impact lead time and lead time variability have on inventory levels.
- What an effective inventory management policy is.
- How buyers and suppliers use *supply contracts* to improve supply chain performance.
- What approaches can be used to forecast future demand.

2.1 INTRODUCTION

In many industries and supply chains, inventory is one of the dominant costs. In the United States, for example, over a trillion dollars is invested in inventory. For many managers, effective supply chain management is synonymous with reducing inventory levels in the supply chain. Of course, this is a very simplistic view of supply chain management—in fact, the goal of effective inventory management in the supply chain is to have the correct inventory at the right place at the right time to minimize system costs while satisfying customer service requirements. Unfortunately, managing inventory in complex supply chains is typically difficult, and inventory-related decisions can have a significant impact on the customer service level and supply chain systemwide cost.

As we discussed in Chapter 1, a typical supply chain consists of suppliers and manufacturers, who convert raw materials into finished products, and distribution centers and warehouses, from which finished products are distributed to customers. Inventory can appear in many places in the supply chain, and in several forms:

- Raw material inventory.
- Work-in-process (WIP) inventory.
- Finished product inventory.

Each of these needs its own inventory control mechanism or approach. Unfortunately, determining these mechanisms is difficult because efficient production, distribution, and inventory control strategies that reduce systemwide costs and improve service levels must take into account the interactions of the various levels in the supply chain. Nevertheless, the benefits of determining these inventory control mechanisms can be enormous.

EXAMPLE 2-1

General Motors (GM) has one of the largest production and distribution networks in the world. In 1984 GM's distribution network consisted of 20,000 supplier plants, 133 parts plants, 31 assembly plants, and 11,000 dealers. Freight transportation costs were about $4.1 billion with 60 percent for material shipments. In addition, GM inventory was valued at $7.4 billion, of which 70 percent was WIP and the rest was finished vehicles. GM has implemented a decision tool capable of reducing the combined corporate cost of inventory and transportation. Indeed, by adjusting shipment sizes (i.e., inventory policy) and routes (i.e., transportation strategy), costs could be reduced by about 26 percent annually [25].

If inventory is typically expensive and difficult to manage, why hold it at all? Inventory is held for a variety of reasons, and inventory control mechanisms need to take these reasons into account. Inventory is held due to

1. **Unexpected changes in customer demand.** Customer demand has always been hard to predict, and uncertainty in customer demand has increased in the last few years due to
   a. The short life cycle of an increasing number of products. This implies that historical data about customer demand may not be available or may be quite limited (see Chapter 1).
   b. The presence of many competing products in the marketplace. This proliferation of products makes it increasingly difficult to predict demand for a specific model. Indeed, while it is relatively easy to forecast demand across product groups—that is, to forecast demand for all products competing in the same market—it is much more difficult to estimate demand for individual products. We discuss this in more detail in Section 2.3 and in Chapters 6 and 11.
2. **The presence in many situations of a significant uncertainty** in the quantity and quality of the supply, supplier costs, and delivery times.
3. **Lead times.** Even if there is no uncertainty in demand or supply, there is a need to hold inventory due to delivery lead times.
4. **Economies of scale offered by transportation companies** that encourage firms to transport large quantities of items, and therefore hold large inventories. Indeed, many of the transportation providers try to encourage large-size shipments by offering all sorts of discounts to shippers (see Chapter 3). Similarly, incentives provided by manufacturers to distributors and retailers motivate buyers to purchase large quantities during manufacturers' promotional periods and hence lead to high inventory levels.

Unfortunately, although it is clear why inventory is held, holding the right amount at the right time in the appropriate place is frequently difficult:

- In 1993, Dell Computer's stock plunged after the company predicted a loss. Dell acknowledged that the company was sharply off in its forecast of demand, resulting in inventory write-downs [254].
- In 1993, Liz Claiborne experienced an unexpected earnings decline, as a consequence of higher-than-anticipated excess inventories [255].
- In 1994, IBM struggled with shortages in the ThinkPad line due to ineffective inventory management [256].
- In 2001, Cisco took a $ 2.25 billion excess inventory charge due to declining sales.

These examples raise two critical issues in inventory management and demand forecasting. Since demand is uncertain in most situations, the demand forecast is critical for determining what to order, and when to order it. But what is the relationship between forecast demand and the optimal order quantity? Should the order quantity be equal to, greater than, or smaller than forecast demand? And, if order quantity is different than forecast demand, by how much? We explore these issues throughout the rest of this chapter.

The strategy, approach, or set of techniques used to determine how to manage inventory is known as a firm's *inventory policy*. To decide on an effective inventory policy, managers have to take many characteristics of the supply chain into account:

1. First and foremost is customer demand, which may be known in advance or may be random. In the latter case, forecasting tools may be used in situations in which historical data are available to estimate the average customer demand, as well as the amount of variability in customer demand (often measured as the standard deviation).
2. Replenishment lead time, which may be known at the time the order is placed, or may be uncertain.
3. The number of different products being considered. These products compete on budget or space and hence the inventory policy of one product affects the others.

4. The length of the planning horizon.
5. Costs, including order cost and inventory holding cost.
   a. Typically, order cost consists of two components: the cost of the product and the transportation cost. The product cost may exhibit economies of scale; that is, the larger the order quantity, the smaller the per-unit price.
   b. Inventory holding cost, or inventory carrying cost, consists of
      i. State taxes, property taxes, and insurance on inventories.
      ii. Maintenance costs.
      iii. Obsolescence cost, which derives from the risk that an item will lose some of its value because of changes in the market.
      iv. Opportunity costs, which represent the return on investment that one would receive had money been invested in something else (e.g., the stock market) instead of inventory.
6. Service level requirements. In situations where customer demand is uncertain, it is often impossible to meet customer orders 100 percent of the time, so management needs to specify an acceptable level of service.

2.2 SINGLE STAGE INVENTORY CONTROL

We start by considering inventory management in a single supply chain stage. There are a variety of techniques and approaches that can be effective for managing inventory in a single stage, depending on the characteristics of that stage.

2.2.1 The Economic Lot Size Model

The classic *economic lot size model,* introduced by Ford W. Harris in 1915, is a simple model that illustrates the trade-offs between ordering and storage costs. Consider a warehouse facing constant demand for a *single* item. The warehouse orders from the supplier, who is assumed to have an unlimited quantity of the product. The model assumes the following:

- Demand is constant at a rate of D items per day.
- Order quantities are fixed at Q items per order; that is, each time the warehouse places an order, it is for Q items.
- A fixed cost (setup cost), K, is incurred every time the warehouse places an order.
- An inventory carrying cost, h, also referred to as a *holding cost,* is accrued per unit held in inventory per day that the unit is held.
- The lead time, the time that elapses between the placement of an order and its receipt, is zero.
- Initial inventory is zero.
- The planning horizon is long (infinite).

Our goal is to find the optimal order policy that minimizes annual purchasing and carrying costs while meeting all demand (that is, without shortage).

This is an extremely simplified version of a real inventory system. The assumption of a known fixed demand over a long horizon is clearly unrealistic. Replenishment of products very likely takes several days, and the requirement of a fixed order quantity is restrictive. Surprisingly, the insight derived from this model will help us to develop inventory policies that are effective for more complex realistic systems.

It is easy to see that in an optimal policy for the model described above, orders should be received at the warehouse precisely when the inventory level drops to zero. This is called the *zero inventory ordering property,* which can be observed by considering a policy in which orders are placed and received when the inventory level is not zero. Clearly, a cheaper policy would involve waiting until the inventory is zero before ordering, thus saving on holding costs.

To find the optimal ordering policy in the economic lot size model, we consider the inventory level as a function of time; see Figure 2-3. This is the so-called saw-toothed inventory pattern. We refer to the time between two successive replenishments as a *cycle* time. Thus, total inventory cost in a cycle of length T is

$$K + \frac{hTQ}{2}$$

since the fixed cost is charged once per order and holding cost can be viewed as the product of the per-unit, per-time-period holding cost, h; the average inventory level, $Q/2$; and the length of the cycle, T.

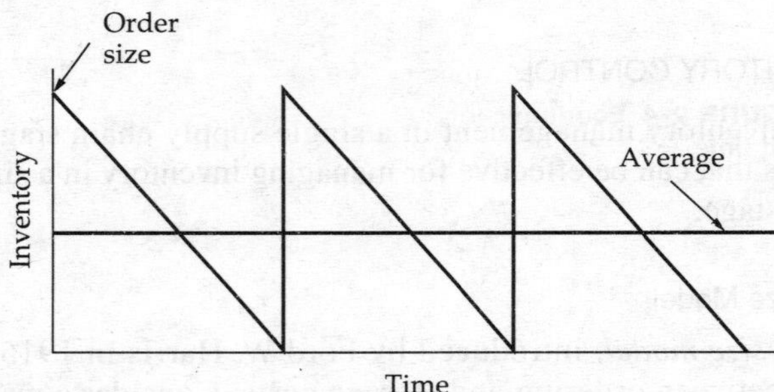

FIGURE 2-3 Inventory level as a function of time.

Since the inventory level changes from Q to 0 during a cycle of length T, and demand is constant at a rate of D units per unit time, it must be that $Q = TD$. Thus, we can divide the cost above by T, or, equivalently, Q/D, to get the average total cost per unit of time:

$$\frac{KD}{Q} + \frac{hQ}{2}$$

Using simple calculus, it is easy to show that the order quantity Q^* that minimizes the cost function above is

$$Q^* = \sqrt{\frac{2KD}{h}}$$

The simple model provides two important insights:

1. An optimal policy balances inventory holding cost per unit time with setup cost per unit time. Indeed, setup cost per unit time $= KD/Q$, while holding cost per unit time $= hQ/2$ (see Figure 2-4). Thus, as one increases the order quantity Q, inventory holding costs per unit of time increase while setup costs per unit of time decrease. The optimal order quantity is achieved at the point at which inventory setup cost per unit of time (KD/Q) equals inventory holding cost per unit of time ($hQ/2$). That is:

TABLE 2-1

SENSITIVITY ANALYSIS

b	0.5	0.8	0.9	1	1.1	1.2	1.5	2
Increase in cost	25%	2.5%	0.5%	0	0.4%	1.6%	8.9%	25%

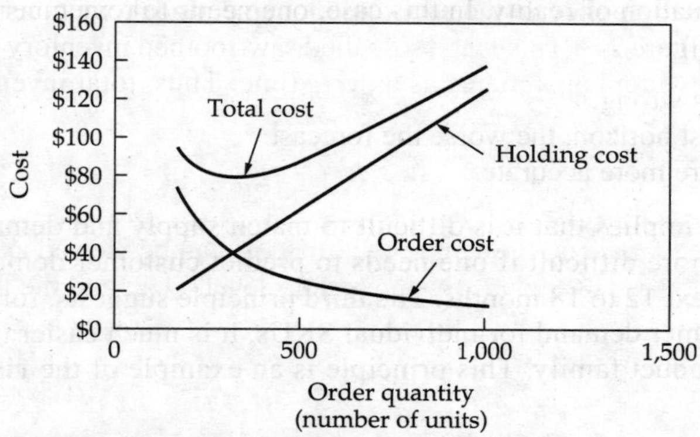

FIGURE 2-4 Economic lot size model: total cost per unit time.

$$\frac{KD}{Q} = \frac{hQ}{2}$$

or

$$Q^* = \sqrt{\frac{2KD}{h}}$$

2. Total inventory cost is insensitive to order quantities; that is, changes in order quantities have a relatively small impact on annual setup costs and inventory holding costs. To illustrate this issue, consider a decision maker that places an order quantity Q that is a multiple b of the optimal order quantity Q^*. In other words, for a given b, the quantity ordered is $Q = bQ^*$. Thus, $b = 1$ implies that the decision maker orders the economic order quantity. If $b = 1.2$ ($b = 0.8$), the decision maker orders 20 percent more (less) than the optimal order quantity. Table 2-1 presents the impact of changes in b on total system cost. For example, if the decision maker orders 20 percent more than the optimal order quantity ($b = 1.2$), then the increase in total inventory cost relative to the optimal total cost is no more than 1.6 percent.

EXAMPLE 2-2

Consider a hardware supply warehouse that is contractually obligated to deliver 1,000 units of a specialized fastener to a local manufacturing company each week. Each time the warehouse places an order for these items from its supplier, an ordering and transportation fee of Rs.20 is charged to the warehouse. The warehouse pays Rs.1.00 for each fastener and charges the local firm Rs.5.00 for each fastener. Annual holding cost is 25 percent of inventory value, or Rs.0.25 per year. The warehouse manager would like to know how much to order when inventory gets to zero.

To answer this question, we can use the formula defined above. Annual demand (assuming the manufacturing plant operates for 50 weeks a year) is 50,000 units, annual holding cost is Rs.0.25 per unit, and fixed setup cost per unit is Rs.20.00. Each time the warehouse places an order, the optimal order quantity is thus 2,828.

2.2.2 The Effect of Demand Uncertainty

The previous model illustrates the trade-offs between setup costs and inventory holding costs. It ignores, however, issues such as demand uncertainty and forecasting. Indeed, many companies treat the world as if it were predictable, making production and inventory decisions based on forecasts of the demand made far in advance of the selling season. Although these companies are aware of demand uncertainty when they create a forecast, they design their planning processes as if the initial forecast was an accurate representation of reality. In this case, one needs to remember the following principles of all forecasts (see [170]):

1. The forecast is always wrong.
2. The longer the forecast horizon, the worse the forecast.
3. Aggregate forecasts are more accurate.

Thus, the first principle implies that it is difficult to match supply and demand, and the second one implies that it is even more difficult if one needs to predict customer demand for a long period of time, for example, the next 12 to 18 months. The third principle suggests, for instance, that while it is difficult to predict customer demand for individual SKUs, it is much easier to predict demand across all SKUs within one product family. This principle is an example of the **risk pooling** concept (see Section 2.3).

2.2.3 Single Period Models

To better understand the impact of demand uncertainty, we consider a series of increasingly detailed and complex situations. To start, we consider a product that has a short lifecycle and hence the firm has only one ordering opportunity. Thus, before demand occurs, the firm must decide how much to stock in order to meet demand. If the firm stocks too much, it will be stuck with excess inventory it has to dispose of. If the firm stocks too little, it will forgo some sales, and thus some profits.

EXAMPLE 2-3 EVMs

Elections are important but highly cumbersome exercises in big democracies like India. Traditionally, for casting of votes, there used to be a huge amount of preparation, involving printing, storing, transportation, security and counting of ballot papers. The management of ballot paper was a tedious, costly and time-consuming affair. Looking at the criticality of the process, often a large number of excess ballot papers had to be printed. The waste was sometimes upto 70% of total printed ballots when we add the safety stock of ballots printed before the poll and the uncasted votes, which were often around 50% in India. Maintenance of this critical inventory was a classic case of wasteful expenditure in the form of the most critical inventory. Gradually, the Election Commission introduced the Electronics Voting Machines (EVMs) in place of traditional ballot boxes. In collaboration with the Election Commission and other experts in the area, two public sector undertakings viz., Bharat Electronics Ltd., Bangalore and Electronic Corporation of India Ltd., Hyderabad designed and later produced it on a mass scale. The preparation, transportation, use and security of EVMs are much easier than the traditional ballot papers. There is a possibility of maintaining the memory of EVMs, which can be retrieved even after a decade. Due to these machines, the efficiency of the whole system has improved significantly in terms of accuracy, speed and effort [277, 285, 298].

Using historical data, the firm can typically identify a variety of demand scenarios and determine a likelihood or probability that each of these scenarios will occur. Observe that given a specific inventory policy, the firm can determine the profit associated with a particular scenario. Thus, given a specific order quantity, the firm can weight each scenario's profit by the likelihood that it will occur and hence determine the average, or expected, profit for a particular ordering quantity. It is thus natural for the firm to order the quantity that maximizes the average profit.

EXAMPLE 2-4

Consider a company that designs, produces, and sells summer fashion items such as swimsuits. About six months before summer, the company must commit itself to specific production quantities for all its products. Since there is no clear indication of how the market will respond to the new designs, the company needs to use various tools to predict demand for each design, and plan production and supply accordingly. In this setting, the trade-offs are clear: overestimating customer demand will result in unsold inventory, while underestimating customer demand will lead to inventory stockouts and loss of potential customers.

To assist management in these decisions, the marketing department uses historical data from the last five years, current economic conditions, and other factors to construct a *probabilistic forecast* of the demand for swimsuits. They have identified several possible scenarios for sales in the coming season, based on such factors as possible weather patterns and competitors' behavior, and assigned each a probability, or chance of occurring. For example, the marketing department believes that a scenario that leads to 8,000 unit sales has an 11 percent chance of happening; other scenarios leading to different sales levels have different probabilities of occurring. These scenarios are illustrated in Figure 2-5. This probabilistic forecast suggests that average demand is about 13,000 units, but there is a probability that demand will be either larger than average or smaller than average.

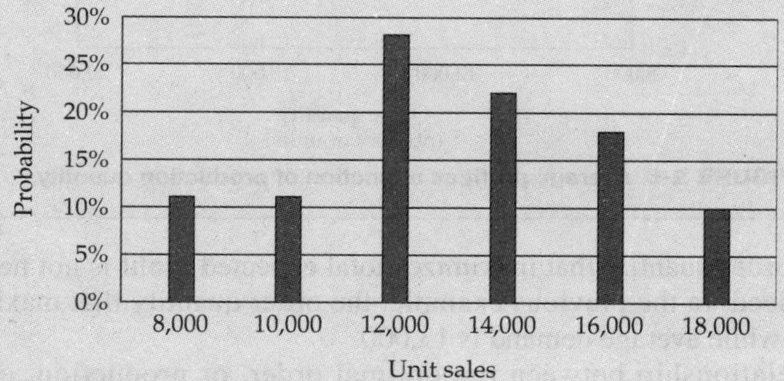

FIGURE 2-5 **Probabilistic forecast.**

We have the following additional information:

- To start production, the manufacturer has to invest Rs.100,000 independent of the amount produced. We refer to this cost as the *fixed production cost*.
- The variable production cost per unit equals Rs.80.
- During the summer season, the selling price of a swimsuit is Rs.125 per unit.
- Any swimsuit not sold during the summer season is sold to a discount store for Rs. 20. We refer to this value as the *salvage value*.

To identify the best production quantity, the firm needs to understand the relationship between the production quantity, customer demand, and profit.

Suppose the manufacturer produces 10,000 units while demand ends at 12,000 swimsuits. It is easily verified that profit equals revenue from summer sales minus the variable production cost minus the fixed production cost. That is:

$$\begin{aligned}\text{Profit} &= 125(10{,}000) - 80(10{,}000) - 100{,}000\\ &= 350{,}000\end{aligned}$$

On the other hand, if the company produces 10,000 swimsuits and demand is only 8,000 units, profit equals revenue from summer sales plus salvage value minus the variable production cost minus the fixed production cost. That is:

$$\begin{aligned}\text{Profit} &= 125(8{,}000) + 20(2{,}000) - 80(10{,}000) - 100{,}000\\ &= 140{,}000\end{aligned}$$

Notice that based on the marketing department's forecast, the probability that demand is 8,000 units is 11 percent while the probability that demand is 12,000 units is 27 percent. Thus, producing 10,000 swimsuits leads to a profit of

EXAMPLE 2-4 *Continued*

Rs. 350,000 with probability of 27 percent and a profit of Rs.140,000 with probability of 11 percent. In similar fashion, one can calculate the profit associated with each scenario given that the manufacturer produces 10,000 swimsuits. This allows us to determine the *expected* (or average) profit associated with producing 10,000 units. This expected profit is the total profit of all the scenarios weighted by the probability that each scenario will occur.

We, of course, would like to find the order quantity that maximizes average profit. Figure 2-6 plots the average profit as a function of the production quantity. It shows that the optimal production quantity, or the quantity that maximizes average profit, is about 12,000.

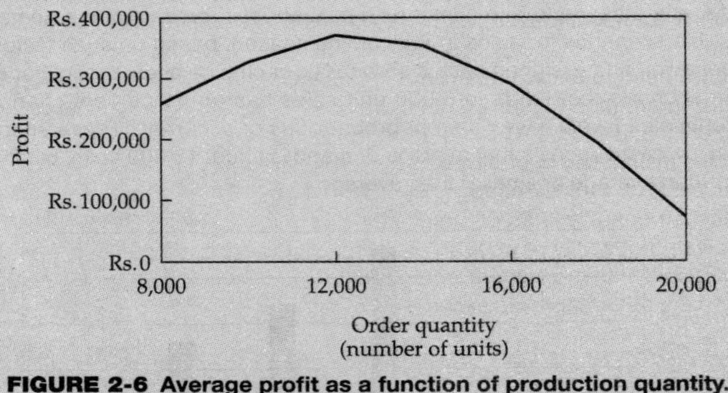

FIGURE 2-6 Average profit as a function of production quantity.

Interestingly, the order quantity that maximizes total expected profit is not necessarily equal to the average demand. Indeed, in the previous example, the order quantity that maximizes total expected profit is 12,000 units while average demand is 13,000.

So what is the relationship between the optimal order, or production, quantity and average demand? Should the optimal order quantity always be less than average demand, as in the previous example? To answer these questions, we compare the marginal profit and the marginal cost of ordering an additional unit. If an additional unit is sold, the marginal profit is the difference between the selling price per unit and the variable ordering (or production) cost per unit, and if an additional unit is not sold during the selling season, the marginal cost is the difference between the variable production cost and the salvage value per unit. If the cost of not selling an additional unit is larger than the profit from selling an additional unit, the optimal quantity in general will be less than average demand, while if the reverse is true, the optimal order quantity in general will be greater than the average demand.

EXAMPLE 2-5

Let's return to our example. In this example, average demand is 13,000 units. We saw previously that the optimal order quantity is around 12,000 units. Why is this the case?

For this purpose, evaluate the *marginal* profit and the marginal cost of producing an additional swimsuit. If this swimsuit is sold during the summer season, then the marginal profit is equal to Rs. 45. If the additional swimsuit is not sold during the summer season, the marginal cost is equal to Rs. 60. Thus, the cost of not selling this additional swimsuit during the summer season is larger than the profit obtained from selling it during the season, and hence the optimal production quantity is less than the average demand.

Of course, this is only true if maximizing average profit is in fact the goal of the firm. As with other types of investments, investment in inventory carries downside risks if sales do not meet expectations, and upside rewards if demand exceeds expectations. Interestingly, it is possible to characterize the upside potential and downside risks in our model and thus assist management in inventory investment decisions.

EXAMPLE 2-6

Once again, consider the previous example. Figure 2-6 plots the average profit as a function of the production quantity. As mentioned above, it shows that the optimal production quantity, that is, the quantity that maximizes average profit, is about 12,000. The figure also indicates that producing 9,000 units or producing 16,000 units will lead to about the same average profit of Rs. 294,000. If, for some reason, we had to choose between producing 9,000 units and 16,000 units, which one should we choose?

To answer this question, we need to better understand the *risk* associated with certain decisions. For this purpose, we construct a frequency histogram (see Figure 2-7) that provides information about potential profit for the two given production quantities, 9,000 units and 16,000 units. For instance, consider profit when the production quantity is 16,000 units. The graph shows that the distribution of profit is not symmetrical. Losses of Rs. 220,000 happen about 11 percent of the time while profits of at least Rs. 410,000 happen 50 percent of the time. On the other hand, a frequency histogram of the profit when the production quantity is 9,000 units shows that the distribution has only two possible outcomes. Profit is either Rs. 200,000 with probability of about 11 percent, or Rs. 305,000 with probability of about 89 percent. Thus, while producing 16,000 units has the same average profit as producing 9,000 units, the possible *risk* on the one hand, and possible *reward* on the other hand, increases as we increase the production size.

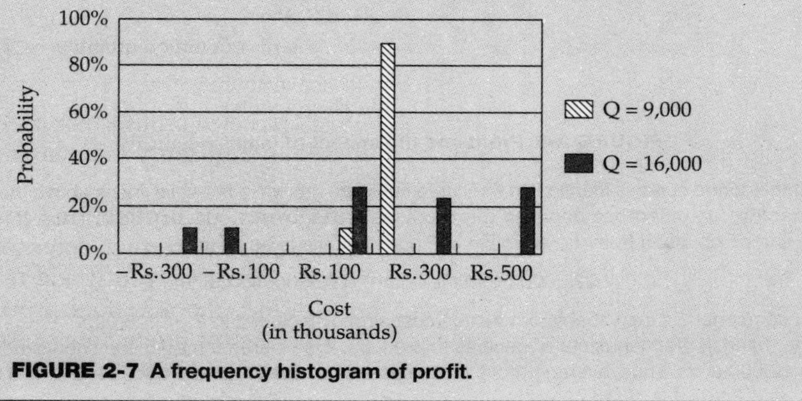

FIGURE 2-7 A frequency histogram of profit.

To summarize:

- The optimal order quantity is not necessarily equal to forecast, or average, demand. Indeed, the optimal quantity depends on the relationship between marginal profit achieved from selling an additional unit and marginal cost. More importantly, the fixed cost has no impact on the production quantity, only on the decision whether to produce or not. Thus, given a decision to produce, the production quantity is the same independently of the fixed production cost.
- As the order quantity increases, average profit typically increases until the production quantity reaches a certain value, after which the average profit starts decreasing.
- As we increase the production quantity, the risk—that is, the probability of large losses—always increases. At the same time, the probability of large gains also increases. This is the risk/reward trade-off.

2.2.4 Initial Inventory

In the previous model, we considered a situation in which the firm has only a single ordering or production opportunity to meet demand during a short selling season. We next consider a similar situation,

EXAMPLE 2-7

Recall our previous example, and suppose now that the swimsuit under consideration is a model produced last year and that the manufacturer has an initial inventory of 5,000 units. Assuming that demand for this model follows the same pattern of scenarios as before, should the manufacturer start production, and, if so, how many swimsuits should be produced?

If the manufacturer does not produce any additional swimsuits, no more than 5,000 units can be sold and no additional fixed cost will be incurred. However, if the manufacturer decides to produce, a fixed production cost is charged independent of the amount produced.

To address this issue, consider Figure 2-8, in which the solid line represents average profit excluding fixed production cost while the dotted curve represents average profit subtracting out the fixed production cost.

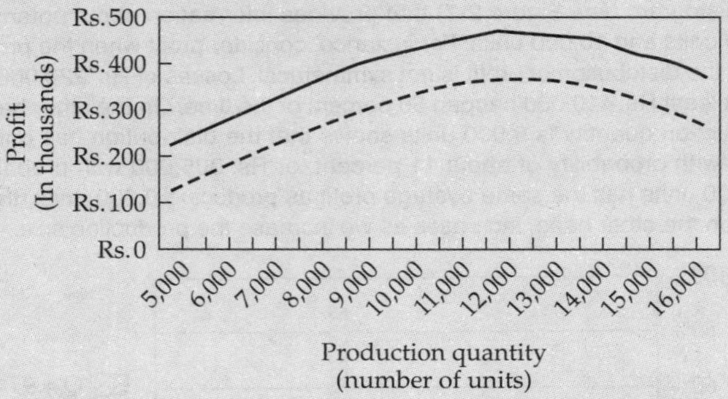

FIGURE 2-8 Profit and the impact of initial inventory.

Notice that the dotted curve is identical to the curve in Figure 2-6 while the solid line is above the dotted line for every production quantity; the difference between the two lines is the fixed production cost. Thus, if nothing is produced, average profit can be obtained from the solid line in Figure 2-8 and is equal to

$$225{,}000 \text{ (from the figure)} + 5{,}000 \times 80 = 625{,}000$$

where the last component is the variable production cost already included in the $225,000.

On the other hand, if the manufacturer decides to produce, it is clear that production should increase inventory from 5,000 units to 12,000 units. Thus, average profit in this case is obtained from the dotted line and is equal to

$$371{,}000 \text{ (from the figure)} + 5{,}000 \times 80 = 771{,}000$$

Since the average profit associated with increasing inventory to 12,000 units is larger than the average profit associated with not producing anything, the optimal policy is to produce 7,000 = 12,000 − 5,000 units.

Consider now the case in which initial inventory is 10,000 units. Following the same analysis used before, it is easy to see that there is no need to produce anything because the average profit associated with an initial inventory of 10,000 is larger than what we would achieve if we produce to increase inventory to 12,000 units. This is true because if we do not produce, we do not pay any fixed cost; if we produce, we need to pay a fixed cost independent of the amount produced.

Thus, if we produce, the most we can make on average is a profit of Rs. 375,000. This is the same average profit that we will have if our initial inventory is about 8,500 units and we decide not to produce anything. Hence, if our initial inventory is below 8,500 units, we produce to raise the inventory level to 12,000 units. On the other hand, if initial inventory is at least 8,500 units, we should not produce anything.

but one in which the firm already has some inventory of the product on hand, perhaps inventory left over from the previous season. If no additional order is placed or produced, the on-hand inventory can be used to meet demand, but, of course, the firm cannot sell more than this initial inventory level. On the other hand, if an order is placed, the fixed cost must be paid, and additional inventory can be acquired. Thus, when initial inventory is available, the trade-off is between having a limited amount of inventory by avoiding paying the fixed cost versus paying the fixed cost and therefore having a higher inventory level.

The previous example motivates a powerful inventory policy used in practice to manage inventory: Whenever the inventory level is reviewed, if it is below a certain value, say, s, we order (or produce) to increase the inventory to level S. Such a policy is referred as an (s, S) policy or a *min max* policy. We typically refer to s as the *reorder point* or the *min* and to S as the *order-up-to level* or the *max*. Finally, observe that if there is no fixed cost, the optimal inventory is characterized by a single number, the order-up-to level; always order enough to raise inventory to the target inventory level.

EXAMPLE 2-8

In the swimsuit production example, the reorder point is 8,500 units and the order-up-to level is 12,000 units. The difference between these two levels is driven by fixed costs associated with ordering, manufacturing, or transportation.

2.2.5 Multiple Order Opportunities

The situations we considered above all focus on a single ordering or production opportunity. This may be the case for fashion items where the selling season is short and there is no second opportunity to reorder products based on realized customer demand. In many practical situations, however, the decision maker may order products repeatedly at any time during the year.

Consider, for instance, a distributor that faces random demand for a product, and meets that demand with product ordered from a manufacturer. Of course, the manufacturer cannot instantaneously satisfy orders placed by the distributor: there is a fixed lead time for delivery whenever the distributor places an order. Since demand is random and the manufacturer has a fixed delivery lead time, the distributor needs to hold inventory, even if no fixed setup cost is charged for ordering the products. There are at least three reasons why the distributor holds inventory:

1. To satisfy demand occurring during lead time. Since orders aren't met immediately, inventory must be on hand to meet customer demand that is realized between the time that the distributor places an order and the time that the ordered inventory arrives.
2. To protect against uncertainty in demand.
3. To balance annual inventory holding costs and annual fixed order costs. We have seen that more frequent orders lead to lower inventory levels and thus lower inventory holding costs, but they also lead to higher annual fixed order costs.

While these issues are intuitively clear, the specific inventory policy that the distributor should apply is not simple. To manage inventory effectively, the distributor needs to decide when and how much to order. We distinguish between two types of policies:

- **Continuous review policy,** in which inventory is reviewed continuously, and an order is placed when the inventory reaches a particular level, or reorder point. This type of policy is most appropriate when inventory can be continuously reviewed—for example, when computerized inventory systems are used.
- **Periodic review policy,** in which the inventory level is reviewed at regular intervals and an appropriate quantity is ordered after each review. This type of policy is most appropriate for systems in which it is impossible or inconvenient to frequently review inventory and place orders if necessary.

2.2.6 Continuous Review Policy

We first consider a system in which inventory is continuously reviewed. Such a review system typically provides a more responsive inventory management strategy than the one associated with a periodic review system (why?).

We make the following additional assumptions.

- Daily demand is random and follows a normal distribution. In other words, we assume that the probabilistic forecast of daily demand follows the famous bell-shaped curve. Note that we can completely describe normal demand by its average and standard deviation.
- Every time the distributor places an order from the manufacturer, the distributor pays a fixed cost, K, plus an amount proportional to the quantity ordered.
- Inventory holding cost is charged per item per unit time.
- Inventory level is continuously reviewed, and if an order is placed, the order arrives after the appropriate lead time.
- If a customer order arrives when there is no inventory on hand to fill the order (i.e., when the distributor is stocked out), the order is lost.
- The distributor specifies a required *service level*. The service level is the probability of not stocking out during lead time. For example, the distributor might want to ensure that the proportion of lead times in which demand is met out of stock is 95 percent. Thus, the required service level is 95 percent in this case.

To characterize the inventory policy that the distributor should use, we need the following information:

AVG = Average daily demand faced by the distributor
STD = Standard deviation of daily demand faced by the distributor
L = Replenishment lead time from the supplier to the distributor in days
h = Cost of holding one unit of the product for one day at the distributor
α = service level. This implies that the probability of stocking out is $1 - \alpha$

In addition, we need to define the concept of *inventory position*. The inventory position at any point in time is the actual inventory at the warehouse plus items ordered by the distributor that have not yet arrived minus items that are backordered.

To describe the policy that the distributor should use, we recall the intuition developed when we considered a single period inventory model with initial inventory. In that model, when inventory was below a certain level, we ordered enough to raise the inventory up to another, higher level. For the continuous review model, we employ a similar approach, known as a (Q, R) policy—whenever inventory level falls to a reorder level R, place an order for Q units.

The reorder level, R, consists of two components. The first is the average inventory during lead time, which is the product of average daily demand and the lead time. This ensures that when the distributor places an order, the system has enough inventory to cover expected demand during lead time. The average demand during lead time is exactly

$$L \times AVG$$

The second component represents the *safety stock,* which is the amount of inventory that the distributor needs to keep at the warehouse and in the pipeline to protect against deviations from average demand during lead time. This quantity is calculated as follows:

TABLE 2-2

SERVICE LEVEL AND THE SERVICE FACTOR, z

Service level	90%	91%	92%	93%	94%	95%	96%	97%	98%	99%	99.9%
z	1.29	1.34	1.41	1.48	1.56	1.65	1.75	1.88	2.05	2.33	3.08

$$z \times STD \times \sqrt{L}$$

where z is a constant, referred to as the **safety factor.** This constant is associated with the service level. Thus, the reorder level is equal to

$$L \times AVG + z \times STD \times \sqrt{L}$$

The safety factor z is chosen from statistical tables to ensure that the probability of stockouts during lead time is exactly $1 - \alpha$. This implies that the reorder level must satisfy:

$$\Pr\{\text{Demand during lead time} \geq L \times AVG + z \times STD \times \sqrt{L}\} = 1 - \alpha$$

Table 2-2 provides a list of z values for different values of the service level α.

What about the order quantity, Q? Although calculating the optimal Q for this model is not easy, the EOQ order quantity we developed previously is very effective for this model. Recall from this model that the order quantity, Q, is calculated as follows:

$$Q = \sqrt{\frac{2K \times AVG}{h}}$$

If there is no variability in customer demand, the distributor would order Q items when the inventory is at level $L \times AVG$ since it takes L days to receive the order. However, there is variability in demand, so the distributor places an order for Q items whenever the inventory position is at the reorder level, R.

Figure 2-9 illustrates the inventory level over time when this type of policy is implemented. What is the average inventory level in this policy? Observe that, between two successive orders, the minimum level of inventory is achieved right before receiving an order, while the maximum level of inventory is achieved immediately after receiving the order. The expected level of inventory before receiving the order is the safety stock

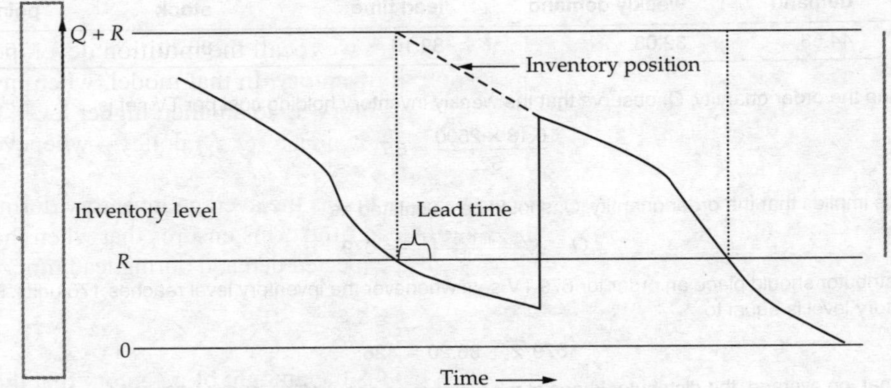

FIGURE 2-9 Inventory level as a function of time in a (Q, R) policy.

EXAMPLE 2-9

Consider a distributor of TV sets that orders from a manufacturer and sells to retailers. Suppose the distributor of the TV sets is trying to set inventory policies at the warehouse for one of the TV models. Assume that whenever the distributor places an order for TV sets, there is a fixed ordering cost of Rs. 45,000 which is independent of the order size. The cost of a TV set to the distributor is Rs. 2500 and annual inventory holding cost is about 18 percent of the product cost. Replenishment time (i.e., lead time) is about two weeks.

Table 2-3 provides data on the number of TV sets sold to retailers in each of the last 12 months. Given that the distributor would like to ensure 97 percent service level, what is the reorder level and the order quantity that the distributor should use?

TABLE 2-3

HISTORICAL DATA

Month	Sept.	Oct.	Nov.	Dec.	Jan.	Feb.	Mar.	Apr.	May	June	July	Aug.
Sales	200	152	100	221	287	176	151	198	246	309	98	156

Table 2-3 implies that average monthly demand is 191.17 and the standard deviation of monthly demand is 66.53. Since lead time is two weeks, we transform the average and the standard deviation to weekly values as follows:

$$\text{Average weekly demand} = \frac{\text{Average monthly demand}}{4.3}$$

while

$$\text{Standard deviation of weekly demand} = \frac{\text{Monthly standard deviation}}{\sqrt{4.3}}$$

These data are provided in Table 2-4. This allows us to calculate average demand during lead time and safety stock using a safety factor $z = 1.9$ (or, more precisely, 1.88) taken from Table 2-2 based on a 97 percent service level. The reorder point is simply the sum of the average demand during lead time plus the safety stock. All these data are presented in Table 2-4.

TABLE 2-4

INVENTORY ANALYSIS

Parameter	Average weekly demand	Standard deviation of weekly demand	Average demand during lead time	Safety stock	Reorder point
Value	44.58	32.08	89.16	86.20	176

To determine the order quantity, Q, observe that the weekly inventory holding cost per TV set is

$$\frac{0.18 \times 2500}{52} = 8.7$$

or Rs.8.70. This implies that the order quantity, Q, should be calculated as

$$Q = \sqrt{\frac{2 \times 45{,}000 \times 44.58}{8.7}} = 679$$

That is, the distributor should place an order for 679 TV sets whenever the inventory level reaches 176 units. Finally, the average inventory level is equal to

$$679/2 + 86.20 = 426$$

which means that, on average, the distributor keeps at the warehouse about 10 (= 426/44.58) weeks of supply.

$$z \times STD \times \sqrt{L}$$

while the expected level of inventory immediately after receiving the order is

$$Q + z \times STD \times \sqrt{L}$$

Thus, the average inventory level is the average of these two values, which is equal to

$$\frac{Q}{2} + z \times STD \times \sqrt{L}$$

2.2.7 Variable Lead Times

In many cases, the assumption that the delivery lead time to the warehouse is fixed and known in advance does not necessarily hold. Indeed, in many practical situations, the lead time to the warehouse may be random or unknown in advance. In these cases, we typically assume that the lead time is normally distributed with average lead time denoted by *AVGL* and standard deviation denoted by *STDL*. In this case, the reorder point, *R*, is calculated as follows:

$$R = AVG \times AVGL + z\sqrt{AVGL \times STD^2 + AVG^2 \times STD^2}$$

where $AVG \times AVGL$ represents average demand during lead time, while

$$\sqrt{AVGL \times STD^2 + AVG^2 \times STDL^2}$$

is the standard deviation of demand during lead time. Thus, the amount of safety stock that has to be kept is equal to

$$z\sqrt{AVGL \times STD^2 + AVG^2 \times STDL^2}$$

As before, the order quantity Q satisfies $Q = \sqrt{\frac{2K \times AVG}{h}}$.

2.2.8 Periodic Review Policy

In many real-life situations, the inventory level is reviewed periodically at regular intervals, and an appropriate quantity is ordered after each review. If these intervals are relatively short (for example, daily), it may make sense to use a modified version of the (Q, R) policy presented above. Unfortunately, the (Q, R) policy can't be directly implemented, since the inventory level may fall below the reorder point when the warehouse places an order. To overcome this problem, define two inventory levels s and S, and during each inventory review, if the inventory position falls below s, order enough to raise the inventory position to S. We call this modified (Q, R) policy an (s, S) policy. Although it is difficult to determine the optimal values for s and S, one very effective approximation is to calculate the Q and R values as if this were a continuous review model, set s equal to R, and S equal to $R + Q$.

If there is a larger time between successive reviews of inventory (weekly or monthly, for example), it may make sense to always order after an inventory level review. Since an order is placed after each inventory review, the fixed cost of placing an order is a sunk cost and hence can be ignored; presumably, the fixed cost was used to determine the review interval. The quantity ordered arrives after the appropriate lead time.

What inventory policy should the warehouse use in this case? Since fixed cost does not play a role in this environment, the inventory policy is characterized by a single parameter, the **base-stock level.** That is, the warehouse determines a target inventory level, the base-stock level, and each review period, the inventory position is reviewed and the warehouse orders enough to raise the inventory position to the base-stock level.

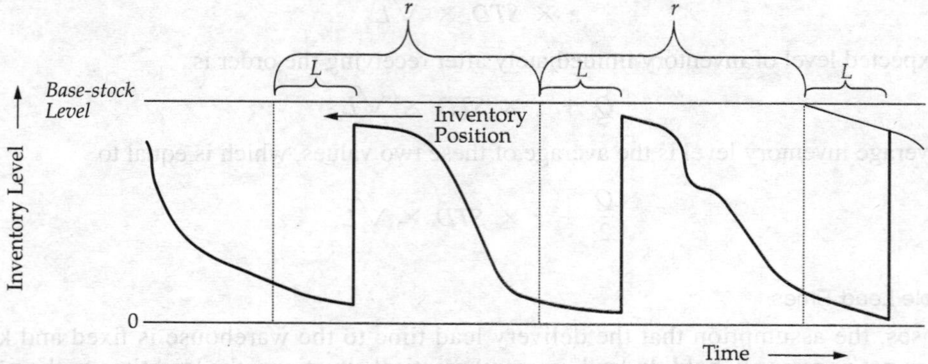

FIGURE 2-10 Inventory level as a function of time in a periodic review policy.

What is an effective base-stock level? For this purpose, let r be the length of the review period—we assume that orders are placed every r periods of time. As before, L is the lead time, AVG is the average daily demand faced by the warehouse, and STD is the standard deviation of this daily demand.

Observe that at the time the warehouse places an order, this order raises the inventory position to the base-stock level. This level of the inventory position should be enough to protect the warehouse against shortages until the next order arrives. Since the next order arrives after a period of $r + L$ days, the current order should be enough to cover demand during a period of $r + L$ days.

Thus, the base-stock level should include two components: average demand during an interval of $r + L$ days, which is equal to

$$(r + L) \times AVG$$

and the safety stock, which is the amount of inventory that the warehouse needs to keep to protect against deviations from average demand during a period of $r + L$ days. This quantity is calculated as follows:

$$z \times STD \times \sqrt{r + L}$$

where z is the safety factor.

Figure 2-10 illustrates the inventory level over time when this type of policy is implemented. What is the average inventory level in this case? As before, the maximum inventory level is achieved imme-

EXAMPLE 2-10

We continue with the previous example and assume that the distributor places an order for TV sets every three weeks. Since lead time is two weeks, the base-stock level needs to cover a period of five weeks. Thus, average demand during that period is

$$44.58 \times 5 = 222.9$$

and the safety stock, for a 97 percent service level, is

$$1.9 \times 32.8 \times \sqrt{5} = 136$$

Hence, the base-stock level should be 223 + 136 = 359. That is, when the distributor places an order every three weeks, he should raise the inventory position to 359 TV sets. The average inventory level in this case equals

$$\frac{3 \times 44.58}{2} + 1.9 \times 32.8 \times \sqrt{5} = 203.17$$

which implies that, on average, the distributor keeps five (= 203.17/44.58) weeks of supply.

diately after receiving an order, while the minimum level of inventory is achieved just before receiving an order. It is easy to see that the expected level of inventory after receiving an order is equal to

$$r \times AVG + z + STD \times \sqrt{r + L}$$

while the expected level of inventory before an order arrives is just the safety stock,

$$z \times STD \times \sqrt{r + L}$$

Hence, the average inventory level is the average of these two values, which is equal to

$$\frac{r \times AVG}{2} + z \times STD \times \sqrt{r + L}$$

2.2.9 Service Level Optimization

So far we have assumed that the objective of this inventory optimization is to determine the optimal inventory policy given a specific service level target. The question, of course, is how the facility should decide on the appropriate level of service. Sometimes this is determined by the downstream customer. In other words, the retailer can require the facility, for example, the supplier, to maintain a specific level of service and the supplier will use that target to manage its own inventory.

In other cases, the facility has the flexibility to choose the appropriate level of service. The trades-offs, presented in Figure 2-11, are clear: everything else being equal, the higher the service level, the higher the inventory level. Similarly, for the same inventory level, the longer the lead time to the

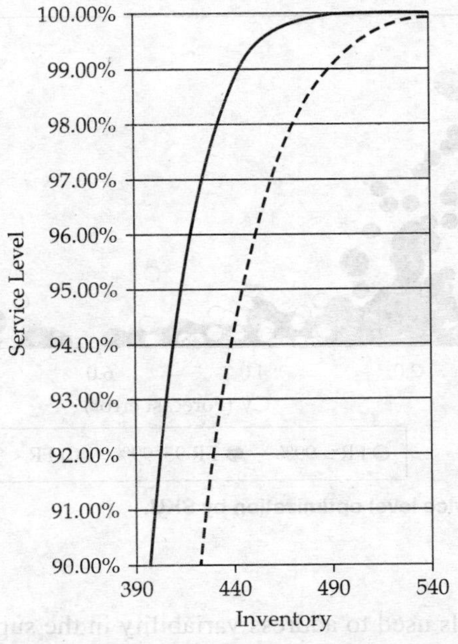

FIGURE 2-11 Service level versus inventory level as a function of lead time.

facility, the lower the level of service provided by the facility. Finally, the marginal impact on service level decreases with inventory level. That is, the lower the inventory level, the higher the impact of a unit of inventory on service level and hence on expected profit.

Thus, one possible strategy, used in retailing, to determine service level for each SKU is to focus on maximizing expected profit across all, or some, of their products. That is, given a target service level across all products, we determine service level for each SKU so as to maximize expected profit. Everything else being equal, service level will be higher for products with

- High profit margin.
- High volume.
- Low variability.
- Short lead time.

The impact of profit optimization on service level is nicely illustrated by Figure 2-12. The vertical axis represents annual sales while the horizontal axis represents demand variability. Each circle is associated with a product and the size of the circle is proportional to profit margin. The target inventory level is 95 percent across all products. As you can see, the service level is higher than 99 percent (brown-colored circles) for many products with high profit margin, high volume, and low variability. On the other hand, service level is lower than 95 percent for products with low profit margin, low volume, and high variability.

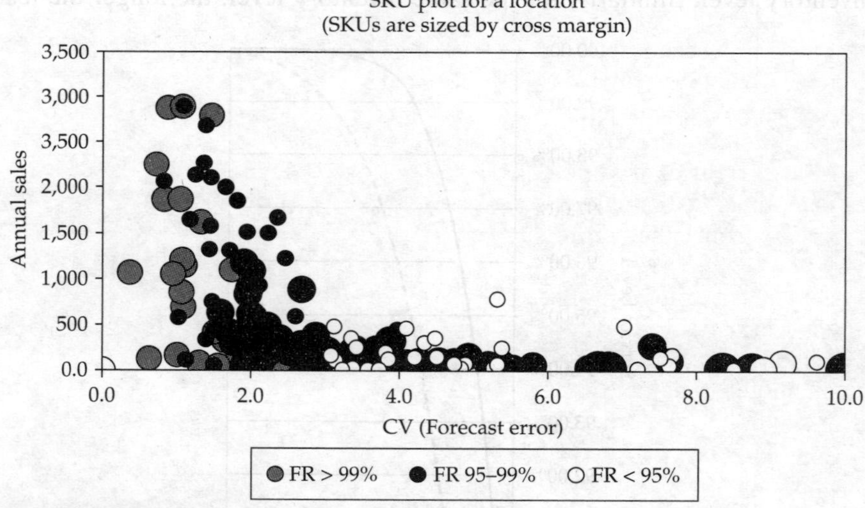

FIGURE 2-12 Service level optimization by SKU.

2.3 RISK POOLING

One of the most powerful tools used to address variability in the supply chain is the concept of **risk pooling.** Risk pooling suggests that demand variability is reduced if one aggregates demand across locations. This is true since, as we aggregate demand across different locations, it becomes more likely that high demand from one customer will be offset by low demand from another. This reduction in variability allows a decrease in safety stock and therefore reduces average inventory.

To understand risk pooling, it is essential to understand the concepts of standard deviation and coefficient of variation of demand. Standard deviation is a measure of how much demand tends to vary around the average, and coefficient of variation is the ratio of standard deviation to average demand:

$$\text{Coefficient of variation} = \frac{\text{Standard deviation}}{\text{Average demand}}$$

It is important at this point to understand the difference between the standard deviation and the coefficient of variation, both of which provide a measure of variability of customer demand. Indeed, while the standard deviation measures the absolute variability of customer demands, the coefficient of variation measures variability relative to average demand.

With this background, to see the power of risk pooling, consider the following case:

CASE: Risk Pooling

ACME, a company that produces and distributes electronic equipment in the Northeast of the United States, faces a distribution problem. The current distribution system partitions the Northeast into two markets, each of which has a single warehouse. One warehouse is located in Paramus, New Jersey, and the second is located in Newton, Massachusetts. Customers, typically retailers, receive items directly from the warehouses; in the current distribution system, each customer is assigned to a single market and receives deliveries from the corresponding warehouse.

The warehouses receive items from a manufacturing facility in Chicago. Lead time for delivery to each of the warehouses is about one week and the manufacturing facility has sufficient production capacity to satisfy any warehouse order. The current distribution strategy provides a 97 percent service level; that is, the inventory policy employed by each warehouse is designed so that the probability of a stockout is 3 percent. Of course, unfilled orders are lost to the competition and thus cannot be satisfied by future deliveries.

Since the original distribution system was designed over seven years ago, the company's newly appointed CEO has decided to review the current logistics and distribution system. ACME handles about 1,500 different products in its supply chain and serves about 10,000 accounts in the Northeast. ACME is considering the following alternative strategy: Replace the two warehouses with a single warehouse located between Paramus and Newton that will serve all customer orders. We will refer to this proposed system as the centralized distribution system. The CEO insists that the same service level, 97 percent, be maintained regardless of the logistics strategy employed.

Obviously, the current distribution system with two warehouses has an important advantage over the single warehouse system because each warehouse is close to a particular subset of customers, decreasing delivery time. However, the proposed change also has an important advantage; it allows ACME to achieve either the same service level of 97 percent with much lower inventory or a higher service level with the same amount of total inventory.

Intuitively this is explained as follows. With random demand, it is very likely that a higher-than-average demand at one retailer will be offset by a lower-than-average demand at another. As the number of retailers served by a warehouse goes up, this likelihood also goes up. Indeed, this is precisely the third principle of all forecasts described at the beginning of Section 2.2.2: aggregate forecasts are more accurate.

How much can ACME reduce inventory if the company decides to switch to the centralized system but maintain the same 97 percent service level?

TABLE 2.5

HISTORICAL DATA FOR PRODUCT A

Week	1	2	3	4	5	6	7	8
Massachusetts	33	45	37	38	55	30	18	58
New Jersey	46	35	41	40	26	48	18	55
Total	79	80	78	78	81	78	36	113

TABLE 2.6

HISTORICAL DATA FOR PRODUCT B

Week	1	2	3	4	5	6	7	8
Massachusetts	0	3	3	0	0	1	3	0
New Jersey	2	4	0	0	3	1	0	0
Total	2	6	3	0	3	2	3	0

To answer that question, we need to perform a more rigorous analysis of the inventory policy that ACME should use in both the current system and the centralized system. We will explain this analysis for two specific products, Product A and Product B, although the analysis must be conducted for all products.

For both products, an order from the factory costs \$60 per order and holding inventory costs are \$0.27 per unit per week. In the current distribution system, the cost of transporting a product from a warehouse to a customer is, on average, \$1.05 per product. It is estimated that in the centralized distribution system, the transportation cost from the central warehouse will be, on average, \$1.10 per product. For this analysis, we assume that delivery lead time is not significantly different in the two systems.

Tables 2-5 and 2-6 provide historical data for Products A and B, respectively. The tables include weekly demand information for each product for the last eight weeks in each market area. Observe that Product B is a slow-moving product: the demand for Product B is fairly small relative to the demand for Product A.

Table 2-7 provides a summary of average weekly demand and the standard deviation of weekly demand for each product. It also presents the *coefficient of variation* of demand faced by each warehouse.

Recall that the standard deviation measures the absolute variability of customer demands, while the coefficient of variation measures variability relative to average demand. For instance, in the case of the two products analyzed here, we observe that Product A has a much larger standard deviation while Product B has a significantly larger coefficient of variation. This distinction between the two products plays an important role in the final analysis.

TABLE 2.7

SUMMARY OF HISTORICAL DATA

Statistics	Product	Average demand	Standard deviation of demand	Coefficient of variation
Massachusetts	A	39.3	13.2	0.34
Massachusetts	B	1.125	1.36	1.21
New Jersey	A	38.6	12.0	0.31
New Jersey	B	1.25	1.58	1.26
Total	A	77.9	20.71	0.27
Total	B	2.375	1.9	0.81

TABLE 2.8
INVENTORY LEVELS

	Product	Average demand during lead time	Safety stock	Reorder point	Q
Massachusetts	A	39.3	25.08	65	132
Massachusetts	B	1.125	2.58	4	25
New Jersey	A	38.6	22.8	62	131
New Jersey	B	1.25	3	5	24
Total	A	77.9	39.35	118	186
Total	B	2.375	3.61	6	33

Finally, note that, for each product, the average demand faced by the warehouse in the centralized distribution system is the sum of the average demand faced by each of the existing warehouses. However, the variability faced by the central warehouse, measured by either the standard deviation or the coefficient of variation, is much smaller than the combined variabilities faced by the two existing warehouses. This has a major impact on inventory levels in the current and proposed systems. These levels, calculated as we have described in previous sections, are shown in Table 2-8.

Notice that the average inventory for Product A at the warehouse in Paramus, New Jersey, is about

$$\text{Safety stock} + Q/2 = 88$$

Similarly, average inventory at the Newton, Massachusetts, warehouse for the same product is about 91 units, while average inventory in the centralized warehouse is about 132 units. Thus, average inventory for Product A is reduced by about 36 percent when ACME shifts from the current system to the new, centralized system—a significant reduction in average inventory.

The average inventory for Product B is 15 at the warehouse in Paramus, 14 at the warehouse in Newton, and 20 at the centralized warehouse. In this case, ACME is going to achieve a reduction of about 43 percent in average inventory level.

This case dramatically illustrates the concept of risk pooling. As mentioned above, the aggregation of demand stemming from risk pooling leads to reduction in demand variability, and thus a decrease in safety stock and average inventory. For example, in the centralized distribution system described above, the warehouse serves all customers, which leads to a reduction in variability measured by either the standard deviation or the coefficient of variation.

We summarize the three critical points we have made about risk pooling:

1. Centralizing inventory reduces both safety stock and average inventory in the system. Intuitively this is explained as follows. In a centralized distribution system, whenever demand from one market area is higher than average while demand in another market area is lower than average, items in the warehouse that were originally allocated for one market can be reallocated to the other. The process of reallocating inventory is not possible in a decentralized distribution system where different warehouses serve different markets.
2. The higher the coefficient of variation, the greater the benefit obtained from centralized systems; that is, the greater the benefit from risk pooling. This is explained as follows. Average inventory includes two components: one proportional to average weekly demand (Q) and the other proportional to the standard deviation of weekly demand (safety stock). Since reduction in average

inventory is achieved mainly through a reduction in safety stock, the higher the coefficient of variation, the larger the impact of safety stock on inventory reduction.

3. The benefits from risk pooling depend on the behavior of demand from one market relative to demand from another. We say that demand from two markets is *positively correlated* if it is very likely that whenever demand from one market is greater then average, demand from the other market is also greater than average. Similarly, when demand from one market is smaller than average, so is demand from the other. Intuitively, the benefit from risk pooling decreases as the correlation between demand from the two markets becomes more positive.

In Chapter 6, we provide different examples of risk pooling. In that chapter, risk pooling is applied by *aggregating demand across products* or *across time,* rather than across customers as we do here.

2.4 CENTRALIZED VERSUS DECENTRALIZED SYSTEMS

The analysis in the previous section raises an important practical issue: What are the trade-offs that we need to consider in comparing centralized distribution systems with decentralized distribution systems?

Safety stock. Clearly, safety stock decreases as a firm moves from a decentralized to a centralized system. The amount of decrease depends on a number of parameters, including the coefficient of variation and the correlation between the demand from the different markets.

Service level. When the centralized and decentralized systems have the same total safety stock, the service level provided by the centralized system is higher. As before, the magnitude of the increase in service level depends on the coefficient of variation and the correlation between the demand from the different markets.

Overhead costs. Typically, these costs are much greater in a decentralized system because there are fewer economies of scale.

Customer lead time. Since the warehouses are much closer to the customers in a decentralized system, response time is much shorter (see Chapter 3).

Transportation costs. The impact on transportation costs depends on the specifics of the situation. On one hand, as we increase the number of warehouses, outbound transportation costs—the costs incurred for delivering the items from the warehouses to the customers—decrease because warehouses are much closer to the market areas. On the other hand, inbound transportation costs—the costs of shipping the products from the supply and manufacturing facilities to the warehouses—increase. Thus, the net impact on total transportation cost is not immediately clear.

2.5 MANAGING INVENTORY IN THE SUPPLY CHAIN

Most of the inventory models and examples considered so far assume a single facility (e.g., a warehouse or a retail outlet) managing its inventory in order to minimize its own cost as much as possible.

In this section, we first consider a multifacility serial supply chain that belongs to a single firm. A serial supply chain is one in which there are a series of stages, each of which supplies a single downstream stage, until the final stage, which meets end customer demand; for example, a single manufacturer that supplies a single wholesaler that in turn satisfies orders from a single distributor. Finally, the distributor supplies a single retailer that meets customer demand.

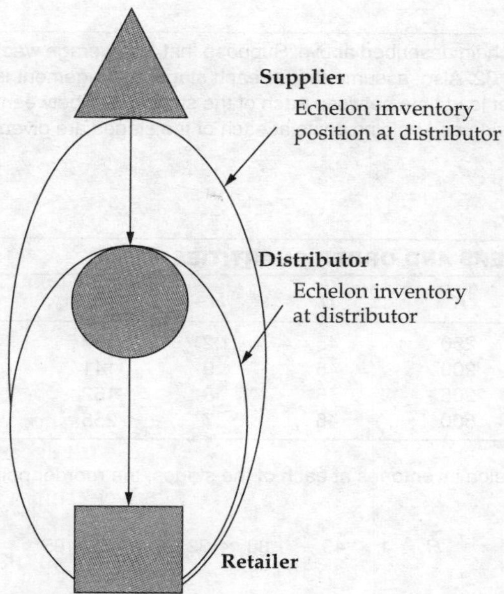

FIGURE 2-13 A serial supply chain.

If this serial supply chain is owned by a single firm, the objective of that firm will be to manage inventory so as to reduce systemwide cost; thus, it is important for the firm to consider the interaction of the various facilities and the impact this interaction has on the inventory policy that should be employed by each facility.

We assume that

1. Inventory decisions are made by a single decision maker whose objective is to minimize systemwide cost.
2. The decision maker has access to inventory information at each of the retailers and at the warehouse.

In this case, an approach based on the concept of the *echelon inventory policy* is an effective way to manage the system (note that it is very difficult to find an optimal policy for this problem, but the policy we describe is very effective).

To understand this policy, it is necessary to introduce the concept of echelon inventory. In a distribution system, each stage or level (i.e., the warehouse or the retailers) often is referred to as an echelon. Thus, the echelon inventory at any stage or level of the system is equal to the inventory on hand at the echelon, plus all *downstream inventory* (downstream means closer to the customer).

For example, look at Figure 2-13; the echelon inventory at the distributor is equal to the inventory at the distributor, plus the inventory in transit to and in stock at the retailer. Similarly, the *echelon inventory position* at the distributor is the echelon inventory at the distributor's warehouse, plus those items ordered by the distributor that have not yet arrived minus all items that are backordered (see Figure 2-13).

This suggests the following effective approach to managing this serial system. First, the retailer inventory is managed using the (Q, R) policy described in Section 2.2.6. The reorder level and order quantity at the retailer are calculated using the formulas discussed in that section:

EXAMPLE 2-11

Consider the four-stage supply chain described above. Suppose that the average weekly demand faced by the retailer is 45, with a standard deviation of 32. Also, assume that at each stage, management is attempting to maintain a service level of 97 percent ($z = 1.88$); that lead time between each of the stages, and between the manufacturer and its supplier, is one week; and that fixed ordering and holding costs at each of the stages are given according to Table 2-9, where we also determine order quantities.

TABLE 2-9

COST PARAMETERS AND ORDER QUANTITIES

	K	*D*	*H*	*Q*
Retailer	250	45	1.2	137
Distributor	200	45	.9	141
Wholesaler	205	45	.8	152
Manufacturer	500	45	.7	255

Next, using the differing echelon inventories at each of the stages, the reorder points are calculated as follows:

For the retailer:

$$R = 1 \times 45 + 1.88 \times 32 \times \sqrt{1} = 105$$

For the distributor:

$$R = 2 \times 45 + 1.88 \times 32 \times \sqrt{2} = 175$$

For the wholesaler:

$$R = 3 \times 45 + 1.88 \times 32 \times \sqrt{3} = 239$$

For the manufacturer:

$$R = 4 \times 45 + 1.88 \times 32 \times \sqrt{4} = 300$$

At each echelon, when the echelon inventory position falls below the reorder point for that echelon, the appropriate Q is ordered.

$$R = L \times AVG + z \times STD \times \sqrt{L}$$

$$Q^* = \sqrt{\frac{2KD}{h}}$$

In this case, the lead time L is the time from when the retailer places an order until the time the order is received, assuming that the warehouse has enough in stock. Whenever the inventory position at a retailer falls below the reorder point R, Q units are ordered. Similarly, a reorder point R and an order quantity Q are calculated for the distributor. In this case, however, the warehouse policy controls its echelon inventory position; whenever the echelon inventory position for the warehouse is below R, an order is placed for Q units.

How should the reorder point associated with the distributor echelon inventory position be calculated? In this case, the reorder point is

$$R = L^e \times AVG + z \times STD \times \sqrt{L^e}$$

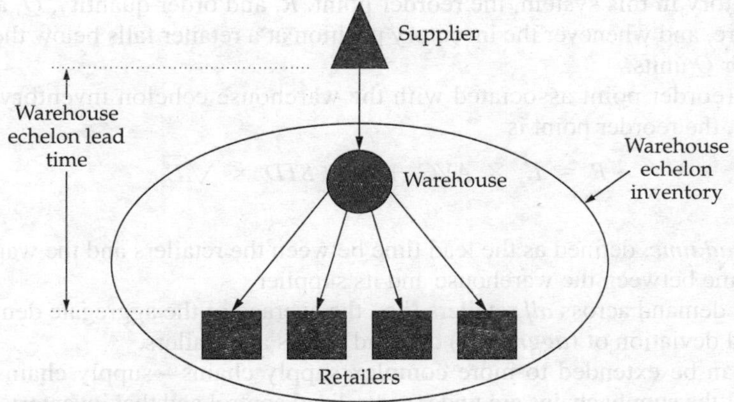

FIGURE 2-14 The warehouse echelon inventory.

where

L^e = *echelon lead time,* defined as the lead time between the retailer and the distributor *plus* the lead time between the distributor and its supplier, the wholesaler

AVG = average demand at the retailer

STD = standard deviation of demand at the retailer

Next, a similar approach is used to manage inventory at the wholesaler and at the manufacturer, where the lead time is modified appropriately, and the appropriate echelon inventory is used.

What if there is more than one facility at a particular stage of the supply chain? For example, what about a two-stage supply chain where a warehouse supplies a set of retailers? Exactly the same approach can be used in this case, except that, now, the echelon inventory at the warehouse is the inventory at the warehouse, plus all of the inventory in transit to and in stock at each of the retailers. Similarly, the echelon inventory position at the warehouse is the echelon inventory at the warehouse, plus those items ordered by the warehouse that have not yet arrived minus all items that are backordered (see Figure 2-14).

EXAMPLE 2-12

Consider the TV distributor from Example 2-9. In that example, we determined the inventory policy for the warehouse. Now suppose that the warehouse supplies a group of retailers. The historical demand data provided in Table 2-3 are the aggregate demand data for the retailers. Finally, the two weeks' lead time is the echelon lead time—the time it takes an order placed by the warehouse to reach a customer. Thus, the distributor needs to ensure that a total of 176 units of inventory, or about four weeks' supply, is somewhere in the system, either in the pipeline to the warehouse, at the warehouse, in transit to the retailers, or at the retailers.

What about the retailers? In this case, we need to perform exactly the same calculations, but this time utilizing the associated lead time from the warehouse to the retailer.

Suppose, for example, that it takes one week for items to get from the warehouse to the retailer. Using the same approach as before to achieve a 97 percent service level, we find that the reorder level, R, for the retailer is 20. Thus, an order is placed whenever the retailer inventory position is 20. Obviously, if other retailers face different demand or lead times, they will have different reorder levels.

To manage inventory in this system, the reorder point, R, and order quantity, Q, are calculated for each retailer as before, and whenever the inventory position at a retailer falls below the reorder point R, an order is placed for Q units.

How should the reorder point associated with the warehouse echelon inventory position be calculated? In this case, the reorder point is

$$R = L^e \times AVG + z \times STD \times \sqrt{L^e}$$

where

L^e = *echelon lead time,* defined as the lead time between the retailers and the warehouse *plus* the lead time between the warehouse and its supplier

AVG = average demand across *all* retailers (i.e., the average of the aggregate demand)

STD = standard deviation of (*aggregate*) demand across all retailers.

This technique can be extended to more complex supply chains—supply chains with additional levels—provided that the supply chains are under centralized control and that inventory information from each of the echelons is available to the decision maker.

2.6 PRACTICAL ISSUES

In a recent survey,[1] materials and inventory managers were asked to identify effective inventory reduction strategies. The top seven strategies in this survey are

1. **Perform periodic inventory review.** In this strategy, see Section 2.2.8, inventory is reviewed at a fixed time interval and every time it is reviewed, a decision is made on the order size. The periodic inventory review policy makes it possible to identify slow-moving and obsolete products and allows management to continuously reduce inventory levels.
2. **Provide tight management of usage rates, lead times, and safety stock.** This allows the firm to make sure inventory is kept at the appropriate level. Such an inventory control process allows the firm to identify, for example, situations in which usage rates decrease for a few months. If no appropriate action is taken, this decrease in usage rates implies an increase in inventory levels over the same period of time.
3. **Reduce safety stock levels.** This can perhaps be accomplished by focusing on lead-time reduction.
4. **Introduce or enhance cycle counting practice.** This process replaces the annual physical inventory count by a system where part of the inventory is counted every day, and each item is counted several times per year.
5. **Follow ABC approach.** In this strategy, items are classified into three categories. Class A items include all high-revenue products, which typically account for about 80 percent of annual (Rs.) sales and represent about 20 percent of inventory SKUs. Class B items include products that account for about 15 percent of annual sales, while Class C products represent low-revenue items, products whose value is no more than 5 percent of sales. Because Class A items account for the major part of the business, a high-frequency periodic review policy (e.g., a weekly review) is appropriate in this case. Similarly, a periodic review policy is applied to control Class B products, although the frequency of review is not as high as that for Class A products. Finally, depending on product value, the firm either keeps no inventory of expensive Class C products or keeps a high inventory of inexpensive Class C products.
6. **Shift more inventory or inventory ownership to suppliers.**

[1] *Inventory Reduction Report,* no. 07-01 (July 2001), pp. 10–12.

7. **Follow quantitative approaches.** These approaches are similar to those described in this chapter that focus on the right balance between inventory holding and ordering costs.

Observe that the focus in the survey was not on reducing cost but on reducing inventory levels. Indeed, in the last few years, we have seen a significant effort by industry to increase the *inventory turnover ratio,* defined as follows:

$$\text{Inventory turnover ratio} = \frac{\text{Annual sales}}{\text{Average inventory level}}$$

This definition implies that an increase in inventory turnover leads to a decrease in average inventory levels. For instance, retailing powerhouse Wal-Mart has the highest inventory turnover ratio of any discount retailer. This suggests that Wal-Mart has a higher level of liquidity, smaller risk of obsolescence, and reduced investment in inventory. Of course, a low inventory level in itself is not always appropriate since it increases the risk of lost sales.

Thus, the question is, what are the appropriate inventory turns that the firm should use in practice? A recent survey of industry practices suggests that the answer does change from year to year and depends, in particular, on the specific industry. Indeed, the survey reports a significant increase in inventory turnover ratios in 2001: about 52.9 percent of the manufacturers participating in the survey increased their turnover. Table 2-10 provides some examples of inventory turnover in different manufacturing companies, by industry, in 2001.

EXAMPLE 2-13 HINDUSTAN LEVER LIMITED (HLL)

Hindustan Lever Ltd. (HLL), renamed Hindustan Unilever Ltd. (HUL) in June 2007, has one of the widest distribution networks in India. It has more than hundred brands, mainly in the fast moving consumer goods (FMCG) category. These are delivered to a very large number of retailers in every nook and corner of India and hundreds of institutional buyers through over 7500 wholesalers. Hindustan Lever is the market leader in home and personal care products, food, beverages and specialty chemicals. Its distribution faced the typical supply chain problem of demand-supply mismatch, which was reflected in repeated cycles of excess inventory and stock-outs. It adopted Adexa iCollaboration suite, an IT-based solution, to move towards replenishment-based distribution system, representing a pull-based approach. Inventory visibility at every level and excellent connectivity through information sharing have helped in arresting this problem of demand-supply mismatch to a large extent [110, 278, 291].

TABLE 2-10

INVENTORY TURNOVER RATIO FOR DIFFERENT MANUFACTURERS

Industry	Upper quartile	Median	Lower quartile
Electronic components and accessories	8.1	4.9	3.3
Electronic computers	22.7	7.0	2.7
Household audio and video equipment	6.3	3.9	2.5
Paper mills	11.7	8.0	5.5
Industrial chemicals	14.1	6.4	4.2
Bakery products	39.7	23.0	12.6
Books: publishing and printing	7.2	2.8	1.5

Source: Based on a survey conducted by Risk Management Associates.

2.7 FORECASTING

Throughout this chapter, we have recounted the problems with forecasting. After all, the three rules of forecasting are

1. The forecast is always wrong.
2. The longer the forecast horizon, the worse the forecast.
3. Aggregate forecasts are more accurate.

Nevertheless, forecasting is a critical tool in the management toolbox. We have seen that by correctly managing inventory, managers can make the best possible use of forecasts, in spite of the inherent difficulties of forecasting. In addition, forecasts aren't just for inventory decision making; decisions about whether to enter a particular market at all, about whether to expand production capacity, or about whether to implement a given promotional plan can all benefit from effective forecasting. In this section, we explore a variety of the techniques that can be used, separately or in combination, to create forecasts. Of course, it would be possible to write an entire book on forecasting (and many such books exist); our goal here is to introduce the different approaches to forecasting and suggest when each of these approaches is appropriate.

Although there are many different forecasting tools and methods, they can be split into four general categories (see [93]):

- **Judgment methods** involve the collection of expert opinions.
- **Market research methods** involve qualitative studies of consumer behavior.
- **Time-series methods** are mathematical methods in which future performance is extrapolated from past performance.
- **Causal methods** are mathematical methods in which forecasts are generated based on a variety of system variables.

Below, we discuss these methods in more detail.

2.7.1 Judgment Methods

Judgment methods strive to assemble the opinions of a variety of experts in a systematic way. For example, salespeople (or dealers) frequently have a good understanding of expected sales, since they are close to the market. A **sales-force composite** can be assembled that combines each salesperson's sales estimate in a logical way.

Panels of experts can be assembled in order to reach a consensus. This approach assumes that by communicating and openly sharing information, a superior forecast can be agreed upon. These experts can be external experts, or internal experts, from a variety of functional areas within a company.

The **Delphi method** is a structured technique for reaching a consensus with a panel of experts without gathering them in a single location. Indeed, the technique is designed to eliminate the danger of one or a few strong-willed individuals dominating the decision-making process. In the Delphi method, each member of the group of experts is surveyed for his or her opinion, typically in writing. The opinions are compiled and summarized, and each individual is given the opportunity to change his or her opinion after seeing the summary. This process is repeated until consensus is achieved.

Recall, for example, the swimsuit production case presented throughout this chapter. In that case, a swimsuit manufacturer used a probabilistic forecast to make production and inventory decisions. This forecast consisted of several scenarios, each with an assigned probability of occurring. In all likelihood, the marketing department used one or more of the judgment methods listed above to develop this probabilistic forecast.

2.7.2 Market Research Methods

Market testing and **market surveys** can be valuable tools for developing forecasts, particularly of newly introduced products. In market testing, focus groups of potential customers are assembled and tested for their response to products, and this response is extrapolated to the entire market to estimate the demand for products. Market surveys involve gathering these data from a variety of potential customers, typically through interviews, telephone-based surveys, and written surveys.

2.7.3 Time-Series Methods

Time-series methods use a variety of past data (that is, past values of the value being predicted) to estimate future data. There are a variety of techniques that are commonly used, each of which has different advantages and disadvantages. We explore the relationship between time-series forecasting methods and the bullwhip effect in Chapter 5.

Below, we discuss some common time-series methods (see [170] for more details):

Moving average. Each forecast is the average of some number of previous demand points. The key here is to select the number of points in the moving average so that the effect of irregularities in the data is minimized. See Chapter 5 for the impact of the moving average forecast on the bullwhip effect.

Exponential smoothing. Each forecast is a weighted average of the previous forecast and the last demand point. Thus, this method is similar to the moving average, except that it is a weighted average of all past data points, with more recent points receiving more weight.

Methods for data with trends. The previous two approaches assume that there is no trend in the data. If there is a trend, methods such as **regression analysis** and **Holt's method** are more useful, as they specifically account for trends in the data. Regression analysis fits a straight line to data points, while Holt's method combines the concept of exponential smoothing with the ability to follow a linear trend in the data.

Methods for seasonal data. A variety of techniques account for seasonal changes in demand. For example, **seasonal decomposition** methods remove the seasonal patterns from the data and then apply the approaches listed above on these edited data. Similarly, **Winter's method** is a version of exponential smoothing that accounts for trends and seasonality.

More complex methods. A variety of more complex methods have been proposed. However, these more complex methods are typically not used in practice, and, indeed, there is some evidence that complex methods don't outperform more simple methods [170].

2.7.4 Causal Methods

Recall that in the time-series methods described above, forecasts are based entirely on previous values of the data being predicted. In contrast, causal methods generate forecasts based on data *other than the data being predicted*. More specifically, the forecast is a function of some other pieces of data. For example, the causal sales forecast for the next quarter may be a function of inflation, GNP, the unemployment rate, the weather, or anything besides the sales in this quarter.

2.7.5 Selecting the Appropriate Forecasting Technique

With so many forecasting techniques available, which one is appropriate for a given situation? Chambers, Mullick, and Smith (CMS), in their seminal *Harvard Business Review* article [45], pose three questions that help with this decision:

- **What is the purpose of the forecast? How is it to be used?** If gross sales estimates are sufficient, a less complex technique may be appropriate, whereas if detailed estimates are required, more advanced techniques may be necessary.
- **What are the dynamics of the system for which the forecast will be made?** Is the system sensitive to the type of economic data that would indicate that a causal model makes sense? Is the demand seasonal, or trending upwards or downwards? All of these impact the choice of forecasting tool.
- **How important is the past in estimating the future?** If the past is very important, time-series methods make sense. If significant systemwide changes render the past less important, judgment or market research methods may be indicated.

CMS also point out that at different stages of the product life cycle, different forecast techniques are appropriate. In the product development phase, market research methods may indicate the potential sales of different products and designs. In the testing and introduction phases, additional market research may be valuable, and judgment methods can be useful for predicting future demand of the products. In the rapid growth phase of the product life cycle, time-series data may be the most valuable.

In addition, once a product becomes mature, time-series analysis will be valuable, as will causal methods, which predict long-term sales performance based on estimates of economic data.

Finally, the quality of forecasts can frequently be improved by combining a variety of the techniques described in this section. Georgoff and Murdick observe that "the results of combined forecasts greatly surpass most individual projections, techniques, should read and analysis by experts"[93]. This is particularly true since it is generally difficult to tell *a priori* which of several available forecasting techniques will work best for a given situation.

SUMMARY

Matching supply and demand in the supply chain is a critical challenge. To reduce cost and provide the required service level, it is important to take into account inventory holding and setup costs, lead time, and lead time variability and forecast demand. Unfortunately, the so-called *first rule* of inventory management states that *forecast demand is always wrong*. Thus, a single number, forecast demand, is not enough when determining an effective inventory policy. Indeed, the inventory management strategies described in this chapter also take into account information about demand variability.

The *second rule* of inventory management is that *the longer the forecast horizon, the worse is the forecast.* This implies that the accuracy of weekly forecast decreases as the forecast horizon increases.

The *third rule* of inventory management is that *aggregate demand information is always more accurate than disaggregate data*. That is, aggregate demand data have much smaller variability. This is exactly the basis for the risk pooling concept that enables lower inventory level without affecting service level.

Of course, although forecasting has many weaknesses, it is important to develop a forecast that is as effective as possible. There are a variety of approaches that are useful for improving forecasts.

In this chapter, we discussed inventory management in systems with a central manager. Of course, in many cases, different managers or companies own or operate different parts of the supply chain. In Chapter 4, we discuss contracts and strategies to manage inventory effectively in these decentralized systems.

DISCUSSION QUESTIONS

1. Answer the following questions about the case at the start of the chapter.

a. Based on the spreadsheet data, how would you characterize Steel Works' products? What about Steel Works' customers? Given your answer and the information in the case what does this suggest?

b. What does the coefficient of variation tell us? Can you determine the coefficient of variation for the DuraBend™ and DuraFlex™ product lines?

c. How much inventory has Steel Works been holding? How much should they have been holding?

d. Although no data is given for the Custom Products division, are there any obvious opportunities that are suggested by the information in the case?

2. How can firms cope with huge variability in customer demand?

3. What is the relationship between service and inventory levels?

4. What is the impact of lead time, and lead time variability, on inventory levels?

5. What factors should management consider when determining a target service level?

6. Consider the (Q, R) policy analyzed in Section 2.2.6. Explain why the expected level of inventory before receiving the order is

$$z \times STD \times \sqrt{L}$$

while the expected level of inventory immediately after receiving the order is

$$Q + z \times STD \times \sqrt{L}$$

7. Consider the base-stock policy analyzed in Section 2.2.8. Explain why the expected level of inventory after receiving an order is equal to

$$r \times AVG + z \times STD \times \sqrt{r + L}$$

while the expected level of inventory before an order arrives is

$$z \times STD \times \sqrt{r + L}$$

8. Imagine that you operate a department store. List five products you sell, and order them from lowest target service level to highest target service level. Justify your ordering.

9. Consider a supply chain consisting of a single manufacturing facility, a cross-dock, and two retail outlets. Items are shipped from the manufacturing facility to the cross-dock facility and from there to the retail outlets. Let L_1 be the lead time from the factory to the cross-dock facility and L_2 be the lead time from the cross-dock facility to each retail outlet. Let $L = L_1 + L_2$. In the analysis below, we fix L and vary L_1 and L_2.

a. Compare the amount of safety stock in two systems, one in which lead time from the cross-dock facility to a retail outlet is zero (i.e., $L_1 = L$ and $L_2 = 0$) and a second system in which the lead time from the factory to the cross-dock facility is equal to zero (i.e., $L_1 = 0$ and $L_2 = L$).

b. To reduce safety stock, should the cross-dock facility be closer to the factory or the retail outlets? For this purpose, analyze the impact of increasing L_1, and therefore decreasing L_2, on total safety stock.

10. Suppose you are selecting a supplier. Would you prefer a supplier with a short but highly variable delivery lead time or a supplier with a longer but less variable lead time?

11. Although we typically model inventory-related costs as either fixed or variable, in the real world the situation is more complex. Discuss some inventory-related costs that are fixed in the short term but may be considered variable if a longer time horizon is considered.

12. When is a model such as the *economic lot sizing* model, which ignores randomness, useful?

13. What are the penalties of facing highly variable demand? Are there any advantages?

14. Give a specific example of risk pooling (a) across locations, (b) across time, and (c) across products. You may select a local auto or FMCG supply chain.

15. When would you expect demand for a product in two stores to be positively correlated? When would you expect it to be negatively correlated?

16. Consider the first Walkman™ model introduced by Sony. Discuss which forecasting approach would be most useful at the start, in the middle, and toward the end of the product life cycle. Now, consider a more recent Apple iPod model. How would your assessment of the appropriate forecasting techniques change?

17. **Technical question:** KLF Electronics is an American manufacturer of electronic equipment. The company has a single manufacturing facility in San Jose, California. KLF Electronics distributes its products through five regional warehouses located in Atlanta, Boston, Chicago, Dallas, and Los Angeles. In the current distribution system, the United States is partitioned into five major markets, each of which is served by a single regional warehouse. Customers, typically retail outlets, receive items directly from the regional warehouse in their market. That is, in the current distribution system, each customer is assigned to a single market and receives deliveries from one regional warehouse.

The warehouses receive items from the manufacturing facility. Typically, it takes about two weeks to satisfy an order placed by any of the regional warehouses. Currently, KLF provides their customers with a service level of about 90 percent. In recent years, KLF has seen a significant increase in competition and huge pressure from their customers to improve the service level and reduce costs. To improve the service level and reduce costs, KLF would like to consider an alternative distribution strategy in which the five regional warehouses are replaced with a single, central warehouse that will be in charge of all customer orders. This warehouse should be one of the existing warehouses. The company CEO insists that whatever distribution strategy is used, KLF will design the strategy so that service level is increased to about 97 percent.

Answer the following three questions:

a. A detailed analysis of customer demand in the five market areas reveals that the demand in the five regions is very similar; that is, it is common that if weekly demand in one region is above average, so is the weekly demand in the other regions. How does this observation affect the attractiveness of the new system?

b. To perform a rigorous analysis, you have identified a typical product, Product A. Table 2-11 provides historical data and includes weekly demand for this product for the last 12 weeks in each of the market areas. An order (placed by a warehouse to the factory) costs $5,550 (per order), and holding inventory costs $1.25 per unit per week. In the current distribution system, the cost of transporting a product from the manufacturing facility to a warehouse is given in

TABLE 2-11

HISTORICAL DATA

	Week											
	1	2	3	4	5	6	7	8	9	10	11	12
Atlanta	33	45	37	38	55	30	18	58	47	37	23	55
Boston	26	35	41	40	46	48	55	18	62	44	30	45
Chicago	44	34	22	55	48	72	62	28	27	95	35	45
Dallas	27	42	35	40	51	64	70	65	55	43	38	47
Los Angeles	32	43	54	40	46	74	40	35	45	38	48	56

TABLE 2-12

TRANSPORTATION COSTS PER UNIT PRODUCT

Warehouse	Inbound	Outbound
Atlanta	12	13
Boston	11.50	13
Chicago	11	13
Dallas	9	13
Los Angeles	7	13

TABLE 2-13

TRANSPORTATION COSTS PER UNIT IN CENTRALIZED SYSTEM

Warehouse	Atlanta	Boston	Chicago	Dallas	Los Angeles
Atlanta	13	14	14	15	17
Boston	14	13	8	15	17
Chicago	14	8	13	15	16
Dallas	15	15	15	13	8
Los Angeles	17	17	16	8	13

Table 2-12 (see the column "Inbound"). Table 2-12 also provides information about transportation cost per unit from each warehouse to the stores in its market area (see the column "Outbound"). Finally, Table 2-13 provides information about transportation costs per unit product from each existing regional warehouse to all other market areas, assuming this regional warehouse becomes the central warehouse.

Suppose you are to compare the two systems for Product A only; what is your recommendation? To answer this question, you should compare costs and average inventory levels for the two strategies assuming demands occur according to the historical data. Also, you should determine which regional warehouse will be used as the centralized warehouse.

c. It is proposed that in the centralized distribution strategy, that is, the one with a single warehouse, products will be distributed using UPS Ground Service, which guarantees that products will arrive at the warehouse in three days (0.5 week). Of course, in this case, transportation cost for shipping a unit product from a manufacturing facility to the warehouse increases. In fact, in this case, transportation costs increase by 50 percent. Thus, for instance, shipping one unit from the manufacturing facility to Atlanta will cost $18.Would you recommend using this strategy? Explain your answer.

CASE: Sport Obermeyer

Aspen, Colorado

Wally Obermeyer deftly balanced his office keys and a large printout of forecasting data as he wheeled his mountain bike through the front entrance of Sport Obermeyer's headquarters in Aspen, Colorado. It was a crisp November morning in 1992; Wally paused for just a moment to savor the fresh air and beauty of the surrounding mountains before closing the door behind him.

Wally had arrived at work early to start one of the most critical tasks Sport Obermeyer, a fashion skiwear manufacturer, faced each year—committing to specific production quantities for each skiwear item the company would offer in the coming year's line. The task required carefully blending analysis, experience, intuition, and sheer speculation. This morning Sport Obermeyer would start to make firm commitments for producing its 1993–1994 line of fashion skiwear with scant information about how the market would react to the line. In fact, no clear indications had yet emerged about how end-consumers were responding to the company's current 1992–1993 line. Despite the attraction of waiting for market information, Wally knew that further procrastination would delay delivery to retailers and that late delivery would reduce the exposure consumers would have to Obermeyer products.

As usual, Obermeyer's new line offered strong designs, but the ultimate success of the line was highly dependent on how well the company was able to predict market response to different styles and colors. Feedback from retailers on the 1993–1994 line wouldn't begin to surface until the Las Vegas trade show next March, long after many of Obermeyer's products had entered production. Wally mused:

> How appropriate that our fate is always determined in Las Vegas. Like most fashion apparel manufacturers, we face a "fashion gamble" each year. Every fall we start manufacturing well in advance of the selling season, knowing full well that market trends may change in the meantime. Good gamblers calculate the odds before putting their money down. Similarly, whether we win or lose the fashion gamble on a particular ski parka depends on how accurately we predict each parka's salability.

Inaccurate forecasts of retailer demand had become a growing problem at Obermeyer: in recent years greater product variety and more intense competition had made accurate predictions increasingly difficult. Two scenarios resulted—both painful. On one hand, at the end of each season, the company was saddled with excess merchandise for those styles and colors that retailers had not purchased; styles with the worst selling records were sold at deep discounts, often well below their manufactured cost. On the other hand, the company frequently ran out of its most popular items; although popular products were clearly desirable, considerable income was lost each year because of the company's inability to predict which products would become best-sellers.

Wally sat down at his desk and reflected on the results of the day-long "Buying Committee" meeting he had organized the previous day. This year Wally had changed the company's usual practice of having the committee, which comprised six key Obermeyer managers, make production commitments based on the group's consensus. Instead, hoping to gather more complete information, he had asked each member independently to forecast retailer demand for each Obermeyer product. Now it was up to him to make use of the forecasts generated by the individuals in the group. He winced as he noted the discrepancies between different committee members' forecasts. How could he best use the results of yesterday's efforts to make appropriate production commitments for the coming year's line?

A second issue Wally faced was how to allocate production between factories in Hong Kong and China. Last year, almost a third of Obermeyer's parkas had been made in China, all by independent subcontractors in Shenzhen. This year, the company planned to produce half of its parkas in China, continuing production by subcontractors, and starting production in a new plant in Lo Village, Guangdong. Labor costs in China were extremely low, yet Wally had some concerns about the quality and reliability of Chinese operations. He also knew that plants in China typically required larger minimum order quantities than those in Hong Kong and were subject to stringent quota restrictions by the U.S. government. How should he incorporate all of these differences into a well-founded decision about where to source each product?

Tsuen Wan, New Territories, Hong Kong

Raymond Tse, managing director, Obersport Limited, was anxiously awaiting Sport Obermeyer's orders for the 1993–1994 line. Once the orders arrived, he would have to translate them quickly into requirements for specific components and then place appropriate component orders with vendors. Any delay would cause problems: increased pressure on his relationships with vendors, overtime at his or his subcontractors' factories, or even late delivery to Sport Obermeyer.

Obersport Ltd. was a joint venture established in 1985 by Klaus Obermeyer and Raymond Tse to coordinate production of Sport Obermeyer products in the Far East. (See Figure 2-15.) Obersport was responsible for fabric and component sourcing for Sport Obermeyer's entire production in the Far East. The materials were then cut and sewn either in Raymond Tse's own "Alpine" factories or in independent subcontractors located in Hong Kong, Macau, and China. Raymond was owner and president of Alpine Ltd., which included skiwear manufacturing plants in Hong Kong as well as a recently established facility in China. Sport Obermeyer's orders represented about 80 percent of Alpine's annual production volume.

Lo Village, Guangdong, China

Raymond Tse and his cousin, Shiu Chuen Tse, gazed with pride and delight at the recently completed factory complex. Located among a wide expanse of rice paddies at the perimeter of Lo Village, the facility would eventually provide jobs, housing, and recreational facilities for more than 300 workers. This facility was Alpine's first direct investment in manufacturing capacity in China.

Shiu Chuen had lived in Lo Village all of his life—the Tse family had resided there for generations. Raymond's parents, former landowners

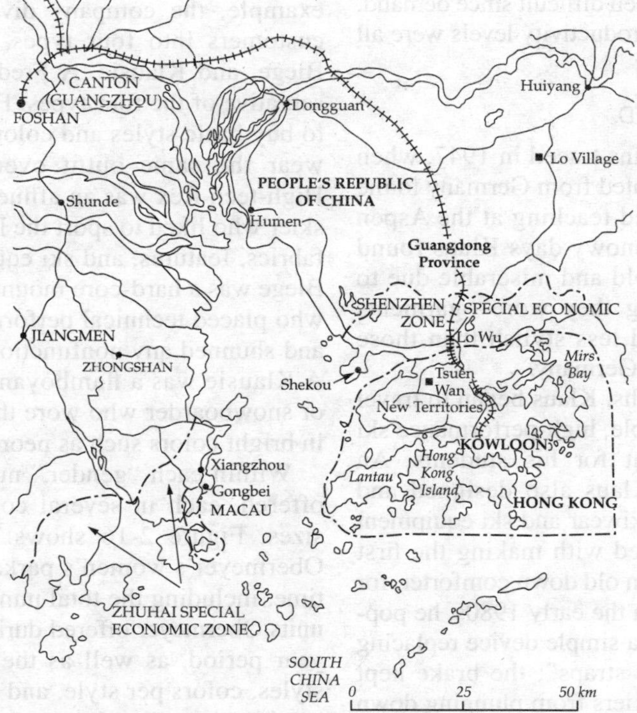

FIGURE 2-15 Map of facilities (Hong Kong and Guangdong).

in the village, had moved to Hong Kong before Raymond was born, returning to the village for several years when Raymond was a young boy during the Japanese occupation of Hong Kong in World War II. In 1991, Raymond Tse had visited Lo Village for the first time in over 40 years. The villagers were delighted to see him. In addition to their personal joy at seeing Raymond, they hoped to convince him to bring some of his wealth and managerial talent to Lo Village. After discussions with people in the community, Raymond decided to build the factory, so far investing over US$1 million in the facility.

Working with Alpine's Hong Kong management, Shiu Chuen had hired 200 workers for the factory's first full year of operation. The workers had come from the local community as well as distant towns in neighboring provinces; most had now arrived and were in training in the plant. Shiu Chuen hoped he had planned appropriately for the orders Alpine's customers would assign to the plant this year; planning had been difficult since demand, worker skill levels, and productivity levels were all hard to predict.

SPORT OBERMEYER, LTD.

Sport Obermeyer's origins traced in 1947, when Klaus Obermeyer emigrated from Germany to the United States and started teaching at the Aspen Ski School. On frigid, snowy days Klaus found many of his students cold and miserable due to the impractical clothing they wore—garments both less protective and less stylish than those skiers wore in his native Germany.

During summer months, Klaus began to travel to Germany to find durable, high-performance ski clothing and equipment for his students. An engineer by training, Klaus also designed and introduced a variety of skiwear and ski equipment products; he was credited with making the first goose-down vest out of an old down comforter, for example, in the 1950s. In the early 1980s, he popularized the "ski brake," a simple device replacing cumbersome "run-away straps"; the brake kept skis that had fallen off skiers from plunging down the slopes. Over the years, Sport Obermeyer developed into a preeminent competitor in the U.S. skiwear market: estimated sales in 1992 were $32.8 million. The company held a commanding 45 percent share of the children's skiwear market and an 11 percent share of the adult skiwear market. Columbia Sportswear was a lower-price, high-volume-per-style competitor whose sales had increased rapidly during the previous three years. By 1992 Columbia had captured about 23 percent of the adult ski-jacket market.

Obermeyer offered a broad line of fashion ski apparel, including parkas, vests, ski suits, shells, ski pants, sweaters, turtlenecks, and accessories. Parkas were considered the most critical design component of a collection; the other garments were fashioned to match their style and color.

Obermeyer products were offered in five different "genders": men's, women's, boys', girls', and preschoolers'. The company segmented each "gender" market according to price, type of skier, and how "fashion-forward" the market was. For example, the company divided its adult male customers into four types, dubbed Fred, Rex, Biege, and Klausie. A Fred was the most conservative of the four types; Freds had a tendency to buy basic styles and colors and were likely to wear the same outfit over multiple seasons. High-tech Rex was an affluent, image-conscious skier who liked to sport the latest technologies in fabrics, features, and ski equipment. In contrast, Biege was a hard-core mountaineering-type skier who placed technical performance above all else and shunned any nonfunctional design elements. A Klausie was a flamboyant, high-profile skier or snowboarder who wore the latest styles, often in bright colors such as neon pink or lime green.

Within each "gender," numerous styles were offered, each in several colors and a range of sizes. Figure 2-16 shows how the variety of Obermeyer's women's parkas had changed over time, including the total number of stockkeeping units Obermeyer offered during the preceding 16-year period, as well as the average number of styles, colors per style, and sizes per style-color combination offered.

Obermeyer competed by offering an excellent price/value relationship, where value was defined as both functionality and style, and targeted the middle to high end of the skiwear market. Unlike some of its competitors who made outerwear for both skiing and casual "street wear," Obermeyer sold the vast majority (over 85 percent) of its products to customers for use while skiing. Functionality was critical to the serious skier: products had to be warm and waterproof, yet not constrain the skier's ability to move his or her arms and legs freely.

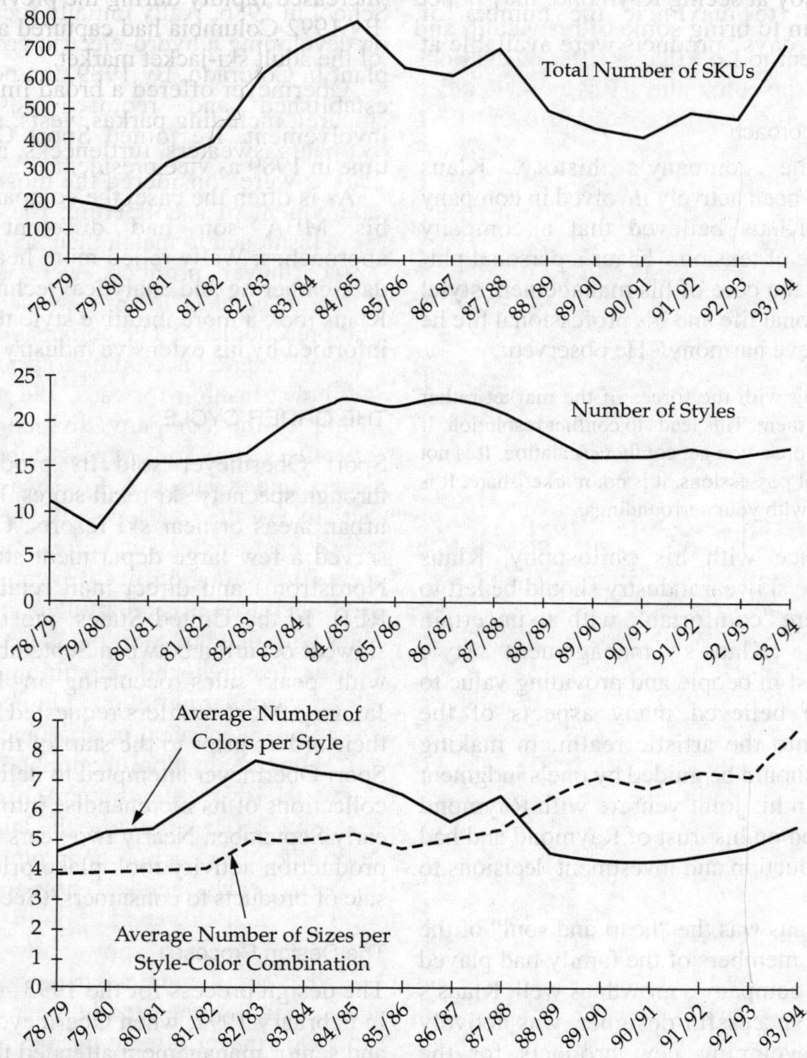

FIGURE 2-16 Product variety, Obermeyer women's parkas.

Note:

An example of a "style" is a Stardust parka.

An example of a "style-color combination" is a red Stardust parka.

An example of an "SKU" (stockkeeping unit) is a size 8, petite, red Stardust parka.

Management believed that the effective implementation of its product strategy relied on several logistics-related activities, including delivering matching collections of products to retailers at the same time (to allow consumers to view and purchase coordinated items at the same time) and delivering products to retail stores early in the selling season (to maximize the number of "squarefootage days" products were available at retail).

Management Approach

Throughout the company's history, Klaus Obermeyer had been actively involved in company management. Klaus believed that a company should run "free of tension." Klaus's personal philosophy was at the core of his management style; in both his personal life and his professional life he sought to "achieve harmony." He observed:

> We're blending with the forces of the market rather than opposing them. This leads to conflict resolution. If you oppose a force, you get conflict escalation. It is not money, it is not possessions, it is not market share. It is to be at peace with your surroundings.

In accordance with his philosophy, Klaus believed that the skiwear industry should be left to people who were "comfortable with an uncertain bottom line." Klaus's management style emphasized trust in people and providing value to customers. He believed many aspects of the business fell into the artistic realm; in making decisions, one should be guided by one's judgment and intuition. In his joint venture with Raymond Tse, Klaus relied on his trust of Raymond and had always left production and investment decisions to Raymond.

Although Klaus was the "heart and soul" of the company, other members of the family had played key roles in the company's growth as well. Klaus's wife, Nome, a successful designer, was actively involved in developing new products for the company. In Klaus's judgment, Nome had a "feel" for fashion—Klaus had relied heavily on her judgment in assessing the relative popularity of various designs.

In recent years, Klaus's son Wally had become actively involved in managing the company's internal operations. After completing high school, Wally combined working part time for the company with ski-patrolling on Aspen Mountain for six years, before entering college in 1980. After graduating from the Harvard Business School in 1986, Wally initially focused his efforts on developing a hydro-electric power-generating plant in Colorado. By 1989, the power plant was established and required less day-to-day involvement. He joined Sport Obermeyer full time in 1989 as vice president.

As is often the case, the company founder and his MBA son had different management approaches: Wally relied more heavily on formal data-gathering and analytical techniques, whereas Klaus took a more intuitive style that was heavily informed by his extensive industry experience.

THE ORDER CYCLE

Sport Obermeyer sold its products primarily through specialty ski-retail stores, located either in urban areas or near ski resorts. Obermeyer also served a few large department stores (including Nordstrom) and direct mail retailers (including REI). In the United States, most retail sales of skiwear occurred between September and January, with peak sales occurring in December and January. Most retailers requested full delivery of their orders prior to the start of the retail season; Sport Obermeyer attempted to deliver coordinated collections of its merchandise into retail stores by early September. Nearly two years of planning and production activity took place prior to the actual sale of products to consumers. (See Table 2-14.)

The Design Process

The design process for the 1993–1994 line began in February 1992, when Obermeyer's design team and senior management attended the annual international outdoorswear show in Munich, Germany, where they viewed current European offerings. "Europe is more fashion-forward than the United States," Klaus noted. "Current European styles are

TABLE 2-14

PLANNING AND PRODUCTION CYCLE, OBERMEYER 1993–1994 LINE

Month	Design activities	Order receipt and production planning	Materials management	Production	Retail activities
Jan 92					
Feb 92	Design process begins				
Mar 92	Las Vegas show for 92–93.				
Apr 92					
May 92	Concepts finalized				
Jun 92					
Jul 92	Sketches sent to Obersport		Order greige fabric		
Aug 92				Prototype production	
Sep 92	Designs finalized			Prototype production	
Oct 92				Sample production	
Nov 92		Place *first* production order with Obersport	Receive first order • Calculate fabric and component requirements • Order components • Place print/dye orders	Sample production	
Dec 92				Sample production	
Jan 93			Chinese New Year vac.	Chinese New Year vac.	
Feb 93				Full-scale production	
Mar 93		Las Vegas Show for 93–94 line (80% of retailers' initial orders received) Place *second* production order with Obersport	Receive second order • Calculate fabric and component requirements • Order components • Place print/dye orders	Full-scale production	
Apr 93		Additional retailer orders received		Full-scale production	
May 93		Additional retailer orders received		Full-scale production	
Jun 93		Additional retailer orders received		Full-scale production Ship finished goods	
Jul 93				Full-scale production Ship finished goods	
Aug 93				Full-scale production Air freight finished goods	93–94 line delivered to retail
Sep 93					Retail selling period
Oct 93					Retail selling period
Nov 93					Retail selling period
Dec 93		Retailer replenishment orders received			Peak retail selling period
Jan 94		Retailer replenishment orders received			Peak retail selling period
Feb 94		Retailer replenishment orders received			Retail selling period
Mar 94					Retail selling period
Apr 94					Retail selling period

often good indicators of future American fashions." In addition, each year, a major trade show for ski equipment and apparel was held in Las Vegas. The March 1992 Las Vegas show had provided additional input to the design process for the 1993–1994 line. By May 1992, the design concepts were finalized; sketches were sent to Obersport for prototype production in July. Prototypes were usually made from leftover fabric from the previous year since the prototype garments would be used only internally by Obermeyer management for decision-making purposes. Obermeyer refined the designs based on the prototypes and finalized designs by September 1992.

Sample Production

As soon as designs were finalized, Obersport began production of sample garments—small quantities of each style-color combination for the sales force to show to retailers. In contrast to prototypes, samples were made with the actual fabric to be used for final production; dyeing and printing subcontractors were willing to process small material batches for sample-making purposes. Sales representatives started to show samples to retailers during the week-long Las Vegas show, typically held in March, and then took them to retail sites throughout the rest of the spring.

Raw Material Sourcing and Production

Concurrent with sample production, Obersport determined fabric and component requirements for Obermeyers's initial production order (typically about half of Obermeyer's annual production) based on Obermeyer's bills of material. It was important that Obersport place dyeing /printing instructions and component orders quickly since some suppliers' lead times were as long as 90 days. Cutting and sewing of Obermeyer's first production order would begin in February 1993.

Retailer Ordering Process

During the Las Vegas trade show, most retailers placed their orders; Obermeyer usually received orders representing 80 percent of its annual volume by the week following the Las Vegas show. With this information in hand, Obermeyer could forecast its total demand with great accuracy (see Figure 2-17). After completing its forecast, Obermeyer placed its second and final production order. The remainder of retailers' regular (nonreplenishment) orders were received in April and May. As noted below, retailers also placed replenishment orders for popular items during the peak retail sales season.

Shipment to Obermeyer Warehouse

During June and July, Obermeyer garments were transported by ship from Obersport's Hong Kong warehouse to Seattle, from which they were trucked to Obermeyer's Denver warehouse. (Shipment took approximately six weeks.) Most goods produced in August were air-shipped to Denver to ensure timely delivery to retailers. In addition, for goods manufactured in China, air freighting was often essential due to strict quota restrictions in certain product categories. The U.S. government limited the number of units that could be imported from China into the United States. Government officials at the U.S. port of entry reviewed imports; products violating quota restrictions were sent back to the country of origin. Since quota restrictions were imposed on the total amount of a product category all companies imported from China, individual companies often rushed to get their products into the country before other firms had "used up" the available quota.

Shipment to Retail; Retail Replenishment Orders

Toward the end of August, Obermeyer shipped orders to retailers via small-package carriers such as UPS and RPS. Retail sales built gradually during September, October, and November, peaking in December and January. By December or January, retailers who identified items of which they expected to sell more than they currently had in stock often requested replenishment of those items from Obermeyer. This demand was filled if Obermeyer had the item in stock.

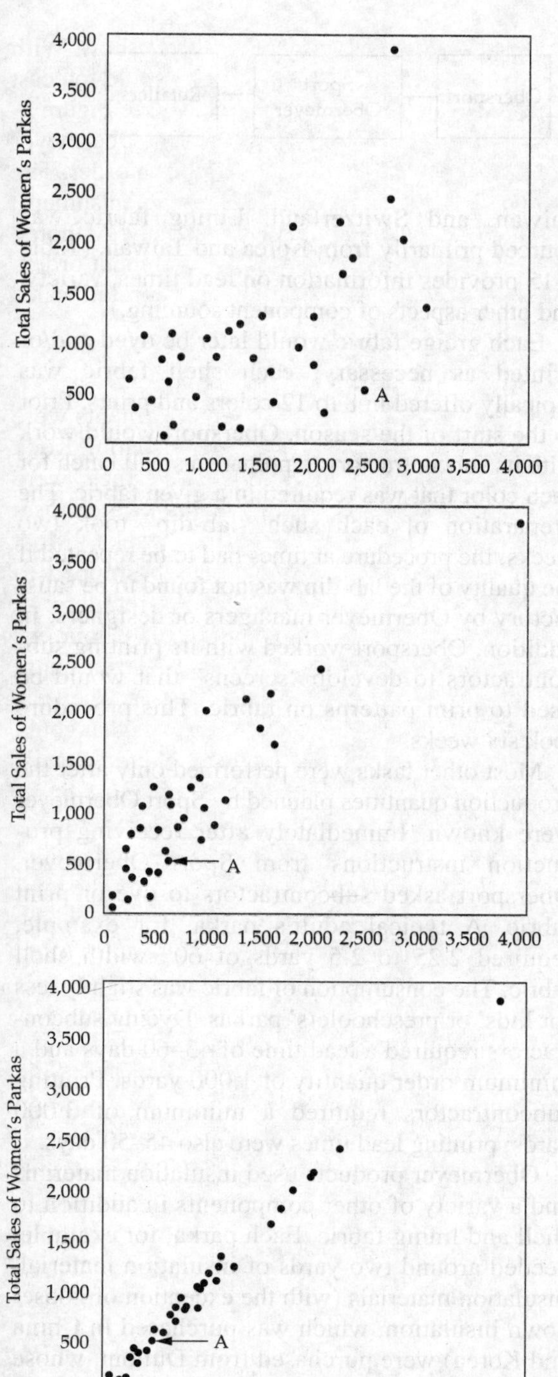

Initial Forecast

Each data point represents the forecast and actual season sales for a particular parka (at the style-color level). For example, parka A had an initial forecast of 2,500 units and season sales of 510 units.

Updated Forecast, Incorporating First 20% of Sales Data

After observing 20% of demand, the revised forecast for parka A was 575 units.

Final Forecast, Incorporating First 80% of Sales Data

After observing 80% of demand, the final forecast for parka A was 500 units.

FIGURE 2-17 How demand forecasts improve with increasing information.

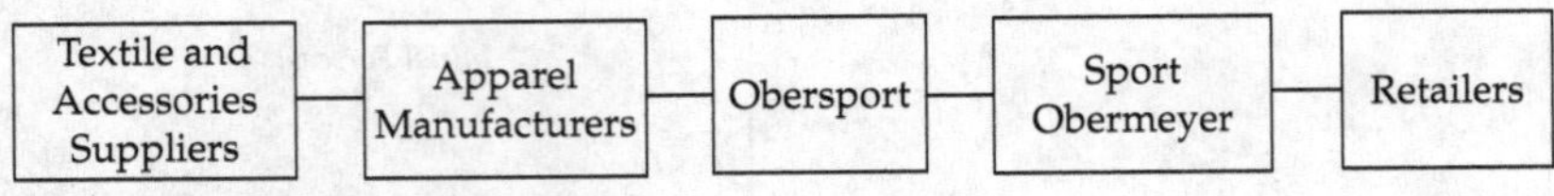

FIGURE 2-18 The supply chain.

By February Obermeyer started to offer replenishment items to retailers at a discount. Similarly, retailers started marking down prices on remaining stock in an attempt to clear their shelves by the end of the season. As the season progressed, retailers offered deeper discounts; items remaining at the end of the season were held over to the following year and sold at a loss. Obermeyer used a variety of methods to liquidate inventory at year-end, including selling large shipping containers of garments well below manufacturing cost to markets in South America and engaging in barter trade (for example, trading parkas in lieu of money for products or services used by the company, such as hotel rooms or air flights).

THE SUPPLY CHAIN

Obermeyer sourced most of its outerwear products through Obersport. (See Figure 2-18.) In recent years, Wally had worked with Obersport to "pre-position" (purchase prior to the season and hold in inventory) greige fabric[2] as part of a wider effort to cope with manufacturing lead times. To preposition the fabric, Obermeyer would contract with fabric suppliers to manufacture a specified amount of fabric of a given type each month; Obermeyer would later specify how it wanted the fabric to be dyed and/or printed. Obermeyer had to take possession of all fabric it contracted for, whether or not it was actually needed. Different types of fabrics were purchased for use as shell (outer) fabric and lining fabric. Approximately 10 types of shell fabrics were required each year. Obersport purchased shell fabric from vendors in the United States, Japan, Korea, Germany, Austria, Taiwan, and Switzerland. Lining fabric was sourced primarily from Korea and Taiwan. (Table 2-15 provides information on lead times, variety, and other aspects of component sourcing.)

Each greige fabric would later be dyed and/or printed as necessary; each shell fabric was typically offered in 8 to 12 colors and prints. Prior to the start of the season, Obersport would work with its subcontractors to prepare a small batch for each color that was required in a given fabric. The preparation of each such "lab-dip" took two weeks; the procedure at times had to be repeated if the quality of the lab-dip was not found to be satisfactory by Obermeyer managers or designers. In addition, Obersport worked with its printing subcontractors to develop "screens" that would be used to print patterns on fabric. This procedure took six weeks.

Most other tasks were performed only after the production quantities planned by Sport Obermeyer were known. Immediately after receiving production instructions from Sport Obermeyer, Obersport asked subcontractors to dye or print fabric. A typical adult's parka, for example, required 2.25 to 2.5 yards of 60" width shell fabric. The consumption of fabric was slightly less for kids' or preschoolers' parkas. Dyeing subcontractors required a lead time of 45–60 days and a minimum order quantity of 1,000 yards. Printing subcontractors required a minimum of 3,000 yards; printing lead times were also 45–50 days.

Obermeyer products used insulation materials and a variety of other components in addition to shell and lining fabric. Each parka, for example, needed around two yards of insulation material. Insulation materials (with the exception of goose-down insulation, which was purchased in China and Korea) were purchased from DuPont, whose licensees in Hong Kong, Taiwan, Korea, and China could provide them within two weeks. At

[2]Greige fabric is a fabric that has been woven or knitted but not yet dyed or printed.

TABLE 2-15

PROCUREMENT INFORMATION FOR OBERMEYER'S PARKA COMPONENTS

Component	Variety	Country of origin	Procurement lead time	Minimums	Usage per parka	Avg. % of total parka material cost
Greige Shell Fabric	10	Japan, USA, Switzerland, Germany, Austria, Korea, Taiwan	45–90 days	5,000–10,000 yards	2.2–2.5 yards per adult parka 1.5–2 yards per child's parka	30
Finishing of Shell Fabric	8–12 color-prints per fabric	Finishing takes place in country of origin (see above)	Dyeing or Printing: 45–60 days	Dyeing: 1,000 yards Printing: 3,000 yards per design, at least 1,000 yards per color in any design	2.25–2.5 yards per adult parka 1.5–2 yards per child's parka	13
Finished Lining Fabric	6	Nylon: Korea, Taiwan Fleece: Korea, Taiwan, USA	45–60 days	600–1,000 yards	2–2.5 yards per adult parka 1.25–1.75 yards per child's parka	13
Insulation	3–4 different weights used (from 80–240 grams/meter)	Hong Kong, Korea, Taiwan, China	2–3 weeks	50–100 yards	~2 yards per adult parka ~1.2–1.5 yards per child's parka	16
Zippers	400 standard tape colors 4 teeth gauges 4–5 teeth colors 2–3 teeth materials 5–6 slider types	Hong Kong, Japan	Standard (from Hong Kong): 60 days Custom (from Japan): 90+ days,	500 yards (standard colors) 1,000 yards (custom colors)	~1 yard	12
Thread	80 colors	Hong Kong	30 days	5,000 yards	2,000–3,000 yards	2
Logo Patches, Drawcords, Hang Tags, etc.	Various	Mostly from Hong Kong	15–30 days	Various	Various	10
Snaps (undyed)	10	Germany, Italy, Hong Kong	1–2 months	1,000 pieces	5–10 pieces	3
Dyeing of Snaps	50 colors	Hong Kong	15–30 days	1,000 pieces per color	5–10 pieces	1
						100

TABLE 2-16

SAMPLE—PARKA ASSEMBLY OPERATIONS FOR THE ROCOCO WOMEN'S PARKA

	HK$/Piece	Operation
1	$0.05	Male belt loop (×1).
2	$0.20	Sew front shoulder seam with invisible stitching. Quilt all over: lining (×5), front placket (×1), and collar (×2).
3	$0.50	Invisible-stitch front bellow facing (×2).
4	$0.50	Double top-stitch front bellow facing (×2).
5	$0.70	Zig-zag stitch front bellow seam (×2).
6	$2.40	Set double-jetted zipped pocket (×2) and insert D-ring (×1).
7	$0.25	Five-stitch overlock pocket bag (×2).
8	$1.00	Invisible-stitch the bottom facing of bellow, sew front shoulder pleat (×2), insert front body facing.
9	$0.40	1/4" double stitch the front and back shoulder seam (×4).
10	$0.30	Single top stitch (the middle of double top-stitching) the front and back shoulder seam (×4).
11	$4.50	Turn over the body and attach collar, sew zipper; invisible-stitch bottom and sleeve opening, leave a small opening at the bottom of left front zipper.
12	$1.00	1/4" double stitch the front zipper seam from bottom to collar top.
13	$0.50	Invisible stitch the back bellow seam (×2).
14	$0.50	1/4" double stitch the back bellow seam.
15	$0.70	Zig-zag stitch back bellow seam (×2).
16	$1.00	Join under facing of back bellow seam with invisible stitching (×2). Join front and back shoulder seam with invisible stitching (×4).
17	$0.50	Close side seam with invisible stitching, match seaming (×6).
18	$0.25	Three-stitch overlock the side seam.
19	$1.00	Sew sleeve opening, bottom hem with invisible stitching.
20	$0.80	Invisible stitch front placket seam, then 1/4" double top-stitch the placket seam.
21	$1.10	Invisible stitch the sleeve seam (×4); invisible stitch sleeve panel seam, sew pleats at sleeve panel seam (×2).
22	$0.90	1/4" double top-stitch raglan sleeve seam and sleeve panel seam (×6).
23	$0.70	Single lockstitch raglan sleeve seam and sleeve panel seam, double stitch the center of sleeve panel seam (×6).
24	$0.70	Invisible stitch the armhole seam (×2), match the notch of armhole seam (×2).
25	$0.50	Double stitch armhole seam (×2).
26	$0.40	Single lockstitch raglan sleeve seam and sleeve panel seat, double stitch the center of sleeve panel seam (×6).
27	$0.60	Single lockstitch to close bottom hem facing (×1), insert the drawstring to bottom hem.
28	$0.60	Invisible stitch sleeve opening, insert/sew elastic to sleeve opening (×2).
29	$1.00	Sew collar facing (×1), invisible stitch the collar top, close bottom of collar, insert belt loop, change thread.
30	$0.25	1/4" double needle stitch at middle part of placket (×1).
31	$0.35	Zig-zag stitch at the center of double needle stitch at placket (×1).
32	$0.80	Running stitch to close the end of filled placket (×1).
33	$0.20	Sew main label, and insert the label at side seam, and then sew size label.
34	$0.80	Sew the inside pocket: pocket with zipper at left, pocket with Velcro at right.
35	$0.20	Set front facing with 1/16" edge stitching (×2).
36	$1.70	Three-stitch overlock lining pocket bag (×2).
37	$1.60	Sew triangular stitching at ends of zipper facing, invisible stitch at zipper facing seam, turn out and 1/16" edge-stitching (×1).
38	$1.30	Sew 13 top stitching at the lining body.
39	$1.40	Five-stitch overlock the lining body.
40	$0.80	Set shoulder pad (×2).

Total Average Labor Cost for the Rococo parka = HK$78. (Column does not add—some operations were performed multiple times to completely assemble one parka.)

*For this parka, the subcomponents described in steps 1 and 2 were completed by outside subcontractors.

TABLE 2-17

COMPARISON OF OPERATIONS IN HONG KONG AND CHINA

Topic	Hong Kong	China
Hourly wage	HK$30	RMB 0.91
Exchange rate	HK$7.8 = US$1	RMB (Renminbi) 5.7 = US$1
Working hours	8 hours/day, 6 days/week	9 hours/day, 6.5 days/week
	⇒ Total = 48 hours/week	⇒ Total = 58.5 hours/week
	Maximum overtime allowed = 200 hours/year	During peak production periods, workers work 13 hours/day, 6.5 days/week
Weekly (nonpeak) output/worker	19 parkas	12 parkas
Actual labor content per parka (including repair work)	~2.35 hours	~3.6 hours
Paid labor time per parka (including repair work)	~2.53 hours/parka	~4.88 hours/parka
Labor cost/garment	HK$75.6	RMB 4.45
Line configuration	10–12 people/line	40 people/line
Training	Cross-trained	Trained for single operation only
Minimum order quantity	600 units in same style	1,200 units in same style
Repair rate	1–2%	~10%
Challenges	• Wage Rate • Workforce: • Low unemployment (~2%) • Younger workers prefer office jobs	• Workforce: • Less quality and cleanliness conscious • Training requirements

the beginning of each year, Obersport gave DuPont an estimate of its annual requirement for each type of insulation.

Obersport also had to ensure the availability of a variety of other components such as D-rings, buckles, snaps, buttons, zippers, pull-strings with attached castings, and various labels and tags. Buckles, D-rings, pull-strings, and buttons were procured locally in Hong Kong and had a 15- to 30-day lead time. Many snaps were purchased from German vendors; since snap lead times were long, Obersport kept an inventory of snaps and dyed them locally as needed. Labels and tags had short lead times and were relatively inexpensive; Obersport generally carried excess stock of these materials.

TABLE 2-18

COST INFORMATION FOR ROCOCO PARKA (MADE IN HONG KONG)

Obermeyer Landed Cost	
Cost FOB Obersport[a]	$49.90
Agent's Fee (to Obersport, 7%)	$3.49
Freight (Ocean Carrier)[b]	$1.40
Duty, Insurance, and Miscellaneous	$5.29
Total Landed Cost	**$60.08**
Cost FOB Obersport:	
Material	$30.00
Labor	$10.00
Hong Kong Quota, Obersport Profit and Overhead	$9.90
Total	$49.90

All figures in US Dollars.
[a]FOB (free on board) Obersport means that Obermeyer paid for freight and owned the products while they were in-transit.
[b]If transportation by air, cost would be approximately $5.00 per parka.

TABLE 2-19

ESTIMATED COST INFORMATION FOR ROCOCO PARKA (IF ASSEMBLED IN CHINA)

Obermeyer landed cost	
Cost FOB Obersport[a]	$42.64
Agent's fee (to Obersport, 7%)	$2.98
Freight (Ocean Carrier)[b]	$1.40
Duty, insurance, and miscellaneous	$4.90
Total landed cost	**$51.92**
Cost FOB Obersport:	
Material	$30.00
Labor	$0.78
Transportation within China and China Overhead	$2.00
China Quota, Obersport Profit and Overhead	$9.90
Total	$42.68

All figures in US Dollars.
[a]FOB (free on board) Obersport means that Obermeyer paid for freight and owned the products while they were in-transit.
[b]If transportation by air, cost would be approximately $5.00 per parka.

Most zippers were purchased from YKK, a large Japanese zipper manufacturer. Obersport used a wide variety of zipper types each year. Zippers varied by length, tape color, and slider shape as well as the gauge, color, and material of the zipper teeth. Approximately 60 percent of Obersport's zipper requirements were sourced from YKK's Hong Kong factory, where standard zippers were manufactured. The lead time for these zippers was 60 days. The remainder was nonstandard zippers, which were sourced from Japan with at least 90-day lead times—sometimes longer. YKK required a minimum order quantity of 500 yards if the dyeing color was a standard color from its catalog; if not, the minimum order quantity was 1,000 yards. All production materials were received by Obersport; materials for any given style were then collected and dispatched to the factory where the particular style was to be cut and sewn. Obermeyer products were produced in a number of different factories in Hong Kong and China.

Cut and Sew

A typical Obermeyer product required many cutting and sewing steps. (Table 2-16 shows the sequence of sewing operations for the Rococo parka.) The allocation of operations to workers differed from one factory to another depending on the workers' level of skill and the degree of worker cross-training. Workers in Hong Kong worked about 50 percent faster than their Chinese counterparts. In addition to being more highly skilled, Hong Kong workers were typically trained in a broader range of tasks. Thus, a parka line in Hong Kong that required 10 workers to complete all operations might require 40 workers in China. Longer production lines in China led to greater imbalance in these lines; hence, a Hong Kong sewer's actual output during a given period of time was nearly twice that of a Chinese worker. (See Table 2-17 for a comparison of Hong Kong and China operations. The cost components of the Rococo parka, which was produced in Hong Kong, are shown in Table 2-18. Table 2-19 shows the estimated cost of producing the Rococo in China. Obermeyer sold the Rococo parka to retailers at a wholesale price of $112.50; retailers then priced the parka at $225.)

Workers were paid on a piece-rate basis in both China and Hong Kong: the piece rate was calculated to be consistent with competitive wages rates in the respective communities. Wages in China were much lower than in Hong Kong; an average sewer in a Guangdong sewing factory earned US$0.16 per hour compared with US$3.84 per hour in the Alpine factory in Hong Kong.

Workers in Hong Kong were also able to ramp up production faster than the Chinese workers. This ability, coupled with shorter production lines, enabled the Hong Kong factory to produce smaller order quantities efficiently. For parkas, the minimum production quantity for a style was 1,200 units in China and 600 units in Hong Kong.

Obermeyer produced about 200,000 parkas each year. The maximum capacity available to the company for cutting and sewing was 30,000 units a month; this included the production capacity at all factories available to make Sport Obermeyer products.

Obersport was responsible for monitoring production and quality at all subcontractor factories.

Workers from Obersport inspected randomly selected pieces from each subcontractor's production before the units were shipped to the United States.

PRODUCTION PLANNING

Wally's immediate concern was to determine an appropriate production commitment for the first half of Obermeyer's projected demand for the 1993–1994 season. He had estimated that Obermeyer earned 24 percent of wholesale price (pre-tax) on each parka it sold, and that units left unsold at the end of the season were sold at a loss that averaged 8 percent of wholesale price. Thus, for example, on a parka style such as the Rococo, which had a wholesale selling price of $112.50, Obermeyer's expected profit on each parka sold was approximately 24%($112.50) = $27, and its expected loss on each parka left unsold was approximately 8%($112.50) = $9.

A Sample Problem

To build his intuition about how to make production decisions, he decided to look at a smaller version of the company's problem. He looked at the Buying Committee's forecasts for the sample of 10 women's parkas[3] (see Table 2-20.) Since these 10 styles represented about 10 percent of Obermeyer's total demand, to make this smaller version representative of the larger problem, he assumed he had cutting and sewing capacity of 3,000 units per month (10 percent of actual capacity) during the seven-month production period. Using these assumptions, Wally needed to commit 10,000 units for the first phase of production. The remaining 10,000 units could be deferred until after the Las Vegas show.

Wally studied the Buying Committee's forecasts, wondering how he could estimate the risk associated with early production of each style. Was there some way he could use the differences among each member's forecast as a measure of demand uncertainty? An examination of demand from previous years indicated that forecast accuracy was the highest for those styles for which the Buying Committee had the highest level of agreement. (Technically, he found that the

[3]When the Buying Committee convened, Wally had asked each member to forecast sales so that each member's total forecast summed to a specified aggregate figure (for parkas, 200,000 units). Similarly, the forecasts in the sample problem had been scaled to sum to 20,000 units.

TABLE 2.20

SAMPLE BUYING COMMITTEE FORECASTS, 10 STYLES OF WOMEN'S PARKAS

		Individual forecasts								
Style	Price[a]	Laura	Carolyn	Greg	Wendy	Tom	Wally	Average forecast	Standard deviation	2 × standard deviation
Gail	$110	900	1,000	900	1,300	800	1,200	1,017	194	388
Isis	$99	800	700	1,000	1,600	950	1,200	1,042	323	646
Entice	$80	1,200	1,600	1,500	1,550	950	1,350	1,358	248	496
Assault	$90	2,500	1,900	2,700	2,450	2,800	2,800	2,525	340	680
Teri	$123	800	900	1,000	1,100	950	1,850	1,100	381	762
Electra	$173	2,500	1,900	1,900	2,800	1,800	2,000	2,150	404	807
Stephanie	$133	600	900	1,000	1,100	950	2,125	1,113	524	1,048
Seduced	$73	4,600	4,300	3,900	4,000	4,300	3,000	4,017	556	1,113
Anita	$93	4,400	3,300	3,500	1,500	4,200	2,875	3,296	1,047	2,094
Daphne	$148	1,700	3,500	2,600	2,600	2,300	1,600	2,383	697	1,349
Totals		20,000	20,000	20,000	20,000	20,000	20,000	20,000		

[a]Obermeyer's wholesale price.
Note:
Laura Kornashiewicz was marketing director; Carolyn Gray was customer service manager; Greg Hunter was production manager; Wendy Hemphill was production coordinator; Tom Tweed was a sales representative; Wally Obermeyer was vice president.

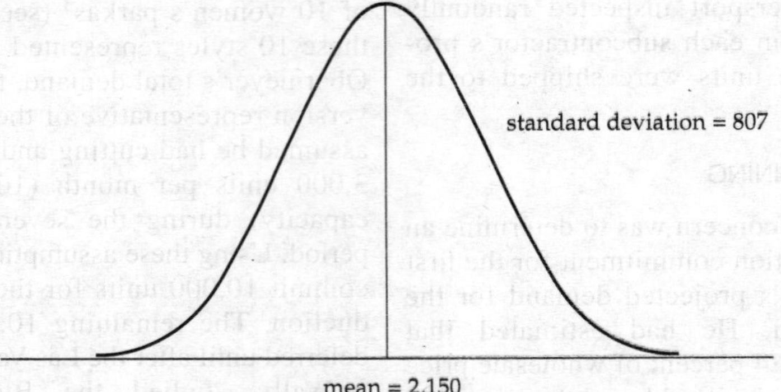

FIGURE 2-19 Forecast distribution for the Electra parka.

standard deviation of demand for a style was approximately twice the standard deviation of the Buying Committee's forecasts for that style.) With this in mind, he constructed a forecast distribution for each style as a normal random variable with the mean equal to the average of the Buying Committee member's forecasts and standard deviation twice that of the Buying Committee's forecasts (see Figure 2-19).

Where to Produce

To complete the planning decision, Wally would also need to decide which styles to make in Hong Kong and which would be better to produce in China. This year, Obermeyer expected to produce about half of all its products in China. Longer term, Wally wondered whether producing in China would constrain Obermeyer's ability to manage production and inventory risks. Would China's larger minimum order sizes limit the company's ability to increase the range of products it offered or to manage inventory risk? Was Obermeyer's trend toward increased production in China too risky given the uncertainty in China's trade relationship with the United States?

CASE DISCUSSION QUESTIONS

1. Using the sample data given in Table 2-20, make a recommendation for how many units of each style Wally should make during the initial phase of production. Assume that all of the 10 styles in the sample problem are made in Hong Kong and that Wally's initial production commitment must be at least 10,000 units. Ignore price differences among styles in your initial analysis.
2. Can you come up with a measure of risk associated with your ordering policy? This measure should be quantifiable.
3. Repeat your methodology and assume now that all 10 styles are made in China. What is the difference (if any) between the two initial production commitments?
4. What operational changes would you recommend to Wally to improve performance?
5. How should Wally think (both short-term and long-term) about sourcing in Hong Kong versus China? What kind of sourcing policy do you recommend?

CHAPTER 3

Network Planning

CASE: The Bis Corporation

The Bis Corporation is a company that produces and distributes paints. Currently, eight manufacturing plants located in cities such as Atlanta and Denver serve about 2,000 retail stores including Home Depot, Wal-Mart as well Bis-owned stores. The current distribution system is a single-tier network where all products are shipped from the plants to 17 warehouses, located all over the United States, and from there to retail accounts.

The company was established in 1964 as a family venture and grew in the 1970s and 1980s at a fairly steady rate. Bis is now owned by 12 shareholders and run by a newly appointed CEO.

Bis produces and sells about 4,000 different SKUs (stockkeeping units) at a similar price and the gross margin in the paint industry is about 20 percent. Despite high profitability, the new CEO is concerned that the supply chain is not the most efficient one. Specifically, the CEO pointed out that inbound truck utilization, inventory turns, and service levels are just too low. In a recent shareholder meeting, he pointed out that the current production and distribution strategy used by Bis was designed about 20 years ago and was never modified. It consists of the following steps:

- Produce and store at the manufacturing plants.
- Pick, load, and ship to a warehouse center.
- Unload and store at the warehouse.
- Pick, load, and deliver to stores.

Thus, the shareholders decided to look for outside help in modifying their logistics network and supply chain strategy. Your company was able to secure the engagement, after six months of continuous work by the sales division. The commitment you made when you received the engagement was to improve the effectiveness and to align the cost of service with account profitability. In your original proposal, you mentioned that "this will be accomplished by reengineering the production, inventory, and logistics functions." It seems that the concept of reengineering the entire supply chain, together with your commitment not only to the design but also to the implementation of the new strategy, is what made your proposal attractive to Bis shareholders.

Your team has identified three important issues that need to be addressed:

1. *What is the best network configuration that the Bis Corporation should use?* An important observation made early on in the analysis was that the single-tier network currently used by Bis forces low truck utilization and hence high transportation cost. It was thus proposed that Bis needs to consider replacing the logistics network with a two-tier distribution network that includes primary and secondary warehouses. In such a network, primary warehouses receive products from the plants

Source: Bis is a fictional company. The material in this case is loosely based on our experience with several companies.

and transfer inventory to secondary warehouses. The secondary warehouses in turn will serve the retail outlets. Since the number of primary warehouses is relatively small, it can potentially allow for high truck utilization and hence reduction in transportation cost. The challenge is to identify the number, locations, and size of the primary and secondary warehouses.

2. *Given the new network configuration, where should the company position inventory? How much?* Specifically, with 4,000 SKUs in this supply chain, it is not clear how inventory should be positioned. Should inventory of every SKU be positioned at every facility or should some SKUs perhaps be stocked only at the primary warehouses while others only at the secondary facilities?
3. *Which plant should produce which product?* Should each plant specialize in a few products and thus be able to produce large batches and hence reduce production cost or should plants be flexible and able to serve all retailers in close proximity, thus focusing on reducing distribution costs?

To identify the best network configuration, you have grouped the retail outlets into 550 zones and the different products into five product families. The data collected include the following:

1. Demand in 2004 by SKU per product family for each customer zone.
2. Annual production capacity (in SKUs) at each manufacturing plant.
3. Maximum capacity (SKUs) for each warehouse, new and existing.
4. Transportation costs per product family per mile for distributing products from the manufacturing plants and from the warehouses.
5. Setup cost for establishing a warehouse as well as the cost of closing an existing facility.
6. Potential locations for new warehouses.

Customer service is of particular concern to Bis because there are a number of competing products in the markets. No specific dollar figure can be attached to a specific level of service; however, the CEO insists that to remain competitive, delivery time should be no more than one day for most of the retail outlets.

The Bis Corporation has just finished a comprehensive market study that shows significant volume growth in its markets. This growth is estimated to be uniform across the different zones, but it varies from product family to product family. The estimated yearly growth for 2006 and 2007 is given in Table 3-1.

The variable production cost at the eight manufacturing facilities varies by product and by manufacturing plant. The CEO and company shareholders oppose building a new manufacturing plant because of the costs and risks involved. They are willing, however, to change the focus of different facilities so that each manufacturing facility produces the appropriate product based not only on manufacturing cost, as is currently done, but also on the entire supply chain costs, including transportation costs.

The Bis Corporation would like to address the following issues:

1. Should Bis switch from the current distribution network to a two-tier logistics network? How many primary and secondary distribution centers should be established and where should they be located?
2. Does the model used in this process truly represent Bis's logistics network? How can the Bis Corporation validate the model? What is

TABLE 3-1

ESTIMATED YEARLY GROWTH

Family	1	2	3	4	5
Multiplier	1.07	1.03	1.06	1.05	1.06

the impact of aggregating customers and products on the model accuracy?
3. What is the optimal inventory positioning strategy within the network? Should each facility keep stock of all SKUs?
4. Should Bis manufacturing strategy change to one in which each facility specializes in a few products. What is the impact of transportation cost on the manufacturing strategy?

By the end of this chapter, you should be able to understand the following issues:

- How a company can develop a model representing its logistics network.
- How a company can validate this model.
- How aggregating customers and products affects the accuracy of the model.
- How a company decides on where to position inventory.
- What the impact is of demand uncertainty and variability on inventory positioning.
- How a company sources products from its different plants in an environment with multiple facilities capable of producing multiple products.
- How a company knows whether, when, and where to expand its production capacity.

3.1 INTRODUCTION

The physical supply chain consists of suppliers, plants, warehouses, distribution centers, and retail outlets as well as raw materials, work-in-process inventory, and finished products that flow between the facilities. In Chapter 2, we discussed a variety of approaches for managing inventory in an *existing* supply chain. In this chapter, we take a step back and focus on what we call *network planning*—the process by which the firm structures and manages the supply chain in order to

- Find the right balance between inventory, transportation, and manufacturing costs.
- Match supply and demand under uncertainty by positioning and managing inventory effectively.
- Utilize resources effectively by sourcing products from the most appropriate manufacturing facility.

Of course, this is a complex process that requires a hierarchical approach in which decisions on network design, inventory positioning and management, and resource utilization are combined to reduce cost and increase service level. It is useful to divide the network planning process into three steps:

1. **Network design.** This includes decisions on the number, locations, and size of manufacturing plants and warehouses, the assignment of retail outlets to warehouses, and so forth. Major sourcing decisions also are made at this point and the typical planning horizon is a few years.
2. **Inventory positioning.** This includes identifying stocking points as well as selecting facilities that will produce to stock and thus keep inventory, and facilities that will produce to order and hence keep no inventory. These decisions are, of course, closely related to the inventory management strategies discussed in Chapter 2.
3. **Resource allocation.** Given the structure of the logistics network and the location of stocking points, the objective in this step is to determine whether production and packaging of different products is done at the right facility. What should be the plants' sourcing strategies? How much capacity should each plant have to meet seasonal demand?

In this chapter, we will analyze each of these steps and provide examples of the processes involved.

3.2 NETWORK DESIGN

Network design determines the physical configuration and infrastructure of the supply chain. As explained in Chapter 1, network design is a strategic decision that has a long-lasting effect on the firm. It involves decisions relating to plant and warehouse location as well as distribution and sourcing.

The supply chain infrastructure typically needs to be reevaluated due to changes in demand patterns, product mix, production processes, sourcing strategies, or the cost of running facilities. In addition, mergers and acquisitions may mandate the integration of different logistics networks.

In the discussion below, we concentrate on the following key strategic decisions:

1. Determining the appropriate number of facilities such as plants and warehouses.
2. Determining the location of each facility.
3. Determining the size of each facility.
4. Allocating space for products in each facility.
5. Determining sourcing requirements.
6. Determining distribution strategies, that is, the allocation of customers to each warehouse.

EXAMPLE 3.1 FCI

The Food Corporation of India (FCI) has played a major role in the public food distribution system in India. With an annual procurement and distribution of 30 to 40 million tones of foodgrains from local purchase centers, called *mandies*, it is perhaps the largest institutional buyer in the world. It was setup by the Government of India in 1964 to manage a strategic position in food grain trade, including procurement, storage, preservation, bulk transportation and finally distribution. The major objectives of FCI are provision of effective price support to farmers, distribution of food-grains through public distribution system (PDS), maintenance of satisfactory level of buffer stock of food-grain for national food security, and market intervenance in case of a need for price stabilization. Its distribution network ensures a steady food grain supply to about 5 lakhs Fair Price Shops (FPS) under PDS, which covers a mammoth 67 million cardholders. FCI also ensures steady supply of grains to a number of welfare schemes of state and central government for below poverty line (BPL) and above poverty line (APL) population of the nation. There are not many examples in supply chain area where such a large procurement and distribution system is being managed for over last 43 years with a larger perspective of socio-economic development of a nation [274, 288].

The objective is to design or reconfigure the logistics network in order to minimize annual systemwide cost, including production and purchasing costs, inventory holding costs, facility costs (storage, handling, and fixed costs), and transportation costs, subject to a variety of *service level* requirements.

In this setting, the trade-offs are clear. Increasing the number of warehouses typically yields

- An improvement in service level due to the reduction in average travel time to the customers.
- An increase in inventory costs due to increased safety stocks required to protect each warehouse against uncertainties in customer demands.
- An increase in overhead and setup costs.
- A reduction in outbound transportation costs: transportation costs from the warehouses to the customers.
- An increase in inbound transportation costs: transportation costs from the suppliers and/or manufacturers to the warehouses.

In essence, the firm must balance the costs of opening new warehouses with the advantages of being *close* to the customer. Thus, warehouse location decisions are crucial determinants of whether the supply chain is an efficient channel for the distribution of products.

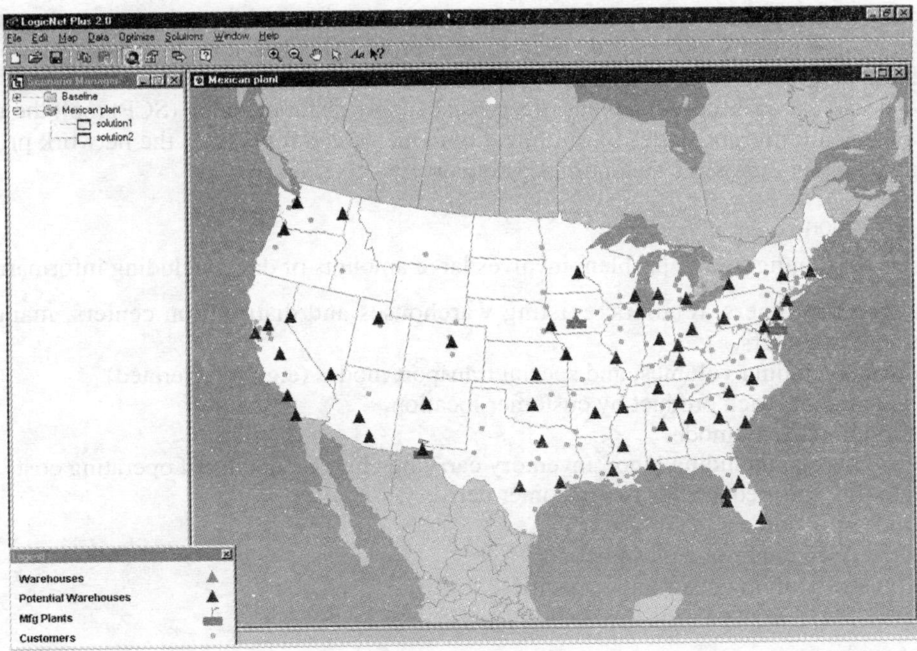

FIGURE 3-1 **The SCP screen representing data prior to optimization.**

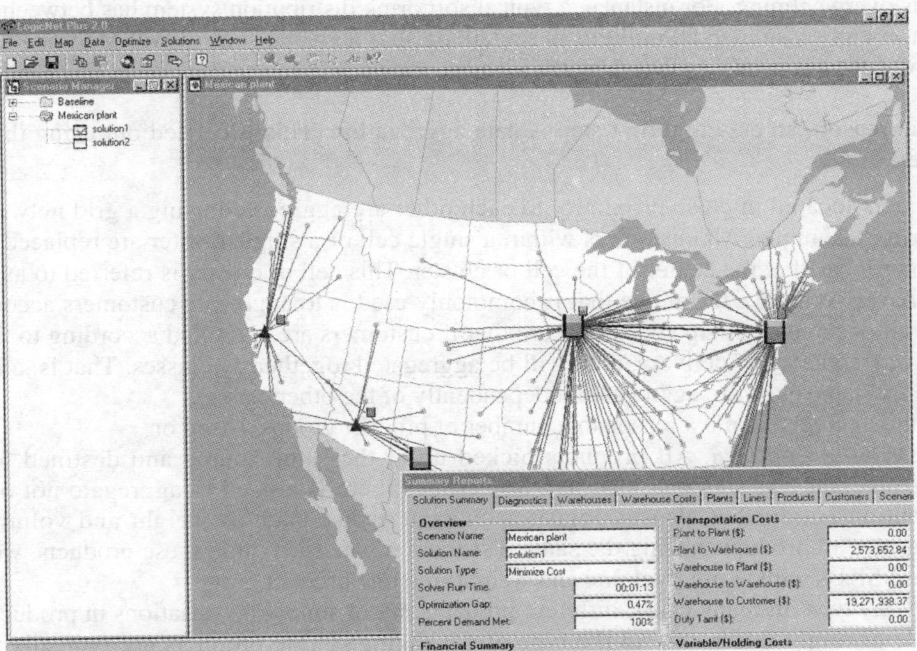

FIGURE 3-2 **The SCP screen representing the optimized logistics network.**

We describe below some of the issues related to data collection and the calculation of costs required for the optimization models. Some of the information provided is based on logistics textbooks such as [19, 120, 208].

Figures 3-1 and 3-2 present two screens of a typical supply chain planning (SCP) tool; the user would see these screens at different stages of optimization. One screen represents the network prior to optimization and the other represents the optimized network.

3.2.1 Data Collection

A typical network configuration problem involves large amounts of data, including information on

1. Locations of customers, retailers, existing warehouses and distribution centers, manufacturing facilities, and suppliers.
2. All products, including volumes, and special transport modes (e.g., refrigerated).
3. Annual demand for each product by customer location.
4. Transportation rates by mode.
5. Warehousing costs, including labor, inventory carrying charges, and fixed operating costs.
6. Shipment sizes and frequencies for customer delivery.
7. Order processing costs.
8. Customer service requirements and goals.
9. Production and sourcing costs and capacities.

3.2.2 Data Aggregation

A quick look at the above list suggests that the amount of data involved in any optimization model for this problem is overwhelming. For instance, a typical soft drink distribution system has between 10,000 and 120,000 accounts (customers). Similarly, in a retail logistics network, such as Wal-Mart or JC Penney, the number of different products that flow through the network is in the thousands or even hundreds of thousands.

For that reason, an essential first step is data aggregation. This is carried out using the following procedure:

1. Customers located in close proximity to each other are aggregated using a grid network or other clustering technique. All customers within a single cell or a single cluster are replaced by a single customer located at the center of the cell or cluster. This cell or cluster is referred to as a customer zone. A very effective technique that is commonly used is to aggregate customers according to the five-digit or three-digit zip code. Observe that if customers are classified according to their service levels or frequency of delivery, they will be aggregated together by classes. That is, all customers within the same class are aggregated independently of the other classes.
2. Items are aggregated into a reasonable number of product groups, based on
   a. *Distribution pattern*. All products picked up at the same source and destined to the same customers are aggregated together. Sometimes there is a need to aggregate not only by distribution pattern but also by logistics characteristics, such as weight and volume. That is, consider all products having the same distribution pattern. Within these products, we aggregate those SKUs with similar volume and weight into one product group.
   b. *Product type*. In many cases, different products might simply be variations in product models or style or might differ only in the type of packaging. These products are typically aggregated together.

EXAMPLE 3-2

To illustrate the impact of aggregation on variability, consider an example in which two customers (e.g., retail outlets) are aggregated. Table 3-2 provides data on demand generated by these customers over the last seven years.

TABLE 3-2

HISTORICAL DATA FOR THE TWO CUSTOMERS

	Year						
	2000	**2001**	**2002**	**2003**	**2004**	**2005**	**2006**
Customer 1	22,346	28,549	19,567	25,457	31,986	21,897	19,854
Customer 2	17,835	21,765	19,875	24,346	22,876	14,653	24,987
Total	40,181	50,314	39,442	49,803	54,862	36,550	44,841

Assuming that these data correctly represent the distribution of next year's demand for each customer, Table 3-3 provides a summary of average annual demand, the standard deviation of annual demand, and the coefficient of variation for each customer and for the aggregated one. For a discussion on the difference between the standard deviation and the coefficient of variation, see Chapter 2.

TABLE 3-3

SUMMARY OF HISTORICAL DATA

	Statistics		
	Average annual demand	**Standard deviation annual demand**	**Coefficient of variation**
Customer 1	24,237	4,658	0.192
Customer 2	20,905	3,427	0.173
Total	45,142	6,757	0.150

Note that the average annual demand for the aggregated customer is the sum of the average demand generated by each customer. However, the variability faced by the aggregated customer, measured using either the standard deviation or the coefficient of variation, is smaller than the combined variabilities faced by the two existing customers. Coefficent of variation is the ratio of standard deviation and average demand for the same period.

An important consideration, of course, is the impact on the model's effectiveness of replacing the original detailed data with the aggregated data. We address this question in two ways.

1. Even if the technology exists to solve the logistics network design problem with the original data, it may still be useful to aggregate data because our ability to forecast customer demand at the account and product levels is usually poor. Because of the reduction in variability achieved through aggregation, forecast demand is significantly more accurate at the aggregated level.
2. Various researchers report that aggregating customers into about 150 to 200 zones usually results in no more than a 1 percent error in the estimation of total transportationcosts; see [19] and [113].

In practice, the following approach is typically used when aggregating the data:

- Aggregate demand points into at least 200 zones. If customers are classified into classes according to their service levels or frequency of delivery, each class will have at least 200 aggregated points.

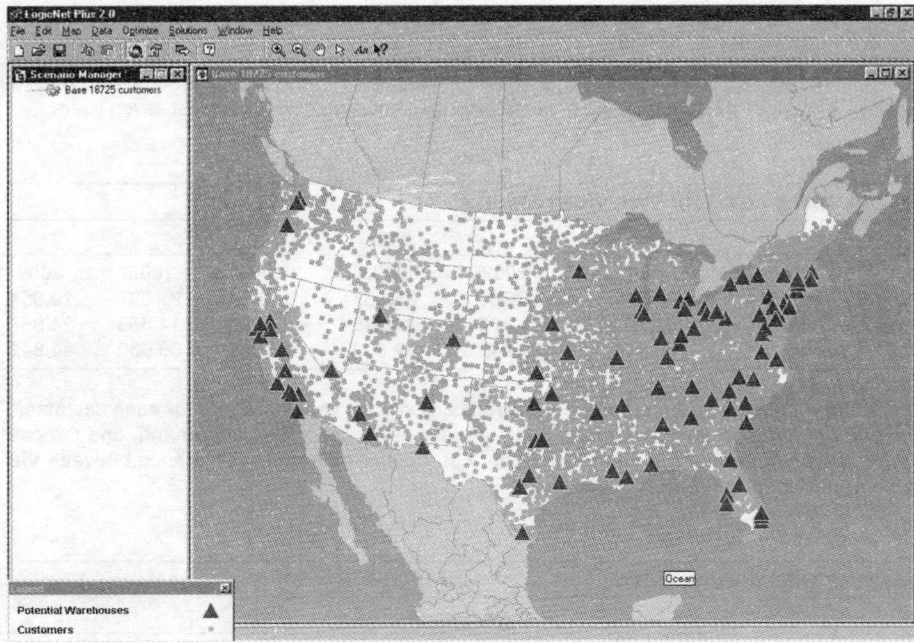

FIGURE 3-3 The SCP screen representing data prior to aggregation.

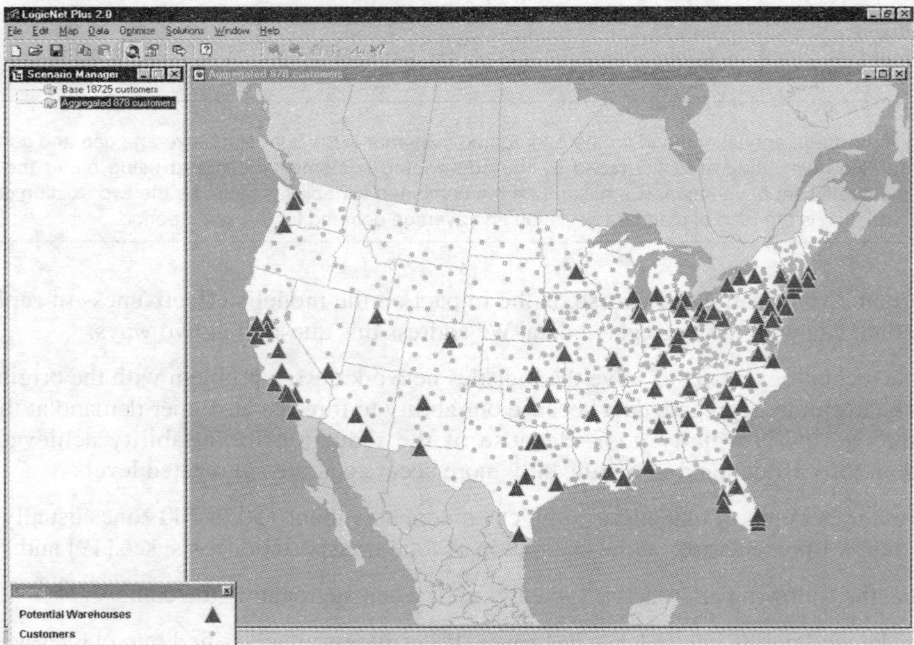

FIGURE 3-4 The SCP screen representing data after aggregation.

Total cost: $5,796,000
Total customers: 18,000

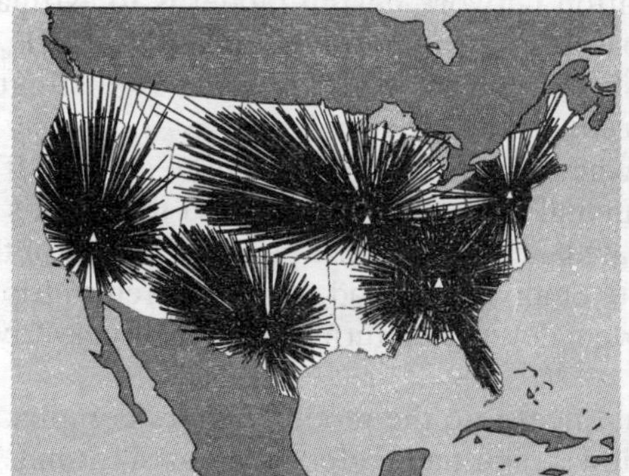

Total cost: $5,793,000
Total customers: 800

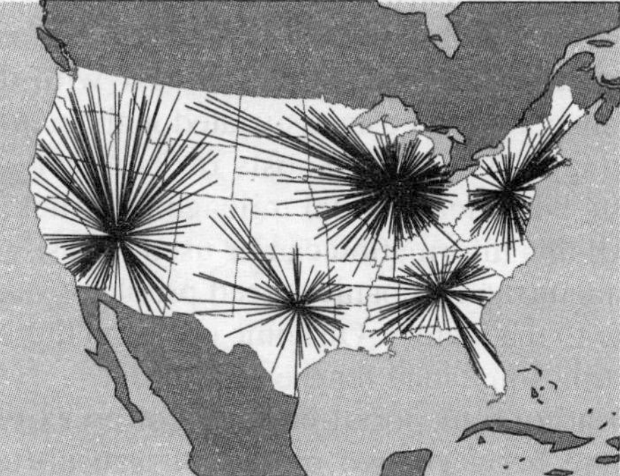

Cost difference < 0.05%

FIGURE 3-5 **The impact of customer aggregation on model accuracy.**

- Make sure each zone has approximately an equal amount of total demand. This implies that the zones may be of different geographic sizes.
- Place the aggregated points at the center of the zone.
- Aggregate the products into 20 to 50 product groups.

Figure 3-3 presents information about 3,220 customers all located in North America while Figure 3-4 shows the same data after aggregation using a three-digit zip code resulting in 217 aggregated points.

Finally, Figure 3-5 presents the impact of customer aggregation in a supply chain with a single manufacturing facility and a single product. The original supply chain has 18,000 demand points aggregated down using three-digit zip codes to 800 zones. As you can see, the cost difference between the original supply chain and the aggregated one is smaller than 0.05 percent. Similarly, Figure 3-6 tests the impact of product aggregation in a supply chain with 5 plants, 25 potential locations for warehouses, and 46 products aggregated down to 4 products. Again, the difference in cost between the original model and the aggregated one is less than 0.03 percent.

Total cost: $104,564,000
Total products: 46

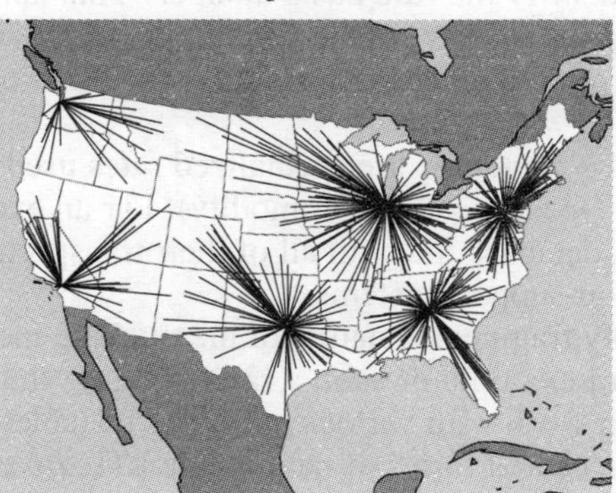

Total cost: $104,599,000
Total products: 4

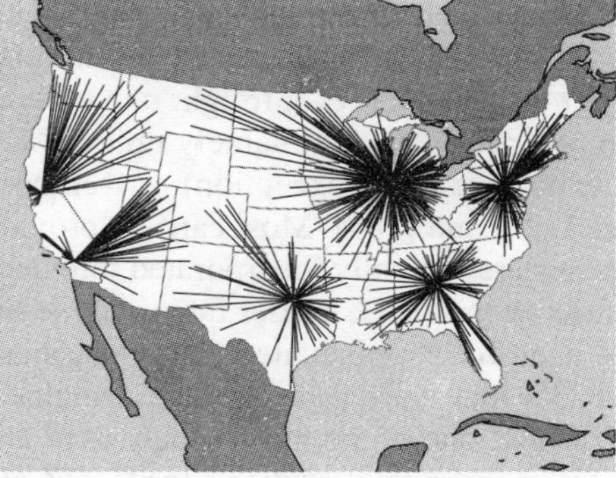

Cost difference: 0.03%

FIGURE 3-6 **The impact of product aggregation on model accuracy.**

3.2.3 Transportation Rates

The next step in constructing an effective distribution network design model is to estimate transportation costs. An important characteristic of most transportation rates, including truck, rail, and others, is that the rates are almost linear with distance but not with volume. We distinguish here between transportation costs associated with an *internal* and an *external* fleet.

Estimating transportation costs for company-owned trucks is typically quite simple. It involves annual costs per truck, annual mileage per truck, annual amount delivered, and the truck's effective capacity. All this information can be used to easily calculate cost per mile per SKU. Some of the Indian auto manufacturing companies faced problems due to empty truck-load during the return trip from the dealer's site to the factory. On some occasion there were delays in return trips as the truck-drivers spent time in getting some load for the return trip.

Incorporating transportation rates for an external fleet into the model is more complex. We distinguish here between two modes of transportation: truckload, referred to as TL, and less than truckload, referred to as LTL.

In the United States, TL carriers subdivide the country into zones. Almost every state is a single zone, except for certain big states, such as Florida or New York, which are partitioned into two zones. The carriers then provide their clients with zone-to-zone table costs. Indian transporters follow a similar approach. This database provides the cost per mile per truckload between any two zones. For example, to calculate TL cost from Chicago, Illinois, to Boston, Massachusetts, one needs to get the cost per mile for this pair and multiply it by the distance from Chicago to Boston. An important property of the TL cost structure is that it is not symmetric; that is, it is typically more expensive to ship a fully loaded truck from Illinois to New York than from New York to Illinois.

In the LTL industry, the rates typically belong to one of three basic types of freight rates: *class, exception,* and *commodity.* The class rates are standard rates that can be found for almost all products or commodities shipped. They are found with the help of a *classification tariff* that gives each shipment a *rating* or a *class*. For instance, the railroad classification includes 31 classes, ranging from 400 to 13, that are obtained from the widely used *Uniform Freight Classification*. The National Motor Freight Classification, on the other hand, includes only 23 classes, ranging from 500 to 35. In all cases, the higher the rating or class, the greater the relative charge for transporting the commodity. There are many factors involved in determining a product's specific class. These include product density, ease or difficulty of handling and transporting, and liability for damage.

Once the rating is established, it is necessary to identify the *rate basis number*. This number is the approximate distance between the load's origin and destination. With the commodity rating or class and the rate basis number, the specific rate per hundred pounds (hundredweight, or cwt) can be obtained from a carrier tariff table (i.e., a freight rate table).

The two other freight rates, namely *exception* and *commodity,* are specialized rates used to provide either less expensive rates (exception) or commodity-specific rates (commodity). For an excellent discussion, see [120] and [184]. Most carriers provide a database file with all of their transportation rates; these databases are typically incorporated into decision-support systems.

The proliferation of LTL carrier rates and the highly fragmented nature of the trucking industry have created the need for sophisticated rating engines. An example of such a rating engine that is widely used is SMC3's RateWare [see 264]. This engine can work with various carrier tariff tables as well as SMC3's CzarLite, one of the most widely used and accepted forms of nationwide LTL zip code–based rates. Unlike an individual carrier's tariff, CZAR-Lite offers a market-based price list derived from studies of LTL pricing on a regional, interregional, and national basis. This provides shippers with a fair

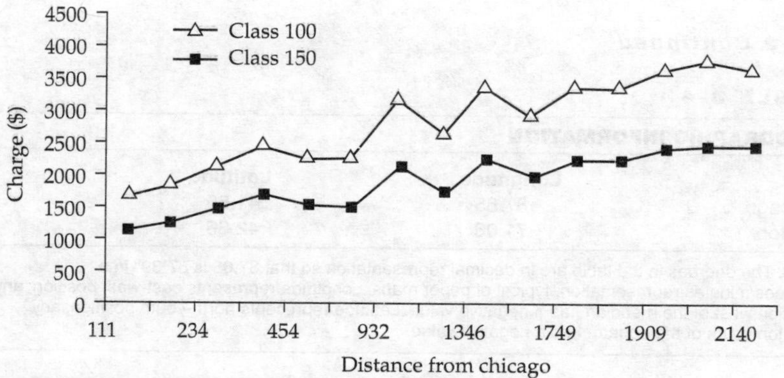

FIGURE 3-7 Transportation rates for shipping 4,000 lb.

pricing system and prevents any individual carrier's operational and marketing bias from overtly influencing the shipper choice. Consequently, CZAR-Lite rates are often used as a base for negotiating LTL contracts between shippers, carriers, and third-party logistics providers.

In Figure 3-7 we provide LTL cost charged by one carrier for shipping 4,000 pounds as a function of the distance from Chicago. The cost is given for two classes: class 100 and class 150. As you can see, in this case, the transportation cost function is not linear with distance.

3.2.4 Mileage Estimation

As explained in the previous subsection, the cost of transporting products from a specific source to a specific destination is a function of the distance between these two points. Thus, we need a tool that allows us to estimate distances. We can estimate distances using either street network or straight-line distances. Specifically, suppose we want to estimate the distance between two points, a and b. For this purpose, we need to obtain lon_a and lat_a, the longitude and latitude of point a (and similarly for point b). Then, the straight-line distance in miles from a to b, D_{ab} is calculated as follows:

$$D_{ab} = 69\sqrt{(lon_a - lon_b)^2 + (lat_a - lat_b)^2}$$

The value 69 is approximately the number of miles per *degree* of latitude in the continental United States because longitude and latitude are given in degrees. This equation is accurate for short distances only; it does not take into account the curvature of the earth. To measure fairly long distances and correct for the earth's curvature, we use the approximation suggested by the U.S. Geological Survey see [126];

$$D_{ab} = 2(69)\sin^{-1}\sqrt{(\sin(\frac{lat_a - lat_b}{2}))^2 + \cos(lat_a) \times \cos(lat_b) \times (\sin(\frac{lon_a - lon_b}{2}))^2}$$

EXAMPLE 3-3

Consider a manufacturer shipping a single fully loaded truck from Chicago, Illinois, to Boston, Massachusetts. The manufacturer is using a TL carrier whose rate is 105 cents per mile per truckload. To calculate transportation cost for this shipment, we need geographic data. Table 3-4 provides information about the longitude and latitude of each city.

Application of the equation in Table 3-4 leads to a straight-line distance from Chicago to Boston equal to 855 miles. Multiplying this number by the circuity factor, 1.14 in this case, leads to an estimate of the actual road distance equal to 974 miles. This number should be compared with the actual road distance, which is 965 miles. Thus, based on our estimate of the road distance, the transportation cost in this case is $1,023.

EXAMPLE 3-3 *Continued*

TABLE 3-4

GEOGRAPHIC INFORMATION

City	Longitude	Latitude
Chicago	−87.65	41.85
Boston	−71.06	42.36

Note: The degrees in the table are in decimal representation so that 87.65 is 87°39" in a degrees/minutes representation, typical of paper maps. Longitude represents east-west position; any position west of the meridian has a negative value. Latitude represents north-south position; any location south of the equator has a negative value.

These equations result in very accurate distance calculations; in both cases, however, the equations underestimate the actual road distance. To correct for this, we multiply D_{ab} by a *circuity* factor, ρ. Typically, in a metropolitan area, $\rho = 1.3$, while $\rho = 1.14$ for the continental United States.

Applications in which exact distances are more appropriate can typically be obtained from geographic information systems (GIS). However, this approach typically slows down the operation of SCP tools dramatically, and the approximation technique described above usually provides enough accuracy for many applications.

3.2.5 Warehouse Costs

Warehousing and distribution center costs include three main components:

1. *Handling costs*. These include labor and utility costs that are proportional to annual flow through the warehouse.
2. *Fixed costs*. These capture all cost components that are not proportional to the amount of material that flows through the warehouse. The fixed cost is typically proportional to warehouse size (capacity) but in a nonlinear way (see Figure 3-8). As the figure shows, this cost is fixed in certain ranges of the warehouse size.

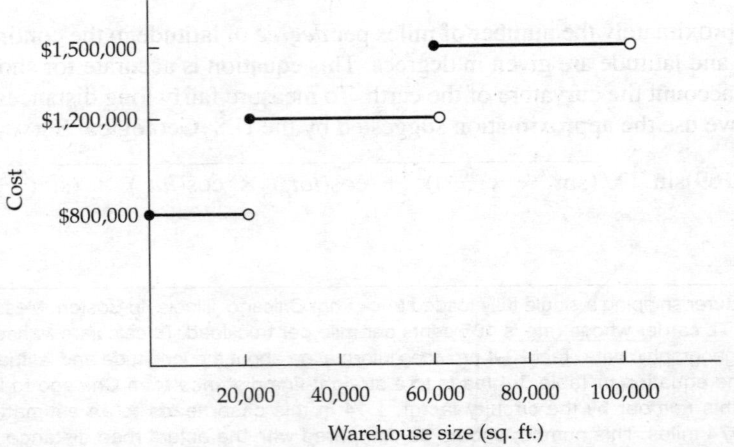

FIGURE 3-8 Warehouse fixed costs as a function of the warehouse capacity.

3. *Storage costs*. These represent inventory holding costs, which are proportional to *average* positive inventory levels.

Thus, estimating the warehouse handling costs is fairly easy while estimating the other two cost values is quite difficult. To see this difference, suppose that during the entire year, 1,000 units of product are required by a particular customer. These 1,000 units are not required to flow through the warehouse *at the same time,* so the average inventory level will likely be significantly lower than 1,000 units. Thus, when constructing the data for the SCP tool, we need to convert these annual flows into actual inventory amounts over time. Similarly, annual flow and average inventory associated with this product tell us nothing about how much space is needed for the product in the warehouse. This is true because the amount of space that the warehouse needs is proportional to peak inventory, not annual flow or average inventory.

An effective way to overcome this difficulty is to utilize the *inventory turnover ratio*. This is defined as follows:

$$\text{Inventory turnover ratio} = \frac{\text{Annual sales}}{\text{Average inventory level}}$$

Specifically, in our case the inventory turnover ratio is the ratio of the total annual outflow from the warehouse to the average inventory level. Thus, if the ratio is λ, then the average inventory level is total annual flow divided by λ. Multiplying the average inventory level by the inventory holding cost gives the annual storage costs. Finally, to calculate the fixed cost, we need to estimate the warehouse capacity. This is done in the next subsection.

3.2.6 Warehouse Capacities

Another important input to the distribution network design model is the actual warehouse capacity. It is not immediately obvious, however, how to estimate the actual space required, given the specific annual flow of material through the warehouse. Again, the inventory turnover ratio suggests an appropriate approach. As before, annual flow through a warehouse divided by the inventory turnover ratio allows us to calculate the average inventory level. Assuming a regular shipment and delivery schedule, such as that given in Figure 3-9, it follows that the required storage space is approximately *twice* that amount. In practice, of course, every pallet stored in the warehouse requires an empty space to allow for access and handling; thus, considering this space as well as space for aisles, picking, sorting, and processing facilities, and AGVs (automatic guided vehicles), we typically multiply the required storage space by a factor (>1). This factor depends on the specific application and allows users to assess the amount of

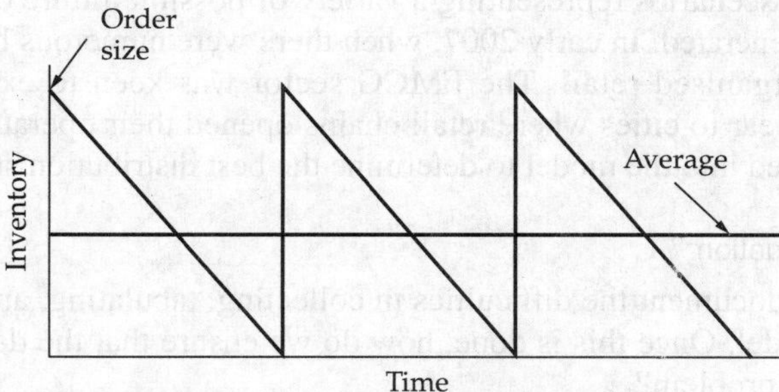

FIGURE 3-9 Inventory level as a function of time.

space available in the warehouse more accurately. A typical factor used in practice is three. This factor would be used in the following way. Consider a situation where the annual flow through the warehouse is 1,000 units and the inventory turnover ratio is 10.0. This implies that the average inventory level is about 100 units and, hence, if each unit takes 10 square feet of floor space, the required space for the products is 2,000 square feet. Therefore, the total space required for the warehouse is about 6,000 square feet.

3.2.7 Potential Warehouse Locations

It is also important to effectively identify potential locations for new warehouses. Typically, these locations must satisfy a variety of conditions:

- Geographical and infrastructure conditions.
- Natural resources and labor availability.
- Local industry and tax regulations.
- Public interest.

As a result, only a limited number of locations would meet all the requirements. These are the potential location sites for the new facilities.

3.2.8 Service Level Requirements

There are various ways to define service levels in this context. For example, we might specify a maximum distance between each customer and the warehouse serving it. This ensures that a warehouse will be able to serve its customers within a reasonable time. Sometimes we must recognize that for some customers, such as those in rural or isolated areas, it is harder to provide the same level of service that most other customers receive. In this case, it is often helpful to define the service level as the proportion of customers whose distance to their assigned warehouse is no more than a given distance. For instance, we might require that 95 percent of the customers be situated within 200 miles of the warehouses serving them.

3.2.9 Future Demand

As observed in Chapter 1, decisions at the strategic level, which include network design, have a long-lasting effect on the firm. In particular, decisions regarding the number, location, and size of warehouses have an impact on the firm for at least the next three to five years. This implies that changes in customer demand over the next few years should be taken into account when designing the network. This is most commonly addressed using a scenario-based approach incorporating net present value calculations. For example, various possible scenarios representing a variety of possible future demand patterns over the planning horizon can be generated. In early 2007, when there were numerous business activities related to expansion of Indian organised retail. The FMCG sector was keen to explore different sites for warehouses, which were near to cities where retail chains opened their operation. These scenarios can then be directly incorporated into the model to determine the best distribution strategy.

3.2.10 Model and Data Validation

The previous subsections document the difficulties in collecting, tabulating, and cleaning the data for a network configuration model. Once this is done, how do we ensure that the data and model accurately reflect the network design problem?

The process used to address this issue is known as model and data validation. This is typically done by reconstructing the existing network configuration using the model and collected data, and comparing the output of the model to existing data.

The importance of validation cannot be overstated. Valuable output of the model configured to duplicate current operating conditions includes all costs—warehousing, inventory, production, and transportation—generated under the current network con- figuration. These data can be compared to the company's accounting information. This is often the best way to identify errors in the data, problematic assumptions, modeling flaws, and so forth.

In one project we are aware of, for example, the transportation costs calculated during the validation process were consistently underestimating the costs suggested by the accounting data. After a careful review of the distribution practices, the consultants concluded that the effective truck capacity was only about 30 percent of the truck's physical capacity; that is, trucks were being sent out with very little load. Thus, the validation process not only helped calibrate some of the parameters used in the model but also suggested potential improvements in the utilization of the existing network.

It is often also helpful to make local or small changes in the network configuration to see how the system estimates their impact on costs and service levels. Specifically, this step involves posing a variety of what-if questions. This includes estimating the impact of closing an existing warehouse on system performance. Or, to give another example, it allows the user to change the flow of material through the existing network and see the changes in the costs. Often, managers have good intuition about what the effect of these small-scale changes on the system should be, so they can more easily identify errors in the model. Intuition about the effect of radical redesign of the entire system is often much less reliable. To summarize, the model validation process typically involves answering the following questions:

- Does the model make sense?
- Are the data consistent?
- Can the model results be fully explained?
- Did you perform sensitivity analysis?

Validation is critical for determining the validity of the model and data, but the process has other benefits. In particular, it helps the user make the connection between the current operations, which were modeled during the validation process, and possible improvements after optimization.

3.2.11 Solution Techniques

Once the data are collected, tabulated, and verified, the next step is to optimize the configuration of the logistics network. In practice, two techniques are employed:

1. Mathematical optimization techniques that include
   - Exact algorithms that are guaranteed to find optimal solutions, that is, least-cost solutions,
   - Heuristic algorithms that find *good* solutions, not necessarily optimal solutions.
2. Simulation models that provide a mechanism to evaluate specified design alternatives created by the designer.

Heuristics and the Need for Exact Algorithms We will start our discussion by considering mathematical optimization techniques. In order to understand the effectiveness of heuristic algorithms and the need for exact algorithms, consider the following example developed by Geoffrion and Van Roy in [92].

EXAMPLE 3-4

Consider the following distribution system:

- Single product.
- Two plants, referred to as plant *p*1 and plant *p*2.
- Plant *p*2 has an annual capacity of 60,000 units.
- The two plants have the same production costs.
- Two existing warehouses, referred to as warehouse *w*1 and warehouse *w*2, have identical warehouse handling costs.
- Three markets areas, *c*1, *c*2, and *c*3, with demands of 50,000, 100,000, and 50,000, respectively.
- Table 3-5 provides distribution cost per unit. For instance, distributing one unit from plant *p*1 to warehouse *w*2 costs Rs. 5.

TABLE 3-5

DISTRIBUTION COSTS PER UNIT

Facility warehouse	*p*1	*p*2	*c*1	*c*2	*c*3
*w*1	0	4	3	4	5
*w*2	5	2	2	1	2

Our objective is to find a distribution strategy that specifies the flow of products from the suppliers through the warehouses to the market areas without violating the plant *p*2 production capacity constraint, that satisfies market area demands, and that minimizes total distribution costs. Observe that this problem is significantly easier to solve than the logistics network configuration problem discussed earlier. Here we assume that facility location is not an issue, and we merely attempt to find an effective distribution strategy. For this purpose, consider the following two intuitive heuristics:

Heuristic 1

For each market, we choose the cheapest warehouse-to-source demand. Thus, *c*1, *c*2, and *c*3 would be supplied by *w*2. Then, for this warehouse, choose the cheapest plant; that is, distribute 60,000 units from *p*2 and the remaining 140,000 from *p*1. The total cost is

$$2 \times 50{,}000 + 1 \times 100{,}000 + 2 \times 50{,}000 + 2 \times 60{,}000 + 5 \times 140{,}000 = \text{Rs.}1{,}120{,}000$$

Heuristic 2

For each market area, choose the warehouse where the total delivery costs to and from the warehouse are the lowest; that is, consider inbound and outbound distribution costs. Thus, for market area *c*1, consider the paths $p1 \rightarrow w1 \rightarrow c1$, $p1 \rightarrow w2 \rightarrow c1$, $p2 \rightarrow w1 \rightarrow c1$, $p2 \rightarrow w2 \rightarrow c1$.

Among all these alternatives, the cheapest is $p1 \rightarrow w1 \rightarrow c1$, so choose *w*1 for *c*1. Using a similar analysis, we choose *w*2 for *c*2 and *w*2 for *c*3.

This implies that warehouse *w*1 delivers a total of 50,000 units while warehouse *w*2 delivers a total of 150,000 units. The best inbound flow pattern is to supply 50,000 from plant *p*1 to warehouse *w*1, supply 60,000 units from plant *p*2 to warehouse *w*2, and supply 90,000 from plant *p*1 to warehouse *w*2. The total cost for this strategy is Rs. 920,000.

Unfortunately, the two heuristics described earlier do not produce the best, or least-cost, strategy. To find the best distribution strategy, consider the following *optimization model*. Indeed, the distribution problem described earlier can be framed as the following linear programming problem.[1]

For this purpose, let

- *x*(*p*1,*w*1), *x*(*p*1,*w*2), *x*(*p*2,*w*1), and *x*(*p*2,*w*2) be the flows from the plants to the warehouses.
- *x*(*w*1, *c*1), *x*(*w*1, *c*2), and *x*(*w*1, *c*3) be the flows from warehouse *w*1 to customer zones *c*1, *c*2, and *c*3.
- *x*(*w*2, *c*1), *x*(*w*2, *c*2), and *x*(*w*2, *c*3) be the flows from warehouse *w*2 to customer zones *c*1, *c*2, and *c*3.

[1]This part of the section requires a basic knowledge of linear programming. It can be skipped without loss of continuity.

EXAMPLE 3-4 *Continued*

The linear programming problem we need to solve is

$$\text{Minimize } \{0x(p1, w1) + 5x(p1, w2) + 4x(p2, w1) + 2x(p2, w2) + 3x(w1, c1) + 4x(w1, c2) + 5x(w1, c3) + 2x(w2, c1) + 1x(w2, c2) + 2x(w2, c3)\}$$

subject to the following constraints:

$$x(p2, w1) + x(p2, w2) \leq 60{,}000$$
$$x(p1, w1) + x(p2, w1) = x(w1, c1) + x(w1, c2) + x(w1, c3)$$
$$x(p1, w2) + x(p2, w2) = x(w2, c1) + x(w2, c2) + x(w2, c3)$$
$$x(w1, c1) + x(w2, c1) = 50{,}000$$
$$x(w1, c2) + x(w2, c2) = 100{,}000$$
$$x(w1, c3) + x(w2, c3) = 50{,}000$$

All flows are greater than or equal to zero.

One can easily construct an Excel model for this problem and use the Excel linear programming solver to find the optimal strategy. For more information on how to construct the Excel model, see [135]. This strategy is described in Table 3-6.

TABLE 3-6

OPTIMAL DISTRIBUTION STRATEGY

Facility warehouse	p1	p2	c1	c2	c3
w1	140,000	0	50,000	40,000	50,000
w2	0	60,000	0	60,000	0

The total cost for the optimal strategy is Rs. 740,000.

This example clearly illustrates the value of optimization-based techniques. *These tools can determine strategies that will significantly reduce the total system cost.* Of course, the logistics network configuration model that we would like to analyze and solve is typically more complex than the simple example described above. One key difference is the need to establish optimal locations for warehouses, distribution centers, and cross-dock facilities. Unfortunately, these decisions render linear programming inappropriate and require the use of a technique called *integer programming*. This is true because linear programming deals with continuous variables, while a decision on whether or not to open a warehouse at a specific city is a binary variable—0 if we do not open a warehouse in that location and 1 otherwise.

Thus, the logistics network configuration model is an integer programming model. Unfortunately, integer programming models are significantly more difficult to solve. The interested reader is referred to [30] and [223] for a discussion of exact algorithms for the logistics network configuration problem.

Simulation Models and Optimization Techniques The mathematical optimization techniques described earlier have some important limitations. They deal with static models—typically by considering annual, or average, demand—and they do not take into account changes over time. Simulation-based tools take into account the dynamics of the system and are capable of characterizing system performance for a *given design*. Thus, it is up to the user to provide the simulation model with a number of design alternatives.

This implies that simulation models allow the user to perform a microlevel analysis. Indeed, the simulation model may include (see [106])

1. Individual ordering pattern.
2. Specific inventory policies.
3. Inventory movements inside the warehouse.

Unfortunately, simulation models only model a prespecified logistics network design. In other words, given a particular configuration of warehouses, retailers, and so forth, a simulation model can be used to help estimate the costs associated with operating that configuration. If a different configuration is considered (e.g., a few of the customers are to be served by a different warehouse), the model has to be rerun.

As you will see in more detail in Chapter 14, simulation is not an optimization tool. It is useful in characterizing the performance of a particular configuration, but not in determining an effective configuration from a large set of potential configurations. In addition, a detailed simulation model that incorporates information about individual customer ordering patterns, specific inventory and production policies, daily distribution strategies, and so on, may require enormous computational time to achieve a desired level of accuracy in system performance. This implies that typically one can consider *very few* alternatives using a simulation tool.

Thus, if system dynamics is not a key issue, a static model is appropriate and mathematical optimization techniques can be applied. In our experience, this type of model accounts for almost all the network configuration models used in practice. When detailed system dynamics is an important issue, it makes sense to utilize the following two-stage approach, suggested by Hax and Candea [106], which takes advantage of the strengths of both simulation- and optimization-based approaches:

1. Use an optimization model to generate a number of least-cost solutions at the macrolevel, taking into account the most important cost components.
2. Use a simulation model to evaluate the solutions generated in the first phase.

3.2.12 Key Features of a Network Configuration SCP

One of the key requirements of any supply chain planning tool for network design is flexibility. In this context, we define *flexibility* as the ability of the system to incorporate a large set of preexisting network characteristics. Indeed, depending on the particular application, a whole spectrum of design options may be appropriate. At one end of this spectrum is the complete reoptimization of the existing network. This means that each warehouse can be either opened or closed and all transportation flows can be redirected. At the other end of the spectrum, it may be necessary to incorporate the following features in the optimization model:

1. *Customer-specific service level requirements.*
2. *Existing warehouses.* In most cases, warehouses already exist and their leases have not yet expired. Therefore, the model should not permit the closing of these warehouses.
3. *Expansion of existing warehouses.* Existing warehouses may be expandable.
4. *Specific flow patterns.* In a variety of situations, specific flow patterns (e.g., from a particular warehouse to a set of customers) should not be changed, or perhaps more likely, a certain manufacturing location does not or cannot produce certain SKUs.

5. *Warehouse-to-warehouse flow*. In some cases, material may flow from one warehouse to another warehouse.
6. *Production and bill of materials*. In some cases, assembly is required and needs to be captured by the model. For this purpose, the user needs to provide information on the components used to assemble finished goods. In addition, production information down to the line level can be included in the model.

It is not enough for the supply chain planning tool to incorporate all of the features described above. It also must have the capability to deal with all these issues with little or no reduction in its *effectiveness*. The latter requirement is directly related to the so-called *robustness* of the tool. This stipulates that the relative quality of the solution generated by the tool (i.e., cost and service level) should be independent of the specific environment, the variability of the data, or the particular setting. If a particular SCP tool is not robust, it is difficult to determine how effective it will be for a particular problem.

3.3 INVENTORY POSITIONING AND LOGISTICS COORDINATION

The importance of inventory positioning, and the need for the coordination of inventory decisions and transportation policies, has long been evident. Unfortunately, managing inventory in complex supply chains is typically difficult, and may have a significant impact on the customer service level and supply chain systemwide cost.

In Chapter 2, we discussed inventory in detail. Recall that inventory appears in several forms:

- Raw material inventory.
- Work-in-process (WIP) inventory.
- Finished product inventory.

Each of these needs its own inventory control mechanism. Unfortunately, determining these mechanisms is difficult because efficient production, distribution, and inventory control strategies that reduce systemwide costs and improve service levels must take into account the interactions of the various levels in the supply chain. Nevertheless, the benefits of determining these inventory control mechanisms can be enormous. In Chapter 2, we discussed a variety of mechanisms and approaches, focusing on those that addressed the issue of demand uncertainty in its various forms.

3.3.1 Strategic Safety Stock

The bulk of the analysis in Chapter 2 focused on a single facility (e.g., a warehouse or a retail outlet) managing its inventory in order to minimize its own cost as much as possible, or a single firm that operates multiple facilities and has decided to keep inventory at each of them. In this section, we continue to explore a multifacility supply chain that belongs to a single firm. The objective of the firm is to manage inventory so as to reduce systemwide cost; thus, it is important to consider the interaction of the various facilities and the impact this interaction has on the inventory policy that should be employed by each facility.

One way to manage the inventory for whatever product is produced in a facility is to wait for specific orders to arrive before starting to manufacture them. We call such a facility a make-to-order facility, and contrast it to the make-to-stock facilities we have discussed in previous chapters. An important question that arises when managing inventory in a complex supply chain is *where to keep safety stock*—in other words, which facilities should produce to stock and which should produce to order? The answer to this question clearly depends on the desired service level, the supply network, lead times as well as a variety of operational issues and constraints. Thus, management needs to focus on a strategic model that allows the firm to position safety stock effectively in its supply chain. This is a difficult optimization problem that requires techniques and approaches beyond the level of this text.

To understand the issues involved, consider the following model. Consider a single-product, single-facility periodic review inventory model. Let

- SI be the amount of time that passes from when an order is placed until the facility receives a shipment; this time is referred to as *incoming service time*.
- S be the *committed service time* made by the facility to its own customers.
- T be the *processing time* at the facility.

Of course, we must assume that $SI + T > S$, since otherwise, no inventory is needed in the facility.

We assume that the facility manages its inventory following a periodic review policy (described in Chapter 2) and that demand is normally distributed with the characteristics described in Chapter 2 (technically, we say that the demand is independent and identically distributed across time periods following a normal distribution). Given deterministic SI, S, and T, and with no setup costs, the level of safety stock that the facility needs to keep is

$$zh\sqrt{SI + T - S}$$

where z is the safety stock factor associated with a specified level of service and h is the inventory holding cost. The value $SI + T - S$ is referred to as the facility *net lead time.*

Now, consider the following two-stage supply chain with facility, or stage, 2 feeding facility 1, which serves the end customer. Define SI_1, S_1, and T_1 to be the incoming service time, committed service time, and processing time of facility 1, and do the same for facility 2. Thus, S_1 is the committed service time to the end customer, S_2 is the commitment that facility 2 makes to facility 1, and, hence, $S_2 = SI_1$. Finally, SI_2 is the supplier commitment to facility 2. All of these relationships are depicted in Figure 3-10.

The objective is to minimize total supply chain cost without requiring a new service commitment from external suppliers. Observe that if we reduce the committed service time from facility 2 to facility 1, we can impact required inventory at both facility 1 and facility 2. In fact, in this case, inventory at facility 1 is reduced but inventory at the second facility is increased. Thus, the overall objective is to choose the committed service time at each facility, and, therefore, the location and amount of inventory, so as to minimize total, or, more precisely, systemwide, safety stock cost.

To illustrate the trade-offs and the impact of strategically positioning safety stock in the supply chain, consider the following case.

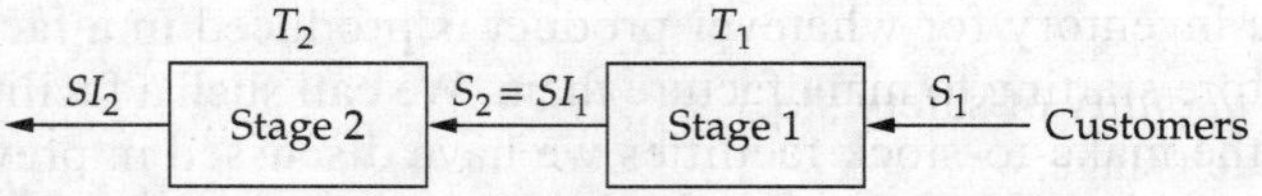

T_2 T_1

SI_2 ← Stage 2 ← $S_2 = SI_1$ ← Stage 1 ← S_1 ← Customers

FIGURE 3-10 The relationship between the two facilities in the model.

CASE: ElecComp Inc.

ElecComp Inc. is a large contract manufacturer of circuit boards and other high-tech parts. The company sells about 27,000 high-value products whose life cycle is relatively short. Competition in this industry forces ElecComp to commit to short lead times to its customers; this committed service time to the customers is typically much shorter than manufacturing lead time. Unfortunately, the manufacturing process is quite complex including a complex sequence of assemblies at different stages.

Because of the long manufacturing lead time and the pressure to provide customers with a short response time, ElecComp kept inventory of finished products for many of its SKUs. Thus, the company managed its supply chain based on long-term forecast, the so-called push-based supply chain strategy. This make-to-stock environment required the company to build safety stock and resulted in huge financial and shortage risks.

Executives at ElecComp had long recognized that this push-based supply chain strategy was not the appropriate strategy for their supply chain. Unfortunately, because of the long lead time, a pull-based supply chain strategy, in which manufacturing and assembly are done based on realized demand, was not appropriate either.

Thus, ElecComp focused on developing a new supply chain strategy whose objectives are

1. Reducing inventory and financial risks.
2. Providing customers with competitive response times.

This could be achieved by

- Determining the optimal *location* of inventory across the various stages of the manufacturing and assembly process.
- Calculating the optimal *quantity* of safety stock for each component at each stage.

The focus of redesigning ElecComp's supply chain was on a hybrid strategy in which a portion of the supply chain is managed based on push, that is, a make-to-stock environment, while the remaining portion of the supply chain is managed based on pull, that is, a make-to-order strategy. Observe that the supply chain stages that produce to stock will be the locations where the company keeps safety stock, while the make-to-order stages will keep no stock at all. Hence, the challenge was to identify the location in the supply chain in which the strategy switched from a push-based, that is, a make-to-stock, strategy to a pull-based, that is, a make-to-order, supply chain strategy. This location is referred to as the *push-pull boundary*.

ElectComp developed and implemented the new push-pull supply chain strategy, and the impact was dramatic. For the same customer lead times, safety stock was reduced by 40 to 60 percent, depending on product line. More importantly, with the new supply chain structure, ElecComp concluded that they could cut lead times to their customers by 50 percent and still enjoy a 30 percent reduction in safety stock.

To understand the analysis and the benefit experienced by ElecComp, consider Figure 3-11 in which a finished product (part 1) is assembled in a Dallas facility from two components, one produced in the Montgomery facility and one in a different facility in Dallas. Each box provides information about the value of the product produced by that facility; numbers under each box are the processing time at that stage; bins represent safety stock. Transit times between facilities are provided as well. Finally, each facility provides committed response time to the downstream facilities. For instance, the assembly facility quotes a 30-day response time to its customers. This implies that any order can be satisfied in no more than 30 days. The Montgomery facility quotes an 88-day response time to the assembly facility. As a result, the assembly facility needs to keep inventory of finished products in order to satisfy customer orders within its 30-day committed service time.

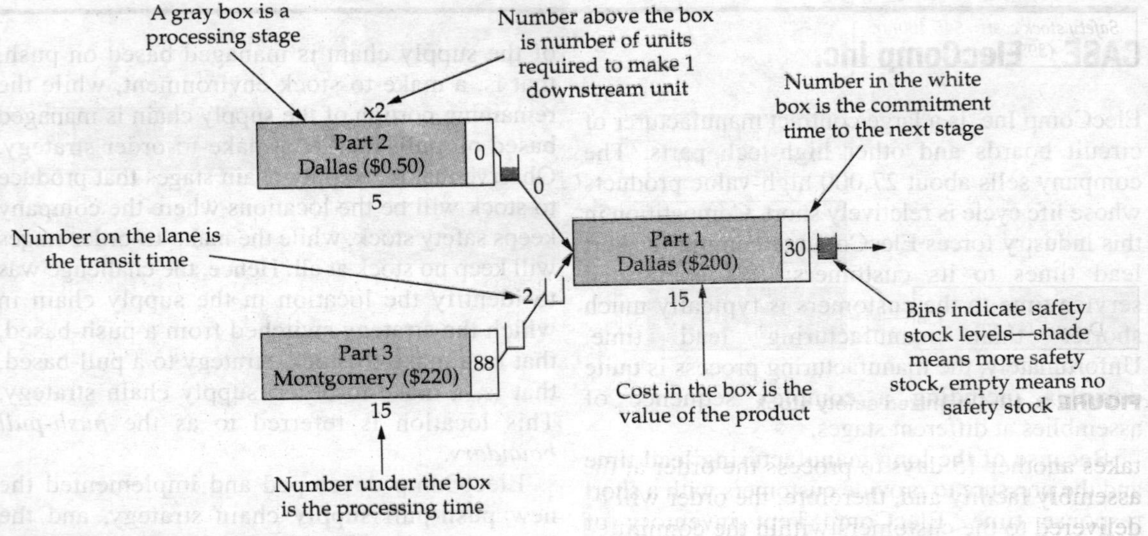

FIGURE 3-11 How to read the diagrams.

Observe that if somehow ElecComp can reduce the committed service time from the Montgomery facility to the assembly facility from 88 days to, say, 50 or perhaps 40 days, the assembly facility will be able to reduce its finished goods inventory while the Montgomery facility will need to start building inventory. Of course, ElecComp's objective is to minimize systemwide inventory and manufacturing costs; this is precisely what Inventory Analyst™ from LogicTools (www.logic-tools.com) allows users to do. By looking at the entire supply chain, the tool determines the appropriate inventory level at each stage.

For instance, if the Montgomery facility reduces its committed lead time to 13 days, then the assembly facility does not need any inventory of finished goods. Any customer order will trigger an order for parts 2 and 3. Part 2 will be available immediately, since the facility producing part 2 holds inventory, while part 3 will be available at the assembly facility in 15 days: 13 days' committed response time by the manufacturing facility plus 2 days' transportation lead time. It

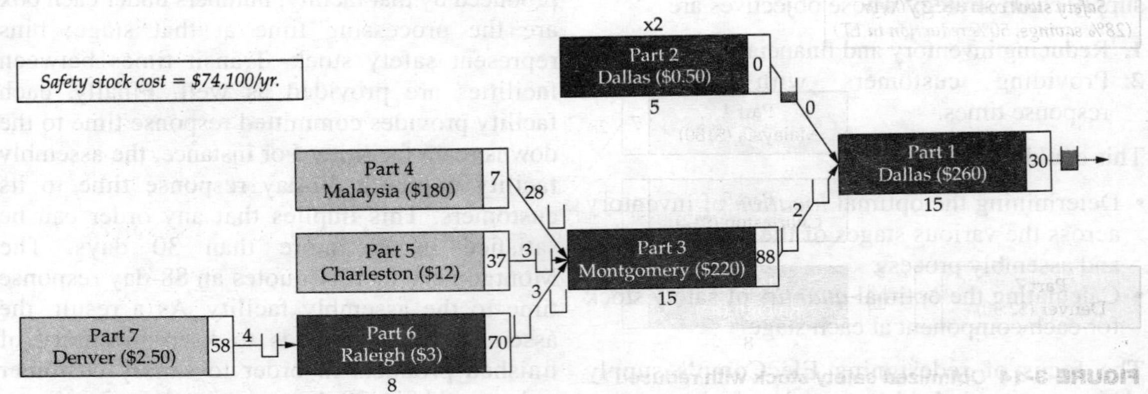

FIGURE 3-12 Current safety stock location.

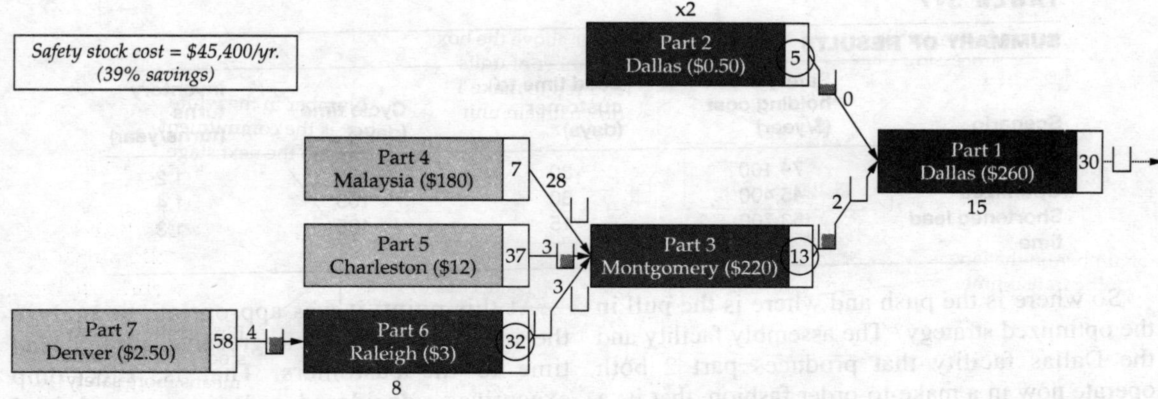

FIGURE 3-13 Optimized safety stock.

takes another 15 days to process the order at the assembly facility and, therefore, the order will be delivered to the customers within the committed service time. Thus, in this case, the assembly facility produces to order, that is, a pull-based strategy, while the Montgomery facility needs to keep inventory and hence is managed based on push, that is, a make-to-stock strategy.

Now that the trade-offs are clear, consider the product structure depicted in Figure 3-12. Light gray boxes (parts 4, 5, and 7) represent outside suppliers while black boxes represent internal stages within ElecComp's supply chain. Observe that the assembly facility commits a 30-day response time to the customers and keeps inventory of finished goods. More precisely, the assembly facility and the facility manufacturing part 2 both produce to stock. All other stages produce to order.

Figure 3-13 depicts the optimized supply chain that provides customers with the same 30-day response time. Observe that by adjusting committed service time of various internal facilities, the assembly system starts producing to order and keeps no finished goods inventory. On the other hand, the Raleigh and Montgomery facilities need to reduce their committed service time and hence keep inventory.

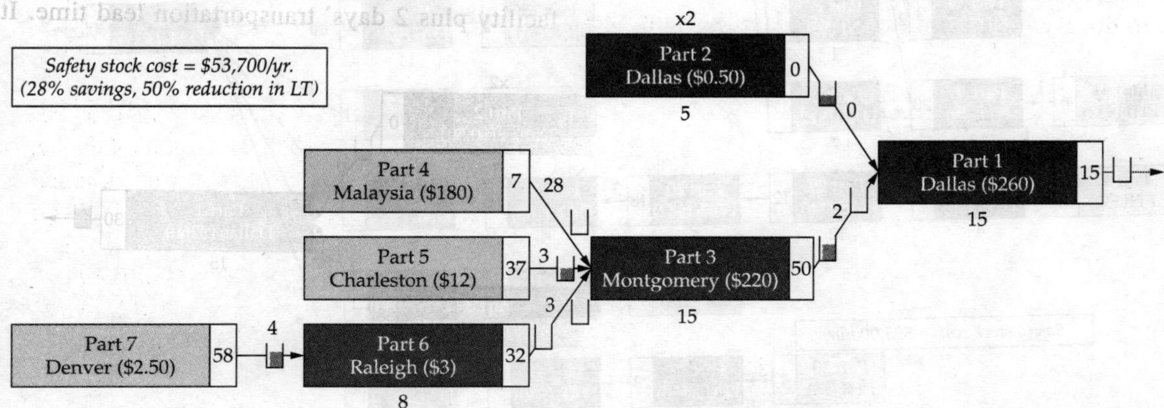

FIGURE 3-14 Optimized safety stock with reduced lead time.

TABLE 3-7

SUMMARY OF RESULTS

Scenario	Safety stock holding cost ($/year)	Lead time to customer (days)	Cycle time (days)	Inventory turns (turns/year)
Current	74,100	30	105	1.2
Optimized	45,400	30	105	1.4
Shortened lead time	53,700	15	105	1.3

So where is the push and where is the pull in the optimized strategy? The assembly facility and the Dallas facility that produces part 2 both operate now in a make-to-order fashion, that is, a pull strategy, while the Montgomery facility operates in a make-to-stock fashion, a push-based strategy. The impact on the supply chain is a 39 percent reduction in safety stock!

At this point, it was appropriate to analyze the impact of a more aggressive quoted lead time to the customers. That is, ElecComp executives considered reducing quoted lead times to the customers from 30 days to 15 days. Figure 3-14 depicts the optimized supply chain strategy in this case. The impact was clear. Relative to the baseline (Figure 3-12), inventory

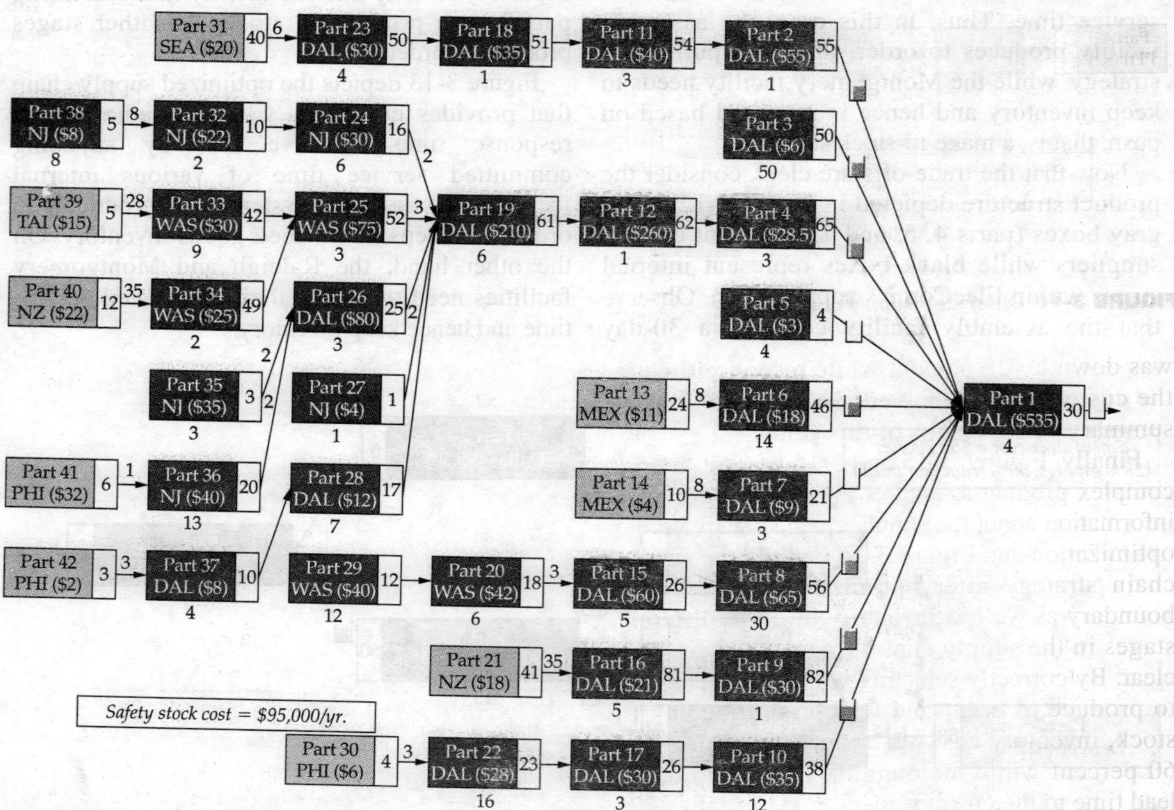

FIGURE 3-15 Current supply chain.

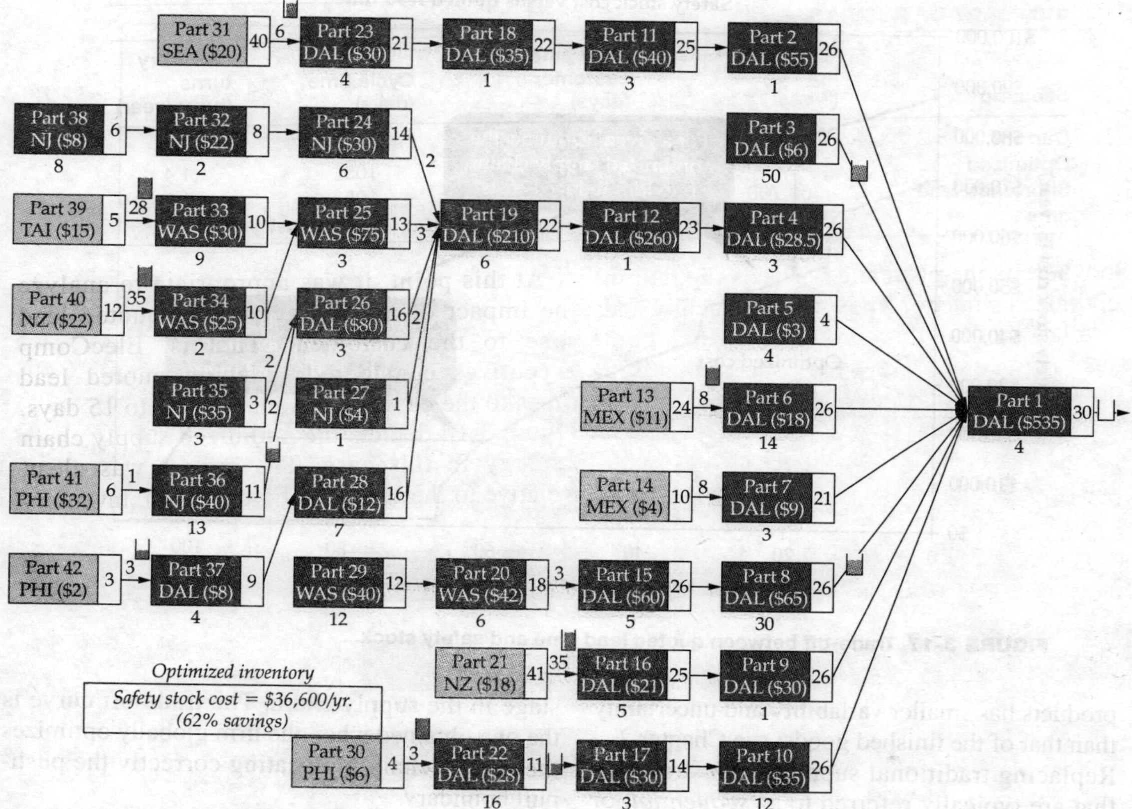

FIGURE 3-16 Optimized supply chain.

was down by 28 percent while response time to the customers was halved. See Table 3-7 for a summary of the results of this study.

Finally, Figures 3-15 and 3-16 present a more complex product structure. Figure 3-15 provides information about the supply chain strategy before optimization and Figure 3-16 depicts the supply chain strategy after optimizing the push-pull boundary as well as inventory levels at different stages in the supply chain. Again, the benefit is clear. By correctly selecting which stage is going to produce to order and which is producing to stock, inventory cost was reduced by more than 60 percent while maintaining the same quoted lead time to the customers.

To summarize, using a multistage inventory optimization technology (Inventory Analyst™ from LogicTools), ElecComp was able to significantly reduce inventory cost while maintaining and sometimes significantly decreasing quoted service times to the customers. This was achieved by

1. Identifying the push-pull boundary; that is, identifying supply chain stages that should operate in a make-to-stock fashion and hence keep safety stock. The remaining supply chain stages operate in a make-to-order fashion and thus keep no inventory. This is done by pushing inventory to less costly locations in the supply chain.
2. Taking advantage of the risk pooling concept. This concept suggests that demand for a component used by a number of finished

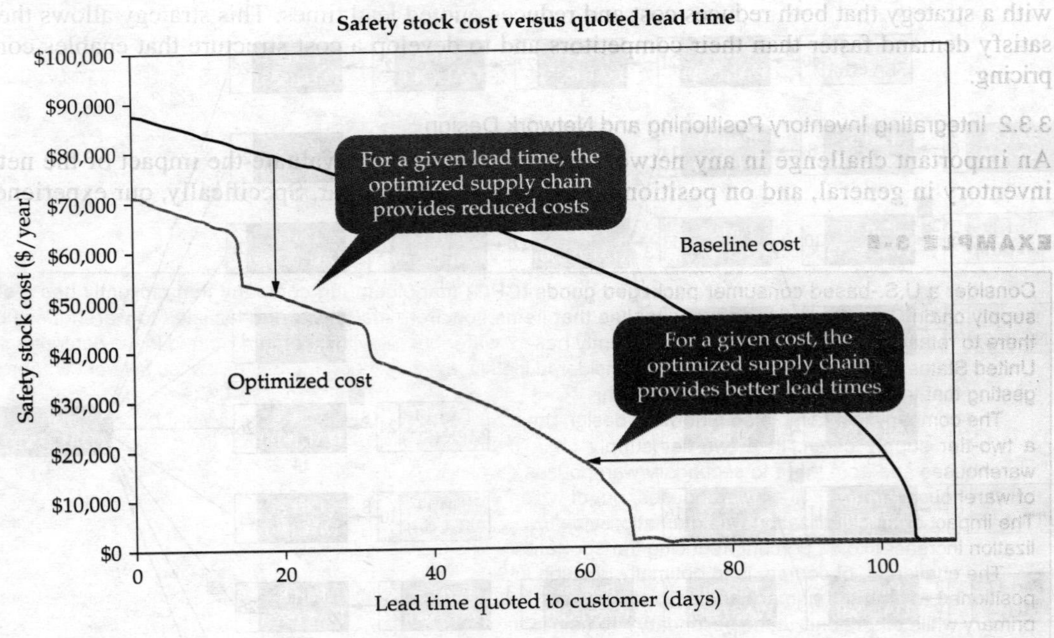

FIGURE 3-17 Trade-off between quoted lead time and safety stock.

products has smaller variability and uncertainty than that of the finished goods; see Chapter 2.

3. Replacing traditional supply chain strategies that are typically referred to as *sequential,* or *local, optimization* by a *globally optimized supply chain strategy*. In a sequential, or local, optimization strategy, each stage tries to optimize its profit with very little regard to the impact of its decisions on other stages in the same supply chain. On the other hand, in a global supply chain strategy, the entire supply chain strategy is integrated, so that strategies are selected for each stage that will maximize supply chain performance.

To better understand the impact of the new supply chain paradigm employed by ElecComp, consider Figure 3-17, where we plot total inventory cost against quoted lead time to the customers. The black trade-off curve represents the traditional relationship between cost and quoted lead time to the customers. This curve is a result of locally optimizing decisions at each stage in the supply chain. The trade-off curve is the one obtained when the firm globally optimizes the supply chain by locating correctly the push-pull boundary.

Observe that this shift of the trade-off curve, due to optimally locating the push-pull boundary, implies

1. For the same quoted lead time, the company can significantly reduce cost.

or

2. For the same cost, the firm can significantly reduce lead time.

Finally, notice that the curve representing the traditional relationship between cost and customer quoted lead time is smooth while the new trade-off curve representing the impact of optimally locating the push-pull boundary is not, with jumps in various places. These jumps represent situations in which the location of the push-pull boundary changes and significant cost savings are achieved.

Firms employing a new supply chain paradigm like the one described in the case above typically end up with a strategy that both reduces cost and reduces quoted lead times. This strategy allows the firms to satisfy demand faster than their competitors and to develop a cost structure that enables competitive pricing.

3.3.2 Integrating Inventory Positioning and Network Design

An important challenge in any network design project is to evaluate the impact of the network on inventory in general, and on positioning inventory in particular. Specifically, our experience is that

EXAMPLE 3-5

Consider a U.S.-based consumer packaged goods (CPG) manufacturing company that currently has a single-tier supply chain. The single-tier network implies that items flow from manufacturing facilities to warehouses and from there to retail outlets. The supply chain currently has 17 warehouses, with 6 of them located in the central region of the United States. The current supply chain is considered inefficient since inbound truck utilization is about 63 percent, suggesting that transportation cost is just too high.

The company just completed a network design project whose objective was to transform the single-tier network into a two-tier supply chain. In a two-tier supply chain, items are shipped from manufacturing facilities to primary warehouses and from there to secondary warehouses and finally to retail outlets. The new design reduced the number of warehouses from 17 to 14 warehouses, out of which 5 are primary warehouses and 9 are secondary warehouses. The impact on truck utilization was dramatic; since trucks can be shipped to primary warehouses fully loaded, truck utilization increased to 82 percent, reducing transportation costs by about 13 percent.

The challenge, of course, is to optimally position inventory in the new supply chain. That is, should every SKU be positioned at both the primary and secondary warehouses, or, perhaps, should some SKUs be positioned only at the primary while others only at the secondary? To help in the process, consider Figure 3-18, which presents information on customer demand for 4,000 different SKUs. The vertical coordinate provides information on average weekly sales, while the horizontal coordinate provides information on demand variability measured by the coefficient of variation (see Chapter 2 for details).

Observe that products can be classified into three different categories:

- High-variability–low-volume products.
- Low-variability–high-volume products.
- Low-variability–low-volume products.

The supply chain strategy should be different for different product categories. For example, inventory risk is the main challenge for high-variability–low-volume products. Thus, these products should be positioned mainly at the primary warehouses so that demand from many retail outlets can be aggregated, reducing inventory costs.

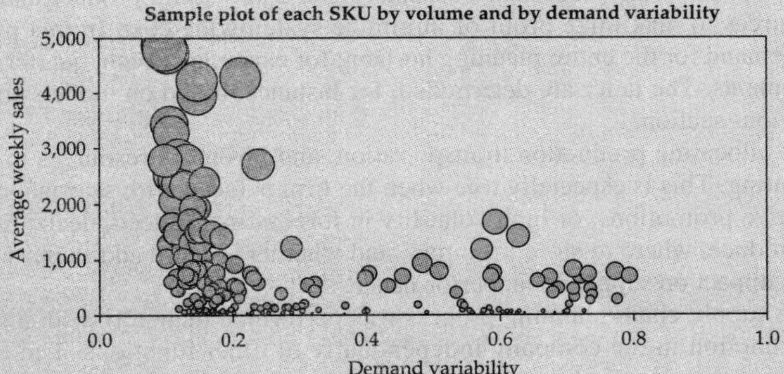

FIGURE 3-18 Sample plot of each SKU by volume and demand variability.

EXAMPLE 3-5 *Continued*

On the other hand, low-variability–high-volume products should be positioned close to the retail outlets, at the secondary warehouses, since this allows the supply chain to ship fully loaded tracks as close as possible to the customers, thus reducing transportation costs.

Finally, positioning low-variability–low-volume products requires a bit more analysis since other characteristics are important, such as profit margins, and so forth.

many companies try to keep as much inventory close to the customers, hold some inventory at every location, and hold as much raw material as possible. Clearly, the focus of this strategy is on local optimizations, where each facility in the supply chain optimizes its own objective with very little regard to the impact of its decisions on other facilities in the supply chain. This typically yields

- Low inventory turns.
- Inconsistent service levels across locations and products.
- The need to expedite shipments, with resulting increased transportation costs.

The discussions above suggest that positioning inventory in the supply chain should be done using models that consider the entire supply chain. The next example illustrates the process and some of the results.

The analysis in Example 3-4 leads to an important intuition. Demand uncertainty is a critical factor for high-variability–low-volume products and, hence, the supply chain strategy will position inventory at the primary warehouses so as to take advantage of risk pooling. Thus, in this case, the strategy is a **pull** strategy. On the other hand, for low-variability–high-volume products, the focus is on economies of scale in transportation costs and, hence, these products are positioned as close as possible to the customers to reduce transportation costs, a **push**-based strategy. This framework is very similar to the framework developed in Section 6.2.4 under a more general setting.

3.4 RESOURCE ALLOCATION

Given a fixed logistics network, the firm needs to decide on a monthly, quarterly, or annual basis how to utilize resources effectively. This is done by developing a supply chain master plan. *Supply chain master planning* is defined as the process of coordinating and allocating production and distribution strategies and resources to maximize profit or minimize systemwide cost. In this process, the firm considers forecast demand for the entire planning horizon; for example, month, quarter, year, as well as safety stock requirements. The latter are determined, for instance, based on models similar to the one analyzed in the previous section.

The challenge of allocating production, transportation, and inventory resources in order to satisfy demand can be daunting. This is especially true when the firm is faced with seasonal demand, limited capacities, competitive promotions, or high volatility in forecasting. Indeed, decisions such as when and how much to produce, where to store inventory, and whether to lease additional warehouse space may have enormous impact on supply chain performance.

Traditionally, the supply chain planning process was performed manually with a spreadsheet and was done by each function in the company independently of other functions. The production plan would be determined at the plant, independently from the inventory plan, and would typically require the two plans to be somehow coordinated at a later time. This implies that divisions typically end up "optimizing" just one parameter, usually production costs.

In modern supply chains, however, it is well understood that this sequential process is not effective. For example, focusing only on production costs typically implies that each manufacturing facility produces just a few SKUs, thus producing large batches and reducing fixed costs. Unfortunately, this may increase transportation costs as the specific facility producing a certain product may be far from the demand market. Alternatively, reducing transportation costs will typically require each manufacturing facility to produce many SKUs and, hence, customers can be served by the closest facility.

Finding the right balance between the two cost components requires replacing the sequential planning process by a process that takes into account the interaction between the various levels of the supply chain and identifies a strategy that maximizes supply chain performance. This is referred to as global optimization and it requires an optimization-based decision-support system. These systems, which model the supply chain as large-scale mixed-integer linear programs, are analytical tools capable of considering the complexity and dynamic nature of the supply chain.

These types of decision-support tools require some or all of the following data:

- Facility locations: plants, distribution centers, and demand points.
- Transportation resources including internal fleet and common carriers.
- Products and product information.
- Production line information such as minimum lot size, capacity, costs, and so forth.
- Warehouse capacities and other information such as certain technology (refrigerators) that a specific warehouse has and, hence, can store certain products.
- Demand forecast by location, product, and time.

Depending on the objective of the planning process, the output can focus on either of the following:

- **Sourcing strategies.** Where should each product be produced during the planning horizon?
- **Supply chain master plan.** What are the production quantities, shipment size, and storage requirements by product, location, and time period?

In some applications, the supply chain master plan serves as an input for a detailed production scheduling system. In this case, the production scheduling system employs information about production quantities and due dates received from the supply chain master plan. This information is used to propose a detailed manufacturing sequence and schedule. This allows the planner to integrate the back end of the supply chain, that is, manufacturing and production, and the front end of the supply chain, that is, demand planning and order replenishment; see Figure 3-19. This diagram illustrates an important issue. The focus of order replenishment systems is on service level. Similarly, the focus of tactical planning, that is, the process by which the firm generates a supply chain master plan, is on cost minimization or profit maximization. Finally, the focus in the detailed manufacturing scheduling

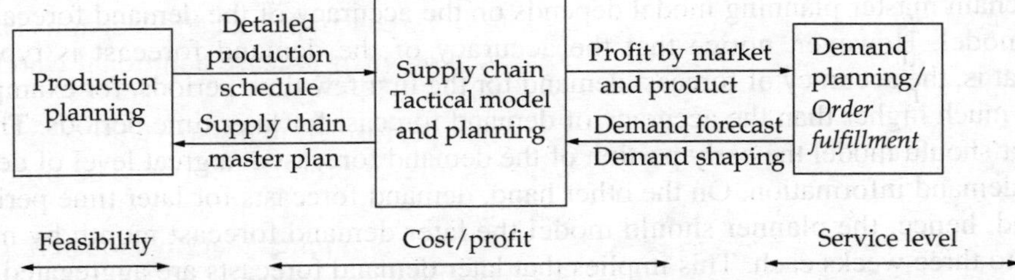

FIGURE 3-19 The extended supply chain: from manufacturing to order fulfillment.

portion of the supply chain is on *feasibility*. That is, the focus is on generating a detailed production schedule that satisfies all production constraints and meets all the due date requirements generated by the supply chain master plan.

Of course, the output from the tactical planning process, that is, the supply chain master plan, is shared with supply chain participants to improve coordination and collaboration. For example, the distribution center managers can now better use this information to plan their labor and shipping needs. Similarly, plant managers use the plan to make sure they have a sufficient supply of raw materials.

In addition, supply chain master planning tools can identify potential supply chain bottlenecks *early* in the planning process, allowing the planner to answer questions such as

- Will leased warehouse space alleviate capacity problems?
- When and where should the inventory for seasonal or promotional demand be built and stored?
- Can capacity problems be alleviated by rearranging warehouse territories?
- What impact do changes in the forecast have on the supply chain?
- What will be the impact of running overtime at the plants or outsourcing production?
- What plant should replenish each warehouse?
- Should the firm ship by sea or by air? Shipping by sea implies long lead times and therefore requires high inventory levels. On the other hand, using air carriers reduces lead times and, hence, inventory levels but significantly increases transportation cost.
- Should we rebalance inventory between warehouses or replenish from the plants to meet unexpected regional changes in demand?

Another important capability that tactical planning tools have is the ability to analyze demand plans and resource utilization to maximize profit. This enables balancing the effect of promotions, new product introductions, and other planned changes in demand patterns and supply chain costs. Planners now are able to analyze the impact of various pricing strategies as well as identify markets, stores, or customers that do not provide the desired profit margins.

Naturally, one has to decide whether to focus on cost minimization or on profit maximization. While the answer to this question may vary from instance to instance, it is clear that cost minimization is important when the structure of the supply chain is fixed or at times of a recession and therefore oversupply. In this case, the focus is on satisfying all demand at the lowest cost by allocating resources effectively. On the other hand, profit maximization is important at times of growth, that is, at a time when demand exceeds supply. In this case, capacity can be limited because of the use of limited natural resources or because of expensive manufacturing processes that are hard to expand, as is the case in the chemical and electronic industries. In these cases, deciding whom to serve and for how much is more critical than cost savings.

Finally, an effective supply chain master planning tool also must be able to help the planners improve the accuracy of the supply chain model. This, of course, is counterintuitive since the accuracy of the supply chain master planning model depends on the accuracy of the demand forecast that is an input to the model. However, notice that the accuracy of the demand forecast is typically time dependent. That is, the accuracy of forecast demand for the first few time periods, for example, the first four weeks, is much higher than the accuracy of demand forecast for later time periods. This suggests that the planner should model the early portion of the demand forecast at a great level of detail, that is, apply weekly demand information. On the other hand, demand forecasts for later time periods are not as accurate and, hence, the planner should model the later demand forecast month by month or by groups of two to three weeks each. This implies that later demand forecasts are aggregated into longer time buckets and, hence, due to the risk pooling concept, the accuracy of the forecast improves.

In summary, supply chain master planning helps address fundamental trade-offs in the supply chain such as production setup cost versus transportation costs or production lot sizes versus capacities. It takes into account supply chain costs such as production, supply, warehousing, transportation, taxes, and inventory as well as capacities and changes in the parameters over time.

EXAMPLE 3-6

This example illustrates how supply chain master planning can be used dynamically and consistently to help a large food manufacturer manage the supply chain. The food manufacturer makes production and distribution decisions at the division level. Even at the division level, the problems tend to be large-scale. Indeed, a typical division may include hundreds of products, multiple plants, many production lines within a plant, multiple warehouses (including overflow facilities), bill-of-material structures to account for different packaging options, and a 52-week demand forecast for each product for each region. The forecast accounts for seasonality and planned promotions. The annual forecast is important because a promotion late in the year may require production resources relatively early in the year. Production and warehousing capacities are tight and products have limited shelf life that need to be integrated into the analysis. Finally, the scope of the plan spans many functional areas, including purchasing, production, transportation, distribution, and inventory management.

Traditionally, the supply chain planning process was performed manually with a spreadsheet and was done by each function in the company. That is, the production plan would be done at the plant, independently from the inventory plan, and would typically require the two plans to be somehow coordinated at a later time. This implies that divisions typically end up "optimizing" just one parameter, usually production costs. The tactical planning SCP introduced in the company allows the planners to reduce systemwide cost and better utilize resources such as manufacturing and warehousing. Indeed, a detailed comparison of the plan generated by the tactical tool with the spreadsheet strategy suggests that the optimization-based tool is capable of reducing total costs across the entire supply chain. See Figure 3-20 for illustrative results.

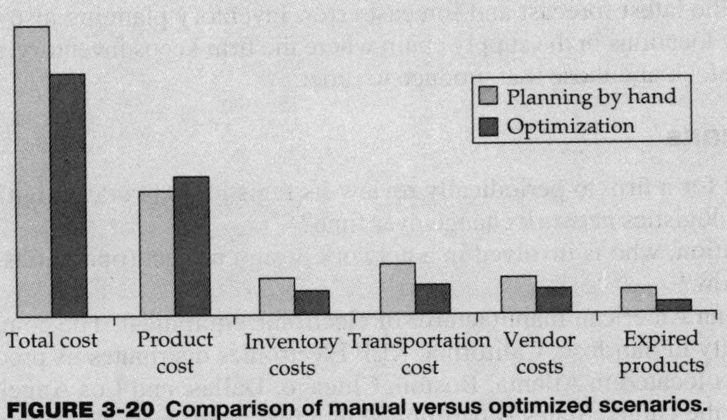

FIGURE 3-20 Comparison of manual versus optimized scenarios.

SUMMARY

Optimizing supply chain performance is difficult because of conflicting objectives, demand and supply uncertainties, and supply chain dynamics. However, through network planning, which combines network design, inventory positioning, and resource allocation, the firm can globally optimize supply chain performance. This is achieved by considering the entire network, taking into account production, warehousing, transportation, and inventory costs as well as service level requirements.

TABLE 3-8
NETWORK PLANNING CHARACTERISTICS

	Network design	Inventory positioning and management	Resource allocation
Decision focus	Infrastructure	Safety stock	Production Distribution
Planning horizon	Years	Months	Months
Aggregation level	Family	Item	Classes
Frequency	Yearly	Monthly/weekly	Monthly/weekly
ROI	High	Medium	Medium
Implementation	Very short	Short	Short
Users	Very few	Few	Few

Table 3-8 summarizes the key dimensions of each of the planning activities, network design, inventory positioning/management, and resource allocation. The table shows that network design involves long-term plans, typically over years; is done at a high level; and can yield high returns. The planning horizon for resource allocation (supply chain master planning) is months or quarter, the frequency of replanning is high, for example, every few weeks, and it typically delivers quick results as well. Inventory planning is focused on short-term uncertainty in demand, lead time, processing time, or supply. The frequency of replanning is high, for example, monthly planning to determine appropriate safety stock based on the latest forecast and forecast error. Inventory planning also can be used more strategically to identify locations in the supply chain where the firm keeps inventory, as well as identify stages that produce to stock and those that produce to order.

DISCUSSION QUESTIONS

1. Why is it important for a firm to periodically review its logistics network design? How do a firm's requirements for its logistics network change over time?
2. Within the organization, who is involved in a network design project (operations, sales, marketing executives, etc.)? How?
3. KLF Electronics is an American manufacturer of electronic equipment. The company has a single manufacturing facility in San Jose, California. KLF Electronics distributes its products through five regional warehouses located in Atlanta, Boston, Chicago, Dallas, and Los Angeles. In the current distribution system, the United States is partitioned into five major markets, each of which is served by a single regional warehouse. Customers, typically retail outlets, receive items directly from the regional warehouse in their market area. That is, in the current distribution system, each customer is assigned to a single market and receives deliveries from one regional warehouse. The warehouses receive items from the manufacturing facility. Typically, it takes about two weeks to satisfy an order placed by any of the regional warehouses. In recent years, KLF has seen a significant increase in competition and huge pressure from their customers to improve service level and reduce costs. To improve service level and reduce costs, KLF would like to consider an alternative distribution strategy in which the five regional warehouses are replaced with a single, central warehouse that will be in charge of all customer orders.

Describe how you would design a new logistics network consisting of only a single warehouse. Provide an outline of such an analysis: What are the main steps? Specifically, what data would you need? What are the advantages and disadvantages of the newly suggested distribution strategy relative to the existing distribution strategy?

4. In selecting potential warehouse sites, it is important to consider issues such as geographical and infrastructure conditions, natural resources and labor availability, local industry and tax regulations, and public interest. For each of the following industries, give specific examples of how the issues listed above could affect the choice of potential warehouse sites:
   a. Automobile manufacturing
   b. Pharmaceuticals
   c. Books
   d. Aircraft manufacturing
   e. Book distribution
   f. Furniture manufacturing and distribution
   g. PC manufacturing
   h. A typical Indian retail mall.
5. Consider the pharmaceutical and the chemical industries. In the pharmaceutical industry, products have high margins and overnight delivery typically is used. On the other hand, in the chemical industry, products have low margins and outbound transportation cost is more expensive than inbound transportation. What is the effect of these characteristics on the number of warehouses for firms in these industries? Where do you expect to see more warehouses: in the chemical industry or the pharmaceutical industry?
6. In Section 3.2.3, we observe that the TL transportation rate structure is asymmetric. Why?
7. Discuss some specific items that make up the handling costs, fixed costs, and storage costs associated with a warehouse.
8. What is the difference between using an exact optimization technique and a heuristic to solve a problem?
9. What is simulation, and how does it help solve difficult logistics problems?

CASE: H. C. Starck, Inc.

1. THE ARRIVAL

Tom Carroll was a Fellow in MIT's Leaders for Manufacturing program. On June 1st, 1999, after completing a difficult academic year, Tom arrived at H. C. Starck, Inc., to start on his six-month internship. He knew that his work would involve reducing lead times, but did not know any specifics. His first meeting was with Lee Sallade, Director of Operations. Figure 3-21 presents an abbreviated organizational chart for H. C. Starck. Lee explained that the sales group was pressuring him to reduce lead times—defined here as the time from when the customer places the order, until the product is shipped. The general feeling was that this metric was running at 8 to 14 weeks, mostly due to the long manufacturing time, but there was no hard data. The sales department felt that if lead time could be reduced to three weeks, they would have a substantial advantage in the

Source: Copyright © 2000 Massachusetts Institute of Technology. This case was prepared by LFM Fellow Thomas J. Carroll under the direction of Professors Stephen C. Graves and Thomas W. Eagar as the basis for class discussion rather than to illustrate either effective or ineffective handling of an administrative situation. The case is based on the author's LFM internship at the H. C. Starck, Inc. during July–Dec., 1999.

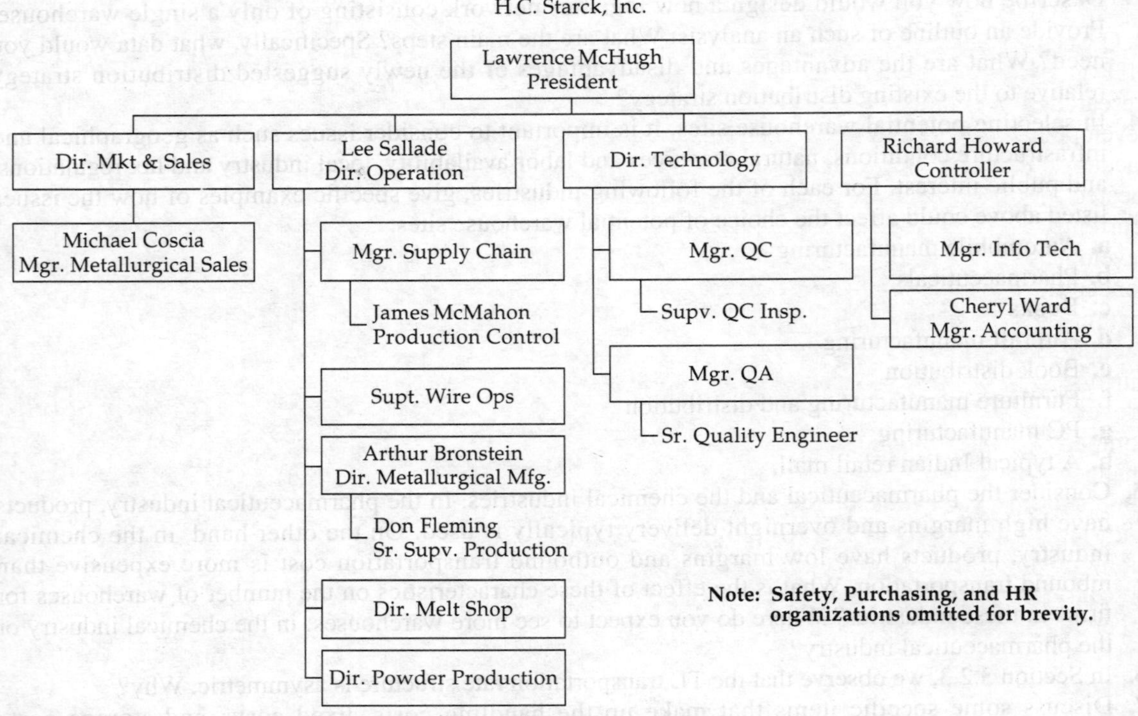

FIGURE 3-21 Abbreviated H. C. Starck organizational chart.

marketplace, and would realize incremental sales volume. Lee agreed that lead time was important, but cautioned about focusing solely on lead time, and not overall cycle time, which is the length of time it takes material to physically flow through the manufacturing process:

> We need to reduce cycle time as well as lead time. Larry *[the company president]* got burned once on a lead-time reduction project. The distributors ended up taking all the benefit. You should talk to him about that.

Lee explained that cycle time and inventory were important, but were difficult to influence since the company held such a high level of tantalum inventory:

> Making Ta ingot from scrap gives us a cost advantage compared to making it from good Ta powder. We have the technology to process and refine scrap that other companies do not. We buy scrap before we need it, because the supply is so erratic. We ran out once in 1996, and we don't want that to happen again. Sometimes we buy more than is needed, just to ensure an uninterrupted supply.

Lee also stressed the idea of managing with data. He was concerned that many operational decisions were based on 'industrial mythology,' and that rigorous data collection and analysis could help to break out of this mode of operation. Tom spent some more time discussing the operation with Lee, and left the meeting with a clear project goal: Reduce customer lead time to three weeks or less for all metallurgical products, without increasing inventory. While the goal was clear, the method was not. According to Lee: "We're not really sure how to achieve this. That is why we hired a smart MIT student like you!" Tom had a lot of work to do, and was eager to apply his newly learned skills.

2. THE COMPANY

H. C. Starck, Inc., traces its roots back to 1940, when MIT graduate Richard Morse founded National Research Corporation (NRC) as a process-development company focused on exploiting vacuum technology. The company was originally located at 70 Memorial Drive in Cambridge (currently MIT building E51). Early processes developed at NRC include 'Minute Maid' frozen concentrated orange juice, and 'Holiday Brand' instant coffee. In the 1950's, NRC applied its vacuum technology to the production of high-purity metals, and in 1959 entered the tantalum processing business. Morse left in 1960, and the company went through a series of ownership changes, starting with the acquisition by Norton in 1963. Norton divested its interest in NRC in 1976, with H. C. Starck AG (a German company specializing in refractory metals) acquiring 50 percent, and a venture capital group acquiring the other 50 percent. Bayer AG purchased the majority of H. C. Starck AG in 1986; Bayer Corp USA purchased the remaining 50 percent of H. C. Starck, Inc., shortly thereafter. At this point, HCST was focused primarily on the reduction of tantalum, and production of tantalum powders. It wasn't until HCST acquired the tantalum mill and wire products from Fansteel in 1989 that it entered the metallurgical products market in a large way. The H. C. Starck International Group also has Ta reduction and powder manufacturing operations in Japan, Thailand, and Germany, but the Newton, MA, location is the only plant with melting and mill capability.

3. TANTALUM

Tantalum (Ta) was discovered in 1802 by Ekeberg, but many chemists thought niobium and tantalum were identical elements until Rowe in 1844, and Marignac, in 1866, showed that niobic and tantalic acids were two different acids. The first relatively pure ductile tantalum was produced by von Bolton in 1903. Tantalum ores are found in Australia, Brazil, Mozambique, Thailand, Portugal, Nigeria, Zaire, and Canada. Separation of tantalum from niobium requires several complicated steps. Several methods are used to commercially produce the element, including reduction of potassium fluorotantalate with sodium.

Tantalum is a gray, heavy, and very hard metal. Tantalum is almost completely immune to chemical attack at temperatures below 150°C, and is attacked only by hydrofluoric acid, acidic solutions containing the fluoride ion, and free sulfur trioxide. Alkalis corrode it only very slowly. At high temperatures, tantalum becomes much more reactive. The element has a melting point (about 3000°C) exceeded only by tungsten and rhenium. Tantalum is used to make a variety of alloys with desirable properties such as high melting point, high strength, and good ductility. Tantalum is used to make electrolytic capacitors and vacuum furnace parts, which account for about 60 percent of its use. The metal is also widely used to fabricate chemical process equipment, nuclear reactors, and aircraft and missile parts. Tantalum is completely immune to body liquids and is a nonirritating material. It has, therefore, found wide use in making

TABLE 3-9

TANTALUM PRICES

Form	Price per pound
Tantalite ore (contained pentoxide basis)	$ 35–45
Capacitor-grade powder	$135–240
Capacitor wire	$180–250
Sheet	$100–150

(Prices are from 1998 USGS data)

surgical appliances. Tantalum oxide is used to make special glass with high index of refraction for camera lenses. The metal has many other uses, with a total worldwide annual consumption of about 550 tons.

Tantalum is very expensive, as shown in Table 3-9. Compare this to $0.65/lb for aluminum and $5/troy oz ($73/lb) for silver (The Wall Street Journal, June 23, 1999). It is expensive stuff!

4. H. C. STARCK, INC., IN THE TANTALUM SUPPLY CHAIN

Tantalum-containing tin slags and mined ore are processed and refined to the tantalum "double salt," K_2TaF_7, by H. C. Starck AG. This free-flowing white powder is shipped from Germany in pallet-sized containers to the four Ta powder production operations worldwide. The "double salt" is reacted with molten sodium and then cooled to form particles of elemental tantalum dispersed in a solid salt mass. The large mass is mechanically broken up, and the salts are leached out through several steps, leaving pure tantalum powder. Figure 3-22 diagrams a simplified version of the Ta supply chain. A large portion of the powder is further refined and graded, and sold for the production of sintered tantalum capacitors. Some of the powder is sintered into bars for the production of wire, also mostly for capacitors. Ta powder that is under or over the desired particle size is scrapped, and sent to the melt shop for recycling. Also, any scrap from the sintering or wire forming operations is collected and recycled.

The melt shop receives the above-mentioned scrap, as well as scrap from the metallurgical products divisions, scrap purchased on the open market, scrap generated by customers, and occasionally Ta ingots purchased from government reserves. (The United States and Russia have recently been reducing their strategic metal reserves, and periodically sell excess inventory at auction.) The scrap is processed and blended to

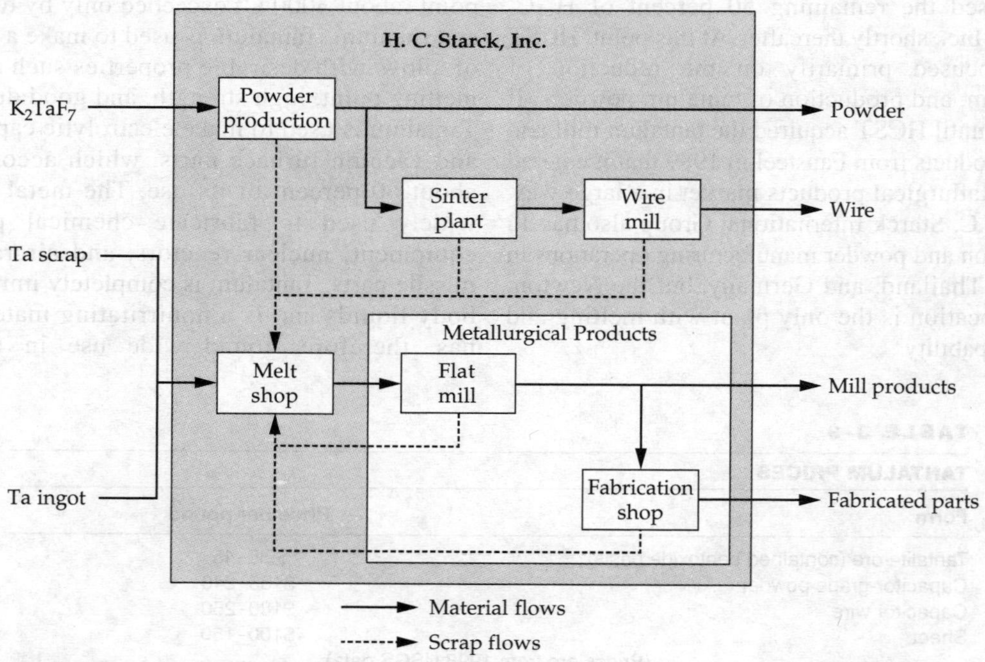

FIGURE 3-22 H. C. Starck, Inc., in the tantalum supply chain.

achieve the desired chemistry, and is then melted into ingots in an electron-beam vacuum furnace. The eight-inch- diameter round ingots are cold-forged to a four-inch- thick 'sheet bar,' which is the starting material for the Metallurgical Products division.

5. METALLURGICAL PRODUCTS

The metallurgical products (MP) division of HCST comprises two basic functional areas, rolling and fabrication. The rolling plant has three mills that reduce the incoming four-inch-thick 'sheet bar' to the final gauge thickness, and a variety of equipment to perform functions such as cleaning, cutting to size, and annealing. The rolling plant produces only flat shapes. The fabrication area includes a sheet-metal shop, a machine shop, and several tube-welding lines. The fabrication shop takes flat stock from the rolling plant, and produces more complex finished products.

All incoming four-inch-thick sheet bars first undergo a 'breakdown' rolling process on the large mill. This mill can produce pieces up to 36 inches wide, and as thin as 0.015 inch. A 12-inch-wide foil mill can start with materials as thick as 0.030 inch, and is used for most production with a final gauge of 0.014 inch or less. There is also a 16-inch-wide intermediate mill, but it is only used for very small custom jobs. Don Fleming, Sr. Supervisor of Production for the rolling plant, has been with HCST for just over a year but has extensive experience from another rolling plant. Don describes the process:

> When we roll a bar down from 4 inches, it develops 'fishtailing' and edge cracks. We need to stop rolling and trim it all around when we get to 1/4 inch thick, to prevent these cracks from propagating. This typically results in a trim loss of 20 percent. If the final gauge is going to be thicker than 1/16 inch, we'll also anneal at this point.

As a metal is cold-rolled, it becomes work hardened. A piece of tantalum that starts out soft and ductile can be reduced up to 95 percent in cross-sectional area, but will become hard and brittle beyond this amount of reduction. By annealing the metal at over 1000° C, the grain structure has a chance to recrystallize to a stress-free state. This restores the original softness and ductility, allowing the piece to be rolled further. Before annealing, the piece of metal must be chemically cleaned. The high annealing temperatures would allow any surface contaminants (notably carbon, oxygen, nitrogen, and hydrogen from the atmosphere and hydrocarbon lubricants) to diffuse interstitially into the metal, causing embrittlement. This cycle of roll-clean-anneal may be repeated several times, as described in Figure 3-23. Don continues his explanation:

> If the final gauge will be less than 1/16 inch, then it will get rolled down to 1/8 inch before we anneal it. We can roll sheet down to 0.015 inch on the large mill. Anything thinner than that goes to the foil mill. Even though we use the same mill, the rolling process is different depending on the gauge. 'Breakdown' is done on the large mill in a free-rolling mode, and brings it to as thin as 1/8 inch. From 1/8 inch down is 'finish' rolling, which is done in tension. Also, we use a different set of work rolls for breakdown and finish—it takes a full shift to convert the large mill between the two processes.

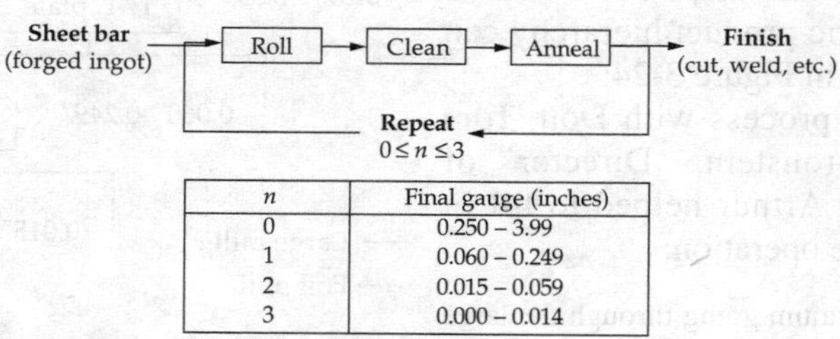

n	Final gauge (inches)
0	0.250 – 3.99
1	0.060 – 0.249
2	0.015 – 0.059
3	0.000 – 0.014

FIGURE 3-23 Basic production process.

TABLE 3-10

LARGE MILL PRODUCTION REPORT

(pounds)	1998 Breakdown	1998 Finish	1999 Breakdown	1999 Finish
Jan.	28,936	12,307	36,255	8,686
Feb.	68,001	10,828	46,175	18,106
Mar.	38,210	24,529	75,256	15,500
Apr.	78,514	22,122	16,978	14,112
May	61,782	20,155	28,539	18,219
June	43,176	24,277	28,103	25,586
July	57,216	15,880		
Aug.	7,838	9,296		
Sept.	28,394	15,981		
Oct.	44,151	11,383		
Nov.	23,73	16,287		
Dec.	46,591	9,792		
YTD	526,540	182,837	231,306	100,209

During 'free rolling,' the workpiece moves through the mill simply by the action of the working rolls. Since the piece is not connected to anything, its entire length can be rolled. In tension rolling, a titanium 'leader' is attached to each end of the workpiece with a spiral spring (much like the pages of a spiral-bound notebook are attached together). The leader is coiled up on an arbor at each end of the mill. Tension applied to the workpiece helps to 'pull' it through the working rolls. Since the spring connection cannot go through the work rolls, there is a yield loss at each end of the piece. This yield, together with the typical side trim yields, averages 10 percent.

This series of rolling operations is the start of every product in the portfolio. By arranging the products by final gauge, and then mapping the number of individual rolling steps and standard stopping points, a generic product hierarchy can be constructed as shown in Figure 3-24.

After discussing the process with Don, Tom met with Arthur Bronstein, Director of Metallurgical Products. Arthur helped to fill in some of the details of the operation:

The average piece of tantalum going through the large rolling mill for breakdown rolling is 570 pounds, and it takes 55 minutes to process it, including piece-to-piece setup. For finish rolling, the average piece is 450 pounds, and it takes two hours to complete. The changeover between breakdown and finish takes a full eight-hour shift. The large mill is staffed with two operators both during rolling and changeover. The fully loaded wage rate is about $25/hour, and we typically run 5 percent to 10 percent overtime.

Arthur also gave Tom a spreadsheet with the mill's production report for last year, and the current year-to-date, shown here in Table 3-10. The large mill ran on a two-week cycle, with about one week of breakdown followed by one

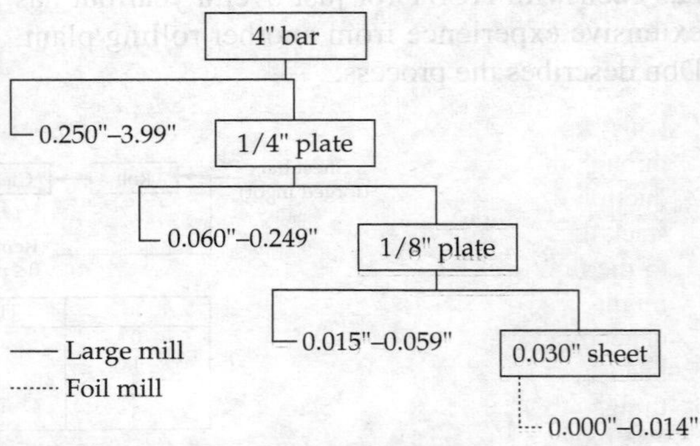

FIGURE 3-24 Generic product hierarchy.

week of finish rolling. This schedule was run three shifts per day (i.e., 24 hours), five days per week, with just four weeks per year shut down for holidays and maintenance. The large mill averaged 85 percent uptime over the course of the year. Arthur wondered if this were the optimal schedule, or if more frequent changeovers would be beneficial.

6. SCHEDULING

H. C. Starck had installed a new ERP system (SAP's R/3) at the beginning of 1999, and was currently using the system to record all transactions. Production planning and scheduling, however, continued to be performed manually. Jim McMahon, Supervisor of Production Control and a 20-year HCST veteran, explains the raw material ordering method.

> I get the sales forecast, and covert it into a production forecast. I set the ingot orders by month for a year at a time, and revise the orders a few times per year. Getting the ingots is the real chore—the melt shop only has so much capacity. Also, sales orders typically come in spikes, and are very unpredictable.

In addition to the sales forecast variability, there was also some production variability. Jim estimated that the mill met its planned schedule about 90 percent of the time, and the melt shop about 80 percent of the time. Most of the schedule misses were due to equipment failures. In addition to raw material ordering, Jim also manually performed shop floor scheduling. The SAP scheduling utility was not used.

> I just know what is going on—all the orders come through me. Paul *[Jim's assistant]* or I generate a production order as soon as we get a sales order. Then I stack them up on my desk, until it is time to release it to the floor. If it isn't due for another eight weeks, I might keep it here four weeks before releasing it, depending on the loading in the shop at the time. I've been here enough years that I just know how long things will take. I don't have faith in SAP because I don't think the recipes are right.

In fact, the recipes were a problem. One indicator of the problem was standard cost. Standard costs were calculated from the recipes, and for some products these costs were lower than for the raw material used to make them—a logical impossibility. The engineering department was working to review and fix these problems, but it was a painstakingly slow process. A particularly problematic product to schedule was tubing. Tubing was produced by rolling flat sheet into a tube, and sealing the resulting seam by gas-tungsten arc welding. The plant could produce and inspect about 1,500 feet of tubing per day, working two shifts. Tube orders tended to be unpredictable and large—an order totaling 1,000 feet would be considered typical. Also, due to the extremely high material cost, nearly all orders were cut-to-length. In addition to the length, bending to a shape (for example, a u-bend for a heat exchanger application), or having caps welded on one end, further customized many orders. Jim explained the problem:

> The big problem in tubing is the erratic schedule, big peaks and valleys. This has been helped somewhat by 'blanket orders,' which allow us to do some smoothing.

In a "blanket order," a customer would commit to buy a quantity of a certain product, say 5,000 feet of $^3/_4$-inch diameter × 0.015-inch wall thickness tubing, by the end of the year. Then the plant would build the 5,000-foot tube inventory at standard 20-foot lengths. Randomly throughout the year, the customers would issue 'releases' against the blanket order. A typical release might ask for 50 tubes at 9-foot-9-inches each, to be shipped in six weeks. The tubes would be cut from stock, and shipped. In this example, the scrap rate works out well; 25 of the 20-foot standard sections could be cut to make the 50 tubes, with less than 3 percent scrap. Oftentimes, however, the scrap rate was much worse. If the above example had been for slightly longer tubes, say 50 pieces at 10 feet 9 inches each, then 50 of the standard 20-foot pieces would be cut to fill the order, with 50 pieces at 9 feet 3 inches each left over. These were set aside in the hope that they would eventually be used on another order, leading to an accumulation of odd-sized pieces. Sections shorter than two feet were scrapped.

7. SALES AND MARKETING

Mike Coscia, Manager of Marketing and Sales, Metallurgical Products, discussed the sales incentives:

> Our corporate profit sharing bonus is based on four goals: Sales volume, Return on Assets, Quality, and Safety. We've hit the maximum payout each of the last two years, and we're shooting to do it again this year. Reducing lead time is a great thing to do, in that it may help us make more sales, and will improve ROA, but it doesn't directly affect our bonus.

Still, he agreed that lead-time reduction was important:

> Tantalum is 4x the price of Zirconium or Hasteloy. If the customers can't get the tantalum in time, they might substitute one of the other alloys. If it works, they'll never switch back.

Mike was skeptical about our ability to achieve the goal of three-week lead time.

> I don't think we can get there. Our sales volumes are 10 times what they were 15 years ago, but the process hasn't changed. Sometimes I think the best thing sales can do is not take an order. We've just started to load the forecast data into SAP. Production planning is still done manually. There seems to be an 'information black hole'—orders go to the mill, but the demand data doesn't seem to make it back upstream to the melt shop.

There was a team started a few months ago to look at order processing, with the goal of getting all the paperwork from customer to production in less than two weeks, 80 percent of the time. Mike expressed frustration with the new SAP R/3 system:

> I don't understand why it takes so long, especially now that we have SAP. Why is there a physical piece of paper that travels from Sales to Production? Why can't this be automated through SAP? I know SAP can do this, but there are a lot of complaints about the system, and fear of doing it wrong.

As one way around the "information black hole," Sales, Production Control, and Operations had recently instituted a 'drumbeat' meeting each morning at 8:00 a.m. This meeting focused on achieving on-time delivery, by each morning reviewing the status of all the shipments that were due in the next week. Any that were at risk of being late were expedited through the plant. The meeting did keep everyone up-to-date on order status, but an unintended effect was that most jobs were bypassed until they made it to the 'drumbeat list,' then it was a race to get them completed on time.

8. FINANCE

Cheryl Ward was HCST's Manager of Accounting, and had led the implementation of the financial module of SAP:

> SAP has made a fundamental change in how we collect financial data. The manufacturing people used to give weekly time sheets and material tickets to accounting, who entered the data, and made sure that it all made sense. Now, the manufacturing people enter the data directly into SAP, as a real-time transaction. This is a big cultural change.

It took a couple of months, but the operators on the manufacturing floor became proficient at making the transactions, with fairly high accuracy and reliability. While the transaction recording was going well, the behind-the-scenes calculations performed by SAP were not. One example of this involved the anneal oven. Each shop order was being charged for eight hours of oven time. Parts do take approximately eight hours to anneal; however, many parts can be in the oven simultaneously. The system was not set up to account for this, leading to errors in both allocation of overhead (and therefore product costs), and also in the scheduling system (one of the reasons it was not used). From a financial standpoint, these errors led to large cost allocation variances that were adjusted at the end of the accounting period. Even six months into the implementation, the adjustments were sometimes as large as 100 percent of the actual values. Rick Howard, HCST's Controller, discussed inventory:

> Inventory is very expensive—we seem to have years of inventory. Since scrap is such an important raw material for us, we consider it a strategic purchase—we buy it even when we don't really need it. Tantalum is a thinly traded market, so we take it when we can get it, if for nothing else than to keep it out of the hands of our competitors. Reducing inventory in the plant won't really save us money—it will just push the inventory back in the pipeline to scrap. Scrap is valued at $75 per pound, heavy gauge material (thicker than $^1/_4$ inch) at $100 per pound, and thinner gauges average $125 per pound, so, there is not a huge savings for holding material earlier in the pipeline. We're going to hold the inventory somewhere in the system; it might as well be at strategic points near the end.

Rick pointed out that as a subsidiary of Bayer, HCST's cost of capital was a favorable 9 percent. Rick also expressed concern about a Chinese company that recently started selling Ta wire. While their quality was not very good, their sales price was roughly equal to HCST's production cost. Rick was worried that the Chinese would eventually improve their quality, and then might enter the mill products market.

9. THE PRESIDENT

Tom also met with Larry McHugh, President of H. C. Starck, Inc. Larry described one of his experiences with cycle-time reduction at another company:

> I'm not a big fan of lead time and service level projects. These will help your business when you are supplying end customers, but not when you are supplying intermediates, like we are. We already have a majority of the worldwide chemical process industry Ta market. Some of our customers whine about long deliveries, but most would not buy more even if we improved it. I think quicker deliveries might give us an advantage in some of the smaller segments, such as furnace parts and sputtering targets. Before I came to H. C. Starck, I ran operations at another company. We spent a pile of money implementing Goldratt's "The Goal" management method. We really took it to heart, and substantially reduced cycle times, but gained no benefit. Our product was sold through regional distributors—they ended up taking all the inventory savings. You could argue that with the improved performance, we could have recruited more distributors, but with the geographic exclusions, and with others being locked up by our competitors, there was really no way to change. So we spent a bunch of money, with nothing to show for it. I don't want that to happen here. The one area where this really may help is with inventory. If you can figure a way to cut our inventories, then that may really save some money.

10. LEAD TIME AND INVENTORY DATA

By this time, Tom's head was spinning with conflicting opinions and advice from each of the different players. Everyone seemed to have an opinion, but few people had much supporting data. Tom decided it was time to collect some hard data on which to base his recommendation. While the SAP R/3 system was not being used for planning or scheduling, it was being used to record all the accounting transactions, including order creation and all material movements. Transactions were recorded in near real time, usually within a few hours of when they physically occurred, and often within minutes. Even though some of the values calculated by recipes were unreliable, the data resulting from manually entered transactions were quite accurate. Figure 3-25 shows lead-time data from a customer perspective—how long does it take from order to delivery? (Initial compliance for using SAP to record transactions was poor, so data for January and February were ignored.) The data showed that the average lead time was under 7 weeks, not 12, as was commonly quoted. Many of the longest orders were actually "blanket orders" with no releases against them yet.

At the start of the project, the generally accepted belief was that the customer lead time was long due to the long manufacturing time. Figure 3-26 shows this manufacturing lead time,

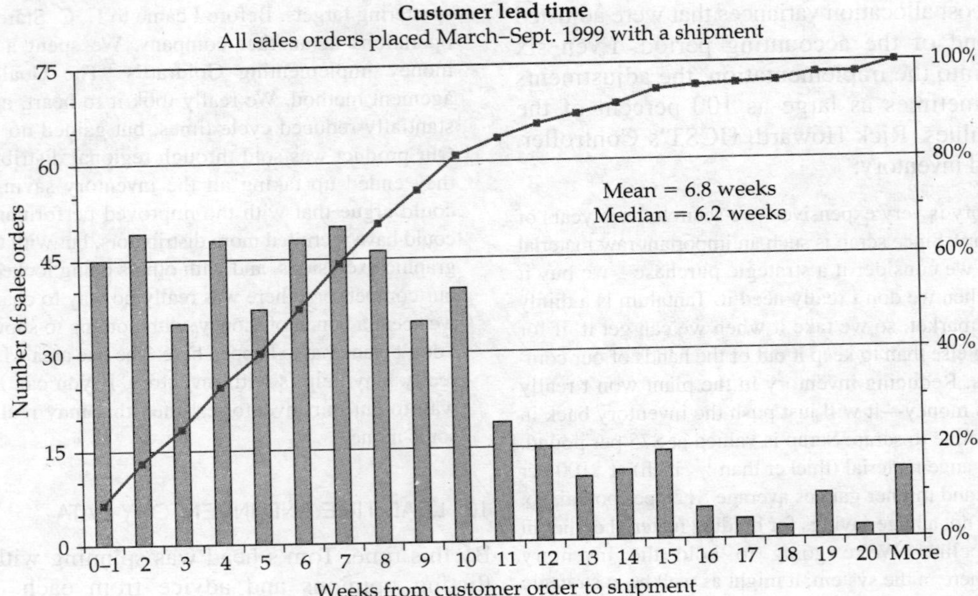

FIGURE 3-25 Customer lead time.

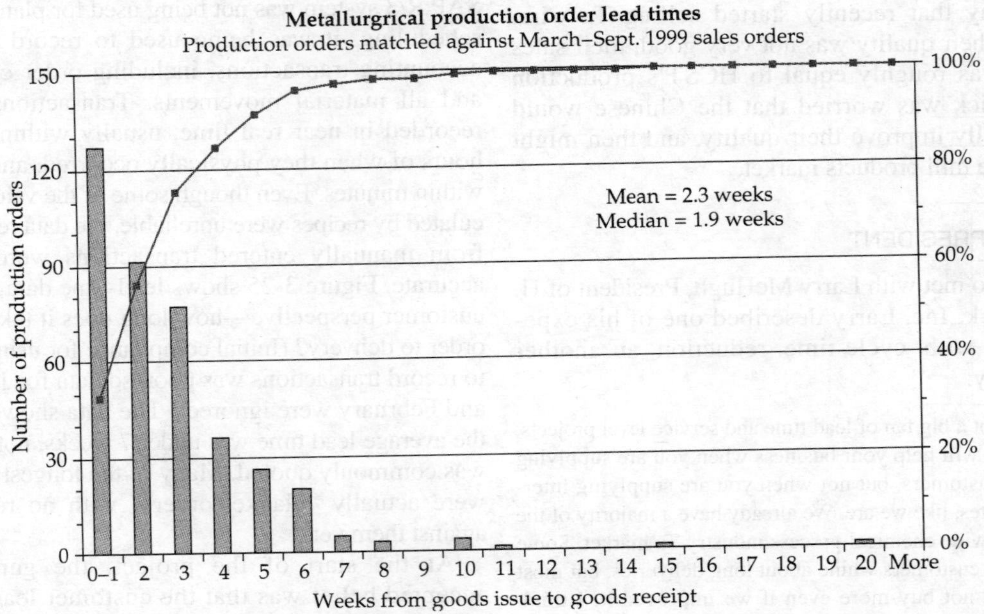

FIGURE 3-26 Manufacturing lead time.

counting the time from 'goods issue' to 'goods receipt.' 'Goods issue' is the transaction that occurs when the input material is physically issued to the shop floor, and 'goods receipt' is the transaction that is completed after all manufacturing and inspection steps are complete, and the material physically moves to the stockroom, to be shelved or packaged for shipment. This graph shows that, on average, final items are manufactured in just over two weeks, with 75 percent complete in three weeks. How could it be that manufacturing averaged just over two weeks, but order-to-delivery averaged nearly seven weeks? What happened to the other five weeks? One possibility is that there was a shortage of material, with no raw-material inventories from which to produce.

Figure 3-27 shows inventory levels. They appear to be more than adequate to ensure a high level of availability. If neither manufacturing time nor inventory levels were the cause of the long customer lead times, what could it be? Before Tom's arrival, it was felt that a lot of time was wasted getting the customers' orders to the shop floor. A group had been meeting for several weeks looking at the issue, and had started some process

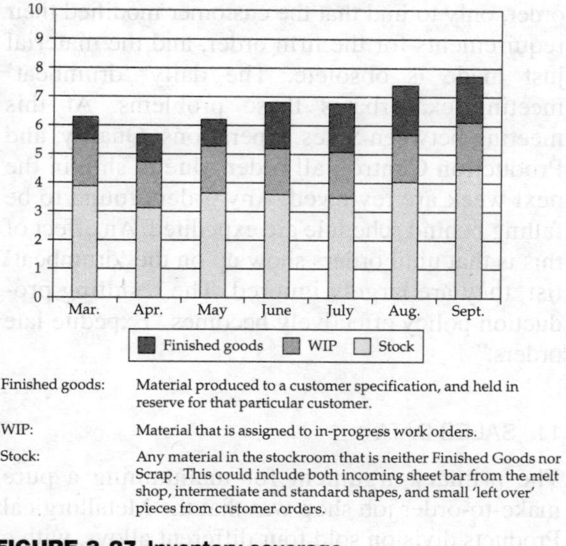

10
9
8
7
6
5
4
3
2
1
0
Mar.
Apr.
May
June
July
Aug.
Sept.
Finished goods
WIP
Stock
Finished goods: Material produced to a customer specification, and held in reserve for that particular customer.
WIP: Material that is assigned to in-progress work orders.
Stock: Any material in the stockroom that is neither Finished Goods nor Scrap. This could include both incoming sheet bar from the melt shop, intermediate and standard shapes, and small 'left over' pieces from customer orders.

FIGURE 3-27 Inventory coverage.

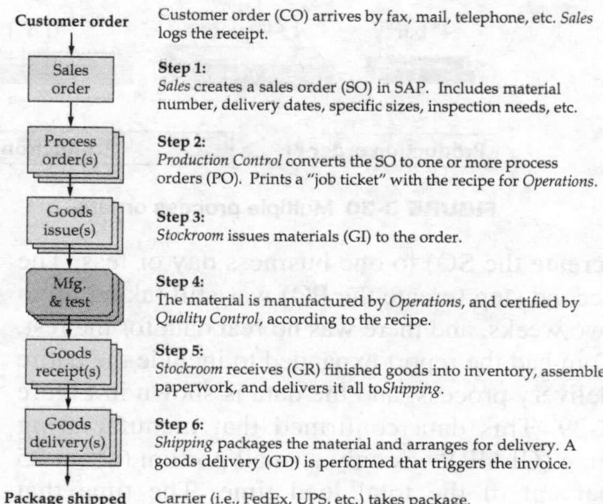

Customer order
Customer order (CO) arrives by fax, mail, telephone, etc. Sales logs the receipt.
Sales order
Step 1:
Sales creates a sales order (SO) in SAP. Includes material number, delivery dates, specific sizes, inspection needs, etc.
Process order(s)
Step 2:
Production Control converts the SO to one or more process orders (PO). Prints a "job ticket" with the recipe for Operations.
Goods issue(s)
Step 3:
Stockroom issues materials (GI) to the order.
Mfg. & test
Step 4:
The material is manufactured by Operations, and certified by Quality Control, according to the recipe.
Goods receipt(s)
Step 5:
Stockroom receives (GR) finished goods into inventory, assembles paperwork, and delivers it all toShipping.
Goods delivery(s)
Step 6:
Shipping packages the material and arranges for delivery. A goods delivery (GD) is performed that triggers the invoice.
Package shipped
Carrier (i.e., FedEx, UPS, etc.) takes package.

FIGURE 3-28 Order flow diagram.

mapping. In theory, the information flow was controlled by SAP R/3 as shown in Figure 3-28. In reality, SAP was often ignored, and a manual paper-based process was used to transmit the order from Sales to Operations.

A custom ABAP (SAP's programming language) report had been created to look at the first two steps in the process, and procedures had been implemented that reduced the first step

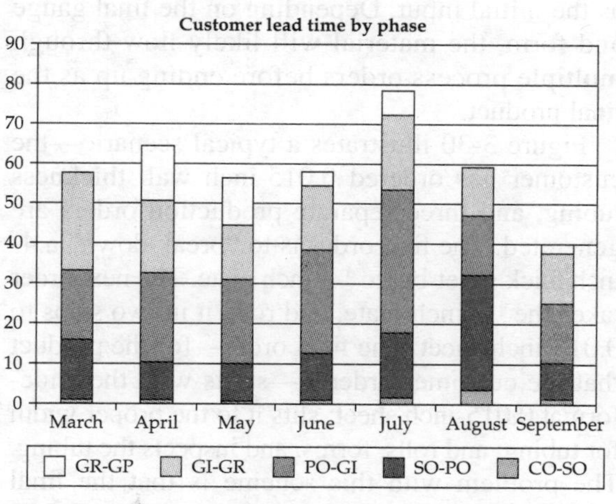

FIGURE 3-29 Customer lead time—by order phase.

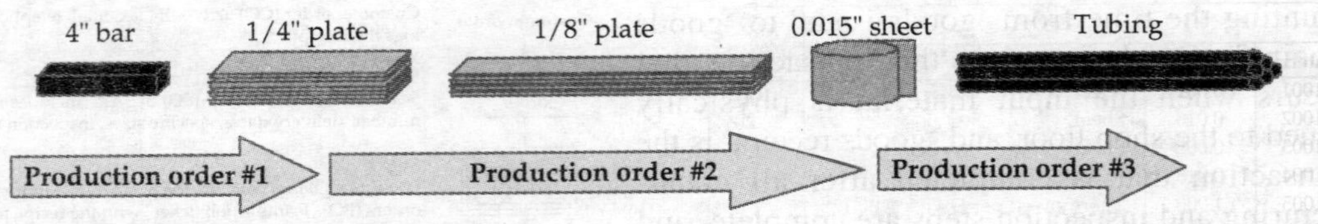

FIGURE 3-30 Multiple process orders.

(create the SO) to one business day or less. The second step (create the PO) was still taking up to two weeks, and there was no real data for the rest. Tom had the report expanded to include the entire delivery process, and the data is shown in Figure 3-29. This data confirmed that manufacturing time (GI-GR) was only a small portion (about 25 percent of the total lead time. The time that finished material sat waiting to be shipped was also relatively small—most orders were shipped as soon as they were built. The problem lay in the SO to GI phase—all that time between when the sales department entered the order in to SAP, and when the plant actually started manufacturing. (The large increase in SO-PO in August can be attributed to the annual two-week plant shutdown.) This long lag time can be partially explained by the slow manual process of transmitting orders, and partially by the current production policy. The typical production routing used a make-to-order policy, with either 4- inch sheet bar or $^1/_4$-inch plate from a stock inventory as the initial input. Depending on the final gauge and form, the material will likely flow through multiple process orders before ending up as the final product.

Figure 3-30 illustrates a typical scenario—the customer has ordered 0.015-inch wall thickness tubing, and three separate production orders are generated. The first order is to "break down" a 4-inch thick sheet-bar to $^1/_4$-inch plate. The next order takes the $^1/_4$-inch plate, and rolls it in two steps to 0.015-inch sheet. The final order—for the product that the customer ordered—starts with the wide-format 0.015-inch sheet; slits it to the proper width for tubing; and rolls, forms, and inspects the tubing. The problem with this scheme is that the final process order, the one that makes the product for the customer, cannot be started until the previous steps, that create the necessary intermediate material, are completed. Figure 3-26 measured only the manufacturing lead time for customer-ordered items, in this case, equivalent to the in-process time of production order #3, which produced the tubing from the 0.015-inch gauge sheet.

Compounding this are certain ordering and expediting schemes. As a way to cut customer lead times, the sales department enters hard orders on probable sales, so that when the actual customer order arrives, the material is already partially through the manufacturing process. Sometimes this works well, but often it causes one of two problems. Since SAP requires that orders have a delivery date, sales makes up a date. If the date is too far into the future, the order may be ignored by Operations. If the date is too close, Operations may build and ship the material before the customer wants it, or completes the probable order, only to find that the customer modified their requirements for the firm order, and the material just made is obsolete. The daily 'drumbeat' meeting exacerbates these problems. At this meeting between Sales, Operations, Quality, and Production Control, all orders due to ship in the next week are reviewed. Any orders found to be falling behind schedule are expedited. An effect of this is that until orders show up on the 'drumbeat' list, they are largely ignored. The resulting production policy effectively becomes "Expedite late orders."

11. SALES DATA

The primary argument for maintaining a pure make-to-order job shop was that the Metallurgical Products division sold four different alloys, with a

			1999/Invoiced sales—pounds per month								
Material	Gauge	Description	Jan.	Feb.	Mar.	Apr.	May	June	July	Aug.	Sept.
1001	0.005	Sheet - 1.0"× 23.75"	171	0	0	20	0	0	0	17	0
1002	0.010	Sheet	20	56	287	179	41	204	560	143	276
1003	0.005	Sheet	263	576	584	812	617	969	572	359	909
1004	0.015	Sheet	68	611	1,263	167	1,917	803	321	377	404
1005	1.000	Thermowell per Dwg # ABC12	0	0	0	0	0	0	0	0	2
1006	0.150	Sheet	101	0	0	0	0	0	0	0	0
1007	0.060	Plate	0	146	32	117	129	414	581	26	191
1008	0.040	Sheet	321	101	191	486	8	98	263	176	690
1009	0.030	Sheet	0	122	614	275	422	360	686	246	177
1010	0.020	Sheet	0	54	102	183	45	54	126	92	119
1011	0.002	Foil	618	1,079	1,215	1,188	1,020	290	1,590	849	1,017
1012	0.125	Plate	228	8	32	90	432	17	8	0	450
1013	0.150	Plate	1,100	0	0	0	0	35	0	0	0
1014	0.250	Plate	6	12	0	770	0	752	0	0	174
1015	0.375	Plate	0	0	0	0	0	0	375	0	0
1016	0.500	Tube—0.50" OD	3	0	0	51	6	54	33	27	33
1017	0.750	Tube—3/4"	0	0	0	8	12	558	0	0	12
1018	0.015	Tube—1.0" OD	8	0	0	0	0	230	0	41	0
1019	0.020	Tube—1.5" OD	0	0	0	0	0	0	0	11	0
1020	0.500	Tube—.50" OD	44	3	0	0	0	0	35	0	0
1021	0.020	Tube—5/8" OD	0	6	0	0	0	8	0	0	0
1022	0.102	Sheet	0	27	33	0	0	0	0	0	0
1023	0.010	Sheet—1.0" × 23.75"	0	99	14	18	0	0	0	0	0
1024	0.060	Plate—7/8" × 39.125"	15	0	24	0	0	0	0	15	0
1025	1.125	Ring—6.25" OD × 4.5" ID	45	0	0	0	0	0	0	0	0
1026	1.000	Ring—4.0" OD × 2.5" ID	12	0	0	0	0	0	0	0	0
1027	0.015	Sputter Target—2.0" × 5.0"	0	105	0	0	0	0	0	0	0
1028	0.500	Ring—10" OD × 8.5" ID	0	189	0	48	293	93	0	0	174
1029	0.500	Disk—10" dia	275	0	353	0	581	0	530	414	1,017
1030	0.250	Plate—5.25" × 10.25"	0	0	0	57	0	18	0	17	0
1031	0.500	Disc—6" Dia	0	0	0	15	0	0	0	0	0
1032	0.010	Tube—2" OD	0	0	0	14	0	12	12	0	0
1033	0.8 mm	Disc—314 mm Dia	0	0	0	0	20	0	0	0	0
1034	0.375	Disk—9.625" dia	0	0	0	0	57	0	0	0	0
1035	0.015	Tube—1.0" w/end cap	0	0	0	0	0	2	0	0	0
1036	0.125	Ring—12-3/4" OD × 9-3/8" ID	0	0	0	0	23	0	0	0	0
1037	0.125	Plate—3.5" × 13.2"	0	0	0	0	0	0	0	0	33

FIGURE 3-31 Invoiced sales for alloy #1.

total of over 600 unique part numbers on the books. The extreme product diversity and unpredictable line-item demand seemed to preclude any make-to-stock possibility. A review of the sales data for the first nine months of the year, however, seemed to indicate that the product diversity was actually much less than originally thought. (For brevity, we will consider only two of the four alloys—these two were chosen as illustrations because they have very different demand profiles, and together they account for 80 percent of the total demand.) While each alloy has 100 to 200 unique part numbers, Figures 3-31 and 3-32 show that less than half of these were sold over the course of nine months, and many of these only sold once or twice. Demand seems to be concentrated in just a few parts.

12. CASE WRAP-UP

Having spent two months learning about the operation, building relationships, and trying to make small operational gains, Tom spent a few minutes reviewing the situation. The Metallurgical Products department at HCST was scheduled as a make-to-order job shop, with customer lead-time performance averaging seven weeks. Order expediting is the rule rather than the

Material	Gauge	Description	1999/Invoiced sales—pounds per month								
			Jan.	Feb.	Mar.	Apr.	May	June	July	Aug.	Sept.
2001	0.045	Repair Disc 4" Dia	0	0	0	0	0	0	0	0	13
2002	0.045	Repair Disc 2 1/2" Dia	0	0	0	9	0	0	0	0	0
2003	0.045	Repair Disc 1" Dia	0	0	0	0	0	2	0	0	0
2004	0.045	Repair Disc .75" Dia	0	0	2	0	0	0	1	0	0
2005	0.015	Endcap to fit 1" OD	0	0	0	0	0	0	0	0	0
2006	0.045	3/4" Repair Disk	0	4	4	0	9	4	9	0	5
2007	0.045	1" Repair Disk	0	6	7	0	0	8	0	2	1
2008	0.045	1 1/2" Repair Disk	0	4	4	8	0	0	4	0	4
2009	0.045	2" Repair Disk	0	4	5	4	10	10	0	4	0
2010	0.045	2-1/2" Repair Disk	0	6	7	0	0	0	4	0	4
2011	0.045	3" Repair Disk	0	0	0	9	0	0	10	0	5
2012	0.045	4" Repair Disk	0	8	6	15	0	84	7	9	8
2013	0.045	5" Repair Disk	10	0	0	0	0	12	0	11	0
2014	0.045	6" Repair Disk	0	12	0	0	8	0	0	6	32
2015	0.045	3/4" Patch Kit	0	0	2	0	0	1	0	0	3
2016	0.045	1" Patch Kit	0	0	2	0	1	0	1	0	3
2017	0.045	1 1/2" Patch Kit	0	0	1	0	2	1	1	0	6
2018	0.045	2" Patch Kit	0	0	0	0	0	1	0	0	5
2019	0.045	2 1/2" Patch Kit	0	0	0	0	0	1	1	0	4
2020	0.045	3" Patch Kit	0	0	0	0	5	1	0	0	6
2021	0.045	4" Patch Kit	0	0	0	0	9	0	5	0	16
2022	0.045	6" Patch Kit	0	0	0	0	9	0	0	0	0
2023	0.045	5" Patch Kit	0	7	0	0	5	0	0	0	0
2024	0.005	Sheet—Annealed	0	6	0	0	6	0	0	0	0
2025	0.002	Foil Annealed	551	0	0	0	0	0	0	0	0
2026	0.010	Sheet Annealed	0	0	435	0	251	412	0	0	0
2027	0.060	Plate Annealed	0	0	277	323	60	0	504	12	205
2028	0.045	Sheet Unnanealed	67	0	0	0	0	0	0	0	0
2029	0.045	Sheet Annealed	137	122	430	18	37	16	0	368	5
2030	0.375	Plate Annealed	0	0	0	23	0	0	0	0	0
2031	0.020	Sheet Annealed	761	521	826	671	889	1,004	3,975	27	7
2032	0.025	Plate Annealed	0	69	24	0	0	0	0	0	0
2033	0.150	Plate Annealed	0	0	0	0	41	0	0	0	0
2034	0.125	Plate Annealed	0	35	78	63	34	0	0	208	0
2035	0.030	Sheet Annealed	1,638	116	1,138	634	524	579	1,672	703	517
2036	0.015	Sheet Annealed	108	0	13	56	0	27	0	0	1
2037	0.015	Welded Tube .50" OD	0	0	6	0	0	23	7	0	0
2038	0.025	Welded Tube 1.5" OD	0	0	0	0	0	2	0	0	0
2039	0.020	Welded Tube .50" OD	0	0	181	142	0	0	0	0	0
2040	0.025	Welded Tube .75" OD	296	936	2,989	1,366	2,468	989	657	528	1,392
2041	0.020	Welded Tube .75" OD	0	50	316	3	379	0	2,856	0	0
2042	0.025	Welded Tube .75" OD	0	0	0	0	0	32	0	0	5
2043	0.015	Welded Tube 1"-1.49 OD	0	0	480	444	0	77	118	343	0
2044	0.020	Welded Tube 10." OD	0	0	0	32	241	108	4	0	0
2045	0.030	Welded Tube 1.0" OD	0	0	370	0	0	1	0	0	41
2046	0.015	Welded Tube 1.5" OD	0	0	0	0	40	0	133	0	0
2047	0.030	Welded Tube 1.50" OD	0	255	100	0	0	0	0	0	0
2048	0.030	Custom Sheet Annealed	0	1	1	0	0	0	0	0	0
2049	0.020	Custom Sheet Annealed	0	0	0	0	0	35	0	0	0
2050	0.015	Welded Tube 1" OD With Cap	0	0	0	1,003	0	0	176	0	0
2051	0.022	Welded Tube 1.25" OD	0	0	0	1,014	0	0	0	0	0
2052	0.035	Tube 1.25" OD	0	0	302	0	0	0	0	0	0
2053	0.020	Disc 66mm OD	0	0	0	0	0	0	0	0	0
2054	0.118	Tube .815" od × 3mm wall	0	0	0	8	8	0	0	0	0
2055	0.118	Tube .614" od × 3mm wall	0	0	0	6	0	0	0	0	0

FIGURE 3-32 Invoiced sales for alloy #2.

exception, and in fact a daily meeting occurs to enable the expediting. The plant carries an average of six months' inventory, yet few items are sold from stock, or even made in a single production step from stock. Nearly all work passes through some of the standard gauges of 4 inch, $^1/_4$ inch, $^1/_8$ inch, and 0.030 inch, yet no standard stock is held at these sizes other than a small amount at $^1/_4$ inch, and small leftover pieces at the other gauges. The Sales group was pressing hard to reduce customer lead times to under three weeks. The goal seemed attainable since production orders averaged just over two weeks, but something needed to be done to speed the time between when an order was received and operations began working on producing the final product. It seemed as though maintaining stocks of some of the standard intermediate sizes would help customer lead times, since end items could be produced in a single production operation, but which items should be stocked, and at what levels? Also, not everyone in the organization was convinced that reduction of customer lead time was a priority—some were more focused on inventory reduction, while others felt that inventory levels were not that important. Tom had four months left to come up with a plan and implement it—what was he going to do?

CASE DISCUSSION QUESTIONS

1. Why are the lead times so long?
2. How might Starck reduce or affect the lead times?
3. What are the costs from reducing the lead times? What are the benefits from reducing the lead times?

This is a relatively long and involved case. You should use your judgment about how best to approach it, given that you have limited time. You should be able to diagnose what is going on and identify key tactics to pursue, and we do not expect you to develop an elaborate analysis of the data given herein (although this is certainly fine to do if you have the time).

CHAPTER 4

Supply Contracts

CASE: American Tool Works

American Tool Works (ATW) is a leading U.S. manufacturer of high-quality power and hand tools, such as electric drills, hammers, and so forth. The company has manufacturing facilities all over the world, and its main markets are in Europe and North America. Products are sold through distributors and dealers or directly to home owners and tradesmen.

ATW enjoys a very successful partnership with its distributors and dealers. This channel provides about 80 percent of its revenue, and, as a result, is the focus of the new management team that took over in 2004. The relationship between ATW and its distributors and dealers may take two forms:

- Large distributors tend to have a vendor-managed-inventory (VMI) agreement with ATW. In this situation, ATW monitors the inventory levels of various products at the distributors' facilities, and makes additional shipments as necessary.
- Midsize and small distributors do not have the technical capability to participate in the VMI relationship, since they don't have the technology to automatically transfer the necessary sales and inventory information to ATW.

Many of these distributors sell not only ATW products, but many products from firms that compete with ATW.

The large distributors are typically pleased by the performance of the VMI agreement. ATW Supply Chain VP Dave Morrison recently instituted a series of meetings with ATW's key large dealers. In these conversations, the dealers emphasized the following:

- Their salespeople can direct demand to either ATW products or competitors' products. That is, buyers typically ask the distributors' sales team for advice on product/brand combination.
- Currently, distributors' sales team make decisions based on
  - Comfort level with different products/brand.
  - Promotional items.
  - Profit margin.
- ATW products' stock levels at the distributor do not effect sales since, in VMI, shipments are received frequently—a few times a week.
- For many products, space is limited due to indoor storage requirements. VMI considerably reduces inventory levels and thus the required space while maintaining or increasing service levels.

Dave also met with a number of small distributors. They identified three reasons for buying ATW products: name recognition, quality, and sales support. As in the case of large distributors, they also suggested that their salespeople can direct demand to certain product/brand combinations. Interestingly, they qualified their statement as follows:

- Sixty percent of sales are prespecified by the buyer and the distributor has no impact on the brand/ product chosen by the contractor.
- The remaining 40 percent can be heavily steered by the distributor's sales force.
- When the sales force steers demand, it is done based on on-site inventory level.
- ATW's competitors use a variety of different approaches to increase sales at these small distributors. One encourages some dealers to increase inventory of tools with a promise to buy the tools back if they don't sell. One implemented a sales incentive program in which money contributed by both the manufacturer and the distributor is put into an account that is divided between the salespeople once a year.

After concluding his talks with the dealers, Dave felt very confident with the performance of the VMI program. However, he had the sense that there were both a tremendous opportunity to increase sales to smaller dealers and, at the same time, a risk that his competitors would steal some of ATW's business with small and midsize dealers.

By the end of the chapter, you should be able to answer the following questions:

- What can ATW do to increase inventory at small and midsize dealers?
- What can ATW do to increase sales at small and midsize dealers?
- Why are ATW's competitors using the two approaches described in the case when they deal with small and midsize dealers?
- Should ATW adopt these approaches?
- Should ATW try different approaches? What are the possible approaches they should consider?

4.1 INTRODUCTION

In the last few years, we have seen significant increase in the level of outsourcing; companies outsource everything from the manufacturing of specific components to the design and assembly of the entire product. For example, in the electronics industry, there has been a marked increase in purchasing volume as a percentage of the firm's total sales. For instance, between 1998 and 2000, outsourcing in the electronics industry increased from 15 percent of all components to 40 percent [216].

Interestingly, many brand-name manufacturers now outsource both the entire design and manufacturing of some of their products. For instance, it is expected that in 2005, about 30 percent of digital cameras, 65 percent of MP3 players, and about 70 percent of PDAs will be the work of original design manufacturers (ODM), that will be sold to consumers by brand manufacturers; see [68].

One important driver is the search for low-cost countries that allow manufacturers to significantly reduce labor cost. At the same time, many companies in the Far East developed significant capability to design and manufacture high-quality, low-cost products. These developments suggest both an opportunity and a challenge.

EXAMPLE 4.1 CONTRACT FARMING

Thai agro products are in great demand in many countries. In order to improve their global competitiveness by bringing down cost, many agro-industries in Thailand have started contract farming in the neighboring countries like Laos and Cambodia. This is due to cheap production cost. The selected agro products are grown in these countries in accordance with a contact with the farmers or their agents. After harvest, the produce is shipped back to the agro industries in Thailand for processing, packaging and marketing. Through contact farming, the cost of growing raw agro-products has gone down considerably.

Indeed, the increase in the level of outsourcing implies that the procurement function becomes critical for an OEM to remain in control of its destiny. As a result, many OEMs focus on closely collaborating with the suppliers of their *strategic components or products*. In most cases, this requires effective supply contracts that try to coordinate the supply chain.

A different approach has been applied by OEMs for *nonstrategic components*. In this case, products can be purchased from a variety of suppliers, and flexibility to market conditions is perceived as more important than a permanent relationship with the suppliers. Indeed, *commodity products,* for example, electricity, computer memory, steel, oil, grain or cotton, are typically available from a large number of suppliers and can be purchased in spot markets. Because these are highly standard products, switching from one supplier to another is not considered a major problem.

In the following, we discuss effective supply contracts for both strategic and nonstrategic components.

4.2 STRATEGIC COMPONENTS

Effective procurement strategies require the development of relationships with suppliers. These relationships can take many forms, both formal and informal, but often, to ensure adequate supplies and timely deliveries, buyers and suppliers typically agree on supply contracts. These contracts address issues that arise between a buyer and a supplier, whether the buyer is a manufacturer purchasing raw materials from a supplier, an OEM purchasing components, or a retailer purchasing goods. In a typical supply contract, the buyer and supplier will agree on

- Pricing and volume discounts.
- Minimum and maximum purchase quantities.
- Delivery lead times.
- Product or material quality.
- Product return policies.

EXAMPLE 4.2 RELIANCE RETAIL

Reliance Industries Limited (RIL) is a name synonymous with unprecedented corporate growth in India especially in the area of petrochemical, polyester yarn and fiber products. When RIL Chairman, Mukesh Ambani thought of diversifying into retail, he had a mega plan in his mind. It involves multi-format retail chains. His working principle is 'farm to fork,' which simply aims at eliminating middlemen and thus cutting down the cost. Reliance Fresh, a wing of Reliance Retail is operationalizing the disintermediation in the inbound side of its supply chain through direct procurement from farmers rather than sourcing through mandies, which is a common practice in India. Contract farming is another way to rope in farmers in the mainstream of the retail supply chains. When implemented, farmers may be assisted with high-quality seeds, fertilizers and other supports. They are likely to still get a better price than what they were getting earlier from the middlemen. In return, they have to follow the requirements of the retail chains, ensure good quality and meet schedules. Established small retailers and middlemen are naturally aggrieved and there has been some initial resistance from them in few states in India [296].

As we will see, supply contracts are very powerful tools that can be used for far more than to ensure adequate supply and demand for goods.

4.2.1 Supply Contracts

To illustrate the importance and impact of different types of supply contracts on supply chain performance, consider a typical two-stage supply chain consisting of a buyer and a supplier. The sequence of events in such a supply chain is as follows. The buyer starts by generating a forecast, determines how many units to order from the supplier, and places an order to the supplier so as to optimize his own profit;

the supplier reacts to the order placed by the buyer. Thus, in this supply chain, the supplier has a make-to-order (MTO) supply chain while the buyer is purchasing items prior to knowing customer demand, based on a forecast.

Evidently, this sequence of events represents a sequential decision-making process and, thus, the supply chain is referred to as a **sequential supply chain**. In such a sequential supply chain, each party determines its own course of action independent of the impact of its decisions on other parties. Obviously, this cannot be an effective strategy for supply chain partners since it does not identify what's best for the entire supply chain.

To illustrate the challenges faced by sequential supply chains and the importance and impact of different types of supply contracts on supply chain performance, consider the following set of examples, based on the swimsuit case analyzed in Chapter 2.

EXAMPLE 4-3

Consider once again the swimsuit example discussed in Section 2.2.2. In this case, we assume that there are two companies involved in the supply chain: a retailer who faces customer demand and a manufacturer who produces and sells swimsuits to the retailer. Demand for swimsuits follows the same pattern of scenarios as before, and the retailer pricing and costing information are the same:

- During the summer season, a swimsuit is sold to customers at Rs.125 per unit.
- The wholesale price paid by the retailer to the manufacturer is Rs.80 per unit.
- Any swimsuit not sold during the summer season is sold to a discount store for Rs. 20.

For the manufacturer, we have the following information:

- Fixed production cost is Rs.100,000.
- The variable production cost per unit equals Rs. 35.

Observe that the retailer's marginal profit is the same as the marginal profit of the manufacturer, Rs.45. Also, notice that, excluding the fixed production cost, the retailer's selling price, salvage value, and variable cost are the same as the selling price, salvage value, and production cost in the original example in Chapter 2. This implies that the retailer's marginal profit for selling a unit during the season, Rs. 45, is smaller than the marginal loss, Rs.60, associated with each unit sold at the end of the season to discount stores.

How much should the retailer order from the manufacturer? Recall our conclusion at the end of the swimsuit case study: the optimal order quantity depends on marginal profit and marginal loss but not on the fixed cost. Indeed, the solid line in Figure 4-1 represents average profit for the retailer and it suggests that the retailer's optimal policy is to order 12,000 units for an average profit of Rs. 470,700. If the retailer places this order, the manufacturer's profit is 12,000(80 − 35) −100,000 = Rs. 440,000.

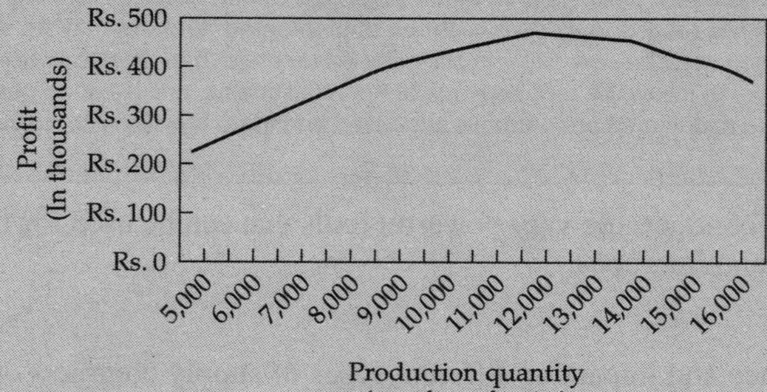

FIGURE 4-1 The retailer's expected profit as a function of order quantity.

Observe that, in the example above, the buyer assumes all of the risk of having more inventory than sales, while the supplier takes no risk. Indeed, since the supplier takes no risk, he would like the buyer to order as much as possible, while the buyer limits his order quantity because of the huge financial risk. Of course, *since the buyer limits his order quantity, there is a* ***significant increase in the likelihood of out of stock***. If the supplier is willing and able to share some of the risk with the buyer, it may be profitable for the buyer to order more items, thereby reducing out-of-stock probability and increasing profit for both the supplier and the buyer.

It turns out that a variety of supply contracts enable this **risk sharing,** and therefore increase profits for both supply chain entities.

Buy-Back Contracts In this contract, the seller agrees to buy back unsold goods from the buyer for some agreed-upon price higher than the salvage value. Clearly, this gives the buyer incentive to order more units, since the risk associated with unsold units is decreased. On the other hand, the supplier's risk clearly increases. Thus, the contract is designed such that the increase in order quantity placed by the buyer, and hence the decrease in the likelihood of out of stock, more than compensates the supplier for the increase in risk. Let's return to the swimsuit example.

EXAMPLE 4-4

Suppose the manufacturer offers to buy unsold swimsuits from the retailer for Rs. 55. In this case, the retailer marginal profit, Rs. 45, is greater than its marginal loss, Rs. 35, thus motivating the retailer to order more than average demand. Indeed, under this contract, the solid line in Figure 4-2 illustrates the retailer's average profit, while the dotted line represents the manufacturer's average profit. The figure shows that, in this case, the retailer has an incentive to increase its order quantity to 14,000 units, for a profit of Rs. 513,800, while the manufacturer's average profit increases to Rs. 471,900. Thus, the total average profit for the two parties increases from Rs. 910,700 (= Rs. 470,700 + Rs. 440,000) in the sequential supply chain to Rs. 985,700 (= Rs. 513,800 + Rs. 471,900) when a buy-back contract is used.

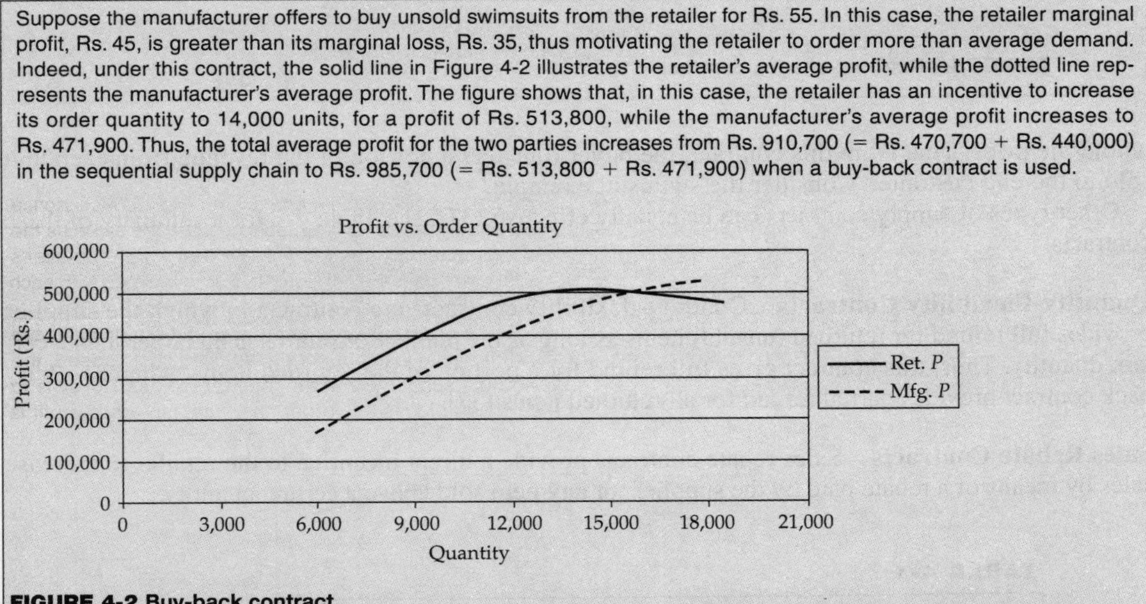

FIGURE 4-2 **Buy-back contract.**

Revenue-Sharing Contracts Observe that, in the sequential supply chain, one important reason for the buyer to order a limited number of units is the high wholesale price. If somehow the buyer can convince the supplier to reduce the wholesale price, then clearly the buyer will have an incentive to order more units. Of course, a reduction in wholesale price will decrease the supplier's profit if it is unable to sell more units. This is addressed by revenue-sharing contracts. In a revenue-sharing contract, the buyer shares some of its revenue with the seller, in return for a discount on the

EXAMPLE 4-5

Suppose the swimsuit manufacturer and retailer have a revenue-sharing contract, in which the manufacturer agrees to decrease the wholesale price from Rs. 80 to Rs. 60, and, in return, the retailer provides 15 percent of the product revenue to the manufacturer. Under this contract, the solid line in Figure 4-3 illustrates the retailer's average profit while the dotted line represents the manufacturer's average profit. The figure shows that, in this case, the retailer has an incentive to increase his order quantity to 14,000 (as in the buy-back contract) for a profit of Rs. 504,325, and this order increase leads to increased manufacturer's profit of Rs. 481,375, in spite of lower wholesale prices. Thus, the supply chain total profit is Rs. 985,700 (= Rs. 504,325 + Rs. 481,375). That is, the reduction in the wholesale price coupled with revenue sharing leads to increased profits for both parties.

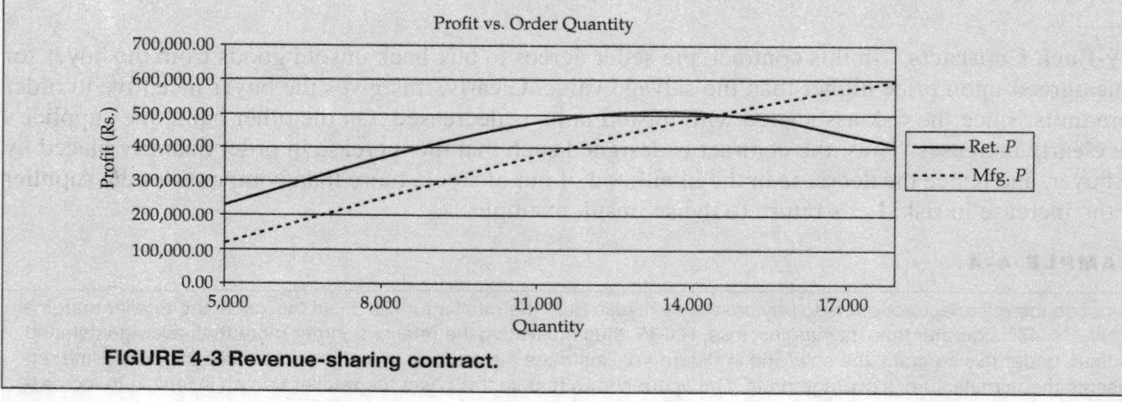

FIGURE 4-3 Revenue-sharing contract.

wholesale price. That is, in this contract, the buyer transfers a portion of the revenue from each unit sold to the end customer. Consider the swimsuit example.

Other types of supply contracts can be equally effective [37]; see Table 4-1 for a summary of these contracts.

Quantity-Flexibility Contracts Quantity-flexibility contracts are contracts in which the supplier provides full refund for returned (unsold) items as long as the number of returns is no larger than a certain quantity. Thus, this contract gives full refund for a portion of the returned items, whereas a buy-back contract provides partial refund for all returned items [37].

Sales Rebate Contracts Sales rebate contracts provide a direct incentive to the retailer to increase sales by means of a rebate paid by the supplier for any item sold above a certain quantity.

TABLE 4-1

CONTRACTS FOR STRATEGIC COMPONENTS

Contract	Characteristics
1. Buy-back	Partial refund for all unsold goods
2. Revenue-sharing	Buyer shares revenue with supplier in return for discount wholesale price
3. Quantity-flexibility	Full refund for a limited number of unsold goods
4. Sales rebate	Incentives for meeting target sales

Global Optimization The various contracts described above raise an important question: What is the most profit both the supplier and the buyer can hope to achieve? To answer this question, we take a completely different approach. What if an unbiased decision maker is allowed to identify the best strategy for the entire supply chain? This unbiased decision maker would consider the two supply chain partners, the supplier and the buyer, as two members of the same organization. That is, the transfer of money between the parties is ignored and the unbiased decision maker will maximize supply chain profit.

EXAMPLE 4-6

In the swimsuit example, the only relevant data in this case are the selling price, Rs.125; the salvage value, Rs. 20; the variable production costs, Rs. 35; and the fixed production cost. In this case, the cost that the retailer charges the manufacturer is meaningless, since we are only interested in external costs and revenues. Evidently, in this case, the supply chain marginal profit, 90 = 125 − 35, is significantly higher than the marginal loss, 15 = 35 − 20, and, hence, the supply chain will produce more than average demand. Indeed, Figure 4-4 suggests that, in this global optimization strategy, the optimal production quantity is 16,000 units, which implies an expected supply chain profit of Rs.1,014,500.

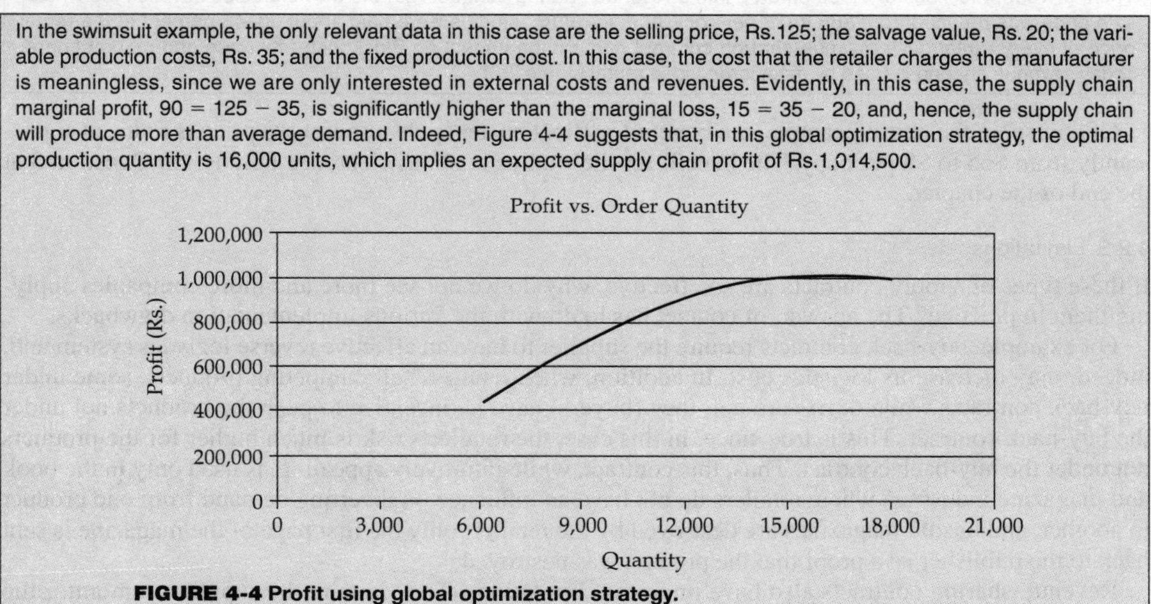

FIGURE 4-4 Profit using global optimization strategy.

Of course, this kind of unbiased decision maker doesn't usually exist. However, effective supply contracts provide incentives for supply chain partners to replace traditional strategies, in which each partner optimizes its own profit, with **global optimization,** where supply chain profit is maximized. The difficulty with global optimization is that it requires the firm to surrender decision-making power to an unbiased decision maker.

This is precisely why supply contracts are so important. *They help firms achieve global optimization, without the need for an unbiased decision maker, by allowing buyers and suppliers to share the risk and the potential benefit.* Indeed, it can be shown that *carefully designed supply contracts achieve the exact same profit as global optimization*.

In addition, from an implementation point of view, the main drawback of global optimization is that it does not provide a mechanism to allocate supply chain profit between the partners. It only provides information on the best, or optimal, set of actions that need to be taken by the supply chain to improve profit. Supply contracts allocate this profit among supply chain members.

More importantly, effective supply contracts allocate profit to each partner in such a way that no partner can improve his profit by deciding to deviate from the optimal set of decisions. That is, there is no incentive for either the buyer or the seller to deviate from the set of actions that will achieve the global optimal solution.

The following example illustrates the impact of supply contracts in practice.

EXAMPLE 4-7

Until 1998, video rental stores used to purchase copies of newly released movies from the movie studios for about $65 and rent them to customers for $3. Because of the high purchase price, rental stores did not buy enough copies to cover peak demand, which typically occurs during the first 10 weeks after a movie is released on video. The result was low customer service level; in a 1998 survey, about 20 percent of customers could not get their first choice of movie. Then, in 1998, Blockbuster Video entered into a revenue-sharing contract with the movie studios in which the wholesale price was reduced from $65 to $8 per copy, and, in return, studios were paid about 30–45 percent of the rental price of every rental. This revenue-sharing contract had a huge impact on Blockbuster revenue and market share. Today, revenue sharing is used by most large video rental stores [38].

Of course, in the above example, the benefit for Blockbuster is clear; purchase price is reduced significantly from $65 to $8 per copy. The benefit for the studios is not as clear; see Discussion Question 3 at the end of the chapter.

4.2.2 Limitations

If these types of supply contracts are so effective, why do we not see more and more companies applying them in practice? The answer, of course, has to do with the various implementation drawbacks.

For example, buy-back contracts require the supplier to have an effective reverse logistics system and, indeed, may increase its logistics cost. In addition, when retailers sell competing products, some under buy-back contracts while others are not, they (buyers) have an incentive to push the products not under the buy-back contract. This is true since, in this case, the retailer's risk is much higher for the products not under the buy-back contract. Thus, this contract, while intuitively appealing, is used only in the book and magazine industries where retailers do not have an influence on diverting demand from one product to another, and unsold magazines are destroyed by the retailer; only the first page of the magazine is sent back to the publisher as a proof that the product was destroyed.

Revenue-sharing contracts also have important limitations. They require the supplier to monitor the buyer's revenue and thus increase administrative cost. The importance of monitoring the revenue is nicely illustrated by two recent lawsuits.

EXAMPLE 4-8

A lawsuit brought by three independent video retailers who complained they had been excluded from receiving the benefits of revenue sharing was dismissed by the judge in June 2002. The reason: the independent retailers did not have the information infrastructure that would have allowed the studios to monitor revenue.

Of course, information technology is not enough; building trust between the supplier and the buyer is not only important but also difficult to achieve, as is nicely illustrated by the following example.

EXAMPLE 4-9

In January 2003, the Walt Disney Company sued Blockbuster, accusing them of cheating its video unit of approximately $120 million under a four-year revenue-sharing agreement (*New York Times*, January 4, 2003).

Another important limitation is that, in revenue sharing, buyers have an incentive to push competing products with higher profit margins. That is, revenue-sharing contracts typically reduce the buyer's profit margin since some of the revenue is transferred to the supplier. Thus, the buyer has an incentive to push other products, in particular, similar products from competing suppliers with whom the buyer has no revenue-sharing agreement.

4.3 CONTRACTS FOR MAKE-TO-STOCK/MAKE-TO-ORDER SUPPLY CHAINS

A key assumption in all the contracts discussed so far is that the supplier has a make-to-order supply chain. This implies that, in the sequential supply chain analyzed earlier, the supplier takes no risk while the buyer takes all the risk. The contracts described earlier suggest mechanisms for transferring some of the risk from the buyer to the supplier. An important question, thus, is what the appropriate contracts are when the supplier has a make-to-stock (MTS) supply chain.

To better understand some of the issues involved, consider the following example.

EXAMPLE 4-10

Ericsson sells telecommunication network equipment to AT&T and purchases components from a variety of suppliers such as Flextronics. Due to significant differences in component lead times, the manufacturing strategy used by Ericsson is different than the one applied by Flextronics. Specifically, Flextronics has an MTS environment dictated in part by component lead times, while Ericsson makes production decisions only after receiving an order from AT&T. See [181, 182].

Observe that Ericsson assembles products after receiving orders from its customer, AT&T, while Flextronics produces to stock and needs to build capacity in advance of receiving orders from Ericsson. This implies that, in this supply chain, the supplier takes all the risk while the buyer takes no risk. The issues that arise in this type of relationship are nicely illustrated in the following example.

EXAMPLE 4-11

Consider the supply chain for fashion products such as ski jackets. In this case, the selling season starts in September and is over by December. The sequence of events in this supply chain is as follows. Production starts 12 months before the selling season, before distributors place any orders with the manufacturer. The distributor places orders with the manufacturer six months after the beginning of production. At that time, the manufacturer has completed producing the products while the distributor has received firm orders from retailers. Thus, the manufacturer produces ski jackets prior to receiving distributor orders. Demand for ski jackets follows the same pattern of scenarios as before (see Example 4-1), and the distributor's pricing and cost information is

- The distributor sells ski jackets to retailers for Rs.125 per unit.
- The distributor pays the manufacturer Rs. 80 per unit.

For the manufacturer, we have the following information:

- Fixed production cost is Rs.100,000.
- The variable production cost per unit equals Rs. 55.
- Any ski jacket not purchased by the distributors is sold to a discount store for Rs. 20.

Observe that the manufacturer's marginal profit is Rs. 25 while the marginal loss from each unit produced but not purchased by the distributor is Rs. 60. Since the marginal loss is greater than the marginal profit, the distributor should produce less than average demand, that is, less than 13,000 units. How much should the manufacturer produce? Figure 4-5 represents the manufacturer's average profit as a function of the number of units produced, and it suggests that the manufacturer's optimal policy is to produce 12,000 units for an average profit of Rs.160,400. The distributor's average profit in this case is Rs. 510,300.

EXAMPLE 4-11 *Continued*

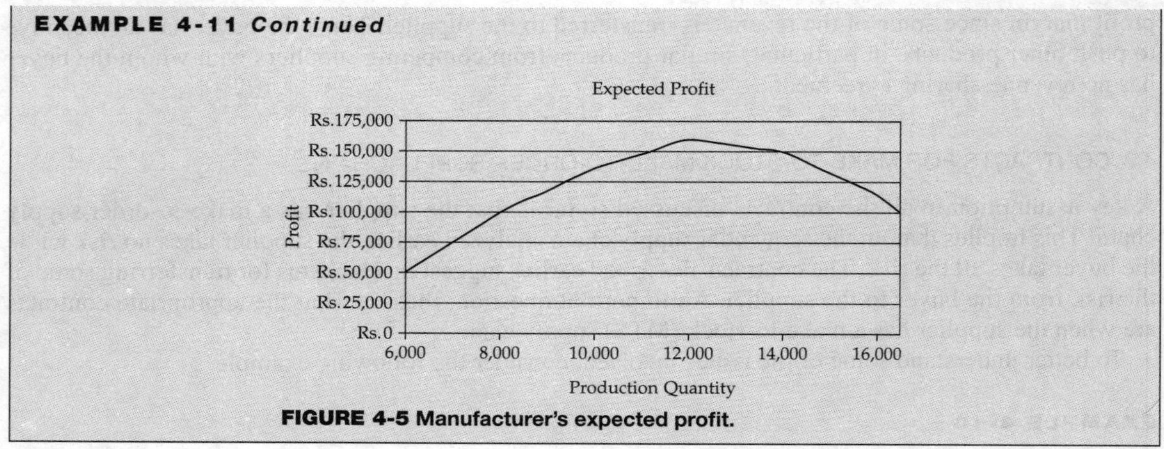

FIGURE 4-5 Manufacturer's expected profit.

Observe that, unlike the swimsuit example, here the manufacturer assumes all of the risk of building more capacity than sales, while the distributor takes no risk. Indeed, since the distributor takes no risk, it would like the manufacturer to build as much capacity as possible, while the manufacturer limits its production quantity because of the huge financial risk.

Again, a variety of supply contracts enable risk sharing and hence reduce manufacturer's risk and motivate the manufacturer to increase production capacities. This increases profit for both the supplier and the distributor.

Pay-Back Contracts In this contract, the buyer agrees to pay some agreed-upon price for any unit produced by the manufacturer but not purchased by the distributor. Clearly, this gives the manufacturer incentive to produce more units, since the risk associated with unused capacity is decreased. On the other hand, the distributor's risk clearly increases. Thus, the contract is designed such that the increase in production quantities more than compensates the distributor for the increase in risk. Let's return to the ski jacket example.

Cost-Sharing Contracts Observe that, in the sequential supply chain, one important reason why the manufacturer does not produce enough is the high production cost. If somehow the manufacturer can convince the distributor to share some of the production cost, then, clearly, the manufacturer will have an incentive to produce more units. Of course, paying part of the production cost will decrease

EXAMPLE 4-12

Suppose the distributor offers to pay Rs.18 for each unit produced by the manufacturer but not purchased by the distributor.

In this case, the manufacturer's marginal loss is 55 − 20 − 18 = Rs.17 while marginal profit is still Rs. 25. Thus, the manufacturer has an incentive to produce more than average demand. Figure 4-6 illustrates the manufacturer's average profit while Figure 4-7 represents the distributor's average profit. The figures show that, in this case, the manufacturer has an incentive to increase its production quantity to 14,000 units, for a profit of Rs.180,280, while the distributor's average profit increases to Rs. 525,420. Thus, the total average profit for the two parties increases from Rs. 670,000 (= Rs.160,400 + Rs. 510,300) in the sequential supply chain to Rs. 705,700 (= Rs.180,280 + Rs. 525,420) when a pay-back contract is used.

EXAMPLE 4-12 *Continued*

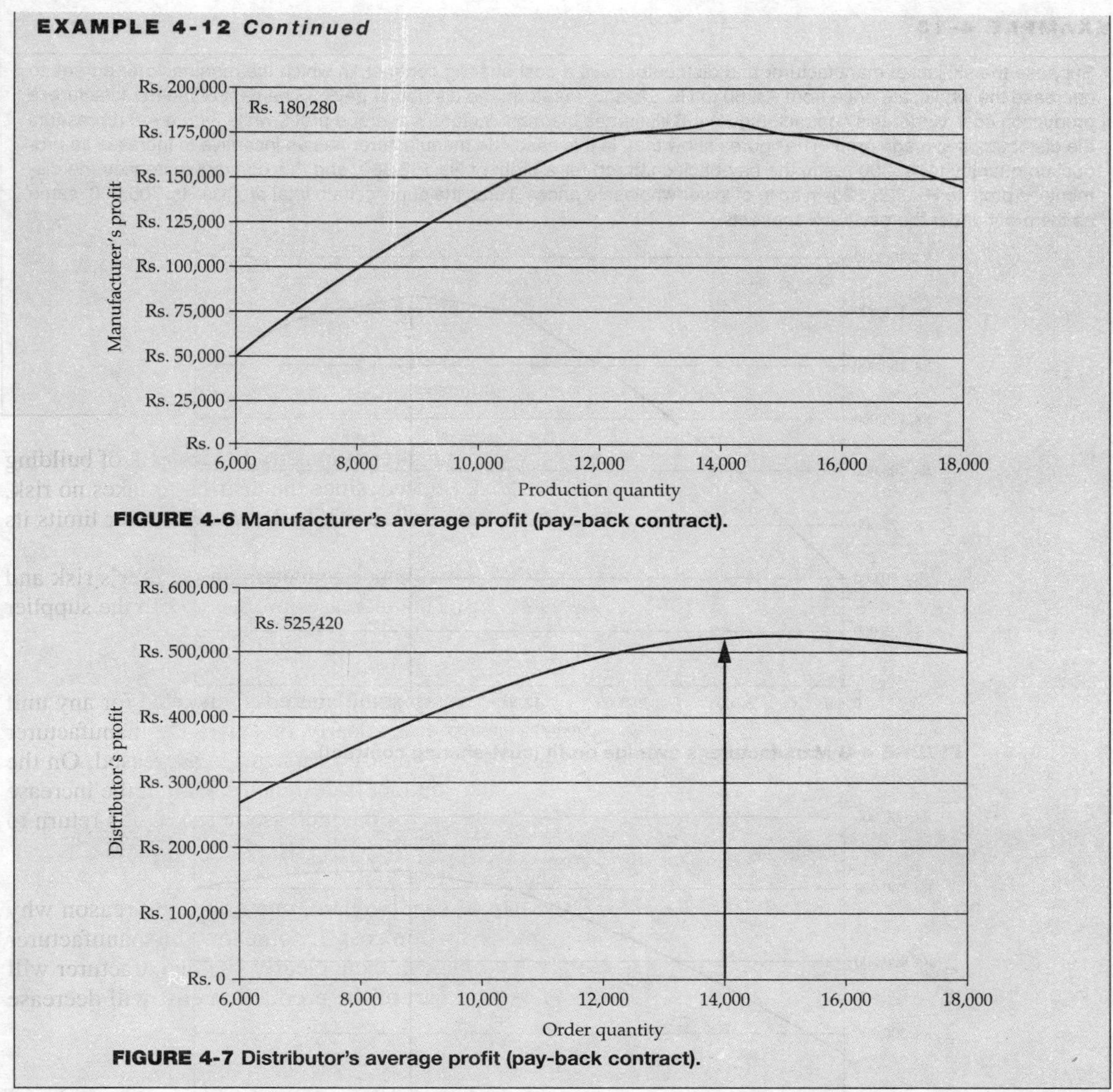

FIGURE 4-6 Manufacturer's average profit (pay-back contract).

FIGURE 4-7 Distributor's average profit (pay-back contract).

the distributor's profit if it is unable to sell more units. This is addressed through cost-sharing contracts. In a cost-sharing contract, the buyer shares some of the production cost with the manufacturer, in return for a discount on the wholesale price. Consider the ski jacket example.

One problem with the cost-sharing contract is that it requires the manufacturer to share its production cost information with the distributor; something manufacturers are reluctant to do. So, how is this contract implemented in practice? Typically, the issue is addressed through an agreement in which the distributor purchases one or more components that the manufacturer needs. The components remain on the distributor's books but are shipped to the manufacturer's facility for the production of the finished good.

EXAMPLE 4-13

Suppose the ski jacket manufacturer and distributor have a cost-sharing contract, in which the manufacturer agrees to decrease the wholesale price from Rs. 80 to Rs. 62, and, in return, the distributor pays 33 percent of the manufacturer's production cost. Under this contract, Figure 4-8 illustrates the manufacturer's average profit, while Figure 4-9 represents the distributor's average profit. The figures show that, in this case, the manufacturer has an incentive to increase its production quantity to 14,000 (as in the pay-back contract) for a profit of Rs.182,380, and this contract increases the distributor's profit to Rs. 523,320, in spite of lower wholesale prices. Thus, the supply chain total profit is Rs. 705,700, same as the profit under the pay-back contracts.

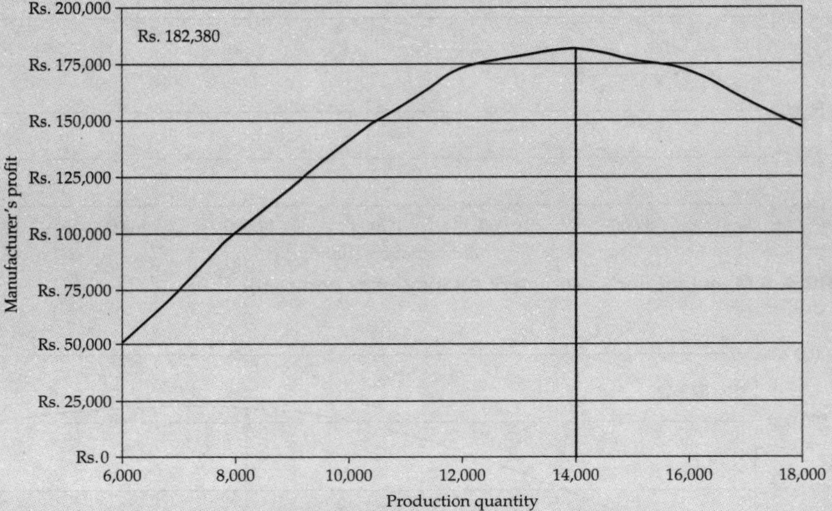

FIGURE 4-8 Manufacturer's average profit (cost-sharing contract).

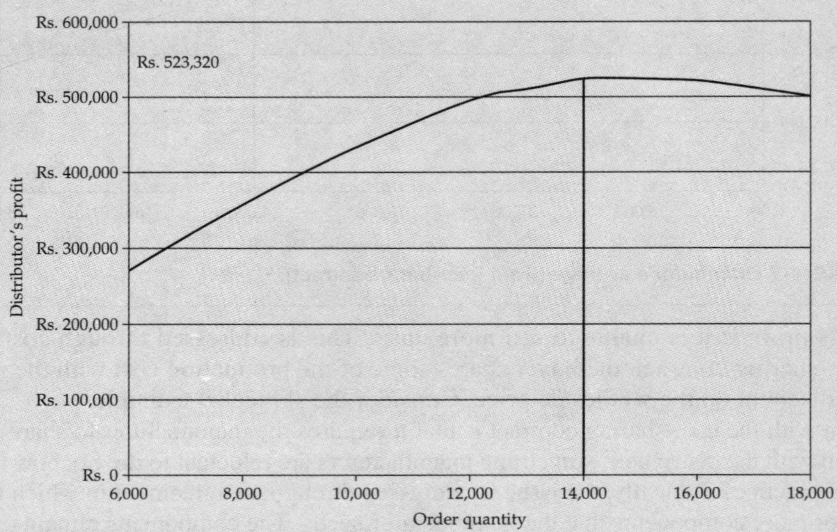

FIGURE 4-9 Distributor's average profit (cost-sharing contract).

EXAMPLE 4-14

A large OEM in the electronics industry contracts with a manufacturing partner (CM) responsible for the design and manufacturing of parts used by the OEM. The OEM uses its buying power to purchase key components, used by the CM, from the CM's supplier. These components are given to the CM either on consignment, that is, the OEM still owns the parts at the CM, or in a buy-sell arrangement where the OEM sells to the CM. The OEM's buying power implies that they can receive a better price than the CM receives from the supplier. In addition, this strategy guarantees that any competitors of the OEM who buy parts from the same CM do not benefit from the OEM's buying power.

Finally, it is easy to see that, in the ski-jacket example, both pay-back and cost-sharing contracts achieve the maximum possible profit in this supply chain. That is, the parameters of the contracts were selected so that supply chain profit in each case is the same as in global optimization.

EXAMPLE 4-15

In the ski-jacket example, the only relevant data when we globally optimize the supply chain are the selling price, Rs.125; the salvage value, Rs. 20; the variable production costs, Rs.55; and the fixed production cost. In this case, the cost that the distributor pays the manufacturer is meaningless, since we are only interested in external costs and revenues. Evidently, in this case, the supply chain marginal profit, 70 = 125 − 55, is significantly higher than the marginal loss, 35 = 55 − 20, and, hence, the supply chain will produce more than average demand. Indeed, Figure 4-10 suggests that, in this global optimization strategy, the optimal production quantity is 14,000 units, which implies an expected supply chain profit of Rs.705,700, exactly the same profit as under pay-back and cost sharing contracts.

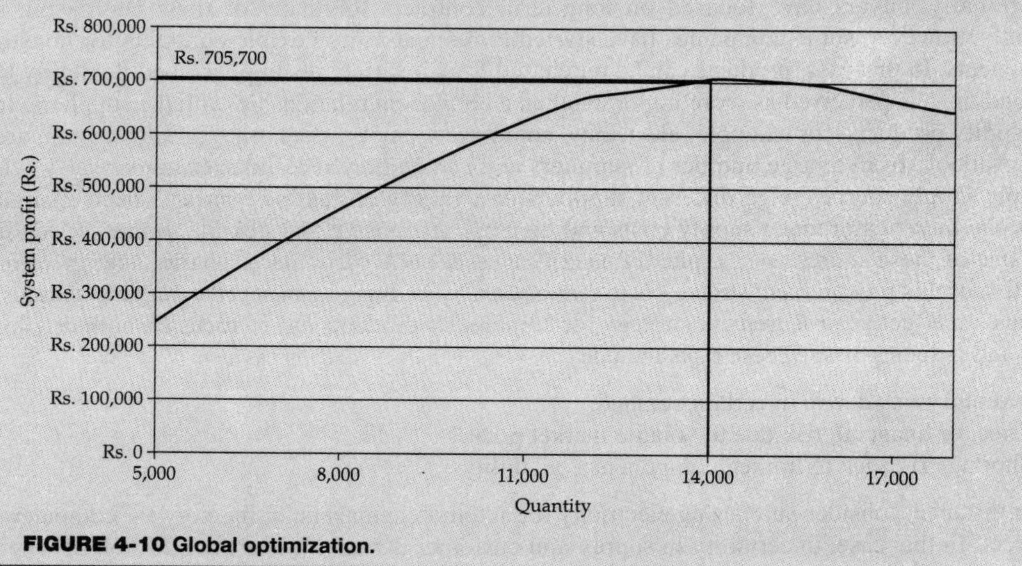

FIGURE 4-10 Global optimization.

4.4 CONTRACTS WITH ASYMMETRIC INFORMATION

An important assumption made in the discussion so far is that the buyer and the supplier share the same demand forecast. It is easy to see, however, that when the supplier needs to build capacity based on forecast received from manufacturers, the buyer has an incentive to inflate its forecast. Indeed, as observed in [247], "forecasts by electronics and telecom companies are often inflated."

To better understand the issue, consider Example 4-8. In this example, Flextronics built production capacity based on forecast received from Ericsson, the company that has the relationship with the end customer, AT&T. A forecast received by Flextronics from Ericsson may be inflated, but there is no way to verify it. Indeed, since there is always a positive probability that the forecast is higher than realized demand, the supplier cannot argue that this gap is due to inflated forecasts.

Thus, the question is whether one can design contracts that achieve credible information sharing.

Interestingly, this question is answered in the affirmative [182]. Indeed, the following two contracts achieve credible information sharing.

- **Capacity reservation contracts:** Manufacturer pays to reserve a certain level of capacity with the supplier. The reservation price is a menu of prices designed by the supplier to motivate the manufacturer to reveal its true forecast. That is, by choosing the amount of capacity to reserve with the supplier, the manufacturer signals its true forecast.
- **Advance purchase contracts:** Supplier charges the advance purchase price for firms' orders placed prior to building capacity and a different price for any additional order placed when demand is realized. Again, the initial firm commitment made by the manufacturer provides the suppliers information about the manufacturer's true forecast.

4.5 CONTRACTS FOR NONSTRATEGIC COMPONENTS

Traditionally, buyers have focused on long-term contracts for many of their purchasing needs. Recently, however, some companies have started looking at more flexible contracts for nonstrategic components. In this case, products can be purchased from a variety of suppliers, and flexibility to market conditions is perceived as more important than a permanent relationship with the suppliers. Indeed, commodity products, for example, electricity, computer memory, steel, oil, grain, or cotton, are typically available from a large number of suppliers and can be purchased in spot markets. By selecting multiple supply sources (e.g., different suppliers or a variety of flexible contracts from a single supplier), the buyer can reduce supply costs and be more responsive and flexible to market conditions. Each one of these sources will typically be critical under one particular scenario, and, therefore, the objective of this procurement strategy is to reduce cost by hedging against unfavorable situations.

Thus, an effective procurement strategy for commodity products has to focus on both driving costs down and reducing risks. These risks include

- Inventory risk due to uncertain demand.
- Price, or financial, risk due to volatile market price.
- Shortage risk due to limited component availability.

For instance, consider purchasing electricity for automobile makers, or memory for computer manufacturers. In this case, uncertainty in supply and customer demand raises the question of whether to purchase supply now or wait for better market conditions in the future. Purchasing now implies inventory risks associated with inventory shortages or unsold products. Relying on the spot market leads to price risk as well as shortage risk of not finding enough supply of components.

Despite the nonstrategic nature of commodity products, it is critical to identify effective procurement strategies for these components, since companies may be completely dependent on them. At the same time, uncertainty in supply and customer demand raises the question of whether to purchase supply now or wait for better market conditions in the future.

Long-Term Contracts Also called *forward* or *fixed commitment* contracts, long-term contracts eliminate financial risk. These contracts specify a fixed amount of supply to be delivered at some point in the future; the supplier and the buyer agree on both the price and the quantity to be delivered to the buyer. Thus, in this case, the buyer bears no financial risk while taking huge inventory risks due to uncertainty in demand and the inability to adjust order quantities.

EXAMPLE 4-16 ORGANIZED HATCHERIES

The supply chain of hatcheries is professionally managed in many parts of India. There are many players in the business of selling eggs, day-old chicks, broilers, and feed for chicks. Organized hatcheries own commercial farms and aim for complete vertical integration to have a total control over the entire supply chain. They have long-term contracts with the feedstock suppliers to manage the problem, which is due to occasional non-availability of feedstock and recurrent fluctuation in the prices. On the distribution side, a majority of them have negotiated for long-term contracts with hotels and restaurants for a steady supply of dressed chicken and eggs. With the organized retail growing fast in India, this sector has got a vast new market to perform in.

Flexible, or Option, Contract One way to reduce inventory risk is through *option* contracts, in which the buyer prepays a relatively small fraction of the product price upfront, in return for a commitment from the supplier to reserve capacity up to a certain level. The initial payment is typically referred to as a *reservation price* or *premium*. If the buyer does not *exercise* the option, the initial payment is lost. The buyer can purchase any amount of supply up to the option level by paying an additional price, agreed to at the time the contract is signed, for each unit purchased. This additional price is referred to as the *execution price* or *exercise price*. Of course, the total price (reservation plus execution price) paid by the buyer for each purchased unit is typically higher than the unit price in a long-term contract.

Evidently, option contracts provide the buyer with flexibility to adjust order quantities depending on realized demand and, hence, these contracts reduce inventory risks. Thus, these contracts shift risks from the buyer to the supplier since the supplier is now exposed to customer demand uncertainty. This is in contrast to long-term contracts in which the buyer takes all the risk.

A related strategy used in practice to share risks between suppliers and buyers is through *flexibility* contracts. In these contracts, a fixed amount of supply is determined when the contract is signed, but the amount to be delivered (and paid for) can differ by no more than a given percentage determined upon signing the contract.

Spot Purchase Buyers look for additional supply in the open market. Firms may use an independent e-market or a private e-market to select suppliers; see Chapter 9. The focus is on using the marketplace to find new suppliers and forcing competition to reduce product price.

Portfolio Contract Recently, innovative companies (e.g., HP; see below) have applied a portfolio approach to supply contracts. In this case, *buyers* sign multiple contracts at the same time in order to optimize their expected profit and reduce their risk. The contracts differ in price and level of flexibility, thus allowing the buyer to hedge against inventory, shortage, and spot price risk. This approach is, of course, particularly meaningful for commodity products since a large pool of suppliers is available, each offering a different type of contract. Thus, the buyer may be interested in selecting several different complementary contracts so as to reduce expected procurement and inventory holding costs.

To find an effective contract, the buyer needs to identify the appropriate *mix* of low-price yet low-flexibility (long-term) contracts, reasonable price but better flexibility (option) contracts, or unknown price and quantity supply but no commitment (spot market). Specifically, the buyer must optimize between the differ-

TABLE 4-2

CONTRACTS FOR NONSTRATEGIC COMPONENTS

Contract	Characteristics
1. Long-term	Fixed commitment made in advance
2. Flexible or option	Prepay for the option to purchase
3. Spot market	Immediate purchase
4. Portfolio	Combine the first three contract options strategically

ent contracts: How much to commit from the long-term contract? We refer to this commitment as the **base commitment** level. How much capacity to buy from companies selling option contracts? We refer to this as the **option** level. And finally, how much supply should be left uncommitted? If demand is high, the buyer looks for additional supply in the spot market.

An example of the portfolio approach is Hewlett-Packard's (HP) strategy for the procurement of electricity or memory products. About 50 percent of HP's procurement cost is invested in long-term contracts, 35 percent in option contracts, and the remaining in the spot market. See Table 4-2 for a summary of these contracts.

How does this portfolio approach address risk? Observe that if demand is much higher than anticipated and the base commitment level plus the option level do not provide enough protection, the firm must use the spot market for additional supply. Unfortunately, this is typically the worst time to buy in the spot market, since prices are high due to shortages. Thus, the buyer can select a trade-off level between price risk, shortage risk, and inventory risk by carefully selecting the level of long-term commitment and the option level. For instance, for the same option level, the higher the initial contract commitment, the smaller the price risk but the higher the inventory risk taken by the buyer. On the other hand, the smaller the level of the base commitment, the higher the price and shortage risks due to the likelihood of using the spot market. Similarly, for the same level of base commitment, the higher the option level, the higher the risk assumed by the supplier since the buyer may exercise only a small fraction of the option level. These trade-offs are summarized in Table 4-3, where in parentheses we identify the party that takes on most of the risk.

SUMMARY

Relationships between suppliers and buyers can take many forms, both formal and informal, but often, to ensure adequate supplies and timely deliveries, buyers and suppliers typically agree on supply con-

TABLE 4-3

RISK TRADE-OFF IN PORTFOLIO CONTRACTS

Option level		Base commitment level: Low	Base commitment level: High
	High	Inventory risk (supplier)	N/A*
	Low	Price and shortage risks (buyer)	Inventory risk (buyer)

*For a given situation, either the option level or the base commitment level may be high, but not both.

tracts. In this chapter we argued that these contracts can be used as powerful tools to achieve global optimization, to better manage the trade-off between cost and risk for commodity products, and to motivate supply chain parties to reveal their true forecast of customer demand.

DISCUSSION QUESTIONS

1. When is a buy-back contract appropriate? When is a payback contract appropriate? What about an option contract? How are they related? Argue that buy-back and pay-back contracts are special types of options contracts.
2. Consider a single manufacturer and a single supplier. Six months before demand is realized, the manufacturer has to sign a supply contract with the supplier. The sequence of events is as follows. Procurement contracts are signed in February and demand is realized during a short period of 10 weeks that starts in August.

   Components are delivered from the supplier to the manufacturer at the beginning of August and the manufacturer produces items to customer orders. Thus, we can ignore any inventory holding cost. We will assume that unsold items at the end of the 10-week selling period have zero value. The objective is to identify a procurement strategy so as to maximize expected profit.

   Specifically, consider a manufacturer that needs to find supply sources for electricity. The manufacturer produces and sells products to end customers at a unit price, Rs.20, and we assume that the only contributor to the production cost is the cost of electricity. To simplify the example, we assume that a unit of electricity is required to produce a unit of finished good. The manufacturer thus has information on the distribution of the demand for electricity. More precisely, she knows that demand for electricity follows the probabilistic forecast described in Table 4-4.

   Two power companies are available for supply:

   - Company 1 offers a fixed commitment contract with the following conditions: power is bought in advance at a price Rs.10 per unit.
   - Company 2 offers an option contract with reservation price of Rs.6 per unit paid in advance and then Rs.6 per unit paid for each unit delivered.

   What is the procurement strategy that should be used by the manufacturer?

TABLE 4-4

Demand	Probability
800	11%
1,000	11%
1,200	28%
1,400	22%
1,600	18%
1,800	10%

3. In Example 4-7, we discuss the revenue-sharing contract between Blockbuster Video and the movie studios. In this case, the benefit for Blockbuster is clear: purchase price is reduced significantly from \$65 to \$8 per copy. What are the benefits for the studios? (*Hint:* Think about the studio's cost structure).
4. Again, consider the revenue-sharing contract between Blockbuster Video and the movie studios. This contract has been extremely profitable for both sides. Since economists have explored revenue-

sharing contracts for many years, why do you think Blockbuster and the movie studios took until 1998 to implement a revenue-sharing contract?

5. In this chapter, we discuss a variety of supply contracts for strategic components, both in make-to-stock and make-to-order systems, which can be used to coordinate the supply chain.

   a. Why do make-to-stock and make-to-order systems require different types of supply contracts?
   b. Consider contracts for make-to-stock systems. What are the advantages and disadvantages of each type of contract? Why would you select one over the others?
   c. Consider contracts for make-to-order systems. What are the advantages and disadvantages of each type of contract? Why would you select one over the others?

6. In Appendix C, we describe the inventory.xls spreadsheet that you will find on the CD that accompanies this text. Use this spreadsheet and the following data to answer the questions below:

Distributor sells for	Rs. 100.00
Salvage	Rs. 20.00
Fixed production cost	Rs.130,000.00
Variable production cost	Rs. 35.00

   a. If a buy-back contract is used and the manufacturer sells the product to the distributor for $65, what is the buy-back amount that is required for the supply chain profit to equal the globally optimal profit?
   b. If a revenue-sharing contract is used, what is an appropriate price for the manufacturer to charge the distributor, and what is an appropriate revenue-sharing level, so that the supply chain profit equals the globally optimal profit?

7. In this chapter, we discussed two classes of supply contracts for strategic components, one of which is appropriate when the manufacturer manufactures goods after the distributor orders them, but the distributor orders before he observes demand, while the other is appropriate when the manufacturer manufactures goods before the distributor orders them, but the distributor orders after he observes demand. Discuss another possible situation, and describe how supply contracts might be beneficial to the supply chain in this new situation.

8. In the portfolio approach described in Section 4.5, the supplier takes on all the risk when the option level is high and the base commitment level is low. Why would suppliers agree to take on that risk?

9.[1] Consider the following demand scenario:

Quantity	Probability
2,000	3%
2,100	8%
2,200	15%
2,300	30%
2,400	17%
2,500	12%
2,600	10%
2,700	5%

[1] Prepared by Stephen Shum.

Suppose the manufacturer produces at a cost of Rs. 20/unit. The distributor sells to end customers for Rs. 50/unit during season, unsold units are sold for Rs.10/unit after season.

a. What is the system optimal production quantity and expected profit under global optimization?

b. Suppose the manufacturer is make-to-order; that is, the timing of events is as follows:

- The distributor orders before it receives demand from end customers.
- The manufacturer produces the amount ordered by the distributor.
- Customer demand is observed.

  i. Suppose the manufacturer sells to the distributor at Rs. 40/unit, how much will the distributor order? What is the expected profit for the manufacturer and distributor?

  ii. Find an option contract such that both the manufacturer and distributor enjoy a higher expected profit than (b)(i). What is the expected profit for the manufacturer and the distributor?

c. Suppose the manufacturer is make-to-stock; that is, the timing of events is as follows:

- The manufacturer produces a certain amount.
- The distributor observes demand.
- The distributor orders from the manufacturer.

  i. Using the same wholesale price contract as part (b)(i), calculate the production/ inventory level of the manufacturer. What is the expected profit for the manufacturer and distributor? Compare your results with part (b)(i).

  ii. Find a cost-sharing contract such that both the manufacturer and distributor enjoy a higher expected profit that that in (c)(i), and calculate their expected profits.

10.[2] Using the data of Question 9, suppose the manufacturer has an inflated demand forecast as follows:

Quantity	Probability
2,200	5%
2,300	6%
2,400	10%
2,500	17%
2,600	30%
2,700	17%
2,800	12%
2,900	3%

a. Suppose the manufacturer is make-to-order (timing of events as in 9(b)). Using your contract in Question 9(b)(ii), find the order quantity, and expected profits of the distributor and of the manufacturer. Compare your answers with 9(b)(ii).

b. Suppose the manufacturer is make-to-stock (timing of events as in 9(c)). Using your contract in Question 9(c)(ii), find the production quantity, expected profits of the manufacturer and of the distributor. Compare your answers with 9(c)(ii).

c. If you are the distributor and you have the choice of revealing the true demand forecast or inflated demand forecast to the manufacturer, what will you do in each case? Explain.

---

[2] Prepared by Stephen Shum.

CHAPTER 5

The Value of Information

CASE: Barilla SpA (A)

Giorgio Maggiali was becoming increasingly frustrated. As director of logistics for the world's largest pasta producer, Barilla SpA (Societa per Aziont translates as "Society for Stockholders" and is interpreted as "Inc."), Maggiali was acutely aware of the growing burden that demand fluctuations imposed on the company's manufacturing and distribution system. Since his appointment in 1988 as Director of Logistics, he had been trying to make headway on an innovative idea proposed by Brando Vitali, who had served as Barilla's director of logistics before Maggiali. The idea, which Vitali called just-in-time distribution (JITD), was modeled after the popular "just-in-time" manufacturing concept. In essence, Vitali proposed that, rather than follow the traditional practice of delivering product to Barilla's distributors on the basis of whatever orders those distributors placed with the company, Barilla's own logistics organization would instead specify the "appropriate" delivery quantities—those that would more effectively meet the end consumer's needs yet also would distribute the workload on Barilla's manufacturing and logistics systems more evenly.

For two years Maggiali, a strong supporter of Vitali's proposal, had tried to implement the idea, but now, in the spring of 1990, little progress had been made. It seemed that Barilla's customers were simply unwilling to give up their authority to place orders as they pleased; some were even reluctant to provide the detailed sales data upon which Barilla could make delivery decisions and improve its demand forecasts. Perhaps more disconcerting was the internal resistance from Barilla's own sales and marketing organizations, which saw the concept as infeasible or dangerous, or both. Perhaps it was time to discard the idea as simply unworkable. If not, how might Maggiali increase the chances that the idea would be accepted?

COMPANY BACKGROUND

Barilla was founded in 1875 when Pietro Barilla opened a small shop in Parma, Italy, on Via Vittorio Emanuele. Adjoining the shop was the small "laboratory" Pietro used to make the pasta and bread products he sold in his store. Pietro's son Ricardo led the company through a significant period of growth and, in the 1940s, passed the company to his own sons, Pietro and Gianni. Over time Barilla evolved from its modest beginnings into a large, vertically integrated corporation with flour mills, pasta plants, and bakery-product factories located throughout Italy.

In a crowded field of more than 2,000 Italian pasta manufacturers, Pietro and Gianni Barilla differentiated their company with a high-quality product supported by innovative marketing pro-

Source: This case was written by Janice H. Hammond of Harvard Business School.

grams. Barilla revolutionized the Italian pasta industry's marketing practices by creating a strong brand name and image for its pasta, selling pasta in a sealed cardboard box with a recognizable color pattern rather than in bulk, and investing in large-scale advertising programs. In 1968, to support the double-digit sales growth the company had experienced during the 1960s, Pietro and Gianni Barilla began construction of a .25-million-square-meter state-of-the-art pasta plant in Pedrignano, a rural town 5 km outside Parma.

The cost of this massive facility—the largest and most technologically advanced pasta plant in the world—drove the Barillas deeply into debt. In 1971 the brothers sold the company to the U.S. multinational firm W. R. Grace, Inc. Grace brought additional capital investment and professional management practices to the company and launched an important new Mulino Bianco ("White Mill") line of bakery products. Throughout the 1970s, facing difficult economic conditions and new Italian legislation that both capped retail pasta prices and increased the cost-of-living allowances for employees, Grace struggled to make its Barilla acquisition pay off. In 1979, Grace sold the company back to Pietro Barilla, who by then had secured the necessary funds to purchase it.

The capital investments and organizational changes that Grace had brought to Barilla, combined with improving market conditions, helped Pietro Barilla launch a successful return to the company. During the 1980s, Barilla enjoyed an annual growth rate of over 21 percent (see Table 5-1). Growth was realized through the expansion of existing businesses, both in Italy and other European countries, as well as through acquisition of new, related businesses.

By 1990 Barilla had become the largest pasta manufacturer in the world, making 35 percent of the pasta sold in Italy and 22 percent of the pasta sold in Europe. Barilla's share in Italy comprised its three brands: The traditional Barilla brand represented 32 percent of the market; the remaining 3 percent of market share was divided between its Voiello brand (a traditional Neapolitan pasta competing in the high- priced segment of the semolina pasta market) and its Braibanti brand (a high-quality, traditional Parmesan pasta made from eggs and semolina). About half of Barilla's pasta was sold in northern Italy and half in the south, where Barilla held a smaller share of the market than in the north but where the market was larger. In addition, Barilla held a 29 percent share of the Italian bakery products market.

In 1990 Barilla was organized into seven divisions: three pasta divisions (Barilla, Voiello, and Braibanti), the Bakery Products Division (manufacturing medium- to long-shelf-life bakery products), the Fresh Bread Division (manufacturing very-short shelf-life bakery products), the Catering Division (distributing cakes and frozen croissants to bars and pastry shops), and the International Division. Barilla's corporate headquarters were located adjacent to the Pedrignano pasta plant.

TABLE 5-1

BARILLA SALES, 1960–1991

Year	Barilla sales (lire in billions*)	Italian wholesale price index
1960	15	10.8
1970	47	41.5
1980	344	57.5
1981	456	67.6
1982	609	76.9
1983	728	84.4
1984	1,034	93.2
1985	1,204	100.0
1986	1,381	99.0
1987	1,634	102.0
1988	1,775	106.5
1989	2,068	121.7
1990†	2,390	128.0

*In 1990, 1,198 lire = US$1.00.

†1990 figures are estimates.

Source: Based on company documents and *International Financial Statistics Yearbook, International Monetary Fund.*

TABLE 5-2

PER CAPITA CONSUMPTION OF PASTA AND BAKERY PRODUCTS, IN KILOGRAMS, 1990

Country	Bread	Breakfast cereals	Pasta	Biscuits
Belgium	85.5	1.0	1.7	5.2
Denmark	29.9	3.7	1.6	5.5
France	68.8	0.6	5.9	6.5
Germany (West)	61.3	0.7	5.2	3.1
Greece	70.0		6.2	8.0
Ireland	58.4	7.7		17.9
Italy	130.9	0.2	17.8	5.9
Netherlands	60.5	1.0	1.4	2.8
Portugal	70.0		5.7	4.6
Spain	87.3	0.3	2.8	5.2
United Kingdom	43.6	7.0	3.6	13.0
Average	70.3	2.5	5.2	7.1

Adapted from *European Marketing Data and Statistics* 1992, Euromonitor Plc 1992, p. 323.

INDUSTRY BACKGROUND

The origins of pasta are unknown. Some believe it originated in China and was first brought to Italy by Marco Polo in the 13th century. Others claim that pasta's origins were rooted in Italy, citing as proof a bas relief on a third-century tomb located near Rome that depicts a pasta roller and cutter. "Regardless of its origins," Barilla marketing literature pronounced, "since time immemorial, Italians have adored pasta." Per capita pasta consumption in Italy averaged nearly 18 kilos per year, greatly exceeding that of other western European countries (see Table 5-2). There was limited seasonality in pasta demand—for example, special pasta types were used for pasta salads in the summer while egg pasta and lasagna were very popular for Easter meals.

In the late 1980s the Italian pasta market as a whole was relatively flat, growing less than 1 percent per year. By 1990 the Italian pasta market was estimated at 3.5 trillion lire. Semolina pasta and fresh pasta were the only growth segments of the Italian pasta market. In contrast, the export market was experiencing record growth; pasta exports from Italy to other European countries were expected to rise as much as 20 to 25 percent per year in the early 1990s. Barilla's management estimated that two-thirds of this increase would be attributed to the new flow of exported pasta to eastern

TABLE 5-3

BARILLA PLANT LOCATIONS AND PRODUCTS MANUFACTURED, 1989

Index	Plant location	Products
1	Braibanti	Pasta
2	Cagliari	Pasta
3	Foggia	Pasta
4	Matera	Pasta
5	Pedrignano	Pasta, noodles, biscuits
6	Viale Barilla	Tortellini, noodles, fresh pasta
7	Caserta	Pasta, rusks, breadsticks
8	Grissin Bon	Breadsticks
9	Rubbiano	Rusks, breadsticks
10	Milano	Panettone, cakes, croissants
11	Pomezia	Croissants
12	Mantova	Biscuits, cakes
13	Melfi	Snacks
14	Ascoli	Snacks, sliced loafs
15	Rodolfi	Sauces
16	Altamura	Flour mill
17	Castelplanio	Flour mill
18	Ferrara	Flour mill
19	Matera	Flour mill
20	Termoli	Flour mill
21	Milano	Fresh bread
22	Milano	Fresh bread
23	Altopascio	Fresh bread
24	Padova	Fresh bread
25	Torino	Fresh bread

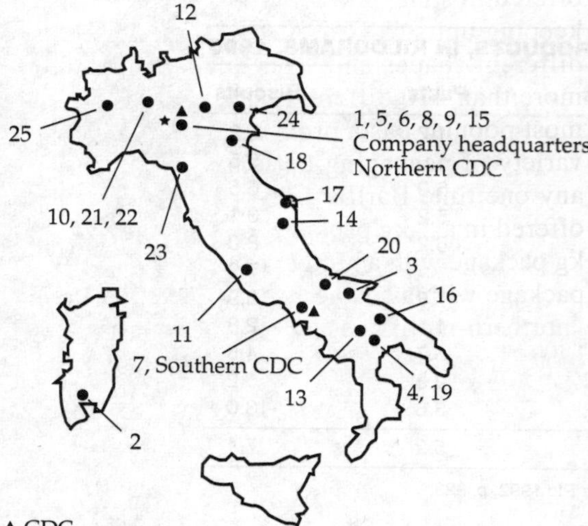

FIGURE 5-1 Map of Barilla plant locations and products manufactured.

European countries seeking low-priced basic food products. Barilla managers viewed the eastern European market as an excellent export opportunity, with the potential to encompass a full range of pasta products.

PLANT NETWORK

Barilla owned and operated an extensive network of plants located throughout Italy (see Table 5-3 and Figure 5-1), including large flour mills, pasta plants, and fresh bread plants, as well as plants producing specialty products such as panettone (Christmas cake) and croissants. Barilla maintained state-of-the-art research and development (R&D) facilities and a pilot production plant in Pedrignano for developing and testing new products and production processes.

Pasta Manufacturing

The pasta-making process is similar to the process by which paper is made. In Barilla plants, flour and water (and for some products, eggs and/or spinach meal) were mixed to form dough, which was then rolled into a long, thin continuous sheet by sequential pairs of rollers set at increasingly closer tolerances. After being rolled to the desired thickness, the dough sheet was forced through a bronze extruding die screen; the die's design gave the pasta its distinctive shape. After passing through the extruder, Barilla workers cut the pasta to a specified length. The cut pieces were then hung over dowels (or placed onto trays) and moved slowly through a long tunnel kiln that snaked across the factory floor. The temperature and humidity in the kiln were precisely specified for each size and shape of pasta and had to be tightly controlled to ensure a high-quality product. To keep changeover costs low and product quality high, Barilla followed a carefully chosen production sequence that minimized the incremental changes in kiln temperature and humidity between pasta shapes. After completing the four-hour drying process, the pasta was weighed and packaged.

At Barilla, raw ingredients were transformed into packaged pasta on fully automated 120-meter-long production lines. In the Pedrignano plant, the largest and most technologically advanced of Barilla's plants, 11 lines produced 9,000 quintals (900,000 kilos) of pasta each day. Barilla employees used bicycles to travel within this enormous facility.

Barilla's pasta plants were specialized by the type of pasta produced in the plant. The primary distinctions were based on the composition of the pasta—for example, whether it was made with or without eggs or spinach and whether it was sold as dry or fresh pasta. All of Barilla's non-egg pasta was made with flour ground from *grano duro* (high-protein "hard" wheat), the highest-quality flour for making traditional pasta products. Semolina, for example, is a finely ground durum wheat flour. Barilla used flours made from *grano tenero* (tender wheat), such as farina, for more delicate products such as egg pasta and bakery products. Barilla's flour mills ground flour from both types of wheat.

Even within the same family of pasta products, individual products were assigned to plants based on the size and shape of the pasta. "Short" pasta products, such as macaroni or fusilli, and "long" products, such as spaghetti or capellini, were made in separate facilities because of the different sizes of equipment required.

CHANNELS OF DISTRIBUTION

Barilla divided its entire product line into two general categories:

- "Fresh" products, including fresh pasta products, which had 21-day shelf lives, and fresh bread, which had a one-day shelf life.
- "Dry" products, including dry pasta, and longer shelf-life bakery products such as cookies, biscuits, flour, bread sticks, and dry toasts. Dry products represented about 75 percent of Barilla's sales and had either "long" shelf lives of 18 to 24 months (e.g., pasta and dried toasts) or "medium" shelf lives of 10 to 12 weeks (e.g., cookies). In total, Barilla's "dry" products were offered in some 800 different packaged stock-keeping units (SKUs). Pasta was made in 200 different shapes and sizes and was offered in more than 470 different packaged SKUs. The most popular pasta products were offered in a variety of packaging options; for example, at any one time Barilla's #5 spaghetti might be offered in a 5-kg package, a 2-kg package, a 1-kg package with a northern Italian motif, a 1-kg package with a southern Italian motif, a 0.5-kg "northern-motif" package, a 0.5-kg "southern-motif" package, a display pallet, and a special promotional package with a free bottle of Barilla pasta sauce.

Most Barilla products were shipped from the plants in which they were made to one of two Barilla central distribution centers (CDCs): the northern CDC in Pedrignano or the southern CDC on the outskirts of Naples. See Figure 5-2.

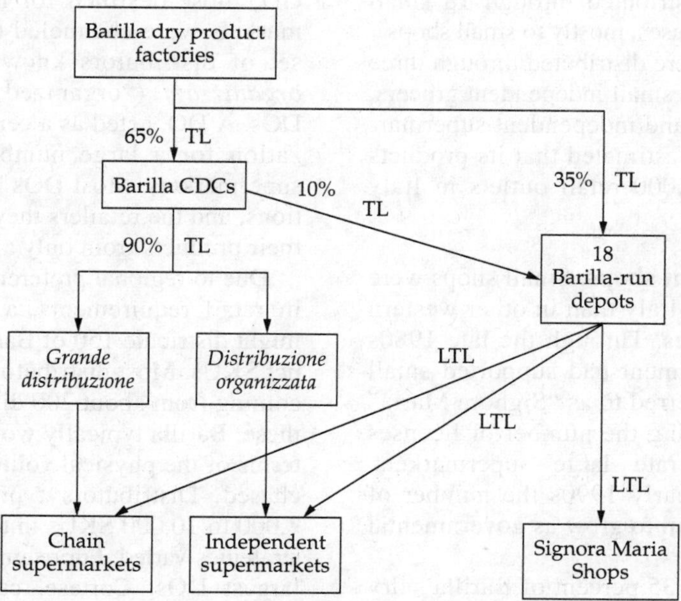

TL = Delivery in truckload quantities.
LTL = Delivery in less-than-truckload quantities.

Note: Shipping percentages are based on product weight.

FIGURE 5-2 Barilla distribution patterns.

(Certain products, such as fresh bread, did not flow through the CDCs.) Other fresh products were moved quickly through the distribution system; fresh product inventory was typically held only three days in each of the CDCs. In contrast, each CDC held about a month's worth of dry product inventory.

Barilla maintained separate distribution systems for its fresh and dry products because of their differences in perishability and retail service requirements. Fresh products were purchased from the two CDCs by independent agents *(concessionari)* who then channeled the products through 70 regional warehouses located throughout Italy. Nearly two thirds of Barilla's dry products were destined for supermarkets; these products were shipped first to one of Barilla's CDCs, where they were purchased by distributors. The distributors in turn shipped the product to supermarkets. Brando Vitali's JITD proposal focused solely on dry products sold through distributors. The remainder of the dry products was distributed through 18 small Barilla-owned warehouses, mostly to small shops.

Barilla products were distributed through three types of retail outlets: small independent grocers, supermarket chains, and independent supermarkets. In sum, Barilla estimated that its products were offered in 100,000 retail outlets in Italy alone.

1. **Small independent shops.** Small shops were more prevalent in Italy than in other western European countries. Through the late 1980s the Italian government had supported small grocers (often referred to as "Signora Maria" shops) by restricting the number of licenses provided to operate large supermarkets. However, in the early 1990s the number of supermarkets began to grow as governmental restrictions abated.

   Approximately 35 percent of Barilla's dry products (30 percent in the north of Italy and 40 percent in the south) were distributed from Barilla's internally owned regional warehouses to small independent shops, which typically held over two weeks of inventory at the store level. Small shop owners purchased products through brokers who dealt with Barilla purchasing and distribution personnel.

2. **Supermarkets.** The remaining dry products were distributed through outside distributors to supermarkets—70 percent to supermarket chains and 30 percent to independent supermarkets. A supermarket typically held from 10 to 12 days of dry product inventory within the stores, and on average carried a total of 4,800 dry product SKUs. Although Barilla offered many pasta products in multiple types of packages, most retailers would carry a product in only one (and at most two) packaging options.

   Dry products destined for a supermarket chain were distributed through the chain's own distribution organization, known as a *grande distribuzione* ("grand distributor"), or GD; those destined for independent supermarkets were channeled through a different set of distributors known as *distribuzione organizzata* ("organized distributors"), or DOs. A DO. acted as a central buying organization for a large number of independent supermarkets. Most DOs had regional operations, and the retailers they served usually got their products from only a single DO.

   Due to regional preferences and differences in retail requirements, a typical distributor might distribute 150 of Barilla's 800 dry product SKUs. Most distributors handled products coming from about 200 different suppliers; of these, Barilla typically would be the largest in terms of the physical volume of products purchased. Distributors typically carried from 7,000 to 10,000 SKUs in total. However, their strategies varied. For example, one of Barilla's largest DOs, Cortese, carried only 100 of Barilla's dry products and carried a total of only 5,000 SKUs.

   Both GDs and DOs purchased products from the Barilla CDCs, maintained inventory in their own warehouses, and then filled supermarket orders from their warehouse inventory. A distributor's warehouse typically held a two-week supply of Barilla dry products in inventory.

Many supermarkets placed daily orders with distributors; the store manager would walk up and down the store aisles and note each product that needed to be replenished and the number of boxes required (more sophisticated retailers used handheld computers to record order quantities as they checked the shelves). The order would then be transmitted to the store's distributor; orders were typically received at the store 24 to 48 hours after receipt of the order at the distribution center.

SALES AND MARKETING

Barilla enjoyed a strong brand image in Italy. Its marketing and sales strategy was based upon a combination of advertising and promotions.

Advertising

Barilla brands were heavily advertised. Advertising copy differentiated Barilla pasta from basic commodity "noodles" by positioning the brand as the highest quality, most sophisticated pasta product available. One ad campaign was built on the phrase "Barilla: a great collection of premium Italian pasta." The "collection" dimension was illustrated by showing individual uncooked pasta shapes against a black background, as though they were jewels, evoking a sense of luxury and sophistication. Unlike other pasta manufacturers, Barilla avoided images of traditional Italian folklore, preferring modern, sophisticated settings in major Italian cities.

Advertising themes were supported by sponsorships of well-known athletes and celebrities. For example, Barilla engaged tennis stars Steffi Graf to promote Barilla products in Germany and Stefan Edberg in the Scandinavian countries. Luminaries such as actor Paul Newman were also used to promote Barilla products. In addition, Barilla advertising focused on developing and strengthening loyal relationships with Italian families by using messages such as "Where there is Barilla, there is a home."

Trade Promotions

Barilla's sales strategy relied on the use of trade promotions to push its products into the grocery distribution network. A Barilla sales executive explained the logic of the promotion-based strategy:

> We sell to a very old-fashioned distribution system. The buyers expect frequent trade promotions, which they then pass along to their own customers. So a store will know right away if another store is buying Barilla pasta at a discount. You have to understand how important pasta is in Italy. Everyone knows the price of pasta. If a store is selling pasta at a discount one week, consumers notice the reduced price immediately.

Barilla divided each year into 10 or 12 "canvass" periods, typically four to five weeks in length, each corresponding to a promotional program. During any canvass period, a Barilla distributor could buy as many products as desired to meet current and future needs. Incentives for Barilla sales representatives were based on achieving the sales targets set for each canvass period. Different product categories were offered during different canvass periods, with the discount depending on the margin structure of the category. Typical promotional discounts were 1.4 percent for semolina pasta, 4 percent for egg pasta, 4 percent for biscuits, 8 percent for sauces, and 10 percent for breadsticks.

Barilla also offered volume discounts. For example, Barilla paid for transportation, thus providing incentives of 2 to 3 percent for orders in full truckload quantities. In addition, a sales representative might offer a buyer a 1,000 lire per carton discount (representing a 4 percent discount) if the buyer purchased a minimum of three truckloads of Barilla egg pasta.

Sales Representatives

Barilla sales representatives serving DOs spent an estimated 90 percent of their time working at the store level. In the store, sales reps helped merchandise Barilla products and set up in-store promotions; took note of competitive information, including competitors' prices, stockouts, and new product introductions; and discussed Barilla products and ordering strategies with store management. In addition, each sales rep spent a half day in a regularly scheduled weekly meeting with the distributor's buyer, helping the distributor place its weekly order, explaining promotions and discounts, and settling problems such as returns and deletions associated with the last delivery. Each rep carried a portable computer for inputting distributor orders. The rep also would spend a few hours a week at the CDC, discussing new products and prices, covering problems concerning the previous week's deliveries, and settling disputes about different discounts and deal structures.

In contrast, a very small sales force served the GDs. The GD sales force rarely visited GD warehouses and usually sent their orders to Barilla via fax.

DISTRIBUTION

Distributor Ordering Procedures

Most distributors—GDs and DOs alike—checked their inventory levels and placed orders with Barilla once a week. Barilla products would then be shipped to the distributor over the course of the week that started 8 days after the order was placed and ended 14 days after the order was placed—the average lead time was 10 days. For example, a large distributor that ordered every Tuesday might order several truckloads to be delivered from the following Wednesday through the following Tuesday. Distributors' sales volumes varied; small distributors might order only one truckload a week, whereas the largest warranted deliveries of as many as five truckloads a week.

Most distributors used simple periodic review inventory systems. For example, a distributor might review inventory levels of Barilla products each Tuesday; the distributor would then place orders for those products whose levels fell below the reorder level. Nearly all of the distributors had computer-supported ordering systems, but few had forecasting systems or sophisticated analytical tools for determining order quantities.

Impetus for the JITD Program

As the 1980s progressed, Barilla increasingly felt the effects of fluctuating demand. Orders for Barilla dry products often swung wildly from week to week (see Figure 5-3). Such extreme demand variability strained Barilla's manufacturing and logistics operations. For example, the specific sequence of pasta production necessitated by the tight heat and humidity specifications in the tunnel kiln made it difficult to quickly produce a particular pasta that had been sold out owing to unexpectedly high demand. On the other hand, holding sufficient finished goods inventories to meet distributors' order requirements was extremely expensive when weekly demand fluctuated so widely and was so unpredictable.

Some manufacturing and logistics personnel favored asking distributors or retailers to carry additional inventory to check the fluctuation in distributors' orders, noting that with their current inventory levels, many distributors' service levels to the retailers were unacceptable (see Figure 5-4 for sample distributor inventory levels and stockout rates). Others felt that the distributors and retailers were already carrying too much inventory. In the late 1980s a Barilla logistics manager discussed retail inventory pressure:

> Our customers are changing. And do you know why they are changing? As I see it, they are realizing they do not have enough room in their stores and warehouses to carry the very large inventories manufacturers would like them to. Think of shelf space in retail outlets. You cannot easily increase it. Yet manufacturers are continuously introducing new products, and they want retailers to display each product on the fronts of their shelves! That would be impossible even if supermarkets were made from rubber![1]

[1]Claudio Ferrozzi, *The Pedrignano Warehouse*(Milan: GEA, 1988).

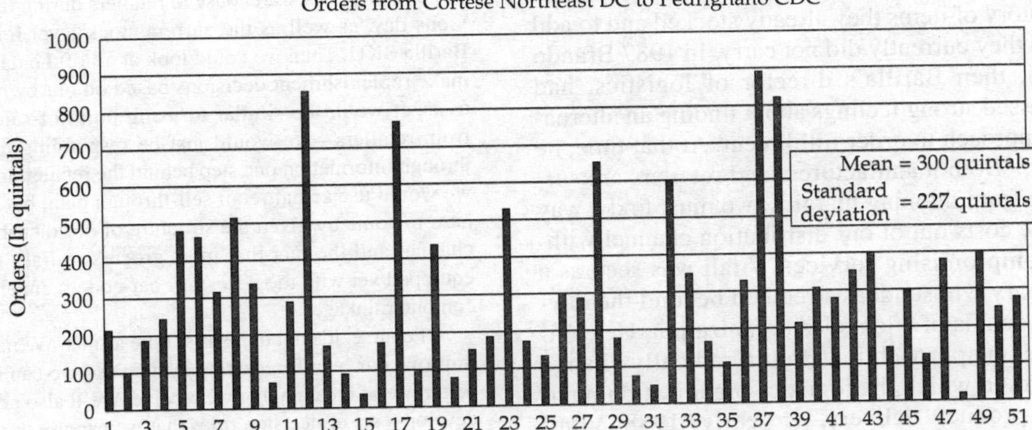

FIGURE 5-3 Weekly demand for Barilla dry products from Cortese's Northeast Distribution Center to the Pedrignano CDC, 1989.

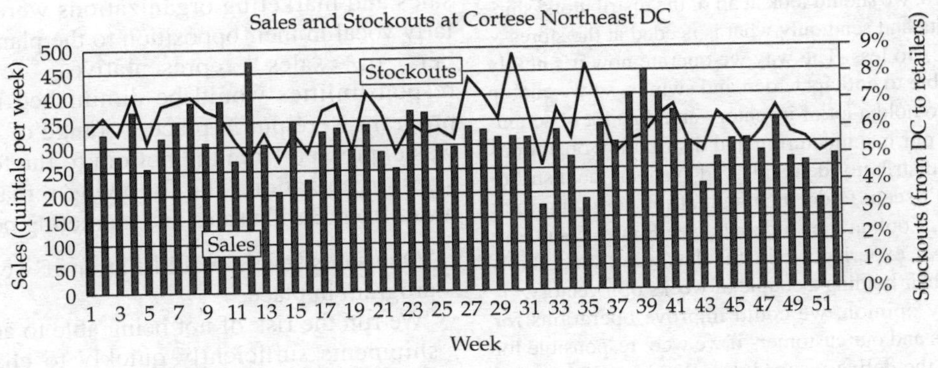

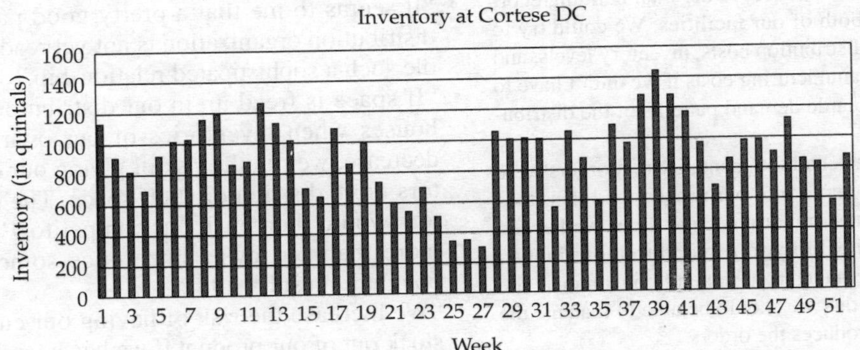

FIGURE 5-4 Sample stockout and inventory levels, Cortese's Northeast Distribution Center, 1989.

Distributors felt similar pressure to increase the inventory of items they already stocked and to add items they currently did not carry. In 1987 Brando Vitali, then Barilla's director of logistics, had expressed strong feelings about finding an alternative approach to order fulfillment. At that time, he noted, "Both manufacturers and retailers are suffering from thinning margins; we must find a way to take costs out of our distribution channel without compromising service." Vitali was seen as a visionary whose ideas stretched beyond the day-today details of a logistics organization. He envisioned an approach that would radically change the way in which the logistics organization managed product delivery. In early 1988 Vitali explained his plan:

> I envision a simple approach: rather than send product to the distributors according to their internal planning processes, we should look at all of the distributors' shipment data and send only what is needed at the stores—no more, no less. The way we operate now it's nearly impossible to anticipate demand swings, so we end up having to hold a lot of inventory and do a lot of scrambling in our manufacturing and distribution operations to meet distributor demand. And even so, the distributors don't seem to do such a great job servicing their retailers. Look at the stockouts (see Figure 5-4) these DOs have experienced in the last year. And that's despite their holding a couple of weeks of inventory.
>
> In my opinion, we could improve operations for ourselves and our customers if we were responsible for creating the delivery schedules. We'd be able to ship product only as it is needed, rather than building enormous stocks in both of our facilities. We could try to reduce our own distribution costs, inventory levels, and ultimately our manufacturing costs if we didn't have to respond to the volatile demand patterns of the distributors.
>
> We have always had the mentality that orders were an unchangeable input into our process and therefore that one of the most important capabilities we needed to achieve was flexibility to respond to those inputs. But in reality, demand from the end consumer is the input and I think that we should be able to manage the input filter that produces the orders.
>
> How would this work? Every day each distributor would provide us data on what Barilla products it had shipped out of its warehouse to retailers during the previous day, as well as the current stock level for each Barilla SKU. Then we could look at all of the data and make replenishment decisions based on our own forecasts. It would be similar to using point-of-sale data from retailers—we would just be responding to see-through information one step behind the retailer. Ideally, we would use actual retail sell-through data, but that's hard to come by given the structure of our distribution channel and the fact that most grocers in Italy aren't equipped yet with the necessary bar-code scanners and computer linkages.
>
> Of course, it's not quite as simple as that. We need to improve our own forecasting systems so we can make better use of the data that we receive. We'll also need to develop a set of decision rules that we can use to determine what to send after we've made a new forecast.

Vitali's proposal, "just-in-time distribution," met with significant resistance within Barilla. The sales and marketing organizations were particularly vocal in their opposition to the plan. A number of sales representatives felt their responsibilities would be diminished if such a program were put in place. A range of concerns was expressed from the bottom to the top of the sales organization. The following remarks were heard from Barilla sales and marketing personnel:

- "Our sales levels would flatten if we put this program in place."
- "We run the risk of not being able to adjust our shipments sufficiently quickly to changes in selling patterns or increased promotions."
- "It seems to me that a pretty good part of the distribution organization is not yet ready to handle such a sophisticated relationship."
- "If space is freed up in our distributors' warehouses when inventories of our own product decrease, we run the risk of giving our competitors more distributor shelf space. The distributors would then push our competitors' product more than our own, since once something is bought it must be sold."
- "We increase the risk of having our customers stock out of our product if we have disruption in our supply process. What if we have a strike or some other disturbance?"

- "We wouldn't be able to run trade promotions with JITD. How can we get the trade to push Barilla product to retailers if we don't offer some sort of incentive?"
- "It's not clear that costs would even be reduced. If a DO decreases its stock, we at Barilla may have to increase our own inventory of those products for which we cannot change production schedules due to our lack of manufacturing flexibility."

Vitali countered the concerns of the sales organization:

> I think JITD should be considered a selling tool, rather than a threat to sales. We're offering the customer additional service at no extra cost. In addition, the program will improve Barilla's visibility with the trade and make distributors more dependent on us—it should improve the relationships between Barilla and the distributors rather than harm them. And what's more, the information regarding the supply at the distributors' warehouses provides us with objective data that would permit us to improve our own planning procedures.

Giorgio Maggiali, head of materials management for Barilla's fresh products group, was appointed director of logistics in late 1988 when Vitali was promoted to head one of the company's new divisions. Maggiali was a hands-on manager, known for his orientation to action. Shortly after his appointment, Maggiali appointed a recent college graduate, Vincenzo Battistini, to help him develop and implement the JITD program.

Maggiali recounted his frustrations in implementing the JITD program:

> In 1988 we developed the basic ideas for the approach we wanted to use and tried to convince several of our distributors to sign on. They weren't even interested in talking about it; the manager of one of our largest distributors pretty much summed up a lot of the responses we had when he cut off a conversation saying, "Managing stock is my job; I don't need you to see my warehouse or my figures. I could improve my inventory and service levels myself if you would deliver my orders more quickly. I'll make you a proposal—I'll place the order and you deliver within 36 hours." He didn't understand that we just can't respond to wildly changing orders without more notice than that. Another distributor expressed concerns about becoming too closely linked to Barilla. "We would be giving Barilla the power to push product into our warehouses just so Barilla can reduce its costs." Still another asked, "What makes you think that you could manage my inventories any better than I can?"
>
> We were finally able to convince a couple of our distributors to have in-depth discussions about the JITD proposal. Our first discussion was with Marconi, a large, fairly old-fashioned GD. First Battistini and I visited Marconi's logistics department and presented our plan. We made it clear that we planned to provide them with such good service that they could both decrease their inventories and improve their fill rate to their stores. The logistics group thought it sounded great and was interested in conducting an experimental run of the program. But as soon as Marconi's buyers heard about it, all hell broke loose. First the buyers started to voice their own concerns; then, after talking to their Barilla sales reps, they started to repeat some of our own sales department's objections as well. Marconi finally agreed to sell us the data we wanted, but otherwise things would continue as before with Marconi making decisions about replenishment quantities and timing. This clearly wasn't the type of relationship we were looking for, so we talked to other distributors, but they weren't much more responsive.
>
> We need to regroup now and decide where to go with JITD. Is this type of program feasible in our environment? If so, what kind of customer should we target? And how do we convince them to sign up?

The Barilla case raises two important issues:

- Variations in distributors' order patterns have caused severe operational inefficiencies and cost penalties for Barilla. The extreme variability in orders that Barilla receives is surprising considering the distribution of demand for pasta in Italy. Indeed, while variability in aggregate demand for pasta is quite small, orders placed by the distributors have a huge variability.
- In the proposed JITD strategy, Barilla will be in charge of the channel between the CDCs and the distributors and decide on the timing and size of shipments to its distributors. Thus, unlike traditional

supply chains in which distributors place orders and manufacturers try to satisfy these orders as much as possible, in JITD "Barilla's own logistics organization would specify the appropriate delivery quantities—those that would more effectively meet the end consumer's needs yet would also more evenly distribute the workload on Barilla's manufacturing and logistics systems." This strategy is referred to as *vendor managed inventory (VMI)*.

By the end of this chapter, you should be able to answer the following questions:

- What are the reasons for the increase in variability in Barilla's supply chain?
- How can the firm cope with the increase in variability?
- What is the impact of transferring demand information across the supply chain?
- Can the VMI strategy solve the operational problems faced by Barilla?
- How can the supply chain meet conflicting goals of different partners and facilities?

5.1 INTRODUCTION

We live in the "Information Age." Data warehouses, web services, XML, wireless, the Internet, and portals are just a few of the technologies dominating the business page of the daily newspaper. In Chapters 14 and 15, we examine these technologies in detail and look at the issues surrounding their implementation. In this chapter, we consider the value of using any type of information technology; we deal specifically with the potential availability of more and more information throughout the supply chain and the implications this availability has on effective design and management of the integrated supply chain.

The implications of this abundance of available information are enormous. The supply chain pundits and consultants like to use the phrase *In modern supply chains, information replaces inventory.* We don't dispute this idea, but its meaning is vague. After all, at some point the customer needs products, not just information! Nevertheless, information changes the way supply chains can and should be effectively managed, and these changes may lead to, among other things, lower inventories. Indeed, our objective in this chapter is to characterize how information affects the design and operation of the supply chain. We show that by effectively harnessing the information now available, one can design and operate the supply chain much more efficiently and effectively than ever before.

It should be apparent to the reader that having accurate information about inventory levels, orders, production, and delivery status throughout the supply chain should not make the managers of a supply chain less effective than if this information were not available. After all, they could choose to ignore it. As we will see, however, this information provides a tremendous opportunity to improve the way the supply chain is designed and managed. Unfortunately, using this information effectively does make the design and management of the supply chain more complex because many more issues must be considered.

We argue here that this abundant information

- Helps reduce variability in the supply chain.
- Helps suppliers make better forecasts, accounting for promotions and market changes.
- Enables the coordination of manufacturing and distribution systems and strategies.
- Enables retailers to better serve their customers by offering tools for locating desired items.
- Enables retailers to react and adapt to supply problems more rapidly.
- Enables lead time reductions.

We provide examples that illustrate that, unfortunately, in various industries, supply chain partners do not agree to share information, inflate their forecasts, or abuse the information shared. Thus, after

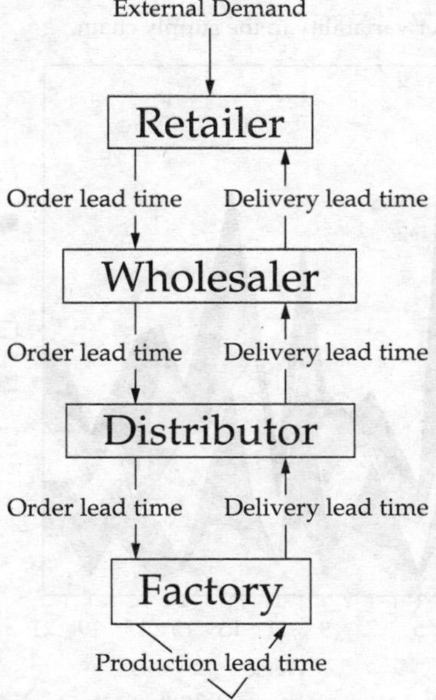

FIGURE 5-5 The supply chain.

discussing and demonstrating the benefits of information sharing, we discuss incentive mechanisms that motivate supply chain parties to share information with each other.

The chapter is based on the seminal work in [139] and [140] as well as the recent work in [48] and [49]. In the next section, we follow the review article [47].

5.2 THE BULLWHIP EFFECT

In recent years, many suppliers and retailers have observed that, while customer demand for specific products does not vary much, inventory and back-order levels fluctuate considerably across their supply chain. For instance, in examining the demand for Pampers disposable diapers, executives at Procter & Gamble noticed an interesting phenomenon. As expected, retail sales of the product were fairly uniform; there is no particular day or month in which the demand is significantly higher or lower than any other. However, the executives noticed that distributors' orders placed to the factory fluctuated much more than retail sales. In addition, P&G's orders to its suppliers fluctuated even more. This increase in variability as we travel up in the supply chain is referred to as the *bullwhip effect*.

Figure 5-5 illustrates a simple four-stage supply chain: a single retailer, a single wholesaler, a single distributor, and a single factory. The retailer observes customer demand and places orders to the wholesaler. The wholesaler receives products from the distributor, who places orders to the factory. Figure 5-6 provides a graphical representation of orders, as a function of time, placed by different facilities. The figure clearly shows the increase in variability across the supply chain.

To understand the impact of the increase in variability on the supply chain, consider the second stage in our example, the wholesaler. The wholesaler receives orders from the retailer and places orders to his supplier, the distributor. To determine these order quantities, the wholesaler must forecast the retailer's demand. If the wholesaler does not have access to the customer's demand data, he must use orders placed by the retailer to perform his forecasting.

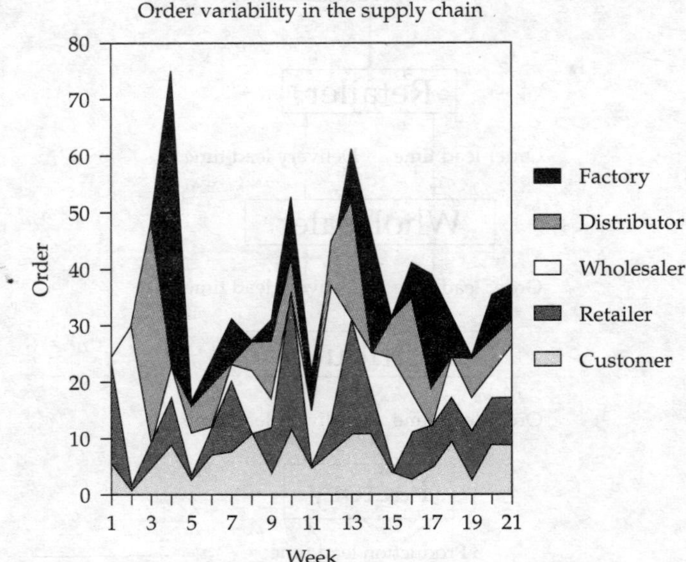

FIGURE 5-6 The increase in variability in the supply chain.

Since variability in orders placed by the retailer is significantly higher than variability in customer demand, as Figure 5-6 shows, the wholesaler is forced to carry more safety stock than the retailer or else to maintain higher capacity than the retailer in order to meet the same service level as the retailer.

This analysis can be carried over to the distributor as well as the factory, resulting in even higher inventory levels and therefore higher costs at these facilities.

Consider, for example, a simple widget supply chain. A single factory, Widget-Makers Inc., supplies a single retailer, the WidgetStore. Average annual widget demand at the WidgetStore is 5,200 units, and shipments are made from WidgetMakers to the store each week. If the variability in orders placed by the WidgetStore is low, so that the shipment every week is about 100 units, WidgetMakers' production capacity and weekly shipping capacity need be only about 100 units. If weekly variability is very high, so that during certain weeks WidgetMakers must make and ship 400 units and some weeks no units at all, it is easy to see that production and shipping capacity must be much higher and that some weeks this capacity will be idle. Alternatively, WidgetMakers could build up inventory during weeks with low demand and supply these items during weeks with high demand, thus increasing inventory holding costs.

Thus, it is important to identify techniques and tools that will allow us to control the bullwhip effect; that is, to control the increase in variability in the supply chain. For this purpose, we need to first understand the main factors contributing to the increase in variability in the supply chain.

1. *Demand forecasting*. Traditional inventory management techniques (see Chapter 2) practiced at each level in the supply chain lead to the bullwhip effect. To explain the connection between forecasting and the bullwhip effect, we need to revisit inventory control strategies in supply chains. As discussed in Chapter 2, an attractive policy used in practice by each stage of the supply chain is the *periodic review policy* where the inventory policy is characterized by a single parameter, the **base-stock level**. That is, the warehouse determines a target inventory level, the base-stock level,

and each review period, the inventory position is reviewed, and the warehouse orders enough to raise the inventory position to the base-stock level.

The base-stock level is typically set equal to the average demand during lead time and review period plus a multiple of the standard deviation of demand during lead time and review period. The latter quantity is referred to as *safety stock*. Typically, managers use *standard forecast smoothing techniques* to estimate average demand and demand variability. An important characteristic of all forecasting techniques is that as more data are observed, the estimates of the mean and the standard deviation (or variability) of customer demands are regularly modified. Since safety stock, as well as the base-stock level, strongly depends on these estimates, the user is forced to change order quantities, thus increasing variability.

2. *Lead time*. It is easy to see that the increase in variability is magnified with increasing lead time. For this purpose, recall from Chapter 2 that to calculate safety stock levels and base-stock levels, we in effect multiply estimates of the average and standard deviation of the daily customer demands by the sum of the lead time and the review period. Thus, with longer lead times, a small change in the estimate of demand variability implies a significant change in safety stock and base-stock level, leading to a significant change in order quantities. This, of course, leads to an increase in variability.
3. *Batch ordering*. The impact of batch ordering is quite simple to understand. If the retailer uses batch ordering, as happens when using a (Q, R) inventory policy or a min-max policy, then the wholesaler will observe a large order, followed by several periods of no orders, followed by another large order, and so on. Thus, the wholesaler sees a distorted and highly variable pattern of orders.

   It is useful to remind the reader that firms use batch ordering for a number of reasons. First, as pointed out in Chapter 2, a firm that is faced with fixed ordering costs needs to apply the (Q, R) or (s, S) inventory policies, which lead to batch ordering. Second, as transportation costs become more significant, retailers may order quantities that allow them to take advantage of transportation discounts (e.g., full-truckload quantities). This may lead to some weeks with large orders, and some with no orders at all. Finally, the quarterly or yearly sales quotas or incentives observed in many businesses also can result in unusually large orders observed on a periodic basis.
4. *Price fluctuation*. Price fluctuation also can lead to the bullwhip effect. If prices fluctuate, retailers often attempt to *stock up* when prices are lower. This is accentuated by the prevailing practice in many industries of offering promotions and discounts at certain times or for certain quantities. This practice, referred to as *forward buying*, implies that retailers purchase large quantities during distributors' and manufacturers' discount and promotion time and order relatively small quantities at other time periods.
5. *Inflated orders*. Inflated orders placed by retailers during shortage periods tend to magnify the bullwhip effect. Such orders are common when retailers and distributors suspect that a product will be in short supply, and therefore anticipate receiving supply proportional to the amount ordered. When the period of shortage is over, the retailer goes back to its standard orders, leading to all kinds of distortions and variations in demand estimates.

5.2.1 Quantifying the Bullwhip Effect[2]

So far, we have discussed factors contributing to the increase in variability in the supply chain. To better understand and control the bullwhip effect, we also would find it useful to *quantify* the bullwhip effect; that is, quantify the increase in variability that occurs at every stage of the supply chain. This

[2] This section can be skipped without loss of continuity.

would be useful not only to demonstrate the magnitude of the increase in variability but also to show the relationship between the forecasting technique, the lead time, and the increase in variability.

To quantify the increase in variability for a simple supply chain, consider a two-stage supply chain with a retailer who observes customer demand and places an order to a manufacturer. Suppose that the retailer faces a fixed lead time, so that an order placed by the retailer at the end of period t is received at the start of period $t + L$. Also, suppose the retailer follows a simple periodic review policy (see Chapter 2) in which the retailer reviews inventory every period and places an order to bring its inventory level up to a target level. Observe that, in this case, the review period is one.

Hence, as discussed in Chapter 2, Section 2.2.7, the base-stock level is calculated as

$$L \times AVG + z \times STD \times \sqrt{L}$$

where *AVG* and *STD* are the average and standard deviation of daily (or weekly) customer demand. The constant z is the safety factor and is chosen from statistical tables to ensure that the probability of no stockouts during lead time is equal to the specified level of service.

To implement this inventory policy, the retailer must estimate the average and standard deviation of demand based on its observed customer demand. Thus, in practice, the order-up-to point may change from day to day according to changes in the current estimate of the average and the standard deviation.

Specifically, the order-up-to point in period t, y_t, is estimated from the observed demand as

$$y_t = \hat{\mu}_t L + z\sqrt{L}\, S_t$$

where $\hat{\mu}_t$ and S_t are the estimated average and standard deviation of daily customer demand at time t.

Suppose the retailer uses one of the simplest forecasting techniques: the moving average. In other words, in each period, the retailer estimates the mean demand as an average of the previous p observations of demand. The retailer estimates the standard deviation of demand in a similar manner. That is, if D_i represents customer demand in period i, then

$$\hat{\mu}_t = \frac{\sum_{i=t-p}^{t-1} D_i}{p}$$

and

$$S_t^2 = \frac{\sum_{i=t-p}^{t-1} (D_i - \hat{\mu}_t)^2}{p - 1}$$

Note that the expressions above imply that, in every period, the retailer calculates a new mean and standard deviation based on the p most recent observations of demand. Then, since the estimates of the mean and standard deviation change every period, the target inventory level also will change in every period.

In this case, we can quantify the increase in variability; that is, we can calculate the variability faced by the manufacturer and compare it to the variability faced by the retailer. If the variance of the customer demand seen by the retailer is *Var* (*D*), then the variance of the orders placed by that retailer to the manufacturer, *Var* (*Q*), relative to the variance of customer demand satisfies

$$\frac{Var\,(Q)}{Var\,(D)} \geq 1 + \frac{2L}{p} + \frac{2L^2}{p^2}$$

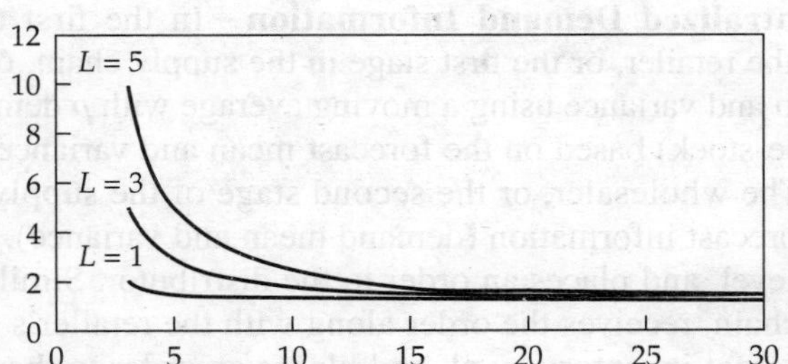

FIGURE 5-7 A lower bound on the increase in variability given as a function of *p*.

Figure 5-7 shows the lower bound on the increase in variability as a function of p for various values of the lead time, L. In particular, when p is large and L is small, the bullwhip effect due to forecasting error is negligible. The bullwhip effect is magnified as we increase the lead time and decrease p.

For instance, suppose the retailer estimates the mean demand based on the last five demand observations, that is, $p = 5$. Suppose also that an order placed by the retailer at the end of period t is received at the start of period $t + 1$. This implies that the lead time (more precisely, the lead time plus the review period) equals 1, that is, $L = 1$. In this case, the variance of the orders placed by the retailer to the manufacturer will be at least 40 percent larger than the variance of the customer demand seen by the retailer, that is,

$$\frac{Var\ (Q)}{Var\ (Q)} \geq 1.4$$

Next, consider the same retailer, but now assume, as is typically the case in the retail industry, that the retailer uses 10 demand observations (i.e., $p = 10$) to estimate the mean and standard deviation of demand. Then the variance of the orders placed by the retailer to the manufacturer will be at least 1.2 times the variance of the customer demand seen by the retailer. In other words, by increasing the number of observations used in the moving average forecast, the retailer can significantly reduce the variability of the orders it places to the manufacturer.

5.2.2 The Impact of Centralized Information on the Bullwhip Effect

One of the most frequent suggestions for reducing the bullwhip effect is to centralize demand information within a supply chain, that is, to provide each stage of the supply chain with complete information on the actual customer demand. To understand why centralized demand information can reduce the bullwhip effect, note that if demand information is centralized, each stage of the supply chain can use the actual customer demand data to create more accurate forecasts, rather than relying on the orders received from the previous stage, which can vary significantly more than the actual customer demand.

In this subsection, we consider the value of sharing customer demand information within a supply chain. For this purpose, consider again the initial four-stage supply chain, pictured in Figure 5-5, with a single retailer, wholesaler, distributor, and factory. To determine the impact of centralized demand information on the bullwhip effect, we distinguish between two types of supply chains: one with centralized demand information and a second with decentralized demand information. These systems are described below.

Supply Chain with Centralized Demand Information In the first type of supply chain, the *centralized supply chain,* the retailer, or the first stage in the supply chain, observes customer demand, forecasts the demand mean and variance using a moving average with p demand observations, finds his target inventory level (base-stock) based on the forecast mean and variance of demand, and places an order to the wholesaler. The wholesaler, or the second stage of the supply chain, receives the order along with the retailer's forecast information (demand mean and variance), uses this forecast to determine its target inventory level, and places an order to the distributor. Similarly, the distributor, or the third stage of the supply chain, receives the order along with the retailer's forecast demand, uses this forecast to determine its target inventory level, and places an order to the fourth stage of the supply chain, the factory.

In this centralized supply chain, each stage of the supply chain receives the retailer's forecast mean demand and follows a base-stock inventory policy based on this mean demand. Therefore, in this case, we have centralized the demand information, the forecasting technique, and the inventory policy.

Following the analysis above, it is not difficult to show that the variance of the orders placed by the kth stage of the supply chain, $Var\,(Q^k)$, relative to the variance of the customer demand, $Var\,(D)$, is just

$$\frac{Var\,(Q^k)}{Var\,(D)} \geq 1 + \frac{2\sum_{i=1}^{k} L_i}{p} + \frac{2\left(\sum_{i=1}^{k} L_i\right)^2}{p^2}$$

where L_i is the lead time between stage i and stage $i + 1$. That is, the lead time L_i implies that an order placed by facility i at the end of period t arrives at that facility at the beginning of period $t + L_i$. For example, if an order placed by the retailer to the wholesaler at the end of period t arrives at the beginning of period $t + 2$, then $L_1 = 2$. Similarly, if the lead time from the wholesaler to the distributor is two periods, then $L_2 = 2$, and if the lead time from the distributor to the factory is also two periods, then $L_3 = 2$. In this case, the total lead time from the retailer to the factory is

$$L_1 + L_2 + L_3 = 6 \text{ periods}$$

This expression for the variance of the orders placed by the kth stage of the supply chain is very similar to the expression for the variability of the orders placed by the retailer given in the previous section, with the single-stage lead time L replaced by the k-stage lead time $\sum_{i=1}^{k} L_i$. Thus, we see that *the variance of the orders placed by a given stage of a supply chain is an increasing function of the total lead time between that stage and the retailer.* This implies that the variance of the orders becomes larger as we move up the supply chain, so that the orders placed by the second stage of the supply chain are more variable than the orders placed by the retailer (the first stage) and the orders placed by the third stage will be more variable than the orders placed by the second stage, and so on.

Decentralized Demand Information The second type of supply chain that we consider is the *decentralized supply chain*. In this case, the retailer does not make its forecast mean and variance of demand available to the remainder of the supply chain. Instead, the wholesaler must estimate the demand mean and variance based on the orders received from the retailer. Again we assume that the wholesaler uses a moving average with p observations—these are the latest p orders placed by the retailer—to forecast the demand mean and variance. It then uses this forecast to determine the target inventory level and places an order to the supplier, the distributor. Similarly, the distributor uses a moving average with p observations of the orders placed by the wholesaler to forecast the mean and standard deviation of demand and uses these forecasts to determine the target inventory level. The distributor's target level is used to place orders to the fourth stage of the supply chain.

It turns out that in this system, the variance of the orders placed by the kth stage of the supply chain, $Var\ (Q^k)$, relative to the variance of the customer demand, $Var\ (D)$ satisfies

$$\frac{Var\ (Q^k)}{Var\ (D)} \geq \prod_{i=1}^{k}\left(1 + \frac{2L_i}{p} + \frac{2L_i^2}{p^2}\right)$$

where, as before, L_i is the lead time between stages i and $i + 1$.

Note that this expression for the variance of the orders placed by the kth stage of the supply chain is very similar to the expression for the variability of orders placed by the retailer in the centralized case, but now the variance increases multiplicatively at each stage of the supply chain. Again, the variance of the orders becomes larger as we move up the supply chain so that the orders placed by the wholesaler are more variable than the orders placed by the retailer.

Managerial Insights on the Value of Centralized Information We have already seen that, for either type of supply chain, centralized or decentralized, the variance of the order quantities becomes larger as we move up the supply chain so that the orders placed by the wholesaler are more variable than the orders placed by the retailer, and so on. The difference in the two types of supply chains is in terms of how much the variability grows as we move from stage to stage.

The results above indicate that the variance of the orders grows additively in the total lead time for the centralized supply chain, while the increase is multiplicative for the decentralized supply chain. In other words, a decentralized supply chain, in which only the retailer knows the customer demand, can lead to significantly higher variability than a centralized supply chain, in which customer demand information is available at each stage of the supply chain, particularly when lead times are long. We therefore conclude that *centralizing demand information can significantly reduce the bullwhip effect.*

This reduction is illustrated nicely in Figure 5-8, which shows the ratio between variability of orders placed by stage k, for $k = 3$ and $k = 5$, and variability of customers' demands for the centralized and decentralized systems when $L_i = 1$ for each i. It also shows the ratio between variability in orders placed by the retailer and variability in customers' demands ($k = 1$).

Thus, it is now clear that by sharing demand information with each stage of the supply chain, we can significantly reduce the bullwhip effect. Indeed, when demand information is centralized, each stage of the supply chain can use the actual customer demand data to estimate the average demand. On the other

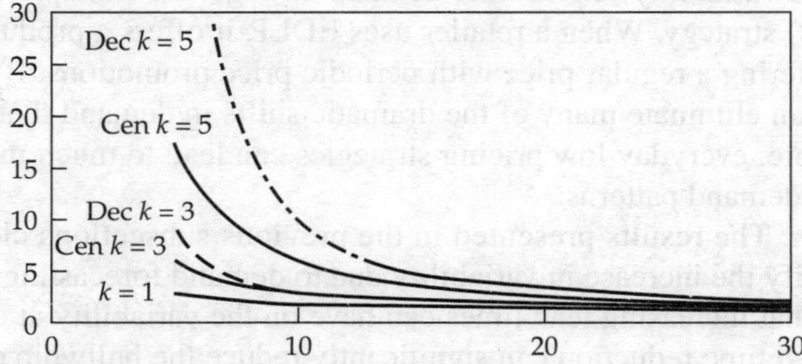

FIGURE 5-8 Increase in variability for centralized and decentralized systems.

hand, when demand information is not shared, each stage must use the orders placed by the previous stage to estimate the average demand. As we have already seen, these orders are more variable than the actual customer demand data, and thus the forecasts created using these orders are more variable, leading to more variable orders.

Finally, it is important to point out that the bullwhip effect exists even when demand information is completely centralized and all stages of the supply chain use the same forecasting technique and inventory policy. In other words, if every stage of the supply chain follows a simple base-stock policy and if each stage uses the same customer demand data and forecasting technique to predict the expected demand, then we will still see the bullwhip effect. However, the analysis indicates that if information is not centralized—that is, if each stage of the supply chain is not provided with customer demand information—then the increase in variability can be significantly larger. Thus, we conclude that *centralizing demand information can significantly reduce, but will not eliminate, the bullwhip effect.*

5.2.3 Methods for Coping with the Bullwhip Effect

Our ability to identify and quantify the causes of the bullwhip effect leads to a number of suggestions for reducing the bullwhip effect or for eliminating its impact. These include reducing uncertainty, reducing the variability of the customer demand process, reducing lead times, and engaging in strategic partnerships. These issues are discussed briefly below.

1. *Reducing uncertainty.* One of the most frequent suggestions for decreasing or eliminating the bullwhip effect is to reduce uncertainty throughout the supply chain by centralizing demand information, that is, by providing each stage of the supply chain with complete information on actual customer demand. The results presented in the previous subsection demonstrate that centralizing demand information can reduce the bullwhip effect.

   Note, however, that even if each stage uses the same demand data, each may still employ different forecasting methods and different buying practices, both of which may contribute to the bullwhip effect. In addition, the results presented in the previous subsection indicate that even when each stage uses the same demand data, the same forecasting method, and the same ordering policy, the bullwhip effect will continue to exist.
2. *Reducing variability.* The bullwhip effect can be diminished by reducing the variability inherent in the customer demand process. For example, if we can reduce the variability of the customer demand seen by the retailer, then even if the bullwhip effect occurs, the variability of the demand seen by the wholesaler also will be reduced.

   We can reduce the variability of customer demand through, for example, the use of an "everyday low pricing" (EDLP) strategy. When a retailer uses EDLP, it offers a product at a single consistent price, rather than offering a regular price with periodic price promotions. By eliminating price promotions, a retailer can eliminate many of the dramatic shifts in demand that occur along with these promotions. Therefore, everyday low pricing strategies can lead to much more stable—that is, less variable—customer demand patterns.
3. *Lead-time reduction.* The results presented in the previous subsections clearly indicate that lead times serve to magnify the increase in variability due to demand forecasting. We have demonstrated the dramatic effect that increasing lead times can have on the variability at each stage of the supply chain. Therefore, lead time reduction can significantly reduce the bullwhip effect throughout a supply chain.

Observe that lead times typically include two components: order lead times (i.e., the time it takes to produce and ship the item) and information lead times (i.e., the time it takes to process an order). This distinction is important since order lead times can be reduced through the use of cross-docking, while information lead time can be reduced through the use of electronic data interchange (EDI).

4. *Strategic partnerships.* The bullwhip effect can be eliminated by engaging in any of a number of strategic partnerships. These strategic partnerships change the way information is shared and inventory is managed within a supply chain, possibly eliminating the impact of the bullwhip effect. For example, in vendor managed inventory (VMI, see Chapter 8), the manufacturer manages the inventory of its product at the retailer outlet, and therefore determines for itself how much inventory to keep on hand and how much to ship to the retailer in every period. Therefore, in VMI the manufacturer does not rely on the orders placed by a retailer, thus avoiding the bullwhip effect entirely.

EXAMPLE 5-1 ABC INDUSTRIES

ABC Industries (name changed) is a well known consumer goods supply chain in India dealing with over 125 SKUs like different edible oils, food products, fabric care products and hair oils. Its gigantic network is reflected by its 32 warehouses and 3500 distributors, who in turn cater to over 1.6 million domestic retail outlets. The distribution levels were heavily skewed towards the end of the planning period, which used to be one month. This resulted in desynchronized production-distribution system, which showed repeated instances of inventory buildups, expired products, stockouts, over-packed warehouses, inter-warehouse transfer, and demurrage, contributing to high operating cost within its supply chain. ABC implemented a well know ERP system to streamline the integration and synchronization of its supply chain. Forecasting accuracy improved by 14%, distribution skewness reduced, planning cycle reduced from 30 days to 15 days, internal and pipe-line inventory level reduced with less frequent stockouts.

5.3 INFORMATION SHARING AND INCENTIVES

The previous analysis indicates that centralizing demand information can dramatically reduce the variability seen by the upstream stages in a supply chain. Therefore, it is clear that these upstream stages would benefit from a partnership that provides an incentive for the retailer to make customer demand data available to the rest of the supply chain. In fact, the previous analysis suggests that upstream facilities are better off receiving the true forecasts generated by OEMs and retailers.

Unfortunately, this is not the case in certain industries. For example, according to *BusinessWeek* [247], "Forecasts by electronics and telecom companies are often inflated." One problem in this industry, of course, is that OEMs typically use an assemble-to-order strategy, while their contract manufacturers typically have to build capacity due to long lead time, in advance to receiving orders from the OEM. Such an asymmetry implies that all the risk is taken by the supplier and hence the supplier does not necessarily build enough capacity (see Chapter 4 for further discussion). One possible response by the OEMs is to inflate their forecast so that the supplier is motivated to build more capacity. However, such an inflated forecast may cause the supplier to ignore the forecast altogether.

Two contracts have been discussed in the literature and shown to provide incentives for the buyers to reveal their true forecasts, see [182]:

- **Capacity reservation contracts,** in which the supplier provides the OEM with a menu specifying different level of capacities he is willing to build and the corresponding price for each one. It turns out that to motivate the OEM to reveal its true information, the per-unit price charged by the supplier decreases with the level of capacity.
- **Advance purchase contracts,** in which the contract manufacturer charges an advance purchase price for orders placed prior to building capacity and a different (higher) price for any additional order placed when demand is realized.

EXAMPLE 5-2

The following article illustrates the dangers of sharing information.

Of all the people Mike Dreese met at 1997's Gavin in the Pines convention—a big recording-industry show held in New Hampshire that year—it was the rep from rackjobber Handleman Co. that made the biggest impression. Dreese recalls watching this guy strut, practically beating his chest as he boasted about the fantastic information his company was getting on regional sales of CDs. Now Handleman, the largest buyer of music in the country, knew exactly what genres of music were selling where and when, the rep gloated. The data helped the company know exactly what to stock in the record bins it serviced in giant mass-market retailers like Wal-Mart and Kmart. By combining these new data with its own figures, Handleman could determine just how many units of, say, Korn's debut album or the latest from 2 Skinnee J's it should place in the racks at the Wal-Mart on Route 1A in Lynn, Mass. And this new bounty of information came from one source: SoundScan Inc., a private company that electronically tracks and tallies every single record sold by some 85% of music retailers in the country. SoundScan then crunches the numbers and sells reports to the record labels, promoters, and managers.

Mike Dreese couldn't believe it. He knew where some of the information was coming from. It was coming from him. Every Sunday night for the past six years, he'd steadfastly reported, direct from his IBM AS/400 minicomputer, the sales of his now-20-store record chain, Newbury Comics—location by location, label by label, artist by artist—to SoundScan's powerful server in Hartsdale, N.Y.

From the start, Dreese had concerns about releasing his numbers electronically through a third party, even though he says that SoundScan founders Mike Shalett and Mike Fine had assured him that his figures would go to the record labels only in aggregate form. But now he'd heard a Handleman rep say that the information Newbury Comics was giving to SoundScan was helping the giant retailers that it competes with every day. "The rep indicated that Handleman had this wonderful way of getting information to help them program Wal-Mart's CD bins," says Dreese, leaning across his battered metal desk, which he bought used in the late 1980s for 30 bucks. "It made me realize to what an extent a company like Wal-Mart was benefiting from the precise regional data that it could never compile on its own."

Dreese had to act—but not too hastily. After 19 years in the business, he knew better than to casually risk the promotional support—the price-and-position dollars, the artist appearances, the cooperative advertising—that the labels bestowed on retailers that reported to SoundScan. And he wasn't about to do himself in on an impulse. So he waited and thought and reconsidered. But, Dreese says, about three months after he'd returned from the Gavin convention in Holderness, N.H., he picked up the phone and called SoundScan. "I asked them if they had in fact ever engaged in consulting arrangements with retailers," he says, "and they said in fact that they had."

Dreese knew what he had to do. "The letter I sent was your basic bombshell letter," he says. "It just said, 'As per our contract, as of June 1998, we will no longer be a SoundScan reporter.'"

Mike Dreese had pulled the plug.

This was not the way it was supposed to be. Sharing information, the conventional wisdom goes, gives your business a competitive edge—no matter what industry you're in and no matter where you fall in the supply chain. And any technology that can facilitate that sharing (be it point-of-sale systems linked to modems, as in the case of the music industry, or radio-frequency transponders connected to PCs, as in the case of the beef industry) only sharpens your chances for success.

Source: Thea Singer, "Sharer Beware," *Inc.*, March 1, 1999.

A related challenge that firms face when sharing their information with supply chain partners is how to guarantee that their information does not help their competitors. To better understand this issue, consider the following example.

So, what went wrong? Indeed, since information sharing is so critical for effective supply chain management, why did SoundScan Inc., a major player in the music industry, and Newbury Comics have such a breakup? The answer has to do with the misalignment of incentives in the supply chain. As the example indicates, Newbury Comics benefited from price support received from the record labels in exchange for providing the data. They were assured that only aggregated data would be sent to the record labels.

However, if the data aggregator is engaged in consulting with various retailers, these data can be a powerful tool that can help these retailers better manage their inventory and distribution channels.

5.4 EFFECTIVE FORECASTS

Information leads to more effective forecasts. The more factors that predictions of future demand can take into account, the more accurate these predictions can be. See Chapter 2 for a more detailed discussion of forecasts.

For example, consider retailer forecasts. These are typically based on an analysis of previous sales at the retailer. However, future customer demand is clearly influenced by such issues as pricing, promotions, and the release of new products. Some of these issues are controlled by the retailer, but some are controlled by the distributor, wholesaler, manufacturer, or competitors. If this information is available to the retailer's forecasters, the forecasts obviously will be more accurate.

Similarly, distributor and manufacturer forecasts are influenced by factors under retailer control. For example, the retailer may design promotions or set pricing. Also, the retailer may introduce new products into the stores, altering demand patterns. In addition, because a manufacturer or distributor has fewer products to consider than the retailer, he may have more information about these products. For example, sales may be closely tied to some event. If a retailer is aware of this, he can increase inventories or raise prices to take advantage of this fact.

For all of these reasons, many supply chains are moving toward cooperative forecasting systems. In these supply chains, sophisticated information systems enable an iterative forecasting process, in which all of the participants in the supply chain collaborate to arrive at an agreed-upon forecast. This implies that all components of the supply chain share and use the same forecasting tool, leading to a decrease in the bullwhip effect (see Chapters 5 and 15).

EXAMPLE 5-3

In fall 1996, Warner-Lambert, the consumer goods manufacturer, and Wal-Mart, the department store, began a pilot study of the collaborative planning, forecasting, and replenishment (CPFR) system. This software system facilitates collaboration in forecasting efforts between retailers and manufacturers. CPFR makes it easy to exchange drafts of forecasts as well as details of future sales promotions and past sales trends. The software "makes it easy for each side to review related messages and append new ones." Other companies, including Procter & Gamble, intend to adopt the CPFR system, and software companies intend to launch competing versions of this software. These systems go under the general name of *collaborative systems* [242].

5.5 INFORMATION FOR THE COORDINATION OF SYSTEMS

Within any supply chain are many systems, including various manufacturing, storage, transportation, and retail systems. We have seen that managing any one of these systems involves a series of complex trade-offs. For example, to efficiently run a manufacturing operation, setup and operating costs must be balanced with the costs of inventory and raw materials. Similarly, we have seen in Chapter 2 that inventory level is a delicate balance between holding costs, order setup costs, and required service level. We also have seen in Chapter 3 that there is a balance between inventory costs and transportation costs, because transportation typically involves quantity discounts of one type or another.

However, all of these systems are connected. Specifically, the outputs from one system within the supply chain are the inputs to the next system. For example, the outputs from the manufacturing operation may be the inputs to a transportation or storage system, or both. Thus, trying to find the best set of trade-offs for any one stage isn't sufficient. We need to consider the entire system and coordinate decisions.

This will be true whether or not there is a common owner for several of the systems in the supply chain. If there is, it is clearly in this owner's best interest to ensure that the overall cost is reduced, although this could lead to an increase in costs in one system if larger decreases occur elsewhere. Even if there is no common owner, however, the various systems still need some kind of coordination to operate effectively. The issue, of course, is whose best interest is it to reduce *overall* system cost and how will these savings be shared among the system owners?

To explain this, observe that when the system is not coordinated—that is, each facility in the supply chain does what is best for that facility—the result, as we discussed in Chapter 1, is *local optimization*. Each component of the supply chain optimizes its own operation without due respect to the impact of its policy on other components in the supply chain.

The alternative to this approach is *global optimization,* which implies that one identifies what is best for the entire system. In this case, two issues need to be addressed:

1. Who will optimize?
2. How will the savings obtained through the coordinated strategy be split between the different supply chain facilities?

These issues can be addressed in various ways. For example, in Chapter 4 we discuss the use of supply contracts, and in Chapter 8 we discuss these issues as part of a detailed discussion on strategic partnerships.

To coordinate these facets of the supply chain, information must be available. Specifically, the knowledge of production status and costs, transportation availability and quantity discounts, inventory costs, inventory levels, and various capacities and customer demand is necessary to coordinate systems, especially in cost-effective ways.

EXAMPLE 5-4 BAJAJ AUTO LIMITED (BAJAJ)

Bajaj Auto enjoyed one of the dream situations in its segment in 80s, when the majority of its two-wheeler scooter models were being sold at a very high premium. Stockout was a normal thing for Bajaj scooters. Due to high quality of Bajaj scooters and limited options, customers were ready to wait for their turn to come even after one year. The success of Bajaj lies in strong brand, efficient and automated production lines, and strong supply chain network. Its outbound supply chain now spreads in over 50 countries. It consists of over 450 local dealers and more than 1,200 service stations.

Bajaj launched "Project 110 percent" to improve its topline by 100 percent and bottomline by 10 percent through improvement in core business processes and supply chain initiatives. As a measure, it initially implemented SAP ERP solution, which was later upgraded to mySAP Enterprise Portal to make it web-enabled. Through this initiative, their dealers got connected in a real-time mode to the Bajaj main line of planning, coordination and replenishment. Instead of sending faxes, now a dealer places online order to Bajaj and can monitor the order position as well as track its shipment. Bajaj gets continuous update on customer requirement through their dealers in this network. Through improved forecasting and sales planning, and information sharing in the distribution channel, Bajaj has largely contained the Bullwhip effect, and this is now reflected in lesser inventory at all levels [70].

5.6 LOCATING DESIRED PRODUCTS

There is more than one way to meet customer demand. Typically, for a make-to-stock system, we think of meeting customer demand from retail inventory if at all possible. However, there are other ways to meet customer demand.

For example, suppose you go to a retailer to buy a large appliance and it is not available. Perhaps you will go to the retailer's competitor down the street. But what if the retailer searches a database and promises to have the item delivered to your house within 24 hours. You will probably feel like you've received great customer service, even though the retailer is out of stock of the item you wanted. Thus, being able to locate and deliver goods is sometimes as effective as having them in stock. But if the goods are located at the retailer's competitor, it is not clear whether this competitor would be willing to transfer the item. We discuss these kinds of issues in detail in Chapter 7, Section 7.2.3, "Inventory Pooling," and Chapter 8, Section 8.5, "Distributor Integration."

5.7 LEAD-TIME REDUCTION

The importance of lead-time reduction cannot be overstated. It typically leads to

1. The ability to quickly fill customer orders that can't be filled from stock.
2. Reduction in the bullwhip effect.
3. More accurate forecasts due to a decreased forecast horizon.
4. Reduction in finished goods inventory levels (see Chapter 2). This is true because one can stock raw materials and packaging material (or subassembly) inventories to reduce finished goods cycle time.

For all of these reasons, many firms are actively searching for suppliers with shorter lead times, and many potential customers consider lead time a very important criterion for vendor selection.

Much of the manufacturing revolution of the past 20 years led to reduced lead times; see [112]. Similarly, in Chapter 6 we discuss distribution network designs that reduce lead times; these designs can exist only because of the availability of information about the status of the entire supply chain. However, as discussed earlier, effective information systems (e.g., EDI) cut lead times by reducing that portion of the lead time linked to order processing, paperwork, stock picking, transportation delays, and so on. Often these can be a substantial portion of the lead time, especially if there are many different stages in the supply chain and this information is transmitted one stage at a time. Clearly, if a retailer order *rapidly* propagates up the supply chain through the tiers of suppliers as far back as is necessary to meet the order, lead time can be greatly reduced.

Similarly, transferring point-of-sale (POS) data from the retailer to its supplier can help reduce lead times significantly because the supplier can anticipate an incoming order by studying POS data. These issues are covered in depth in Chapter 8, where we discuss strategic partnering between retailers and suppliers.

5.8 INFORMATION AND SUPPLY CHAIN TRADE-OFFS

As observed in Chapter 1, a major challenge in supply chain management is replacing sequential planning processes with global optimization. In sequential planning, each stage of the supply chain optimizes its profit with no regard to the impact of its decisions on other supply chain stages. In contrast, in global optimization, the objective is to **coordinate** supply chain activities so as to maximize **supply chain performance**.

Unfortunately, as we discuss in detail below, the managers of different stages in the supply chain have conflicting goals, and it is exactly these conflicts that necessitate the integration and coordination of the different stages in the supply chain. Even within one stage, trade-offs have to be made between reducing inventory or transportation costs, or between increasing product variety or reducing inventory levels.

By carefully using the available information, the supply chain can move toward global optimization, and, as a result, reduce systemwide cost while accounting for these conflicting goals and various trade-offs. This is easier to do in a centralized system, but even in a decentralized system, it may be necessary to find incentives to bring about the integration of supply chain facilities.

5.8.1 Conflicting Objectives in the Supply Chain[3]

We begin with the raw material suppliers. To operate and plan efficiently, these suppliers would like to see stable volume requirements, with little variation in the mix of required materials. In addition, they prefer flexible delivery times, so that they can deliver efficiently to more than one customer. Finally, most suppliers would like to see large volume demands, so that they can take advantage of economies of scope and scale.

Manufacturing management also has its own wish list. High production costs frequently limit the number of expensive changeovers as well as quality problems that may occur at the start of production runs. Typically, manufacturing management wants to achieve high productivity through production efficiencies, leading in turn to low production costs. These goals are facilitated if the demand pattern is known far into the future and has little variability.

The materials, warehousing, and outbound logistics management also have lists of criteria. These include minimizing transportation costs by taking advantage of quantity discounts, minimizing inventory levels, and quickly replenishing stock. Finally, to satisfy their customers, retailers need short order lead times and efficient and accurate order delivery. The customers in turn demand in-stock items, enormous variety, and low prices.

5.8.2 Designing the Supply Chain for Conflicting Goals

In the past, for some of these goals to be met, others had to be sacrificed. The supply chain was viewed as a set of trade-offs that had to be made. Typically, high inventory levels and shipping costs, and less product variety, enabled manufacturers and retailers to come closer to meeting their goals. At the same time, customers' expectations were not as high as they are today. As we know, these expectations have increased dramatically in recent times as customers demand high variety and low cost, even as increased pressure to control inventory and transportation costs also has become prevalent. Fortunately, the large amount of information now available allows supply chains to be designed so that they come closer to meeting all of these apparently conflicting goals. In effect, some of the trade-offs that were considered several years ago to be inherent in any supply chain may not be trade-offs at all.

In the following subsections, we discuss many of these perceived trade-offs and how, through the use of advanced information technology and creative network design, they don't have to be trade-offs at all in a modern supply chain—or, at the very least, their impact can be reduced.

The Lot Size–Inventory Trade-Off As we have seen, manufacturers would like to have large lot sizes. Per-unit setup costs are reduced, manufacturing expertise for a particular product increases, and processes are easier to control. Unfortunately, typical demand doesn't come in large lot sizes, so large lot sizes lead to high inventory. Indeed, much of the focus of the "manufacturing revolution" of the 1980s involved switching to manufacturing systems with smaller lot sizes.

Setup time reduction, kanban and CONWIP (constant work in progress) systems, and other "modern manufacturing practices" were typically geared toward reducing inventories and improving system

[3] This section is based on the recent work of Lee and Billington [119].

responsiveness. Although traditionally viewed in a manufacturing context, this approach to manufacturing has implications across the entire supply chain. Retailers and distributors would like short delivery lead times and wide product variety to respond to the needs of their customers. These advanced manufacturing systems make it possible for manufacturers to meet these needs by enabling them to respond more rapidly to customer needs.

This is especially true if information is available to ensure that the manufacturer has as much time as possible to react to the needs of downstream supply chain members. Similarly, if distributors or retailers have the ability to observe factory status and manufacturer inventory, they can quote lead times to customers more accurately. In addition, these systems enable retailers and distributors to develop an understanding of, and confidence in, the manufacturers' ability. This confidence allows the distributors and retailers to reduce the inventory they hold in anticipation of manufacturing problems.

The Inventory–Transportation Cost Trade-Off There is a similar trade-off between inventory and transportation costs. To see this, we need to review the nature of transportation costs, which we explored in more detail in Chapter 3. First, consider a company that operates its own fleet of trucks. Each truck has some fixed cost of operation (e.g., depreciation, driver time) and some variable cost (e.g., gas). If a truck is always full when it makes a delivery, the cost of operating the truck is spread out over the largest possible number of items. Since, in the end, the same total number of goods is always delivered (more or less equal to customer demand), carrying full truckloads minimizes transportation costs.

Similarly, if an outside firm is used for shipping, the firm typically provides quantity discounts. Also, it is usually cheaper to ship in quantities of full truckloads (TL shipping) than partial (less than) truckloads (LTL shipping). Thus, in this case too, operating full trucks minimizes transportation costs.

In many cases, however, demand is in units of far less than a single truckload. Thus, when items are delivered in full truckloads, they typically have to wait for longer periods of time before they are consumed, leading to higher inventory costs.

Unfortunately, this trade-off can't be eliminated completely. However, we can use advanced information technology to reduce this effect. For example, advanced production control systems can be used to manufacture items as late as possible to ensure full truckloads. Similarly, distribution control systems may allow a materials manager to combine shipments of different products from warehouses to stores in order to fill trucks. This requires knowledge of orders and demand forecasts, as well as supplier delivery schedules. Cross-docking, described earlier in the chapter, also helps to control this trade-off by allowing the retailer to combine shipments from many different manufacturers onto one truck destined for a particular location.

Indeed, recent advances in decision-support systems allow the supply chain to find the appropriate balance between transportation and inventory costs by taking into account all aspects of the supply chain. Regardless of the transportation strategy selected, competition in the transportation industry will force costs down. This effect is enhanced by advanced transportation modes and carrier selection programs that ensure that the most cost-effective approach is used for each particular delivery, lowering overall transportation costs.

The Lead Time–Transportation Cost Trade-Off Total lead time is made up of time devoted to processing orders, to procuring and manufacturing items, and to transporting items between the various stages of the supply chain. As we mentioned above, transportation costs are lowest when large quantities of items are transported between stages of the supply chain. However, lead times often can be reduced if items are transported immediately after they are manufactured or arrive from suppliers. Thus, there is a trade-off between holding items until enough accumulate to reduce transportation costs and shipping them immediately to reduce lead time.

Again, this trade-off cannot be completely eliminated, but information can be used to reduce its effect. Transportation costs can be controlled as described in the previous section, reducing the need to hold items until a sufficient number accumulate. In addition, improved forecasting techniques and information systems reduce the other components of lead time, so that it may not be essential to reduce the transportation component.

The Product Variety–Inventory Trade-Off Evidently product variety greatly increases the complexity of supply chain management. Manufacturers that make a multitude of different products with smaller lot sizes find their manufacturing costs increase and their manufacturing efficiency decreases. To maintain the same lead times as a company may have had with fewer products, smaller amounts will probably be shipped so warehouses will need to hold a larger variety of products; thus, increasing product variety increases both transportation and warehousing costs. Finally, because it is usually difficult to accurately forecast the demand for each product, because all are competing for the same customers, higher inventory levels must be maintained to ensure the same service level.

The main issue that a firm supplying a variety of products needs to address is how to match supply and demand effectively. For instance, consider a manufacturer of winter ski jackets. Typically, 12 months before the selling season, the firm introduces a number of designs that it will sell in the winter. Unfortunately, it is not clear how many ski jackets to produce from each design; therefore, it is not clear how to plan production.

One way to support the required product variety efficiently is to apply the concept called *delayed differentiation,* which we discuss in Section 6.2 and Chapter 11. In a supply chain in which delayed differentiation is utilized, *generic products* are shipped as far as possible down the supply chain before variety is added. This could mean that a single product is received in the distribution center, and there it is modified or customized according to customer demand as seen by the warehouse.

Observe that, by doing so, we are again using the concept of risk pooling introduced in Chapter 2. Indeed, by shipping a generic product to the warehouses, we have aggregated customer demand across all products. As we have seen, this implies a more accurate demand forecast with a much smaller variability, leading to reduced safety stock. This process of aggregating demand across products is similar to the process of aggregating across retailers (see Chapter 2).

Delayed differentiation is one example of *design for logistics,* a concept we will discuss in much more detail in Chapter 11.

The Cost–Customer Service Trade-Off All of these trade-offs are examples of the cost–customer service trade-off. Reducing inventories, manufacturing costs, and transportation costs typically comes at the expense of customer service. In the preceding subsections, we have seen that the level of customer service can be maintained while decreasing these costs by using information and appropriate supply chain designs. Implicitly, we have defined customer service as the ability of a retailer to meet a customer's demand from stock.

Of course, customer service could mean the ability of a retailer to meet a customer's demand quickly. We have discussed how transshipping may make this possible without increasing inventory. In addition, direct shipping from warehouses to the homes of retail customers is another way to achieve this. For example, Sears delivers a large proportion of the large appliances that it sells directly from warehouses to the end customer. This controls inventory cost at retail stores and allows warehouses to take direct advantage of risk pooling effects. For this kind of system to work, information about warehouse inventories must be available at the stores, and order information should be rapidly transmitted to the warehouse. This is just one example of a system in which available information and appropriate supply chain design lead to decreased costs and increased service. In this case, costs are lower when the inventory is stored in a centralized warehouse than when there is a larger inventory in the store. At the same time, customer service is improved because customers have a larger inventory to choose from and appliances are immediately delivered to their homes.

Finally, it is important to point out that so far we have emphasized how supply chain technology and management can be applied to increase customer service levels *defined in some traditional sense* and reduce costs. However, advanced supply chain management techniques and information systems could be used to give customers a kind of service that they have never been able to realize before, and for which suppliers could charge a premium. One such example is the concept of *mass customization,* which involves delivering highly personalized goods and services to customers at reasonable prices and at high volume. Although this may not have been economically feasible in the past, improving logistics and information systems now make this possible. The concept of mass customization is explained in more detail in Chapter 11.

5.9 DECREASING MARGINAL VALUE OF INFORMATION

We end this chapter with a caveat. Throughout the chapter, we have discussed the benefits of information. Of course, obtaining and sharing information are not free. RFID, databases, communications systems, analysis tools, and managers' time all have significant associated costs. Indeed, many firms are struggling with exactly how to use the data they collect through loyalty programs, RFID readers, and so on.

Even businesses that understand the value of global optimization need to explore the cost of exchanging information versus the benefit of doing so. Many times, it may not be necessary to exchange all of the available information, or to exchange information continuously. Indeed, in many cases, there is a decreasing marginal value of information, in the sense that once key pieces of information have been exchanged, there is little benefit in exchanging additional information.

For example, researchers have considered how often distributors and manufacturers need to exchange information. They have found, for example, that in one particular supply chain, if the distributor orders weekly, most of the benefits from sharing demand information can be achieved by sharing information two to four times a week. The additional benefits achieved by sharing information more than four times a week are minimal. In other words, the marginal benefit of sharing information is decreasing in the number of times information is shared.

Also, researchers have found that in multistage decentralized manufacturing supply chains, many of the performance benefits of detailed information sharing can be achieved if only a small amount of information is exchanged between supply chain participants. For example, in one specific supply chain, in many cases, almost three-quarters of the cost benefits of completely sharing manufacturing and order status information exchange can be achieved by periodically exchanging very limited estimates of when jobs will complete processing—there is limited additional benefit in exchanging more detailed information. In other words, the marginal benefit of sharing information is decreasing in the level of detail of the exchanged information.

In general, of course, exchanging more detailed information or more frequent information is costly. Thus, supply chain participants need to understand the costs and benefits of particular pieces of information, focusing on how often this information is collected, how much of this information needs to be stored, how much of this information needs to be shared, and in what form it needs to shared, since all of these things have associated costs along with their associated benefits.

SUMMARY

The bullwhip effect suggests that variability in demand increases as one moves up in the supply chain. This increase in variability causes significant operational inefficiencies; for example, it forces every facility in the supply chain to increase inventory significantly. Indeed, in [139] the authors estimate that in certain industries, such as the pharmaceutical industry, this distorted information can cause the total inventory in the supply chain to exceed 100 days of supply. Thus, it is important to identify strategies to efficiently cope with the bullwhip effect. In this chapter, we have identified specific techniques to "counteract" the bullwhip effect, one of which is information sharing, that is, centralized demand information. We also have highlighted important challenges when supply chain partners share information, including incentives to share credible forecasts and alignments of expectations associated with the use of information.

Finally, we looked at the interaction of various supply chain stages. Typically, operating a supply chain is viewed as a series of trade-offs both within and between the different stages. We concluded that information is the key enabler of integrating the different supply chain stages and discussed how information can be used to reduce the necessity of many of these trade-offs. Chapter 6 provides more information on this and related topics.

DISCUSSION QUESTIONS

1. Answer these questions about the Barilla case study:
   a. Diagnose the underlying causes of the difficulties that the JITD program was created to solve. What are the benefits of this program?
   b. What conflicts or barriers internal to Barilla does the JITD program create? What causes these conflicts? As Giorgio Maggiali, how would you deal with this?
   c. As one of Barilla's customers, what would your response to JITD be? Why?
   d. In the environment in which Barilla operated in 1990, do you believe JITD would be feasible? Effective? If so, which customers would you target next? How would you convince them that the JITD program was worth trying? If not, what alternatives would you suggest to combat some of the difficulties that Barilla's operating system faces?
   e. Compare the JITD strategy proposed by Barilla to the celebrated JIT strategy developed by Toyota and others.
2. Discuss how each of the following helps to alleviate the bullwhip effect:
   a. E-commerce and the Internet.
   b. Express delivery.
   c. Collaborative forecasts.
   d. Everyday low pricing.
   e. Vendor-managed inventory (VMI).
   f. Supply contracts.
3. What are the advantages to retailers of sharing inventory? For instance, suppose you go to a car dealer to find a blue model, and he doesn't have that model in stock. Typically, he will obtain the model from another local dealer. What are the disadvantages to the retailer?

4. Name a few local supply chains where lead time is too long. Discuss five ways that the lead times within a supply chain can be reduced.
5. Consider the supply chain for breakfast cereal. Discuss the competing objectives of the farmers who make the raw materials, the manufacturing division of the company that makes the cereal, the logistics division of the company that makes the cereal, the marketing division of the company that makes the cereal, the distribution arm of the grocery chain that sells the cereal, and the manager of an individual grocery store that sells the cereal.
6. Consider Example 5-1 and discuss strategies that could help Newbury Comics and SoundScan Inc. solve the misalignment problem.

CASE: Reebok NFL Replica Jerseys: A Case for Postponement

"This time of year is a little too exciting for us. I have a warehouse full of jerseys out there and retailers are screaming for the teams and players I don't have! Every year, it seems like we have the right mix of inventory going into the season, and then some team that no one expected to do well gets off to a 4-0 start, and the team everyone expected to contend for the Super Bowl is losing games. Suddenly I have 1000s of jerseys I can't sell and 1000s of orders I can't fill."

Tony is responsible for the inventory of NFL replica jerseys that Reebok maintains in their central distribution center. It is early October, and the NFL season is well underway. "No wonder we call this the chase; I feel like I have been running for months; I'm exhausted. I wish there was some way to plan inventory that would allow me to react faster to hot players and teams. But with player demand changing so much from year to year, I really can't increase inventory; in fact I like to minimize inventory at year-end."

BACKGROUND

Reebok International Ltd. is headquartered in Canton, Mass. The company employs approximately 7,400 people, and is widely known for their sports apparel and footwear brands. Reebok was a small British shoe company in 1979, when Paul Fireman acquired the exclusive North American license to sell Reebok shoes.[4] In 1985 Reebok USA acquired the original British Reebok, and Reebok International went public. Reebok in 2003 had total revenues of $3485 M and realized income from operations of $157 M. Paul Fireman continues to be the chairman and CEO.

In December 2000 Reebok signed a 10-year contract with the National Football League (NFL) that granted an exclusive license to Reebok to manufacture, market, and sell NFL licensed merchandise including on-field uniforms, sideline apparel, practice apparel, footwear, and an NFL-branded apparel line. The National Football League is the premier professional league for American football, consisting of 32 teams. Teams are organized in two conferences, the American Football Conference (AFC) and the National Football Conference (NFC), and in four divisions within each conference.

The history of American football traces back to 1869.[5] The Arizona Cardinals are the oldest continuing operation in pro football, dating back to 1899. In 2003, the Super Bowl between the Tampa Bay Buccaneers and the Oakland Raiders received over 139M viewers, making it the most

Source: Copyright 2005, John C. W. Parsons. This case was prepared by John C. W. Parsons under the direction of Professor Stephen C. Graves as the basis for class discussion rather than to illustrate either effective or ineffective handling of an administrative situation. The case is based on the author's MLog thesis, "Using a Newsvendor Model for Demand Planning of NFL Replica Jerseys" supervised by Professor Stephen C. Graves, June 2004.

[4] www.reebok.com/useng/history/1890.htm.

[5] www.nfl.com/history.

watched television program in history. From its humble beginnings, the NFL has grown into a very successful league.

LICENSED APPAREL BUSINESS

The Licensed Apparel Business is a high margin and lucrative business. In granting an exclusive license to Reebok, the NFL expects Reebok to provide a very high level of service to its customers, the sports retailers who ultimately sell to the public. However, demand is influenced by many uncontrollable factors and is extremely hard to predict; forecasting which items will sell is akin to forecasting who will be the Most Valuable Player in next year's Super Bowl.

Reebok has a history of delivering quality products. One retailer states, "The Reebok line is great. We're excited and anxious at the same time. [In the past] the fear was that one team jersey could be found from five different manufacturers at five different stores in the mall. Now the [question] is, will the consumer have to pay an extra $20 for a team jersey because it is from Reebok?"[6]

Yet other retailers worry about having a sole source for these products. "As a top-tier retailer in apparel, we'll only have access to that one brand," says another retailer. "I think that Reebok makes great product. We just hope they can deliver because we won't have options B, C, or D to go to."[7]

Of particular importance is Reebok's ability to deliver *hot-market* items, a concern for retailers in all areas of the licensed business. "I think with one major partner in Reebok we are in a better position for hot-market items. . . . Reebok will be able to take a larger position in blanks on jerseys and fleece and feel more confident that they can meet the demands of retailers."[8]

A *hot-market* item, in the context of the NFL replica jersey business, is an item that was either not expected to sell well before the season or an unknown item that had no prior sales expectations. Early reviews of Reebok show that their performance has been satisfactory. "To be fair, in hot markets delivery is always going to be an issue. Whether you have 12 companies or one, it will always be an issue. And I have to say, this year, Reebok has been pretty much on-time with their deliveries."[9]

Reebok developed its expertise in Licensed Apparel through acquisition and expansion. In 2001 Reebok purchased a relatively small licensed apparel business, LogoAthletic, located in Indianpolis. LogoAthletic had extensive experience and expertise in sports apparel, as well as past relationships with the NFL. As a consequence, Reebok decided to locate its Licensed Apparel management at the former LogoAthletic facilities in Indianapolis.

DEMAND FOR NFL REPLICA JERSEYS

The NFL replica jersey consists of a 5-ounce nylon diamond back mesh body, a nylon dazzle sleeves/yoke in the team color and white, and a 8.6-ounce polyester flat knit rib collar, and stripe knit inserts for select teams. Each team's jersey is a distinct combination of style, cuts, and colors (team color, white, and alternate) along with the team logo, (see Figure 5-9 for examples).

Although the consumer demand for jerseys is year- round, the NFL season drives much of the demand. Sales are highest in August and September in anticipation of the season. As the season starts, certain teams and players get a sales bump due to their performances. For example, in 2003 the Kansas City Chiefs started the season with a series of wins, and their jerseys became *hot-market* items, creating shortages. Previously unknown players sold unexpectedly well: Dante Hall made several outstanding plays in the first four games, creating a hot-market for his jersey.

[6] Cara Griffin, "NFL's New World Order," *Sporting Goods Business* 35, no. 1 (Jan. 2002) p. 56.
[7] *Ibid.*
[8] *Ibid.*
[9] *Ibid.*

FIGURE 5-9 Examples of NFL replica jerseys.

Later in the season, consumer demand is driven by holiday presents and the anticipation of the playoffs. During the playoffs the demand is strongly correlated to weekly performance. A team that loses sees its sales disappear, while teams that win and continue to play experience strong sales. The two Super Bowl teams sell much higher than normal up to the game. The Super Bowl winner continues to sell for one to two weeks following the championship, but then sales decline rapidly until the start of the next season.

Most player trades and free agent signings occur during the off season of February to April. Consumers react to these player movements by demanding the newest superstar jersey for their favorite team. For instance, when Warren Sapp signed with the Oakland Raiders in March 2004, retailers expected Reebok to start shipping his jersey immediately.

SALES CYCLE

The annual sales cycle starts in January/February. Reebok offers retailers a discount to place early orders that result in retailers placing approximately 20 percent of annual orders for planned delivery in May. Reebok uses the advance-order information to plan purchases from their suppliers for the upcoming season.

There is limited ordering by the retailers between February and April except for some order adjustments; for instance, retailers place orders for short lead-time delivery to meet unexpected demand due to player movements, for example, the signing of Terrell Owens by Philadelphia in 2004.

Retail orders placed between May and August are primarily to position inventory in the retail distribution centers (DCs) to meet the in-season replenishment requirements from the retail outlets;

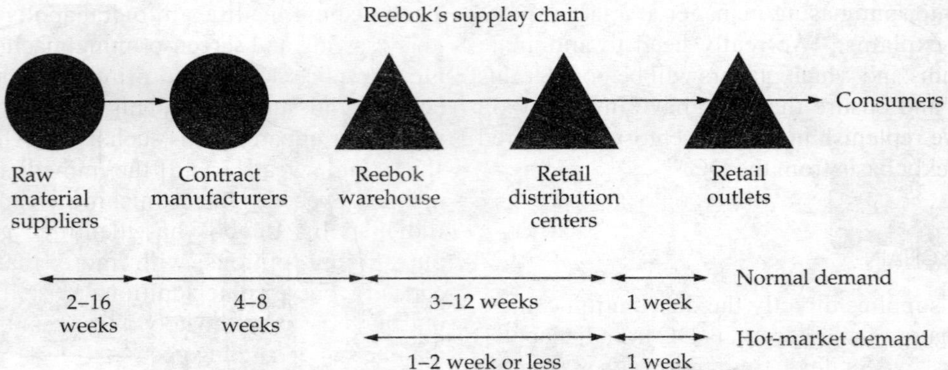

FIGURE 5-10 **Reebok's supply chain.**

the lead-time expectations at this point are 3 to 4 weeks. By the end of August, Reebok has shipped 50 percent of anticipated sales to retailers.

The in-season replenishment period between September and January is known as "The Chase." For the jerseys that are selling according to the preseason forecasts, retailers use their DC inventory to replenish the stock at their stores. But the retailers need to place replenishment orders with Reebok for strong sellers to restock their DC inventories. This is the time when consumers react to player and team performance and create hot markets. Retailers need to adjust their inventories to "chase" the hot-market items, and they expect Reebok to supply product to chase the hot markets. Unknown players become superstars, and former superstars become nonfactor players. There is an opportunity for retailers to sell through high volumes of product if they can stock the correct players to match the consumer demand.

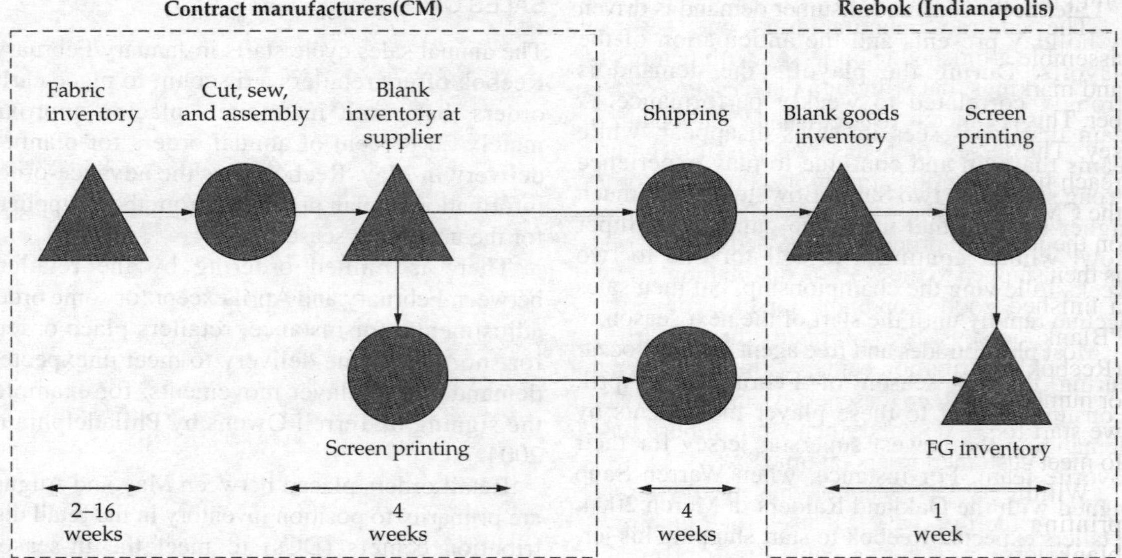

FIGURE 5-11 **Reebok's supply chain—detail.**

A senior purchasing manager at a large sports retailer explains, "We really need to anticipate what teams and which players will be popular this season, and ensure that they have inventory on hand. We replenish in-store inventory as required on a weekly basis from the DC."

SUPPLY CHAIN

Reebok supplies directly the distribution centers for its major retailers from its DC in Indianapolis. Retailers expect lead times between 3 and 12 weeks for replenishment of normal demand, but expect much shorter lead times of 1 to 2 weeks when faced with hot-market demand.

Figures 5-10 and 5-11 provide a high-level depiction of Reebok's supply chain. Reebok sources all jerseys from offshore contract manufacturers (CM) with a manufacturing lead time of 30 days. Reebok procures the fabric and raw materials that are held in inventory by each CM. Internal contracts are in place to ensure sufficient levels of raw material inventory to provide capability to produce any team on demand, if required. Shipping takes two months for ocean shipping or one week via air.

The contract manufacturers cut, sew, and assemble a finished team jersey with team colors and markings, but without a player name or number. This is called a "team finished" or "blank" jersey. The jersey then has two possible paths to reach finished goods inventory. For some orders, the CM screen-prints the player name and number on the jersey to produce a "dressed" jersey, which is then shipped to the Reebok distribution center as a finished good. For blank jerseys Tony stated, "Blank jerseys are shipped directly to the (Reebok) distribution center with no player name or number. We keep these jerseys in inventory until we start to see demand, then we will burn blanks to meet customer orders on time."

Within its DC, Reebok has its own screen printing facility, which it uses for finishing the blank jerseys. It has a capacity to print about 10,000 jerseys per day during the peak season. The finishing facilities in Indianapolis consist of many sewing and screen-printing machines, capable of embroidering and printing to the highest commercial standards. (This capacity is shared with other apparel items such as NBA jerseys, T-shirts, and sweatshirts. If the immediate requirements exceed the finishing capacity in Indianapolis, Reebok has identified good local outsourcing options with more than enough capacity, but at some additional cost. The cost to outsource is approximately 10 percent higher than the internal decorating cost.)

The inventory of blank jerseys in Indianapolis has two primary purposes: to fill demand for players that are ordered in small quantities and to respond quickly to higher-than-expected demand for popular players. The CM and Reebok have an agreed minimum order level of 1,728 units for the dressed jersey for any player. A player with demand less than this level will be supplied through the use of blank jerseys that are printed in Indianapolis. A typical NFL team has only a handful of players with demand sufficient to warrant production by the CM.

Reebok also uses blank jerseys during the off-season to meet immediate demand for players that unexpectedly change teams. Monty, production manager, cites a recent example, "When Warren Sapp signed with the Oakland Raiders in March (2004), retailers expected us to start shipping his jersey immediately. We can't wait three months to get jerseys from our suppliers; we had to start printing immediately. It is a good thing we had extra Raiders jerseys in stock."

PURCHASE PLANNING

Reebok's purchasing cycle starts much before the sales cycle, namely in July, 14 months before the beginning of the target NFL season. For example, the purchasing cycle for the September 2004 season started in July 2003. Reebok places purchase orders on its CMs twice per month from July to October, with delivery planned for April. All jerseys ordered during this time are typically for blank jerseys, due to the uncertainty about the roster for the following season. Reebok expects the CM to manufacture the jerseys immediately and hold the blank jerseys in inventory. If Reebok requires the jerseys in the current year, then a request can be made to the CM to expedite those jerseys for immediate delivery.

During January and February, Reebok places orders against known demand, namely the advanced orders from the retailers. Reebok makes purchases during March and April based on a combination of known orders and forecasts. Reebok continues to place orders in May and June to position inventory at its DC in Indianapolis in anticipation of retailer orders for the coming season. From March to June is the most difficult time of year for Reebok's planners: the advance orders have been filled, but Reebok must decide its inventory based on its forecast of the demand for the upcoming season.

PLANNING PROBLEM

As noted above, the March to June time window is the most critical time in the purchase cycle. Reebok has already placed its orders to cover the preseason orders from the retailers, and now must place the majority of its orders based on its forecast for the upcoming season. In this section, we present an illustrative example, namely the planning problem for the New England Patriots for the 2003 season.[10]

Reebok sells jerseys to retailers at a wholesale price of \$24.00 per jersey. The retail price is in excess of \$50. Reebok's costs depend on the CM; the average costs for a blank jersey and for a dressed jersey, delivered to Indianapolis, are \$9.50 and \$10.90, respectively. The cost to decorate a blank jersey in Indianapolis is about \$2.40.

Reebok has several options for jerseys that it cannot sell to retailers and that are leftover at the end of the season. Reebok can sell to discounters but needs to do so carefully to protect its retail channels. Reebok also can hold unsold jerseys in its DC and hope to sell them during the next season. There is significant risk with this option, especially for dressed jerseys, due to free-agent signings, trades, and retirements. Also, teams often change the style or color of their uniforms. In either case, Reebok can be stuck with outdated jerseys with very little value.

Reebok's general practice is to sell leftover dressed jerseys at a discount but hold blank jerseys for the next season, for teams that are not expected to make any changes to their jerseys. The average price that Reebok gets from a discounter for a dressed jersey is \$7.00. Reebok estimates its annual holding cost for a blank jersey to be 11 percent, which reflects both the capital cost for the inventory and the costs for storage and handling; thus, the cost to hold any unsold blank Patriots jerseys until next season is \$1.045 per jersey. The New England Patriots redesigned their uniforms a few years ago, and there is no indication that any changes are coming in the near future.

Forecasting demand is a challenge. Reebok develops forecasts based on a combination of factors: past sales, team and player performances, market intelligence, advanced orders, informed guesses. Furthermore, the forecast is continually revised as the sales cycle unfolds, and as Reebok gets more information on the current season.

In February 2003, following the initial order placement of retailers, enough information was available to generate a team and player level forecast. Table 5-4 provides this forecast for the New England Patriots.

At the time, the six named players were the most popular in terms of jersey sales; furthermore, these six players each had a demand forecast that was sufficient to cover the CM's minimum order quantity. Whereas Reebok did expect demand for other players (e.g., Ted Johnson, #52), this demand was even harder to forecast and was not likely to exceed the CM's minimum order quantity. Hence, Reebok developed an aggregate forecast of more than 23,000 jerseys for all other players.

[10] These are not the actual cost, revenue, or volume numbers. All numbers have been disguised.

TABLE 5-4

DEMAND FORECASTS

Description	Mean	Standard deviation
New England Patriot Total	87,680	19,211
Brady, Tom, #12	30,763	13,843
Law, TY, #24	10,569	4,756
Brown, Troy, #80	8,159	3,671
Vinatieri, Adam, #04	7,270	4,362
Bruschi, Tedy, #54	5,526	3,316
Smith, Antowain, #32	2,118	1,271
Other players	23,275	10,474

CASE DISCUSSION QUESTIONS

1. Given the uncertainty associated with player demand, how should Reebok approach inventory planning for NFL replica jerseys?
2. What should Reebok's goal be? Should Reebok minimize inventory at the end of the season? Or maximize profits? Can Reebok achieve both? What service level should Reebok provide to its customers?
3. Are the models in Section 2.2.2 helpful here? What is the cost of underage for a dressed jersey? What is the cost of overage for a dressed jersey? How might Reebok decide between dressed jerseys and blank jerseys?
4. Using the forecast for the New England Patriots, what is the optimal quantity to order for each player? For blank jerseys? What profit do you expect for Reebok? How much and what type of inventory is expected to be leftover at the end of the season? What service level?

CHAPTER 6

Supply Chain Integration

CASE: Dell Inc.: Improving the Flexibility of the Desktop PC Supply Chain

It was June 2005, seemingly a good time for Dell Inc. Since the dot-com bubble burst in 2001, the price of the company's stock had roughly doubled. Both the company's revenue and net income were reaching new heights. In spite of the confidence and optimism, however, Dell's desktop PC manufacturing division found that its manufacturing costs had continued to surge. Tom Wilson, one of the division's directors, revealed: "The recent increase in Level 5 manufacturing is alarming to us at Dell. From Dell's perspective, this adds cost to our overall manufacturing process. We are not able to take as much advantage as we should of the lower cost structure of our contract manufacturers. Instead, we have to rely more heavily on the 3rd-party integrators (3PIs). Not only do we get lower-quality products because we currently don't require 3PIs to perform integration unit testing, we also have difficulty forecasting for the 3PIs how much manufacturing capacity they should have available to support Dell's demand."

Source: This case study was written based on MIT Leaders for Manufacturing (LFM) Class of 2006 Fellow Johnson Wu's master thesis and co-developed with his thesis advisors Prof. Charles Fine and Prof. David Simchi-Levi and LFM Program Director Dr. Donald Rosenfield.

HISTORY OF THE PC INDUSTRY

In the 1960s, the first so-called personal computers (PCs)—non-mainframe computers—such as the LINC and the PDP-8 became available. They were expensive (around $50,000) and bulky (many were about the size of a refrigerator). However, they were called "personal computers" because they were small and cheap enough for individual laboratories and research projects. These computers also had their own operating systems so users could interact with them directly.

The first microcomputers hit the market in the mid-1970s. Usually, computer enthusiasts purchased them in order to learn how to program, and used them to run simple office or productivity applications or play games. The emergence of the single-chip microprocessor led to substantially lower computer prices, and, for the first time, a broad spectrum of buyers from the general public. The first widely and successfully sold desktop computer was the Apple II introduced in 1977 by Apple Computer.

In the 1980s, computers became increasingly cheaper and gained great popularity among home and business users. This trend was partly driven by the launch of the IBM PC and its associated software, which enabled the use of a spreadsheet, a word processor, presentation graphics, and a simple database application on a single relatively low-cost machine. In 1982, *Time* magazine named the personal computer its Man of the Year. Laptop computers truly the size of a notebook. also became available in the 1980s. The first commercially available portable computer was the Osborne 1 in 1981, which used the CP/M operating system. Although it was large and heavy by today's standards, with a tiny CRT monitor, it had a near-revolutionary impact on business, as professionals were able to take their computer and data with them for the first time. However, it was not possible to run the Osborne on batteries; it had to be plugged in.

Personal computers became more powerful and capable of handling more complex tasks in the 1990s. By this time, they were becoming more like multi-user computers or mainframes. During this decade, desktop computers were widely advertised for their ability to support graphics and multimedia, and this power led to increased usage of desktop computers by movie studios, universities, and governments.

By the end of the 1980s, laptop computers, truly the size of a notebook, were becoming popular among business people. By 2005, high-end PCs focused more on greater reliability and more powerful multitasking capability.

DELL'S COMPANY BACKGROUND AND ITS DIRECT MODEL

Dell was founded by Michael Dell in his University of Texas–Austin dorm room in 1984 based on a simple business model: eliminating the retailers from the sales channel and selling directly to customers. By using this model to deliver customized systems to customers with lower-than-market-average prices, Dell soon started to enjoy business success, joining the ranks of the top-five computer system makers worldwide in 1993, and became Number 1 in 2001. With three major manufacturing facilities in the United State (Austin, Texas; Nashville, Tennessee; Winston-Salem, North Carolina) and facilities in Brazil, China, Malaysia, and Ireland, Dell's revenue for the last four quarters totaled $56 billion. Dell employs 65,200 people worldwide.[1]

In addition to personal computers, Dell's current product offerings include a variety of consumer electronics: workstations, servers, storage, monitors, printers, handhelds, LCD TVs, projectors, and so forth. Some of these products are manufactured by Dell factory associates; other products are manufactured by other companies but sold under the Dell brand.

Throughout the company's history, Dell's fundamental business model has not changed: selling directly to customers has become Dell's key strategy and strength. The direct business model includes no retailers and starts and ends with the customer: a customer orders online or via phone a computer system according to his preferred configuration, Dell manufacturers this computer system, and Dell ships directly to the customer. Dell has been able to keep manufacturing costs lower than competitors' costs because it not only saves money by shipping directly to customers, but it also only builds to order, so raw material inventory is low. The direct model also reduces the time from customer order to receipt of the system. Moreover, the direct model provides a single point of accountability so Dell can more easily design its customer service model in order to provide the necessary resources to satisfy its customers.

CONTRACT MANUFACTURING

By 2005, most PC makers utilized contract manufacturers to produce high-tech electronic products. The phenomenon of contract manufacturing began in the 1980s. To take advantage of labor cost differences, many original equipment manufacturers (OEMs) initiated business engagements with contract manufacturers (CMs). When the contract manufacturing business model was first implemented, CMs were responsible for producing materials or unassembled components in less expensive regions and shipping them to the OEMs' factories in the United State or Europe for product assembly. By the late 1990s, however, more and more contract manufacturers began to perform some level of manufacturing/assembly for

[1] Dell Company Web site, Company Facts.

their customers. This helped fuel the growth of contract manufacturing. According to Alameda, California–based Technology Forecasters Inc., in 1998, the contract manufacturing industry was worth $90 billion. By 2001, this figure almost doubled to $178 billion.[2] OEMs chose to let contract manufacturers own and manage part of the manufacturing process for the following reasons:[3]

1. Capability: The OEM cannot make the item or easily acquire this capability and must seek a supplier.
2. Manufacturing competitiveness: The supplier has a lower cost, faster availability, and so forth.
3. Technology: The supplier's version of the item is better.

By 2005, almost all the desktop PCs sold in the United States were initially produced by contract manufacturers in China. In a typical contract manufacturing transaction, the OEM approaches the contract manufacturer with a product design. The two negotiate and agree on the price, property of materials, subtier suppliers, and sometimes even the manufacturing process. The contract manufacturer then acts as the OEM's factory. Most contract manufacturers for both desktop and laptop PC products have factories in China or other parts of Asia. Depending on the degree of manufacturing competency and cost, some contract manufacturers do everything from manufacturing all the way to shipping fully assembled products on behalf of the OEM. Therefore, by 2005, most American PC makers had become "fabless," and Dell was one of the few American companies that still retained manufacturing facilities in the United States.

In Dell's case, because customers can customize some components of their PCs when placing an order, manufacturing a fully finished product and shipping it by ocean from the contract manufacturer's facility in China to the customers in the United States would be time-prohibitive, and manufacturing a finished product and air-

[2] Drew Wilson, "Contract Manufacturing Revs Up for 2000," *The Electronics Industry Yearbook/2000,* p. 88.

[3] Charles H. Fine and Dan Whitney, "Is the Make-Buy Decision Process a Core Competence?" MIT CTPID Working Paper, 1996.

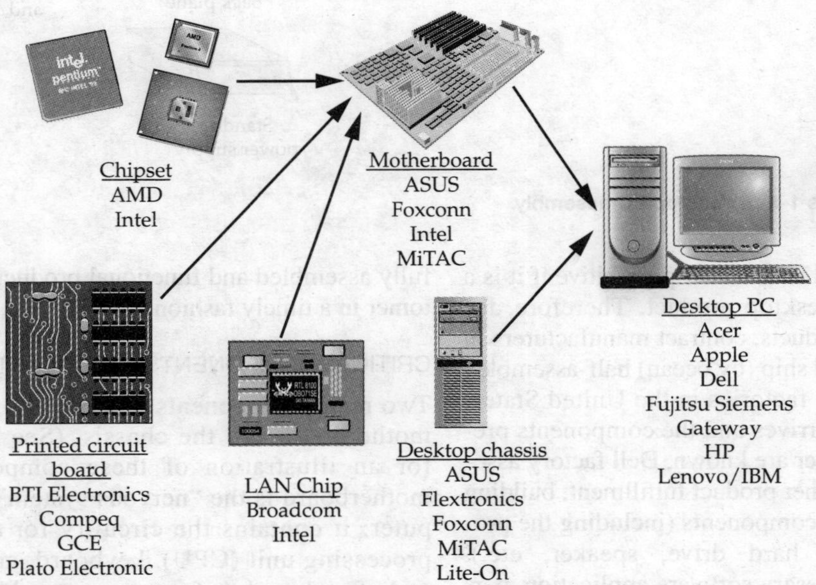

FIGURE 6-1 Critical components of a desktop PC and major component manufacturers.

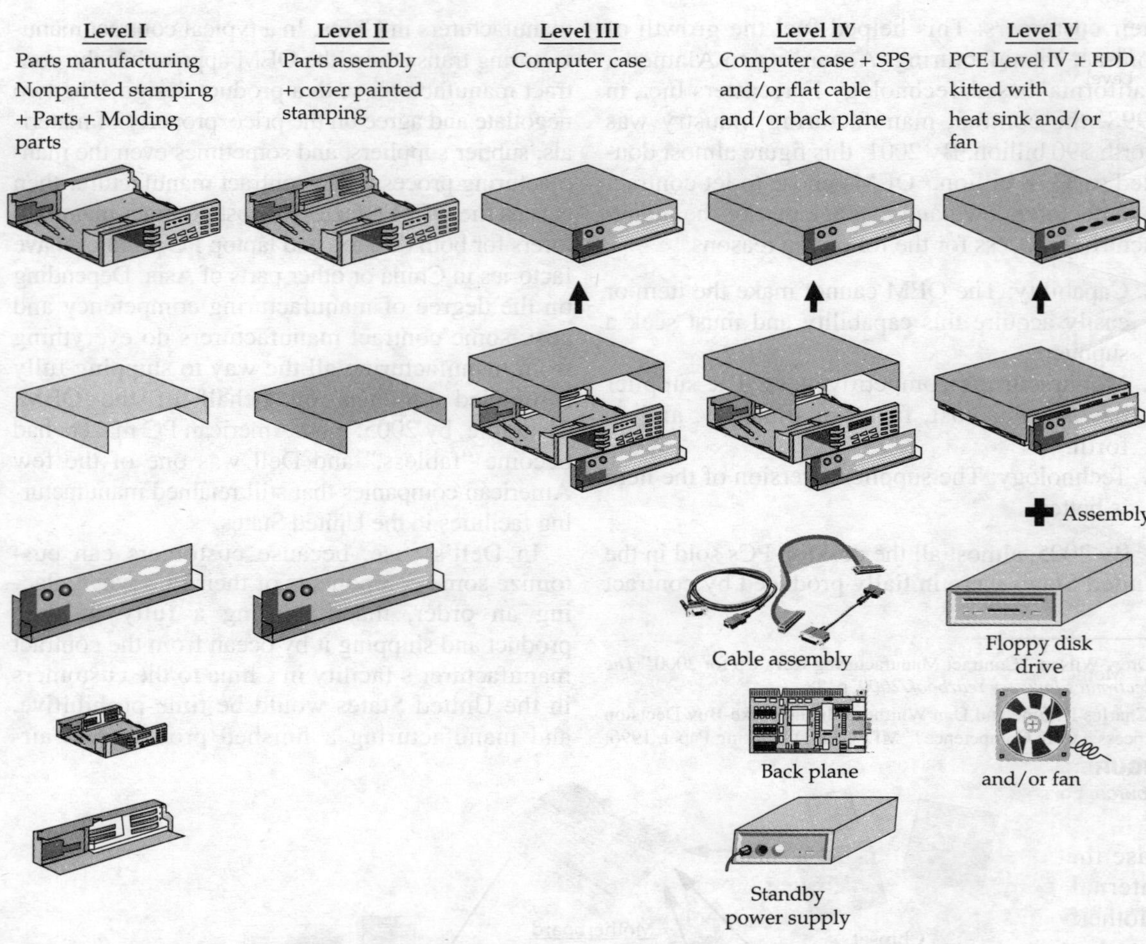

FIGURE 6-2 Levels 1–5 of desktop PC assembly.

freighting it would be too cost-prohibitive if it is a heavy or bulky desktop product. Therefore, for Dell's desktop products, contract manufacturers in China produce and ship (by ocean) half-assembled products to Dell's factories in the United States. Once the supply arrives and the components preferred by a customer are known, Dell factory associates perform further product fulfillment: building in the customized components (including the processor, memory, hard drive, speaker, etc.), installing the necessary software application, performing final unit testing, and then delivering the fully assembled and functional product to the customer in a timely fashion.

CRITICAL COMPONENTS OF A DESKTOP PC

Two major components of a desktop PC are the motherboard and the chassis. (See Figure 6-1 for an illustration of these components.) A motherboard is the "nervous system" of a computer: it contains the circuitry for the central processing unit (CPU), keyboard, and monitor and often has slots for accepting additional circuitry. A chassis is the enclosure or framework

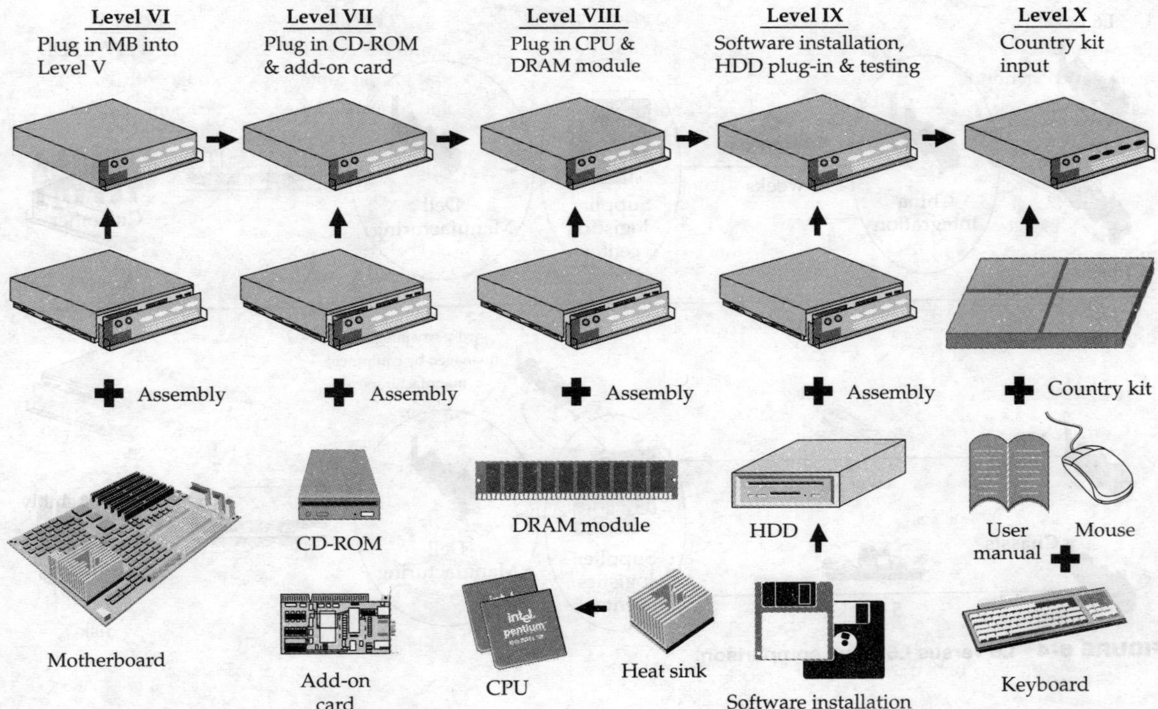

FIGURE 6-3 Levels 6–10 of desktop PC assembly.
Source: Foxconn Company presentation.

case that contains and protects all of the vital internal components from dust or moisture. Motherboards are typically screwed manually to the bottom of the chassis case, with the input/output (I/O) ports exposed on the side of the chassis. The chassis also contains the power supply unit.

A motherboard contains three critical components: chipset, printed circuit board (PCB), and local area network (LAN) chip. A PCB is the base of a motherboard; it consists of etched conductors attached to a sheet of insulator. Various components are soldered to the circuit board. A chipset is a group of integrated circuits that contains the northbridge and southbridge. The northbridge communicates with the CPU and memory; the southbridge communicates with the slower devices, such as the Peripheral Component Interconnect (PCI) bus, real-time clock, power management, and so forth. A LAN chip enables a computer to communicate with the Internet via Ethernet or Wi-Fi technology.

LEVEL 5 VERSUS LEVEL 6 MANUFACTURING

In desktop PC manufacturing, the degree of assembly can be broken down into 10 levels. The higher the level, the more fully integrated it is. Figures 6-2 and 6-3 depict the 10 levels of desktop PC assembly. This scale also can apply to the manufacturing of servers and storage.

Level 5 (L5) includes the assembly of desktop PC chassis, floppy disk drive, and fan. Depending on the chassis configuration, it also can include the power supply in some cases. In Level 6 (L6), along with these components, the motherboard is

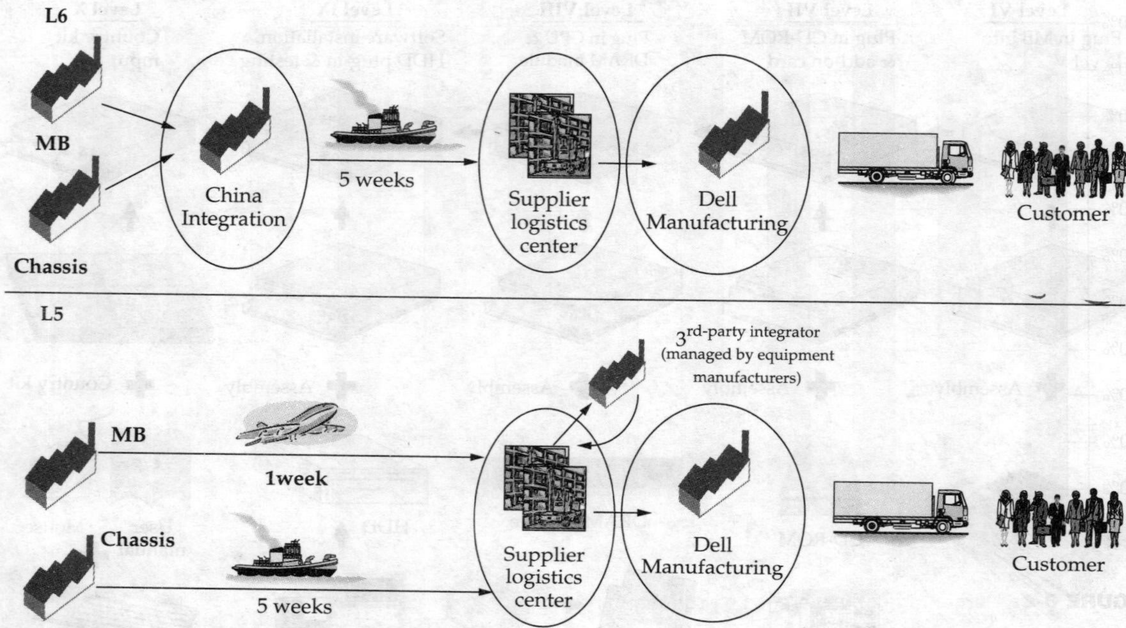

FIGURE 6-4 L6 versus L5 value comparison.

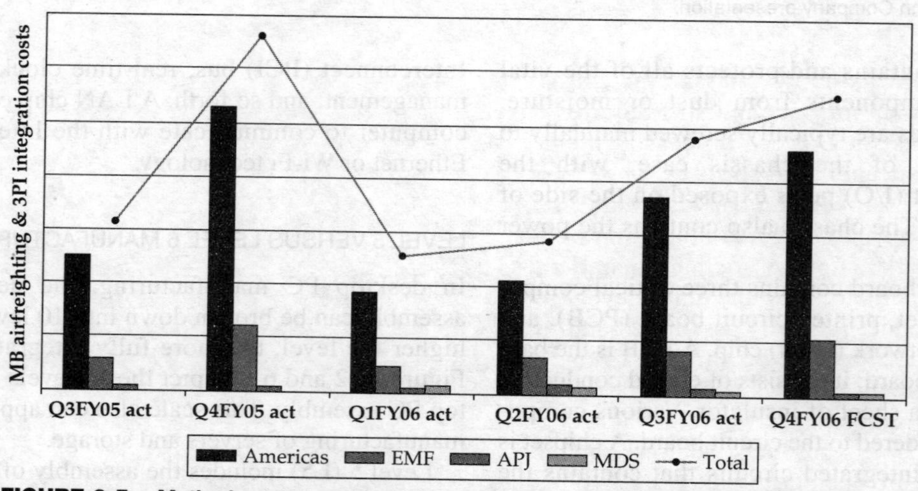

FIGURE 6-5 Motherboard air-freighting and 3PI integration costs (Q3FY05–Q4FY06).
Note: Data from Dell's Worldwide Procurement (WWP) organization. AMF includes 3PI integration cost. EMF (European Manufacturing Facility) and APJ (Asia Pacific Japan) don't as intergration is done in Dell factory. In Dell's financial year Q1FY05 is February–April 2004; Q4FY06 is November 2005–January 2006.

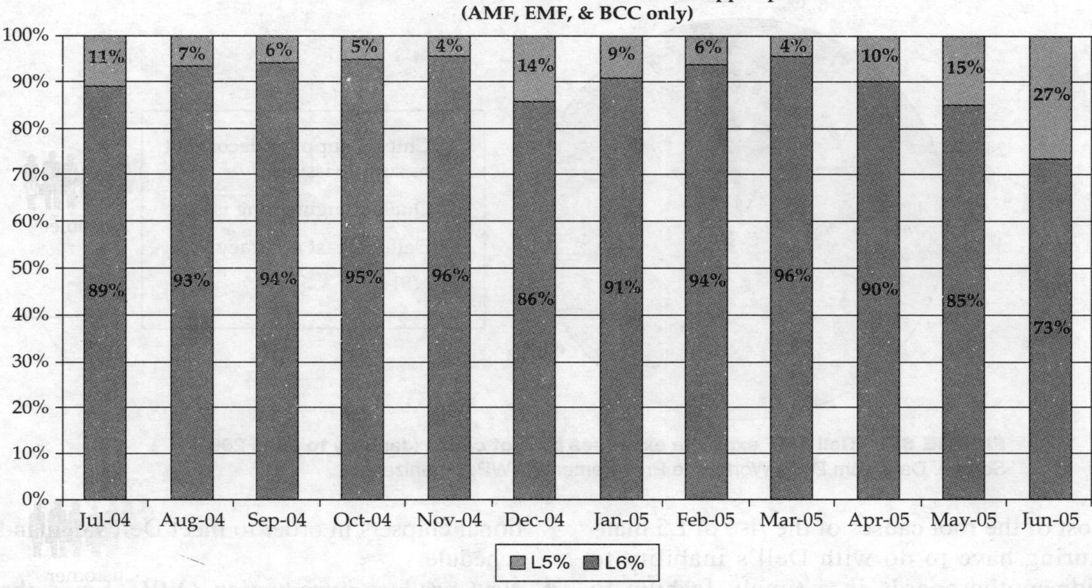

FIGURE 6-6 Percentage of L5 versus L6 production from July 2004 to June 2005.

also installed into the chassis. In other words, when a supplier performs Level 6 manufacturing, the supplier installs the motherboard in the chassis—an activity not performed in Level 5 manufacturing.

When a contract manufacturer in China produces an L6 desktop PC chassis, the chassis is not a functional unit yet and still requires customized parts such as the processor, memory, hard drive, speaker, and so forth. The contract manufacturer ships the L6 chassis from China to Dell's factories in the United States and Ireland, and then Dell factory associates install these customized parts to make the unit "Level 10." A Level 10 product is a fully assembled and functional product that can be shipped to the customer. Figure 6-4 shows the similarities and differences between the L5 and L6 value chains.

Some of Dell's products, such as handhelds and printers, are manufactured to Level 10 by the contract manufacturers. This means that Dell does not have dedicated manufacturing resources or capability to manufacture these products. Rather, the contract manufacturers produce these products, include the user manuals in the packaging, and ship the products to Dell's merge centers. These products are then "merged" with PCs manufactured by Dell factory associates into the same shipment, so the customer can receive a single shipment with all of the items in the order. Dell uses this shipping strategy to create a more satisfying customer experience.

ROOT CAUSES OF INCREASING L5 MANUFACTURING

L5 manufacturing has higher overall manufacturing and logistics cost than L6. Dell's rising manufacturing cost, caused by an increase in the utilization of L5 manufacturing, can be seen in Figure 6-5. Furthermore, as can be seen in Figure 6-6, the level of L5 manufacturing (relative to L6) started to increase quite significantly in March 2005. The L5 percent in June (27 percent) was more than six times the L5 percent in March (4 percent).

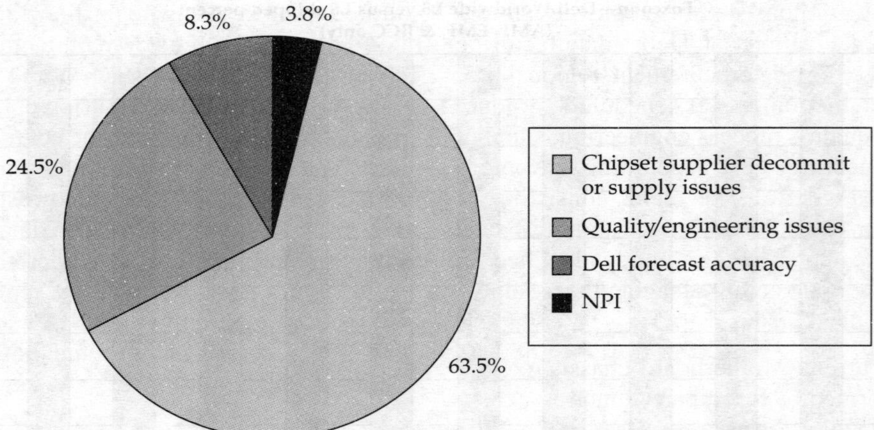

FIGURE 6-7 Dell AMF expedite expenses by root cause (January to June 2005)
Source: Data from Dell's Worldwide Procurement (WWP) organization.

Most of the root causes of the rise of L5 manufacturing have to do with Dell's inability to provide motherboards in a timely fashion to contract manufacturers. These causes can be summarized as follows:

1. *Chipset supplier decommit or supply issues.* When a chipset supplier is unable to deliver the previously agreed quantity of chipsets, it creates a disruption in the desktop PC supply chain. According to the data gathered in the first half of 2005, this accounted for more than 60 percent of the L5 manufacturing, as motherboards were not available for L6 manufacturing.
2. *Quality/engineering issues.* These issues lead to dysfunctional or problematic motherboards that need to be repaired or replaced by a new supply, which can subsequently create an additional unexpected demand of motherboards that were not part of the forecast agreed to by Dell's chipset supplier.
3. *Dell forecast accuracy.* When the actual demand surpasses the forecast, Dell needs to source extra chipsets or risk the possibility of not meeting customer demand. Since the lead time for manufacturing, assembling, testing, and delivering a chipset is on average 13 weeks, such a long lead time makes it difficult for the chipset supplier to provide the additional chipsets in order to meet Dell's demand schedule.
4. *New product introduction (NPI).* Since the actual demand of a newly released PC product can be especially volatile, the forecast uncertainty can create a need to air-freight extra motherboards normally not required when the product is in a mature stage with a stable level of demand and a constant level of L6 manufacturing. The volatile demand can lead to an increase of L5 manufacturing (motherboard-chassis assembly in the United State in order to reduce the time to market for a newly launched product). However, as Figure 6-7 indicates, the amount Dell spends on expediting motherboards under this particular circumstance is rather small—only 3.8 percent.

Figure 6-7 shows the breakdown of motherboard air-freight costs by root cause from Dell AMF (America Manufacturing Facility).

DELL BPI TEAM'S METHODOLOGY: FOCUSING ON COMPLEXITY MANAGEMENT

In order to solve the problem of continuously rising manufacturing cost induced by an increasing level of L5, a task force was assembled at Dell. The cross-functional business process improvement (BPI) team consisted of employees from a variety of organizations at Dell: manufacturing /operations, worldwide procurement, regional procurement, production master schedulers, production control, quality, process engineering, supplier quality engineering, cost accounting, inventory control, and logistics. The team, consisting of members from the different organizations affected by the chipset supply shortage, jointly identified six manufacturing options for managing the assembly work in the United State:

1. Keep as current. Motherboard-chassis integration performed by a 3rd party integrator (3PI) managed by the contract manufacturers.
2. Dell America Operations (DAO) cellular integration. Enable the Dell factory work cells to perform L5 to L10 manufacturing work.
3. Offline integration at the supplier logistics center (SLC). Keep the current L6 to L10 manufacturing process unchanged; handle mother board-chassis integration work at an SLC.
4. Offline integration at a Dell-leased building. Keep the current L6 to L10 manufacturing process unchanged; handle motherboard-chassis integration work at a separate building leased by Dell.
5. 3PI managed directly by Dell.
6. L6 from equipment manufacturers' Mexico plants. Many CMs have manufacturing facilities in which they produce for their other customers. Dell can potentially negotiate with the CMs to dedicate a portion of the CM's manufacturing capacity to support Dell's business.

The BPI team determined that it would survey of the various departments impacted at Dell to quantify the complexity and cost of managing each of the six manufacturing options. The categories of the survey were established by the team based on the attributes or business processes that would be impacted by the change of manufacturing method. The survey was sent to the content expert within each affected department. These experts were involved in the day-to-day business processes and planning and would be the best source of information regarding the impact on their departments of each manufacturing option. Table 6-1 illustrates the result of the survey.

On the basis of manufacturing complexity, the original option (1) of having the contract manufacturers manage the 3PI had a medium complexity score. Option 3A received the lowest complexity score because overall Dell believed having its own factory associates assemble motherboards into L5 chassis in an SLC would only require Dell to install new equipment at the SLC, so the capital expenditure would be low and not impact the existing manufacturing process in the Dell factory. (Note that the complexity of Option 3A is only a point less than Option 4—Dell-managed 3PI.) At the other end of the complexity spectrum is Option 5. This option was the most complex because it would require Dell's biregional procurement organization (in Austin, Texas, and Shanghai, China) to coordinate and entirely revamp its business processes of managing the L6 chassis from Mexico. (At the time of this case study, all the L6 chassis came from only the Chinese factories of the contract manufacturers.) The lack of a robust transportation and customs infrastructure in Mexico also contributed to the high complexity score.

On the basis of manufacturing cost, the original option (1) of motherboard-chassis assembly in a CM-managed 3PI has the highest manufacturing cost. This high cost is driven by the process complexity involved: there are many changing hands handling the inventory from one part of the process to the next, as evidenced by the following testimony from a Dell quality engineer: "In our current manufacturing option, the motherboards air-freighted from China are first stored in the SLC and then transported to the 3PI site for integration with the chassis. The chassis are then sent back to the SLC before being pulled into our Dell factories. There are many stakeholders that 'touch' the process: CMs, SLC management, 3PI staff, CM staff managing the 3PI production, and Dell factory associates and process engineers. There are just too many cooks in the kitchen trying to accomplish the same thing. We need a

TABLE 6-1

COMPLEXITY AND COST ANALYSIS OF THE SIX POTENTIAL MANUFACTURING OPTIONS

	Option 1	Option 2 (original)	Option 2 (revised)	Option 3A	Option 3B	Option 4	Option 5
Worldwide procurement	10	1	1	1	1	5	10
Regional procurement	8	5	5	5	5	5	10
Master scheduler	5	5	5	5	5	5	5
Production control	5	10	10	7	7	7	5
Operations	1	10	10	5	5	1	1
DAO quality	5	10	10	5	5	1	1
Processing engineering	1	10	10	5	5	1	1
Supplier quality Engineering (regional)	10	1	1	1	1	5	7
Supplier quality Engineering (global)	1	1	1	1	1	1	10
Cost accounting	5	1	1	10	10	10	1
Inventory control	1	5	5	5	7	10	1
Logistics	5	1	1	5	5	5	10
Total:	57	60	60	55	57	56	62
Cost per box	$10.07	$7.00	$7.90	$7.54	$7.70	$7.61	$7.00

Notes: The "cost per box" data has been modified to respect Dell's data confidentiality.

Option 1: CM-managed 3PI (original baseline).
Option 2: Integration at DAO work cells.
Option 3A: Integration at SLC/hub.
Option 3B: Integration at Dell-leased building.
Option 4: Dell-managed 3PI.
Option 5: Integrated chassis from CM factories in Mexico.

cleaner and more straight-forward process. This will not only make it easier to manage the process, but it will also improve our relationships with the CMs and 3PIs since the current process creates many confusing and frustrating situations, as well as last-minute fires related to motherboard quality issues."

With all this information in mind, Tom Wilson and the rest of the BPI team had to select and implement a solution that would deliver advantages to Dell from both a cost angle and an operational complexity perspective. The team pondered the following questions:

1. Why does L5 incur higher manufacturing and logistics costs than L6? What are some of the costs that are incurred in L5 but not in L6? Are there any costs that apply to only L6 but not L5?
2. Which of the six proposed manufacturing solutions should Dell implement, based on the survey result (Table 6-1)? Why? What are the pros and cons of this recommendation?
3. How easily sustainable is your recommendation for the previous question if the chipset supply shortage further deteriorates?
4. How good is the methodology employed by the BPI team to determine the optimal manufacturing option for Dell? Are there more effective approaches?
5. How can Dell effectively address the root causes contributing to the increase of L5 manufacturing?

By the end of this chapter, you should be able to answer the following questions:

- What is a push strategy? A pull strategy? A push–pull strategy? How would you characterize Dell's supply chain strategy?
- When should the firm use push? pull? or push–pull? What are the key drivers when selecting the appropriate strategy?
- What does it take to implement a push–pull strategy? What is the impact? What would it cost?
- What is the impact of the Internet on the supply chain strategy employed by the traditional retailers and the online stores? In particular, what is the impact on distribution and fulfillment strategies?

6.1 INTRODUCTION

In Chapter 1, we observed that supply chain management revolves around *efficient integration of suppliers, manufacturers, warehouses, and stores.* The challenge in supply chain integration, of course, is to coordinate activities across the supply chain so that the enterprise can improve performance: reduce cost, increase service level, reduce the bullwhip effect, better utilize resources, and effectively respond to changes in the marketplace. As many companies have recently realized, these challenges are met not only by coordinating production, transportation, and inventory decisions, but, more generally, by integrating the **front end** of the supply chain, customer demand, to the **back end** of the supply chain, the production and manufacturing portion of the supply chain. The objective of this chapter is to illustrate the opportunities and the challenges associated with supply chain integration. We consider

- Various supply chain strategies, including push, pull, and a relatively new paradigm, the push–pull strategy.
- A framework for matching products and industries with supply chain strategies.
- Demand-driven supply chain strategies.
- The impact of the Internet on supply chain integration.

Obviously, the availability of information plays an important role in supply chain integration. In some cases, the supply chain must be designed to make this information available. In other cases, the supply chain strategy must be designed to *take advantage* of information that is already available. And, in many cases, an expensive network must be designed to compensate for the lack of information.

6.2 PUSH, PULL, AND PUSH–PULL SYSTEMS

Traditional supply chain strategies are often categorized as push or pull strategies. Probably, this stems from the manufacturing revolution of the 1980s, in which manufacturing systems were divided into these categories. Interestingly, in the last few years, a number of companies have employed a hybrid approach, the push–pull supply chain paradigm. In this section, we explain each one of the strategies.

6.2.1 Push-Based Supply Chain

In a *push-based supply chain,* production and distribution decisions are based on long-term forecasts. Typically, the manufacturer bases demand forecasts on orders received from the retailer's warehouses. It therefore takes much longer for a push-based supply chain to react to the changing marketplace, which can lead to

- The inability to meet changing demand patterns.
- The obsolescence of supply chain inventory as demand for certain products disappears.

In addition, we saw in Chapter 5 that the variability of orders received from the retailers and the warehouses is much larger than the variability in customer demand, due to the bullwhip effect. This increase in variability leads to

- Excessive inventories due to the need for large safety stocks (see Chapter 2).
- Larger and more variable production batches.
- Unacceptable service levels.
- Product obsolescence.

Specifically, the bullwhip effect leads to inefficient resource utilization, because planning and managing are much more difficult. For instance, it is not clear how a manufacturer should determine production capacity. Should it be based on peak demand, which implies that most of the time the manufacturer has expensive resources sitting idle, or should it be based on average demand, which requires extra—and expensive—capacity during periods of peak demand? Similarly, it is not clear how to plan transportation capacity: based on peak demand or average demand. Thus, in a push-based supply chain, we often find increased transportation costs, high inventory levels, and/or high manufacturing costs, due to the need for emergency production changeovers.

6.2.2 Pull-Based Supply Chain

In a *pull-based supply chain*, production and distribution are demand driven so that they are coordinated with true customer demand rather than forecast demand [17]. In a pure pull system, the firm does not hold any inventory and only responds to *specific* orders. This is enabled by fast information flow mechanisms to transfer information about customer demand (e.g., POS data) to the various supply chain participants. Pull systems are intuitively attractive since they lead to

- A decrease in lead times achieved through the ability to better anticipate incoming orders from the retailers.
- A decrease in inventory at the retailers since inventory levels at these facilities increase with lead times (see Chapter 2).
- A decrease in variability in the system and, in particular, variability faced by manufacturers (see the discussion in Section 5.2.3) due to lead-time reduction.
- Decreased inventory at the manufacturer due to the reduction in variability.

EXAMPLE 6-1

A major apparel manufacturer recently changed its supply chain strategy to a pull-based system. Retailers order from this manufacturer about once a month, but transfer POS data much more frequently, for example, daily or weekly. These data allow the manufacturer to continuously adjust production quantities according to true customer demand.

Thus, in a pull-based supply chain, we typically see a significant reduction in system inventory level, enhanced ability to manage resources, and a reduction in system costs when compared with the equivalent push-based system.

On the other hand, pull-based systems are often difficult to implement when lead times are so long that it is impractical to react to demand information. Also, in pull- based systems, it is frequently more difficult to take advantage of economies of scale in manufacturing and transportation since systems are not planned far ahead in time. These advantages and disadvantages of push and pull supply chains have led companies to look for a new supply chain strategy that takes advantage of the best of both. Frequently, this is a **push–pull** supply chain strategy.

6.2.3 Push–Pull Supply Chain

In a *push–pull* strategy, some stages of the supply chain, typically the initial stages are operated in a push-based manner, while the remaining stages employ a pull-based strategy. The interface between the push-based stages and the pull-based stages is known as the **push–pull boundary**.

To better understand this strategy, consider the **supply chain time line** defined as the time that elapses between the procurement of raw material, that is, the beginning of the time line, and the delivery of an order to the customer, that is, the end of the time line. The push–pull boundary is located somewhere along the time line and it indicates the point in time when the firm switches from managing the supply chain using one strategy, typically a push strategy, to managing it using a different strategy, typically a pull strategy. This is illustrated in Figure 6-8.

Consider a PC manufacturer who builds to stock and thus makes all production and distribution decisions based on forecast. This is a typical push system. By contrast, an example of a push–pull strategy is one in which the manufacturer builds to order. This implies that component inventory is managed based on forecast, but final assembly is in response to a specific customer request. Thus, the push portion of the manufacturer's supply chain is that portion prior to assembly, while the pull part of the supply chain starts with assembly and is performed based on actual customer demand. The push–pull boundary is at the beginning of assembly.

Observe that, in this case, the manufacturer takes advantage of the fact that *aggregate forecasts are more accurate* (see Chapter 2). Indeed, demand for a component is an aggregation of demand for all finished products that use this component. Since aggregate forecasts are more accurate, uncertainty in component demand is much smaller than uncertainty in finished goods demand and this leads to safety stock reduction. Dell Computers has used this strategy very effectively and is an excellent example of the impact of the push–pull strategy on supply chain performance.

Postponement, or delayed differentiation in product design (see Chapter 11), is also an excellent example of a push–pull strategy. In postponement, the firm designs the product and the manufacturing process so that decisions about which specific product is being manufactured can be delayed as long as possible. The manufacturing process starts by producing a generic or family product, which is differentiated to a specific end-product when demand is revealed. The portion of the supply chain prior to product differentiation is typically operated using a push-based strategy. In other words, the generic product is built and transported based on a long-term (aggregate) forecast. Since demand for the generic product is an aggregation of demand for all its corresponding end-products, forecasts are more accurate and

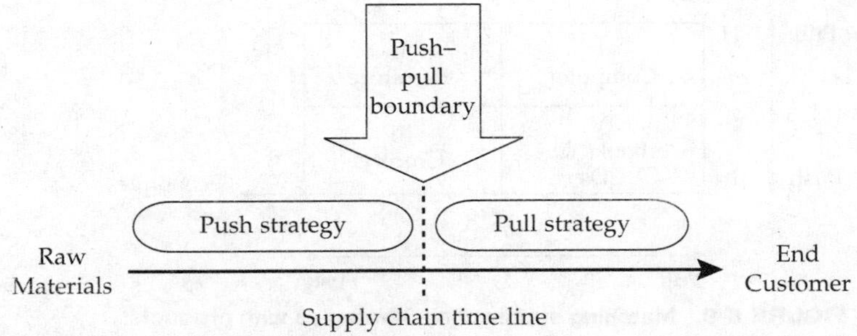

FIGURE 6-8 Push–pull supply chains.

thus inventory levels are reduced. In contrast, customer demand for a specific end-product typically has a high level of uncertainty and thus product differentiation occurs only in response to individual demand. Thus, the portion of the supply chain starting from the time of differentiation is pull-based.

EXAMPLE 6-2 MOBILE RECHARGE COUPONS

Till early 2006, Indian pre-paid mobile phone users were offered different denominations of recharge coupons for recharging their mobiles phones for talk-time at the retailer shop. Due to different variety of denominations, the supply chain of recharge coupons was overloaded with these coupons at different levels such as service provider, distributor, retailer etc. Despite huge inventory, customers always complained for non-availability of other denominations that they were looking for. This was due to working capital limitation of a large number of small retailers who could not afford to keep sufficient inventory of all denominations or maintain frequent replenishment from distributors.

Of late, service providers have come up with e-recharge system, through which a retailer can refill the customer's mobile talk-time account with any denomination through electronic-mode. This completely arrested the existing twin problem of physical inventory for some denominations along with stock-out situation for remaining denominations. The technological possibility of having a single machine at the retailer level to electronically generate the coupons of any denomination of any service provider has revitalized this industry. The delayed differentiation in deciding the denomination till the time the customer places an order is one of the finest examples of moving the push-pull boundary towards the customer end in the supply chain, which has solved the twin problem of inventory and stock-outs.

6.2.4 Identifying the Appropriate Supply Chain Strategy

What is the appropriate supply chain strategy for a particular product? Should the firm use a push-based supply chain strategy, a pull-based strategy, or a push–pull strategy? Figure 6-9 provides a framework for matching supply chain strategies with products and industries. The vertical axis provides information on uncertainty in customer demand, while the horizontal axis represents the importance of economies of scale, in either production or distribution.

Everything else being equal, higher demand uncertainty leads to a preference for managing the supply chain based on realized demand: a pull strategy. Alternatively, smaller demand uncertainty leads to an interest in managing the supply chain based on a long-term forecast: a push strategy.

Similarly, everything else being equal, the higher the importance of economies of scale in reducing cost, the greater the value of aggregating demand, and thus the greater the importance of managing the supply chain based on long-term forecast, a push-based strategy. If economies of scale are not important, aggregation does not reduce cost, so a pull-based strategy makes more sense.

In Figure 6-9, we partition the region spanned by these two dimensions into four boxes. Box I represents industries (or, more precisely, products) that are characterized by high uncertainty and by

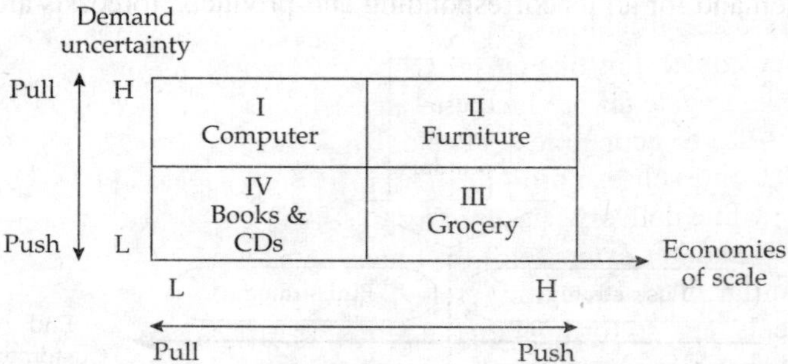

FIGURE 6-9 Matching supply chain strategies with products: the impact of demand uncertainty and economies of scale.

situations in which economies of scale in production, assembly, or distribution are not important, such as the computer industry. Our framework suggests that a pull-based supply chain strategy is appropriate for these industries and products. This is exactly the strategy employed by Dell Inc.

Box III represents products that are characterized by low demand uncertainty and high economies of scale. Products in the grocery industry such as beer, pasta, and soup belong to that category. Demand for these products is quite stable, while reducing transportation cost by shipping full truckloads is critical for controlling supply chain cost. In this case, a pull strategy is not appropriate. Indeed, a traditional, push-based retail strategy is appropriate, because managing inventory based on long-term forecasts does not increase inventory holding costs while delivery costs are reduced by leveraging economies of scale.

Boxes I and III represent situations in which it is relatively easy to identify an efficient supply chain strategy. In the remaining two cases, there is a mismatch between the strategies suggested by the two attributes, uncertainty and the importance of economies of scale. Indeed, in these boxes, uncertainty "pulls" the supply chain toward one strategy, while economies of scale "push" the supply chain in a different direction.

For instance, box IV represents products characterized by low demand uncertainty, indicating a push-based supply chain, and low economies of scale, suggesting a pull- based supply chain strategy. Many high-volume/fast-moving books and CDs fall in this category. In this case, a more careful analysis is required, since both traditional retail push strategies and more innovative push–pull strategies may be appropriate, depending on the specific costs and uncertainties. We discuss this choice in more detail in Section 6.4.

Finally, box II represents products and industries for which uncertainty in demand is high while economies of scale are important in reducing production and/or delivery costs. The furniture industry is an excellent example of this situation. Indeed, a typical furniture retailer offers a large number of similar products distinguished by shape, color, fabric, and so forth, and, as a result, demand uncertainty is very high. Unfortunately, these are bulky products and hence delivery costs are also high.

Thus, in this case, there is a need to distinguish between the production and the distribution strategies. The production strategy has to follow a pull-based strategy since it is impossible to make production decisions based on long-term forecasts. On the other hand, the distribution strategy needs to take advantage of economies of scale in order to reduce transportation cost. This is exactly the strategy employed by many retailers that do not keep any inventory of furniture. When a customer places an order, it is sent to the manufacturer, who orders the fabric and produces to order. Once the product is ready, it is shipped, typically using truckload carriers, together with many other products to the retail store and from there to the customer. For this purpose, the manufacturer typically has a fixed delivery schedule and this is used to aggregate all products that are delivered to stores in the same region, thus reducing transportation costs due to economies of scale. Hence, the supply chain strategy followed by furniture manufacturers is, in some sense, a **pull–push** strategy where production is done based on realized demand, a pull strategy, while delivery is according to a fixed schedule, a push strategy.

The automobile industry is another example of the conditions of box II. A typical car manufacturer offers a large number of similar products distinguished by functionality, motor power, shape, color, number of doors, sports wheels, and so forth, and, as a result, demand uncertainty for a particular configuration is very high. Delivery costs are quite high as well. Traditionally, this industry has employed a push-based supply chain strategy, building inventory for the dealer distribution systems. Thus, the automobile industry does not currently follow the model developed in Figure 6-9.

Recently, however, GM announced a dramatic vision for restructuring the way it is designing, building, and selling its products [257]. The goal is to allow customers to customize and order cars online and have the cars delivered *to the customer's door* in less than 10 days. GM is moving exactly in the direction predicted by our model, toward a build-to-order strategy.

Unfortunately, lead times in the automobile industry are currently long: 50 to 60 days on average. To achieve its vision, GM has to redesign the entire supply chain, including the way it partners with suppliers, the way it manufactures products, and the way it distributes products. Reducing lead times to 10 days or below also may require a significant reduction in the number of options and configurations offered to buyers.

6.2.5 Implementing a Push–Pull Strategy

The framework developed in the previous section attempts to characterize the appropriate level of pull and push for different products. For instance, a high degree of pull is appropriate for products that belong to box I in Figure 6-9. Of course, achieving the design of the pull system depends on many factors, including product complexity, manufacturing lead times, and supplier–manufacturer relationships. Similarly, there are many ways to implement a push–pull strategy, depending on the location of the push–pull boundary. For instance, Dell locates the push–pull boundary at the assembly point, while furniture manufacturers locate the boundary at the production point.

EXAMPLE 6-3

Consider the automobile industry, known for its long transportation lead times. Prior to its latest effort to implement a make-to-order strategy, there were previous attempts to implement a push– pull strategy. In 1994, GM announced the establishment of a regional distribution center in Orlando, Florida, where an inventory of about 1,500 Cadillacs was maintained. Dealers could order cars they did not have in their lot from the distribution center, and the cars would be delivered within 24 hours. Thus, GM was attempting to employ a push–pull strategy in which inventory at its regional distribution center was managed based on long-term forecasts while delivery to dealers was based on realized demand. This implies that the push–pull boundary was located at the manufacturer's distribution center.

As discussed in Chapter 12, two major issues contributed to the failure of this strategy. First, the regional warehouse shifted inventory costs from the dealers to GM, since it allowed dealers to reduce inventory levels. Second, the regional distribution center equalized small and large dealers. If all dealers have access to the regional warehouse, then there is no difference between small and large dealers. Thus, it is difficult to see why large dealers would be interested in participating in such an arrangement.

The discussion so far suggests that the push strategy is applied to that portion of the supply chain where demand uncertainty is relatively small and, thus, managing this portion based on long-term forecast is appropriate. On the other hand, the pull strategy is applied to the portion of the supply chain time line where uncertainty is high and, hence, it is important to manage this portion based on realized demand. This distinction between the two portions of the supply chain has an important impact on the objectives of the supply chain strategy, as well as on organizational skills required to manage the system effectively.

Since uncertainty in the push portion of the supply chain is relatively small, service level is not an issue, so the focus can be on **cost minimization**. In addition, this portion of the supply chain is characterized not only by low demand uncertainty and economies of scale in production and/or transportation, but also by long lead times and complex supply chain structures, including product assembly at various levels. Thus, cost minimization is achieved by better utilizing resources such as

TABLE 6-2

CHARACTERISTICS OF THE PUSH AND PULL PORTIONS OF THE SUPPLY CHAIN

Portion	Push	Pull
Objective	Minimize cost	Maximize service level
Complexity	High	Low
Focus	Resource allocation	Responsiveness
Lead time	Long	Short
Processes	Supply chain planning	Order fulfillment

production and distribution capacities while minimizing inventory, transportation, and production costs.

On the other hand, the pull portion of the supply chain is characterized by high uncertainty, simple supply chain structure, and a short cycle time. Hence, the focus here is on service level. Specifically, high service level is achieved by deploying a **flexible** and **responsive** supply chain, that is, a supply chain that can adapt quickly to changes in customer demand.

This implies that different processes need to be used in different portions of the supply chain. Since the focus in the pull part of the supply chain is on service level, **order fulfillment** processes are typically applied. Similarly, since the focus of the push part of the supply chain is on cost and resource utilization, supply chain **planning** processes are used here to develop an effective strategy for the next few weeks or months. In Chapter 3, we provide a detailed discussion of supply chain planning. Table 6-2 summarizes the characteristics of the push and pull portions of the supply chain.

EXAMPLE 6-4

Consider a supplier of fashion skiwear such as Sport Obermeyer [83]. Every year the company introduces many new designs, or products, for which forecast demand is highly uncertain. One strategy used successfully by Sport Obermeyer involves distinguishing between high-risk and low-risk designs. Low-risk products, that is, those for which uncertainty and price are low, are produced in advance using long-term forecasts and focusing on cost minimization, a push-based strategy. But decisions on production quantities for high-risk products are delayed until there is a clear market signal on customer demand for each style, a pull strategy. Since fabric lead times are long, the manufacturer typically orders fabric for high-risk products well in advance of receiving information about market demand, based only on long-term forecasts.

In this case, the manufacturer takes advantage of the same principle applied by Dell Inc.: that aggregate forecasts are more accurate. Since demand for fabrics is an aggregation of demand for all products that use that fabric, demand uncertainty is low and thus fabric inventory is managed based on push strategy. Thus, Sport Obermayer uses a push–pull strategy for the high-risk products and a push strategy for the low-risk products.

Notice that the push portion and the pull portion of the supply chain interact only at the push–pull boundary. This is the point along the supply chain time line where there is a need to coordinate the two supply chain strategies, typically through **buffer inventory**. However, this inventory plays a different role in each portion. In the push portion, buffer inventory at the boundary is part of the output generated by the tactical planning process, while in the pull part it represents the input to the fulfillment process.

Thus, the interface between the push portion of the supply chain and the pull portion of the supply chain is forecast demand. This forecast, which is based on historical data obtained from the pull portion, is used to drive the supply chain planning process and determines the buffer inventory.

6.3 THE IMPACT OF LEAD TIME

The previous discussion motivates a closer look at the impact of lead time on the supply chain strategy. Intuitively, the longer the lead time, the more important it is to implement a push-based strategy. Indeed, it is typically difficult to implement a pull strategy when lead times are so long that it is hard to react to demand information.

In Figure 6-10, we consider the impact of lead time and demand uncertainty on supply chain strategy.

Box A represents products with short lead time and high demand uncertainty, suggesting that a pull strategy should be applied as much as possible. Again, the PC industry is a good example of these types of products and the application of a high degree of pull. Box B represents items with long supply lead time and low demand uncertainty. Examples include many items in the grocery industry. Again, in this case, the appropriate supply chain strategy is push.

The situation is more challenging for products having the characteristics of boxes C and D. For instance, box C includes products with short supply lead time and highly predictable demand. Good examples are products in the grocery industry with short life cycle, for example, bread or dairy products. It is interesting to observe how the retail industry takes advantage of the short lead time and low demand uncertainty for these products. Indeed, in these types of situations, retailers and supermarkets use a strategy referred to as *continuous replenishment*. In such a strategy, suppliers receive POS data and use these data to prepare shipments at previously agreed-upon intervals to maintain specific levels of inventory; see Chapter 8 for a detailed discussion. Thus, since customer demand drives production and distribution decisions in this supply chain, this strategy is a pull strategy at the production and distribution stages and push at the retail outlets.

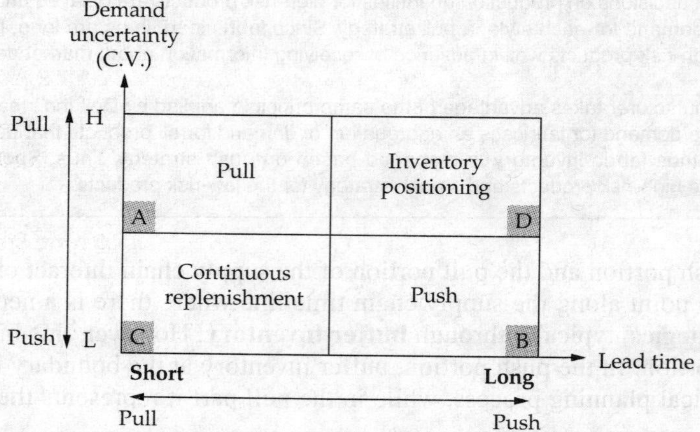

FIGURE 6-10 Matching supply chain strategies with products: the impact of lead time and demand uncertainty.

Finally, the most difficult supply chains to manage are those associated with box D, where lead times are long and demand is not predictable. Inventory is critical in this type of environment, but this requires positioning inventory strategically in the supply chain (see Chapter 3, Section 3.3). Different stages of the supply chain are managed in different ways, depending, among other things, on economies of scale; those stages that keep inventory are managed based on push and others are managed based on pull. As we will in see in the next example, sometimes the entire supply chain is managed based on push.

EXAMPLE 6-5

A large manufacturer of metal components has a manufacturing facility in China, a central distribution center in China, and many regional and country warehouses serving different markets. Customers include automotive manufacturing companies such as GM, Ford, Toyota, and others. The commitment the manufacturer makes to the OEM is that any order will be released from the closest warehouse in less than eight days. Important characteristics of this supply chain include

- The same component is used across multiple assemblies
- Lead times for raw material and finished goods (from the China distribution center to the regional and country warehouses) are quite long.

Recently, the firm realized that its supply chain is not effective, with too much inventory and at the same time low service levels. A careful examination of the current supply chain strategy used by the firm suggests that, because of the tight committed response time to end customers, most inventory was kept close to the customers, at regional and country DCs. Thus, inventory is managed using local optimization: each facility stocks up inventory with little regard to the impact of its decision on supply chain performance. The end result of this strategy is a supply chain with a low inventory turnover ratio of about 3.5.

To overcome these challenges, the manufacturer decided to change the way they position inventory in their supply chain (specifically, the firm applied techniques similar to those described in Section 3.3). The results of this process are described in Figure 6-11, where you can see both the baseline and the supply chain after the change. Each pie represents inventory at a different location, where brown and black colors are associated with cycle stock and safety stock, respectively. As you can see, most of the safety stock in the optimized supply chain is positioned as plant raw material and at the regional DCs. The reason, in both cases, is risk pooling (see Chapter 2). Indeed, raw material inventory takes advantage of the risk pooling concepts by aggregating demand across all finished products that use the same component. The regional DCs take advantage of the risk pooling concept by aggregating demand across many country DCs. The net impact of correctly positioning inventory in this supply chain was a significant inventory reduction and an increase to 4.6 turns a year.

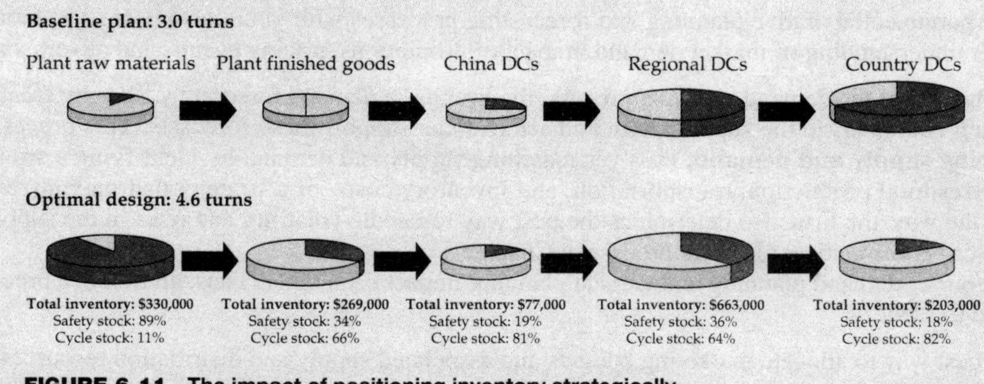

FIGURE 6-11 The impact of positioning inventory strategically.

6.4 DEMAND-DRIVEN STRATEGIES

The framework we have developed in this chapter requires integrating demand information into the supply chain planning process. This information is generated by applying two different processes:

- **Demand forecast:** A process in which historical demand data are used to develop long-term estimates of expected demand, that is, forecasts (see Chapter 2 for details).
- **Demand shaping:** A process in which the firm determines the impact of various marketing plans such as promotion, pricing discounts, rebates, new product introduction, and product withdrawal on demand forecasts.

Of course, in either case, the forecast is not completely accurate, and hence an important output from the demand-forecast and demand-shaping processes is an estimate of the **accuracy** of the forecast, the so-called **forecast error,** measured according to its **standard deviation**. This information provides insight into the likelihood that demand will be higher (or lower) than the forecast.

High demand forecast error has a detrimental impact on supply chain performance, resulting in lost sales, obsolete inventory, and inefficient utilization of resources. Can the firm employ supply chain strategies to increase forecast accuracy and thus decrease forecast error? We identify the following approaches:

- Select the push–pull boundary so that demand is aggregated over one or more of the following dimensions:
  —Demand is aggregated across products.
  —Demand is aggregated across geography.
  —Demand is aggregated across time.
  The objective is clear. Since aggregate forecasts are more accurate, the result is improved forecast accuracy.
- Use market analysis and demographic and economic trends to improve forecast accuracy (see Chapter 2 for details).
- Determine the optimal assortment of products by store so as to reduce the number of SKUs competing in the same market. Indeed, we are familiar with a large retailer who used to keep in each store more than 30 different types of garbage cans. It was relatively easy to predict aggregate demand across all SKUs in the garbage can category, but very difficult to predict demand for an individual SKU.
- Incorporate collaborative planning and forecasting processes with your customers so as to achieve a better understanding of market demand, impact of promotions, pricing events, and advertising.

At the end of the demand planning process, the firm has a demand forecast by SKU by location. The next step is to analyze the supply chain and see if it can support these forecasts. This process, called **balancing supply and demand,** involves matching supply and demand by identifying a strategy that minimizes total production, transportation, and inventory costs, or a strategy that maximizes profits. Along the way, the firm also determines the best way to handle volatility and risks in the supply chain. We describe this tactical planning process in Chapter 3.

Of course, demand planning and tactical planning impact each other. Thus, an iterative process must be used to identify

- The best way to allocate marketing budgets and associated supply and distribution resources.
- The impact of deviations from forecast demand.

- The impact of changes in supply chain lead times.
- The impact of competitors' promotional activities on demand and supply chain strategies.

The importance of the iterative process is demonstrated by the following example.

EXAMPLE 6-6

A classic example of the perils of not including supply chain analysis in market plans is the story of Campbell's Soup's winter promotion. In one unfortunate season, the marketing department decided to promote chicken noodle soup in the winter. Of course, there is a seasonal spike in the demand for soup in winter anyway. By itself, this seasonal spike requires preparing and storing chicken and ingredients in huge quantities in the spring and fall in order to meet the demand. In addition, due to the promotion, production had to start early and use overtime capacity in order to meet the demand. Unfortunately, the cost of the excess production and inventory requirements far exceeded the revenue from the promotions [51].

6.5 THE IMPACT OF THE INTERNET ON SUPPLY CHAIN STRATEGIES

The influence of the Internet and e-commerce on the economy in general, and business practice in particular, has been tremendous. Changes are happening rapidly. For instance, the direct-business model employed by industry giants such as Dell Inc. and Amazon.com enables customers to order products over the Internet and thus allows companies to sell their products without relying on third-party distributors. Similarly, many companies reported that business-to-business e-commerce provides convenience and cost reduction.

In parallel, the Internet and the emerging e-business models have produced expectations that many supply chain problems will be resolved merely by using these new technology and business models. E-business strategies were supposed to reduce cost, increase service level, and increase flexibility and, of course, profits, albeit sometime in the future. In reality, these expectations have frequently gone unmet, as many of the new e-businesses have not been successful. In many cases, the downfall of some of the highest-profile Internet businesses has been attributed to their logistics strategies. Several examples follow.

EXAMPLE 6-7

The furniture industry seemed ripe for modernization and e-business when executives from living.com purchased Shaw Furniture Gallery, the 10th largest furniture store in North Carolina, in March of 1999. The purchase was intended to provide living.com with access to top-line furniture manufacturers. After an investment of $70 million in capital and a spot as the exclusive Amazon.com furniture link, living.com declared bankruptcy on August 29, 2000. Reasons for the failure included the investment in a new information system that did not function correctly and the switch to a carrier that had no experience with furniture delivery, leading to a stunning 30 percent return rate.

EXAMPLE 6-8

Furniture.com, launched in January 1999, offered thousands of products from many furniture makers, although only a few brand names. The company had $22 million in sales in the first nine months of 2000 and one million visitors a month to its Web site. Its downfall in November 2000 was due to logistics details, and, in particular, inefficient delivery processes. Initially, Furniture.com used carriers to ship its products from a central warehouse to the customers. Since transportation costs were too high, the firm formed an alliance with six regional distributors. Unfortunately, these relationships were hard to maintain and left many problems unsolved, including handling of repairs and returns.

Some companies, of course, are extremely successful in developing new business models that allow them to increase profits significantly and capture a sizeable market share. These companies use the Internet as the driver of business change.

EXAMPLE 6-9

Founded in 1989, Peapod is based in Skokie, Illinois, and is considered one of America's leading online grocers. As a highly experienced online grocer, the company serves more than 130,000 customers. In 1999, Peapod had sales of $73 million and generated a loss of $29 million. Peapod's mounting losses and inability to secure additional funding resulted in a buyout of a majority of its stock in April 2000 by Royal Ahold, the international food company. Peapod thus escaped the fate of Shoplink.com, Streamline.com, and Priceline's WebHouse Club, all of which left the online grocery business at about the same time. These failures are generally attributed to high delivery costs.

EXAMPLE 6-10

What started in 1995 as Earth's biggest bookstore is rapidly becoming Earth's biggest store. Amazon.com's main site offers millions of books, CDs, DVDs, videos, toys, tools, and electronics. In addition, Amazon.com conducts auctions for items ranging from art to real estate and provides schedulers, address books, and online greeting cards. Amazon also owns stakes in online sellers of pet supplies, prescription drugs, cars, groceries, and more. Indeed Amazon.com has become a model for Internet companies by placing market share ahead of profits and making acquisitions funded by its meteoric market capitalization. In 1996, the company had $16M in sales and a $6M loss; in 1999, it had $1.6B in sales and a $720M loss; in 2000, it had $2.7B in sales and a $1.4B loss; and in 2005, revenue reached $8.49B with total profit of $359M, quite a remarkable transformation.

Despite its downturn in 2001 and the write-off of $2.25B in excess inventory, Cisco is a good model of a company that makes innovative use of the Internet.

EXAMPLE 6-11

According to Peter Solvik, who is CIO of Cisco, "Cisco's Internet-based business model has been instrumental in its ability to quadruple in size from 1994 to 1998 ($1.3 billion to over $8 billion), hire approximately 1,000 new employees per quarter while increasing their productivity, and save $560M annually in business expenses." Over 80 percent of Cisco's customer business is performed over the Internet, and this is only a small part of the entire picture. Indeed, to differentiate itself from the competition in what is essentially a commodity business, Cisco acquires companies that have leading technology and integrates these companies rapidly with its systems. It also sells network solutions, not just components, to its customers. This requires coordination of hardware, software, and service components in many sales. The ability to provide these services and integrate comes from Cisco's single-enterprise system. This system provides the backbone for all activities in the company and not only connects customers and employees but also chip manufacturers, component distributors, contract manufacturers, logistics companies, and systems integrators. These participants can perform like one company because they all rely on the same Web-based data sources. All of Cisco's suppliers see the same demand and do not rely on their own forecasts based on information flowing from multiple points in the supply chain. Cisco also built a dynamic replenishment system to help reduce supplier inventory. Cisco's average turns in 1999 were 10, compared with an average of 4 for competitors. Inventory turns for commodity items are even more impressive: they reach 25–35 turns a year.

The previous examples raise an important question: Why is it that, in some cases, these new business models fail, while, in other cases, they are incredibly successful? If Amazon, Dell, and Cisco can use the Internet to develop such effective business models, what inhibits other firms from adopting similar techniques?

To answer this question, we require a better understanding of Internet-based supply chain strategies.

6.5.1 What Is E-Business?

To better understand the impact of the Internet on supply chains, we start by introducing our definition of e-business and e-commerce.

E-business is a collection of business models and processes motivated by Internet technology and focusing on improvement of extended enterprise performance.

E-commerce is the ability to perform major commerce transactions electronically.

These definitions lead to several observations. First, e-commerce is only part of e-business. Second, Internet technology is the force behind the business change. Finally, the focus in e-business is on the extended enterprise, that is, intra-organizational, business-to-consumer (B2C), and business-to-business (B2B) transactions. B2C refers to businesses that are "direct to customer," especially retail activities over the Internet, and includes products, insurance, banking, and so forth. B2B refers to business conducted over the Internet predominantly between businesses. This includes both electronic sourcing (the so-called eSourcing) and reverse auction as well as collaboration with suppliers and vendors to achieve common goals.

Many companies have recognized that the Internet can have a huge impact on supply chain performance. Indeed, these companies have observed that the Internet can help them move away from the traditional push strategies employed by most supply chains. Initially, the move was toward a pull strategy, but, eventually, many companies ended up with a push–pull supply chain.

6.5.2 The Grocery Industry

Consider the grocery industry. A typical supermarket employs a push-based strategy where inventory at the warehouses and stores is based on a forecast. When Peapod was founded 17 years ago, the idea was to establish a pure pull strategy with no inventory and no facilities. When a customer ordered groceries, Peapod would pick the products at a nearby supermarket. This strategy had significant service problems since stockout rates were very high (about 8 to 10 percent). In 1999, Peapod changed its business model to a push–pull strategy by setting up a number of warehouses; stockout rates are now less than 2 percent. Observe that, in this case, the push part is the portion of the Peapod supply chain prior to satisfying customer demand and the pull part starts from a customer order. Also note that since a Peapod warehouse covers a large geographical area, clearly larger than the one covered by an individual supermarket, demand is aggregated over many customers and locations, resulting in better forecasts and inventory reduction.

Of course, in the online grocery industry, there are other challenges, including reducing transportation costs and responding in a very short period of time, that is, typically within 12 hours in a tight delivery window. Unfortunately, no current online grocers have the density of customers that will allow them to control transportation costs, and therefore compete successfully with traditional supermarkets. This is the reason why most online grocers have failed. Indeed, the framework developed in the previous section suggests that this industry is characterized by a low level of demand uncertainty for many products and high economies of scale in transportation cost, implying that a push-based strategy is more appropriate.

6.5.3 The Book Industry

The book industry is another excellent example of the evolution of supply chain strategies from push to pull and then to push–pull. Until recently, Barnes and Noble had a typical push supply chain. When Amazon.com was established about 10 years ago, their supply chain was a pure pull system with no warehouses and no stock. Indeed, at that time, Ingram Book Group supplied most of Amazon's customer demand.

Ingram Book can aggregate across many customers and suppliers and take advantage of economies of scale. Thus, the pull model employed by Amazon.com was an appropriate strategy when Amazon.com was building its brand name. As volume and demand increased, two issues became clear. First, Amazon.com's service level was affected by Ingram Book's distribution capacity, which was shared by many booksellers. Indeed, during periods of peak holiday demand, Amazon.com could not meet its service level goals. Second, using Ingram Book in the first few years allowed Amazon.com to avoid inventory costs but significantly reduced profit margins. As demand increased, it became evident that Ingram Book did not provide any advantage for many of the book categories, because Amazon.com's ability to aggregate across large geographical areas allowed the company to reduce uncertainties and hence inventory costs by itself, without using a distributor.

As Amazon.com discovered these issues, the company changed its philosophy, and now Amazon.com has several warehouses around the country where most of the titles are stocked. Thus, inventory at the warehouses is managed based on a push strategy, while demand is satisfied based on individual requests, a pull strategy. In fact, Amazon strategy is a bit more sophisticated; slow-moving, low-volume books and CDs are not stocked at all at Amazon distribution centers; Amazon orders those when demand arrives. Thus, Amazon distinguishes between fast-moving, high-volume and slow-moving, low-volume books. In the latter case, the company is using a pull-based strategy, while in the former, it uses a push–pull strategy (why?).

6.5.4 The Retail Industry

The retail industry was, in general, late to respond to competition from virtual stores and to recognize the opportunities provided by the Internet. Recently, however, the landscape has changed, as many so-called brick-and-mortar companies are adding an Internet shopping component to their offering. Enter click-and-mortar giants Wal-Mart, Kmart, Target, and Barnes and Noble, among others. These retailers recognize the advantage they have over pure Internet companies. Indeed, they already have the distribution and warehousing infrastructure in place. Thus, they have established virtual retail stores, serviced by their existing warehousing and distribution structures.

As a result of going online, click-and-mortar firms have changed their approach to stocking inventory. High-volume, fast-moving products, whose demand can be accurately matched with supply based on long-term forecasts, are stocked in stores, while low-volume, slow-moving products are stocked centrally for online purchasing. The low-volume products have highly uncertain demand levels, and thus require high levels of safety stock. Centralized stocking reduces uncertainties by aggregating demand across geographical locations, and thus reduces inventory levels. The analysis implies that these retailers use a push strategy for high-volume, fast-moving products and a push–pull strategy for low-volume, slow-moving products.

Of course, the move from brick-and-mortar to click-and-mortar is not an easy one, and may require skills that the brick-and-mortar companies don't have.

EXAMPLE 6-12

Wal-Mart has always prided itself on its distribution operations. Thus, it was a huge surprise when the company announced that it planned to hire an outside firm to handle order fulfillment and warehousing for its online store, Wal-Mart.com, which the retailer launched in the fall of 1999. Fingerhut Business Services filled orders behind the scenes at Wal-Mart's cyberstore. Indeed, with a background in handling individual orders, Fingerhut has emerged as a major provider of third-party distribution services to other retailers and e-tailers interested in home delivery. Fingerhut provided Internet order fulfillment, warehousing, shipment, payment processing, customer service, and merchandise returns for Wal-Mart.com when the service was launched.

6.5.5 Impact on Transportation and Fulfillment

This review of the evolution of supply chain strategies in various industries suggests the following insight: The Internet and the associated new supply chain paradigms introduce a shift in fulfillment strategies: from cases and bulk shipments to single items and smaller-size shipments, and from shipping to a small number of stores to serving highly geographically dispersed customers. This shift also has increased the importance and the complexity of reverse logistics.

Table 6-3 summarizes the impact of the Internet on fulfillment strategies. Specifically, the new developments in supply chain strategies are very good news for the parcel and LTL industries. Both pull and push–pull systems rely heavily on individual (e.g., parcel) shipments rather than bulk shipments. This is especially true in the business-to-consumer area, where a new term has been coined: e-fulfillment. Another impact of e-fulfillment on the transportation industry is the significant increase in reverse logistics. Indeed, in the business-to-consumer arena, e-fulfillment typically means that the supplier needs to handle many returns, each of which consists of a small shipment. This is true, since online retailers need to build customer trust through generous return terms. Parcel shipping is already set up to handle these returns, a major issue in B2C and, in many cases, in B2B commerce. This is a challenge for the LTL industry, which traditionally has not been very involved in door-to-door services.

E-fulfillment logistics requires short lead time, the ability to serve globally dispersed customers, and the ability to reverse the flow easily from B2C to C2B. Only parcel shipping can do all that. Indeed, one important advantage of the parcel industry is the existence of an excellent information infrastructure that enables real-time tracking. Thus, the future looks promising for the parcel shipping industry and, in particular, for those carriers and consolidators who work to modify their own systems in order to integrate it with their customers' supply chains.

TABLE 6-3

TRADITIONAL FULFILLMENT VERSUS E-FULFILLMENT

	Traditional fulfillment	E-fulfillment
Supply chain strategy	Push	Push–pull
Shipment	Bulk	Parcel
Reverse logistics	Small part of the business	Important and highly complex
Delivery destination	Small number of stores	Large number of geographically dispersed customers
Lead times	Relatively long	Relatively short

SUMMARY

In recent years, many companies have improved performance, reducing cost, increasing service levels, reducing the bullwhip effect, and improving responsiveness to changes in the marketplace, by integrating the supply chain. In many cases, this was facilitated by the implementation of push–pull strategies and by a focus on demand-driven strategies. In particular, the Internet has created the opportunity to revolutionize supply chain strategies. Indeed, the success of giants such as Dell Inc. and Cisco and the significant market capitalization of young companies such as Amazon.com can be attributed to sophisticated Internet-based supply chain strategies.

At the same time, the collapse of many Internet companies sends an alarming message that e-business presents not only opportunities but also great challenges. Key to these challenges is the ability to identify the appropriate supply chain strategy for a particular company and individual products. Indeed, the premise on which many of the Internet companies were built—that, in the new economy, there is no need for either physical infrastructure or inventory—has, in many cases, been disastrous. The new supply chain paradigm, push–pull strategy, advocates holding inventory, although it pushes the inventory upstream in the supply chain.

DISCUSSION QUESTIONS

1. Discuss the advantages of a push-based supply chain. What about a pull-based supply chain?
2. What is an example of a product with a primarily push-based supply chain? A product with a primarily pull-based supply chain?
3. What are the advantages of moving the push–pull boundary earlier in a supply chain? What about later?
4. Amazon.com, Peapod, Dell, and many furniture manufacturers use push–pull supply chain strategies. Describe how each of these companies takes advantage of the risk-pooling concept.
5. Explain Amazon's strategy for slow-moving, low-volume products and fast-moving, high-volume items.
6. Discuss some additional examples of each of the four categories in Figure 6-9.
7. Is it possible for the appropriate supply chain (push, pull, or push–pull) to change during a product's life cycle? If not, explain why? If it is possible, what are some specific examples of products for which the appropriate supply chain changed?
8. Is e-fulfillment a new concept? What is the difference between online and catalog selling? Consider, for instance, Land's End, a company that has both channels.
9. Explain how demand for a product like televisions can be shaped? How does this compare to the ways in which demand for a product like canned soup can be shaped?
10. Other than the examples listed in Section 6.5, what are some more examples of failed Internet supply chain strategies? Successful Internet supply chain strategies?
11. Answer the questions at the end of the case study "Dell Inc.: Improving the Flexibility of the Desktop PC Supply Chain."

CASE: The Great Inventory Correction

John Chambers likened it to a 100-year flood, although the problem was dearth, not plenitude. The swift evaporation of technology demand that began in the latter part of 2000 was indeed exceptional, as the CEO of Cisco Systems famously suggested. Chipmakers and PC companies suddenly found themselves with a glut of inventory and capacity. Networking and telecom equipment makers were particularly hard hit; Cisco, more irrationally exuberant than most, was forced to write off a staggering $2.25 billion worth of gear. Throughout the first half of 2001, a procession of high-tech companies including such bellwethers as Nortel Networks, Lucent Technologies, Corning, and JDS Uniphase announced huge write-downs of unsalable inventory.

Today, high-tech companies are still loaded with rapidly depreciating goods. At one end of the food chain, the cyclical semiconductor industry is suffering through its deepest trough in demand since 1998, the year of the Asian crisis. In the middle, electronics contract manufacturers and their suppliers, customers, and distributors are trying to figure out who owns which surplus components. At the other end of the chain, PC makers are waging price wars, and the gray market in networking equipment is thriving. Flood of the century or not, tech companies are taking steps to limit their exposure to the next traumatic event. Some are revising their inventory models; others are implementing supply chain software and setting up Web supplier hubs. Everyone wants tighter collaboration with suppliers and timelier information from customers. Tech companies are trying, in short, to make their supply chains shorter, transparent, and as flexible as possible.

NEW LOGIC

Check out the recent earnings releases of semiconductor makers (not the pro forma kind) and you'll find a litany of inventory write-downs: Agere Systems, $270 million; Micron Technology, $260 million; Vitesse Semiconductor, $50.6 million; Alliance Semiconductor, $50 million; Xilinx, $32 million. Worldwide, chip sales in June were down 30.7 percent from a year ago, according to the Semiconductor Industry Association, and analysts predict a decline in 2001 revenues of more than 20 percent—the steepest ever.

"I've been in the chip industry for 20 years," says Nathan Sarkisian, "and I've never seen anything like it." Sarkisian is senior vice president and CFO of Altera Corp., a San Jose, California–based chipmaker with 2000 revenues of $1.4 billion. "We grew roughly 65 percent last year with less than four months' supply of inventory throughout most of the year," he recalls. "That's pretty good when you think about semiconductor product cycles."

But in the fatal fourth quarter, units shipped to distributors fell 25 percent short of expectations. The slide continued into 2001, thanks to declining demand from Altera's major customers, communications companies. For Q2 2001, revenues were down 25 percent sequentially and 37 percent from Q2 2000. Altera was eventually forced to write down a whopping $115 million worth of inventory.

Going forward, Altera wants to ensure that future market dips won't savage the bottom line, and to that end it's revising its inventory model, for starters.

Altera designs programmable logic devices (PLDs). It's a "fabless" chipmaker, outsourcing manufacturing to giant foundry Taiwan Semiconductor Manufacturing Corp. Previously, it would build its mainstream PLDs through to finished goods, stockpiling them in Asian facilities in anticipation of customer demand. "We own the inventory as soon as it leaves the fab," notes Sarkisian. Also, it would essentially build new products on spec, producing quantities well beyond what the customer needed for prototyping. The virtues of this model are highlighted in Altera's annual report: "We, our distributors, and subcontract manufacturers—not our customers—hold stocks of inventory, thereby enhancing the cost advantage of PLDs for our customers."

Now, Altera will continue to build its mainstream products to stock, but only in die banks (stores of chips before packaging and testing). "By building die, we have taken out the biggest portion of the manufacturing lead time, but the inventory is in its most flexible form, with a minimum of value added," says Sarkisian. Only when orders are confirmed will Altera's subcontractors package, test, and ship the PLDs.

The lead time for these products will be measured in weeks. For Altera's mature products, "we will be strictly build-to-order," says Sarkisian, and the lead time for those will be measured in months. Finally, new products will no longer be built on spec; a customer order will be required.

VISIBLE IMPROVEMENTS

Chipmakers are at the mercy of the laws of physics. It takes anywhere from three to seven weeks to turn a raw silicon disk into a wafer with

Source: Edward Teach, *CFO Magazine,* September 1, 2001.

hundreds of chips, depending on the complexity of the chip and how much a customer is willing to pay, says Jim Kupec, president of United Microelectronics Corp. USA, a division of Taiwan-based foundry UMC. Additional time is required to separate, package, and test the chips. And in the real world, "things get spoiled in the fab," says Arnold Maltz, associate professor of supply chain management at Arizona State University College of Business. "Every now and then, somebody brings the wrong batch. Capacity isn't always available. Then you have the mismatch of supply and demand." In a 1999 study of major U.S. chipmakers, Maltz and his fellow researchers found that the average cycle time for semiconductors, from the fab to the customer, was 117 days—plenty of time for demand to change direction.

To reduce its exposure, a chip company can postpone adding value to die bank inventory. It also can seek better information from its customers, as Altera is now doing. "We're asking customers to give us more visibility in their inventories and build plans," says Sarkisian. That may seem like an obvious solution, but it isn't always available, says Maltz, because "there's some concern on the customer side that you're giving away strategic information." Nevertheless, Altera recently took two big steps toward greater visibility, announcing joint ventures with Nortel and Motorola to collaborate on product development.

Chipmakers also can shrink cycle times around wafer fabrication using supply chain management (SCM) software. Altera's i2 Technologies system, which is linked to its fabs, suppliers, and distributors, has cut weekly planning cycle time from 10 days to 1 day and reduced the long-term planning cycle time from four weeks to one week. About 85 percent of production is automatically scheduled by the system. "i2 runs our foundries," says Tom Murchie, vice president of operations. "It starts wafers by technology process, by fab, and by the strategic inventory targets we've chosen."

UMC's customers can forecast collaboratively with the foundry via its MyUMC Web portal, using i2 augmented by an available-to-promise order system. "What [MyUMC] does is automatically take a request for a customer's order, then almost instantaneously find the best manufacturing slot," explains Kupec.

FREAK SHOW

Other kinds of tech companies are using SCM planning tools, from such vendors as i2, Manugistics Group, and SAP. Cisco, for instance, uses Manugistics to run its Web supplier hub. At server maker Sun Microsystems, a combination of i2 and Rapt Inc. software enables "short, predictable lead times with the lowest possible costs," says Helen Yang, vice president of supply management.

But if SCM software is so great, why didn't it prevent the inventory glut? One reason is that not everyone uses it: Only about 20 percent of companies with more than $500 million in annual revenues have installed SCM tools, according to AMR Research.

A more compelling reason, however, is that software can't eliminate the problem of garbage in, garbage out. Supply chain planning tools rely on algorithms to crunch a mix of historical data, production numbers, and "guesswork," says Kevin O'Marah, service director for supply chain strategies at AMR. "How good is your guess? You're speculating on trends going forward."

This is feasible in mature industries, says O'Marah, but high tech, with its volatile swings in demand, is a very different story. In semiconductors, long cycle times mean that companies are always making a bet on an uncertain future. And at Cisco, "growth changed from 40 percent to negative 10 percent. That's a real freak show!" exclaims O'Marah. "Can you imagine a forecasting system even encompassing this scenario?"

"We recognize that forecasts will not be accurate," says Yang. "The game is how fast we can respond to changes."

O'Marah blames habit, in part, for the inventory overhang. Component shortages have plagued electronics manufacturing for the past decade, he points out, "and the habit of market leaders is to lock up allocations available for components. It's a reasonable way to think."

"When a new technology comes along—a faster chip, a new bus—there are constraints in supply," says Karen Peterson, research director at Gartner. "A lot of the [original equipment manufacturers] or contract manufacturers will lie about what they need. If I'm an OEM, I may say I need 200 percent more than I think I need. It's going to put my priority higher [with the supplier]."

Double ordering of chips, capacitors, and resistors from manufacturers and distributors also contributed to the glut, adds Pamela Gordon, president of Technology Forecasters, an Alameda, California– based consulting firm for the electronics manufacturing services (EMS) industries. Those parts were in particularly short supply in 2000, she says. As for other kinds of high-tech equipment, such as networking and telecom gear, Gordon faults manufacturers for not doing sufficient due diligence on shaky customers, dot-com or otherwise.

DON'T KNOW MUCH ABOUT HISTORY

"The telecom guys thought, 'We can do no wrong,'" says Dan Pleshko, vice president of global procurement and strategic supply-chain management at Flextronics International Corp. "They forgot to look at history, at business cycles. The PC guys had been through a couple of cycles. They had been through pain."

Flextronics, one of the world's largest EMS companies, with $12 billion in revenues, had an unusually good vantage point of the inventory glut. The Singapore-based company makes everything from printed circuit boards to cell phones for a variety of high-tech clients, including Cisco, Lucent, Nortel, and Ericsson. In 2000, the company's inventories ballooned from $470 million at the beginning of the year to $1.7 billion at year's end.

As orders poured in, Flextronics and other EMS companies could see the magnitude of the aggregated supply they were producing. Couldn't they have warned their clients? "In general, I don't think any of [the EMS companies] did that before," says Pleshko. "I think that will happen going forward."

Pleshko says Flextronics wants to obtain a better understanding with customers of consumer demand and product life cycles. Also, "we're moving very aggressively to a supplier-managed inventory environment," he says. The company wants to establish material hubs, where suppliers' facilities are located close to Flextronics's factories. "Compaq, Dell, and IBM have done this already," says Pleshko. "The EMS guys are just coming up to speed."

Meanwhile, there have been some disputes over the ownership of inventory in the EMS world. Some distributors have complained, for example, that they were being stuck with surplus parts. But that's a reversal of the situation in 2000, when "everyone was looking under every rock to find parts," says Pleshko. "When times were good, distributors were making a lot of money. They forgot."

THE CRYSTAL BALL

Times are bad, and tech companies are still working down inventories. They await an upturn of the business cycle, a new thing that will drive computer sales—Microsoft's Windows XP operating system, for instance, or an unforeseen killer app—and the start in 2002 of an especially robust three-year PC replacement cycle (companies stocked up because of the year 2000 problem).

Meanwhile, two computer companies are better positioned than most to weather the downturn, thanks to superior supply chain management. One is Dell Computer. With its build-to-order business model, Dell is the lowest-cost PC maker; it never has more than a few days' inventory on hand.

The other company is IBM. True, a third of Big Blue's revenues come from annuity-like businesses such as services and software. And even with its diversified risk, IBM isn't immune to the downturn. Sales were relatively flat in the second quarter ($21.6 billion), and IBM has warned that its chip sales will fall in the second half of the year. But IBM's inventories also have remained flat. Overall, they are at their lowest level since 1988, according to Steve Ward, general manager for IBM's Global Industrial Sector. That may owe something to old-fashioned vertical integration. Still, AMR's O'Marah and others regard IBM's supply chain management as among the best in the business.

Lean inventories are "absolutely critical," says Ward. "In parts of our business, the value of components drops about 1.5 percent per month." IBM does build some items to order, but mostly it builds fast, on a pull or just-in-time basis. "Our suppliers have visibility to how much inventory we have," says Ward.

An SAP system provides crucial automation, but other practices also promote smaller inventories. For example, IBM has reduced the number of different parts by emphasizing commonality across platforms and products. Thus, for example, the flat screens used on ThinkPads and the flat-panel monitors sold for PCs are the same.

The number of suppliers is kept small, too. Purchasing is structured by commodities, with a market expert assigned full-time to each commodity. IBM buys all of its production parts electronically, via the Internet and EDI. "That means we can have much faster transactions, moving to much faster collaboration with suppliers," says Ward.

How far into the future does IBM peer? Ward says the company maintains a "very detailed" forecast for the next 90 days out, updated weekly and rolled out through all suppliers; a "fairly detailed" forecast for 90 days to a year; and a "strategic" forecast for longer periods. "I can't tell you right now what kind of hard file [disk] we're going to put in our ThinkPads two years from now," says Ward, "but I know how many we'll need."

The principal sources of inputs for those predictions are, of course, IBM's salespeople. They may not have quite the sobriety of their white-shirt-and-black-tie forebears, but they know their customers' businesses inside out, boasts Ward. Managers meet frequently to discuss and anticipate demand ("is this a conceptual need, or has it been confirmed by the customer?").

A rationally exuberant sales force—these days, that's about as close to a crystal ball as a high-tech company can get.

CASE DISCUSSION QUESTIONS

1. How has Altera modified its strategy? Why?
2. Do you think Altera's new strategy will be successful? What are some advantages and disadvantages of the new strategy?
3. How do you anticipate Altera's customers will react to this new strategy? What are advantages and disadvantages for Altera's customers?
4. What information does Flextronics have that its clients do not? Why? How can Flextronics leverage this information?
5. How does IBM manage its suppliers in order to make its pull strategy more effective?

In 1996 and 1997 Amazon grew quickly. To support the increased traffic and sales while continuing to meet outstanding service levels, the company built up its infrastructure and systems.[vii]

- Distribution center capacity grew from 50,000 to 285,000 square feet, including a 70% expansion of the Seattle distribution center (DC), and the launch of a second DC in Delaware in November 1997. The new DC positioned Amazon closer to its East Coast customers and publishers, which enabled the company to decrease order fulfillment lead times and lessen its dependence on its main supplier Ingram.[viii] "Now, with distribution centers on both coasts, we can dramatically reduce order-to-mailbox time for Amazon.com customers everywhere," Bezos noted at that time.[ix]
- Amazon increased the number of titles held in its DCs to over 200,000 at the end of 1997 and reduced promised delivery times on those titles.[x]
- In parallel, major efforts were made in software development to support back-office operations. According to Jeff Bezos, "80% of the company's investment in software development since its founding in 1995 has not gone into its famously user-friendly screens, but to back-office logistics."[xi]

In 1998, Amazon expanded its product lines, launching its Music store in June 1998 and Video and DVD stores in November 1998. For these new categories, Amazon relied on the same procurement model, establishing relationships with music, video, and DVD wholesalers. Nonetheless, with the additional product lines, the inventory turns dropped from 56 in 1997 to 24.8 in 1998 (see Table 7-1).

1999: Building Additional Fulfillment Infrastructure

By late 1998, the company was beginning to face tougher competition from players like Buy.com (which aggressively undercut prices), Barnesand Noble.com, and CDNow, all of which offered similar features as Amazon. To remain the "e-tailing" leader, Amazon decided to pursue a "Get Big Fast" strategy intended to increase its revenue per customer. Amazon started adding new product lines and features at a fast pace (Table 7-2 provides a timeline of key developments). To support its transformation and its projected triple-digit growth, Amazon adapted its supply chain and distribution network.

Amazon first had to decide how many DCs it should have and where to locate them. Amazon executives turned to outside experts and used i2 Technologies' Supply Chain Strategist software package.[xii] This software identified regions to consider for its distribution facilities based on factors such as supplier and customer locations, inbound and outbound freight rates, warehousing expenses, labor, and other cost factors. After selecting the major regions, Amazon's management narrowed its search based on additional factors such as tax rates, employment levels and the availability of suitable distribution facilities to lease.[xiii]

Amazon's first pick was a DC near Reno, Nevada, intended to serve the southern California market with two- to three-day lead-times. It leased a 322,560-square-foot highly mechanized facility in Fernley, Nevada, formerly used by Stanley Tools.[xiv] (See Figure 7-1 for a map of the distribution centers' locations.)

Amazon next leased a DC in Coffeyville, Kansas, intended to serve customers in the Chicago, St. Louis, Dallas, and Minneapolis areas. The company expanded the existing facility, previously used by Golden Books, from 460,000 square feet to 750,000 square feet.[xv]

Three other facilities were added in 1999 to reduce shipping times to key markets in the Midwest and the Southeast: a 770,000-square-foot facility located in Campbellsville, Kentucky, previously used by Fruit of the Loom; a 600,000-square-foot DC in Lexington, Kentucky, previously used by W. T. Young Storage Co.; and an 800,000-square-foot DC located in McDonough, Georgia.[xvi]

TABLE 7-2

AMAZON'S TIMELINE OF KEY DEVELOPMENTS.

Dates	Amazon.com	Amazon.co.uk	Amazon.de	Amazon.fr
July 1995	Launch of Books category			
June 1998	Launch of Music category			
Oct. 1998		Launch of Books category	Launch of Books category	
Nov. 1998	Launch of Video category			
Feb. 1999	46% stake in Drugstore.com offering 15,000 healthcare products			
Mar. 1999	Launch of Auctions 50% stake in internet pet company in Pets.com			
July 1999	Launch of Electronics and Toys 49% stake in internet sports company Gear.com			
Oct. 1999	Launch of zshops (third-party sellers selling their products on Amazon.com)	Launch of Music category	Launch of Music category	
Nov. 1999	Launch of Software and Video Games categories Launch of Home Improvement, Tools, and Hardware categories Acquisition of tools and equipment catalog company Tool Crib of the North	Launch of Auctions Launch of zshops	Launch of Auctions Launch of zshops	
Jan. 2000	Creation of a drugstore.com shopping "tab" at Amazon.com			
Mar. 2000		Launch of Video category	Launch of Video category	
Apr. 2000	Launch of Lawn and Patio categories Launch of Health and Beauty categories			
May 2000	Launch of Kitchen category			
July 2000		Launch of Software and Video Games categories	Launch of Software and Video Games categories	
August 2000	Amazon.com partners with ToysRUs. Under the agreements, ToysRUs identifies, buys and manages inventory, while Amazon handles site development, order fulfillment and customer service			Launch of Books, Music, and Video Categories
Sept. 2000	Launch of Computer category			

TABLE 7-2 CONTINUED.

Dates	Amazon.com	Amazon.co.uk	Amazon.de	Amazon.fr
Nov. 2000	Launch of Cell phones and Services category Launch of Used products Launch of e-books store (electronic books customers can download) Launch of Amazon.jp in Japan			
April 2001	Amazon.com launched Borders.com as a co-branded Web site powered by Amazon.com			
May 2001		Launch of Electronics category	Launch of Electronics category	Launch of Software and Video Games categories
Aug. 2001	Agreement with electronics retailer Circuit City. In-store pick up available to Amazon customers	Strategic alliance made with UK specialist bookseller Waterstone. Waterstone online books selling relunched, powered by Amazon e-commerce platform Launch of Toys and Kids store		
Sept. 2001	Amazon.com partners with Target to open a Target store at Amazon.com Launch of Travel store	Launch of Travel store		
Oct. 2001	Launch of Magazine subscriptions store			
Mar. 2002		Launch of Marketplace (used products)	Launch of Marketplace (used products)	
April 2002	Agreement with Borders Inc to provide Amazon customers the option of picking up Books, CDs and DVDs in Borders stores nationwide			
June 2002	Launch of Amazon. ca in Canada			
Sept. 2002	Launch of Office products through Office Depot alliance			
Nov. 2002	Launch of Apparel category		Launch of Magazine subscriptions store	
Dec. 2002	Amazon announced the relaunch of Cdnow Web site on Amazon's e-commerce platform.			
April 2003		Launch of Kitchen and Home store	Launch of Kitchen and Home store	

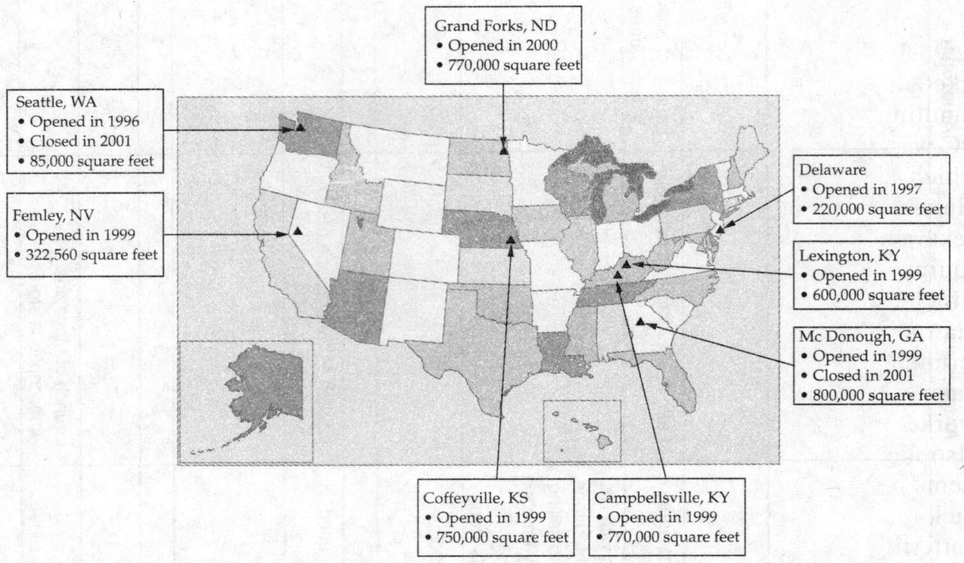

FIGURE 7-1 Map of Amazon's distribution centers location in the US at the end of 2001.
Source: Case writer adapted.

The addition of 3.2 million square feet of distribution capability cost Amazon $320 million, but increased its capacity to pack, wrap, and ship to nearly a million boxes a day. According to Jeff Bezos, "This has been the fastest expansion of distribution capacity in peacetime history."[xvii]

Next, Amazon had to decide which product types each of the new DCs should carry. By the end of 1999, Amazon offered its customers a range of merchandise that had very different characteristics. For example, some items (such as barbeque grills) were quite large whereas others (such as CDs) were quite small; some items had mainly regional demand whereas others had broadly distributed, nation-wide demand; and some had strong seasonal demand patterns, whereas others had more uniform demand patterns over the year. Toys were a particularly challenging category: new toys had to be ordered from suppliers as early as eight months before their release dates, demand for many toys was highly unpredictable, and seasonality was extreme: approximately 65% of toys were sold in the Christmas season compared to 30% of books. However, the executives decided that rather than create specialized distribution facilities for different product categories, for the most part, each DC would handle the full array of items. Tom Taylor noted, "The decision that distribution centers should carry a mix of products was based on transportation cost, time to deliver to consumers, and the cost of dealing with multi-item orders."[xviii] (About 35 percent of Amazon orders included multiple items,[xix] for example, a multi-category order might include a book, a CD and a toy.) Taylor continued, "All distribution centers carry all type of product categories, apart from the Delaware distribution center, which could not handle large sized products like toys. And, since Lexington and Campbellsville are not far from each other, we decided to put the smaller sized items in Campbellsville and the larger ones in Lexington. This made sense, since larger sized items are never shipped with smaller sized items. For example, a barbecue grill and a CD will always be sent to the customer in two separate shipments."

Another decision regarded the equipment in new DCs. Amazon's operations team decided to take advantage of some of the latest materials-handling technologies for its warehouses. Each DC was equipped with a "pick-to-light" system, which employed lights that were sequentially illuminated to show workers which items to pick next, and how many. In addition, the DCs were equipped with radio-frequency technology, which directed workers to warehouse locations via radio signals sent to the worker's handheld terminal. Voice technology, which allowed computers to "verbally" communicate instructions to workers, was tested in a trial phase. The DCs also maintained "pick profiles" for fast-selling items based on item size, velocity and location pick rates, pick zones, and picking and storage patterns. The pick profiles were used to build pick lists for employees that specified optimal combinations of customer orders for picking and shipping.[xx] Each pick list contained approximately 100 items, each identifiable through its title, Amazon Standard Identification Number (ASIN), and storage-slot location. All items contained on the same pick list were stored and located in the same zone in the DC; zone sizes varied based on the DC's volume.

The system created two types of pick lists: one type containing only items for single-item orders and the other type containing only items for multi-item orders. Single-item orders were relatively simple to process: each item on the pick list was picked in the specified sequence and placed in a bin with its associated paperwork; then the full bin was sent directly to packaging, where each item was packaged individually. Multi-item orders required an additional step: after the items in the orders were picked and placed in a bin (the "pre-sortation" step), the items in the same customer order were grouped (the "sortation" step). To group the items into orders, sorters placed the items into sortation slots temporarily assigned to the customer orders on the pick list; then the items in each slot were withdrawn from the slot and packaged together.

Finally, to maintain high levels of quality and productivity in its distribution centers, Amazon developed key metrics to measure worker performance, including number of items picked per hour, free replacement rate,[2] inventory accuracy, number of hours from order confirmation to shipment, and cost per unit shipped. Performance information was routinely shared with individual workers.

Just before the Christmas 1999 season, the new distribution center network was up and running. Using the new network as well as the help of all employees from nonessential activities at that period like Marketing, Editorial, and Catalogue, Amazon delivered more than 99 percent of its orders in time for Christmas 1999. In the fourth quarter alone of 1999, Amazon shipped about 20 million items and acquired more than 2.5 million first-time customers.[xxi]

The company's mantra "deliver at any cost" allowed Amazon to achieve its growth but at great expense: it lost $323 million on $676 million in revenues in the fourth quarter.

2000–2002: Optimizing the Customer Fulfillment Network

In early 2000, Wall Street began to put profit pressure on all dotcoms, including Amazon. Amazon's stock price, which had reached a record high of $106.69 in December 1999, began to fell dramatically (Figure 7-2 details Amazon's stock price history). In this context, Jeff Bezos acknowledged the need for profitability and "a stronger focus on operational excellence, which means treating customers right but at lower cost."[xxii]

In September 1999, Jeff Wilke was hired to the position of Vice President of Operations at

[2] Free replacement rate refers to the number of shipments which Amazon re-sent free of charge because a previous shipment either did not arrive or contained the wrong items, divided by the total number of shipments.

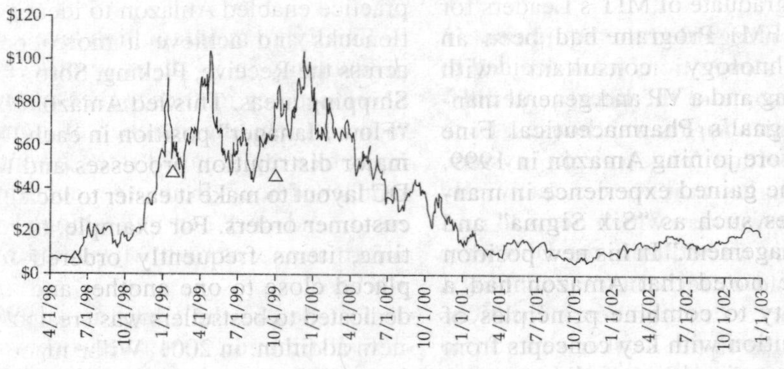

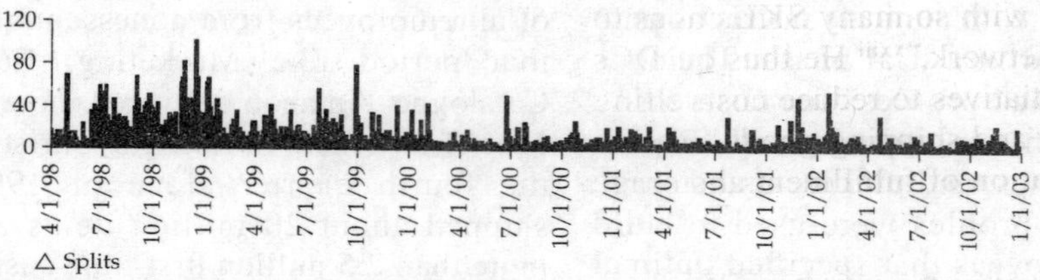

FIGURE 7-2 Amazon's daily stock price history and volume (millions of shares) from March 1998 to December 2002.
Source: Case writer adapted from Datastream International.

Quarter	Gross margin	Fulfillment cost	Shipping cost
Q100	22.3%	17.3%	
Q200	23.5%	15.1%	
Q300	26.2%	15.1%	
Q400	23.1%	13.5%	
Q101	26.1%	14.1%	
Q201	26.9%	12.8%	
Q301	25.4%	12.8%	
Q401	24.6%	9.8%	15.2%
Q102	26.3%	10.6%	
Q202	27.1%	10.7%	
Q302	25.4%	10.6%	
Q402	23.5%	8.9%	12.5%

Notes:

Gross Margin = Net sales − Cost of sales;

Cost of sales = Cost of merchandise + Inbound and outbound shipping cost + Cost to package product.

Fulfillment costs do not include shipping cost, which are included in the cost of sales

FIGURE 7-3 Evolution of fulfillment and shipping costs as a percentage of revenue.
Source: Case writer adapted.

Amazon. Wilke, a graduate of MIT's Leaders for Manufacturing (LFM) Program had been an Information Technology consultant with Andersen Consulting and a VP and general manager of Allied Signal's Pharmaceutical Fine Chemicals unit before joining Amazon in 1999. At Allied Signal, he gained experience in management techniques such as "Six Sigma" and "Total Quality Management." In his new position at Amazon, Wilke noted that Amazon had a "unique opportunity to combine principles of world-class distribution with key concepts from world-class manufacturing because they 'assemble' so many orders with so many SKUs as part of such a complex network."[xxiii] He thus quickly launched several initiatives to reduce costs associated with stocking and shipping goods (Figure 7-3 reports the evolution of fulfillment and shipping costs).

Streamlining US Distribution Centers' Processes

Wilke's first achievement was to teach the US DC's staff to use Six Sigma DMAIC (Define, Measure, Analyze, Improve, and Control) reviews as a tool to reduce variation and defects. In 2001, this approach was used to improve inventory-record accuracy. For example, a DMAIC review enabled Wilke to discover weaknesses in the way temporary employees' work was supervised. In the past, when temps were brought into Amazon's fulfillment centers to stock items, there was no extra layer of verification to make sure they were putting things in the right place. The DMAIC review led to changes in the fulfillment auditing process to cut temps' mistakes. This was just one in a series of improvements that helped reduce inventory-record accuracy errors by 50 percent in a year's time.[xxiv]

Second, Wilke encouraged DC staff to simulate holiday season conditions. For example, during non-holiday periods a DC might close 15 out of the 20 doors available for supplier truck deliveries or use only part of the available automated equipment to simulate high-pressure holiday conditions. The experience gained from such practice enabled Amazon to identify process bottlenecks and achieve a more continuous flow across the Receive, Picking, Sorting, Packing, and Shipping areas. This led Amazon to create a new "Flow Manager" position in each DC to redesign major distribution processes and to reconfigure DC layout to make it easier to locate, sort and ship customer orders. For example, to reduce picking time, items frequently ordered together were placed close to one another and a specific area dedicated to bestsellers was created.

In addition, in 2001, Wilke made arrangements for additional storage capacity to be added to the system during the holiday season. For example, he leased six off-site facilities totaling approximately 1.1 million square feet of space to support the storage and fulfillment functions of the US DCs.

Inventory Costs

Another focus of Wilke's team was inventory optimization in the fulfillment network. Having products at the right place, in the right amount and at the right time would decrease Amazon's inventory carrying costs significantly and prevent the company from making split shipments. A split shipment occurred when a customer order contained multiple items and Amazon was forced to send the order in two or more separate shipments because the items ordered were not all located in the same fulfillment center. Since Amazon typically paid for the additional shipment costs, it avoided split shipments whenever possible.

To improve inventory management, Wilke's team

- Refined the software used to forecast customer demand by improving its ability to anticipate seasonal and regional demands, thus reducing the risk of buying too much or too little merchandise. "We rewrote much of the software so that we could pinpoint demand in different regions," noted Cayce Roy, VP of US Fulfillment.[xxv]

- Established buying rules to better allocate volumes among wholesalers and direct vendors. Mike Siefert, General Manager for the books product line at that time, noted: "Wholesalers were now used as a safety net for out-of-stock items, for slow velocity titles and to respond to a quick surge in demand on a specific title."
- Integrated its suppliers' management systems with its own inventory, warehouse, and transportation systems. For instance, Amazon introduced the available-to-promise capabilities to its customers by tying Ingram's inventory to its customer interface. Available-to-promise functionality allowed Amazon to display on its Web site an accurate time frame for a customer's order to ship. Items in stock at an Amazon DC were listed as available in 24 hours. If an item was not in stock at an Amazon DC but was in stock at an Ingram DC, the Web site would typically display availability in 2–3 days, the time needed for Ingram to ship the order to Amazon and for Amazon to ship to the customer. Upon receipt of a customer order, if an ordered item was not in stock at one of its own DCs, Amazon would send it to Ingram electronically; Ingram would then ship the item usually the same or next day, to an Amazon distribution center. Piloted with Ingram, the available-to-promise functionality was later rolled out to other wholesalers and publishers that had the ability to give information on their inventory, at the item level, every hour.
- Implemented a set of "cascading" buying rules that determined which supplier offered the best price and delivery options for each item Amazon ordered. Amazon's systems would check product availability at suppliers: If the item was in stock at the supplier offering the best price, Amazon would order it. If not, the system would identify the supplier offering the next best price and check its product availability on that item.

In parallel, Wilke's team considered other options to avoid holding inventory. For each product category, Amazon used its specially tailored software to evaluate multiple fulfillment options, including the following:

- Having wholesalers "drop ship" orders, that is, ship an order directly to the customer without first shipping the product through an Amazon DC. For a drop shipment order, Amazon processed the order and customer payment, and placed an order with a wholesaler that would deliver the products directly to the customer's address. Amazon first developed drop-shipment in the books product line with Ingram for single-item orders in 2001. According to Mike Siefert, "Amazon is good at polling multiple products and shipping them to customers, so it made sense from a cost perspective for Amazon to select wholesalers to manage single book orders." Drop shipment enabled customers to get their orders within 2 to 3 days. Second, the program was expanded to other items, such as electronics or computers, which were costly or difficult for Amazon to store or handle. Third, Amazon started using drop shipping as a "capacity valve" to augment Amazon's own DC capacity, and integrated drop shippers in its software. The algorithm allocating volume among drop shippers and Amazon DCs was based on the price of the item (if the item price was under \$10, the 7% discount differential between buying direct vs. from wholesalers was too low to warrant drop shipping), DC variable cost and the cost of shipping to the customer, In the fourth quarter 2002, more than 10% of orders were drop shipped.[xxvi] In some cases, Amazon used a drop shipment even if the necessary inventory was in an Amazon DC—the company's objective was to find the most efficient, effective fulfillment method for each order.
- Partnering with other companies, with Amazon handling order fulfillment in exchange for fees and a percentage of sales, while the partner covered the cost of inventory. For example, in August 2000, Amazon partnered with ToysR'Us and created a co-branded online store selling toys and baby products. Amazon maintained the on-line "store" and handled the order

processing, order fulfillment, and customer service; ToysR'Us managed merchandising, buying, and owned the inventory, which was housed in Amazon's distribution facilities. This model allowed Amazon to transfer the financial risk of toys inventory obsolescence to its more toy-savvy partner.

Delivery Processes

To reduce shipping costs, Jeff Wilke's team developed a method called "postal injection" or "zone-skipping," in which Amazon arranged for full truckloads of orders to be driven from its DCs to major cities, thereby bypassing the postal service's sorting hubs.[xxvii] Postal injection eliminated processing steps and travel distances for the U.S. Postal Service and UPS, reducing Amazon's shipping costs for orders sent via postal injection by an estimated 5% to 17%.[xxviii]

Other Company Initiatives to Gain Profitability

On January 31, 2001, in an effort to reduce costs. Amazon.com announced it would reduce its headcount by 15%—eliminating 1,300 jobs—and consolidate its fulfillment and customer service operations by closing two distribution centers (in Georgia and Seattle) and a call center in Seattle.

Meanwhile, Amazon continued to seek ways to boost customer revenues. Amazon began to offer a 30% across-the-board discount on all books priced over $20 in July 2001, and extended the 30% discount to books priced over $15 in April 2002. It also announced free shipping on all orders over $99 in November 2001, extending free shipping to all orders over $49 in June 2002 and to all orders over $25 in August 2002.[xxix] In exchange for free delivery, Amazon's customers typically agreed to wait an extra three to five days to receive their orders.

In the fourth quarter of 2001, Amazon had managed to cut $22 million, or 17%, from expenses associated with filling orders and became profitable for the first time. In 2002, Amazon.com reached a record of $3.9 billion in sales, representing an increase of 26% over 2001. Operating income improved to $64 million, or 2% of net sales, compared to a 2001 operating loss of $412 million. Third-party seller transactions (new, used, and refurbished items sold on Amazon.com pages by individuals and businesses) grew to 21% of worldwide units in fourth quarter of 2002. Inventory turns increased to 17 in 2002, up from 14.6 in 2001.

A. Online Spending by Country, 2001 Actual

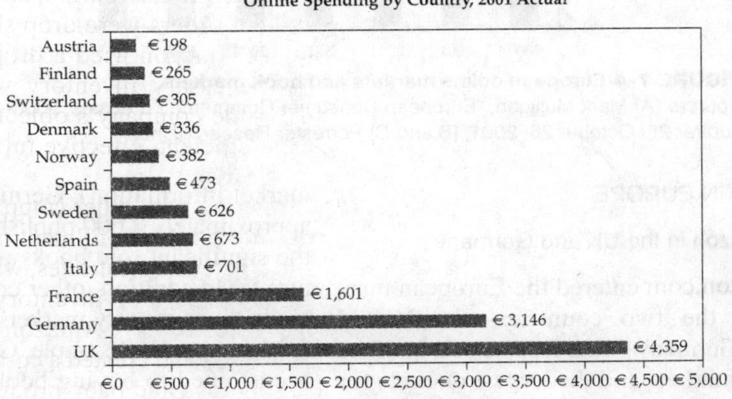

B. Book Sales in Europe in 1999

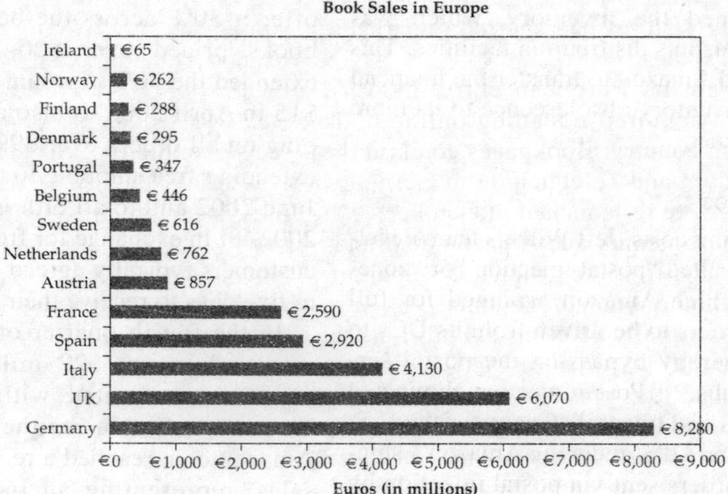

C. Projected Evolution of German online book sales from 2000 to 2006

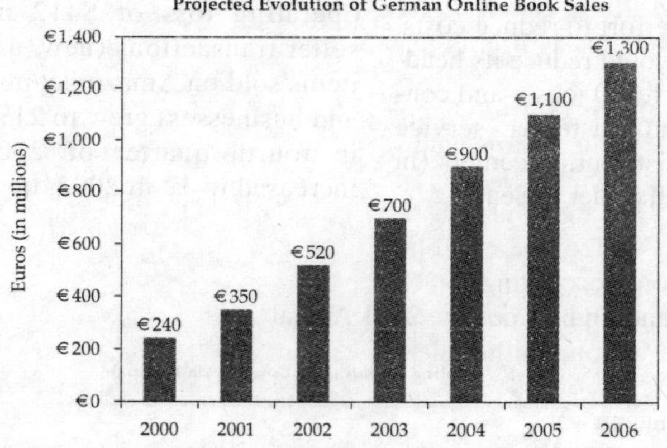

FIGURE 7-4 European online markets and book markets.
Source: (A) Mark Mulligan, "European Consumer Commerce Forecasts, 2000–2006," *Jupiter* 26, October 26, 2001; (B and C) Forrester Research, Inc.

AMAZON.COM IN EUROPE

Launching Amazon in the UK and Germany

In 1998, Amazon.com entered the European market, targeting the two countries—the United Kingdom and Germany—that represented both the largest online markets and the largest markets for books in Europe (Figure 7-4 compares European market information). Germany, for example, had approximately 2,000 publishing houses, indicating the significant role books played in German culture.[xxx] In addition, other country-specific factors made these country markets particularly attractive for Amazon. For example, German customers were accustomed to buying books through mail-order companies. In the UK, the end in 1995 of government-regulated fixed retail book prices and the consequent development of new distribution channels such as specialty stores had spurred remarkable growth in books sales.

To accelerate its European entry, in April 1998 Amazon acquired a leading online book retailer in each country: Bookpages.co.uk in the United Kingdom and Telebuch.de in Germany. The two sites were re-launched in October 1998 under the Amazon.co.uk and Amazon.de brands (see Figure 7-5). Like their US parent, Amazon.co.uk and Amazon.de started as pure book retailers, initially offering 1.4 million UK titles plus 200,000 US titles on the UK site and 335,000 German titles plus 374,000 US titles on the German site. In the fall of 1999, duplicating the US "Get Big Fast" strategy, Amazon.co.uk and Amazon.de began incorporating a wider variety of products, including Music in October 1999, and Auctions and zShops in November 1999. Between 2000 and 2002, more product lines were added to the two sites at a rapid pace, as shown in Table 7-2.

Despite competition from Bertelsmann's BOL.co.uk and BOL.de and Barnesandnoble.com, Amazon quickly became the leading online bookseller in the UK and Germany. In 1999, Amazon.co.uk and Amazon.de combined sales reached $167.7 million (accounting for 10% of Amazon's total revenues) and Amazon.co.uk and Amazon.de each had over one million active customers.

Launching Amazon in France

In September 2000, Amazon continued its expansion overseas with the opening of Amazon.fr. To enter the French market, Amazon did not acquire an online bookseller prior to its launch, but built the site from scratch. This included the time-consuming tasks of building a database containing all the products to be displayed on the Web site, setting up accounts with hundreds of publishers and distributors and setting up the French warehouse. Moreover, unlike in the UK and Germany, Amazon, facing tough competition from already established competitors like Fnac.com (the online site of the leading French retailer of books, media, and other consumer products), Alapage.com (a branch of France Telecom) and BOL (the Bertelsmann-owned online bookseller), decided to launch the Books, Music, Video, and DVD product lines at the same time.

At the end of 2000, the international segment of Amazon comprising the UK, German, and the newly launched French and Japan (launched in November 2000) sites reached $381 million in sales, accounting for 13.8% of the company's total revenue. International sales grew 74% in 2001 to reach $661 million. With 21% of sales, International was beginning to represent a significant portion of Amazon's total revenue.

Amazon's Challenges in Europe: Globalization and Localization

During its first years in Europe, Amazon had faced several challenges that led to particular operational and organizational choices.

A series of challenges pertained to cultural differences among countries targeted. Explained Diego Piacent.ini, Senior Vice President and General Manager, Amazon.com Europe:

> The key to achieving international e-commerce success lies in understanding one simple fact: customers everywhere want better selection, more convenience, and better service. After recognizing this fact, online retailers will soon understand that the major challenge to international expansion is the ability to bring these universal benefits to customers around the world while honoring local customs.[xxxi]

As a result, Amazon recognized the European market as an aggregate of regional markets and chose to fully comply with their legal and cultural specificities. In practice, this implied significant tailoring of Amazon.com's traditional value chain to local needs.

First, Amazon decided to maintain dedicated Web sites for each of the three customer bases. Although Web site functionalities such as browsing and searching were identical, language, editorial content, and items displayed online were unique to each country. In addition, Amazon built

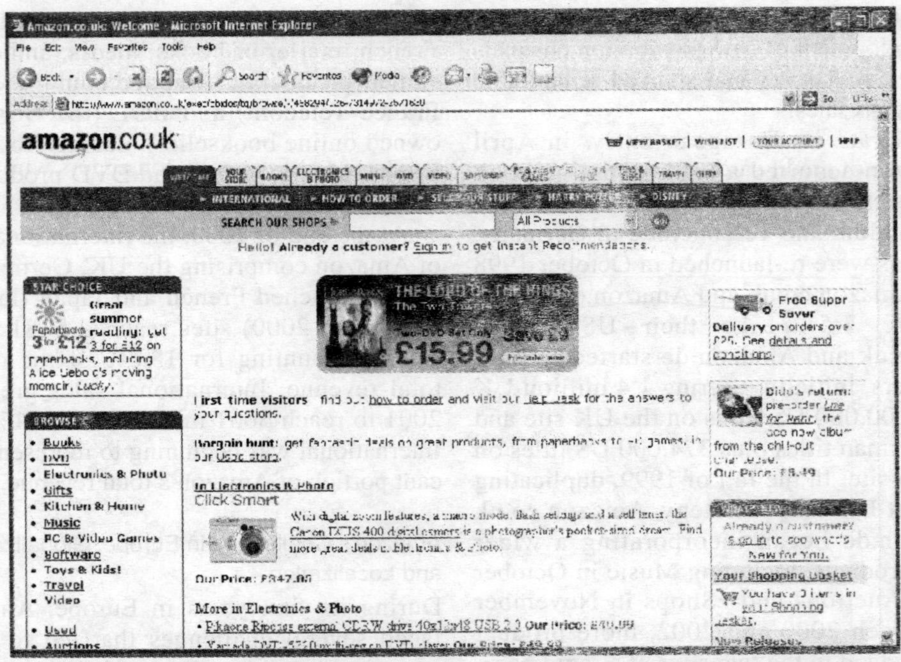

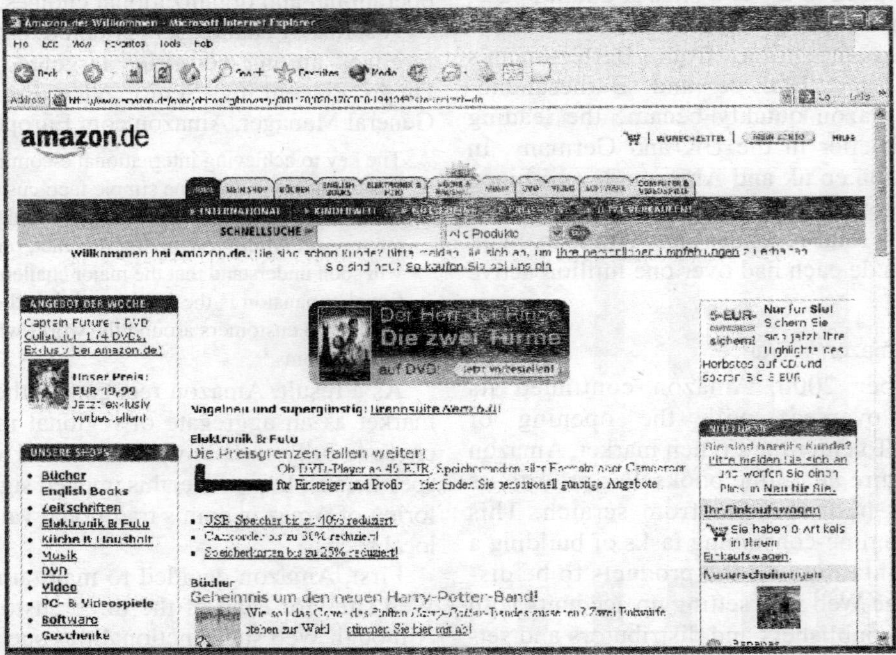

FIGURE 7-5 Amazon.co.uk and Amazon.de homepages in 2003.
Source: Amazon.co.uk and Amazon.de.

dedicated 24-hours-a-day customer centers with native-language-speaking customer service representatives who adequately understood the needs of European shoppers.

Second, Amazon needed to address selling regulations in each country. In Germany and France, book list prices were fixed and could not be discounted by retailers. In France, retailers could not

A. European use of credit cards for online purchases. (Percentage of European consumers who ordered on line in previous three months who responded affirmatively to the question: "Did you use a credit card for your most recent purchase online?")

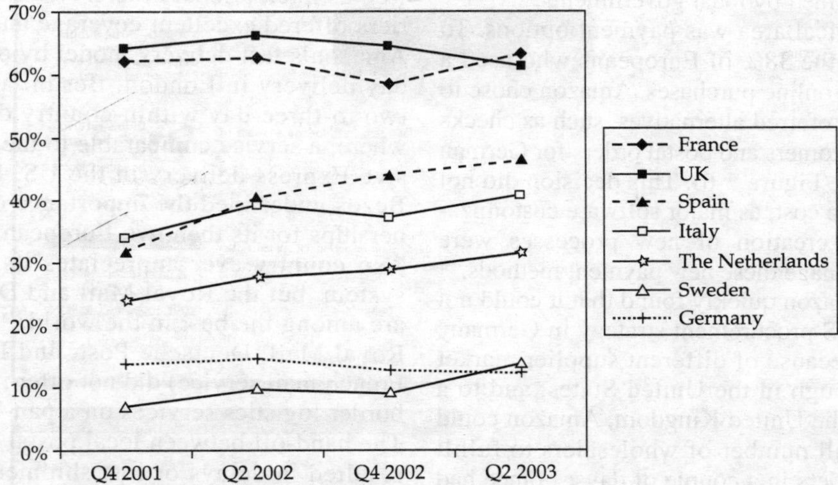

B. European payment methods for online purchases

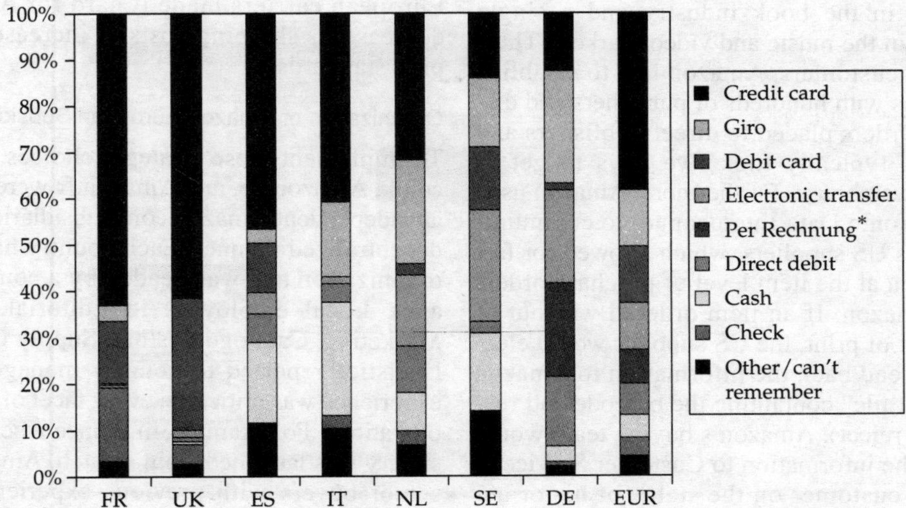

FIGURE 7-6 Europe's online payment methods.
Source: Forrester Research, "Europe's Online Payment Potpourri," by Joost van Krujsdijk, October 2003.

sell items at a lower price than their on-invoice purchasing price. In order to comply with the local laws while keeping a competitive offering, Amazon introduced free shipping in 2001. Moreover, taking full advantage of the flexibility of country laws, Amazon set up promotional activities such as clearance sales permitted on "slow moving" book inventory during a specific time frame defined by local governments.

A third critical area was payment options. To reach beyond the 38% of Europeans who used a credit card for online purchases, Amazon chose to offer locally preferred alternatives, such as checks for French customers and postal orders for German customers (see Figure 7-6). This decision did not come without a cost, as major software customization and the creation of new processes were required to manage these new payment methods.

Fourth, Amazon quickly found that it could not replicate its US procurement strategy in Germany and France because of different supplier market factors. Although in the United States, and to a lesser extent the United Kingdom, Amazon could rely on a small number of wholesalers to fulfill most of its orders in a couple of days, France had no wholesalers in media (books, music, and video) markets and Germany had only a single wholesaler in the book industry and a single wholesaler in the music and video markets. Thus, to serve its customers, Amazon had to establish relationships with hundreds of publishers and distributors. Orders placed to direct publishers and distributors typically took five days to get to Amazon's warehouse. Furthermore, Amazon used EDI (Electronic Data Interchange) to communicate with its US suppliers, which allowed for fast confirmation at the item level of purchase orders sent by Amazon. If an item ordered was out of stock or out of print, the US supplier would electronically send back the information to Amazon (in a "reject file" containing the barcode and reason for the reject). Amazon's buying team would then send the information to Customer Service to update the customer on the status of his or her order and to the Catalogue department to update the Web site information. EDI penetration was low among book, music, and video distributors in Europe where most vendors still used e-mail and even fax. As a result, Amazon did not know whether all the items ordered were going to be fulfilled until the order was physically received in the distribution center.

Finally, Amazon relied on national postal service carriers in Europe to deliver its domestic as well as international orders. National postal carriers offered excellent coverage and suited well Amazon's fast delivery model by offering next-day delivery in London, Berlin, and Paris and two to-three-day within-country delivery elsewhere, a service comparable to the more expensive Express delivery in the US. In 2000, Jeff Bezos underlined the importance of these partnerships for its then two European subsidiaries: "No country ever appreciates its local postal system, but the Royal Mail and Deutsche Post are among the best in the world."[xxxii] However, Royal Mail, Deutsche Post, and La Poste (the French mail service) did not offer reliable cross-border logistics services on a pan-Europe basis. The hand-off between local postal carriers often resulted in delays or lost shipments, affecting negatively customer experience. Finally, the lack of domestic postal competitors or pan-European carriers made it hard for Amazon to decrease its shipping costs or increase its shipping standards.

Organization of Amazon European Subsidiaries

To implement these strategic choices, Amazon.co.uk, Amazon.de, and Amazon.fr were managed as independent Amazon.com subsidiaries run in a decentralized manner. Each country had its own organization and was headed by a country manager. Local employees in Editorial, Finance, Marketing, Catalogue listing, Supply Chain, and Logistics reported to country managers. Local experience was critical in every facet of Amazon's operations. For example, in France where the subsidiary was launched from scratch, Amazon hired senior buyers with previous experience in the French media industry to establish supplier relationships.

FIGURE 7-7 Amazon's European distribution centers.
Source: Adapted from <http://www.lib.utexas.edu/maps/europe/Europe_ref_2003.jpg>, accessed on February 17, 2005.

Each subsidiary owned and operated a dedicated warehouse. In the United Kingdom, a distribution center located in the Marston Gate logistics park, situated 200 kilometers north of London, delivered all customer orders placed on the UK Web site. This location was chosen primarily for its low labor costs. Amazon.de's DC was located in Bad Hersfeld, near Frankfurt. Centrally located, Bad Hersfeld allowed Amazon to reach any place in Germany in less than 5 hours. This translated into overnight service via Deutsche Post for most German locations. The UK and Germany DCs each had over 400,000 square feet in storage capacity and were highly automated. Amazon.fr's distribution center was built in Orleans, 150 km south of Paris. Its storage capacity was 225,000 square feet and, unlike the other two distribution centers, all tasks were performed manually. Figure 7-7 shows the locations of the three European DCs.

By 2001, Amazon.com embarked on a major cost-cutting and restructuring effort to reach profitability. One facet of this program was to consolidate certain functions in Amazon's European subsidiaries. In February 2001, Amazon transferred the company's European customer service operation from the Netherlands to existing customer service centers in the UK and Germany. An Amazon spokeswoman explained the rationale for this change: "The functions that these people are doing are still needed. We found that we do not need three different centers to serve our customer base. It just made much more sense."[xxxiii] During 2001, Amazon decided to unify the marketing and branding functions of the three subsidiaries at the European level, with a purpose to build an identical set of values for the Amazon brand. Other important steps included rolling out common Human Resource evaluation forms. Finally, Allan Lyall became European Operations Director, a newly created position in 2001. Initially, his role encompassed the management of the three European DCs, but it expanded in 2002 to include Transportation, Supply Chain Operations, EDI, operations excellence, and capacity engineering.

Going Forward

By 2002 International revenues were \$1.2 billion (35% of Amazon's total revenue). International was Amazon's fastest growing segment—its 77% growth rate was fueled by the popularity of free shipping, offered to customers of all three sites, and the launch of marketplace activities in the UK and Germany.

Going forward, Amazon executives in Seattle planned to roll out some product categories and functionalities already available in US. This would include developing marketplace activities, and partnering with merchants in selected categories to increase Amazon's selection. Amazon also was evaluating opportunities to expand in other European countries. Amazon Europe needed to build up its infrastructure to support this ambitious vision.

In June 2002, Tom Taylor was transferred from Seattle to London to address some of these issues. Taylor described his mission simply: "Europe will be where the US stands in 2 years after product category expansion and as marketplace develops. This will require a new organization and a new set of skills."

Tom Taylor's Background

Tom Taylor's professional experience started in 1985 at General Motors where he was a Design engineer in the Brake Division. During his frequent interactions with the operations team, he developed a passion for manufacturing. In 1991, he graduated from MIT's LFM program and returned to General Motors as a first line supervisor in a plant of Delphi Systems, a GM subsidiary. In 1992, he was promoted to Manufacturing Planner. In 1994, he decided to join K2, a company manufacturing skis, located in Seattle. Initially a process engineer in charge of adapting operations processes to a new generation of skis, he quickly was promoted to Plant Manager. Facing tough competition from countries with lower labor costs, K2 decided to relocate its manufacturing operations in China, and Taylor became Plant Manager in China. Before June 2000, Taylor had attempted several times to join Amazon without success, his manufacturing profile apparently being of little interest to Amazon at that time. In June 2000, having decided to return to the US, Taylor tried once more to join Amazon, this time successfully. He was hired by Jeff Wilke, Amazon.com's SVP of Operations, who was looking to hire manufacturing specialists. Wilke's vision was to apply process improvement and standardization concepts to Amazon's operations. Taylor's first assignment was to manage the two oldest DCs (located in Seattle and Delaware), which were still operated manually. At the end of 2000, Jeff Wilke organized the operations department into two divisions, respectively covering the eastern half and the western half of the country. Taylor became Eastern Operations Director, in charge of four DCs: Delaware, McDonough in Georgia, and Campbellsville and Lexington in Kentucky. In the course of the next year and a half, he focused on improving those DCs' productivity and ensuring they could handle holiday season peaks. In June 2002, Taylor was promoted to Director of European Supply Chain Operations.

Tom Taylor's early focus in Europe was to look for standardization and synergies among operations processes across the three different countries. This first required the critical step of defining and implementing comparable metrics (such as vendor lead-time, fulfillment rate) across countries to develop better insights into their operations activity. Tom's approach was two-fold: based on his knowledge of US systems and processes, he picked "easy win" areas where porting US techniques to Europe would provide immediate impact. In addition, he leveraged the power of his newly created European Supply Chain Operations Group to obtain adequate resources from the central Amazon IT department in Seattle.

Within a year, Taylor's team had raised the proportion of high velocity items in stock, created and implemented vendor scorecards, improved the accuracy of forecasting tools, reduced suppliers' lead times, decreased customer order backlogs, and developed a process that provided the distribution centers with a clear listing of receipts and shipments due in the following weeks. For example, to reduce the customer order backlog (orders for which shipments had not yet been generated), Tom's team first built a comprehensive daily report for each of the three countries presenting a breakdown of backlogs according to the type of issue(s) preventing Amazon from fulfilling orders within the timeframe promised the customer. Issues were classified by type: supply chain type (e.g., a purchase order had been placed to a wholesaler/publisher but the order had not been received by Amazon), DC type (e.g., the item had been received but not yet recorded in stock), or customer type (e.g., the customer had placed an order using a check as payment method but Amazon had not received the check). Tom's team assigned owners for each backlog type, who analyzed their backlog type's root causes and defined and implemented standardized processes and tools to resolve the underlying issues.

Assessing the EDN Opportunity

In the longer term, Taylor wondered which infrastructure would best support Amazon Europe's growth potential. Amazon's decentralized fulfillment model seemed to offer opportunities for rationalization and cost savings. One of the most obvious targets was redundant inventory of "common" products (such as CDs by international pop and rock stars and US books) currently carried in more than one of European DCs. The rollout of non-media, less- country-specific lines of products (such as consumer electronics, Home and Kitchen products) made this issue even more interesting. Did Amazon need three independent distribution centers in the UK, Germany, and France or could it build a European distribution network (EDN) where the location of inventory would be strategically, rather than geographically, determined?

Intrigued by this opportunity, Taylor had laid out possible benefits of an EDN to Amazon Europe. First, it could significantly expand product selection of current sites through fulfillment from other DCs. For example, the French site could add Home and Kitchen products (currently available on the UK site) to its selection and fulfill the orders from the UK DC. Instead of creating a local dedicated buying team and replicating inventory, France could rely on the existing UK buying team and inventory held in the UK. Second, it would facilitate global sourcing from lowest cost vendors and allow inventory planning at the global network level. Third, it would reduce the risk of relying on a single DC to serve a large base of customers. Indeed, historical records showed that each European DC had experienced a systems failure at least once. Fourth, it could improve customers' experience by enabling Amazon to select the appropriate DC to fulfill a customer order. For example, orders of UK products from customers located in Switzerland or Spain could have a shorter shipping time if served from the German DC instead of the UK DC. An EDN would help Amazon balance the load across its DCs. As Allan Lyall noted, "If a warehouse had a huge backlog

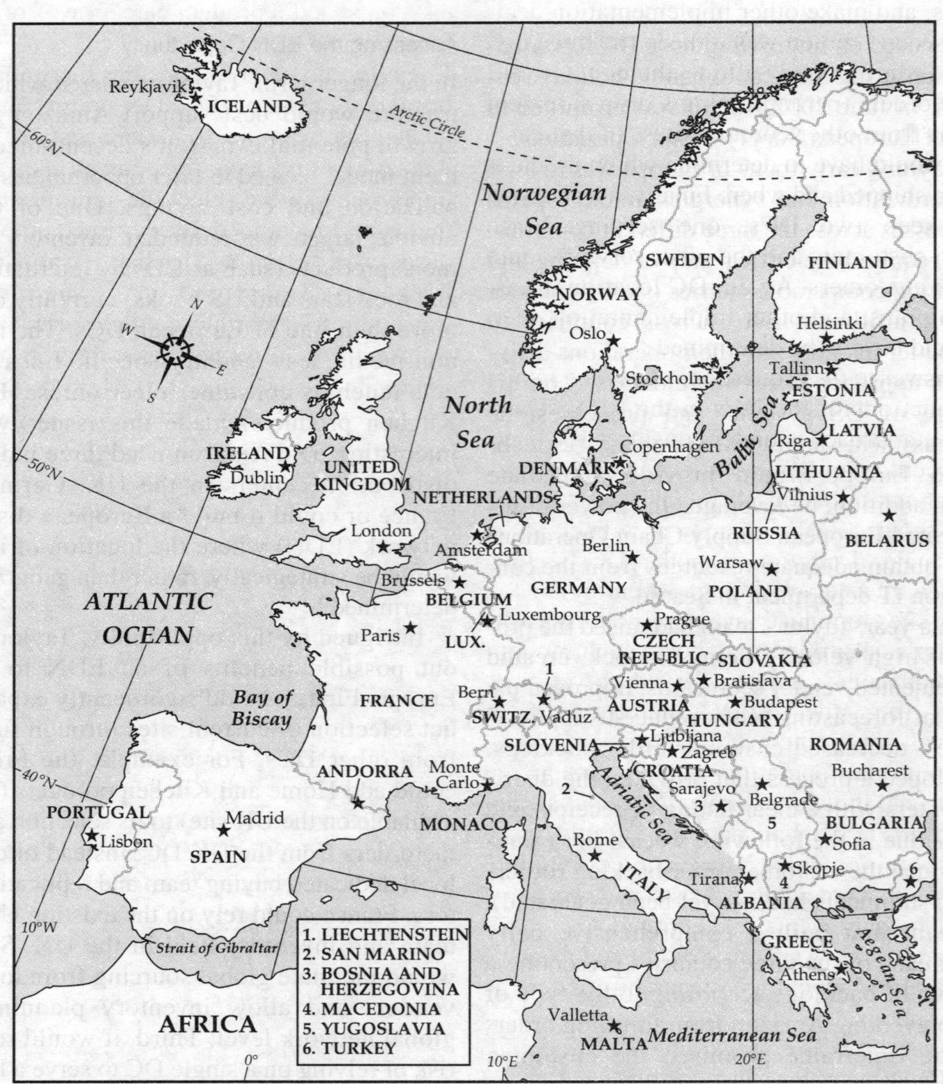

FIGURE 7-8 Map of Europe.
Source: "European Countries" from the Houghton Mifflin Education Place web site <http://www.eduplace.com/ss/maps/pdf/eur_country.pdf>, accessed on February 24, 2005. Copyright © Houghton Mifflin Company. Reprinted by permission of Houghton Mifflin Company. All rights reserved.

affecting delivery promise times, Amazon could reallocate customer orders to another DC." Fifth, should Amazon decide to expand into other European countries, it could supply them from current DCs instead of setting up local distribution operations.

Facing the map of Europe (see Figure 7-8), Tom Taylor considered and evaluated alternatives to design the EDN. One option was to link the different sites to a single European distribution center. Under this option, Amazon would have to determine the DC location, formulate transportation plans, and make other implementation decisions. A second option was to keep the three distribution centers and allow them to fulfill customer orders (perhaps using a drop shipment approach) from other country sites. In that case, Amazon would have to determine which products to be drop shipped and when. Finally, a last option was to keep two DCs, one serving North European customers and the other serving South European customers. Again, DC location, transportation plans, and other implementation decisions would have to be determined.

The answer to these questions depended in part on the functions of the DCs in the EDN. There were three approaches under consideration: one, Amazon could continue with its current strategy of holding inventory in all three DCs, with the function of the EDN primarily as a back-up in case of a major disruption to another DC. Second, Amazon could selectively share inventory among European sites to reduce inventory-holding costs. For example, a product category, such as consumer electronics, could be served only from a single DC (e.g., the UK DC, thereby reducing stock levels in France and Germany). Third, Amazon Europe's operations could be integrated fully, with the three sites' inventories physically mixed based on demand patterns and inventory and transportation costs. These choices required analyses of demand patterns, costs, transportation options, IT requirements, and current DC capabilities. In additions, Amazon would need to make decisions about inventory ownership under the different options.

Other questions arose regarding the location of the EDN's DCs. With over two-thirds[xxxiv] of the UK's orders delivered to customers located south of the Marston Gate DC, should Amazon keep the French DC? If Amazon expanded into other European countries, should it fulfill these orders from an existing DC or should Amazon consider a new location for a new DC or hub?

Tom Taylor also had to define an implementation plan. Would he start by dissociating DCs from country Web sites? Would he start by doing tests on specific product categories from specific locations?

Taylor also had to consider the impact of the implementation of the EDN on internal departments. For example, to build a sustainable EDN, Amazon would have to redesign its transportation processes and select the appropriate carriers that would meet its delivery-time and price standards. According to Siobhan Farnon, Director, European Transportation: "The immediate impact on transportation would most likely be a reduction in delivery service levels. Most customers located in the UK, Germany, and France are used to next-day delivery, even when choosing the standard shipping option."

To address this issue, the transportation team would have to work collaboratively with customer service to educate customers to associate a different shipping price to the delivery service level chosen. Currently, Amazon.fr and Amazon.de offered only a standard shipping option, which promised delivery in two to three business days. Nonetheless, customers in Germany and France were accustomed to getting overnight service due to the proximity of the local DCs to the customer base and the short delivery times by La Poste and Deutsche Post. Amazon.co.uk offered standard and free shipping for domestic deliveries; about 45% of UK customers chose free shipping.

Another opportunity would be to leverage EDN volume to implement "postal injection." Amazon thought it would need to allocate about twelve hours to travel from a hub in Germany to a hub in the UK (or from the UK to France or from France to Germany); thus, it expected to be able to fulfill most customer orders between those countries in two, or possibly three, days. Going forward, Amazon could seek better terms from a pan-European carrier capable of meeting Amazon's delivery time requirements. Allan Lyall expected competitive forces to drive Deutsche Post and/or other carriers to develop capabilities within three to five years that would allow them to provide Amazon with appropriate pan-European services.

Amazon hoped that under an EDN, its procurement department would be able to centralize its purchases and extract higher volume discounts from suppliers. However, suppliers of common media products were extremely concentrated. For example, Universal, Warner, Sony, BMG, and EMI made up approximately 80% of total music sales (and about 80% of Amazon's music sales) in the UK, Germany, and France. Nonetheless, negotiations on terms and conditions with each of these and many other vendors had always been conducted at the country level because the suppliers were organized in country subsidiaries, each managed independently. For example, Amazon's vendor management team in Germany would conduct negotiations with Sony Germany and Amazon's vendor management team in France would negotiate with Sony France. Amazon's relationships with Warner provided another example of this fragmentation—across its global operations, Amazon had six different relationships with Warner Home Video. Mike Siefert, European Buying Manager noted: "Most vendors in Europe are very archaic in the way they are set up, but the good news is that they want to be forward thinking—probably because Amazon Europe is big enough now to have a negotiation power."

The EDN would also require a better coordination among departments and a clear HR plan. In the short term, people working in the functions affected by the implementation of the EDN would have to learn to work collaboratively to leverage the opportunities and savings the EDN offered. In the longer term, network optimization could lead to reduction of staff in the operations team comparable to what happened in the US in 2001. For example, Amazon could consider centralizing the buying teams in one location to be in charge of the buying activity for all Europe. This would imply relocating employees to another location and would require training of "European," rather than country-specific, buyers. Centralized buying raised other issues: Would it make sense to implement an infrastructure in which UK suppliers would send items to the German warehouse to ship it back to customers located in the UK?

Making the Case for an EDN

Faced with all these options, Taylor realized that his team would have to lay out a strong business case.

Taylor would have to give answers to concerns from managers working in Retail functions at Amazon. Is Amazon doing the right thing for its customers as well as for the company? Would the customer experience deteriorate? Would Amazon be able to detect fast moving items or other demand trends for each country if buying was to be consolidated at the European level?

Moreover, as always for the European subsidiaries, IT resources would be a constraint. IT resources, managed in the United States, limited the number of new projects rolled out by Amazon every year. The project of establishing a European distribution network would be in competition with other cost saving projects. The level of importance given to this project would depend on the return on investment put forth in the project's business case. There was no time to waste. Did the EDN make sense in the context of strong growth? If so, which option should Taylor choose?

i. <http://www.bizinfocentral.com/affiliate/Book/>. About Amazon.com section (accessed March 30, 2004).

ii. Pankaj Ghemawat, "Leadership Online: Barnes & Noble vs. Amazon.com (A)," HBS Case No. 9-798-063 (Boston: Harvard Business School Publishing, 2000).

iii. Interview with Mike Siefert, European Supply Chain Manager, Amazon.com

iv. Pankaj Ghemawat, "Leadership Online: Barnes & Noble vs. Amazon.com (A)," HBS Case No. 9-798-063 (Boston: Harvard Business School Publishing, 2000).

v. *Ibid.*

vi. *Ibid.*

vii. "Earth's biggest bookstore' comes to Delaware," November 18, 1997. <http://www.state.de.us

/dedo/news/1997/amazon.htm> (accessed March 30, 2004).

viii. Anthony Bianco, "Virtual Bookstores Start to Get Real: The 'sell all, carry few' strategy won't work forever," *Business Week* (October 27, 1997).

ix. Saul Hansell, "Amazon's Risky Christmas," *The New York Times,* November 28, 1999.

x. Anthony Bianco, "Virtual Bookstores Start to Get Real: The 'sell all carry few' strategy won't work forever," *Business Week* (October 27, 1997).

xi. *Ibid.*

xii. James Aaron Cooke, "Clicks and Mortar," *Logistics Management and Distribution Report* 39, no. 1 (January 1, 2000).

xiii. *Ibid.*

xiv. "Amazon.com–New distribution center," *News-bytes News Network,* January 8, 1999.

xv. "Amazon.com to Open Kansas Distribution Center, "*Internetnews.com,* April 15, 1999. http://www.internetnews.com/ec-news/article.php/99121.

xvi. Beth Cox, "Amazon.com to Open Two Kentucky Distribution Centers," *Internetnews.com,* May 27, 1999. <http://www.internetnews.com/ec-news/article.php/128321> (accessed December 17, 2004).

xvii. "Amazon.com: More Than a Merchant," by Miguel Helft, The Industry Standard, 01/18/00,<http://www.nwfusion.com/news/2000/0118amazonprof.html>(accessed December 20, 2004).

xviii. Interview with Tom Taylor, Director of European Supply Chain Operations, Amazon.com

xix. Greg Sandoval, "How lean can Amazon get?" *CNet News.com,* April 19, 2002. <http://news.com.com/How+lean+can+Amazon+get%3F/2100-1017_3-886784.html> (accessed December 17, 2004).

xx. James Aaron Cooke, "Clicks and Mortar," *Logistics Management and Distribution Report* 39, no. 1 (January 1, 2000).

xxi. Amazon.com, <http://phx.corporate ir.net/phoenix.zhtml?c=97664&p=IROL-NewsText&t= Regular &id=231842&> (accessed December 17, 2004).

xxii. "Jeff Bezos: There's No Shift in the Model," *Business Week Online,* August 2000. <http://www.businessweek.com/2000/00 08/b3669094.htm> (accessed July 8, 2004).

xxiii. http://www.amazon.com/exec/obidos/tg/feature/-/165151/102-5368591-9733717 (accessed December 20, 2004).

xxiv. Chip Bayers, "The last laugh," *Business 2.0* 3, no.9 (September 2002).

xxv. Sandoyal, Greg. "How Lean Can Amazon Get?" CNET News.com (April 19, 2002), <http://news.com.com/How+lean+can+Amazon+get/2100-1017_3-886784.html> (accessed December 17, 2004>.

xxvi. "Event Brief of Amazon.com Conference Call – Final," Nov. 7, 2002, Fair Disclosure Wire, (c) CCBN and FDCH e-Media.

xxvii. Robert Hof and Heather Green, "How Amazon Cleared That Hurdle: To earn a profit, it cut costs and started growing again," *Business Week* (February 4, 2002): 60.

xxviii. Nick Wingfield, "Survival Strategy: Amazon Takes Page from Wal-Mart to Prosper on Web," *Wall Street Journal,* November 22, 2002.

xxix. Beth Cox, "Amazon Expands Free Shipping Again" *Internetnews.com* (August 26, 2002).http://www.internetnews.com/ecnews/article.php/1452161 (accessed July 8, 2004).

xxx. Diego Piacentini, "Helping E-Commerce Sites Achieve International Success," <http:/usinfo.state.gov/journals/ites/0500/ije/amazon2.htm> (accessed July 8, 2004).

xxxi. *Ibid.*

xxxii. Malcolm Wheatley, "Amazon.com Sees Supply-chain as Crucial to Its Future," *Global Logistics & Supply Chain Strategies* (September 2000). <http://www.supplychain-brain.com/archies.9.00. Amazon.htm?adcode=5> (accessed July 8, 2004).

xxxiii. "Amazon.com to consolidate European service centers," News Story by Todd R. Weiss, FEBRUARY 09, 2001, Computerworld.com,<http://www.computerworld.com/industrytopics/retail/story/0,10801,57582,00.html> (accessed December 20, 2004).

xxxiv. Interview with Allan Lyall, European Operations Director, Amazon.com.

By the end of this chapter, you should be able to understand the following issues:

- **Best practices in distribution strategies.**
- **How to reconfigure the distribution network.**
- **The impact of concepts such as inventory pooling and transshipment strategies.**

7.1 INTRODUCTION

As discussed in other chapters, supply chain management revolves around *efficient integration* of the various entities of the supply chain in order to improve performance. Indeed, a fully effective supply chain requires the integration of the **front end** of the supply chain, customer demand, with the **back end** of the supply chain, the production and manufacturing processes.

Of course, depending on the situation, the firm may have opportunities to focus on various portions of the supply chain and to derive significant improvements in performance. In this chapter, we focus on the distribution function. Obviously, after products are manufactured, packaged, and so forth, they need to be stored and transported (sometimes stored in several places and transported several times) until they reach the end of the supply chain, either by being directly delivered to a customer or by being delivered to a retailer where they are purchased by customers. The objective of this chapter is to illustrate various possible distribution strategies, and the opportunities and challenges associated with these strategies.

Fundamentally, there are two possible distribution strategies. Items can be **directly shipped** from the supplier or manufacturer to the retail stores or end customer, or one or more **intermediate inventory storage points** (typically warehouses and/or distribution centers) can be used. Warehouses can be used in a variety of different ways, depending, among other things, on the manufacturing strategy (make-to-stock versus make-to-order), the number of warehouses, the inventory policy, the inventory turnover ratio, whether these are internal warehouses owned by the firm or by an outside distributor, and whether the supply chain is owned by a single firm or by a variety of firms. The bulk of this chapter is devoted to exploring a variety of intermediate inventory storage point strategies, but we first consider direct shipment.

7.2 DIRECT SHIPMENT DISTRIBUTION STRATEGIES

Direct shipment strategies exist to bypass warehouses and distribution centers. Employing direct shipment, the manufacturer or supplier delivers goods directly to retail stores.

The advantages of this strategy are that

- The retailer avoids the expenses of operating a distribution center.
- Lead times are reduced.

This type of distribution strategy also has a number of important disadvantages:

- Risk-pooling effects, which we described in Chapter 2, are negated because there is no central warehouse.
- The manufacturer and distributor transportation costs increase because it must send smaller trucks to more locations.

For these reasons, direct shipment is common when the retail store requires fully loaded trucks, which implies that the warehouse does not help in reducing transportation cost. It is most often mandated by powerful retailers or used in situations where lead time is critical. Sometimes, the manufacturer is reluctant to be involved with direct shipping but may have no choice in order to keep the business. Direct shipment is also prevalent in the grocery industry, where lead times are critical because of perishable goods.

EXAMPLE 7-1

JC Penney has successfully implemented a direct shipping strategy. JC Penney sells general merchandise through nearly a thousand stores and millions of catalogs. With 200,000 items from more than 20,000 suppliers, managing the flow of goods is a formidable task. Each individual store retains total accountability for sales, inventory, and profit and is responsible for sales forecasts and releasing orders. Orders are communicated to buyers who coordinate the shipment with distribution personnel to ensure quick response, and an internal control and tracking system is used to monitor the flow of materials. In most cases, products are shipped directly to Penney's stores.

EXAMPLE 7-2 DABUR DISTRIBUTION NETWOK

Dabur India Limited (DIL) manages one of the oldest and leading FMCG supply chains in India. Dabur, as a company is over 100 years old and deals with a diversified product range in "natural and herbal" personal and healthcare products, such as Dabur Chawanprash, Dabur Amla, Vatika, Hajmola, Real Juice etc. It procures raw material worth around Rs.5000 million from a wide base of vendors. The company has an envious distribution network for its 600 SKUs, which is delivered through 2100 stockiest to several thousand retail outlets covering every nook and corner of India. In 2006-07, to improve its distribution system, Dabur launched its unique 'Retail Excellence' program, DARE (Driving Achievement of Retail Excellence). This has major objectives as channel focus, activating key customers, improving rural focus, rewarding distribution efficiency, maximizing brand impact and building information capabilities. Dabur, which has mastered its distribution network with millions of small retailers in India, has to replicate its success when organized retail will play a bigger role in Indian FMCG supply chains [59, 276, 282, 283, 284, 287, 293].

EXAMPLE 7-3 GODREJ INTEGRATION

Godrej India Limited (GIL) has focused on the integration of its supply chain with great passion and planning. Its five factories are connected to four regional warehouses and 1200 distributors through an IT-based platform called *Sampark*, meaning 'connectivity' in local language. Through a customized ERP package, dealers share their billing and inventory information with the central unit of Godrej *via* internet. Dealers get pricing and other information from Godrej through this platform. To extend this network further to over 50,000 retailers, Godrej has implemented another progamme called *Sampurna*, meaning 'complete' [69].

7.3 INTERMEDIATE INVENTORY STORAGE POINT STRATEGIES

As mentioned above, there are a variety of characteristics that can be used to distinguish between different intermediate inventory storage point strategies. One of the most fundamental involves the length of time that inventory is stored at warehouses and distribution centers. In a traditional warehousing strategy, the distribution centers and warehouses hold stock inventory and provide their downstream customers (whether they are additional warehouses in the supply chain or retailers) with inventory as needed. In a **cross-docking** strategy, warehouses and distribution centers serve as transfer points for inventory, but no inventory is held at these transfer points. Centralized pooling and transshipment strategies may be useful when there is a large variety of different products, so that demand for specific end products is relatively small, and difficult to predict.

7.3.1 Traditional Warehousing

In Chapter 2, we discussed inventory management and risk pooling, and how these are impacted by the use of warehouses. We investigated the value of employing a warehouse in order to facilitate risk pooling, and we considered effective approaches for managing inventory in a supply chain with one or more warehouses. Of course, there are a variety of other issues and decisions in a traditional warehousing system.

Centralized versus Decentralized Management In a centralized system, decisions are made at a central location for the entire supply network. Typically, the objective is to minimize the total cost of the system subject to satisfying some service-level requirements. This is clearly the case when the network is owned by a single entity, but it is also true in a centralized system that includes many different organizations. In this case, the savings, or profits, need to be allocated across the network using some contractual mechanism. We have already seen that centralized control leads to global optimization. Similarly, in a decentralized system, each facility identifies its most effective strategy without considering the impact on the other facilities in the supply chain. Thus, a decentralized system leads to local optimization.

It is easy to see that, at least theoretically, a centralized distribution network will be at least as effective as a decentralized one because the centralized decision makers can make all of the decisions that decentralized decision makers would make, but also have the option of considering the interplay of decisions made at different locations in the supply network.

Unfortunately, in a logistics system in which each facility can access only its own information (or has only limited access to the information about other facilities), a centralized strategy is not possible. With advances in information technologies, however, all facilities in a centralized system can have access to the same data. Indeed, in Chapter 15, we discuss the concept of *single point of contact*. In this case, information can be accessed from anywhere in the supply chain and is the same no matter what mode of inquiry is used or who is seeking the information. Thus, centralized systems allow the sharing of information and, more importantly, the utilization of this information in ways that reduce the bullwhip effect (see Chapter 5) and improve forecasts. Finally, they allow the use of coordinated strategies across the entire supply chain—strategies that reduce systemwide costs and improve service levels.

Sometimes, of course, a system cannot be centralized "naturally." The retailers, manufacturers, and distributors might all have different owners and different objectives. In these cases, it is often helpful to form partnerships to approach the advantages of a centralized system. We discuss these kinds of partnerships in Chapter 8. Also, detailed supply contracts can be useful, and we discuss these in more detail in Chapter 4.

Central versus Local Facilities Another critical decision in supply chain design involves whether to use centralized or local production and warehousing facilities. Centralized facilities imply both fewer warehouses and fewer distribution centers, and these facilities are located further from customers. Models that help the firm decide on the number, location, and size of each facility are discussed in Chapter 3. Here we summarize additional important considerations:

Safety stock. Consolidating warehouses allows the vendor to take advantage of risk pooling. In general, this means that the more centralized an operation is, the lower are the safety stock levels.

Overhead. Economies of scale suggest that operating a few large central warehouses leads to lower total overhead cost relative to operating many smaller warehouses.

Economies of scale. In many manufacturing operations, economies of scale can be realized if manufacturing is consolidated. It is often much more expensive to operate many small manufacturing facilities than to operate a few large facilities with the same total capacity.

Lead time. Lead time to market often can be reduced if a large number of warehouses are located closer to the market areas.

Service. This depends on how *service* is defined. As we indicated above, centralized warehousing enables the utilization of risk pooling, which means that more orders can be met with a lower total inventory level. On the other hand, shipping time from the warehouse to the retailer will be longer than in a decentralized system.

Transportation costs. Transportation costs are directly related to the number of warehouses used. As the number of warehouses increases, transportation costs between the production facilities and the warehouses also increase because total distance traveled is greater and, more importantly, quantity discounts are less likely to apply. However, transportation costs from the warehouses to the retailers are likely to fall because the warehouses tend to be much closer to the market areas.

Of course, it is possible that in an effective distribution strategy, some products will be stored in a central facility while others will be kept in various local warehouses. For instance, very expensive products with low customer demand and high demand uncertainty may be stocked at a central warehouse while low-cost products facing high customer demand and low demand uncertainty may be stocked at many local warehouses. In the former, the objective is to take advantage of risk pooling by using a centralized warehouse and hence reduce inventory levels, while in the latter, the objective is to ship fully loaded trucks across the supply chain and hence reduce transportation cost. See Chapter 3, Section 3.3.2, for a detailed discussion.

In addition, the use of centralized or local production and warehousing facilities is not necessarily an either-or decision. There are degrees of local and centralized operation, with varying degrees of the advantages and disadvantages listed above. Finally, advanced information systems help each type of system maintain some of the advantages of the other type. For example, safety stock levels can be reduced when transshipment between facilities is possible and the technology can identify available inventory.

7.3.2 Cross-Docking

Cross-docking is a strategy that Wal-Mart made famous. In this system, warehouses function as inventory coordination points rather than as inventory storage points. In typical cross-docking systems, goods arrive at warehouses from the manufacturer, are transferred to vehicles serving the retailers, and are delivered to the retailers as rapidly as possible. Goods spend very little time in storage at the warehouse—often less than 12 hours. This system limits inventory costs and decreases lead times by decreasing storage time.

Of course, cross-docking systems require a significant start-up investment and are very difficult to manage:

1. Distribution centers, retailers, and suppliers must be linked with advanced information systems to ensure that all pickups and deliveries are made within the required time windows.
2. A fast and responsive transportation system is necessary for a cross-docking system to work.
3. Forecasts are critical, necessitating the sharing of information.
4. Cross-docking strategies are effective *only* for large distribution systems in which a large number of vehicles are delivering and picking up goods at the cross-dock facilities at any one time. In such systems, there is enough volume every day to allow shipments of fully loaded trucks from the suppliers to the warehouses. Since these systems typically include many retailers, demand is sufficient so items that arrive at the cross-docking facilities can be delivered immediately to the retail outlets in full truckload quantities.

EXAMPLE 7-4

The tremendous market growth of Wal-Mart over the past 15 to 20 years highlights the importance of an effective strategy that coordinates inventory replenishment and transportation policies [229]. Over this time period, Wal-Mart developed into the largest and highest-profit retailer in the world. A number of major components in Wal-Mart's competitive strategy were critical to its success, but perhaps the most important has been its enthusiastic use of cross-docking. Wal-Mart delivers about 85 percent of its goods utilizing cross-docking techniques, as opposed to about 50 percent for Kmart. To facilitate cross-docking, Wal-Mart operates a private satellite communications system that sends point-of-sale (POS) data to all of its vendors, allowing them to have a clear picture of sales at all of its stores. In addition, Wal-Mart has a dedicated fleet of 2,000 trucks and, on average, stores are replenished twice a week. Cross-docking enables Wal-Mart to achieve economies of scale by purchasing full truckloads. It reduces the need for safety stocks and has cut the cost of sales by 3 percent compared to the industry average, a major factor explaining Wal-Mart's large profit margins.

7.3.3 Inventory Pooling

We begin our discussion of inventory pooling with an example.

EXAMPLE 7-5

In 1994, General Motors started to test a program in Florida that was intended to reduce the amount of time Cadillac buyers needed to wait for new cars. According to the *Wall Street Journal*:

> Under the program, which begins in mid-September, about 1,500 Cadillacs will be parked at a regional distribution center in Orlando, Fla., to await delivery to dealers statewide within 24 hours. . . . GM hopes improving customer service will boost sales of Cadillacs . . . Research shows we lose 10% to 11% of sales because the car is not available . . . GM says the test program will increase Cadillac sales by 10%.

Why would GM initiate such a program, known as an *inventory pooling* program? Why would dealers participate in such a program? GM's motivation is clear: as we have seen throughout this book, a centralized distribution system performs better than decentralized systems. Indeed, for the same inventory level, a centralized system provides a higher service level, and hence higher sales—this is precisely the risk-pooling concept discussed in Chapter 2. In addition, recall the concept of the push–pull supply chain. By pooling inventory at the central warehouse in Orlando and pulling from it after customers order a particular vehicle, GM is moving from a push supply chain, in which dealers have to order before demand is realized, to a push–pull supply chain, in which dealers pull from regional distribution centers. This implies that the end consumers will see better customer service in this type of system, as more cars are available to them.

It isn't clear, however, if GM will sell more cars to GM dealers in this type of system. Since inventory is pooled, the total number of cars ordered by dealers will not necessarily increase, even as customer service increases. In the long run, will this benefit GM? We shed light on this question in Example 7-6.

What about the dealers? On one hand, the dealers have access to more inventory, and can thus potentially sell more. On the other hand, this sort of centralized inventory does tend to "level the playing field" between dealers. Small dealers with limited inventory would favor such a system since they now have an enormous amount of inventory available in less than 24 hours to their customers. Large dealers,

EXAMPLE 7-6

Consider two retailers facing random demand for a single product. In this simplified example, the retailers are identical, with the same costs and characteristics; this implies that issues such as the difference between the retailer sizes do not play a role in the analysis. We compare two systems, the centralized and the decentralized systems. In the centralized pooled system, the retailers together operate a joint inventory facility and take items out of the pooled inventory to meet demand. In the decentralized system, each retailer individually orders from the manufacturer to meet demand. Thus, in both systems, inventory is owned by the retailers. The two systems are illustrated in Figure 7-9.

We consider a single period of random demand. The probabilistic forecast of demand faced by each retailer is depicted in Figure 7-10. Finally, the wholesale price is $80 per unit, the selling price is $125 per unit, salvage value is $20 per unit, and production cost equals $35 per unit.

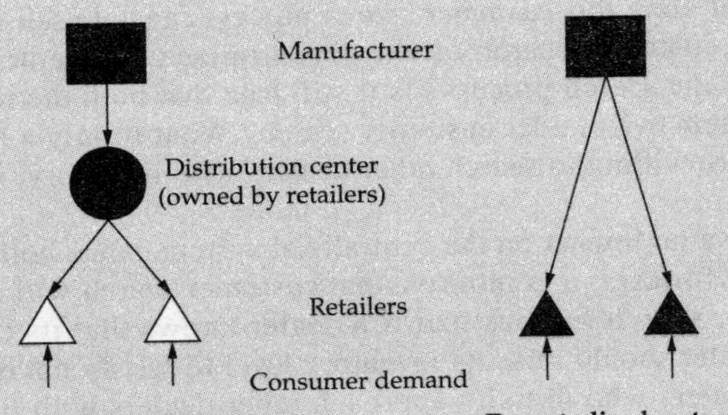

FIGURE 7-9 The centralized and decentralized systems.

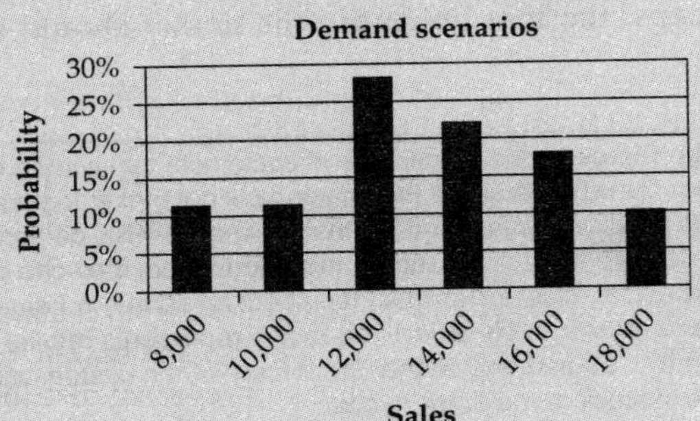

FIGURE 7-10 Probabilistic demand faced by each retailer.

however, typically compete in the market using their available inventory, and, hence, this sort of system will wipe out their advantage.

To better understand the issues involved with inventory pooling, consider the following example.

We apply the same analysis as in Section 2.2.2 to each retailer in the decentralized system to determine that each dealer will order 12,000 units with an expected profit per dealer of $470,000 and an expected sales of 11,340 units. Since each dealer orders 12,000 units, the manufacturer's profit is $1,080,000 in this system. In the centralized system, because of the risk pooling concept, the two dealers together will order 26,000 units, and their total expected profit is $1,009,392 on joint expected sales of 24,470 units, as compared to $940,000 and 22,680 units in the simple decentralized system. Note that orders are higher than in the decentralized system since pooling has lessened the downside risk of ordering more units (at least one of the retailers is likely to have higher-than-average demand). Finally, since the dealers order more items, the manufacturer's profit goes up to $1,170,000, compared to the manufacturer's profit in the decentralized system of $1,080,000.

Thus, the example suggests, as expected, that both the manufacturer and the dealers prefer the centralized system. However, the previous example makes an important assumption that does not hold in practice: if a customer arrives when a dealer does not have inventory, the customer disappears and this unit of demand is lost. This is clearly not always true. Indeed, loyal customers faced with no inventory at a dealer will be likely to switch to another dealer to search whether this dealer has inventory. From the manufacturer's point of view, this *customer search* process can help sell more products.

What is the impact of customer search on the decentralized and centralized systems? Can the dealers take advantage of the search process? Is it still true that both the manufacturer and dealers prefer the centralized system even under customer search? What if only a fraction of the customers are loyal customers and are willing to search other dealers with inventory; is one system better than the other?

Clearly, search will have no impact on the centralized system, since both retailers have access to the same inventory pool. However, it is intuitive that customer search will impact the decentralized system. Indeed, customer search implies that if a dealer knows that its competitors do not keep enough inventory, this dealer should raise its inventory level to satisfy not only its own demand, but also the demand of customers who initially approach other dealers with limited inventory. On the other hand, if this dealer somehow learned that its competitors keep a significant amount of inventory, then this dealer is not likely to see customers who switch from a competitor and hence will reduce its inventory level. Thus, a dealer's strategy depends on its competitor's strategy. The more inventory the competitor keeps, the less inventory the dealer should order. Conversely, the less

EXAMPLE 7-7

Let's return to our example. We let α represent the percentage of customers that search the system— in other words, the percentage of customers who check the other retailer if their demand is not met at the first retailer. Using this information, each retailer can determine what its effective demand will be (that is, what its initial demand and the searched demand will total) if the other retailer orders a specific amount. Based on this information, they can calculate how much they should order given any order by their competitors. This is known as their best response. In Figure (7-11), the black curve represents retailer two's best response to retailer one's order, and brown represents retailer one's best response to retailer two's orders, for a system in which $\alpha = 90$ percent, so that 90 percent of the customers whose demand is not met at a retailer checks to see if the item is in stock at the other retailer:

Observe (black curve) that as retailer one increases its inventory, retailer two's inventory decreases, up to a certain amount. The same is true for retailer one's inventory as a function of retailer two's policy.

EXAMPLE 7-7 ***Continued***

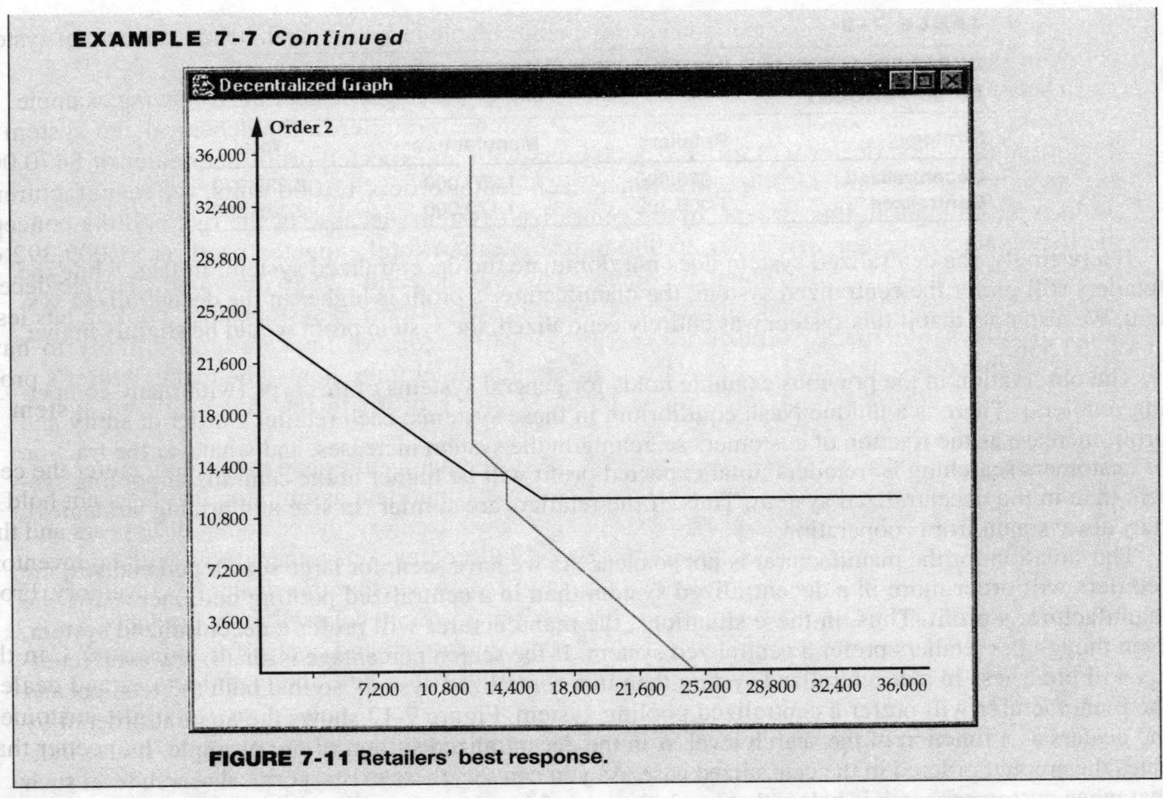

FIGURE 7-11 Retailers' best response.

inventory the competitor has, the more the dealer will order. The problem, of course, is that dealers do know their competitor's strategy and, hence, it is not clear how they decide on their inventory level. Thus, it is not clear what the impact of search on the manufacturer is.

This question is addressed using concepts from **game theory,** and, in particular, the concept of **Nash equilibrium.** If two competitors are making decisions, we say that they have reached Nash equilibrium if they have both made a decision, in this case decided on an amount to order, and neither can improve his or her expected profit by changing the order amount if the other dealer doesn't change his order amount. For example, if both dealers have decided to order a certain amount, these decisions constitute a Nash equilibrium if one of the dealers can't increase his expected profit by ordering more items, unless the other dealer orders fewer items.

Notice also that if retailer one orders about 20,000 units, retailer two will respond by ordering about 12,000 units (black curve); however, if this is the case, then retailer one should modify its strategy and reduce its order quantity (brown curve). The only case where no retailer has an incentive to modify its strategy is when they order the amounts associated with the intersection of the two curves. This is the Nash equilibrium for this system and it is a unique Nash equilibrium. Thus, the optimal order quantity for each retailer is 13,900, and the total expected profit for each retailer is $489,460 (for a total expected profit of $978,920). The expected sales (by retailer) is 12,604 (so that total expected sales is 25,208), and the total amount ordered from the manufacturer is 27,800, implying that the manufacturer's profit is $1,251,000. In Table 7-3, we compare centralized and decentralized system performance with a 90 percent search rate.

TABLE 7-3

DECENTRALIZED AND CENTRALIZED SYSTEMS FOR SEARCH LEVEL OF 90 PERCENT

Strategy	Retailers	Manufacturer	Total
Decentralized	978,920	1,251,000	2,229,920
Centralized	1,009,392	1,170,000	2,179,392

Interestingly, the centralized system does not dominate the decentralized system. In fact, while the retailers still prefer the centralized system, the manufacturer's profit is higher in the decentralized system. We also note that if this system was entirely centralized, the system profit would be slightly higher, at $2,263,536.

The observation in the previous example holds for general systems of this type (with many competing retailers). There is a unique Nash equilibrium in these systems; each retailer's order quantity and profit increase as the fraction of customers searching in the system increases, and whatever the fraction of customers searching is, retailers' total expected profit will be higher in the centralized pooling system than in the decentralized system. Thus, if the retailers are similar (in size and pricing strategies), they always gain from cooperation.

The situation for the manufacturer is not so clear. As we have seen, for large search percentages, the retailers will order more in a decentralized system than in a centralized pooling one, increasing the manufacturer's profit. Thus, in these situations, the manufacturer will prefer a decentralized system, even though the retailers prefer a centralized system. If the search percentage is small, however, retailers will order less in a decentralized system than in a centralized system, so that both the retailers and the manufacturer will prefer a centralized pooling system. Figure 7-12 shows the amount ordered by the dealers as a function of the search level, α in the decentralized system of our example. It also indicates the amount ordered in the centralized case. As you can see, there exists a critical search level such that when customer search is below that level, the manufacturer prefers the centralized system and, otherwise, the manufacturer prefers the decentralized system.

Thus, manufacturers always prefer a higher search level. How can this be achieved? Two common approaches are marketing strategies to increase brand loyalty and information technology initiatives to increase communication between retailers.

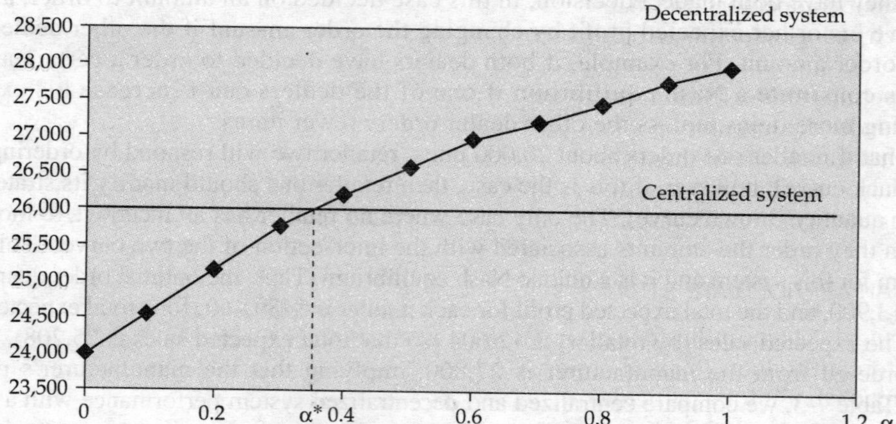

FIGURE 7-12 Amount ordered by dealers as a function of the search level.

Clearly, if brand loyalty increases, customers will more likely search for a particular brand at another retailer if their first choice does not have the product in inventory. Acura, for example, for many years offered a $500 rebate to existing Acura customers who chose to replace their current Acura with a new one. This program clearly provided an incentive for customers to visit multiple Acura dealers if necessary to find the car they were searching for.

Information technology enhances communication between dealers, and between dealers and customers, thus increasing the ease with which customers can search in the system, and therefore the likelihood that customers will search in the system. Ford and Honda, for example, have both developed information systems that provide each dealer with information on inventory levels of other dealers in the United State. When a dealer is unable to satisfy demand, he is able to check the availability of the car at a nearby dealer. Similarly, services like Auto-By-Tel, CarPoint, and GMBuyPower enable customers to specify the car that they wish to purchase, and to be presented with a list of dealers who have that particular model in stock. Dealers opt into this type of system and typically pay a fee to join.

7.4 TRANSSHIPMENT

Sometimes, it isn't necessary to literally have a centralized inventory deposit to take advantage of inventory pooling. Indeed, the growth of rapid transportation options and advanced information systems has made transshipment an important option to consider when selecting supply chain strategies, and another way to implement inventory pooling strategies. By *transshipment*, we mean the shipment of items between different facilities *at the same level in the supply chain* to meet some immediate need.

Most often, transshipment is considered at the retail level. As we mentioned above, transshipment capability allows the retailer to meet customer demand from *the inventory of other retailers*. To do this, the retailer must know what other retailers have in inventory and must have a rapid way to ship the items either to the store where the customer originally tried to make the purchase or to the customer's home. These requirements can be met only with advanced information systems, which allow a retailer to see what other retailers have in stock and facilitate rapid shipping between retailers.

It is easy to see that if the appropriate information systems exist, shipment costs are reasonable, and all of the retailers have the same owner, transshipment makes sense. In this case, the system is effectively taking advantage of the risk-pooling concept, even if no central warehouse exists, because one can view inventory in different retail outlets as part of a large, single pool.

Retailers that are independently owned and operated may want to avoid transshipment because they will be helping their competitors. In Chapter 8, we consider the issues associated with *distributor integration,* in which independent distributors cooperate in various ways, including transshipment of needed goods.

If these competing retailers still agree to transship, then they are faced with similar questions to those discussed under the inventory pooling model. That is, if dealers agree to transship, it is not clear how much inventory each one of them should keep, since a retailer's strategy depends on its competitor's strategy. It turns out that the techniques and results similar to those we presented when describing inventory pooling also hold in this case.

7.5 SELECTING AN APPROPRIATE STRATEGY

Very few major supply chains utilize one of these strategies exclusively. Typically, different approaches are used for different products, making it necessary to analyze the supply chain and determine the appropriate approach to use for a particular product or product family.

TABLE 7-4

DISTRIBUTION STRATEGIES

Strategy → Attribute ↓	Direct shipment	Cross-docking	Inventory at warehouses
Risk pooling			Take advantage
Transportation costs		Reduced inbound costs	Reduced inbound costs
Holding costs	No warehouse costs	No holding costs	
Allocation		Delayed	Delayed

To evaluate these concepts, we proceed with a simple question: What are the factors that influence distribution strategies? Obviously, customer demand and location, service level, and costs, including transportation and inventory costs, all play a role. It is important to note the interplay of inventory and transportation costs (see Chapters 2 and 3). Both transportation and inventory costs depend on shipment size, but in opposite ways. Increasing lot sizes reduces the delivery frequency and enables the shipper to take advantage of price breaks in shipping volume, therefore reducing transportation costs. However, large lot sizes increase inventory cost per item because items remain in inventory for a longer period of time until they are consumed.

Demand variability also has an impact on the distribution strategy. Indeed, as we observed in Chapter 2, demand variability has a huge impact on cost; the larger the variability, the more safety stock needed. Thus, stock held at the warehouses provides protection against demand variability and uncertainty, and due to *risk pooling*, the more warehouses a distributor has, the more safety stock is needed. On the other hand, if the warehouses are not used for inventory storage, as in the cross-docking strategy, or if there are no warehouses at all, as in direct shipping, more safety stock is required in the distribution system. This is true because, in both cases, *each store* needs to keep enough safety stock. This effect is mitigated, however, by distribution strategies that enable better demand forecasts and smaller safety stocks, and transshipment and pooling strategies. Any assessment of different strategies also must consider lead time and volume requirements, customer requirements and behavior, end product variety, and the capital investment involved in the various alternatives.

Table 7-4 summarizes and compares direct shipping, warehouse inventory, and cross-docking strategies. The inventory-at-warehouses strategy refers to the classical distribution strategy in which inventory is kept at the warehouses. The allocation row in the table refers to the point at which the allocation of different products to different retail outlets needs to be made. Clearly, in direct shipment, allocation decisions have to be made earlier than in the other two, so forecast horizons need to be longer.

SUMMARY

In recent years, many companies have improved performance, reducing cost, increasing service levels, reducing the bullwhip effect, and improving responsiveness to changes in the marketplace, by integrating the supply chain. It is critical, however, to implement effective distribution strategies regardless of the total level of supply chain integration. Depending on the details of the situation, direct shipping or distribution strategies utilizing intermediate inventory storage points such as warehouses or distribution centers might be more appropriate. Even if intermediate inventory storage points are utilized, additional decisions need to be made. Should there be many or only a few warehouses or DCs? Should inventory be held at these locations, or merely transshipped? As a retailer, does it make sense to participate in a centralized inventory pooling system? What about a transshipment system? All of these decisions depend on the nature and characteristics of costs, products, and customers.

DISCUSSION QUESTIONS

1. Consider a large discount store. Discuss some products and suppliers for which the discount store should use a cross-docking strategy; some products and suppliers better suited to a direct-shipment strategy; and, finally, some products and suppliers for which the discount store should utilize a change to; "traditional warehousing strategy."
2. Consider the following supply chains. For each one, list specific advantages of centralized and decentralized management, and centralized and local facilities:
   - **a.** Milk and dairy products
   - **b.** Newspapers
   - **c.** MP3 players
   - **d.** Cars
   - **e.** Jeans
3. What companies or supply chains can you think of that use an inventory pooling strategy?
4. What companies or supply chains can you think of that use transshipment strategies?
5. List two similarities between inventory pooling and transshipment strategies. List two differences. Why might one or the other be appropriate for a particular supply chain?
6. Discuss how companies or dealers can encourage search.
7. Discuss how dealers might discourage search. Why might dealers want to discourage search?
8. Answer the following questions about the Amazon case at the start of the chapter
   - **a.** What expansion options should Amazon Europe select? Expand into other countries? Launch Marketplace activities?
   - **b.** What distribution network configuration should Amazon Europe adopt?

CHAPTER **8**

Strategic Alliances

CASE: How Kimberly-Clark Keeps Client Costco in Diapers

One morning, a Costco store in Los Angeles began running a little low on size-one and size-two Huggies. Crisis loomed.

So what did Costco managers do? Nothing. They didn't have to, thanks to a special arrangement with Kimberly-Clark Corp., the company that makes the diapers.

Under this deal, responsibility for replenishing stock falls on the manufacturer, not Costco. In return, the big retailer shares detailed information about individual stores' sales. So, long before babies in Los Angeles would ever notice it, diaper dearth was averted by a Kimberly-Clark data analyst working at a computer hundreds of miles away in Neenah, Wisconsin.

"When they were doing their own ordering, they didn't have as good a grasp" of inventory, says the Kimberly-Clark data analyst, Michael Fafnis. Now, a special computer link with Costco allows Mr. Fafnis to make snap decisions about where to ship more Huggies and other Kimberly-Clark products.

Just a few years ago, the sharing of such data between a major retailer and a key supplier would have been unthinkable. But the arrangement between Costco Wholesale Corp. and Kimberly-Clark underscores a sweeping change in American retailing. Across the country, powerful retailers fromWal-Mart Stores Inc. to Target Corp. to J.C. Penney Co. are pressuring their suppliers to take a more active role in shepherding products from the factory to store shelves.

CHANGING SIZES

In some cases, that means requiring suppliers to shoulder the costs of warehousing excess merchandise. In others, it means pushing suppliers to change product or package sizes. In the case of Costco and Kimberly-Clark, whose coordinated plan is officially called "vendor-managed inventory," Kimberly-Clark oversees and pays for everything involved with managing Costco's inventory except the actual shelf-stockers in store aisles.

Whatever the arrangement and the terminology, the major focus for these big retailers is the same: Cutting costs along the so-called supply chain, which comprises every step from lumber mill to store shelf. The assumption is that suppliers themselves are in the best position to spot inefficiencies and fix them.

For consumers, it all translates to lower prices at the cash register. Indeed, big companies' increasing

---

Source: Emily Nelson and Ann Zimmerman. *The Wall Street Journal,* Eastern Edition, September 7, 2000.

focus on the supply chain is one reason U.S. prices for general merchandise—goods from laundry detergent to wool sweaters—fell 1.5 percent in 1998 and again last year and are falling at the same rate this year, according to Richard Berner, chief U.S. economist at Morgan Stanley DeanWitter. "Supply-chain management has had a major impact," says Mr. Berner, who compiled his analysis from government data.

RETURN TO UNISEX

There is also a potential downside for consumers: Fewer choices in brands and types of packages. For example, two years ago, Kimberly-Clark stopped making separate diapers for boys and girls and reverted to unisex-only. Less variety makes for easier inventory-tracking in its factories and trucks, the Dallas-based company says.

To a great extent, better cooperation between retailers and suppliers has been made possible by improved technology—such as the computer link Kimberly-Clark uses. It's also a consequence of the greater strength of major retailers as they consolidate and expand globally. Many economists say that closer retailer–supplier coordination on the supply chain is the model of the future and will ultimately determine which companies succeed in the new millennium.

"A shopper buys a roll of Bounty paper towel, and that would trigger someone cutting a tree in Georgia," says Steve David, who heads supply-chain work for Procter & Gamble Co., the Cincinnati consumer-products giant. "That's the holy grail."

These days, P&G stations about 250 people in Fayetteville, Ark., minutes from Wal-Mart's headquarters in Bentonville, solely to promote its products to the discount chain and ensure they move as quickly as possible to store shelves. The two giants share some inventory data.

The price of inefficiencies on the supply chain is high. Revlon Inc. this year slowed its product shipments because store shelves were backed up with older inventory. Kmart Corp.'s new chief executive, Charles Conaway, has publicly blamed the retailer's sagging profits in part on a weak supply chain infrastructure. Last month, he said he expects to spend $1.4 billion over the next two years to update Kmart's technology, including systems for coordinating with suppliers. And earlier this year, Estee Lauder Cos. hired away Compaq Computer Corp.'s executive in charge of supply chain to bolster that operation at the cosmetics concern.

By several accounts, the close collaboration between Costco and Kimberly-Clark serves as a model for other merchandisers, and also helps explain strong recent sales gains by the two companies. In the past two years, Kimberly-Clark gradually expanded the program and now manages inventory for some 44 retailers of its products. The consumer-products company says it wrung $200 million in costs from its supply chain during that period, and it vows to squeeze out another $75 million this year.

"This is what the information age has brought to this industry," says Wayne Sanders, chairman and chief executive officer of Kimberly-Clark. "It gives us a competitive advantage." In fact, Kimberly-Clark says the cost savings it achieves on its supply chain are one reason its Huggies—and not rival P&G's Pampers—are sold at Costco stores in most areas of the country.

"If a company finds a way to lower its costs, it gets those deals," says Richard Dicerchio, Costco's chief operating officer. A spokeswoman for P&G says its supply chain is very efficient, and Costco carries many of its other products.

To oversee ordering for the retailers whose inventory it manages, Kimberly-Clark employs a staff of 24 people, including Mr. Fafnis. A Kimberly- Clark spokeswoman says the benefits of the program "more than offset" additional labor costs. Last year, Kimberly-Clark posted a 51 percent rise in net income to $1.67 billion on $13 billion in sales, capping three years of improving results.

For Costco, the benefits of such close cooperation with a major supplier are equally clear:

Costco saves money not only on staffing in its inventory department, but also on storage. Before Kimberly-Clark began managing Costco's inventory, in late 1997, the retailer would keep an average of a month's supply of Kimberly-Clark products in its warehouses. Now, because Kimberly-Clark has proven it can replenish supplies more efficiently, Costco needs to keep only a two-week supply.

What's more, Costco says its shelves are less likely to go empty under the new system. That's important for both retailer and supplier, because consumer studies indicate that a majority of customers will walk out of a store empty-handed if they can't find a particular item they need. P&G, for example, estimates that an average retailer's loss from out-of-stocks runs about 11 percent of annual sales.

For Costco, which keeps its costs down by typically offering just one brand-name product and its own private-label Kirkland Signature product in each category, maintaining supplies on shelves is crucial. "If we're out of stock, it means we're out of a category, so the chance of a loss of a sale is greater," Mr. Dicerchio says.

Susanne Shallon of Redondo Beach, Calif., says she always buys size-four Huggies for her 22-month-old daughter, Beth, and Pull-Ups for her five-year-old son, Emil, at a nearby Costco because the store is well-stocked. "It's good to have the confidence that when I go into the store, the product will be on hand," she says.

A "Pull" Product

For now, Kimberly-Clark manages inventory in Costco stores everywhere but the Northeast. Kimberly-Clark recently sent analysts to Costco headquarters in Issaquah, Wash., to push for a possible next stage: expanding to the Northeast and collaborating on forecasts, not just recorded sales.

James Sinegal, CEO of Costco, says the chain has always managed its inventory well, but "we want to take things to a higher level." Costco has been a star performer among U.S. retailers, posting double-digit sales growth every year since 1996. Its sales rose 13 percent to $26.98 billion in the fiscal year ended Aug. 29, 1999.

At Costco, diapers are known as a "pull" product—meaning that shoppers make a trip to the store specifically to buy them. Parents are also particularly price-conscious, so the pressure is on for the retailer to keep diapers in stock and to make it as cheap as possible to do so.

For Mr. Fafnis, the 34-year-old Kimberly-Clark data analyst responsible for overseeing stock at 155 Costco stores across the Western U.S., that means arriving at his cubicle at 7:30 each morning to a stack of spreadsheets that show exactly how many boxes of Huggies, Kleenex tissues, and Scott paper towels sit on the shelves. He's privy to more sales and inventory detail than many Costco executives can see.

His mission: to keep each store's inventory as low as possible without risking empty shelves. That allows him very little margin for error, as it takes an average of a week from the time he types an order into his computer until a truck pulls up to a Costco store.

Scanning the spreadsheets one morning a few months ago, Mr. Fafnis, who studies baseball statistics as a hobby, quickly spots the potential problem in Los Angeles. The store's supply of size-one and size-two Huggies is down to 188 packages; in the past week, 74 were sold. That means the store could drop below its safety stock—typically, two weeks' worth of inventory—within days. The computer spits out a suggested order, but Mr. Fafnis cuts it by a few packages. As the father of a two-year-old Huggies wearer, he has a certain instinct for the market. "When the next truck pulls in, you want to be right at your safety stock. That's the ideal situation," Mr. Fafnis says.

Mr. Fafnis, who has never been inside a Costco (there aren't any in Wisconsin), tries to tailor orders to shoppers' whims and the needs of particular neighborhoods. On a bulletin board in his cubicle, he posts a list of special requests heavily marked with orange highlighter. For example, a store in Reno, Nev., can receive deliveries only early Monday mornings to get around city noise ordinances.

After Mr. Fafnis enters orders in his computer, a Kimberly-Clark transportation analyst at the company's logistics center in Knoxville, Tenn., calls up the same computer file and assigns the order to a trucking company.

A CANCELED ORDER

Complaints are handled by Kimberly-Clark customer service analyst Rachel Pope, who sits a few cubicles away from Mr. Fafnis. One afternoon, a Costco merchandise manager calls to say that a store in Spokane, Wash., is under construction and doesn't want its delivery. Ms. Pope phones the logistics center in Knoxville, which tells her the truck destined for Spokane is already at a loading dock in Ogden, Utah. She reaches the driver, via conference call, just before he begins filling the truck. "This was close," she says.

The drive for efficiency creates new problems. Last year, Costco store managers complained that some deliveries were incomplete. Kimberly-Clark managers visited 13 Costco stores and spotted some drivers accidentally unloading items intended for a later stop. Now, Kimberly-Clark uses a simple cardboard divider to separate each store's order.

Scouting store shelves for out-of-stocks is Donna Imes, Kimberly-Clark's saleswoman for Costco. Ms. Imes, who lives near Costco's headquarters, typically logs in to her home computer at 4:30 every morning, scanning reports from Mr. Fafnis. She walks every aisle of at least five Costco stores a week, taking notes in a spiral-ring pad about displays and competitors' prices and chatting up store managers and customers.

Recently, when Ms. Imes saw shoppers stowing diapers on the bottom rung of their carts, she called Huggies brand managers to caution them not to make the packages wider. Noticing that a particular store often ran low on Depend incontinence underwear at the beginning of the month, a Costco manager told Ms. Imes that residents of a retirement center next door always shopped then. So she alerted Mr. Fafnis, who programmed his computer accordingly.

The importance of supply chain hasn't been lost on Kimberly-Clark itself, which is trying to apply the same principles to its own suppliers. These days, it keeps less than a month's supply of diapers in its own warehouses, down nearly 50 percent over the past two years.

For now, raw-material shipments remain the weak link. Advances are small, focusing on such details as how the company stocks Velcro tabs for its diapers. Two years ago, Kimberly-Clark began sharing its production plans with Velcro USA Inc. via weekly e-mails. That cut Velcro inventory 60 percent, saving several million dollars.

Kimberly-Clark says it's trying to cut costs further. Jim Steffen, the company's president of U.S. consumer sales, regularly reminds his staff that the retailer is the customer. "The last time I looked," he says, "we didn't own any stores."

By the end of this chapter, you should be able to answer the following questions:

- Why are major retailers moving toward relationships in which the supplier manages inventory levels at the retailer?
- When should a company handle its logistics needs in-house, and when should external sources be used?
- What other types of business partnerships can be used to improve supply chain performance?
- Can pressures such as the ones described in this case be used to a company's advantage?

8.1 INTRODUCTION

One of the paradoxes of business today is that at the same time that complex business practices (such as the ones we have discussed in the preceding chapters) are becoming essential for firms to survive and thrive, the necessary financial and managerial resources to implement these practices are becoming increasingly scarce. This is one reason why it may not always be effective to perform all of these key business functions in-house. Frequently, a company may find it effective to use other firms with special resources and technical knowledge to perform these functions. Even if a firm has the available resources to perform a particular task, another firm in the supply chain may sometimes be better suited to perform that task simply because its relative location in the supply chain better positions it to do so.

Often, a combination of position in the supply chain, resources, and expertise determines the most appropriate firm in the supply chain to perform a particular function. Of course, it is not enough to *know* who in the supply chain should perform a particular function—steps must be taken so that the function is actually performed by the appropriate firm. For example, in some of the situations, labor intensive activities have been outsourced to India and China due to lower wages of unskilled and semi-skilled workforce in these countries. Electronic hardware outsourcing to Taiwan and software intensive jobs to India are due to reasons such as availability of manufacturing facility or skilled manpower.

As with any business function, there are four basic ways for a firm to ensure that a logistics-related business function is completed [144]:

1. **Internal activities.** A firm can perform the activity using internal resources and expertise, if they are available. As we will discuss more completely in the next section, if this activity is one of the *core strengths* of the firm, this may be the best way to perform the activity.
2. **Acquisitions.** If a firm doesn't have the expertise or specialized resources internally, it can acquire another firm that does. For some of the recent acquisitions in India, such as Corus by Tata Steel, one of the reasons experts give is the availability of many modern technologies of Corus to Tata. In some cases, it has helped the acquiring firm in getting wider accessibility to new markets. This certainly gives the acquiring firm full control over the way the particular business function is performed, but it has several possible drawbacks. For one thing, acquiring a successful company can be difficult and expensive. The culture of the acquired company may clash with that of the acquiring company, and the effectiveness of the acquired company could be lost in the assimilation process. The acquired company may have previously dealt with the acquiring company's competitors, and it could lose this business. This may hurt its overall effectiveness. For these reasons, as well as many others, an acquisition may not be appropriate.
3. **Arm's-length transactions.** Most business transactions are of this type. A firm needs a specific item or service, such as the delivery of a load of items, the maintenance of a vehicle, or the design and installation of logistics management software, and purchases or leases the item or service. Many times, an arm's-length transaction is the most effective and appropriate arrangement. Of course, the goals and strategies of the supplier might not match those of the buyer. In general, this kind of short-term arrangement fulfills a particular business need but doesn't lead to long-term strategic advantages.
4. **Strategic alliances.** These are typically multifaceted, goal-oriented, long-term partnerships between two companies in which both risks and rewards are shared. In many cases, the problems of outright acquisition can be avoided while at the same time mutual goals can lead to the commitment of many more resources than in the case of arm's-length transactions. Strategic alliances typically lead to long-term strategic benefits for both partners.

This chapter focuses on *strategic alliances* related to supply chain management. In the next section, we introduce a framework for analyzing the advantages and disadvantages of strategic alliances. In Sections 8.3, 8.4, and 8.5, the three most important types of supply chain–related strategic alliances are discussed in greater detail: third-party logistics (3PL), retailer–supplier partnerships (RSP), and distributor integration (DI).

8.2 A FRAMEWORK FOR STRATEGIC ALLIANCES

There are many difficult strategic issues that play a part in the selection of appropriate *strategic alliances*. Jordan Lewis [125] has introduced an effective general framework for analyzing strategic alliances. This framework, which we briefly introduce in this section, is very helpful for considering the kinds of supply chain–related strategic alliances that we address in the rest of this chapter.

To determine whether a particular strategic alliance is appropriate for your firm, consider how the alliance will help address the following issues:

Adding value to products. A partnership with the appropriate firm can help add value to existing products. For example, partnerships that improve time to market, distribution times, or repair times help to increase the perceived value of a particular firm. Similarly, partnerships between companies with complementary product lines can add value to both companies' products.

Improving market access. Partnerships that lead to better advertising or increased access to new market channels can be beneficial. For example, complementary consumer product manufacturers can cooperate to address the needs of major retailers, increasing sales for everyone.

Strengthening operations. Alliances between appropriate firms can help to improve operations by lowering system costs and cycle times. Facilities and resources can be used more efficiently and effectively. For example, companies with complementary seasonal products can effectively use warehouses and trucks year-round.

Adding technological strength. Partnerships in which technology is shared can help add to the skills base of both partners. Also, the difficult transitions between old and new technologies can be facilitated by the expertise of one of the partners. For example, a supplier may need a particular enhanced information system to work with a certain customer. Partnering with a firm that already has expertise in this system makes it easier to address difficult technological issues.

Enhancing strategic growth. Many new opportunities have high entry barriers. Partnerships might enable firms to pool expertise and resources to overcome these barriers and explore new opportunities.

Enhancing organizational skills. Alliances provide a tremendous opportunity for organizational learning. In addition to learning from one another, partners are forced to learn more about themselves and to become more flexible so that these alliances work.

Building financial strength. In addition to addressing these competitive issues, alliances can help to build financial strength. Income can be increased and administrative costs can be shared between partners or even reduced owing to the expertise of one or both of the partners. Of course, alliances also limit investment exposure by sharing risk.

Strategic alliances have their downsides. The list above is useful for determining these. Each company has its *core strengths* or competencies—specific talents that differentiate the company from its competitors and give it an advantage in the eyes of its customers. These core strengths must not be weakened by the alliance, which can happen if resources are diverted from these strengths or if technological or strategic strengths are compromised to make the partnership successful. Similarly, key differences with competitors must not be diminished. This is possible if key technology is shared or if entry barriers are reduced for the competition.

Determining these core strengths is clearly very important; unfortunately, it is also very difficult; what they are depends on the nature of the business and of the firm. Core strengths don't necessarily correspond to a large investment of resources, and they may be intangible items such as management skills or brand image. To determine a firm's core strengths, consider how the firm's internal capabilities contribute to differentiating it from its competition in each of the seven key items listed above. Now, how will *strategic alliances* help or hurt in each of these areas? See more on this topic in Chapter 9 where we discuss outsourcing decisions.

The following example illustrates the advantages and disadvantages of strategic alliances. Consider how IBM, Intel, and Microsoft benefited and were hurt by the relationships described in this example.

EXAMPLE 8-1

Although not specifically related to logistics, the example of the IBM personal computer (PC) highlights the advantages and the disadvantages of outsourcing key business functions. When IBM decided to enter the PC market in late 1981, the company did not have the infrastructure in place to design and build a personal computer. Rather than take the time to develop these capabilities, IBM outsourced almost all the major components of the PC. For example, the microprocessor was designed and built by Intel and the operating system was provided by a small company in Seattle called Microsoft. IBM was able to release this computer to market within 15 months of beginning its design by tapping the expertise and resources of other companies. Furthermore, within three years IBM replaced Apple Computer as the number one supplier of personal computers. By 1985 IBM's market share was more than 40 percent. However, the downside to IBM's strategy soon became clear, as competitors such as Compaq were able to enter the market by utilizing the same suppliers as IBM. Furthermore, when IBM tried to regain control of the market by introducing its PS/2 line of computers, featuring a new, proprietary design and an operating system called OS/2, other companies did not follow IBM's lead, and the original architecture remained dominant in the market. By the end of 1995, IBM's market share had fallen to less than 8 percent, behind market leader Compaq's 10 percent [50]. Finally, in 2005, IBM sold its personal computer division to Lenovo Group.

EXAMPLE 8-2 BACKWARD INTEGRATION IN TATA MOTORS

Tata Motor is relatively a late entrant in small and medium size car segment in India. Its first indigenously developed *Indica* model was launched in December 1998. The market was very upbeat about this model, which is reflected in a record of over 100,000 fully paid bookings within the first week. The success can be attributed to strong brand image of group-company and a strong supply chain network to deliver the product at a competitive price. Over its strong competitors, like Maruti, Ford Motors, General Motors, Hyundai, etc, Tata has an unparallel edge. It can leverage the backward integration with tier 1, tier 2 and in some cases tier 3 suppliers. For example, steel, which constitutes the major share of raw material cost, is sourced from Tata's own flagship company—Tata Steel. Maruti, its major competitor, sources steel from POSCO, Nippon steel, Bhushan Steel, etc. Another important raw material is paints. Nerolac Paints, which is a JV between Tata and Kansai Paints of Japan supports Tata Motor in its supply. This level of backward integration is not very common in the auto sector across the globe [275].

Although strategic alliances are becoming increasingly prevalent in all walks of business, three types are particularly significant in supply chain management. Third party logistics (3PL), retailer–supplier partnerships (RSP), and distributor integration (DI) are discussed in detail in the next three sections. As you read about these issues, try to place them in the framework described above.

8.3 THIRD-PARTY LOGISTICS

The use of third-party logistics (3PL) providers to take over some or all of a company's logistics responsibilities is becoming more prevalent. Indeed, the third-party logistics industry, which essentially began in the 1980s, has grown over the past decade or so from a $31 billion industry to an $85 billion industry (at the end of 2004), taking in about 8 percent of all of the money spent on logistics in the United State [265].

8.3.1 What Is 3PL?

Third-party logistics is simply the use of an outside company to perform all or part of the firm's materials management and product distribution functions. 3PL relationships are typically more complex than traditional logistics supplier relationships: they are true strategic alliances.

Although companies have used outside firms to provide particular services, such as trucking and warehousing, for many years, these relationships had two typical characteristics: they were *transaction based* and the companies hired were often *single-function* specific. Modern 3PL arrangements involve long-term commitments and often multiple functions or process management. For example, Ryder Dedicated Logistics currently has a multiyear agreement to design, manage, and operate all of Whirlpool Corporation's inbound logistics [136, 266]. Safe Express also provides 3PL services to many firms in India.

3PL providers come in all sizes and shapes, from small companies with a few million dollars in revenues to huge companies with revenues in the billions. Most of these companies can manage many stages of the supply chain. Some third-party logistics providers own assets such as trucks and warehouses; others may provide coordination services but not own assets on their own. Non-asset-owning third-party logistics firms are sometimes called fourth-party logistics providers (4PL).

Surprisingly, the use of third-party logistics is most prevalent among large companies. Firms such as 3M, Eastman Kodak, Dow Chemical, Time Warner, and Sears Roebuck are turning over large portions of their logistics operations to outside suppliers. Third-party logistics providers are finding it hard to persuade small companies to employ their services, although this may change as the use of 3PL becomes more prevalent and as 3PL providers make a larger effort to develop relationships with smaller companies [28].

8.3.2 Advantages and Disadvantages of 3PL

Most of the general advantages and disadvantages of strategic alliances described in Section 8.2 apply here.

Focus on Core Strengths The most frequently cited benefit of using 3PL providers is that it allows a company to focus on its core competencies. With corporate resources becoming increasingly limited, it is often difficult to be an expert in every facet of the business. Logistics outsourcers provide a company with the opportunity to focus on that company's particular area of expertise, leaving the logistics expertise to the logistics companies. (Of course, if logistics is one of the company's areas of expertise, then outsourcing may not make sense.)

Provide Technological Flexibility The ever-increasing need for technological flexibility is another important advantage of the use of 3PL providers. As requirements change and technology advances, and technology such as RFID becomes more prevalent, the better 3PL providers constantly update their information technology and equipment. Often individual companies do not have the time, resources, or

EXAMPLE 8-3

The partnership between Ryder Dedicated Logistics and General Motors' Saturn division is a good example of these benefits. Saturn focuses on automobile manufacturing and Ryder manages most of Saturn's other logistics considerations. Ryder deals with vendors; delivers parts to the Saturn factory in Spring Hill, Tennessee; and delivers finished vehicles to the dealers. Saturn orders parts using electronic data interchange (EDI) and sends the same information to Ryder. Ryder makes all the necessary pickups from 300 different suppliers in the United States, Canada, and Mexico, using special *decision-support software* to effectively plan routes to minimize transportation costs [61].

EXAMPLE 8-4

British Petroleum (BP) and Chevron Corp. also wished to stick to their core competencies. To do this, they formed Atlas Supply, a partnership of about 80 suppliers, to deliver items such as spark plugs, tires, window-washing fluid, belts, and antifreeze to their 6,500 service stations. Rather than use the distribution networks of either BP or Chevron or create a new one, Atlas outsourced all logistics to GATX, which is responsible for running five distribution centers and maintaining inventory of 6,500 SKUs at each service station. Each service station orders supplies through its oil company, which forwards the order to Atlas and then to GATX. Each station has a pre-assigned ordering day to avoid system bottlenecks. GATX systems determine appropriate routes and configurations and transmit orders to the DC. The next day, the DC selects and packs the orders, and trucks are loaded in the appropriate order based on the delivery schedule. As deliveries are made, returns and deliveries from Atlas suppliers are picked up. GATX electronically informs Atlas, Chevron, and BP of the status of all deliveries. The companies save enough on transportation costs alone to justify this partnership, and the two oil companies have managed to reduce the number of DCs from 13 to 5 and significantly improve service levels [5].

expertise to constantly update their technology. Different retailers may have different, and changing, delivery and information technology requirements, and meeting these requirements may be essential to a company's survival. Third-party logistics providers often can meet these requirements in a quicker, more cost-effective way [104]. Also, third-party providers already may have the capability to meet the needs of a firm's potential customers, allowing the firm access to certain retailers that might not otherwise be possible or cost-effective.

Provide Other Flexibilities Third parties also may provide greater flexibility to a company. One example is flexibility in geographic locations. Increasingly, suppliers are requiring rapid replenishment, which in turn may require regional warehousing. By utilizing third-party providers for this warehousing, a company can meet customer requirements without committing capital and limiting flexibility by constructing a new facility or committing to a long-term lease. Also, flexibility in service offerings may

EXAMPLE 8-5

Working with the Simmons Company, a mattress manufacturer, Ryder Dedicated Logistics provided new technology that allowed Simmons to completely change the way it does business. Before its involvement with Ryder, Simmons warehoused between 20,000 and 50,000 mattresses at each of its manufacturing facilities to meet customer demand in a timely fashion. Now, Ryder maintains an on-site logistics manager at Simmons' manufacturing plant. When orders arrive, the logistics manager uses special software to design an optimal sequence and route to deliver the mattresses to customers. This logistics plan is then transmitted to the factory floor, where the mattresses are manufactured, in the exact quantity, style, and sequence required—all in time for the shipment. This logistics partnership has virtually eliminated the need for Simmons to hold inventory at all [61].

EXAMPLE 8-6

SonicAir, a division of UPS, provides an even more sophisticated third-party service. This company serves specialized customers who supply equipment for which every hour of downtime is very expensive; SonicAir rapidly delivers service parts where they are needed. SonicAir maintains 67 warehouses and uses specialized software to determine the appropriate inventory level for each part at each warehouse. When an order is placed, the system determines the best way to deliver the part and sends it out, usually on the next flight, where it is delivered by one of the company's ground couriers. This service enables customers to store fewer parts at each field service bureau than would otherwise be necessary—and still provide the same level of service. With some parts valued at hundreds of thousands of dollars, this is clearly a cost savings to the customer. At the same time, this business is very profitable for SonicAir because customers are willing to pay well for this level of service [61].

be achieved through the use of third parties, which may be equipped to offer retail customers a much larger variety of services than the hiring firm. In some cases, the volume of customers demanding these services may be low to the firm, but higher to the 3PL provider, who may be working for several different firms across different industries [237]. In addition, flexibility in resource and workforce size can be achieved through outsourcing. Managers can change what would be fixed costs into variable costs, in order to react more quickly to changing business conditions.

Important Disadvantages of 3PL The most obvious disadvantage of the use of 3PL providers is the *loss of control* inherent in outsourcing a particular function. This is especially true for outbound logistics where 3PL company employees themselves might interact with a firm's customers. Many third-party logistics firms work very hard to address these concerns. Efforts include painting company logos on the sides of trucks, dressing 3PL employees in the uniforms of the hiring company, and providing extensive reporting on each customer interaction.

Also, if logistics is one of the core competencies of a firm, it makes no sense to outsource these activities to a supplier who may not be as capable as the firm's in-house expertise. For example, Wal-Mart built and manages its own distribution centers and Caterpillar runs its parts supply operations. These are competitive advantages and core competencies of these firms, so outsourcing is unnecessary. In particular, if certain logistics activities are within the core competencies of the firm and others are not, it might be wise to employ 3PL providers for only those areas that outside providers can handle better than the hiring firm. For example, if VMI replenishment strategies and materials handling are core competencies of a company but transportation is not, a 3PL firm could be contacted to handle shipments from the dock to the customer exclusively. Similarly, pharmaceutical companies build and own DCs for controlled drugs, but often use public warehouses located closer to the customer for items that are less expensive and easier to control [10].

8.3.3 3PL Issues and Requirements

A third-party logistics contract is typically a major and complex business decision. Other than the pros and cons listed above, there are many considerations that are critical in deciding whether an agreement should be entered into with a particular 3PL provider.

1. **Know your own costs.** Among the most basic issues to consider in selecting a 3PL provider is to know your own costs so they can be compared with the cost of using an outsourcing firm. Often it is necessary to use activity-based costing techniques, which involve tracing overhead and direct costs back to specific products and services [104].
2. **Customer orientation of the 3PL.** Of course, it is not enough to select a provider based on cost alone. Many of the advantages listed above involve intangibles such as flexibility. Therefore, the strategic logistics plan of the company and how a 3PL provider would fit into this plan must be considered carefully. A survey of 3PL providers [136] identified the following characteristics as most critical to the success of a 3PL agreement. The most important was the customer orientation of the provider; that is, the value of a 3PL relationship is directly related to the ability of the provider to understand the needs of the hiring firm and to adapt its services to the special requirements of that firm. The second most important factor was reliability. The flexibility of the provider, or its ability to react to the changing needs of the hiring firm and the needs of that firm's customers, was third. Significantly further down the list were cost savings.
3. **Specialization of the 3PL.** When choosing a potential 3PL provider, some experts suggest that companies should consider firms whose roots lie in the particular area of logistics that is most

relevant to the logistics requirements in question. For example, Roadway Logistics, Menlo Logistics, Blue Dart and Yellow Logistics evolved from major LTL carriers; Exel Logistics, GATX, and USCO started as warehouse managers; and UPS and Federal Express have expertise in the timely handling of small packages. Some firms have even more specialized requirements, and these should be considered carefully when choosing a 3PL partner [6]. Sometimes, a firm can use one of its trusted core carriers as its third-party logistics provider. For example, Schneider National, a firm that already worked closely with Baxter Healthcare Corp., agreed a few years ago to take over Baxter's dedicated fleet routes [148].

4. **Asset-owning versus non-asset-owning 3PL.** There are also advantages and disadvantages to utilizing an asset-owning versus a non-asset-owning 3PL company. Asset-owning companies have significant size, access to human resources, a large customer base, economies of scope and scale, and systems in place, but they may tend to favor their own divisions in awarding work, to be bureaucratic, and to have a long decision-making cycle. Non-asset-owning companies may bemore flexible and able to tailor services and have the freedom to mix and match providers. They also may have low overhead costs and specialized industry expertise at the same time, but limited resources and lower bargaining power [10].

8.3.4 3PL Implementation Issues

Once a potential partner has been selected, the process has only begun. Agreements need to be reached and appropriate efforts must be made by both companies to initiate the relationship effectively. Experts point to one lesson in particular that has come from failed 3PL agreements: Devote enough time to start-up considerations; that is, starting the relationship effectively during the first six months to a year is both the most difficult and the most critical part of any 3PL alliance. The company purchasing the services must identify exactly what it needs for the relationship to be successful, and be able to provide specific performance measures and requirements to the 3PL firm.

The logistics provider, in turn, must consider and discuss these requirements honestly and completely, including their realism and relevance [28]. Both parties must be committed to devoting the time and effort needed to making a success of the relationship. It is critical that both parties remember that this is a mutually beneficial third-party alliance, with shared risk and reward. The parties are partners—neither party can take a "transaction pricing" mentality [9].

In general, *effective communication* is essential for any outsourcing project to succeed. First, within the hiring company, managers must communicate to each other and to their employees exactly why they are outsourcing and what they expect from the outsourcing process, so that all relevant departments are on the "same page" and can become appropriately involved. Obviously, communication between the firm and the 3PL provider is also critical. It is easy to speak in generalities, but specific communication is essential if both companies are to benefit from the outsourcing arrangement [28].

On a technological level, it is usually necessary to enable communications between the 3PL supplier's systems and those of the hiring customer. Along the same line, a firm should avoid 3PL providers who utilize proprietary information systems, because these are much more difficult to integrate with other systems.

Other important issues to discuss with potential 3PL providers include the following:

- The third party and its service providers must respect the confidentiality of the data that you provide them.
- Specific performance measures must be agreed upon.

- Specific criteria regarding subcontractors should be discussed.
- Arbitration issues should be considered before entering into a contract.
- Escape clauses should be negotiated into the contract.
- Methods of ensuring that performance goals are being met should be discussed [9].

8.4 RETAILER–SUPPLIER PARTNERSHIPS

The formation of strategic alliances between retailers and their suppliers is becoming ubiquitous in many industries. We saw in Chapter 5 that variation in demand to suppliers from retailers in traditional retailer–supplier relationships is far greater than the variation in demand seen by retailers. In addition, suppliers have far better knowledge of their lead times and production capacities than retailers do. Thus, as margins get tighter and customer satisfaction becomes even more important, it makes sense to create cooperative efforts between suppliers and retailers in order to leverage the knowledge of both parties. These are called retailer–supplier partnership (RSP) and we describe some examples in the next sections.

8.4.1 Types of RSP

The types of retailer–supplier partnerships can be viewed on a continuum. At one end is information sharing, which helps the vendor plan more efficiently, and at the other is a consignment scheme, where the vendor completely manages and owns the inventory until the retailer sells it.

In a basic *quick response* strategy, suppliers receive POS data from retailers and use this information to synchronize their production and inventory activities with actual sales at the retailer. In this strategy, the retailer still prepares individual orders, but the POS data are used by the supplier to improve forecasting and scheduling and to reduce lead time.

EXAMPLE 8-7

Among the first companies to utilize this scheme was Milliken and Company, a textile and chemicals company. Milliken worked with several clothing suppliers and major department stores, all of which agreed to use POS data from the department stores to "synchronize" their ordering and manufacturing plans. The lead time from order receipt at Milliken's textile plants to final clothing receipt at the department stores was reduced from 18 weeks to 3 weeks [215].

In a *continuous replenishment* strategy, sometimes called *rapid replenishment*, vendors receive POS data and use these data to prepare shipments at previously agreed-upon intervals to maintain specific levels of inventory. In an advanced form of continuous replenishment, suppliers may gradually decrease inventory levels at the retail store or distribution center as long as service levels are met. Thus, in a structured way, inventory levels are continuously improved. In addition, the inventory levels need not be simple levels, but could be based on sophisticated models that change the appropriate level based on seasonal demand, promotions, and changing consumer demand [174].

In a *vendor-managed inventory (VMI)* system, sometimes called a *vendor-managed replenishment (VMR)* system, the supplier decides on the appropriate inventory levels of each of the products (within previously agreed-upon bounds) and the appropriate inventory policies to maintain these levels. In the initial stages, vendor suggestions must be approved by the retailer, but eventually the goal of many VMI programs is to eliminate retailer oversight on specific orders. This type of relationship is perhaps most famously exemplified by Wal-Mart and Procter & Gamble, whose partnership, begun in 1985, has dramatically improved P&G's on-time deliveries to Wal-Mart while increasing inventory turns [34]. Other discount stores followed suit, including Kmart, which by 1992 had developed over 200 VMI partners [215]. These VMI projects have in general been successful: projects at Dillard Department Stores, JCPenney, and Wal-Mart have shown sales increases of 20 to 25 percent, and 30 percent inventory turnover improvements [34].

The main characteristics of RSP are summarized in Table 8-1.

EXAMPLE 8-8

First Brands, Inc., the maker of such products as Glad sandwich bags, has successfully partnered with Kmart. In 1991, the company entered Kmart's Partners in Merchandise Flow program, in which vendors are responsible for ensuring appropriate inventory levels to Kmart at all times, at Kmart's insistence. Initially, Kmart provided a three-year sales history, followed later by daily POS data to First Brands, which uses special software to convert these data into a production and delivery plan to each of Kmart's 13 distribution centers [60].

8.4.2 Requirements for RSP

The most important requirement for an effective retailer–supplier partnership, especially one toward the VMI end of the partnership spectrum, is *advanced information systems,* on both the supplier and retailer sides of the supply chain. Electronic data interchange, EDI, or Internet-based private exchanges—to relay POS information to the supplier and delivery information to the retailer—are essential to cut down on data transfer time and entry mistakes. Bar coding and scanning are essential to maintain data accuracy. And inventory, production control, and planning systems must be online, accurate, and integrated to take advantage of the additional information available.

As in all initiatives that can radically change the way a company operates, top management commitment is required for the project to succeed. This is especially true because information that has been kept confidential up to this point will now have to be shared with suppliers and customers, and cost allocation issues will have to be considered at a very high level (this is covered in more detail below). It is also true because such a partnership may shift power within the organization from one group to another. For instance, when a VMI partnership is implemented, the day-to-day contacts with retailers shift from sales and marketing personnel to logistics personnel. This implies that incentives for and compensation of the sales force have to be modified since the retailer's inventory levels are driven by

TABLE 8-1

MAIN CHARACTERISTICS OF RSP

Criteria → Type ↓	Decision maker	Inventory ownership	New skills employed by vendors
Quick response	Retailer	Retailer	Forecasting skills
Continuous replenishment	Contractually agreed-to levels	Either party	Forecasting and inventory control
Advanced continuous replenishment	Contractually agreed-to and continuously improved levels	Either party	Forecasting and inventory control
VMI	Vendor	Either party	Retail management

supply chain needs, not by pricing and discount strategies. This change in power may require significant involvement of top management.

Finally, RSP requires the partners to develop a certain level of trust without which the alliance is going to fail. In VMI, for example, suppliers need to demonstrate that they can manage the entire supply chain; that is, they can manage not only their own inventory but also that of the retailer. Similarly, in quick response, confidential information is provided to the supplier, which typically serves many competing retailers. In addition, strategic partnering in many cases results in significant reduction in inventory at the retailer outlet. The supplier needs to make sure that the additional available space is not used to benefit the supplier's competitors. Furthermore, the top management at the supplier must understand that the immediate effect of decreased inventory at the retailer will be a *one-time loss in sales revenue*.

8.4.3 Inventory Ownership in RSP

Several important issues must be considered when entering into a retailer–supplier partnership. One major issue is the decision concerning who makes the replenishment decisions. This places the partnership on the continuum of strategic partnership possibilities described above. This can be done in stages, first with information and, later, decision making, which is shared between the partners. Inventory ownership issues are critical to the success of this kind of strategic alliance effort, especially one involving vendor-managed inventory. Originally, ownership of goods transferred to the retailer when goods were received. Now, some VMI partnerships are moving to a consignment relationship in which the supplier owns the goods until they are sold. The benefit of this kind of relationship to the retailer is obvious: lower inventory costs. Furthermore, since the supplier owns the inventory, it will be more concerned with managing it as effectively as possible.

One possible criticism of the original VMI scheme is that the vendor has an incentive to move to the retailer as much inventory as the contract allows. If this is a fast-moving item and the partners had agreed upon two weeks of inventory, this may be exactly what the retailer wants to see in stock. If, however, this is a more complex problem of inventory management, the vendor needs to have an incentive to keep inventories as low as possible, subject to some agreed-upon service level. For example, Wal-Mart no longer owns the stock for many of the items it carries, including most of its grocery purchases. It only owns them briefly as they are being passed through the checkout scanner [36].

It is less clear, however, why this consignment arrangement is beneficial to the supplier since the supplier owns inventory for a longer period of time. Many times, as in the case of Wal-Mart, the supplier has no choice because the market dictates this kind of arrangement. Even if this is not the case, such an arrangement is beneficial to the supplier because it allows the supplier to coordinate distribution and production, thus reducing total cost. To better understand this issue, recall from Chapter 5 the discussion of the difference between *global optimization* and *local optimization*. In the traditional supply chain, each facility does what is best for that facility; that is, the retailer manages its own inventory without regard to the impact on the supplier. The supplier in turn identifies a policy that will optimize its own cost subject to satisfaction of the retailer demand. In VMI, one tries to optimize the entire system by coordinating production and distribution. In addition, the supplier can further decrease total cost by coordinating production and distribution for several retailers. This is precisely why global optimization allows for significant reductions in total system costs. Sometimes, depending on the relative power of the supplier and the retailer, the supply contract must be negotiated so that the supplier and the retailer share *overall system savings*. Retailers also must take this into account when comparing the cost of competing vendors: Different logistics schemes have different costs.

EXAMPLE 8-9

Ace Hardware, a retail hardware dealer co-op, has successfully implemented a consignment VMI scheme for lumber and building materials. In this program, Ace maintains financial ownership of these goods at the retailer, but the retailer has custodial ownership that makes it responsible if the product is damaged or destroyed [6]. The program is considered extremely successful, with service levels increasing from 92 to 96 percent on VMI items. Ace would eventually like to expand it to other product lines [8].

In addition to inventory and ownership issues, advanced strategic alliances can cover many different areas. Issues such as joint forecasting, meshed planning cycles, and even joint product development are sometimes considered [194].

8.4.4 Issues in RSP Implementation

For any agreement to be a success, performance measurement criteria also must be agreed to. These criteria should include nonfinancial measures as well as the traditional financial measures. For example, nonfinancial measures could include point-of-sale (POS) accuracy, inventory accuracy, shipment and delivery accuracy, lead times, and customer fill rates. When information is being shared between retailers and suppliers, *confidentiality* becomes an issue. Specifically, a retailer who deals with several suppliers within the same product category may find that category information is important to the supplier in making accurate forecasts and stocking decisions. Similarly, there may be a relationship between stocking decisions made by several suppliers. How can these potential conflicts be managed, with the retailer maintaining the confidentiality of each partner?

When entering any kind of strategic alliance, it is important for both parties to realize that there will initially be problems that can only be worked out through *communication* and *cooperation*. For example, when First Brands started partnering with Kmart, Kmart often claimed that its supplier was not living up to its agreement to keep two weeks of inventory on hand at all times. It turned out that the problem arose from different forecasting methods employed by the two companies. This problem was eventually solved by direct communication between Kmart's forecasting experts and those from First Brands—this type of communication would have occurred through salespeople before the VMI partnership began [60].

In many cases, the supplier in a partnership commits to fast response to emergencies and situational changes at the retailer. If the manufacturing technology or capacity do not currently exist at the supplier, they may need to be added. For example, VF Mills, the maker of Wrangler jeans and a pioneer of quick response methods in the clothing industry, had to completely reengineer its production processes, including retraining and additional capital investment [34].

8.4.5 Steps in RSP Implementation

The important points listed above can be summarized in the following steps in VMI implementation [114]:

1. Initially, the contractual terms of the agreement must be negotiated. These include decisions concerning ownership and when it is to be transferred, credit terms, ordering responsibilities, and performance measures such as service or inventory levels, when appropriate.
2. Next, the following three tasks must be executed:
   - If they do not exist, integrated information systems must be developed for both supplier and retailer. These information systems must provide easy access to both parties.

- Effective forecasting techniques to be used by the vendor and the retailer must be developed.
- A tactical decision support tool to assist in *coordinating* inventory management and transportation policies must be developed. The systems developed, of course, will depend on the particular nature of the partnership.

8.4.6 Advantages and Disadvantages of RSP

One advantage of VMI relationships is nicely illustrated by the following example.

EXAMPLE 8-10

Whitehall Robbins (WR), which makes over-the-counter drugs such as Advil, has an RSP relationship with Kmart. Like First Brands, WR initially disagreed with Kmart about forecasts. In this case, it turned out that WR forecasts were more accurate because the company has a much more extensive knowledge of its products than Kmart does. For example, Kmart's Chap Stick forecasts did not take the seasonality of the product into account. In addition, WR planners can take production issues, such as planned downtime, into account when planning shipments.

Also, WR benefits in another way. In the past, Kmart would order large quantities of seasonal items at the beginning of the season, often linked to a promotion. This practice often led to returns because it was difficult for Kmart to accurately forecast the amount it would sell. Now WR supplies weekly demand at an "everyday low cost," so large orders and preseason promotions have been eliminated, which in turn has greatly reduced returns. Inventory turns for seasonal items have gone from 3 to more than 10 and for nonseasonal items from 12–15 to 17–20 [60].

Thus, in general, a huge advantage of RSPs is the knowledge the supplier has about order quantities, implying an ability to control the bullwhip effect (see Chapter 5).

This of course varies from one type of partnership to another. In quick response, for instance, this knowledge is achieved through transfer of customer demand information that allows the supplier to reduce lead time, while in VMI the retailer provides demand information and the supplier makes ordering decisions, thus completely controlling the variability in order quantities. Of course, this knowledge can be leveraged to reduce overall system costs and improve overall system service levels. The benefits to the supplier in terms of better service levels, decreased managerial expenses, and decreased inventory costs are obvious. The vendor should be able to reduce forecast uncertainties and thus better coordinate production and distribution. To be more specific, reduced forecast uncertainties lead to reduced safety stocks, reduced storage and delivery costs, and increased service levels [114], as we noted in our discussion of the bullwhip effect in Chapter 5.

In addition to the important benefits listed above, implementing a strategic partnership provides a variety of side benefits. It provides a good opportunity for the reengineering of the retailer–supplier relationship. For example, redundant order entries can be eliminated, manual tasks can be automated, tasks such as ticketing merchandise and designing displays can be reassigned for systemwide efficiency, and unnecessary control steps can be eliminated from the process [34]. Many of these advantages stem from the same changes and technology needed to implement partnerships in the first place.

Many of the problems with retailer–supplier partnerships have been discussed above and are summarized here.

- It is necessary to employ advanced technology, which is often expensive.
- It is essential to develop trust in what once may have been an adversarial supplier– retailer relationship.
- In a strategic partnership, the supplier often has much more responsibility than formerly. This may force the supplier to add personnel to meet this responsibility.

- Finally, and perhaps most critically, expenses at the supplier often increase as managerial responsibilities increase. Also, inventory may initially be shifted back to the supplier; if a consignment arrangement is used, inventory costs in general may increase for the supplier. Thus, it may be necessary to work out a contractual relationship in which the retailer shares decreased system inventory costs with the supplier.

Float is another issue with any EDI implementation, and it needs to be carefully considered when committing to a VMI partnership. Retailers who have become accustomed to waiting 30 to 90 days to pay for goods may now have to pay upon delivery. Even if they pay only when their goods are sold, this could be much sooner than their usual period of float [88].

8.4.7 Successes and Failures

We have cited several examples of RSP in the sections above. We include several other examples of successes—and one example of a failure—next.

EXAMPLE 8-11

Western Publishing is using VMI for its Golden Books line of children's books at several retailers, including more than 2,000 Wal-Mart locations. In this program, POS data automatically trigger reorders when inventory falls below a reorder point. This inventory is delivered either to a distribution center or, in many cases, directly to a store. In this case, ownership of the books shifts to the retailer once deliveries have been made. In the case of Toys "R" Us, Western Publishing has even managed the entire book section for the retailer, including inventory from suppliers other than Western Publishing. The company has generated significant additional sales in both cases, although the program has increased costs significantly: These are costs related to the additional inventory management duties, as well as the extra freight costs incurred by shipping directly to stores. Nonetheless, management believes that VMI has provided a net benefit for the company [6].

EXAMPLE 8-12

After Wal-Mart included supplier Mead-Johnson in its VMI program, the results were dramatic. Mead-Johnson has complete POS information to which it reacts instead of orders. Since this program was implemented, inventory turns at Wal-Mart have gone from under 10 to more than 100, and at Mead-Johnson from 12 to 52. Similarly, Scott Paper Company has been managing inventory in 25 of its customer distribution centers. In this effort, inventory turns at the customers have increased from about 19 to somewhere between 35 and 55, inventory levels have been reduced, and service levels have improved. One caveat can be drawn from the experiences of Schering-Plough Healthcare Products (SPHP) with Kmart's Partners in the Merchandise Flow Program. In the first year of implementation, SPHP did see decreased stockouts at Kmart, but not substantially improved sales or profits. By patiently continuing with the program, however, SPHP eventually did realize substantial benefits in these areas [239].

EXAMPLE 8-13

VF Corporation's Market Response System provides another success story of VMI. The company, which has many well-known brand names (e.g., Wrangler, Lee, the North Face, and Nautica), began its program in 1989. Currently, about 40 percent of its production is handled through some type of automatic replenishment scheme. This is particularly notable because the program encompasses 350 different retailers, 40,000 store locations, and more than 15 million levels of replenishment. Each division uses automatic software to manage the huge influx of data, and special techniques developed at VF to cluster the data so that they are more manageable. VF's program is considered one of the most successful in the apparel industry [209].

EXAMPLE 8-14

Spartan Stores, a grocery chain, shut down its VMI effort about one year after its inception. In examining the reasons for the failure of the program, some important ingredients for a successful VMI program became clear. One problem was that buyers were not spending any less time on reorders than they had before because they didn't trust the suppliers enough to stop their careful monitoring of the inventories and deliveries of the VMI items. Buyers intervened at the slightest hint of trouble. Further, the suppliers didn't do much to allay these fears. The problems were not with the suppliers' forecasts; instead, they were due to the suppliers' inability to deal with product promotions, which are a key part of the grocery business. Because suppliers were unable to account for promotions appropriately, delivery levels were often unacceptably low during these periods of peak demand. In addition, Spartan executives felt that the inventory levels achieved by the VMI program were no lower than the levels the company could have achieved with a well-managed traditional supplier program. It should be noted that Spartan considered the VMI program successful with some suppliers. These were the suppliers with better forecasting skills. In addition, Spartan intends to maintain the continuous replenishment programs, in which inventory levels automatically trigger fixed delivery quantities with some of its suppliers [156].

8.5 DISTRIBUTOR INTEGRATION

For years, business experts have advised manufacturers, particularly industrial manufacturers, to treat their distributors like partners [172]. Typically, this meant appreciating the value of the distributors and their relationship with the end users, and providing them with the necessary support to be successful. Distributors have a wealth of information about customer needs and wants, and successful manufacturers use this information when developing new products and product lines. Similarly, distributors typically rely on manufacturers to supply the necessary parts and expertise.

EXAMPLE 8-15

The former chairman and CEO of Caterpillar Corporation, Donald Fites, credits Caterpillar dealers with much of his company's recent success. Fites points out that dealers are much closer to customers than to the corporation, and can respond more rapidly to customer needs. They arrange financing when the product is purchased and carefully monitor, repair, and service the product. Fites says that "the dealer creates the image of a company that doesn't just stand behind its products but with its products anywhere in the world." Caterpillar believes that its dealer network gives the company a tremendous advantage over its competition, especially the big Japanese construction and mining equipment manufacturers such as Komatsu and Hitachi [84].

This view of distributors is changing, however, as customer service needs present new challenges, and information technology rises to meet these challenges. Even a strong and effective distributor network can't always meet the needs of customers. A rush order might be impossible to meet from inventory or the customer might require some specialized technical expertise that the distributor does not have.

In the past, these issues were addressed by adding inventory and personnel, either to each distributor or to the manufacturer. Modern information technology leads to a third solution, in which distributors are integrated so that the expertise and inventory located at one distributor is available to the others.

8.5.1 Types of Distributor Integration

Distributor integration (DI) can be used to address both inventory-related and service-related issues. In terms of inventory, DI can be used to create a large pool of inventory across the entire distributor network, lowering total inventory costs while raising service levels. Similarly, DI can be used to meet a customer's specialized technical service requests by steering these requests to the distributors best suited to address them. In Chapter 7, we discussed various issues associated specifically with the pooling of dealer inventory in Section 7.3.3. We explore a variety of other issues associated with dealer integration here.

As we have pointed out in previous chapters, increased inventory is traditionally used to meet unusual rush orders and to provide spare parts quickly to facilitate repairs. In more sophisticated companies, risk-pooling concepts might be used to keep inventory earlier in the supply chain, where it can be distributed as needed. In a DI arrangement, each distributor can check the inventories of other distributors to locate a needed product or part. Dealers are contractually bound to exchange the part under certain conditions and for agreed-upon remuneration. This type of arrangement improves service levels at each of the distributors and lowers the total system inventory required. Of course, this type of arrangement is possible only because sophisticated information systems allow distributors to review each others' inventory and integrated logistics systems allow parts to be delivered cheaply and efficiently.

EXAMPLE 8-16

Machine tool builder Okuma America Corporation has implemented a DI system. Okuma carries many expensive machine tools and repair parts, but the high cost of carrying the full line makes it impossible for Okuma's 46 distributors in North and South America to do so. Instead Okuma requires each of its dealers to carry a minimum number of machine tools and parts. The company manages the entire system so that each tool and part is in stock somewhere in the system, either in one of the company's two warehouses or at one of the distributors. A system called Okumalink allows each of the distributors to check the warehouse inventories and to communicate with other distributors in finding a required part. Once a part is found, the company ensures that it is delivered quickly to the requesting dealer. There are plans to upgrade the system so that each distributor has full knowledge of the inventory held by all distributors. Since the system's implementation, inventory costs throughout the system have been reduced, the chance that a distributor will lose a sale because of inventory shortages has decreased, and customer satisfaction has increased [173].

Similarly, DI can be used to improve each distributor's perceived technical ability and ability to respond to unusual customer requests. In this kind of alliance, different distributors build expertise in different areas. A customer's specific request is routed to the distributor with the most expertise. For example, Otra, a large Dutch holding company with about 70 electrical wholesale subsidiaries, has designated some of them as *centers of excellence* in particular areas, such as warehouse layouts or point-of-sale materials. The other subsidiaries, as well as customers, are directed to these centers of excellence to meet particular requests [173].

8.5.2 Issues in Distributor Integration

There are two major issues involved in implementing a DI alliance. First, distributors may be skeptical of the rewards of participating in such a system. There is the chance that they will feel they are providing some of their expertise in inventory control to less skilled partners, especially when some of the distributors are larger and have bigger inventories than others. In addition, participating distributors will be forced to rely upon other distributors, some of whom they may not know, to help them provide good customer service.

This new kind of relationship also tends to take certain responsibilities and areas of expertise away from certain distributors and concentrate them on a few distributors. It is not surprising that distributors might be nervous about losing these skills and abilities. This explains why establishing a DI relationship requires a large commitment of resources and effort on the part of the manufacturing company.

Distributors must feel sure that this is a long-term alliance. Organizers must work hard to build trust among the participants. Finally, the manufacturer may have to provide pledges and guarantees to ensure distributor commitment.

EXAMPLE 8-17

Dunlop-Enerka is a Dutch company that supplies conveyer belts to mining and manufacturing companies worldwide. Traditionally, the company met maintenance and repair requirements by storing vast quantities of inventory at distributors throughout Europe. To reduce inventories, the company installed a computer-based information system, Dunlocomm, to monitor inventory at the warehouses of each of its distributors. When a part is needed, a distributor uses the system to order the part and arrange for its delivery. To ensure distributor participation, Dunlop-Enerka guaranteed 24-hour delivery of each part to each distributor—if a part wasn't in stock, Dunlop-Enerka custom manufactured and shipped it within the available time window. This guarantee reassured distributors enough so they committed to the system and, over time, inventory throughout the system dropped by 20 percent [173].

SUMMARY

In this chapter, we examined various types of partnerships that can be used to manage the supply chain more effectively. We started off by discussing the different paths a firm can take to ensure that particular supply chain–related issues are addressed, including performing them internally or outsourcing them completely. Obviously, many different strategic and tactical issues play a part in the selection of the most appropriate strategy.

We discussed a framework that can help in selecting the most appropriate way to address a particular logistics issue. Increasingly, third-party logistics providers are taking over some of a firm's logistics responsibilities. There are both advantages and disadvantages to outsourcing the logistics function, as well as many important issues to consider once the decision has been made and a 3PL agreement is being implemented. Retailer–supplier partnerships, in which the supplier manages a portion of the retailer's business—typically retail inventories—also are becoming common. There is a spectrum of possible types of retailer–supplier partnerships, ranging from agreements that cover only information sharing, to agreements in which the supplier has complete control over the retailer's inventory policy.

We considered various issues and concerns relating to the implementation of these types of arrangement. Finally, we discussed a class of alliances, called distributor integration, in which manufacturers coordinate the efforts of their (potentially competing) distributors to create risk-pooling opportunities across the various distributors and to enable different distributors to develop different areas of expertise.

DISCUSSION QUESTIONS

1. Consider a manager developing a logistics strategy. Discuss specific situations for which the best approach would be to
   - **a.** Employ internal logistics expertise.
   - **b.** Acquire a company with this expertise.
   - **c.** Develop a strategy, and then employ specific suppliers to carry out well-defined portions of the strategy.
   - **d.** Develop the strategy with a third-party logistics provider.

2. Why is the third-party logistics industry growing so rapidly?
3. In this chapter, we discuss three types of retailer supplier partnerships: *quick response, continuous replenishment,* and *vendor-managed inventory (VMI).* For each type, discuss situations where that type would be preferred over the other two. For instance, compare quick response to continuous replenishment: under what conditions is one preferred over the other?
4. Consider the quick response partnership. Suppose the retailer places an order at the beginning of each month but transfers POS data to the supplier every week. What is the impact of the manufacturer's weekly production capacity on the benefit from information sharing? That is, under what situations is information sharing most beneficial: high weekly production capacity or low capacity? How should the supplier use the weekly demand data received from the retailer?
5. Discuss the various possibilities for inventory ownership policies in a VMI arrangement. What are the advantages and disadvantages of each of these policies?
6. Recall Example 8-13, the story of Spartan Stores' failed VMI effort. Discuss how Spartan might have done things differently in order to help the program succeed.

CASE: Audio Duplication Services, Inc. (ADS)

Audio Duplication Services is a compact disc and cassette duplication and distribution company. Its major customers, the big record companies, use ADS to duplicate and distribute CDs and cassettes. ADS stores the master tapes and, when a customer requests it, makes a certain number of copies and delivers them to its customers' customers, music stores and other points of sale such as the department stores Wal-Mart and Kmart and electronics stores such as Circuit City and Best Buy. ADS is one of six big players in the audio duplication market. ADS has about 20 percent of the $5 billion market, while its two biggest competitors share another 40 percent. Managers at ADS are currently trying to understand and react to some difficult supply chain–related issues.

- Some of the big national retailers are putting pressure on ADS's customers, the record companies, to manage inventory in the following way, known as a vendor-managed inventory, or VMI, agreement. The record companies will be put in charge of deciding how much of each album, CD, and cassette title is delivered to each store and when each delivery is made. To help with these decisions, the record companies will be provided with continuously updated point-of-sale (POS) data from each of the stores. Also, the record companies will own the inventory until it is sold, at which point payment will be transferred from the retailers to the record companies. Since ADS provides the record companies with duplication and distribution services, the record companies have asked ADS to help with the logistics of the VMI agreement.
- In the past, ADS has shipped to the distribution centers of large national retailers, and the retailers have arranged for distribution to the individual stores. Now, the retailers are providing strong incentives to ship directly to individual stores. Of course, this means higher expenses for ADS.
- In general, ADS's shipping costs are increasing. Currently, ADS has a shipping manager who arranges with different shippers to make deliveries on a shipment-by-shipment basis. Perhaps there is a better way to manage these deliveries, either by purchasing a fleet of trucks and doing the shipping in house or by outsourcing the entire shipping function to a third party. Maybe something between these two extremes will be best.

Source: ADS is a fictional company. The material in this case is loosely based on the authors' experience with several companies.

Of course, ADS is facing even bigger issues, such as the future of the audio duplication industry as online audio distribution technologies become more prevalent. In any event, each record company periodically reviews its contract with its audio duplication service, so management must address each of the above issues effectively for the company to remain successful.

CASE DISCUSSION QUESTIONS

1. Why are ADS's customers' customers moving toward VMI arrangements?
2. How will this impact ADS's business? How can ADS management take advantage of this situation?
3. How should ADS manage logistics?
4. Why are the large national retailers moving toward a direct shipment model?

CASE: The Smith Group

The Smith Group is a leading U.S. manufacturer of high-quality power and hand tools, such as electric drills, hammers, and so forth, and a major competitor to ATW, the company described in the case at the start of Chapter 4. Like ATW, Smith enjoys a very successful partnership with their distributors and dealers, who provide the majority of their revenue, and like ATW, Smith has always had VMI agreements with their large distributors.

Smith's small distributors, however, have not traditionally had electronic data transfer capability necessary to implement VMI. To overcome this, however, Smith implemented a Kanban system with many of the small distributors. In this approach, the Smith Group is imitating the Kanban approach developed by Toyota to govern the flow of material through a plant. In the Kanban system used by Toyota, production is triggered by a demand through the use of cards. This is also the approach taken by Smith. When delivery trucks arrive at a distributor's facility, they collect all the cards that were detached from items sold by the distributors. This provides the Smith Group with information about the customer demand that they can use in their production and distribution planning.

The Kanban approach designed by the Smith Group is a clever way of implementing an approach similar to the VMI strategy without the need for electronic data transfer:

- The system provides Smith with almost **real-time information** about customer demand without the need for EDI.
- A careful analysis of the card system used by the Smith Group suggests that it effectively manages inventory at the distributor level. Indeed, in this periodic review environment, the optimal inventory policy is known to be a base-stock policy. Interes-tingly, the card system implies that **inventory is managed based on a base-stock level, thus effectively reducing distributors' inventory cost.**
- The system may allow the Smith Group to switch to a make-to-order environment further reducing inventory cost on the manufacturing side. In fact, the key concept behind the Kanban approach developed by Toyota is a pull-based process. The make-to-order strategy will make the Smith Group supply chain a pull-based system, and hence a more responsive supply chain.

CASE DISCUSSION QUESTIONS

1. What is the advantage to the Smith Group of implementing the Kanban system described in the case?
2. Explain how the card system implies that inventory is managed on a base-stock level.
3. How might the system allow the Smith Group to switch to a make-to-order environment?
4. What is the risk of the Kanban system for the Smith Group?
5. If the Kanban system is going to allow the Smith Group to reduce its inventory, what is the impact on the distributor? What are the distributors going to do with the extra space?

CASE: MARUTI UDYOG LIMITED

BACKGROUND

The history of Indian auto sector is characterized by an initiative taken in February 1981, when through an act of Parliament, the Government of India (GoI) allowed Suzuki Motor Company (SMC), now, renamed Suzuki Motor Corporation, of Japan to hold 26 per cent stake in Maruti Udyog Limited (MUL). This was through a joint venture signed between GoI and Suzuki in October 1982. At that time, the auto industry was going through a major technological stagnation, low production, limited variety, high cost of operations and low productivity. Therefore, the three major objectives of this initiative were: (i) modernization of auto sector, (ii) large volume production, and (iii) development and production of fuel-efficient vehicles. Within 13 months of its inception, the first car came out of Maruti's Gurgaon plant in December 1983. During the initial days, Maruti's did not face any stiff competition in the market from two local players, Premier Automobiles and Hindustan Motors, which were having a market share of around 40,000 units per year.

Suzuki exercised its option to increase its stake in MUL by 40% in 1987. In 1991, a new phase of liberalization and globalization started in India. Soon after, in 1992 Suzuki further increased its stake to 50%, through which the basic nature of company changed into a non-Government company. Later, in 2002 SMC increased its stake to 54%.

The Maruti vision statement aims at the leadership position in the Indian automobile industry by creating customer delight and shareholder's wealth and thus becoming a pride of the nation www.maruti.co.in. Maruti looked at the small car segment with a clear focus on customer, 3Fs (fast, flexible and first mover), innovation, networking including partnership, and open learning environment. To back all such initiatives, there was always a strong supply chain orientation, involving alignment of supplier, employees and dealers to execute its core supply chain practices.

Maruti's journey started with many challenges. The Government policy was for Maruti to substantially increase its local content over a period of time. In the initial stage, Maruti was to produce around 30% value of the finished car. Suzuki was to transfer the technology. It was also envisioned that for 60% of the remaining 70% of the car value, there would be local procurements. This required development of local vendors, capable of delivering high quality, which was the hallmark of its Japanese joint venture partner—Suzuki. Keeping the cost of the car low and maintaining high customer service level were the two key concerns to retain its market leadership. Indian customers in this segment of cars are very cost conscious. Therefore, Maruti quickly look up many supply chain initiatives, which helped in developing MUL into a continuously improving organization with an ability to quickly adapt to changes. On one hand, its journey towards lean supply chain required many efforts aimed at inventory reduction and on the other hand, the customer orientation made it necessary to remain agile in the market place. In early 90s, there were some signals of conflict between the joint venture partners. Suzuki had an expansion and modernization plan of Rs. 22 billion. There were apprehensions that Suzuki was deliberately attempting to withhold some technology so that it could later be used to its advantage. The conflict got resolved around 1996, when the Government approved the Suzuki plan.

MARUTI: THE PRESENT

Maruti has ensured its complete presence in India through 16 regional sales offices and 700 dealers spread in all parts of the nation. Out of these 700 dealers, over 500 are networked through extranet, which supports its Dealer Management System (DMS). MUL, now a Rs. 14,6530 million auto giant of India, owns around 297 acre of facility in a close vicinity of India's national capital city

Delhi. The manufacturing base located at the three assembly lines in Gurgaon has an installed capacity of 3.5 lakhs units per annum with an annual production capability of six lakh cars. Another one lakh cars now comes from its manufacturing base at Manesar, which was operationalised in February 2007. This itself speaks volumes about the very high productivity of MUL. It has a decent portfolio of eleven brands of cars. During year 2005−06, its market share in the Indian passenger car market was about 54 per cent, which constituted a sale of 5,61,822 vehicles, including exports of 34784 units www.maruti.co.in.

VENDOR MANAGEMENT AT MARUTI

Maruti sources 75 to 80 per cent of its component requirements from locally developed vendors. Strategic relationship with its vendors has yielded fascinating results to Maruti. Localization is the mandate given to it since its inception. MUL had provided a lot of incentives to its vendors to establish their facility near to its plant. These incentives include availability of subsidized land for establishing plant, bank guarantee for loan, reliable power supply generated by MUL itself, etc. Vendor development and strategic partnership with vendors are keys to success of localization. Localization can succeed only when the local vendors are in a position to match the global player on low cost, high quality and technical support.

On the raw material side, the primary items are steel coils and paints. While paints are locally procured, steel procurement had a major import composition from Japan and Korea. Attempts are on to increase the local composition in the procurement of steel coils and reduce the associated cost. To improve the situation, rater than limited tendering system and adhering to lowest bidder, attempts are also made to go ahead with a quotation-based system with a flexibility to negotiate price [201].

For the components, MUL plays a collaborative role with the vendors by assisting them in periodically improving their processes. Through interaction, training, regular audits and follow-ups MUL has helped its vendors to reduce line rejections and warranty cost. It seeks to align the vendors' interest with their own manufacturing and service standards. Cost reduction strategies are aligned with long-term strategic relationship with vendors. Yield Improvement Programme (YIM) of MUL aims at meeting the increasing demand. Upgradation of vendor's production system and foreign collaboration has helped to bring in efficiency and bring down cost of production and delivery to Maruti. Purchase agreement with the vendor involves delivery and payment conditions so as to minimize future risks. Vendors located nearby are saved from packaging as they supply directly to the MUL assembly line.

Maruti supports its vendors to integrate with the World-Wide Purchase (WWP) system, in which the vendor becomes the sole supplier for a Suzuki product all over the world [201]. With an increase in sale volume, the vendor is generally better placed to reduce cost of supply. Another major effort that has helped Maruti supply chain in cost cutting is VA/VE initiative, which has a support of over 250 engineers. Value Analysis (VA) or Value Engineering (VE) aims at value improvement programme. Value in this context is the ratio of function and cost. Value improvement is possible when either at the same cost the functionality of a component improves or for the same functionality, the cost of the component goes down. Therefore, the VA/VE effort requires conscious R&D and product redesign strategies.

In 1992, MUL's total inventory was 57 days of stock. It had come down to 19 days of stock in 2003−2004 [96, 154]. Maruti introduced an Automated Material Receipt System (AMRS). With this, the system helped the inventory reduction to two days. Thereafter, a target was set to bring it further down to one day. However, this required introducing Business Process Re-engineering (BPR). Material Receipt System (MRS) at Maruti was automated through bar-coded consignment and a WiFi-enabled handheld device with the officer to update the stock in real-time mode [236]. The barcodes of the received consignment are read and with this, a Material Receipt Voucher Machine generates receipts for the suppliers, which has all the information like receiver name, nature of material received, date of receipt, quantity, etc. Vendors are allowed entry into the operations area of MUL about an hour before scheduled time.

As compared to earlier system, there was a significant saving in time of clearance from an average of one minute to five seconds. The reengineering effort also resulted in reduction in manpower for this purpose, as now only one person is sufficient to perform these operations. The reduction in processing time is one of the many measures to cut down the procurement lead time, which has a direct bearing on days of inventory. Maruti, now manages less than one day of inventory. To make this type of lean system functional, the supply chain needs reliable vendors, who are located nearby and have capability to cope with frequent replenishment requirements of Maruti.

Standardization of parts has also helped Maruti to achieve the wonder of risk pooling, which has ultimately resulted in reduction in average inventory and overall inventory cost. A majority of its models have common parts, which has significantly helped its vendors and logistics service providers as it gives them the benefit of economies of scale and risk management.

VENDOR RATIONALIZATION

Maruti has consciously put efforts in developing vendors through long-term strategic partnerships. Contrary to the normal practice in India, generally no formal tendering is done for procurement. This is possible only when there are limited numbers of reliable vendors. It pruned its vendor base of around 370 in March 2000 to 299 in March 2003 and further to 220 by the end of 2003−04. It has a plan to bring this down to a level of 100 key vendors [103, 201]. Low vendor-base is effective in meeting the long-term objective of cost reduction and quality improvement as now both Maruti and its vendors can work closer to meet these goals. Building vendor capability through technology transfer, training, guarantee for loans, lease finance for equipment, and collaboration are the primary objectives of the vendor rationalization programme. Timely payment to vendors on a weekly basis is a common practice. In March 2003, thirteen of its key vendors were their joint venture companies. At that time, over 100 vendors had a collaborative relationship with the foreign company for support in advance facilities, technical data and know-how [201]. In the fiscal year 2002, the top ten local vendors accounted for approximately 34% aggregate purchases of components from vendors in India.

VENDOR MANAGED INVENTORY

Maruti's approach to Vendor Managed Inventory (VMI) system is through strategic partnership with its vendors. It supports collaborative planning, mandated cost and activity transfer to the suppliers, and automated replenishment. Collaborative planning and related information sharing with vendor are the prerequisites of VMI as in their absence, the supplier cannot have the visibility of production plan and therefore cannot be expected to maintain and manage inventory in a blind situation of planning. Vendors are mandated to own the activity and costs related to management of inventory even at the buyer (MUL) site. Automated replenishment system is the final objective of any VMI system, in which the execution against the replenishment strategy is done automatically through an IT-enabled system on the basis of daily changes in inventory and demand at the replenished site. For the VMI system to improve, Maruti needs to focus on accurate date sharing with its vendors, utilize business intelligence systems to support automated replenishment, and make its Collaborative Planning Forecasting & Replenishment (CPFR) system more mature. Rather than vendor oriented matrices, it has to develop and utilize supply chain-oriented performance matrices. Based on continuous monitoring and joint effort, some of the initial bottlenecks could be overcome.

e-NAGARE SYSTEM

e-Nagare system was implemented in January 2003 to tackle the problem of material accumulation due to multiple sourcing, losses of procurement information and sub-model variations, and to help to achieve systematic levelized production with synchronized supplies. Nagare means drum in local language. e-Nagare is an electronic version of Kanban system, which has helped in reducing the average inventory through 'just in time' philosophy.

A typical planning system involves making plans at three important levels: (i) an annual production plan, (ii) a fortnight production plan involving a plan each on 1st and 15th of the month followed by a firm delivery schedule sent to suppliers for the 5th and 20th of the month, respectively and (iii) a firm daily schedule. An e-Nagare system is useful in daily schedule for large voluminous items from local vendors where transit time is just few hours. The vendors of Maruti are connected through extranet to Maruti and they share all data relevant for current production. An yearly schedule is broken down into months and weeks and then passed on to the production department, which then schedules its production according to this. For example, an order for a particular day, say, 19 February, involves checking the schedule two days before that date, i.e. on17 February and then an order is placed. In the process, a supplier gets around one day to meet the changes in the schedule. Suppliers are also provided the same copy of the monthly schedule, which is used by the own production department. The high level of information sharing helps to counter the amplification in demand variability, typically called the Bullwhip effect in a supply chain.

The order may be placed *via* the extranet or on-line portal [236]. After considering the previous day production, available inventory, demand forecast and perceived internal changes in production plan, it calculates and communicates the order for the day-after-tomorrow requirement to the vendors. Most of the vendors are using flexible manufacturing systems (FMS) as it helps automation and provides flexibility to cope with the changes in the requirements by Maruti. By implementing this system the inventory levels were initially reduced to seven days and now has come down to less than a day.

LOGISTICS

Around 70% of the total number of Maruti vendors, who contribute to around 80% of the supplies value are located within a radius of 100 kms radius to Maruti factory. They can use the services of a third party logistics provider (3PL) to aggregate the supplies from a few other suppliers in a milk-run system and achieve the advantage of consolidation in the form of FTL. This also helps in maintaining a frequent replenishment system. Some of the outstation suppliers maintain their local warehouse in the vicinity of a Maruti factory to manage bulk shipment from their outstation production units.

For its excellent business performance MUL has been ranked the best for four consecutive years from 2000 to 2003 by J.D. Power Asia Pacific on the India Customer Satisfaction Index study [96, 97, 98, 102, 103, 115, 117, 154, 155, 168, 201, 202, 213, 236].

CHAPTER 9

Procurement and Outsourcing Strategies

CASE: Zara

On January 15, 2002, José María Castellano Ríos, chief executive officer of the Spanish apparel company Inditex, stepped to the podium at the Jacob Javits Convention Center in New York City to accept the International Retailer of the Year award from the National Retail Federation. The year just closed had been a tumultuous one on the international scene, and for retailers it had been a down year. Retail consolidations and bankruptcies were occurring at a fast pace. Yet Inditex and its flagship company Zara had managed yet another year of impressive growth and strong profitability. Indeed, 2001 had in many respects been a landmark year for Inditex, for founder Amancio Ortega Gaona and for Castellano.

Source: Professors Nelson Fraiman and Medini Singh of Columbia Business School, together with Linda Arrington and Carolyn Paris, prepared this case as the basis for class discussion rather than to illustrate either effective or ineffective handling of a business situation. This case was prepared under the auspices of the W. Edwards Deming Center. It was sponsored by the Chazen Institute and the Center for International Business Education.

The authors wish to thank José María Castellano Ríos of Inditex and Luis Bastida and Francisco González of BBVA for making this project possible.

HISTORY OF ZARA

Amancio Ortega Gaona, a native of Galicia, had worked as a clerk at a ladies' apparel retailer before starting his own housecoat manufacturing business in 1963. He opened the first Zara store in La Coruña in 1975; by 1989, there were 82 Zara stores in Spain, and Ortega began international expansion with Zara stores in Portugal, Paris and New York. Zara's parent company Inditex took on 4 other formats, Pull & Bear, Massimo Dutti, Bershka and Stradivarius,[1] and in 2001 had launched Oysho, an intimate apparel and swimwear brand. See Table 9-1 for selected financial information. The brand names Zara, Pull & Bear, Bershka and Oysho were invented, generic names suitable for "export"; and by fiscal 2000, over half of Inditex sales were outside Spain.

During 2000–2001, Inditex received widespread favorable press and analyst coverage, touting

[1]Pull & Bear (6.6 percent of 2000 sales) was launched in 1991 as a men's basic, casual line, with women's apparel added in 1998. Inditex purchased an interest in Massimo Dutti (7.8 percent of 2000 sales), a men's shirt company, in 1991 and acquired 100 percent in 1995, in the meantime evolving it into a more classic and upscale line for men and women. In 1998, Bershka (5.2 percent of 2000 sales), a "club" look line for teenage girls, was launched, and a 90 percent interest in Stradivarius (2.8 percent of 2000 sales), a line of day or street wear for teenage girls, was acquired in 1999. See Figure 9-1 for position of various Inditex products.

TABLE 9-1

SELECTED FINANCIAL INFORMATION FOR INDITEX

(Euro in millions)	Fiscal Year				
	1996	**1997**	**1998**	**1999**	**2000**
Income Statement Data					
Net Sales	€1,008.5	€1,217.4	€1,614.7	€2,035.1	€2,614.7
Growth	*16.8%*	*20.7%*	*32.6%*	*26.0%*	*28.5%*
Gross Profit	487.5	599.1	814.8	1046.7	1337.7
Gross Margin	*48.3%*	*49.2%*	*50.5%*	*51.4%*	*51.2%*
Operating Income	152.4	192.8	242.1	299.6	390.3
Operating Margin	*15.1%*	*15.8%*	*15.0%*	*14.7%*	*14.9%*
Net Income	72.7	117.4	153.1	204.7	259.2
Balance Sheet Data					
Assets					
Cash & Equivalents	€79.6	€134.8	€151.7	€164.5	€203.9
Account Receivables	NA	NA	75.0	121.6	145.1
Inventories	NA	NA	157.6	188.5	245.1
Other Current Assets	110.7	139.2	7.1	7.3	6.2
Long-term Assets	597.7	669.2	915.1	1168.8	1395.7
Goodwill	0	1.7	1.2	98.1	89.1
Deferred Charges	32.3	32.3	18.6	24.1	22.5
Total Assets	820.3	977.2	1,326.3	1,772.9	2,107.6
Liabilities					
Short-term Debt	55.9	43.0	88.3	116.3	96.9
Other Current Liabilities	178.2	229.9	356.3	435.4	573.4
Long-term Debt	168	164.1	186.3	290.9	231.8.
Other Long-term Liabilities	3.3	10.3	22.0	37.1	34.6
Total Liabilities	405.4	447.3	652.9	879.7	936.7
Shareholders' Equity	414.9	529.9	673.4	893.2	1170.9
Total L&SE	820.3	977.2	1,326.3	1,772.9	2,107.6
Financial Statistics					
Days Inventory (fye)			35.6	33.8	34.2
Net Working Capital	(123.4)	(133.7)	(204.9)	(234.3)	(273.9)
Operating Statistics					
Total Retail Sales (millions)	€1,525.5	€1,998.8	€2,606.5		
Average Sales per Store (millions)	€2.04	€2.17	€2.41		
Total Retail Stores	*748*	*922*	*1,080*		
Average Sales per Sq. Meter	€4,752.34	€4,534.69	€4,853.82		
Total Selling Sq. Meters	*321,000*	*441,000*	*537,000*		
Same Store Sales	11.0%	5.0%	9.0%		

Inditex—Net Sales & EBIT by concept

(Euro in millions)	Net Sales		
	1998	**1999**	**2000**
Zara	€1,304.2	€1,603.4	€2,044.7
Pull & Bear	131.9	143.8	172.6
Massimo Dutti	120.5	144.2	184.0
Bershka	22.3	82.1	134.9
Stradivarius	N/A	26.3	72.5

TABLE 9-1 ***Continued***

(Euro in millions)	EBIT		
	1998	**1999**	**2000**
Zara	€213.0	€248.4	€327.9
Pull & Bear	15.0	17.1	24.1
Massimo Dutti	14.2	17.4	20.3
Bershka	(3.7)	7.1	8.4
Stradivarius	N/A	1.7	(3.2)

Source: Inditex May 2001 Offering Memorandum.

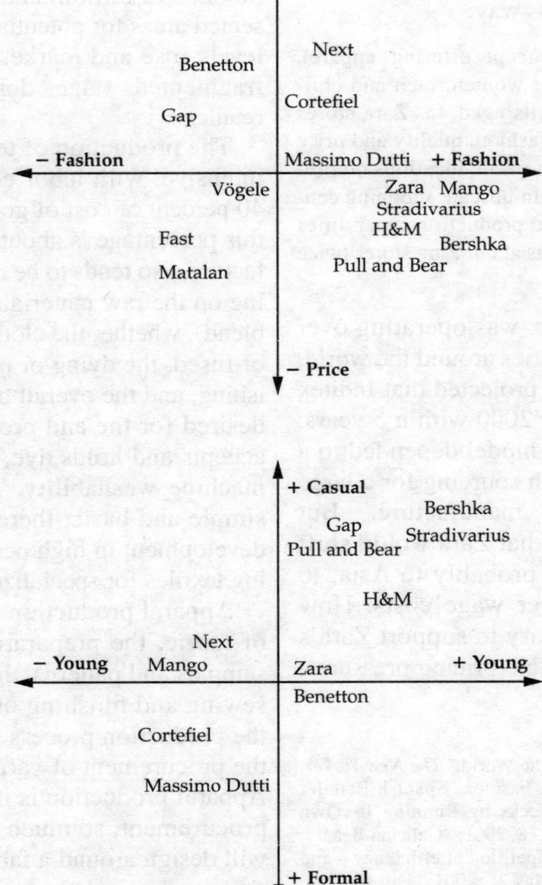

FIGURE 9-1 Inditex's product positioning.

Inditex's success and attributing it to Zara's unique integrated business model.[2] Its success had led to Zara being described as "possibly the most innovative and devastating retailer in the world" by Daniel R. Piette, Chairman and CEO, LV Capital. Inditex made an initial public offering of stock in May 2001, and was by then the world's third largest clothing retailer. Ortega's stake in Inditex was worth billions, but Ortega remained a famously privately man, still living near La Coruña and involved in running Inditex.

Zara offered clothing for women (about 58 percent of sales), men (about 22 percent and children (about 20 percent). In its offering document, Inditex described Zara in this way:

> Zara is a high-fashion concept offering apparel, footwear and accessories for women, men and children, from newborns to adults aged 45. Zara stores offer a compelling blend of fashion, quality and price offered in attractive stores in prime locations on premier commercial streets and in upscale shopping centers. Our in-house design and production capabilities enable us to offer fresh designs at our Zara stores twice a week throughout the year.

At year-end 2001 Inditex was operating over 1200 stores in over 35 countries around the world, under 6 fascia, and analysts projected that Inditex stores would easily number 2000 within 5 years. Zara's vertically integrated model depended to a great extent on local Spanish sourcing for a large proportion of garment manufacture. But Castellano had considered that Zara would shift more production offshore, probably to Asia, to take advantage of the lower wage costs. How much of a shift was necessary to support Zara's expansion and to meet possible pricing pressures, and how much of a shift could be made without undermining Zara's success—were critical issues facing Inditex.

THE TEXTILE AND APPAREL INDUSTRY

In 1999, the global textile and apparel industry accounted for 5.7 percent of the production value of world manufacturing output and more than 14 percent of world employment. The clothing market in the major countries was estimated at about $580 billion, with the U.S. accounting for about $180 billion and Western Europe about $225 billion. Eastern Europe (about $14 billion), Latin America (about $45 billion) and some parts of Asia represented areas for potential market growth as income levels rose and markets matured out of a highly fragmented stage dominated by independent retailers.

The production of textiles is relatively capital intensive, with labor costs accounting for about 40 percent of cost of goods sold, while for apparel this percentage is about 60 percent. Textile manufacture also tends to be highly specialized, depending on the raw materials (natural or synthetic or a blend), whether the cloth is woven, knitted, matted or fused, the dying or printing, treatment and finishing, and the overall performance characteristics desired for the end product, such as how well it accepts and holds dye, how well it insulates and machine washability. Though some fabrics are simple and basic, there is constant research and development in high performance textiles, including textiles for specialized industrial uses.

Apparel production involves the procurement of fabric, the preparation of designs, including samples and patterns, the cutting of fabric and the sewing and finishing of garments. For knitwear, the production process is modified to incorporate the procurement of yarn and the knitting process. Apparel production is intimately related to fabric procurement, so much so that apparel designers will design around a fabric or will design the fabric for a particular garment.

In terms of production, the apparel industry could be roughly broken down into three tiers of

[2] "The Most Devastating Retailer in the World," *The New Yorker,* September 18, 2000; "Just-in-Time Fashion: Spanish Retailer Zara Makes Low-Cost Lines in Weeks by Running Its Own Show," *The Wall Street Journal,* May 18, 2001; "Galician Beauty: Spanish clothier Zara beats the competition at efficiency—and just about everything else," *Forbes,* May 28, 2001; "Fast Fashion: How a secretive Spanish tycoon has defied the postwar tide of globalization, bringing factory jobs from Latin America and Asia back to Continental Europe," *Newsweek,* September 27, 2001.

quality, with some correspondence to sourcing of production:

- **i.** a high quality segment encompassing items that incorporate fashion elements and emphasize quality of material and workmanship, such as ladies' suits;
- **ii.** a medium quality segment for more basic items where quality of material and workmanship had to be acceptable but where there was little differentiation among producers and relatively little in terms of a time-sensitive fashion component (cardigans and khakis);
- **iii.** and a low quality segment (e.g., men's underwear) where products had commodity-like characteristics and competed principally on price.

The low wage countries had grown their production volume mostly in the medium and low quality segments, but were increasing their share of high quality production. Fifty percent of Europe's exports but only 20 percent of its imports were concentrated in the high quality segment.

The apparel industry was unusual in that many segments of it did not really benefit from economies of scale (volume production of identical goods) in the traditional sense; maintaining margin by more precisely meeting high quality demand was more important to profitability. For the more mechanized parts of production—fabric production, including knitting by machine, and cutting—setup time was not too significant. More importantly, except for commodity-like garments, the ability to manage small batch production to meet the ever-changing tastes of consumers placed a premium on flexibility and responsiveness of the production system. Sewing and finishing services were still done mostly manually and tended to be highly specialized and the most labor intensive part of the process, as reflected in the large participation of small and medium enterprises in the apparel industry. Also relevant was the preponderance of women, with their relatively lower wage levels, among apparel production workers.

Given the labor-intensive quality of apparel production, it was not surprising that relative wage levels had been a significant driver of production sourcing. Along with the analysis of wage levels, however, firms weighed other important factors: raw materials quality and availability, skills requirements and worker productivity, transportation time and cost and other components of lead time, political and foreign exchange risk, regulatory issues and social responsibility concerns. A complex system of quotas and tariffs had also been an important part of the sourcing equation, resulting in a number of distortions in the supply chain, such as transshipment of goods through Hong Kong to avoid quotas on products from China. China's entry into the World Trade Organization, as well as the staged dismantling of the textile and apparel quota system—to be complete by 2005—were expected to increase China production but also result in the reduction of trade barriers affecting, e.g., import of goods from the E.U. into Latin American countries. In the meantime, the regional reduction of trade barriers had fostered increased manufacture in Eastern Europe, Turkey and Northern Africa in support of European markets and Mexican, Caribbean and Central American manufacture in support of the U.S. market.

THE TEXTILE AND APPAREL INDUSTRY IN THE E.U. AND IN SPAIN

The textile and apparel industry in the E.U. employed about 2 million people in 1999, accounting for 7.6 percent of total E.U. manufacturing employment, and generated a turnover of 178 billion euros. Italy had the largest percentage of the E.U. textile and apparel business, at 31 percent, with the U.K. at 15 percent, Germany at 14 percent, France at 13 percent, Spain at 9 percent and Portugal at 6 percent. The E.U. was the second largest exporter of textiles and clothing in the world, but stronger as an exporter of textiles than of clothing. In particular, the E.U. countries were leaders in the development of high-tech fibers and related technologies.

The industry was known for its fragmentation and the importance of subcontracting within regional clusters of small and independent but collaborative firms, such as in northern Italy, but there were also some large firms, like Inditex, managing or tapping into the subcontracting networks to run manufacturing on a larger scale.[3] This "industrial district" structure of the textile and apparel industry in the E.U., run on low overhead but at a high skill level, implied a different type of scale or network economy, shared across a group of firms; whether or not all firms within the system had common ownership was not as important as how well the components worked together.

In apparel, the E.U's special strength was design-driven manufacturing, where design stayed close to the customer and was bound up with production. Of particular importance was the close relationship between clothing companies and textile companies, which permitted collaboration on fabric design. On the other end of the production chain, there was a significant volume of outsourcing of labor-intensive operations ("outward processing transactions" (OPT)) to Eastern European and Mediterranean rim countries, which were near enough to provide rapid turnaround and could be relatively easily monitored for quality control.

The Spanish textile and apparel industry was comprised mostly of many very small firms, and had traditionally not been strong in R&D or technological innovation, nor had it needed to be in order to compete in the domestic market. However, during the 1990's Spain experienced greater prosperity, with rising wage levels, and its domestic customer base had become more sophisticated. Spanish consumers cared a lot about fashion and quality in clothing purchases, with price less of a consideration, but given general wage levels, luxury name brand apparel had been out of the reach of most shoppers.[4]

Ortega's home province of Galicia is in the rainy northwestern corner of Spain. A hilly and picturesque land alongside the Atlantic Ocean, with a Celtic heritage, its weather is often overcast or foggy. Galicia's economy had been rooted in farming, fishing and mining. Galicia had generally been poorer, and experienced higher levels of unemployment, than other parts of Spain, and in the early part of the 20th century, many people emigrated from Galicia to Argentina, Uruguay and Cuba. Reducing unemployment and improving skills levels had been priorities of the Galician regional government and labor organizations. The principal city of La Coruña (A Coruña in the regional dialect Gallego) had a modern and convenient airport, and there were frequent flights to Madrid and Barcelona, but La Coruña was not a major international port city.

Though Galicia had not been known as a center of textile and clothing manufacture on an industrial level, in the 1980's the region began an aggressive push to evolve traditional dressmaking skills and participate in the sector by promoting a concept of "Galician fashion." By 1998 it was estimated that 29 thousand people (most of them women) worked for about 760 firms in Galicia involved in the textile and apparel business. Many of the firms (over 450) were small workshops or cooperatives, with an average of 15 workers each, and 75 percent of production consisted of the assembly line production of garments and 16 percent of knitwear production. There were also several large firms headquartered in Galicia: Adolfo Domingues, Caramelo, Mafecco and Zara. Galicia's share of national production in the textile and clothing sector increased from 7 percent to 14 percent from

[3]See *The Competitiveness of the European Textile Industry*, by Maurizio Giuli (South Bank University—London 1997), citing the "industrial district" model of production.

[4]According to a 1999 report of the U.S. and Foreign Commercial Service and U.S. Department of State, 6 out of 10 Spanish women rated quality, 3 out of 10 rated fashion, and only 1 out of 10 rated price, as the most important determinant in a clothing purchase.

1991 to 1997, employment generated by Galician clothing firms represented 10.5 percent of the total jobs created by this sector in Spain for that period, and exports from the region increased ten-fold from 1991 to 1998.

THE ZARA MODEL

Zara's Planning and Design Cycle

The Zara timeline for a season began, as for other apparel manufacturers, a year or so in advance of the start of the corresponding season. There were two seasons, with the spring/summer collection scheduled to arrive in stores beginning in January/February and the fall/winter collection scheduled to arrive in stores beginning in August/September (reversed for the Southern hemisphere). About a year in advance designers began to work to define dominant themes and colors, and then to put together an initial collection.

Zara had 200 designers on staff. While designers were catwalk-influenced and expected to adapt haute couture style for the mass market, "they are not themselves encouraged to be ivory tower aesthetes making distinctive fashion statements," according to María Pérez, head of the Design department. "Zara produces about 11 thousand styles each year—perhaps 5 times as many as a comparable retailer would typically produce, and all in relatively small batches to begin with," she said. "This encourages them to experiment, but always within a commercial orientation."

The designers worked in large open spaces at Zara's headquarters, with one design center for each of the women's, men's and children's lines. Designers often prepared sketches by hand but eventually worked on a CAD system to illustrate the design and associated specifications. The design centers were light and modern, with pop music playing in the background.

The store specialists worked in the same rooms, reviewing daily detailed printouts of store sales and speaking to store managers by phone to gather informal feedback. Each store specialist was responsible for a group of stores by region and visited them periodically. Each store manager was likely to have retailing experience and was chosen for her commercial design sense and feel for market trends, because it was the job of the store managers to feed market information from the stores back into the design and production decision-making. Communications and workflow within the design center were very fluid.

Patterns and Samples

In some cases designs were sent out to third party suppliers for them to prepare samples (a 2–3 month process), or the paper pattern and then a sample garment were prepared in-house, with Zara's pattern-makers and the seamstresses who made up the samples working in the same large, open design center. Patterns once finalized could be made available to the computers that would guide the cutting tools. Based on samples, the initial collection for the season was finalized and shown within Zara.

Production Sourcing and Scheduling

Once the initial collection for a season had been approved, the related fabric procurement and production planning started. Where garments were third party sourced (about half of the total), commitments for production were made roughly 6 months prior to the scheduled store delivery, while garments for in-house production were scheduled for manufacture so that they would be ready in time for scheduled delivery to the stores. Of the outsourced production, about 60 percent came from Europe and 30 percent from Asia, with the balance from the rest of the world.

The decision to source with external suppliers or to manufacture in-house was based on a number of considerations, including expertise, relative cost and, especially, time sensitivity. Inditex owned 21 Zara factories, each of which was separately managed. Factory managers' bids were assessed against third party supplier bids to make sure that in-house manufacturing stayed competitive. In general, garments with fashion styling tended to be manufactured in-house while basics and knits tended to be outsourced.

Zara committed about 15–25 percent of its season inventory—the more basic items—six months in advance of the season, compared with 40–60 percent for most apparel retailers. By the beginning of the season about 50–60 percent of its season inventory had been committed (either already manufactured or subject to firm commitment with specifications), compared to what Zara estimated was closer to 80 percent committed for most apparel retailers. About a quarter of the season's collection was made available at the start of the season, with the inventory in the stores at the beginning of the season tending to be more heavily weighted toward basic items and including the initial fashion collection, both of which were produced based on regular lead time commitments maximizing third party supplier sourcing. In-house manufacturing was reserved more for current (in-season) production. Altogether, in-house production was weighted 85 percent to in-season production and 15 percent to the next season's production.

In-house Manufacture

In-house manufacture entailed two basic steps: fabric procurement and garment assembly and finishing. Inditex owned a fabric sourcing company in Barcelona (Comditel), several textile production companies and a share in a fabric finishing company, Fibracolor. Comditel managed about 40 percent of fabric procurement, with a specialty in greige goods (undyed fabrics, often woven cotton, which can be dyed or printed to order). Setup time for dying or printing was about 4 or 5 days, with the whole process taking about a week. For synthetics and more fashion fabrics, Zara relied mostly on external sourcing.

Based on decisions about which styles were to be produced and in what sizes, the Zara factories cut the fabric. A "mattress" of layered fabric was laid out on long tables, vacuum sealed and cut by machine based on a computer layout of pattern pieces. The layout itself was arranged by people working at computer terminals who specialized in appropriate layout with minimum waste; Zara managers had determined that these skilled workers were able, within 15 or 20 minutes, to arrange layout with higher utilization than could be achieved solely with computer algorithms, though the computer-generated layouts, which took only a few seconds to generate, were used for benchmarking. The cut fabric pieces were marked and bundled for sewing.

Sewing was subcontracted to a network of 400 smaller firms within Galicia and northern Portugal. Within this rural area, where wages were low and unemployment high, Zara's subcontracted sewing work enabled many women to work, including on a part-time basis. Zara reserved time with its sewing subcontractors but was not limited in terms of garment specifications given in advance.

Deliveries between the Zara factories and the subcontractors occurred many times a week, with subcontractors picking up new work as they left off completed work. Overall turnaround time for sewing ran a week or two. Pressing, tagging and final inspection of completed garments occurred upon their return to the Zara factories. Assuming it had the fabric in stock, Zara was in a position, with its in-house design, pattern-making and cutting capabilities, and its network of sewing subcontractors, to go from start to finish on a style production within as little as 10 days.

In-Season Production

Zara committed only 50–60 percent of production in advance of the season, with the remainder manufactured on a rolling basis during the season. It was the in-house portion of the in-season production that easily could be modified in response to market demand. If an item was not selling, further production could be eliminated. If an item sold well, more units could be made up within a week or so, assuming the fabric was available. Zara would produce more to meet demand to the extent of fabric in stock, but no more. Miguel Díaz Miranda, Vice-President of Manufacturing, explained:

The size of the production run—"scale," in the traditional sense—is not an issue. We recoup our costs on the garments through markup because people will pay a premium for the right garment at the right time. It is the product that drives the customer.

For an expected very strong demand, we'll take a bigger risk on the fabric purchasing decision. Sometimes we make a decision that from an economic point of view might not seem sound, but we know that. For example, we might have an item that was selling very well, but if we think that we are saturating the market with that look we will stop manufacturing it and create unsatisfied demand on purpose. From a strictly economic point of view, that is ridiculous. But the culture we are creating with our customers is: you better get it today because you might not find it tomorrow.

According to Zara's management, echoed by analysts and the press, it was the ability to respond in-season that gave Zara a different fashion risk profile from other apparel retailers. When the initial collection had items that were performing poorly in stores, Zara could respond with alternative offerings, while most apparel retailers could only respond with increased markdowns and more aggressive (costly) advertising to move unpopular merchandise. For Zara, in-season replenishment did not require incremental capacity to be found or much higher costs incurred at the last minute; instead the close-to-sale-time manufacturing permitted an ongoing reallocation of resources in the ordinary course and with minimal disruption. In-house manufacturing capacity had been reserved and was available, but exactly *what* was to be manufactured could be determined within a few weeks of when the garments would appear for sale in the stores. "We were able to tilt the in-store inventory from equestrian themes to black within 2 weeks of the September 11 terrorist attacks," said Hugo Alvarez Gallego, of the Inditex capital markets group.

Distribution

Distribution of both outsourced and in-house manufactured garments was centralized at Zara's 500,000 square meter distribution center in Arteixo. The distribution center was centrally located among fourteen manufacturing plants. Garments moved along two hundred and eleven kilometers of track from the cluster of factories located there to the distribution center. Hanging garments were arranged on coded bars that sorted automatically by style within the distribution center; stock-picking of hanging garments was done manually. Folded garments were sorted on a carousel, with each garment dropped down a chute toward a box for its destination store based on its bar code.

About 2.5 million garments could move through the distribution center each week. Though the distribution center in Arteixo was utilized at only 50 percent capacity at the end of 2001, based on the company's growth plans of 20–25 percent per year, more distribution capacity needed to come on-line, and the company was building a second distribution center in Zaragoza, in the interior of the northeastern area of Spain.

Shipments were made out of the distribution center twice a week, by truck to Europe and by airfreight to stores outside Europe, so that stores received goods within 24–36 hours of shipment in Europe and within 1–2 days outside Europe. No inventory was held centrally, and there was almost no inventory at the stores that was not on the selling floor.

Retailing

Store managers asked for the items from a collection that they wanted at their stores, but the final allocations of inventory were made centrally, taking into account current store sales and inventory information, and sometimes included new items not requested by the store manager. Stores received new inventory several times a week. "The freshness in assortment is very important for fashion forward merchandise. It creates an exciting anticipation on the part of our customers. They know when the trucks are expected at their local store so that they can be the first to see the new merchandise," reported Josefina Lucía Bengochea Martín, a store manager in Barcelona. "Our customers come into our stores on average of 17 times a year; that number would be 3 or 4 for our competitors" commented José María Castellano.

Items that were not sold could be returned for possible reallocation to other stores or for outlet sale. Sale periods were heavily regulated in Europe; only items previously in stock could be marked down. In general, Zara tried to minimize the volume of merchandise moved at end-of-season sale prices, since under their system there was no need for a large inventory clearance. Zara experienced 15–20 percent markdown sale of season volume, compared to 30–40 percent for much of the industry. Zara did not advertise, but instead relied on word of mouth. Typical expenditure for retail advertising is 3–4 percent of sales; at Inditex it ran at 0.3 percent, almost all of that for simple newspaper notices of the sales periods.

The Stores

Zara stores were uniform, including as to lighting, fixtures and window display, as well as the arrangements of garments, with a targeted floorspace of 1200 square meters (see Figure 9-2). There was a model store located at Zara headquarters that was kept up-to-date in terms of current product selection. Store locations were upscale in prime high street areas such as the Champs Elysees in Paris, Regent Street in London and Lexington Avenue in New York City, and the store design, displays and windows emphasized an upscale, fashion forward message. The uncluttered arrangement of goods in uncrowded spaces coordinated by color made the experience of shopping more like that in high-end luxury stores, and quite different from that offered by the "value" marketers.

Pricing Strategy

Zara contrasted its pricing strategy to many others in its business, which set price equal to cost plus a target margin. "Zara prices are based on comparables within the target market, subject to covering costs plus a target margin," said Pablo Alvarez, Vice-President of Marketing. For example, a coat in Madrid, Spain, could be priced for €100, and the same coat in New York's Lexington Avenue store could be priced $185 (a sample price-tag is shown in Figure 9-3.

During its long expansion through 2001, Zara printed price tags for multiple jurisdictions showing on the single tag all of its different prices by country. This simplified the tagging procedure and also permitted goods to be moved from store to store without retagging and also permitted goods to be transshipped between one country to another without retagging. However at the beginning of 2002 Zara switched to a system of local price marking in the stores, using a device that read the bar code and printed the appropriate local price.

Growth Strategy

Zara's growth had been outward from its base in Spain, with the locations for new stores chosen selectively to stake out sequentially new territories that could be supported within the Zara model. Most of the stores were company-owned, although in some markets (e.q., the Middle East) Zara had opened a small number of stores through franchises and in some other markets (e.g., Japan) Zara had opened stores through alliances. Zara did not establish local distribution centers and warehouses when it entered a market, or engage in store-opening promotions.

Zara had about 450 stores in 33 countries (see Table 9-2) and was opening about 10 stores a month in 2002. Though Zara had stores in New York City, Miami, and Puerto Rico, Inditex management indicated that significant expansion in the U.S. market was not a near-term priority. "In our view, the U.S. is over-retailed, and the U.S. consumer, outside of the coasts and big cities, has very basic fashion tastes," said José María Castellano Ríos "The market for high volume styles typical of American fashion, like chinos, is saturated. Also in America you usually have to advertise. We have plenty to do closer to home."

A SOURCING DILEMMA

As Castellano stepped to the podium he reflected on how far Zara had come since he joined the company from IBM in 1984. He felt

FIGURE 9-2 The display and store layout in a Zara store.

FIGURE 9-3 Sample Zara price tags.

comfortable that Zara was on the right track for a continuation of the measured and organic growth off its business model and unique positioning based in Galicia. However, he and other members of his management team, together with Ortega, constantly revisited Zara's strategy.

One element of the strategy before him now was production sourcing. To provide some cushion in its margins, particularly in view of possible pricing pressure as the Euro took hold in Europe, Zara had announced that the proportion of outsourced manufacture would grow, initially to 60 percent, to take advantage of increased low cost production coming on-line, principally in China. This seemed like a moderate, conservative step toward adopting the conventional wisdom that higher margins could be built off lower wage costs, but perhaps away from the "Zara model" of local, vertically integrated production. But how low could local, in-season production go without negatively impacting Zara's fashion-forward image, and ultimately, the competitive advantage that drove its margins?

TABLE 9-2

ZARA—STORE LOCATIONS: 2000

	Company-owned	Franchise	Joint venture	Total
Spain	220			220
Portugal	32			32
Belgium	12			12
France	63			63
United Kingdom	7			7
Germany			6	6
Poland		2		2
Greece	15			15
Cyprus		2		2
Israel		9		9
Lebanon		2		2
Turkey	4			4
Japan			6	6
United States	6			6
Canada	3			3
Mexico	23			23
Argentina	8			8
Venezuela	4			4
Brazil	5			5
Chile	2			2
Uruguay	2			2
Kuwait		2		2
Dubai		2		2
Saudi Arabia		5		5
Bahrain		1		1
Qatar		1		1
Andorra		1		1
Austria	3			3
Denmark	1			1
Total	410	27	12	449

Source: Inditex May 2001 Offering Memorandum.

TABLE 9-3

RELATIVE WAGE LEVELS

	Hourly labor costs (US $)	
	Textiles	**Clothing**
India	$0.60	$0.39
China	0.62	0.43
Tunisia	1.76	NA
Morocco	1.89	1.36
Hungary	2.98	2.12
Portugal	4.51	3.70
Spain	8.49	6.79
USA	12.97	10.12
Italy	15.81	13.60

TABLE 9-3 ***Continued***

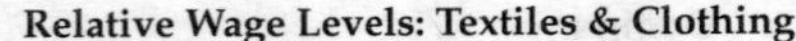

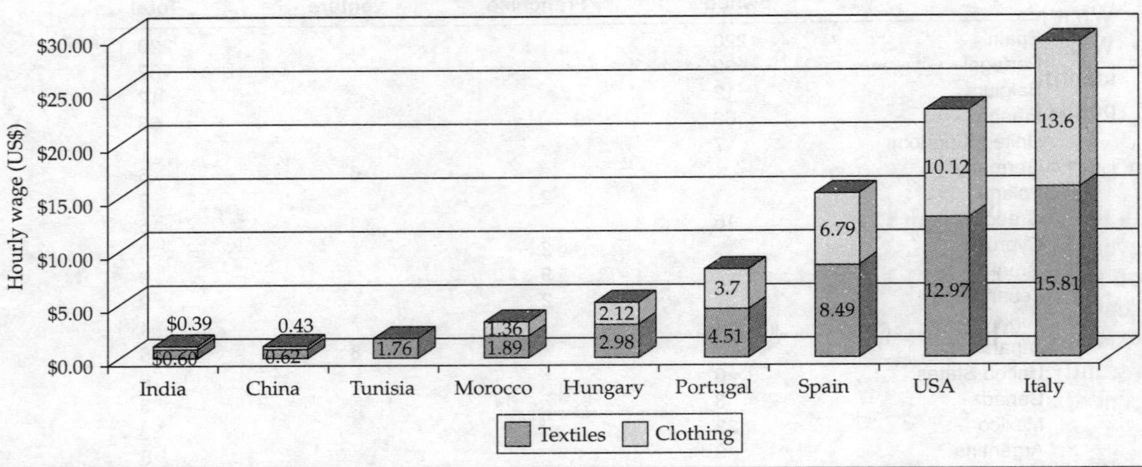

Source: European Commission: 1998 statistics.

TABLE 9-4

PRODUCTION MOVEMENT

	Production allocation		
	1998	**1999**	**2000**
In-house	53%	50%	44%
External	47%	50%	56%
	100%	100%	100%

	Origin of production		
	1998	**1999**	**2000**
Spain	29%	25%	20%
Portugal	27%	24%	22%
European Union	10%	9%	5%
Rest of Europe	8%	11%	15%
Asia	19%	23%	29%
Rest of World	7%	8%	9%
	100%	100%	100%

Source: Company reports.

By the end of this chapter, you should be able to answer the following questions:

- What are the roles that outsourcing and procurement play in the supply chain? What are the risks and benefits associated with outsourcing many of a firm's activities?

- What are the key issues involved in deciding what to make internally and what to buy from outside suppliers?
- When a firm outsources a particular process, how can it ensure timely supply of components?
- What is the impact of the Internet on the procurement process?
- What procurement strategy should a company use for individual products? Is there a framework that identifies the procurement strategy that the firm needs to consider for each product? What are the key points that should be considered when making these decisions?

9.1 INTRODUCTION

In the 90s, outsourcing was the focus of many industrial manufacturers; firms considered outsourcing everything from the procurement function to production and manufacturing. Executives were focused on stock value, and huge pressure was placed on the organization to increase profits. Of course, one "easy" way to increase profit is by reducing costs through outsourcing. Indeed, in the mid 90s there was a significant increase in purchasing volume as a percentage of the firm's total sales. More recently, between 1998 and 2000, outsourcing in the electronics industry has increased from 15 percent of all components to 40 percent [216].

Consider, for instance, the athletic shoe industry, a fashion industry with products that require significant investment in technology [195]. No company in this industry has been as successful as Nike, a company that outsources almost all of its manufacturing activities. As observed by Quinn and Hilmer, Nike, the largest supplier of athletic shoes in the world, focuses mainly on research and development on the one hand and marketing, sales, and distribution on the other. Indeed, this strategy allowed Nike to grow in the 90s at an annual rate of about 20 percent [195].

Cisco's success story is even more striking. According to Peter Solvik, CIO of Cisco, "Cisco's Internet-based business model has been instrumental in its ability to quadruple in size from 1994 to 1998 ($1.3 billion to over $8 billion), hire approximately 1,000 new employees per quarter while increasing their productivity, and save $560M annually in business expenses." Specializing in enterprise network solutions, Cisco used, according to John Chambers, Cisco CEO, a "global virtual manufacturing strategy." As he explains, "First, we have established manufacturing plants all over the world. We have also developed close arrangements with major suppliers. So when we work together with our suppliers, and if we do our job right, the customer cannot tell the difference between my own plants and my suppliers in Taiwan and elsewhere" [134]. This approach was enabled by Cisco's single-enterprise system, which provides the backbone for all activities in the company, and connects not only customers and employees, but also chip manufacturers, component distributors, contract manufacturers, logistics companies, and systems integrators. These participants can perform like one company because they all rely on the same Web-based data sources. All its suppliers see the same demand and do not rely on their own forecasts based on information flowing from multiple points in the supply chain. Cisco also built a dynamic replenishment system to help reduce supplier inventory. Cisco's average turns in 1999 were 10 compared with an average of 4 for competitors. Inventory turns for commodity items are even more impressive; they reach 25–35 turns a year.

Apple Computers also outsources most of its manufacturing activities; in fact, the company outsources 70 percent of its components, including major products such as printers. As Quinn and Hilmer point out, "Apple focused its internal resources on its own disk operating system and the supporting macro software to give Apple products their unique look and feel" [195].

In the last few years, U.S. and European companies not only outsource their manufacturing activities, but increasingly their product design [68]:

- Taiwanese companies now design and manufacture most laptops sold around the world.
- Brands such as Hewlett-Packard and PalmOne collaborate with Asian suppliers on the design of their personal digital assistants (PDAs).

So, why do many technology companies outsource manufacturing, and even innovation, to Asian manufacturers? What are the risks involved? Should outsourcing strategies depend on product characteristics, such as product clockspeed, and if so how?

To answer these questions, we first discuss the *buy/make* decision process. We identify the advantages and the risks associated with outsourcing and present a framework for optimizing buy/make decisions.

EXAMPLE 9-1 BAJAJ AUTO LIMITED (BAJAJ)

Through a web-based enterprise portal, Bajaj Auto, India's giant in two and three-wheeler auto manufacturing, has integrated its procurement and inbound operations. Bajaj, vendors can know the different schedules related to production of different models. It helps them in order execution with more accuracy and shorter lead time. They receive an online receipt note in the form of a token for the delivered material. They can use web-based invoicing and can check their outstanding payment through the portal [70].

After presenting this framework, we discuss effective procurement strategies. We argue that procurement strategies vary from item to item within the same organization depending on the product and market characteristics associated with that product. Thus, we introduce a framework for identifying the appropriate procurement strategy and show that the procurement strategy is tightly linked to the firm's outsourcing strategy.

Finally, we discuss the procurement process itself, which can be a very expensive process for many buyers. Indeed, since 1995, when the first online marketplace was established, the procurement landscape has changed considerably with the introduction of independent (also referred to as public), private, and consortium-based e-marketplaces. These developments increase both the opportunities and challenges faced by many buyers.

9.2 OUTSOURCING BENEFITS AND RISKS

Throughout the 90s, strategic outsourcing, outsourcing the manufacturing of key components, was used as a tool to rapidly cut costs. In their recent study, Lakenan, Boyd, and Frey [134] reviewed eight major contract equipment manufacturers (CEMs)—Solectron, Flextronics, SCI Systems, Jabil Circuit, Celestica, ACT Manufacturing, Plexus, and Sanmina—which were the main suppliers to companies such as Dell, Marconi, NEC Computers, Nortel, and Silicon Graphics. The aggregated revenue for the eight CEMs quadrupled between 1996 and 2000 while their capital expenditure grew 11-fold [134].

Some of the motivations for outsourcing are [134, 195]

Economies of scale. An important objective in outsourcing is to reduce manufacturing costs through the aggregation of orders from many different buyers. Indeed, the aggregation allows suppliers to take advantage of economies of scale, both in purchasing and in manufacturing.

Risk pooling. Outsourcing allows buyers to transfer demand uncertainty to the CEM. One advantage that the CEMs have is that they aggregate demand from many buying companies and thus reduce uncertainty through the risk-pooling effect. The CEMs can thus reduce component inventory levels while maintaining or even increasing service level.

Reduce capital investment. Another important objective in outsourcing is to transfer not only demand uncertainty to the CEM but also capital investment. Of course, the CEM can make this investment because it is implicitly shared between many of the CEM's customers.

Focus on core competency. By carefully choosing what to outsource, the buyer is able to focus on its core strength, that is, the specific talent, skills, and knowledge sets that differentiate the company from its competitors and give it an advantage in the eye of the customers. For instance, Nike focuses on innovation, marketing, distribution, and sales, not on manufacturing [195].

Increased flexibility. Here we refer to three issues: (i) The ability to better react to changes in customer demand, (ii) the ability to use the supplier's technical knowledge to accelerate product development cycle time, and (iii) the ability to gain access to new technologies and innovation. These are critical issues in industries where technologies change very frequently, for example, high-tech, or when products have a short life cycle, for example, fashion products.

These benefits come with new and considerable risks. Consider how IBM benefited and was hurt by outsourcing.

EXAMPLE 9-2

When IBM decided to enter the PC market, in late 1981, the company did not have the infrastructure in place to design and build a personal computer. Rather than take the time to develop these capabilities, IBM outsourced almost all of the major components of the PC. For example, the microprocessor was designed and built by Intel and the operating system was provided by a small company in Seattle called Microsoft. IBM was able to get this computer to market within 15 months of starting the design by tapping into the expertise and resources of these companies. Furthermore, within three years, IBM replaced Apple as the number-one supplier of personal computers, and by 1985, IBM had over 40 percent of market share. However, the downside to IBM's strategy soon became clear, as competitors such as Compaq were able to enter the market by utilizing the same suppliers as IBM. Furthermore, when IBM tried to regain control of the market by introducing its PS/2 line of computers, featuring a new, proprietary design and an operating system called OS/2, other companies did not follow IBM's lead, and the original architecture remained dominant in the market. By the end of 1995, IBM's market share had fallen to less than 8 percent, behind market leader Compaq's 10 percent [50].

Similarly, outsourcing ended up leading to problems for Cisco.

EXAMPLE 9-3

In 2000, Cisco was forced to announce a $2.2 billion write-down for obsolete inventory and 8,500 employees were laid off. This was the result of a significant reduction in demand for telecommunication infrastructure to which Cisco was not able to respond effectively. Interestingly, other, smaller networking companies saw the downturn coming and downgraded their forecasts and hence their inventory months earlier. Of course, Cisco's problem is its virtual global manufacturing network. The virtual global network resulted in long supply lead time for key components and this would have impacted delivery to customers. So, Cisco decided to carry component inventory that was ordered long in advance of the downturn. And competition on limited supplier capacities forced Cisco to sign long-term contracts with its suppliers, resulting in the huge inventory write-down [23].

The IBM personal computer example and the more recent Cisco example reveal two substantial risks associated with outsourcing. These include [80, 134, 195].

Loss of competitive knowledge. Outsourcing critical components to suppliers may open up opportunities for competitors (as in the IBM PC example). Similarly, outsourcing implies that companies lose their ability to introduce new designs based on their own agenda rather than the supplier's agenda [195]. Finally, outsourcing the manufacturing of various components to different suppliers may prevent the development of new insights, innovations, and solutions that typically require cross-functional teamwork [195].

Conflicting objectives. Suppliers and buyers typically have different and conflicting objectives. For instance, increased flexibility is a key objective when buyers outsource the manufacturing of various components. This implies an ability to better match supply and demand by adjusting production rates as needed. Unfortunately, this objective is in direct conflict with the suppliers' objectives of long-term, firm, and stable commitment from the buyer. Indeed, this is an important issue for suppliers since, unlike the buyers, their profit margins are relatively small and, hence, they have to focus on cost reduction rather than flexibility. In good times, when demand is high, this conflict can be addressed by buyers who are willing to make long-term commitments to purchase minimum quantities specified by a contract (as in the Cisco example). However, in a slow economy, when there is a significant decline in demand, these long-term commitments entail huge financial risks for the buyers [134]. Similarly, product design issues are affected by the conflicting objectives of suppliers and buyers. Again, buyers, insisting on flexibility, would like to solve design problems as fast as possible, while suppliers focus on cost reduction that typically implies slow responsiveness to design changes.

9.3 A FRAMEWORK FOR BUY/MAKE DECISIONS

How can the firm decide on which component to manufacture and which to outsource? Consultants and supply chain pundits typically suggest focusing on core competencies, but how can the firm identify what is in the core, and hence should be made internally, and what is outside the core, and hence should be purchased from outside suppliers?

Below we introduce a framework developed by Fine and Whitney [80]. To introduce the framework, they classify the reasons for outsourcing into two major categories:

Dependency on capacity. In this case, the firm has the knowledge and the skills required to produce the component but for various reasons decides to outsource.

Dependency on knowledge. In this type of dependency, the company does not have the people, skills, and knowledge required to produce the component and outsources in order to have access to these capabilities. Of course, the company has to have the knowledge and skills to evaluate customer needs and convert these into key requirements and characteristics that the component should have.

To illustrate these two concepts, Fine and Whitney consider outsourcing decisions at Toyota. As a successful Japanese car manufacturer, the company designs and makes about 30 percent of its car components. The details are quite revealing:

- Toyota has both the knowledge and the capacity to produce its engines and indeed 100 percent of the engines are produced internally.
- For transmissions, the company has the knowledge and indeed designs all the components but depends on its suppliers' capacities, since 70 percent of the components are outsourced.
- Vehicle electronic systems are designed and produced by Toyota's suppliers. Thus, in this case, the firm has a dependency on both capacity and knowledge.

Fine and Whitney observe that "Toyota seems to vary its outsourcing practice depending on the strategic role of the components and subsystems." The more strategically important the component is, the smaller the dependency on knowledge or capacity. This suggests the need for a better understanding of product architecture when considering what to outsource.

For this purpose, and following Ulrich [240] and Swaminathan [233], we distinguish between integral and modular products. A modular product can be made by combining different components. A personal computer is an excellent example of a modular product in which the customers specify memory and hard-drive sizes, monitor, software, and so forth. Other examples that are frequently cited include home stereo equipment and high-end bicycles. The definition of modular products implies [78]

- Components are independent of each other.
- Components are interchangeable.
- Standard interfaces are used.
- A component can be designed or upgraded with little or no regard to other components.
- Customer preference determines the product configuration.

An integral product, on the other hand, is a product made up from components whose functionalities are tightly related. Thus,

- Integral products are not made from off-the-shelf components.
- Integral products are designed as a system by taking a top-down design approach.
- Integral products are evaluated based on system performance, not based on component performance.
- Components in integral products perform multiple functions.

Of course, in real life, very few products are either modular or integral. Indeed, the degree of modularity or integrality may vary with personal computers being on one end of the spectrum, that is, highly modular products, and airplanes being on the other end of the spectrum, that is, highly integral products. For instance, a car is a product that includes many modular components, for example, the stereo system or other electronic systems, and many integral components, for example, the engine.

Table 9-5 presents a simple framework for make/buy decisions, developed in Fine [78] and Fine and Whitney [80].

This framework considers both modular and integral products, and the firm's dependency on knowledge and capacity. For modular products, capturing knowledge is important, whereas having the production capacity in-house is less critical. For example, for a PC manufacturer, capturing knowledge may refer to the design of the various components. Thus, if the firm has the knowledge, outsourcing the manufacturing process provides an opportunity to reduce cost. On the other hand, if the firm has neither knowledge nor capacity, outsourcing may be a risky strategy as the knowledge developed by the supplier may be transferred to a competitor's products. For integral products, capturing both knowledge

TABLE 9-5

A FRAMEWORK FOR MAKE/BUY DECISIONS

Product	Dependency on knowledge and capacity	Independent for knowledge, dependent for capacity	Independent for knowledge and capacity
Modular	Outsourcing is risky	Outsourcing is an opportunity	Opportunity to reduce cost through outsourcing
Integral	Outsourcing is very risky	Outsourcing is an option	Keep production internal

and capacity is important as long as it is possible to have both. This implies that if the firm has both the knowledge and the capacity, then in-house production is appropriate. On the other hand, if the firm does not have both, perhaps it is in the wrong business.

The previous framework provides a general approach for make/buy decisions but doesn't help with component-level outsourcing strategies. How should a firm determine whether a specific component should be outsourced or made internally? This question is considered in Fine et al. [79], where the authors develop a hierarchical model that includes five criteria:

1. **Customer importance.** How important is the component to the customer? What is the impact of the component on customer experience? Does the component affect customer choice? In short, what is the value customers attached to the component?
2. **Component clockspeed.** How fast does the component's technology change relative to other components in the system?
3. **Competitive position.** Does the firm have a competitive advantage producing this component?
4. **Capable suppliers.** How many capable suppliers exist?
5. **Architecture.** How modular or integral is this element to the overall architecture of the system?

Depending on these criteria, the decision may be to outsource, keep in-house, acquire capability, develop strategic partnering with a supplier, or help develop supplier capabilities. For example,

1. When the component is important to the customer (first criterion), the clockspeed is fast (second), and the firm has a competitive advantage (third), clearly keeping the component manufacturing in-house is appropriate independent of the number of suppliers (fourth) and the component architecture (fifth).
2. When the component is not important to the customer, the clockspeed is slow, and the firm does not have competitive advantage, outsourcing is appropriate independent of the last two criteria.
3. If customer value is high, clockspeed is fast, and the competitive position is weak, the firm should either invest to develop in-house capability, acquire a supplier, or develop strategic partnering depending on the number of suppliers in the market.
4. Finally, if customer value is high, clockspeed is slow, and competitive position is weak, the strategy depends on the component architecture. When the architecture is modular, outsourcing is appropriate. On the other hand, when the component is an integral part of the entire system, joint development with suppliers, or even the development of in-house capability, is the right course of action.

9.4 PROCUREMENT STRATEGIES

Until recently procurement was considered a clerical function with very little added value to the organization. Today, procurement is used as a competitive weapon that distinguishes successful, highly profitable companies from others within the same industry. Indeed, a survey of electronics companies identified 19 percentage point gaps in profitability between the least and the most successful companies, a full 13 percentage points of which were accounted for by the lower cost of goods sold. In this industry, 60–70 percent of the cost of goods sold is attributed to the cost of purchased goods and services [129].

To better understand the impact of procurement on business performance, we review the net profit margins of three companies in various industries. In 2005, Pfizer's profit margin was about 24 percent, compared to Dell's 5 percent and Boeing's 2.8 percent. Thus, reducing procurement cost by exactly one percentage point of revenue would have translated directly into the bottom line, that is, net profit. To achieve the same impact on net profit through higher sales, Pfizer would need to increase its revenue by 4.17 (0.01/0.24) percentage points, Dell by 20 percentage points, and Boeing by 35.7 percentage points. The implications are clear! The smaller the profit margins, the more important it is to focus on reducing procurement costs.

EXAMPLE 9-4

In 2001, General Motors's revenue was $177.3 billion, annual spending on parts was $143.8 billion, and net profit margin was 0.3 percent. A 0.5 percent reduction in annual spending would have increased profit by $0.72 billion. To achieve the same increase in profit through higher sales, General Motors would have had to increase revenue by a startling $240 billion, clearly an impossible challenge [152].

The example illustrates the impact of effective procurement strategies on the bottom line. The appropriate procurement strategy depends on the type of products the firm is purchasing and the level of risk and uncertainty involved. In the automotive industry, for example, it is clear that the procurement strategy that should be applied to vehicle electronic systems is quite different than the one applied to transmission systems or to tooling equipment and machines. Indeed, these items have different characteristics, for example, the level of risk, technology knowledge, available capacity, initial investment required, logistics challenges, and so forth.

So, how can the firm develop an effective purchasing strategy? What are the capabilities needed for a successful procurement function? What are the drivers of effective procurement strategies? And how can the firm ensure continuous supply of material without increasing its risks?

The first serious attempt to answer these questions was made by Peter Kraljic in his seminal article, "Purchasing Must Become Supply Management" [132]. In his article, Kraljic argues that the firm's supply strategy should depend on two dimensions: (1) profit impact and (2) supply risk. According to Kraljic's framework, supply risk "is assessed in terms of availability, number of suppliers, competitive demand, make-or-buy opportunities, and storage risks and substitution opportunities." On the other hand, profit impact "is determined in terms of the volume purchased, percentage of total purchased cost, or impact on product quality or business growth" [132].

These two dimensions give rise to *Kraljic's supply matrix,* see Figure 9-4, where the horizontal coordinate represents profit impact and the vertical coordinate represents supply risks. The two axes define four quadrants.

The top-right quadrant represents strategic items where supply risk and impact on profit are high. Examples of components in that category include car engines and transmission systems. These are the items that have the highest impact on customer experience and their price is a large portion of the system cost. These are also the components that typically have a single supplier [42]. Clearly, the most appropriate supply strategy for these items is to focus on long-term partnerships with suppliers.

The bottom-right quadrant represents items with high impact on profit but low supply risk, what Kraljic calls leverage items. These are items that have many suppliers, and a small percentage of cost savings will have a large impact on the bottom line [42, 178]. Thus, focusing on cost reduction by, for example, forcing competition between suppliers is the appropriate procurement strategy.

The top-left quadrant represents high supply-risk but low profit-impact items. These components, referred to as bottleneck components, do not contribute a large portion of the product cost, but their supply is risky. Thus, unlike leverage items, in this case suppliers have a power position [42, 125]. For

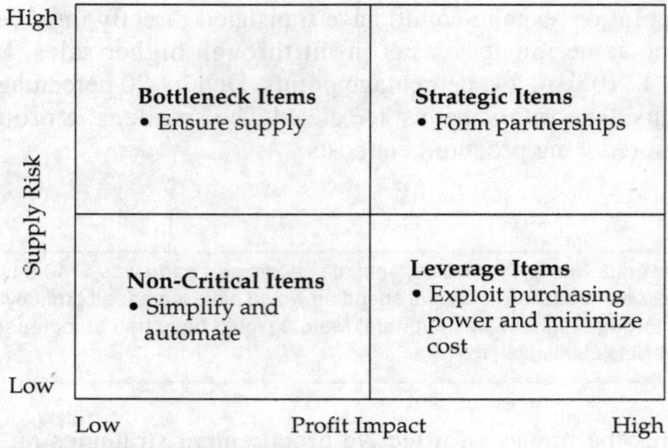

FIGURE 9-4 Kraljic's supply matrix.

these bottleneck items, ensuring continuous supply, even possibly at a premium cost, is important. This can be done through long-term contracts or by carrying stock (or both).

Finally, for noncritical items, the objective is to simplify and automate the procurement process as much as possible. In this case, a decentralized procurement policy is appropriate; for example, a policy where authorized employees order directly, without going through a formal requisition and approval process [180].

The implication of the supply matrix is clear. Each one of the four product categories requires a different procurement strategy. For example, long-term contracts may be appropriate for bottleneck items to ensure continuous supply of components. On the other hand, spot purchasing, or allowing employees to purchase items using approved (online) catalogs, may be appropriate for noncritical items. Strategic items should be the focus of top management, and purchasing decisions regarding these items may require a combination of analytical techniques such as those described in Chapter 3, supply contracts such as those described in Chapter 4, strategic partnering such as those described in Chapter 8, and risk mitigation strategies such as those described in Chapter 10.

9.4.1 Supplier Footprint

Many industries have changed their supply strategies in the last three decades. In the 1980s, American automotive manufacturing companies focused on suppliers either in the United States or in Germany. This changed in the 1990s, with a shift to suppliers in Mexico, Spain, and Portugal. Finally, in the last few years, these OEMs have again changed their supplier footprint with a significant move to China. Similar trends have been observed in the high-tech industry. In the 1980s, the focus of U.S. high-tech companies was on sourcing in the United States; in the 1990s, on Singapore and Malaysia, and recently on Taiwan and mainland China.

The challenge is therefore to develop a framework that helps organizations determine the appropriate supplier footprint. Intuitively, the strategy should depend on the type of product or component purchased, the ability to forecast, the impact on profit, the technology, product clockspeed, and so forth.

For this purpose, we start our discussion by introducing the concept of functional and innovative products proposed by Marshall L. Fisher in his article "What Is the Right Supply Chain for Your Products?" [82]. Table 9-6 depicts the key characteristics of the two product categories.

As you can see, functional products are associated with slow product clockspeed, predictable demand, and low profit margins. Examples include diapers, soup, milk, and tires. On the other hand, innovative products such as fashion items, cosmetics, or high-tech products are associated with fast product clockspeed, unpredictable demand, and high profit margins.

As observed by Fisher, the supply chain strategy that should be applied to innovative products is quite different than the supply chain strategy for functional products. Following our terminology, and the discussion in Chapter 6, it is clear that the appropriate supply chain strategy for functional products is push, where the focus is on efficiency, cost reduction, and supply chain planning. On the other hand, the appropriate supply chain strategy for innovative products is pull, because of the high profit margins, fast clockspeed, and unpredictable demand. Indeed, here the focus is on responsiveness, maximizing service level, and order fulfillment (see Section 6.2.5 and Table 6-2.)

The implications of the different supply chain strategies for procurement are clear. When the firm, say a retailer, procures functional products, the focus should be on *minimizing total landed cost,* that is, the total cost of purchasing and delivering the product to its final destination. This cost includes

- Unit cost
- Transportation cost
- Inventory holding cost
- Handling cost
- Duties and taxation
- Cost of financing

On the other hand, when procuring innovative products, focusing on total landed cost is the wrong strategy. Because of the fast clockspeed, high margins, and high forecast error, the focus in this case should be *on reducing lead times and on supply flexibility.*

Thus, when a retailer or a distributor procures functional products, sourcing from low-cost countries, for example, mainland China and Taiwan, is appropriate. On the other hand, when sourcing innovative products, the focus is on suppliers close to the market area, that is, where the products are sold. Alternatively, short lead time may be achieved using air shipments, and, in this case, the tradeoffs are unit cost versus transportation cost.

Of course, the analysis so far has focused on procuring finished goods; this is appropriate for retailers and distributors or even OEMs that outsource all manufacturing activities to contract manufacturers. But what should the sourcing strategy be for components?

For this purpose, we combine the insights from Kraljic's supply matrix model and Fisher's framework. Indeed, Fisher's framework emphasizes the demand side while Kraljic emphasizes the supply side. Thus, our framework considers four criteria:

TABLE 9-6

CHARACTERISTICS OF FUNCTIONAL VERSUS INNOVATIVE PRODUCTS

	Functional products	Innovative products
Product clockspeed	Slow	Fast
Demand characteristics	Predictable	Unpredictable
Profit margin	Low	High
Product variety	Low	High
Average forecast error at the time production is committed	Low	High
Average stockout rate	Low	High

- **Component forecast accuracy.**
- **Component supply risk.**
- **Component financial impact.**
- **Component clockspeed.**

The only criterion that needs some discussion is component forecast accuracy. Observe that the component forecast accuracy is not necessarily the same as the finished product forecast accuracy. For example, if the same component is used in multiple finished goods, the risk pooling concept discussed in Chapter 2 implies higher forecast accuracy at the component level.

Depending on these criteria, the decision may be to focus the sourcing strategy on minimizing total landed costs, lead time reduction, or increasing flexibility. For example, when component forecast accuracy is high, supply risk is low, financial impact is high, and clockspeed is slow, a cost-based sourcing strategy is appropriate. That is, in this case, focusing on minimizing total landed cost should be the main objective of the procurement strategy. This typically implies sourcing from low-cost countries, for example, Asia-Pacific countries.

In contrast, when component forecast accuracy is low, financial risk is high, and clockspeed is fast, a sourcing strategy based on lead time reduction is appropriate. If, in addition, supply risk is high, dual sourcing, flexibility, and lead time reduction are the focus of the sourcing strategy. Of course, it is not clear how one achieves all these objectives. One solution is to apply the portfolio approach described in Chapter 4. This approach combines long-term contract (short lead time through carrying inventory), option contracts (flexibility), and spot market (multiple supply sources), as is illustrated in the following example.

EXAMPLE 9-5

In 2000, Hewlett-Packard was faced with an important challenge. Demand for flash memory grew exponentially and, as a result, the price of flash memory and its supply were uncertain. This, together with HP's high demand uncertainty for flash memory, implies significant financial and supply risk. Specifically, if HP commits to purchase a large amount of inventory, they are exposed to huge financial risk through obsolescence cost. If, on the other hand, they do not have enough supply, then they are exposed to both supply risk and financial risk, since purchasing from the spot market during shortage periods leads to premium payments. HP's solution was the portfolio strategy, where they combined fixed commitment, option contracts, and spot purchasing [169].

Figure 9-5 summarizes the framework in more detail. It provides a qualitative approach for evaluating a component sourcing strategy by integrating the impact of the four criteria. To evaluate the framework, consider the procurement of car seats in the automotive industry. Car seats are typically used in a variety of models, so forecast accuracy is high; there are many suppliers, so supply risk is low but profit impact is high; finally, technology clockspeed is slow. The level of supply risk and the financial impact imply that these items belong to the leverage category. Together with the high forecast accuracy and slow clockspeed, they suggest a focus on minimizing total landed cost.

9.5 E-PROCUREMENT

In the mid to late 90s, business-to-business automation was considered a trend that would have a profound impact on supply chain performance. Between 1998 and 2000, hundreds of e-markets were established in dozens of industries, from chemicals and steel to utilities and human resources. These marketplaces promised, among other things, increased market reach for both buyers and suppliers,

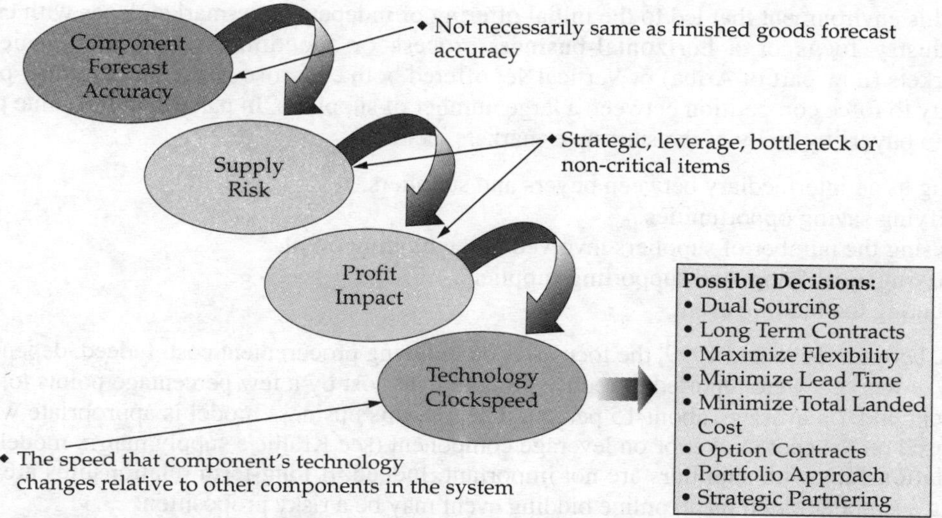

FIGURE 9-5 **A qualitative approach for evaluating component sourcing strategy.**

reduced procurement costs, and paperless transactions. Indeed, companies such as Ariba and CommerceOne were founded on the premise that e-procurement software that automates the requisitioning process will be able to reduce processing cost per order from as high as $150 per order to as low as $5 per order [224].

To better understand the huge expectations from e-procurement as well as the need for a new business model that will allow manufacturers and suppliers to improve supply chain performance, consider the business environment in the mid 90s. At that time, many manufacturers were desperately looking to outsource their procurement functions. These companies recognized that the procurement process is highly complex, requires significant expertise, and is very costly. Indeed, business-to-business transactions represent an enormous portion of the economy (much larger than business-to-consumer transactions), and the business-to-business marketplace is frequently highly fragmented, with a large number of suppliers competing in the same marketplace and offering similar products.

EXAMPLE 9-6 ePROCUREMENT BY ANDHRA PRADESH GOVERNMENT

Indian southern state Andhra Pradesh has used its eProcurment system for an aggregated transaction worth Rs. 37,000 crores from 18,028 tenders through a comprehensive infrastructure for tendering and procurement from companies of different sizes, platforms, and locations. 12 government departments, 18 public sector undertakings, 62 urban local bodies, and 5 universities are using this facility. The initiative has helped in the better management of its procurement process along with lesser time to finish the process, which otherwise is very time-consuming in government departments in India [286, 290].

Of course, a fragmented marketplace provides both opportunities and challenges. Indeed, buyers recognize that by forcing many suppliers that offer similar products to compete against each other, procurement costs can be significantly reduced. Unfortunately, to achieve these lower costs, buyers need significant expertise in the procurement process, which many of them did not have.

It is this environment that led to the initial offering of independent e-marketplaces with either a vertical-industry focus or a horizontal-business-process or functional focus. Companies such as FreeMarkets (now part of Ariba) or VerticalNet offered both expertise in the procurement process and the ability to force competition between a large number of suppliers. In particular, the value proposition offered to buyers by many of the start-up e-markets included

- Serving as an intermediary between buyers and suppliers.
- Identifying saving opportunities.
- Increasing the number of suppliers involved in the bidding event.
- Identifying, qualifying, and supporting suppliers.
- Conducting the bidding event.

Thus, between 1996 and 1999, the focus was on reducing procurement cost. Indeed, depending on the industry, e-markets were reported to reduce procurement cost by a few percentage points to as much as 40 percent and, on average, about 15 percent. Clearly, this business model is appropriate when buyers are focused on the spot market or on leverage component (see Kraljic's supply matrix model) and long-term relationships with suppliers are not important. Indeed, if long-term relationships are important, selecting a supplier based on an online bidding event may be a risky proposition.

The problem, of course, was that the value proposition for the suppliers was not as clear. Clearly, e-markets allow relatively small suppliers to expand their market horizon and reach buyers that they could not have reached otherwise. E-markets allow suppliers, particularly in fragmented industries, to access spot markets where buyers are looking not for long-term relationships but rather for a great price at an acceptable quality. Equally important, these markets allow suppliers to reduce marketing and sales costs and thus increase their ability to compete on price. Finally, e-markets allow suppliers to better utilize their available capacities and inventories. The natural question to ask is whether these benefits compensate for a reduction in revenue by on average 15 percent, and sometimes as high as 40 percent. At the same time, it is not clear that many suppliers feel comfortable competing on price alone. Thus, suppliers, especially those with brand-name recognition, may resist selling their services through e-markets.

What about the e-markets themselves? How do they generate revenue? Initially, many of the markets charged a *transaction fee* paid by either the buyer, the suppliers, or both. This fee was typically a percentage of the price paid by the buyer and varied from 1 to 5 percent [126]. As pointed out in [126], transaction fees pose serious challenges to the market maker because

1. Sellers resist paying a fee to the company whose main objective is to reduce the purchase price.
2. The revenue model needs to be flexible enough so that transaction fees are charged to the party that is more motivated to secure the engagement. For instance, if demand is much larger than supply, buyers are more motivated than sellers and hence the transaction fee should be paid by the buyers.
3. Buyers also resist paying a fee in addition to the purchase price.

Finally, low barriers to entry created a fragmented industry flooded with participants. For instance, just in the chemical industry, there were about 30 e-markets, including CheMatch, e-Chemicals, ChemB2B.com, ChemCross, OneChem, ChemicalDesk, ChemRound, and Chemdex [55]. Low margins and inability to build scale resulted in a major shake-up of this industry.

These challenges have motivated a continuous evolution of the e-markets' business model. Many exchanges have changed the way they charge their clients. Indeed, two other types of charge mechanisms have been used by some e-markets. These include a *licensing fee* and a *subscription fee*. In the former case, the software vendor licenses its software so that the company can automate the access to the marketplace. In the latter case, the marketplace charges a membership fee that depends on the size of the company, the number of employees who use the system, and the number of purchase orders [126].

At the same time, many e-markets have completely modified their value proposition. Initially, the focus of the value proposition was on market reach for buyers and sellers as well as lower purchase cost. The landscape has completely changed in the last few years with the introduction of four types of markets:

Value-added independent (public) e-markets. Independent e-markets have expanded their value proposition by offering additional services such as inventory management, supply chain planning, and financial services [119]. For instance, Instill.com focuses on the food service industry and provides an infrastructure that links together operators, that is, restaurants, distributors, and manufacturers. This e-marketplace provides value to its customers by offering not only procurement services but also forecasting, collaboration, and replenishment tools.

Pefa.com, to give another example, services the European fresh fish market. It offers buyers access to "a large number of independent fresh fish auctions." The benefits to buyers are evident:

- Provide visibility on price from many European ports.
- Provide information on product quality.

Private e-markets. In the last few years, many companies have established their own private e-market to allow them to run reverse auctions and online supplier negotiation. In a reverse auction, suppliers submit bids and the buyer selects the winning bid(s) typically based on cost. In many cases, this process allows buyers to consolidate their purchasing power across the entire corporation. For instance, the Subway restaurant franchise with 16,000 members in over 70 countries has a private e-market that allows the different restaurants to purchase from over 100 suppliers. Motorola, to give another example, has implemented supplier negotiation software that allows the firm to conduct bids, negotiate, and select an effective procurement strategy. Since the implementation of the Emptoris technology in 2002, over 1,000 of Motorola's supplier representatives have used the new procurement system [162].

Consortia-based e-markets. These e-markets are very similar to the public e-markets except that they are established by a number of companies within the same industry. Examples include Covisint (see below) in the automotive industry, Exostar in the aerospace industry, Trade-Ranger in the oil industry, and Converge and E2Open in the electronic industry. The objective of these consortia-based e-markets is not only to aggregate activities and use the buying power of consortia members but, more importantly, to provide suppliers with a standard system that supports all the consortia's buyers and hence allows suppliers to reduce cost and become more efficient. Interestingly, in the last three years, some of the consortia have decided to exit the auction business, for example, Covisint and E2Open, and focus on technology that enables business collaboration between trading partners and hence provide tools used by buyers and suppliers in a secure environment.

Content-based e-markets. These include two types of markets. The first focuses on maintenance, repair, and operations (MRO) goods while the second focuses on industry-specific products. As its name suggests, the focus of the e-marketplace is on content, which is achieved by integrating catalogs from many industrial suppliers. To achieve scale and increase efficiencies, content-based e-markets unify suppliers' catalogs and provide effective tools for searching and comparing suppliers' products.

For example, Aspect Development (now part of i2) offers electronics parts catalogs that integrate with CAD systems.

To emphasize the difference between private and consortia-based e-markets, consider the automotive industry.

EXAMPLE 9-7

Covisint was established in early 2000 by Detroit's big-three automakers. Later on, Renault, Nissan, Mitsubishi, and Peugeot joined the marketplace. Interestingly, not all automakers have signed on. For example, focusing on its own suppliers and processes, Volkswagen established its own private e-market, VWgroupsupply.com. Volkswagen's e-market not only provides similar capabilities to that of Covisint's, but also provides suppliers with real-time information on production plans so that suppliers can better utilize their production capacities and other resources. In both cases, the e-marketplaces do not focus on reducing purchase costs but rather on improving supply chain processes and thus supply chain efficiencies. For instance, both are integrating design activities within the marketplace so that if an automaker's engineer changes the design of a component, the relevant suppliers are involved in the process and can respond quickly, cutting cycle time and, effectively, reducing cost, to the design change. Of course, one important challenge faced by Covisint is whether competing automakers will be willing to risk their most sensitive procurement standards and processes by using the consortia [101]. Similarly, it is not clear that tier 1 suppliers in the automotive industry will accept a system owned by the OEM for their own purchasing needs, since information about the price they pay to their own suppliers may be revealed. By the end of 2003, Covisint sold its auction business to FreeMarket. Today, Covisint specializes in two areas, automotive and health care, and in both cases the focus is on enabling collaboration and improving decision making processes.

These issues are not unique to the automotive industry, as is illustrated by the following example from the electronics industry.

EXAMPLE 9-8

Celestica and Solectron are competitors with similar products and customers but different procurement strategies. In 1999, Celestica established a private e-marketplace for its 10,000 suppliers. The company uses its private marketplace to provide its suppliers with production data. Demand forecast data received by Celestica from its customers are transferred to its suppliers through the private portal so that suppliers can coordinate the back end of Celestica's supply chain, that is, the suppliers' production activities, with the front end of Celestica's supply chain, that is, its customer demand forecast. Unlike Celestica, Solectron is using a public e-marketplace. According to Bud Mathaisel, CIO of Solectron, it could cost more than $80 million to build and support an integrated private marketplace for its 8,000 suppliers. By focusing on a public marketplace, Solectron can take advantage of standard data and standard business processes provided by the exchange and thus reduce cost [241].

SUMMARY

In this chapter, we examined outsourcing and procurement strategies. Outsourcing has both benefits and risks, and we considered a framework for making buy/make decisions. These decisions should depend on whether a particular component is modular or integral, and whether or not a firm has the expertise and capacity to manufacture a particular component or product. Of course, decisions about individual components depend on a variety of criteria, including customer importance, technology clockspeed, competitive position, number of suppliers, and product architecture.

Similarly, procurement strategies vary from component to component. We identified four categories of components—strategic, leverage, bottleneck, and noncritical items—and the associated procurement strategies. This framework motivates a clear strategy for supplier selection, that is, offshoring versus onshoring. Indeed, we emphasized four categories important in selecting suppliers: component forecast accuracy, clockspeed, supply risk, and financial impact.

DISCUSSION QUESTIONS

1. Answer the following questions about the case at the beginning of this chapter:
   a. Describe Zara's current sourcing strategy. How is it a competitive advantage for the firm?
   b. What specific challenges are a result of Zara's rapid inventory turnover? What portions of Zara's replenishment strategy make it easier to manage?
   c. Will Zara's current sourcing strategy continue to be useful as it expands? How should this strategy change? What are the risks associated with this new strategy?
2. Discuss the impact of the product life cycle on the buy/make framework developed in Section 9.3.
3. Apply the hierarchical model discussed in Section 9.3 to IBM's decision in the early 1980s to outsource the production of microprocessors for its PCs to Intel.
4. Consider a consumer product manufacturer such as Procter & Gamble. Analyze whether the company should outsource the production of products such as shampoo. Is your recommendation consistent with P&G's strategy? If not, explain the reason for the difference between your strategy and what is done by P&G.
5. Discuss the appropriate sourcing strategy for a component with low customer importance, fast clockspeed, and no competitive advantage.
6. Apply the Kraljic matrix model to the Cisco virtual manufacturing strategy.
7. Provide examples of three types of items identified in the Kraljic matrix model: leverage, bottleneck, and noncritical items.
8. Analyze component procurement strategy as a function of the product life cycle. Specifically, identify the appropriate strategy when a product is at a growth stage (introduction), maturity (steady state), and end-of-life.
9. According to Bill Paulk, IBM's vice president of e-marketplaces, "IBM has saved about $1.7 billion since 1993 by being able to divulge sensitive price and inventory information over a private exchange built for 25,000 suppliers and customers." As the host of the exchange, the company helped defray the cost of connecting suppliers. The payoff: On-time delivery to customers soared from about 50 percent to close to 90 percent, "which helped justify the cost," Paulk says. In 1999, IBM invested in E2open, a consortia-based e-marketplace for the electronics industry. Why do you think IBM needs both a private exchange and a consortia-based e-marketplace?

CASE: Solectron: From Contract Manufacturer to Global Supply Chain Integrator

Most people think we're a manufacturing company. We're good at manufacturing, but we're really a service company.

—Koichi Nishimura, Solectron CEO[1]

In mid-2001, Solectron Corporation was confronting issues that it had never before faced in its twenty-four year history. The company was the world's premier supply chain integrator, with

[1] Bill Roberts, "CEO of the Year Koichi Nishimura, Contract Manufacturing Visionary," *Electronic Business, December 1999.*

$18.7 billion in annual revenue.[2] Since going public in 1989, its stock had appreciated by a factor of 280 times by the time it peaked in October 2000.

The economic downturn of 2001 hit the company hard. While revenues for the first quarter of fiscal 2001 (ending December 1, 2000) were twice that of the same quarter in the previous year, quarter-to-quarter revenue decreased each quarter during fiscal 2001, with a 27 percent decrease from Q2 to Q3. The company had large amounts of excess inventory. Collections suffered, and receivables jumping significantly (Table 9-7).

By September, the stock had fallen 77 percent from its high, and market capitalization was just 40 percent of annual revenues (Figure 9-6).[3] The company had laid off 20,000 of its 80,000 workers and closed facilities.[4] What should they do now?

THE ELECTRONICS MANUFACTURING SERVICES INDUSTRY

The electronics manufacturing services industry (EMS, also referred to as contract manufacturing) grew out of a large number of small job shops that manufactured assemblies for clients, The clients, original equipment manufacturers (OEMs), would often use these shops to supplement their own production capabilities, or to offload production that did not contribute to their competitive advantage, such as cables or simple printed circuit boards. In the 1970s and early 1980s, production was relatively low volume, as consumer electronic products did not require extremely high production levels.

As the personal computer became a mass-market product in the 1980s, a few contract manufacturers grew rapidly, led by SCI Systems. The rise in PC use also drove related markets, such as those for printers and memory devices. In the 1990s the industry continued its rapid growth, driven by the development of the Internet, with its demand for networking equipment such as routers and servers. The exploding demand for mobile phones and other wireless devices, as well as other electronic tools such as personal digital assistants, also contributed to the heavy demand for manufacturing capacity during this period. Solectron grew rapidly during the 1980s and 1990s, becoming the dominant company in the industry by the mid-1990s.

In 2000, the EMS industry was estimated to be $103 billion, or about 13 percent of the total cost of goods sold of OEM companies. The penetration rate was forecasted to increase to 22 percent, or $231 billion by 2005, for an overall industry compounded annual growth rate (CAGR) of 18 percent. The same forecast anticipated that the top tier EMS companies should grow at a disproportionately high rate, averaging 25 percent per year for the five-year period.[5] The industry consisted of several large public companies, the largest of which was Solectron, and included Sanmina/SCI Systems, Flextronics, Plexus, Jabil Circuit, and Celestica, and hundreds of smaller companies, most of whom were privately held.

---

[2]For the fiscal year ended August 31, 2001.

[3]As of September 10, before the terrorist attacks of September 11 that drove the stock price further down.

[4]Aaron Elstein and Scott Thurm, "Telecoms' Rout May Hit Firms They Hire," *The Wall Street Journal*, August 10, 2001, C1.

[5]Ellen Chae and Todd Bailey, "Annual EMS Industry Update," *Prudential Financial,* August 2001, 7. Forecasts from IDC, Technology Forecasters, and Prudential. These estimates incorporate the effects of the weakness in demand for electronic products in 2001, but were made before the events of September 11.

Source: Research Associate David Hoyt prepared this case under the supervision of Professor Hau Lee as the basis for class discussion rather than to illustrate either effective or ineffective handling of an administrative situation. The case was prepared in cooperation with Solectron Corporation. The data presented is for teaching purposes only, and certain facts may have been changed to enhance the teaching objective. Before using any facts presented in this case for other purposes, the reader should verify them with Solectron. The case was edited by Mary Petrusewicz.

TABLE 9-7

SELECTED FINANCIAL DATA

(All dollar values in millions)

	2001	2000	1999	1998	1997
Revenue[a]	18,692	14,138	9,669	6,102	3,694
Cost of sales	17,206	12,862	8,733	5,436	3,266
Gross profit	1,486	1,275	936	667	428
Operating expenses	(1,585)[b]	(571)	(420)	(298)	(192)
Operating income (loss)	(98)	704	516	369	236
Taxes, interest, other	26	(217)	(166)	(118)	(78)
Net income (loss)	(124)	497	350	251	158
Total assets	12,930	10,376	5,421	2,411	1,876
Inventory	3,209	3,787	1,197	789	495
Accounts receivable (net)	2,444	2,146	1,283	670	419
Employees at year-end	60,800	57,000	33,00	22,000	17,000
Square footage at year-end (millions)	11	10	7	5,5	3
	Q4 2001	**Q3 2001**	**Q2 2001**	**Q1 2001**	**Q4 2000**
Revenue	3,595	3,983	5,419	5,696	4,736
Cost of sales	3,387	3,678	4,930	5,211	4,323
Gross profit	208	308	488	485	413
Operating expenses	(314)	(277)	(295)	(209)	(170)
Restructuring and impairment	(207)	(285)	—	—	—
Operating income (loss)	(313)	(254)	193	276	243
Taxes, interest, other	63	68	(71)	(85)	(72)
Net income	(250)	(186)	122	191	171
Ending backlog ($ billion)	2.2	2.5	4.4	5.8	4.9
New orders ($ billion)	3.3	2.1	4.0	6.5	6.5
Total assets	12,930	13,293	14,605	14,027	10,376
Inventory	3,209	4,201	4,882	4,584	3,787
Inventory turns	3.7	3.2	4.2	5.0	5.5
Accounts receivable (net)	2,444	2,391	3,188	2,688	2,146
Days receivable outstanding	61	63	49	42	38
Employees at period end	60,800	65,800	79,800	71,900	65,000

Source: Solectron Corporation.

Accounting calendar: Q4 2001 ended August 31, 2001
Q3 2001 ended June 1, 2001
Q2 2001 ended March 2, 2001
Q1 2001 ended December 1, 2000
Q4 2000 ended August 25, 2000

[a]Results from 2000, 1999 and 1998 include acquisitions made during 2000 and accounted for by a pooling of interests. These acquisitions are not included in 1997 results. In 1998, they accounted for $813 million of revenue and $52 million of net income.

[b]Includes acquisition, restructuring and impairment costs of $547 ($207 in Q4, $285 in Q3, and $55 in Q2).

OVERVIEW OF SOLECTRON CORPORATION

Solectron Corporation was founded in 1977 to make solar energy products as part of the solar energy boom of the mid-1970s.[6] The company struggled financially, and began to build assemblies, primarily printed circuit boards (PCBs) for

[6]The company's name is a combination of "solar" and "electronics."

Solectron's weekly stock prices and volumes for the ten years ended September 26, 2001 were:

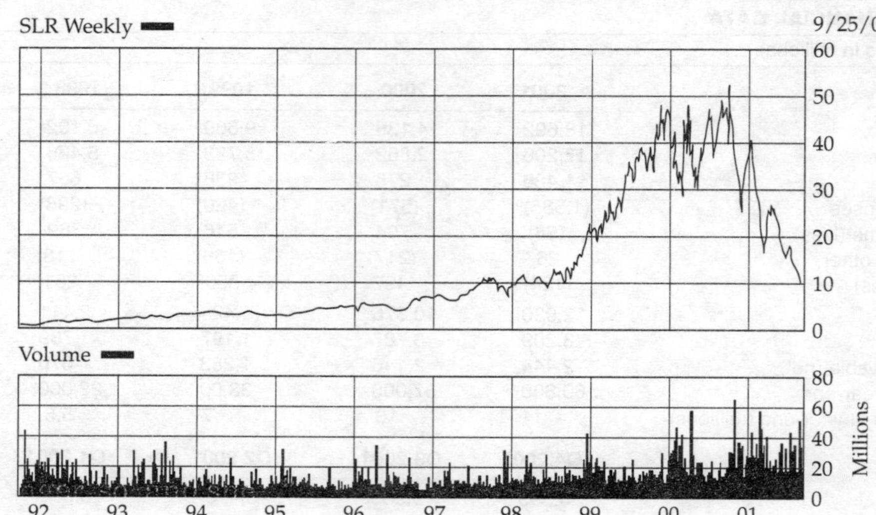

FIGURE 9-6 Solectron stock price.
Source: www.bigcharts.com; with permission.

other electronics firms. Located in Milpitas, California, Solectron was close to the fast-growing Silicon Valley electronics industry, and thus had ready access to a large number of potential clients for its manufacturing services. Starting in the early 1980s, it focused its complete attention on contract manufacturing, and changed the PCB job shop business into an important industry, providing high quality electronics manufacturing services.

An essential element of the company's strategy was an intense focus on quality and a company culture that reinforced this focus in all areas of business. Solectron won the prestigious Malcolm Baldrige National Quality Award in 1991, and again in 1997 (its first year of eligibility after the first win, making it the first repeat winner in the award's history), and by 2001 had won more than 250 quality and service awards from its customers. The Baldrige application process had been a cornerstone of the company's operations since 1989, helping focus the company's attention on quality and customer satisfaction.

In the early 1990s, the company began a program of strategic acquisitions, in which it purchased the manufacturing facilities of its customers, and received long-term contracts to supply those customers. Under Solectron, these facilities could also be used to supply multiple customers, increasing the plant utilization. The company made many such acquisitions fueling its rapid growth. In 1994, it passed $1 billion in annual revenue. In 1998, it became the first company in the EMS industry to be added to the S&P 500.

Solectron manufactured a wide range of products for its customers in many business segments, including:

- Networking (27 percent of FY2000 revenues)—hubs, modems, NICs, remote access, routers, switches.
- Telecommunications (29 percent)—access equipment, base stations, IP telephony equipment, mobile phones, pagers, switching equipment, transmission equipment, video conferencing equipment.

- Computers (25 percent, PCs/Notebooks 16 percent, Workstations and Servers 9 percent)—docking stations, Internet access devices, mainframes, midrange servers, notebooks, PC servers, PCs, retail systems, supercomputers, workstations.
- Computer Peripherals (7 percent)—disk and tape drives, tax machines, laser and inkjet printers, projector engines.
- `Others (12 percent)—avionics, consumer electronics, GPS, medical electronics, semiconductor equipment, test/industrial controls.[7]

The company was heavily dependent on its largest customers; 72 percent of sales in FY2000 came from the top ten customers, led by Ericsson at 13 percent and Cisco at 12 percent. Others in the top ten included Compaq, HP, and IBM.[8]

As Solectron grew, it expanded its services. In 1996, it began quick-turnaround prototype services as the result of its acquisition of Fine Pitch Technologies. By the end of the decade, it had three strategic business units: Technology Solutions, which provided technology building blocks that helped customers minimize time-to-market for new products; Global Manufacturing, which provided design, new product introduction, and manufacturing and distribution services; and Global Services, which provided repair, upgrade, and maintenance, as well as logistics, return management, warehousing, and many other post-manufacture support activities. A Global Materials Services group supported all three business units by providing sourcing, procurement, and other common supply base management resources.

CULTURE AND QUALITY

Solectron's corporate culture, and its overriding emphasis on quality, was an essential element of its success. The company's core values and beliefs were thoroughly ingrained in Solectron's management and strategic planning processes (Exhibit 9-1, page 319).

Early Cultural Development

The cultural development started in 1978, when Dr. Winston Chen, a long-time IBM executive, joined the company as president. At the time, electronics companies that contracted their printed circuit board (PCB) assemblies to outside manufacturers chose vendors based on low price and fast delivery, and did not expect high quality. Dr. Chen challenged this practice, insisting that only by achieving the highest quality standards could one achieve the lowest cost.

Harkening back to his IBM days, Dr. Chen used two basic principles to run the company: superior customer service, and respect for the individual. In order to fully implement these principles, he established systems that provided rapid feedback of required information, and the freedom for employees to act in order to fulfill these objectives. For instance, he established a process for measuring customer satisfaction weekly, by asking all customers to provide assessments according to five criteria: quality, responsiveness, communication, service, and technical support. The results were reviewed by management every week, and posted weekly at each production line. Chen commented, "We don't tell people, 'You're good,' or 'You're bad.' We say, 'Here's what the customers say.' That's a very powerful tool."[9]

The company also developed weekly profit and loss statements for each production line, which were distributed to all line managers. Chen noted, "If you really want to respect individuals, you've got to let them know how they're doing—and let them know soon enough so they can do something about it. Ultimately, the measures that matter are customer satisfaction and profit and loss."[10] In

[7]Solectron Web, site, http://www.solectron.com/about/index.html. Percentage shares from Solectron's 2000 Annual Report, 8.

[8]Solectron 2000 Annual Report, 20. In FY1999, the top ten accounted for 74% of sales, led by Compaq (12%) and Cisco (11%). In FY1998, the top ten accounted for 68%, led by HP (11%) and Cisco (10%).

[9]Alex Markels, "The Wisdom of Chairman Ko," *Fast Company*, November 1999.

[10]Ibid.

1984, when Chen became CEO, his vision was to "revive American manufacturing competitiveness and become the best manufacturing company in the world."

Solectron's operations utilized a highly diverse group of employees, which the company called "associates." Many associates were recent immigrants. The contract manufacturing industry, Solectron included, typically paid relatively low wages to its production workers. Yet, the company could not achieve its vision unless these people were highly motivated and unified toward a common purpose. The Solectron culture provided that unification.

In 1988, Dr. Chen convinced one of his former IBM colleagues, Dr. Koichi Nishimura, to join the company as chief operating officer. By this time, the company had grown to $93 million in revenue, with solid profits. Dr. Nishimura's approach was to never be satisfied, continually question existing practices, and strive for continuous improvement. This applied to all aspects of business, whether it was the time required to prepare financial reports, improvements in production quality, or increased customer satisfaction.

The Baldrige Award, and the Focus on Quality

Soon after arriving at Solectron, Dr. Nishimura learned of the Malcolm Baldrige National Quality Award, which had been instituted by Congress in 1987 to promote excellence in the nation's manufacturing and service sector. He decided that the award's evaluation process was similar to Solectron's principles, and that it could be a benchmark for continuous improvement. The company applied for the 1989 award, but did not receive a site visit, which is a required step for all finalists. However, it did receive a report from the evaluators recommending improvements in many aspects of the company's operations.

Dr. Nishimura was delighted with this "free consulting," and implemented the recommended improvements. After failing to get a site visit again the next year, Nishimura commented, "We weren't trying to win the award, we were simply trying to build a quality company. And the award was the template."[11]

In 1991, Solectron did get a visit from the Baldrige Award examiners. The company received a large amount of advice for improvement—and won the award. It was the first time the award had been given to a company in the contract manufacturing industry.

Baldrige Award winners are ineligible for the prize for five years, but Solectron felt that the application process was so valuable that it prepared internal evaluations based on the Baldrige Award every eighteen months. Nishimura noted that "[this] keeps us focused on continuously improving things for our customers. That's the only way to be the best."[12] In 1997, the first year it was eligible to reapply, Solectron again won the Baldrige Award—the first repeat winner in the award's history.

Day-to-Day Practice

Cultural practices at Solectron had several components, each of which reinforced the others, and most of which were directly related to the company's stated mission.

The emphasis on continual improvement, and the process of creating and reinforcing values, was institutionalized throughout the organization. For example, 7:30 A.M. meetings on Tuesday, Wednesday, and Thursday had been an institution since the early days of the company. The meetings were attended by about thirty to fifty people, ranging from engineers and program managers to site management personnel. Each meeting began with a site overview of the quality results from two days before the meeting (the most recent results available). Progress toward site quality plans objectives was also reviewed at each meeting. The remainder of the Tuesday meeting was devoted to an internal customer satisfaction review, or management train-

[11]Ibid.

[12]Ibid.

ing provided by a combination of company executives and external guest speakers.

The Wednesday meeting was highly focused on quality, and was a forum for process improvement and knowledge sharing. The emphasis was on prevention of problems rather than correction, through the use of self-directed work teams (SDWT) and the company's Quality Improvement Process (QIP).[13] SDWT members made presentations at the 7:30 A.M. meetings. The meeting also served as a forum for recognizing excellent performance. When a team received a recognition award from a customer, Solectron's president presented a check to be shared equally by the members of the team, and publicly recognized the team at the meeting.

The focus of the Thursday morning meeting was customer satisfaction and program management. Solectron asked each customer to grade its performance every week on quality, delivery, communication, and service. At the Thursday meeting this data was reviewed, problems discussed, and improvement plans presented. Decisions were made by consensus of the site management team. Consensus decision-making was intended to strengthen teamwork, which was a strong Solectron value, and heavily emphasized by top management.

Symbolism was also used to unite the workforce. For instance, all employees, from the CEO to a beginning assembler, wore identical white smocks with the company logo.[14] While the smocks were justified on the basis of electrostatic discharge control, their larger purpose was to help all associates feel part of one family. Signs with the company beliefs and the "Five Ss" were also prominently displayed in Solectron facilities.

Culture and Acquisition Integration

Through the 1990s, Solectron's growth strategy included acquiring manufacturing operations from its customers. By late 2000, the workforce was over 80,000 people, many of whom had joined Solectron as the result of acquisitions. Integrating employees was essential to the success of the acquisition, since success was highly dependent on the ability of Solectron to harness the intelligence, know-how, and experience of the new employees. The company culture was an important part of that integration.

The company assigned an integration team to work with the acquired operation composed of four to eight people representing the major functional areas (e.g., finance, human resources, operations, materials, and information technology). The team became involved in the early stages of the due diligence process, long before the acquisition decision was finalized. The business integration process utilized an extensive checklist, and included all major functional areas covering activities from just prior to the announcement of the transaction all the way through the first 100 days after the transaction closed (Table 9-8). When the decision was made to proceed with an acquisition, a detailed integration plan was created. The development of this plan included participation by the acquired operation, ensuring that it was a part of the process. The Solectron integration team worked with the acquired company for three to six months after the acquisition was finalized, training the new employees and acting as a Solectron resource.[15]

EVOLUTION FROM CONTRACT MANUFACTURER TO GLOBAL SUPPLY CHAIN INTEGRATOR

Solectron grew from a contract manufacturer into a global supply chain integrator as it increased the size and the scope of services it offered. The OEMs' vision for their use of outside services evolved concurrently, so that by 2001 they outsourced activities that they would never have considered only a few years before (Exhibit 9-2, page 320).

---

[13]QIP teams were cross-functional, and addressed specific problems or opportunities for improvement. They developed action plans based on the company's objectives for customer satisfaction, quality, and flexibility.

[14]Visitors are issued blue smocks, so that they can be identified.

[15]"Solectron's Acquisitions Get Careful Attention," *Electronic Buyers' News,* July 24, 2000. Available online at http://www.ebnonline.com/story/OEG20000721S0011.

TABLE 9-8

BUSINESS INTEGRATION TEMPLATE.

A small portion of the acquisition business integration checklist:

FUNCTION:
- AM ACCOUNT MANAGEMENT
- COM CORPORATE COMMUNICATIONS
- FAC FACILITIES/EH&S
- FIN FINANCE
- HR HUMAN RESOURCES
- IT ITSS
- MAT MATERIALS
- NPI NPI/TECHNOLOGY
- OPS OPERATIONS
- PM PROGRAM MGMT
- QA QUALITY

H = Required by Day 1
M = Required by Day 100
L = Can wait until Day 1000+

LEGEND:
R = RED (Far below expectations; potential showstopper)
Y = YELLOW (Behind plan; needs more focus)
G = GREEN (On target)
X = Complete
/ = Not applicable

LOG	NO	PROCESS	PRIORITY L/M/H	SLR LEAD	(XXX) LEAD	DUE DATE	SOLUTION: IDENTIFIED	SOLUTION: VERIFIED	SOLUTION: DOCUMENTED	SOLUTION: SIGNED OFF	SOLUTION: IMPLEMENTED	COMMENT	ACTUAL COMP DATE
		Account Management Tasks											
AM	1	Cust. Acct. list review/comparison											
AM	2	New entity communication to cust.											
AM	3	SLR letter to all customers											
AM	4	Develop account structure											
AM	5	Review quotes											
AM	6	Review contracts											
AM	7	Review forecasting methodology											
AM	8	Prepare training materials											
AM	9	CSI Process training											
AM	10	Account management training											
		Facilities Tasks											
FAC	1	*Establish facilities maintenance services (janitorial, landscape, maintenance)*											
FAC	2	*Establish services contracts as needed (security, mail, café, coolers, etc.)*											
FAC	3	*Lease contracts other than building lease*											
FAC	4	*Solectron address*											
FAC	5	*Road and building signage*											
FAC	6	*Solectron philosophy visuals-local language (tenets banners map case)*											
FAC	7	*Transfer or set up Utilities contracts (elec, gas, vacuum, air, etc)*											
FAC	8	*Insure insurance coverage set up as required*											
FAC	9	*Badging & facility access*											
FAC	10	*Transfer or execute building lease*											
		Finance Tasks											
FIN	1	*Accounts Payable*											
FIN	2	*Account Receivable*											
FIN	3	*Assignment of applicable leases*											

Source: Solectron Corporation.

One Solectron executive described this evolution by comparing it to the change in bridge design as steel replaced wood.

> At first, people duplicated the designs of wooden bridges, just replacing the material. As they learned more, they began to modify the designs to take advantage of the properties of steel. Bridges still looked like they traditionally looked, but the modified designs couldn't have been built in wood. Finally, engineers developed entirely new approaches to bridge design, which couldn't have been imagined previously. That's where we are today. The manufacturing and information technology that we have today allows a fundamental change in the way our customers operate.[16]

When it first offered contract manufacturing services, Solectron provided little more than substitution for capabilities that its customers already possessed. Customers were driven by two forces: cash flow and resource allocation. They looked to outsourcing if they could cut costs, or if they needed extra short-term capacity to meet peak demand. Customers would often maintain a level of internal capability appropriate for ongoing needs, outsourcing when peak demand exceeded this level.

Because customers maintained some production internally, and might only outsource some assemblies, customers were often in a stronger position than Solectron when negotiating with parts suppliers. As a result, customers often consigned kits of parts that Solectron assembled. Solectron differentiated itself from other PCB assembly companies primarily because of its focus on quality.

As Solectron added more customers and took on more business from existing customers, its total volume increased. Eventually, it was in a stronger position to negotiate with parts suppliers than were its customers, and began to take on additional purchasing, parts inventory, and kitting responsibility. Solectron could then offer customers capability that they couldn't get themselves: reduced prices due to greater volume purchasing. Rather than outsourcing as a way to access relatively inexpensive, skilled labor, it became a source of tactical advantage. Tactical turnkey assembly meant that OEMs specified what was needed, and Solectron bought the materials, built the product, and shipped it to the customer.

Technological Developments

The development of surface mount technology (SMT) offered an important opportunity. In the 1970s and through much of the 1980s, PCB assemblies were constructed by inserting components into holes in the boards and soldering the components. Pin-through-hole (PTH) was an inexpensive method for low-volume assembly, but only a limited number of the relatively bulky components could be placed on a PCB, and they could only be placed on one side of the board. In 1983, Solectron began building a new type of PCB assembly, in which components were pasted directly onto the planar surface of the board. This surface mount technology used much smaller components, and enabled components to be placed on both sides of the PCB, greatly increasing the density of the circuit that could be placed on an individual board.

The advantages of SMT came at a price. The capital cost of SMT equipment was much higher than the equipment needed for PTH assemblies. At the time, few products were needed in truly high volume. In the early 1980s, mobile phones were not yet in production, and even personal computers were not mass-produced. Most OEMs could not justify the capital cost of SMT, even though they could benefit from the technology.

Solectron, however, could amortize the cost of SMT equipment across the volume of many customers, providing capability that OEMs could not economically acquire. By 1992, most new designs used SMT, relying heavily on Solectron and other contract manufacturers for production.

---

[16]Arthur Chait, corporate vice president of worldwide marketing, teleconference, July 30, 2001.

New Business Model

In 1992, Solectron introduced a new business model when it purchased manufacturing sites from IBM. As part of the asset acquisitions, Solectron received long-term supply contracts. This approach enabled OEMs to make the strategic decision to concentrate their efforts and resources on their core competencies, generally product definition, engineering, and marketing, and to use Solectron to perform procurement and production, which were its core competencies. Since they no longer maintained internal production capabilities, this was a strategic, rather than tactical decision for the OEMs.

IBM's Bordeaux, France, plant, an early acquisition in 1992, was illustrative of the success of the model. The 27,000 square meter facility had struggled to be profitable, and IBM placed all the people it could think of, such as sales staff and software developers, in the plant to fill the empty space. Still, employee numbers had shrunk to 1,000, of which only 500 worked in manufacturing, and only half of those were making PCBs. By early 2001, under Solectron, the plant employed 4,200 employees building mobile phone switching gear for Ericsson, networking equipment for Cisco, bar-code readers, and medical instruments, Products built for IBM utilized only a small fraction of the plant's capacity. The IBM plant manager, who stayed on as a Solectron employee after the sale, noted that it was almost like working at a completely different factory. "It's unbelievable; it's booming."[17]

This model was repeated many times, and Solectron rapidly grew. It acquired manufacturing facilities from customers, and used those facilities to fulfill long-term supply contracts. It also used the acquired facilities to produce products for other customers. This allowed for risk pooling, as fluctuating demands from different companies were smoothed, and safety stock levels of common component inventory could be reduced (compared with levels required if stocked individually by each company).

Over the next few years, Solectron acquired facilities in such strategic divestitures from more than twenty companies, including Hewlett Packard, Texas Instruments, NCR, Nortel Networks, Sony, Ericsson, Cisco Systems, Philips Electronics, and Mitsubishi.

As Solectron took over production for several major companies in the same industry (e.g., Cisco and Nortel), the economies of scale escalated further, since these companies shared similar processes and many common parts. Solectron also increased its visibility of these industries through the aggregated forecasts of each major player. However, the demand projections made by each OEM were still subject to demand information distortion, and might not reflect the true demands of the ultimate customer.

Consolidation and Relocation In addition to acquiring facilities from OEMs, there was consolidation within the EMS industry in the late 1990s, driven by the increasingly close relationships between OEMs and their suppliers. OEM companies preferred to establish strategic relationships with a few top tier EMS suppliers, who could fulfill their worldwide needs. In July 2001, Sanmina, then the fifth largest EMS, acquired SCI, the fourth largest, and twice the size of Sanmina. Solectron acquired two top-ten companies, NatSteel Electronics in November 2000, and C-Mac Industries in August 2001, as well as the Bluegum Group, the largest EMS firm in Australia.[18]

There was also a trend for the top companies to move production of high volume, predictable products to low-cost regions such as Asia (excluding Japan), Mexico, and central Europe. By mid-2001, Solectron had 30 percent of its production in such areas, with the goal of increasing to 70 percent.[19] This had two benefits—decreasing production costs, and moving production capacity closer to future high growth markets.

---

[17] Michael J. Ybarra, "Vineyards and Surface Mount Technology," *Upside*, April 2001, 116–119.

[18] Petri Lehtivaara, "The Electronics Manufacturing Services Industry," Case GM 863, International Institute for Management Development, October 1, 2001.

[19] Chae and Bailey, 16.

Through acquisitions, Solectron had developed a global network of facilities located strategically close to its customers and to emerging markets. This enabled it to introduce products in its new product introduction centers and then rapidly transfer production to the facilities best suited to volume production, either due to the low cost structure of the volume production site or its proximity to the end user, depending on the needs of the OEM customer. Load could also be balanced across the network, and production of a particular product could be transferred between sites as it passed through different phases of its life cycle, in order to maximize profitability.

Information Systems The development of the World Wide Web and tools for communication between information systems in different companies allowed Solectron to use technology to improve its operation and enabled its customers to optimize their supply chain in a fundamentally different way. Internally, the company invested heavily in information technology for the management of its worldwide network of facilities and suppliers. Its Global Enterprise and Resource System consisted of an enterprise resource planning system combined with additional applications such as product data management, shop floor control, warehouse management, materials database, rapid "what if" tools, financial analysis and reporting, and human resources. The company established a Web-enabled extranet that allowed the sharing of information with customers, suppliers, and partners. This helped integrate the supply chain by giving all parties equal access to certain information for planning and decision analysis. This visibility of critical information helped to minimize the "bull whip" effect that often occurred when making decisions in an uncertain environment when demand signals were not aligned (Figure 9-7).[20]

[20]Brian Fukumoto, corporate director of business transformation, e-mail communication, October 28, 2001.

Supply Chain Management

For its customers who fully utilized this approach, Solectron took responsibility for end-to-end supply chain management. The customer was responsible for the basic research and development of products, but Solectron played an important role in the actual product design. Solectron did all parts procurement, assembly, and testing, and delivered the product to the location specified by the customer. Solectron also took responsibility for service and technical support, as well as for recycling the product after its useful life. In short, Solectron was responsible for the entire product lifecycle planning. The customer focused its efforts on research, product definition, marketing, and sales.

From the OEMs' perspective, the major driver was no longer whether to make or buy a given assembly, but the larger question of where to get materials. The critical issue was the total cost of getting the item they needed, fully built and ready to go to the customer, when and where it was needed. This took much more into account than just procurement and manufacturing, as worldwide logistics became extremely important. If parts were sourced from one part of the world to be used in products for a customer in another part of the world, the transportation costs, tax, and duty for the parts might be greater than the labor cost of the assembly.

Previously the barrier to entry had been the capital cost of SMT equipment; now there were many companies with this equipment. Solectron's competitive edge now resided in the ability to execute quickly and across international borders, using its global network of facilities. The expertise was now in more than manufacturing; it was also in developing a global network of suppliers, and in moving goods efficiently around the world. Often more time and money would be spent on logistics than on assembling components.

The company's operations in Romania exemplified this situation. The Romanian operation had begun in 2000. The facility was used primarily to manufacture items destined for customers in central Europe, a region expected to grow rapidly due

The GEARS Application Architecture is shown below:

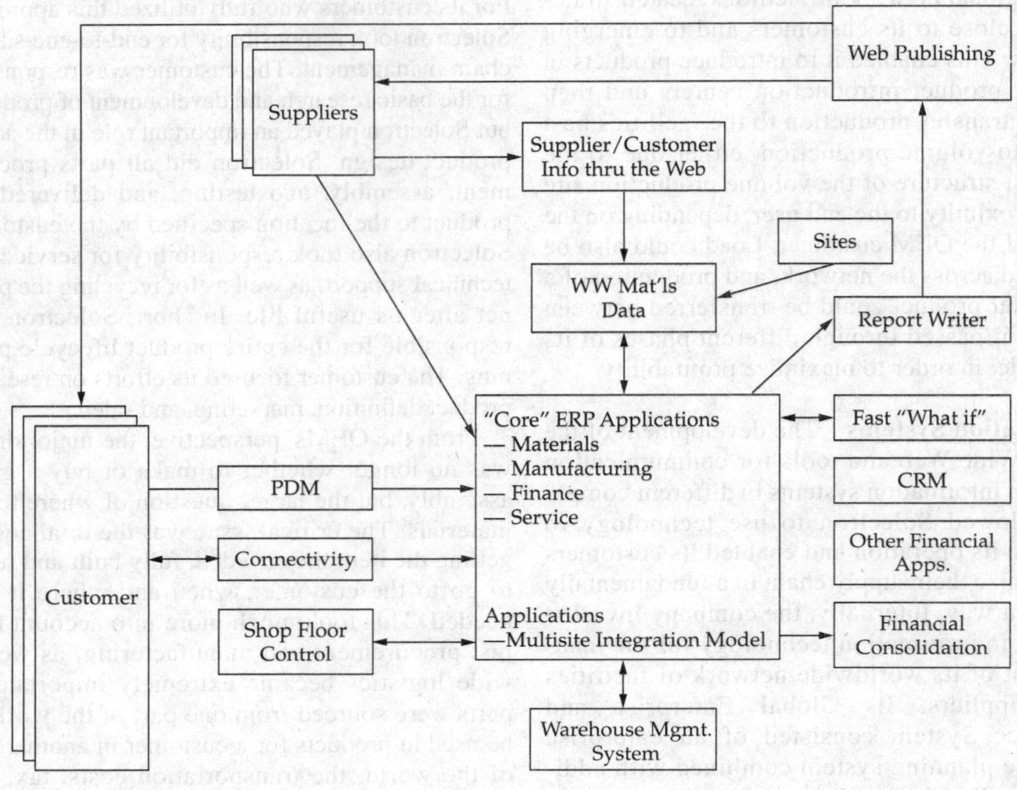

FIGURE 9-7 Global Enterprise and Resource System (GEARS).

to pent-up demand for electronic products. Labor was inexpensive, at about $.50 per hour, and Romania had an excellent workforce with a strong work ethic. However, it took a full day to get materials to the factory from western European countries, and two days to get completed products out of the country. Thus, there was a trade-off between labor and logistics costs due to infrastructure maturity.

Organization for Global Supply Chain Integration

To facilitate end-to-end supply chain management, the company organized into three business units: Technology Solutions, Global Manufacturing, and Global Services. The Global Materials Services group supported the business units.

Technology Solutions The Technology Solutions business unit provided modular and embedded systems design and manufacturing systems, offering a wide range of memory and I/O products, as well as embedded boards and systems that provided OEM customers with technology building blocks that could be used to quickly get products to market. This unit was built around the Solectron's largest wholly owned subsidiaries,

Force Computers (acquired in 1997), and SMART Modular Computers (acquired in 1999). In 2000, the Technology Solutions business unit had revenues of $1.5 billion, or 11 percent of the company's total sales.

Global Manufacturing The Global Manufacturing business unit provided manufacturing services to Solectron's customers. This was the largest of the business units, with revenues in 2000 of $12.4 billion, or 88 percent of the company's sales. In addition to the traditional contract manufacturing services, this unit provided new product introduction services and pre-manufacturing capabilities such as design for manufacturing, concurrent engineering, and prototyping.[21]

Solectron's work with start-up companies, which was housed in the Global Manufacturing business unit, reflected one aspect of these services. In 1996, Solectron acquired Fine Pitch Technologies specifically to work with small emerging companies that required quick-turnaround prototyping and a high level of engineering support in order to launch products. Fine Pitch was designed to provide a level of support that was not available from larger EMS firms, and to provide a path to volume production. However, the company had to carefully choose which start-ups to work with, as there were many more that wanted to establish relationships with Solectron than the company could service. Each of these relationships was a strategic investment, as the payoff would come later as the start-up grew. Solectron evaluated the suitability of these relationships much as a venture capital investor would, and chose only those that had a good strategic fit and offered the potential for high growth. Brocade Communications and Juniper Networks were two examples of companies that based their operations around Solectron's services.

[21]Concurrent engineering is continual product development after the product is already in production.

Global Services The Global Services business unit offered product repair, upgrades, and maintenance services through factory and service centers worldwide. It also provided services such as warehousing, logistics, returns management, engineering change management and end-of-life management. In 2001 this was a small part of the business, with 2000 revenues of just $233 million—less than 2 percent of the company's revenues. However, it was growing rapidly and promised to be an important area of future growth. Its revenues in 2000 were nearly three times the 1999 sales.

Global Materials Services These three business units were supported by the Global Materials Services group, which interacted with suppliers, handled procurement, was responsible for optimizing inventories, prepared market forecasts, and provided worldwide logistics support.

SITUATION IN THE FALL OF 2001

The technology business boomed in the late 1990s and into 2000, particularly the telecommunications and networking sectors. Solectron benefited, as it supplied many of the leading firms. In the fall of 2000, the company realized that a supply glut was likely, as each of their large customers, such as Cisco, Ericsson, and Lucent, expected explosive growth. Solectron added the forecasts from each competitor, and realized that they totaled far more than any realistic market size, even under the most optimistic scenario. It tried to restrain excessive orders from the OEMs, and went so far as to demand up-front payments with some orders. The OEMs insisted that their production plans be met, promising to pay for excess materials.[22] The strong culture to be the best and to continuously improve, and the ingrained belief in "customer first," made it extremely difficult to resist the pressure to increase production.

[22]Pele Engardino, "Why the Supply Chain Broke Down," *Business Week,* March 19, 2001, 41.

The economy began to soften in late 2000, and by early 2001 it was clear that demand was falling, particularly in industries with important Solectron customers such as telecommunications. The business turned seemingly overnight from one of severe allocation and struggle to keep up with demand to one of extreme overcapacity and excess supply. New orders decreased from $6.5 billion in the quarter ending December 1, 2000 to $2.1 billion in the quarter ending June 1, 2001. Revenue peaked at $5.7 billion in the quarter ending December 1, 2000, and declined 36.9 percent to $3.6 billion in the quarter ending August 31, 2001. Backlog, which had been at $5.8 billion on December 1, 2000, was just $2.2 billion on August 31, 2001. The stock price fell dramatically.

The rapid change in the business environment led to large inventory increases, as Solectron was unable to stop the orders it had placed with its 4,000 suppliers. Inventory rose by more than $1 billion during the six months ending March 2, 2001. The company was able to decrease inventory by more than $1.6 billion from the peak level over the next six months, however, by returning excess material to OEM customers and returning to its previous JIT practices, which had not been followed during the buildup driven by its attempt to meet increased OEM production demands.

Solectron also announced a restructuring that included workforce reductions and facility closures. The company formed a high-level cross-functional team to validate the value proposition at each Solectron site, develop restructuring goals and plans, and monitor progress. The team evaluated new cost structures, more efficient organizational designs, and improved customer relationship management processes. By October 2001, the workforce had been reduced from its peak of 80,000 to less than 60,000. The number of SMT lines had been cut from 1,100 to less than 700, and floorspace had been reduced from 14 million to less than 11 million square feet.[23] Restructuring charges of $285 million were booked in Q3 (May), and another $207 million in Q4 (August). Two facilities acquired as part of the Natsteel acquisition, one in Hungary and one in Mexico, were closed and production moved to other plants.[24]

Despite the short-term slow-down, and the painful steps that were taken, Solectron remained optimistic for the long-term. The use of outsourcing as an OEM strategy continued to accelerate. OEMs were increasingly attracted to Solectron's value proposition as a global supply chain integrator. The company believed that the economic and industrial climate favored the concentration of business in a small number of large suppliers of services to the OEM market. It expected dramatic growth in Asia (excluding Japan), which it expected to grow from a very small consumer to one-third to one-half of the total worldwide electronics market. It also expected that pent-up demand, combined with a rapidly developing disposable income, would lead to large markets in central and eastern Europe.

However, it struggled with the question of how to weather the current storm and ensure that it was properly positioned for the future.

STUDY QUESTIONS

1. How has Solectron's value to its customers evolved over time?
2. How has global expansion contributed to Solectron's ability to move from a contract manufacturing supplier to a supply chain integrator?
3. How has the company been able to successfully integrate its acquisitions?
4. What was the impact of the company's culture on the success of the company, on the business downturn of 2001, and on its ability to respond to the business downturn?
5. What additional products and services should Solectron provide to its customers in the future?
6. What should the company do in the short term? In the long term?

[23]Brian Fukumoto, e-mail communication, October 28, 2001.

[24]Chae and Bailey, 15–16. Restructuring charges from company financial releases.

EXHIBIT 9-1 SOLECTRON'S VISION, MISSION, BELIEFS, AND "5 Ss"

MISSION[a]

"Our mission is to provide worldwide responsiveness to our customers by offering the highest quality, lowest total cost, customized, integrated design, supply-chain and manufacturing solutions through long-term partnerships based on integrity and ethical business practices."

BELIEFS

Customer First	Strengthen customer partnerships by providing products and services of the greatest value through innovation and excellence.
Respect for the Individual	Emphasize associate dignity, equality, and individual growth.
Quality	Execute with excellence; drive to six-sigma capability in all key processes; exceed customer expectations.
Supplier Partnerships	Emphasize communication, training, measurement, and recognition.
Business Ethics	Conduct business with uncompromising integrity.
Shareholder Value	Optimize business results though continuous improvement.
Social Responsibility	Be an asset to the community.

VISION

"Be the best and continuously improve."

THE FIVE Ss

When traveling to benchmark Japanese companies in 1988, Dr. Saeed Zohouri, the company's vice president of technology, observed a sign at a Yamaha motorcycle factory describing the "Five S" practices.[b] They were embraced by Dr. Nishimura, who felt that they were useful for achieving his vision of combining the best of Japanese techniques with American innovation.

Seiri (Organization)

- Distinguish between those things that are needed and not needed.
- Keep only needed materials at the job site.
- Throw away all unneeded items immediately.

Seiton (Orderliness)

- Put things in the right order in the designated area.
- Store all materials and information in an orderly fashion at all times.
  - Tidy
  - Ready to use
  - Organized according to frequency of use
- A place for everything and everything in its place.

Seiso (Cleanliness)

- Problems are more visible when everything is neat and clean.
- Find minor defects while "sweeping clean."

Seiketsu (Standardized Cleanup)

- Clean tools, equipment, and job site immediately after use.
- Equipment that is kept clean runs better.

Shitsuke (Discipline)

- Use and follow standard procedures.

- Follow company rules and regulations.
- Follow safety procedures at all times.

Source: Solectron Corporation.

[a]Revised 1997.

[b]Dr. Zohouri later became Solectron's chief operating officer.

EXHIBIT 9-2 THE OUTSOURCING DECISION

The decision to outsource was a major strategic decision for an OEM, and one whose pros and cons had to be carefully considered to determine if outsourcing would really improve the OEM's performance and maximize its value. While outsourcing could bring strategic benefits, it had costs—the changes were traumatic and difficult to reverse for an OEM that had traditionally done its own manufacturing. Outsourcing affected thousands of workers, and it opened critical aspects of a company's business to the scrutiny of supply partners and other external forces, and potentially exposed them to disruptive intervention.*

Therefore, in making the decision to outsource, it was essential to understand how the true cost of internal production compared with the costs of acquiring the material from others. This involved three types of analysis:

- Strategic. Does owning or enjoying preferential access to the production asset have any strategic importance? How does the company's manufacturing strategy meet the needs of its overall business strategy? For instance, ownership of design and manufacturing assets gives Intel fast product ramp-up and protects the company's intellectual property.
- Operational. What are the performance targets and the needs of manufacturing and the supply chain (such as lead times and unit costs)? For instance, Dell configured its supply chain to meet its overall business strategy of delivering customized computers shortly after orders were placed.
- Organizational. How does the business achieve results? It is difficult for established companies to transform their supply chains.

Solectron identified three benefits that OEMs could gain by outsourcing.** The central theme was that outsourcing allowed OEMs to allocate their resources on core competences, such as research and development and marketing. These three benefits were time-to-market, economics, and technology.

TIME-TO-MARKET

The speed with which a company could bring products to market became an increasingly competitive issue in the 1990s. Early market entrants were able to command a dominant market share, and achieve the corresponding financial rewards. By working with an EMS company that could help get the product to market quickly, and rapidly ramp up production, OEMs were able to decrease the time-to-market for their products.

ECONOMICS

EMS companies were able to achieve far greater asset utilization than OEMs, since they could use the same assets to produce products for many companies. This resulted in significant cost savings for the OEMs. In addition, the risks of product changes, short product life cycles, and other sources of inefficiencies were reduced because the EMS company could balance the effect of schedule changes with production demand from other products and customers.

TECHNOLOGY

Manufacturing process became increasingly more complicated and expensive throughout the 1990s. The impact of SMT has been previously described, but the issue was continually present as product and manufacturing technologies rapidly developed. Access to the latest manufacturing technology might be impossible for most OEMs, because of both cost and complexity. However, an EMS would be able to offer the technology to meet the production needs of many customers, and develop the required skills to effectively utilize the new processes. Thus, outsourcing offered the potential for an OEM to access important new technologies without incurring high start-up costs (both economic and in training), nor paying excessive production costs.

*This section based on Brian Fukumoto, e-mail communication, October 28, 2001.

**Advantages from: http://www.solectron.com/gscf/benefits.html, September 12, 2001.

CHAPTER **10**

Global Logistics and Risk Management

CASE: Wal-Mart Changes Tactics to Meet International Tastes

São Bernardo, Brazil. Wal-Mart Stores Inc. is finding out that what plays in Peoria isn't necessarily a hit in suburban São Paulo.

Tanks of live trout are out; sushi is in. American footballs have been replaced by soccer balls. The fixings for *feijoada,* a medley of beef and pork in black bean stew, are now displayed on the deli counter. American-style jeans priced at $19.99 have been dropped in favor of $9.99 knock-offs.

But adapting to local tastes may have been the easy part. Three years after embarking on a blitz to bring "everyday low prices" to the emerging markets of Brazil and Argentina, Wal-Mart is finding the going tougher than expected.

Brutal competition, markets that don't play to Wal-Mart's ability to achieve efficiency through economies of scale, and some of its own mistakes have produced red ink. Moreover, the company's insistence on doing things "the Wal-Mart way" has apparently alienated some local suppliers and employees.

DEEP POCKETS

No one is counting Wal-Mart out, of course. With sales of nearly $105 billion last year and profits of $3.1 billion, the Bentonville, Arkansas, behemoth has deep pockets. And it has revised its merchandising in Brazil and Argentina and made other changes. Its four newest stores are smaller than the initial outlets in São Paulo and Buenos Aires and are in mid-size cities where competition isn't so fierce.

Bob L. Martin, Wal-Mart's head of international operations, is confident that the company will eventually become the dominant retailer in South America. "There is low-hanging fruit all over the place," he says. "The market is ripe and wide open for us." He adds that Wal-Mart plans to add eight stores in both Argentina and Brazil next year, doubling the number now in each country.

A lot is riding on Wal-Mart's global expansion drive, which is targeting not only South America but also China and Indonesia, two other markets full of promise and pitfalls. With opportunities for growth dwindling at home, the company is opening fewer than 100 domestic stores a year, down from as many as 150 in the early 1990s. The current rate of openings can't generate the profit gains that Wal-Mart wants, and its main hopes lie overseas.

Source: Jonathan Friedland and Louise Lee. *The Wall Street Journal,* Online Edition, October 8, 1997. Copyright 1997 by Dow Jones & Company, Inc. Reproduced with permission of Dow Jones & Company, Inc. in the format textbook via Copyright Clearance Center.

"If we're good enough in international, we can duplicate Wal-Mart," chief executive David D. Glass said in an interview in June. "We have very high expectations."

A SMALL OPERATION SO FAR

So far, though, the six-year-old international operation is relatively tiny; it accounted for only 4.8 percent of Wal-Mart's 1996 sales. Most of the company's international revenue comes from Canada, where Wal-Mart purchased 120 stores from Woolworth Corp. in 1994, and from Mexico, where earlier this year it bought a controlling stake in Cifra, SA, its partner, and now has about 390 stores. Last year, the international unit had an operating profit of $24 million, its first, compared with a $16 million loss in 1995. Mr. Martin says he expects further improvement this year. Mr. Glass said he expects international growth to account for a third of Wal-Mart's annual increase in sales and profits within three to five years.

The performance of Wal-Mart's 16 South American stores may well indicate the future outlook. In Canada and Mexico, many customers were familiar with the company from cross-border shopping trips, and by acquiring local retailers, Wal-Mart quickly reached the size necessary to hold down costs. In South America and Asia, by contrast, Wal-Mart is building from scratch in markets already dominated by savvy local and foreign competitors such as Grupo Pão de Acucar SA of Brazil and Carrefour SA of France.

LOSSES FORECAST

Wal-Mart doesn't break out financial data on its South American Operations. However, retail analysts, citing the accounts of Wal-Mart's Brazilian partner, Lojas Americanas SA, expectWal-Mart to lose $20 million to $30 million in Brazil this year, on top of an estimated $48 million in losses since starting up in South America in 1995. In Argentina, where the company doesn't have a partner, Wal-Mart executives concede that it is losing money but say its performance meets expectations. The company expects operations in both countries to be profitable by early 1999.

"What counts is that we are finding great customer acceptance," Mr. Martin says. Wal-Mart says its supercenter in Osasco, Brazil, was the top-grossing store in the entire company last year. And at a recent supercenter opening in the mid-size Brazilian city of Ribeirão Prêto, shoppers practically beat down the doors to scoop up bargain-priced microwave ovens and television sets.

But such enthusiasm is hard to sustain. At an older supercenter in Avellaneda, a suburb of Buenos Aires, a few shoppers are in the store during peak hours one Sunday. Hugo and Mariana Faojo help explain why. Browsing in the shoe section, the young couple say they see little difference between the goods at Wal-Mart and those at nearby Carrefour. For groceries, they prefer Supermercados Jumbo SA, a Chilean-owned chain, where they say they find high-quality products and fresh meats. Clothes and household goods, Wal-Mart's mainstays, are similar in quality and price to those at Carrefour, says Mr. Faojo, a government surveyor.

Not only did Carrefour arrive first—it now has a total of about 60 stores in Argentina and Brazil—but it is maneuvering with prices and promotions to keep Wal-Mart off balance. When Thomas Gallegos, who manages Wal-Mart's new store here, prints up fliers advertising bargains, the nearby Carrefour responds in just a few hours by offering the same product for a few cents less—and its fliers are handed out at the entrance to the Wal-Mart parking lot. "Geez, the competition is aggressive," says Mr. Gallegos, who previously ran a Wal-Mart in Harlingen, Texas.

Carrefour, which, like Wal-Mart in the United States, drives hard bargains with its suppliers, can afford to play low-ball because it has the critical mass that Wal-Mart lacks here. And it holds down its overhead by stocking a far-narrower selection of merchandise; for example, the Carrefour in La Plata, Argentina, stocks 22,000 items, while the Wal-Mart next door carries 58,000.

Mr. Martin contends that Carrefour's advantage is ephemeral and that customers value Wal-Mart's broader choice. "It's costing them something to fight us," he adds. Carrefour didn't respond to requests for an interview.

DISTRIBUTION PROBLEMS

Right now, however, Wal-Mart's effort to stock such a wide variety of merchandise is hurting it. Squeezing out costs in the supply chain is crucial to its "everyday low pricing" formula. In the United States, the company runs like a well-oiled machine, maintaining a highly sophisticated inventory-management system and its own network of distribution centers.

But timely delivery of merchandise is a relative concept in the bumper-to-bumper traffic of São Paulo, where Wal-Mart depends on suppliers or contract truckers to deliver most of its goods directly to stores. Because it doesn't own its distribution system, it can't control deliveries nearly as well as it does in the United States, vendors say. Stores here sometimes process 300 deliveries daily, compared with seven a day at U.S. locations, and some shipments have mysteriously disappeared somewhere between the port and the store.

"The biggest issue Wal-Mart has is shipping product on time and getting it on the shelf," says Jim Russel, a national account manager for Colgate-Palmolive Co. in Bentonville. Wal-Mart recently built a warehouse in Argentina and one in Brazil that it says will eventually reduce its distribution problems.

But logistics aren't the only issue. Some local suppliers have difficulty meeting Wal-Mart's specifications for easy-to-handle packaging and quality control, forcing the retailer to rely so heavily on imported goods that it could have problems if Brazil's economic stabilization policies falter. Eleven South American suppliers have taken umbrage at Wal-Mart's aggressive pricing policies and for a time refused to sell goods to the chain.

Wal-Mart also has sought to drive hard bargains with divisions of its major suppliers back in the United States. The pitch hasn't been altogether successful. Wal-Mart doesn't get special deals just because it's a big U.S. customer, some large domestic suppliers say.

VARIOUS MISTAKES

Wal-Mart's troubles in South America stem partly from its own mistakes. Analysts say it failed to do its homework before plunging in. In addition to the live trout and American footballs, the company initially imported items such as cordless tools, which few South Americans use, and leaf blowers, which are useless in a concrete jungle such as São Paulo.

And merchandise flubs weren't the only mistakes. In Brazil, Wal-Mart brought in stock-handling equipment that didn't work with standardized local pallets. It also installed a computerized bookkeeping system that failed to take into account Brazil's wildly complicated tax system. Vincente Trius, who heads Wal-Mart's Brazilian operations, says, however, that the company hasn't lost money as a result of tax miscalculations.

Wal-Mart has also been slow to adapt to Brazil's fast-changing credit culture. Not until last February did the company start accepting postdated checks, which have become the most common form of credit since Brazil stabilized its currency in 1995. Pão de Acucar, whose Extra hypermarkets compete with Wal-Mart, has been taking postdated checks since they first became popular and has installed a sophisticated credit-checking system at its registers. Wal-Mart is hurrying to do so, too.

The six South American Sam's Club locations, the members-only warehouse stores that sell merchandise in bulk, got off to a slow start largely because shoppers weren't used to paying a membership fee and don't have enough room at home to store bulk purchases. In Argentina the clubs have faced another barrier: Small-business customers are reluctant to sign up for fear Wal-Mart could provide tax information to the authorities on their purchases.

Wal-Mart won't disclose Sam's Club membership data in South America. But it now offers shoppers free one-day memberships tied to specific purchases. Mr. Martin says that Wal-Mart is "disappointed" in the club's performance in Argentina but that it is improving in Brazil. The company says it plans more Sam's outlets in South America but hasn't disclosed details.

PROBLEMS CALLED TEMPORARY

Wal-Mart's Mr. Glass characterized the missteps as temporary problems and inevitable in entering a new market. "It's a lengthy process to go to South America, recruit good managers, bring them to Wal-Mart, and train them and indoctrinate them and teach them what you want to teach them," he said in June. "It's slow going early on, and you spend a lot of money. You pay a lot of tuition to learn what you need to learn."

Wal-Mart says that it is developing a strong group of young executives and hasn't suffered high turnover. But Francisco de Narvaez, the owner of Argentine supermarket chain Casa Tia SA, says some managers have left because Wal-Mart "didn't listen to their senior-level local employees." In the past six months, Wal-Mart has hired two managers who had worked at its Mexican operations to take over two São Paulo locations.

Mr. Trius, a Spanish-born executive who earlier turned around Dairy Farm Ltd.'s Spanish supermarket chain, says he believes the criticisms of Wal-Mart's South American operations go too far. "If Joe Blow was to open in Brazil with the same concept and within two years had everything in place, people would say, 'What an incredible job,'" he says. "People expected us to snap our fingers and be Wal-Mart in the United States overnight. To me, the criticisms are more related to expectations than to reality."

By the end of this chapter, you should be able to answer the following questions:

- Other than a need to expand, what other reasons would Wal-Mart have for opening stores globally?
- Why would it be beneficial for Wal-Mart to have suppliers in different countries?
- Why would Wal-Mart want strong centralized control of its stores? Why would Wal-Mart want strong local control of stores?
- What pitfalls and opportunities other than those mentioned in *The Wall Street Journal* article would Wal-Mart face over the next few years?
- What are the sources of risks faced by the global supply chain and how can the firm mitigate the various risks?

10.1 INTRODUCTION

It is readily apparent that global operations and supply chains are becoming increasingly significant. Dornier et al. [65] collected the following statistics, which help to indicate the magnitude of this trend:

- About one-fifth of the output of U.S. firms is produced overseas.
- One-quarter of U.S. imports are between foreign affiliates and U.S. parent companies.
- Since the late 1980s, over half of U.S. companies increased the number of countries in which they operate.

In many ways, international supply chain management is the same as domestic supply chain management spread over a larger geographic area. However, as we will discuss in the remainder of this chapter, international supply chain networks can provide a wealth of additional opportunities if they are managed effectively. At the same time, there are many additional potential problems and pitfalls to be aware of.

International supply chains can run the gamut from a primarily domestic business with some international suppliers to a truly integrated global supply chain. Some of the advantages and disadvantages that we will discuss apply equally to all of the systems in the following list, while others apply only to the most complex integrated systems.

International distribution systems. In this type of system, manufacturing still occurs domestically, but distribution and typically some marketing take place overseas.

International suppliers. In this system, raw materials and components are furnished by foreign suppliers, but final assembly is performed domestically. In some cases, the final product is then shipped to foreign markets.

Offshore manufacturing. In this type of system, the product is typically sourced and manufactured in a single foreign location, and then shipped back to domestic warehouses for sale and distribution.

Fully integrated global supply chain. Here products are supplied, manufactured, and distributed from various facilities located throughout the world. In a truly global supply chain, it may appear that the supply chain was designed without regard to national boundaries. Of course, this is far from the truth! As we shall see, the true value of a global supply chain is realized by taking advantage of these national boundaries.

Clearly, a supply chain can fit more than one of these categories. Throughout the following discussion, consider how each of the issues discussed applies differently to firms, depending on their position in this global supply chain spectrum.

In any event, many firms cannot help but become involved in global supply chain issues. Dornier et al. [65] identified the following forces that collectively drive the trend toward globalization:

- Global market forces.
- Technological forces.
- Global cost forces.
- Political and economic forces.

10.1.1 Global Market Forces

Global market forces involve the pressures created by foreign competitors, as well as the opportunities created by foreign customers. Even if companies don't do business overseas, the presence of foreign competitors in home markets can affect their business significantly. To defend domestic markets successfully, companies may find it necessary to move into foreign markets. Sometimes the threat of a presence is sufficient, as in the dry breakfast cereal business, dominated by Kellogg Co. in the United States and Nestlé in Europe. Apparently, failed attempts in the past to penetrate each other's home markets, combined with the threat of retaliation, are enough to maintain the status quo.

In addition, much of the demand growth available to companies is in foreign and emerging markets. Recently, companies have made great sacrifices (particularly in terms of proprietary technology) and taken on considerable business risk to become involved in ventures in mainland China. Indeed, the United States is accounting for less and less of the total consumption of goods in the world.

One cause of this increasing demand for products throughout the world is the global proliferation of information. Television introduces products to Europeans. Japanese vacation abroad. Businesses send

EXAMPLE 10-1

In Brazil thousands of people move from preindustrial villages to rapidly growing cities. Once there, their first goal is to install television sets, even as they continue to "make sacrificial offerings of fruit and fresh-killed chickens to Macumban spirits by the candlelight" [143].

overnight mail between continents. The Internet provides instant international exposure, as well as the ability to purchase goods in one country that will be delivered in another without leaving home or office.

As Kenichi Ohmae, head of management consulting firm McKinsey's Japanese office, points out, people have "all become global citizens, and so must the companies that want to sell us things" [177]. Products are universally desired, and many companies are willing to sell them globally. This is clearly a self-amplifying trend for an industry, because, as companies become global, their competitors also must become global in order to compete. Thus, many companies are becoming global citizens with universal products and the opportunity to hire talented employees worldwide.

Along similar lines, particular markets often serve to drive technological advances in some areas. By participating in these competitive markets, companies are forced to develop and enhance leading-edge technologies and products. These products can then be used to increase or maintain market position in other areas or regions where the markets are not as competitive. To be a leader in software, for example, you have to compete in the U.S. market. Similarly, the German machine tools market and the Japanese consumer electronics market are hotly contested.

10.1.2 Technological Forces

Technological forces are related to the products themselves. Various subcomponents and technologies are available in different regions and locations around the world, and many successful firms need to have the ability to use these resources quickly and effectively. To achieve this, it may be necessary for firms to locate research, design, and production facilities close to these regions. This is often particularly useful if suppliers are involved in the design process, as discussed in Chapter 11. The same logic applies to collaborations and interfirm development projects. To gain access to markets or technology, companies in different regions frequently collaborate, resulting in the location of joint facilities close to one of the partners.

Along similar lines, global location of research-and-development facilities is becoming more common, primarily for two reasons. First, as product cycles become shorter and time more important, companies have discovered how useful it is to locate research facilities close to manufacturing facilities. This helps transfer technology from research facilities to manufacturing facilities, and speeds up the resolution of problems that inevitably arise during this transfer. In addition, specific technical expertise may be available in certain areas or regions. For example, a few years ago, Microsoft opened a research lab in Cambridge, England, to take advantage of the expertise available in Europe.

10.1.3 Global Cost Forces

Cost forces often dictate global location decisions. In the past, the low cost of unskilled labor was a decisive factor in determining factory location. Recently, studies have found that in many cases, the costs of cheaper unskilled labor were more than offset by the increase in other costs associated with operating facilities in remote locations. In some cases, of course, cheaper labor is sufficient justification for overseas manufacturing. More recently, however, other global cost forces have become more significant. For example, cheaper *skilled labor* is drawing an increasing number of companies overseas.

Many of the analyses and programs that U.S. consulting firms undertook to address the Year 2000 problem (in which computer programs might fail when the year changed from 1999 to 2000) were done in India, where programming skills are much cheaper.

We have discussed how a supplier and the manufacturer supply chain must often be tightly integrated to deliver certain products effectively. Often this can be accomplished most cost-effectively if the various participants are located close together. This may necessitate establishing integrated supply chains in different markets. Finally, the capital costs of building a new facility often dominate labor costs. Many governments are willing to provide tax breaks or cost-sharing arrangements to lower the cost of the new facility. In addition, supplier price breaks and cost-sharing joint ventures may dictate these types of decisions.

10.1.4 Political and Economic Forces

Political and economic forces may greatly affect the drive toward globalization. In Section 10.2.1, we will discuss exchange rate fluctuation and the operational approaches to dealing with this issue. There are also several other political and economic factors. For example, regional trade agreements may drive companies to expand into one of the countries in the regional group. It may be to a company's advantage to obtain raw materials from or to manufacture within European, Pacific Rim, or North American trading blocs. In some cases, production processes may even be redesigned to avoid tariffs; for example, almost-finished goods may be shipped into a trading bloc to avoid tariffs on "finished goods."

Similarly, various trade protection mechanisms can affect international supply chain decisions. Tariffs and quotas affect what can be imported, and may lead a company to decide to manufacture within the market country or region. More subtle regulations, including local content requirements, affect supply chains. To address local content requirements, for example, TI and Intel, both U.S. firms, make microprocessors in Europe, and various Japanese automakers produce cars in Europe. Even voluntary export restrictions can affect the supply chain: Japanese manufacturers began to manufacture more expensive cars after agreeing voluntarily to limit exports to the United States. Recall that this is why brands such as Infiniti and Lexus came into existence. Government procurement policies can affect the ability of international companies to be successful in various markets. In the United States, for example, the Department of Defense gives as much as a 50 percent advantage to U.S. companies in the bidding on contracts.

EXAMPLE 10-2 TIPCO FOOD, THAILAND

Thailand has the largest global market share of around 45% in processed pineapple. Tipco Food is one the largest Thai exporters of this product with a whopping figure of Baht 3.7 billion. In 2006–07, due to the weakening of the US dollar ($) against most of the global currencies, including Baht, Tipco's global supply chain came under tremendous threat. The exchange rate has crumbled as follows: late 2006–Baht 41 per dollar; early 2007–Baht 37 per dollar; July 2007–Baht 33 per dollar. For the same quantity of export, the revenue inflow has gone down by about one fifth of its value a few months back. Most of these export-oriented supply chains have become non-competitive in the global market. As a protective measure, these export-oriented firms are focusing on local market to boost their sales [20].

10.2 RISK MANAGEMENT

We have looked at the various forces that drive companies to develop global supply chains. Of course, many of the advantages of sourcing, manufacturing, and selling globally are immediately obvious. The world is converging in many instances toward standardized products.

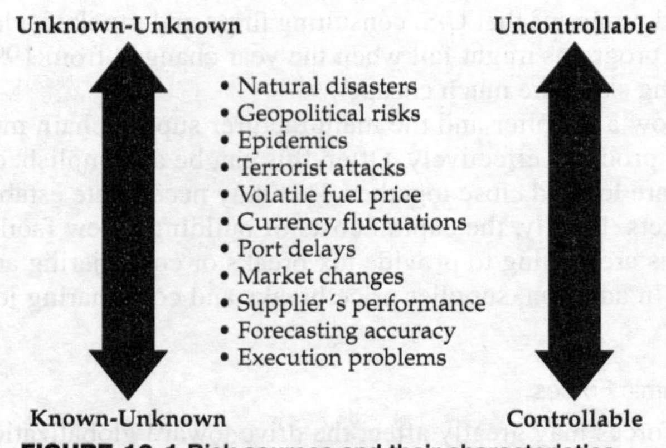

FIGURE 10-1 Risk sources and their characteristics.

This implies that more and more, vast markets have opened up for products—far greater than anything managers in the past could have imagined. By taking advantage of this trend, companies can realize vast economies of scale in terms of production, management, distribution, marketing, and so forth [143].

Indeed, as we discussed in the previous section, costs can be lowered with a larger number of options for sourcing raw material, labor, and outsourcing opportunities and a greater number of potential manufacturing sites. At the same time, the increase in potential markets allows for an increase in sales and profits. These advantages are due to the increase in the size and scope of the supply chain—they are independent of the specific characteristics of the global supply chain.

Unfortunately, all these advantages and opportunities associated with global supply chains come with significant increase in the level of risks faced by today's global companies. Indeed, outsourcing and offshoring imply that the supply chain is geographically more diverse and hence more exposed to various risks. Similarly, recent trends toward cost reduction, lean manufacturing, and just-in-time imply that in a progressive supply chain, low inventory levels are maintained. However, in the event of an unforeseen disaster, adherence to this type of strategy could result in a shutdown of production lines because of lack of raw material or parts inventory.

Thus, in this section, we examine the various risks inherent in global supply chains and techniques to mitigate these risks.

10.2.1 Many Sources of Risks

Global supply chains are exposed to similar risks to those faced by domestic supply chains, as well as other risks that are more global in nature. Figure 10-1 provides a nonexhaustive list of the various types of risks faced by global companies.[1] Natural disasters, geopolitical risks, epidemics, or terrorist attacks can shut down production lines because of lack of parts inventory. Indeed, this actually happened to some auto manufacturers in the wake of the September 11, 2001, terrorist attack.

Unfortunately, it is very difficult to prepare for mega-disasters such as hurricanes Katrina (2005) or Andrew (1992) because there is little experience to draw on [56]. Similarly, a SARS epidemic

[1]The figure is inspired by [35].

like the one in 2003 could shut down the flow of components and products from the Far East to the rest of the world but again is difficult to prepare for because of lack of data. Following former Secretary of Defense Donald Rumsfeld, we refer to these types of risks as the *unknown-unknown* since these are risks associated with scenarios where one cannot identify likelihood of occurrence.

At the other spectrum in Figure 10-1, we find sources of risks such as supplier performance, forecast accuracy, and operational problems. These are risks that can be quantified and hence we refer to those as the *known-unknown*. For example, using historical data the firm can characterize forecast error, mean time between machine failure, and supplier lead-time performance.

Of course, due to their nature, the unknown-unknown are difficult to control while the known-unknown are more controllable. Between the two extremes are various types of risks that can be controlled to a certain extent. For example, risk associated with volatile fuel price can be managed through long-term contracts while fluctuating exchange rates can be managed through a variety of hedging strategies as we discuss below.

Indeed, currency fluctuations pose a significant risk in today's global operations. They change the relative value of production and the relative profit of selling a product in a particular country. Relative costs change so that manufacturing, storing, distributing, or selling in a particular region at a particular price can change from being extremely profitable to a total loss. The same is true domestically. In many cases, certain regions within the same country may be less expensive for storage or manufacturing than others. However, the cost differences between domestic regions are not typically as dramatic as those across countries and, more importantly, they don't change as frequently.

It should be stressed that although managers typically think of exchange rates as affecting the dollar value of assets and liabilities denominated in foreign currencies, it is the *operating exposure* described in the previous paragraphs that can have the most dramatic effect on annual operating profit. This operating exposure reflects the fact that, in the short run, changes in currency exchange rates do not necessarily reflect changes in relative inflation rates between countries. Thus, over the short term, regional operations can become relatively more or less expensive in terms of dollars. Note that this operating exposure is not only a function of a firm's global supply chain, but also its competition's global supply chain. If a competitor's relative costs decrease more, a firm can be underpriced in the market [142].

Indeed, Dornier et al. [65] identified several factors that affect the impact of operating exposure on a firm. *Customer reactions* influence how a firm adjusts prices in various markets in response to changes in operating expenses. As discussed above, *competitor reactions* also influence how a firm can react to changes in the relative cost of doing business. Competitors can react to price increases by raising their own prices to increase profitability or gain market share. As we discuss in the next section, *supplier reactions*—the ability of suppliers to respond with flexibility to varying demands—is a strong factor in the effectiveness of certain strategies that help firms address the risk of operating exposure. Finally, *government reactions* play a large role on the global stage. Governments can intervene to stabilize currencies or even directly support endangered firms by providing subsidies or tariffs. In addition, other political instabilities also can affect multinational companies. Tax situations can change rapidly because political factors dictate different treatment of corporations, particularly foreign corporations, in various regions.

Likewise, foreign companies can enter domestic markets. These companies may even use domestic profits to subsidize low-priced goods in foreign markets. This could even affect companies that have decided not to compete on the global stage.

So what are the methods that the global firm can use to mitigate many of the risks described in this subsection? In the next two subsections, we consider strategies for dealing with both the unknown-unknown, and the classes of risk further towards the known-unknown end of the risk spectrum.

10.2.2 Managing the Unknown-Unknown

Are there strategies that the firm can use to deal with the unknown-unknown? Unfortunately, these are the sources of risks that may create a mega-disaster that not only can wipe out years of profit but also can force a company to exit a certain region or a specific market.

We discuss in this section the following methods for managing supply chain risks and in particular strategies for managing the unknown-unknown.

- Invest in redundancy.
- Increase velocity in sensing and responding.
- Create an adaptive supply chain community.

As we will illustrate below, an effective use of these methods allows the supply chain to recover from a misfortune, thus creating the so-called *resilient supply chain*. Each of these methods focuses on a different supply chain dimension. Redundancy is built at the design stage; sensing and responding require accurate information in a timely fashion; finally, an adaptive supply chain is a supply chain in which all its elements share similar culture, work toward the same objectives, and benefit from financial gains.

Redundancy A key challenge in risk management is to design the supply chain so that it can effectively respond to unforeseen events, the unknown-unknown, without significantly increasing costs. This can be done through careful analysis of supply chain cost trade-offs so that the appropriate level of redundancy is built into the supply chain.

EXAMPLE 10-3

In 2001, a U.S.-based consumer packaged goods (CPG) company had a global supply chain with about 40 manufacturing facilities all over the world. Demand for its products, household goods, was spread over many countries. The company grew organically and through acquisition. Management realized that it was time to rationalize its network and close nonproductive manufacturing facilitates. Initial analysis indicated that the firm can reduce cost by about $40M a year by shutting down 17 of its existing manufacturing facilities, and leaving 23 plants operating, while still satisfying market demand all over the world.

Unfortunately, this new lean supply chain design suffered from two important weaknesses. First, the new design left no plant in North America or Europe, thus creating long and variable supply lead times. Such lead times require a significant increase in inventory levels. More importantly, the remaining manufacturing facilities in Asia and Latin America were fully utilized and, hence, any disruption of supply from these countries, due to epidemics or geopolitical problems, would make it impossible to satisfy many market areas. So how can one design the supply chain taking into account epidemics or geopolitical problems that are difficult to quantify?

The approach the firm took was to analyze the cost trade-offs. These trade-offs are illustrated in Figure 10-2 where the x-coordinate represents the number of plants that remain open and the y-coordinate, the various cost components, including variable production cost, fixed cost, transportation, duties, and inventory costs. The top line is the total cost, that is, the sum of various cost components. As you can see, closing 17 plants and leaving 23 open will minimize supply chain costs. However, observe that the total cost function is quite flat around the optimal strategy. Indeed, increasing the number of open plants from 23 to 30 facilities will increase total cost by less than $2.5M while at the same time increasing redundancy significantly. Thus, even though we cannot quantify the risks associated with epidemics or geopolitical problems, we can prepare the supply chain for supply disruption by investing in redundancy without significantly increasing supply chain costs.

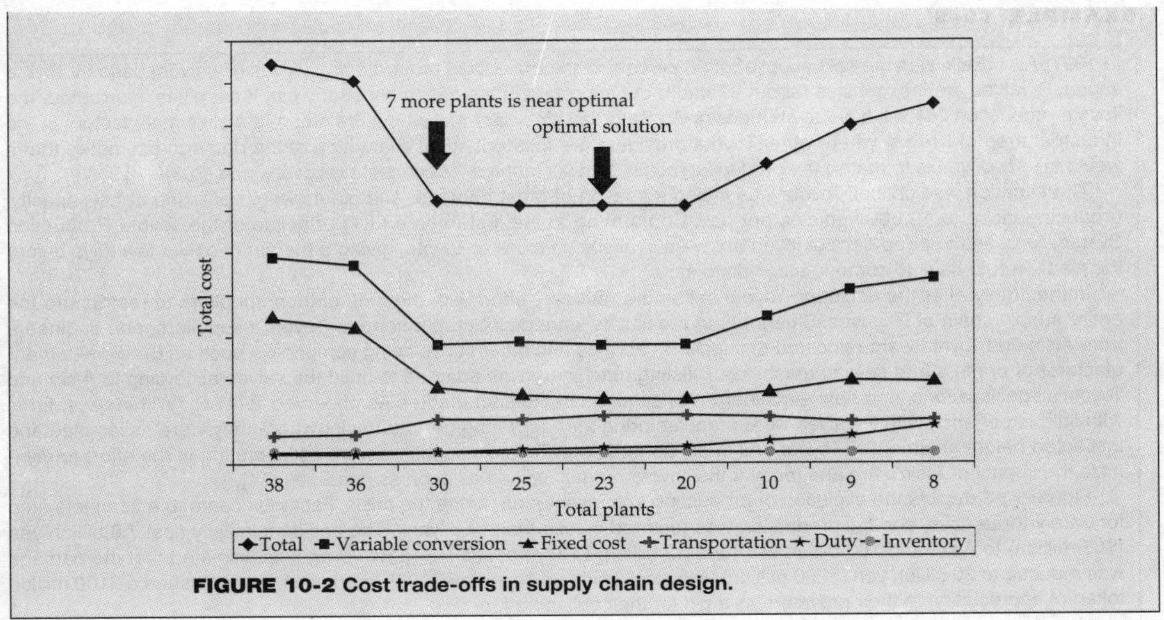

FIGURE 10-2 Cost trade-offs in supply chain design.

Sensing and Responding The following case illustrates how speed in sensing and responding can help the firm overcome unexpected supply problems. Indeed, it also illustrates how failure to sense, and therefore respond to, changes in the supply chain can force a company to exit a specific market.

EXAMPLE 10-4

In 2001, the Philips semiconductor factory in Albuquerque, New Mexico, provided several types of radio frequency chips used in mobile telephones. Major customers included OEMs such as Ericsson and Nokia. On Friday, March 17, 2000, at 8 p.m., Mother Nature, in the form of lightning, struck the Philips semiconductor plant. Fire, smoke, and water used during the fire exhaustion destroyed almost all the silicon stock in the factory. As a result, the plant was shut down for months.

Three days after the fire, Nokia detected delays in incoming orders from the Albuquerque plant. In the initial contacts, Philips reported they expected the plant to be shut for only one week. Fearing the worst, Nokia decided to send engineers to New Mexico to evaluate the damage. When the engineers did not get access to the plant, Nokia raised red flags and increased the frequency of monitoring incoming orders from the plant from weekly to daily. On March 31, two weeks after the fire, Philips confirmed to Nokia that months of orders will be disrupted.

Nokia's response to the news was decisive. The company changed product design so they could use chips from other suppliers. These suppliers committed a five-day lead time. Unfortunately, this was not enough; one of the five components provided by Philips was impossible to source from other suppliers. So Nokia convinced Philips to provide this component from two Philips factories in China and the Netherlands.

Ericsson's experience was quite different. It took the news to reach upper management about four weeks, even though Philips informed Ericsson of the fire three days after the incident. More importantly, only five weeks after the fire, Ericsson realized the severity of the situation. By that time, the alternative supply of chips was already taken by Nokia. The impact on Ericsson was devastating. $400M in potential sales was lost; part of the loss was covered by insurance. This, together with other problems such as component shortages, the wrong product mix, and marketing problems, caused a $1.68B loss to Ericsson Cell Phone Division in 2000 and forced the company to exit the cell phone market [43].

Source: Adapted with permission from F. Cela Diaz, "An Integrative Framework for Architecting Supply Chains." MS thesis, Massachusetts Institute of technology, 2005.

EXAMPLE 10-5

In 1997, Aisin Seiki was the sole supplier of 98 percent of the brake fluid proportioning valves (P-valves) used by Toyota Japan. P-valves are inexpensive (about $7 each) but important in the assembly of any car. If supply is interrupted, the Toyota production line will have to shut down. On Saturday, February 1, 1997, a fire stopped Aisin's main factory in the industrial area of Kariya, where other Toyota providers are located. Initial evaluation of the damage estimated that it would take two weeks to restart the production again, and six months for complete recovery, see [203].

The situation was critical. Toyota was facing a season of great demand, and plants were operating at full capacity, producing close to 15,500 vehicles per day. Conforming to the just-in-time (JIT) principle of the Toyota Production System, only two to three days of inventory were available in stock at Toyota, giving a margin of only a few days before the plants would have to come to a complete stop.

Immediately after the accident, Toyota initiated a recovery effort with the help of their suppliers to restructure the entire supply chain of P-valves. Blueprints of the valves were distributed among all Toyota's suppliers, and engineers from Aisin and Toyota were relocated to suppliers' facilities and other surrounding companies, such as Brother—a manufacturer of printers and sewing machines. Existing machinery was adapted to build the valves according to Aisin and Toyota's specifications, and new machinery was acquired in the spot market. As observed in [174], "Within days, firms with little experience with P-valves were manufacturing and delivering parts to Aisin, where they were assembled and inspected before shipment to Toyota." All in all, about 200 of Toyota's suppliers were collaborating in the effort to minimize the impact of Aisin's fire and recover the Toyota production line as soon as possible [174].

Figure 10-3 depicts the evolution of production and inventories during the crisis. Factories came to a complete stop for barely three days, and full production was restored in less than one week. The accident initially cost 7.8 billion yen ($65 million) to Aisin and 160 billion yen (or $1.3 billion) to Toyota; see [174]. However, it is estimated that the damage was reduced to 30 billion yen ($250 million) with extra shifts and overtime [203]. In addition, Toyota issued a $100 million token of appreciation to their providers as a gift for their collaboration.

Source: Adapted with permission from F. Cela Diaz, "An Integrative Framework for Architecting Supply Chains." MS thesis, Massachusetts Institute of Technology, 2005. Much of his analysis is based on data in [175], [151], and [13].

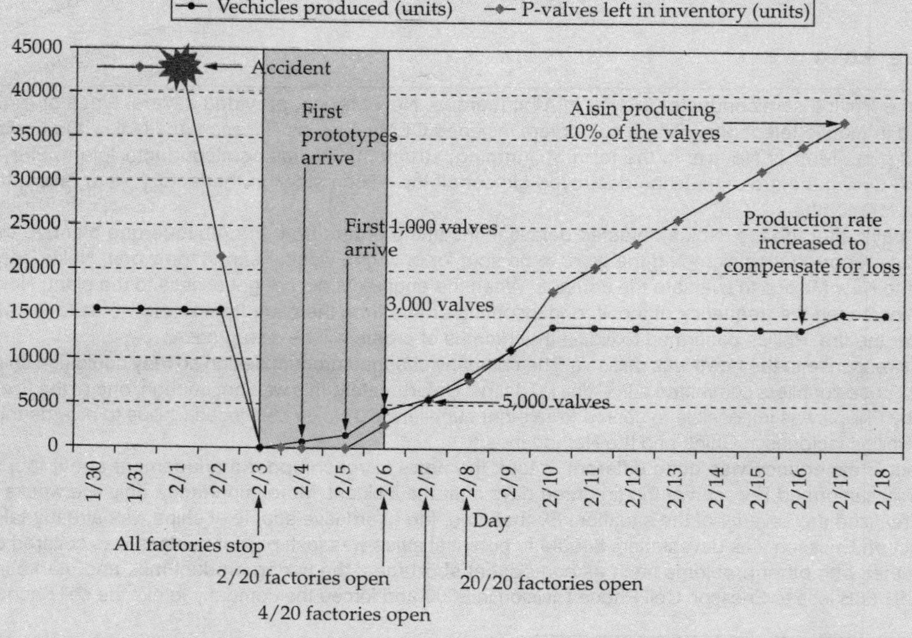

FIGURE 10-3 Vehicle production and P-valve inventory levels.

Adaptability This is, no doubt, the most difficult risk management method to implement effectively. It requires all supply chain elements to share the same culture, work towards the same objectives and benefit from financial gains. Indeed, it creates a community of supply chain partners that morph and reorganize to better react to sudden crisis. The next example illustrates the impact of the adaptive supply chain in a powerful way.

The example thus illustrates how Toyota's suppliers self-organized to address a sudden disruption in the supply of a key component. However, it raises three important questions. Does a single-sourcing strategy make sense for such a key component? Even if a single-sourcing strategy is appropriate, should not Toyota carry large amounts of inventory for such a low-cost but key component? And finally, what are the underlying mechanisms that exist in Toyota's supply chain and help the firm quickly recover from the sudden supply disruption?

According to Kiyoshi Kinoshita, Toyota's general manager of production control, single sourcing and holding almost no inventory was a calculated risk [203]. Toyota's single sourcing allows Aisin to achieve economies of scale in P-valve production, and offer high quality at very low costs to Toyota [174].

The third question is discussed in detail in [174]. They observe that key to understanding the ability of the supply chain to adapt to the new environment is the just-in-time (JIT) philosophy followed by Toyota and its suppliers almost religiously. Indeed, the essence of JIT is to control the amount of work-in-process (WIP) inventory at a relatively low level. Such a low level of WIP inventory promotes high quality and a quick identification of problems in the production line. Indeed, in JIT, every worker has the authority to stop the line in order to correct any problem. This also implies that JIT with low inventory levels fosters problem-solving capability [174].

These are the qualities that were essential to the quick adaptability of Toyota's supply chain. Once Toyota identified the Aisin fire as a problem, it stopped not only its production line, but the entire supply chain. This stop of the line forced supply chain partners to deal with the challenge [174].

10.2.3 Managing Global Risks

We now turn our attention to the other risks faced by global supply chains, including those risks that can be, to a certain extent, quantified and controlled (that is, the intermediate risks identified in Figure 10-1). Bruce Kogut [130] identified three ways a global supply chain can be employed to address global risks: speculative, hedge, and flexible strategies.

Speculative Strategies Using *speculative strategies,* a company bets on a single scenario, with often spectacular results if the scenario is realized, and dismal ones if it is not. For example, in the late 1970s and early 1980s, Japanese automakers bet that if they did all of their manufacturing in Japan, rising labor costs would be more than offset by exchange rate benefits, rising productivity, and increased levels of investment and productivity. For a while these bets paid off, but then rising labor costs and unfavorable exchange rates began to hurt manufacturers, and it became necessary to build plants overseas. Of course, if it had remained favorable to do all the manufacturing in Japan, the Japanese manufacturers would have "won the bet" because building new facilities is time-consuming and expensive.

Hedge Strategies Using *hedge strategies,* a company designs the supply chain in such a way that any losses in part of the supply chain will be offset by gains in another part. For example, Volkswagen operates plants in the United States, Brazil, Mexico, and Germany, all of which are important markets for Volkswagen products. Depending on macroeconomic conditions, certain plants may be more profitable at various times than others. Hedge strategies, *by design,* are simultaneously successful in some locations and unsuccessful in others.

Flexible Strategies When properly employed, *flexible strategies* enable a company to take advantage of different scenarios. Typically, flexible supply chains are designed with multiple suppliers and excess manufacturing capacity in different countries. In addition, factories are designed to be flexible, so that products can be moved at minimal cost from region to region as economic conditions demand.

When considering the implementation of a flexible strategy, managers have to answer several questions:

1. Is there enough variability in the system to justify the use of flexible strategies? Clearly, the more variability in international conditions, the more a company can benefit from utilizing flexible strategies.
2. Do the benefits of spreading production over various facilities justify the costs, which may include loss of economies of scale in terms of manufacturing and supply?
3. Does the company have the appropriate coordination and management mechanisms in place to take rapid advantage of flexible strategies?

If the supply chain is appropriately designed, several approaches can be utilized to implement flexible strategies effectively:

Production shifting. Flexible factories and excess capacity and suppliers can be used to shift production from region to region to take advantage of current circumstances. As exchange rates, labor cost, and so on, change, manufacturing can be relocated.

Information sharing. Having an increased presence in many regions and markets often will increase the availability of information, which can be used to anticipate market changes and find new opportunities.

Global coordination. Having multiple facilities worldwide provides a firm with a certain amount of market leverage that it might otherwise lack. If a foreign competitor attacks one of your main markets, you can attack back. Of course, various international laws and political pressures place limits on this type of retaliation.

Political leverage. The opportunity to move operations rapidly gives firms a measure of political leverage in overseas operations. For example, if governments are lax in enforcing contracts or international law, or present expensive tax alternatives, firms can move their operations. In many cases, the implicit threat of movement is sufficient to prevent local politicians from taking unfavorable actions.

EXAMPLE 10-6

When Michelin began to target North American markets aggressively, Goodyear was able to drop its tire prices in Europe. This forced Michelin to slow its overseas investment program.

10.2.4 Requirements for Global Strategy Implementation

Any company, even a huge global company, is not immediately ready for integrated global supply chain management on this scale. Michael McGrath and Richard Hoole [158] discuss important developments that are necessary to set the stage for this kind of massive global integration. These developments are outlined below for each of the **five basic functions of firms:** product development, purchasing, production, demand management, and order fulfillment.

1. **Product development.** It is important to design products that can be modified easily for major markets, and which can be manufactured in various facilities. As we discuss in the next section, this is not always possible, but it is certainly helpful in those cases where it is achievable. While it is dangerous to design a product to be the "average" of what several markets require, it may be possible to design a base product or products that can be more easily adapted to several different markets. An international design team may be helpful in this regard.
2. **Purchasing.** A company will find it useful to have management teams responsible for the purchase of important materials from many vendors around the world. In this way, it is much easier to ensure that the quality and delivery options from various suppliers are compatible, and that a qualified team is present to compare the pricing of various suppliers. Also, these teams can work to guarantee that sufficient suppliers in different regions are at hand to ensure the flexibility necessary to take full advantage of the global supply chain.
3. **Production.** As we discussed above, excess capacity and plants in several regions are essential if firms are to take full advantage of the global supply chain by shifting production as conditions warrant. To utilize this kind of strategy, however, effective communications systems must be in place so that this global supply chain can be managed effectively. Centralized management is thus essential to this system, which implies that centralized information must be available. Indeed, knowledge of the current status of factories, supplies, and inventory is essential when making the types of decisions described above. In addition, since factories are typically supplying each other in a complex supply chain, it is important that interfactory communication is solid and that centralized management makes each factory aware of the system status.
4. **Demand management.** Often demand management, which involves setting marketing and sales plans based on projected demand and available product, is carried out on a regional basis. For the supply chain to be managed in an integrated way, demand management clearly has to have at least some centralized component. On the other hand, much of this sensitive, market-based information is best supplied by analysts located in each region. Thus, once again communication is a critical component of the success of global supply chain management.
5. **Order fulfillment.** To successfully implement a truly flexible supply chain management system, a centralized system must be in place so that regional customers can receive deliveries from the global supply chain with the same efficiency as they do from local or regionally based supply chains. All the flexibility in the world is of little use if it makes the system so cumbersome and unpleasant that customers turn elsewhere. We discuss the kinds of advanced information systems that this centralized order fulfillment requires in Chapter 14.

Only when a company is sufficiently prepared to implement flexible strategies can it take advantage of all that the global supply chain has to offer.

10.3 ISSUES IN INTERNATIONAL SUPPLY CHAIN MANAGEMENT

In this section, we discuss other important issues of international supply chains that were not appropriate for the previous sections.

10.3.1 International versus Regional Products

The preceding discussion suggests that the ideal company builds "universal products" that can be sold in many markets. In many cases, however, this is not that simple. Ohmae [177] pointed out that there are several categories of products, each of which has different "international requirements."

Region-specific products. Some products have to be designed and manufactured specifically for certain regions. For example, automobile designs are often region specific. The 1998 Honda Accord has two basic body styles: a smaller body style tailored to European and Japanese tastes and a larger body style catering to American tastes. Of course, even if regional designs are different, effective supply chain management can take advantage of common components or subassemblies within the different designs. We discuss this issue in detail in Chapter 11.

EXAMPLE 10-7

Nissan designates "lead-country" status to each of its car models. For example, the Maxima and Pathfinder are designed for American tastes, often by American design studios. Similar designs are developed primarily for Japanese and European markets. Once regional product managers ensure that vehicles meet lead-country requirements, other regional product managers suggest slight changes that might promote local sales. But the focus is on developing cars for regions. Otherwise, Nissan fears "the trap of pleasing no one well by pleasing everyone half way." There is no effective way to average size, color, and other aesthetic and substantive differences in cars across regions without ending up with a model that no customers in that region particularly like. Of course, if models can be modified slightly to increase sales in other regions, it helps, but that isn't the primary focus [177].

True global products. These products are truly global, in the sense that no modification is necessary for global sales. For example, Coca-Cola is essentially the same throughout the world, as are Levi's jeans and McDonald's burgers. Similarly, luxury brands such as Coach and Gucci are essentially the same worldwide. It should be noted, however, that some of these brands and products, such as Coke and McDonald's, depend on very specific regional manufacturing and bottling facilities and distribution networks, while others are essentially distributed and sold in the same way throughout the world [143].

The difference between region-specific products and global products does not imply that one is inherently better than the other. However, it is important to consider carefully which of the two product types is more appropriate for a particular situation because employing strategies for regional products that are designed for global products, or vice versa, can lead to disastrous results.

10.3.2 Local Autonomy versus Central Control

Centralized control can be important in taking advantage of some of the strategies we have discussed, but in many cases it makes sense to allow local autonomy in the supply chain. Sometimes, after independent regional operations have proven to be successful, headquarters can't resist the temptation to tamper with the system, and performance suffers.

In addition, it is important to temper expectations for regional business depending on the characteristics of the region involved. For example, companies typically experience, in the short term, relatively low returns in Japan, medium returns in Germany, and higher returns in the United States. Indeed, those companies that are successful in Japan had often settled initially for low returns [177].

However, managers may be tempted to follow local conventional wisdom, and thus miss some of the opportunities derived from the knowledge acquired in the operation of a global supply chain.

EXAMPLE 10-8

When it first introduced the decongestant Contac 600 to Japanese markets, SmithKline Corporation was advised to use the traditional approach, involving more than 1,000 distributors with which the firm would have little contact. Rather than accept this advice, SmithKline used 35 wholesalers, with whom it remained in close contact. SmithKline had used this approach successfully elsewhere. Despite the naysayers, the introduction was highly successful [143].

10.3.3 Miscellaneous Dangers

To be sure, there are many potential dangers that firms must face as they expand their supply chains globally. Exchange rate fluctuations, discussed earlier as an opportunity, can just as easily be a risk if not properly managed. It may be harder to administer offshore facilities, especially in less-developed countries. Similarly, the promise of cheap labor may mask the threat of reduced productivity [151]. Expensive training may be required, but even then productivity may not reach domestic levels.

Often local collaboration occurs in the global supply chain. In this case, collaborators can ultimately become competitors.

EXAMPLE 10-9

- Hitachi, which used to manufacture under license from Motorola, now makes its own microprocessors.
- Toshiba, which manufactured copiers for 3M, is now a major supplier of copiers under the Toshiba brand name.
- Sunrise Plywood and Furniture, of Taiwan, was for many years a partner of Mission Furniture in California. Now it is one of Mission's major competitors [151].

Similar dangers exist with foreign governments. To deal with China and gain access to that country's huge markets, many companies are handing over critical manufacturing and engineering expertise to the Chinese government or to Chinese partners. It is only a matter of time until these Chinese companies, or other companies selected by the government, begin to compete under favorable terms with their original partners. The only question is whether the overseas firms that gave away their technology will still be able to compete successfully in the Chinese market, or if they will lose this opportunity even as Chinese companies begin to compete on the world stage.

EXAMPLE 10-10

Royal Dutch Shell and its Japanese partners, Mitsui and Mitsubishi, have been investing for over a decade in the development of oil fields in Russia's far east. The oil exploration project has run into environmental problems and cost far exceeded the original projection. Surprisingly, now that development is almost over, oil prices are at an all-time high, and huge revenue is expected, the partners sold a majority stake in the project to Gazprom, Russia's state-owned gas company. The assumption in the West is that Russia flexed its muscles and forced the three partners to transfer ownership, threatening dire consequences for any environmental problems [15].

Indeed, this serves to highlight only one of the dangers that foreign governments pose to the international supply chain. Although world markets are becoming more open all the time, the world is far from becoming a giant free trade zone. At any time, the threat of *protectionism* might appear, and if the global supply chain is not set up with some kind of counter to this threat, companies will not be able to do much about it. Sometimes the threat comes not from the foreign government, but from the domestic government, dealing with the concerns of smaller local firms.

EXAMPLE 10-11

In 1986, Taiwan had a $15.7 billion trade surplus with the United States, heightening domestic pressure on the U.S. government to impose trade restrictions on Taiwanese products. This occurred despite the fact that the vast majority of Taiwanese imports were parts to supply American companies such as GE, IBM, Hewlett-Packard, and Mattel, which had moved manufacturing offshore to take advantage of lower costs. In response, Taiwan was forced to increase the value of its currency relative to the U.S. dollar, thus effectively removing much of the cost advantage of manufacturing to Taiwan [151].

10.4 REGIONAL DIFFERENCES IN LOGISTICS

In the previous sections, we discussed the general advantages, disadvantages, and strategies for utilizing global supply chains effectively. Of course, it is important to be aware of the cultural, infrastructural, and economic differences between regions when decisions are made about particular foreign links in the global supply chain. Wood et al. [243] identified several categories of differences that managers must consider when designing international supply chains. In particular, major differences can be highlighted between the so-called *triad,* or First World, nations, Japan, the United States, and the nations of western Europe; *emerging nations* such as Thailand, Taiwan, China, Brazil, Argentina, and the countries of eastern Europe; and the *Third World* nations. These differences are summarized in Table 10-1 and analyzed below.

10.4.1 Cultural Differences

Cultural differences can critically affect the way international subsidiaries interpret the goals and pronouncements of management. Wood et al. [243] highlighted beliefs and values, customs, and language, all of which play a big role in global business and can strongly affect negotiation and communication.

Language consists not only of words but also of expressions, gestures, and context. Many times, the words appear to be translated correctly, but the meaning is not. We've all heard stories of American businesspeople using the wrong gestures in Asia, leading to disastrous consequences. It is important to utilize appropriate resources to make sure that communication is effective.

Beliefs, or specific values about something, can differ widely from culture to culture. The belief that effective communication is important, for instance, can vary from culture to culture. Similarly, values, or more general conceptions, can vary. For example, American manufacturers value "efficiency" in ways that some other cultures do not [243]. Also, some cultures may value time more than others, so that late delivery may be viewed in some places as a serious problem, while in others it is not particularly important.

Customs, of course, vary greatly from country to country. In many cases, it is important for the businessperson to adhere to local customs to avoid offending anyone. For example, the practice of gift giving varies greatly from country to country.

10.4.2 Infrastructure

In First World countries, the manufacturing and logistics infrastructure is highly developed. Highway systems, ports, communication and information systems, and advanced manufacturing techniques

TABLE 10-1

MAJOR DIFFERENCES BETWEEN DIFFERENT REGIONS

	First World	Emerging	Third World
Infrastructure	Highly developed	Under development	Insufficient to support advanced logistics
Supplier operating standards	High	Variable	Typically not considered
Information system availability	Generally available	Support system not available	Not available
Human resources	Available	Available with some searching	Often difficult to find

allow the development of advanced supply chains. Regional differences do exist, primarily for geographical, political, or historical reasons. For example, road widths, bridge heights, and communications protocols may differ from region to region, but, in general, techniques have been developed to overcome these differences.

Regardless of the infrastructure, geography also affects supply chain decisions, even within First World countries. In the United States, for example, where large distances often exist between major cities, more inventory might be held than in countries such as Belgium, where the distance between cities is small.

Similarly, relative economic conditions have affected the mix of logistics and supply chain components in many First World countries. For example, countries with relatively cheap land and cheap labor, such as France, have built many large, "low-tech" warehouses, while the Scandinavian countries have developed warehouse automation because labor in those countries is so expensive [76].

In the emerging nations, the supply chain infrastructure is usually not fully in place. Most domestic companies in emerging nations see logistics as a necessary expense and not a strategic advantage, so they limit investments in logistics infrastructure. In many cases, gross national income in an emerging nation may not yet be sufficient to fully implement an advanced logistics infrastructure. In addition, the focus of infrastructure development may have been on exports instead of building a system appropriate for imports and exports. This is true in China [243]. Nonetheless, these nations are "emerging" because they have begun to address these issues. For example, many countries have national transportation policies in place, and are beginning or continuing to implement them.

In the Third World, the infrastructure is generally insufficient to support advanced logistics operations. Roads are often in poor shape. Warehousing facilities are frequently unavailable. Distribution systems may be nonexistent. In general, specific supply chain decisions have to be considered carefully, because many of the things taken for granted in the triad or emerging nations may not exist here.

10.4.3 Performance Expectation and Evaluation

Although regional differences remain among First World nations, operating standards are generally uniform and high. For example, overnight carriers are expected to make deliveries overnight. Contracts are legally binding documents. Environmental regulations and constraints typically are present, and companies are expected to obey them. However, the approaches to developing and enforcing relationships do differ from region to region. For example, European and American companies use formal partnership contracts more frequently than Japanese firms, which tend to favor informal partnership agreements built over time [36].

In emerging nations, operating standards typically vary greatly. Some firms may have—and meet—high expectations, and place great value on contracts and agreements. Others, however, might not be so scrupulous. Research and negotiation are essential to successful deal making in the emerging nations. In addition, the government typically plays a large role in business, so foreign partners and corporations often must be ready to respond to the government's changing whims.

In the Third World, traditional performance measures have no meaning. Shortages are common and customer service measures that are used in the West (e.g., stock availability, speed of service, and service consistency) are irrelevant; given this situation, a firm has little control of the timing and availability of inventory [243].

10.4.4 Information System Availability

Within the triad nations, computer technology has increased at more or less the same rate across different nations. In most cases, POS data, automation tools, personal computers, and other information system tools are just as available in Spain as in California.

Of course, there may be incompatibilities in various systems. For example, European EDI standards may vary from country to country and industry to industry. In addition, legal standards relating to data protection and document authentication vary from country to country. Nevertheless, efforts are underway to overcome these hurdles, and technology exists to overcome the technical incompatibilities [164].

Support systems in the emerging nations may not be in place to implement efficient information systems. Communications networks may be incomplete and not reliable enough to support the traffic. Technical support expertise may not be available to utilize and maintain the equipment. However, governments in these nations typically have plans or programs in place to address these issues.

Advanced information technology is simply not available in Third World countries. Systems such as EDI and bar coding cannot be supported in this type of environment. Even the value of a personal computer is limited because of inefficient communications systems. In addition, data on the economy and population typically are unavailable.

10.4.5 Human Resources

Within most First World countries, technically and managerially competent workers are available. As Wood et al. [243] pointed out, "Cultural differences aside, a logistics manager from Japan would be functionally at home in a counterpart's position in America." Unskilled labor, however, is relatively expensive in these regions.

While it may be true that skilled managerial and technical personnel are frequently not available in emerging nations, sometimes this is not the case. It might take some searching, but employees with the appropriate skills often can be found. In particular, the eastern European countries have generally well-educated populations [100]. In addition, the wages of skilled workers in emerging nations are generally competitive on the world market. On the other hand, many Chinese managers used to be selected for political reasons, rather than technical or managerial expertise, so experience in this case may not be an appropriate indicator of ability [100].

Although it may be possible to find employees that are appropriate to the available technology level, it is often difficult to find trained logistics professionals and managers familiar with modern management techniques in Third World countries. Thus, training becomes especially important in this type of environment.

SUMMARY

In this chapter, we examined issues specific to *global* supply chain management. First, we discussed various types of international supply chains, covering the spectrum from primarily domestic supply chains with some international product distribution all the way to fully integrated global supply chains. We then examined the various forces compelling companies to develop international supply chains. Both advantages and risks are inherent in global supply chains. These risks run the gamut from unknown-unknown risks to known-unknown risks. We discussed a variety of approaches to dealing with unknown-unknown risks, and a set of strategies for addressing many of the other risks. In particular, we focused on the advantages of having a truly flexible global supply chain to address the inherent risks in operating a global company. However, even with a flexible supply chain, the strategies and approaches used to address these risks will work only if the appropriate infrastructure is in place.

We next surveyed some of the many issues in global supply chain management, including the concepts of international and regional products, and the issue of centralized versus decentralized control in an international context. We concluded with a discussion of regional logistics differences that influence the design of effective supply chains in different parts of the world.

DISCUSSION QUESTIONS

1. Discuss situations in which each of these supply chains might be the appropriate choice for a firm:
   a. International distribution systems.
   b. International suppliers.
   c. Offshore manufacturing.
   d. Fully integrated global supply chain.
2. Discuss a recent example of an unknown-unknown risk that proved damaging to a supply chain. Explain specifically how each of the following strategies might have mitigated this risk:
   a. Invest in redundancy.
   b. Increase velocity in sensing and responding.
   c. Create an adaptive supply chain community.
3. You are the CEO of a small electronics manufacturing firm that is about to develop a global strategy. Would you prefer a speculative strategy, a hedge strategy, or a flexible strategy? Would your answer to this question change if you were the CEO of a large electronics firm?
4. Discuss some examples of regional products and of true global products. What is it about the products that makes them better suited to being regional or global products?
5. You are the manager of a regional bakery. Contrast the issues you would face if your firm is located in each of the following countries:
   a. Belgium
   b. Russia
   c. Singapore
   d. Canada
   e. Argentina
   f. Nigeria
6. Answer these questions about the case at the beginning of this chapter:
   a. Other than a need to expand, what other reasons would Wal-Mart have for opening stores globally?
   b. Why would it be beneficial for Wal-Mart to have suppliers in different countries?
   c. Why would Wal-Mart want strong centralized control of its stores? Why would Wal-Mart want strong local control of stores?
   d. What pitfalls and opportunities, other than those mentioned in this case, will Wal-Mart face over the next few years?

CHAPTER 11

Coordinated Product and Supply Chain Design

CASE: Hewlett-Packard: DeskJet Printer Supply Chain

Brent Cartier, manager for special projects in the Materials Department of Hewlett-Packard (HP) Company's Vancouver Division, clicked off another mile. It had been a long week and it looked like it would be a long weekend as well, based on the preparation that needed to be done for Monday's meeting with group management on worldwide inventory levels for the DeskJet Printer product line. Even when he was busy, he always took time for the 25-mile bike ride to work—it helped reduce stress in times like this.

The DeskJet printer was introduced in 1988 and had become one of HP's most successful products. Sales had grown steadily, reaching a level of over 600,000 units in 1990 ($400 million). Unfortunately, inventory growth had tracked sales growth closely. Already, HP's distribution centers had been filled with pallets of the DeskJet printer. Worse yet, the organization in Europe was claiming that inventory levels there needed to be raised even further to maintain satisfactory product availability.

Each quarter, representatives from the production, materials, and distribution organizations in Europe, Asia-Pacific, and North America met to discuss "the I-word"—as they referred to it—but their conflicting goals prevented them from reaching consensus on the issues. Each organization had a different approach to the problem. Production had not wanted to get involved, claiming it was "just a materials issue," but had taken the time to rant about the continued proliferation of models and options. The distribution organization's pet peeve was forecast accuracy. They didn't feel that the distribution organization should have to track and store warehouses of inventory, just because the Vancouver Division couldn't build the right products in the right quantities. The European distribution organization had even gone so far as to suggest that they charge the cost of the extra warehouse space that they were renting back to the Vancouver Division directly, instead of allocating it among all the products that they shipped. Finally, Brent's boss, David Arkadia, the materials manager at the Vancouver Division, had summarized the perspective of group management at the last meeting when he said, "The word is coming down from corporate: We can't run our business

Source: This case was written by Laura Kopczak and Professor Hau Lee of the Department of Industrial Engineering and Engineering Management at Stanford University.

with this level of unproductive assets. We're just going to have to meet customer needs with less inventory."

As Brent saw it, there were two main issues. The first issue was to find the best way to satisfy customer needs in terms of product availability while minimizing inventory. The second and stickier issue involved how to get agreement among the various parties that they had the right level of inventory. They needed to develop a consistent method for setting and implementing inventory goals and get everyone to sign off on it and use it. It was not going to be easy. The situation was especially urgent in Europe. His mind was still filled with the faxed picture that he had received the previous day, showing the dip in product availability levels for some versions of the product at the European Distribution Center (DC), yet he was sure that loads and loads of DeskJets had been shipped to Europe in the past months. His voice mail had been filled with angry messages from the sales offices, and yet the European DC was telling Vancouver that it had run out of space to store Vancouver's products.

Brent parked his bike and headed for the company showers. His morning shower was another ritual—this was the time he had to review his plans for the day and play out different scenarios. Perhaps a solution would come to him . . .

BACKGROUND

Hewlett-Packard Company was founded in 1939 by William Hewlett and David Packard, with headquarters in Palo Alto, California. It grew steadily over the next 50 years, diversifying from its base in electronic test and measurement equipment into computers and peripherals products, which now dominated its sales. In 1990 HP had over 50 operations worldwide, with revenues of $13.2 billion and net income of $739 million.

HP was organized partially by product group and partially by function. The Peripherals Group was the second largest of HP's six product groups, with 1990 revenues of $4.1 billion. Each of the group's divisions acted as a strategic business unit for a specific set of products. Products included printers, plotters, magnetic disk and tape drives, terminals, and network products.

The Peripherals Group had set technological standards with many of its products, with innovations such as the disposable print head used in its ink-jet printers and moving-paper plotters. While these innovations contributed to its success, the Peripherals Group was also recognized for its ability to identify and profitably exploit market opportunities, as in the case of its most successful product, the LaserJet printer.

THE RETAIL PRINTER MARKET

Worldwide sales of small workgroup/personal printers in 1990 were about 17 million units, amounting to $10 billion. The market tracked personal computer sales closely; the market was mature in the United States and western Europe but was still developing in eastern Europe and in the Asia-Pacific region. Small workgroup/personal printers were sold almost exclusively through resellers. The reseller channels were changing rapidly, particularly in the United States. Traditionally, printers had been sold through computer dealers, but as personal computers became commodity products, more and more sales were flowing through superstores and consumer mass merchandisers such as Kmart and Price Club.

The retail printer market was composed of three technology segments: impact/dot matrix (40 percent), ink-jet (20 percent), and laser (40 percent). Dot matrix was the oldest technology and was viewed as noisy and of lower print quality compared to the other two types. The dot-matrix printer market share was expected to fall to 10 percent during the next few years as the technology was replaced by either ink-jet or laser printers in all applications except multipart forms and wide-carriage printing. Prior to 1989 most customers were not aware of ink-jet technology. However, customers were discovering that ink-jet print quality was almost as good as laser print quality—and at a much more affordable price. Sales had increased dramatically. In the monochrome market, it remained to be seen which technology would eventually dominate at the low end. Much would depend on the pace at which technology developed in both areas and on the relative costs.

HP and Canon pioneered ink-jet technology separately at their respective corporate laboratories during the early 1980s. The key technological breakthroughs had been ink formulation and the disposable printhead. HP had introduced its first disposable head model, the ThinkJet printer, in the late 1980s, while Canon had just introduced one in 1990.

HP led the ink-jet market in the United States, while Canon led the market in Japan. European competitors included Epson, Mannesmann-Tally, Siemens, and Olivetti, though only Olivetti had introduced a printer with a disposable print head by 1991. Some dot-matrix printer companies were also starting to offer ink-jet printer products.

Ink-jet printers were rapidly becoming commodity products. The end customer, choosing between two ink-jet printers of equal speed and print quality, increasingly used general business criteria such as cost, reliability, quality, and availability to decide. Product loyalty continued to decrease.

THE VANCOUVER DIVISION AND ITS QUEST FOR ZERO INVENTORY

In 1990 the Vancouver Division's mission statement read: "Our Mission Is to Become the Recognized World Leader in Low-Cost Premium-Quality Printers for Printed Communications by Business Personal Computer Users in Offices and Homes."

The Vancouver Division, located in Vancouver, Washington, was established in 1979. HP saw an opportunity to provide personal printers for the relatively new, fast-growing personal computer market. HP consolidated personal printer activities from four divisions (Fort Collins, Colorado; Boise, Idaho; Sunnyvale, California; and Corvallis, Oregon) to the Vancouver site. The new division became part of HP's Peripherals Group and was chartered with the design and manufacturing of ink-jet printers.

As Bob Foucoult, the production manager and one of Vancouver's first employees, recalled, "Management was pulled from all over HP and plopped down in Vancouver. There was no cohesive staff and no cohesive set of business practices—perhaps that's why we were so open to new ideas."

The manufacturing organization realized early on that a fast, high-volume manufacturing process would be required for success in the printer market. With the current (1979) 8- to 12-week manufacturing cycle time and 3.5 months of inventory, the Vancouver Division would be doomed to fail. They looked within HP for knowledge of high-volume processes, but found none. HP, being an instrument company, only had experience building low-volume, highly customized products using batch processes.

One day in mid-1981 two Vancouver managers happened to take seats on a plane next to two professors: Richard Schoenberger (Nebraska University) and Robert Hall (Indiana University). Schoenberger had just written a rough draft for a paper called "Driving the Productivity Machine" about a manufacturing process being used in Japan: *kanban*. Vancouver's management recognized the promise of this "new" manufacturing concept and Robert Hall recognized an opportunity to have his ideas tested in the United States. They decided to work together.

Within a year Vancouver had converted the factory to stockless production just-in-time (JIT) and had reduced inventory from 3.5 months to 0.9 month, with a drastic reduction in cycle time. Vancouver became a showcase factory for the *kanban* process; between 1982 and 1985 more than 2,000 executives from within and outside HP toured the process. Vancouver impressed visitors by having them sign a raw printed circuit board as they arrived, then presenting them with a finished printer, made with that PC board using the standard process, an hour and a half later.

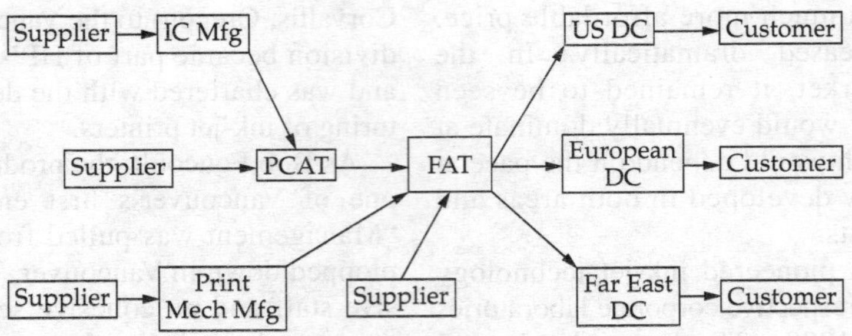

FIGURE 11-1 The Vancouver supply chain.

There was one key element missing, however. As Bob Foucoult puts it, "We were all dressed up but had no one to take us to the dance." Vancouver had not yet introduced a successful, high-volume product that would take full advantage of the advanced production line. Vancouver had introduced products based on HP's latest ink-jet technology but, as with any new technology, they had to gain experience to work the bugs out. The early models had poor resolution and required special paper for printing, resulting in limited success in the marketplace. In 1988 things started to change. Vancouver introduced the DeskJet printer, a new model with near-letter-quality resolution that used standard paper. The introduction was a wild success. Since the manufacturing process had been in place and had been thoroughly exercised, all that was needed was to "flip the switch." HP's knowledge and implementation of the ink-jet technology, combined with its streamlined manufacturing process, gave it the edge needed to become the market leader in the ink-jet printer market.

THE DESKJET SUPPLY CHAIN

The network of suppliers, manufacturing sites, distribution centers (DCs), dealers, and customers for the DeskJet product comprised the DeskJet supply chain (Figure 11-1). Manufacturing was done by HP in Vancouver. There were two key stages in the manufacturing process: (1) printed circuit board assembly and test (PCAT) and (2) final assembly and test (FAT). PCAT involved the assembly and testing of electronic components such as ASICs (application-specific integrated circuits), ROM (read-only memory), and raw printed circuit boards to make logic boards and printhead driver boards for the printers. FAT involved the assembly of other subassemblies such as motors, cables, keypads, plastic chassis and "skins," gears, and the printed circuit assemblies from PCAT to produce a working printer, as well as the final testing of the printer. The components needed for PCAT and FAT were sourced from other HP divisions as well as from external suppliers worldwide.

Selling the DeskJet in Europe required customizing the printer to meet the language and power supply requirements of the local countries, a process known as "localization." Specifically, the localization of the DeskJet for different countries involved assembling the appropriate power supply module, which reflected the correct voltage requirements (110 or 220) and power cord terminator (plug), and packaging it with the working printer and a manual written in the appropriate language. The design of the product was such that the assembly of the power supply module had to be done as part of the final assembly and test process, and therefore the localization of the printer

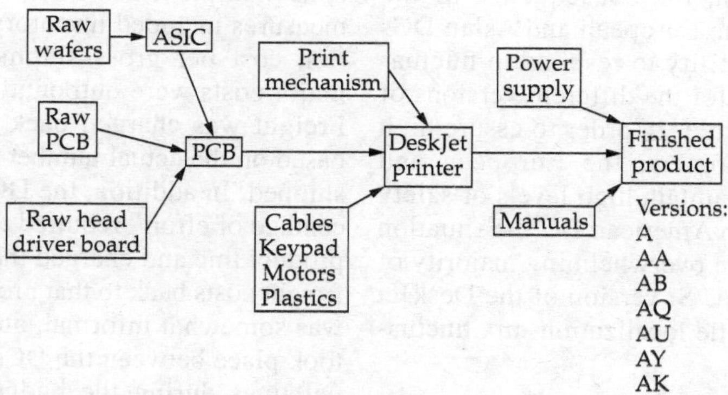

FIGURE 11-2 Bill of material in the Vancouver supply chain.

was performed at the factory. Hence, the finished products of the factory consisted of printers destined for all of the different countries. These products were then sorted into three groups destined for the three distribution centers: North America, Europe, and Asia-Pacific. Figure 11-2 details the bill of materials and the various options available.

Outgoing products were shipped to the three distribution centers by ocean. In Vancouver, inventories of the components and raw materials were maintained to meet production requirements, but otherwise, no significant buffer inventories between the PCAT and FAT stages were kept. Management had continued to prefer to maintain no finished goods inventory at the factory, a tradition that was started in 1985 as described in the previous section.

The total factory cycle time through the PCAT and FAT stages was about a week. The transportation time from Vancouver to the U.S. DC, located in San Jose, California, was about a day, whereas it took four to five weeks to ship the printers to Europe and Asia. The long shipment time to the DCs in Europe and Asia was due to ocean transit and the time to clear customs and duties at ports of entry.

The printer industry was highly competitive. Customers of HP's computer products (resellers) wanted to carry as little inventory as possible, yet maintaining a high level of availability to end users (consumers) was critical to them. Consequently there had been increasing pressure for HP as a manufacturer to provide high levels of availability at the DCs for the resellers. In response, management had decided to operate the DCs in a make-to-stock mode in order to provide very high levels of availability to the dealers. Target inventory levels, equal to the forecasted sales plus some safety stock level, were set at the three DCs.

As mentioned earlier, Vancouver prided itself as an almost "stockless" factory. Hence, in contrast to distribution, manufacturing of the DeskJet printer operated in a pull mode. Production plans were set weekly to replenish the DCs "just in time" to maintain the target inventory levels. To ensure material availability, safety stocks were also set up for incoming materials at the factory.

There were three major sources of uncertainty that could affect the supply chain: (1) delivery of incoming materials (late shipments, wrong parts, etc.), (2) internal process (process yields and machine downtimes), and (3) demand. The first two sources of uncertainties resulted in delays in the manufacturing lead time to replenish the stocks at the DCs. Demand uncertainties could lead to inventory buildup or back orders at the DCs. Since finished printers were shipped from

Vancouver by ocean, the consequence of the long lead time for the European and Asian DCs was that the DC's ability to respond to fluctuations in the demand for the different versions of the product was limited. In order to assure high availability to customers, the European and Asian DCs had to maintain high levels of safety stocks. For the North American DC the situation was simpler; since an overwhelming majority of demand was for the U.S. version of the DeskJet printer, there was little localization-mix fluctuation.

THE DISTRIBUTION PROCESS

At HP, while a typical DC shipped hundreds of different peripheral and computer products, a small number of products accounted for a large share of the unit volume. The DeskJet printer was one of these high-volume products.

The Operations Manager of each regional DC reported to a Worldwide Distribution Manager, who reported directly to HP's Vice President of Marketing, and by dotted line to the Peripherals Group Manager (peripherals made up the bulk of shipments through distribution centers). Each Operations Manager had a staff of six functional managers, representing Finance, MIS, Quality, Marketing, Physical Distribution, and Distribution Services. The first three functions were similar to their respective functions in a manufacturing organization. Marketing was responsible for interactions with customers. Physical Distribution was responsible for the "physical process," that is, from receiving through shipping. Distribution Services was responsible for planning and procurement.

The major performance measures for a typical DC included line item fill rate (LIFR) and order fill rate (OFR). LIFR was calculated as the total number of customer order line items filled on time divided by the total number of customer line items attempted. (Each time HP tried to pull material for a line item, it was counted as an attempt.) OFR was a similar measure, but was based on orders completed, where an order contains multiple line items. Secondary performance measures included inventory levels and distribution cost per gross shipment dollar. The two major costs were outbound freight and salaries. Freight was charged back to the product lines based on the actual number of pounds of product shipped. In addition, the DC estimated the "percentage of effort" required to support a particular product line and charged that percentage of nonfreight costs back to that product line. The system was somewhat informal, and major negotiations took place between the DCs and the major product lines during the budget-setting process to determine the percentage allocation that was appropriate for each product line.

The DCs had traditionally envisioned their process as a simple, straight-line, standardized process. There were four process steps:

1. Receive (complete) products from various suppliers and stock them.
2. Pick the various products needed to fill a customer order.
3. Shrink-wrap the complete order and label it.
4. Ship the order by the appropriate carrier.

The DeskJet printer fit well into the standard process. In contrast, other products, such as personal computers and monitors, required special processing, called "integration," which included addition of the appropriate keyboard and manual for the destination country. Although this extra processing didn't require much additional labor, it was difficult to accommodate in the standard process and disrupted the material flow. Furthermore, the DCs' materials management systems supported distribution (passthrough processing of "end-items" in the form of individual models and options) and did not support manufacturing (assembly of components into a final product). There were no MRP (material resource planning) or BOM (bill of materials) explosion systems, and the DCs did not have adequate people trained in component procurement.

There was considerable frustration within the distribution organization regarding the support of

TABLE 11-1

SOME SAMPLE DESKJET DEMAND DATA: EUROPE

Option	Nov.	Dec.	Jan.	Feb.	Mar.	Apr.	May	June	July	Aug.	Sept.	Oct.
A	80	0	60	90	21	48	0	9	20	54	84	42
AA	400	255	408	645	210	87	432	816	430	630	456	273
AB	20,572	20,895	19,252	11,052	19,864	20,316	13,336	10,578	6,096	14,496	23,712	9,792
AQ	4,008	2,196	4,761	1,953	1,008	2,358	1,676	540	2,310	2,046	1,797	2,961
AU	4,564	3,207	7,485	4,908	5,295	90	0	5,004	4,385	5,103	4,302	6,153
AY	248	450	378	306	219	204	248	484	164	384	384	234
Total	29,872	27,003	32,344	18,954	26,617	23,103	15,692	17,431	13,405	22,692	30,735	19,455

assembly processes. In general, top management stressed the DC's role as a warehouse and the need to continue to "do what they were best at—distribution." Tom Beal, the U.S. DC materials manager, expressed the general concern when he said, "We have to decide what our core competency is and what value we add. We need to decide whether we are in the business of warehousing or integration, then adopt strategies to support our business. If we want to take on manufacturing processes (here), we have to put processes in place to support them."

THE INVENTORY AND SERVICE CRISIS

To limit the amount of inventory throughout the DeskJet supply chain and at the same time provide the high level of service needed had been quite a challenge to Vancouver's management. The manufacturing group in Vancouver had worked hard on supplier management to reduce the uncertainties caused by delivery variabilities of incoming materials, on improving process yields, and on reducing downtimes at the plant. The progress made had been admirable. However, improvement of forecast accuracy remained a formidable task.

The magnitude of forecast errors was especially alarming in Europe. It was becoming quite common to have product shortages for model demands from some countries, while inventory of some other models kept piling up. In the past, the target inventory levels at the DCs were based on safety stocks that were a result of some judgmental rule of thumb. It seemed like the increasing difficulty of getting accurate forecasts meant that the safety stock rules would have to be revisited.

David Arkadia had solicited the help of a young inventory expert from corporate HP, Dr. Billy Corrington, to help him put in place a scientifically based safety stock system that would be responsive to forecast errors and replenishment lead times. Billy had formed a team consisting of Laura Rock, an industrial engineer, Jim Bailey, the planning supervisor, and José Fernandez, the purchasing supervisor from Vancouver, to overhaul the safety stock management system. They were to recommend a method for calculating appropriate safety stock levels for the various models and options at the three DCs. Gathering appropriate data turned out to be a task that the team spent a lot of time at. They now felt that they had a good sample of demand data (see Table 11-1) and were developing the safety stock methodology. Brent was hoping that this new methodology would solve the inventory and service problem. It would be nice if he could tell his management that all this inventory and service mess was due to their lack of a sound safety stock methodology, and Billy's expertise would then be their savior.

One issue that continually came up was the choice of inventory carrying cost to be used in safety stock analyses. Estimates within the company ranged from 12 percent (HP's cost of debt plus some warehousing expenses) to 60 percent (based on the return on investment [ROI] expected of new product development projects). Another issue was the choice of target line item fill rate to be used. The company target was 98 percent, a number that had been "developed" by marketing.

As faxes and phone calls about the worsening situation at the European DC kept pouring in, Brent also began receiving other suggestions from his colleagues that were more aggressive in nature. Talks about Vancouver's setting up a sister plant in Europe had surfaced. Would the volume in Europe be large enough to justify such a site? Where should it be located? Brent knew that the European sales and marketing folks would like such an idea. He also liked the idea of having a European plant to take care of the inventory and service problem in Europe. Maybe that would put a halt to his recent loss of sleep.

There was certainly a group that advocated more and more inventory. It was simple logic, according to them. "When it comes down to real dollars, inventory costs do not enter into the P&L statements, but lost sales hurt our revenues. Don't talk to us about inventory–service trade-offs. Period."

Kay Johnson, the Traffic Department supervisor, had long suggested the use of air shipment to transport the printers to Europe. "Shortening the lead time means faster reaction time to unexpected changes in product mix. That should mean lower inventory and higher product availability. I tell you, air freight is expensive, but it is worth it."

Brent recalled his conversation at lunch with a summer intern from Stanford University. The enthusiastic student was lecturing Brent that he should always try to tackle the "root of the problem." Going to the root of the problem, according to the intern, is what the professors taught at school, and was also what a number of quality gurus preached. "The root of the problem is that you have a horrible forecasting system. There is no easy way out. You've got to invest in getting the system fixed. Now, I know this marketing professor at Stanford who could help you. Have you ever heard of the Box-Jenkins method?" Brent also remembered how he lost his appetite at that lunch, as he was listening to the student who was so eager to volunteer his advice.

WHAT NEXT?

Brent reviewed his schedule for the day. At 11:00 he planned to meet with Billy, Laura, Jim, and José to review the recommended inventory levels they had calculated using the safety stock model. He was somewhat concerned about what level of change the model would recommend. If it suggested small changes, management might not feel the model was useful, but if it suggested large changes, they might not accept it either.

After lunch he would meet briefly with the materials and manufacturing managers to review the results and sketch out their recommendations. At 2:00 he would talk with the U.S. DC materials manager by phone. That night he could reach Singapore and Saturday morning he could reach Germany. Hopefully he could get buyoff from everyone. He wondered, too, if there wasn't some other approach that he should be considering. He knew that whatever numbers he came up with would be too high.

By the end of this chapter, you should be able to answer the following questions:

- What are the frameworks, tools and concepts that companies can use as they think about the product engineering process and its impact on supply chain performance?
- How can design for logistics concepts be used to control logistics costs and make the supply chain more efficient?
- What is delayed differentiation and how can Hewlett-Packard use delayed differentiation to address the problems described in the case above? How can the advantages of delayed differentiation be quantified?
- When should suppliers be involved in the new product development process?

- What is mass customization? Does supply chain management play a role in the development of an effective mass customization strategy?

For many years, manufacturing engineering was the last stop in the product engineering process. The researchers and design engineers worked on developing a product that worked, and perhaps one that used materials as inexpensively as possible. Then manufacturing engineers were charged with determining how to make this design efficiently. In the 1980s, this paradigm began to change. Management began to realize that product and process design were key product cost drivers, and that taking the manufacturing process into account early in the design process was the only way to make the manufacturing process efficient. Thus, the concept of design for manufacturing (DFM) was born.

Recently, a similar transformation has begun in the area of supply chain management. We have discussed appropriate strategies for supply chain design and operation, assuming that *product design decisions were already made* by the time the supply chain is designed. Designing the supply chain, we have assumed, involves determining the best way to supply existing products using existing manufacturing processes. In the last few years, however, managers have started to realize that by taking supply chain concerns into account in the product and process design phase, it becomes possible to operate a much more efficient supply chain. Obviously, this is analogous to the DFM practice of taking manufacturing into account during the product design phase.

For most of this chapter, we discuss various approaches that leverage product design in order to manage the supply chain more effectively. Before we get to specific design issues, we begin with a general framework that integrates the development chain introduced in Chapter 1 with the supply chain.

11.1 A GENERAL FRAMEWORK

Recall that in Chapter 1, we introduced the concept of the development chain, the set of activities and processes associated with new product introduction. Indeed, although for much of this text we have focused on the supply chain, in many organizations we find two interacting chains:

- The **supply chain,** which focuses on the flow of physical products from suppliers through manufacturing and distribution all the way to retail outlets and customers, and
- The **development chain,** which focuses on new product introduction and involves product architecture, make/buy decisions, earlier supplier involvement, strategic partnering, supplier footprint, and supply contracts.

Clearly, these two chains will intersect as products move from development to production, and just as clearly, decisions made in the development chain will impact the efficiency of the supply chain. Unfortunately, in most organizations, different managers are responsible for the different activities that are part of these chains. Typically, the VP of engineering is responsible for the development chain, the VP of manufacturing for the production portion of the chains, and the VP of supply chain or logistics for the fulfillment of customer demand. What's more, each of these managers frequently has performance incentives that focus on his or her individual responsibilities, often ignoring the impact of his or her decisions on the other portion of the development and supply chains. Unless carefully addressed, the typical impact of these organizational and incentive structures is a misalignment of product design and supply chain strategies.

Keep in mind that each chain has different characteristics. For example, key characteristics of the supply chain include

- **Demand uncertainty and variability,** in particular, the bullwhip effect discussed in Chapter 5.
- **Economies of scale** in production and transportation (see Chapters 2 and 3).
- **Lead time,** in particular due to globalization (see Chapters 9 and 10).

Of course, each of these dimensions has a significant impact on the appropriate supply chain strategy, and, thus, in Chapter 6, we developed a framework to match these dimensions with supply chain strategies (see Sections 6.2 and 6.3).

The development chain provides a different set of challenges. It can be characterized by

- **Technology clockspeed,** that is, the speed by which technology changes in a particular industry. This clearly has an impact on product design and hence on the development chain.
- **Make/buy decisions,** or decisions regarding what to make internally and what to buy from outside suppliers. (For more details, see our discussion in Chapter 9.)
- **Product structure,** that is, the level of modularity or integrality that a product must have. Later in this chapter, we discuss the concept of modularity in products in more detail, but for the purposes of this section, it is sufficient to say that a highly modular product is assembled from a variety of modules, and for each module there may be several options. In this way, the bulk of manufacturing can be completed before the selection of modules and assembly into the final product takes place.

Clearly, each of these characteristics has a significant impact on the supply chain strategy that the firm must use. Indeed, the supply chain strategy for a fast clockspeed product, for example, PCs or laser printers, is quite different than the supply chain strategy for a slow clockspeed product, for example, airplanes. Similarly, the level of outsourcing, the supplier footprint, and product architecture also have an impact on the supply chain strategy.

Concepts such as the development supply chain and technology clockspeed are directly related the work of Marshall Fisher. In his seminal article, "What Is the Right Supply Chain for Your Product?" [82], Professor Fisher distinguishes between two extreme product types, **innovative products** and **functional products**. Functional products are characterized by slow technology clockspeed, low product variety, and typically low profit margins. Examples include grocery products such as soup and beer, tires, office equipment, and so forth. Innovative products, on the other hand, are characterized by fast technology clockspeed and short product life cycle, high product variety, and relatively high margins.

So, *what is the appropriate supply chain strategy and the product design strategy for each product type?* Obviously, products with fast clockspeed (innovative products) require a different approach than products with slow clockspeed (functional products). At the same time, both the supply chain strategy and the product design strategy must take into account the level of demand uncertainty.

Figure 11-3 provides a framework for matching product design and supply chain strategies with the characteristics of the development chain (clockspeed) and the supply chain (demand uncertainty). The horizontal axis provides information on demand uncertainty while the vertical axis represents product introduction frequency, or product clockspeed.

As we have already observed in Chapter 6, everything else being equal, higher demand uncertainty leads to a preference for managing the supply chain based on a pull strategy. Alternatively, smaller demand uncertainty leads to an interest in managing the supply chain using a push strategy. Recall the characteristics of push and pull supply chain strategies. In a push strategy, the focus is on predictable demand, leveraging high economies of scale, and achieving cost efficiency. In contrast, in a pull supply chain, the focus is on reacting to unpredictable demand, dealing with low economy of scale, and achieving responsiveness, which in part is achieved by aggressively reducing lead times.

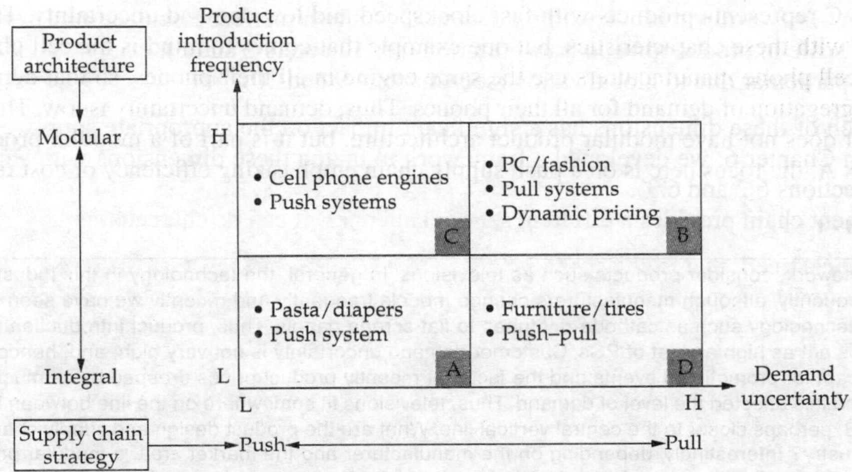

FIGURE 11-3 The impact of demand uncertainty and product introduction frequency on product design and supply chain strategy.

Similarly, everything else being equal, high product introduction frequency (fast clock speed) suggests a focus on modular product architecture since this allows the independent development of product subcomponents so that final feature set selection and product differentiation are postponed as much as possible, sometimes until demand is realized. (We discuss these ideas in significantly more detail later in this chapter in Section 11.2.4.) On the other hand, speeding up product development and postponing differentiation, and thus product modularity, is not that important when product introduction frequency is low (i.e., for slow clockspeed products).

In Figure 11-3, we partition the region spanned by these two dimensions, demand uncertainty and product introduction frequency, into four boxes. Box A represents products that are characterized by predictable demand and slow product introduction frequency. Examples include products such as diapers, soup, and pasta. Our framework suggests that, in this case, the focus is on a push strategy, supply chain efficiency, and high inventory turns.

Box B represents products with fast clockspeed and highly unpredictable demand. Many high-tech products such as PCs, printers, and cell phones as well as fashion items belong to this category. Here, the focus is on responsiveness, on pull strategy as well as modular product architecture. Thus, products in this category require a supply chain that values responsiveness over cost—the Zara case study in Chapter 9 illustrates how this can be done through excess capacity and reduction of lead time to customers. In many cases, dynamic pricing strategies also are utilized to better match supply and demand, as we discuss in Chapter 13.

Box D represents products with slow clockspeed but high demand uncertainty. These are the products and industries where a combination of push and pull is essential. And, similarly to box B, these are also situations where lead time reduction, if possible, is important. Examples of products in this category include high-end furniture, chemical products such as agrochemicals, commodity and specialty chemicals, and products such as (large-diameter) tires used in the mining industry where volume is relatively small and, hence, demand is highly unpredictable.

Finally, box C represents products with fast clockspeed and low demand uncertainty. There are not many products with these characteristics, but one example that comes to mind is the cell phone engine. Indeed, many cell phone manufacturers use the same engine in all their phones, so that demand for the engine is an aggregation of demand for all their phones. Thus, demand uncertainty is low. The cell phone engine by itself does not have modular product architecture, but it is part of a modular product. Again, similarly to box A, the focus here is on a push supply chain emphasizing efficiency or cost reduction.

EXAMPLE 11-1

To test our framework, consider products such as televisions. In general, the technology in this industry does not change very frequently, although manufacturers change models frequently and recently we have seen a significant move from old technology such as cathode-ray tubes to flat-screen panels. Thus, product introduction frequency is high but perhaps not as high as that of PCs. Customer demand uncertainty is not very high, and, hence, demand is predictable, except for promotional events and the fact that recently product prices dropped by as much as 10 percent a month and this affected the level of demand. Thus, televisions fit somewhere on the line between boxes B and D in Figure 11-3, perhaps closer to the central vertical line. What are the product design and supply chain strategies used in this industry? Interestingly, depending on the manufacturer and the market area, a modular product architecture and lead time reduction strategies. Indeed, while most manufacturing is done in China, the business strategy depends on the final destination. Sophisticated TV manufacturers ship components to poor countries and assemble the products at the market based on customer demand. This push–pull strategy requires modular design and allows manufacturers to reduce cost and satisfy legal requirements that sometime demand assembly by local companies. On the other hand, for the U.S. market, the focus recently has been on lead time reduction from the old 90-day lead time from manufacturing to arrival at the stores to about 30 days. Such short lead times reduce inventory significantly, and the supply chain is thus less vulnerable to the impact of a 10 percent monthly drop in product price [16].

In the next section, we discuss a series of concepts introduced by Professor Hau Lee [137] and known collectively as design for logistics (DFL). These concepts suggest product and process design approaches that help to control logistics costs and increase customer service levels.

Following that, we discuss the advantages of including suppliers in the product design process. This discussion is based on an extensive report issued by the Global Procurement and Supply Chain Benchmarking Initiative at Michigan State University, which is titled "Executive Summary: Supplier Integration into New Product Development: A Strategy for Competitive Advantage"[166].

Finally, we discuss the concept of mass customization, developed by Joseph Pine II with several coauthors. In particular, we focus on the ways in which advanced logistics and supply chain practices help to enable this exciting new business model.

11.2 DESIGN FOR LOGISTICS

11.2.1 Overview

Transportation and inventory costs, as we have seen, are often critical supply chain cost drivers, particularly when inventory levels must be kept fairly high to ensure high service levels. These are exactly the issues that DFL addresses, using the following three key components [137]:

- Economic packaging and transportation.
- Concurrent and parallel processing.
- Standardization

Each of these components addresses the issue of inventory or transportation costs and service levels in complementary ways. They are discussed in detail in the following subsections.

11.2.2 Economic Packaging and Transportation

Of the various DFL concepts, perhaps the most obvious involves designing products so that they can be efficiently packed and stored. Products that can be packed more compactly are cheaper to transport, particularly if delivery trucks "cube out" before they "weigh out." In other words, if the space taken up by a product and not its weight constrains how much can fit in a delivery vehicle, products that can be stored more compactly can be transported less expensively.

EXAMPLE 11-2 INDIAN OIL SOLVES LPG DISTRIBUTION PROBLEMS

INDIAN OIL CORPORATION (IOCL) faced a problem in managing its rail shipment of LPG to various bottling plants in 1983. Generally, there were complaints of either huge shortage or over-shipments in its supply chain. The issue was critical to the core business of IOCL and therefore, several rounds of internal brainstorming were done. Discussions also followed with explosives experts and related government officials. Finally, IOCL came out with its famous concept of road shipment of LPG through specially mounted bullets on trailer trucks. Initially, it started with a fleet of around 200 trucks. This was after extensive work on the design aspects of these trucks. The project, which started on a pilot scale is now the backbone of LPG distribution in the country. This also enabled the oil sector to make supplies based on flexible requirements. It reduced the problems of short and over shipments, thus containing the backlogs in the markets and railway demurrage.

EXAMPLE 11-3

Swedish furniture retailer Ikea, with about $18 billion in sales, is the world's largest furniture retailer. Started in Sweden by Ingvar Kamprad, Ikea currently has 220 stores in 33 countries [121, 258]. It has grown so dramatically by "reinventing the furniture business" [149]. Traditionally, furniture sales were split between department stores and small, locally owned shops. Typically, customers would place an order, and delivery could take place up to two months after the order was placed.

Ikea changed that formula by displaying all of its 10,000 products in large warehouse-like spaces in out-of-town stores and keeping all of these items in the warehouse. This was accomplished by designing products so that they can be packed compactly and efficiently in kits, which customers take from the stores and assemble at home. These kits are easy and cheap to transport, so products can be manufactured efficiently in a small number of factories and then shipped relatively cheaply to stores all over the world. Since Ikea has so many stores, each of which is very large, the company is able to take advantage of vast economies of scale. This has enabled the firm to sell good-quality furniture at prices lower than that of its competitors [149].

Ikea continues to work toward improved design and packaging to continue its dramatic growth—"recently the company figured out how to shave one-third off the width of bookcase packing boxes by making the back panels a separate assembly piece" [188].

There are other reasons to design products to pack compactly. For example, many major retailers favor products that take up less storage space and stack easily. Efficient storage reduces certain components of inventory cost because handling costs typically decrease, space per product (and thus rent per product) decreases, and revenue per square foot can increase. For example, many of the large plastic items available in discount stores, such as garbage pails, are designed to stack, so that they take up less shelf (or floor) space in the store. Thus, while it might not be enough to design packaging efficiently after the product design is completed, it may be valuable to redesign the product itself in order to take these issues into account.

EXAMPLE 11-4

Recently Rubbermaid won several design awards from *BusinessWeek* magazine. When describing why the Clear Classics food storage containers won an award, the writers mention that "Wal-Mart loves products designed to fit 14-by-14-inch shelves," which is one of the reasons these products were so successful. In addition, when describing the children's Icy Rider sled designed by Rubbermaid (which also won the award), the writers state, "Of course, not all products sold in Wal-Mart can fit into 14-by-14 shelving. But if designers create them to stack and save space, they have a shot of selling toWal-Mart . . . After researching Wal-Mart's needs, Rubbermaid made the Icy Rider thin and stackable" [175].

Similarly, it is often possible to ship goods in bulk and only complete final packaging at the warehouse or even at the retailer. This may save on transportation costs because bulk goods tend to be shipped more efficiently.

EXAMPLE 11-5

The Hawaiian sugar industry switched over to bulk transportation after World War II, when costs began to increase. They estimate that the cost of transporting a bulk ton of sugar is about $0.77 today, whereas the cost of transporting the same quantity of sugar in bags would be about $20.00 [62].

In some cases, final packaging can even be delayed until the goods are actually sold. For example, many grocery stores now sell flour, cereal, honey, liquid soap, rice, beans, grains and many other goods in bulk, allowing consumers to package as much as they want.

Recall that cross-docking (see Chapter 7) involves moving goods from one truck (e.g., from the supplier) to another set of trucks (e.g., perhaps going to individual retail stores). In some cases, boxes or pallets are taken off an incoming truck and moved directly to an outgoing one. However, it is often necessary to repackage some of the products. In many cases, bulk pallets of single items come in from suppliers, but mixed pallets with many different items have to go out to individual retailers. In this case, goods must be repacked at the cross-dock point, so more identification or labeling also might be needed if packages are broken up [217]. In general, packaging and products that are designed to facilitate this type of cross-docking operation by making repacking easier will clearly help to lower logistics costs.

11.2.3 Concurrent and Parallel Processing

In the previous section, we focused on simple ways that redesign of the product and packaging could help control logistics costs. In this subsection, we will focus on modifying the manufacturing *process*—which also may require modification of the product design.

We have seen that many difficulties in operating supply chains are due to long manufacturing lead times. Most manufacturing processes consist of manufacturing steps performed in sequence. The requirements of short start-up times and ever-shorter product life cycles often dictate that certain manufacturing steps be performed in different locations to take advantage of existing equipment or expertise. *Concurrent and parallel processing* involves modifying the manufacturing process so that steps that were previously performed in a sequence can be completed at the same time. This obviously helps reduce manufacturing lead time, lower inventory costs through improved forecasting, and reduce safety stock requirements, among other benefits.

A key to keeping the manufacturing process parallel is the concept of decoupling. If many of the components of the product can be decoupled, or physically separated, during manufacturing, it is possible that these components can be manufactured in parallel. If manufacturing each of the individual components takes the same amount of time in the newly decoupled design, but the manufacturing steps are performed in parallel, lead time will decrease. Even if some of these modular components take slightly more time to manufacture, the overall lead time may still decrease since various components are being manufactured in parallel. An added advantage of this manufacturing strategy of decoupling is that it may be possible to design different inventory strategies for the various decoupled components. If the supply of raw materials or manufacturing yield is uncertain for a particular component, a higher inventory level can be held of that single component, rather than for the entire end product.

EXAMPLE 11-6

A European manufacturer produces network printers for the European market in alliance with a manufacturer in the Far East. The main printer PC board is designed and assembled in Europe. It is then shipped to Asia, where it is integrated with the main printer housing in a process that involves building the printer, including the motor, printhead, housing, and so forth, around the board. The finished product is then shipped to Europe. The manufacturer is concerned with the long production and transportation lead times, which make it essential to maintain a large safety stock in Europe. However, much of the long manufacturing lead time is due to the sequential manufacturing process. Redesigning the printer manufacturing process and product so that the board can be integrated with the rest of the printer at the end of the manufacturing process will decrease lead times by allowing parallel manufacturing in Europe and the Far East. In addition, moving final assembly to Europe can serve to further increase responsiveness and decrease lead times. The two manufacturing processes are diagrammed in Figure 11-4 [137].

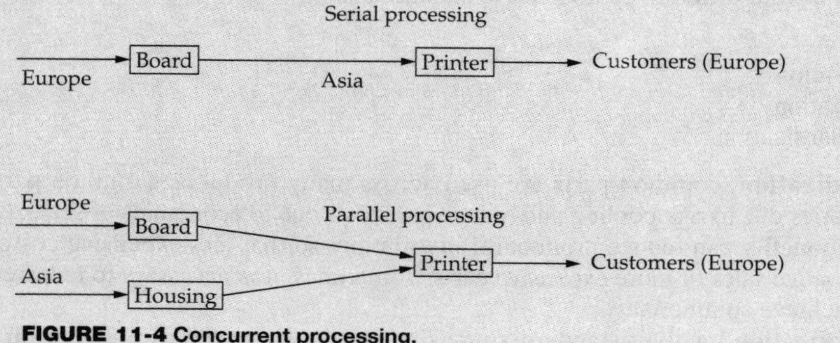

FIGURE 11-4 Concurrent processing.

11.2.4 Standardization

As we have discussed above, it is possible in some cases to shorten lead times (e.g., by taking advantage of parallel processing) in order to reduce inventory levels and increase forecast accuracy. Sometimes, however, it is impossible to reduce the lead time beyond a certain point. In these cases, it may be possible to achieve the same objectives by taking advantage of standardization.

Recall the third principle of forecasting described in Chapter 2: aggregate demand information is always more accurate than disaggregate data. Thus, we can better forecast demand for a continent than a country or for a product family (e.g., ski jackets) than a specific product (or style). Unfortunately, in a traditional manufacturing environment, aggregate forecasts are not of much use—the manufacturing manager has to know exactly what needs to be made before starting the process. However, by effectively using standardization, it may be possible to make effective use of the information in aggregate forecasts. Specifically, approaches based on product and process commonality make it possible to delay decisions about which specific product will be manufactured until after some of the manufacturing or purchasing decisions have been made. Thus, these decisions can be made on an aggregate level, using the more accurate aggregate forecasts.

Professor Jayashankar Swaminathan has developed a wide-ranging framework for effective implementation of standardization through the use of the correct operational strategy [233]. Swaminathan suggests that product modularity and process modularity are the key drivers that enable a standardization strategy that lowers inventory costs and increases forecast accuracy.

Following Swaminathan, we define the following concepts:

A modular product is a product assembled from a variety of modules such that, for each module, there are a number of options. The classic example of a modular product is the personal computer, which can be customized by combining different video cards, hard drives, memory chips, and so forth. Recall that this concept of modularity is also important for the implementation of *concurrent and parallel processing,* which was described in the previous subsection.

A modular process is a manufacturing process consisting of discrete operations, so that inventory can be stored in partially manufactured form between operations. Products are differentiated by completing a different subset of operations during the manufacturing process. Observe that modular products are not necessarily made of modular processes, as it may not be possible to store intermediate, or semifinished, inventories.

Swaminathan identifies four different approaches to standardization:

- Part standardization
- Process standardization
- Product standardization
- Procurement standardization

In **part standardization,** common parts are used across many products. Common parts reduce required part inventories due to risk pooling and reduce part costs due to economies of scale. Of course, excessive part commonality can reduce product differentiation, so that less expensive customization options might cannibalize sales of more expensive parts. Sometimes, it is necessary to redesign product lines or families to achieve commonality.

Process standardization involves standardizing as much of the process as possible for different products, and then customizing the products as late as possible. In this case, products and manufacturing processes are designed so that decisions about which specific product is manufactured—differentiation—can be delayed until after manufacturing is under way. The manufacturing process starts by making a *generic* or *family* product that is later differentiated into a specific end-product. For this reason, this approach is also known as *postponement* or *delayed product differentiation* [137]. By delaying differentiation, production starts can be based on aggregate forecasts. Thus, design for delayed product differentiation can be effectively used to address the uncertainty in final demand even if forecasts cannot be improved.

It is usually necessary to redesign products specifically for delayed differentiation. For example, it may be necessary to resequence the manufacturing process to take advantage of process standardization. *Resequencing* refers to modifying the order of product manufacturing steps so that those operations that result in the differentiation of specific items or products are postponed as much as possible. One famous and dramatic example of a firm utilizing resequencing to improve its supply chain operation is Benetton Corporation.

EXAMPLE 11-7

Benetton is a major supplier of knitwear, Europe's largest clothing manufacturer, and the world's largest consumer of wool in the garment sector [259], supplying hundreds of shops. The nature of the fashion industry is that consumer preferences change rapidly. However, because of the long manufacturing lead time, store owners frequently had to place orders for wool sweaters up to seven months in advance of when the sweaters would appear in their stores. The wool sweater manufacturing process typically consists of acquiring yarn, dyeing it, finishing it, manufacturing the garment parts, and then joining those parts into a completed sweater. Unfortunately, this left little flexibility to respond to the changing tastes of consumers. To address this issue, Benetton revised the manufacturing process, postponing the dyeing of the garments until *after* the sweater was completely assembled. Thus, color choices could be delayed until after more forecasting and sales information were received. Hence, because of the postponement of the dyeing process, yarn purchasing and manufacturing plans could be based on aggregate forecasts for product families, rather than forecasts for specific sweater/color combinations. This revised process made sweater manufacturing about 10 percent more expensive and required the purchasing of new equipment and the retraining of employees. However, Benetton was more than adequately compensated by improved forecasts, lower surplus inventories, and, in many cases, higher sales [222].

A U.S. disk drive manufacturer provides another notable example. Notice in this example that although lower levels of inventory need to be held to achieve specific service levels, the per-unit inventory cost tends to be more expensive.

EXAMPLE 11-8

A major U.S. manufacturer of mass storage devices makes different unique hard-drive products for each of a variety of customers. Orders are placed to be delivered by a certain time and, since lead times are very long, the manufacturer has to keep a variety of products in process in order to meet promised delivery dates. Since variability of demand is high and each product is unique, the manufacturer has to maintain high levels of in-process inventory to meet demand reliably. The manufacturing process involves a brief generic segment, through which products intended for all customers must go, and then an extensive customization portion. Clearly, the ideal point to hold inventory is before customization begins. Unfortunately, however, the majority of manufacturing time, due particularly to time-consuming testing, occurs after differentiation has started. This testing has to take place after differentiation starts because a particular circuit board has to be added to the assembly for the testing to take place, and this circuit board is different for each customer. In order to delay differentiation, it is possible to insert a generic circuit board into the assembly, complete much of the testing, remove the generic circuit board, and add the customer-specific boards later. In this way, disk drive differentiation can be delayed until more order information is available. Clearly, this will decrease the level of required in-process inventory needed to meet demand reliably. However, this will add some additional manufacturing steps. In particular, the generic board has to be added and removed. Thus, it is necessary to compare the manufacturing inefficiencies caused by adding and removing this circuit board with the gains in inventory savings. The manufacturing processes are illustrated in Figure 11-5 [137].

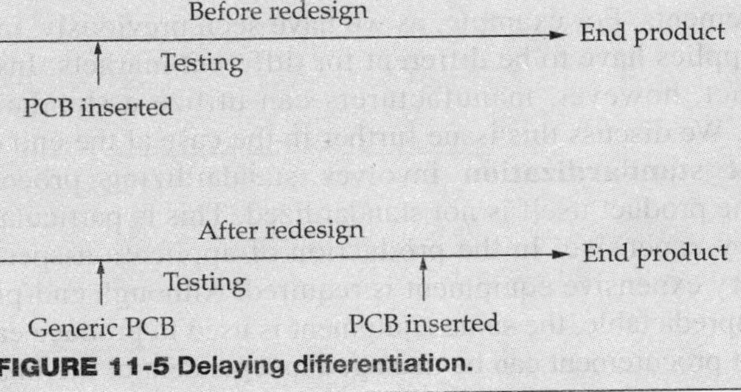

FIGURE 11-5 Delaying differentiation.

Part and process standardization are frequently connected. Sometimes part standardization is necessary for implementing process standardization.

EXAMPLE 11-9

A major printer manufacturer was preparing to introduce a new color printer into the market. Demand for the new printer and an existing printer was expected to be highly variable and negatively correlated. The manufacturing processes for the two products were similar, except that different circuit boards and printhead assemblies were used. Differences in head assemblies and circuit boards led to very different manufacturing processes. To implement process standardization, that is, delayed differentiation, it is necessary to ensure that the manufacturing processes are similar until the final step. To do this, the printers have been redesigned so that both products share a common circuit board and printhead. This ensures that differentiation can be delayed as much as possible. Thus, part standardization enables process standardization in this case [137].

In some cases, the concepts of resequencing and commonality allow the final manufacturing steps to be completed at distribution centers (DCs) or warehouses instead of at the factory. One of the advantages of this approach is that if DCs are much closer to the demand than the factories, products can be differentiated closer to the demand, thus increasing the firm's ability to respond to rapidly changing markets. This is one of the approaches we will discuss in more detail in Section 11.2.8, when we analyze the case from the beginning of this chapter.

Sometimes, processes can be redesigned so that the differentiating steps don't have to be performed in a manufacturing facility or distribution center at all, but can take place in the retailer after the sale is made. Often this is accomplished by focusing on modularity during the design phase, placing functionality in *modules* that can be easily added to a product. For example, many laser printers and copiers are packaged in their most basic version. Along with the printer, each retail store stocks separately packaged modules that add features to the printer or copier, such as advanced paper handling, stapling, and so forth. Obviously, this can greatly lower required inventory since only extended features can be stocked in module form, instead of entire printers.

In **product standardization,** a large variety of products may be offered, but only a few kept in inventory. When a product not kept in stock is ordered, the order may be filled by a product that offers a superset of the features required by a customer. This process, known as *downward substitution,* is common in many industries. For example, in the semiconductor industry, it is quite common to sell a higher-speed or a higher-functionality chip as a lower-speed/functionality chip when the low-end chip is out of stock. Similarly, car rental agencies and hotels frequently fill reservations with higher-end vehicles or rooms when the lower-end vehicles or rooms are not available. Sometimes, it may be possible to redesign products so that one product can be adjusted to meet several end-customer requirements. For example, as we have seen previously, many products are similar, except that power supplies have to be different for different markets. Instead of manufacturing two versions of a product, however, manufacturers can utilize a standardized product, with a switchable power supply. We discuss this issue further in the case at the end of this chapter.

Finally, **procurement standardization** involves standardizing processing equipment and approaches, even when the product itself is not standardized. This is particularly valuable when processing equipment is very expensive. In the production of application-specific integrated circuits (ASICs), for example, very expensive equipment is required. Although end-products are highly customized and demand is unpredictable, the same equipment is used to produce each of the possible end-products. Thus, equipment procurement can be managed independent of the final demand.

11.2.5 Selecting a Standardization Strategy

To help with the selection of the appropriate standardization strategy, Swaminathan [233] proposed a framework based on the observation that the firm's choice of standardization strategy is a function of the firm's ability to modularize its products and processes. Table 11-2 illustrates the proposed strategic choices under different conditions.

- If process and product are modular, process standardization will help to maximize effective forecast accuracy and minimize inventory costs.
- If the product is modular, but the process is not, it is not possible to delay differentiation. However, part standardization is likely to be effective.
- If the process is modular but the product is not, procurement standardization may decrease equipment expenses.
- If neither the process nor the product is modular, some benefits may still result from focusing on product standardization.

TABLE 11-2

OPERATIONAL STRATEGIES FOR STANDARDIZATION

		Process	
		Nonmodular	*Modular*
Product	*Modular*	Part standardization	Process standardization
	Nonmodular	Product standardization	Procurement standardization

11.2.6 Important Considerations

The various strategies described above are designed to deal with inaccurate forecasts and product variety; frequently, it may not be possible or cost-effective to implement these strategies in the context of a particular product or a specific supply chain. Even if implementing a particular strategy is theoretically possible, in many cases the expenses resulting from product and packaging redesign will exceed the savings under the new system. In addition, capital expenditures are likely to be required to retool assembly lines. Sometimes, as we discussed above, it may even be necessary to add manufacturing capability at distribution centers. Typically, the value of these types of changes is higher at the start of the product life cycle, when expenditures can be amortized over the entire life of the product. It is possible that DFL initiatives that make a great deal of sense at the start of the product life cycle don't pay for themselves when implemented later [137].

It also may be more expensive to manufacture a product with a new process. In many of the examples mentioned above, the products and manufacturing processes became more expensive. It is therefore necessary to estimate the savings produced by a more effectively designed product or process, and compare these savings to the increased cost of manufacturing. Many of the benefits of implementing such a system are very difficult to quantify; increased flexibility, more efficient customer service, and decreased market response times may be hard to place a value on, which only serves to make the analysis more difficult. To add to the difficulty, engineers are often forced to take a broader perspective than they have been trained to take when they are making these kinds of decisions.

To add to these complications, process modifications such as resequencing will cause the level of inventory in many cases to go down, but the per unit value of inventory being held will be higher. In the sweater example, it may be possible to hold less wool in inventory because it doesn't have to be dyed before it is assembled. However, much of this wool will be held in the form of sweaters, which have a higher value than dyed wool. Of course, if manufacturing or customizing steps are postponed, the generic products may have a lower value than customized products, so value is added later in the supply chain than it would be otherwise.

Finally, in some cases, tariffs and duties are lower for semifinished or nonconfigured goods than for final products [137]. Thus, implementing a strategy of completing the manufacturing process in a local distribution center may help to lower costs associated with tariffs and duties.

All of these issues have to be taken into consideration when implementing a specific design for logistics strategy. Nevertheless, it is clear that in many cases, DFL can help to improve customer service and greatly reduce the costs of operating the supply chain.

11.2.7 The Push–Pull Boundary

Recall our discussion of the push–pull boundary in Chapter 6. In push-based systems, production decisions are based on long-term forecasts, while in pull-based supply chains, production is demand driven. We listed many advantages of pull-based systems and concluded that compared to push-based systems, pull-based systems typically lead to a reduction in supply chain lead times, inventory levels, and system costs, while simultaneously making it easier to manage system resources.

Unfortunately, it is not always practical to implement a pull-based system throughout the entire supply chain. Lead times may be too long, or it may be necessary to take advantage of economies of scale in production or transportation. The standardization strategies we have been discussing in this section can be viewed as a method to combine push and pull systems within a single supply chain into what we called, in Chapter 6, a push–pull system. Indeed, that portion of the supply chain prior to product differentiation is typically a push-based supply chain. That is, the undifferentiated product is built and transported based on long-term forecasts. In contrast, differentiation occurs as a response to market demand. Thus, the portion of the supply chain starting from the time of differentiation is a pull-based supply chain.

For instance, in the Benetton example, Example 11-6, uncolored sweaters are made to forecast, but dyeing takes place as a reaction to customer demand. We call the point of differentiation the **push–pull boundary,** since this is the point where the system changes from a push-based system to a pull-based system.

One way to view the push–pull boundary concept is through the third rule of inventory management, discussed in Chapter 2. Since aggregate demand information is more accurate than disaggregate data, the push portion of the supply chain includes only activities and decisions made prior to product differentiation. These activities and decisions are based on aggregate demand data.

Clearly, then, an additional advantage of postponement is that it allows firms to realize many of the advantages of pull-based systems, while at the same time allowing for the economies of scale inherent in push-based systems. Often, when implementing a standardization strategy, if there is more than one possible differentiation point, it may be useful to think in terms of locating the push–pull boundary in order to achieve a balance between the advantages of the push- and the pull-based systems.

EXAMPLE 11-10 ASIAN PAINTS USES DTM

With a small beginning in 1942, Asian Paints today is the India's largest producer of paints with about 45% market share and ranks among top ten decorative coating companies of the world, with revenue of Rs. 36.7 billion (around US $ 851 million). It has seven major manufacturing facilities in India. The largest one at Sriperumbudur is being expanded to an estimated capacity of 100,000 liters per year and another one is coming up in Rohtak in Haryana, a northern state of in India. Its global presence spans 29 manufacturing facilities in many countries across globe.

Asian Paints has demonstrated one of the finest executions of supply chain innovation. Most of its 150000 dealers stock a single base color. Customers can place their order either by coming personally to select the shades from a computerized catalogue or a shade booklet or through a communication mode like the telephone. After the customer decides the final shade and its quantity, the dealer uses his computerized Dealer Tinting Machine (DTM) to blend shades into the base paint, which comes from Asian Paints. The paint is delivered within few minutes. This is one of the finest examples of delayed product differentiation in the supply chain domain as the final product differentiation is being made just after the actual demand is fully known. The approach has unburdened the dealers from their perennial problem of excess stock of some shades and stock out of other ones [33, 250].

11.2.8 Case Analysis

Consider the Hewlett-Packard case that you read at the beginning of this chapter. Although several problems and issues are outlined in the case, we will focus on analyzing the inventory problems in the European distribution center. In particular, HP faces long delivery lead times of about four to five weeks from its production facility in Vancouver, Washington, to Europe. The Vancouver plant is a high-speed, high-volume facility where manufacturing takes about a week.

In particular, HP is concerned with high inventory levels and inventory imbalance in Europe. One of the characteristics of the DeskJet product line is that it is customized for local markets, a process called *localization*. This involves adding labeling and documentation in the correct language and customizing the power supply for the correct voltage level and plug. Customization is done in Vancouver many weeks before the products arrive in Europe. Furthermore, once the printers arrive in Europe, inventory imbalance might occur in the following sense: The European DC often finds itself with too much inventory of printers customized for certain markets, and not enough inventory of printers customized for others.

What are the causes of these problems? Based on the case and material we have discussed in previous chapters, the following issues are clear:

- There is significant uncertainty about how to set the correct inventory level.
- The many different localization options make inventory difficult to manage.
- Long lead times lead to difficulty in forecasting and high safety stocks.
- Uncertainty in the many local markets makes forecasting difficult.
- Maintaining cooperation between the various HP divisions is challenging.

In the short term, the first issue can be addressed by rationalizing safety stock utilizing the methods we discussed in Chapter 2. To address these problems in the longer term, the following solutions have been proposed:

- Switch to air shipments of printers from Vancouver.
- Build a European factory.
- Hold more inventory at the European DC.
- Improve forecasting practices.

Unfortunately, there are significant problems with each of these suggestions. Air shipments are prohibitively expensive in this competitive, low-margin business. European volumes are not sufficient to justify building a new factory. Inventory is already a problem; more would simply magnify the problem. Finally, it is unclear how to improve forecasts.

Thus, HP management is motivated to consider another option: process standardization or *postponement*. Specifically, this option involves shipping "unlocalized" printers to the European DC and localizing them after observing local demand. The question is, what are the inventory savings of such a strategy? To address this issue, we utilize the inventory management policies detailed in Chapter 2.

Recall that we can calculate required safety stock for each of the customized products by noting that safety stock must equal $z \times STD \times \sqrt{L}$, where z is selected to maintain the required service level (see Table 2-2). In the analysis below, we assume that lead time is five weeks, and we require a 98 percent service level. By dividing this quantity by average demand, we determine the number of weeks of safety stock required. Thus, the first six rows of Table 11-3 contain the results of these calculations for each of the customization options specified in Table 11-1. The second-to-last row totals all of the required safety stock. We see that by utilizing effective inventory management strategies and the current distribution system, HP needs over three-and-a-half weeks of safety stock on hand to meet the 98 percent service level requirement. The table also shows the effect of postponing localization until after demand is observed. In this case, the DC keeps safety stock of only the generic printer, customizing the printers as demand is realized. This allows the DC to focus on aggregate demand levels and, therefore, as we saw in the section on risk pooling in Chapter 2, aggregate demand has a much smaller standard deviation than individual demand. The standard deviation of the aggregate demand is calculated in the last row of the table. This new standard deviation is used to determine safety stock for the generic model. Observe that this new system, in which localization is postponed, requires less safety stock than the currently existing system.

The dollar savings in inventory carrying cost obviously depend on the rate of carrying cost used. For example, if carrying cost is taken to be 30 percent and a product value of $400 is assumed, annual savings are about $800,000. In addition, there are other benefits to implementing a postponement strategy. These include

- The value of inventory in transit, and thus insurance costs, goes down.
- It may be possible to reduce freight handling costs.

TABLE 11-3

INVENTORY ANALYSIS

Parameter	Average monthly demand	Standard deviation of monthly demand	Average weekly demand	Standard deviation of weekly demand	Safety stock	Weeks of safety stock
A	42.3	32.4	9.8	15.6	71.5	7.4
AA	420.2	203.9	97.7	98.3	450.6	4.6
AB	15,830.1	5,624.6	3,681.4	2,712.4	12,433.5	3.4
AQ	2,301.2	1,168.5	535.1	563.5	2,583.0	4.8
AU	4,208.0	2,204.6	978.6	1,063.2	4,873.6	5.0
AY	306.8	103.1	71.3	49.7	227.8	3.2
Total	23,108.6		5,373.9		20,640.0	3.8
Generic	23,108.6	6,244	5,373.9	3,011.1	13,802.6	2.6

- Some of the localization materials can be locally sourced, reducing costs and meeting "local content" requirements.

On the other hand, there are costs associated with implementing this process standardization strategy. First, the product and packaging have to be redesigned so that localization can be delayed. This entails expense and requires research-and-development work on a product that is already working well. Also, the European distribution center has to be modified to facilitate localization there. Recall that, in addition to capital investments, the mind-set of the distribution operation—"Distribution, not manufacturing, is our core competency"—has to be changed.

Hewlett-Packard did indeed implement such a strategy, with great success. Inventory declined while service levels rose, leading to significant cost savings and increased profitability. To achieve these results, the printer was redesigned for localization and the distribution center took on more work and responsibilities.

11.3 SUPPLIER INTEGRATION INTO NEW PRODUCT DEVELOPMENT

Another key supply chain issue involves the selection of appropriate suppliers for components of the new product. Traditionally, this has been done after design and manufacturing engineers have determined the final design for a product. Recently, a study by the Global Procurement and Supply Chain Benchmarking Initiative, at Michigan State University [166], found that firms often realize tremendous benefits from involving suppliers in the design process. Benefits include a decline in purchased material costs, an increase in purchased material quality, a decline in development time and cost and in manufacturing cost, and an increase in final product technology levels.

In addition to the competitive forces that drive managers to seek out all types of supply chain efficiencies, several competitive forces are specifically encouraging managers to find opportunities to work with suppliers during the product design process. These forces include the continuing focus on strategies that encourage companies to focus on their core competencies and outsource other business capabilities, and to continually reduce the length of product life cycles. Both of these forces encourage companies to develop processes that make the design process more efficient. Taking advantage of supplier competencies is certainly one way to do this.

11.3.1 The Spectrum of Supplier Integration

The supplier integration study [166] notes that there is no single "appropriate level" of supplier integration. Instead, they develop the notion of a *spectrum of supplier integration*. In particular, they identify a series of steps from least to most supplier responsibility as follows:

None. The supplier is not involved in design. Materials and subassemblies are supplied according to customer specifications and design.

White box. This level of integration is informal. The buyer "consults" with the supplier informally when designing products and specifications, although there is no formal collaboration.

Grey box. This represents formal supplier integration. Collaborative teams are formed between the buyer's and the supplier's engineers, and joint development occurs.

Black box. The buyer gives the supplier a set of interface requirements and the supplier independently designs and develops the required component.

Of course, just because the black-box approach is at one end of the continuum doesn't mean that it is the best approach in all cases. Instead, firms must develop a strategy that helps them determine the appropriate level of supplier integration for different situations. The Global Procurement and Supply Chain Benchmarking Initiative has developed a strategic planning process to help firms make this determination [166]. The first several steps of the process are summarized below:

- Determine internal core competencies.
- Determine current and future new product developments.
- Identify external development and manufacturing needs.

These three steps help management determine what is going to be procured from suppliers and what level of supplier expertise is appropriate. If future products have components that require expertise that the firm does not possess, and development of these components can be separated from other phases of product development, then taking a black-box approach makes sense. If this separation is not possible, then it makes more sense to use the grey-box development. If the buyer has some design expertise but wants to ensure that the supplier can adequately manufacture the component, perhaps a white-box approach is appropriate.

11.3.2 Keys to Effective Supplier Integration

Simply selecting an appropriate level of supplier integration is not sufficient. Much work goes into ensuring that the relationship is a success. The next steps of the strategic planning process [166] help to ensure this success:

- Select suppliers and build relationships with them.
- Align objectives with selected suppliers.

Selecting suppliers in general involves various considerations such as manufacturing capacity and response time. Since supplier integration partners typically supply components (in addition to cooperating in their design), all of the traditional considerations still apply. In addition, the special nature of supplier integration presents an additional set of supplier requirements.

The same study identifies many of these, including

- The capability to participate in the design process.
- The willingness to participate in the design process, including the ability to reach agreements on intellectual property and confidentiality issues.
- The ability to commit sufficient personnel and time to the process. This may include colocating personnel if appropriate.
- Sufficient resources to commit to the supplier integration process.

Of course, the relative importance of these requirements depends on the particular project and type of integration. Once suppliers are identified, it is critical to work on building relationships with them. For example, firms have found it useful to involve suppliers early in the design process. Companies that do so report greater gains than those that involve suppliers only after design concepts have been generated. Sharing future plans and technologies with suppliers helps to build this relationship, as does a joint continuous improvement goal. Separate organizational groups dedicated to managing the relationship are also useful. In all of these cases, the goals of the purchasing firm revolve around building long-term, effective relationships with trusted suppliers. These will naturally lead to the alignment of buyer and supplier objectives, which will result in more effective integration.

11.3.3 A "Bookshelf" of Technologies and Suppliers

The Michigan State group also developed the idea of a "bookshelf" of technologies and suppliers within the context of supplier integration. This involves monitoring the development of relevant new technologies and following the suppliers that have demonstrated expertise in these technologies. Then, when appropriate, a buyer firm can quickly introduce these technologies into new products by integrating the supplier design team with its own. This enables a firm to balance the advantages and disadvantages of being on the cutting edge of new technology. On one hand, there is no need to use the technology immediately in order to gain experience with it: suppliers are developing this knowledge with other customers. On the other hand, the danger of being slow to introduce cutting-edge technology and concepts is lessened. The bookshelf concept is a dramatic example of the power of supplier integration.

11.4 MASS CUSTOMIZATION

11.4.1 What Is Mass Customization?

In his book *Mass Customization* [189], Joseph Pine II introduced a concept that is becoming important to more and more businesses: *mass customization*. In this section, we will first review the concept and then discuss how logistics and supply chain networks play an important role in the implementation of related ideas.

Mass customization has evolved from the two prevailing manufacturing paradigms of the 20th century: craft production and mass production. Mass production involves the efficient production of a large quantity of a small variety of goods. Spurred by the Industrial Revolution, so-called *mechanistic firms* developed in which management put a high priority on automating and measuring tasks. A very bureaucratic management structure, with rigid, functionally defined groups and tasks, and tightly supervised employees, is common. This kind of organization enables tight control and predictability, which tends to lead to high degrees of efficiency. The quality of a small number of items can be quite high and prices can be kept relatively low. This is particularly critical for commodity products, where firms have typically competed on price and, more recently, on quality.

Craft production, on the other hand, involves highly skilled and flexible workers, often craftsmen in the manufacturing setting, who are governed by personal or professional standards, and motivated by the desire to create unique and interesting products or services. These workers, found in so-called *organic organizations*, are typically trained through apprenticeships and experience; the organization is flexible and continually changing. This type of organization is able to produce highly differentiated and specialized goods, but it is very difficult to regulate and control. As a consequence, the quality and production rates of these goods are hard to measure and reproduce, and they are typically much more expensive to manufacture [190].

In the past, managers often had to make a decision between these two types of organizations with their inherent trade-offs. For some products, a low-cost, low-variety strategy was appropriate while for others, a higher-cost, higher-variety, more adaptable strategy was more effective. The development of mass customization demonstrates that it is not always necessary to make this trade-off.

Mass customization involves the delivery of a wide variety of customized goods or services quickly and efficiently at low cost. Thus, it captures many of the advantages of both the mass production and craft production systems described above. Although not appropriate for all products (e.g., commodity products may not benefit from differentiation), mass customization gives firms important competitive advantages and helps to drive new business models.

11.4.2 Making Mass Customization Work

Pine points out [190] that the key to making mass customization work is highly skilled and autonomous workers, processes, and modular units, so that managers can coordinate and reconfigure these modules to meet specific customer requests and demands.

Each module continually strives to upgrade its capabilities; a module's success depends on how effectively, quickly, and efficiently it completes its task, and how good it is at expanding its capabilities. Managers are charged with determining how these capabilities "fit together" efficiently. Thus, management's success depends on how effectively it can develop, maintain, and creatively combine the links between modules in different ways to meet different customer requests, and on the creation of a work environment that encourages the development of a variety of different modules.

Since each unit has highly specialized skills, workers can develop expertise and efficiency in the manner of mass production. Since these units or modules can be assembled in many ways, the differentiation of craft production is achievable. Pine calls this type of organization a *dynamic network.*

There are several key attributes that a company, or, more specifically, the *systems within a company that link different modules,* must possess to implement mass customization successfully [190]. They are

Instantaneousness. Modules and processes must be linked together very quickly. This allows rapid response to various customer demands.

Costless. The linkages must add little if any cost to the processes. This attribute allows mass customization to be a low-cost alternative.

Seamless. The linkages and individual modules should be invisible to the customer, so customer service doesn't suffer.

Frictionless. Networks or collections of modules must be formed with little overhead. Communication must work instantly, without taking time for the team building; this is necessary in so many other types of environments.

With these attributes in place, it becomes possible to design and implement a dynamic, flexible firm that can respond to varying customer needs quickly and efficiently.

EXAMPLE 11-11

National Bicycle is a subsidiary of Matsushita that sells bicycles under the Panasonic and National brand names in Japan. Several years ago, management found that sales were not at acceptable levels, primarily because the company was unable to predict and satisfy varying customer demand. In the year before beginning the mass customization efforts, 20 percent of bicycles from the previous year remained in inventory. Rather than market to a particular niche or try to improve forecasts, National became a mass customizer.

The company developed a highly flexible bicycle frame manufacturing facility, noting that painting and the installation and tuning of components were separate functions that could be performed by other "modules" in its manufacturing facility. Next, they installed a sophisticated custom-order system called the Panasonic Order System at retailers. This system includes a unique machine that measures customer weight and size, and the appropriate dimensions of the frame, position of the seat, and extension of the bar stem. The customers also can select model type, color patterns, and various components. Information from the dealer is instantaneously transmitted to the factory, where a computer-aided design (CAD) system produces technical details in three minutes. The information is transmitted automatically to the appropriate modules, where manufacturing is completed. The bike is then delivered to consumers two weeks later.

Thus, by noting that the production process could be separated into independent production modules in a seamless and essentially costless manner, and by installing sophisticated information systems, National Bicycle was able to increase sales and customer satisfaction without significantly increasing manufacturing costs [81].

11.4.3 Mass Customization and Supply Chain Management

Clearly, many of the advanced supply chain management approaches and techniques that we have discussed in this and earlier chapters are essential if mass customization is to be successfully implemented. This is particularly true if the components in the network stretch across several companies.

The same information technology that is so critical for effective supply chain management is also critical for coordinating the different modules in the dynamic network and ensuring that together they meet customer requirements. The required system attributes listed above make effective information systems mandatory. Similarly, in many cases, the modules in the dynamic network exist across different firms. This makes concepts such as strategic partnerships and supplier integration essential for the success of mass customization. Finally, as many of the printer-related examples indicate, postponement can play a key role in implementing mass customization. For instance, postponing regional differentiation until products have reached regional distribution centers facilitates regional customization. As the following example illustrates, postponing differentiation until orders have been received allows customer-specific customization.

EXAMPLE 11-12

Dell Computer has become one of the dominant players in the PC industry—it sells more systems globally than any computer company [260]—by adopting a unique strategy based on mass customization. Dell never builds a PC for a customer until the customer's order has been placed. This allows the customer to specify unique requirements, and Dell builds the computer to these requirements. A growing majority of orders come in over the Internet. The order-taking system interfaces with Dell's own supply chain control system, which ensures that inventory is where it needs to be for the computer to be quickly manufactured. In addition, Dell stores very little inventory. Instead, Dell's suppliers have built warehouses close to Dell's facilities, and Dell orders parts on a just-in-time basis. By implementing these strategies, Dell has been able to provide customers with exactly what they want very quickly. In addition, inventory costs are low and Dell minimizes the danger of parts obsolescence in the rapidly changing computer industry. In this way, Dell has become one of the dominant players in the desktop PC, laptop, and server markets.

Dell has utilized many of the important concepts we have discussed to achieve its goals. The company is driven by advanced information systems that do everything from taking many of the orders (over the Web) to managing inventory in the supply chain. Strategic partnerships have been established with many of Dell's suppliers. Dell is even establishing supplier integration partnerships with some of its key suppliers (e.g., 3Com, the network equipment supplier) to ensure that new computers and networking devices are compatible. Finally, Dell has utilized the concept of postponement, deferring final assembly of computers until orders have been received, to achieve mass customization [160].

SUMMARY

In this chapter, we focused on various ways that product design interacts with supply chain management. First, we considered various design for logistics concepts, in which product design is used to lower the costs of logistics. Products designed for efficient packaging and storage obviously cost less to transport and store. Designing products so that certain manufacturing steps can be completed in parallel can cut down on manufacturing lead time, leading to a reduction in safety stocks and increased responsiveness to market changes. Finally, standardization enables risk pooling across products, leading to lower inventories, and allows firms to use the information contained in aggregate forecasts more effectively.

Another critical design/supply chain interaction involves integrating suppliers into the product design and development process. We discussed different ways that suppliers can be integrated into the development process and considered guidelines for managing this integration effectively.

Finally, advanced supply chain management helps to facilitate mass customization. Mass customization involves the delivery of a wide variety of customized goods or services quickly and efficiently at low cost. Obviously, this approach helps to provide firms with important competitive advantages and, just as obviously, effective supply chain management is critical if mass customization is to be successful.

DISCUSSION QUESTIONS

1. List two low clock speed products, two medium clock speed products, and two fast clock speed products.
2. How does a low clock speed impact the product design strategy? How about a fast clock speed?
3. Give an example of a product appropriate for each of the boxes in Figure 11-3.
4. Discuss some examples of products that are designed to lower shipping and storage costs.
5. How does the proliferation of products, models, and options make the supply chain more difficult to manage?
6. What are the advantages of downward substitution? What are the disadvantages?
7. What are some products or industries that have been damaged by excessive part standardization?
8. Discuss some examples of modular and nonmodular products and processes.
9. How do standardization strategies help managers deal with demand variability and the difficulty of making accurate forecasts?
10. What are the advantages and disadvantages of integrating suppliers into the product development process?
11. You are the CEO of a medium-sized apparel manufacturer, and you are considering a mass customization strategy for some of your products. How will you decide which, if any, of your products are appropriate candidates for mass customization?

CASE: Hewlett-Packard Company: Network Printer Design for Universality

INTRODUCTION

Sarah Donohoe, manufacturing engineering manager of the network laser printer division at Hewlett-Packard Company (HP), listened intently to her colleagues at the project review meeting for the development of their latest new product. With Sarah at the meeting were Jane Schushinski, marketing manager; Leo Linbeck, head of product design; and David Hooper, the controller of the division.

The main topic for this meeting was the decision of whether or not to use a universal power supply for the next generation of network laser printer, code-named Rainbow. Previously, printers in the North American and the European market have distinct power supplies and the associated fusers in the main engine of the printer. For North American printers, a 110-volt power supply was installed. For European printers, a 220-volt power supply was added. This printer engine was built by HP's manufacturing partner in Japan. Due to the long lead time for engine manufacturing, HP had to specify the requirements of the two types of printers at least 14 weeks ahead. The time that it takes the Japanese partner to commit the printers for shipment, the transportation times, and customs clearance totals about four weeks. Hence, if a universal power supply is used, then HP would have the flexibility of postponing the specification of the printer engine by at least two months in the planning process. Consequently, the production team believed that a universal power supply can enable HP to better respond to the changing demand in the individual markets and reduce its inventory costs.

Linbeck had begun the meeting by reviewing a fax he had received from the Japanese partner. "We have been asking our partner for a universal power supply and fuser for a long time, and now, when we are about to finalize our design of the next generation network printer, they are telling us that designing the new power supply is finally feasible and can be completed within the time constraints we have set for delivering the product to market on time. However, we must make the decision within the next two weeks so our Japanese partner can line up its design engineers to work on the project." Hooper summed up finance's position as follows, "I do not know what other costs or benefits to the supply chain will be derived from this new change, but what I do know is that our Japanese partner quoted that universal power supply would increase costs by $30 per unit."

As the conversation progressed around the room, Hooper's words became more and more indicative of the group's feelings as a whole. The only hard number available for analyzing the costs and benefits of the change was the $30 increase as quoted by the Japanese partner. If the team was to implement the change, they would have to convince management that the benefits outweighed the costs. Unfortunately, as the meeting went on, quantifying the advantages and disadvantages appeared more and more difficult.

THE HEWLETT-PACKARD COMPANY

Hewlett Packard was one of Silicon Valley's legends. Established by two Stanford University graduates, William Hewlett and David Packard, in 1939, the company initially prided itself on supplying superior engineering tools, designed for engineers by engineers. As the company grew and diversified, the strong belief in technological innovation as the key to competitive advantage persisted.

Innovation was the key to HP's strategy. In 1957, Packard expressed his belief in the importance of this capability:

> Improvement is accomplished by better methods, better techniques, better machinery and equipment and by people continually finding better ways to do their jobs and to work together as a team. I will never see the day when there is not yet room for improvement.

Through time, HP's focus on innovation had brought the world products such as the hand-held calculator and the ink-jet printer. In 1992, the company continued to invest heavily in technology, spending $1.6 billion, or 10 percent of revenue, on research and development. The high levels of investment have paid off: For three straight years, over half of HP's orders had been for products introduced within the last two years.

CHANGING MARKET CONDITIONS

In the early 1990s, while technological innovation continued to drive the company's success, many business units were being forced to compete on other dimensions. In consumer product lines, low prices, broad availability, and ease of use had become competitive requirements. Lew Platt, HP's current president and chief executive officer, once acknowledged the importance of improving customer service and responsiveness:

> We're not doing as good a job in order fulfillment as we need to. In fact it's where we get our lowest marks from customers. We have to be a lot easier to do business with. Improvement in order fulfillment will strengthen HP's competitiveness, increase customer satisfaction, and reduce expenses, so this is an area of great urgency. Along with improving profitability, it's our top priority.

In addition, product life cycles were continually shrinking, making time to market the difference between maximizing market opportunities and missing them. Nowhere were these demands more important than in the laser printer division.

Source: This case was written by Professor Hau L. Lee, based on an original case written by Steven Pious and Toni Cupal. It is intended as the basis for class discussion rather than to illustrate either effective or ineffective handling of an administrative situation. The product and individuals' names have been disguised.

HP held a dominant 57 percent of the worldwide laser printer market, but several formidable competitors, including Apple, Fuji-Xerox, Kyocera, Oki, and Compaq, had recently entered the market; life cycles had fallen to under three years; and the quality of competitive products made consumers willing to switch brands if HP's price was too far above the market average or if the product was not easily available.

To meet these challenges, HP had aggressively worked to improve its product development process. Cross-functional teams that brought specialists from all functional areas together to create a new product were becoming standard. The primary benefit of such teams was their ability to identify and eliminate potential problems early in the design cycle while the financial and time-to-market costs of changing the product design were low. As intended, the different perspectives of the team members often gave rise to heated debates over design decisions.

THE NETWORK PRINTER DIVISION SUPPLY CHAIN

The laser products as a group constitute a major and rapidly rising portion of HP's revenue. In 1992 the revenue of laser products was $3 billion, but was projected to reach close to $8 billion by 1998. The network printer is a high-end laser printer that has networking capabilities and special functionalities. Rainbow, the network printer under development, is a product with much more configurable options and features for the printer, such as memory, stapling ability, firmware, system software, fax modems, paper handling, linkage to print server, scanner, and printer stand. It will be priced between $5,000 to $6,000.

The network printer division at HP currently outsources the procurement and assembly of the product's main engine to a Japanese partner. The components, including the power supply and fuser unit, were fully integrated with a printed circuit board from HP's Boise factory into the printer engine at the partner's factory. Monopoly control of one of the key components allowed this partner to require a 14-week lead time from HP.

The design team of Rainbow recognized that the multiple thousands of configurable options for the new product would be a nightmare for forecasting and production planning. Consequently, special efforts were spent in the design of the products so that most of the customization of the products, like the installation of paper input units, cabinet stands, fax modems, paper output units, stapler upgrade package, memory, and print server linkage, can all be carried out at the distribution centers (DCs). Hence, all these options can be installed as accessories at the DCs. In addition, the localization of the product through the inclusion of driver software disks, manuals, power cords, and front panels (with the correct mix of languages) are also done at the DCs.

Hence, the supply chain process involves the transportation of the base printer, almost exclusively by boat, from the partner's facility to HP's DCs in either North America or Europe. The shipment process lasted one month. The demand for a network printer in Asia and Latin America was still minimal compared with the demand in North America or Europe. Similarly, all necessary accessories and localization materials are also shipped to the DCs from the respective suppliers. Both the printers and other materials are stocked at the DCs. When customer orders from resellers arrive, the printers are customized and localized, followed by appropriate labeling and packaging. Final transportation time, typically via truck, to the resellers in each region, the United States or Europe, ranges from a few days to approximately a week.

THE UNIVERSAL POWER SUPPLY DECISION

The Marketing Perspective

Jane Schushinski, marketing manager:

> I think changing to a universal power supply is a fantastic idea if it does not add cost to the product. Customers will not pay for features that they don't need, and universal power supply is irrelevant to them—the network printer is not like a portable hair

dryer that they would carry with them to travel around the world.

The biggest difficulty we have in marketing is not will there be demand for our product, but how much and where. HP makes great printers. We have always been the leader in innovation, reliability, and service. Rainbow is just the first of our series of new network printer line, and we expect to sell 25,000 per month of the product worldwide, with North America having about 60 percent of the market.

What hurts us is our inability to accurately forecast the mix of demands in geographical regions. We may think that Europe will need 10,000 units and North America 2,000 when the numbers may turn out to be 15 and 15,000 respectively. The problem lies in market conditions where increased competition and constantly changing technical innovations can drastically change the demand for a product in a few weeks. In addition, there are a lot of firms trying to compete on price. This too changes demand. Predicting these changes is quite difficult.

Finally, the long lead time from Japan causes my marketing staff to pull their hair out. We have to specify the market for the printer four and a half months ahead of delivery. We estimate that the entire life cycle of the product is at most 18 months. Four-and-a-half-months lead time in an 18-month market—it's ridiculous! The last thing that we want is a repeat of the VIPER debacle. That episode has my hair turning prematurely gray. We had so much of that product laying around we started calling our factory the "snake pit!"

It is easy to see why we love the universal power supply. With the universal power supply, we only need to estimate worldwide product demand four months ahead of time instead of numbers for each market. We can make the determination of individual market demands much later, and this postponement will help us create more accurate forecasts and help prevent expensive localization errors.

The VIPER was an earlier-generation HP laser printer. While the printer itself was very successful, the VIPER's story illustrates the difficulties with demand uncertainties. The VIPER was developed in the same manner as the new printer being considered. The main components of the VIPER were sourced from Japan and resulted in the same three-and-a-half-month lead time to the factories. The product required a dedicated power supply and fuser, 110V or 220V, and these were not interchangeable. Specification of the dedicated power supply, at the beginning of the three and a half months, committed the product either to the North American or the European market.

HP had not forecasted the correct mix of European and North American VIPER demand. The printer was sold out in Europe while demand in the United States was less than anticipated—HP filled a warehouse with unwanted North American printers that could not be used to satisfy demands for the European market without incurring heavy costs of disassembling the printer and reconfiguring the power supply and fuser in the engine. Eventually, heavy discounting, or "fire sales," was needed to rid the excess inventory, incurring very high cost. Buyers in the North American market now expected HP to reduce printer prices over time. Inadvertently, HP had undercut its ability to command premium prices in the market.

The Product Development Perspective

The product life cycle of printers can be divided into three stages: ramp-up, maturity, and end of life. The ramp-up period is the time from the initial introduction of the product until HP's production volume levels off. During this stage the product is usually the only printer on the market providing its distinctive features. The maturity stage reflects a period of increasing competition. Comparable printers will be introduced and price will become a more influential aspect of the product market. In the last stage, end of life, there is fierce competition on all fronts. Retail profits at this stage reach their lowest point as margins are squeezed. It is here that HP aims to introduce its next generation product.

When there is an imbalance of demand in North America and Europe, the division can live with the consequence of having excess inventory in one continent and shortages in another, or ship the excess from one continent to another (an operation known as "transshipment"), where the printer is reconfigured and sold.

In the end-of-life-stage, in addition to transshipping the products across the continent to correct for some of the imbalances, the division can also discount the product to create demand, dismantle the product and sell the parts to HP's service division in Roseville, or just write the product off.

Leo Linbeck's office was stacked high with what must have represented every available trade journal related to printing technology. From behind his HP workstation, he explained his point of view regarding the universal power supply:

> While Jane gains "responsiveness," I'm staring at a $30-per-unit cost increase. With the pressure to lower material costs, the design team would find it hard to justify this seemingly unnecessary increase in material cost. Although the printer engine costs about $1,000 each, so that $30 may not seem that much, every single dollar increase in material cost is a decrease of a dollar in our profit. That is why our design group is getting so much heat to get the material cost down. My concern is that we have no way to reliably predict how much value the so-called benefits of universal power supply truly represent.
>
> Now, I'm the first to admit that I'm no marketing expert, but it's pretty clear to me that if we could just learn to forecast demand better, this universal supply would literally be a worthless idea. Maybe pumping $30 per unit into improving the forecasting process makes more sense than sending it out the door in a cardboard box. At least in the first case we have some hope of recovering it again.
>
> I do agree with Jane's point regarding the benefits late in the product life cycle. Currently, reconfiguring the product with a different power supply is a real pain. We have to purchase new power supplies rated at the correct voltage, ship the printers across the Atlantic from the undersold region, swap the power supply, change the fuser electronic circuit and the fuser bulb, and, finally, distribute the product to retailers. The old power supplies have to be disposed of. To make matters worse, there are all kinds of regulatory issues that surface. A universal power supply eliminates all rework that is now required, but whether the gains it provides outweigh the increase in materials cost remains unclear.
>
> Whichever way we end up going, one thing is certain. We cannot delay our development schedule in order to make this decision. We need to decide on a strategy quickly and GO!

As early as 1991, in order to improve their cost position and speed up time to market, the printer divisions in Boise had implemented two new product development metrics. First, they had instituted cost reduction goals for each new generation of printer. The costs captured in this measure included labor, material, and manufacturing overhead. The second metric, called break-even time (BET), had been mandated by upper management. It measured the time from project initiation to break even, defined as the point where total discounted cash outflow equaled total discounted cash inflow.

The Finance Perspective

Neatly arranged on David Hooper's desk were the latest sets of pro-forma income statements and balance sheets for the new project. Pointing out the effect of the universal power supply on income, he noted,

> If we incorporate the universal power supply and sell 450,000 units of Rainbow, it will cost us approximately $13.5 million in additional material costs. If we are not able to pass this increase along to the customer, or at least our retailers, that comes straight out of our bottom line.
>
> I sure agree that there will be benefits from universal power supply. May be we should take a hard look at the costs of stockouts and inventory.
>
> Demand fluctuates during each of the three life-cycle periods and so do the costs of making or missing a sale. We typically estimate that for each lost sale we actually forgo multiple times our profit margin. The reason for this is that if a customer buys a competitive brand due to our inability to keep the resellers on stock, there is a chance that he will stay with that brand when he purchases a printer in the future. This effect might cover three or four generations of printers. Moreover, we may lose the profits from the sales of consumables such as toner cartridges and perhaps even other HP peripheral products.
>
> The cost of stockouts when the product is first introduced into the market is even higher, as the potential word-of-mouth and publicity effects can damage the future sales and ultimate success of the product. On the

other hand, the cost of stockouts at the end-of-life stage is probably considerably lower, as there is less fear of adverse effect on future sales, and the resellers might in some cases steer the customer to wait for the new, incoming, replacement product.

Although the cost of stockouts in the ramp-up stage is the highest, it is also this stage when we know the least about the market response to our new product, and our forecast errors are usually much greater. I understand that Sara's material planning people had done some homework and found that the standard deviation of our monthly forecast error (a new measure of forecast accuracy that the group has started to measure) was close to 40 percent of the average monthly demand in both markets in the mature and end-of-life stages. Their perception is that the corresponding percentage is 80–90 percent in the ramp-up stage.

The other major cost that I have to monitor is inventory. My financial analysts have estimated that our annual holding cost rate is approximately 30 percent, which covers warehousing, insurance, cost of capital, and shrinkage.

The Manufacturing Perspective

Sara Donohoe, manufacturing engineering manager, commented,

I think the universal power supply is a great idea. This innovation will improve our flexibility to respond to orders in two key ways. The first is the obvious gain of delaying the regional allocation decision by two and a half months. I'm sure marketing has expounded on this ad infinitum. The second gain is more subtle. You see, while transshipment has always been possible in theory, we have avoided it whenever possible. Let me explain.

At the ramp-up stage, we always try to stockpile our DC's with loads of printers so that we don't ever run out of stock, and, given the high cost of shortage at this stage, this seems reasonable. There is not much of a need for transshipment. In the mature phase, if we keep doing what everyone at HP does and keep enough safety stock to meet the standard service target of around 98 percent then again, the chance of our needing transshipment is still small. However, I am not sure if we want to keep having 98 percent service goals at the end-of-life stage, and indeed that is when transshipments will be most needed.

The whole idea behind transshipment is to adjust inventories in response to market demand. To do this effectively, you need to move the product quickly. Unfortunately, to send a printer by air across the Atlantic costs us $75. Sea shipment reduces costs significantly to approximately $15/unit, but a month out on the ocean does not do much for responsiveness, which is exactly what you're trying to achieve! In addition to the transportation cost, we know how tedious and complex it is to reconfigure the power supply and fuser. I would put my conservative estimate of the activity-based cost for reconfiguration to be at least $250 per printer.

As you might imagine, the quality people go nuts when they find out we're doing this. How can you establish a controlled process if you only do something once a year? Even worse, since the rework involves electrical components, safety standards require the reconfiguration process to be certified by Underwriter's Laboratory. If you've ever dealt with UL, you'll realize how much trouble you'd have getting a process like this approved.

The universal power supply would allow us to avoid this mess, making transshipment a distinct possibility. The cost of reconfiguration is almost zero. It is at least a possibility, although I'm not sure who would coordinate it or decide when to ship . . . our friends in distribution, I guess.

My only real concern with developing the universal supply is the potential power play that could emerge at the time of allocation of the production build to the two regions. Again, I would like some visibility and control over how many units I can count on receiving.

The Distribution Perspective

Rob Seigel runs the North America distribution center. Rob worked in a variety of positions before he moved to management and his present position.

Given a universal product, transshipment won't present a big problem for the DC; it's just another shipment to us and we can easily "localize" the product by adding manuals and plug adapters at the DC. Personally, however, I feel like it's a great way to chew up company profits. I can just see us sending 1,000 units to Germany in February only to have them ship another 1,000 back to me in March. Both actions may seem to make sense at the time the decision was made, but in the end the company's out hundreds of thousands of dollars!

Who is going to make the decision to shift inventory from DC to DC? I can see a real firefight if one DC wants more but the other is unwilling to give up its excess. We all have pressures for high customer service and even if I have some excesses now, that does not mean that I may not need it next month. Sending the product to Europe helps their performance, but what about mine? I hope I do not have to do it! One thing I don't have time for is spending half of my day on the phone to Germany trying to negotiate a transfer.

I guess, though, if we can avoid what happened with the VIPER we have got to be better off. That was an interesting time. See that warehouse, pretty big. It was so full we stopped leaving the aisles clear and just stacked printers solid, from floor to ceiling, all the way from front to back. I would pay money to prevent that from happening again. All other work grinds to a halt when a crisis like that emerges.

THE DECISION

The team had decision-making authority, but they would have to defend their decision to upper management. From past experience, they knew that if they decided to adopt the universal power supply, management would want to ensure they had performed adequate analyses of all the costs and benefits of such a decision, as well as some estimate of the risks involved. In addition, some consideration of how the decision would impact future generations of products will have to be made.

CASE DISCUSSION QUESTIONS

1. In what way is a universal power supply a postponement strategy?
2. What are the costs and benefits of a universal power supply (feel free to make assumptions)?
3. How would such costs and benefits be different over the product life cycle?
4. Besides deciding on a universal power supply, what other operational improvements can you suggest to HP Boise?
5. What would be your recommendations about the adoption of a universal power supply?

CHAPTER 12

Customer Value

CASE: Made to Measure

On a Saturday afternoon in August, Carolyn Thurmond walked into a J.C. Penney store in Atlanta's Northlake Mall and bought a white Stafford wrinkle-free dress shirt for her husband, size 17 neck, 34/35 sleeve.

On Monday morning, a computer technician in Hong Kong downloaded a record of the sale. By Wednesday afternoon, a factory worker in Taiwan had packed an identical replacement shirt into a bundle to be shipped back to the Atlanta store.

This speedy process, part of a streamlined supply chain and production system for dress shirts that was years in the making, has put Penney at the forefront of the continuing revolution in U.S. retailing. In an industry where the goal is speedy turnaround of merchandise, Penney stores now hold almost no extra inventory of house-brand dress shirts. Less than a decade ago, Penney would have had thousands of them warehoused across the U.S., tying up capital and slowly going out of style.

The new process is one from which Penney is conspicuously absent. The entire program is designed and operated by TAL Apparel Ltd., a closely held Hong Kong shirt maker. TAL collects point-of-sale data for Penney's shirts directly from its stores in North America, then runs the numbers through a computer model it designed. The Hong Kong company then decides how many shirts to make, and in what styles, colors, and sizes. The manufacturer sends the shirts directly to each Penney store, bypassing the retailer's warehouses—and corporate decision makers.

TAL is a no-name giant, the maker of one in eight dress shirts sold in the U.S. Its close relationship with U.S. retailers is part of a power shift taking place in global manufacturing. As retailers strive to cut costs and keep pace with consumer tastes, they are coming to depend more on suppliers that can respond swiftly to their changing needs. This opens opportunities for savvy manufacturers, and TAL has rushed in, even starting to take over such critical areas as sales forecasting and inventory management.

On the weekend Ms. Thurmond made her purchase, the same Atlanta store sold two sage-colored shirts of similar size but of another Penney house brand, Crazy Horse. That left none of this size and color in stock at the store. Based on past sales data, TAL's computers determined that the ideal inventory level for that brand, style, color, and size at that particular store was two. Without consulting Penney, a TAL factory in Taiwan made two new shirts. It sent one by ship, but to get one in the store quickly, it dispatched one by air. TAL paid the shipping but sent a bill for the shirts to Penney.

Source: Gabriel Kahn. *The Wall Street Journal,* Eastern Edition, September 11, 2003.

Instead of asking Penney what it would like to buy, "I tell them how many shirts they just bought," says Harry Lee, TAL's managing director.

TAL was born in 1947 after Chinese border guards blocked Mr. Lee's uncle, C. C. Lee, from importing state-of-the-art weaving machines to Shanghai for fear they would hurt the local textile industry. So the uncle set up shop in Hong Kong, then under British rule. With low-cost Asian manufacturing, TAL thrived. It supplies labels such as J. Crew, Calvin Klein, Banana Republic, Tommy Hilfiger, Liz Claiborne, Ralph Lauren, and Brooks Brothers. Harry Lee, 60 years old, joined the family business 30 years ago after earning a Ph.D. in electrical engineering in the U.S. and serving a stint at Bell Labs.

Now, TAL is negotiating a deal to manage Brooks Brothers' shirt inventory the same way it does Penney's. For Lands' End, TAL stitches made-to-measure pants in Malaysia and flies them straight to U.S. customers, with a shipping invoice that carries the Lands' End logo.

These retailers have been willing to cede some functions once seen as central because TAL can do them better and more cheaply. Rodney Birkins Jr., vice president for sourcing of J.C. Penney Private Brands Inc., describes as "phenomenal" the added efficiency Penney has been able to achieve with TAL. Before it started working with TAL a decade ago, Penney would routinely hold up to six months of inventory in its warehouses and three months' worth at stores. Now, for the Stafford and Crazy Horse shirt lines that TAL handles, "it's zero," Mr. Birkins says.

With decisions made at the factory, TAL can respond instantly to changes in consumer demand: stepping up production if there is a spike in sales or dialing it down if there's a slump. The system "directly links the manufacturer to the customer," says Mr. Birkins. "That is the future."

Retailers across the board have sought to lower the amount of inventory they hold, both to cut costs and to reduce goods sold at a markdown. That means working more closely with suppliers. Wal-Mart Stores Inc. has pioneered a system that opens its computer system to suppliers all over the world. Suppliers can track how their items are selling overall and even at individual stores. They can anticipate demand and communicate better with Wal-Mart buyers. But Wal-Mart still handles all the warehousing and distribution, and it stops short of allowing its suppliers to place their own orders.

The degree of power Penney turned over to TAL is radical. "You are giving away a pretty important function when you outsource your inventory management," says Wai-Chan Chan, a principal with McKinsey & Co. in Hong Kong. "That's something that not a lot of retailers want to part with."

Penney, too, was reluctant, and took the step only after building up trust over years of working with TAL. But Penney now has let TAL take the arrangement a step further: designing new shirt styles and handling their market testing.

TAL's design teams in New York and Dallas come up with a new style, and within a month its factories churn out 100,000 new shirts. For a test, these are offered for sale at 50 Penney stores. Not nearly all will sell, but offering a wide array of colors and sizes helps to provide a true test of consumer sentiment. After analyzing sales data for a month, TAL—not Penney—decides how many of the new shirts to make and in what colors.

Because TAL manages the entire process, from design to ordering yarn, it can bring a new style from the testing stage to full retail rollout in four months, much faster than Penney could on its own.

The system in effect lets consumers, not marketing managers, pick the styles. "When you can put something on the floor that the customer has already voted on is when we make a lot of money," says Penney's Mr. Birkins.

Like the retailer, TAL changed its methods in response to economic pressures. TAL has seen the price of its shirts fall almost 20 percent over five years as low-cost textile manufacturing exploded in China's Guangdong province. It could jump even more in 2005, when textile-importing nations such as the U.S. must complete a phaseout of import quotas for countries in the World Trade Organization. Most of TAL's manufacturing is in places with higher wages than Guangdong, such as Thailand, Malaysia, Taiwan, and Hong Kong. So "our customers need a reason to buy from us," Mr. Lee says.

TAL learned the supply-chain business the hard way. In 1988, a U.S. wholesaler that handled its shirts, Damon Holdings Inc., failed. Mr. Lee, fearing a loss of sales and figuring he understood the wholesaling business, bought Damon. The result was "a big shock." A manager TAL had put in charge of Damon went on a buying spree, and soon its warehouses were crammed with two years' worth of shirt inventory that was going out of style. Shirts that cost $10 to make had to be sold for $3. By the time TAL closed Damon in 1991, it had lost $50 million.

But the experience started Mr. Lee thinking about a way to do business more efficiently, by linking his Asian factories directly with U.S. stores. "The failure gave us a head start," he says.

Around the same time, TAL had begun supplying Penney with house-brand shirts. Mr. Lee saw that Penney was holding up to nine months of inventory, twice what most competitors kept. "You didn't have to be a genius to realize you can do a lot better than that," he says. Visiting Penney headquarters in Plano, Texas, he floated a radical solution: Why not have TAL supply shirts directly to Penney stores instead of sending bulk orders to a Penney warehouse?

Mr. Birkins was skeptical. But he saw that savings could be huge. It cost Penney 29 cents a shirt to have its warehouse workers sort out orders in the U.S. TAL could do it for 14 cents.

And such a system would let Penney respond more quickly to consumer demand. This had been a problem for the retailer, which often needed months to restock hot-selling styles. Stores ended up missing sales of these styles while holding less-popular models that they had to move at a discount.

Mr. Birkins pitched the idea to his Penney bosses. It met a brick wall. Each division found fault with it. Executives who ran warehousing said the plan could prove disastrous if TAL didn't deliver on time or to the right stores. Technology people worried that the computer systems wouldn't be compatible. The plan sat for several years, until a senior Penney manager began a push to improve efficiency by reducing inventory across the board. "We used that as our wedge," Mr. Birkins says. "That turned it."

It took TAL a year to set up the system in Asia. Mr. Lee then began by supplying a single Penney store in Kansas City, Mo. He enlisted a Chinese numerologist to choose an auspicious day: June 20, 1997. Factory workers toasted the occasion with champagne. Things went smoothly, and within months, TAL was delivering shirts directly to all of Penney's stores in North America. Inventory levels dropped.

There was one clear downside: If a store sold out of a style of shirts, it couldn't quickly get some more from a regional warehouse. So TAL agreed to sometimes send shirts to stores by air freight—a costly step but one TAL would take to keep the customer happy.

Soon Mr. Lee saw another opportunity. Penney's sales forecasts often missed, sometimes overestimating shirt needs by as much as two months' worth. Sales forecasting is one of the most difficult tasks for retailers, yet one that's increasingly important to get right as inventories get tighter. Penney blames the problem on older-generation software.

Convinced he could do better, Mr. Lee pitched an even more outlandish idea: Why not let TAL staff in Hong Kong forecast how many shirts Penney's stores would need each week? This time, Penney executives were listening.

Mr. Lee was operating on a simple premise. If he could get sales data straight from the stores, he could take the consumer's pulse and respond instantly, ordering more fabric and increasing production where needed. Penney buyers would just be in the way. "I can do all the pieces of the puzzle," he says.

He hired dozens of programmers, who designed a computer model to estimate an ideal inventory of house-brand shirts for each of Penney's 1,040 North American stores, by style, color, and size. Penney provided him with goals for how often stores' inventory should be replenished, then stepped back and let him do the rest. "It's on autopilot," says Mr. Birkins, "and TAL is the autopilot."

TAL's computer model began to outpace the Penney system still used for the retailer's other merchandise. For some shirt models, stores could now keep half as much in stock as they had previously.

The system hasn't been flawless. Ming Chen, a manager at TAL's Taiwan factory, recalls a few occasions when TAL underestimated Penney's needs significantly. She says the factory "sacrificed other customers" to rush out Penney's order first and sent some shirts by air freight to be sure they arrived on time. Costing 10 times as much as ocean shipping, sending shirts by air was "a painful decision," she says. "But sometimes you have to decide which customers you're going to take care of."

Sitting in his Hong Kong headquarters, in a neighborhood whose factories have given way to office space, Mr. Lee is thinking of ways to push his idea to the next level. He would like to form a joint venture with Penney that would manage the supply chain for some other manufacturers that supply the retailer. TAL has already started doing this with underwear. "Why not consolidate it all here?" he asks.

Mr. Birkins says Penney is seriously considering the idea.

By the end of this chapter, you should be able to answer the following questions:

- What is customer value?
- How is customer value measured?
- How do you match the supply chain to product characteristics and sales strategy?
- How is information technology used to enhance customer value in the supply chain?
- How does supply chain management contribute to customer value?
- How can a company add value to its offering in order to compete?

12.1 INTRODUCTION

In today's customer-driven market, it is not the product or service itself that matters most, but the perceived value to the customer of the entire relationship with a company. The way companies measure the quality of their product and services has evolved from internal quality assurance to external customer satisfaction and from there to *customer value*. Internal quality measures, such as the number of production defects, dominated company goals in the era of supply-driven manufacturing. The ability to provide customers with quality product was the main goal. External customer satisfaction measures were focused on developing an understanding of the company's current customers, their use of a company's products, and their impression of its service. This provided valuable information about current customers and generated ideas for areas for improvement within the company. The current emphasis on customer value goes a step further by establishing the reasons a customer chooses one company's product over another's, and looking at the entire range of product, services, and intangibles that constitute the company's image and brand.

Thinking in terms of customer value promotes a broader look at a company's offerings and its customers. It requires learning why customers purchase, continue to purchase, or defect from a company. What are their preferences and needs and how can they be satisfied? Which customers are profitable and have potential for revenue growth, and which customers may lead to losses? Assumptions about customer value need to be examined carefully to make sure the trade-offs made are the correct ones. Some examples include:

- Does the customer value low prices more than superior customer support services?
- Does the customer prefer next-day delivery or lower prices?
- Does the customer prefer to purchase the item in a store that specializes in this type of item or from a large mega-store that provides one-stop shopping opportunities?

These are critical questions for any business, and should be the driving force behind business strategy and performance measures.

EXAMPLE 12-1 NIRMA

In a highly competitive detergents and toilet soaps market of India, **Nirma** is known for delivering customer value by focusing on low cost. It has adopted numerous value analysis activities to cut down the cost at competitive quality. The flat distribution network pioneered by Nirma is considered one of the lowest cost FMCG distribution networks in India. With a network of over two million retail outlets, Nirma boasts of having the patronage of more than 40 million loyal consumers in India [295].

Indeed, *logistics,* previously considered a back-office function, has evolved into the highly visible discipline of supply chain management partly because of this change in perspective. Supply chain management is naturally an important component in fulfilling customer needs and providing value. Equally important, supply chain management determines the availability of products, how fast they will arrive in the market, and at what cost. Our definition of *supply chain management* (see Chapter 1) implies that the ability to respond to customer requirements is the most basic function of this discipline. This function refers not only to the physical attributes of product distribution, but also to related information, such as production or delivery status, and the ability to access this information.

Supply chain management also can impact the important customer value of price by significantly reducing costs. Dell's strategy of reducing its supply chain costs by postponing the final product assembly until after the purchase (i.e., by building to order) has allowed Dell to underprice its competitors in the personal computer industry. Wal-Mart has been able to lower costs by introducing the cross-docking strategy and by engaging in strategic partnering with its suppliers. Finally, the policy of everyday low prices applied by Wal-Mart and other retailers also is motivated in large part by supply chain efficiencies.

EXAMPLE 12-2

The downfall of Kmart is attributed in part to its strategy of competing on price with Wal-Mart. Wal-Mart's goal since the early 80s was to provide customers with access to goods when and where they want them, and to develop cost structures that enable competitive pricing. The key to achieving this goal was to make supply chain efficiencies the centerpiece of its strategy. On the other hand, Kmart's strong desire to keep up earnings discouraged investments in supply chain efficiencies and, in particular, in information technology. By the late 90s, it became clear that Kmart's supply chain was not as efficient as that of Wal-Mart [225].

The example suggests the importance of linking pricing strategies with supply chain efficiencies. We discuss this issue in Chapter 13.

Customer value drives changes and improvements in the supply chain, some forced by customer and competitor activities and others undertaken to achieve competitive advantage. Furthermore, large manufacturers, distributors, or retailers place certain requirements on their suppliers that force them to adopt supply chains that will make these requests feasible. Specifically, Wal-Mart requires many of its suppliers to practice vendor-managed inventory. More recently, in January 2005, Wal-Mart went live with RFID technology and mandated its use for its suppliers, with the goal of improving replenishment times and decreasing the amount of out-of-stock items, see Chapter 15. Large manufacturers such as Hewlett-Packard and Lucent Technologies require that their parts manufacturers have 100 percent availability of stock for the parts they use. In return, they are willing to commit to a single supplier for the product or service, or at least commit to a minimum volume of purchases from a primary supplier.

Customer value is also important for determining the type of supply chain required to serve the customer and what services are required to retain customers. A company's supply chain strategy is determined by the type of products or services it offers and the value of various elements of this offering to the customer. For example, if customers value one-stop shopping, that would entail carrying a large number of products and options, even if that is costly in terms of inventory management. If customers value innovative products, then companies who produce them need to apply their supply chain to supply these products efficiently while demand lasts. If a company offers personal customization of its products, then its supply chain needs to be flexible enough to provide the infrastructure for this offering. Thus, the supply chain needs to be considered in any product and sales strategy and could, in itself, provide competitive advantages leading to increased customer value.

Finally, the "Made to Measure" case study illustrates the importance of providing innovative services to customers, in this case managing the entire product supply chain. The case also illustrates the importance of developing supply chain management as a core competency and leveraging it to succeed in an extremely competitive business.

12.2 THE DIMENSIONS OF CUSTOMER VALUE

We have defined customer value as the way the customer perceives the entire company's offerings, including products, services, and other intangibles. The customer perception can be broken into several dimensions:

- Conformance to requirements.
- Product selection.
- Price and brand.
- Value-added services.
- Relationships and experiences.

The list of dimensions starts with the essentials—the first three items above—and goes on to more sophisticated types of features that may not always be critical. However, the less-critical features can be mined for ideas to create a unique way to add value and differentiation to a company's offering. In this section, we suggest how each dimension is affected by supply chain management and how, in turn, it needs to take into account the customer values inherent in each dimension.

12.2.1 Conformance to Requirements

The ability to offer what the customer wants and needs is a basic requirement to which supply chain management contributes by creating availability and selection. Marshall Fisher calls it the *market mediation* function of the supply chain [82]. This function is distinct from the supply chain physical function of converting raw materials into goods and shipping them through the chain to the customer. The costs associated with the market mediation function occur when there are differences between supply and demand. If the supply exceeds demand, there are inventory costs throughout the supply chain; if demand exceeds supply, there are lost sales and possibly market share.

If product demand is predictable, as in *functional items* such as diapers, soup, or milk, market mediation is not a major issue. Clearly, efficient supply chains for functional items can reduce costs by focusing on reducing inventory, transportation, and other costs. This is the strategy Campbell Soup and Procter & Gamble employ for their supply chains.

However, when dealing with fashion items or other high-variability items, the nature of demand can create large costs due to lost sales or excess inventory. These high-variability products require responsive supply chains, which stress short lead times, flexibility, and speed over cost efficiencies. When the supply chain strategy does not match the product characteristics, there are major implications in the ability to conform to the market, as illustrated in the following example.

EXAMPLE 12-3

Zara is part of Inditex, which is one of the world's largest fashion distributors, with eight sales formats and 2,951 stores in 64 countries. The first Zara shop opened its doors in 1975 in La Coruña (Spain), the city that saw the group's early beginnings and is now home to its central offices. Its stores can now be found in the most important shopping districts of more than 400 cities in Europe, the Americas, Asia, and Africa.

Zara stores are managed with the founder Amancio Ortega's philosophy that "you need to have five fingers touching the factory and five touching the customer." Zara's super responsive supply chain can design, produce, deliver a new garment, and put it on display in its over 650 stores worldwide in 15 days. This ability to provide a large variety of the latest designs quickly and in limited quantities enables it to collect 85 percent of the full ticket price while the industry average is 60 to 70 percent. As a result, its net margins are much higher than the competition's.

Zara does many things in an unconventional way and defies industry trends.

- It keeps half of its production in house instead of outsourcing, as is common.
- It intentionally leaves extra capacity in its warehouses.
- It manufactures and produces in small batches rather than try to achieve economies of scale.
- It manages all design, warehousing, distribution, and logistics itself instead of using third parties.
- It holds its retail stores to a rigid timetable for placing orders and receiving stock.
- It puts price tags on items before they are shipped rather than at each store.
- It leaves large empty areas in the stores and tolerates, even encourages, stock-outs.

According to [75], Zara's Success is due to conformance to a system that is built on three principles:

- **Closing the communication loop.** The supply chain is organized so it can track material and product in real time but also close the information loop both for hard data and anecdotal.
- **Sticking to a rhythm across the supply chain.** Zara is willing to spend money on anything that will make its supply chain fast and responsive.
- **Leveraging capital assets to increase supply chain flexibility.** It uses the investment in production and distribution facilities to make the supply chain responsive to new and changing demand patterns. For instance, it produces the more complicated product in house and outsources the simple ones.

Conformance to requirements also is achieved through attention to **customer access,** the ability to easily find and purchase a product. For companies such as McDonald's, Starbucks, and Walgreens, access involves prime real estate. Providing mail, phone, and Web access in addition to, or instead of, stores can enhance the customer's ability to purchase the product conveniently. Finally, **access** includes the perception of providing the consumers with a store or Web site layout that makes it easy to find and purchase the product they are seeking [57]. Grainger's success in integrating the Web with its older business channels is a good example of the ability to provide customers with the access they need to a company's services.

EXAMPLE 12-4

The business that William W. Grainger founded in 1927 has been one of the success stories of the Internet. Grainger wanted to provide an efficient solution to the need for a speedy and consistent supply of electric motors. The MotorBook, as it was originally called, was the basis for today's Grainger® Catalog. The product line has since expanded to over 220,000 MRO supplies and parts. Grainger is the largest firm in the market for industrial products, with 1999 revenues of $4.5 billion. In 1995, Grainger started its Web initiative with a variety of goals:

- Provide customers with access to all the products Grainger makes available, over 220,000, and not just the 86,500 that could be presented in the paper catalog.
- Provide customers with much better tools for searching, locating, and selecting the product that best suits their needs.
- Deliver products the same day from the branch closest to the customer who placed the order, or ship them from one of Grainger's five regional distribution centers and have them delivered the next day.

Grainger faces a variety of challenges:

- Grainger offers 65 million different price points so no "one price fits all" and the Internet needs to honor each business account's unique pricing structure.
- Servicing business accounts requires checking credit and establishing payment guidelines.
- Real-time inventory availability—many customers looking for parts cannot wait and need immediate service.
- Compensating the sales force—Grainger decided to pay commissions on Internet orders, thus getting a buy-in from their sales reps, who have relationships with the customers and can encourage customers to use the Web, which is more cost-effective than other channels.

The initiative had a huge impact on Grainger. In 1999, Grainger spent $20 million for the development, marketing, and customer service of grainger.com, which led to $100 million worth of orders. In the first half of 2000, Grainger generated $120 million in revenue with the size of the average order on the Web site being $250, compared with $140 for branch and phone orders [219].

12.2.2 Product Selection

Many products come in a large variety of options, styles, colors, and shapes. For instance, a car may come in five styles, 10 different exterior colors, 10 interior colors, and with automatic or manual transmission—a total of 1,000 configurations. The difficulty is that distributors and retailers need to stock most of the various configurations and combinations of products. As explained in Chapter 2, this proliferation of options makes it difficult to predict customer demand for a specific model, thus forcing retailers and distributors to build large and diverse inventories.

The contribution of product proliferation to customer value is difficult to analyze and understand. Three successful business trends exist:

- Specializing in offering one type of product. Examples include companies such as Starbucks and Subway.
- Mega-stores that allow one-stop shopping for a large variety of products. Examples include Wal-Mart and Target.
- Mega-stores that specialize in one product area. Examples here include Home Depot, Office Max, and Staples.

These trends also have emerged on the Internet, where some sites have been successful in offering a large variety of different products while others specialize in a single offering. For instance, ballsonline.com specializes in sports balls of all types, theworldofgolf.com in all things golf, while amazon.com is a virtual shopping mall with many shopping options beyond books.

One interesting aspect of the Internet is "the long tail" phenomenon that occurs in the almost limitless market of supply and demand that has been opened by the Internet. In this market, as described in *The*

Long Tail, by Chris Anderson [7], the lack of physical or local restrictions allows retailers to focus and make revenue on the less popular items in their catalogues. These items appear as a tail when ranking books or DVDs by popularity. In fact, companies such as Amazon, Netflix, and Raphsody made between a quarter and half of their revenues in 2005 on titles not carried by traditional retailers such as Wal-Mart, which carries only the most popular titles. See Figure 12-1 for a comparison of Rhapsody and Wal-Mart in 2004 and 2005.

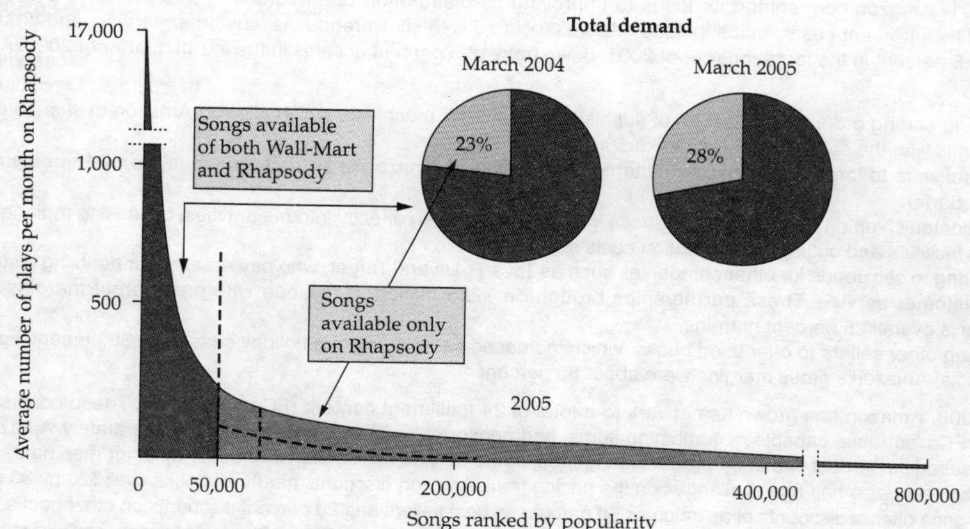

FIGURE 12-1 The Rhapsody data—2004 versus 2005.
Source: Chris Anderson [7].

The PC industry has seen significant changes in the way products are sold. In the mid-1980s, PCs were sold through specialized stores such as Egghead. At the beginning of the 1990s, PCs were sold in department stores such as Sears. More recently, however, the direct business model has caught on. Nevertheless, Dell, the leader in the direct business model, announced in July 2006 that it is opening its own retail stores in order to compete with Apple. This suggests that there may be a need for a company to sell its products through various outlets to reach the largest number of customers. In fact, companies such as Circuit City enable customers to shop on the Web and pick up the items at the store.

As observed earlier, the proliferation of products and the difficulty in predicting demand for a specific model force retailers and distributors to hold large inventories.

There are several ways to control the inventory problem of a large variety of configurations or products.

1. The approach pioneered by Dell is the **build-to-order model,** where the configuration is determined only when the order comes in. This is an effective way to implement the push–pull strategy discussed in Chapter 6 by employing the concept of postponement introduced in Chapter 11. An interesting way to implement this strategy is described in the following example.
2. A different strategy, suitable for products with long manufacturing lead times, such as vehicles, is to keep **larger inventories at major distribution centers**. These distribution centers allow the

EXAMPLE 12-5

Amazon.com is the most famous and successful e-tailer. It started in 1995 by selling a huge variety of books and later added music and videos. More recently, Amazon started selling toys, electronics, and other merchandise. Amazon's fulfillment strategy has evolved over time. Initially, the company did not hold any inventory. When a customer ordered a book, Amazon would transfer the order to Ingram Books. In 1999, however, Amazon established its own seven large warehouses, referred to as fulfillment centers (one warehouse was later closed) and started shipping directly to the customers. Today, Amazon has 16 fulfillment centers in the United States.

In 2001, Amazon.com shifted its focus to improving its distribution operations in a push towards profit. It has improved its fulfillment costs, which include costs associated with six warehouses, customer service, and credit card fees, to 9.8 percent in the fourth quarter of 2001, down from 13.5 percent of sales in the fourth quarter of 2000. Amazon did this by

- Improving sorting order and utilization of sophisticated packing machines, which allowed Amazon to ship 35 percent more units with the same number of workers as the previous year.
- Using software to forecast purchasing patterns, which allowed Amazon to slash inventory levels by 18 percent in the fourth quarter.
- Consolidated shipping of 40 percent of goods into full trucks driven directly into major cities, bypassing regional postal sorting facilities and cutting transportation costs significantly.
- Partnering to sell goods for other companies such as Toys 'R' Us and Target, who pay Amazon for handling distribution and customer service. These partnerships brought in $225 million in revenue with gross profit margins double Amazon's overall 25 percent margins.
- Allowing other sellers to offer used books, which increased sales during the holiday season by 38 percent. For these products, Amazon's gross margins were about 85 percent.

By 2006, Amazon has grown its network to a total of 24 fulfillment centers (FCs) worldwide. These consist of two types of FCs: sortable, capable of combining items, and nonsortable, for larger items shipped separately. Amazon also has increased its product line to 34 product categories, some fulfilled by Amazon and some by other merchants.

Amazon.com also has had challenges on the pricing front: Amazon discounts nearly all books over $20 by 30 percent. Amazon once offered discounts of as much as 50 percent on best sellers and 20 percent discounts on other books. Early in 2001, the company started to raise book prices—with 5 percent to 10 percent discounts more common—only to reverse the increases as sales fell. In the book business, few other retailers have offered discounts, other than for best sellers. There is good reason Amazon can afford to cut book prices: the average book may sit on the shelf of a store for six months or a year before it is bought. The cost of this inventory in a chain of hundreds of stores is huge. Amazon, on the other hand, can keep just one or two copies in its warehouse—and still make the title available to the whole country—and restock as quickly as customers buy books [111].

manufacturer to reduce inventory levels by taking advantage of risk pooling (see Chapter 2 and the discussion of inventory pooling in Section 7.2.3) and delivering the vehicles quickly to customers. General Motors has initiated this approach with its Cadillac unit in Florida. Dealers can order cars that they do not have on their lot from a regional warehouse that can ship the car out in a day. Of course, two major issues need to be raised when considering this strategy:

- *Inventory costs of cars at the regional warehouse*. Is the manufacturer (i.e., General Motors) going to pay for the inventory at the regional warehouse? If it is, then there is an incentive for the dealers to reduce inventory in their lots and reduce their cost while increasing that of the manufacturer.
- Equalizing small and large dealers. If all dealers have access to the regional warehouse, then there is no difference between the different dealers. Thus, it is difficult to see why large dealers would be interested in participating in such an arrangement, especially if they are going to pay for inventory at the regional warehouse.

3. Another possibility is to offer **a fixed set of options that cover most customer requirements**. For instance, Honda offers a limited number of options on its cars. Dell offers few options for modems

or software that can be installed on its machines, although the overall number of possible configurations remains quite high. Indeed, large product variety is not required in all cases. For example, a dysfunctional level of variety exists in many grocery products—28 varieties of toothpaste, to give one example [82]. It is not clear whether this variety actually adds any value for the customer.

12.2.3 Price and Brand

Price of products and the level of service are essential parts of customer value. Although the price may not be the only factor a customer considers, there may be a narrow price range that is acceptable for certain products. For instance, for commodity products—even relatively sophisticated items such as personal computers are commodities—there is very little flexibility in price. Therefore, companies achieve cost advantages through innovations in their supply chains. As we have seen in Dell's direct business model, allowing clients to configure their own systems and building a supporting supply chain not only improve customer value but also reduce costs.

Wal-Mart has been a supply chain innovator, which has enabled it to provide low-cost merchandise and undercut its competition (see Example 12-1). In addition, we have seen that the "everyday low pricing" policy applied by retailers such as Wal-Mart and manufacturers such as Procter & Gamble is an important tool in reducing the bullwhip effect (see Chapter 5). This policy appeals to customers who do not have to worry about buying at the wrong time, and to the retailer and manufacturer who do not need to plan for demand variations as a result of promotions.

An important factor affecting the product price is its brand. In today's market, there are fewer salespeople and more customers looking for supermarket-style shopping [205]. This is true across a wide variety of retail environments, from auto superstores to e-tailers.

EXAMPLE 12-6

Consider prices for books and CDs sold on the Internet. A study conducted in 2000 found "substantial and systematic differences in price across retailers on the Internet. Prices posted on the Internet differ by an average of 33 percent for books and 25 percent for CDs." More importantly, Internet retailers with the lowest price do not necessarily sell more. For instance, the research found that Books.com had a lower price than Amazon.com in 99 percent of the cases, yet Amazon had about 80 percent of the market at the time of the study, while Books.com had about 2 percent. One way to explain this behavior is through "trust consumers have for the various Internet retailers and the associated value of branding" [31].

Interestingly, the Internet and its impact on consumer behavior have increased the importance of brand names, because a brand name is a guarantee of quality in the buyer's mind. Brand names such as Mercedes cars, Rolex watches, and Coach purses can be promoted for high quality and prestige and command much higher prices than products that lack this aura. Furthermore, the higher price in itself may be a large part of the prestige and perceived quality. The product's high margins will require a focus on service level, and hence the supply chain needs to be more responsive; the increase in supply chain cost will be offset by the higher margin.

EXAMPLE 12-7

One of the key elements in the rise of Federal Express as the most successful small package carrier is that it was the first carrier to narrow its focus to overnight delivery, thereby owning the word "overnight" in the market. Even though there are cheaper alternatives, customers are willing to pay a premium to ship by Federal Express because of the brand name and the perception of dependability it conveys [205].

In many industries, "product" typically means both the "physical product" and associated "services." Typically, pricing the physical product is not as difficult as pricing services. At the same time, it is quite difficult to compare different services and, as a result, variability in pricing increases. This suggests opportunities for companies that develop new offerings and services that are more difficult to turn into commodities. As we will see below, there is a challenge in turning these opportunities into offerings that customers are actually willing to pay for.

In Chapter 13, we examine strategic pricing, where companies can employ sophisticated analysis to align customer service preferences with supply chain costs.

12.2.4 Value-Added Services

Many companies cannot compete on product price alone in an economy that has an overabundance of supply. Therefore, they need to consider other sources of income. This drives companies toward value-added offerings that differentiate them from competitors and provide them with more profitable pricing structures.

Value-added services, such as support and maintenance, can be a major factor in the purchase of some products, especially technical products. Indeed, many companies are now adding more services around their products [128]. This is due in part to the following:

1. The commoditization of products, where only the price matters and all other features are identical, reducing profitability and competitive advantage from the sale of products alone.
2. The need to get closer to the customer.
3. The increase in information technology capabilities that make this offering possible.

A sophisticated service offering is illustrated in the following example.

EXAMPLE 12-8

Goodyear Tire & Rubber Co. provides truck manufacturer Navistar International Transportation Corp. with an automated supply chain service that includes delivering mounted tires sequenced for just-in-time use on automated assembly lines. Goodyear has a 13-person information technology group dedicated to the tire maker's materials management division. This division acts as systems integrator on supply chain projects it takes on with wheel manufacturer Accuride, Inc., in Henderson, Kentucky. Under a joint venture called AOT, Inc., Goodyear and Accuride furnish entire wheel assemblies, painted and ready for use, to Mitsubishi Motor Co. and Ford Motor Co. as well as Navistar. Those assemblies include Goodyear's or competitors' tires, depending on customer specifications [128].

A recent example of a market with a low entry barrier and many companies initially competing mostly on price is the business-to-business e-marketplace. It only took a few years for many of these market makers to realize that they need to extend their service offerings; they now provide a variety of additional services, including financial, logistics, and supply chain services (see Chapter 9 for more detail).

As observed in the previous section, pricing services is not an easy task. For many years, companies such as IBM did not charge for their services, although the company's slogan was "IBM Means Service." Today, service provides most of IBM's income. Companies that have not stressed customer support, such as Microsoft, are enhancing their capabilities in this area. In many cases, there is a charge associated with receiving support, such as a one-time call fee or a service agreement. Service and support not only can generate additional revenue, but, more importantly, they can bring the company closer to the customer and provide insight on how to improve its offering, tailor support, and find the next idea to add value to its products and services.

An important value-added service is information access. Allowing customers access to their own data—such as pending orders, payment history, and typical orders—enhances their experience with the company. For example, it is well known that customers value the ability to know the status of an order, sometimes even more than the actual turnaround time. This capability provides reliability and enables planning. FedEx pioneered the package tracking systems that are now standard in this industry. As we will see below, this not only enhances service, but also can result in large savings for the provider of the information by handing over to its customers some of the data entry and inquiry functions from its own employees.

The ability of customers to access information is becoming an essential requirement in supply chain management, as visibility of information is what an increasing number of customers expect. The Internet enables these capabilities and companies will need to invest in information systems that support it. In Chapter 14, we consider these issues in more detail.

12.2.5 Relationships and Experiences

The final level of customer value is an increased connection between the firm and its customers through development of a relationship. This makes it more difficult for customers to switch to another provider, since a relationship requires an investment of time from both the customer and the provider. For example, Dell configures PCs and supports them for large customers. When Dell manages the entire PC purchase for a large customer, including special custom features, it becomes more difficult for the customer to switch to another vendor.

The learning relationship, where companies build specific user profiles and utilize this information to enhance sales as well as retain customers [192], is another example of a relationship providing customer value. Companies such as Individual Inc., which builds tailored information services, and USAA, which uses its databases to offer customers other services and products, are examples of this kind of organization.

EXAMPLE 12-9

Founded in 1989 by brothers Andrew and Thomas Parkinson, Peapod has grown to be one of America's leading Internet grocers. Peapod is a wholly owned subsidiary of international food provider Royal Ahold and works in partnership with Ahold USA supermarket companies, including Stop & Shop and Giant Food. The company, which operates in Boston, southern Connecticut, Washington, Chicago, and Long Island, New York, serves over 103,000 members. Shoppers browse through Peapod's offerings on its Internet site through a personalized interface based on their location. Peapod's computers are linked directly to the databases of the supermarkets from which it purchases the groceries. The shoppers can create their own virtual supermarket by accessing the information according to category and creating customized shopping lists that can be saved for repeated use. At the end of each shopping session, Peapod has the opportunity to learn about its service by asking, "How did we do on the last order?" and using the relatively high response rate of its customers (35 percent) to institute requested changes to its services [192].

The approach used by Peapod Inc. is an example of the *one-to-one enterprise* concept suggested by Peppers and Rogers in [185]. Companies learn about each customer through databases and interactive communications, and sell to one customer as many products and services as possible throughout the lifetime of the customer's patronage. Indeed, Peapod is using its databases to suggest new offerings to customers, tracking the customer's preferences and needs, and further tailoring the company's offering to the customer.

The learning process can take time, but this will make it difficult for competitors to emulate the strategy. In addition, it typically ensures that a customer who considers switching to another provider will have to take into account the investment in time and money required to make the switch.

Indeed, some Internet sites, such as Amazon.com, are applying new modes of learning, with suggestions to customers based on their own previous purchases or those of customers who make similar purchases. Of course, one issue with an Internet service that provides customer reviews and suggestions is that a customer can distinguish between a Web site where they purchase the product and the Web site in which they receive information about the product. That is, it is not clear that a service offering in which a Web site provides suggestion tools and customer reviews may convince the consumer to purchase the product at that site. The consumer may well receive information from one site and make the purchase on another [31].

A different approach, tailored toward large customers and designed to make it difficult to switch to another vendor, was introduced by Dell. It offers large corporations custom PC configurations loaded with specific software, tags, and other special requirements. Dell also has tailored its Web site so that different types of users can access it according to their needs. In many ways, this approach is a more extensive application of mass customization, which we discussed in Chapter 11.

Beyond relationships, some companies are also designing, promoting, and selling unique experiences to their customers, which, according to Pine and Gilmore [191], is a way to differentiate and thrive in a customer-driven economy. The authors define experience as an offering distinct from customer service:

> An experience occurs when a company intentionally uses services as the stage, and goods as props, to engage individual customers in a way that creates memorable events [191].

Examples include airline frequent flyer programs, theme parks, Saturn owner gatherings, and Lexus weekend brunch and car wash events.

EXAMPLE 12-10

As an extension of its brand experience, Apple operates retail stores in the United States, Canada, Japan, and the United Kingdom. The stores carry most of Apple's products as well as many third-party products and offer on-site support and repair for Apple hardware and software. The first stores were opened in May 2001 and were designed for two purposes: to stem the tide of Apple's declining share of the computer market and to counter a poor record of marketing Apple products by third-party retail outlets. As noted in [89], the design of the stores takes into account

1. Creating an experience. This is accomplished through the striking glass staircase, store design, and attention to the line of sight so that it feels more like walking into a hands-on museum than walking into a retail store.
2. Honoring context. The store is organized by the context in which people use the products. With digital cameras, photo printers, and Apple's iPhoto software set up together, customers can envision using these products in their own lives. By acknowledging this context in the design of the store, Apple encourages its customers to dream about possibilities.
3. Prioritizing its messages. The store is visually spare with product packages kept below eye level and relatively few products on display. The store focuses on a handful of important messages.
4. Instituting consistency. The Apple personality comes through every time the customer encounters the brand, whether on television, in print or outdoor advertising, or through interacting with one of Apple's products. The Apple stores are no different, and Apple is able to project that personality across all these channels by maintaining rigorous consistency of design.
5. Designing for change. The front window displays are rigged using simple flat panels mounted on tracks and cables. This system allows the displays to be changed quickly and easily while still allowing a diverse range of possibilities for grabbing the attention of passersby.
6. Not forgetting the human element. The people who staff the store form an integral part of the overall experience. Apple Store employees don't look like run-of-the-mill retail workers. Instead of name tags, they have business cards. And they all carry iPods on their belts, creating the impression that they don't just work for Apple—they live the lifestyle Apple is selling to customers. Apple's retail workers are brand emissaries [89].

The Internet provides other opportunities for creating experiences that have not yet been fully explored. One of the strengths of the Internet is the creation of collaborative communities that can be used to develop relationships between people with similar interests or the desire to collaborate. One such technology is "eRoom," which is a virtual workspace in which multiple parties can view and work with almost any form of unstructured data, such as drawings and presentations that are far too big for e-mail. These can be placed in an eRoom and discussed and walked through with clients or prospects via teleconference and Web demo. In addition, participants can trade comments within eRoom with no phone contact at all. Since the room is always there, it works for everyone's schedule. Companies use the same technology to create "communities of interest," some of which involve only its own employees, others a mix of internal staff and outside partners [141].

As with the initial introduction of services, companies do not yet charge for experiences. Before a company can charge for this offering, experiences must be seen by the customer as worth the price. This requires a large investment in making the experience valuable in itself. Disney's theme parks are the prime example of a successful experience that many are willing to pay for. The parks also can be viewed as a means of selling Disney's products—movies and various spin-off toys and accessories.

The ability to provide sophisticated customer interactions (e.g., relationships and experiences) is very different from the ability to manufacture and distribute products. This suggests the emergence of firms that specialize in providing the former. Patricia Seybold in *The Customer Revolution* [219] states that thriving when a customer is in control requires that businesses transform into completely customer-centric entities. She outlines eight steps to delivering a great total customer experience:

1. Create a compelling brand personality—a distinct offering that customers can identify with.
2. Deliver a seamless experience across channels and touch points. In other words, make sure that customers' experience and information are the same no matter what access method they choose to use at a certain point.
3. Care about customers and their outcomes.
4. Measure what matters to customers: the quality of the customer's experience as opposed to internal company measures.
5. Hone operational excellence.
6. Value customers' time.
7. Place customer's information requirements and needs at the core. This requires the ability to be proactive; for instance, reminding customers of maintenance requirements and training opportunities.
8. Design to morph—the ability to change practices based on customer requirements.

Supply chain performance is critical in most of the points above—it can play a role in the branding as well as the seamless experience and operational excellence required to deliver leading customer experience. The "Made to Measure" case study at the beginning of this chapter clearly illustrates many of the points above from creation of a distinct offering to its customers; consolidation of information systems; willingness to pay for expensive freight to handle exceptions; operational excellence; saving its customer the time and expense of running the supply chain, as well as reducing inventory levels; and, finally, the ability to change based on the requirements.

12.2.6 Dimensions and Achieving Excellence

Our analysis of customer value dimensions clearly shows that companies need to select their customer value goals since the supply chain, market segmentation, and skill sets required to succeed depend on this choice. In the *The Myth of Excellence* [57], the authors analyze many companies along the lines of how they rank on price, product, service, access, and relationship. Their conclusion is that companies cannot excel along all these dimensions (thus the name of the book). Their analysis shows that, in order to succeed, a company needs to be dominating in one attribute, differentiate itself on another, and be adequate in all the rest. Some of their examples:

1. Wal-Mart stands out on price, as in its motto "Always low prices, Always," and secondarily in large brand selection.
2. Target competes by emphasizing brand selection before price.
3. Nike Stores emphasize experience first and product second.
4. McDonald's provides access first (they have stores almost everywhere) and service second.
5. American Express emphasizes service first and access as a second attribute.

12.3 CUSTOMER VALUE MEASURES

Because customer value is based on customer perceptions, it requires measures that start with the customer. Typical measures include service level and customer satisfaction. Seybold [219] goes a step further and suggests managing companies by additional customer value measures such as growth in number of active customers, customer retention, defections, referrals, acquisition costs, and share of customer's spending.

Our objective in this section is to introduce various basic measures of customer value, as well as supply chain performance measures. The latter are important since supply chain performance is an important contributor to customer value.

1. **Service level.** Service level is the typical measure used to quantify a company's market conformance. In practice, the definition of service level can vary from company to company, but *service level* is usually related to the ability to satisfy a customer's delivery date, for instance, the percent of all orders sent on or before the promised delivery date. Many companies consider this measure so critical to their ability to succeed in today's markets that they invest heavily in decision-support systems that allow them to quote delivery dates accurately by analyzing information from the entire supply chain.

   There is a direct relationship between the ability to achieve a certain level of service and supply chain cost and performance. For instance, demand variability and manufacturing and information lead times determine the amount of inventory that needs to be kept in the supply chain. Clearly, when setting the level of service that should be used for a particular offering, it is important to understand customer value. For instance, customers may value low cost, information about the delivery date, and the ability to customize the product more than they value immediate delivery itself. This is definitely the case for Dell's customers, who prefer to wait the additional time it takes to build and deliver the PC, rather than purchase off-the-shelf.
2. **Customer satisfaction.** Customer satisfaction surveys are used to measure sales department and personnel performance as well as to provide feedback for necessary improvements in products and services. In addition, as in the Peapod example, there are other innovative ways to receive information about customer satisfaction. However, customer surveys may not be the best way to learn about customer value. As Reichheld [200] points out, relying on customer satisfaction surveys can often be misleading. These surveys are easy to manipulate and are typically measured at the selling point while nothing is said about retaining the customer.

Indeed, more important than what customers say about their satisfaction is *customer loyalty*, which is easier to measure than customer satisfaction. This can be accomplished by analyzing customer repurchase patterns based on internal databases.

EXAMPLE 12-11

Lexus is a consistent winner of auto satisfaction awards, but it refuses to consider surveys as the best measure of satisfaction. To Lexus, the only meaningful measure of satisfaction is repurchase loyalty. Lexus considers the repurchase activities of cars and services as the only measure for its dealers' success. Each Lexus dealership has a satellite dish that keeps information flowing back and forth to headquarters, where these measures are constantly tracked [200].

An additional option is to learn from customer defections. Unfortunately, identifying those customers is not an easy task because dissatisfied customers seldom cancel an account completely. Instead, they gradually shift their spending, making a partial defection. However, if this type of tracking is possible, it may provide the key to increasing customer value.

Another example is Charles Schwab (see [219]). The online broker tracks customer asset accumulation, customer satisfaction, customer retention, and employee retention. These are the measures on which managers and employees receive incentives.

3. **Supply chain performance measures.** As we have seen, supply chain performance affects the ability to provide customer value, especially in the most basic dimension of availability of products. Therefore, there is a need to develop independent criteria to measure supply chain performance. The need for well-defined measures in the supply chain stems from the presence of many partners in the process and the requirement of a common language. This is precisely the motivation behind standardization initiatives such as the Supply-Chain Council's reference models.

The Supply-Chain Council was organized in 1996 by Pittiglio Rabin Todd & McGrath (PRTM) and AMR Research, and initially included 69 voluntary member companies. In 2006, the Supply-Chain Council had closer to 1,000 corporate members worldwide and has established numerous international chapters. The Supply-Chain Council's membership consists primarily of practitioners representing a broad cross section of industries, including manufacturers, services, distributors, and retailers; see [261].

The first model introduced was the Supply Chain Operations Reference (SCOR) model, which uses a *process reference model* that includes analyzing the current state of a company's processes and its goals, quantifying operational performance, and comparing it to benchmark data. For this purpose, SCOR has developed a set of metrics for supply chain performance; its members are in the process of forming industry groups to collect best-practice information that companies can use to evaluate their supply chain performance. Table 12-1 lists examples of metrics used to evaluate supply chain performance in SCOR, based on [159].

Once a specific company's metrics are calculated,they are compared to those of industry benchmarks such as average and best-in-class. This enables identifying the company's advantages as well as opportunities for supply chain improvement. Examples of these metrics are reported in the "Overall Business Performance" survey conducted by PRTM [90]:

- **Total supply chain management costs:** This includes the total cost to manage order processing, acquire materials, manage inventory, and manage supply chain finance and information systems. The survey found that leading companies have total costs between 4 and 5 percent of sales. Median performers spend 5 to 6 percent more.

TABLE 12-1

SCOR LEVEL 1 METRICS

Perspectives	Metrics	Measure
Supply chain reliability	On-time delivery	Percentage
	Order fulfillment lead time	Days
	Fill rate	Percentage
	Perfect order fulfillment	Percentage
Flexibility and responsiveness	Supply chain response time	Days
	Upside production flexibility	Days
Expenses	Supply chain management cost	Percentage
	Warranty cost as percentage of revenue	Percentage
	Value added per employee	Dollars
Assets/utilization	Total inventory days of supply	Days
	Cash-to-cash cycle time	Days
	Net asset turns	Turns

- **Cash-to-cash cycle time:** The number of days between paying for raw materials and getting paid for product, as calculated by inventory days of supply plus days of sales outstanding minus average payment period for material. The survey shows that best in class have less than a 30-day cycle time, while median performers can be up to 100 days.
- **Upside production flexibility:** The number of days required to achieve an unplanned, sustainable, 20 percent increase in production. This measure is now under two weeks for best in class and even less than a week for some industries. The main constraint is material availability and not internal manufacturing or labor constraints.
- **Delivery performance to request:** The percentage of orders that are fulfilled on or before the customer's requested date. The survey indicated that best-of-class performance is at least 94 percent and in some industries approaches 100 percent. The median performance ranges from 69 percent to 81 percent.

More recently, the Supply Chain Council introduced the Design Chain Operations Reference (DCOR) model that provides a framework that links business process, metrics, best practices, and technology features into a unified structure to support communication among design chain partners and to improve the effectiveness of the extended supply chain including the development chain. The original DCOR, inspired by SCOR, was developed by the Business Process Management organization of Hewlett-Packard and conveyed to the Supply-Chain Council in 2004.

While the SCOR model is organized around the management processes of plan, source, make, deliver, and return, DCOR is organized around the processes of plan, research, design, integrate, and amend. It spans product development, research, and development but does not attempt to describe every business process or activity. Where SCOR addresses the process categories of make to stock, make to order, and engineer to order product, DCOR is focused on product refresh, new product, and new technology as its key execution processes.

The SCOR model is a good example of a set of supply chain metrics and provides a means to compare performance to other companies in the same industry or in others. It has the additional advantage of possibly becoming an industry standard. The DCOR model goes a step further by including supply chain decisions in the design phase.

Despite the widespread use of these models, every company needs to understand its own unique environment and determine its measures based on that insight. For instance, Dell measures inventory velocity, and not the more standard inventory turns.

12.4 INFORMATION TECHNOLOGY AND CUSTOMER VALUE

Information technology has produced many valuable benefits for customers and businesses. We will briefly review three aspects below. The first is exchange of information between customers and businesses, the second is the use of information by companies to learn more about their customers so that they can better tailor their services, and the third is enhanced business-to-business capabilities.

1. **Customer benefits.** Customer service has changed for many reasons. One of the most dramatic is the opening of corporate, government, and educational databases to the customer. This started with kiosks and voice mail and has accelerated significantly with the uniform data access tools of the Internet. These innovations have had the effect of increasing customer value while reducing costs for the supplier of the information. Banks were the first to realize that by installing automated teller machines (ATMs), they could reduce their workforce. Voice mail was at first derided as dehumanizing, preventing interactions with a live person, but it actually allowed unmediated access to a user's accounts at any time of the day from almost anywhere. The Internet has expanded these capabilities and allows users to access their accounts and perform transactions from any location at any time. This opening of the information boundaries between customer and company is part of the new customer value equation, where the information is part of the product.

   The Internet also has had some less obvious effects [26]:

   - *Increased importance of intangibles.* Customers have become accustomed to ordering even high-priced products from unseen salespeople over the phone or Internet. This increases the importance of brand names and other intangibles, such as service capabilities or community experience in purchasing decisions.
   - *Increased ability to connect and disconnect.* The Internet makes it easier not only to identify business partners and connect to them but also to disconnect and find new partners. Increasing availability of information, including performance measures and data, reduces the need to develop long-term trust relationships. Companies can rely on accessible, published track records to make decisions on quality of service. This ability is mainly important when there is not a considerable initial investment in setting up the partnership. If there is, then frequent changes of partners may have a major impact on cost and available resources.
   - *Increased customer expectations.* The ability to compare and the ease of performing various transactions over the phone and the Internet have raised expectations of similar services from every type of business as well as for business-to-business interactions.
   - *Tailored experience.* The ability to provide each customer an individual experience is an important part of the Internet. Amazon.com saves the customer's information and recommends books and other items based on previous purchases. Mass customization can allow users to store their individual preferences or sizes and order custom-fit clothes and shoes from various vendors without having to reenter the information.

2. **Business benefits.** One way to enhance customer value is to use the information captured in the supply chain to create new offerings for customers. The information now available allows companies to "sense and respond" to customers' desires rather than simply make and sell products and services. Indeed, as

we have seen, learning about customers takes time, requires some of the customers' time, and eventually makes switching vendors more difficult. The learning process takes many forms from sophisticated data mining methods used to correlate purchasing patterns, to learning about each individual customer by keeping detailed data of preferences and purchases. The method applied depends on the industry and business model. Retailers would use the first method while service companies, as in the example below, would be more likely to track individual customer preferences and requirements.

EXAMPLE 12-12

In the 1930s, it was difficult for military personnel to obtain reasonably priced insurance, so a group of officers formed United Services Automobile Association (USAA) to provide insurance for military officers. USAA still offers services only to active and former military officers and their families and handles all transactions by mail and phone. USAA has used its extensive databases to expand into financial and shopping services for its members. When a customer calls USAA, the information about him or her can be accessed and updated and the customer can be offered a variety of services to match his or her needs. For instance, if a customer owns a boat purchased or financed through USAA, he or she could receive an offer to acquire insurance [192].

3. **Business-to-business benefits.** The "Made to Measure" case study at the start of the chapter illustrates how information technology allows suppliers to provide new services to its customers. Other examples include Dell's establishment of its private e-marketplace (see Chapter 6) and use of the Internet to improve supply chain collaboration by providing demand information and production data to its suppliers. Thus, these developments make it possible to outsource important parts of a company's business, but still keep close control over what it produces or services. For instance, strategic partnering relies heavily on information sharing and enables the partners to achieve supply chain efficiencies (see Chapters 5 and 8).

EXAMPLE 12-13

Dell's Direct Business Model

Michael Dell started a computer business in his dormitory room in 1984 with this simple insight: He could bypass the dealer channel through which personal computers were being sold and instead sell directly to customers and build their personal computers (PCs) to order. This idea, now called the *direct business model,* eliminated the cost of inventory and the reselling expenses. The model had other benefits that were not apparent when Dell founded his company, Dell Computer Corporation. "You actually get to have a relationship with the customer," Michael Dell explains, "and this creates valuable information which, in turn, allows us to leverage our relationships with both suppliers and customers. Couple that information with technology, and you have the infrastructure to revolutionize the fundamental business models of major global companies."

Dell Computer's model involves building computers based on components that are available in the market. The decision not to manufacture the computer components has relieved Dell of the burden of owning assets, research and development risks, and managing a large number of employees. Spreading the development and manufacturing risk among several suppliers allowed Dell to grow much faster than if these functions were performed inside the company.

Dell's use of technology and information to blur the traditional boundaries in the supply chain between suppliers, manufacturers, and end users has been named *virtual integration*. In a traditional computer company, such as Digital Computer, processes were *vertically integrated*, with all the research, development, manufacturing, and distribution capabilities in-house. This allowed for a high level of communication and ability to develop products based on the company's interaction with its clients. The disadvantage was the high risk and costs of development and the ownership of assets in a volatile industry. To achieve the advantages of an integrated company, Dell treats suppliers and service providers as if they were inside the company. Their systems are linked in real time to Dell's system and their employees

EXAMPLE 12-13 *Continued*

participate in design teams and product launches. Technology enhances the economic incentives to collaborate because it makes it possible to share design databases and methodologies and speed the time to market.

Dell measures *inventory velocity,* the reciprocal of the average amount of time a product spends in inventory. For this purpose, each component is marked with a date stamp. Accumulating inventory in the fast-moving PC industry is a high-risk proposition since the components can become obsolete very quickly. In some cases, such as Sony monitors, Dell does not keep any inventory but has UPS or Airborne Express pick up the monitors from Sony's Mexican factory, the computer from Dell's Austin, Texas, facility, and then match and deliver them to the customers. Dell suppliers benefit from the real-time information about demand and a commitment from Dell for a certain level of purchases. The results are impressive. While Compaq, IBM, and Hewlett-Packard all announced plans in late 1998 to emulate portions of Dell's business model, with various build-to-order plans, all have had difficulty in making the transition. Most are moving to a target inventory level of four weeks, while Dell maintains just eight days of inventory, allowing it to turn over inventory 46 times a year.

On the customer side, Dell has segmented its customer base so that it can offer value-added services to different customers. Dell configures PCs and supports them for large customers. It will also load standard software and place asset stickers on the machines based on customer requests. For some clients, Dell has an on-site team that assists in PC purchasing and servicing. "The whole idea behind virtual integration is that it lets you meet customers' needs faster and more efficiently than any other model." Furthermore, it allows Dell to be efficient and responsive to change at the same time. By spending time with customers and following technological trends, Dell tries to be a few steps ahead of the change, and even create and shape it.

Source: Based on [147].

Other examples of information sharing between businesses can be found in [173]. The authors describe various arrangements between manufacturers and distributors for sharing information on inventory that results in cost reduction. These arrangements, motivated by the risk-pooling concept introduced in Chapter 2, allow manufacturers and distributors to reduce overall inventory by sharing information about inventory in all locations and allowing any member of the channel to share the inventory.

SUMMARY

Creating customer value is the driving force behind a company's goals, and supply chain management is one of the important means. Supply chain management strategy affects customer value; its considerations affect every aspect of customer value and must be part of any strategy or plan, not an afterthought. It is important to choose the appropriate supply chain strategy to match customer value with the company's market. Excellence in supply chain management translates into customer value in many dimensions, from availability and selection to influencing the price at which a product can be sold.

The supply chain strategy in the Dell example was the business model, and it created the customer value of low prices. The TAL case study showed that the ability to manage the customer's inventory created a strong differentiator in a highly competitive commodity business. Zara creates a fast-turning supply chain close to its markets in order to stay current and keep shoppers coming back for new merchandise.

Customer access to information about the availability of products and the status of orders and deliveries is becoming an essential capability. This also creates opportunities to learn about customers and their preferences, and to create new modes of interaction. Dell uses this information to enhance its services, TAL uses the access to the customer to better predict trends, and Zara has a simple but effective feedback loop.

Adding services, relationships, and experiences is a way for companies to differentiate their offerings in the market and learn about their customers. It also makes it difficult for the customers to switch to another service provider.

Measuring customer value is at the heart of company goals and objectives, but identifying the appropriate measure is not an easy task. Dell measures inventory velocity, the reciprocal of the average amount of time a product spends in inventory, and not the usual inventory turns.

The ability to provide sophisticated customer interactions (for example, relationships and experiences) is very different from the ability to manufacture and distribute products. Because a distinctive expertise is required for each function, companies will gain by specializing. We observe this trend in consumer product industries, where firms such as Nike and Sara Lee lend their name to products produced by many manufacturing companies.

There is no real customer value without a close relationship with customers. Today, this is possible not only through direct interaction, but also through information and communications technology. By allowing customers to state their preferences and learning from them—a true two-way interaction—a firm can develop the means to achieve greater customer value and therefore loyalty. We have seen that successful companies all value this capability and build it into their business and supply chain model.

DISCUSSION QUESTIONS

1. Discuss the trade-off between product quality and price in traditional and online retailing.
2. Consider dynamic pricing strategies and their impact on profit. Explain why dynamic pricing provides significant profit benefit over (the best) fixed-price strategy as
   a. Available capacity decreases.
   b. Demand uncertainty increases.
   c. Seasonality in demand pattern increases.
3. Discuss how supply chain management decisions impact the ability to excel in certain dimensions. Specifically, consider
   a. Conformance to requirements.
   b. Product selection.
   c. Price and brand.
   d. Value-added services.
   e. Relationships and experiences.
4. What is the dominant customer value the following companies bring?
   a. Starbucks
   b. The Gap
   c. Expedia.com
5. What additional experience opportunities does the Internet enable?
6. What measures would you use in a business like Amazon.com to evaluate the company's performance? The supply chain?

CHAPTER 13

Smart Pricing

CASE: Starbucks Economics: Solving the Mystery of the Elusive "Short" Cappuccino

Here's a little secret that Starbucks doesn't want you to know: They will serve you a better, stronger cappuccino if you want one, and they will charge you less for it. Ask for it in any Starbucks and the barista will comply without batting an eye. The puzzle is to work out why.

The drink in question is the elusive "short cappuccino"—at 8 ounces, a third smaller than the smallest size on the official menu, the "tall," and dwarfed by what Starbucks calls the "customer-preferred" size, the "Venti," which weighs in at 20 ounces and more than 200 calories before you add the sugar.

The short cappuccino has the same amount of espresso as the 12-ounce tall, meaning a bolder coffee taste, and also a better one. The World Barista Championship rules, for example, define a traditional cappuccino as a "five- to six-ounce beverage." This is also the size of cappuccino served by many continental cafés. Within reason, the shorter the cappuccino, the better.

The problem with large cappuccinos is that it's impossible to make the fine-bubbled milk froth ("microfoam," in the lingo) in large quantities, no matter how skilled the barista. A 20-ounce cappuccino is an oxymoron. Having sampled the short cappuccino in a number of Starbucks across the world, I can confirm that it is a better drink than the buckets of warm milk—topped with a veneer of froth—that the coffee chain advertises on its menus.

This secret cappuccino is cheaper, too—at my local Starbucks, $2.35 instead of $2.65. But why does this cheaper, better drink—along with its sisters, the short latte and the short coffee—languish unadvertised? The official line from Starbucks is that there is no room on the menu board, although this doesn't explain why the short cappuccino is also unmentioned on the comprehensive Starbucks Web site, nor why the baristas will serve you in a whisper rather than the usual practice of singing your order to the heavens.

Economics has the answer: This is the Starbucks way of sidestepping a painful dilemma over how high to set prices. Price too low and the margins disappear; too high and the customers do. Any business that is able to charge one price to price-sensitive customers and a higher price to the rest will avoid some of that awkward trade-off.

It's not hard to identify the price-blind customers in Starbucks. They're the ones buying enough latte to bathe Cleopatra. The major costs of staff time, space in the queue, and packaging are similar for any size of drink. So, larger drinks carry a substantially higher markup, according to Brian McManus, an assistant professor at the Olin

Source: Tim Harford, *Slate Magazine,* January 6, 2006, www. slate. com/id/2133754.

School of Business who has studied the coffee market.

The difficulty is that if some of your products are cheap, you may lose money from customers who would willingly have paid more. So, businesses try to discourage their more lavish customers from trading down by making their cheap products look or sound unattractive, or, in the case of Starbucks, making the cheap product invisible. The British supermarket Tesco has a "value" line of products with infamously ugly packaging, not because good designers are unavailable but because the supermarket wants to scare away customers who would willingly spend more. "The bottom end of any market tends to get distorted," says McManus. "The more market power firms have, the less attractive they make the cheaper products."

That observation is important. A firm in a perfectly competitive market would suffer if it sabotaged its cheapest products because rivals would jump at the opportunity to steal alienated customers. Starbucks, with its coffee supremacy, can afford this kind of price discrimination, thanks to loyal, or just plain lazy, customers.

The practice is hundreds of years old. The French economist Emile Dupuit wrote about the early days of the railways, when third-class carriages were built without roofs, even though roofs were cheap: "What the company is trying to do is prevent the passengers who can pay the second-class fare from traveling third class; it hits the poor, not because it wants to hurt them, but to frighten the rich."

The modern equivalent is the airport departure lounge. Airports could create nicer spaces, but that would frustrate the ability of airlines to charge substantial premiums for club-class departure lounges.

Starbucks' gambit is much simpler and more audacious: Offer the cheaper product but make sure that it is available only to those customers who face the uncertainty and embarrassment of having to request it specifically. Fortunately, the tactic is easily circumvented: If you'd like a better coffee for less, just ask.

By the end of this chapter, you should be able to answer the following questions:

- Why do companies like Starbucks try to differentiate between different customers?
- How can other companies do this? What are the dangers of doing this?
- How can firms take advantage of the fact that different customers are willing to pay different amounts for the same product?
- What are manufacturers trying to achieve by offering rebates? If all of the rebates are redeemed, is it still worthwhile to manufacturers to offer them? To retailers?
- What are firms trying to achieve by controlling pricing?
- How can dynamic pricing help firms to efficiently utilize capacity?
- What lessons can firms draw from the success of airline revenue management?

13.1 INTRODUCTION

For most of this text, we have considered a variety of approaches for dealing with end customer demand and the variability of that demand, but we've always implicitly assumed that the demand is beyond the firm's control. In reality, this is far from true. Advertising, displays, and promotional tools all can be used to change the demand level to some extent. Most importantly, pricing is an important tool to impact demand. Indeed, progressive companies use pricing as an important lever to effectively manage the supply chain by managing the demand level.

No company underscores the impact of pricing strategies on effective supply chain management more than Dell. The exact same product is sold at different prices on Dell's Web site depending on whether the purchase is made by a private consumer; a small, medium, or large business; the federal government; or an education or health care provider. What's more, the price for the same product for the same market is not fixed [2]—it can change rapidly over time, and options that are less expensive than others one day may be more expensive than others the next. Dell is not alone in its use of a sophisticated pricing strategy. Consider:

- IBM is investigating software that will allow it to adjust prices according to demand [161].
- A particular model of Nikon Coolpix Digital Camera is sold either online or in stores for about $600. However, the manufacturer provides a rebate of $100 independently of where the camera is purchased. Similarly, a particular model of Sharp digital camcorder is sold for about $500 at retail or virtual stores. Sharp provides a rebate to the customer of $100 independently of where the product was purchased.
- Boise Cascade Office Products sells many products online. Boise Cascade states that prices for the 12,000 items ordered most frequently online might change as often as daily [123].

This observation raises a variety of questions. What are these companies doing? Why does Dell charge a different price for different consumers? At different times? If Dell can do it, can it work for other companies? What is the impact of the mail-in rebate? In fact, shouldn't Nikon and Sharp just reduce the wholesale price paid by the retailers instead of asking the consumer to mail in the coupon? And, finally, what is wrong with a traditional fixed-price policy?

A careful review of these companies suggests that they have one thing in common: they are trying to boost profit by using what are known as smart pricing or revenue management techniques, techniques that were first pioneered by the airline, hotel, and rental car industries. In the airline industry, revenue management increased revenue significantly; American Airlines estimates that revenue management provides incremental revenue of $1 billion annually [53]. In fact, if it were not for the combined contributions of revenue management and airline schedule planning systems, American Airlines would have been profitable only one year in the last decade [54].

13.2 PRICE AND DEMAND

All things being equal, demand for a product will typically go up as the product's price goes down. There are exceptions to this rule (in the case where consumers consider price a signal of quality, for example), but these are few and far between. Of course, certain products might be more or less sensitive to price change depending on their particular characteristics, but this general decrease in demand with increasing price, the property known as the "downward-sloping demand curve," almost always holds. This presents an interesting problem to managers when they are trying to determine the optimal price for their products: if demand goes up as price goes down, and if revenue is the product of demand and price (as it clearly is), what is the best price to charge for a particular product? In general, this is a difficult problem to solve. To find the best price, a manager needs to be able to characterize the relationship between pricing and demand for each product that he or she sells, and then utilize this characterization to determine the optimal price for each product. Notice that this may involve many complexities. For example, vast quantities of data may need to be analyzed, and competitors' behavior may need to be captured in this relationship. In spite of these difficulties, however, many firms do manage to at least approximate this relationship. In the example below, we assume this relationship is known, and then determine the optimal price.

EXAMPLE 13-1

Consider a retailer selling a single item. Based on past experience, management estimates the relationship between demand, D, and price, p, by the linear function $D = 1{,}000 - 0.5p$. This implies that when the price is $1,600, there is demand for 200 of the items, while if the price is $1,200, there is demand for 400 of the items. Notice that revenue equals price times demand at that price. Thus, the revenue at different price levels can be calculated, and is displayed in Table 13-1.

TABLE 13-1

PRICE VERSUS REVENUE FOR EXAMPLE 13-1

Price	Demand	Revenue
$ 250	875	$218,750
$ 500	750	$375,000
$ 750	625	$468,750
$1,000	500	$500,000
$1,250	375	$468,750
$1,500	250	$375,000

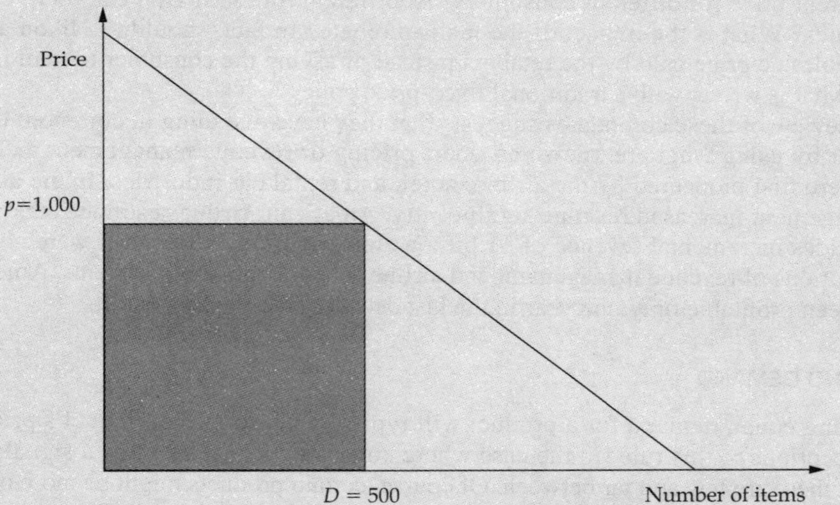

FIGURE 13-1 Demand–price curve for Example 13-1.

Thus, when items are priced at a level of $1,000, revenue equals $1{,}000 \times 500 = 500{,}000$, the maximum revenue. Figure 13-1 depicts the demand–price curve, where the shaded area represents total revenue.

13.3 MARKDOWNS

Of course, although in the example above we assumed that demand is a deterministic function of price, in truth this is rarely the case. In most cases, demand is random, and, as we discussed in Chapter 2, we need to set inventory levels based on estimates of future demand. This implies that sometimes at the end of a selling season, there is remaining inventory. Thus, firms frequently employ a **markdown,** or

sale, to dispose of this excess inventory. To understand the concept of a markdown, demand needs to be viewed in a slightly different way. Rather than considering aggregate demand, which, as we know, decreases as price increases, think of the individual customers that make up that aggregate demand. Each of these customers has a maximum price that he or she is willing to pay for the product—this is known as the *reservation price*.

EXAMPLE 13-2

Consider the same product described in the previous example, with the relationship between demand, D, and price, p, given by the linear function $D = 1{,}000 - 0.5p$. (See Figure 13-1.) We already saw that when the price is $1,200, 400 of the items will be sold. This means that 400 customers have a reservation price at or above $1,200—when the price is below their reservation price, they will buy. Similarly, if the price is $600, demand will be for 700 units as is illustrated in Figure 13.2. In other words, there are 700 customers with reservation prices at or above $600.

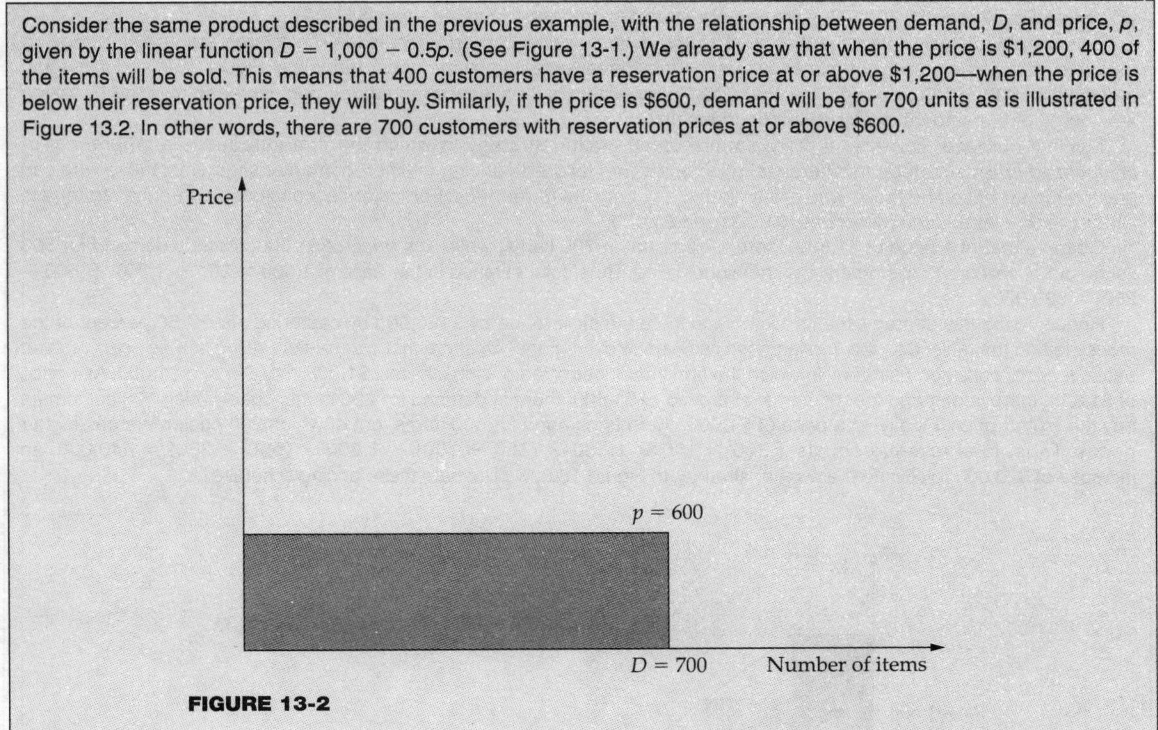

FIGURE 13-2

Clearly, the lower the price, the more customers with a reservation price at or above that price. The concept of markdowns, or sales, is therefore to sell the product to customers whose reservation prices were below the original price, but above the sale price. Traditionally, retailers tried to avoid markdowns. As Robert Philips [186, p. 242] points out, "many retailers considered markdowns to be . . . evidence of mistakes in purchasing, pricing, or marketing." Indeed, the low-price (low-reservation-price) customers were seen as less desirable or profitable, but useful to get rid of the excess inventory.

13.4 PRICE DIFFERENTIATION

We have seen that markdowns help firms get rid of excess inventory. However, progressive retailers noticed a very important fact: in many cases, even sales prices are profitable, and the customers who are willing to buy at the sales price were different than the customers who were willing to buy at the original price. For example, in fashion, some customers are very fashion conscious. These customers are eager to buy at the start of the selling season, and willing to pay more to have fashionable items first. Other

EXAMPLE 13-3

Recall the product discussed in the previous examples, where the relationship between demand, D, and price, p, is given by the linear function $D = 1{,}000 - 0.5p$. We saw previously that when items are priced at a level of \$1,000, revenue equals 1,000 × 500 = 500,000, which at first glance seems to be the best pricing strategy. Figure 13-1 depicts the demand–price curve, where the shaded area represents total revenue. Since \$1,000 is the price that maximizes revenue, at first glance this seems like the best pricing strategy. However, observe that, according to the demand–price curve, the retailer charges many customers who are willing to pay a higher price only \$1,000. In fact, there are about 200 customers among the 500 who are willing to pay \$1,600 per item. Out of these 200 customers, there are about 100 who are willing to pay \$1,800. All of these customers are charged the same price, \$1,000.

This simple analysis illustrates that by charging a single price, management is leaving a large amount of money on the table. In fact, the amount of money left on the table is represented by the upper triangle in Figure 13-1 and it is equal to (why?) (2,000 − 1,000) × 500/2 = 250,000. The question is thus: how can management increase revenue by taking advantage of the amount of money left on the table?

For this purpose, consider a more sophisticated pricing strategy in which the firm introduces a *differential* or *customized* pricing strategy. In differential pricing, the firm tailors its pricing to different market segments: those who can pay the higher price and those who are willing to pay only the lower price. For instance, consider a two-price strategy in which the firm introduces two prices, \$1,600 and \$1,000.

Observe that at a price of \$1,600, there is demand for 200 items, while at a price of \$1,000, there is demand for 500 items, out of which 200 customers pay the higher price. Thus, total revenue in this case is 1,600 × 200 + 1,000 × (500 − 200) = 620,000.

Hence, using this strategy, the firm is able to increase its revenue by \$120,000 by capturing almost 50 percent of the money left on the table. Can the firm increase its revenue even more? Observe that a three-tier pricing strategy can do even better. Indeed, consider a strategy in which the firm introduces three pricing classes: \$1,800, \$1,600, and \$1,000. At a price of \$1,800, there is demand for 100 items; at a price of \$1,600, there is demand for 200 items, out of which 100 customers pay the higher price. Finally, at a price of \$1,000, there is demand for 500 items, out of which 200 customers pay higher prices. Thus, total revenue equals 1,800 × 100 + 1,600 × (200 − 100) + 1,000 × (500 − 200) = 640,000, an increase of \$20,000 relative to the two-tier strategy. In Figure 13-3, we illustrate these pricing schemes.

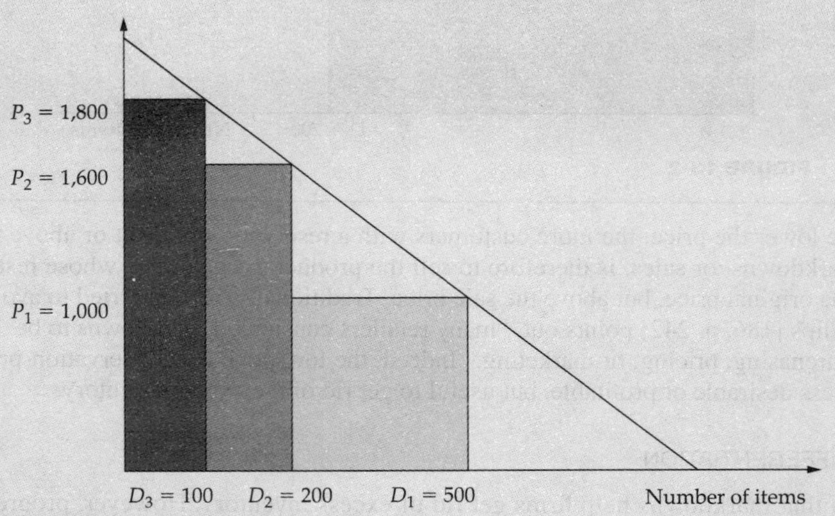

FIGURE 13-3 Three-tier pricing strategy.

customers are value-conscious. These customers are willing to wait until the end of the sales season but are unwilling to pay the same high prices as the fashionable customers. If these different customers are charged different prices, then perhaps revenue can be increased. This practice of charging different prices to different sets of customers is known as *price differentiation*. Consider the following example.

Of course, an important question remains: how can a firm successfully charge different prices to different customers? In Section 13.6, we discuss that question in detail. In the next section, we explore that question specifically in the context of traditional revenue management in the airline, hotel, and car rental industries—these were, after all, the success stories that motivated managers in other industries to focus on pricing as a valuable tool.

13.5 REVENUE MANAGEMENT

Revenue management techniques have received significant attention in recent years from companies trying to improve profitability. These methods, which integrate pricing and inventory strategies to influence market demand, provide controls for companies to improve the bottom line. Revenue management has been described as "selling the right inventory unit to the right type of customer, at the right time, and for the right price" [127].

As observed earlier, revenue management techniques have been traditionally applied in the airline, hotel, and rental car industries. A number of characteristics are common to all these applications. These include (see [127])

1. The existence of perishable products, that is, products that expire or are irrelevant after a certain date.
2. Fluctuating demand.
3. Fixed capacity of the system.
4. Segmentation of the market based, for instance, on sensitivity to price or service time.
5. Products sold in advance.

These approaches were pioneered by American Airlines in the 1980s. After airline deregulation, the established air carriers faced new competition from upstart airlines, most noticeably PeopleExpress. For the first time, airlines were facing fare competitions. To counter these new threats, American Airlines turned to the techniques of revenue management, employing differentiated pricing to "leave less money on the table." This was widely successful; PeopleExpress soon went out of business, and the techniques were soon adopted by the other major airlines, and then hotel and rental car companies. (For a detailed review of the history of revenue management, see [186].)

In general, revenue management involves the targeting of specific products and prices at specific industry segments. In other words, airline revenue management focuses on implementing the price differentiation described in the previous section. In the airline industry, the key to price differentiation and thus airline revenue management is the classification of airline passengers into two segments: leisure travelers and business travelers. Leisure customers are highly sensitive to price but not generally sensitive to the duration of the trip. They also may be willing to book nonrefundable tickets far ahead of time. On the other hand, business travelers are not particularly price-sensitive, but highly sensitive to trip duration. Similarly, business travelers need high flexibility so that they can adjust their travel plans as needed, while, typically, leisure travelers do not need that level of flexibility. This suggests the framework developed by Duadel and Vialle [66] for differentiating between customers, which we introduce in Figure 13-4.

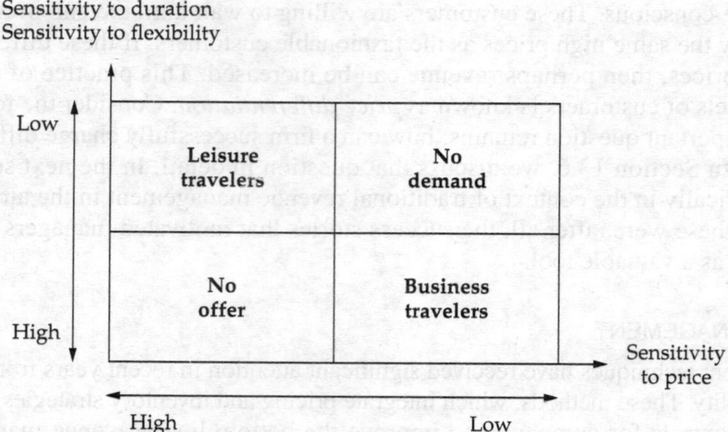

FIGURE 13-4 Customer differentiation in the airline industry.

The airline then strives to offer different tickets (that is, different in terms of pricing, timing, and flexibility) to these different customers. In other words, the airlines "build fences" to prevent business travelers from moving from the top-left box to the bottom-right box. This is done by requiring weekend stays and early booking. Of course, the more fare classes, the more fences need to be built between the different market segments.

Once these distinctions have been made, revenue management strategies focus on determining how many of each type of ticket to offer, and how much to price for each ticket. For historical reasons, this decision is divided into two parts. Since the 1960s, airlines have used computerized reservation systems to book flights. When revenue management was introduced, it was designed so that it could be used with these relatively inflexible systems.

For this to be possible, revenue management at airlines has two key steps:

1. **Market segmentation.** For a specific time and flight (origin to destination), different products are designed and priced to target different market segments. These products feature different restrictions; they may be, for example, nonrefundable, or only available up to 21 days before the flight.
2. **Booking control.** Given products and prices, the booking control system allocates available seats to fare classes, in general by setting limits on the number of seats that can be allocated to lower fare classes.

Designing product offerings and managing booking control are very difficult problems that require sophisticated algorithms and techniques. The basic concept, however, is quite simple. Seats are allocated to fare classes so that the marginal revenue from each of the classes is equal.

EXAMPLE 13-4

Consider a simplified example, in which an airline is allocating two types of seats on a flight. The leisure fare is $100 per ticket, the business fare is $250 per ticket, and there are 80 seats on the plane. The airlines assume that they can sell as many seats as they make available at the leisure fare, but the business fare is random and follows the demand distribution shown in Figure 13-5.

Based on this demand distribution, the expected revenue for each number of allocated seats can be determined (similar to the way we calculated our inventory values in Chapter 2), and the expected marginal revenue (the revenue

EXAMPLE 13-4 *Continued*

associated with allocating one additional seat) also can be calculated, as show in black in Figure 13-6. As we would expect, this marginal revenue decreases as the number of allocated seats increases. The marginal revenue associated with leisure class seats is shown in brown in Figure 13-6. Since there is unlimited demand for these seats, the marginal revenue is constant.

The marginal revenue of the two products is equal at 18 seats; therefore, 18 seats should be allocated to business class.

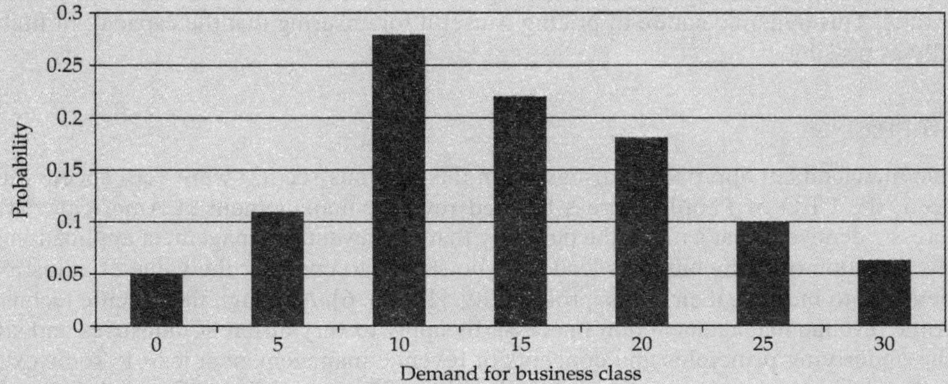

FIGURE 13-5 Demand distribution for Example 13-4.

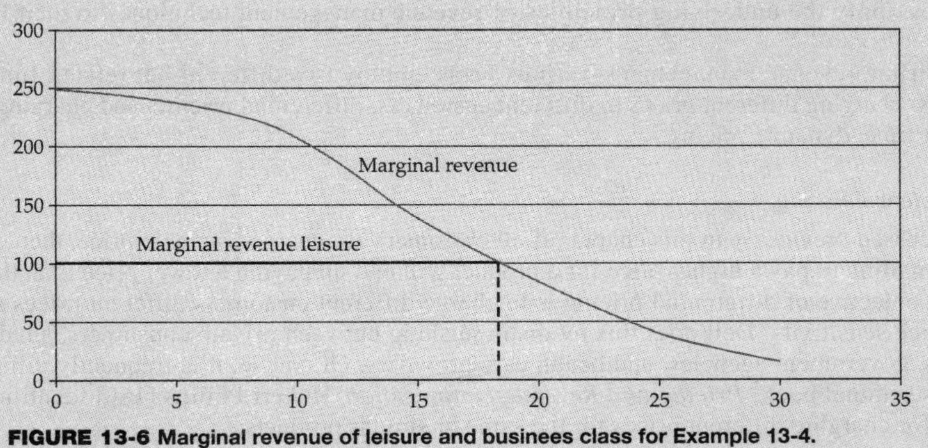

FIGURE 13-6 Marginal revenue of leisure and businees class for Example 13-4.

Of course, real-world airline revenue management problems are much more complex, with a variety of flight classes, different hierarchies of classes, and more complex demand information. Nevertheless, the basic concept of equating marginal revenues of fare classes is at the heart of these systems.

Another challenge faced by many revenue management systems concerns what is known as *network management*. In a typical airline network, a particular leg of a flight can be part of many ultimate origin–destination pairs. For example, a flight leg from San Francisco to Chicago can be part of a San Francisco–Chicago flight, but also a San Francisco–Pittsburgh flight, a San Francisco–Detroit flight, and many others. The revenue management system needs to account for this by allocating seats to particular flights in addition to all of the other concerns we have discussed. This makes the problem even more difficult, and very sophisticated techniques have to be used to solve these problems.

Notice another key issue about airline revenue management: we have focused on differential pricing, with the goal of charging customers with lower price sensitivity (higher reservation prices) more. Just as importantly, airlines employ prices that change over time. A flight from San Francisco to Chicago might be expensive on some days and times, but less expensive on others when demand is lower. Similarly, if a plane is not filling up, the airline might increase the allocation of lower-price fares to that flight over time. This dynamic nature of pricing is useful for ensuring that the capacity of flights is utilized as fully as possible.

13.6 SMART PRICING

The revenue management approaches discussed in the previous section were very successful for airlines. Indeed, the CEO of PeopleExpress blamed revenue management at American Airlines for PeopleExpress's demise. What's more, the publicity that this revenue management application garnered received the attention of many business leaders, who started to consider the value of adjusting prices, and thus demand, to increase their firms' profitability. [186, p. 6]. Although the specific techniques and tools of airline revenue management don't necessarily apply to very different industries and situations, many of the underlying principles and concepts of revenue management at least to some extent do.

Indeed, the pricing strategies applied by Dell, Nikon, Sharp, and Boise Cascade Office Products have one thing in common. These companies use price as a tool to influence customer demand and, hence, they apply the underlying principles of revenue management techniques to their respective industries.

As in airline revenue management, various firms employ two different but related fundamental approaches: charging different prices to different customers, differential pricing, and charging different prices over time, dynamic pricing.

13.6.1 Differential Pricing

As we discussed previously in this chapter, if all customers are charged a single price, then customers who were willing to pay a higher price for a product will end up paying a lower price than they would have—the objective of differential pricing is to charge different customers different prices according to their price sensitivity. Dell does this by distinguishing between private consumers, small or large businesses, government agencies, and health care providers. Of course, it is frequently difficult to do this. In his seminal book, *Pricing and Revenue Optimization,* Robert Philips [186] identifies several strategies for charging different prices for the same or similar products:

Group pricing. The practice of giving discounts to specific groups of customers is very common in many industries. Senior citizen discounts at diners, software discounts to universities, student discounts at movie theaters, and "ladies night" at bars are all examples of group pricing. Of course, these types of discounts will work only for groups in which there is a correlation between group members and price sensitivity.

Channel pricing. This is the practice of charging different prices for the same product sold through different channels. For example, many firms sell certain products at different prices on their Web sites and in their retail stores. Airlines may sell tickets at different prices on their Web sites versus

SUMMARY

Progressive supply chain managers have recently begun to focus on the fact that demand is not something out of their control. Indeed, pricing and promotion can be used to influence the level of demand. Traditionally, fashion retailers have used price markdowns to sell off excess inventory at the end of the season. However, in the mid-1980s, airline executives began to use a set of more sophisticated approaches to manipulating demand. These approaches are collectively known as revenue management, and they have two goals. The first is to differentiate demand, so that customers who are willing to pay a higher price do so, thus maximizing revenues. The second is to use pricing to adjust aggregate demand so that capacity and demand can be matched in a way that maximizes profit.

Inspired by the widespread success of revenue management in the airline industry, managers in many industries began to explore the value of focusing on smart pricing. Managers are using a variety of techniques to both offer differential pricing and set dynamic prices to effectively match supply and demand in the supply chain. The Internet and e-business in many cases make smart pricing more effective, and as these sales channels grow, the focus on effective pricing continues to grow. Of course, smart pricing is not without its dangers. If customers feel like they have been unfairly treated, smart pricing techniques can ultimately hurt the business.

DISCUSSION QUESTIONS

1. Consider a retailer selling a single item. Based on past experience, management estimates the relationship between demand, D, and price, p, by the linear function $D = 2{,}000 - 0.6p$. At what price is revenue maximized. What if the retailer can charge two different prices? Can you find a set of prices that will increase profit in this case?
2. Find a specific example of each of the following. Explain the benefit to the firm in each case:
   a. Group pricing
   b. Channel pricing
   c. Regional pricing
   d. Time-based differentiation
   e. Product versioning
   f. Coupons and rebates
3. In this chapter, we discussed the success of revenue management in the airline industry. If this is the case, why are so many airlines in financial trouble?
4. Consider dynamic pricing strategies and their impact on profit. Explain why dynamic pricing provides significant profit benefit over (the best) fixed-price strategy as
   a. Available capacity decreases.
   b. Demand uncertainty increases.
   c. Seasonality in demand pattern increases.
5. Identify two companies for whom regular sales might make sense. Identify two for whom an everyday-low-price strategy might be more sensible. Explain your choices.
6. Discuss why it is not necessarily correct to consider a retailer markdown indicative of an ordering mistake by the retailer.
7. Consider a bicycle retailer. When might it make sense for the retailer to lower prices, and when might it make sense to raise prices? Why?
8. Consider the strategy that Coca-Cola was considering employing to dynamically change prices based on external temperature. Discuss the advantages and disadvantages of this strategy. If Coke decided to adopt this strategy, how might they best go about overcoming consumer resistance?

CASE: The Great Rebate Runaround

Ah, the holiday shopping season: Santa Claus, reindeer—and rebate hell. Those annoying mail-in offers are everywhere these days. Shoppers hate collecting all the paperwork, filling out the forms, and mailing it all in to claim their $10 or $100. But no matter how annoying rebates are for consumers, the country's retailers and manufacturers love them.

From PC powerhouse Dell to national chains Circuit City and OfficeMax to the Listerine mouthwash sold at Rite Aid drugstores, rebates are proliferating. Nearly one-third of all computer gear is now sold with some form of rebate, along with more than 20% of digital cameras, camcorders, and LCD TVs, says market researcher NPD Group.

Hal Stinchfield, a 30-year veteran of the rebate business, calculates that some 400 million rebates are offered each year. Their total face value: $6 billion, he estimates. Office-products retailer Staples says it and its vendors alone pay $3.5 million in rebates each week.

TAX ON THE DISORGANIZED

Why the rage for rebates? The industry's open secret is that fully 40% of all rebates never get redeemed because consumers fail to apply for them or their applications are rejected, estimates Peter S. Kastner, a director of consulting firm Vericours. That translates into more than $2 billion of extra revenue for retailers and their suppliers each year. What rebates do is get consumers to focus on the discounted price of a product, then buy it at full price.

"The game is obviously that anything less than 100% redemption is free money," says Paula Rosenblum, director of retail research at consulting firm Aberdeen Group.

The impact on a company's bottom line can be startling. Consider TiVo. The company caught Wall Street off guard by sharply reducing its first-quarter loss to $857,000, from $9.1 million in the same period last year. One reason: About 50,000 of TiVo's 104,000 new subscribers failed to redeem mail-in rebate offers, reducing the company's expected rebate expense by $5 million. TiVo says it generally sees lower redemption rates during the Christmas shopping season, when consumers may be too distracted to file for rebates on time.

Credit this bonanza for retailers and suppliers partly to human nature. Many consumers are just too lazy, forgetful, or busy to apply for rebates: Call it a tax on the disorganized. Others think the 50 cents, $50—or even $200—is just not worth the hassle of collecting.

"I WAS FROSTED"

But many consumers—and state and federal authorities—suspect that companies design the rules to keep redemption rates down. They say companies count on complex rules, filing periods of as little as a week, repeated requests for copies of receipts, and long delays in sending out checks to discourage consumers from even attempting to retrieve their money. When the check does arrive, it sometimes gets tossed in the trash because it looks like junk mail.

These obstacles don't stop Chuck Gleason. A rebate junkie, he has redeemed dozens of rebates on the high-tech and electronics gizmos he buys. But getting his money, he says, sometimes drives him crazy.

On Nov. 7, 2004, for example, the 57-year-old director of operations for a Portland (Ore.) metal-recycling company bought a TiVo digital video recorder for $300. TiVo promised that a $100 rebate would arrive in six to eight weeks if Gleason mailed in his receipt and the universal product code on the box and kept his TiVo subscription for at least 30 days.

Source: Brian Grow, *BusinessWeek Online,* November 23, 2005, www.businessweek.com/maginanial/D5_49/b3962ø74.htm.

Gleason sent in the paperwork the very next day, and nothing happened. By February there was still no sign of his $100, despite repeated follow-ups, so he threatened to file complaints with state and federal officials. But TiVo's rebate processor, Parago, left him even more exasperated: "Because your issue requires further research, your e-mail has been forwarded to a special team," said an e-mail from a customer-service agent named Sophie.

Finally, on Mar. 29, more than 14 weeks after he bought his DVR, his check arrived. "I was frosted," he says.

"BREAKAGE" AND "SLIPPAGE"

Citing privacy restrictions, TiVo officials declined to discuss the case. But the company says it regrets any inconvenience and recently changed its rebate process to include a printable sign-up form at tivo.com to cut down on handwriting errors. Parago also declined to discuss the incident but said errors are rare among the "tens of millions" of rebates it processes each year.

Indeed, processors and companies offering rebates insist that there is no intentional effort to deny them, a move that Stinchfield, who is the chief executive of Orono (Minn.) consulting firm Promotional Marketing Insights, says would be akin to "brand suicide." Rather, companies say, the rules are aimed at stopping fraud. Rebate processors won't provide estimates for the amount of fraud they encounter, but Young America Corp., the nation's largest processor, says it now monitors 10,000 addresses suspected of submitting bogus rebates.

The quest for buyers who don't end up collecting a rebate has spawned special industry lingo. Purchases by consumers who never file for their rebates are called "breakage." Wireless companies that pay 100% rebates on some cell phones, for example, rely in part on "breakage" to make money. Rebate checks that are never cashed are called "slippage."

COMPLAINTS HAVE SOARED

One processor, TCA Fulfillment Services in New Rochelle, N.Y., published a "Rebate Redemption Guide" for its corporate customers several years ago. It cited the low redemption rates that companies could expect after hiring TCA: just 10% for a $10 rebate on a $100 product, and just 35% for a $50 rebate on a $200 product. "If you are using another fulfillment company, add 20% to these redemption rates," says the chart.

Lewisville (Tex.)-based Parago bought TCA's customer list last December and disavows that guide. It says it can't estimate current rates because clients don't provide the company with sales data. TCA founder Frank Giordano did not respond to several calls and a letter requesting comment.

Consumer-product makers such as Procter & Gamble pioneered rebates in the 1970s as a nifty way to advertise small discounts without actually marking the products down. In the'90s, their popularity soared as computer makers and consumer-electronics companies pitched them as a way to move piles of PCs, cell phones, and televisions before they became obsolete. The value of rebates jumped, too, from a couple of bucks to $100 or more.

With more companies plugging rebates—and more dollars at stake for consumers—complaints have soared. Gripes filed with the Council of Better Business Bureaus have tripled since 2001, from 964 to 3,641 last year. But processors say that number is still tiny compared with the vast number of claims they handle.

REGULATORY SCRUTINY

David S. Bookbinder files many of the complaints. Each year the 40-year-old computer technician claims more than 100 mail-in rebates. He figures those deals save him—and customers of his computer-repair business, Total PC Support, in Revere, Mass.—as much as $2,500. After eight weeks of waiting, he usually calls customer-service numbers to hunt down his check. If the representative alleges that paperwork was wrong or asks for more time, he automatically files complaints with the Better Business Bureau, the Federal Trade Commission, and the state attorney general.

Regulators are intensifying their scrutiny of the industry. In October, New York Attorney General Eliot Spitzer settled a case with Samsung Electronics America. The company agreed to pay $200,000 to 4,100 consumers who were denied rebates because they lived in apartment buildings. Samsung's rebate program, according to Spitzer's office, allowed only one rebate per address, and the form didn't have a space to list apartment numbers. Samsung did not respond to requests for comment.

Meanwhile, in Connecticut, officials are investigating ads that list prices only after rebates—a marketing scheme prohibited in the state. Attorney General Richard Blumenthal won't disclose the names of the retailers. "If consumers are compelled to jump through hoops to receive the rebate, or are denied rebates for illogical or arbitrary reasons, that adds fuel to our investigation," he says.

"NO INCENTIVE"

Some regulators are using novel tactics. On Nov. 7, Massachusetts officials filed suit against Young America to demand that it submit to an audit of $43 million in uncashed rebate checks. The company, headquartered in Young America, Minn., kept that amount of money from 1995 to mid-2002 in return for charging its clients lower fees, it says. Massachusetts officials believe that keeping uncashed checks could be an incentive to deny legitimate redemption claims. "It's almost like the old bait and switch," says Massachusetts State Treasurer Timothy P. Cahill.

Young America is fighting back. In written responses to questions from *BusinessWeek,* CEO Roger D. Andersen stands by the company's policy and says retailers and suppliers sometimes prefer that it keep uncashed checks. That keeps Young America from having to send them back and then turn around and collect its fee from clients.

"Young America receives the same fees whether a submission is valid or invalid," he says. "We have no incentive to increase invalid rates."

UNIFORM RULES

The backlash against mail-in rebates is pushing some companies to drop them. Best Buy plans to phase them out in two years. At Staples, mail-in rebates were the No.1 customer complaint for years, says Jim Sherlock, director of sales and merchandising. So a year ago, the Framingham (Mass.) company switched to an online system called EasyRebates that customers use to file for rebates and track their progress.

Staples says waiting times for payments have been cut from about 10 weeks to as little as four, and rebate complaints dropped by 25%. "Breakage" also dropped by as much as 10%, but that decline in unclaimed rebates is offset by better fraud prevention, it says.

The fulfillment houses are also overhauling their systems. While it won't disclose figures, Parago says it has invested "tens of millions" of dollars in computer technology. So now, computers, not customer-service agents, validate most of the claims. Then consumers receive e-mail updates and can check Web sites such as RebatesHQ.com to monitor claims. Before, says Parago Chief Financial Officer Juli C. Spottiswood, getting a rebate update was a "big black hole."

With billions of dollars at stake, bids to set uniform rules for rebates have met a ferocious response. Last year, California State Senator Liz Figueroa introduced a bill requiring companies to grant customers at least 30 days to apply for a rebate, mail checks within 60 days of receiving an application, and standardize the paperwork and personal data needed for a claim.

"REGULATION IS WARRANTED"

Telecom giants SBC Communications and T-Mobile and the California Manufacturers &

Technology Assn. quickly mobilized. They argued that Figueroa's bill would drive up costs and increase fraud by cutting down on the proof required for a rebate. After passing the California House and Senate, the bill was vetoed by Governor Arnold Schwarzenneger.

Now, Figueroa, a Democrat, is evaluating whether to reintroduce the bill in January. "This is an area where regulation is warranted," she maintains.

Despite the crackdowns and efforts at reforms, redeeming rebates will probably never be much fun. "In a perfect world, consumers would love mail-in rebates to go away," says Stephen Baker, director of industry analysis at NPD. "However, they want the best price that they can get. Those two things are fundamentally going to be at odds."

CASE DISCUSSION QUESTIONS

1. This article describes one reason manufacturers might want to offer rebates rather than decrease wholesale price. Explain why this can be viewed as an example of customized pricing.
2. Even if all rebates were redeemed, why might manufacturers still want to offer rebates rather than decrease wholesale prices?
3. Why do you suppose that Best Buy, rather than one of Best Buy's big suppliers such as Sony or Panasonic, is considering eliminating rebates?

CHAPTER 14

Information Technology and Business Processes

CASE: Supply Chain Whirl

Five years ago, Whirlpool began an effort to turn around its global supply chain. The company is seeing results, but it's not done yet.

The supply chain at Whirlpool Corp. in 2000 was broken. Indeed, a manager there at the time quipped that among the four major appliance makers in the U.S., Whirlpool ranked fifth in delivery performance.

"We had too much inventory, too little inventory, wrong inventory, right inventory/wrong place, any combination of those things," says J. B. Hoyt, who was then supply chain project director. He says a sales vice president approached him one day and said he'd accept even worse performance from supply systems if they would just be consistent rather than wildly bouncing back and forth between good and poor production and shipping plans.

So in 2001, Benton Harbor, Mich.–based Whirlpool embarked on a multiproject global overhaul of its supply chain systems. The metaproject remains a work in progress today, with a number of systems yet to be rolled out and some major technical issues to be resolved. But managers at Whirlpool say its success to date—including huge improvements in customer service and reduced supply chain costs—is providing the psychological and financial impetus to drive the remaining systems work.

Whirlpool CIO Esat Sezer says that by 2000, the company had grown by acquisition and geographic expansion to the point that old systems, stitched together by spreadsheets and manual procedures, couldn't cope with the exploding complexity. "Our supply chain was becoming a competitive disadvantage for us," he says. Availability—the percentage of time a product is in the right place at the right time—was an unacceptably low 83 percent, even as inventories remained too high overall.

The homegrown supply systems were primitive and not well integrated with the company's SAP ERP system, which had been installed in 1999, or with a legacy production scheduling system, Sezer says. And they weren't integrated with the systems of major wholesale customers or suppliers of parts and materials. "The plans we were creating weren't linking back into reality," he says.

In particular, Sezer says, supply chain systems weren't fine-grained enough, nor were they very good at juggling priorities and constraints except through slow and cumbersome manual methods. Often, they would optimize locally—a single

Source: Gray H. Anthes, "Supply Chain Whirl," *Computer World*, June 6, 2005.

product line at one location, for example—but not for the supply chain as a whole.

Here's what Whirlpool was using for its North American supply chain in 2000:

- A homegrown production scheduling system, the Whirlpool Manufacturing Control System (WMCS), which was developed in the mid-1980s and extensively modified over the years.
- SAP AG's R/3 ERP system, which was installed in 1999 and used for transaction-processing applications such as accounting and order processing.
- i2 Technologies Inc.'s Demand Planner (now called Demand Manager), which was installed in 1997 and used for demand forecasting.
- A system for distribution planning that was custom-developed for Whirlpool in the 1980s that used optimization software from ILOG Inc.

Then, in 2001, Whirlpool began to implement an advanced planning and scheduling (APS) system. It included a suite of supply chain integration and optimization tools from i2—Supply Chain Planner for Master Scheduling, Deployment Planning, and Inventory Planning. Those three modules, the heart of Whirlpool's efforts to fix its supply chain, went live in three phases over 2001 and 2002.

In mid-2002, Whirlpool installed the i2 TradeMatrix Collaborative Planning, Forecasting and Replenishment (CPFR) system, a Web-based collaboration tool for sharing and combining the sales forecasts of Whirlpool and its major trade partners—Sears, Roebuck and Co., Lowe's Cos., and Best Buy Co.

The rollout of a component for Web-based collaboration with suppliers, based on SAP's Inventory Collaboration Hub, is just getting under way. And Whirlpool continues to use the old WMCS for production scheduling but plans to replace that with SAP's Production Planning module.

IT'S AVAILABLE

By all accounts, the supply chain overhaul was a smashing success for the $13 billion company. CPFR cut forecasting errors in half. APS boosted availability in North America from 83 percent to 93 percent (it's at 97 percent today), reduced finished-goods inventories by more than 20 percent, and trimmed 5 percent from freight and warehouse costs. Whirlpool declined to discuss the cost of the projects.

Managers at Whirlpool give much of the credit for the success of these projects to a close partnership between the IT department and the business units. Says Hoyt, "It was one of the first times the IT community didn't say, 'OK, here's your tool.' We said the tool had to do x, y and z. We did the requirements analysis together."

Whirlpool considered standardizing completely on SAP for all ERP and supply chain systems in North America, but i2 ultimately got the nod for the APS system, the critical part needed to fix the company's availability and inventory problems. "There was a lot of back and forth, but after a long harangue and discussion of our business requirements, we settled on the i2 tool set in North America," Hoyt says.

But while i2 was seen as being more capable than SAP for handling the fine-grained optimization, constraint-based planning, and prioritization that the business units wanted, it was far from ideal from an IT perspective. The APS system would cost IT, whose budget is about $190 million, more than an all-SAP supply chain because there would be less integration, more systems interfaces, and more skills to maintain in-house. Plus, IT was worried about i2's deteriorating financial condition.

Whirlpool had already standardized on IBM AIX application servers and zSeries mainframe database servers for supply chain systems and had put systems for all its global operations in a single data center in Benton Harbor. Now it was time to standardize on software.

So in 2001, a mandate came from the CIO, via Whirlpool's Executive Committee, that supply chain modernizations henceforth would be based entirely on SAP. In particular, new systems planned for Europe for 2003 and Latin America would use SAP's Advanced Planner and Optimizer rather than the more capable but costly i2-based APS system used in North America. And they were to use SAP's NetWeaver for Web collaboration with suppliers and trade partners rather than North America's TradeMatrix CPFR.

Vivek Mehta, a lead supply chain analyst at Whirlpool, says SAP may catch up with i2 in its optimization capabilities, but in the meantime, i2's financial condition is worrisome. "There were 10 guys at i2 that we interacted with, and some of them are gone now," he says. "There's lack of continuity."

"We have this challenge, where the IT organization is pushing for everything to be SAP, but the business, on the other hand, is going for whatever brings them value," Mehta says. "They are now used to the optimal plan, the high service levels, the lower inventories. So if we bring in something and say their availability will go down by a couple of points, no way will they buy that."

Sezer says Whirlpool will probably replace i2 with SAP "eventually" but is in no hurry. "We'd like to get the return out of that investment before making any platform decisions," he says.

Sezer says that in the four years since Whirlpool standardized on IBM and SAP as "strategic partners," revenue has increased on average $1 billion per year and IT expenses have fallen 6 percent per year. He says there are several joint development projects under way involving all three companies.

But for the time being, the combination of SAP and i2 works well for Whirlpool, far better than the legacy tools of a few years ago. Sezer says the company's supply chain is now a competitive advantage. "On a global scale, to be able to manage all your operating platforms, I'm not aware that any of our competitors have that today," he says.

Specifically, in this chapter we will address the following questions:

- What is the impact of business process change on IT implementation?
- What are the goals of IT from the perspective of supply chain management?
- What IT components are needed to achieve the goals of supply chain management?
- What are the supply chain component systems and how should they be approached?
- What are decision support systems and how do they support supply chain management?
- What criteria should be used to select decision support systems?
- What drives the selection of best of breed systems?

14.1 INTRODUCTION

Information technology (IT) is an important enabler of effective supply chain management, which typically spans the entire enterprise and beyond, encompassing suppliers on one end and customers on the other. Therefore, our discussion of IT for supply chains will include both systems that are internal to an individual company as well as external systems, which facilitate information transfer *between* various companies and individuals.

Indeed, as we have observed in Chapter 3, when applying supply chain strategies that reduce cost and lead times and increase service level, the timeliness and availability of relevant information are critical. In addition, an increasing number of companies are providing value-added IT-based services to their customers as a way of differentiating themselves in the marketplace and developing strong long-term relationships with their customers. Of course, once these kinds of services are offered by even one company within an industry, they can very quickly become a basic requirement for all others.

A common theme of our IT discussion and the first section in this chapter is the importance of combining business process (BP) changes with IT improvements. A recent study by MIT, PRTM, and SAP suggests that there is a strong link between IT strategy, sound business processes, and supply chain performance.

This is complemented by a discussion of an important supply chain process called sales and operations planning and what kind of IT solutions can assist with making this process work more effectively.

In Chapter 15, we will cover the technology issues related to standards, infrastructure, and electronic commerce in more detail. In this chapter, we will review the basic goals of supply chain IT and the specific system components related to supply chain management. We will explore decision support and business intelligence technologies and how they relate to supply chain planning. Finally, we will discuss several ways of analyzing how to make decisions and integrate supply chain functionality into current systems or the IT situation.

14.2 THE IMPORTANCE OF BUSINESS PROCESSES

A recent study by MIT, PRTM and SAP, see [107], and a wealth of anecdotal evidence, as in the Whirlpool case study, suggest that there is a link between IT strategy, sound business processes, and supply chain performance. Unfortunately, until the [107] study, there has been little hard evidence to establish the link. Interestingly, in this study, the authors use data from about 75 different supply chains to argue that companies that invest mostly in business processes do better than those who invest in IT only and lack the appropriate business processes. Indeed, the data suggest that investments only in technology without the appropriate business processes lead to negative returns.

Specifically, the objective of the study was to find whether or not there is a direct correlation between the maturity of the business process, the amount of investment in IT infrastructure, and supply chain performance.

To address these issues, there were two challenges:

- Identify measures to characterize supply chain effectiveness.
- Develop measures to characterize the level of maturity of the business process and the information technology employed by the company.

Of course, it is relatively easy to measure supply chain performance. Indeed, in the last few years, many companies have used key performance indicators (KPI) to identify opportunities and challenges in their supply chains. In fact, this has been the main motivation behind many of the benchmarking methodologies developed recently, for example, the Supply-Chain Operations Reference (SCOR) model developed by the Supply Chain Council.

Unfortunately, measuring the level of maturity of the business process or the information technology infrastructure that a company possesses is much more difficult. What makes this a real challenge, however, is the fact that different portions of the company's business can be at different levels of maturity. In fact, even the same portion of the business may be out of balance in the sense that the maturity of the business process and the information technology do not complement each other very well. Thus, in [107], the authors developed two sets of questions: one to characterize the level of business maturity and the second to characterize the level of maturity of the information technology.

The overall level of maturity of the firm's business processes is based on the SCOR model. There are **four categories of business processes:**

Level I: Disconnected processes. Companies at this level are characterized by the proliferation of many independent processes. Companies are organized functionally with no or a low degree of integration. Supply chain planning is typically done for each site independently of other sites. Characteristics of this level include:

- Functional (silo) strategies.
- Lack of clear, consistent supply chain management processes.
- No measurements, or measurements not aligned with company objectives.

Level II: Internal integration. At this level, companies are organized functionally, with a high degree of integration. Decisions are made through the integration of key functional areas, that is, sales, manufacturing, and logistics. Common forecasts are applied throughout the organization. Characteristics of this level include:

- Integration of some functional information to decrease inventory and improve efficiency.
- Documented processes that are followed across the entire organization.
- Key measurements that are used departmentally.

Level III: Intracompany integration and limited external integration. At this level, companies are cross-functionally organized. Organizations at this stage involve key suppliers and customers in decision-making processes. Characteristics of this level include:

- Decisions optimized across the internal supply chain.
- Sophisticated processes that involve all affected internal organizations.
- Key suppliers and customers included in supply chain planning.

Level IV: Multi-enterprise integration. Organizations at this level apply multi-enterprise processes, use common business objectives, and have an extensive knowledge of the suppliers' and customers' business environments. Collaboration links trading partners and enables them to operate as one virtual corporation. Characteristics of this stage include:

- Collaboration across the entire supply chain.
- Internal and external collaborative supply chain management focus on key service and financial goals.
- Measures directly linking supply chain results to company goals.

The different levels of business processes need to be supported by a corresponding information technology infrastructure; these are the **four different categories of IT systems** applied in the study:

Level I: Batch processes, independent systems, and redundant data across the organization. Focus is on spreadsheet and manual manipulation of data for decision making.

Level II: Shared data across the supply chain. Decisions are made using planning tools that apply data across the supply chain; for example, demand planning module that applies expert knowledge, advanced algorithms, and statistical methods for forecasting.

Level III: Complete visibility of internal data. Key suppliers and customers have access to some of these data; for example, forecast is shared with key suppliers. Processes, not only data, are shared across the supply chain.

Level IV: Data and processes are shared internally and externally.

To characterize the linkage between supply chain performance and the maturity of business processes and IT infrastructure, the research team collected and analyzed data from 60 companies worldwide providing detailed (and confidential) information on 75 different supply chains. The research team included people from SAP and PRTM and data were collected in 2002–2003.

The team collected data from the various supply chains by sending questionnaires focusing on supply chain planning processes and systems. The team applied the SCOR model to assess the current state of a supply chain's business processes. In this model, seven planning areas were evaluated:

- **Strategic planning:** Network design, inventory positioning, and manufacturing strategy.
- **Demand planning:** Demand forecasts and promotional planning.
- **Supply planning:** Coordination of manufacturing, inventory, and transportation activities across the supply chain.
- **Supply–demand balancing:** Trade-off between supplier's capability and customer demand is considered; pricing and promotional activities are applied systematically to better match supply and demand.
- **Procurement planning:** Materials and commodities sourcing strategy.
- **Manufacturing planning:** Single site versus enterprisewide strategy.
- **Delivery planning:** Commitments to customers are based on forecast, available capacity, or real-time inventory and manufacturing information.

For each planning area, the team identified both systems and processes according to the maturity level defined in the previous section. Specifically, the team used the data collected from the 75 supply chains to determine the maturity of processes and systems along each one of the seven dimensions. Thus, the maturity of a supply chain business process is determined as the average of the seven scores on each of the planning dimensions. Consequently, the business process maturity level of a supply chain is a number between 1 and 4. A supply chain's system maturity is determined in the same way.

We refer to a company as having a mature business process (system) if its business process (system) maturity level is at least two. Finally, we define best-in-class systems (BICS) to be the top 20 percent IT mature supply chains, that is, these are the 20 percent of the supply chains with the top system maturity level. Of course, not all of those have mature business processes.

Using these definitions and based on the empirical study, the results were as follows:

- **Companies with mature business processes have lower inventory levels.** Figure 14-1 suggests that companies with mature business processes have significantly reduced the number of days of supply of inventory, cash-to-cash cycle time, inventory carrying cost, and total obsolescence cost, measured as a percentage of revenue. For example, process-mature companies with top systems performance—that is, BICS companies that are process mature—were able to reduce inventory carrying cost by 35 percent. This leads to the second key finding.
- **Improvements in certain areas demand IT investments.** Consider fill rate levels; see Figure 14-2. Note that only make-to-stock (MTS) companies are included since this does not apply to make-to-order and configure-to-order companies. This implies that IT infrastructure provides a huge competitive advantage with respect to fill rate. To obtain better insight into this finding, consider a participant in the research, a global toy producer that faces thousands of order entries a minute during the high season of its business, the fourth quarter. Each order has to be allocated to the right warehouse, and product substitution has to be taken into account. This environment demands a significant investment in IT infrastructure to provide the appropriate level of fill rate.
- **BICS companies with mature processes achieve superior financial performance.** One of the most significant findings of the study underscores the importance of investments both in systems and processes. Indeed, Figure 14-3 suggests that companies with mature business processes and best-in-class IT systems have on average 14 percent net profit compared to the 8 percent market average; that is, they have 75 percent higher profitability.

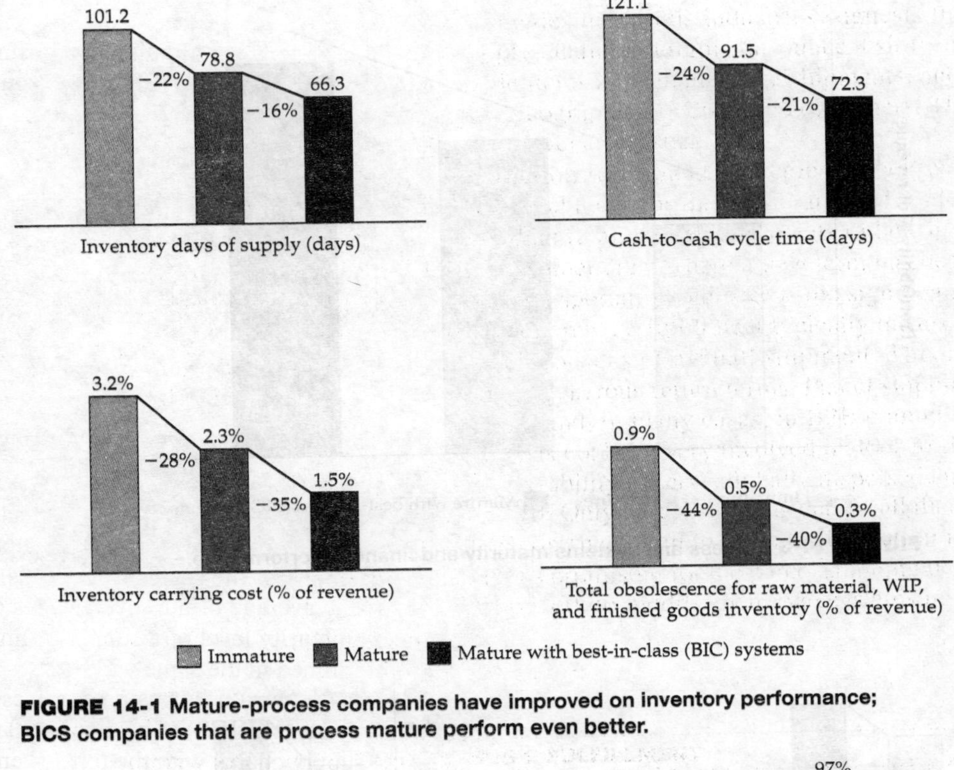

FIGURE 14-1 Mature-process companies have improved on inventory performance; BICS companies that are process mature perform even better.

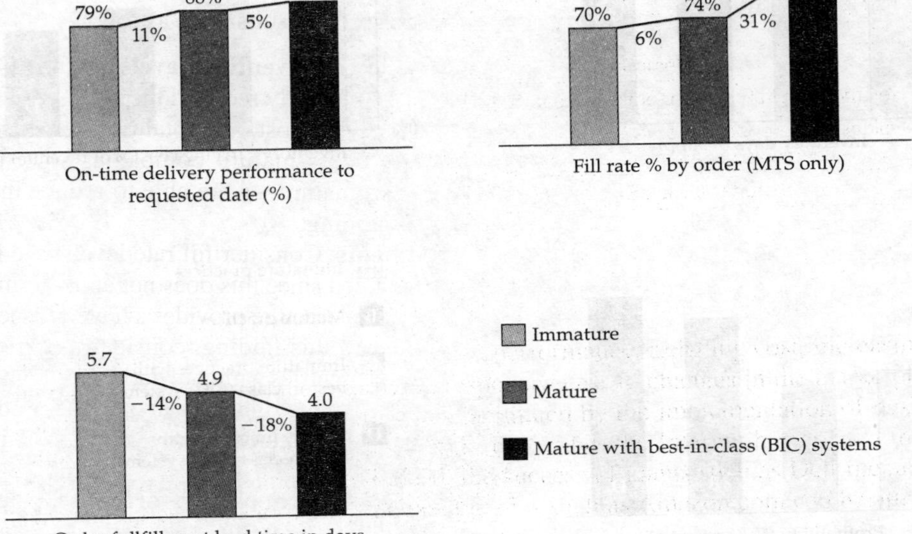

FIGURE 14-2 On-time delivery, fill rate level, and order fulfillment lead time.

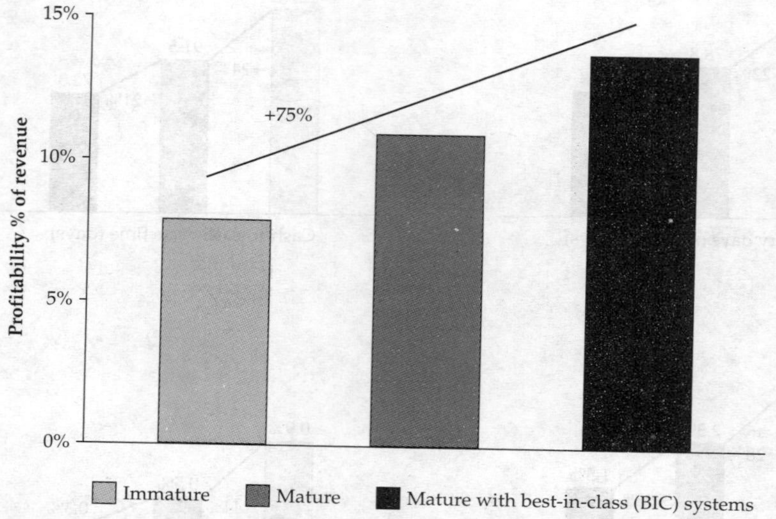

FIGURE 14-3 Process and systems maturity and financial performance.

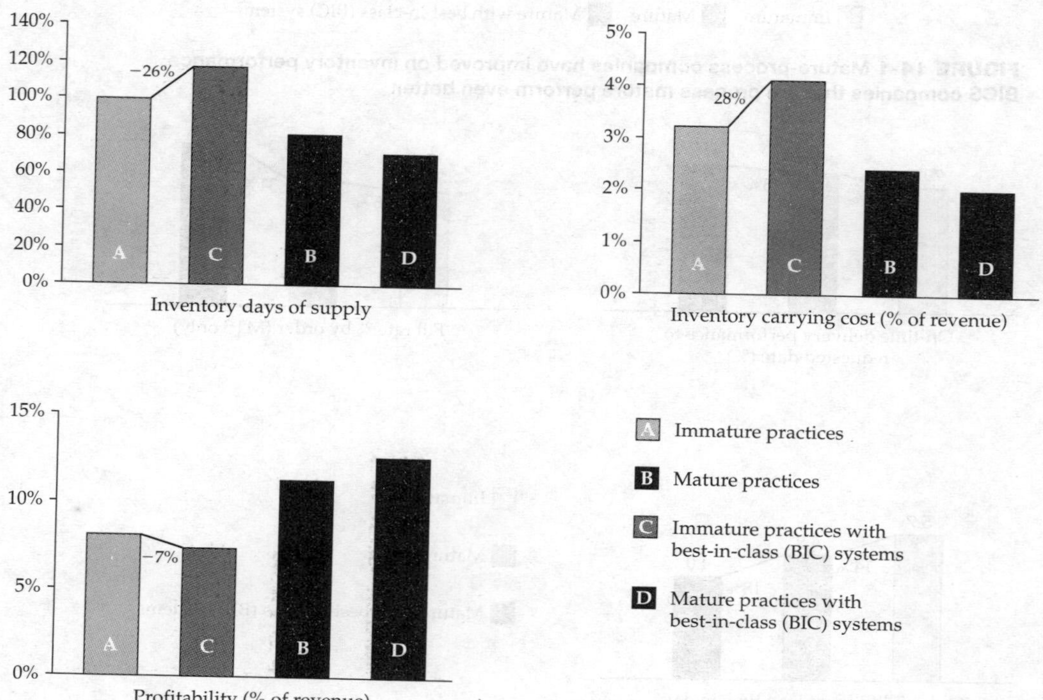

FIGURE 14-4 Impact of investment in IT infrastructure.

- **Investing only in IT infrastructure leads to significant inefficiencies.** One of the most surprising findings of the study was that companies who have invested only in IT infrastructure but not in supporting business processes suffer significant inefficiencies; see Figure 14-4. As the figure indicates, BICS companies, that is, the top 20 percent IT mature companies, who are process immature have higher days of supply, higher inventory carrying costs, and lower profit than process-immature companies that did not invest in IT infrastructure. For example, BICS companies with immature business processes have 26 percent higher inventory days of supply, 28 percent higher inventory carrying costs, and 7 percent lower average profit. The bottom line seems to be that just implementing IT systems without the supporting business processes is a waste of money.
- **Priority in IT investments depends on your objectives.** A frequently asked question is what is the impact of various IT technologies on different performance criteria such as order fulfillment lead time, inventory levels, or cash-to-cash cycle time? Interestingly, the results indicate that companies that support their demand planning process with a corresponding software module, that is, demand planning module, shorten their order fulfillment lead time by 47 percent and reduce cash-to-cash cycle time by 49 percent. Impact on inventory levels measured in terms of days of supply is quite minimal, less than 10 percent reduction. On the other hand, supporting the supply planning process with IT systems reduces inventory (days of supply) by about 40 percent.

The previous analysis can be nicely summarized in Figure 14-5. The vertical axis provides information about the maturity level of the business processes while the horizontal axis provides information on the maturity level of the IT systems. The following paragraphs discuss what the boxes in Figure 14-5 represent.

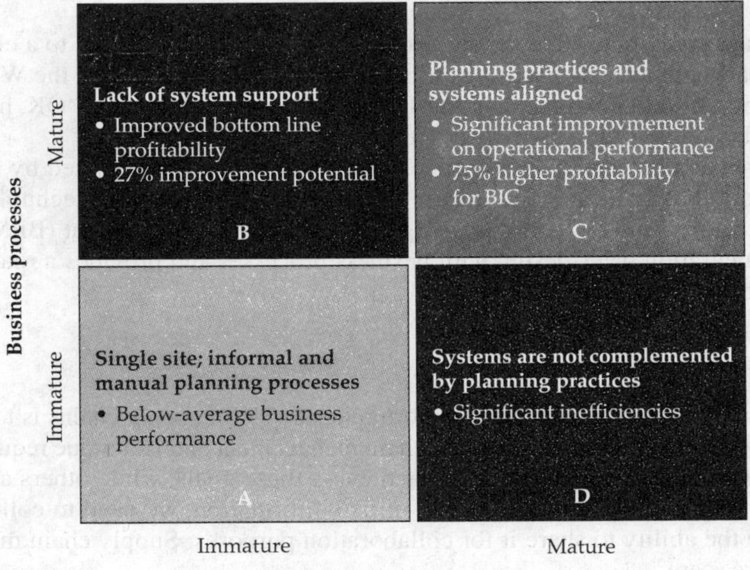

FIGURE 14-5 Linking processes and systems with operational and financial performance.

Box A represents companies (or, more precisely, supply chains) that are characterized by immature business processes and IT systems. The study suggests that these supply chains suffer from below-average business performance. This includes high inventory levels, high cash-to-cash cycle time, and low profitability, to give a few examples.

Box B represents supply chains with mature business processes and immature systems. Companies in this category perform significantly better than those who did not invest in either processes or systems, but they leave a lot on the table. Specifically, the study suggests that these supply chains can increase profit (measured as a percentage of revenue) by, on average, 27 percent by investing in IT; that is, by transferring their IT systems through the stages of excellence to become mature systems. Of course, such an investment in IT may require adjusting the business processes.

Box C represents supply chains with mature systems and processes. These supply chains enjoy significant improvements in operational performance. More importantly, supply chain leaders, that is, supply chains that have mature processes and are BICS,—those that are in the top 20 percent of IT maturity—enjoy 75 percent higher profit relative to other companies. Indeed, a remarkable performance!

Finally, Box D represents supply chains with mature IT systems but not processes. Surprisingly, the study reveals that these companies perform even worse than those with immature systems and processes. This, of course, requires a more careful analysis. Indeed, everything else being equal, one would expect that the higher maturity level of the firm's IT systems would yield higher supply chain performance. The study suggests that this is not the case.

There are several explanations for this dichotomy. First, IT infrastructure typically requires significant investment accompanied by expensive support staff. At the same time, IT provides only information; without a process that is able to effectively transform information into knowledge and decisions, the supply chain will react to this vast amount of data in a greedy fashion, generating an ineffective strategy.

The Whirlpool case study notes that the success of these projects is credited to a close partnership between the IT department and the business units. Indeed, according to Hoyt, the Whirlpool supply chain project director, "It was one of the first times the IT community didn't say, 'OK, here's your tool.' We said the tool had to do x, y and z. We did the requirements analysis together."

The importance of combining business process with IT has been recognized by the industry. In Chapter 15, we also will discuss in detail a new infrastructure and software technology called service-oriented architecture (SOA) and the related business process management (BPM) technologies that enable better integration of IT design with business processes and provides a roadmap and technology solutions for this purpose.

14.3 GOALS OF SUPPLY CHAIN IT

A different perspective on the challenges and opportunities of IT for supply chains is to consider some of the desired goals of IT as they relate to supply chain management and its unique requirements. Some companies and industries are currently far from achieving these goals, while others are well on their way to accomplishing many of them. In order to utilize information, we need to collect it, access it, analyze it, and have the ability to share it for collaboration purposes. Supply chain management system goals in these areas are

- Collect information on each product from production to delivery or purchase point, and provide complete visibility for all parties involved.

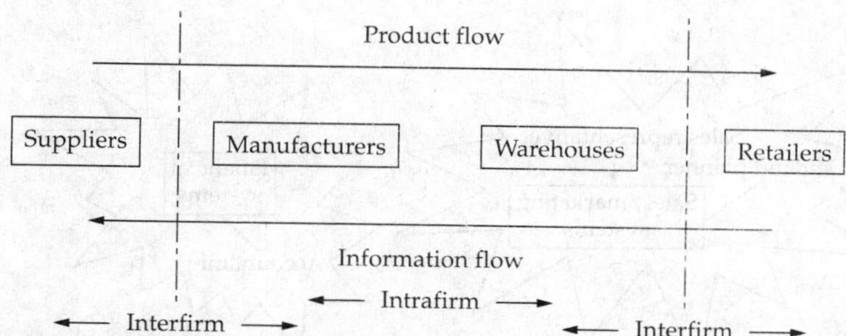

FIGURE 14-6 Flow of information and goods in the supply chain.

- Access any data in the system from a *single point of contact*.
- Analyze, plan activities, and make trade-offs based on information from the entire supply chain.
- Collaborate with supply chain partners. As we have seen in previous chapters, collaboration allows companies to manage uncertainty, for example, through information sharing, and ultimately achieve global optimization.

The primary goal of IT in the supply chain is to link the point of production seamlessly with the point of delivery or purchase. The idea is to have an information trail that follows the product's physical trail. This allows planning, tracking, and estimating lead times based on real data. Any party that has an interest in the whereabouts of the product should be able to have access to this information. As we can see in Figure 14-6, information and products flow from the supplier to the manufacturer, internally through the manufacturer's distribution system, and then on to the retailers.

Below we discuss each goal:

- **Collect information:** Evidently, the retailer needs to know the status of its orders and the suppliers need to be able to anticipate an incoming order from the manufacturer. This entails access to data that reside in other companies' information systems as well as across functions and geographic locations inside a company. Furthermore, the participants need to see data in their own terms; that is, if suppliers of cotton are looking at the demand for Q-Tips, they need it translated into pounds of cotton consumed. Therefore, translation tables such as bills of material are required throughout the system.

  The availability of information regarding the status of products and material is the basis on which intelligent supply chain decisions can be made. Furthermore, it is not sufficient to simply track products across the supply chain; there is also a need to alert diverse systems to the implications of this movement. If there is a delay in a delivery that will affect production schedules, the appropriate systems need to be notified so they can make the proper adjustments by either delaying the schedules or seeking alternative sources. This goal requires standardization of product identification (e.g., bar coding) across companies and industries. For example, Federal Express has implemented a tracking system that provides ongoing information on the whereabouts of any package handled by the company and makes this information available internally as well as to customers. Radio frequency identification (RFID) technology, discussed in detail in Chapter 15, is an attempt to address this issue in the extended supply chain.
- **Access to data:** Here we introduce the important concept of single point of contact. The goal is that all the available information, either information provided to a customer or required internally, can be accessed in one stop and be consistent, regardless of the mode of inquiry used (e.g., phone, fax, Internet, kiosk) or who is making the inquiry. This requirement is complicated by the fact that to satisfy a customer's query, information may be required that resides in various locations within one company and, in

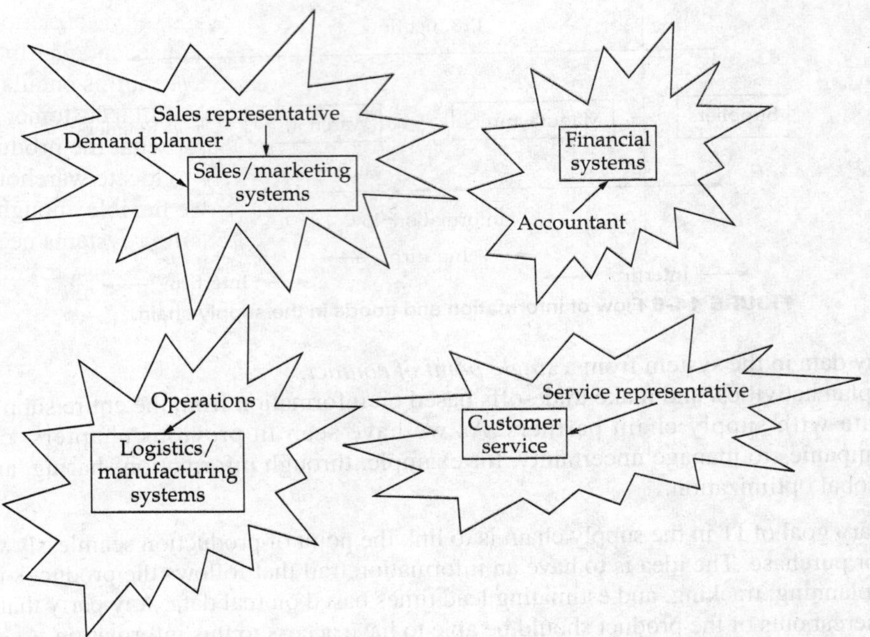

FIGURE 14-7 Current information systems.

some cases, across several companies. In many companies, information systems tend to be islands, depending on their functions within the company. Customer service will work with one system, accounting with another, while the manufacturing and distribution systems are completely separate (see Figure 14-7). Occasionally there may be a transfer of some crucial information that needs to be accessed across systems, but if the transfer is not done in real time, then the systems never have exactly the same data. The customer service representative receiving an order may not be able to provide shipping status information, and the plant may not be able to inquire about current outstanding orders. Ideally, everyone who needs to use certain data should have access to the same real-time data through any interface device (see Figure 14-8).

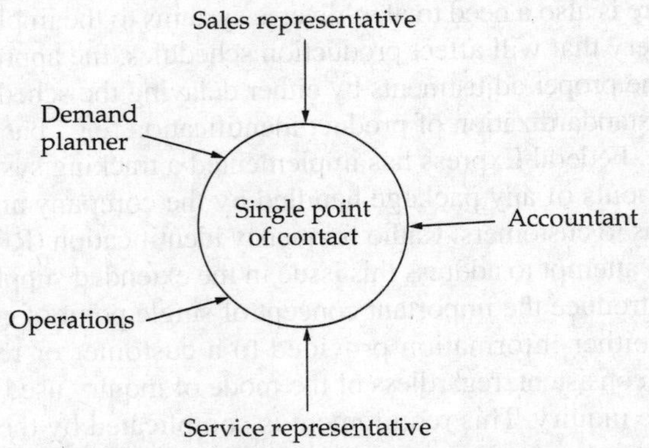

FIGURE 14-8 New generation of information systems.

- **Analysis based on supply chain data:** The third goal is related to analyzing the data, especially in a way that takes into account the global supply chain picture. In addition, the information system must be utilized to find the most efficient ways to produce, assemble, warehouse, and distribute products—in other words, the best way to operate the supply chain. As we have seen, this entails various levels of decision making: from operational decisions involving the way to fulfill a customer order, to tactical decisions related to which warehouse to stock with what product, or what the production plan for the next three months should be, to strategic decisions about where to locate warehouses, and what products to develop and produce. To facilitate this, systems need to be flexible enough to accommodate changes in supply chain strategies. To achieve this kind of flexibility, systems need to be highly configurable and new standards need to be developed. We will discuss these issues in detail below.
- **Collaborate with supply chain partners:** The ability to collaborate with supply chain partners is essential to a company's success. Indeed, as observed in Chapter 1, an important objective in supply chain management is replacing sequential processes with global optimization. This requires not only sophisticated alignment of IT systems but also the integration of business processes. Depending on its supply chain role, a company may be required to either integrate with a customer's procurement system or require its own suppliers to link into its own systems or collaborative platforms, or both. The level and type of collaboration vary between industries. For instance, collaborative forecasting was initiated in the consumer packaged goods industry, while supplier integration is more common in the hi-tech industry where outsourcing of critical components requires systems that support the product and logistics coordination.

  In recent years, collaboration has become the focus of supply chain systems. The ability to link and work effectively with suppliers has produced new systems called supplier relationship management (SRM). In addition, the various exchanges that were developed during the Internet boom of the late 90s are becoming collaboration platforms, whether private or public. On the other end of the supply chain, customer relationship management (CRM) systems are evolving to provide better contact and understanding of customer needs. A specialized supply chain standard for collaboration between suppliers and vendors called collaborative planning, forecasting, and replenishment (CPFR) is described in detail in Chapter 15.

  The four goals of supply chain management do not all have to be achieved at the same time, and are not necessarily dependent on each other. They can be targeted in parallel, with the order of importance depending on the industry, company size, internal priorities, and return on investment considerations. For instance, a bank could not survive without single-point-of-contact capability, a delivery company without a sophisticated tracking system, and a high-tech manufacturer without a production planning system.

Enterprise resource planning (ERP) systems are installed in most companies today and cover the first two requirements to a large extent. They provide a common infrastructure throughout the company with role-based access to data. Web-based portals often provide the entry point into these systems for internal use as well as for customers, suppliers, and partners. The portal can simplify access to data by providing a single point of contact as well as a collaboration platform. Furthermore, portals are moving toward an abstract point of access that AMR Research names "The unbound portal"; see [221]. This portal will be accessible from whatever device or interface system the user is accessing at a certain point and not only on the Internet as portals are currently deployed.

The following retail case study nicely illustrates the way to achieve these goals using information technology.

CASE: 7-Eleven Stocks Up on Tech Savvy

Standing in front of a refrigerated case at the 7-Eleven store in Rockwall, Texas, on a Friday morning, store manager Sherry Neal considered a seemingly mundane, but in fact important, decision: how many chicken salad sandwiches to order for the next day.

To aid her decision, Neal held a new lightweight wireless tablet with a colorful screen chock-full of information. She noted that she had two sandwiches that were due to expire that day and six the next. Using the gadget's built-in keyboard, she recorded the inventory information into an electronic form.

On the same screen, she saw that the National Weather Service was forecasting seasonably warm and fair weather for the next five days. Having observed customer behavior as an employee of 7-Eleven since 1979, Neal knew good weather was likely to mean good business over the upcoming weekend. Another part of the screen told her how many chicken salad sandwiches her store had sold on each of the last four Saturdays.

The display also provided information that let her see she had been selling out of the increasingly popular sandwiches the last few days.

"I've got to be more aggressive," she concluded as she used the gadget to order four more sandwiches, predicting that six would sell on Friday and another six on Saturday. She transmitted the order wirelessly to the store's back-office server, then onto the corporate network and data center, and eventually to 7-Eleven's fresh food distributor, where the sandwiches were made, loaded onto a truck, and delivered to the store around midnight.

Thanks to innovative technology that permeates every layer of the world's largest convenience chain store, 7-Eleven knows exactly how many chicken salad sandwiches it sold in each of its 5,800 North American stores today, yesterday, last week, last month, and last year. Better yet, it can predict with great accuracy how many of the item each store will sell tomorrow, and it can do the same for each of the roughly 2,500 products sold in its stores.

The hundreds of millions of dollars 7-Eleven has invested in technology over the past 10 years appear to be paying off. The profitable company, whose stock has soared above $30 since trading for less than $6 in early 2003, boasts 35 consecutive quarters of same-store sales increases and last year reported $12.2 billion in revenue.

7-Eleven hasn't always flourished. It struggled in the late 1980s after an ill-conceived acquisition of gasoline refiner Citgo and an ill-timed leveraged buyout aggravated by the October 1987 stock market crash. Help arrived in 1991 when 7-Eleven's Japan licensee, Ito-Yokado, became the company's majority shareholder and shared its retailing approach with the entire company.

ITEM BY ITEM

The innovative demand-chain approach to retailing that Ito-Yokado used to great success at Seven-Eleven Japan is known as "tanpin kanri," meaning item-by-item management, as opposed to category-by-category management. In traditional retailing, the emphasis is on how, say, beverages as a class are selling. In tanpin kanri, the emphasis is on how a particular beverage, such as Dr Pepper, is selling. The idea is to pay attention to the fine details of customers' buying preferences and let them dictate which products are carried in the store—and, ultimately, which products are developed.

In Japan, the strategy turned Seven-Eleven stores into hot spots to shop, especially when it comes to trendy snacks and freshly made food. In

Source: TheDeal.com, "Item by Item," http://news.com.com/7-Eleven+stocks+up+on+tech+savvy/2100-1022_3-5841919.html, posted August 23, 2005. Used by permission of TheDeal.com.

North America, customers are likely to visit a 7-Eleven store a few times a week, but in Japan they show up several times a day for breakfast, lunch, dinner, and snacks. People are often looking for something new to taste, and delivering appetizing new food items is the key to keeping customers coming back in Japan and in North America.

Technology plays a crucial role in gathering, analyzing, and distributing information in tanpin kanri and in its North American incarnation, known as retailer initiative. Before 7-Eleven introduced retailer initiative to North American stores, in 1994, the company had no accurate way of knowing which products its stores were selling. The company only knew which products it had bought from suppliers.

"Suppliers used to decide how much of their products to place on the shelves," recalls Margaret Chabris, public relations director at 7-Eleven and an employee at the company since 1978. "Decisions were made in the manufacturers' best interests, not necessarily the customers' best interests."

Keith Morrow, 7-Eleven's chief information officer and vice president of information systems, puts it even more plainly: "To take the shelves back from suppliers and vendors causes us to place a heavy reliance on automation and technology. We need actionable information in the store to place orders, or we just become order takers from our suppliers."

Today, the retailer initiative strategy underlies all technology at 7-Eleven. "Our philosophy is that decisions about what should be in the store are best made at the store at the moment of truth by people in the store on a real-time basis," says Morrow, who joined the company in early 2001. "Information lets us shape the store and what's in it around the demand curve of the customer who comes into the store, based on what they're doing day to day, minute by minute, not based on some focus group or marketing research or nonscientific guess of what a customer might do."

WHAT CUSTOMERS WANT

The ability to respond quickly to customers' ever-changing tastes is paramount in the convenience store business. "The customer will reward those stores who know what they want," says Jeff Lenard of the National Association of Convenience Stores. He points out that competition for the convenience store customer has intensified over the past few years as many types of stores—pet stores, toy stores, drugstores, video rental outfits, and even consumer electronics stores—have begun selling cold beverages and snacks.

"Over the last several years, 7-Eleven has been a leader and an innovator in using technology to serve customers," he says. "It may not be something customers see, but they see it because the store better knows what they want."

When it comes to collecting information on customer preferences and "using the information both tactically for ordering and strategically for merchandising, 7-Eleven is far ahead of any of its peers," says John Heinbockel, a Goldman, Sachs analyst who covers the company. "Other convenience store chains have only just gotten around to point-of-sale scanning in the last couple of years. They don't have the texture and the data that 7-Eleven has item by item, store by store, day by day, for the last decade."

The Mobile Operations Terminal, or MOT, from NEC that helped Neal order chicken salad sandwiches is one of two new wireless tools 7-Eleven is installing in stores this year to slash the time and labor it takes to count inventory and order new products. The other is the MC3000 color handheld scanner from Symbol Technologies, used to collect data on every item as it comes off the delivery truck. Both devices use the standard Microsoft Windows CE operating system, and both run on Microsoft .Net.

The MOT is a far cry from inventory and ordering methods 7-Eleven store managers used in the past. Displaying the mix of desperation and industry that often accompany a lack of automation, these included tearing off tabs from bound notebooks, color-coding information by hand, keeping track of frozen sandwiches and their expiration dates on sheets of paper, and, in a pinch, even making sandwiches on the premises following instructions from corporate management.

The company's wireless tools aren't the only recent upgrade. Last year 7-Eleven spent $93 million on technology. In its 5,300 U.S. stores, the company installed new ProLiant servers from Hewlett-Packard, wireless local area networks, and software for computer-based training. The company also introduced a software ordering system for fresh food, a fast-growing and increasingly important product category for 7-Eleven.

The new technology installed in 7-Eleven stores works under a Windows-based proprietary system, known as the retail information system, or RIS, which has been under development since the mid-1990s. It supports the retailer initiative strategy by providing timely sales data that enables each store to tailor its product assortment to its customers. RIS also helps store operators see which items are selling well and which are not, allowing them to make room for more popular products and for new items. RIS also reduces the risk involved in introducing new products because sales data is available for evaluation within 24 hours of a product's introduction.

SHARING DATA

7-Eleven shares some of its data analysis with a handful of key suppliers, such as Anheuser-Busch, Kraft Foods, and PepsiCo in a partnering program called 7-Exchange. The 7-Exchange data system for category management, which suppliers access through a secure Web site, can provide insights that lead to new products or new packaging.

"We worked with Anheuser-Busch when we noticed a significant shift in consumer behavior around beverage package size," Morrow recalls. "Through analytics, we knew that the customer preference was migrating from take-home multipacks of beer and soft drinks to larger-size single servings."

A case study helped lead the beverage giant to reduce the multipacks and increase the size of single cans.

Information from the 7-Exchange system can also alert participating companies to a potential missed opportunity. Recently, Kraft Foods noticed that some 7-Eleven stores weren't carrying Nabisco's popular new three-ounce Big Bag line of Oreos and other cookies and crackers as widely as other stores were.

"We contacted our field group and sent them to talk to store managers and show them how well the Big Bag line was selling elsewhere," says Randy Watkins, Kraft Foods national account manager. "It's the store manager's decision whether to purchase or not, but we gave them the information to allow them to make what we thought was a good Retailer Initiative decision."

7-Eleven also has used technology to open up the doors to small suppliers. Although most of the larger suppliers exchange information with the convenience store chain through traditional electronic data interchange–based transmissions, smaller suppliers use a Web portal, called the Web Vendor Terminal, to communicate with the company. The beauty of the Internet-based system, Morrow explains, is that thousands of smaller suppliers that don't have EDI can accept orders from the stores, allowing them to carry very specific ethnic or local items, such as panini grill sandwiches and self-serve espresso in a Manhattan store that opened this summer.

Technology enables 7-Eleven to "micromarket," Lenard says. "What works in Dallas may not work for customers in New York and California, so using technology to really target what each store and each set of customers needs is critical."

TRIAL AND ERROR

Not all of 7-Eleven's tech initiatives have succeeded. Many people expected self-service checkout, which big-box stores such as Wal-Mart Stores and Home Depot are offering increasingly, to appeal to convenience store customers. But in trials, the company found that "less than 4 percent of our customer base had a preference to talk to the machine rather than with the store clerk," Morrow says.

This contrasts with the growing popularity of the ATM-like virtual commerce, or v-com, kiosks installed in more than 1,000 of 7-Eleven's U.S. stores. "With services like getting a check cashed, the bias goes the other way," Morrow explains. "People prefer to do financial transactions with a machine because it's more secure and more private. With v-com, you don't have to talk to a person about getting a money order or who you're giving money to."

Another technology that 7-Eleven has yet to embrace is radio frequency identification, which is used to tag items for inventory tracking. Other big retailers, most notably Wal-Mart, use RFID to keep tabs on inventory, but Morrow believes it isn't yet suitable in the item-by-item business of convenience stores.

"The cost and reliability of RFID are prohibitive at the item level and will be for years," he says. "It doesn't make sense to put a 50-cent tag on a sandwich that costs $2."

However, RFID is being used for contactless payment acceptance at 7-Eleven stores. The technology is expected to be installed in all U.S. stores by early 2006. The latest initiative allows a 7-Eleven customer making a purchase to pass a credit card embedded with an RFID chip near a specialized scanner to pay without handing over the credit card to a clerk for swiping.

The tech innovations that do fly at 7-Eleven are often the result of extensive pilot programs to test viability and customer response. For example, 7-Eleven began experimenting with virtual commerce in 1998. The pair of wireless gadgets the company is deploying this year is no exception. At the pilot program in the Rockwall, Texas, store, manager Neal used various versions of the scanner and MOT for 15 months. She seems delighted with the finished products she received recently. And she seems pleased with her newfound power.

"With the new system, I can order exactly what I want." And that is exactly what 7-Eleven wants.

This case nicely illustrates the achievement of the four goals described above:

- 7-Eleven has collected data item by item, store by store, day by day, for the last decade while other retailers are only collecting point of sale data at best.
- The Mobile Operations Terminal, a lightweight wireless tablet with a colorful screen, allows access to the item information in the store and allows recording of inventory changes. This allows for the same information to be accessed throughout the system.
- The retail information system installed in the stores provides timely sales data that enable each store to tailor its product assortment to its customers. The system helps store operators see which items are selling well and which are not, allowing them to make room for more popular products and for new items. It also reduces the risk involved in introducing new products because sales data are available for evaluation within 24 hours of a product's introduction.
- Finally, collaboration with suppliers is enabled through sharing of 7-Eleven's data analysis through a program called 7-Exchange. The 7-Exchange data system for category management, which suppliers access through a secure Web site, can provide insights that lead to new products or new packaging.

14.4 SUPPLY CHAIN MANAGEMENT SYSTEM COMPONENTS

The infrastructure and access issues, which ERP systems attempt to resolve, bring all business functions together to make an enterprise more efficient. They do not, however, help answer the fundamental questions of what should be made, where, when, and for whom. This is the role played by human planners with the aid of various analytical tools such as decision-support systems (DSSs).

Decision-support systems range from spreadsheets, in which users perform their own analysis, to expert systems, which attempt to incorporate the knowledge of experts in various fields and suggest possible alternatives. The appropriate DSS for a particular situation depends on the nature of the problem, the planning horizon, and the type of decisions that need to be made. In addition, there is frequently a trade-off between generic tools that are not problem-specific and allow analysis of many different kinds of data, and often more expensive systems that are tailored to a specific application.

Within the various disciplines that make up supply chain management, DSS are used to address various problems, from strategic problems such as network planning discussed in Chapter 3 to tactical problems such as the assignment of products to warehouses and manufacturing facilities, all the way through to day-to-day operational problems such as production scheduling, delivery mode selection, and vehicle routing. The inherent size and complexity of many of these systems make DSS essential for effective decision making.

The DSS that various companies and industries employ depends, among other things, on manufacturing characteristics, demand fluctuation, transportation costs, and inventory costs. For instance, if a company's predominant cost is transportation, the first DSS implementation would be a fleet routing system or network design. On the other hand, if there is a high variability in demand and complex manufacturing processes requiring setups when switching between products, demand planning and production scheduling systems may be the most urgent.

Different systems typically support the strategic, tactical, and operational levels. Some of the supply chain components predominantly support one level, while others may support more than one, depending on how they are defined and utilized.

14.4.1 Decision-Support Systems

To successfully use a DSS, appropriate performance measures need to be selected. For example, reducing total cost may be a goal, but in some cases improving customer service level may be more pertinent. DSS interfaces usually allow the user to select the relative importance of different objectives.

Once data have been collected, they must be analyzed and presented. Depending on the DSS and the particular decision being made, there are many different ways to analyze the data. It is important for the decision makers to *understand* how the DSS analyzes the data in order to assess the validity and accuracy of the decision-support system's recommendations. It is up to the decision maker to determine which analysis is most appropriate.

There are two main ways to analyze data. The first is using business analytic tools that are general-purpose methods on data that are extracted from ERP and other systems. These systems typically use the following techniques:

Queries. Often vast quantities of data make manual analysis difficult. Decisions are often facilitated by simply allowing decision makers to ask specific questions about the data, such as "How many clients do we service in California?" and "How many clients purchased over $3,000 of a certain product by state?"

Statistical analysis. Sometimes asking questions is not enough. In this case, statistical techniques can sometimes be used to determine trends and patterns in the data. For example, statistical data such as the average inventory in a warehouse, the average number of stops and length of a route, and the variability of customer demand often can be useful to decision makers.

Data mining. Recently, as corporate databases have become larger and more all encompassing, new tools have been developed to look for "hidden" patterns, trends, and relationships in the data. Data mining, for example, produced the marketing gem that men purchase beer and diapers on Friday

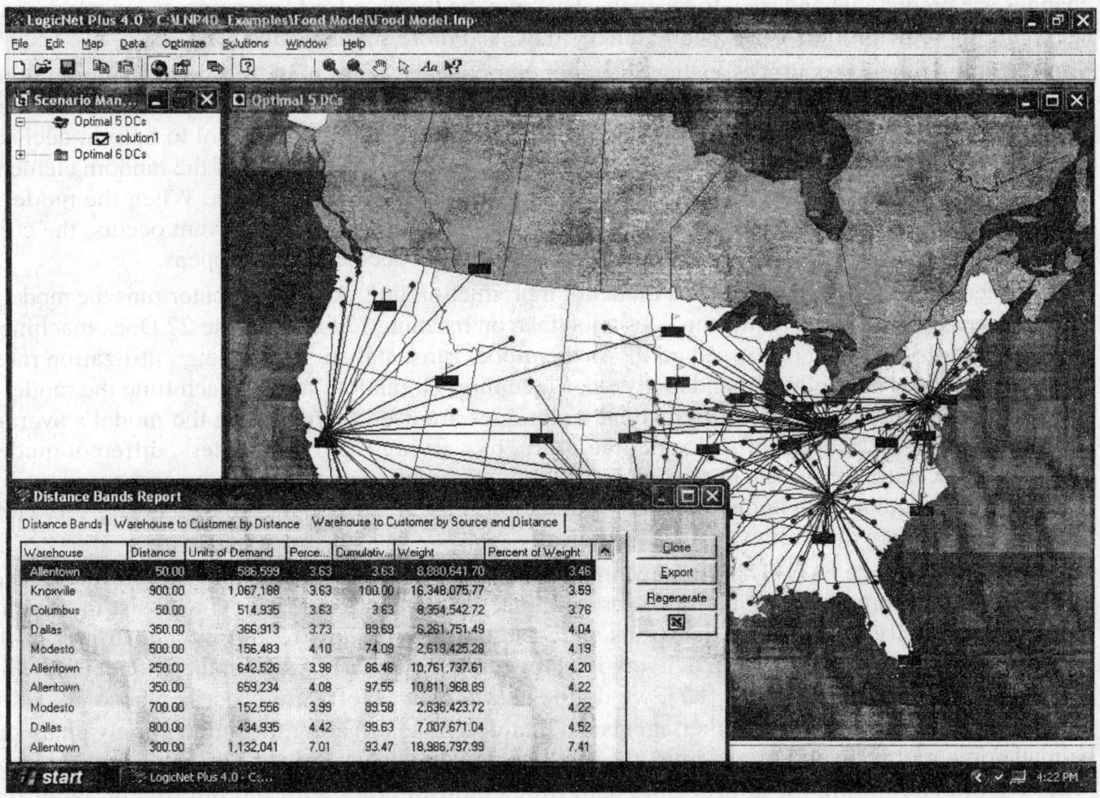

FIGURE 14-9 A typical GIS interface for supply chain management.

afternoon, suggesting to retailers that these items should be displayed close to each other in the store.

Online analytical processing (OLAP) tools. Online analytical processing tools provide an intuitive way to view corporate data, typically stored in data warehouses. OLAP tools aggregate data along common business dimensions and let users navigate through the hierarchies and dimensions by drilling down, up, or across levels. OLAP tools also provide sophisticated statistical tools to analyze these data and tools to present them. Mostly they are generic tools—more sophisticated than spreadsheets and easier to use than database tools—for the analysis of large amounts of data.

The second way to analyze data is to use DSS that provide specialized interfaces that display and report based on the specific problem being solved. For instance, see Figure 14-9 for an interface that uses geographic information systems and scenario management. These DSS employ analytical tools that have some specific embedded knowledge of the problem being solved. Since these problems are usually complex, the DSS employs its problem knowledge to find efficient solutions.

These systems typically use the following type of analytics:

Calculators. Simple decision-support tools can facilitate specialized calculations such as accounting costs. In many cases, more than simple calculations may not be warranted, especially if the changes are predictable and easy to evaluate. This may be the case for forecasting or inventory management, for some product types, while others may need more sophisticated tools.

Simulation. All business processes have random components. Sales may take one value or another. A machine may or may not fail. Often these random, or stochastic, elements of a problem make analyzing it very difficult. In these cases, *simulation* is frequently an effective tool to help in decision making. In simulation, a model of the process is created on a computer. Each of the random elements of the model (e.g., sales, failures) is specified with a probability distribution. When the model is "run," the computer simulates carrying out the process. Each time a random event occurs, the computer uses the specified probability distribution to randomly "decide" what happens.

Consider, for example, a simulation model of a production line. As the computer runs the model, a series of decisions is made. How long does a job take on machine 1? On machine 2? Does machine 3 break while job 4 is being processed on it? As the model runs, statistical data (e.g., utilization rates, completion times) are collected and analyzed. Since this is a random model, each time the model is run, the results may be different. Statistical techniques are used to determine the model's average outcome and the variability of this outcome. Also, by varying input parameters, different models and decisions can be compared. For example, different distribution systems can be compared, utilizing the same simulated customer demand. Simulation is often a useful tool to understand very complex systems that are difficult to analyze analytically.

Artificial intelligence (AI). These are techniques that try to create systems that exhibit intelligence by incorporating some form of learning. For example, *intelligent agents* use AI to assist in decision making, especially in real-time decisions such as determining how to supply a customer in the shortest possible time or to quote a delivery lead time as the customer waits on the phone. Following Fox, Chionglo, and Barbuceanu [87], we define an *agent* as a software process whose goal is to communicate and interact with other agents, so that decisions affecting the entire supply chain can be made on a global level. For example, the intelligent agent that assists the customer service representative in determining the appropriate lead time could interact with the intelligent agent that schedules production to help ensure that the lead time is met [246].

Indeed, a number of DSS for supply chain management can be viewed as using intelligent agents to plan and execute different activities in the supply chain. These systems are characterized by the following interrelated issues [87]:

- The activities allocated to each intelligent agent (i.e., software processor).
- The level and nature of interactions between the different agents.
- The level of knowledge embedded within each agent.

For instance, a real-time supply chain planning tool involves the following components: intelligent agents that are located at each facility collect information and enable planning and scheduling for the facility. In this case, facilities include manufacturing plants and distribution centers. Each agent interacts with other agents so that they can balance excess capacity at different plants, find missing parts, or coordinate production and distribution. A central planning agent communicates with agents that are located at each facility to collect status information and relate central planning decisions. The type and level of decisions made by the agents—as opposed to human operators—and the frequency and level of communications between agents depend on the specific implementation.

Expert systems also fall under the umbrella of artificial intelligence. These systems capture an expert's knowledge in a database and use it to solve problems. Expert systems rely on an extensive database of knowledge, usually expressed as a set of rules. Solving a problem involves applying the rules in the knowledge base and producing a conclusion that has the ability to explain how it was reached. Within the context of a decision-support system, this kind of expert system might suggest alternative solutions that the human decision maker has neither the time nor expertise to recognize. Although not extensively used in logistics practice, these systems have an important role because of their capability to capture and explain expert reasoning.

Mathematical models and algorithms. Mathematical tools, often from the discipline of operations research, can be applied to the data to determine potential solutions to problems. For example, these tools may generate the best set of locations for new warehouses, an efficient route for a truck to take, or an effective inventory policy for a retail store. These algorithms fall into two categories:

- *Exact algorithms.* Given a particular problem, these algorithms will find a solution that is mathematically the "best possible solution," also called the optimal solution. In general, these kinds of optimization algorithms may take a long time to run, especially if a problem is complex. In many cases, it is impossible to find the optimal, or very best, solution. In other cases, it may be possible but not worth the effort. This happens because the input data to these algorithms are often approximated or aggregated, so *exact solutions to approximate problems may be worth no more than approximate solutions to approximate problems*.
- *Heuristics.* These are algorithms that provide good, but not necessarily optimal, solutions to problems. Heuristics typically run much faster than exact algorithms. Most DSS that use mathematical algorithms employ heuristics. A good heuristic will rapidly provide a solution that is very close to the optimal solution. Heuristic design often involves a trade-off between the quality of a solution and speed. It is often useful if, in addition to the solution, the heuristic provides an estimate of *how far the heuristic solution is from the optimal solution*.

The analytical tools used in practice are typically a hybrid of many of the tools described above. Almost all decision-support systems employ a combination of tools, and many will allow further analysis using generic tools such as spreadsheets. In addition, some of the tools listed above may be embedded in generic tools (e.g., spreadsheets).

There are many factors that dictate the appropriate analytical tools to use for a particular decision-support system. These include

- The type of problem being considered.
- The required accuracy of the solution—there may be no need to find the optimal solution.
- Problem complexity—some tools may not be appropriate for very complex problems, while others may be an overkill for relatively simple problems.
- The number and type of quantifiable output measures.
- The required speed of the DSS—for operational systems such as lead-time quotation and vehicle routing, speed may be essential.
- The number of objectives or goals of the decision maker—for example, a DSS for truck routing may need to find a solution with the minimum number of vehicles and the least total distance traveled.

Table 14-1 shows a number of problems and the analytical tools that are appropriate for them.

14.4.2 IT for Supply Chain Excellence

In this section, we describe the main IT capabilities required for supply chain excellence as well as the relationships between them. These capabilities are described in Figure 14-10 and, as you can see, they are grouped into four layers.

TABLE 14-1
APPLICATIONS AND ANALYTICAL TOOLS

Problem	Tools used
Marketing	Query, statistics, data mining
Routing	Heuristics, exact algorithms
Production scheduling	Simulation, heuristics, dispatch rules
Logistics network configuration	Simulation, heuristics, exact algorithms
Mode selection	Heuristics, exact algorithms

1. **Strategic network design** allows planners to pick the optimal number, location, and size of warehouses and/or plants; to determine optimal sourcing strategy, that is, which plant/vendor should produce which product; and to determine the best distribution channels, that is, which warehouses should service which customers. The objective is to minimize total costs, including sourcing, production, transportation, warehousing, and inventory, by identifying the optimal trade-offs between the number of facilities and service levels. The planning horizon for these systems is typically a few months to a few years using aggregated data and long-term forecasts.

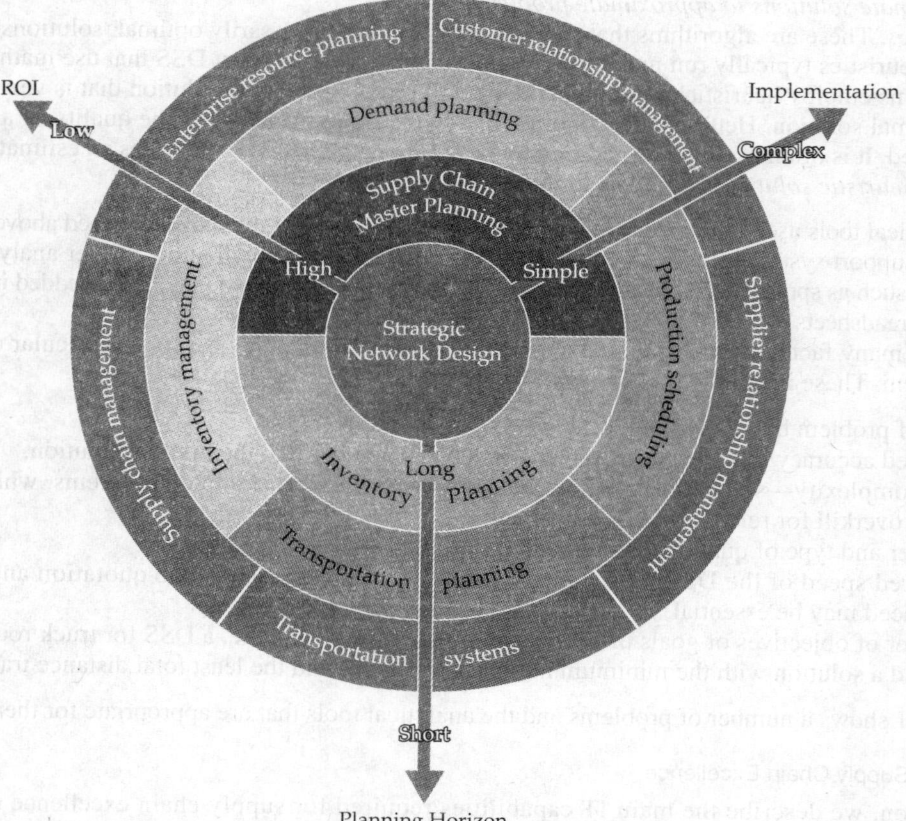

FIGURE 14-10 Capabilities required to achieve supply chain excellence.

2. **Tactical planning** determines resource allocation over shorter planning periods such as weeks or months. These systems include
   - *Supply chain master planning* coordinates production, distribution strategies, and storage requirements by efficiently allocating supply chain resources to maximize profit or minimize systemwide cost. This allows companies to plan ahead for seasonality, promotions, and tight capacities.
   - *Inventory planning* determines the optimal amount of safety stock and how to best position inventory in the supply chain.

Strategic network design and tactical planning collectively represent the **network planning** process described in Chapter 3. Optimization is applied in all these cases to generate effective strategies.

3. **Operational planning** systems enable efficiencies in procurement, production, distribution, inventory, and transportation for short-term planning. The planning horizon is typically daily to weekly and the focus is on one function; that is, each system focuses on only one function, for example, production. Therefore, these systems focus on generating feasible strategies, not optimized solutions, because of the lack of integration with other functions, the detailed level of the analysis, and the short planning horizon. Operational planning systems include four components:
   - *Demand planning* generates demand forecasts based on various historical and other pertinent information. It also allows users to analyze the impact of promotions, new product introduction, and other business plans. The method used is mostly statistical analysis.
   - *Production scheduling* generates detailed production schedules based on the supply chain master plan or demand forecasts. The method used is constraint-based feasibility analysis that satisfies all production constraints.
   - *Inventory management* generates inventory plans for the various facilities in the supply chain based on average demand, demand variability, and source material lead times. The methods used are statistical and computational.
   - *Transportation planning* produces transportation routes and schedules based on availability of transportation on a lane, cost, and customer delivery schedules. There are a large variety of transportation planning options, so these systems can vary from fleet planning, transportation mode selection to routing and distribution planning.

   Because of the nature of operational planning, the methods used are mostly heuristic.

4. **Operational execution** systems provide the data, transaction processing, user access, and infrastructure for running a company. These systems tend to be real-time in the sense that the data are current and are constantly being updated by users and events. These systems include five components:
   - *Enterprise resource planning* traditionally spans manufacturing, human resources, and financials but is now the backbone of most companies' IT infrastructure. These systems are expanding to include new functionality covered by other components we discuss. They are also providing Web-based access and services and becoming more open to integration of other components.
   - *Customer relationship management* involves systems that update and track interaction with customers. These systems connect to order tracking and other back-end systems to provide better information for customers and the service representatives who are trying to assist them.
   - *Supplier relationship management* provides the interface to suppliers for procurement, transaction exchange as well as collaborative activities.

- *Supply chain management* systems provide tracking of distribution activities in plants and warehouses as well as the event management that tracks exceptions based on performance measures. In addition, they provide lead-time quotations based on current supply chain status—called available-to-promise (ATP) or capable-to-promise (CTP).
- *Transportation systems* provide internal and external access and tracking of goods in transport. There may be some ability to route and plan at this level, but it would be on a smaller scale in terms of scope and horizon than the transportation planning systems.

Figure 14-10 illustrates the difference between the various layers of capabilities:

- **Planning horizon** for strategic network design is much longer than for an operational system. Indeed, companies typically make long-term investments in facilities over a few years. On the other hand, supply chain master planning develops a strategy for a few months to a year. Finally, operational systems have a very short horizon of days to weeks.
- **Return on investment** for strategic systems can be very high since the decisions impact large capital investments and major distribution decisions. Typically, companies report 5 to 15 percent cost reduction due to strategic network design implementation. Consider now operational planning and execution, which can have a significant cost impact as well. Unfortunately, they may require a much larger investment for much smaller gain.
- **Implementation complexity** of a strategic network design is not high since the tools that are used and the processes employed do not need to integrate with other systems or processes. Similarly, strategic network design does not require real-time updates and few people in the company interact with it. Operational systems, on the other hand, are notoriously difficult to implement and integrate and require real-time data and extensive training.

14.5 SALES AND OPERATIONS PLANNING

Some of the concepts described above can be illustrated through an important supply chain management process called **sales and operation planning** (S&OP). S&OP is a business process that continuously balances supply and demand. It is cross-functional integrating sales, marketing, new product launch, manufacturing, and distribution into a single plan and typically involves analysis of aggregated volume such as product families. S&OP practice started in the mid-80s and has focused mainly on demand planning and analysis. The process typically involves monthly meetings where demand forecasts and supply capacity constraints are compared and feasible execution plans are identified. Most companies use demand planning software and spreadsheet analysis of data collected from various ERP, CRM, and manufacturing systems.

CASE: S&OP "Evolution" at Adtran

Adtran is a $500 million designer and manufacturer of componentry for the telecom industry, headquartered in Huntsville, AL. Adtran's case was typical in that it often takes a crisis or "wake up" moment to lead fundamental change; in Adtrans' case, that was rising inventories and decreasing customer satisfaction that reached levels that required a change. That situation was driven in large part by the complex environment the company faces: short product life

Source: SC Digest, "Thomas Dadmun VP Supply Chain Operations Adtran," News and Views, www.scdigest.com/assets/newsviews/05=10=28=2.cfm, October 28, 2005.

cycles, difficult to forecast products, many engineering changes, short order delivery cycles with long supplier lead times, little or no ability to "shape" demand. Combined with forecast accuracy of less than 50 percent, and "we had a 'perfect storm' that was leading to hits on the bottom line," Dadmun said.

Particularly vexing were the various "walls of silence" that restricted the flow of information; for example, little or no information about why the forecast was missed. "We'd ask, 'Why did we miss the forecast?'" Dadmun said. "'Because customers didn't order' would be the response. But why didn't they order? That we didn't know."

There were also walls of silence between the supply side and marketing, and the supply and sales side and engineering. "Only engineering really knew what dates they were going to hit in terms of new product introductions," Dadmun noted. "Often, we were building supply capabilities and revenue plans that didn't reflect the true schedule."

Faced with this situation, Dadmun helped drive a number of initiatives to improve results. This included forming a multi-functional team across supply, sales, marketing, and engineering to look at the problem; investing in new supply chain technology; and ultimately starting an effective S&OP process.

There were some key moves. First, to get buy-in, Adtran worked with the vendor (i2) to back-test forecasting results with its demand planning tool for 20 of the company's top SKUs over the past 2–3 years. The surprising insight: the tool's base line forecast simply based on history, etc. was better for 18 of the 20 SKUs than the forecast team's results—an observation that quickly generated interest and support from execs and others.

Adtran also brought in some outside consultants to help them benchmark against best practice in the area. This also worked to show Adtran execs that they were not operating at close to an industry-leading level. "It delivered a wake-up call," Dadmun noted.

Dadmun also helped convince the organization that while an improved baseline forecast coming out of a new demand planning tool would help, it wasn't enough. "That's still a rear view mirror view," he commented. "You need additional input from sales, marketing, and engineering to see the upcoming curves and exit ramps."

The S&OP "evolution" at Adtran is designed in three phases.

Phase 1 (complete):

- Implement supply-side technology to better understand supply capacity and constraints
- Implement demand planning technology
- Launch an integrated S&OP process, with goal of developing a true consensus forecast and integrated financial plan
- Assignment of "process captains," now out of sales/marketing, for each division
- Use of a pre-meeting before the actual S&OP meeting to review the data, work out issues, identify other needed information, etc. so that the main meeting can focus on building the plan
- Focus on "exception management"

Phase 2 (in process):

- Use of an online S&OP "dashboard" that provides a detailed view of forecasts and actual results, and allows rapid drill down into supporting information
- Focus on identifying when and how the forecast and plan went wrong
- Further reduce the "walls of silence" through both process and technology

Phase 3 (planned):

- Facilitate more true root cause analysis, especially in trying to learn at a detailed customer level why a forecast was inaccurate.

Among the real keys to achieving S&OP success is "to really start with the end in mind," Dadmun noted. "You really have to define what you want to come out at the end. This is essential, and not as easy as you might think."

Other Lessons Learned Include:

- There is no change without some suffering—be prepared to have poor processes and results exposed to execs and peers
- Develop early proof points, perhaps in a pilot mode, to create buy-in
- Benchmark to be able to say "I've seen it done."
- Use some outside experts/consultants—if this is new territory for your company, partner with others that have been down the path
- Work hard to develop other internal champions besides yourself
- Celebrate success—when one planner hit 72 percent accuracy, the highest level, they took the whole team out to dinner

"We have to be able to get to the point where we can drill into the demand side of the equation with the same level of detail and insight that we can on the supply side," Dadmun added.

The Adtran case study is typical of current S&OP practices, which focus on demand planning, bringing together sales and marketing to agree on a forecast, and meetings that enable balancing production capacity with demand.

Obviously, achieving the level of S&OP process success described in the case of Adtran is quite challenging. Still, the process does not include optimization, inventory considerations, and what-if capabilities and is not tied to ERP/APS solutions since it was mostly executed through spreadsheet analysis. However, in most cases, data are too complex and there are too many options to analyze in a spreadsheet and there is a need to create a repeatable and visible process that is integrated with ERP systems. Therefore, there are opportunities to deploy IT to support the process.

Recently, a new phase of S&OP has emerged. In this phase, S&OP is aided by new technology platforms that allow easier integration of data and the ability to optimize and not focus solely on the forecast. Figure 14-11 describes the way a $5 billion manufacturer sees its S&OP process and

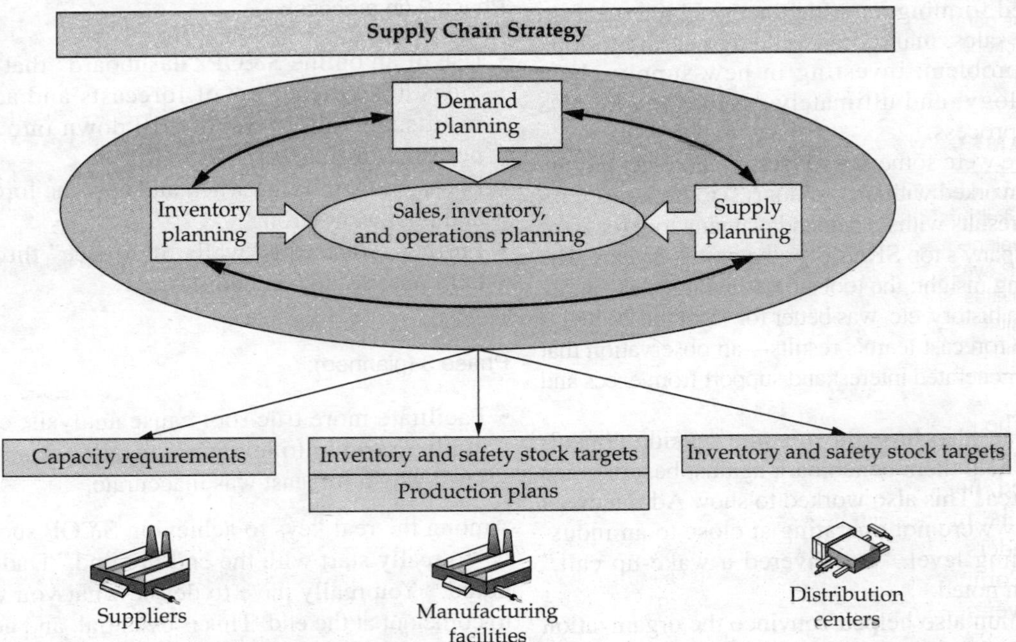

FIGURE 14-11 Advanced S&OP process.

is using its SAP implementation to deliver this system. The key is the integration of the different activities into the S&OP process. The first element is the traditional demand planning for product profiling and forecasting. The second is the supply planning for internal and external capacity checking. The third element is inventory planning to determine overall inventory targets and perform safety stock optimization and service level optimization. S&OP is focused on alignment of supply and demand as well as direction setting.

Integrating these processes is a challenge that many companies have and where new technologies for business process management and composite application described in Chapter 15 will have an impact on a company's capabilities.

14.6 INTEGRATING SUPPLY CHAIN INFORMATION TECHNOLOGY

How do all the elements of information technology (IT) come together? Supply chain management is extremely complex, so there is no simple or cheap solution to the issues we have raised. Many companies do not think it is cost-effective to introduce certain IT innovations because they are not sure there will be a significant return on investment. Trucking companies do not purchase sophisticated tracking systems because few clients would actually want to receive such detailed information. Warehouse managers do not invest in RFID technology because it is too expensive.

EXAMPLE 14.1 MAHINDRA & MAHINDRA

Mahindra & Mahindra Limited (M&M) has shown excellent operational performance in the area of farm equipment machinery. It has integrated its supply chain with the use of IT tools like ERP and RFID. The ERP solution has helped it in reducing inventory and lead-time by switching over to a pull-based replenishment in its supply chain. The planning is responsive to the fluctuation in the market demand. It uses RFID technology for various purposes like tracking the process parameters during high temperature pre-treatment and electro-deposition process on the product despite chemical reactions involved in the process. All relevant information related to parts or bodyshells can now be captured during the production and assembly process [271, 294, 297].

EXAMPLE 14.2 DMS AT MARUTI

Maruti has rolled out its Dealer Management System (DMS) to strategically integrate its operations planning with the market through a battery of 700 strong dealers, out of which over 500 are hooked to this system. The system has been developed in phases with the support of WIPRO at a cost of about Rs. 220 million. The DMS system is integrated to the ERP system of the Maruti. It generates the entire information starting from customer enquiry to sales and post-sales activities, like servicing the car. The complete history of a car during and after the sales, including detail of last service is available through this system. The DMS system provides total integration platform of the outbound of Maruti's supply chain [236].

The key is to analyze what each component can contribute to the enterprise and then plan the investment according to the specific needs of the company and the demands of the industry. It should be noted, however, that the holistic solution is frequently greater than the arithmetic sum of the parts—that is, installation of a warehouse control system and a transportation management system can do wonders for customer service performance.

Companies need to decide whether to automate their internal processes or agree to some industry conventions—which usually happens when investing in an ERP system from one of the major vendors (e.g., SAP and Oracle). As more and more companies share information such as order entry, requisition, bills of material, and so forth, and take part in joint planning, one can expect standard approaches to sharing this information will lower everyone's cost of doing business. In supply chain management, no single standard has yet emerged, as each ERP vendor continues to set its own de facto standards.

In the next section, we discuss implementation of ERP and DSS. What are the priorities in implementation? What should a company invest in first? Finally, we will review the "best of breed" compared with the single-vendor package dilemma and illustrate the dilemma through the case studies in this chapter.

14.6.1 Implementation of ERP and DSS

Implementation of a system that supports supply chain integration involves infrastructure and decision-support systems. The ERP systems that are typically part of the infrastructure are different in many ways from the supply chain DSS. Table 14-2 compares enterprise resource planning (ERP) and decision-support systems based on various implementation issues.

The question is what strategy should a company use in deciding what system to implement and when. The IT goals for supply chain management, described in Section 14.3, suggest that a company first must install an ERP system so that the data will be accessible and complete. Only then can it start analysis of its entire supply chain processes using various DSS tools. This may be the ideal, but in reality the data needed to achieve supply chain efficiencies already exist—maybe not in a single easy-to-access database, but it is worth the time it takes to assemble the database compared to the cost of waiting for installation of the ERP system.

These issues are illustrated in Table 14-2. An ERP implementation is typically much longer than a DSS implementation. The value of an ERP system to the enterprise involves the first two goals—visibility and single point of contact—and, while these can imply improved operations, DSSs impact the ability to perform strategic and tactical planning as well. This means that DSS projects have a much better ROI. Finally, DSS installations are typically cheaper and easier to implement and they affect a smaller number of highly trained users compared with those of an ERP system, which has a large number of users who require less extensive training.

Indeed, as we saw in the Whirlpool case study at the beginning of this chapter, companies do not necessarily wait for an ERP implementation to proceed with DSS implementations. Indeed, in many cases it makes sense to first deploy a DSS that provides a more immediate and observable return. Of course, companies examine their financial and human resources before they decide on the order and the number of projects they will tackle at a time.

The type of DSS implemented depends on the industry and the potential impact on the business. Table 14-3 includes some examples from various industries. In the soft drink industry, where distribution is a major cost factor, priorities are different than those of a computer manufacturer, which has a complex manufacturing process with many different products and whose distribution cost is only a

TABLE 14-2

ERP AND DSS FOR SUPPLY CHAIN MANAGEMENT

Implementation issue	ERP	DSS
Length	18–48 months	6–12 months
Value	Operational	Strategic, tactical, operational
ROI	2–5-year payback	1-year payback
Users	All end users	Small group
Training	Simple	Complex

TABLE 14-3

PRIORITIES WHEN IMPLEMENTING DSS

Industry	DSS
Soft drink distributor	Network and transportation
Computer manufacturer	Demand and manufacturing
Consumer products	Demand and distribution
Apparel	Demand, capacity, and distribution

fraction of product cost. Thus, in the latter case, the manufacturer can utilize expensive shipping solutions.

14.6.2 "Best of Breed" versus Single-Vendor ERP Solutions

Supply chain IT solutions consist of many pieces that need to be assembled in order to achieve a competitive edge. They include infrastructure (ERP) and various systems to support decision making (DSS). Two extreme approaches can be taken: The first is to purchase the ERP and supply chain DSS as a total solution from one vendor; the second is to build a "best of breed" solution, which purchases the best-fit solution in each category from a different vendor, thus producing a system that better fits each function in the company. While the best-of-breed solution is more complex and takes longer to implement, it may be an investment that provides greater long-term flexibility and better solutions to the company's problems. Of course, the long period of implementation also can cause the solution to be less useful at the end and cause difficulty maintaining IT staff and enthusiasm for the project. Many companies choose an interim approach that includes a dominant ERP provider; the functionality that cannot be provided by the vendor, or does not suit the company, is provided through best-of-breed or in-house systems.

EXAMPLE 14.3 DABUR'S JOURNEY WITH ERP

Dabur, a leading FMCG company of India, has faced ups and downs in its journey towards ERP implementation. In 1999, it started with Baan ERP for its manufacturing and later in April 2001 under "Project Synergy", it rolled out Mfg Pro. ERP for its outbound supply chain involving Carrying and Forwarding Agents (CFAs) and mother warehouses. These were supported by an in-house developed ASP and SQL platform data-warehouse, which runs on the corporate intranet for information management of backorder, inventory, sale, receivables etc. After acquisition of Balsara, another FMCG in India, Dabur's problem in information management started mounting due to a diversified IT platform. ERP demands seamless integration of different business functions and IT modules. The company therefore decided to have a consistent system and for that purpose it decided in favor of SAP R3 as a single platform all across the business functions. Within six month, it went live with a big-bang on 1 April 2006. Another major IT initiative of Dabur is the launch of e-procurement services from FreeMarket (now known as Ariba). The future plan to integrate stockists in the Dabur ERP is critical to its information system automation in the distribution channel [58,276, 282, 283, 284, 287, 293].

Finally, there are companies (e.g., Wal-Mart) that still prefer in-house, proprietary software development [39]. This probably makes sense for extremely large companies with expert IT departments and systems that already serve the company well. More recently, with the advent of new technologies discussed in Chapter 15 that provide easier business-oriented development and integration, there may be a push back toward more internal or software integrator development rather than reliance on ERP vendors.

Table 14-4 summarizes the pros and cons of these ERP versus best-of-breed approaches.

TABLE 14-4

"BEST OF BREED" VERSUS SINGLE VENDOR AND PROPRIETARY

Implementation issue	Best of breed	Single vendor	Proprietary
Length	2–4 years	12–24 months	Not known
Cost	Higher	Lower	Depends on expertise
Flexibility	Higher	Lower	Highest
Complexity	Higher	Lower	Highest
Quality of solution	Higher	Lower	Not sure
Fit to enterprise	Higher	Lower	Highest
Staff training	Longer	Shorter	Shortest

SUMMARY

Success in supply chain management IT depends on a combination of applying business processes and new technologies in a way that is most effective for the business. We show evidence that companies who apply both business processes and technology outperform their peers.

We identified the four major goals for IT:

1. Information availability on each product from production to delivery point.
2. Single point of contact.
3. Decision making based on total supply chain information.
4. Collaboration with supply chain partners.

How are the four major goals achieved? More importantly, what is the impact of achieving these goals on the logistics manager?

First, standardization of processes, communications, data, and interfaces brings about cheaper and easier methods to implement the basic infrastructure. IT infrastructure will become more accessible for companies of any size and in the future will work across companies in an almost seamless way. This will allow access to IT and integration of the systems at every level of the supply chain—therefore, there will be more information and tracking of products at each level. New technologies such as RFID will allow products to be tagged and tracked through the supply chain and will be as easy to locate as a Federal Express package.

Second, data display and access in various forms are becoming more integrated in systems that do not require any specialized knowledge. This makes system interfaces more intuitive and relevant to the task at hand. Portal interfaces described in this chapter are one such example.

Third, various systems will interact in a way that will blur the current boundaries; SOA will allow easier integration and, as a result, systems purchased as "best of breed" by different people at various levels in the organization will become better integrated and use common interfaces. Similarly, there will be a proliferation of applications that can plug into a company's enterprise system to provide specialized functionality. The third goal will be achieved through development of decision-support systems and intelligent agents that are more sophisticated, rely on real-time data, and are interoperable.

Finally, electronic commerce is changing the way we work, interact, and do business. E-commerce provides an interface to businesses and government that allows meaningful data comparison, and transactions that follow through with error checking and correction capability. It enables access to data that exist in government, educational, and private databases and the ability to modify or correct these data.

Private (and public) e-marketplaces now allow buyers to integrate their suppliers into their information systems.

In the future, businesses will be able to expand their intercompany transactions into more sophisticated applications that can perform some basic processes and pass the information on to other applications. In a process as complicated as supply chain management, systems that not only perform their own function but also alert others in the system will be especially beneficial to fulfill the four goals we have outlined.

These topics are addressed in detail in Chapter 15.

We end with a quote from Lou Gerstner, former IBM CEO (see [146]): "The payoff from information technology is going to be in making transactions and processes more effective and efficient, so it's not about creating a new economy, it's not about creating new models of behavior or new models of industry. It's about taking a tool, a powerful tool, and saying, 'How can I make my supply chain more effective and efficient, how can I make my purchasing process more efficient, how can I make my internal employee communications more effective and efficient, how can I as a government deliver services to constituents more efficiently and more effectively?'"

DISCUSSION QUESTIONS

1. What are the major challenges facing supply chains that can be aided by IT?
2. What is the impact of business processes on supply chain management IT?
3. How can ERP vendors take advantage of Internet technology?
4. Compare the capabilities required to achieve supply chain excellence (see Figure 14-10) according to
   - **a.** Decision focus.
   - **b.** Data aggregation level.
   - **c.** Time to implement.
   - **d.** The number of users involved in the analysis.
5. Identify five supply chains in your country which are supported by ERP. Discuss their business performance before and after the implementation.

CHAPTER 15

Technology Standards

CASE: Pacorini Stays on Top of Global Logistics Market with IBM SOA Solution

Manufacturing and distribution organizations worldwide today are able to provide their customers with the goods they want, when they want them, processed and delivered in quality condition—thanks in part to efficient logistics companies such as the Pacorini Group (Pacorini). Based in Trieste, Italy, Pacorini provides delivery of coffee, metals, foods, and general cargo. The company processes these goods for quality control and schedules them to arrive just when they are needed in the customer's supply chain management (SCM) process. A highly regarded international company, Pacorini has 22 locations and 550 full-time employees; it comprises several different companies across three continents and 11 countries.

Historically, Pacorini's integrated, end-to-end SCM solutions created the logistics industry in Italy and have inspired many competitors worldwide. As a market leader in the delivery of green coffee, Pacorini has maintained its competitive position up to now by offering timely customer service. However, although it used advanced technologies and leading SCM software, the company's internal business processes were not integrated. It was a challenge to manage siloed information, and to provide consistent customer service in a 24 × 7 world. Consequently, Pacorini was concerned about its ability to stay ahead of its competition.

"From order management to warehouse management, purchase orders, work orders, custom duties and accounting, Pacorini's legacy systems were not integrated with customer and employee interfaces," says Cristian Paravano, Pacorini CIO. "When customers wanted to know the status of their orders, they phoned a customer service representative, who then would research the question on multiple diverse systems and then either fax or phone the answer to the customer. We needed to construct an integrated framework to enable employees to retrieve or transmit information from a single point of entry. That would streamline our internal processes, lowering costs and shortening response times."

OVERHAULING BUSINESS PROCESSES

Pacorini did change, in a major way. Starting with an analysis of its current business processes to define priority tasks and link them together using streamlined workflows, Pacorini then built a framework of integrated online processes. The company put into place a service oriented architecture (SOA) to construct information retrieval and work processes using repeatable information services, customized to fit every task in a consistent manner.

Source: IBM Case Study, June 20, 2006. Used by permission of IBM.

IMPLEMENTING THE SOLUTION, STEP BY STEP

Based on an IBM solution, the company has implemented an order-enabled portal solution for both internal and external customers. It has also deployed a system-to-system order management solution with its largest coffee customer in Italy. Pacorini is now in the process of applying the communications standards it developed with its largest customer to 9 of its other top 10 customers. In the future it will extend this solution to customers in metals, freight forwarding, and distribution areas.

Online ordering will enable the company to automate approximately 30,000 transactions this year, a projected savings of equivalent to four full-time employees. Eventually, Pacorini will extend a full range of business services to internal and external customers, including document management, electronic bill presentment, and online inventory information.

When this goal is reached, both customers and employees will be able to monitor order fulfillment throughout its various stages. "We can manage potential problems with customers, warnings, rights, and many other controls that before were handled using phone calls, e-mails, and faxes," says Paravano. "With WebSphere business integration software, it's possible to deploy, govern, and monitor a process," says Paravano. "These are the components that go into supplying outstanding service to customers."

Paravano continues, "This is a project that will continue into the future as we discover more and more ways to be efficient and please customers."

SAVING MONEY WITH BPM AND SOA

With its entire order management process integrated and automated, employees can manage orders more efficiently while providing consistent and highly accurate order information.

Building incremental efficiencies using standard work processes and repeatable information services also means cost reductions for IT support as well as better business process management. "Service oriented architecture and business process management go hand in hand," says Paravano. "In each country, in each location, and with each customer, we use many different information service components to build consistent business processes. This provides us with the flexibility we need to respond to customer and market demands as well as lower operating costs."

Cost reductions in turn mean better competitive positioning. Some of Pacorini's markets such as green coffee and metals are mature, offering small profit margins and providing low barriers to entry, so gaining greater efficiencies and reducing costs are critical to competition. "Automating and integrating our business helps us consolidate our position in the market," says Paravano. "We feel sure that we have a competitive advantage that comes from the rich functionality of IBM products and IBM's roadmap, which leads to full integration through service oriented architecture."

In this chapter, we will answer the following questions:

- How do technology standards impact supply chain management improvements?
- What are the important standards and technology trends?
- How does business process management relate to Web services technologies?
- What is RFID and how will it impact supply chain performance?

15.1 INTRODUCTION

The objective of this chapter is to review IT-related standards, new technology platforms, and other evolving technology standards important for effective supply chain management. Indeed, these technology standards are important in supply chain management because of the dynamic cross-company nature of the technology requirements, as can be seen from the Pacorini case study above.

In the last few years, there have been some important changes in the IT world and related technology that greatly affect supply chain management. The most important technology development has been radio frequency identification (RFID), a sophisticated replacement for bar codes. This technology is still in the early stages of adoption and some of its advanced features are not yet implemented, but it has received widespread support and has important backers in industry with giants such as HP, the Department of Defense, and Wal-Mart.

At the same time, the IT landscape has changed considerably with the consolidation of the market to a few large players. These players are trying to set standards for the infrastructure platform and partner with as many developers as possible with the hope of becoming the predominant player, and thus providing ease of integration and adoption.

Finally, the Internet has motivated new approaches to system design. The most prominent of these approaches is service-oriented architecture (SOA), which is a collection of independent services that communicate with each other based on defined standards. SOA is typically combined with business process management (BPM), which refers to activities performed by businesses to optimize and adapt their processes.

As we describe in Chapter 14, the infrastructure and standards decisions are some of the most important components of an IT strategy. In this chapter, we review the details of standards and infrastructure and then focus on some supply chain–specific standards, particularly next-generation platforms such as SOA and RFID, which form the basis of many current tracking and replenishment activities.

15.2 IT STANDARDS

The push toward IT standards is a strong and growing trend. Although some issues are specific to logistics and supply chain management, most developments are occurring across industries and application areas. The IT field is evolving to a high level of standardization for the following reasons:

- *Market forces:* Corporate users need standards in order to reduce the cost of system development and maintenance.
- *Interconnectivity:* The need to connect different systems and work across networks has pushed the development of standards.
- *New software models:* The Internet has produced the need for software that has new development and deployment characteristics.
- *Economies of scale:* Standards reduce the price of system components, development, integration, and maintenance.

In the last three decades, the standardization of IT has gone through four major phases, as can be seen in Figure 15-1:

- **Proprietary:** Computer development until the early 80s involved proprietary systems, mostly mainframe computers that were accessed through key punches and later terminals with no processing capabilities (so-called dumb terminals). There was little communication between systems with few options such as private networks or physical media.
- **Stand alone:** The IBM personal computer (PC) software and hardware, introduced in the early 80s, became the first standard platform, called Wintel, the Microsoft Windows and Intel standard. This

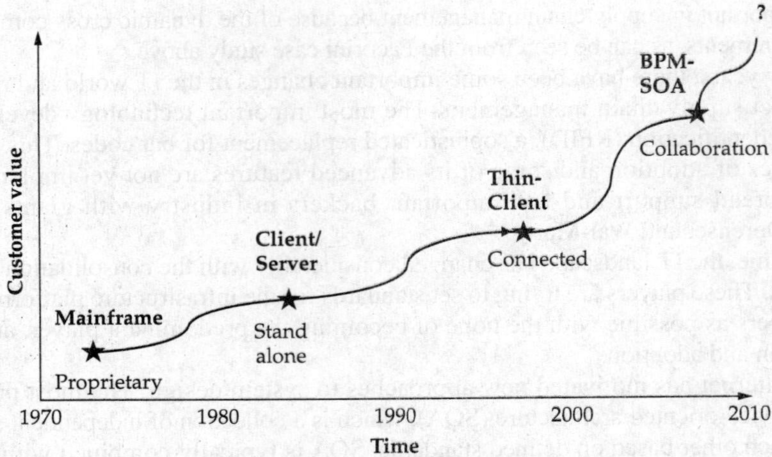

FIGURE 15-1 Software standards and the next inflection point.
Source: Inspired by [193].

eventually created a large user base and an expanded market for applications. Communication standards also were developed mostly for local networks—Ethernet and IBM token ring were the leading contenders. For business networks, some standards were developed, but mostly private networks were used for file transfers. Electronic data interchange (EDI), a common transaction format, was introduced at this time. It allowed companies to electronically transmit data that used to be handled in paper form. We will expand on EDI in Section 15.3.3, "Electronic Commerce."

As an outgrowth of the popularity of PCs, the client/server was developed, integrating PC capabilities and standards with business systems, by applying the PC computing powers to create a more sophisticated client-controlled interface.

- **Connected:** The Internet provided the missing link in communications and display standards beyond the local network. Initially developed by the U.S. government and used primarily in research institutes, the development of the browser in the early 90s created a standard and accessible interface and spread to universities, individuals, and later industry. Another benefit was that the Internet enabled forms of communication that heretofore existed internally in many companies to work across companies and to become as ubiquitous as phone calls. The most obvious example is electronic mail, but this is by no means the only form. File and information transfer between individuals and companies was greatly simplified by the Internet. The Internet then spawned expanded electronic commerce from shopping, bidding, and exchanges to shipment tracking and extended collaboration between companies on joint forecasts, transportation, and other activities.

  At the same time, due in large part to year 2000 fears, many companies replaced their legacy systems with client/server-based enterprise resource planning (ERP) systems, which have become the standard backbone of company IT. The first generation ERP systems focused mainly on finance and human resource applications. This was followed by additional functionality in areas such as manufacturing and distribution. More recently, ERP vendors started adding supply chain capabilities.
- **Collaboration:** The next phase of standards, which is currently being developed, will address collaboration, a more sophisticated form of communication between companies. The technology to support this phase is built around SOA and BPM technologies. All the major software companies are supporting this concept and competing to develop platforms for implementation.

The new phase of collaboration also has increased the importance of ERP systems and their ability to support SOA and BPM technology. We will address this in detail in Section 15.4.

Of course, it is difficult to identify the source of the next IT inflection. Indeed, it is worth pointing out that in the previous phases, successful developments came about quite unexpectedly and, hence, it is hard to predict which new standard will emerge and succeed.

15.3 INFORMATION TECHNOLOGY INFRASTRUCTURE

Information technology infrastructure is a critical factor in the success or failure of any system implementation. The infrastructure forms the base for data collection, transactions, system access, and communications. IT infrastructure typically consists of the following components:

- Interface/presentation devices
- Communications
- Databases
- System architecture

15.3.1 Interface Devices

Personal computers, voice mail, terminals, Internet devices, bar-code scanners, and personal digital assistants (PDAs) are some of the most common interface devices. A key trend in IT is toward uniform access capability anytime and anywhere, and interface devices clearly play a major role in this area. The Internet browser is fast becoming the interface of choice for information access, although it is still not as sophisticated as Windows in displaying forms and graphical data. In addition, other devices such as PDAs and phones also are competing as access devices to user systems. Supply chain management requires a standard way to track products in order to provide participants with the information they need to perform efficiently. For instance, it is important to record point-of-sale information, especially if these data are accessible by the supplier, as in vendor-managed inventory systems.

The Uniform Code Council created the bar code system, Universal Product Code (UPC), in 1973, and it has been used extensively for scanning and recording information about products. Automatic data capture interfaces, such as bar-code readers and radio frequency (RF) tags, are standardized and commonly used. RF tags on products or packaging are used to locate items, particularly in large warehouses. The same technology, together with wireless communication devices and GPS capabilities, enables tracking of tagged cargo while in shipment. A more recent innovation will eventually replace the UPC—this is the radio frequency identification (RFID) tag, on which we devote Section 15.5.

15.3.2 System Architecture

System architecture encompasses the way the components—databases, interface devices, and communications—are configured. We include this topic in the section on information technology infrastructure because the design of the communications networks and choice of systems depend on the implementation of these systems.

Legacy systems evolved as departmental solutions using mainframe or minicomputers that were accessed through "dumb" terminals (see Figure 15-2). The PC was initially used apart from a company's main systems for special applications such as word processing or spreadsheets. Eventually the PCs in an office were connected by means of local area networks (LANs) so users could share files,

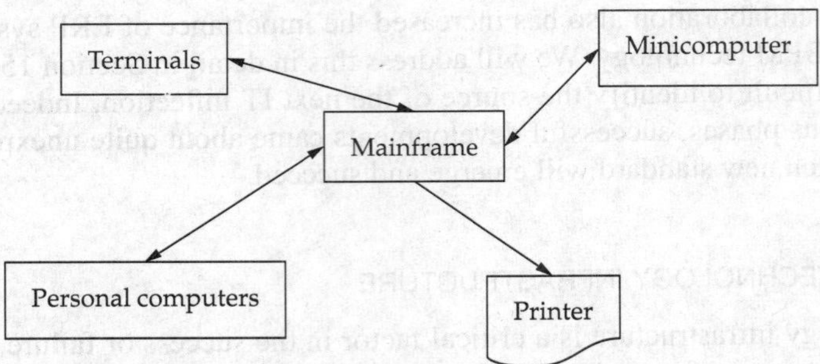

FIGURE 15-2 Legacy system architecture.

e-mail, and other applications. These networks were then extended across companies with wide area networks (WANs) that connected the dispersed offices of a company. Finally, new systems were developed to take advantage of the PC's computing power and friendly graphic interface. In these systems, the PC is typically called the "client" and the main processor is the "server." *Client/server computing* is a form of distributed processing whereby some processes are performed centrally for many users while others are performed locally on a user's PC.

Most current system design involves client/server structure (see Figure 15-3), although the sophistication and price of the client, the number and type of servers, and various other design parameters vary greatly from system to system. Examples of servers include database servers that allow Structured Query Language (SQL) requests from users, transaction-processing monitors, directory/security servers, and communications servers. See [95] for an introduction to client/server concepts.

The Internet is a form of client/server where the local PC browser processes the HTML (hypertext markup language) pages and Java applets (i.e., small applications) that are retrieved from servers—in this case from all over the world. The client/server model is now evolving toward a Web-centric model where the client is a Web browser connected to a Web server.

The power of the client/server concept is in distributing functions among specialist servers that perform them efficiently; it is also easier to add new modules and functions. The disadvantage is the added complexity of navigating between servers and making sure that data are processed correctly and updated across the network. The implementation of client/server systems also has given impetus to the trend toward standardization because each server needs to be able to communicate tasks and processes across the network. This feature is called *interoperability,* which means two systems are capable of interacting in a sophisticated way that is a built-in feature of their design. Many interfaces between sys-

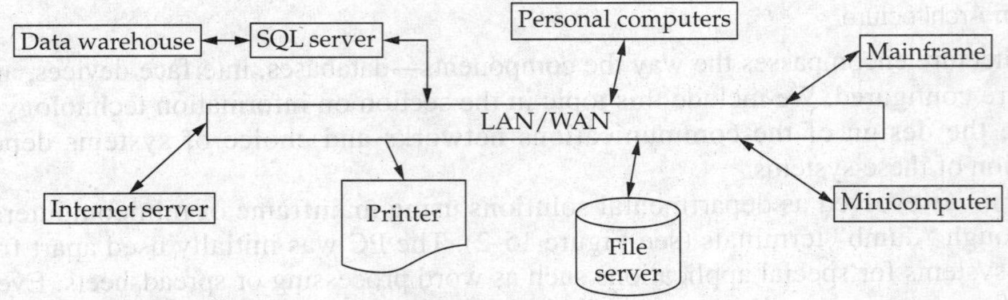

FIGURE 15-3 Client/server system architecture.

tems are created through file transfers or other temporary schemes because the systems use different file formats and communications schemes. When standards for intrasystem operation become common, tools will be available to perform these interfaces and provide full data and process-sharing interface mechanisms.

The applications that reside between the server and the client are collectively called *middleware,* literally the slash (/) in the term *client/server*. These are typically tools that facilitate communication between different system architectures, communication protocols, hardware architectures, and so forth. The parts of an application that reside on a server, client, or as middleware depend on specific implementations. This is the three-tiered architecture model now favored by many client/server designers.

Middleware can be important in the implementation of supply chain systems since, in many cases, the information for the planning tool exists in a number of locations and forms across the company. The appropriate middleware can be used to collect the data and format it in a way that can be used by various planning tools. That is how many supply chain applications are currently implemented. For instance, a telecommunications company may have billing information for the company's various services, such as long distance and wireless, stored on different systems. A customer service representative might have to search multiple locations for a customer's bills if the customer purchased more than one service. Middleware would perform the function of looking through the databases and combining the information. When these types of processes are applied between companies over the Internet, they are called enterprise applicationl integration (EAI).

A more advanced generation of system infrastructure attempts to provide interconnectivity and collaboration platforms between companies. The technology to achieve this is called service-oriented architecture (SOA) and will be addressed in detail in Section 15.4.

15.3.3 Electronic Commerce[1]

Electronic commerce (e-commerce) refers to the replacement of physical processes with electronic ones and the creation of new models for collaboration with customers and suppliers. E-commerce can be used to facilitate the interaction between different companies as well as the interaction of individuals within companies. Examples include purchasing over the Internet, exchanges, order tracking, and e-mail.

E-commerce has been in existence for many years, using private networks for corporations (e.g., WANs) and public ones at universities and government agencies. The acceptance of Internet standards has accelerated the adoption of e-commerce, especially between individual buyers and companies but also between companies. The initial use of the Internet, showcasing marketing material, has expanded to allow user status and tracking inquiries as well as product purchases. Companies allow users to access their databases to troubleshoot product problems, thus saving the company money in support calls.

Companies use Internet standards internally—*intranets*—as well as externally—*extranets* and *exchanges*. The difference between Internets, intranets, and extranets is explained mostly by who is allowed access to the system. Intranets allow companies to implement internal applications without having to develop custom interfaces and avoid incompatible types of hardware and special dial-in procedures. Internet applications typically allow unlimited access but extranets allow limited access by restricting partners and customers from outside the company to certain applications and data. Internet

[1] While there is a difference between the definition of e-business and e-commerce in general (see Chapter 6), in practice these terms are used interchangeably.

standards have been used in recent years to create exchanges—private and public—that allow participants to trade or exchange information.

Another concept that has developed around internal company use of the Internet is the portal—a role-based entry into a company's systems. A portal aggregates all the applications and sources of information employees need in order to perform their job into a single desktop environment, typically through the Web browser. This capability not only empowers an employee to be productive individually, but also makes it simpler for employees to interact with others, whether within the company or outside. Portals require integration technology for structured and unstructured data sources, including databases, Java classes, Web services, and XML. As more organizations begin to deploy an enterprise portal framework, they are looking at ways to reduce the time and cost associated with building portals. The ability for end users to aggregate content and provide faster access to more information sources is critical to the success of building and maintaining portals.

EXAMPLE 15-1

At office-furniture maker Herman Miller Inc., approximately 300 employees who spend most of their days in contact with suppliers use a customizable portal that gives them fast access to news and information. This allows the employees to deal with business partners more effectively, because they don't have to hunt for or combine various bits of data. The company was originally attracted to the technology from Top Tier Software (which was acquired by SAP in March 2001) because it provided a way for suppliers to interact with Herman Miller's enterprise resource planning system.

Once the company saw how effective a portal interface could make employees, it began to roll it out for internal use as well. Today the company has several separate portals for various types of employees, but it is considering evolving its Web site into a sort of "superportal" that will then lead customers, suppliers, and employees to different subportals, depending on their needs. The benefits of collaboration are tremendous. For example, employees can decide what kind of alerts they want to have fed to their screens ("supplier X is three days late with a delivery") and then drill into data to identify the cause of the problem and the potential ramifications. The system has not been a panacea, however. While the technology is very good at sifting through structured data such as those contained in databases, it is far less effective in handling unstructured data, such as correspondence, computer-aided design drawings, and the like. SAP recently combined its portals division with another business unit that dealt with online marketplaces, where unstructured data predominate, so, over time, all that functionality can be brought to bear in a single product [141].

Electronic commerce can happen at several levels of sophistication, from one-way communication such as Web browsing, to direct database access for retrieving personal data or creating transactions such as making online purchases or managing a bank account. More advanced applications typically employ electronic data interchange (EDI) and, more recently, XML-based processes for data exchange. XML is a general standard that does not address the issue of terminology in a specific industry. This is being addressed in one case by a high-tech company industry consortium called RosettaNet (see [267]) that views itself as an e-business equivalent of the Rosetta stone, which carried the same message in three different languages, enabling translation from hieroglyphics. The RosettaNet-based initiative is aimed at producing a flexible standard governing online business collaboration between manufacturers and suppliers. RosettaNet defines dictionaries and partner interface processes, which handle multiple data transactions among partners. It is being used by some high-tech vendors but has proven expensive to implement. This could change if the standard is adopted widely and vendors provide systems that support it.

Finally, the ability to share processes electronically is particularly applicable to supply chain management. An example of an application for sharing processes is collaborative planning, forecasting, and replenishment (CPFR), a Web-based standard that enhances vendor-managed inventory and continuous replenishment by incorporating joint forecasting. With CPFR, parties electronically exchange a series of written comments and supporting data that include past sales trends, scheduled promotions, and forecasts. This allows the participants to coordinate joint forecasts by concentrating on differences in forecast numbers. The parties try to find the cause of the differences and come up with joint and improved figures. As we emphasized in Chapter 5, multiple forecasts can have very expensive supply chain implications. Indeed, forecast sharing among supply chain partners can result in a significant decrease in inventory levels since it tends to reduce the bullwhip effect. To do this, systems need to be designed to allow data verification and ensure standard practices of coordination.

Collaborative planning, forecasting, and replenishment was developed by the Voluntary Interindustry Commerce Standards Association (VICS) committee, made up of retailers, manufacturers, and solution providers. This group has developed a set of business processes that entities in a supply chain can use for collaborating along a number of buyer/seller functions, toward improving supply chain performance. According to the committee, its mission is to create collaborative relationships between buyers and sellers through co-managed processes and shared information. By integrating demand- and supply-side processes, CPFR will improve efficiencies, increase sales, reduce fixed assets and working capital, and reduce inventory for the entire supply chain while satisfying consumer needs.

The VICS committee created the CPFR Voluntary Guidelines to explain the business processes, supporting technology, and change management issues associated with implementing CPFR. The CPFR Guidelines gained VICS board approval in June 1998. The committee published the CPFR Roadmap in November 1999, explaining how manufacturers and retailers can implement a CPFR partnership. This Roadmap, see [269], includes the following nine steps:

1. Develop guidelines for the relationships.
2. Develop a joint business plan.
3. Create a sales forecast.
4. Identify exceptions for the sales forecast.
5. Collaborate on exception items.
6. Create an order forecast.
7. Identify exceptions for the order forecast.
8. Resolve/collaborate on exception items.
9. Generate orders.

EXAMPLE 15-2

Henkel is a large German company with over 57,000 employees worldwide and over 11 billion euros in sales. Henkel manufactures over 10,000 products, including detergents, cosmetics, adhesives, and many others. Eroski is the leading food retailer in Spain, with over four billion euros in sales each year. Eroski is one of Henkel's largest Spanish customers. In December 1998, the two companies decided to undertake collaborative planning and forecasting (CPFR) in order to address customer service and stockout issues relating to Henkel products in Eroski stores. The effort initially focused on detergents, with a goal of improving customer service, reducing lost sales, and increasing the turnover rate. Using commercially available software, the two companies collaborated on business and promotional plans and sales forecasts. The process was started in December 1999, and the companies have seen dramatic improvement in the quality of forecasts. Before the process started, half of the sales forecasts had an average error of over 50 percent. Several months after the implementation, 75 percent of the forecasts showed an error of less than 20 percent. Similar improvements were seen in stockout levels. One of the challenges of implementing CPFR between these two firms was involving business organizations in the forecasting process that had not been involved in the past. For example, Henkel customer service personnel had to develop close working relationships with Eroski sales forecasters. Once initial reluctance was overcome, the benefits of this process were quickly realized. Forecasts could be developed that combined Eroski's knowledge of the dynamics of individual retail outlets and the impact of promotion at these outlets, with Henkel's knowledge of the individual products and the impact of external factors on these product sales [108].

15.4 SERVICE-ORIENTED ARCHITECTURE (SOA)

Service-oriented architecture (SOA) is defined as "a standards-based approach to managing services, made available by different software packages for business process orchestration that delivers flexible reuse and reconfiguration." [221]

The importance of SOA is that it is the architecture adopted by all the major business software vendors as the base of their development tools and platforms and is also used widely by systems integrators to develop custom applications. In addition, SOA has three valuable contributions [179]:

1. **SOA-based integration.** Integration has traditionally been done point to point or using enterprise application integration (EAI). These types of integrations tend to be hard to maintain and use proprietary technology with a separate infrastructure. SOA-based integration uses standards and the business process execution language that makes maintenance much simpler and easier to learn.
2. **Composite application development.** The use of business process management (BPM) to develop a top-down approach to application development and the composition of ready-made components that are reusable and have built-in integration (services) make them easy to use and maintain.
3. **Modernizing legacy applications.** Many IT departments spend 70 to 80 percent of their budget maintaining mainframe or other legacy applications. Using SOA, companies can define the business processes and start separating the business logic from the application.

SOA is strongly linked with BPM and, as we saw in Chapter 14, the ability to define and improve business processes is essential for the success of IT investments. Business Process Management [see bpm.com] provides the discipline and tools for business users to define end to end processes, identify performance goals and manage them. BPM's roots are in workflow, but it differs in a few significant ways because of the end-to-end nature of the processes, higher visibility and built in support for making changes. BPM does not require SOA, although it will perform better if there is easier access to enterprise services. BPM systems typically provide graphical interfaces for defining the processes and linking in services. Another technology typically deployed with BPM is Business Rules Management Systems (BRMS), which enable a business user to maintain rules and link them to the process.

SOA and BPM drive a layered approach where business process tools use business services or composites to design the application. The lower levels provide orchestration, implementation services, and the actual applications, as you can see in more detail in Figure 15-4.

Because interfaces are platform-independent, a client from any device using any platform or *operating system* in any coding language can, in theory, access or use the service. This set of services will reside in a repository on a network and can communicate with each other. Some examples of services include certain business functions such as processing a payment order, calculating or updating currency exchange rates, authenticating users, and displaying an address on a map.

Each one of the four major software vendors has adopted SOA and defined a strategy related to implementation on its business process platform. In Table 15-1, we summarize the approach of the four major software vendors. This is defined along the lines of strategy, composite platform, repository, and ecosystem.

15.4.1 Technology Base: IBM and Microsoft

Microsoft's focus is on the development platforms for SOA software development. It provides, along with Java, the standards and services required to implement SOA. Both major platforms, **Java 2 Enterprise Edition (J2EE)** and **Microsoft .NET,** focus on a similar vision of the future of Web

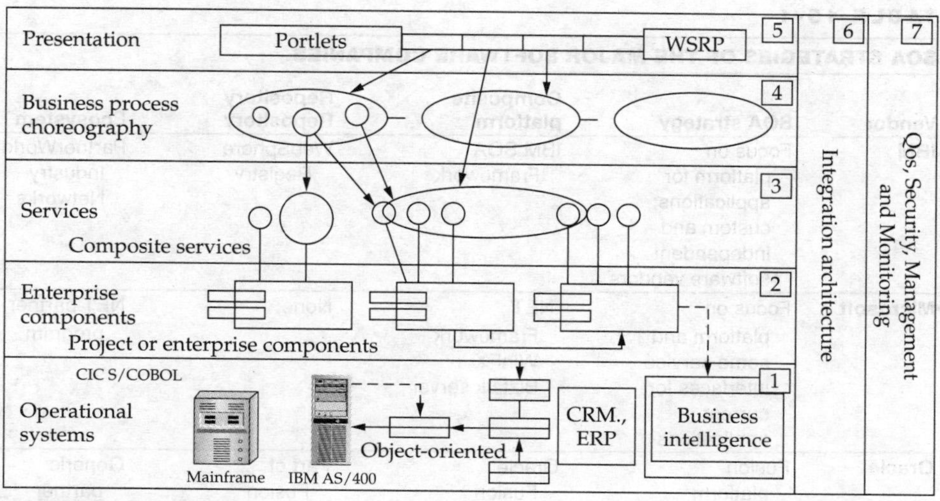

FIGURE 15-4 SOA layers.
Source: [262].

services, and have been building similar technology frameworks for developers. Both the Java and .NET platforms rely on the same set of established standards such as

- *eXtensible markup language* (XML), a language that facilitates direct communication among computers on the Internet. Unlike the older *hypertext markup language* (HTML), which provides HTML tags giving instructions to a Web browser about how to display information, XML tags give instructions to a Web browser about the category of information.
- *Universal description, discovery, and integration* (UDDI), a Web-based distributed directory that enables businesses to list themselves on the Internet and discover each other, similar to a traditional phone book.
- *Web services description language* (WDSL), an XML-formatted language that UDDI uses, which was developed jointly by Microsoft and **IBM** and is used to describe a Web service's capabilities as collections of communication endpoints capable of exchanging messages.
- *Simple object access protocol* (SOAP), an XML-based messaging protocol used to encode the information in Web service request and response messages before sending them over a network. SOAP messages are independent of any operating system or protocol and may be transported using a variety of Internet protocols.
- *Business Process Execution Language* (BPEL), a specification that defines how Web services can be combined to orchestrate long-lasting business processes. It has been submitted for standardization by a group led by IBM and Microsoft. BPEL, an XML-based language that allows developers to formally describe a business process such as the steps involved in processing a loan application or making a purchase request, could become a key standard for application integration and business-to-business processing, and will likely be the basis of Microsoft and IBM's future application integration products.

IBM also is focused on the technology platform and less on the applications. Through its strong middleware technology such as WebSphere, it is positioned to be a supplier of components and services for the creation of custom applications. It also partners with independent software vendors (ISVs) who

TABLE 15-1

SOA STRATEGIES OF THE MAJOR SOFTWARE COMPANIES

Vendor	SOA strategy	Composite platform	Repository Repository	Ecosystem
IBM	Focus on platform for applications; custom and independent software vendors	IBM SOA Framework	WebSphere Registry	PartnerWorld Industry Networks
Microsoft	Focus on platform and some service interfaces for current applications	.NET Framework + WinFX + Biztalk server	None	NET partner program
Oracle	Fusion platform	Oracle Fusion middleware	Part of Fusion architecture	Generic partner program
SAP	Enterprise service applications on the NetWeaver platform	NetWeaver composite applications	Part of NetWeaver architecture	NetWeaver partner program

Source: Adapted from [91].

provide off-the-shelf applications using IBM technology. The Pecorini case study at the beginning of the chapter provides such an example.

15.4.2 ERP Vendor Platform: SAP and Oracle

ERP companies such as SAP and Oracle are now competing with their own SOA platforms and trying to create a community of developers around them. The SAP strategy, see [244], is intended to tie developers to its platform and create innovation around it that will drive adoption. Oracle is more focused on integrating the many software vendor packages it has acquired in the last few years under one platform. It also provides development tools similar to IBM and Microsoft.

SAP's enterprise SOA elevates the design, composition, and deployment of Web services to an enterprise level to address business requirements. An enterprise service is typically a series of Web services combined with simple business logic that can be accessed and used repeatedly to support a particular business process. Aggregating Web services into business-level enterprise services provides more meaningful building blocks for the task of automating enterprise-scale business scenarios.

Enterprise services allow firms to efficiently develop composite applications, which are applications that compose functionality and information from existing systems to support new business processes or scenarios. All enterprise services communicate using Web services standards, can be described in a central repository, and are created and managed by tools provided by SAP NetWeaver, which provides the foundation.

SAP NetWeaver is a collection of infrastructure and integration technologies that will underpin SAP's applications, mySAP ERP, SRM, CRM, and so on, and allow them to flexibly interoperate with one another and with pieces of applications from other software vendors. In essence, the elements of NetWeaver include an application server, integration server, Web portal, business intelligence software, master data management system, and composite application development environment. The plan is that NetWeaver will eventually replace the three-tier client/server architecture used by the current ERP suite.

Oracle is a traditional application development vendor that has grown since 2005 through the acquisition of several applications vendors including Peoplesoft (which already included JD Edwards), customer relationship management vendor Siebel as well as supply chain application vendors such as Demantra for demand planning and G-log for transportation. It has created a platform called Oracle Fusion around which these applications will eventually standardize. Oracle also has strong middleware applications including JDeveloper, BPEL Process Manager, Enterprise Service Bus, Oracle Web Services Manager, Business Rules, and Oracle Business Activity Monitoring. Oracle also has established a composition platform that supports BPEL processes, thus orchestrating the execution of services and events.

Oracle products enable IT professionals to tailor the composition environment from programming code to orchestrating business processes. However, Oracle's impact beyond its installed base is not strong and, as with Microsoft, its strength is with traditional technology-based developers. [91]

EXAMPLE 15-3 ASIAN PAINTS PORTFOLIO OF IT PRODUCTS

Asian Paints, the largest paint manufacturer of India manages its supply chain with a wide-range of IT-solutions. It has focused on Top Operating Performance (TOP) for its supply chain excellence. Its IT portfolio includes world class solutions like SAP for the ERP, Optiva for Customer Relationship Management (CRM), Factory Planner, Demand Planner and Supply Chain Planer from i2 and many more. Asian Paints has undertaken massive process redesign, standardization and benchmarking exercises to focus on process integration and compatibility of IT solutions [33, 250].

15.4.3 Conclusion

The technical nature of this discussion should not obscure the basic understanding that SOA changes the method and possibilities of designing application software. The main elements of SOA, as defined in the beginning of this section, are [221]

1. It is an application architecture with standard ways to integrate services.
2. Services are defined using a standard description language and have evocable interfaces. Simple examples are "check the credit rating for this customer," "map this address," and "transfer this purchase order to the customer."
3. The services can be part of business processes and there are applications that help users describe these.
4. Processes, transactions, and special functional components all have to be exposed as services, allowing composite, diverse applications to be exposed as well.
5. Each interaction should be independent of each and every other interaction and the interconnect protocols of the communicating devices. This allows for diverse platforms that can be integrated. The platform and language of the application do not make any difference as long as the services are exposed for calling this application.

SOA will allow business users to combine information from various applications and use it for analysis or collaboration. This is particularly important in supply chain management, where the information required typically spans several applications and companies.

15.5 RADIO FREQUENCY IDENTIFICATION (RFID)[2]

15.5.1 Introduction

Radio frequency identification (RFID) is a technology that deploys tags emitting radio signals and devices, called readers, that pick up the signal. The tags can be active or passive, that is, they either broadcast information or respond when queried by a reader. They can be read-only or read/write and one-time or reusable. They can be used to read an electronic product code (EPC), a unique number that identifies a specific item in the supply chain, as well as to record information in order to direct workflow along an assembly line or to monitor and record environmental changes. An essential component of the widespread acceptance of RFID is the EPCglobal network, which will allow password protected access to the Internet of RFID data anywhere in the supply chain.

The proliferation of RFID and full implementation of the technology will take many years and the EPCglobal network has not yet even been accepted as the standard. In addition, a few challenges remain. These include common international standards for tags, technical problems with tag scanning accuracy, and reduction in the cost of tags. One example is the reliability of tags, which, according to industry analysts [29], are functioning at only 80 percent success rates. Antennas sometimes separate from their tags, and even when the tags stay intact, tag readers are not always reliable. There are also problems reading tags through metal or liquids and interference from nylon conveyor belts. Other issues with RFID that have not been resolved relate to policy issues such as privacy concerns.

Nevertheless, specific mandates by channel masters such as Wal-Mart are going to accelerate the immediate use of RFID, even if it is at the so-called slap-and-ship level only. This technique involves putting a tag on a case or pallet heading out of the warehouse. The tags are scanned at the supplier's loading dock and a "ship notice" is e-mailed to Wal-Mart, who compares it to the incoming shipments. Even this limited application has advantages in speeded order payment and chargeback resolution [212].

All these exciting developments have already created a thriving and fast-growing market for RFID technology and services. Many companies are experimenting with various applications of RFID as well as preparing to comply with the mandates from industry giants such as Wal-Mart and the world's largest procurement agency, the U.S. Department of Defense (DoD). These applications include using RFID to improve manufacturing processes, manage SKUs in distribution centers, and track products or containers. According to the Wireless Data Research Group (WDRG), the market for RFID hardware, software, and services has increased from more than $1 billion in 2003 to a predicted $3.1 billion in 2007 [133].

EXAMPLE 15-4 MARUTI USES RFID

Maruti Udyog Limited (MUL), leader in small car segment in India, has a new plant at Manesar in the Indian state of Haryana. Here, RFID-enabled pallets are being used with products on the shop-floor. The shop-floor operations are managed and monitored through the use of RFID tags. Production-related instructions are written on RFID tags and as the assembly moves along the different operations in the shop-floor, the operator can read the specific operation to be performed at his machine or work station. The machining and other operations parameters may be recorded on the RFID tag before it moves to the next station. RFID technology is useful in tracking the root causes of quality problem as the RFID tags can record the entire history of a product coming out of the assembly line [236].

---

[2] Based on David Simchi-Levi, "The Impact of RFID on Supply Chain Efficiency," chap. 8 in Claus Heinrich, *RFID and Beyond: Growing Your Business Through Real World Awareness* (New York: Wiley, 2005). Reprinted with permission of John Wiley & Sons, Inc.

Most of the current applications *are within the four walls* where the benefit from RFID is evident and implementation is relatively easy. The question, of course, is how does one achieve efficiencies beyond a single facility? That is, how can RFID technology be used to improve supply chain efficiencies? The supply chain pundits and technology experts like to say that RFID will increase supply chain efficiency through better visibility and the acceleration of processes in the supply chain. We, of course, do not dispute these ideas, but the meaning is vague; visibility and accelerated processes allow the supply chain to respond better, but what are the business processes that make this possible? Clearly, these processes need to take into account not only supply chain complexity but also economies of scale as well as variability and uncertainty. Indeed, as observed in Chapter 14, it is only through a combination of technology and business processes that the supply chain can achieve significant improvements.

Thus, the objective of this section is to propose a framework and a process for using RFID to improve supply chain performance. In our analysis, we will focus on the advantage that RFID provides over point-of-sale (POS) data as well as issues associated with supply chain collaboration, technology cost, and who pays for the technology.

15.5.2 RFID Applications

Two important drivers motivate companies to start experimenting with RFID applications. One is the mandate by some major channel masters and procurement agencies and the second is the immediate benefits that can be gained from implementing the technology.

An important decision that suppliers and manufacturers need to make when considering RFID is the level of implementation: pallet/case or individual item. Item-level tagging will be required to achieve many of the benefits of RFID such as preventing counterfeiting and theft. Unfortunately, because of the cost of the tags, item-level tagging will first be implemented only for high-value items such as cars and ink cartridges.

Current information systems manage data about products at an aggregated level such as number of items or cases. Thus, tracking single products or cases by implementing RFID will require new information technology (IT) to support it even at the case level. Of course, the largest benefit can be achieved from implementing RFID at the product level. For example, with RFID, you could store information in your database about when a particular package of beef was packed, which cow it came from, which farm it was from, and where it was slaughtered. Such data could be provided in real time across the supply chain as palettes roll into the warehouse or items roll off the shelves. Modeling these data will be a huge technical challenge on its own, and writing applications to understand and use this level of information or even palette-level information will be a major issue that companies will have to deal with [29].

Some of the mandated applications within the next few years include those discussed in the following examples.

EXAMPLE 15-5

WAL-MART STORES INC.

In January 2005, Wal-Mart went live with RFID technology and mandated its use for its suppliers. At first, Wal-Mart had more than 100 suppliers tagging products. It now has more than three times that number involved, feeding RFID-tagged goods to 500 Wal-Mart facilities through five distribution centers. The company expects the number of stores capable of handling RFID-tagged items to double to 1,000 by January 2007, with 600 suppliers employing the technology by then. The company has already seen a return on investment, such as out-of-stock items that are RFID-tagged being replenished three times faster than before, and the amount of out-of-stock items that have to be manually filled cut by 10 percent.

EXAMPLE 15-6

DEPARTMENT OF DEFENSE

Pentagon suppliers must place RFID tags on cases or pallets shipped to the DoD by January 2005 for certain products and depots, which are expanded in 2006 (see [270]).

EXAMPLE 15-7

FOOD AND DRUG ADMINISTRATION

The FDA recommends that all pharmaceutical producers, wholesalers, and retailers begin developing plans to place RFID tags on pallets, cases, and unit items by 2007 [212].

There are already some existing applications of RFID, mostly implemented in one facility or one process. The following are some examples. We start with package tracking.

Package Tracking

EXAMPLE 15-8

UK BREWERIES

In late May 2004, Trenstar, a Denver-based logistics company, signed a deal with Coors UK, and now has partnerships with the three largest brewing companies in Britain to manage their keg shipments. Previously, the breweries owned their own kegs and managed their shipments and returns—a costly and labor-intensive process. Trenstar bought the kegs from these companies and outfitted each with an RFID tag. The breweries now contract the keg coordination with Trenstar, which provides detailed audit trails of exactly where the kegs are and when they're due back. The biggest benefit to brewers from RFID is the reduction of asset loss since they lose on average 5 to 6 percent of their kegs every year. That has been cut by more than half.

RFID implementation by the British breweries also had some positive unintended consequences. Because the technology provided an audit trail for each keg, the breweries were able to claim tax credits on the amount of beer left in each keg. Typically, a brewery is taxed on the amount of beer shipped out. With an airtight audit trail now in place, breweries weigh the kegs upon their return and receive tax credits on the bottom swill or, if the keg was defective, the full keg. Companies save roughly $1 to $12 per keg, depending on how much beer is left in the container [41].

Product tracking

EXAMPLE 15-9

MICHELIN NORTH AMERICA INC.

Michelin North America implanted RFID tags on some tires to track their performance over a period of time. Michelin engineers have developed an RFID transponder that is embedded into the tire during manufacturing and allows the tire's identification number to be associated with a vehicle identification number (VIN), making tires uniquely identifiable with an individual vehicle and telling when and where the tire was made, maximum inflation pressure, tire size, and so forth The information can be obtained using a small handheld reader that scans the tag, much like a bar code on a package at a grocery store.

There are three main uses for tire electronics, including identification, operating conditions that include tire pressure monitoring systems, and vehicle performance, where a tire can actually sense road conditions and adjust vehicle's performance through communication between the tire and the vehicle's operating systems.

Outside of storing valuable information, RFID technology also can provide added logistics benefits, providing companies with improved shipping performance through the reduction of manual inspections, saving numerous work hours and improving efficiency. In addition, RFID can reduce the time needed to process returns while increasing shipping accuracy and reducing lost sales [163].

EXAMPLE 15-10 ABHISHEK INDUSTRIES (AI)

Abhishek Industries (AI), a flagship Company of Trident Group of Industries in India, is a Rs.15 billion global enterprise, spanning across 37 countries, and a products portfolio involving terry towels, non terry products, yarn, writing and printing paper, and chemicals. AI is using RFID for the semi-finished goods's tracking at its Ludhiana terry towel plant. The RFID system is integrated with their existing SAP R/3 ERP system. The integrated system has provided greater visibility and traceability of material resulting in its closer control [271, 280, 302].

Store

EXAMPLE 15-11

MARKS AND SPENCER (M&S)

M&S has been one of the early UK pioneers in using RFID tags in the retail sector and first trialed the tracking technology on a selection of men's clothing in its High Wycombe store in 2003. The RFID tags are contained in throwaway paper labels attached to, but not embedded in, a variety of men's and women's clothing items in stores. M&S uses mobile scanners to scan garment tags on the shop floor, and portals at distribution centers and the loading bays of stores allow rails of hanging garments to be pushed through and read at speed.

M&S plans to extend the item-level RFID tagging of clothing items following successful trials in 42 stores. Item-level RFID tagging of certain ranges of clothing will now be rolled out to a further 80 stores in the spring of 2007. The clothes include a variety of complex sizing items such as men's suits and women's trousers and skirts.

The retailer is aiming to use RFID tags to help achieve its goal of 100 percent stock accuracy by ensuring the right goods and sizes are in the right stores to meet demand [157].

Manufacturing

EXAMPLE 15-12

CLUB CARD INC.

A Georgia maker of golf cars and utility vehicles implemented RFID use in the manufacturing process of a new high-end car called the Precedent. The process begins by permanently installing an active RFID tag on every assembly carriage of the Precedent. At each stop on the assembly line, the carriage passes a reader that sends the car's identifying data to a proprietary manufacturing execution system. The software determines which custom options should be installed in the vehicle and which machine requirements, such as torque, must be completed. Before the car leaves the post, workers make sure the tasks for the location have been completed. This process replaces use of printed instructions and cuts the time of building a new Precedent from 88 minutes to 45. The expenditure for the system was below $100,000 [212].

Warehouse Management

EXAMPLE 15-13

GILLETTE

In 2003 Gillette launched a major EPC trial in its packaging and distribution center located in Fort Devens, Massachusetts. The company is tracking all cases and pallets of its female shaving systems within this facility. It now knows where every case of Venus razors is in its pack center, how long a case was there, where it was stored, and when it was shipped. The goal of the pilot is to develop systems and business processes needed to sustain extraordinary levels of efficiency and productivity. When the company rolls out the Wal-Mart tagging requirement, it also will be able to eliminate manual case counting, scanning, and other expenses [207].

Product Launch

EXAMPLE 15-14

GILLETTE

Gillette's launch of its Fusion razor in March 2006 was completely EPC-supported, placing RFID smart labels on all cases and pallets of the razors shipped to the 400 RFID-enabled retail locations of its two customers involved in the pilot. Gillette also placed tags on the Fusion promotional displays it sent the retailers, which got onto the shelves in three days after being sent from Gillette's distribution center. This process typically takes 14 days for a new product launch.

The swiftness of the Fusion launch is attributed to the added visibility the tagged goods provided the company. This visibility began as the goods arrived at the retailers' distribution centers and ended, most importantly, at the retailers' box-crushing machines, where reads of the Fusion case tags allowed Gillette to infer that all contents had been placed on shelves. In cases where the retailer's EPC feedback network showed the Fusion razors or promotional displays had reached a retail store's back room, but no read events were recorded showing the goods being brought to the sales floor in a timely manner, Gillette contacted the managers of those stores and requested the razors and displays be brought out.

Gillette forecasts a 25 percent return on its RFID investment over the next 10 years through increased sales and productivity savings. The company's success at getting the Fusion razors onto shelves more than 90 percent faster than normal indicates the significant impact RFID can make as an enabler of more efficient supply chain operations [176].

15.5.3. RFID and Point-of-Sale Data

The data commonly used by retailers and their suppliers to forecast demand are point-of-sale (POS) data. POS data, taken from cash registers, measure what is actually sold. Specifically, this is the historical data used by many demand planning tools to forecast demand. Unfortunately, POS data do not measure real demand because of lost sales due to out-of-stock items.

Indeed, a large number of sales are lost due to misplaced items or items not on the shelves where buyers can find them. Out-of-stock is conservatively estimated to be 7 percent of sales [14], but the truth is that no one knows the real value. For example, Raman, Dehoratius, and Ton [196] document many DC and store-level execution problems that lead to customers not being able to find products in the store. Some of the drivers of the execution problems are related to store and DC replenishment processes such as scanning errors, items not moved from storage to shelf, the wrong item picked at the DC, and items from the DC not verified in the store. Large variety, cramped storage, and high inventory make it hard to maintain accuracy and replenish shelves. This leads to misplaced SKUs and significant discrepancies between physical inventory levels and information system inventory records

This is, of course, a huge opportunity for RFID, which will provide much more accurate information on the available inventory. For instance, companies that comply with Wal-Mart's mandate will receive information that is much more detailed than POS [4]. It will include the following events:

- Received at Wal-Mart DC.
- Departed DC.
- Received at store.
- Departed store stock room (arrived on shelf).
- Case (or tag) destroyed.

This information can provide the following immediate benefits:

- Better control over overage, shortage, and damage claims management and ability to better assign responsibility to the supplier, the carrier, or Wal-Mart.
- Better control over product recall.
- Use of the data to improve processes through collaboration between suppliers and Wal-Mart.

But the true advantage of RFID information over POS data is that, *for the first time, lost sales can be quantified*. Since the retailer knows what is sold, what is in inventory, and when the shelves are not stocked, it will be possible to determine *realized* demand based on *actual sales plus lost sales*. This analysis will require new statistical and forecasting techniques that will take advantage of the new information.

15.5.4 Business Benefits

RFID implementation will improve both the accuracy and speed of data collection. The accuracy is achieved through reduction of errors in scanning as well as better prevention of theft, diversion, and ability to efficiently track expiration dates for spoilage. The speed is related to less handling required, ease of performing an inventory count in a facility through multi-object scanning, and so on. This combined with new processes will lead to an acceleration of the supply chain that will result in new supply chain efficiencies.

Retailers are expected to be the main beneficiaries of RFID implementation. According to a study by A. T. Kearney [14], retailers expect benefits in three primary areas:

1. **Reduced inventory:** A one-time cash savings of about 5 percent of total system inventory. This is achieved through reduction in order cycle time and improved visibility, leading to better forecasts. Reduction in order cycle time yields reduction in both cycle stock and safety stock while improved forecast yields safety stock reduction.
2. **Store and warehouse labor reduction:** An annual reduction of store and warehouse labor expenses of 7.5 percent.
3. **Reduction in out of stock:** A yearly recurring gain of 7 cents per dollar of sales due to fewer out-of-stock items and less theft.

Overall, a retailer with a wall-to-wall RFID system that includes readers and actionable real-time information feeding corporate databases could save 32 cents on every dollar in sales, taking into account the cost of implementation [14].

Companies are struggling with estimating the cost of implementing RFID, which is significantly different for manufacturers and retailers. The estimated direct costs for RFID implementation includes

- **Tagging:** This is a recurring cost incurred by manufacturers. Most companies that sell RFID tags do not quote prices because pricing is based on volume, the amount of memory on the tag, and the packaging of the tag (whether it's encased in plastic or embedded in a label, for instance) [21]. Generally speaking, a 96-bit EPC tag costs from 20 to 40 U.S. cents, with higher costs for thermal transfer and other special requirements.[3] The tagging is done during production so the companies will use tags on all cases, even ones going to customers who do not require them. Therefore, the cost for a company that ships 20 million cases a year will be up to $4 million this year and will eventually decrease.
- **Readers:** This is mostly a fixed cost that retailers and manufacturers will incur. Preliminary estimates for large retailers include a cost of $400,000 for a distribution center and $100,000 per store [14]. The only ongoing (variable) cost is for hardware and software maintenance.
- **Information systems:** Long-term benefits from RFID will result, as we will describe below, when information systems will learn to handle the type of real-time, item-level information that RFID provides.

---

[3] www.rfidjournal.com/faq/20/85.

Manufacturers also can benefit from RFID depending on the type of business. The immediate benefits from internal implementation include

1. **Inventory visibility:** Better tracking of inventory throughout its facilities.
2. **Labor efficiency:** Reduced cycle counting, bar code scanning, and manual recording.
3. **Improved fulfillment:** Reduced shrinkage, improved dock and truck utilization, and improved product traceability.

Long term, both manufacturers and retailers will benefit from significant reduction in the **bullwhip effect** (the increase in *variability as one moves up in the supply chain,* see Chapter 5). Indeed, as observed in Chapter 5, complete visibility throughout the supply chain such as the one provided by RFID will reduce supply chain variability. This will not only allow reduction in inventory levels but also lead to better utilization of resources, for example, manufacturing and transportation resources. At the same time, reduction in the bullwhip effect also benefits retailers as service levels are improved. Indirectly, manufacturers will benefit from reduction of out of stocks by retailers. A reduction of out of stock by 50 percent will provide suppliers with a revenue gain of 5 percent [212].

Indeed, for manufacturing companies selling a low volume of expensive goods such as drugs and general merchandise, the benefits are quite high [14]. On the other hand, for manufacturers of high-volume, low-cost products such as food and grocery, the benefits from RFID are not as clear. This is due to two reasons:

1. These industries already have efficient supply chains through the implementation of a variety of technologies and processes.
2. Uncertainty in these industries is relatively small and hence demand is highly predictable.

It is therefore *likely that these high-volume, low-cost manufacturers will implement RFID at the case and pallet level* until the technology matures and the price of tags decreases considerably. This means that RFID benefits such as preventing store thefts and providing the ability to read a customer's shopping cart will take a long time to materialize.

However, there are many benefits that can be achieved with case-level implementation. For example, Gillette sees the following business benefits from implementing RFID at this level [207]:

1. Reduce the number of pallet touch points, resulting in efficiencies and labor savings.
2. Eliminate manual case and pallet scanning.
3. Do away with manual case counting.
4. Cut back in label printing and application.
5. Shorten the time it takes to check an order before shipping.
6. Improve order accuracy.
7. Reduce negotiations with retailers over missing product.
8. Curtail shrinkage at DCs, at warehouses, and in transit.
9. Improve forecasting.
10. Lower overall inventory levels.
11. Increase on-shelf availability of products.
12. Improve customer service levels.

Observe that items 1 through 8 will result from the physical implementation and do not require the development of new business processes. However, items 9 through 12 require supply chain coordination and new supply chain processes in order to be realized.

15.5.5 Supply Chain Efficiency

Information received from RFID systems throughout the supply chain can provide almost instant real-time visibility of inventory and in-transit product status. This can help improve the performance of inventory, transportation, and replenishment systems that rely on this information.

In a supply chain with zero lead time, no capacity limits, and no economies of scale, RFID technology would lead to immediate supply reaction to every demand instance. Thus, in such an ideal supply chain, production and transportation lots are of unit size and the supply chain is managed based on the status of each facility. Specifically, in such an environment, when a customer removes a product from the shelf, the DC will ship the product to the retail store and this will trigger production of an additional unit.

This is precisely the concept of **lean manufacturing,** where each manufacturing facility reacts to demand from its downstream facility, that is, a pull-based strategy, and not to forecast, that is, a push-based strategy. Thus, in an ideal supply chain, the main benefit from RFID technology is the ability to enjoy the benefits associated with lean manufacturing strategies.

Of course, in real-world supply chains, responding to a demand event is not that simple. First, demand can be replenished from a DC, transferred from a nearby store, or satisfied through an emergency shipment from the manufacturing facility. These alternatives provide opportunities to better manage the supply chain, and become a challenge as supply chain complexity increases. More importantly, supply chains possess setup time and cost, long lead times, and significant economies of scale in manufacturing and transportation that make reaction to individual demand triggers impractical.

Therefore, even though RFID provides real-time data, it is not always wise to respond in real time to every event. Specifically, RFID technology does not imply that it is possible to implement pure pull strategies. So how can supply chains take into account economies of scale and lead times as they use RFID data? The answer has to do with a hybrid approach in which planning and execution systems are integrated to provide the right balance between pull supply chains demanded by RFID technology and push strategies required due to lead times and economies of scale.

SUMMARY

Advances in standards make a significant contribution to the ability to improve supply chain performance. In the 90s, the evolution of the Internet was a major factor in supply chain changes. In the next 10 years, the two major standards are SOA and RFID.

SOA provides the backbone for building more adaptable systems that can operate across different technology infrastructures. It is still at the stage where the basic technology is being developed and deployed, but it will most certainly have a large impact on how systems are developed. The related business process technologies will make it easier to define and execute new processes and therefore become more flexible.

RFID is a revolutionary technology that will significantly impact the way supply chains are managed and lead to greater efficiency. RFID tags will not merely replace bar codes but will allow real-time tracking of products, or at least cases and pallets. In particular, it will enable a large reduction of lost sales that is very costly for companies. However, achieving these efficiencies will require new information systems that can take advantage of the real-time and detailed product location information provided by the RFID technology.

DISCUSSION QUESTIONS

1. What is the impact of SOA technology on SCM? Specifically, how can a transportation company use this technology to either improve service or provide new services?
2. What is the importance of standards in managing a global supply chain?
3. How would you suggest taking advantage of RFID to manage promotions?
4. How do you see a future supply chain when all items are tagged?

CHAPTER 16

Local Issues in Supply Chain Management

CASE: Amazing Story of Mumbai Dabbawalahs

BACKGROUND OF MUMBAI CITY

Mumbai, as a city is unique in many ways. It is often referred to as the financial capital of India. Mumbai contributes around 40% of all income tax collections, 60% of all customs duty collections and 20% of excise duty collections of the nation which is a clear indicator of its economic contribution to India. Historically, seven islands of Mumbai were joined together, resulting in one mainland of about 436 square kilometers in area. The city is located on the western coast of India, which is surrounded by the Arabian Sea. Geographically, it is marked by a long stretch in one direction (Figure 16.1). Over 15 millions people from different ethnic backgrounds live in Mumbai. Over a period of time the city has expanded considerably and this has created considerable pressure on the civil amenities and infrastructure. The working population generally commutes quite a long distance from home to work place and often takes more than an hour in commuting. Local people generally rely on public transport to travel, which is mainly due to traffic congestion, lack of parking space and not so good road condition. However, the local rail provides the lifeline to the city. The Western and Central Railways are the main operators and cater to the over six millions daily commuters of this metropolitan city.

MUMBAI DABBAWALAHS

Who are these *dabbawalahs*? The word *dabbawalah* or *tifinwalahs* stands for one who carries lunch-boxes. *Mumbai dabbawalahs* have demonstrated to the business world one of the most amazing distribution networks, which they have been operating since 1890s, the time when India was under the British rule. Mumbai has always attracted people from different parts of India as it provides many opportunities for work. Indians traditionally love home-cooked food. People from different communities have different taste and preference of food. During early days, there was hardly any culture of canteens or fast food centers. Mr. Mahadeo Havaji Bacche (Mahadeo) sensed an opportunity here and developed the lunch-box delivery services with about 100 uneducated-unemployed people, who were called the 'Bombay *dabbawalahs*'. In course of time, the name of this city changed to 'Mumbai' and thereafter 'Bombay *dabbawalahs*' became 'Mumbai *dabbawalahs*.' As the Mumbai population grew, the operations of Mumbai *dabbawalah* also expanded. The number of *dabbawalahs* kept growing, except during 1980-1990, when there were closures of some mills in Mumbai. In 1954, they organized themselves with the formation of Nutan Mumbai Tiffin Box Suppliers' Charity Trust. By the year 2000, they were delivering almost 2,00,000 lunch-boxes a day. Taking return trip also into account, there are 4,00,000 manual transactions involved with customers each day. The total turnover exceeds Rs. 36 crores per annum. Now they are operating with around 5000 *dabbawalahs*, who are responsible for the success of this supply network. In 1998, the interest in the Mumbai *dabbawalah's* distribution system came into the limelight when Forbes global Magazine ranked its operational excellence at a Six Sigma level with an accuracy rating of 99.999999. This in other words means that the *dabbawalahs* made one error or less in six million transactions. Forbes Global Magazine noted, "Mumbai's "*tiffenwalahs*" have achieved a level of service to which Western businesses can only aspire. "Efficient organization" is not the first thought that comes to mind in India, but when the profit motive is given free rein, anything is possible. To appreciate Indian efficiency at its best, watch the *tiffinwalahs* at work."

Organization: The organizational structure of Mumbai *dabbawalah's* is very simple. There are thirteen positions at the top, starting from the President and followed by the Vice President, Secretary, Treasurer, and nine Directors. At the field level, there are around 5000 *dabbawalahs*, who are coordinated and supported by few *Makadams*. They help in training new *dabbawalahs*, resolving disputes, maintaining the payment-receipt records, acquiring and communicating with new customers, and most importantly sorting lunch boxes. There has never been a strike by the workers as they are treated as shareholders. Work for them is service to God. Most importantly, the teamwork and coordination are at their best. There are three golden rules for ensuring discipline in the system: (i) every *dabbawalah* has to wear a white cap during working hour, (ii) they cannot take alcohol during duty, and (iii) they have to carry their identity card. The purpose is to keep their identity known and visible to public. Local Mumbai people are generally aware of the importance and urgency involved in the working of these *dabbawalahs*. For traffic crossing and train loading they get natural support from these locals. During loading period in the morning, railway provides sorting area on the platform for the *dabbawalahs*. They also get special railway compartment during 10.00 to 11.30 AM in trains going south. In a way, the working of these *dabbawalahs* has intermingled with the culture of Mumbai. There are not many parallels of this type that one can find even in the well-managed business world.

OPERATIONS OF MUMBAI DABBAWALAH

Office going people, school children and businessmen in Mumbai generally leave home in early hour of the day and travel long distance to reach to their respective work place. Mostly they prefer home-cooked food during lunch. Mumbai *dabbawalahs* are ready to provide the services of bringing the lunch-box from home to the work place and back. The pick-up of the lunch box with hot home-cooked food from home is around 10.30 in the morning. And then starts the excellence model of distribution system of Mumbai *dabbawalahs*. An illustration of the movement of the lunchbox is shown in Table 16.1 and Figure 16.1.

The reasons why *dabbawalahs* are important lie in the five major aspects of their functioning. These are:

1. very low cost of operations,
2. error-free distribution of lunch-boxes,
3. highest level of customer satisfaction,
4. highly motivated workforce and
5. minimum use of modern technology.

It is not difficult to imagine that these five aspects at one place can always make a lethal combination needed in the success of any business.

Cost of Operation: The cost of operation of the distribution network of the Mumbai *dabbawalah* is amazingly low. Monthly charge for a customer is around Rs. 300 per lunch box and an annual

TABLE 16-1

AN ILLUSTRATIVE MOVEMENT OF LUNCH BOXES

Time and Place	Activity
10:34-11:20 am: Andheri Station.	This is the most crucial time as lunch boxes are to be loaded in a wooden crate filled with lunch in the train. Generally, they choose to occupy the last compartment of the train.
11:20 – 12:30 pm: Church Gate Station	Unloading at the destination station and re-arrangement of lunch boxes takes place as per the destination area and destination building code
11:20 - 1:15 (At all Destination Stations)	Lunch time at the destination point
1:15 – 2:00 pm (At all Destination Stations)	Reverse logistics starts with pick up of the lunch box from the office
2:00 – 2:30 pm (At Destination Station)	Segregation is done as per the destination code
2:48 – 3:30 pm (In train)	Return journey by train
3:30 – 4:00 pm: The originating station	Final sorting and dispatch to the origin area

bonus during festival season. In some cases, due to very long distance covered or due to big size of a lunch box the monthly charge may be little higher. Despite this, the total revenue generated is around Rs. 360 million.

Low cost of operation has helped in their expansion, customer retention, and thereby generating economy of scale. *Dabbawalahs* do not use any motor vehicle for the lunch-box movement. For a long distance travel, say, for example, home pick-up at Andheri and office drop at Churchgate (Figure 16.1), local suburban train services are used. The use of this mass transport system is very economical as the fare for a daily commuter on these local trains is quite low. Not only cost, but also the time to travel is the minimum possible, as compared to other modes of transport. Movement of lunch-boxes from home to the nearest originating suburban station is through bicycle, hand-pulled wooden cart or in many cases *dabbawalahs* carry these packed lunch-boxes in their hand held bags. Most of these *dabbawalahs* are semi-literate or illiterate with an average of grade eight pass qualification. They earn around Rs. 5000 to Rs. 8000 per month through a system that they call profit sharing. In addition, they get Deepawali (an important festival in India) bonus that they receive from customers.

Error-free Distribution: How is it possible to achieve an almost error-free delivery within this complex network? When we talk of error in the context of six sigma, it relates to CTQs (Critical-to-Quality). CTQs for Mumbai *dabbawalahs* are those service quality characteristics, which are critical for the customers. For their customer, there are three important CTQs. Everyone will like to have his own lunch-box and no one else's. Second, it should be delivered neither too early nor too late. If delivered too early, the food would not remain warm and fresh. If delivered late, lunchtime would be over. Third, the cost of this service should be low as a higher cost would dissuade customers from using this service. Error-free delivery has been achieved with the help of a unique codification system for the lunch-boxes.

Coding System for the Lunch boxes: As an illustration, the coding of lunch-box from Vile Parle to Churchgate is shown in Figure 16.2. The coding system is unique, very simple and *ad hoc* but serves its purpose. The coding has a flow logic, which ensures complete traceability and defines flow directions in both situations of forward logistics and reverse logistics of lunch boxes. Even a semi-literate or an illiterate *dabbawalah* with little training can recognize the coordinates of destination office and originating station through a simple combination of alphabets, numbers and color codes.

The flow logic of the coding is simple yet effective. At the point of aggregation and sorting, a symbol A, B, C, D… indicates the start point of the forward distribution node. For example, at

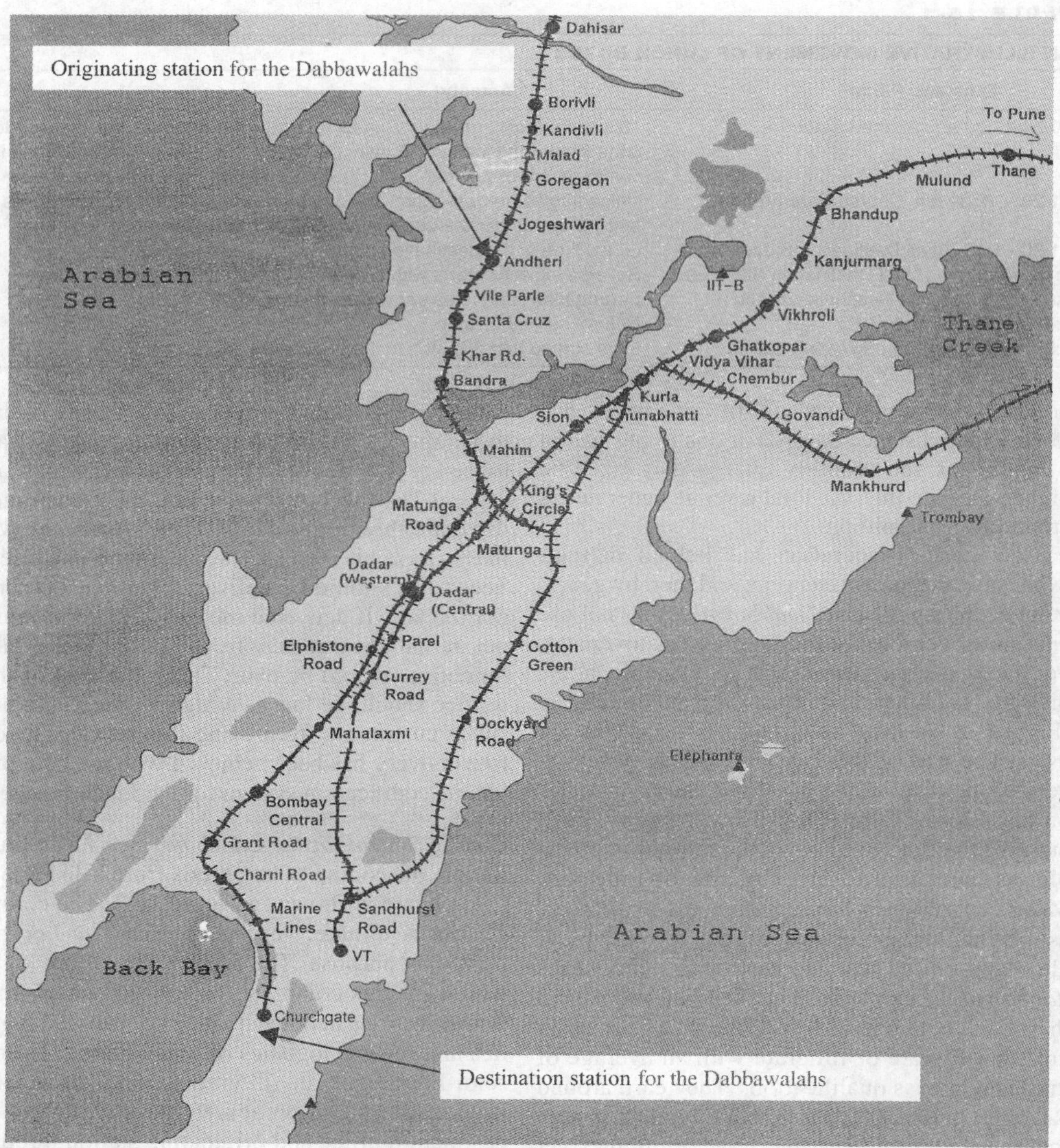

FIGURE 16.1 Suburban Railway Map of Mumbai illustrating the Originating and Destination Stations

Note: Map not drawn to scale.

aggregation and sorting node D, all the lunch boxes from homes having D residential station would be brought. In the reverse logistics, or return trip when empty lunch boxes are coming back from offices to home, this code automatically becomes the destination code. Distribution

Code for Tiffin Box	Legends	Meaning
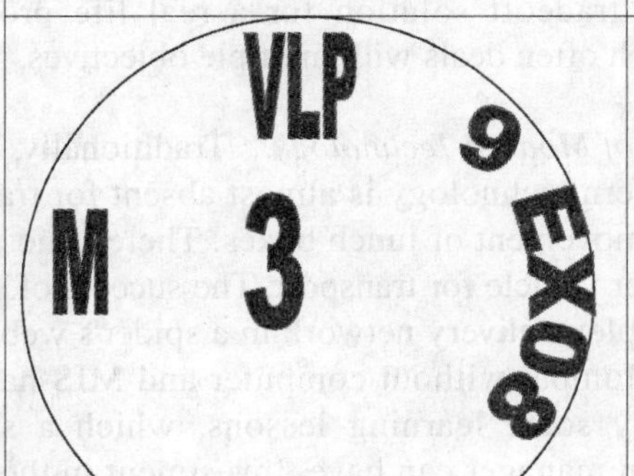 VLP 9 EX08 M 3	VLP	Vile Parle (suburb in Mumbai)
	9EX08	Code for Dabbawalahs at destination
	EX	Express Towers (building name)
	08	Floor no.
	M	Code for Dabbawalahs at residential station
	3	Code for destination station, e.g. Churchgate station (Nariman Point)

FIGURE 16.2 Coding Scheme of Lunch Boxes

in the forward flow has a destination code for distribution. This is indicated by zones of destination.

Distribution Network Design: The coding system effectively gets operationalized through a unique combination of "milk-run" and "hub and spoke" type of distribution network, which at times looks like a "Just in Time" system. How does it work to a cost advantage and operational efficiency? Think about the collection of lunch-boxes in the morning—the first activity of the chain. For example, a *dabbawalah* goes to houses allocated to him, one after another. He almost runs while he collects from one home to another. Housewives generally keep lunch-box ready as these *dabbawalahs* are never ready to wait. In the process, one *dabbawalah* collects around 20 lunch boxes. Here, the challenge is to cover a wide catchments area as each collection point may be little away from its preceding or succeeding point. So, this supports wide coverage, optimal utilization of *dabbawalah's* capacity, time-flexibility in starting the day's operation by a *dabbawalah* so as to meet the target collection, and operational ease. If we compare this with a milkman delivering milk or a newsvendor delivering newspaper in a residential colony, the approach is similar. Intuitively, they adopt the shortest path to cover all the houses on their route with a start, originating from his own residence to a finish or the final destination, which in case of *dabbawalah* is the originating railway platform. This portion of the distribution-network of Mumbai *dabbawalah* resembles a 'milk-run' system. From point to the destination railway station, the movement is in suburban trains. This results in cost advantage, time saving, road congestion avoidance, safety and ease of movement in the long distance involved. Mass transport system like railways are generally very cost effective as compared to other options. How about the distribution network beyond the destination railway station? All lunch-boxes, which are loaded in the train at different railways stations but coded for a particular railway station, say Vile Parle, are off-loaded here. From this railway station, the distribution of the lunch boxes is done in manner similar to the 'hub and spoke' system. This supports volume flexibility, operational ease, short response time, and cost advantage. This distination railway platform is now hub of the distribution point and different *dabbawalahs* take their lunch box load for different office buildings. Generally, many offices are located in one building. Consolidation of distribution is needed now. All lunch boxes of one multistoried building or few adjoining offices are sorted according to the coding system on the lunch boxes. It displays the building or office premise code very prominently [Figure 16.2]. This element of the lunch-box code is the basis of movement now onwards. The movement paths henceforth resemble spokes in different directions emanating from the off-loaded point on the platform. Interestingly, adaptation of these configurations is not by an elegant design but by intuition and experience. Nothing can fully substitute intuition and experience in a business decision. Probably, a very cumbersome and well designed mathematical model would have also minimized the four objectives, which *dabbawalahs* have achieved—total cost of transportation, total time taken to deliver the lunch boxes, error rate or wrong delivery in the system, and total distance travelled in the whole movement plan. With the dynamic changes in the number of customers and their requirements, route constraints, etc, *dabbawalahs* generally strike at the best tradeoff solution for a real life problem, which often deals with multiple objectives.

Use of Modern Technology: Traditionally, use of modern technology is almost absent for tracking the movement of lunch boxes. There is no use of motor vehicle for transport. The success of such a complex delivery network in a spider's web route of Mumbai without computer and MIS has certainly some learning lessons, which a supply chain manager can have. Investment in the technology and its maintenance must be weighed against the benefits not only to the users like *dabbawalahs* but one should also look at the ultimate incremental benefit and cost to the customers. It is therefore no surprise that once the incoming calls are free in India and the majority of mobile service providers have come out with life-time incoming free connection with nominal initial charges, these *dabbawalahs* are getting initiated to this type of communication mode. More recently, they have introduced booking for delivery through SMS and their website. These involves negligible operating expenses. But they still use orthodox push-carts, cycles and head carrier for local distances as any other mode would increase the cost substantially.

The commitment, friendliness and customer-orientation are the hallmark to the operational efficiency of Mumbai *dabbawalah's* distribution system, which is well reflected in their unprecedented growth and customer loyalty [44, 105, 171, 235, 249. 273].

Many local issues are important in the design and operation of a supply chain. Local needs may give rise to unique supply chain solutions. Based on this case, many discussion points emerge for a supply chain manager. Some of these are listed below. In this chapter we will specially address the following questions:

- How does the local issue create a need for new supply chain strategy?

- How does the supply chain work in emergency situation when not much planning is possible, for example during an earthquake like Tsunami, 9/11 type of attack, etc.?
- Why there is a need to focus on reverse logistics?
- How is organized retail affecting the supply chains of developing nations, like India?

16.1 INTRODUCTION

In the earlier chapters, we have discussed many approaches to manage a supply chain. Many local issues play an important role in designing the supply chain. For developing nations, the supply chain efficiency is adversely affected due to infrastructural problems like road, power, water etc. Availability of modern port and air carrier system helps supply chains to perform effectively. For example, India is one of the fastest developing economies of the world. Its seventy percent population lives in very small towns or villages. Infrastructural problems like mode of transport and availability of power sometimes adversely affect the supply chains of consumer goods. Stock out are not very rare. As a last mile problem, the remotest end of a very established FMCG supply chain starts faltering nearer to the customer. Collaborative planning forecasting and replenishment becomes crippled due to absence of a good IT network and probably lack of a cost-effective mode to deal with this situation. Then, it poses a serious challenge to the supply chain managers dealing in these areas.

Despite problems in deploying classical supply chain management approaches some improvised solutions have always been effective. The following example of Amul illustrates the point.

EXAMPLE 16-1 AMUL

In the domain of cold chain management, India's Anand Milk Union Ltd, popularly known as Amul has demonstrated one of the finest examples to the world. It has been working under tremendous infrastructural constraints related to maintenance of low temperature during storage, transportation, processing and retail. Since its inception as a dairy cooperative movement in 1946, Amul is one of the most well-known brands in India. The apex cooperative organization, GCMMF (Gujarat Co-operative Milk Marketing Federation Ltd.) is a unique experiment in itself as it is owned by some 2.6 million milk producers in Indian state of Gujarat. Collection of around 450,000 liters of milk, converting them into high quality, value added product like pasteurized milk under different categories—ice cream, butter, cheese, yogurt, sweets, etc, and delivering these to every household through a battery of 47 depots, over 3,500 distributors and 5 lakh retail outlets across the length and breadth of India, is indeed a demonstration of supply chain management acumen and skill. Despite being a cooperative movement, Amul has banked on professional supply chain management practices. It has provided a role model for rural development. Collection of 2.38 billion liters of milk per year with a daily average of 6.5 million liters has resulted in sales turnover of Rs. 42778 million (around $1050 million) in the year 2006-07. The Amul model has facilitated the populary known white revolution in India to bring the nation to the top of the club of largest milk and milk product producer in the world [183, 272, 279].

16.2 SUPPLY CHAIN ISSUES DURING NATURAL DISASTERS AND OTHER CALAMITIES

Natural disasters do not come announced. Neither do terrorist attacks like 9/11 in US, Parliament attack in India, and bomb blasts in many parts of the world. These are not very uncommon these days. All these calamities require preparedness and pre-planning for delivering relief material and conducting rescue operations. Like fire stations, centralized relief centers can be designated. Their procurement and distribution should be as swift as possible. While natural disasters cannot be avoided, with speed and agility the damages to life and property can certainly be minimized.

Sometimes, during these disasters, over-supply is a problem. This was the case in the Tsunami hit Andaman & Nicobar Islands and coastal areas of Southern states on the Eastern side of India on 26 December 2004. The supply chain for distribution of relief material was established wherein relief material was collected from different places under respective District Administration. On a war footing these items were to be transported through different modes like rail and air. Besides foodstuff and drinking water, there were gensets, pumps, blankets and tents. The over-supply to Car Nicobar Air base could not be distributed because of little onward requirement. The relief material was once again air-lifted to other coastal regions. The supply chains to all the areas needed to be very quickly planned for need-based distribution among them. How to manage a distribution network in a disaster like earth-quake, flood, Tsunami or a terrorist attack is a matter of far greater implication as human lives are at stake. One should address the specific needs of relief supply chains and humanitarian supply chains with more caution and better planning.

EXAMPLE 16-2 DISTRIBUTION SYSTEM DURING NATURAL DISASTERS

On 26 January 2001, a severe earthquake rocked the Indian state of Gujarat with its epicenter at Bhuj and devastated the whole of the Kutch region. The public and government response to this natural disaster was spontaneous. Relief material started pouring in from all parts of India and also from many other countries. All relief material started moving towards Bhuj, leading to heavy traffic congestion and chocked supply. On one hand there were scarcity of supply at the affected people, on the other hand there was an over-supply in the pipe-line. Distribution of relief material was getting affected. While sufficient relief material was around, it was not reaching to the affected people due to congestion, storage and distribution problems. The excess material from Bhuj was removed swiftly and redistributed in many other affected surrounding areas in Kutch region like Morbi, Amreli, etc. Special instructions were issued to re-route the relief supplies to other places and on some occasions advice came in to delay the dispatch. In such cases, several relief materials are perishable products like food and milk. Their handling requires special care. The supply chain of food and basic necessities to the affected areas was restored from the neighboring states and small time farms. The situation was tackled successfully soon but the lessons that were learnt should not be forgotten.

16.3 SUPPLY CHAIN ISSUES FOR SMEs

Small and medium enterprises (SMEs) are playing a major role in any nation's development and in bringing about its economic prosperity. They provide jobs and decentralize the development process of a nation. In India, the importance of SMEs can be well understood by the fact that they contribute to almost 40% of the gross industrial value added in the national economy and around 45% in total exports. The formal concepts of supply chain have not settled well in a majority of supply chain activities involving SMEs in India. Strategic use of IT tools is limited, and there is an over-dependence on a bigger supply chain partner. There are numerous threats too. For example, rationalization of vendor-base has been counter-productive to many SMEs. A majority of the SMEs do not assess the supply chain risks properly and their role in total supply chain planning is minuscule. Despite clear evidences on a direct relationship between use of technology and improved supply chain results, Indian SMEs have not taken advantage of the new modes like electronic markets, electronic data interchange and Internet commerce [71, 72].

Due to lack of transparency in the supply chains of SMEs, the middlemen pocket a majority of the profit. For example, the plight of SMEs for leather and brassware in India has not improved much despite huge export and domestic demand. The leather supply chain in India involves over 3,000 tanneries, mostly SMEs with a total processing capacity of 700,000 tons of hides and skins per year. A majority of the unorganized small players do not possess the high-end technology and automation to deliver quality products at a fast pace. Automation, through use of technology, can significantly improve the competitiveness of this supply chain. But it has to come to all the relevant stages of its supply chains, for example, during recovery of skin as a raw material, tanning and finishing, and production of leather products.

EXAMPLE 16-3 BRASSWARE SMEs IN INDIA

There are more than 1000 SMEs in the brassware cluster at Moradabad district of Indian state Uttar Pradesh. The main markets for their highly skilled craft products are in North America, Europe, Australia, Canada, South Africa, Scandinavia and the Middle East. Its supply chain operates at three levels. It starts with household units that work for the second layer locally called as *karkhanedars*. They are small manufacturers and obtain their orders from the third layer of its supply chain, i.e. large exporters. These large exporters earn maximum profits, while the SMEs still struggle to survive. *Karkhanedars* subcontract a majority of the operations to household units for ingot making, casting, welding, scrapping, polishing, plating and other major activities of brassware production. They involve themselves in minor finishing operations and negotiation with exporters. The supply chain involving SMEs can prosper only when they come in the mainstream and get integrated with supply chain planning and control [71, 72].

16.4 ORGANIZED RETAIL IN INDIA

India is witnessing a tremendous changeover in its retail sector. Organized retail is coming up fast. Major players like Reliance, Bharti, RPG Group, Tata, Aditya Birla, Subhikhsha, etc have mega plans of expansion. The multi format of retail, which is unfolding in India is focused on competitive-offerings to Indian consumers. Many mega marts are coming up with an offering of a tremendously large variety of products and services under one roof. It involves many verticals such as food, beverages, grocery, household consumption items, apparels, footwear, electronic goods, lifestyle products, home appliances, electronics-communication products, services like travel, finance, insurance and banking, services like entertainment and leisure experiences, pharmaceuticals and healthcare products and related services, educational products and related services etc. How can these be delivered unless there is strong backend integration in its supply chain? Many new alignments and business partnerships have to evolve.

EXAMPLE 16-4 RELIANCE RETAIL

On 15 August 2006, Reliance opened its biggest hypermarket under one roof in Ahmedabad, the capital city of state Gujarat in India. It has more than 95,000 products. It has plans to open over 500 similar ones by 2010 [281, 289, 296].

There have been protests by small retailers, which are typically of “mom and pop” type, as they see a future in which their margin and market share both will diminish substantially. The Government is also conscious of these facts. Till mid 2007, the foreign players running cash-and-carry stores can sell to distributors, retailers and hotels among others, but not to consumers. The government has put a restriction of 49 percent FDI restriction for single-brand retailers. This has kept many global players like Tesco and Carrefour on the fence, as they are multi-product retail chains. Wal-Mart, in the same category, has plans to enter in the arena with a 50:50 partnership with a local player Bharti. They envisage Wal-Mart’s role in a majority of backend operations. This sector is fast unfolding with many new developments taking place everyday. However, since the beginning of liberalization in India in 1991, all Governments at the center have endorsed the process of liberalization, privatization and globalization. Therefore, many analysts expect this sector to grow in India with an unprecedented pace [281, 289, 296].

16.5 REVERSE LOGISTICS

Reverse logistics has become very important in the contemporary supply chains due to an endless list of wastes generated every day in the form of TVs, computers, printers, mobile phones, chemical waste, plastics, toys etc who have a limited life. How to deal with these when their useful life with the customer ends? Some options are based on extending the life of the product so that environmental degradation could be delayed. As a first measure, identifying a second hand user is possibly the best option. For example, Maruti, an auto manufacturing company in India has come out with a "true-value-system." A used Maruti car, when it comes to this system undergoes many quality and performance tests and maintenance after which its true value is objectively assessed for a second hand user. Other options are reconfiguration, remanufacture, redesign, recycle, cannibalization, and disposal. Due to a quality defect, even a new product can come back in the supply chain as a warranty claim.

EXAMPLE 16-5 RECALL OF MATTEL TOYS

US toy maker Mattel Inc. is known for its world-class toys featuring popular characters like Barney, Dora, and Diego. In August 2007, it asked its US customers and other sellers to return 967,000 plastic toys and another 533,000 from other countries including Britain, Canada, and Mexico. Customers and retailers of Mattel are also located in many other countries including Asia. The reason for this recall is based on the apprehension that these toys, produced between April 19 to July 6 by a third party Chinese manufacturer, contain excessive lead in the paint applied on these toys. Later, these were reports related to design problem as the actual cause of the defect and recall. But, the damage to Mattel has already taken place. It suffered losses of over US$ 30 million due to recall along with damage to its brand name and stock-out or low sale scenario for quite sometime [20].

The management of reverse logistics is not as simple as its forward supply chain as the forecasting-based planning is often quite inaccurate. Therefore, generally, extra capacity would be needed or one has to look for flexibility in planning the schedules. Sometimes, when there is a product recall, the reverse supply chain gets choked with replacement claims [197, 210].

EXAMPLE 16-6 RECALL OF NOKIA BATTERIES

In August 2007, Nokia mobile phone users in India were asked by the company to return and get replacement for the BL-5C series batteries in these phones due to the apprehension of defects like overheating etc. Worldwide, over 46 million and in India, around one lakh mobile phones had these defective batteries. The recall has had an estimated impact of around $340 million globally along with a negative market sentiment about the brand [32].

Reverse logistics in many supply chains are well organized. For example, Indian soft drink supply chains still use glass bottles, which are recycled before reuse. Paper industry has a well-organized collection network for used-paper, which is ultimately supplied to the manufactures. Used papers can be recycled for producing fresh paper and the process is encouraged. It saves the degradation of forests since paper requires wood as a raw material and hence causes pressure on the environment. Therefore, besides dealing with environmental concerns, reverse logistics should be supportive in recovering the associated economic benefits also [197, 198, 210].

SUMMARY

Local issues require special supply chain solutions. In this chapter local issues especially relevant to India and its neighboring countries have been discussed. During the time of natural calamities, like earthquakes, floods etc, a temporary supply chain architecture has to be created without loss of time. The effectiveness of these supply chains determines the extent to which life and property of common masses can be saved. In the developing nations, SMEs are playing an important role in the growth process. Bringing them in the mainstream of supply chain design and operation will serve the major purpose of sustainable supply chains. Most of these countries are also abuzz with the activities related to onset of the retail revolution. Newer challenges have come up and therefore a fresh strategy would be needed to tackle them. In the era of consumerism and heavy competition, outsourcing manufacturing and services to cheaper destination has become very common. This has created pressure to cut time and cost. Quality defects are an outcome of these pressures. Reverse logistics at the time of product recall and end-of-useful life of a product has therefore posed a serious challenge to supply chain managers.

DISCUSSION QUESTIONS

1 Based on the opening case of the Mumbai *dabbawalahs* in this chapter discuss the following issues:

   (i) What should be the level of automation and use of technology in a supply chain? How is it related to complexity of network, educational and skill level of users, cost of operation, value generation, CTQs, investment and return on investment?
   (ii) Discuss if the level of error-free distribution system evolved by Mumbai *dabbawalahs* is directly deployable in the following scenarios: (i) retail chain operations, (ii) milk distribution system, (iii) lunch box distribution system in your own city, and (iv) postal/courier distribution services. In case you feel that there are some modifications needed, discuss those in detail.
   (iii) "Mumbai *dabbawalah's* distribution system is marked by decentralization at the operational-level. Yet it works as a coordinated chain." Do you agree? Discuss.
   (iv) Explore some other systems where coding plays an important role in the distribution network. What system they follow and why?
   (v) What are the critical success factors for the Mumbai *dabbawalahs*? Discuss.
   (vi) Why do Mumbai *Dabbawalahs* operate in an almost competition free environment? What prevents new players from entering in the same field?
   (vii) One of the important characteristics of distribution systems is scalability. How would you rate Mumbai *dabbawalah* on that?
   (viii) Operationally, Mumbai *dabbawalah* deals with both forward and reverse logistics simultaneously. There are many examples of reverse logistics like collection of empty glass bottles of cold drinks. Give more examples of similar type and explore their operational efficiency.
   (ix) What are the lessons for supply chain managers dealing with distribution networks?
   (x) Develop a SOP (Standard Operating Procedure) document for the Mumbai *dabbawalah*. Use secondary sources, like Internet to collect more information, if needed.

2 Give a few examples of reverse logistics and explain its significance in the contemporary business.

3 Compare the similarity and difference in ten important supply chain issues in developing and developed countries. Are these same? If not, what are the additional challenges for managers in a country like India?

4 How does the socio-political situation of a nation affect the supply chain management? Give examples.

Computerized Beer Game

A.1 INTRODUCTION[1]

If you've taken an operations management course in the last 20 years, you are no doubt familiar with the Beer Game. This role-playing simulation of a simple production and distribution system has been used in countless undergraduate, graduate, and executive education courses since it was first developed at MIT in the 1960s.

The Computerized Beer Game, included with this text, is similar in many respects to the traditional Beer Game. As you will learn in the following pages, however, it has many options and features that enable you to explore a variety of simple and advanced supply chain management concepts that cannot be easily taught using the traditional game.

Windows 95 or later is required to operate the game. To install the software, place the included CD in your CD-ROM drive. If the installation program doesn't run automatically, open Windows Explorer, select the CD, and double click on the setup program. Click the "Games" link and then click the "Risk Pool Game and Computerized Beer Game" link to download the setup file.

A.2 THE TRADITIONAL BEER GAME

For comparative purposes, we will briefly review the traditional manual Beer Game, which is typically played on a large board. Locations on the board represent four components, or stages, of the beer supply chain: the factory, the distributor, the wholesaler, and the retailer. Orders placed by each of the component managers, as well as inventory in transit and at each of the locations, are represented by markers and pennies that are placed at the appropriate locations on the board. External demand is represented by a stack of cards.

One player manages each of the supply chain components. Each week, the retail manger observes external demand (by drawing the next "demand card"), fills as much of this demand as possible, records back orders to be filled, and places an order with the wholesaler. In turn the manager of the wholesaler observes demand form the retailer, fills as much of this demand as possible, records back orders, and places an order with the distributor. The distributor manager repeats this process,

[1]A Web-based version of the Beer Game can be found at the MIT Forum for Supply Chain Innovation, http://supplychain.mit.edu/.

ordering from the factory. Finally, the factory manager, after observing and filling demand and back orders, begins production. Order processing and filling delays are incorporated into the game to represent order processing, transportation, and manufacturing lead times. The rules of the game require all back orders to be filled as soon as possible. At each stage of the supply chain, the manager at that stage has only local information; only the retail manager knows customer demand. The goal of the game is to minimize the total holding and back-order costs at the stage you are managing. Each week a cost of $0.50 for each unit in inventory and $1.00 for each unit of back order is accrued.

A typical game is played 25 to 50 "weeks." During the game, communication between players is limited. Inventory and back-order levels usually vary dramatically from week to week. At the end of the game, the players are asked to estimate customer demand. Except for the retail manager, who knows the demand, players often estimate wildly varying demand. After being informed that demand was constant at four units per week for the first four weeks, and then eight units per week for the remaining weeks, players are often surprised. Instinctively, they blame the other players for following inappropriate strategies.

A.2.1 The Difficulties with the Traditional Beer Game

When the Beer Game was first introduced in the 1960s, the concept of *integrated supply chain management*—as well as advanced information systems that support this concept—was not yet developed. In many cases, the supply chain was managed by different managers at each stage based on their individual intuition, experience, and objectives. Since then, however, both the theory and the practice of supply chain management have improved significantly. Unfortunately, as traditionally played, the Beer Game does not necessarily reflect current supply chain practices. Perhaps more importantly, the Beer Game does not necessarily provide students with insight on how to *better manage the supply chain*.

These weaknesses of the traditional Beer Game can be attributed to several of its characteristics. Our experience with the game suggests that the students typically are so occupied with the mechanics of the game, making sure that they correctly follow the rules of the game, that they have no time to develop an effective strategy. Even if a participant uses a sophisticated strategy, he or she may tend to attribute inventory and back-order problems, as well as higher-than-expected cost, to the other participants' strategies, rather than to search for potential flaws in his or her own strategic decisions.

In addition, the demand pattern exhibited in the Beer Game does not reflect a realistic supply chain scenario. In the traditional game, demand unexpectedly doubles in the fifth week of play and remains at that level until the end of the game. In real life, it is unrealistic to expect that managers of each of the supply chain facilities would not be informed of such a huge change in demand patterns.

Finally, the traditional Beer Game doesn't demonstrate several other important supply chain management issues. For example, in many real-world supply chains, several (or all) of the stages have a single owner. Thus, the real objective is to minimize the total system cost, not individual performance. Unfortunately, in the traditional Beer Game, there is no way to judge how much is lost by managing stages individually.

Many of the difficulties in managing the supply chain that are highlighted by the Beer Game can be addressed by shortening cycle times and centralizing information and decision making. Unfortunately, these approaches to solving many supply chain management problems cannot be demonstrated in the traditional Beer Game—students can learn about them only in the lecture following game play.

The Computerized Beer Game was developed precisely to address the difficulties inherent in the traditional Beer Game. In the following sections, we describe the scenario, the commands and options available, and, finally, several supply chain management concepts that we have taught successfully using the Computerized Beer Game.

A.3 THE SCENARIOS

The Beer Game (computerized and traditional) models the following scenarios. First, consider a simplified beer supply chain, consisting of a single retailer, a single wholesaler that supplies this retailer, a single distributor that supplies the wholesaler, and a single factory with unlimited raw materials that brews the beer and supplies the distributor. Each component in the supply chain has unlimited storage capacity, and there is a fixed supply lead time and order delay time between each component.

Every week, each component in the supply chain tries to meet the demand of the downstream component. Any orders that cannot be met are recorded as back orders and met as soon as possible. No orders will be ignored, and all orders must eventually be met. At each week, each component in the supply chain is charged a \$1.00 shortage cost per back-ordered item. Also at each week, each component owns the inventory at that facility. In addition, the wholesaler owns inventory in transit to the retailer, the distributor owns inventory in transit to the wholesaler, and the factory owns both items being manufactured and items in transit to the distributor. Each location is charged a \$0.50 inventory holding cost per inventory item that it owns. Also, each supply chain member orders some amount from its upstream supplier. An order placed at the end of one week arrives at the supplier at the start of the next week. Once the order arrives, the supplier attempts to fill it with available inventory. Thus, an order placed at the end of week w arrives at the supplier at the start of week $w + 1$. The material is shipped (if it is in stock) at the start of week $w + 1$ and arrives at the supply chain member who placed the order no earlier than the start of week $w + 3$. This implies that the actual order lead time is two weeks. Each supply chain member has no knowledge of the external demand (except, of course, the retailer) or the orders and inventory of the other members. The goal of the retailer, wholesaler, distributor, and factory is to minimize total cost, either individually or for the system.

The Computerized Beer Game has other options that model various situations. These differing options enable the instructor to illustrate and compare concepts such as lead-time reduction, global information sharing, and centralized management. For instance, consider a scenario exactly as described above, except that each supply chain member has full knowledge of the external demand, orders, and inventories of all other supply chain members. In another possible scenario, lead times are reduced form the two weeks described above to only one week.

Finally, in a centralized scenario, the game is changed as follows: The manager of the factory controls the entire supply chain and has information about all of the inventory levels throughout the supply chain, as well as the external demand. Because the system is centralized, stages other than the factory do not place orders; all inventory is moved through the system as quickly as possible. In addition, because there can be no back order at any stage except the first one, the retailer pays a \$4.00 shortage cost for each back-ordered item. This enables a fair comparison between the decentralized scenario described above and the centralized scenario. Because three sets of orders are eliminated, the product moves through this supply chain three weeks faster than in the supply chain described above. These are the main scenarios modeled by the Computerized Beer Game. In the following sections, we describe specifically how to use the software to model these situations.

A.4 PLAYING A ROUND

In this section, we describe how to play a round of the Computerized Beer Game, using the default settings, to model the first scenario described above. In the next section, we describe each of the menu commands in detail, so that a variety of scenarios also can be modeled.

A.4.1 Introducing the Game

When the Computerized Beer Game software is started, the following screen appears:

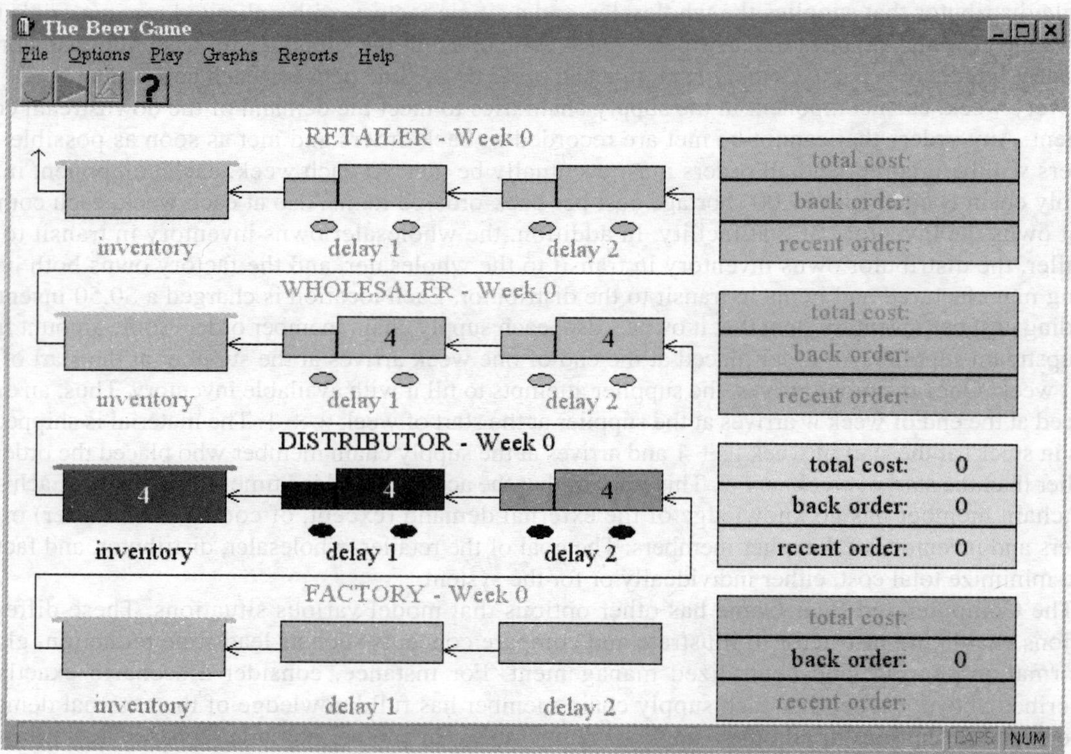

In this simulation, the player takes the role of manager of one of the components of the beer supply chain, either the retailer, the supplier, the distributor, or the factory. This will be called the *interactive* role. The computer takes the remaining roles. On the game display, the interactive role is displayed in color, and the remaining roles are displayed in gray. The information for the interactive roles is also displayed, but the information for other roles is hidden (with the exception of back orders at the supply chain member immediately upstream from the interactive supply chain member and the two outgoing trucks). In the example screen displayed above, the distributor is the interactive role. *Downstream* means the direction of the supply chain leading to the external demand while *upstream* means the direction of the factory. In addition, we refer to components of the supply chain as *facilities*.

Order of Events The simulation is run as a series of weeks. Within each week, first the retailer, then the wholesaler, then the distributor, and finally the factory, executes the following series of events, as the simulation proceeds upstream. For each facility:

Step 1. The contents of *delay 2* are moved to *delay 1*, and the contents of *delay 1* are moved to inventory. *Delay 2* is 0 at this point.

Step 2. Orders from the immediate downstream facility (in the case of the retailer, external customers) are filled to the extent possible. Remember that an order consists of the current order and all accumulated back orders. Remaining orders (equal to current inventory minus the sum of the current orders and back orders) are backlogged, to be met as soon as possible. Except for retailers, which ship orders outside the system, the orders are filled to the *delay 2* location of the immediate downstream facility. This is the start of the two-week delay.

Step 3. Back-order and inventory costs are calculated and added to accumulated total costs from previous periods. This incremental cost is calculated as follows: The total inventory at the facility and in transit to the next downstream facility is multiplied by the holding cost, \$0.50, while the total back order is multiplied by the shortage cost, \$1.00.

Step 4. Orders are placed. If this is the interactive role, the user indicates the desired order amount. If this is one of the automatic roles, the computer places an order using one of several typical inventory control schemes. The schemes can be controlled by the instructor, as we will explain in the next section.

Delays and Order Filling This sequence of events implies several things. First, once the downstream facility places an order at the end of a week, this order will be filled no earlier than the start of the week three weeks later (that is, if the order is placed at the end of week w, the material will be received no earlier than the start of period $w + 3$, a two-week lead time). *Also, once an order is placed at the end of a week, it is not received until the start of the next week. This means that if, for example, the retailer places an order for 5 units at the end of this period, the wholesaler does not even attempt to fill the order until the start of the next period. This period, the wholesaler attempts to fill the order from the previous period.*

Recall also that there is no guarantee that an order will be met, even with this lag. An upstream supplier can fill an order only if it has the necessary inventory. Otherwise it will backlog that order and attempt to fill it as soon as possible. *The exception to this is the factory. There is no limit to production capacity, so the factory's order will always be filled in its entirety after the appropriate delay.*

A.4.2 Understanding the Screen

Each facility in the supply chain is represented on the display. As an example, the *Distributor* is displayed below:

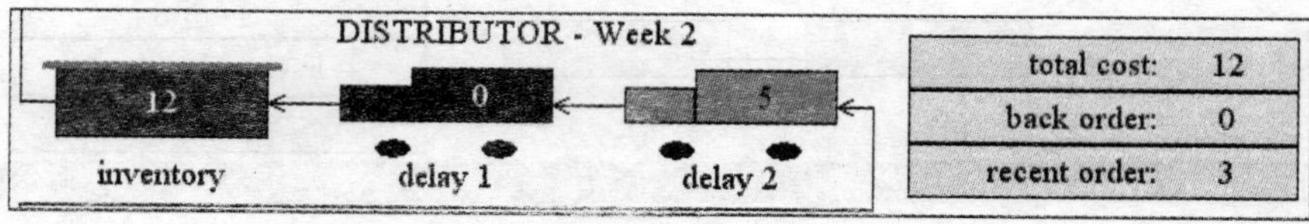

On the left of the screen, the number of items in inventory is displayed. The next two elements (from left to right) represent items in transit to inventory; that is, the numbers in the box labeled *delay 1* represent the number of items that will arrive in inventory in one week, and similarly for *delay* 2. The box on the right lists (1) the total inventory and shortage cost up to the current time; (2) the back order, that is, the demands that have been received at this facility but have not been filled yet due to lack of inventory; and (3) the most recent order placed by this facility, in this example, the *Distributor* to its upstream facility, the *Factory*. Note that in this case, back order refers to orders received by the *Distributor* but not yet met from inventory. To find out the orders placed by the *Distributor* that have been backlogged—that is, not yet met by the factory—check the back order at the *Factory.* Also, the recent order number displayed in the box represents the most recent order sent by the *Distributor* to the *Factory*. This order will arrive at the upstream supplier at the start of the next period.

A.4.3 Playing the Game

To start the game, select **Start** from the **Play** menu, or push the start button on the toolbar. The computer will automatically play the first round for the automatic facilities downstream from the interactive facility. For example, if the *Distributor* is the interactive facility, the computer will play for the *Retailer* and the *Wholesaler,* in that order.

Once this is completed, the first round for the interactive facility is played. Steps 1 and 2 (advance inventories and fill orders, described in the section labeled "Order of Events") are completed. At this point, inventory numbers are updated on the screen, and the Order Entry dialog box appears. The screen looks as follows:

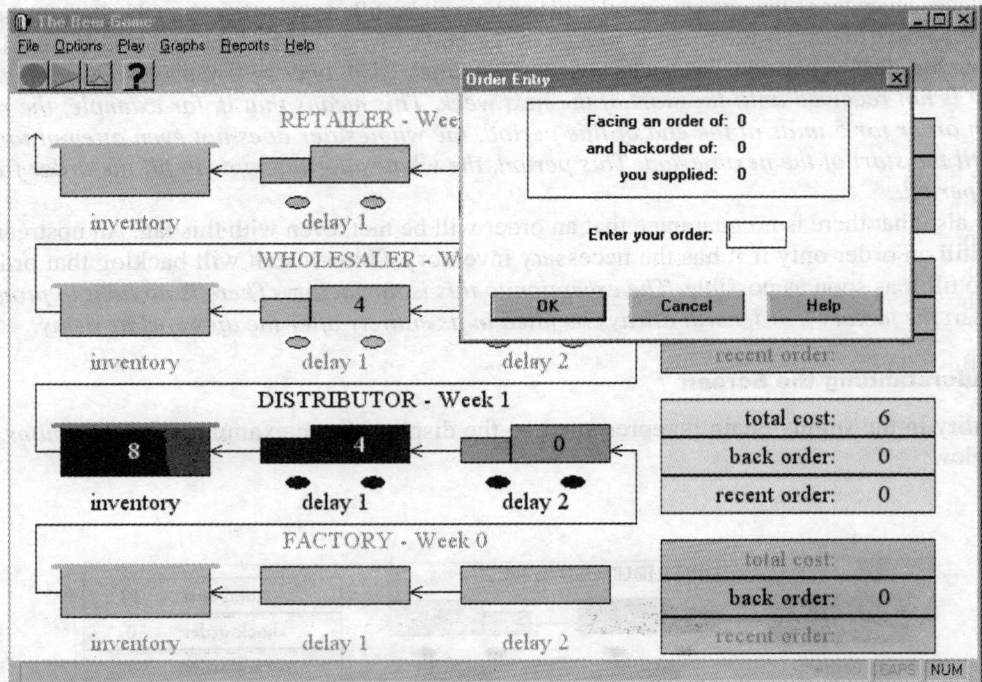

Examine this screen in detail. Recall (you can see this from the previous screen shown on page 460) that the initial inventory was 4, and both *delay 1* and *delay 2* contained 4 units. This holds true for each of the supply chain facilities. Now, steps 1 and 2 have been completed. As you can see from the Order Entry dialog box, there is initially no back order and no order from the *Wholesaler.* Since the starting inventory was 8 (the initial 4 plus 4 from *delay 1*), 8 remain in inventory. *Delay 2* is now empty. In *delay 1* at the *Wholesaler,* there are 4 units, for which the *Distributor* will pay holding costs for this period. This is the first round, so there are no previous orders from the *Distributor* to the *Factory*. Thus, the recent order box reads 0. However, if this was a later round and an order was placed by the *Distributor* to the *Factory* during the previous round, it would appear in the *recent order* box.

The Order Entry dialog box indicates how much total back order and order was faced by the interactive player in this round (again, in our example, the *Distributor*), and how much of it was successfully filled. Note that the back-order box on the right side of the screen indicates the current level of back order, while the dialog box shows the level of back order at the beginning of this round, before the player (in this case, the *Distributor*) attempted to fill downstream orders (in this case, from the *Wholesaler*).

At this point, enter a demand amount. This can be zero or any other integer. Remember that you are trying to balance inventory holding costs and shortage costs. Also, by looking at the back-order box at your supplier (in this example, the *Factory*), you can see how much back order your upstream supplier already has to fill; that is, how many items you have ordered in prior rounds but have not yet received. Once an amount has been entered, the remaining upstream supply chain members play automatically, and the screen is updated. If you enter an order of 3 for the *Distributor,* the remainder of Week 1 play is carried out, and the *Distributor* portion of the screen looks like

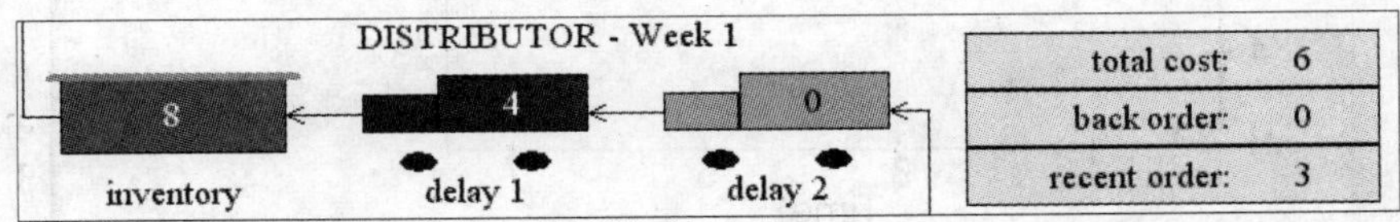

The order of 3 is reflected in the recent order box, and the total cost box reflects holding cost charged due to the 8 units in inventory and the 4 units in *delay 1* at the *Wholesaler*.

To play the next round, select **Next round** from the **Play** menu, or push the *next round button* on the toolbar. The computer again automatically plays the next round for the automatic facility downstream from the interactive facility. Once again, the order entry dialog appears. At this point, both *delay 1* and *delay 2* show an inventory of 0, since the inventory was advanced and *delay 2* was *initially* 0. Recall that after you input an order, the upstream supplier (in this case the *Factory*) will try to meet last period's order of 3. If you order 6 this period and the remaining upstream supply chain members play automatically, the distributor portion of the screen at the end of Week 2 will look like

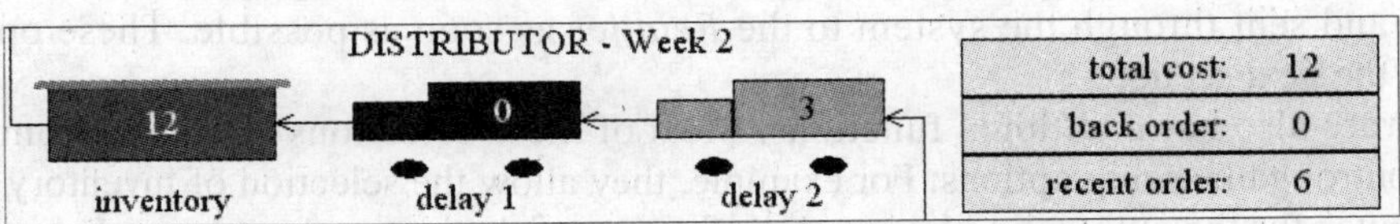

Continue play by selecting **Next round** from the **Play** menu, or pushing the *next round button* at the beginning of each round. At any time, you can view a graph of your performance to date by selecting **Player** from the **Graphs** menu, or pushing the *player graph button.* This graph will display orders, back order, inventory, and total cost over time. A sample graph follows:

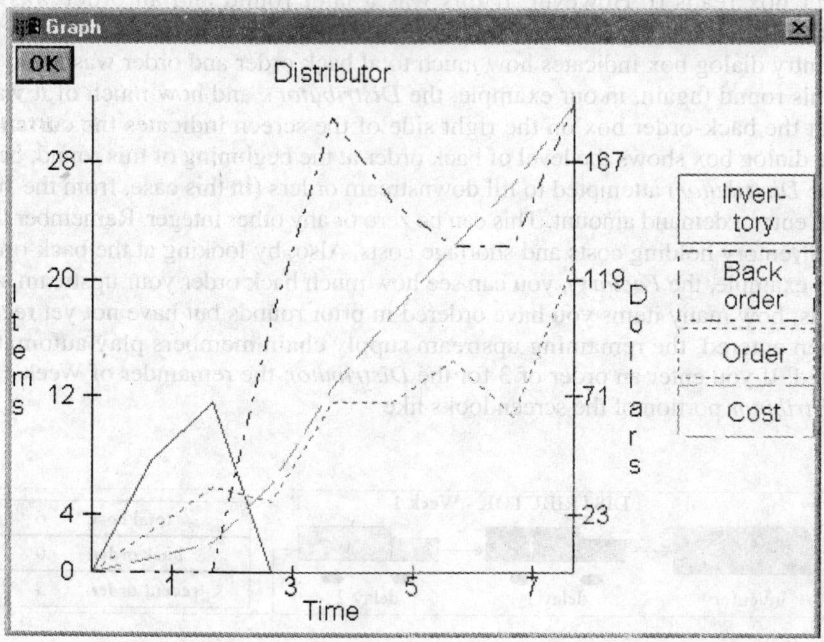

You can also view a list of your orders to date by selecting **Player** from the **Reports** menu.

A.4.4 Other Features

In addition to playing the Computerized Beer Game as we have just described it, it is possible to play the game in three other modes: the *Global Information Mode,* in which inventory levels and orders at all facilities and external demand are available to the interactive player; the *Short Lead Time Mode,* in which lead time through the system is reduced by eliminating *delay 2* at each of the facilities; and the *Centralized Mode,* in which all information is available to the interactive player and orders are placed at the *Factory* and sent through the system to the *Retailer* as soon as possible. These options will be described in the next section.

The software also has additional functions. Most of these selections are made from the **Options** menu and control game setup options. For example, they allow the selection of inventory policies used by the computer for the automatic players and selection of the interactive player. In addition, graphs and reports of the performance of each of the supply chain members and of the system as a whole can be viewed. These options will also described in more detail in the next section.

A.5 OPTIONS AND SETTINGS

This section follows the menu in the Computerized Beer Game, and describes the function of each of the parameters and options that the user can set. In the following subsections, the convention **menu—selection** item is used to describe menu selections.

A.5.1 File Commands

These commands are used to stop and reset play, and exit the system:

File—Reset. This command rests the game. All data from the previous game are lost.

File—Exit. This command exits the Computerized Beer Game and returns you to the Windows environment.

A.5.2 Options Commands

These commands allow the game options to be set, so that different scenarios can be modeled.

Options—Player. This command displays the following Player dialog in order to select the *interactive player.* This is the role that the player will take. The computer takes the other three roles.

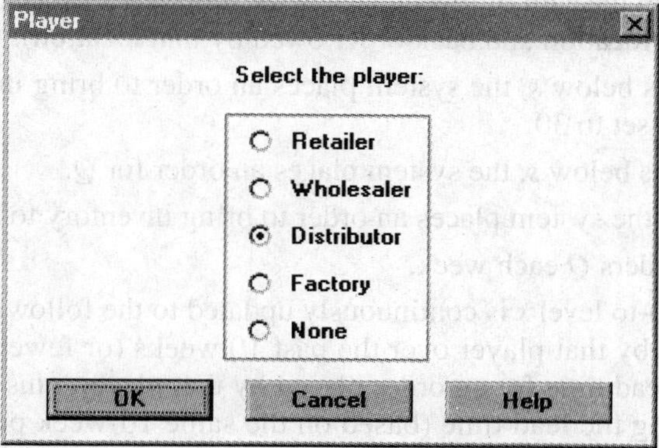

Click on the player button or name to select a player, and then select OK. To cancel the command, select Cancel. Note that if None is selected, the computer will take all of the roles, so that the results can be observed.

Options—Policy. This command displays the following Policy dialog so that policies for each of the automatic players can be selected.

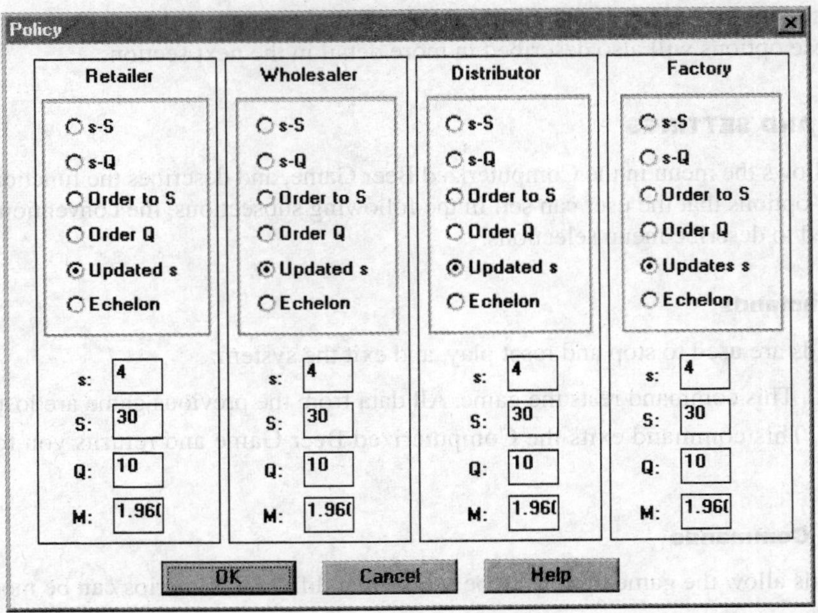

These policies and parameters apply only to computer-controlled players. Different policies can be selected for each of the automatic players. Six policies are available (note that by inventory position in the following, we mean the sum of inventory at a location, back order owed to that location, items being transported to that location and back order owed by that location):

s-S. When inventory falls below *s*, the system places an order to bring inventory to *S*. In this example, *s* is set to 4, and *S* is set to 30.

s-Q. When inventory falls below *s*, the system places an order for *Q*.

Order to S. Each week, the system places an order to bring inventory to *S*.

Order Q. The system orders *Q* each week.

Updated s. The order-up-to level *s* is continuously updated to the following value: the moving average of demand received by that player over the past 10 weeks (or fewer if 10 periods have not yet been played) times the lead time for an order placed by that player, plus *M* times an estimate of the standard deviation during the lead time (based on the same 10-week period). When the inventory level falls below *s*, the system orders up to *s*. However, the maximum possible order size is *S*. Also, the ordering for the first four weeks is adjusted to account for start-up by not ordering (or including in the moving average) demand during the first week at the wholesaler, the first two weeks at the distributor, and the first three weeks at the factory.

Echelon. This is a modified version of the periodic review echelon inventory policy The value of *s* for each of the players is determined as follows. Let *AVG*(*D*) be the 10-week moving average of external customer demand, let *STD*(*D*) be the standard deviation of that external demand, and let $L + r$ equal 3 in the regular game (where the lead time is 2 as previously discussed and the reorder interval is 1 week) and 2 in the short lead time game (described below). Then, at each period at each stage, s is determined as follows:

$$\text{retailer:} \quad s = (L + r) * AVG(D) + M * STD(D) * (L + r)^{.5}$$

$$\text{wholesaler:} \quad s = (L + L + r) * AVG(D) + M * STD(D) * (L + L + r)^{.5}$$

$$\text{distributor:} \quad s = (2 * L + L + r) * AVG(D) + M * STD(D) * (2 * L + L + r)^{.5}$$

$$\text{factory:} \quad s = (3 * L + L + r) * AVG(D) + M * STD(D) * (3 * L + L + r)^{.5}$$

When the inventory position falls below s, the system orders up to s. However, the maximum possible order size is S.

Options—Short Lead Time. This command shortens system lead times by eliminating *delay 2* from the system. Each lead time is thus shortened by one week, and the system display is changed as follows:

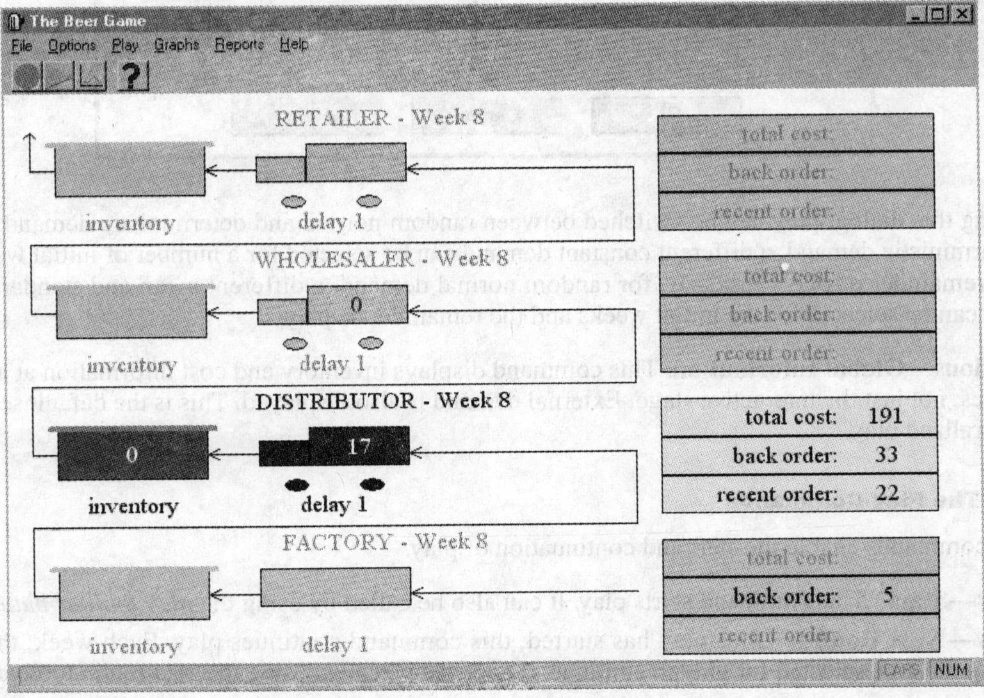

Options—Centralized. This command toggles between standard play and centralized play. In centralized play, the interactive player manages the factory. External demand can be observed and the factory manager can react to it. In addition, when inventory reaches a stage, it is immediately sent forward to the next stage so that inventory is only held by the *Retailer*. This implies that more information is available to the player and that lead time is shortened, since there is no order delay at any stage except the *Factory*.

Options—Demand. This command displays the demand dialog in order to set the external customer demand.

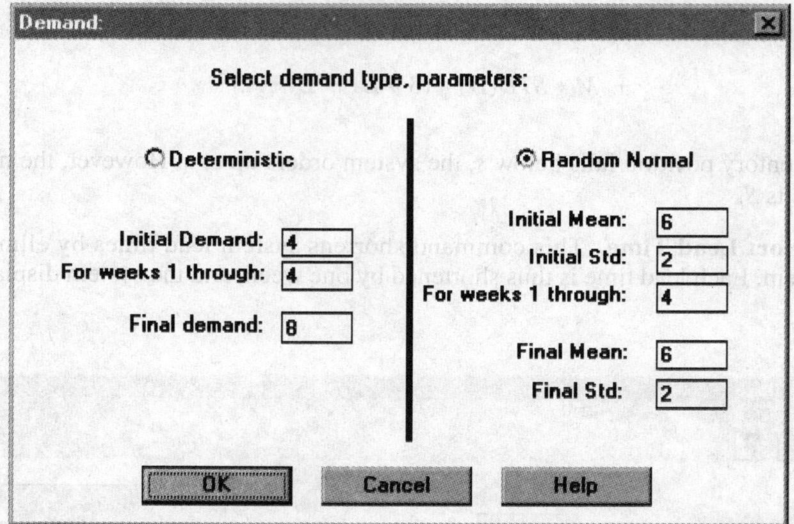

Using this dialog, play can be switched between random normal and deterministic demand. For the deterministic demand, a different constant demand can be selected for a number of initial weeks and the remainder of play. Similarly, for random normal demand, a different mean and standard deviation can be selected for the initial weeks and the remainder of play.

Options—Global Information. This command displays inventory and cost information at all of the stages, not just the interactive stage. External demand is also displayed. This is the default setting for centralized play.

A.5.3. The Play Commands

These commands enable the start and continuation of play.

Play—Start. This command starts play. It can also be called by using the *play toolbar button*.

Play—Next Round. Once play has started, this command continues play. Each week, this command must be selected for play to continue. It also can be called using the *next round* toolbar button.

A.5.4 The Graphs Commands

These commands present status information graphically.

Graphs—Player. This command displays a graph of orders, back orders, inventory, and cost for the current interactive player. This command can also be called using the *graphs* toolbar button. An example follows:

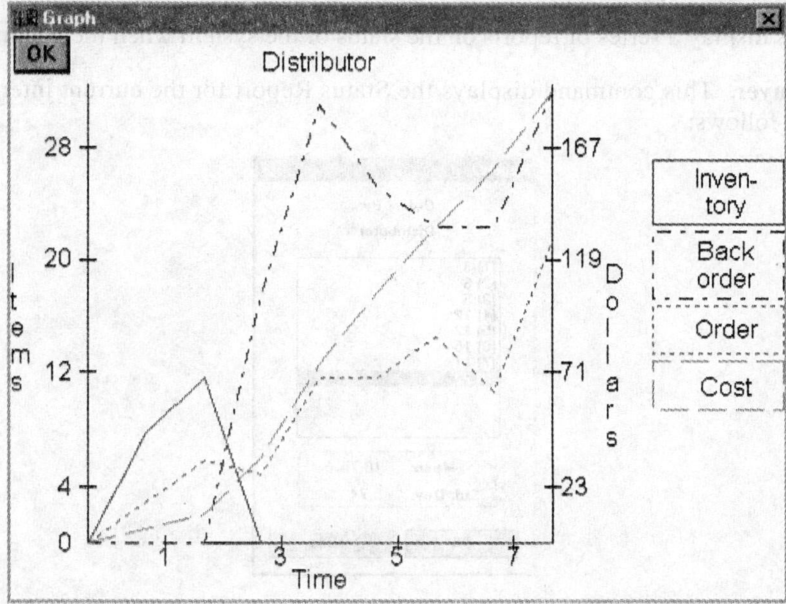

Graphs—Others. When this command is selected, you are first asked to select a player on the following dialog:

Player

Select the player:

- Retailer
- Wholesaler
- Distributor
- Factory
- None

OK Cancel Help

A graph of orders, back orders, inventory, and cost for the selected player is then displayed. This differs from the preceding Graphs—Player command, which displays a graph only for the current interactive player.

Graphs—System. This command displays a graph of orders for each stage.

A.5.5 The Reports Commands

These commands display a series of reports on the status of the system when the command is selected.

Reports—Player. This command displays the Status Report for the current interactive player. A sample report follows:

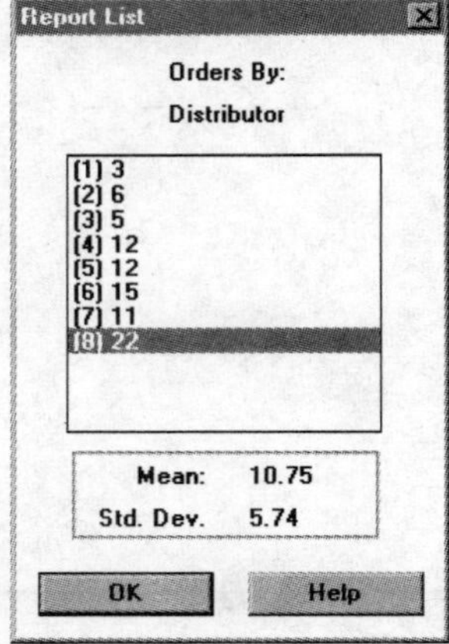

This report lists all orders placed by the player listed at the top of the dialog, as well as the mean and standard deviation of these orders.

Reports—Other. When this command is selected, you are first asked to select a player on the following dialog:

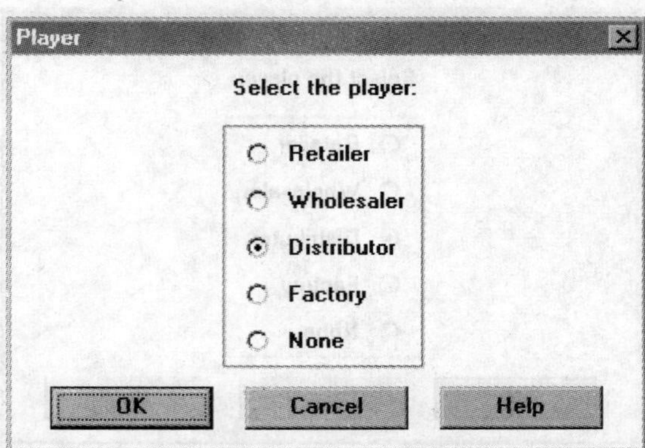

A status report for the selected player is then displayed. This differs from the preceding **Reports—Player** command, which displays a status report only for the current interactive player.

Reports—System. This command displays the System Summary Report:

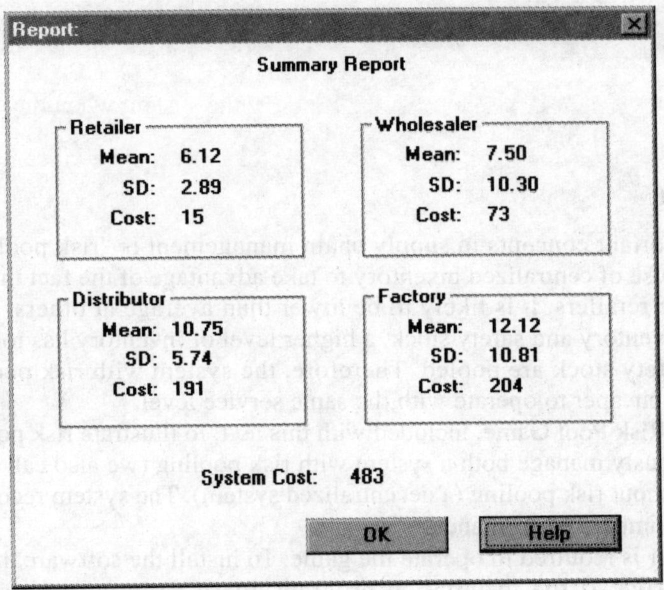

This report summarizes the mean and standard deviation of orders placed by each player up to this point, the total cost experienced by each player, and the total system cost (at the bottom of the dialog).

The Risk Pool Game

B.1 INTRODUCTION

One of the most important concepts in supply chain management is "risk pooling." Recall that risk pooling involves the use of centralized inventory to take advantage of the fact that if demand is higher than average at some retailers, it is likely to be lower than average at others. Thus, if each retailer maintains separate inventory and safety stock, a higher level of inventory has to be maintained than if the inventory and safety stock are pooled. Therefore, the system with risk pooling has less overall inventory and is thus cheaper to operate with the same service level.

We developed the Risk Pool Game, included with this text, to illustrate risk pooling concepts. In the game, you simultaneously manage both a system with risk pooling (we also call this a centralized system) and a system without risk pooling (a decentralized system). The system records the profits of both systems, so you can compare performance.

Windows 95 or later is required to operate the game. To install the software, place the included CD in your CD-ROM drive. If the installation program doesn't run automatically, open Windows Explorer, select the CD, and double click on the setup program. Click the "Games" link and then click the "Risk Pool Game and Computerized Beer Game" link to download the setup file.

B.2 THE SCENARIOS

The Risk Pool Game models the following scenarios. The top half of the screen, the centralized game, consists of the following supply chain: A supplier serves a warehouse, which in turn serves three retailers. It takes two time periods for material to arrive from the supplier at the warehouse. This material can be shipped out during the same period or held in inventory. Once shipped, it takes an additional two periods for material to arrive at the retailers. The retailers then fill all the demand that they can. If demand cannot be met at the time it arrives, it is lost.

The bottom half of the screen represents the decentralized system. Three retailers order separately from the supplier, and the supplier ships material directly to each retailer. This takes four periods from the time the order is placed, the same length of time as the minimum total lead time in the centralized system. As in the centralized system, the retailers fill as much demand as possible—demand that if not met is lost. In each system, total holding cost, materials costs, and revenue are tracked. The goal in both systems is to maximize profit.

B.3 PLAYING SEVERAL ROUNDS

In this section, we describe how to play several rounds of the Risk Pool Game using the default settings. In the next section, we describe each of the menu settings and options so that you can customize the game play.

B.3.1 Introducing the Game

When the Risk Pool Game software is started, the following screen appears:

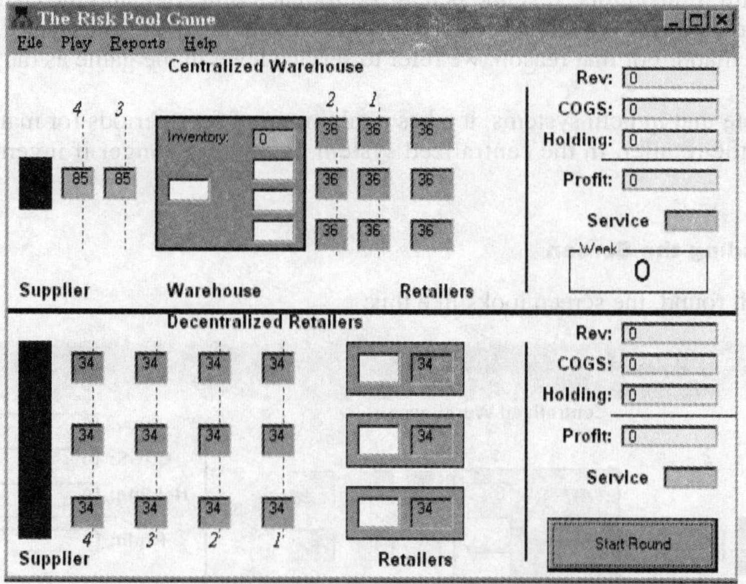

Order of Events During each period or round of the game, several events occur.

Step 1. *To start this step, press the* **Start Round** *button.* The inventory is advanced. In the centralized game, this means that inventory four periods away moves to three periods away, inventory three periods away is added to the warehouse inventory, inventory two periods away is moved to one period away, and inventory one period away is added to retailer inventory. In the decentralized game, inventory four, three, and two periods away is moved, respectively, three, two, and one period away. Inventory one period away is added to retailer inventory.

Step 2. *This step starts automatically.* Demand is met. Each retailer experiences demand and fills as much as possible. Note that the top retailer in both the centralized and decentralized systems faces the same demand; the same is true for the middle and bottom retailers. Also, demand is not back ordered. Demand that cannot be met immediately is lost.

Step 3. *Place orders*. In the centralized system, enter an order for the supplier in the box closest to the supplier. Allocate the warehouse inventory to the three retailers in the three boxes closest to the retailers. Note that the allocation amount must be less than or equal to the total warehouse inventory. In the decentralized system, enter an order for each retailer. The system will present a default selection for each entry. You can keep the default or type in new values. As we describe in the next section, you have control over how the system selects default values. When entries are completed (or the decision has been made to keep the default values), *press the* **Place Orders** *button.*

Step 4. *This step starts automatically*. Orders are filled. The amount ordered is moved into the inventory slots four weeks away. In the centralized system, the amount allocated to each retailer is moved into the inventory slots two weeks away.

Step 5. *This step starts automatically*. Cost, revenue, and service level: A holding cost is charged for each unit in inventory, revenue is realized for each unit sold, and the cost of each item sold is subtracted from revenue. Service level is calculated as the fraction of demand met over total demand. For that reason, we refer to service level in the game as the *fill rate*.

Lead Times Note that in both systems, it takes a minimum of four periods for material that has been ordered to reach the retailer. In the centralized system, it can take longer if inventory is held in the warehouse.

B.3.2 Understanding the Screen

At the start of each round, the screen looks like this:

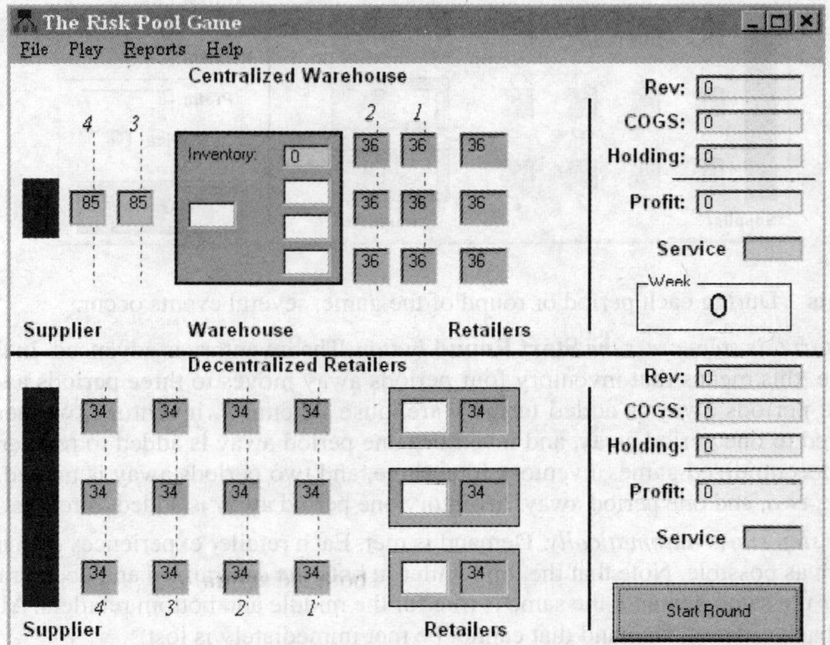

On the top half of the screen, the supplier is represented by the box at the left. The two vertical dotted lines labeled *4* and *3* have boxes on them representing inventory at least four or three periods away from the retailers, respectively. The large middle box represents the warehouse. The top line in the warehouse indicates the inventory contained there; the other boxes are used to enter an order from the supplier and allocation to the warehouse when appropriate. Note that the button in the lower-right-hand corner of the screen initially says *Start Round*. This indicates that it is not the appropriate time to enter the orders and allocation. The two vertical dotted lines to the right of the warehouse are labeled *2* and *1*, indicating inventory two and one period from the retailers, respectively. Note that unlike the *3* and *4* lines to the left of the warehouse, lines *1* and *2* can have up to three inventory boxes, representing inventory going to each of the three retailers. To the right of these lines are the three boxes representing the retailers—the numbers in these boxes represent retailer inventory. The right-hand side of the screen contains cost and profit data. Holding costs and cost of goods sold (COGS) are subtracted from revenue to get profit. Service level and period number are also indicated.

The bottom half of the screen is similar to the top half, except that there is no warehouse. Also, when appropriate, orders are entered directly at the retailers.

The bottom in the lower right-hand corner initially reads *Start Round*. After the round has started, it looks like this:

Place Orders

B.3.3 Playing the Game

The game follows the order of events listed above. To start each round, press the *Start Round* button. Inventory is advanced, and then as much demand as possible is met. At this point, the button in the lower right-hand corner of the screen will change to read *Place Orders*. Do so either by accepting the default choices that are displayed or by typing in new ones. Recall that in the centralized game, you can allocate up to the total amount of inventory in the warehouse to the retailers. Once orders are placed, press the *Place Orders* button. Orders are filled, and cost, revenue, and service level are calculated. You can continue playing for any number of rounds.

B.3.4 Other Features

The game has several other features, which we discuss in detail in the next section. The **Play** menu has options that allow you to set various game parameters. The **Reports** menu allows you to display lists of demands and orders for all of the periods up to the current one.

B.4 OPTIONS AND SETTINGS

This section follows the menu in the Risk Pool Game and describes the function of each of the parameters and options that can be set by the user or instructor. In the following subsections, the convention **menu—selection** item is used to describe menu selections.

B.4.1 File Commands

These commands are used to stop and reset play and exit the system.

File—Reset. This command resets the game. All data from the previous game are lost.

File—Exit. This command exits the game.

B.4.2 Play Commands

These commands control game play and allow various parameters to be set.

Play—Start Round. This command duplicates the *Start Round* button on the lower-right-hand corner of the screen. Selecting it starts each round.

Play—Place Orders. This command duplicates the **Place Orders** button on the lower-right-hand corner of the screen. Select it after entering orders and allocations.

Play—Options. This command displays a submenu with the following choices:

Initial Conditions. This command displays the following dialog box:

Select Initial Inventories

Centralized System

Warehouse Inventory:	0
Store Inventory:	36
Inventory to Stores:	36
Inventory to Warehouse:	85

Decentralized System

Store Inventory:	34
Inventory to Stores:	34

OK Cancel

This enables you to select starting inventories throughout both systems. Note that in the centralized system, each retailer must have the same initial inventory level, and the inventory in transit from the warehouse to the retailer must be the same level for each of the retailers and for both periods. Similar restrictions exist for the decentralized system. After making changes, enter **OK** to accept the changes or **Cancel** to keep the current levels. Note that this option can be used only before the first round is played.

Demand. This command displays the following dialog box:

Random Demand Parameters
Demand Correlation
Strong Negative
None
Strong Positive
Mean: 25
Standard Deviation: 10
OK
Cancel

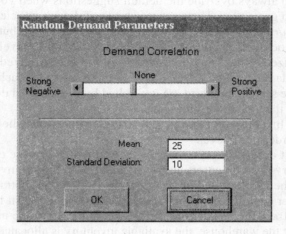

This enables you to control the demand faced by each of the retailers. The demand is normally distributed, with the mean and standard deviation that can be entered on the dialog box. The slider control at the top of the box enables you to control the correlation of the demand at the retailers. If the slider is in the center of its range, demand will be independent. At the right, demand is strongly positively correlated while at the left, demand is strongly negatively correlated. Intermediate positions allow correlation between these extremes.[1] After making changes, select **OK** to accept the changes or **Cancel** to keep the current levels. Note that this option can be used only before the first round is played.

Inventory Policy. This command displays the following dialog box:

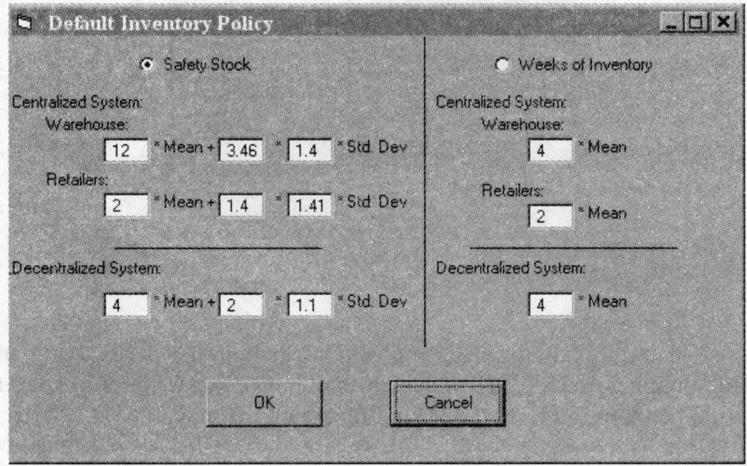

[1]If demand is positively correlated, it is likely that if one retailer has high demand, all of them will; if one retailer has low demand, all of them will. If demand is negatively correlated, it is likely that if one retailer has high demand, at least one other will have low demand.

This enables you to control the inventory policy that displays the default order and allocation quantities. Note that you can always override the default suggestions when you are playing, but having good defaults speeds up game play. There are two types of default policies, the *Safety Stock* policy and the *Weeks of Inventory* policy. Select between them using the radio buttons at the top of the dialog box. The Safety Stock policy allows you to select order-up-to levels for the warehouse and retailers in the centralized system and the retailers in the decentralized system as a function of demand mean and standard deviation. There are three input boxes for each level: the first box is the mean multiplier, and the second and third are multiplied by the standard deviation. These quantities are then summed to get the final order-up-to level.

When the Weeks of Inventory policy is used, a single value multiplied by the mean demand is used to determine the order-up-to level.

To determine default orders, the system does the following: For the centralized system, warehouse echelon inventory (i.e., inventory in transit to the warehouse, inventory at the warehouse, inventory in transit to the retailers, and inventory at the retailers) is subtracted from the order-up-to levels to determine order quantity. Inventory at the retailers and in transit from the warehouse to the retailers is subtracted from the retailer order-up-to level to determine allocations. If insufficient inventory is available at the warehouse, the available inventory is allocated so that the same fraction of desired level is sent to each retailer. For the decentralized system, inventory at each retailer plus inventory in transit to the retailer is raised to the order-up-to level.

After making changes, select **OK** to accept the changes or **Cancel** to keep the current levels. Note that this option can be used at the start of any round.

Costs. This command displays the following dialog:

Change Costs

Holding Cost	1.5
Revenue Per Item	20
Cost Per Item	10

[OK] [Cancel]

You can adjust costs using this dialog. Holding cost is per item per period; cost and revenue are per item. After making changes, select **OK** to accept the changes or **Cancel** to keep the current levels. Note that this option can be used only before the first round is played.

B.4.3 The Reports Commands

These commands display game-related information.

Reports—Orders. This command displays the following report, which lists orders placed by the warehouse in the centralized game and retailers in the decentralized game:

Order Report

Week	Decentralized Retailer 1	Decentralized Retailer 2	Decentralized Retailer 3	Centralized Warehouse
1	0	0	0	0
2	11	10	9	28
3	23	29	2	54
4	6	25	43	74
5	37	25	36	88
6	27	8	15	50
7	26	24	23	73

Done

Select **Done** to hide the report.

Reports—Demands. This command displays the following report, which lists demand faced by the retailers since the start of the game:

Demand History

Week	Retailer 1	Retailer 2	Retailer 3
1	31	30	29
2	28	28	28
3	23	29	2
4	6	25	43
5	37	25	36
6	27	8	15
7	26	24	23
8	24	27	17

Done

Select **Done** to hide the report.

APPPENDIX **C**

Excel Spreadsheet

C.1 INTRODUCTION

We have created an Excel spreadsheet, DMSC3e.xls, that implements many of the examples from Chapter 2 and Chapter 4. *Windows 98* or later and Microsoft Excel 2000 or later are required to use this spreadsheet. To install the software, place the included CD in your CD-ROM drive. If the installation program doesn't run automatically, open Windows Explorer, select the CD, and double-click on the setup program.

Click the "Excel Files" link to open or save the file.

C.2 THE SPREADSHEET

This spreadsheet is quite self-explanatory. It consists of eight sheets, the contents of which are detailed below. We encourage you to experiment with different parameter values and see how these values affect the system.

The sheets are

- **Demand Scenarios.** This sheet contains the probabilistic demand forecast described in the swimsuit examples in Chapter 2 (Examples 2.4 to 2.6)
- **Inventory Calculations.** This sheet contains the single-stage inventory calculations from the swimsuit examples mentioned above.
- **Buy-Back Contract.** This is the two-stage buy-back contract example from Example 4.4 in Chapter 4.
- **Revenue-Sharing Contract.** This is the revenue-sharing contract example from Example 4.5 in Chapter 4.
- **Global Optimization.** This is an example of globally optimizing the two-stage swimsuit production system, as described in Example 4.6 in Chapter 4.
- **Pay-Back Contract.** This is the two-stage ski jacket pay-back contract example from Example 4.12 in Chapter 4.
- **Cost-Sharing Contract.** This is the ski jacket cost-sharing contract example from Example 4.13 in Chapter 4.
- **Global Optimization MTS.** This is an example of globally optimizing the two-stage ski jacket MTS/MTO production system, as described in Example 4.15 in Chapter 4.

APPENDIX D

The Bidding Game

D.1 INTRODUCTION

The Bidding Game provides a platform to experiment with procurement auctions. This platform allows players to take the roles of a single buyer and multiple suppliers. Suppliers compete on price and flexibility, and the buyer contracts with one or more suppliers to maximize expected profit. The game demonstrates the importance of portfolio contracts as well as the impact of a multi-attribute competition among suppliers.

Two versions of the game exist: the Excel version of the game that is included with this book and the Web-based version (see http://supplychain.mit.edu/ProcurementPortal/).
Both were developed by Victor Martinez de Albeniz and David Simchi-Levi. The Web version of the game was also developed by Michael Li. Microsoft Excel 2000 is required to use the Excel version of this game. To install the software, place the included CD in your CD-ROM drive. If the installation program doesn't run automatically, open Windows Explorer, select the CD, and double-click on the setup program.

The game is based on insight from [138].

D.2 THE SCENARIO

A buyer needs to outsource some component for one of its products. We will assume that this component is the only contributor to cost for the buyer. Once the product is manufactured, it is sold to customers at a price p.

Unfortunately, the demand for the product, and thus for the quantity of components needed, is not known at the planning/outsourcing stage. Hence, the buyer must decide on the purchasing of components with some information about the distribution of demand only.

To obtain the flexibility needed by the buyer, an auction is organized with the following format. Each supplier's bid will consist of two parameters:

- A unit reservation fee, or premium, that will be charged for every unit of capacity reserved by the buyer.
- A unit execution fee, or strike, that will be charged for every component requested by the buyer after demand is revealed.

Given bids from each participant in the auction, the buyer reserves capacity at each supplier. Some time later, demand becomes known, and the buyer meets it with the available capacity in its portfolio.

Of course, it will start using the suppliers with smaller execution price and, as capacity in the cheaper sources is exhausted, will move to suppliers with more expensive execution prices.

This game models the auction bidding process. One player (we'll call this player the instructor) takes the role of buyer and the others (the students) take the roles of suppliers. At the creation of the auction, the buyer needs to specify

- The number of suppliers present in the auction. The Excel spreadsheet version of the game requires seven suppliers.
- The number of rounds that will take place. The Excel version allows for multiple rounds.

We will normalize the selling price to $p = 100$ and the cost parameters of each supplier will be selected so that every supplier has the opportunity to make some profit.

Given these parameters, each supplier is confronted with the problem of bidding a reservation price, r, and an execution price, e. For this purpose, the supplier can use a simulator where he or she can test his or her payments, that is, the expected profit (the simulator uses the information on everybody's cost parameters, together with the demand distribution). The specific difficulty at this stage is that suppliers do not know the bids of the other suppliers. In any case, they can use information about the competitors' previous bids and costs. Once the group is ready, it submits a bid to the buyer. At the closing of the current round, the bids of every supplier are revealed to all participants, and either a new round starts or the auction stops, capacity is allocated to every supplier, and the expected payments to each supplier are computed.

D.3 INSTRUCTIONS FOR EXCEL VERSION OF THE GAME

1. The players need to be split into seven supplier groups, plus one buyer (typically the instructor in a class).
2. Each group represents a supplier indexed 1–7 and receives a copy of the game (software).
3. Each supplier has information on execution and reservation costs of all suppliers; they also know the demand distribution as well as the selling price (the price paid by the final customer). All these data are at the top of the screen.
4. Supplier groups use the software to decide on their bid (reservation and execution price); they, of course, do not know what the other bids are (i.e., how other suppliers bid). The software allows them to do what-if analysis by guessing bids of other suppliers and the corresponding capacity allocation (quantity) and profit.
5. The supplier groups must send their initial bids to the buyer (typically, in a class environment, the initial bids are determined out of class and e-mailed to the instructor).
6. Once the buyer has collected the bids, he or she can enter them into the system and show each of the supplier groups how capacity is going to be allocated to each supplier and the corresponding profit of each supplier.
7. The buyer can then ask whether suppliers want to change their bids (they can use the software to make that decision).
8. Go through a few rounds until no supplier group wants to change its bid.

What do the ultimate results tell you about how capacity is allocated and the impact of the process on each supplier?

Bibliography

1. Aberdeen Group, The. "The Supply Risk Management Benchmark Report: Assuring Supply and Mitigating Risk in an Uncertain Economy," September 2005
2. Agrawal, V., and A. Kambil. "Dynamic Pricing Strategies in Electronic Commerce." Working paper, Stern Business School, New York University, 2000
3. Ahn, H.-S.; M. Gumus; and P. Kaminsky. "Pricing and Manufacturing Decisions When Demand Is a Function of Prices in Multiple Periods." To appear in Operations Research, 2007
4. Aimi, G. "Finding the Value in Wal-Mart RFID Mandates: It's in the Information." *AMR Research,* June 22, 2004
5. Andel, T. "There's Power in Numbers." *Transportation & Distribution* 36 (1995), pp. 67–72
6. Andel, T. "Manage Inventory, Own Information." *Transportation & Distribution* 37 (1996), p. 54
7. Anderson, C. *The Long Tail: Why the Future of Business Is Selling Less of More*. New York: Hyperion Books, 2006
8. Andreoli, T. "VMI Confab Examines Value-Added Services." *Discount Store News* 34 (1995), pp. 4–61
9. Anonymous. "Divorce: Third-Party Style." *Distribution* 94 (1995), pp. 46–51
10. Anonymous. "Choosing Service Providers." *Transportation & Distribution* 36 (1995), pp. 74–76
11. Anonymous. "Supply Distruptions May Linger as Quake Aftershock." http://www.eetimes.com, September 22, 1999
12. Anonymous. "Idapta: At the Core of E-Markets." *ASCET* 3 (2001), pp. 145–47
13. Anonymous. "Toyota's Fire Caused Production Cut at 70,000 Units." *Japan Economic Newswire* (via Factiva), February 17, 1998
14. Anonymous. "Meeting the Retail RFID Mandate." *AT Kearney*, November 2003
15. Anonymous. "Don't Mess with Russia." *The Economist,* December 16–22, 2006
16. Anonymous. "High-Definition Television." *The Economist,* November 4–10, 2006
17. Artman, L. B. "The Paradigm Shift from 'Push' to 'Pull' Logistics—What's the Impact on Manufacturing?" Northwestern University, Manufacturing Management Symposium, Evanston, IL, May 1995
18. Baker, W.; M. Marn; and C. Zawada. "Price Smarter on the Net." *Harvard Business Review* 79, no. 2 (2001), pp. 122–27
19. Ballou, R. H. Business *Logistics Management.* 3rd ed. Englewood Cliffs, NJ: Prentice Hall, 1992
20. Bangkok Post: 4 August 2007, p B4.
21. Barias, S. "RFID Bandwagon Rolls On: With Wal-Mart's Deadline Fast Approaching, Shippers Are Learning to Adapt." *Logistics Today,* August 2004
22. Bausch, D. O.; G. G. Brown; and D. Ronen. "Consolidating and Dispatching Truck Shipments of Mobil Heavy Petroleum Products." *Interfaces* 25 (1995), pp. 1–17
23. Berinato, S. "What Went Wrong at Cisco?" *CIO Magazine,* August 1, 2001
24. Billington, C. "HP Cuts Risk with Portfolio Approach." *Purchasing Magazine Online,* February 21, 2002
25. Blumenfeld, D. E.; L. D. Burns; C. F. Daganzo; M. C. Frick; and R. W. Hall. "Reducing Logistics Costs at General Motors." *Interfaces* 17 (1987), pp. 26–47
26. Bovet, D., and Y. Sheffi. "The Brave New World of Supply Chain Management." *Supply Chain Management Review*, Spring 1998, pp. 14–22

27. Bowers, M. R., and A. Agarwal. "Lower In-Process Inventories and Better On-Time Performance at Tanner Companies, Inc." *Interfaces* 25 (1995), pp. 30–43
28. Bowman, R. "A HighWire Act." *Distribution* 94 (1995), pp. 36–39
29. Bradbury, D. "RFID: It's No Supply Chain Saviour—Not Yet Anyway." http://www.silicon.com, September 9, 2004
30. Bramel, J., and D. Simchi-Levi. *The Logic of Logistics: Theory, Algorithms and Applications for Logistics Management.* New York: Springer, 1997
31. Brynjolfsson, E., and M. D. Smith. "Frictionless Commerce? A Comparison of Internet and Conventional Retailers." *Management Science* 46 (2000), pp. 563–85
32. Business Line, 18 August 2007
33. Business Line, Paint Still Perceived a Luxury Product, 28 December, 2003 http://www.apaints.com/AsianPaints.jsp (accessed on 2 Sept 2007)
34. Buzzell, R. D., and G. Ortmeyer. "Channel Partnerships Streamline Distribution." *Sloan Management Review* 36 (1995), p. 85
35. Byrne, M. P. "Best Practice in Global Operations." Presentation at the 2006 MIT Manufacturing Conference, December 6, 2006
36. Byrne, P., and W. Markham. "Global Logistics: Only 10 Percent of Companies Satisfy Customers." *Transportation & Distribution* 34 (1993), pp. 41–45
37. Cachon, G. P. "Supply Coordination with Contracts." In *Handbooks in Operations Research and Management Science,* ed. Steve Graves and Ton de Kok. Amsterdam: North-Holland, 2002
38. Cachon, G. P., and M. A. Lariviere. "Supply Chain Coordination with Revenue Sharing Contracts: Strengths and Limitations." Working paper, the Wharton School, University of Pennsylvania, 2000
39. Caldwell, B. "Walt-Mart Ups the Pace." http://www.informationweek.com, December 9, 1996
40. Camm, J. D.; T. E. Chorman; F. A. Dill; J. R. Evans; D. J. Sweeney; and G. W. Wegryn. "Blending OR/MS, Judgment, and GIS: Restructuring P&G's Supply Chain." *Interfaces* 27 (1997), pp. 128
41. Campbell, A. "RFID Brings Big Gains in Breweries." http://www.RFID-weblog.com, July, 16, 2004
42. Caniels, M. C. J., and C. J. Gelderman. "Purchasing Strategies in Kraljic Matrix—A Power and Dependence Perspective." *Journal of Purchasing and Supply Management* 11 (2005), pp. 141–155
43. Cela Diaz, F. "An Integrative Framework for Architecting Supply Chains." MS Thesis, Massachusetts Institute of Technology, 2005
44. Chakarvarty, SN, Karmali, N, Fast Food, *Forbes Global,* 8 October, 1998
45. Chambers, J. C.; S. K. Mullick; and D. D. Smith. "How to Choose the Right Forecasting Technique." *Harvard Business Review* 49, no. 4 (1971), pp. 45–69
46. Chan, L. M. A.; D. Simchi-Levi; and J. Swann, "Effective Dynamic Pricing Strategies with Stochastic Demand." Working paper, Massachusetts Institute of Technology, 2001
47. Chen, F. Y.; Z. Drezner; J. K. Ryan; and D. Simchi-Levi. "The Bullwhip Effect: Managerial Insights on the Impact of Forecasting and Information on Variability in the Supply Chain." In *Quantitative Models for Supply Chain Management,* ed. S. Tayur, R. Ganeshan, and M. Magazine. Norwell, MA: Kluwer Academic Publishing, 1998, chap. 14
48. Chen, Y. F.; Z. Drezner; J. K. Ryan; and D. Simchi-Levi. "Quantifying the Bullwhip Effect: The Impact of Forecasting, Leadtime and Information." *Management Science* 46 (2000), pp.436–43
49. Chen, F. Y.; J. K. Ryan; and D. Simchi-Levi. "The Impact of Exponential Smoothing Forecasts on the Bullwhip Effect." *Naval Research Logistics* 47 (2000), pp. 269–86
50. Chesbrough, H., and D. Teece. "When Is Virtual Virtuous: Organizing for Innovation." *Harvard Business Review* 74, no. 1 (1996), pp. 65–74
51. Clark, T. "Campbell Soup Company: A Leader in Continuous Replenishment Innovations." Harvard Business School Case 9-195-124, 1994
52. Clemmet, A. "Demanding Supply." *Work Study* 44 (1995), pp. 23–24
53. Cook, T. "SABRE Soars." *ORMS Today,* June 1998, pp. 26–31
54. Cook, T. "Creating Competitive Advantage in the Airline Industry." Seminar sponsored by the MIT Global Airline Industry Program and the MIT Operations Research Center, 2000
55. Copacino, W. C., and R. W. Dik. "Why B2B e-Markets Are Here to Stay. Part I: Public Independent Trading Exchanges." http://Technology Evaluation.Com, March 18, 2002
56. Coy, P. "How Hedge Funds Are Taking On Mother Nature." *BusinessWeek,* January 15, 2006
57. Crawford, F., and R. Mathews. *The Myth of Excellence.* New York: Crown Business, 2001

58. Dabur India Ltd. Annual Report 2006-07 (http://www.dabur.com/en/Investors1/Annual_reports/2006-07/finalannula2007.pdf) (accessed on 28 August 2007)
59. Dabur India Ltd. Annual Report 2006-07 (www.dabur.com/en/Investors1/Annual_reports/2006-07/finalannula2007.pdf)
60. Davis, D. "State of a New Art." *Manufacturing Systems* 13 (1995), pp. 2–10
61. ———. "Third Parties Deliver." *Manufacturing Systems* 13 (1995), pp. 66–68
62. Davis, D., and T. Foster. "Bulk Squeezes Shipping Costs." *Distribution Worldwide* 78, no. 8 (1979), pp. 25–30
63. Deutsch, C. H. "New Software Manages Supply to Match Demand." *New York Times*, December 16, 1996
64. Disabatino, J. "Pricelino.com Reports $1.3 Million Q4 Loss." *Computerworld*, February 4, 2002
65. Dornier, P.; R. Ernst; M. Fender; and P. Kouvelis. *Global Operations and Logistics: Text and Cases*. New York: John Wiley, 1998
66. Duadel, S., and G. Vialle. *Yield Management: Applications to Transport and Other Service Industries*. Paris: ITA, 1994
67. Eid, M. K.; D. J. Seith, and M. A. Tomazic. "Developing a Truly Effective Way to Manage Inventory." Council of Logistics Management Conference, October 5–8. 1997
68. Engardio, P.; B. Einhorn; M. Kripalani; A. Reinhardt; B. Nussbaum; and P. Burrows. "Outsourcing Innovation." *BusinessWeek*, March 21, 2005
69. Express Computer, 09 January 2006 (www.expresscomputeronline.com/20060109/management01/shtml accessed on 29 August 2007
70. Express Computer, 10 May 2004 (http://www.expresscomputeronline.com/20040510/casestudyspecial05/shtml accessed on 29 August 2007
71. Faisal, M.N. (2007) 'Studies in Management of Risk in Supply Chains of Select SME Clusters', Unpublished Ph.D. Thesis, Submitted to Indian Institute of Technology Delhi, New Delhi
72. Faisal, M.N., Banwet, D.K. and Shankar, R. (2007) "Supply Chain Risk Management in SMEs: Analysing the Barriers", to the *International Journal of Management and Enterprise Development*, Vol.4, No. 5, pp. 588-607
73. Federgruen, A., and A. Heching. "Combined Pricing and Inventory Control under Uncertainty." Operations Research 47 (1999), pp. 454–75
74. Feitzinger, E., and H. Lee. "Mass Customization at Hewlett-Packard: The Power of Postponement." Harvard Business Review 75, no. 1 (1977), pp. 116–21
75. Ferdows, K.; M. A. Lewis; and J. A. D. Machuca. "Rapid-Fire Fulfillment." *Harvard Business Review* 82, no. 11 (November 1, 2004), pp. 104–10
76. Fernie, J. "International Comparisons of Supply Chain Management in Grocery Retailing." *Service Industries Journal* 15 (1995), pp. 134–47
77. Figueroa, Claudia. "Local Reps See Temporary Delays after India Quake." http://www.Aparelnews.net, March 9, 2001
78. Fine, C. H. Clock Speed: *Winning Industry Control in the Age of Temporary Advantage*. Reading, MA: Perseus Books, 1998
79. Fine, C. H.; R. Vardan; R. Pethick; and J. El-Hout. "Rapid-Response Capability in Value-Chain Design." *Sloan Management Review* 43, no.2 (2002), pp. 69–75
80. Fine, C. H., and D. E. Whitney. "Is the Make-Buy Decision Process a Core Competence?" Working paper, Massachusetts Institute of Technology, 1996
81. Fisher, M. L. "National Bicycle Industrial Co.: A Case Study." The Wharton School, University of Pennsylvania, 1993
82. Fisher, M. L. "What Is the Right Supply Chain for Your Product?" *Harvard Business Review*, March–April 1997, pp. 105–17
83. Fisher, M. L.; J. Hammond; W. Obermeyer; and A. Raman. "Making Supply Meet Demand in an Uncertain World." *Harvard Business Review*, May–June 1994, pp. 83–93
84. Fites, D. "Make Your Dealers Your Partners." *Harvard Business Review*, March–April 1996, pp. 84–95
85. Flickinger, B. H., and T. E. Baker. "Supply Chain Management in the 1990's." http://www.chesapeake.com/supchain.html
86. Flynn, Laurie. "Intel Posts Sharp Fall in Profit." *New York Times*, April 20, 2006
87. Fox, M.S.; J.F. Chionglo; and M. Barbuceanu. "The Integrated Supply Chain Management System." Working paper, University of Toronto, 1993
88. Gamble, R. "Financially Efficient Partnerships." *Corporate Cashflow* 15 (1994), pp. 29–34

89. Gerrett, J.J. "Six Design Lessons from the Apple Store." *Adaptivepath,* July 9, 2004
90. Geary, S., and J. P. Zonnenberg. "What It Means to Be Best in Class." *Supply Chain Management Review,* July/August 2000, pp. 42–48
91. Genovese, Y.; S. Hayward; J. Thompson; D. M. Smith; and D. W. Cearley. "BPP Changes Infrastructure and the Business Application Vendor Landscape." Gartner Report, September 28, 2006
92. Geoffrion, A., and T. J. Van Roy. "Caution: Common Sense Planning Methods Can Be Hazardous to Your Corporate Health." *Sloan Management* Review 20 (1979), pp. 30–42
93. Georgoff, D. M., and R. G. Murdick. "Managers' Guide to Forecasting." *Harvard Business Review* 64, no. 1 (1986), pp. 1–9
94. Greenhouse, S. "Labor Lockout at West's Ports Roils Business." *New York Times,* October 1 2002
95. Guengerich, S., and V. G. Green. *Introduction to Client/Server Computing*. Dearborn, MI: SME Blue Book Series, 1996
96. Gulyani, S., 2001. Effects of poor transportation on lean production and industrial clustering: Evidence from the Indian auto industry. World Development 29, 1157-1177
97. Gupta, A.K., Govindarajan, V., 2000. Knowledge Flows within Multinational Corporations. Strategic Management Journal 21, 473-496
98. Gupta, A.K.S., Sett, P.K., 2000. Industrial relations law, employment security and collective bargaining in India: myths, realities and hopes. Industrial Relation Journal 31, 144-153
99. Hagel, J., III, and J. S. Brown. "Your Next IT Strategy." *Harvard Business Review* 79, no. 10 (2001)
100. Handfield, R., and B. Withers. "A Comparison of Logistics Management in Hungary, China, Korea, and Japan." *Journal of Business Logistics* 14 (1993), pp. 81–109
101. Hannon, D. "Online Buy Gains Speed." *Purchasing Magazine Online,* February 7, 2002
102. Hakanson, L., Nobel, R., 2000. Technology Characteristics and Reverse Technology Transfer. Management International Review 40, 29-47
103. Halasyam, A.R., 2001. Session VII: Operational Excellence: A Product of Multiple Lever at work. Conference of IMA India. A.R. Hayasyam Director Finance, conference speaker Maruti Udyog Limited, http://www.ima-india.com/autoroundtable/session7.htm (26.05.2003)
104. Harrington, L. "Logistics Asset: Should You Own or Manage?" *Transportation & Distribution* 37 (1996), pp. 51–54
105. Hart, J., The Mumbai working lunch, The Independent, March 19, 2006 http://news.independent.co.uk/world/asia/article352265.ece, Accessed on 15 June 2007
106. Hax, A. C., and D. Candea. *Production and Inventory Management.* Englewood Cliffs, NJ: Prentice Hall, 1984
107. Heinrich, C. E., and D. Simchi-Levi. "Do IT Investments Really Change Financial Performance?" *Supply Chain Management Review,* May 2005, pp. 22–28
108. Henkel-Eroski CPFR Pilot Case Study." Compiled by Thierry Jouenne. Copyright © 2000 by Jowen Editions, 2000. Available at cpfr.org
109. Henkoff, R. "Delivering the Goods." *Fortune,* November 28, 1994, pp. 64–78
110. Hindu Business Line: http://www.thehindubusinessline.com/2004/06/30/stories/2004063002460400.htm
111. Hof, R. "How Amazon Cleared That Hurdle." *BusinessWeek,* February 4, 2002, pp. 60–61
112. Hopp, W., and M. Spearman. *Factory Physics.* Burr Ridge, IL: Richard D. Irwin, 1996
113. House, R. G., and K. G. Jamie. "Measuring the Impact of Alternative Market Classification Systems in Distribution Planning." *Journal of Business Logistics* 2 (1981), pp. 1–31
114. Huang, Y.; A. Federgruen; O. Bakkalbasi; R. Desiraju; and R. Kranski. "Vendor-Managed-Replenishment in an Agile Manufacturing Environment." Working paper. Philips Research
115. Indian Express, 1998. Maruti Union goes on the warpath, Indian Express Newspapers (Bombay) Ltd., http://www.expressindia.com/fe/daily/19980610/16155074.html (03.06.2003)
116. Jacobs, D. A.; M. N. Silan; and B. A. Clemson. "An Analysis of Alternative Locations and Service Areas of American Red Cross Blood Facilities." *Interfaces* 26 (1996), pp. 40–50
117. Jain, S., 2003. Maruti's second skin. 24.11.2003. http://www.rediff.com/money/2003/nov/24guest.htm (03.03.2006)
118. Jakovljevic, P. J. "Understanding SOA, Web Services, BPM, BPEL, and More. Part One: SOA, Web Services, and BPM." http://www.Technologyevaluation.com, December 22, 2004.

119. Johnson, E. M. "Money for Nothing." *CIO Magazine,* September 15, 2000
120. Johnson, J. C., and D. F. Wood. *Contemporary Physical Distribution and Logistics.* 3rd ed. New York: Macmillan, 1986
121. Jones, H. "Ikea's Global Strategy Is a Winning Formula." *Marketing Week* 18, no. 50 (1996), p. 22
122. Kaufman, L. "Wal-Mart's Huge Slice of American Pie." *New York Times,* February 16, 2000
123. Kay, E. "Flexed Pricing." *Datamation* 44, no. 2 (1998), pp. 58–62
124. Keenan, F. "One Smart Cookie." *BusinessWeek E.Biz,* November 20, 2000
125. Kempeners, M., and A. J. van Weele. "Inkoopportfolio: Basis voor inkoop-en marketingstrategie." In *Dynamiek in Commercië 1e Relaties,* ed. H. W. C. Van der Hart and A. J. Van Week. Bunnik, Netherlands: F&G Publishing, 1997
126. Kerrigan, R.; E. V. Roegner; D. D. Swinford; and C. C. Zawada. "B2Basics." McKinsey and Company Report, 2001
127. Kimes, S. E. "A Tool for Capacity-Constrained Service Firms." *Journal of Operations Management* 8 (1989), pp. 348–63
128. King, J. "The Service Advantage." *Computerworld,* October 28, 1998
129. Kluge, J. "Reducing the Cost of Goods Sold." *McKinsey Quarterly,* no.2 (1997), pp. 212–15
130. Kogut, B. "Designing Global Strategies: Profiting from Operational Flexibility." *Sloan Management Review* 27 (1985), pp. 27–38
131. Koloszyc, G. "Retailers, Suppliers Push Joint Sales Forecasting." *Stores,* June 1998
132. Kraljic, P. "Purchasing Must Become Supply Management." Harvard *Business Review,* September– October 1983, pp. 109–17
133. LaFond, A. "RFID Market Update: Revenue Forecasts Down 15 Percent." *Manufacturing.net,* August 10, 2006
134. Lakenan, B.; D. Boyd; and E. Frey. "Why Outsourcing and Its Perils?" *Strategy + Business,* no. 24 (2001)
135. Lawrence, J. A., and B. A. Pasternack. Applied Management Science: *A Computer Integrated Approach for Decision Making.* New York: John Wiley, 1998
136. Leahy, S.; P. Murphy; and R. Poist. "Determinants of Successful Logistical Relationships: A Third Party Provider Perspective." *Transportation Journal* 35 (1995), pp. 5–13
137. Lee, H. "Design for Supply Chain Management: Concepts and Examples." Working paper, Department of Industrial Engineering and Engineering Management, Stanford University, 1992
138. Lee, H. L., and C. Billington. "Managing Supply Chain Inventory: Pitfalls and Opportunities." *Sloan Management Review,* Spring 1992, pp. 65–73
139. Lee, H.; P. Padmanabhan; and S. Whang. "The Paralyzing Curse of the Bullwhip Effect in a Supply Chain." *Sloan Management Review,* Spring 1997, pp. 93–102
140. ———. "Information Distortion in a Supply Chain: The Bullwhip Effect." *Management Science* 43 (1996), pp. 546–58
141. Leibs, S. "Deskbound for Glory." *CFO Magazine,* March 14, 2002
142. Lessard, D., and J. Lightstone. "Volatile Exchange Rates Put Operations at Risk." *Harvard Business Review* 64 (1986), pp. 107–14
143. Levitt, T. "The Globalization of Markets." *Harvard Business Review* 61 (1983), pp. 92–102
144. Lewis, J. *Partnerships for Profit. New York:* Free Press, 1990
145. Lindsey. *A Communication to the AGIS-L List Server*
146. Lohr, S. "He Loves to Win. At I.B.M., He Did," *New York Times,* March 10, 2002
147. Magretta, J. "The Power of Virtual Integration: An Interview with Dell Computer's Michael Dell." *Harvard Business Review,* March–April 1998, pp. 72–84
148. Maltz, A. "Why You Outsource Dictates How." *Transportation & Distribution* 36 (1995), pp. 73–80
149. "Management Brief: Furnishing the World." *The Economist,* November 19, 1994, pp. 79–80.
150. Manrodt, K. B.; M. C. Holcomb; and R. H. Thompson. "What's Missing in Supply Chain Management?" *Supply Chain Management Review,* Fall 1997, pp. 80–86
151. Markides, C., and N. Berg. "Manufacturing Offshore Is Bad Business." *Harvard Business Review* 66 (1988), pp. 113–20
152. Martinez de Albeniz, V. Course presentación material, 2005
153. Martinez de Albeniz, V., and D. Simchi-Levi. "Competition in the Supply Option Market." Working paper, Massachusetts Institute of Technology, 2005

154. Maruti Udyog Ltd., 2004. Annual report, 2003/2004. New Delhi
155. Maruti, 2003. Maruti Culture. http://www.marutiudyog.com/ab/careers.asp?ch=1&ct=9&sc=1 (03.03.2006)
156. Mathews, R. "Spartan Pulls the Plug on VMI." *Progressive Grocer* 74 (1995), pp. 64–65
157. McCue, A. "Marks & Spencer Extends RFID Tagging Nationwide." http://www.silicon.com, November 14, 2006
158. McGrath, M., and R. Hoole. "Manufacturing's New Economies of Scale." *Harvard Business Review* 70 (1992), pp. 94–102
159. McKay, J. "The SCOR Model." Presented in *Designing and Managing the Supply Chain,* an Executive Program at Northwestern University, James L. Allen Center, 1998
160. McWilliams, G. "Whirlwind on the Web." *BusinessWeek*, April 7, 1997, pp. 132–36
161. McWilliams, G. "Dell Fine-Tuned Its Pricing to Gain an Edge in Slow Market." *The Wall Street Journal,* June 8, 2001
162. Metty, T.; R. Harlan; Q. Samelson; T. Moore; T. Morris; R.Sorensen; A. Schneur; O. Raskina; R. Schneur; J. Kanner; K. Potts; and J.Robbins. "Reinventing the Supplier Negotiation Process at Motorola." Interface 35, no. 1 (January–February 2005), pp. 7–23
163. Michelin. "Intelligent Tires: Michelin Outlines New Tecnology at Industry Conference." Press release, Hilton Head, SC, March 9, 2005
164. Mische, M. "EDI in the EC: Easier Said Than Done." *Journal of European Business* 4 (1992), pp. 19–22
165. Mitchell, R. L. "Unilever Crosses the Data Streams." *Computerworld,* December 17, 2001
166. Monczka, R.; G. Ragatz; R. Handfield; R. Trent; and D. Frayer. "Executive Summary: Supplier Integration into New Product Development: A Strategy for Competitive Advantage." *The Global Procurement and Supply Chain Benchmarking Initiative,* Michigan State University, The Eli Broad Graduate School of Management, 1997
167. Mottley, R. "Dead in Nine Months." *American Shipper,* December 1998, pp. 30–33
168. Muthukumar, R., 2004. Operations Management at Maruti. ICFAI Knowledge Centre, Hyderabad, India. Case study distributed by European Case Clearing House, England and USA
169. Nagali, V.; D. Sangheran; J. Hwang; M. Gaskins; C. Baez; M. Pridgen; P. Mackenroth; D. Branvold; A. Kuper; and P. Scholler. "Procurement Risk Management (PRM) at Hewlett-Packard Company." Council of Supply Chain Management Professionals, 2005
170. Nahmias, S. *Production and Operations Analysis.* 3rd ed. Burr Ridge, IL: Irwin/McGraw-Hill, 1997
171. Narayanan, RY, Dabbawala model - a unique Mumbai phenomenon, *Business Line*, August 23, 2006
172. Narus, J., and J. Anderson. "Turn Your Industrial Distributors into Partners." *Harvard Business Review,* March–April 1986, pp. 66–71
173. ———. "Rethinking Distribution: Adaptive Channels." *Harvard Business Review,* July–August 1986, pp. 112–20
174. Nishiguchi, T., and A. Beaudet. "Case Study: The Toyota Group and the Aisin Fire." *Sloan Management Review,* Fall 1998, pp. 49–59
175. Nussbaum, B. "Designs for Living." *BusinessWeek,* June 2, 1997, p. 99
176. O'Connor, M. C. "Gillette Fuses RFID with Product Launch." *RFID Journal,* May 27, 2006
177. Ohmae, K. "Managing in a Borderless World." *Harvard Business Review* 67 (1989), pp. 152–61
178. Olsen, R. F.; and L. M. Ellram. "A Portfolio Approach to Supplier Relationships." *Industrial Marketing Management* 26, no. 2 (1997), pp. 101–13
179. Oracle. "Bringing SOA Value Patterns to Life." Oracle white paper, June 2006
180. Owens, G.; O. Vidal; R. Toole; and D. Favre. "Strategic Sourcing." Accenture report, 2001
181. Özer, Ö. "Strategic Commitments for an Optimal Capacity Decision under Asymmetric Forecast Information." PowerPoint presentation (2003)
182. Özer, Ö., and W. Wei. "Strategic Commitments for an Optimal Capacity Decisions under Asymmetric Forecast Information." *Management Science* 52 (2006); pp. 1239–58
183. Pankaj Chandra, Extraordinary story of Amul, http://www.rediff.com/money/2005/sep/23spec.htm (September 23, 2005)
184. Patton, E. P. "Carrier Rates and Tariffs." In *The Distribution Management Handbook,* ed. J. A Tompkins and D. Harmelink. New York: McGraw-Hill, 1994, chap. 12
185. Peppers, D., and M. Rogers. *Enterprise One to One.* New York: Doubleday, 1997

186. Phillips, R. L. *Pricing and Revenue Optimization.* Stanford, CA: Stanford University Press, 2005
187. Pidd, M. "Just Modeling Through: A Rough Guide to Modeling." *Interfaces* 29, no. 2 (March–April 1999), pp. 118–32
188. Pike, H. "IKEA Still Committed to U.S., Despite Uncertain Economy." *Discount Store News* 33, no. 8 (1994), pp. 17–19
189. Pine, J. B., II. *Mass Customization.* Boston: Harvard University Business School Press, 1993
190. Pine, J. B., II, and Boynton. "Making Mass Customization Work." *Harvard Business Review* 71, no. 5 (1993), pp. 108–19
191. Pine, J. B., II, and J. Gilmore. "Welcome to the Experience Economy." *Harvard Business Review,* July–August 1998, pp. 97–108
192. Pine, J. B., II; D. Peppers; and M. Rogers. "Do You Want to Keep Your Customers Forever?" *Harvard Business Review,* March–April 1995, pp. 103–15
193. Plattner, H. "Design and Innovations in Enterprise Applications." Presented at the MIT Forum for Supply Chain Innovation, September 2006
194. Pollack, E. "Partnership: Buzzword or Best Practice?" *Chain Store Age Executive* 71 (1995), pp. 11A–12A
195. Quinn, J. B., and F. Hilmer. "Strategic Outsourcing." *Sloan Management Review,* 1994, pp. 9–21
196. Raman, A.; N. Dehoratius; and Z. Ton. "Execution: The Missing Link in Retail Operations." *California Management Review* 43, no. 3 (Spring 2001) pp. 136–52
197. Ravi, V., (2006) *Study of select issues of reverse logistics in Indian context.* Unpublished Ph.D. Thesis, Indian Institute of Technology, Delhi
198. Ravi, V., Shankar, R. and Tiwari, M.K. (2005). Productivity improvement of a computer hardware supply chain. *International Journal of Productivity and Performance Management,* 54(4), 239-255
199. Rayport, J. F., and J. J. Sviokla. "Exploiting the Virtual Value Chain." *Harvard Business Review,* November–December 1995, pp. 75–85
200. Reichheld, F. F. "Learning from Customer Defections." *Harvard Business Review,* March–April 1996, pp. 57–69
201. Red Herring Prospectus, 2003, Maruti Udyog Ltd. 2003: IPO, http://www.myiris.com/shares/ipo/draft/MARUDYOG/MARUDYOG.pdf (19.12.2005).
202. Reference for Business, 2003. Osamu Suzuki. http://www.referenceforbusiness.com/biography/SZ/SMC-Osamu-1930.html (24.04.2004)
203. Reitman, V. "To the Rescue: Toyota's Fast Rebound after Fire at Supplier Shows Why It is Tough." *The Wall Street Journal,* May 8, 1997
204. Rich, S. "Saturday Interview—with Doug McGraw; A Hurricane and Espresso. What's Next?" *New York Times,* March 18, 2006
205. Ries, A., and L. Ries. *The 22 Immutable Laws of Branding.* New York: HarperBusiness, 1998
206. Rifkin, G. "Technology Brings the Music Giant a Whole New Spin." *Forbes ASAP*, February 27, 1995, p. 32
207. Roberti, M. "Gilletta Sharpens Its Edge." *RFID Journal,* April 2004
208. Robeson, J. F., and W. C. Copacino, eds. *The Logistics Handbook.* New York: Free Press, 1994
209. Robins, G. "Pushing the Limits of VMI." *Stores* 77 (1995), pp. 42–44
210. Rogers, D.S., and Tibben-Lembke, R.S. (1999). *Going Backwards: Reverse Logistics Trends and Practices.* Reverse Logistics Executive Council: Center for Logistics Management, Pittsburgh, PA
211. Ross, D. F. *Competing through Supply Chain Management.* New York: Chapman & Hall, 1998
212. Rothfeder, J. "What's Wrong with RFID." *CIO Insight,* August 2004, pp. 45–53
213. Sachitanand, N.N., 2000. Where does Maruti go from here? The Hindu. http://www.hindu.com/2000/11/13/stories/0613000b.htm (03.06.2003)
214. SAP. "Stages of Excellence." www.sap.com/scm/
215. Schoneberger, R. J. "Strategic Collaboration: Breaching the Castle Walls." Business Horizons 39 (1996), p. 20
216. Schrader, C. "Speeding Build and Buy Processes across a Collaborative Manufacturing Network." *ASCET* 3 (2001), pp. 82–88
217. Schwind, G. "A Systems Approach to Docks and Cross-Docking." *Material Handling Engineering* 51, no. 2 (1996), pp. 59–62
218. SearchStorage.com staff. http://www.SearchStorage.com, July 11, 2006
219. Seybold, P. B. The Customer Revolution. New York: Crown Business, 2001
220. Shenk, D. Data Smog: *Surviving the Information Glut.* New York: HarperCollins, 1997
221. Shepard, J. "The Future of Enterprise Applications." *AMR Research,* November 9, 2006
222. Signorelli, S., and J. Heskett. "Benetton (A)." Harvard University Business School Case (1984), Case No. 9-685-014

223. Simchi-Levi, D.; X. Chen; and J. Bramel. The Logic of Logistics: *Theory, Algorithms and Applications for Logistics and Supply Chain Management,* 2nd ed. New York: Springer-Verlag, 2004
224. Singh, A. Private communication
225. Sliwa, C. "Beyond IT: Business Strategy Was a Problem, Too." *Computerworld,* January 25, 2002
226. Songini, M. L. "Nike Says Profit Woes IT-Based." *Computerworld,* March 5, 2001
227. Speech of Shri Lalu Prasad: Railway Budget 2006-07: www.indlaw.com/display.aspx?15ea5fb4-d26c-4d34-8a04-ad2ca4e14200; accessed on 26 August 2007)
228. Speech of Shri Lalu Prasad: Railway Budget 2007-08; http://www.indianrailways.gov.in/Budget 2007/budget0708.htm: accessed on 26 August 2007)
229. Stalk, G.; P. Evans; and L. E. Shulman. "Competing on Capabilities: The New Rule of Corporate Strategy." *Harvard Business Review,* March–April 1992, pp. 57–69
230. Stein, T., and J. Sweat. "Killer Supply Chains." http://www.informationweek.com, November 9, 1988
231. Streitfeld, D. "Amazon Pays a Price for Marketing Test." *Washington Post,* October 2000
232. Supply Chain Council. "SCOR Introduction." Release 2.0, August 1, 1997
233. Swaminathan, J. M. "Enabling Customization Using Standardized Operations." *California Management Review* 43, no. 3 (Spring 2001), pp. 125–35
234. Temkin, B. "Preparing for the Coming Shake-Out in Online Markets." *ASCET* 3 (2001), pp. 102–107
235. Thakker, P, Mumbai's amazing dabbawallas, Smart Manager, 11 November, 2005 http://www.rediff.com/money/2005/nov/11spec.htm, Accessed on 15 June 2007
236. Trivedi, G., 2007, IT on Wheels, Real CIO World, Vol 2(15), pp. 26-32
237. Troyer, C., and R. Cooper. "Smart Moves in Supply Chain Integration." *Transportation & Distribution* 36 (1995), pp. 55–62
238. Troyer, T., and D. Denny. "Quick Response Evolution." *Discount Merchandiser* 32 (1992), pp. 104–107
239. Trunnick, P.; H. Richardson; and L. Harrington. "CLM: Breakthroughs of Champions." *Transportation & Distribution* 35 (1994), pp. 41–50
240. Ulrich, K. T. "The Role of Product Architecture in the Manufacturing Firm." Research Policy 24 (1995), pp. 419–40
241. Varon, E. "What You Need to Know about Public and Private Exchange." *CIO Magazine,* September 1, 2001
242. Verity, J. "Clearing the Cobwebs from the Stockroom." *BusinessWeek,* October 21, 1996
243. Wood, D.; A. Barone; P. Murphy; and D. Wardlow. *International Logistics.* New York: Chapman & Hall, 1995
244. Woods, D. and T. Mattern. Enterprise SOA: *Designing IT for Business Innovation.* Sebastopol, CA: O'Reilly Media, 2006
245. Yannis, B. J. "The Emerging Role of Electronic Marketplaces on the Internet." *Comm. ACM* 41, no. 9 (1998), pp. 35–42
246. Zweben, M. "Delivering on Every Promise." *APICS,* March 1996, p. 50
247. *BusinessWeek,* March 19, 2001
248. *Journal of Business Strategy,* October–November 1997
249. Manorama Yearbook 2003, pg 678, ISBN 81-900461-8-7
250. *The Economics Times,* Asian Paints plans largest plant in Haryana, 18 August 2007
251. *The Wall Street Journal,* October 23, 1997
252. *U.S. Surgical Quarterly Report,* July 15, 1993
253. *The Wall Street Journal,* October 7, 1994
254. *The Wall Street Journal,* August 1993. *(Dell Computer ref.)
255. *The Wall Street Journal,* July 15, 1993. *(Liz Claiborne ref.)
256. *The Wall Street Journal,* October 7, 1994. *(IBM ThinkPad ref.)
257. *The Wall Street Journal,* February 22, 2000
258. http://www.ikea-group.ikea.com/corporate/PDF/IKEA_FF_0405_GB.pdf
259. http://www.made-in-italy.com/fashion/fashion_houses/ benetton/intro.htm
260. http://www.dell.com
261. http://www.supply-chain.org
262. http://www-128.ibm.com/developrworks/ web-services/library/ws-soa-design1/
263. http://www.develocity.com/articles/20060801/news.cfm
264. http://www.smc3.com
265. http://www.develocity.com/articles/20051101/enroute.cfm
266. http://phx.corporate-ir.net/phoenix.zhtml?c=108468& p=irol-newsArticle&t=Regular&id=730231&
267. http://www.rosettanet.org

268. http://www.national.com
269. http://www.cpfr.org
270. http://www.dodrfid.org
271. http://dqindia.ciol.com/content/top_stories/2006/106040501.asp
272. http://en.wikipedia.org/wiki/Amul
273. http://en.wikipedia.org/wiki/Dabbawala
274. http://fciweb.nic.in/ (accessed on 25 August 2007)
275. http://rediff.co.in/money/2005/nov/19spec.htm
276. http://smbzone.indiatimes.com/articleshow/ 837644.cms(accessed on 28 August 2007)
277. http://timesofindia.indiatimes.com/articleshow/584717.cms
278. http://www.adexa.com
279. http://www.amul.com/
280. http://www.avaana.com/
281. http://www.business-standard.com/general/ retailer_nextfront.php?Start=11
282. http://www.dabur.com/en/about/ITInitiatives.asp (accessed on 28 August 2007)
283. http://www.dabur.com/EN/Media/default.asp?id=63&showDetail=y&show=this&type=corporate&cMore=yes : (accessed on 28 August 2007)
284. http://www.daburlaltail.com/EN/home/ Navigator%202006-07.pdf (accessed on 28 August 2007):
285. http://www.eci.gov.in/faq/evm.asp
286. http://www.eprocurement.gov.in/default.asp (accessed on 28 August 2007):
287. http://www.expresscomputeronline.com/ 20020225/ebiz1.shtml(accessed on 28 August 2007)
288. http://www.fcinez.com/ (accessed on 25 August 2007)
289. http://www.hindu.com/2006/06/28/stories/ 2006062808151600.htm
290. http://www.hindu.com/2006/09/10/stories/ 2006091007940500.htm (accessed on 28 August 2007):
291. http://www.hll.com/knowus/
292. http://www.indianexpress.com/ie/daily/19981012/28550514p.html (accessed on 20 July 2007)
293. http://www.india-reports.com/retail-weekly/Nov-12-18.aspx(accessed on 28 August 2007)
294. http://www.mahindra.com/index.asp
295. http://www.nirma.co.in/
296. http://www.ril.com/html/business/business_retail.html
297. http://www.sap.com/solutions/businesssuite/scm/pdf/mahindra_50058287S.pdf (accessed on 10 August 2007)
298. http://www.spectrum.ieee.org/may04/4926
299. http://www.tata.com/tata_sons/media/20030311.htm (accessed on 26 August 2007)
300. http://www.timesonline.co.uk/tol/news/world/asia/article1381347.ece (accessed on 20 July 2007)
301. http://www.timesonline.co.uk/tol/news/world/asia/article1381347.ece
302. http://www.tridentindia.com/abt_oview.asp

Index

Page numbers followed by n indicate notes.